AF700411

Illegal Drug and Marijuana Law

Illegal Drug and Marijuana Law

Alex Kreit

Professor of Law
Thomas Jefferson School of Law

CAROLINA ACADEMIC PRESS
Durham, North Carolina

Copyright © 2019
Alex Kreit
All Rights Reserved

ISBN 978-1-61163-789-2
e-ISBN 978-1-5310-1205-2
LCCN 2019944022

Carolina Academic Press
700 Kent Street
Durham, North Carolina 27701
Telephone (919) 489-7486
Fax (919) 493-5668
www.cap-press.com

Printed in the United States of America

To my mother, Sonia Spindt, for always being there for me.

Contents

Table of Cases

Preface

Just two months before my casebook *Controlled Substances: Crime, Regulation, and Policy* was published in January 2013, voters in Colorado and Washington approved the first state marijuana legalization laws. Since then, U.S. drug policy has seen a number of significant changes. As of this writing, ten states have legalized the possession, commercial manufacture, and sale of marijuana; Vermont and Washington, D.C. have legalized marijuana possession and personal cultivation, though not commercial sales. Although marijuana remains a Schedule I controlled substance under federal law, the Department of Justice has for the most part permitted states to implement their legalization laws without interference. Interest in drug policy reform has not been limited to marijuana. Cities and states have started to explore ideas like safe injection sites in response to the opioid crisis, and lawmakers across the country have been reconsidering harsh drug sentencing laws. Finally, the past six years have yielded a number of noteworthy court decisions on drug laws, including U.S. Supreme Court decisions on the federal drug-induced homicide statute and the Controlled Substances Analogue Enforcement Act.

This book, which is in effect the second edition of *Controlled Substances*, covers all of these developments and more. The new title—*Illegal Drug and Marijuana Law*—reflects the shifting legal status of marijuana, which 1/5 of the states now regulate like alcohol rather than as a controlled substance.* *Illegal Drug and Marijuana Law* retains the structure of *Controlled Substances* along with the majority of its cases and articles, although a handful of cuts have been made to make room for new material. Among the most notable new additions are:

- A new chapter on state marijuana legalization laws and the federal response (Chapter 8).
- Expanded coverage of cases and materials related to the opioid crisis, including a new section on the crisis in Chapter 2.

* The term marijuana has a troubling history. "[I]t was popularized in the United States during the 1930s by advocates of prohibition, who sought to exploit prejudice against despised minority groups, especially Mexican immigrants." Martin A. Lee, Smoke Signals: A Social History of Marijuana—Medical, Recreational, and Scientific 6 (2012). Some reject the term marijuana in favor of cannabis, in part because of this history. But the federal Controlled Substances Act and the vast majority of state laws continue to use marijuana (or marihuana), not cannabis. Because this is a law school textbook, and marijuana remains the standard term in most statutes and court decisions, I use the term marijuana in the book's title and text.

- The legal status of hemp following passage of the 2018 Farm Bill.
- The 2018 FIRST STEP Act.
- Stash house stings and the outrageous government conduct defense.
- Drug testing of recipients of public benefits.
- U.S. Supreme Court decisions on the Controlled Substances Analogue Act (*McFadden v. United States*) and the federal drug-induced homicide statute (*Burrage v. United States*).

A course on illegal drug and marijuana law provides a uniquely rich mix of complex legal and policy problems. A close look at the law of drug crimes reveals unusually tough challenges in how to define them, how to prove them, and how to grade them. Is drug possession meant to punish drug ownership or physical contact with drugs? What sort of evidence is sufficient to conclude that a person who possesses drugs intends to distribute them? Should we sentence drug offenders based on the type and quantity of drugs involved in their offense or some other metric? The enforcement of drug laws, meanwhile, provides an ideal vehicle for studying a number of important and often overlooked issues like prosecutorial discretion, the use of informants in modern policing, and racial profiling. Drug prohibition also presents one of the most difficult tests for the theories of punishment. Though we may disagree about how much punishment a thief, a killer, or a drunk driver should receive, few question that theft, murder, and driving under the influence should be against the law. By contrast, many theorists and policy analysts believe that drug criminalization is unjust or unworkable. In the case of marijuana, the debate about prohibition is not just taking place in classrooms and academic conferences, but at ballot boxes across the country.

Yet, while modern drug laws are of central importance to our criminal justice system, they have been strangely absent from the curriculum at most law schools. Every criminal law casebook devotes significant coverage to homicide, property crimes, and rape. But only a handful include a chapter or section on drug offenses. Criminal procedure courses are filled with drug cases. But this is only because so many of the leading Fourth, Fifth, and Sixth Amendment cases happened to involve drug prosecutions. Courses like federal criminal law and international criminal law sometimes include coverage of drug offenses. And there are some schools that offer a seminar or course on drug policy. At most law schools today, however, a student could take every single criminal law-related offering without studying drug law and policy.

Illegal Drug and Marijuana Law aims to help fill this gap in the law school curriculum by giving teachers an accessible, flexible, and engaging textbook with which to design a course on drugs and the law. The book can be used as the primary or exclusive text in a range of law school courses. Whether for a seminar on the war on drugs, an advanced criminal law course on drug crimes, a survey course on controlled substances law, or a summer study abroad course on international drug control, *Illegal Drug and Marijuana Law* is meant for easy adoption.

Before I close, a few formatting notes. My chief objective has been to make this book as readable and user-friendly as possible. To that end, I have minimized the use of ellipses in cases and other source materials. Ellipses appear for omitted material within a sentence or paragraph. But I have opted not to use them where whole paragraphs or the beginning or end of a paragraph have been cut. In a few instances, I have re-ordered paragraphs from source material to enhance readability. I have deleted most in-text citations and the vast majority of footnotes from the cases and materials. Footnotes that have been retained are marked using the original numbering from the source material. A * indicates a footnote that I have written. Finally, in place of the traditional "notes and questions" sections, I use short narrative essays (usually one or two paragraphs) to link and supplement the materials. The book uses a centered straight line to demarcate the end of a case or article and the beginning of author-written text.

If you are a teacher who is thinking of teaching a course on illegal drug and marijuana law, whether using this book or another, I would be glad to discuss ideas with you. I have found learning about and teaching this subject to be incredibly enjoyable and rewarding. I hope that you will as well.

Alex Kreit
akreit@tjsl.edu
San Diego, California
June 2019

Acknowledgments

I am grateful to the law school teachers who used *Controlled Substances: Crime, Regulation, and Policy* (the predecessor to this book) in their classes, and to all of the students who have taken one of my courses on illegal drug and marijuana law. This book has benefited immensely from their feedback, insights, and suggestions.

Thank you to the entire Carolina Academic Press team. I am so fortunate to have such a supportive, dedicated, and understanding publisher.

For their research assistance in preparing *Controlled Substances: Crime, Regulation, and Policy*, I thank Kelly Hayes (Thomas Jefferson School of Law, 2013), Janell Woodbury (Thomas Jefferson School of Law, 2012), Jenna Hackett (Thomas Jefferson School of Law, 2011), Veronica Inezian (Thomas Jefferson School of Law, 2010), and Catherine Deane (Thomas Jefferson School of Law Library). Thanks are also due to Anders Kaye, Bridget Kennedy, and Zara Snapp for their thoughtful comments and advice.

Finally, I am grateful to the following individuals and organizations for their permission to reproduce excerpts from their works in this casebook (listed in order of appearance in this casebook):

Alexander Shulgin and Ann Shulgin, PiHKAL: A Chemical Love Story, Copyright © 1991, 1992, 1995, 1998, 2000, 2003, 2007 by Alexander Shulgin and Ann Shulgin. Reprinted by permission of Transform Press.

Audrey M. Provenzano, *Caring for Ms. L—Overcoming My Fear of Treating Opioid Use Disorder*, 378 New Endland Journal of Medicine 600, © 2018 Massachusetts Medical Society. Reprinted with permission from Massachusetts Medical Society.

Barnard E. Harcourt, *The Collapse of the Harm Principle*, 90 Journal of Criminal Law and Criminology 109 (1999). Reprinted by special permission of Northwestern University School of Law, The Journal of Criminal Law and Criminology.

Douglas Husak, *Illicit Drugs: A Test of Joel Feinberg's* The Moral Limits of the Criminal Law, 10 Libertaria (2008). Reprinted by permission of the author, with special thanks to the author for providing an English-language version of this article.

Ethan A. Nadelmann, *Drug Prohibition in the United States: Costs, Consequences, and Alternatives*, 5 Notre Dame Journal of Law Ethics and Public Policy 783 (1991). Reprinted by permission of the author.

James Q. Wilson, *Against the Legalization of Drugs*, 89 Commentary 21 (1990). Reprinted from COMMENTARY, February 1990, by permission; © 1990 by Commentary, Inc.

Mark A.R. Kleiman & Aaron J. Saiger, *Drug Legalization: The Importance of Asking the Right Question*, 18 Hofstra Law Review 527 (1990). Reprinted with the permission of the Hofstra Law Review Association.

Alex Kreit, *The Decriminalization Option: Should States Consider Moving From a Criminal to a Civil Drug Court Model?*, 2010 University of Chicago Legal Forum 299. Reprinted with permission from the University of Chicago Legal Forum and the University of Chicago Law School.

Peter Reuter, *Can Heroin Maintenance Help Baltimore?*, The Abell Foundation 2009. Reprinted by permission of the author.

Leo Beletsky and Corey S. Davis, *Today's Fentanyl Crisis: Prohibition's Iron Law Revisited*, 46 International Journal of Drug Policy 156 (2017). Reprinted with permission from Elsevier.

Ameet Sarpatwari, Michael S. Sinha, and Aaron S. Kesselheim, *The Opioid Epidemic: Fixing a Broken Pharmaceutical Market*, 11 Harvard Law and Policy Review 463 (2017) Repreinted with permission of the Harvard Law and Policy Review.

Alex Kreit, *Drug Truce*, 77 Ohio State Law Journal 1323 (2016). Reprinted with permission of the author.

Jamie Fellner, *Race, Drugs, and Law Enforcement in the United States*, 20 Stan. L. & Pol'y Rev 257 (2009). Reprinted by permission of the journal.

William J. Stuntz, *The Pathological Politics of Criminal Law*, 100 Michigan Law Review 505 (2001). Reprinted by permission of the Stuntz family.

Michelle Alexander, *The New Jim Crow*, 9 Ohio State Journal of Criminal Law 7 (2011). Reprinted by permission of the author.

Myrna S. Reader, *Single Moms, Battered Women, and Other Sex-Based Anomalies in the Gender-Free World of the Federal Sentencing Guidelines*, 20 Pepperdine Law Review 905 (1993). Reprinted by permission of the author.

L. Buckner Inniss, *A Moving Violation? Hypercriminalized Spaces and Fortuitous Presence in Drug Free School Zones*, 8 Texas Forum on Civil Liberties and Civil Rights 51 (2003). Reprinted by permission of the author.

Scott Burris, Steffanie A. Strathdee, and Jon S. Vernick, *Lethal Injections: The Law, Science, and Politics of Syringe Access for Injection Drug Users*, 37 University of San Francisco Law Review 813 (2003). Reprinted by permission of the University of San Francisco Law Review.

Cortney E. Lollar, *Criminalizing Pregnancy*, 92 Indiana Law Journal 947 (2017). Reprinted by permission of the author.

Kyle O'Dowd, *Weighing the Evidence: Drug Quantity Issues in Mandatory Minimum Cases*, 24 Champion 43 (2000). Reprinted by permission of the National Association of Criminal Defense Lawyers.

Hon. William W. Wilkins, Jr., Phyllis J. Newton and John R. Steer, *Competing Sentencing Policies in a "War on Drugs" Era*, 28 Wake Forest L. Rev. 305 (1993). © Wake Forest Law Review, reprinted by permission.

Stephen J. Schulhofer, *Rethinking Mandatory Minimums*, 28 Wake Forest Law Review 199 (1993). © Wake Forest Law Review, reprinted by permission.

Steven D. Clymer, *Unequal Justice: The Federalization of Criminal Law*, 70 Southern California Law Review 643 (1997). Reprinted with the permission of the Southern California Law Review.

Eric J. Miller, *Embracing Addiction: Drug Courts and the False Promise of Judicial Intervention*, 65 Ohio State Law Journal 1479 (2004). Reprinted by permission of the author and the Ohio State Law Journal.

Ryan S. King and Jill Pasquarella, *Drug Courts: A Review of the Evidence*, The Sentencing Project (2009). Reprinted by permission of The Sentencing Project.

Josh Bowers, *Contraindicated Drug Courts*, 55 UCLA Law Review 783 (2008). Reprinted by permission of the author.

National Association of Criminal Defense Lawyers (2009), *America's Problem-Solving Courts: The Criminal Costs of Treatment and the Case for Reform*. Reprinted by permission of the National Association of Criminal Defense Lawyers.

Nora V. Demleitner, *"Collateral Damage": No Re-Entry for Drug Offenders*, 47 Villanova Law Review 1027 (2002). Reprinted by permission of the Villanova Law Review.

Beth A. Colgan, *Fines, Fees, and Forfeitures*, 4 Reforming Criminal Justice 205 (Erik Luna ed., 2017). Reprinted by permission of the Academy for Justice and the author.

Randy Barnett, *The Harmful Side Effects of Drug Prohibition*, 2009 Utah Law Review 11. Reprinted by permission of the author.

Alexandra Natapoff, *Deregulating Guilt: The Information Culture of the Criminal System*, 30 Cardozo Law Review 965 (2008). Reprinted by permission of the Cardozo Law Review.

Alexandra Natapoff, *Beyond Unreliable: How Snitches Contribute to Wrongful Convictions*, 37 Golden Gate University Law Review 107 (2006). Reprinted by permission of the Golden Gate University Law Review.

Michael L. Rich, *Coerced Informants and Thirteenth Amendment Limitations on the Police-Informant Relationship*, 50 Santa Clara Law Review 681 (2010). Reprinted by permission of the author.

Alex Kreit, *Marijuana Legalization and Pretextual Stops*, 50 UC Davis Law Review 741 (2016). Reprinted by permission of the author.

Robert J. MacCoun, *Testing Drugs Versus Testing For Drug Use: Private Risk Management in the Shadow of Criminal Law*, 56 DePaul Law Review 507 (2007). Reprinted by permission of the author.

Radley Balko, *Overkill: The Rise of Paramilitary Police Raids in America*, The Cato Institute 2006. Reprinted by permission of the Cato Institute.

Erik Luna, *Drug Exceptionalism*, 47 Villanova Law Review 753 (2002). Reprinted by permission of the author and the Villanova Law Review.

Paul Finkelman, *The Second Casualty of War: Civil Liberties and the War on Drugs*, 66 Southern California Law Review 1389 (1993). Reprinted with the permission of the Southern California Law Review.

Thomas M. Quinn and Gerald T. McLaughlin, *The Evolution of Federal Drug Control Legislation*, 22 Catholic University Law Review 586 (1973). Reprinted by permission of the Catholic University Law Review.

Peter J. Cohen, *Medical Marijuana: The Conflict Between Scientific Evidence and Political Ideology*, 2009 Utah Law Review 35. Reprinted by permission of the Cohen family.

Douglas J. Behr, *Did You Forget to Say You're Sorry? Litigating a Show Cause Hearing for a Physician's DEA Registration*, 9 Quinnipiac Health Law Journal 99 (2005). Reprinted by permission of the author.

Corey S. Davis and Derek H. Carr, *The Law and Policy of Opioids for Pain Management, Addiction Treatment, and Overdose Reversal*, 14 Indiana Health Law Review 1 (2017). Reprinted by permission of the Indiana Health Law Review.

Richard C. Ausness, *"There's Danger Here, Cherie!": Liability for the Promotion and Marketing of Drugs and Medical Devices for Off-Label Uses*, 73 Brooklyn Law Review 1253. Reprinted by permission of the author.

Alex Kreit, *Marijuana Legalization*, 1 Reforming Criminal Justice 115 (Erik Luna ed., 2017). Reprinted by permission of the Academy for Justice and the author.

Jonathan P. Caulkins, et al., *Considering Marijuana Legalization: Insights for Vermont and Other Jurisdictions*, RAND Corporation (2015). Reprinted by permission of the RAND Corporation.

Marianne M.J. van Ooyen-Houben, *The Dutche Coffee Shop System, Tensions and Benefits*, 25 Michigan State International Law Review 623 (2017). Reprinted by permission of the author.

Chantal Thomas, *Disciplining Globalization: International Law, Illegal Trade, and the Case of Narcotics*, 24 Michigan Journal of International Law 549 (2003). Reprinted by permission of the author.

United Nations Office on Drugs and Crime, *World Drug Report, 2017.* Reprinted by permission of the United Nations Office on Drugs and Crime.

Peter H. Reuter, *A Report on Global Illicit Drugs Markets 1998-2007: Assessing the Operation of the Global Drug Market, Report 1*, RAND Corporation, Prepared for the European Commission (2009). A Report on Global Illicit Drugs Markets 1998-2007, © European Communities, 2009. Reprinted by permission of the Publications Office of the European Union.

Seth Harp, Note, *Globalization of the U.S. Black Market: Prohibition, the War on Drugs, and the Case of Mexico*, 85 New York University Law Review 1661 (2010). Reprinted by permission of the New York University Law Review.

Laura Calderón, Octavio Rodríguez, and David A. Shirk, *Drug Violence in Mexico: Data and Analysis Through 2017* (2018), University of San Diego Justice in Mexico Project. Reprinted by permission of the University of San Diego Justice in Mexico Project.

Michael Chertoff, *The Nexus Between Drug Trafficking, Terrorism and Organized Crime*, 13 Chapman Law Review 681 (2010). Reprinted by permission of the author.

Daniel Heilmann, *The International Control of Illegal Drugs and the U.N. Treaty Regime: Preventing or Causing Human Rights Violations?*, 19 Cardozo Journal of International and Comparative Law 217 (2011). Reprinted by permission of the Cardozo Journal of International and Comparative Law.

Edward M. Morgan, *Traffic Circles: The Legal Logic of Drug Extraditions*, 31 University of Pennsylvania Journal of International Law 373 (2009). Reprinted by permission of the author.

Joanne Sum-Ping, Note: *A New Approach to Extraterritorial Application of Environmental Statutes?: Uncovering the Effects of Plan Colombia*, 31 Colombia Journal of Environmental Law 139 (2006). Reprinted by permission of the Columbia Journal of Environmental Law.

Raj Bhala, *Fighting Bad Guys with International Trade Law*, 31 University of California Davis Law Review 1 (1997). Reprinted by permission of the author.

Introduction

It is difficult to think of a development that has had a greater impact on our criminal justice system over the past five decades than the war on drugs. More Americans were arrested for a drug offense in 2017 than for any other category of crime tracked by the Federal Bureau of Investigation's Uniform Crime Report. Police made 1.6 million arrests for drug abuse violations, about 15% of all arrests. Of these, 85%—just under 1.4 million—were for simple drug possession. By comparison, in 2017, the police made approximately 1.25 million arrests for property crimes, 990,678 arrests for driving under the influence, and 505,681 arrests for violent crimes.

Drug convictions have contributed to the explosion in our prison population. The United States has the world's highest incarceration rate, with more than 2.3 million people behind bars in state and federal prisons and local jails. Drug offenders make up about one-fifth of this number. Approximately 460,000 people are locked up for drug offenses—97,000 in federal prisons, 208,000 in state prisons, and 157,000 in jails. *See* Peter Wagner and Bernadette Rabuy, *Mass Incarceration: The Whole Pie 2017*, Prison Policy Initiative (March 14, 2017), https://www.prisonpolicy.org/reports/pie2017.html.

Meanwhile, drug investigations have had a dramatic influence on constitutional criminal procedure and policing, leading to (among other things) a rise in the use of informants, pre-textual traffic stops, and no-knock executions of warrants. Some commentators—and even some judges—have gone so far as to argue that courts have developed an implicit "drug exception" to the Constitution.

Although our drug laws are vigorously enforced, the wisdom and morality of drug prohibition remain hotly contested. Some argue that drug use and distribution are consensual, "victimless" activities that should not be criminalized at all. Others view drug prohibition as a moral imperative because of the harms to the community associated with substance abuse. In addition to the debate over whether it is just to criminalize drug transactions, there is widespread disagreement about how to calculate and balance the costs and benefits of prohibition. Does drug prohibition reduce drug use? If so, is the reduction in use substantial enough to be worth the price? This debate is not just playing out in classrooms and at academic conferences. As of June 2019, ten states have enacted laws legalizing the possession, commercial manufacture, and retail sale of marijuana.

Discussions about the role of race and class in our criminal justice system also tend to focus on drug policy. In her book *The New Jim Crow*, Michelle Alexander argues that "[n]othing has contributed more to the systemic mass incarceration of people of color in the United States than the War on Drugs." MICHELLE ALEXANDER, THE NEW JIM CROW 59 (2010).

In addition to the policy issues raised by modern drug prohibition, drug laws can pose challenging legal problems. Almost every attorney who works in criminal law will encounter drug cases throughout her practice—from handling misdemeanor possession cases as a new attorney to navigating a sprawling drug conspiracy case years into practice. As in every area of the law, many drug cases may be straightforward. But even a seemingly run-of-the-mill drug case can sometimes be quite complex. Imagine, for example, that the police find drugs in a hotel room with two occupants, neither of whom claims responsibility for the drugs. Are both occupants guilty of drug possession? Neither?

This book provides an overview of the law and policy of controlled substances. Chapter 1 focuses on drugs and drug use by briefly examining the question of what is a drug and offering perspectives on substance use, abuse and addiction. Chapter 2 introduces some of the key policy questions related to drug prohibition in the United States. Chapter 3 moves from policy to legal doctrine with an overview of drug crimes, including: possession, possession with intent to distribute, manufacture, and additional offenses like drug paraphernalia laws. Chapter 4 addresses drug sentencing and civil sanctions. Chapter 5 deals with the legal and policy issues raised by drug investigations, from the use of informants to racial profiling. Chapter 6 moves from criminal law to administrative law with an examination of the Controlled Substances Act, the federal law under which drugs of abuse are classified and controlled. Chapter 7 focuses on criminal and regulatory provisions related to the recreational use of medicines. Chapter 8 examines state marijuana legalization laws and the conflict between federal and state marijuana laws. Finally, Chapter 9 concludes with a look at international drug control law.

Illegal Drug and Marijuana Law

Chapter 1

Drugs and Drug Use

A. What Is a Drug?

What is a "drug"?

When a politician says she opposes drug legalization, no one thinks she is advocating a return to alcohol prohibition. Legally, alcohol is not classified as a drug. It is exempted from the federal Controlled Substances Act, which was enacted in 1970 to provide a comprehensive and uniform structure for classifying and regulating drugs of abuse. *See* 21 U.S.C. 802(6) (providing that "[t]he term 'controlled substances' . . . does not include distilled spirits, wine, malt beverages, or tobacco"). Yet, one study that aimed to assess "the harms caused by the misuse of drugs" found that "alcohol was the most harmful drug (overall harm score 72), with heroin (55) and crack cocaine (54) in second and third places." David J. Nutt, Leslie A. King, and Lawrence D. Phillips, *Drug Harms in the UK: A Multicriteria Decision Analysis*, 376 The Lancet 1558 (2010).

How about caffeine? There are few restrictions on the sale and use of caffeine in the United States. Indeed, it is perfectly legal to sell caffeinated soft drinks out of vending machines to children. When one company announced plans to sell an inhaler that dispenses breathable caffeine in 2011, however, Senator Charles Schumer (D-NY) attacked the product as "nothing more than a club drug designed to give users the ability to drink until they drop" and wrote to the Food and Drug Administration to ask them to review its safety. Anna Edney, *Caffeine Inhaler a Dangerous 'Club Drug,' Says Senator*, USA Today, Dec. 23, 2011.

In their 1983 book *From Chocolate to Morphine: Everything You Need to Know About Mind-Altering Drugs*, Andrew Weil and Winifred Rosen observed that whether or not we label something as a "drug" can depend a lot on context and cultural attitudes:

> The decision to call some substances drugs and others not is often arbitrary. In the case of medical drugs—substances such as penicillin, used only to treat physical illness—the distinction may be easier to make. But talking about psychoactive drugs—substances that affect mood, perception, and thought—is tricky.
>
> In the first place, foods, drugs, and poisons are not clear-cut categories. Second, people have strong emotional reactions to them. Food is good. Poison is bad. Drugs may be good or bad, and whether they are seen as good or

bad depends on who is looking at them. Many people agree that drugs are good when doctors give them to patients in order to make them better. Some religious groups, such as Christian Scientists, do not share that view, however. They believe that God intends us to deal with illness without drugs.

When people take psychoactive drugs on their own, in order to change their mood or feel pleasure, the question of good or bad gets even thornier. The whole subject of pleasure triggers intense controversy. Should pleasure come as a reward for work or suffering? Should people feel guilty if they experience pleasure without suffering for it in some way? Should work itself be unpleasant? These questions are very important to us, but they do not have easy answers. Different people in different cultures answer them in different ways.

Drug use is universal. Every human culture in every age of history has used one or more psychoactive drugs. (The one exception is the Eskimos, who were unable to grow drug plants and had to wait for white men to bring them alcohol.) In fact, drug-taking is so common that it seems to be a basic human activity. Societies must come to terms with people's fascination with drugs. Usually the use of certain drugs is approved and integrated into the life of a tribe, community, or nation, sometimes in formal rituals and ceremonies. The approval of some drugs for some purposes usually goes hand in hand with the disapproval of other drugs for other purposes. For example, some early Muslim sects encouraged the use of coffee in religious rites, but had strict prohibitions against alcohol. On the other hand, when coffee came to Europe in the seventeenth century, the Roman Catholic Church opposed it as an evil drug but continued to regard wine as a traditional sacrament.

Drug Abuse in America: Problem in Perspective, Second Report
National Commission on Marijuana and Drug Abuse

(1973)

The meaning of the word drug often varies with the context in which it is used. From a strictly scientific point of view, a drug is any substance other than food which by its chemical nature affects the structure or function of the living organism. From this perspective, the term includes some agricultural and industrial chemicals. The physician might define drug as any substance used as a medicine in the treatment of physical or mental disease; when treatment of illness is the referent, the lay public may use the word in the same sense. However, when used in the context of drug "abuse" or the drug "problem," the meaning of "drug" becomes social rather than scientific.

In its social sense, drug is not a neutral term. This point is illustrated by the fact that "drug problem" is frequently used not as a descriptive phrase, but a substitute for the word drug. In our visits to communities throughout this country and other nations, we have noted that local leaders often feel compelled to report not simply that drugs are available or that they are used, but that there is a "drug problem."

This value component of the word drug is reflected in the selective application of this term by the general public. Table 1-1, drawn from a Commission-sponsored National Survey illustrates that the public tends uniformly to regard heroin as a drug, as well as other substances associated with the drug problem, such as marijuana, cocaine, the amphetamines and the barbiturates. Some psychoactive substances, such as alcohol and tobacco, are generally not regarded as drugs at all. In neither public law nor public discussion is alcohol regarded as a drug. It may be called a beverage, a food, a social lubricant or a relaxant, but rarely is it called a drug.

Table 1-1. Substances Regarded as Drugs

	Adults (N = 2411) (percent)	Youth (N = 880) (percent)
Heroin	95	96
Cocaine	88	86
Barbiturates	83	91
Marihuana	80	80
Amphetamines	79	86
Alcohol	39	34
Tobacco	27	16
No opinion	1	1

The imprecision of the term "drug" has had serious social consequences. Because alcohol is excluded, the public is conditioned to regard a martini as something fundamentally different from a marihuana cigarette, a barbiturate capsule or a bag of heroin. Similarly, because the referents of the word "drug" differ so widely in the therapeutic and social contexts, the public is conditioned to believe that "street" drugs act according to entirely different principles than "medical" drugs. The result is that the risks of the former are exaggerated while the risks of the latter are overlooked.

This confusion must be dispelled. Alcohol *is* a drug. All drugs act according to the same general principles. Their effects vary with dose. For each drug there is an effective dose (in terms of the desired effect), a toxic dose and a lethal dose. All drugs have multiple effects. The lower the dose, the more important non-drug factors become in determining drug effect. At high dose levels, and for some individuals at much lower dose levels, all drugs may be dangerous. The individual and social consequences of drug use escalate with frequency and duration of use. American drug policy will never be coherent until it is founded on uniform principles such as these, which apply to *all* drugs.

As the material above discusses, the term "drug" is not amenable to a precise definition and may mean different things to different people and in different contexts. The focus of this book is on drugs that are legally classified as controlled substances under federal law. Controlled substances are the drugs that are likely to come to mind when we think of the war on drugs. The classification of a drug as a controlled substance means that it is against the law to possess, manufacture or distribute the substance for recreational use. Both "street" drugs (like heroin) and prescription drugs that have recreational uses (like OxyContin) are regulated as controlled substances. Strictly medical drugs (like penicillin) or foods that have relatively mild mind-altering effects (like caffeine) are not. Although alcohol and tobacco are drugs used for recreation, both substances are specifically exempted from the federal Controlled Substances Act.

While this book focuses on illegal drugs and marijuana, one of the recurring questions raised by the materials in the chapters to come is what accounts for differences in how the law treats various substances, including alcohol and tobacco. The 1973 Commission on Marijuana and Drug Abuse argued that "[a]lcohol *is* a drug" and that "American drug policy will never be coherent until it is founded on uniform principles . . . , which apply to *all* drugs." But the legal regime that applies to alcohol is, of course, much different from the legal regime that applies to most other drugs. Is this because alcohol is less harmful than other drugs? Is it due to historical accident? Something else?

A writer for the website *Vox* asked himself a question: "What if the media covered alcohol like it does other drugs?" As a thought experiment, he wrote a satirical but factually accurate story about alcohol that tried to capture the "same type of alarmist reporting" that is sometimes part of news coverage of illegal drugs:

> NEW ORLEANS—An ongoing drug epidemic has swept the US, killing hundreds and sickening thousands more on a daily basis.
>
> The widespread use of a substance called "alcohol"—also known as "booze"—has been linked to erratic and even dangerous behavior, ranging from college students running naked down public streets to brutal attacks and robberies.
>
> Federal officials suggest this drug has already been linked to 88,000 deaths each year across the country, including traffic accidents caused by drug-induced impairment, liver damage caused by excessive consumption, and violent behavior. Experts warn that it can also lead to nausea, vomiting, severe headaches, cognitive deficits among children and teens, and even fetal defects in pregnant women.

> Here in New Orleans, the horror of the drug was particularly prominent in the city's French Quarter, where hundreds of young adults could be seen roiling from the effects of the drug. Some collapsed on the ground, dazed from alcohol's effects. Others could be seen vomiting in public—a common result of drinking alcohol. Many could be seen limping and clumsily walking down the street, showcasing the type of impairment that public health officials warn can lead to accidents, especially when someone is behind the wheel of a car.

German Lopez, *Imagine if the Media Covered Alcohol Like Other Drugs*, Vox (June 15, 2015), http://www.vox.com/2015/6/15/8774233/alcohol-dangerous.

B. Perspectives on Substance Use, Abuse and Addiction

There is an extensive range of artistic and scientific commentary on drug use, abuse and addiction.

Some sources recount positive experiences with mind-altering substances. In his 1954 nonfiction book *The Doors of Perception*, for example, novelist Aldous Huxley describes his use of the hallucinogen mescaline as something of a religious experience: "To be shaken out of the ruts of ordinary perception, to be shown for a few timeless hours the outer and inner world, not as they appear to an animal obsessed with survival or to a human being obsessed with words and notions, but as they are apprehended, directly and unconditionally, by Mind at Large—this is an experience of inestimable value to everyone and especially to the intellectual." Others, like Irvine Welsh in his 1993 novel about a group of heroin addicts, *Trainspotting*, paint a decidedly grimmer picture. In the film adaptation, the main character describes withdrawal: "Too ill to sleep. Too tired to stay awake, but the sickness is on its way. Sweat, chills, nausea. Pain and craving. A need like nothing else I've ever known will soon take hold of me. It's on its way."

Psychologists, neuroscientists and physicians may not capture the popular imagination in the same way as novelists or film directors. But the scientific literature on substance use and abuse is equally diverse. Researchers in these fields work to, among other things, examine the pharmacology of different drugs, assess different drug treatment models, and provide diagnostic tools for identifying substance abuse and addiction.

The following excerpts provide a sampling of different perspectives on substance use, abuse, and addiction. As you read through the material, reflect on your own views and experiences. How does your perspective on substance use and abuse shape your beliefs about drug policy? For additional readings, *see, e.g.*, Mike Jay, Artificial Paradises: A Drugs Reader (2000); Rebecca Shannonhouse and Pete Hamill, Under the Influence: The Literature of Addiction (2003).

John Barleycorn
Jack London

(1913)

It all came to me one election day. It was on a warm California afternoon, and I had ridden down into the Valley of the Moon from the ranch to the little village to vote Yes and No to a host of proposed amendments to the Constitution of the State of California. Because of the warmth of the day I had had several drinks before casting my ballot, and divers drinks after casting it. Then I had ridden up through the vine-clad hills and rolling pastures of the ranch, and arrived at the farm-house in time for another drink and supper.

"How did you vote on the suffrage amendment?" Charmian asked.

"I voted for it."

She uttered an exclamation of surprise. For, be it known, in my younger days, despite my ardent democracy, I had been opposed to woman suffrage. In my later and more tolerant years I had been unenthusiastic in my acceptance of it as an inevitable social phenomenon.

"Now just why did you vote for it?" Charmian asked.

I answered. I answered at length. I answered indignantly. The more I answered, the more indignant I became. (No; I was not drunk. The horse I had ridden was well named "The Outlaw." I'd like to see any drunken man ride her.)

And yet—how shall I say?—I was lighted up, I was feeling "good," I was pleasantly jingled.

"When the women get the ballot, they will vote for prohibition," I said. "It is the wives, and sisters, and mothers, and they only, who will drive the nails into the coffin of John Barleycorn—"

"But I thought you were a friend to John Barleycorn," Charmian interpolated.

"I am. I was. I am not. I never am. I am never less his friend than when he is with me and when I seem most his friend. He is the king of liars. He is the frankest truthsayer. He is the august companion with whom one walks with the gods. He is also in league with the Noseless One. His way leads to truth naked, and to death. He gives clear vision, and muddy dreams. He is the enemy of life, and the teacher of wisdom beyond life's wisdom. He is a red-handed killer, and he slays youth."

And Charmian looked at me, and I knew she wondered where I had got it.

I continued to talk. As I say, I was lighted up. In my brain every thought was at home. Every thought, in its little cell, crouched ready-dressed at the door, like prisoners at midnight waiting a jail-break. And every thought was a vision, bright-imaged, sharp-cut, unmistakable. My brain was illuminated by the clear, white light of alcohol. John Barleycorn was on a truth-telling rampage, giving away the choicest secrets on himself. And I was his spokesman. There moved the multitudes of memories of my past life, all orderly arranged like soldiers in some vast review. It was mine to pick and choose. I was a lord of thought, the master of my vocabulary and of the totality of my experience, unerringly capable of selecting my data and building my exposition. For so John Barleycorn tricks and lures, setting the maggots of intelligence gnawing, whispering his fatal intuitions of truth, flinging purple passages into the monotony of one's days.

I outlined my life to Charmian, and expounded the make-up of my constitution. I was no hereditary alcoholic. I had been born with no organic, chemical predisposition toward alcohol. In this matter I was normal in my generation. Alcohol was an acquired taste. It had been painfully acquired. Alcohol had been a dreadfully repugnant thing—more nauseous than any physic. Even now I did not like the taste of it. I drank it only for its "kick." And from the age of five to that of twenty-five I had not learned to care for its kick. Twenty years of unwilling apprenticeship had been required to make my system rebelliously tolerant of alcohol, to make me, in the heart and the deeps of me, desirous of alcohol.

I sketched my first contacts with alcohol, told of my first intoxications and revulsions, and pointed out always the one thing that in the end had won me over—namely, the accessibility of alcohol. Not only had it always been accessible, but every interest of my developing life had drawn me to it. A newsboy on the streets, a sailor, a miner, a wanderer in far lands, always where men came together to exchange ideas, to laugh and boast and dare, to relax, to forget the dull toil of tiresome nights and days, always they came together over alcohol. The saloon was the place of congregation. Men gathered to it as primitive men gathered about the fire of the squatting place or the fire at the mouth of the cave.

I reminded Charmian of the canoe houses from which she had been barred in the South Pacific, where the kinky-haired cannibals escaped from their womenkind and feasted and drank by themselves, the sacred precincts taboo to women under pain of death. As a youth, by way of the saloon I had escaped from the narrowness of woman's influence into the wide free world of men. All ways led to the saloon. The thousand roads of romance and adventure drew together in the saloon, and thence led out and on over the world.

"The point is," I concluded my sermon, "that it is the accessibility of alcohol that has given me my taste for alcohol. I did not care for it. I used to laugh at it. Yet here I am, at the last, possessed with the drinker's desire. It took twenty years to implant that desire; and for ten years more that desire has grown. And the effect of satisfying that desire is anything but good. Temperamentally I am wholesome-hearted and merry. Yet when I walk with John Barleycorn I suffer all the damnation of intellectual pessimism."

"But," I hastened to add (I always hasten to add), "John Barleycorn must have his due. He does tell the truth. That is the curse of it. The so-called truths of life are not true. They are the vital lies by which life lives, and John Barleycorn gives them the lie."

"Which does not make toward life," Charmian said.

"Very true," I answered. "And that is the perfectest hell of it. John Barleycorn makes toward death. That is why I voted for the amendment to-day. I read back in my life and saw how the accessibility of alcohol had given me the taste for it. You see, comparatively few alcoholics are born in a generation. And by alcoholic I mean a man whose chemistry craves alcohol and drives him resistlessly to it. The great majority of habitual drinkers are born not only without desire for alcohol, but with actual repugnance toward it. Not the first, nor the twentieth, nor the hundredth drink, succeeded in giving them the liking. But they learned, just as men learn to smoke; though it is far easier to learn to smoke than to learn to drink. They learned because alcohol was so accessible. The women know the game. They pay for it—the wives and sisters and mothers. And when they come to vote, they will vote for prohibition. And the best of it is that there will be no hardship worked on the coming generation. Not having access to alcohol, not being predisposed toward alcohol, it will never miss alcohol. It will mean life more abundant for the manhood of the young boys born and growing up—ay, and life more abundant for the young girls born and growing up to share the lives of the young men."

"Why not write all this up for the sake of the men and women coming?" Charmian asked. "Why not write it so as to help the wives and sisters and mothers to the way they should vote?"

"The 'Memoirs of an Alcoholic,'" I sneered—or, rather, John Barleycorn sneered; for he sat with me there at table in my pleasant, philanthropic jingle, and it is a trick of John Barleycorn to turn the smile to a sneer without an instant's warning.

"No," said Charmian, ignoring John Barleycorn's roughness, as so many women have learned to do. "You have shown yourself no alcoholic, no dipsomaniac, but merely an habitual drinker, one who has made John Barleycorn's acquaintance through long years of rubbing shoulders with him. Write it up and call it 'Alcoholic Memoirs.'"

The Ethics of Wine Drinking and Tobacco Smoking
Leo Tolstoy

(1891)

What is the explanation of the fact that people use things that stupefy them: vodka, wine, beer, hashish, opium, tobacco, and other things less common: ether, morphia, fly-agaric, etc.? Why did the practice begin? Why has it spread so rapidly, and why is it still spreading among all sorts of people, savage and civilized? How is it that where there is no vodka, wine or beer, we find opium, hashish, fly-agaric, and the like, and that tobacco is used everywhere?

Why do people wish to stupefy themselves?

Ask anyone why he began drinking wine and why he now drinks it. He will reply, "Oh, I like it, and everybody drinks," and he may add, "it cheers me up."

Some—those who have never once taken the trouble to consider whether they do well or ill to drink wine—may add that wine is good for the health and adds to one's strength; that is to say, will make a statement long since proved baseless.

Ask a smoker why he began to use tobacco and why he now smokes, and he also will reply: "To while away the time; everybody smokes."

Similar answers would probably be given by those who use opium, hashish, morphia, or fly-agaric.

"To while away time, to cheer oneself up; everybody does it." But it might be excusable to twiddle one's thumbs, to whistle, to hum tunes, to play a fife or to do something of that sort "to while away the time," "to cheer oneself up," or "because everybody does it"—that is to say, it might be excusable to do something which does not involve wasting Nature's wealth, or spending what has cost great labor to produce, or doing what brings evident harm to oneself and to others.

But to produce tobacco, wine, hashish, and opium, the labor of millions of men is spent, and millions and millions of acres of the best land (often amid a population that is short of land) are employed to grow potatoes, hemp, poppies, vines, and tobacco.

Moreover, the use of these evidently harmful things produces terrible evils known and admitted by everyone, and destroys more people than all the wars and contagious diseases added together. And people know this, so that they cannot really use these things "to while away time," "to cheer themselves up," or because "everybody does it."

There must be some other reason. Continually and everywhere one meets people who love their children and are ready to make all kinds of sacrifices for them, but who yet spend on vodka, wine and beer, or on opium, hashish, or even tobacco, as much as would quite suffice to feed their hungry and poverty-stricken children, or at least as much as would suffice to save them from misery.

Evidently if a man who has to choose between the want and sufferings of a family he loves on the one hand, and abstinence from stupefying things on the other, chooses the former—he must be induced thereto by something more potent than the consideration that everybody does it, or that it is pleasant. Evidently it is done not "to while away time," nor merely "to cheer himself up." He is actuated by some more powerful cause.

The cause of the world-wide consumption of hashish, opium, wine, and tobacco, lies not in the taste, nor in any pleasure, recreation, or mirth they afford, but simply in man's need to hide from himself the demands of conscience.

I was going along the street one day, and passing some cabmen who were talking, I heard one of them say: "Of course when a man's sober he's ashamed to do it!"

When a man is sober he is ashamed of what seems all right when he is drunk. In these words we have the essential underlying cause prompting men to resort to stupefiers. People resort to them either to escape feeling ashamed after having done something contrary to their consciences, or to bring themselves beforehand into a state in which they can commit actions contrary to conscience, but to which their animal nature prompts them.

A man when sober is ashamed to go after a prostitute, ashamed to steal, ashamed to kill. A drunken man is ashamed of none of these things, and therefore if a man wishes to do something his conscience condemns he stupefies himself.

I remember being struck by the evidence of a cook who was tried for murdering a relation of mine, an old lady in whose service he lived. He related that when he had sent away his paramour, the servant-girl, and the time had come to act, he wished to go into the bedroom with a knife, but felt that while sober he could not commit the deed he had planned . . . "when a man's sober he's ashamed." He turned back, drank two tumblers of vodka he had prepared beforehand, and only then felt himself ready, and committed the crime.

Nine-tenths of the crimes are committed in that way: "Drink to keep up your courage."

Half the women who fall do so under the influence of wine. Nearly all visits to disorderly houses are paid by men who are intoxicated. People know this capacity of wine to stifle the voice of conscience, and intentionally use it for that purpose.

Not only do people stupefy themselves to stifle their own consciences, but, knowing how wine acts, they intentionally stupefy others when they wish to make them commit actions contrary to conscience—that is, they arrange to stupefy people in order to deprive them of conscience.

In war, soldiers are usually intoxicated before a hand-to-hand fight. All the French soldiers in the assaults on Sevastopol were drunk.

When a fortified place has been captured but the soldiers do not sack it and slay the defenseless old men and children, orders are often given to make them drunk and then they do what is expected of them.

Everyone knows people who have taken to drink in consequence of some wrongdoing that has tormented their conscience. Anyone can notice that those who lead immoral lives are more attracted than others by stupefying substances. Bands of robbers or thieves, and prostitutes, cannot live without intoxicants.

Everyone knows and admits that the use of stupefying substances is a consequence of the pangs of conscience, and that in certain immoral ways of life stupefying substances are employed to stifle conscience. Everyone knows and admits also that the use of stupefiers does stifle conscience: that a drunken man is capable of deeds of which when sober he would not think for a moment.

Everyone agrees to this, but strange to say when the use of stupefiers does not result in such deeds as thefts, murders, violations, and so forth—when stupefiers are taken not after some terrible crimes, but by men following professions which we do not consider criminal, and when the substances are consumed not in large quantities at once but continually in moderate doses—then it is assumed that stupefying substances have no tendency to stifle conscience.

Thus it is supposed that a well-to-do Russian's glass of vodka before each meal and tumbler of wine with the meal, or a Frenchman's absinthe, or an Englishman's port wine and porter, or a German's lager-beer, or a well-to-do Chinaman's moderate dose of opium, and the smoking of tobacco with them—is done only for pleasure and has no effect whatever on these people's consciences.

It is supposed that if after this customary stupefaction no crime is committed—no theft or murder, but only customary bad and stupid actions—then these actions have occurred of themselves and are not evoked by the stupefaction. It is supposed that if these people have not committed offences against the criminal law they have no need to stifle the voice of conscience, and that the life led by people who habitually stupefy themselves is quite a good life, and would be precisely the same if they did not stupefy themselves. It is supposed that the constant use of stupefiers does not in the least darken their consciences.

Though everybody knows by experience that a man's frame of mind is altered by the use of wine or tobacco, that he is not ashamed of things which but for the stimulant he would be ashamed of, that after each twinge of conscience, however slight, he is inclined to have recourse to some stupefier, and that under the influence of stupefiers it is difficult to reflect on his life and position, and that the constant and regular use of stupefiers produces the same physiological effect as its occasional immoderate use does—yet in spite of all this it seems to men who drink and smoke moderately that they use stupefiers not at all to stifle conscience, but only for the flavor or for pleasure.

But one need only think of the matter seriously and impartially—not trying to excuse oneself—to understand, first, that if the use of stupefiers in large occasional doses stifles man's conscience, their regular use must have a like effect (always first intensifying and then dulling the activity of the brain) whether they are taken in large or small doses. [S]econdly, that all stupefiers have the quality of stifling conscience, and have this always—both when under their influence murders, robberies, and violations are committed, and when under their influence words are spoken which would not have been spoken, or things are thought and felt which but for them would not have been thought and felt; and, thirdly, that if the use of stupefiers is needed to pacify and stifle the consciences of thieves, robbers, and prostitutes, it is also wanted by people engaged in occupations condemned by their own consciences, even though these occupations may be considered proper and honorable by other people.

In a word, it is impossible to avoid understanding that that the use of stupefiers, in large or small amounts, occasionally or regularly, in the higher or lower circles of society, is evoked by and the same cause, the need to stifle the voice of conscience in order not to be aware of the discord existing between one's way of life and the demands of one's conscience.

PiHKAL: A Chemical Love Story
Alexander Shulgin and Ann Shulgin

(1991)

I am a pharmacologist and a chemist. I have spent most of my adult life investigating the actions of drugs; how they are discovered, what they are, what they do, how they can be helpful—or harmful. But my interests lie somewhat outside the mainstream of pharmacology, in the area I have found most fascinating and rewarding, that of the psychedelic drugs. Psychedelics might best be defined as physically non-addictive compounds which temporarily alter the state of one's consciousness.

The prevailing opinion in this country is that there are drugs that have legal status and are either relatively safe or at least have acceptable risks, and there are other drugs that are illegal and have no legitimate place at all in our society. Although this opinion is widely held and vigorously promoted, I sincerely believe that it is wrong. It is an effort to paint things either black or white, when, in this area, as in most of real life, truth is colored grey.

Let me give the reasons for my belief.

Every drug, legal or illegal, provides some reward. Every drug presents some risk. And every drug can be abused. Ultimately, in my opinion, it is up to each of us to measure the reward against the risk and decide which outweighs the other. The rewards cover a wide spectrum. They include such things as curing of disease, the softening of physical and emotional pain, intoxication, and relaxation. Certain drugs—those known as the psychedelics—allow for increased personal insight and expansion of one's mental and emotional horizons.

The risks are equally varied, ranging from physical damage to psychological disruption, dependency, and a violation of the law. Just as there are different rewards with different people, there are also different risks. An adult must make his own decision as to whether or not he should expose himself to a specific drug, be it available by prescription or proscribed by law, by measuring the potential good and bad with his own personal yardstick. And it is here that being well informed plays an indispensable role. My philosophy can be distilled into four words: be informed, then choose.

I personally have chosen some drugs to be of sufficient value to be worth the risks; others, I deem not to be of sufficient value. For instance, I use a moderate amount of alcohol, generally in the form of wine—and at the present time—my liver function tests are completely normal. I do not smoke tobacco. I used to, quite heavily, then gave it up. It was not the health risk that swayed me, but rather the fact that I had become completely dependent upon it. That was, in my view, a case of the price being unacceptably high.

Each such decision is my own, based on what I know of the drug and what I know about myself.

Among the drugs that are currently illegal, I have chosen not to use marijuana, as I feel the light-headed intoxication and benign alteration of consciousness does not adequately compensate for an uncomfortable feeling that I am wasting time.

I have tried heroin. This drug, of course, is one of the major concerns in our society, at the present time. In me, it produces a dreamy peacefulness, with no rough edges of worry, stress or concern. But there is also a loss of motivation, of alertness, and of the urge to get things done. It is not any fear of addiction that causes me to decide against heroin; it is the fact that, under its influence, nothing seems to be particularly important to me.

I have also tried cocaine. This drug, particularly in its notorious "crack" form, is the cause celebre of today. To me, cocaine is an aggressive pusher, a stimulant which gives me a sense of power and of being completely with it, on top of the world. But there is also the inescapable knowledge, underneath, that it is not true power, that I am not really on top of the world, and that, when the drug's effects have disappeared, I will have gained nothing. There is a strange sense of falseness about the state. There is no insight. There is no learning. In its own distinctive way, I find cocaine to be as much an escape drug as heroin. With either one, you escape from who you are, or—even more to the point—from who you are not. In either case you are relieved for a short time from awareness of your inadequacies. I frankly would rather address mine than escape them; there is, ultimately, far greater satisfaction that way.

With the psychedelic drugs, I believe that, for me, the modest risks (an occasional difficult experience or perhaps some body malaise) are more than balanced by the potential for learning. And that is why I have chosen to explore this particular area of pharmacology.

I am completely convinced that there is a wealth of information built into us, with miles of intuitive knowledge tucked away in the genetic material of every one of our cells. Something akin to a library containing uncountable reference volumes, but without any obvious route of entry. And, without some means of access, there is no way to even begin to guess at the extent and quality of what is there. The psychedelic drugs allow exploration of this interior world, and insights into its nature.

Caring for Ms. L—Overcoming My Fear of Treating Opioid Use Disorder

Audrey M. Provenzano, M.D., M.P.H.

378 New England Journal of Medicine 600 (2018)

Ms. L. always showed up 10 minutes early for her appointments, even though I always ran late. Her granddaughter would rest her cheek against Ms. L.'s chest, squishing one eye shut, and scroll through Ms. L.'s phone while they waited. After reviewing her blood sugars, which Ms. L. recorded assiduously in a dog-eared blue diary, we'd talk about smoking cessation. That was a work in progress. "There's just nothing like a cigarette," she'd sigh. "Don't you ever start," she'd admonish her granddaughter, kissing the top of her head.

One day, I knew something was wrong the moment I opened the door. Ms. L. was alone. Sweat dotted her lip and forehead. She closed her eyes and looked away, and tears fell onto her lap. "I need help," she whispered, and it all came out: she had taken a few of the oxycodone pills prescribed for her husband after a leg injury, then a few more from a friend. And like a swimmer pulled into the undertow, she was dragged back into the cold, dark brine of addiction. I tried to hide my shock. I'd known she was in recovery from opioid use disorder (OUD), but it had simply never come up. She hadn't used in decades.

"No one can know that I relapsed," she said. "If my kids find out, they won't let me see my granddaughter." She wanted to try buprenorphine and was frustrated to hear that I could not prescribe it. "Why not?" Annoyed, she rocked in her chair. "I just want to feel normal again, and I know you. I don't want to tell anyone else."

I evaded her question: "I don't have the right kind of license to prescribe it," I said. "Let me refer you to a colleague."

But my incomplete answer gnawed at me. In truth, the reason I didn't have a waiver to prescribe buprenorphine was that I didn't want one. As a new primary care physician, I spent every evening finishing notes and preparing for the next day. Every Friday I left the office utterly depleted, devoid of the energy or motivation it would take to spend a weekend clicking through the required online training.

But more than not wanting to take on the extra work of prescribing a medication for OUD, I did not want to deal with patients who needed it. I knew that for some people with substance use disorders, the relationship with the drug can eclipse all other relationships, leading them to push away family, friends, and caregivers. I had witnessed patients waiting for prescriptions antagonize secretaries and nurses, seen patients try to manipulate toxicology screenings, and heard voices raised in exasperation at colleagues through thin clinic walls. Addiction, according to the American Society of Addiction Medicine, "is characterized by . . . impairment in behavioral control, craving, diminished recognition of significant problems with one's behaviors and interpersonal relationships, and a dysfunctional emotional response." Already overwhelmed, I did not want to take on patients with needs that I did not know how to meet.

One of my colleagues started Ms. L. on buprenorphine treatment. When I saw her again for her diabetes, a space had opened between us. Then she didn't show up to her next appointment. I called her and sent a letter, but she didn't show up to the next one either. Months passed, and then a year.

The night I found out that Ms. L. had died of an overdose, a heavy, wet snow was falling throughout the city, dampening the sound of traffic. In the quiet, I was clicking through the usual computer screens, preparing for clinic in the morning. I saw Ms. L.'s name and stopped. I read the text twice, three times, and then again: "brought in by ambulance . . . unable to revive her." At first I felt horror and revulsion at the thought of her lifeless body on a gurney. Then, profound sadness. I thought about her husband, her children, and especially her granddaughter. I wondered how silent their house must be that snowy night, without Ms. L.'s brassy laugh floating through the hallways.

But it was the shame that kept me awake, listening to the plows pass through the streets. This shame didn't just burn red and hot in my face—it burrowed thick and leaden into my chest and stomach. What if I had treated her myself, instead of referring her? I don't flatter myself that I could have provided her better care—I had complete confidence in my colleague. But Ms. L. and I had had a relationship. She had trusted me. And I'd turned her away.

In the ensuing months, I earned my waiver to prescribe buprenorphine. I still harbored apprehensions about caring for patients with addiction, but I also knew that I could not turn away another Ms. L. I now care for a small panel of patients with OUD. It has not been easy, and I could not provide this care without the support of colleagues with expertise in addiction and social work. I quickly grasped the pharmacology of buprenorphine therapy, but learning how to manage other aspects of addiction care, particularly for patients in early recovery, has been formidable.

One patient, Ms. J., has coexisting alcohol use disorder, chronic pain, and severe anxiety. I have practiced harm reduction for years—maximizing oral therapies in a patient with diabetes who declines to take insulin, for example. But navigating the gray shades of harm reduction in caring for Ms. J., who uses alcohol on an almost daily basis and takes several sedating psychiatric medications in addition to buprenorphine, is an entirely new calculus for me.

Beyond these difficult therapeutic questions, many of my patients with OUD have complex social needs. Before Ms. J., I had never cared for a patient whose visitation rights with her children were predicated on her continuing therapy with me. A few of my patients have had difficulties following clinic guidelines; implementing behavior contracts had not previously been a common part of my practice, and learning how to use them with kindness and respect remains challenging.

Colleagues with years of experience managing substance use often advocate: "Everyone should get waivered. OUD is a chronic disease just like any other—when a patient comes in with hypertension, you don't say, 'Oh, I don't treat that.'" This comparison does not capture the whole picture. Of course OUD is a chronic disease and should be managed in primary care as such. But it's also true that patients with addiction often have acute psychosocial needs. OUD can utterly shatter a life; I have never seen hypertension have such an effect. If we do not recognize, name, and talk about the social issues that must be addressed when caring for patients with OUD, we do a disservice to both patients and caregivers and create a significant barrier to more providers getting waivers. I know, because I was one of them. Everyone in primary care should get a waiver, but that is not enough. We must also advocate for team-based behavioral health and social work resources in every primary care setting to support patients and providers in managing all aspects of OUD, just as we have developed team-based protocols for managing hypertension.

Caring for these patients has become the most meaningful part of my practice. Ms. J., who has tested my clinical judgment almost weekly, has also inspired me with her persistence and courage through a grueling recovery. Buprenorphine has allowed her to feel "normal"—at least most days—and to focus on her sons. Providing some sense of normalcy for patients whose lives are roiled by overdose and estrangement is the most profound therapeutic intervention I've engaged in as a caregiver. I did not know what Ms. L. meant all those years ago when she said that she only wished to feel normal again. I wish that I'd listened more closely. I wish that I had not been afraid.

In 2016, then-Surgeon General Vivek Murthy issued a comprehensive report on substance use and health in the United States. The excerpt from the Surgeon General's report that follows provides a sense of the scope of drug use in the United States, along with a discussion of the diagnostic criteria for a substance use disorder. As you will see, the report uses the term "substance misuse," which it defines as "[t]he use of any substance in a manner, situation, or frequency that can cause harm to users or those around them. For some substances or individuals, any use would constitute misuse (e.g., underage drinking, injection drug use)."

Facing Addiction in America: The Surgeon General's Report on Alcohol, Drugs, and Health

U.S. Department of Health and Human Services,
Office of the Surgeon General
(2016)

How widespread are substance use, misuse, and substance use disorders in the United States? The annual *National Survey on Drug Use and Health* (NSDUH) gathers data on the scope and prevalence of substance use, misuse, and related disorders, as well as utilization of substance use disorder treatment, among Americans aged 12 and older, representing more than 265 million people.

Over 175 million persons aged 12 and older (65.7 percent of this population) reported alcohol use in the past year, with over 66 million (24.9 percent) reporting binge drinking in the past month. More than 36 million (13.5 percent) reported using marijuana in the past year, 12.5 million reported misusing prescription pain relievers, and over 300,000 reported using heroin in the past year. Almost 8 percent of the population met diagnostic criteria for a substance use disorder for alcohol or illicit drugs, and another 1 percent met diagnostic criteria for both an alcohol and illicit drug use disorder. Although 20.8 million people (7.8 percent of the population) met the diagnostic criteria for a substance use disorder in 2015, only 2.2 million individuals (10.4 percent) received any type of treatment. Of those treated, 63.7 percent received treatment in specialty substance use disorder treatment programs.

Past year misuse of prescription psychotherapeutic drugs was reported by 18.9 million individuals in 2015 (7.1 percent of the population). Within this category, prescribed opioid pain relievers (e.g., OxyContin, Vicodin, Lortab) accounted for 12.5 million people, followed by tranquilizers, such as Xanax, reported by 6.1 million people; stimulants, such as Adderall or Ritalin, reported by 5.3 million people; and sedatives, such as Valium, reported by 1.5 million people.

The prevalence of past 30-day use of "any illicit drugs" (a broad category including marijuana/hashish, cocaine/crack, heroin, hallucinogens, inhalants, and prescription psychotherapeutic medications used nonmedically) rose from 9.4 percent in 2013 to 10.2 percent in 2014 among persons aged 12 and older. This 2014 prevalence rate for illicit drugs is significantly higher than it was in any year from 2002 to 2013. However, no significant changes were observed that year specifically in the use of prescription psychotherapeutic drugs, cocaine, or hallucinogens, suggesting that the observed increase was primarily related to increased use of marijuana. Marijuana was the most frequently used illicit drug (35.1 million past year users). The rate for past month marijuana use in 2014 was significantly higher than it was in any year from 2002 to 2013, with the prevalence of past 30-day marijuana use rising from 7.5 percent in 2013 to 8.4 percent in 2014.

Repeated, regular misuse of any of the substances [discussed above] may lead to the development of a substance use disorder. Severe substance use disorders are characterized by compulsive use of substance(s) and impaired control of substance use. Substance use disorder diagnoses are based on criteria specified in the American Psychiatric Association's *Diagnostic and Statistical Manual of Mental Disorders* (DSM). Much of the substance use disorder data included in this *Report* is based on definitions included in the DSM-IV, which described two distinct disorders: substance abuse and substance dependence, with specific diagnostic criteria for each. Anyone meeting one or more of the abuse criteria—which focused largely on the negative consequences associated with substance misuse, such as being unable to fulfill family or work obligations, experiencing legal trouble, or engaging in hazardous behavior as a result of drug use—would receive the "abuse" diagnosis. Anyone with three or more of the dependence criteria, which included symptoms of drug tolerance, withdrawal, escalating and uncontrolled substance use, and the use of the substance to the exclusion of other activities, would receive the "dependence" diagnosis. Notably, addiction is not listed as a formal diagnosis in the DSM. However, substance dependence was often used interchangeably with addiction, and tolerance and withdrawal were considered, by many, cardinal features of addiction.

The DSM-5, which is the fifth and current version of the DSM, integrates the two DSM-IV disorders, substance abuse and substance dependence, into a single disorder called *substance use disorder* with *mild*, *moderate*, and *severe* sub-classifications. Individuals are evaluated for a substance use disorder based on 10 or 11 (depending on the substance) equally weighted diagnostic criteria (Table 1.5). Most of these overlap with those used to diagnose DSM-IV dependence and abuse. Individuals exhibiting fewer than two of the symptoms are not considered to have a substance use disorder. Those exhibiting two or three symptoms are considered to have a "mild" disorder, four or five symptoms constitutes a "moderate" disorder, and six or more symptoms is considered a "severe" substance use disorder.

Table 1.5 Diagnostic Criteria for Substance Use Disorders

Use in larger amounts or for longer than intended
Wanting to cut down or stop using, but not managing to
Spending a lot of time to get, use, or recover from use
Craving
Inability to manage commitments due to use
Continuing to use, even when it causes problems in relationships
Giving up important activities because of use
Continuing to use, even when it puts you in danger
Continuing to use, even when physical or psychological problems may be made worse by use
Increasing tolerance
Withdrawal symptoms

The new diagnostic criteria are likely to reduce the "all or nothing" thinking that has characterized the substance use field. Tolerance and withdrawal remain major clinical symptoms, but they are no longer the deciding factor in whether an individual "has an addiction." Substance use disorders, including addiction, can occur with [a variety of] substances . . . , *not* just those that are able to produce tolerance and withdrawal. It is also important to understand that substance use disorders do not occur immediately but over time, with repeated misuse and development of more symptoms. This means that it is both possible and highly advisable to identify emerging substance use disorders, and to use evidence-based early interventions to stop the addiction process before the disorder becomes more chronic, complex, and difficult to treat.

Chapter 2

Perspectives on Prohibition and Its Alternatives

Should it be a crime to manufacture, sell, or possess certain drugs?

Beliefs about what sort of conduct should be the subject of criminal punishment typically fall into one of two categories: consequentialist and deontological.

Consequentialist arguments are focused on outcomes. Under the chief consequentialist theory of punishment, utilitarianism, punishment is justified if the benefits to society outweigh the costs. This formulation is easy enough to state but exceedingly difficult to apply. This is because there are a wide range of costs and benefits involved in criminal punishment and many of the figures depend on predictions about the future (like how many would-be criminals will be deterred by a given law) or involve considerations that are not easily quantifiable (like the emotional pain experienced by a crime victim or by a child of someone who is incarcerated).

Deontological philosophies, like retribution, are not concerned with results. Retributivists believe that moral blameworthiness justifies punishment, regardless of any costs or benefits to society. As Immanuel Kant famously put it: "Even if a Civil Society resolved to dissolve itself with the consent of all its members . . . the last Murderer lying in the prison ought to be executed before the resolution was carried out." IMMANUEL KANT, THE PHILOSOPHY OF LAW 198 (1887).

Though there are some who subscribe only to one theory of punishment, in practice most discussions about when criminal punishment is justified involve a mixture of utilitarian and retributivist arguments.

Whatever moral philosophy one subscribes to, retributivists and utilitarians alike generally agree that the conduct covered by most criminal statutes calls for criminal punishment. To be sure, there is often strong disagreement about *how much* punishment a robber should receive. But, few object to the existence of criminal laws against robbery (or sexual assault or homicide).

The shape of the debate over drug crimes is much different. Though criminal laws against the possession, distribution, and manufacture of controlled substances are well established, there is a vigorous and ongoing debate over whether this sort of activity should be criminalized at all. In the case of marijuana, this discussion has moved into the realm of mainstream politics. In 2012, voters in Colorado and Washington passed laws legalizing marijuana. Since then, a number of other states have followed suit. (Marijuana legalization laws are covered in detail in Chapter 8.)

The debate over drug prohibition and its alternatives will be a recurring theme throughout this casebook. This chapter provides an introduction to this issue, with materials that sketch out the main arguments for and against criminalizing drugs. The chapter then introduces a handful of additional policy issues that are important to be familiar with before we turn our attention to drug statutes and case law in Chapter 3.

A. Is Drug Criminalization Just?

One common objection to criminal drug laws is that they punish "victimless" conduct. Are the manufacture, use, and sale of drugs truly "victimless"?

In the next case, *Wisconsin v. Hoseman*, a court was asked to decide whether growing marijuana is a "victimless" crime for purposes of a state criminal restitution statute.

Wisconsin v. Hoseman

Court of Appeals of Wisconsin
334 Wis.2d 415 (2011)

Anderson, J.

Seeking to escape responsibility for damages that rendered an 1885 Victorian home uninhabitable, Michael S. Hoseman appeals from a judgment of conviction in which the court included an order that he pay a $25,000 portion of restitution totaling $106,409.63. Hoseman asserts that the manufacture of marijuana is a "victimless" crime; therefore, he reasons the owners of the residence are not "direct victims" of his criminal conduct. We reject Hoseman's argument and affirm that his unauthorized alterations to the residence in order to construct and operate a hydroponic growing operation were at the heart of the extensive damages that made the residence uninhabitable.

Along with four other individuals, Hoseman was charged with a single count of conspiracy to manufacture between 2500 and 10,000 grams of marijuana. The charge arose after law enforcement uncovered a sophisticated marijuana growing operation in Walworth county.

The State and Hoseman reached a plea agreement under which Hoseman pled guilty to a lesser charge of conspiracy to manufacture between 200 and 1000 grams of marijuana. The trial court imposed three years' initial confinement and three years' extended supervision. It also tentatively held Hoseman was jointly and severally liable for restitution of $106,409.63 in property damages.

The underlying facts are not in dispute. The growing operation was set up in an 1885 Victorian home owned by Tom and Lisa Burbey. Initially, the Burbeys had the house on the market for sale but without any potential buyers, they decided to rent out the house. Hoseman, posing as the son of co-conspirator John G. Olson, approached the Burbeys seeking to rent the house as a weekend retreat and represented that the long-range plan was to move to the house and purchase it from the Burbeys. After Tom Burbey finalized the lease, he moved to Las Vegas, Nevada, to join his wife.

Olson provided almost $180,000 in capital for the development of the hydroponic growing operation and Hoseman served as the on-scene architect. Two upstairs bedrooms were converted to grow rooms using nutrients from Canada; hydroponic growing equipment purchased from suppliers in California—including buckets, lights, ballasts, fertilizer and a growing medium. Starting with marijuana seeds from Amsterdam, the original fifty plants were cloned to produce 200 plants with a street value of $300,000 to $500,000. To prepare the two grow rooms, blankets covered all the windows and sheets were stapled to the walls to reflect the grow lights. Hoses and electrical wiring ran up the stairs. Fifty-gallon drums that held the nutrients and residual acids from the operation were drained into toilets and sinks. The exhaust gases from the growing operation were vented directly into the house. For security, closed circuit televisions were mounted in the house to provide coverage of the outside lot.

After not receiving rental payments from Hoseman for several months, Tom Burbey returned to Walworth county to begin an eviction action. Upon arriving at the house, he had to break in because the locks had been changed. After discovering the growing operation, Burbey notified law enforcement.

The Burbeys filed a restitution claim for property damage in the amount of $106,409.63. The damage they documented stated that high humidity from the operation encouraged mold and mildew damage to the walls, fixtures, wood and curtains. The huge barrels of chemicals needed for the operation ruined wood floors, carpeting and an antique rug. There were hundreds of staple holes in the walls as the result of stapling reflective sheets. THC resin saturated many surfaces; there was testimony that the "[s]ticky sappy stuff doesn't wash off that sticks to your hands, it leaves your handprint on it when you touch it and smells like marijuana and stinks like marijuana and never goes away." Draining acidic chemicals into the toilets and sinks created stains; the toilets were also stopped up with plant material. Finally, the furnace was not working, resulting in frozen water pipes. In their claim for restitution, the Burbeys asserted that as a result of the damages, their residence was uninhabitable.

After sentencing, Hoseman and his co-conspirators filed a motion demanding an evidentiary hearing on the Burbeys' claim for restitution. When the hearing began, the co-conspirators objected to the court's authority to hear the claim for restitution, insisting that the Burbeys were not victims of a crime.

> Judge, first of all, in a drug case there—in fact, I had a sentencing before you last week where even the state asserted in a drug case there is no victim. Number one, if this were a burglary matter, sexual assault, homicide, something of that nature, then this person could claim to be a victim. This is a civil matter with civil damages, and they have not asserted in any way.

The Burbeys' attorney responded, the house "was not rented to operate a marijuana greenhouse. It was operated as a residential rental. It was a home. They used my clients' house, water, electricity, heat, all of the equipment, the fixtures, everything in my clients' house for that enterprise. That makes my client[s] [] victim[s]."

The trial court denied the motion, holding that the use of the Burbeys' house was a part of the conspiracy to manufacture marijuana. The court concluded that conducting the criminal enterprise in the Burbeys' house made them victims as defined in Wis. Stat. § 950.02(4)(a)(1), entitling them to restitution under Wis. Stat. § 973.20. The court went on to conduct an evidentiary hearing that lasted over two days. At the conclusion of the hearing, the court determined that restitution damages totaled $106,409.63. It set Hoseman's restitution at $25,000, based on his ability to pay during the six-year term of his sentence. Hoseman appeals.

On appeal, Hoseman continues with his theme that the manufacture of marijuana is a "victimless" crime; specifically, he argues that the Burbeys are not victims under Wis. Stat. § 973.20 and are not allowed to receive restitution. He contends that the term "victim" as defined in the statutes is "a person against whom a crime has been committed" and does not include all of those who suffered pecuniary losses caused by a defendant's crime.

The scope of the trial court's authority to order restitution is a question of statutory interpretation. The interpretation of a statute is a question of law which this court reviews de novo.

Restitution is governed by Wis. Stat. § 973.20. It provides, in relevant part:

> When imposing sentence or ordering probation for any crime . . . for which the defendant was convicted, the court . . . shall order the defendant to make full or partial restitution under this section to any victim of a crime considered at sentencing . . . unless the court finds substantial reason not to do so and states the reason on the record. . . .

Because the restitution statute does not define the term "victim," we turn to Wis. Stat. § 950.02(4)(a), which is a related statute. Section 950.02(4)(a)(1) provides that "victim" means "[a] person against whom a crime has been committed."

Case law arising under the restitution statute informs us that there are two components to the question of whether restitution can be ordered. First, the claimant of restitution must be a "direct victim" of the crime. Second, there must be a causal connection between the defendant's conduct and harm suffered by the claimant.

To answer the first component of the analysis, we are required to determine who is "a person against whom a crime has been committed." In *State v. Vanbeek,* 316 Wis. 2d 527, we discussed who is a "direct victim" of a crime. Vanbeek left a bomb scare note in a lunch room threatening to harm school property, forcing the school district to evacuate students and staff to another location. After Vanbeek was found guilty of making a bomb scare, the school district sought restitution, including the salaries and benefits of teachers and staff. We affirmed the circuit court's order for restitution.

In opposing restitution, "Vanbeek argue[d] that the persons occupying the school were the direct victims of his crime, and that the school district was only collaterally impacted." We rejected his attack:

> This argument misses the mark. Vanbeek conveyed a false threat to destroy school district property, which resulted in an evacuation and a direct loss to the school district. There is no doubt that the conduct involved in the crime considered at sentencing—conveying a threat to destroy school district property by means of explosives—was directed at the school district. Vanbeek left the bomb scare note on school district property and the note threatened to destroy school district property.

Hoseman makes an argument similar to Vanbeek's that the Burbeys were not directly impacted by the manufacture of marijuana:

> [T]he defendant was not convicted of any crime related to the damage of property. The offense of manufacturing with intent to deliver THC is not a crime committed against or directed against the homeowners, and thus, under Wisconsin law, the homeowners should not have been awarded restitution under Wis. Stat. § 973.20.

Like Vanbeek, Hoseman relies on cases that considered "whether the government (on behalf of law enforcement agencies) or police officers were direct victims, and we determined that the government claimant was not a direct victim entitled to restitution." He argues that *State v. Ortiz,* 247 Wis. 2d 836, "hammers home how stringent Wisconsin courts have delineated between direct victims" and "closely related parties." In *Ortiz* we rejected a city's request for restitution of overtime costs incurred in mobilizing a SWAT team to arrest Ortiz who refused to come out of his house. We held that the police officers were the direct victims of Ortiz's criminal conduct and not the city:

> [T]he fact remains that it was the police, not the city, who were the direct and actual victims of Ortiz's crimes. Ortiz did not threaten to injure the city—he threatened to injure the police officers. Ortiz did not fail to comply with an attempt by the city to take him into custody—he failed to comply with the police effort to take him into custody. Ortiz did not obstruct the city—he obstructed the police. And finally, Ortiz's disorderly conduct was not targeted at the city—it was targeted at the police.

Hoseman also relies on *State v. Lee,* 314 Wis. 2d 764, where we held that a police officer who was injured chasing the defendant from the scene of an armed burglary and armed robbery was not a direct victim because he was not the target of the crime of conviction. He argues that *Lee* supports his thesis that because he was not charged with damaging the Burbeys' property, they are not the direct victims of the crime of conviction.

To further support his argument, Hoseman states that "the record does not indicate that there was any direct victim to the crime sentenced upon, in that there was no evidence presented of any purchasers of the defendant's THC product."

The cases Hoseman relies upon are inapposite under the facts of this case; they stand for the proposition that governmental entities are not entitled to restitution for collateral expenses incurred in the normal course of law enforcement. Hoseman is convicted of conspiracy to manufacture marijuana; in furtherance of that conspiracy, Hoseman rented the Burbeys' residence using a ruse, he converted two upstairs rooms into grow rooms for hydroponic growing equipment, he allowed exhaust gases to vent directly into the residence, he ran hoses and electrical wiring up the stairs, and he drained chemicals into the toilets and sinks of the residence. This is not similar to the situation in *Ortiz* where the city tried to ride on the coattails of the police officers who were the targets of Ortiz's criminal conduct. Likewise, this is not similar to *Lee* where the police officer's injury as collateral damage arising after the crime of conviction was committed. What distinguishes this case from those relied upon by Hoseman is the Burbeys, as owners of the residence, were the direct targets of the conspiracy to manufacture marijuana; it was their residence that was altered and made uninhabitable to further the goal of the conspiracy. If the alterations to the Burbeys' residence had not been made, Hoseman and his co-conspirators could not have manufactured marijuana. The alterations are not collateral to the manufacture of marijuana, they are integral. As the Burbeys' attorney so eloquently argued, the house "was not rented to operate a marijuana greenhouse. It was operated as a residential rental. It was a home. They used my clients' house, water, electricity, heat, all of the equipment, the fixtures, everything in my clients' house for that enterprise. That makes my client[s] [] victim[s]."

The Washington Court of Appeals reached the same result in *State v. Coe,* 939 P.2d 715 (Wash. Ct. App. 1997). Like Hoseman, Coe argued "that growing marijuana is a 'victimless' crime and that the State's failure to charge him with vandalism or some other crime that includes an element of property damage makes restitution inappropriate." The court promptly rejected this argument because there was substantial evidence establishing that Coe made "unauthorized alterations to the house's electrical and ventilation systems to facilitate the manufacture of marijuana." Similar to Coe, Hoseman made unauthorized alternations to the residence in order to construct and operate a hydroponic growing operation.

Having concluded that the Burbeys were direct victims of the conspiracy to manufacture marijuana, we turn to the second component of our analysis—whether there is a causal connection between the defendant's entire course of conduct and harm suffered by the claimant.

We have previously summarized the extensive damage to the Burbeys' residence that made it uninhabitable and Hoseman does not seriously challenge the inescapable conclusion that the actions taken in furtherance of the conspiracy to manufacture marijuana caused the damage to the residence.

Hoseman's unauthorized alterations to the residence and unauthorized operation of a marijuana growing operation were integral to the damages that rendered the residence uninhabitable. And Hoseman's conduct of turning an 1885 Victorian home into a twenty-first century hydroponic marijuana growing operation was the substantial factor in causing the damages incurred by the Burbeys.

By the Court.—Judgment affirmed.

It is clear that Hoseman caused damage to the Burbeys' home. But were the Burbeys victims of Hoseman's cultivation of marijuana in the same sense that someone whose wallet is stolen is a victim of theft? It certainly would have been possible for Hoseman to grow marijuana without damaging the Burbeys' home by, for example, growing a smaller number of plants or designing his operation with greater care. Similarly, Hoseman could have caused just as much damage to the Burbeys' home if he had grown a legal plant in the same fashion as he had the marijuana. Why do you think Hoseman was growing marijuana inside of an old Victorian home instead of in an industrial warehouse or on farmland?

The argument that drug crimes should not be punished because they are victimless is rooted in the harm principle. The harm principle posits that criminal punishment should be reserved for conduct that harms others. John Stuart Mill provided the most well-known and enduring description of the harm principle in his 1859 essay *On Liberty.*

On Liberty
John Stuart Mill

(1859)

The object of this Essay is to assert one very simple principle, as entitled to govern absolutely the dealings of society with the individual in the way of compulsion and control, whether the means used be physical force in the form of legal penalties, or the moral coercion of public opinion. That principle is, that the sole end for which mankind are warranted, individually or collectively in interfering with the liberty of action of any of their number, is self-protection. That the only purpose for which power can be rightfully exercised over any member of a civilized community, against his will, is to prevent harm to others. His own good, either physical or moral, is not a sufficient warrant. He cannot rightfully be compelled to do or forbear because it will be better for him to do so, because it will make him happier, because, in the opinions of others, to do so would be wise, or even right. These are good reasons for remonstrating with him, or reasoning with him, or persuading him, or entreating him, but not for compelling him, or visiting him with any evil, in case he do otherwise. To justify that, the conduct from which it is desired to deter him must be calculated to produce evil to some one else. The only part of the conduct of any one, for which he is amenable to society, is that which concerns others. In the part which merely concerns himself, his independence is, of right, absolute. Over himself, over his own body and mind, the individual is sovereign.

It is proper to state that I forego any advantage which could be derived to my argument from the idea of abstract right as a thing independent of utility. I regard utility as the ultimate appeal on all ethical questions; but it must be utility in the largest sense, grounded on the permanent interests of man as a progressive being. Those interests, I contend, authorize the subjection of individual spontaneity to external control, only in respect to those actions of each, which concern the interest of other people. If any one does an act hurtful to others, there is a prima facie case for punishing him, by law, or, where legal penalties are not safely applicable, by general disapprobation. There are also many positive acts for the benefit of others, which he may rightfully be compelled to perform; such as, to give evidence in a court of justice; to bear his fair share in the common defence, or in any other joint work necessary to the interest of the society of which he enjoys the protection; and to perform certain acts of individual beneficence, such as saving a fellow-creature's life, or interposing to protect the defenceless against ill-usage, things which whenever it is obviously a man's duty to do, he may rightfully be made responsible to society for not doing. A person may cause evil to others not only by his actions but by his inaction, and in neither case he is justly accountable to them for the injury. The latter case, it is true, requires a much more cautious exercise of compulsion than the former. To make any one answerable for doing evil to others, is the rule; to make him answerable for not preventing evil, is, comparatively speaking, the exception. Yet there are many cases clear enough and grave enough to justify that exception. In all things which regard the external relations of the individual, he is de jure amenable to those whose interests are concerned, and if need be, to society as their protector. There are often good reasons for not holding him to the responsibility; but these reasons must arise from the special expediencies of the case: either because it is a kind of case in which he is on the whole likely to act better, when left to his own discretion, than when controlled in any way in which society have it in their power to control him; or because the attempt to exercise control would produce other evils, greater than those which it would prevent. When such reasons as these preclude the enforcement of responsibility, the conscience of the agent himself should step into the vacant judgment-seat, and protect those interests of others which have no external protection; judging himself all the more rigidly, because the case does not admit of his being made accountable to the judgment of his fellow creatures.

But there is a sphere of action in which society, as distinguished from the individual, has, if any, only an indirect interest; comprehending all that portion of a person's life and conduct which affects only himself, or, if it also affects others, only with their free, voluntary, and undeceived consent and participation. When I say only himself, I mean directly, and in the first instance: for whatever affects himself, may affect others through himself; and the objection which may be grounded on this contingency, will receive consideration in the sequel. This, then, is the appropriate region of human liberty. It comprises, first, the inward domain of consciousness; demanding liberty of conscience, in the most comprehensive sense; liberty of thought and feeling; absolute freedom of opinion and sentiment on all subjects, practical or speculative, scientific, moral, or theological.

No society in which these liberties are not, on the whole, respected, is free, whatever may be its form of government; and none is completely free in which they do not exist absolute and unqualified. The only freedom which deserves the name, is that of pursuing our own good in our own way, so long as we do not attempt to deprive others of theirs, or impede their efforts to obtain it. Each is the proper guardian of his own health, whether bodily, or mental or spiritual. Mankind are greater gainers by suffering each other to live as seems good to themselves, than by compelling each to live as seems good to the rest.

Though this doctrine is anything but new, and, to some persons, may have the air of a truism, there is no doctrine which stands more directly opposed to the general tendency of existing opinion and practice. Society has expended fully as much effort in the attempt (according to its lights) to compel people to conform to its notions of personal, as of social excellence. The ancient commonwealths thought themselves entitled to practise, and the ancient philosophers countenanced, the regulation of every part of private conduct by public authority, on the ground that the State had a deep interest in the whole bodily and mental discipline of every one of its citizens, a mode of thinking which may have been admissible in small republics surrounded by powerful enemies, in constant peril of being subverted by foreign attack or internal commotion, and to which even a short interval of relaxed energy and self-command might so easily be fatal, that they could not afford to wait for the salutary permanent effects of freedom. In the modern world, the greater size of political communities, and above all, the separation between the spiritual and temporal authority (which placed the direction of men's consciences in other hands than those which controlled their worldly affairs), prevented so great an interference by law in the details of private life; but the engines of moral repression have been wielded more strenuously against divergence from the reigning opinion in self-regarding, than even in social matters; religion, the most powerful of the elements which have entered into the formation of moral feeling, having almost always been governed either by the ambition of a hierarchy, seeking control over every department of human conduct, or by the spirit of Puritanism.

Under the name of preventing intemperance the people of one English colony, and of nearly half the United States, have been interdicted by law from making any use whatever of fermented drinks, except for medical purposes: for prohibition of their sale is in fact, as it is intended to be, prohibition of their use. And though the impracticability of executing the law has caused its repeal in several of the States which had adopted it, including the one from which it derives its name, an attempt has notwithstanding been commenced, and is prosecuted with considerable zeal by many of the professed philanthropists, to agitate for a similar law in this country. The association, or "Alliance" as it terms itself, which has been formed for this purpose, has acquired some notoriety through the publicity given to a correspondence between its Secretary and one of the very few English public men who hold that a politician's opinions ought to be founded on principles. Lord Stanley's share in this correspondence is calculated to strengthen the hopes already built on him, by those who know how rare such qualities as are manifested in some of his public appearances, unhappily are among those who figure in political life. The organ of the Alliance, who would "deeply deplore the recognition of any principle which could be wrested to justify bigotry and persecution," undertakes to point out the "broad and impassable barrier" which divides such principles from those of the association. "All matters relating to thought, opinion, conscience, appear to me," he says, "to be without the sphere of legislation; all pertaining to social act, habit, relation, subject only to a discretionary power vested in the State itself, and not in the individual, to be within it." No mention is made of a third class, different from either of these, viz., acts and habits which are not social, but individual; although it is to this class, surely, that the act of drinking fermented liquors belongs. Selling fermented liquors, however, is trading, and trading is a social act. But the infringement complained of is not on the liberty of the seller, but on that of the buyer and consumer; since the State might just as well forbid him to drink wine, as purposely make it impossible for him to obtain it. The Secretary, however, says, "I claim, as a citizen, a right to legislate whenever my social rights are invaded by the social act of another." And now for the definition of these "social rights." "If anything invades my social rights, certainly the traffic in strong drink does. It destroys my primary right of security, by constantly creating and stimulating social disorder. It invades my right of equality, by deriving a profit from the creation of a misery, I am taxed to support. It impedes my right to free moral and intellectual development, by surrounding my path with dangers, and by weakening and demoralizing society, from which I have a right to claim mutual aid and intercourse." A theory of "social rights," the like of which probably never before found its way into distinct language—being nothing short of this—that it is the absolute social right of every individual, that every other individual shall act in every respect exactly as he ought; that whosoever fails thereof in the smallest particular, violates my social right, and entitles me to demand from the legislature the removal of the grievance. So monstrous a principle is far more dangerous than any single interference with liberty; there is no violation of liberty which it would not justify; it acknowledges no right to any freedom whatever, except perhaps to that of holding opinions in secret, without ever disclosing them; for the moment an opinion which I consider noxious, passes any one's lips, it invades all the "social rights" attributed to me by the Alliance. The doctrine ascribes to all mankind a vested interest in each other's moral, intellectual, and even physical perfection, to be defined by each claimant according to his own standard.

There are two potential responses to those who believe that the harm principle precludes criminal punishment for drug use, manufacture, and sale. First, proponents of drug prohibition might reject the harm principle outright and argue that it is appropriate to use the criminal law to pursue moral goals, such as the advancement of traditional or religious values, even when the targeted activity does not cause harm to others. For example, Steven Calabresi has argued that "[t]oo many people look to the law for guidance regarding what is right and moral for outright, blanket legalization of morals offenses to be desirable." Steven G. Calabresi, *Render Unto Caesar That Which Is Caesar's, and Unto God That Which Is God's*, 31 Harv. J. L. & Pub. Pol'y 495 (2008).

Second, drug prohibitionists might argue that criminal laws against drug activity are perfectly consistent with the harm principle because the sale and use of drugs causes harm. As Barnard Harcourt describes in the excerpt below, today's debate about so-called morals offenses like drug crimes has largely accepted the harm principle. Rather than challenge Mill's assertion that the law should only be used to punish conduct that harms others, most proponents of criminalizing drugs argue that their use and sale are far from victimless.

The Collapse of the Harm Principle
Barnard E. Harcourt

90 Journal of Criminal Law and Criminology 109 (1999)

As we approach the end of the twentieth century, we are witnessing a remarkable development in the debate over the legal enforcement of morality. The harm principle is effectively collapsing under the weight of its own success. Claims of harm have become so pervasive that the harm principle has become meaningless: the harm principle no longer serves the function of a critical principle because non-trivial harm arguments permeate the debate. Today, the issue is no longer whether a moral offense causes harm, but rather what type and what amount of harms the challenged conduct causes, and how the harms compare. On those issues, the harm principle is silent. This is a radical departure from the liberal theoretic, progressive discourse of the 1960s.

[I]n the writings of John Stuart Mill, H.L.A. Hart and Joel Feinberg, the harm principle acted as a necessary but not sufficient condition for legal enforcement. The harm principle was used to exclude certain categories of activities from legal enforcement (necessary condition), but it did not determine what to include (but not sufficient condition), insofar as practical, constitutional or other factors weighed into the ultimate decision whether to regulate a moral offense. Today, although the harm principle formally remains a necessary but not sufficient condition, harm is no longer in fact a necessary condition because non-trivial harm arguments are being made about practically every moral offense. As a result, today, we no longer focus on the existence or non-existence of harm. Instead, we focus on the types of harm, the amounts of harms, and the balance of harms. As to these questions, the harm principle offers no guidance. It does not tell us how to compare harms. It served only as a threshold determination, and that threshold is being satisfied in most categories of moral offense. As a result, the harm principle no longer acts today as a limiting principle with regard to the legal enforcement of morality.

The collapse of the harm principle has significantly altered the map of liberal legal and political theory in the debate over the legal enforcement of morality. To be sure, the liberal criteria themselves have not changed. As in the 1960s, it is still possible today to define "liberalism," in the specific context of the legal enforcement of morality, on the basis of the same three criteria, namely (1) that it is a justifiable reason to limit an individual's freedom of action if their action causes harm to other persons (the harm principle), (2) that it is also a justifiable reason to limit someone's activities in order to prevent serious offense to other persons (the offense principle), and (3) that it is generally not a justifiable reason to limit harmless conduct on the ground that it is immoral. The criteria are the same today.

But the map of liberalism has changed. In the 1960s and '70s, liberalism was predominantly progressive in relation to moral offenses: liberal theory was dominated by progressives, like H.L.A. Hart, Joel Feinberg, and Ronald Dworkin, who were favorably inclined, by and large, toward the relaxation of sexual morality in the area of homosexuality, fornication, and pornography. In the 1960s and '70s, liberalism was opposed, chiefly, by moral conservatives, like Lord Patrick Devlin, who were theoretically illiberal insofar as they espoused legal moralist principles. Today, liberalism is the domain of progressives and conservatives. Conservatives have adopted the harm principle, and increasingly are making harm arguments. As a result, liberal theory itself is no longer formally opposed. Liberal theory has colonized moral conservatism and, it would appear, is being colonized by conservatives in return. The net effect is the emergence of what I will call conservative liberalism.

The harm principle traces back to John Stuart Mill's essay On Liberty. Mill succinctly stated the principle in a now-famous passage in the opening pages of the essay:

> The object of this essay is to assert one very simple principle, as entitled to govern absolutely the dealings of society with the individual in the way of compulsion and control. . . . That principle is that the sole end for which mankind are warranted, individually or collectively, in interfering with the liberty of action of any of their number is self-protection. That the only purpose for which power can be rightfully exercised over any member of a civilized community, against his will, is to prevent harm to others.

Though simple at first blush, the harm principle actually was far more complicated than it looked, and, over the course of the essay, it took on many nuances. The argument in fact became more complex with each restatement. In Mill's short essay, the harm principle metamorphosed from a simple inquiry into harm, to a more complex analysis of interests (self-regarding and other regarding interests), and eventually to a quasi-legal determination of rights. In his final restatement of the harm principle, Mill ultimately defined the concept of harm on the basis of recognized or legal rights. Mill wrote:

> Though society is not founded on a contract . . . the fact of living in society renders it indispensable that each should be bound to observe a certain line of conduct toward the rest. This conduct consists, first, in not injuring the

> interests of one another, or rather certain interests which, either by express legal provision or by tacit understanding, ought to be considered as rights; and secondly, in each person's bearing his share (to be fixed on some equitable principle) of the labors and sacrifices incurred for defending the society or its members from injury and molestation.

As Mill explained elsewhere, the notion of rights embodied in this final restatement rested on a modified utilitarian calculus grounded on the permanent interests of man as a progressive being.

In Mill's writings, then, the original, simple harm principle evolved into a more cumbersome principle. Mill nevertheless applied the principle and justified, on its basis, a large number of regulations and prohibitions. The harm principle, in Mill's own hands, produced a blueprint for a highly regulated society: a society that regulated the sale of potential instruments of crime, that taxed the sale of alcohol and regulated the public consumption of alcohol, that regulated education and even procreation, and that prohibited public intoxication and indecency.

Beginning at least in the 1950s, liberal theorists, most prominently Professors H.L.A. Hart and Joel Feinberg, returned to Mill's original, simple statement of the harm principle. The context was the debate over the legal enforcement of morality. In England, this debate was reignited by the recommendation of the Committee on Homosexual Offences and Prostitution (the "Wolfenden Report") that private homosexual acts between consenting adults no longer be criminalized. In the United States, the debate was reignited by the Supreme Court's struggle over the definition and treatment of obscenity and the drafting of the Model Penal Code. In both countries, the debate was fueled by the perception among liberal theorists that legal moralist principles were experiencing a rejuvenation and were threatening to encroach on liberalism. More than anyone else, Lord Patrick Devlin catalyzed this perceived threat. In his Maccabaean Lecture, delivered to the British Academy in 1959, Lord Devlin argued that purportedly immoral activities, like homosexuality and prostitution, should remain criminal offenses. Lord Devlin published his lecture and other essays under the title *The Enforcement of Morals*, and Devlin soon became associated with the principle of legal moralism—the principle that moral offenses should be regulated because they are immoral.

The Hart-Devlin exchange structured the debate over the legal enforcement of morality, and thus there emerged, in the 1960s, a pairing of two familiar arguments—the harm principle and legal moralism. All the participants at the time recognized, naturally, that this structure was a recurrence of a very similar pairing of arguments that had set the contours of the debate a hundred years earlier. The Hart-Devlin debate replicated, in many ways, the earlier debate between Mill and another famous British jurist, Lord James Fitzjames Stephen. In 1873, in a book entitled *Liberty, Equality, Fraternity*, Lord Stephen had published a scathing attack on Mill's essay and strenuously advocated legal moralism. Stephen described his argument as "absolutely inconsistent with and contradictory to Mr. Mill's." Stephen's argument, like Mill's, was best captured in a now-famous passage: "[T]here are acts of wickedness so gross and outrageous that, self-protection apart, they must be prevented as far as possible at any cost to the offender, and punished, if they occur, with exemplary severity."

Professor Hart immediately underscored the similar structure of the emerging debate. "Though a century divides these two legal writers," Hart observed, referring to Lords Stephen and Devlin, "the similarity in the general tone and sometimes in the detail of their arguments is very great." In his defense, Devlin responded that at the time he delivered the Maccabaean lecture he "did not then know that the same ground had already been covered by Mr. Justice Stephen. . . ." Nevertheless, Devlin conceded that there was "great similarity between [Lord Stephen's] view and mine on the principles that should affect the use of the criminal law for the enforcement of morals." Devlin also noted the similarity between Hart, Mill, and the Wolfenden Report. Referring to the Wolfenden Report, Devlin observed that "this use of the [harm] principle is, as Professor Hart observed, 'strikingly similar' to Mill's doctrine."

Though the paired structure of arguments was similar, it was not exactly the same. In contrast to Stephen's straightforward legal moralist argument, Lord Devlin's argument in *The Enforcement of Morality* was ambiguous and susceptible to competing interpretations. Devlin's argument played on the ambivalence in the notion of harm—at times courting the idea of social harm, at other times aligning more closely with the legal moralism of his predecessor. As a result, the conservative position began to fragment and there developed at least two interpretations of Devlin's argument: the first relied on public harm, the second on legal moralism.

In large part, the source of the ambiguity stemmed from the fact that Devlin defined public morality in terms of harm to society. In several key passages, Devlin strongly suggested that public morality necessarily encompassed conduct that affected society as a whole. Devlin wrote, for instance, that "[t]here is a case for a collective [moral] judgement . . . only if society is affected." "[B]efore a society can put a practice beyond the limits of tolerance," Devlin emphasized, "there must be a deliberate judgement that the practice is injurious to society." In these and numerous other passages, Devlin made clear that public morality would necessarily involve injury to society, and that the injury was precisely "what gives the law its locus standi." This overlap of harm and morality significantly exacerbated the ambiguity in the debate, and the struggle for the meaning of harm.

Under the more extreme reading, Devlin's argument was much closer to the earlier statement of legal moralism in Lord Stephen's book, Liberty, Equality, Fraternity. Certain key passages in Devlin's writings supported this reading, especially the concluding sentence of the Maccabaean lecture:

> So the law must base itself on Christian morals and to the limit of its ability enforce them, not simply because they are the morals of most of us, nor simply because they are the morals which are taught by the established Church—on these points the law recognizes the right to dissent—but for

the compelling reason that without the help of Christian teaching the law will fail.

These were ominous and somewhat bewildering words. "Christian morals." "The law will fail." To what extent was this a prediction of actual social harm or a traditional argument about legal moralism? Could they even be distinguished anymore? Was legal moralism, in reality, a harm argument? In which direction was Devlin going? Unsure, Hart and other liberal theorists returned to Mill's essay On Liberty and to the original, simple statement of the harm principle. Ironically, that rhetorical move would further ambiguate the conception of harm. The simplicity of the original harm principle would veil an intense struggle for the meaning of harm.

In *Law, Liberty, and Morality*, a set of lectures delivered at Stanford University in 1962 in response to Lord Devlin, Hart rehearsed Mill's harm principle, but carefully pared the argument down to its original, simple, and succinct statement. Right after posing the central question of his lectures—"Ought immorality as such to be a crime?"—Hart immediately cited Mill in support of his position. "To this question," Hart responded, "John Stuart Mill gave an emphatic negative answer in his essay *On Liberty* one hundred years ago, and the famous sentence in which he frames this answer expresses the central doctrine of his essay." Then Hart repeated the famous sentence: "He said, 'The only purpose for which power can rightfully be exercised over any member of a civilised community against his will is to prevent harm to others.'" Hart endorsed the simple harm argument, and declared that, "on the narrower issue relevant to the enforcement of morality Mill seems to me to be right."

Similarly, in an early essay in 1973 entitled *Moral Enforcement and the Harm Principle*—an essay which would sketch the contours of his later four-volume treatise on *The Moral Limits of the Criminal Law*—Professor Joel Feinberg rehearsed Mill's harm principle and he, too, pared the principle down to its original, simple formulation. Feinberg emphasized the importance of distinguishing between direct and indirect harm, but went no further, at the time, in developing the harm argument. Feinberg endorsed the argument and wrote that the distinction, "as Mill intended it to be understood, does seem at least roughly serviceable, and unlikely to invite massive social interference in private affairs."

Eleven years later, Feinberg published the first volume of *The Moral Limits of the Criminal Law*, entitled *Harm to Others*. Feinberg explored there the contours of the harm principle and developed fifteen supplementary criteria, or what he called "mediating maxims," to assist in the application of the harm principle. Throughout the four-volume treatise, Feinberg maintained that the harm argument, as refined by the mediating maxims, was one of only two considerations (the other being the offense principle) that were always a good reason for prohibiting purportedly immoral activity.

Feinberg's experience with the harm principle mirrored, in significant ways, Mill's own experience. Like Mill, Feinberg's confidence in the robustness of the original harm principle eroded somewhat over the course of his writings. Whereas Feinberg originally defined liberalism, in his own words, "boldly," relying exclusively on the harm principle (supplemented by an offense principle), Feinberg concluded the fourth and last volume of *The Moral Limits of the Criminal Law* by softening his claims about the critical role of the harm principle. But even under the more cautious version proposed by Feinberg at the end of his treatise, the qualified harm principle still played a dominant role. Feinberg concluded his treatise with the following "cautious" definition of liberalism:

> [W]e can define liberalism cautiously as the view that as a class, harm and offense prevention are far and away the best reasons that can be produced in support of criminal prohibitions, and the only ones that frequently outweigh the case for liberty. They are, in short, the only considerations that are always good reasons for criminalization. The other principles [moralist or paternalist] state considerations that are at most sometimes (but rarely) good reasons, depending for example on exactly what the non-grievance evil is whose prevention is supposed to support criminalization.

As this passage makes clear, the original harm principle remained, even by the end of Feinberg's treatise, one of the two main limits on state regulation of moral offenses.

Gradually, over the course of the 1960s, '70s, and '80s, Mill's famous sentence began to dominate the legal philosophic debate over the enforcement of morality. Harm became the critical principle used to police the line between law and morality within Anglo-American philosophy of law. Most prominent theorists who participated in the debate either relied on the harm principle or made favorable reference to the argument.

Over time, the harm principle essentially prevailed in the legal philosophic debate over the legal enforcement of morality. From one end of the spectrum to the other, there arose a consensus that Hart had carried the day. At the liberal end of the spectrum, Professor Ronald Dworkin reported that Devlin's argument "was widely attacked" and that his thesis was, ultimately, "very implausible." On the other end of the spectrum, Professor Robert George would report that "many . . . perhaps even most [commentators] think that Hart carried the day. . . ." Professor Jeffrie Murphy—who is today a skeptic of the harm principle—captured well the prevailing consensus. "I believed, along with most of the people with whom I talked about legal philosophy," Murphy wrote, "that legal moralism had been properly killed off, that liberalism had once again been vindicated against the forces of superstition and oppression, and that legal philosophy could now move on to new and more important topics."

This is not to suggest that the controversy simply disappeared from philosophic circles. There were attempts to rehabilitate Devlin's position. There were even attempts to radicalize Devlin's argument. And still today, Devlin has supporters. In fact, just this year, Professor Gerald Dworkin published a provocative essay entitled

Devlin Was Right. In the essay, Dworkin sides with Devlin "in believing that there is no principled line following the contours of the distinction between immoral and harmful conduct such that only grounds referring to the latter may be invoked to justify criminalization." Dworkin argues that Devlin was right in criticizing the line between immoral and harmful conduct, and offers his own justification for criminalizing immoral conduct—namely, that the term "wrongful" connotes conduct that "ought not to be done" in the very same way that the terms "harmful" or "offensive" do. Nevertheless, even Gerald Dworkin's provocative essay does not significantly alter the equation. To a certain extent, Dworkin's argument in fact reflects the fragmentation on the conservative side of the debate. In several key passages of his essay, Dworkin seems to premise his argument on the assumption that harmless wrongdoing is simply not possible. If that is true, of course, then his argument collapses into the public harm thesis—and legal moralism is indistinguishable from the harm principle. In any event, and more importantly for present purposes, Dworkin is willing to concede in his essay that he is swimming against the liberal tide. He readily acknowledges that he is practically alone today in defending Lord Devlin. The fact is that, over time, a consensus emerged that the liberal harm principle prevailed in the legal philosophic debate over the enforcement of morality.

As the harm principle began to dominate the legal philosophic debate, the principle also began to dominate criminal law scholarship and legal rhetoric. Most of the leading criminal law scholars either adopted the harm principle or incorporated it in their writings. Herbert Packer, in his famous book published in 1968, entitled *The Limits of the Criminal Sanction*, included the harm principle in his list of limiting criteria that justified the criminal sanction. Although Packer did not focus primarily on the harm principle—focusing instead on the effectiveness and social consequences of policing certain activities—he did incorporate it into his work and argued that "[t]he harm to others formula seems to me to have . . . uses that justify its inclusion in a list of limiting criteria for invocation of the criminal sanction."

The simple harm principle also permeated the rhetoric of the criminal law itself. This was reflected most clearly in the drafting of the Model Penal Code by the American Law Institute, which was begun in 1952 and completed in 1962. Professor Herbert Wechsler, the chief reporter and intellectual father of the Model Penal Code, strongly endorsed harm as the guiding principle of criminal liability. As early as 1955, Wechsler wrote: "All would agree, I think, that there is no defensible foundation for declaring conduct criminal unless it injures or threatens to injure an important human interest. . . ." In his scholarly writings, Wechsler consistently emphasized the harm principle: conduct "is not deemed to be a proper subject of a penal prohibition" unless it "unjustifiably and inexcusably inflicts or threatens substantial harm. . . ." This was, Wechsler emphasized, "a declaration designed to be given weight in the interpretation of the [Model Penal] Code."

The language of the Model Penal Code reflected this emphasis on the harm principle. In the preliminary article, section 1.02, the drafters addressed the purposes of criminal law and stated, as the very first principle, the objective "to forbid and prevent conduct that unjustifiably and inexcusably inflicts or threatens substantial harm to individual or public interests."

The harm principle was also reflected in the definition of crimes, especially moral offenses and public decency crimes. "The Model Penal Code does not attempt to enforce private morality," the drafters explained. "Thus, none of the provisions contained in Article 251 purports to regulate sexual behavior generally."

With regard to each moral offense, the drafters specifically discussed harm. In the case of prostitution, the drafters retained the criminal sanction specifically because of the potential harm in the spread of syphilis and gonorrhea. "Of special importance to the continuation of penal repression," the drafters emphasized, "was the perceived relationship between prostitution and venereal disease." In the case of consensual homosexual activity, the drafters rejected criminal responsibility on the ground of lack of harm. The drafters canvassed the moral grounds for sanctioning sodomy, but ultimately rejected them because of the "absence of harm to the secular interests of the community occasioned by atypical sexuality between consenting adults." With regard to obscenity, the drafters paid special attention to the relationship between obscene materials and overt misbehavior. The drafters noted that "in another era, spiritual error may have been a sufficient ground for penal repression, but in an age of many faiths and none, society tends to look to more objective criteria to determine what is harmful." Even the proposed definition of public drunkenness incorporated the harm (and offense) principles. In the Model Penal Code, the offense of public intoxication "differs from prior law principally in requiring that the person be under the influence of alcohol or other drug 'to the degree that he may endanger himself or other persons or property, or annoy persons in his vicinity.'"

During the course of the last two decades, the proponents of legal enforcement have increasingly deployed the rhetoric of harm. Armed with social science studies, with empirical data, and with anecdotal evidence, the proponents of regulation and prohibition have shed the 1960s rhetoric of legal moralism and adopted, instead, the harm principle. Whether they have been motivated by moral conviction or by sincere adherence to the harm principle, the result is the same: the harm principle has undergone an ideological shift—or, what Professor Balkin would call "ideological drift"—from its progressive origins.

Today, the harm principle is being used increasingly by conservatives who justify laws against prostitution, pornography, public drinking, drugs, and loitering, as well as regulation of homosexual and heterosexual conduct, on the basis of harm to others. The conservative harm arguments are powerful. By endorsing the harm principle and simultaneously making harm arguments, the proponents of legal enforcement have disarmed the progressive position and the traditional progressive reliance on the harm principle. This has significantly changed the structure of the debate over the legal enforcement of morality.

[For example, t]he structure of the debate over the criminalization of the use of psychoactive drugs has . . . changed significantly since the 1960s. The early progressive argument that the use of marijuana was a "victimless crime" was countered in the late 1970s and 1980s by a campaign against drug use that emphasized the harms to society, and justified an all-out war on drugs. The proponents of legal enforcement—in this case modeled on military enforcement—forcefully deployed the harm argument. Here, again, the harm principle experienced an ideological shift from its progressive origins: today, the debate over drug use pits conservative harm arguments against new progressive arguments about "harm reduction."

The progressive position in the 1960s and early 1970s was characterized by the argument that marijuana use was essentially a "victimless" crime. In his 1968 book, *The Limits of the Criminal Sanction*, Herbert Packer emphasized the "fact" that "the available scientific evidence strongly suggests that marijuana is less injurious than alcohol and may even be less injurious than ordinary cigarettes." Packer refuted, one-by-one, the various claims of harm—including the claims that marijuana use stimulates aggression, causes anti-social behavior, and leads to the use of stronger narcotics. "[T]here is a total lack of solid evidence connecting its use with the commission of other crimes in a causative way," Packer argued. Professor John Kaplan, in his 1970 book *Marijuana—The New Prohibition*, similarly offered a point-by-point rebuttal of practically every possible harm argument associated with the use of marijuana. My colleague, Ted Schneyer, suggested that Kaplan's "treatment of these issues is unassailable and, on the basis of existing evidence, Kaplan's conclusion seems warranted—marijuana use can be considered no more harmful to users and other members of society than the use of alcohol." Schneyer remarked that Kaplan's arguments "are applicable . . . to policymaking in the general area of 'victimless' crime." Joel Feinberg placed the case of the use of psychoactive drugs under the rubric of "legal paternalism"—the principle that justifies criminal sanctions where an activity causes possible harm to the actor, but no harm to others.

All that has changed today. The conservative harm arguments disarmed the traditional progressive position. Today, the opponents of drug prohibition—a loosely grouped coalition critical of current anti-drug enforcement policies—argue about "harm reduction." The term "harm reduction" was crafted in the early 1990s as an alternative to "legalization." Ethan Nadelmann, the director of the Lindesmith Center (a drug policy reform center established in New York City with funding from George Soros) and a leading spokesperson for the reform coalition, explains the "harm reduction" argument: we must "[a]ccept that drug use is here to stay and that we have no choice but to learn to live with drugs so that they cause the least possible harm." Rather than continue the war on drugs, Nadelmann argues, "[t]he more sensible and realistic approach today would be one based on the principles of 'harm reduction.' It's a policy that seeks to reduce the negative consequences of both drug use and drug prohibition, acknowledging that both are likely to persist for the foreseeable future." Nadelmann explains:

> What does "harm reduction" mean in practice? . . . "Harm reduction" means designing policies that are likely to do more good than harm, and trying to anticipate the consequences of new policy initiatives. . . . "Harm

> reduction" requires governments to keep public health precepts and objectives front and center in its drug control policies, and to banish the racist and xenophobic impulses that stirred prohibitionist sentiments and laws earlier in this century.... "Harm reduction" means keeping our priorities in order.

In fact, the "harm reduction" movement has cleverly turned the table on the conservative harm arguments, focusing instead on the harms caused by the policies prohibiting drug use. "[M]any, perhaps most, 'drug problems' in the Americas are the results not of drug use per se but of our prohibitionist policies," Nadelmann claims. The greater harms, then, are "the harms that flow from our prohibitionist policies." Nadelmann emphasizes: "[Milton] Friedman, [Thomas] Szasz and I agree on many points, among them that U.S. drug prohibition, like alcohol Prohibition decades ago, generates extraordinary harms."

The concept of "harm reduction" traces its origins to alternative public policies adopted in the late 1970s and early 1980s in the Netherlands and Great Britain. Policies there were designed to render drug use safer and thereby reduce the harms associated with illicit drug use—including the transmission of diseases like AIDS or hepatitis, and the risks of overdose. Policies were also developed to separate out certain drug markets (marijuana and hashish) from others (heroin), and to relax, but still regulate, the possession and sale of small quantities of marijuana. These policies became part of a public health approach to drug use that now includes methadone programs, needle exchange programs, and community outreach programs, in contrast to the more punitive measures associated with the war on drugs. And they are now part of the domestic "harm reduction" agenda.

The counter-argument from proponents of the enforcement of anti-drug laws has been to argue even greater harm. Barry McCaffrey, director of the Office of National Drug Control Policy and better known as the current "Drug Czar," responds to the "harm reduction" argument: "The plain fact is that drug abuse wrecks lives." "[E]ach year drug use contributes to 50,000 deaths and costs our society $110 billion in social costs." McCaffrey also extolls the benefits of prohibition: "In the past 20 years, drug use in the United States decreased by half and casual cocaine use by 70%." McCaffrey's response, in a nut-shell, is that "[a]ddictive drugs were criminalized because they are harmful; they are not harmful because they were criminalized."

In testimony before Congress, McCaffrey has referred to the "harm reduction" movement as "a carefully-camouflaged, well-funded, tightly-knit core of people whose goal is to legalize drug use in the United States. It is critical to understand that whatever they say to gain respectability in social circles, or to gain credibility in the media and academia, their common goal is to legalize drugs." And, in a recent editorial, McCaffrey argues that:

> The so-called harm-reduction approach to drugs confuses people with terminology. All drug policies claim to reduce harm. No reasonable person advocates a position consciously designed to be harmful. The real question is which policies actually decrease harm and increase good. The approach

advocated by people who say they favor "harm reduction" would in fact harm Americans.

As a result, today, both conservatives and progressives are making harm arguments. The debate is over which harms are worse. In that debate, the harm principle is silent.

Bernard E. Harcourt argues that "[c]laims of harm have become so pervasive that the harm principle has become meaningless: the harm principle no longer serves the function of a critical principle because non-trivial harm arguments permeate the debate." Can a meaningful distinction be drawn between harms cited in defense of drug prohibition (such as child neglect due to drug use) and harms that everyone agrees satisfy the harm principle (such as the harm an armed robber causes to her victim)?

Illicit Drugs: A Test of Joel Feinberg's The Moral Limits of the Criminal Law Douglas Husak

10 *Libertaria* (2008)

The test of any theory is its application to practice. A theory is not valuable if it tells us only what we already know. We do not require a theory about the moral limits of the criminal law to tell us that a state may prohibit murder and rape, but may not prohibit political speech or membership in the Catholic Church. A theory is valuable if it provides insights on issues about which we are likely to be confused and undecided.

If so, statutes prohibiting the use of designated drugs provide an ideal test of the liberal theory of law defended by Joel Feinberg's celebrated four-volume treatise on the moral limits of the criminal sanction.

Can prohibitions against drug use for recreational purposes be justified on the ground that drug use causes harm to others? If so, we would have the most secure justification for drug proscriptions that could possibly be provided. But the first and most important point to notice in applying this potential rationale is that the use of a drug *need* not cause harm to anyone, including the user himself. That is, no one need be harmed by my use of a drug—even the most dangerous of the illicit drugs. Therefore, if we are to apply a harm-to-others rationale, statutes proscribing the use of drugs must be conceptualized as examples of *inchoate* offenses. I understand an offense to be *consummate* if it proscribes conduct that is harmful on each and every occasion in which it is performed. More precisely, each act-token of an act-type proscribed by a consummate offense produces a harm or evil. It is not surprising that most of the principles venerated by criminal theorists have been developed with consummate offenses in mind. Core crimes—arson, rape, murder, and the like—are examples of consummate offenses. Each commission of these crimes violates the rights of others and thus causes them harm. Not all offenses, however, are comparable. An offense is inchoate if it proscribes conduct that does *not* cause harm on each and every occasion in which it is performed. More precisely, some act-tokens of the act-type proscribed by an inchoate offense do not produce harm. Even though these statutes are not designed to reduce the occurrence of harm itself, they *are* designed to reduce something that is almost as bad: a *risk* of harm that might materialize. Perhaps illicit drugs should be criminalized because their use increases the probability that a subsequent harm will result.

No state should repeal all inchoate offenses. The crime of attempt, for example, exists and ought to exist in all jurisdictions. Still, several principles are needed to identify the conditions under which the state is justified in prohibiting conduct on the ground that it prevents a risk of harm rather than harm itself. In what follows, I will defend four such principles, and discuss their application to the case of drug prohibitions.

The first two principles are clear and need little elaboration. First, all criminal laws must promote a *substantial* state interest. Since any reasonable person must agree with Feinberg that the prevention of trivial harms cannot justify a penal law, it is apparent that the prevention of trivial risks provides even less of a rationale. I call this constraint the *substantial risk* requirement. Since virtually all behavior involves *some* level of risk, criminal liability to prevent insubstantial risks would threaten to punish all human activity. How should we apply this first principle? In assessing whether the use of any given drug exceeds whatever level of harm is required, we must decide whether the relevant variable is the *aggregate* amount of harm that drug causes, or whether the relevant variable is the amount of harm that drug causes *per incidence of use*. This determination is difficult. On the one hand, it seems strange to conclude that a given drug causes a trivial amount of harm because almost no harm results from particular instances of use. Tobacco causes lots of disease, but only because smokers tend to consume large amounts of tobacco through the course of their lives. On the other hand, it seems equally strange to suppose that a given drug causes massive amounts of harm because people who use it tend to do so frequently. After all, the criminal offense we seek to justify prohibits a single incidence of drug use, even if the offender never elects to use that drug again. I admit, however, that deciding whether to aggregate or to individuate harms for purposes of applying the substantial risk requirement pose one of the many thorny problems that arise in deciding whether proscriptions of illicit drugs may be justified under a harm-to-others rationale.

Second, criminal statutes must directly advance the state's interest. I call this constraint the *empirical* requirement. When applied to inchoate offenses, this requirement entails that the proscription in question must actually decrease the likelihood that a subsequent harm will occur. If enacting the inchoate offense did not make the incidence of the subsequent harm less probable, the state interest in preventing that harm could hardly justify the proscription. In other words, drug proscriptions cannot be justified if they are ineffective or counterproductive.

A third and fourth requirement must be met before an inchoate offense is justified. I call the third condition the *consummate harm* requirement. According to this principle, the state may not proscribe conduct to reduce the risk of a given harm unless the state would be permitted to proscribe conduct that intentionally and directly causes that same harm. In other words, no theory of criminalization should justify an inchoate offense prohibiting an act that creates the risk of some undesirable state of affairs unless a consummate offense prohibiting an act that intentionally and directly causes that very state of affairs would also be justified. The importance of the consummate harm requirement may escape notice because its truth is generally taken for granted. For example, liability for an attempt presupposes that what is attempted is a crime; persons who attempt to perform an act that is not a crime simply have not committed a criminal attempt. If the crime attempted is precluded by a theory of the penal sanction, no one would propose to retain a separate offense of attempting to commit that crime.

The rationale for the consummate harm requirement is straightforward. It cannot be worse to risk bringing about an undesirable state of affairs than to engage in conduct that deliberately and directly brings about that same state of affairs. In any hierarchy of culpable states, recklessness is less culpable than intention (or purpose). If the act of intentionally and directly causing a result should not be criminalized, the state cannot be justified in enacting an inchoate offense to prevent persons from merely creating a risk of that result. For example, since the act of intentionally failing to save money neither is nor ought to be a criminal offense, an inchoate offense designed to prevent persons from engaging in conduct that increases the risk that they will fail to save money would be incompatible with the consummate harm requirement and thus precluded by a theory of criminalization.

Applications of the consummate harm requirement jeopardize the crime of drug use. As I have indicated, when conceptualized under a harm-to-others rationale, these laws are designed to reduce the probability of a subsequent harm. The *nature* of this subsequent harm, however, is not identified by the statute itself. Frankly, the nature of this harm is mysterious. It will prove convenient to give a name to the ultimate harm the offenses of drug possession, use, and distribution are designed to proscribe. To avoid question-begging, I will refer to this elusive harm as *harm X*. No one should be confident about his ability to identify harm X. Many candidates have been proposed. If we hope to specify harm X, we have little alternative but to rely on the opinions of commentators who defend this law. Consider, for example, the opinions of Daniel Lungren, former Attorney General of California. He protests against "legalizing drugs" by predicting that repeal of these proscriptions would increase "homelessness, unemployment, welfare, lost productivity, disability payments, school dropouts, lawsuits, medical care costs, chronic mental illness, accidents, crime, child abuse, and child neglect."

I am skeptical that many of these rationales for drug prohibition would survive a test of criminalization that includes the consummate harm requirement. Let us suppose that Lungren is correct that the failure to punish illicit drug possession would lead to each of the undesirable states of affairs he mentions—even though solid empirical evidence for these claims seldom is provided.[3] Even granting this contested supposition, most of his allegations fail to provide a viable defense of the prohibition. The consummate harm requirement enables us to appreciate what is unpersuasive about many (but not all) of Lungren's allegations. We are not justified in proscribing drug possession because use leads to lost productivity, for example, since conduct that deliberately and directly causes lost productivity neither is nor ought to be criminalized. Since no one proposes to prohibit acts that make workers less productive—such as deliberately quitting one's job and becoming unemployed—it follows that conduct that merely increases the risk of becoming less productive should not be a crime. Proscribing conduct that causes the risk of an undesirable outcome while failing to proscribe conduct that directly and deliberately brings about that very outcome is incompatible with the consummate harm requirement—a requirement that any test of criminalization should include.

But we have not yet completed that part of a theory of criminalization that pertains to inchoate offenses. A fourth principle, which I call the *culpability* constraint, is needed. Criminal laws should not be more extensive than necessary to achieve their objectives. This condition imposes a presumption against overinclusive criminal legislation—a presumption that jeopardizes a great many inchoate offenses. A statute is overinclusive when its justificatory rationale applies to some but not all of the conduct proscribed. Since the purpose of an inchoate offense is to reduce the probability of a subsequent harm, a given offense of risk-imposition is overinclusive when a defendant can breach it *without* increasing the likelihood of that harm. No theory of criminalization should allow such a person to be punished.

Drug proscriptions probably fail the culpability constraint. To support my suspicions, return to Lungren's several attempts to specify what I have called harm X. Recall his allegation that illicit drug use increases child abuse. I admit that this rationale for drug proscriptions satisfies the consummate harm requirement. Still, Lungren's rationale fails to show that existing drug proscriptions are no more extensive than necessary to accomplish their objective. After all, the overwhelming majority of adults can and do use drugs without creating a substantial risk that any children will be abused. Therefore, this statute is overinclusive and presumptively unjustified. A statute punishing all drug users because some drug users increase the risk of child abuse, when the two classes of users are easily distinguished, is more extensive than necessary to accomplish Lungren's objective.

---

3. Does illicit drug use cause greater amounts of crime, for example? Many criminologists think not. Even James Q. Wilson—a steadfast opponent of drug decriminalization—admits that drug prohibitions probably cause more crime than drug use. He contends: "It is not clear that enforcing the laws against drug use would reduce crime. On the contrary, crime may be caused by such enforcement." See James Q. Wilson: "Drugs and Crime," in Michael Tonry and James Q. Wilson, eds: *Drugs and Crime* (Chicago: University of Chicago Press, 1990), p. 522.

It is apparent that a great deal of guesswork is needed to show that given inchoate offenses—like drug proscriptions—fail any or all of the four principles in our test of criminalization. Still, it is clear that many drug offenses are almost certainly overinclusive, with little need for conjecture. Consider statutes prohibiting drug possession or distribution in proximity to a school zone. Although the proscribed acts may seem especially culpable and important to deter, almost none of the cases in which this charge is brought involve sales of drugs to minors. These statutes have been construed so broadly that virtually all drug offenses in urban areas fall within their parameters. It is nearly impossible to find a place in a municipality that is *not* within 1000 feet of a school zone. In one case, a defendant was convicted of this offense even though she distributed drugs within a prison that happened to be near a school. The risk that schoolchildren will use drugs is not increased in this kind of situation. It is difficult to imagine that schoolchildren would break into prison to procure drugs.

How can problems of overinclusion be remedied? Isn't overinclusion inevitable as long as law consists of rules? Many possible solutions to this problem might be defended. I propose that no one should be criminally liable for engaging in conduct that increases the risk of a subsequent harm X unless he acts with culpability about the occurrence of X. Thus, no one would be liable for using a drug because his drug use would increase the risk of child abuse unless he was reckless (or perhaps negligent) about that risk. No one should complain about the overinclusiveness of an inchoate offense if he is culpable with respect to the very harm this statute seeks to prevent. Requiring that defendants are culpable with respect to the subsequent harm these inchoate offenses are designed to prevent would help to justify such laws within a liberal framework that limits the reach of the criminal sanction.

Feinberg offers his only extended discussion of drug prohibitions in his treatment of paternalism. In rejecting "hard paternalism," Feinberg maintains "the state has the right to prevent self-regarding harmful conduct *when but only when* that conduct is substantially nonvoluntary." Unless the person suffers from some cognitive or volitional deficiency, his choice to use drugs is not subject to paternalistic intervention.

Feinberg illustrates his position by presenting three scenarios in which Mr. Roe discusses with Dr. Doe his decision to use a dangerous recreational drug called *x*. In the first example, Roe mistakenly believes that using x will not cause him harm. Feinberg concludes that Roe's decision to use x is nonvoluntary because he does not intend to ingest a substance that will actually harm him. In the second example, Roe is aware that x is harmful but indicates that he actually intends to harm himself. Feinberg claims that Roe's decision is so odd that it creates a presumption of nonvoluntariness. If further examination does not reveal independent evidence of incapacitation, however, Roe should be allowed to proceed. In the third and final example, Roe understands the risks of x, has no desire to harm himself, and states: "I don't care if it causes me physical harm. I'll get a lot of pleasure first, so much pleasure in fact, that it is well worth the risk.'" Feinberg concludes that this latter case is "easy", and he is correct.

To which of these three scenarios do most instances of drug use in the real world conform? I assume that almost no drug user intends to harm himself. If he did, it is hard to see how threats of punishment could be expected to deter him. But do drug users really understand the risks of illicit drug use? Empirical evidence confirms that the vast majority of persons know that drug use may be harmful. Why else would they think that drugs are illegal? In fact, most drug users tend to *over*-estimate rather than *under*estimate the hazards of the substances they consume. And even those few adults who act *in* ignorance seldom act *because* of ignorance. In other words, more accurate information about the hazards of drugs is unlikely to change their behavior. Studies testing the efficacy of educational programs for adolescents support this conclusion. Efforts to present factual information about the risks of specific substances do not reduce the prevalence of drug use and may actually increase it. Drug prohibitionists tend to agree that lack of information by drug users is not at the heart of the problem. As William Bennett, America's first and most famous "drug czar" states: "If ignorance is the problem, knowledge is the cure. I don't believe that for a large number of kids out there who use drugs, that ignorance is the problem." What is true of "kids" is even more likely to be true of adults. If I am correct so far, most illicit drug use by adults conforms to the third scenario—the scenario Feinberg aptly describes as "easy." Like any number of hazardous activities in which persons engage for recreational purposes, drug users typically believe the pleasure is worth the risk. If we reject hard paternalism, drug prohibitions cannot be justified on paternalistic grounds.

Arguably, the most widely accepted rationale for criminalization does not depend on the *effects* or *consequences* of illicit drugs. Instead, punishing drug users might represent a *moral* imperative. William Bennett writes: "I find no merit in the legalizers' case. The simple fact is that drug use is wrong. And the moral argument, in the end, is the most compelling argument." James Q. Wilson expresses this view eloquently. He writes: "Even now, when the dangers of drug use are well-understood, many educated people still discuss the drug problem in almost every way except the right way. They talk about the 'costs' of drug use and the 'socioeconomic factors' that shape that use. They rarely speak plainly—drug use is wrong because it is immoral and it is immoral because it enslaves the mind and destroys the soul." Polls suggest that most people in the United States agree with this moral judgment.

Many legal philosophers would quickly dismiss this rationale out of hand because they do not accept its major premise: *legal moralism*. Feinberg, of course, would join those who reject it. To my mind, however, the ... premise [that recreational drug use is immoral] ... is even less plausible than the first. In other words, I see no reason to believe that the recreational use of illicit drugs is immoral. Of course, I may be mistaken in my belief; debates about morality are notoriously hard to resolve. Because *I* see no reason to believe that the recreational use of illicit drugs is immoral does not show that no such reason exists.

Why should we believe that the recreational use of illicit drugs is immoral? Sometimes, prohibitionists offer historical explanations. They remind Americans of our puritan legacy, of our longstanding suspicion of pleasure and fun, of our alleged "hedonism taboo." But how are these points supposed to advance our inquiry? They cannot be taken seriously as a *justification* for criminalization. Whatever may have been true at an earlier period in our history, no one continues to believe that an activity is immoral simply because it produces pleasure. No one denounces other activities as wrongful—spectator sports and television, for example—on the ground that they are recreational.

How *might* a moral case against recreational drug use be constructed? Someone could believe this activity to be wrongful for either of two kinds of reasons. First, drugs might be thought to be immoral because of the psychological states they cause. In other words, the "high" of drugs might be wrongful for people to experience. This alternative seems improbable. In the first place, it is not altogether clear how a psychological state *could* be immoral to experience. Moreover, the euphoria produced by licit drugs and prescription medications almost never are condemned as wrongful. In addition, psychological states that may be indistinguishable from those caused by drugs—a "runner's high," for example—are not denounced. Therefore, the moral case against drugs is unlikely to be based on the nature of the experiences they cause. A second explanation for the immorality of drug use is more probable. Perhaps the alleged immorality consists in the behavior of persons under the influence of drugs. Specifically, drugs produce risks that users will behave badly. But this case against drugs flounders in light of empirical considerations. Worst-case scenarios aside, few drug users jeopardize the welfare of children, commit crimes, endanger their health to a substantial degree, or otherwise behave in ways that merit blame or condemnation. Since neither of these two explanations of the immorality of drug use seem plausible, it is hard to see how a persuasive case *could* be constructed.

I am not saying that no sensible moral objections have ever been raised against recreational drug use. Instead, I am saying that the *kinds* of moral objections that are plausible provide a poor rationale for criminalization. Let me explain. In my judgment, the most serious moral questions about recreational drug use invoke a conception of human virtue. Philosophers have long disagreed about the details of a theory of human excellence. Greek philosophers and Christian theologians, for example, have offered very different accounts of perfection in human beings. All philosophers, however, agree that the ideal person cultivates his physical and intellectual talents. Drug use, especially when excessive, undermines this aspiration; these users tend to make less of their lives than they might. Heavy drug use might be described as a *handicap*. Those who use drugs excessively for an extended period of time are destined to fall short of an ideal. According to this school of thought, heavy drug use is a moral *vice*—the opposite of a virtue.

Whether *all* recreational drug use is a vice is far more controversial. Philosophers who develop accounts of human excellence disagree about the extent to which the pursuit of pleasure is consistent with the attainment of virtue. Notwithstanding ascetic accounts of virtue—which condemn all pleasurable activities—I see no reason to believe that those who aspire to perfection cannot pursue recreational activities at least occasionally. Perhaps recreational *drug* use, unlike other recreational pursuits, is incompatible with virtue. But this claim needs to be defended rather than assumed.

In any event, the difficulty with this kind of moral position should be evident. No one . . . seriously proposes to criminalize all vice. It is one thing to say that we deserve to be punished when we behave immorally, but quite another to say that we deserve to be punished when we handicap ourselves or fall short of an ideal. Sloth and gluttony are at odds with the development of our physical and intellectual talents, but almost all of us would be subject to punishment if these vices were criminalized. A rationale for criminalization must show that drug use is *wrongful*—not that it is contrary to virtue or excellence. The criminal law establishes a floor beneath which we are not permitted to sink, rather than a ceiling to which we are encouraged to aspire.

A few prohibitionists have risen to the challenge and endeavored to explain why they believe that the recreational use of illicit drugs is immoral, whereas the recreational use of licit drugs is not. James Q. Wilson writes:

> "If we believe—as I do—that dependency on certain mind-altering drugs is a moral issue, and that their illegality rests in part on their immorality, then legalizing them undercuts, if it does not eliminate altogether, the moral message. That message is at the root of the distinction we now make between nicotine and cocaine. Both are highly addictive; both have harmful physical effects. But we treat the two drugs differently, not simply because nicotine is so widely used to be beyond the reach of effective prohibition, but because its use does not destroy the user's essential humanity. Tobacco shortens one's life, cocaine debases it. Nicotine alters one's habits, cocaine alters one's soul."

How are we to understand this attempt to differentiate between the morality of licit and illicit drug use? After all, Wilson does not mention the protection of youth, a rise in crime, a decline in health, or a general deterioration in society to support the distinction he draws. Wilson's reference to the "soul" provides the key to an answer. The use of illicit drugs is said to "alter" or "destroy" the soul. On the basis of this allegation, Wilson is prepared to send illicit drug users to prison, while sparing those who use licit drugs like tobacco and alcohol. How might his argument be assessed? Millions of living Americans and Europeans have used cocaine and heroin. If we examine their souls, would we find them to be altered or destroyed? Would we find the souls of users of licit drugs to be preserved and intact?

I cannot really believe that Wilson is intending to make an empirical claim about what doctors and scientists would discover if they examined the souls of illicit drug users. Instead, I believe he is using religious grounds to object to the use of illicit drugs. Contemporary discussions of drug policy rarely mention religion explicitly. I believe this neglect is unfortunate; religion plays an absolutely central role in shaping contemporary drug policy in the United States today. Attitudes about drugs and drug policy correlate with age, race, geographical location, education, political affiliation, and gender. But no demographic variable correlates nearly as strongly with attitudes about illicit drugs in the United States as religion. Lifetime abstainers frequently mention religion when asked to explain how they have managed to resist the lure of illicit drugs. Polls indicate that a majority of respondents who identify themselves as having "no religion" believe that marijuana should be "made legal." Protestants, by contrast, oppose legalization by a 69–26 margin. The United States is probably more religious than any Western industrialized democracy; it is no coincidence that the United States has the most punitive drug policy. We should not be surprised that issues closely linked to religion are impossible to resolve by rational argument. In this respect, attitudes about drugs resemble those about abortion, where religion plays an even more central role. Religious belief, almost by definition, is the product of faith rather than reason. We live in a secular state in which people should not be punished for behaving in ways that are contrary to the teachings of religion. A justification for punishment must not presuppose that we all share the same religious faith.

One of the frustrating aspects of debating an issue that is influenced by religion is that those who take sides are not always candid about why they hold their opinions. Few are willing to say, "I believe that drug users should be punished because of my religious convictions." Instead, they often disguise the reasons for their beliefs by citing some other liberty-limiting principle. Debates will have no impact as long as we focus on issues that do not really explain why parties to the debate feel as they do. Thus I would like to make one more point before we leave this rationale behind. Prohibitionists pretend to occupy the high moral ground in debates about illicit drug use. Unlike their opponents, they profess to stand up against immorality. Those who oppose criminalization are seemingly placed in the uncomfortable and awkward position of condoning behavior that is suspect from a moral point of view. I contend that the moral high ground should *not* be conceded to those who favor prohibition. Disagreement about the immorality of recreational drug use might be reasonable. But there can be no disagreement about the immorality of punishing people without excellent reasons to do so. Punishment is the most powerful weapon in the state arsenal, and we must always be vigilant to ensure that it is not inflicted without adequate justification. The entire thrust of this paper is that this weapon is invoked without good reason against recreational drug users. If I am correct, prohibitionists are more clearly guilty of immorality than their opponents. The wrongfulness of recreational drug use, if it exists at all, pales against the immorality of punishing drug users. How much harm to drug users and to society are prohibitionists willing to tolerate in their efforts to prevent people from using drugs? I conclude that those who punish drug users perpetrate a far greater immorality than those who use drugs.

Ah Lim v. Washington provides another perspective on the harm principle and its application to drug laws. In *Ah Lim*, the majority suggests that when the government provides robust protections and services to its citizens, it should have more power to limit individual liberty. As the court puts it, "[t]he natural rights of the subject or his rightful exercise of liberty in the pursuit of happiness, depends largely upon the amount of protection which he receives from the government." Are you convinced by this argument?

Ah Lim v. The Territory of Washington

Supreme Court of Washington
1 Wash. 156 (1890)

Dunbar, J.

The defendant was indicted at the August term of the district court for King county, for the crime of smoking opium, as follows, to wit: "The said Ah Lim, on the 27th day of September, A. D. 1889, in the county of King, in the district aforesaid, then and there being, did then and there willfully and unlawfully smoke opium, by then and there burning said opium and inhaling the fumes thereof through an instrument commonly known as an opium pipe, contrary to the form of the statute," etc.

To this indictment the defendant interposed a demurrer specifying several grounds, but the one relied upon by the defendant, and the one to be considered here, is, that the statute upon which the indictment is based is unconstitutional as being in violation of the inalienable right to life, liberty and pursuit of happiness; and that it involves a deprivation of liberty and property, through a limitation upon the means and ways of enjoyment, without due process of law.

[T]he doctrine is well established, that the power of the legislature cannot be restrained by the courts upon considerations of policy or supposed natural equity. Were this power given to the courts, the law, instead of being administered and decided upon uniform principles, would be decided according to the particular bent or inclination of mind of the ruling judge. What would appeal to one judge as natural equity would not be so received by another, and the different views of what constitutes a natural equity would only be equaled in number by the number of judges on the bench, each judge following his own ideas of abstract right, not limited to any well-defined path of investigation, but controlled and impelled only by his personal ideas of what ought or ought not to be allowed in a particular case; pointed in no definite direction, but drifting aimlessly like mariners at sea under a clouded sky with neither compass nor log.

In the case at bar no special constitutional limitation or inhibition is pointed out with which the law in question is in conflict, but it is contended by the defense that the right of liberty and pursuit of happiness is violated by the prohibition of any act which does not involve direct and immediate injury to another.

The state has an undisputed right to, and does provide gymnasium attachments to its schools, and prescribes calisthenic exercises for the muscular development of school children. The object to be obtained is not for the exclusive benefit of the child. The state has an interest in the health of its citizens, and has a right to see to it that its citizens are self-supporting. It is burdened with taxation to build and maintain jails and penitentiaries for the safe keeping of its criminals, and to protect its law-abiding subjects from their ravages. It is taxed to maintain insane asylums for the safe-keeping and care of those who become insane through vicious habits or otherwise. It is compelled to maintain hospitals for its sick, and poorhouses for the indigent and helpless, and surely it ought to have no small interest in, and no small control over, the moral, mental and physical condition of its citizens.

If the state concludes that a given habit is detrimental to either the moral, mental or physical well-being of one of its citizens to such an extent that it is liable to become a burden upon society, it has an undoubted right to restrain the citizen from the commission of that act; and fair and equitable consideration of the rights of other citizens make it not only its right, but its duty, to restrain him. If a man willfully cuts off his hand or maims himself in such a way that he is liable to become a public charge, no one will doubt the right of the state to punish him; and if he smokes opium, thereby destroying his intellect and shattering his nerves, it is difficult to see why a limitation of power should be imposed upon the state in such a case. But it is urged by the defense that a moderate use of opium, or that the moderate use of an opium pipe, is not deleterious, and consequently cannot be prohibited. We answer that this is a question of fact which can only be inquired into by the legislature. Smoking opium is a recognized evil in this country. It is a matter of general information that it is an insidious and dangerous vice, a loathsome, disgusting and degrading habit that is becoming dangerously common with the youth of the country, and that its usual concomitants are imbecility, pauperism and crime. It has been regarded as a proper subject of legislation in every western state, and it is admitted by counsel for the defense in the argument of this case that the statute in relation to the suppression of joints kept for the purpose of smoking opium was constitutional and right.

Granted that this is a proper subject for legislative enactment and control, no limit can be placed on the legislative discretion. It is for the legislature to place on foot the inquiry as to just in what degree the use is injurious; to collate all the information and to make all the needful and necessary calculations. These are questions of fact with which the court cannot deal.

It is common to indulge in a great deal of loose talk about natural rights and liberties, as if these were terms of well-defined and unchangeable meaning. There is no such thing as an absolute or unqualified right or liberty guaranteed to any member of society. Natural rights and liberties of a subject are relative expressions and have relative or changeable meanings. What would be a right of liberty in one state of society would be an undue license in another. The natural rights of the subject or his rightful exercise of liberty in the pursuit of happiness, depends largely upon the amount of protection which he receives from the government. Governments in their earlier existence afforded but little protection to their subjects, consequently the subject had a right to pursue his happiness without much regard to the rights of the government. The reciprocal relations were not large—he yielded up but little and received but little. If he was strong enough to buffet successfully with the world, all well and good; if not, he must live on the charity of individuals or die neglected on the highway. But now all civilized governments make provisions for their unfortunates; and progress in this direction has been wonderful even since noted sages like Blackstone lectured upon the inalienable rights of man. Not only is the protection of individual property becoming more secure, but the vicious are restrained and controlled, and the indigent and unfortunate are maintained at the expense of the government, in comfort and decency, and the natural liberties and rights of the subject must yield up something to each one of these burdens which advancing civilization is imposing upon the state. It is not an encroachment upon the time-honored rights of the individual, but it is simply an adjustment of the relative rights and responsibilities incident to the changing condition of society.

Our conclusion is, that the law in question involves no inalienable right. It may be radical, injudicious and wrong; but, as we have before indicated, these are questions solely for legislative investigation and discretion, and as has been said by Judge Story, "Judges should regard it as their duty to interpret laws and not to wander off into speculations upon their policy."

The judgment of the court below is affirmed.

Scott, J., dissenting.

I cannot agree with the decision rendered in this case. That part of the act upon which the indictment is founded, is, in my opinion, void. It is as follows: "Any person or persons who shall smoke or inhale opium . . . shall be deemed guilty of a misdemeanor," etc.

Legislation . . . has ordinarily been confined to those cases where the act of the person directly and clearly affected the public in some manner. But here a single inhalation of opium, even by a person in the seclusion of his own house, away from the sight and without the knowledge of any other person, constitutes a criminal offense under this statute. And this regardless of the actual effect of the particular act upon the individual, whether beneficial or injurious.

It is admitted that this law can only be sustained upon some one or more of the following grounds, viz.: That smoking or inhaling opium injures the health of the individual, and in this way weakens the state. That it tends to the increase of pauperism. That it destroys the moral sentiment and leads to the commission of crime. In other words, that it has an injurious effect upon the individual, and, consequently, results indirectly in an injury to the community. And it is claimed that we must presume that the legislature had some one or more of these objects in view in enacting the law, although there is nothing upon the face of the act to indicate the legislative intention. This is going to a very great and dangerous extent to sustain legislation, in this most important branch of our social structure.

[I]f the act in question declared that no man should willfully injure himself by smoking or inhaling opium, thereby limiting its scope to such cases where injury resulted, there would be strong, and I think valid, reasons for sustaining it upon some one or more of the grounds mentioned. Every act of the individual which has a direct tendency to render him unfit to perform the duties he owes to society, is a rightful subject of legislation. The principle is a just and legal one. A man has no right to do that which will render himself an imbecile, or a pauper. Society has an interest in the promotion and preservation of the bodily, mental and moral health of each individual citizen. And laws tending to such results should be upheld in all reasonable ways.

A body politic is a social compact by which the whole people covenants with each citizen, and each citizen with the whole people, that all shall be governed by certain laws for the common good. This does not confer power upon the whole people to control rights which are purely and exclusively private, but it does authorize the establishing of laws requiring each citizen to so conduct himself and so use his own property as not unnecessarily to injure another. This is the very essence of government.

It is contended here that the legislature, being the sole and absolute judge of the effect upon the individual, of the act forbidden, has decided every act of smoking or inhaling opium to be injurious to the person so doing, no matter how long or how short the duration, or how great or how small the quantity, or under what conditions or circumstances the same might have been used, and that there is no right of appeal to the courts in this particular. Such a construction of the law makes the legislature the sole judge of the constitutionality of its own acts of this character.

There must be a right of review or control, to some extent, in the courts. Each citizen is entitled to the protection of all the branches of the government. A declaration by the legislature as to what the law shall be, is not necessarily a conclusion reached by the state. The legislature is not the state, although a very important or essential part of it. The power to protect the rights of the citizen from the wrongful effect of such legislation is peculiarly adapted to, and within the province of, the judicial branch of the government[.]

To declare any private act or omission of the citizen to be a crime, which does not result in any injury to the person and could not possibly affect society . . . would be an unwarranted infringement of individual rights, and therefore unconstitutional. Individual desires are too sacred to be ruthlessly violated where only acts are involved which purely appertain to the person, and which do not clearly result in an injury to society, unless, possibly, thus rendered necessary in order to prevent others from like actions which to them are injurious.

A great principle is involved in this character of legislation. Suppose the legislature had forbidden the use of opium in any manner. If the unqualified right to prohibit its use in one way exists, this carries with it the right to prohibit its use entirely. Substitute any other substance, whether commonly used as medicine, food or drink, and still such a statute must be upheld if the courts have no right of review.

It is no answer to say that the legislature would do nothing unreasonable. No man knows as to this. The question is, has it the arbitrary power and right?

I make no question but that the habit of smoking opium may be repulsive and degrading. That its effect would be to shatter the nerves and destroy the intellect; and that it may tend to the increase of pauperism and crime. But there is a vast difference between the commission of a single act, and a confirmed habit. There is a distinction to be recognized between the use and abuse of any article or substance.

It is also a well-known fact that opium, in its different forms, is frequently administered as a medicine with beneficial results; and while it may not be customary to administer it by way of inhalation, yet the legislature should not arbitrarily prevent its use in such a manner. If this act must be held valid it is hard to conceive of any legislative action affecting the personal conduct, or privileges of the individual citizen, that must not be upheld. We have been cited to no law, which has been sustained, that goes to the extent that this one does. It has no reference to the manufacture or sale of the substance. It is not based upon any pernicious example that the commission of the act might be to others. The prohibited act cannot affect the public in any way except through the primary personal injury to the individual, if it occasions him any injury. It looks like a new and extreme step under our government in the field of legislation, if it really was passed for any of the purposes upon which that character of legislation can be sustained, if at all.

In former times laws were sometimes passed limiting individual conduct in ways that are now considered ridiculous. Such as regarding the number of courses permissible at dinner. The length of pikes that might be worn on the shoes, etc. But these were founded on the pique or whims of an exacting and tyrannical aristocracy, rather than on reason. Or, as in the case of the Connecticut blue laws, upon views of propriety or religion that do not now obtain with anything like the former degree of strictness.

Judge Cooley, in his admirable work on Constitutional Limitations . . . says: "In former times sumptuary laws were sometimes passed, and they were even deemed essential in republics to restrain the luxury so fatal to that species of government. But the ideas which suggested such laws are now exploded utterly, and no one would seriously attempt to justify them in the present age. The right of every man to do what he will with his own, not interfering with the reciprocal right of others, is accepted among the fundamentals of our law. The instances of attempt to interfere with it have not been numerous since the early colonial days."

From the best investigation I have been able to give this subject, I am forced to the conclusion that the judgment of the court below should have been reversed, and the defendant discharged.

Are humans capable of dispassionately applying the harm principle? Or are we hardwired to view behavior through a moral lens? In *The Cognitively Illiberal State*, Dan Kahan argues that "[a]s a result of cultural cognition . . . , the promise not to interfere with the liberty of individuals except to prevent harm to others is rendered meaningless: whenever individuals deviate from dominant understandings of virtue, they will be perceived as a source of harm." Assuming that this is correct, does this mean there is no value in attempting to constrain criminal law through the harm principle? Would we be better served by debating the wisdom of drug laws on purely moral terms?

B. Does Drug Criminalization Work?

1. Debating the Costs and Benefits of Prohibition

Those who object to drug criminalization on the grounds that drug transactions are "victimless" conduct that the state should not criminalize would presumably oppose even the most successful prohibition policy. For others, their views on prohibition laws may depend on how well they think the laws work. Of course, the answer to this question can also be strongly influenced by moral intuitions. Someone who finds drug use relatively unobjectionable may think that a reduction in drug use rates is worth very little. This person might support a prohibition model only if it dramatically lowered drug use at a minimal cost. On the other side of the spectrum, there are those who believe that preventing drug use is such a strong moral imperative that they would favor spending large amounts of money to vigorously enforce drug criminalization laws even if the effort only resulted in a modest decline in drug use. Similarly, people may disagree about what our objectives should be in setting drug policy. Should drug laws aim to reduce overall use rates for all illegal drugs or to reduce use among certain populations (e.g., young people) or of certain substances? Or, should drug laws focus on reducing the harms associated with drug abuse first (e.g., drug overdoses) as opposed to reducing drug use rates? Should we strive for an idealized goal like a "drug-free America"? Should we target "process-oriented goals," such as "providing treatment on demand to all users"? Jonathan P. Caulkins and Peter Reuter, *Settling Goals for Drug Policy: Harm Reduction or Use Reduction?*, 92 ADDICTION 1143 (1997).

The consequentialist discussion of the merits of drug criminalization is inevitably complicated by the wide-range of possible objectives and policy options. Even if it were possible to agree on a common objective for our drug laws, any attempt to measure their effectiveness will need to account for a number of considerations beyond drug use rates or drug-related hospital admissions. What value, if any, should be placed on principles like individual choice or privacy in a cost-benefit analysis? How should the unintended consequences of drug criminalization laws—for example, the violence associated with black markets—be measured and factored into the assessment?

With so much room for disagreement over how to define and measure success in drug policy, it should come as no surprise that two people might look at the same set of data and come to different conclusions about what it means. To one person, a five percent reduction in marijuana use and availability at a cost of $1 billion might qualify as a resounding success. Another might consider that same result to be a dismal failure.

In the trio of essays that follows, Ethan Nadelmann, James Q. Wilson, and Mark Kleiman and Aaron Saiger debate the costs and benefits of drug prohibition. The essays are nearly 30 years old and so the specific facts and figures they reference are outdated. But they continue to provide a valuable picture of the types of costs and benefits that feature prominently in the debate over drug prohibition.

The essays are also noteworthy because of their authors. Nadelmann, Wilson, and Kleiman have all been prominent and influential figures in the drug policy field. All three have been both scholars and active participants in policymaking. Nadelmann began his career as a public policy professor at Princeton before going on to help found the Drug Policy Alliance, where he served as Executive Director from 2000 until 2017. Wilson, who died in 2012, was a lifelong academic who also served on a number of government task forces and commissions. Kleiman is currently a public policy professor at New York University and chairman of a consultancy that advised the state of Washington on how to implement its 2012 marijuana legalization law.

Drug Prohibition in the United States: Costs, Consequences, and Alternatives
Ethan A. Nadelmann

5 Notre Dame Journal of Law Ethics and Public Policy 783 (1991)

There is no one legalization option. At one extreme, some libertarians advocate the removal of all criminal sanctions and taxes on the production and sale of all psychoactive substances—with the possible exception of restrictions on sales to children. The alternative extremes are more varied. Some would limit legalization to one of the safest (relatively speaking) of all illicit substances: marijuana. Others prefer a "medical" oversight model similar to today's methadone maintenance programs. The middle ground combines legal availability of some or all illicit drugs with vigorous efforts to restrict consumption by means other than resort to criminal sanctions. Many supporters of this dual approach simultaneously advocate greater efforts to limit tobacco consumption and the abuse of alcohol as well as a transfer of government resources from anti-drug law enforcement to drug prevention and treatment. Indeed, the best model for this view of drug legalization is precisely the tobacco control model advocated by those who want to do everything possible to discourage tobacco consumption short of criminalizing the production, sale, and use of tobacco.

Clearly, neither drug legalization nor enforcement of anti-drug laws promises to "solve" the drug problem. Nor is there any question that legalization presents certain risks. Legalization would almost certainly increase the availability of drugs, decrease their price, and remove the deterrent power of the criminal sanction—all of which invite increases in drug use and abuse. There are at least three reasons, however, why these risks are worth taking. First, drug control strategies that rely primarily on criminal justice measures are significantly and inherently limited in their capacity to curtail drug abuse. Second, many law enforcement efforts are not only of limited value but also highly costly and counterproductive; indeed, many of the drug-related evils that most people identify as part and parcel of "the drug problem" are in fact the costs of drug prohibition policies. Third, the risks of legalization may well be less than most people assume, particularly if intelligent alternative measures are implemented.

Few law enforcement officials any longer contend that their efforts can do much more than they are already doing to reduce drug abuse in the United States. This is true of international drug enforcement efforts, interdiction, and both high-level and street-level domestic drug enforcement efforts.

The United States seeks to limit the export of illicit drugs to this country by a combination of crop eradication and crop substitution programs, financial inducements to growers to abstain from the illicit business, and punitive measures against producers, traffickers, and others involved in the drug traffic. These efforts have met with scant success in the past and show few indications of succeeding in the future. The obstacles are many: marijuana and opium can be grown in a wide variety of locales and even the coca plant "can be grown in virtually any subtropical region of the world which gets between 40 and 240 inches of rain per year, where it never freezes, and where the land is not so swampy as to be waterlogged. In South America this comes to [approximately] 2,500,000 square miles," of which less than 700 square miles are currently being used to cultivate coca. Producers in many countries have reacted to crop eradication programs by engaging in "guerrilla" farming methods, cultivating their crops in relatively inaccessible hinterlands, and camouflaging them with legitimate crops. Some illicit drug-production regions are controlled not by the central government but by drug trafficking gangs or political insurgents, thereby rendering eradication efforts even more difficult and hazardous.

Even where eradication efforts prove relatively successful in an individual country, other countries will emerge as new producers, as has occurred with both the international marijuana and heroin markets during the past two decades and can be expected to follow from planned coca eradication programs. The foreign export price of illicit drugs is such a tiny fraction of the retail price in the United States [approximately 4% with cocaine, 1% with marijuana, and much less than 1% with heroin] that international drug control efforts are not even successful in raising the cost of illicit drugs to U.S. consumers. U.S. efforts to control drugs overseas also confront substantial, and in some cases well-organized, political opposition in foreign countries. Major drug traffickers retain the power to bribe and intimidate government officials into ignoring or even cooperating with their enterprises. Particularly in many Latin American and Asian countries, the illicit drug traffic is an important source of income and employment, bringing in billions of dollars in hard currency each year and providing liveable wages for many hundreds of thousands.

The illicit drug business has been described—not entirely in jest—as the best means ever devised by the United States for exporting the capitalist ethic to potentially revolutionary Third World peasants. By contrast, United States-sponsored eradication efforts risk depriving those same peasants of their livelihoods, thereby stimulating support for communist insurgencies ranging from Peru's Shining Path to the variety of ethnic and communist organizations active in drug-producing countries such as Colombia and Burma. Moreover, many of those involved in producing illicit drugs overseas do not perceive their moral obligation as preventing decadent gringos from consuming cocaine or heroin; rather it is to earn the best living possible for themselves and their families. In the final analysis, there is little the U.S. government can do to change this perception.

Interdiction efforts have shown little success in stemming the flow of cocaine and heroin into the United States. Indeed, during the past decade, the wholesale price of a kilo of cocaine has dropped by 80% even as the retail purity of a gram of cocaine has quintupled from 12 to about 60%; the trend with heroin over the past few years has been similar if less dramatic. Easily transported in a variety of large and small aircraft and sea vessels, carried across the Mexican border by legal and illegal border crossers, hidden in everything from furniture, flowers, and automobiles to private body parts and cadavers, heroin and cocaine shipments are extraordinarily difficult to detect. Despite powerful congressional support for dramatically increasing the role of the military in drug interdiction, military leaders insist that they can do little to make a difference. The Coast Guard and U.S. Customs continue to expand their efforts in this area, but they too concede that they will never seize more than a small percentage of total shipments. Because cocaine and heroin are worth more than their weight in gold, the incentives to transport these drugs to the United States are so great that we can safely assume that there will never be a shortage of those willing to take the risk.

The one success that interdiction efforts can claim concerns marijuana. Because marijuana is far bulkier per dollar of value than either cocaine or heroin, it is harder to conceal and easier to detect. Stepped-up interdiction efforts in recent years appear to have increased its price to the American consumer. The unintended consequences of this success are twofold: the United States has emerged as one of the world's leading producers of marijuana; indeed, U.S. producers are now believed to produce among the finest strains in the world; and many international drug traffickers appear to have redirected their efforts from marijuana to cocaine. The principal consequence of the U.S. drug interdiction effort, many would contend, has been a glut of increasingly potent cocaine and a shortage of comparatively benign marijuana.

Domestic law enforcement efforts have proven increasingly successful in apprehending and imprisoning rapidly growing numbers of illicit drug merchants, ranging from the most sophisticated international traffickers to the most common street-level drug dealers. The principal benefit of law enforcement efforts directed at major drug trafficking organizations is probably the rapidly rising value of drug trafficker assets forfeited to the government. There is, however, little indication that such efforts have any significant impact on the price or availability of illicit drugs. Intensive and highly costly street-level law enforcement efforts such as those mounted by many urban police departments in recent years have resulted in the arrests of thousands of low-level drug dealers and users and helped improve the quality of life in targeted neighborhoods. In most large urban centers, however, these efforts have had little impact on the overall availability of illicit drugs.

The logical conclusion of the foregoing analysis is not that criminal justice efforts to stop drug trafficking do not work at all; rather, it is that even substantial fluctuations in those efforts have little effect on the price, availability, and consumption of illicit drugs. The mere existence of criminal laws combined with minimal levels of enforcement is sufficient to deter many potential users and to reduce the availability and increase the price of drugs. Law enforcement officials acknowledge that they alone cannot solve the drug problem but contend that their role is nonetheless essential to the overall effort to reduce illicit drug use and abuse. What they are less ready to acknowledge, however, is that the very criminalization of the drug market has proven highly costly and counterproductive in much the same way that the national prohibition of alcohol did 60 years ago.

Total government expenditures devoted to enforcement of drug laws amounted to a minimum of $10 billion in 1987. Between 1981 and 1987, federal expenditures on anti-drug law enforcement more than tripled, from less than $1 billion per year to about $3 billion. State and local law enforcement agencies spent an estimated $5 billion, amounting to about one-fifth of their total investigative resources, on drug enforcement activities in 1986. Drug law violators currently account for approximately 10% of the roughly 550,000 inmates in state prisons, more than one-third of the 50,000 federal prison inmates, and a significant (albeit undetermined) proportion of the approximately 300,000 individuals confined in municipal jails. The U.S. Sentencing Commission has predicted that in 15 years the federal prison population will total 100,000 to 150,000 inmates, of whom one-half will be incarcerated for drug law violations.* Nationwide, drug trafficking and drug possession offenses accounted for approximately 135,000 (23%) of the 583,000 individuals convicted of felonies in state courts in 1986. State and local governments spent a minimum of $2 billion last year to incarcerate drug offenders. The costs, in terms of alternative social expenditures foregone and other types of criminals not imprisoned, are perhaps even more severe.

Police have made about 750,000 arrests for violations of the drug laws during each of the last few years. Slightly more than three-quarters of these have been not

* The Sentencing Commission's estimate turned out to be low. In 2006, 15 years after Nadelmann's article was published, there were 176,268 federal prisoners, 93,751 of whom were incarcerated for a drug offense. See William J. Sabol et al., U.S. Dep't of Justice, NCJ 219416, Prisoners in 2006, at 9 (Dec. 2007), https://www.bjs.gov/content/pub/pdf/p06.pdf. [*Footnote by casebook author.*]

for manufacturing or dealing drugs but solely for possession of an illicit drug, typically marijuana. (Those arrested, it is worth noting, represent less than 2% of the 35 to 40 million Americans estimated to have illegally consumed a drug during each of the past years.) On the one hand, these arrests have clogged many urban criminal justice systems: in New York City, drug law violations in 1987 accounted for more than 40% of all felony indictments, up from 25% in 1985; in Washington D.C., the figure was 52% in 1986, up from 13% in 1981. On the other hand, they have distracted criminal justice officials from concentrating greater resources on violent offenses and property crimes. In many cities, urban law enforcement has become virtually synonymous with drug enforcement.

The greatest beneficiaries of the drug laws are organized and unorganized drug traffickers. The criminalization of the drug market effectively imposes a de facto value-added tax that is enforced and occasionally augmented by the law enforcement establishment and collected by the drug traffickers. More than half of all organized crime revenues are believed to derive from the illicit drug business; estimates of the dollar value range between $10 and $50 billion per year. By contrast, annual revenues from cigarette bootlegging, which persists principally because of differences among states in their cigarette tax rates, are estimated at between $200 million and $400 million. If the marijuana, cocaine, and heroin markets were legal, state and federal governments would collect billions of dollars annually in tax revenues. Instead, they expend billions in what amounts to a subsidy of organized criminals.

The connection between drugs and crime is one that continues to resist coherent analysis both because cause and effect are so difficult to distinguish and because the role of the drug prohibition laws in causing and labeling "drug-related crime" is so often ignored. There are five possible connections between drugs and crime, at least three of which would be much diminished if the drug prohibition laws were repealed. First, the production, sale, purchase, and possession of marijuana, cocaine, heroin, and other strictly controlled and banned substances are crimes in and of themselves, which occur billions of times each year in the United States alone. In the absence of drug prohibition laws, these activities would largely cease to be considered crimes. Selling drugs to children would, of course, continue to be criminalized, and other evasions of government regulation of a legal market would continue to be prosecuted, but by and large the connection between drugs and crime that now accounts for all of the criminal justice costs noted above would be severed.

Second, many illicit drug users commit crimes such as robbery and burglary, as well as other vice crimes such as drug dealing, prostitution, and numbers running, to earn enough money to purchase cocaine, heroin, and other illicit drugs—drugs that cost far more than alcohol and tobacco not because they cost much more to produce but because they are illegal. Because legalization would inevitably lead to a reduction in the cost of the drugs that are now illicit, it would also invite a significant reduction in this drug-crime connection.

The third connection between drugs and crime is more coincidental than causal in nature. Although most illicit drug users do not engage in crime aside from their drug use, and although many criminals do not use or abuse illicit drugs or alcohol, substance abuse clearly is much higher among criminals than among noncriminals. A 1986 survey of state prison inmates found that 43% were using illegal drugs on a daily or near daily basis in the month before they committed the crime for which they were incarcerated; it also found that roughly one-half of the inmates who had used an illicit drug did not do so until after their first arrest. Perhaps many of the same factors that lead individuals into lives of crime also push them in the direction of substance abuse. It is possible that legalization would diminish this connection by removing from the criminal subculture the lucrative opportunities that now derive from the illegality of the drug market. But it is also safe to assume that the criminal milieu will continue to claim a disproportionately large share of drug abusers regardless of whether or not drugs are legalized.

The fourth link between drugs and crime is the commission of violent and other crimes by people under the influence of illicit drugs. It is this connection that seems to most infect the popular imagination. Clearly, some drugs do "cause" some people to commit crimes by reducing normal inhibitions, unleashing aggressive and other asocial tendencies, and lessening senses of responsibility. Cocaine, particularly in the form of "crack," has gained such a reputation in recent years, just as heroin did in the 1960s and 1970s and marijuana did in the years before that. Crack cocaine's reputation for inspiring violent behavior may well be more deserved than were those of marijuana and heroin, although the evidence has yet to substantiate media depictions. No illicit drug, however, is as strongly associated with violent behavior as is alcohol. According to Justice Department statistics, 54% of all jail inmates convicted of violent crimes in 1983 reported having used alcohol just prior to committing their offense." The impact of drug legalization on this aspect of the drug-crime connection is the most difficult to assess, largely because changes in the overall level and nature of drug consumption are so difficult to predict.

The fifth connection is the violent, intimidating, and corrupting behavior of the drug traffickers. In many Latin American countries, most notably Colombia, this connection virtually defines the "drug problem." But even within the United States, drug trafficker violence is rapidly becoming a major concern of criminal justice officials and the public at large. The connection is not difficult to explain. Illegal markets tend to breed violence, both because they attract criminally minded and violent individuals and because participants in the market have no resort to legal institutions to resolve their disputes. During Prohibition, violent struggles: between bootlegging gangs and hijackings of booze-laden trucks and sea vessels were frequent and notorious occurrences. Today's equivalents are the booby traps that surround some marijuana fields, the pirates of the Caribbean looking to rob drug-laden vessels en route to the shores of the United States, the machine gun battles and executions of the more sordid drug gangs, and the generally high levels of violence that attend many illicit drug relationships; the victims include not just drug dealers but witnesses, bystanders, and law enforcement officials. Most law enforcement authorities agree that the dramatic increases in urban murder rates during the past few years can be explained almost entirely by the rise in drug dealer killings, mostly of one another. At the same time, the powerful allure of illicit drug dollars is responsible for rising levels of corruption not just in Latin America and the Caribbean but also in federal, state and local criminal justice systems throughout the United States. A drug legalization strategy would certainly deal a severe blow to this link between drugs and crime.

Perhaps the most difficult costs to evaluate are those that relate to the widespread defiance of the drug prohibition laws: the effects of labeling as criminals the tens of millions of people who use drugs illicitly, subjecting them to the risks of criminal sanction, and obliging many of those same people to enter into relationships with drug dealers (who may be criminals in many more senses of the word) in order to purchase their drugs; the cynicism that such laws generate toward other laws and the law in general; and the sense of hostility and suspicion that many otherwise law-abiding individuals feel toward law enforcement officials. It was costs such as these that strongly influenced many of Prohibition's more conservative opponents.

Among the most dangerous consequences of the drug laws are the harms that stem from the unregulated nature of illicit drug production and sale. Many marijuana smokers are worse off for having smoked cannabis that was grown with dangerous fertilizers, sprayed with the herbicide paraquat, or mixed with more dangerous substances. Consumers of heroin and the various synthetic substances sold on the street face even more severe consequences, including fatal overdoses and poisonings from unexpectedly potent or impure drug supplies. In short, nothing resembling an underground Food and Drug Administration has arisen to impose quality control on the illegal drug market and provide users with accurate information on the drugs they consume. More often than not, the quality of a drug addict's life depends greatly on his or her access to reliable supplies. Drug enforcement operations that succeed in temporarily disrupting supply networks are thus a double-edged sword: they encourage some addicts to seek admission into drug treatment programs, but they oblige others to seek out new and hence less reliable suppliers, with the result that more, not fewer, drug-related emergencies and deaths occur.

Repealing the drug prohibition laws clearly promises tremendous advantages. Between reduced government expenditures on enforcing drug laws and new tax revenue from legal drug production and sales, public treasuries would enjoy a net benefit of at least $10 billion per year and possibly much more; thus billions in new revenues would be available, and ideally targeted, for funding much-needed drug treatment programs as well as the types of social and educational programs that often prove most effective in creating incentives for children not to abuse drugs. The quality of urban life would rise significantly. Homicide rates would decline. So would robbery and burglary rates. Organized criminal groups, particularly the up-and-coming ones that have yet to diversify into nondrug areas, would be dealt a devastating setback. The police, prosecutors, and courts would focus their resources on combating the types of crimes that people cannot walk away from. More ghetto residents would turn their backs on criminal careers and seek out legitimate opportunities instead. And the health and quality of life of many drug users and even drug abusers would improve significantly. Internationally, U.S. foreign policymakers would get on with more important and realistic objectives, and foreign governments would reclaim the authority that they have lost to the drug traffickers.

All the benefits of legalization would be for naught, however, if millions more people were to become drug abusers.

Our experience with alcohol and tobacco provides ample warnings. Today, alcohol is consumed by 140 million Americans and tobacco by 50 million. All of the health costs associated with abuse of the illicit drugs pale in comparison with those resulting from tobacco and alcohol abuse.

The impact of legalization on the nature and level of consumption of those drugs that are currently illegal is impossible to predict with any accuracy. On the one hand, legalization implies greater availability, lower prices, and the elimination (particularly for adults) of the deterrent power of the criminal sanction—all of which would suggest higher levels of use. Indeed, some fear that the extent of drug abuse and its attendant costs would rise to those currently associated with alcohol and tobacco. On the other hand, there are many reasons to doubt that a well-designed and implemented policy of controlled drug legalization would yield such costly consequences.

The logic of legalization depends in part upon two assumptions: that most illegal drugs are not as dangerous as is commonly believed; and that those types of drugs and methods of consumption that are most risky are unlikely to prove appealing to many people precisely because they are so obviously dangerous. Consider marijuana. Among the roughly 60 million Americans who have smoked marijuana, not one has died from a marijuana overdose, a striking contrast with alcohol, which is involved in approximately 10,000 overdose deaths annually, half in combination with other drugs. Although there are good health reasons for people not to smoke marijuana daily, and for children, pregnant women, and some others not to smoke at all, there still appears to be little evidence that occasional marijuana consumption does much harm at all. Certainly, it is not healthy to inhale marijuana smoke into one's lungs; indeed, the National Institute on Drug Abuse (NIDA) has declared that "marijuana smoke contains more cancer-causing agents than is found in tobacco smoke." On the other hand, the number of "joints" smoked by all but a very small percentage of marijuana smokers is a tiny fraction of the 20 cigarettes a day smoked by the average cigarette smoker; indeed, the average may be closer to one or two joints per week than one or two per day. Note that the NIDA defines "heavy" marijuana smoker as one who consumes at least two joints "daily." A heavy tobacco smoker, by contrast, smokes about 40 cigarettes per day.

The dangers associated with cocaine, heroin, the hallucinogens, and other illicit substances are greater than those posed by marijuana but not nearly so great as many people seem to think. Consider the case of cocaine. In 1986, NIDA reported that over 20 million Americans had tried cocaine, that 12.2 million had consumed it at least once during 1985, and that nearly 5.8 million had used it within the past month. Among 18- to 25-year-olds, 8.2 million had tried cocaine; 5.3 million had used it within the past year; 2.5 million had used it within the past month; and 250,000 had used it on the average weekly. One could extrapolate from these figures that a quarter of a million young Americans are potential problem users. But one could also conclude that only 3% of those 18- to 25-year-olds who had ever tried the drug fell into that category, and that only 10% of those who had used cocaine monthly were at risk.

All of this is not to say that cocaine is not a potentially dangerous drug, especially when it is injected, smoked in the form of "crack," or consumed in tandem with other powerful substances. Clearly, many tens of thousands of Americans have suffered severely from their abuse of cocaine and a tiny fraction have died. But there is also overwhelming evidence that most users of cocaine do not get into trouble with the drug. So much of the media attention has focused on the relatively small percentage of cocaine users who become addicted that the popular perception of how most people use cocaine has become badly distorted.

With respect to the hallucinogens such as LSD and psilocybic mushrooms, their potential for addiction is virtually nil. The dangers arise primarily from using them irresponsibly on individual occasions. Although many of those who have used hallucinogens have experienced "bad trips," far more have reported positive experiences and very few have suffered any long-term harm. As for the great assortment of stimulants, depressants, and tranquilizers produced illegally or diverted from licit channels, each evidences varying capacities to create addiction, harm the user, or be used safely.

Until recently, no drugs were regarded with as much horror as the opiates, and in particular heroin. As with most drugs, it can be eaten, snorted, smoked, or injected. The custom among most Americans, unfortunately, is the last of these options[.] There is no question that heroin is potentially highly addictive, perhaps as addictive as nicotine. But despite the popular association of heroin use with the most down-and-out inhabitants of urban ghettos, heroin causes relatively little physical harm to the human body. Consumed on an occasional or regular basis under sanitary conditions, its worst side effect, apart from the fact of being addicted, is constipation. That is one reason why many doctors in early 20th-century America saw opiate addiction as preferable to alcoholism and prescribed the former as treatment for the latter where abstinence did not seem a realistic option. It is both insightful and important to think about the illicit drugs as we do about alcohol and tobacco. Like tobacco, some illicit substances are highly addictive but can be consumed on a regular basis for decades without any demonstrable harm. Like alcohol, many of the substances can be, and are, used by most consumers in moderation, with little in the way of harmful effects; but like alcohol they also lend themselves to abuse by a minority of users who become addicted or otherwise harm themselves or others as a consequence. And like both the legal substances, the psychoactive effects of each of the illegal drugs vary greatly from one person to another. To be sure, the pharmacology of the substance is important, as is its purity and the manner in which it is consumed. But much also depends upon not just the physiology and psychology of the consumer but his expectations regarding the drug, his social milieu, and the broader cultural environment, what Harvard University psychiatrist Norman Zinberg called the "set and setting" of the drug. It is factors such as these that might change dramatically, albeit in indeterminate ways, were the illicit drugs made legally available.

It is thus impossible to predict whether or not legalization would lead to much greater levels of drug abuse. The lessons that can be drawn from other societies are mixed. China's experience with the British opium pushers of the 19th century, when millions reportedly became addicted to the drug, offers one worst-case scenario. The devastation of many native American tribes by alcohol presents another. On the other hand, the decriminalization of marijuana by 11 states in the United States during the mid-1970s does not appear to have led to increases in marijuana consumption. In the Netherlands, which went even further in decriminalizing cannabis during the 1970s, consumption has actually declined significantly; in 1976, 3% of 15- and 16-year-olds and 10% of 17- and 18-year-olds used cannabis occasionally; by 1985, the percentages had declined to 2 and 6%, respectively. The policy has succeeded, as the government intended, "in making drug use boring." Finally, late 19-century America is an example of a society in which there were almost no drug laws or even drug regulations but levels of drug use were about what they are today. Drug abuse was regarded as a relatively serious problem, but the criminal justice system was not regarded as part of the solution.

There are, however, strong reasons to believe that none of the currently illicit substances would become as popular as alcohol or tobacco even if they were legalized. Alcohol has long been the principal intoxicant in most societies, including many in which other substances have been legally available. Presumably, its diverse properties account for its popularity: it quenches thirst, goes well with food, often pleases the palate, promotes appetite as well as sociability, and so on. The widespread use of tobacco probably stems not just from its powerful addictive qualities but from the fact that its psychoactive effects are sufficiently subtle that cigarettes can be integrated with most other human activities. None of the illicit substances now popular in the United States share either of these qualities to the same extent, nor is it likely that they would acquire them if they were legalized. Moreover, none of the illicit substances can compete with alcohol's special place in American culture and history, one that it retained even during Prohibition.

Much of the damage caused by illegal drugs today stems from their consumption in particularly potent and dangerous ways. There is good reason to doubt that many Americans would inject cocaine or heroin into their veins even if given the chance to do so legally.

Perhaps the most reassuring reason for believing that repeal of the drug prohibition laws will not lead to tremendous increases in drug abuse levels is the fact that we have learned something from our past experiences with alcohol and tobacco abuse. We now know, for instance, that consumption taxes are an effective method for limiting consumption rates and related costs, especially among young people.

Substantial evidence also suggests that restrictions and bans on advertising, as well as promotion of negative advertising, can make a difference. The same seems to be true of other government measures, including restrictions on time and place of sale, bans on vending machines, prohibitions of consumption in public places, packaging requirements, mandated adjustments in insurance policies, crackdowns on driving while under the influence, and laws holding bartenders and hosts responsible for the drinking of customers and guests. At the same time, we also have come to recognize the great harms that can result when drug control policies are undermined by powerful lobbies such as those that now block efforts to lessen the harms caused by abuse of alcohol and tobacco.

Legalization thus affords far greater opportunities to control drug use and abuse than do current criminalization policies. The current strategy is one in which the type, price, purity, and potency of illicit drugs, as well as the participants in the business, are largely determined by drug dealers, the peculiar competitive dynamics of an illicit market, and the perverse interplay of drug enforcement strategies and drug trafficking tactics.

A drug control policy based predominantly on approaches other than criminal justice thus offers a number of significant advantages over the current criminal justice focus in controlling drug use and abuse. It shifts control of production, distribution, and, to a lesser extent, consumption out of the hands of criminals and into the hands of government and government licenses. It affords consumers the opportunity to make far more informed decisions about the drugs they buy than is currently the case. It dramatically lessens the likelihood that drug consumers will be harmed by impure, unexpectedly potent, or misidentified drugs. It corrects the hypocritical and dangerous message that alcohol and tobacco are somehow safer than many illicit drugs. It reduces by billions of dollars annually government expenditures on drug enforcement and simultaneously raises additional billions in tax revenues. And it allows government the opportunity to shape consumption patterns toward relatively safer psychoactive substances and modes of consumption.

Toward the end of the 1920s, when the debate over repealing Prohibition rapidly gained momentum, numerous scholars, journalists, and private and government commissions undertook thorough evaluations of Prohibition and the potential alternatives. Prominent among these were the Wickersham Commission appointed by President Herbert Hoover and the study of alcohol regulation abroad directed by the leading police scholar in the United States, Raymond Fosdick, and commissioned by John D. Rockefeller. These efforts examined the successes and failings of Prohibition in the United States and evaluated the wide array of alternative regimes for controlling the distribution and use of beer, wine, and liquor. They played a major role in stimulating the public reevaluation of Prohibition and in envisioning alternatives. Precisely the same sorts of efforts are required today.

The controlled drug legalization option is not an all-or-nothing alternative to current policies. Indeed, political realities ensure that any shift toward legalization will evolve gradually, with ample opportunity to halt, reevaluate, and redirect drug policies that begin to prove too costly or counterproductive. The federal government need not play the leading role in devising alternatives; it need only clear the way to allow state and local governments the legal power to implement their own drug legalization policies. The first steps are relatively risk-free: legalization of marijuana, easier availability of illegal and strictly controlled drugs for treatment of pain and other medical purposes, tougher tobacco and alcohol control policies, and a broader and more available array of drug treatment programs.

There is no question that legalization is a risky policy, one that may indeed lead to an increase in the number of people who abuse drugs. But that risk is by no means a certainty. At the same time, current drug control policies are showing little progress and new proposals promise only to be more costly and more repressive. We know that repealing the drug prohibition laws would eliminate or greatly reduce many of the ills that people commonly identify as part and parcel of the "drug problem." Yet that option is repeatedly and vociferously dismissed without any attempt to evaluate it openly and objectively. The past 20 years have demonstrated that a drug policy shaped by rhetoric and fear-mongering can only lead to our current disaster. Unless we are willing to honestly evaluate all our options, including various legalization strategies, there is a good chance that we will never identify the best solutions for our drug problems.

Against the Legalization of Drugs
James Q. Wilson

89 Commentary 21 (1990)

In 1972, the president appointed me chairman of the National Advisory Council for Drug Abuse Prevention. Created by Congress, the Council was charged with providing guidance on how best to coordinate the national war on drugs. (Yes, we called it a war then, too.) In those days, the drug we were chiefly concerned with was heroin. When I took office, heroin use had been increasing dramatically. Everybody was worried that this increase would continue. Such phrases as "heroin epidemic" were commonplace.

That same year, the eminent economist Milton Friedman published an essay in *Newsweek* in which he called for legalizing heroin. His argument was on two grounds: As a matter of ethics, the government has no right to tell people not to use heroin (or to drink or to commit suicide); as a matter of economics, the prohibition of drug use imposes costs on society that far exceed the benefits.

We did not take Friedman's advice. (Government commissions rarely do.) I do not recall that we even discussed legalizing heroin, though we did discuss (but did not take action on) legalizing a drug, cocaine, that many people then argued was benign. Our marching orders were to figure out how to win the war on heroin, not to run up the white flag of surrender.

That was 1972. Today, we have the same number of heroin addicts that we had then—half a million, give or take a few thousand. Having that many heroin addicts is no trivial matter; these people deserve our attention. But not having had an increase in that number for over fifteen years is also something that deserves our attention. What happened to the "heroin epidemic" that many people once thought would overwhelm us?

The facts are clear: A more or less stable pool of heroin addicts has been getting older, with relatively few new recruits. In 1976 the average age of heroin users who appeared in hospital emergency rooms was about twenty-seven; ten years later it was thirty-two. More than two-thirds of all heroin users appearing in emergency rooms are now over the age of thirty. Back in the early 1970s, when heroin got onto the national political agenda, the typical heroin addict was much younger, often a teenager. Household surveys show the same thing—the rate of opiate use (which includes heroin) has been flat for the better part of two decades. More fine-grained studies of inner-city neighborhoods confirm this. John Boyle and Ann Brunswick found that the percentage of young blacks in Harlem who use heroin fell from 8 percent in 1970–71 to about 3 percent in 1975–76.

Why did heroin lose its appeal for young people? When the young blacks in Harlem were asked why they stopped, more than half mentioned "trouble with the law" or "high cost" (and high cost is, of course, directly the result of law enforcement). Two-thirds said that heroin hurt their health; nearly all said they had had a bad experience with it. We need not rely, however, simply on what they said. In New York City in 1973–75, the street price of heroin rose dramatically and its purity sharply declined, probably as a result of the heroin shortage caused by the success of the Turkish government in reducing the supply of opium base and of the French government in closing down heroin-processing laboratories located in and around Marseilles. These were short-lived gains for, just as Friedman predicted, alternative sources of supply—mostly in Mexico—quickly emerged. But the three-year heroin shortage interrupted the easy recruitment of new users.

Health and related problems were no doubt part of the reason for the reduced flow of recruits. Over the preceding years, Harlem youth had watched as more and more heroin users died of overdoses, were poisoned by adulterated doses, or acquired hepatitis from dirty needles. The word got around: Heroin can kill you. By 1974 new hepatitis cases and drug-overdose deaths had dropped to a fraction of what they had been in 1970.

Alas, treatment did not seem to explain much of the cessation in drug use. Treatment programs can and do help heroin addicts, but treatment did not explain the drop in the number of new users (who by definition had never been in treatment) nor even much of the reduction in the number of experienced users.

No one knows how much of the decline to attribute to personal observation as opposed to high prices or reduced supply. But other evidence suggests strongly that price and supply played a large role. In 1972 the National Advisory Council was especially worried by the prospect that U.S. servicemen returning to this country from Vietnam would bring their heroin habits with them. Fortunately, a brilliant study by Lee Robins of Washington University in St. Louis put that fear to rest. She measured drug use of Vietnam veterans shortly after they had returned home. Though many had used heroin regularly while in Southeast Asia, most gave up the habit when back in the United States. The reason: Here, heroin was less available and sanctions on its use were more pronounced. Of course, if a veteran had been willing to pay enough—which might have meant traveling to another city and would certainly have meant making an illegal contact with a disreputable dealer in a threatening neighborhood in order to acquire a (possibly) dangerous dose—he could have sustained his drug habit. Most veterans were unwilling to pay this price, and so their drug use declined or disappeared.

Suppose we had taken Friedman's advice in 1972. What would have happened? We cannot be entirely certain, but at a minimum we would have placed the young heroin addicts (and, above all, the prospective addicts) in a very different position from the one in which they actually found themselves. Heroin would have been legal. Its price would have been reduced by 95 percent (minus whatever we chose to recover in taxes). Now that it could be sold by the same people who make aspirin, its quality would have been assured—no poisons, no adulterants. Sterile hypodermic needles would have been readily available at the neighborhood drugstore, probably at the same counter where the heroin was sold. No need to travel to big cities or unfamiliar neighborhoods—heroin could have been purchased anywhere, perhaps by mail order.

There would no longer have been any financial or medical reason to avoid heroin use. Anybody could have afforded it. We might have tried to prevent children from buying it, but as we have learned from our efforts to prevent minors from buying alcohol and tobacco, young people have a way of penetrating markets theoretically reserved for adults. Returning Vietnam veterans would have discovered that Omaha and Raleigh had been converted into the pharmaceutical equivalent of Saigon.

Under these circumstances, can we doubt for a moment that heroin use would have grown exponentially? Or that a vastly larger supply of new users would have been recruited? Professor Friedman is a Nobel Prize-winning economist whose understanding of market forces is profound. What did he think would happen to consumption under his legalized regime? Here are his words: "Legalizing drugs might increase the number of addicts, but it is not clear that it would. Forbidden fruit is attractive, particularly to the young."

Really? I suppose that we should expect no increase in Porsche sales if we cut the price by 95 percent, no increase in whiskey sales if we cut the price by a comparable amount—because young people only want fast cars and strong liquor when they are "forbidden." Perhaps Friedman's uncharacteristic lapse from the obvious implications of price theory can be explained by a misunderstanding of how drug users are recruited. In his 1972 essay he said that "drug addicts are deliberately made by pushers, who give likely prospects their first few doses free." If drugs were legal it would not pay anybody to produce addicts, because everybody would buy from the cheapest source. But as every drug expert knows, pushers do not produce addicts.

Friends or acquaintances do. In fact, pushers are usually reluctant to deal with nonusers because a nonuser could be an undercover cop. Drug use spreads in the same way any fad or fashion spreads: Somebody who is already a user urges his friends to try, or simply shows already-eager friends how to do it.

But we need not rely on speculation, however plausible, that lowered prices and more abundant supplies would have increased heroin usage. Great Britain once followed such a policy and with almost exactly those results. Until the mid-1960s, British physicians were allowed to prescribe heroin to certain classes of addicts. (Possessing these drugs without a doctor's prescription remained a criminal offense.) For many years this policy worked well enough because the addict patients were typically middle-class people who had become dependent on opiate painkillers while undergoing hospital treatment. There was no drug culture. The British system worked for many years, not because it prevented drug abuse but because there was no problem of drug abuse that would test the system.

All that changed in the 1960s. A few unscrupulous doctors began passing out heroin in wholesale amounts. One doctor prescribed almost six hundred thousand heroin tablets—that is, over thirteen pounds—in just one year. A youthful drug culture emerged with a demand for drugs far different from that of the older addicts. As a result, the British government required doctors to refer users to government-run clinics to receive their heroin.

But the shift to clinics did not curtail the growth in heroin use. Throughout the 1960s the number of addicts increased—the late John Kaplan of Stanford estimated by fivefold—in part as a result of the diversion of heroin from clinic patients to new users on the streets. An addict would bargain with the clinic doctor over how big a dose he would receive. The patient wanted as much as he could get, the doctor wanted to give as little as was needed. The patient had an advantage in this conflict because the doctor could not be certain how much was really needed. Many patients would use some of their "maintenance" dose and sell the remaining part to friends, thereby recruiting new addicts. As the clinics learned of this, they began to shift their treatment away from heroin and toward methadone, an addictive drug that, when taken orally, does not produce a "high" but will block the withdrawal pains associated with heroin abstinence.

Whether what happened in England in the 1960s was a miniepidemic or an epidemic depends on whether one looks at numbers or at rates of change. Compared to the United States, the numbers were small. In 1960 there were sixty-eight heroin addicts known to the British government; by 1968 there were two thousand in treatment and many more who refused treatment. (They would refuse in part because they did not want to get methadone at a clinic if they could get heroin on the street.) Richard Hartnoll estimates that the actual number of addicts in England is five times the number officially registered. At a minimum, the number of British addicts increased by thirtyfold in ten years; the actual increase may have been much larger.

In the early 1980s the numbers began to rise again, and this time nobody doubted that a real epidemic was at hand. The increase was estimated to be 40 percent a year. By 1982 there were thought to be twenty thousand heroin users in London alone. Geoffrey Pearson reports that many cities—Glasgow, Liverpool, Manchester, and Sheffield among them—were now experiencing a drug problem that once had been largely confined to London. The problem, again, was supply. The country was being flooded with cheap, high-quality heroin, first from Iran and then from Southeast Asia.

The United States began the 1960s with a much larger number of heroin addicts and probably a bigger at-risk population than was the case in Great Britain. Even though it would be foolhardy to suppose that the British system, if installed here, would have worked the same way or with the same results, it would be equally foolhardy to suppose that a combination of heroin available from leaky clinics and from street dealers who faced only minimal law-enforcement risks would not have produced a much greater increase in heroin use than we actually experienced. My guess is that if we had allowed either doctors or clinics to prescribe heroin, we would have had far worse results than were produced in Britain, if for no other reason than the vastly larger number of addicts with which we began. We would have had to find some way to police thousands (not scores) of physicians and hundreds (not dozens) of clinics. If the British civil service found it difficult to keep heroin in the hands of addicts and out of the hands of recruits when it was dealing with a few hundred people, how well would the American civil service have accomplished the same tasks when dealing with tens of thousands of people?

Now cocaine, especially in its potent form, crack, is the focus of attention. Now as in 1972 the government is trying to reduce its use. Now as then some people are advocating legalization. Is there any more reason to yield to those arguments today than there was almost two decades ago?

I think not. If we had yielded in 1972 we almost certainly would have had today a permanent population of several million, not several hundred thousand, heroin addicts. If we yield now we will have a far more serious problem with cocaine.

We all have a stake in ensuring that each of us displays a minimal level of dignity, responsibility, and empathy. We cannot, of course, coerce people into goodness, but we can and should insist that some standards must be met if society itself—on which the very existence of the human personality depends—is to persist. Drawing the line that defines those standards is difficult and contentious, but if crack and heroin use do not fall below it, what does?

The advocates of legalization will respond by suggesting that my picture is overdrawn. Ethan Nadelmann of Princeton argues that the risk of legalization is less than most people suppose. Over twenty million Americans between the ages of eighteen and twenty-five have tried cocaine (according to a government survey), but only a quarter million use it daily. From this Nadelmann concludes that at most

3 percent of all young people who try cocaine develop a problem with it. The implication is clear: Make the drug legal and we only have to worry about 3 percent of our youth.

The implication rests on a logical fallacy[.] The fallacy is this: The percentage of occasional cocaine users who become binge users when the drug is illegal (and thus expensive and hard to find) tells us nothing about the percentage who will become dependent when the drug is legal (and thus cheap and abundant). Drs. Gawin and Ellinwood report, in common with several other researchers, that controlled or occasional use of cocaine changes to compulsive and frequent use "when access to the drug increases" or when the user switches from snorting to smoking. More cocaine more potently administered alters, perhaps sharply, the proportion of "controlled" users who become heavy users.

It is possible that some people will not become heavy users even when the drug is readily available in its most potent form. So far there are no scientific grounds for predicting who will and who will not become dependent. Neither socioeconomic background nor personality traits differentiate between casual and intensive users. Thus, the only way to settle the question of who is correct about the effect of easy availability on drug use, Nadelmann or Gawin and Ellinwood, is to try it and see. But the social experiment is so risky as to be no experiment at all, for if cocaine is legalized and if the rate of its abusive use increases dramatically, there is no way to put the genie back in the bottle, and it is not a kindly genie.

Many people who agree that there are risks in legalizing cocaine or heroin still favor it because, they think, we have lost the war on drugs. "Nothing we have done has worked" and the current federal policy is just "more of the same." Whatever the costs of greater drug use, surely they would be less than the costs of our present, failed efforts.

That is exactly what I was told in 1972[.] We did not surrender and we did not lose. We did not win, either. What the nation accomplished then was what most efforts to save people from themselves accomplish: The problem was contained and the number of victims minimized, all at a considerable cost in law enforcement and increased crime. Was the cost worth it? I think so, but others may disagree. What are the lives of would-be addicts worth? I recall some people saying to me then, "Let them kill themselves." I was appalled. Happily, such views did not prevail.

Have we lost today? Not at all. High-rate cocaine use is not commonplace. The National Institute of Drug Abuse (NIDA) reports that less than 5 percent of high-school seniors used cocaine within the last thirty days. Of course this survey misses young people who have dropped out of school and miscounts those who lie on the questionnaire, but even if we inflate the NIDA estimate by some plausible percentage, it is still not much above 5 percent. Medical examiners reported in 1987 that about 1,500 died from cocaine use; hospital emergency rooms reported about 30,000 admissions related to cocaine abuse.

These are not small numbers, but neither are they evidence of a nationwide plague that threatens to engulf us all.

It took about ten years to contain heroin. We have had experience with crack for only about three or four years. Each year we spend perhaps $11 billion on law enforcement (and some of that goes to deal with marijuana) and perhaps $2 billion on treatment. Large sums, but not sums that should lead anyone to say, "We just can't afford this any more."

The illegality of drugs increases crime, partly because some users turn to crime to pay for their habits, partly because some users are stimulated by certain drugs (such as crack or PCP) to act more violently or ruthlessly than they otherwise would, and partly because criminal organizations seeking to control drug supplies use force to manage their markets. These also are serious costs, but no one knows how much they would be reduced if drugs were legalized. Addicts would no longer steal to pay black-market prices for drugs, a real gain. But some, perhaps a great deal, of that gain would be offset by the great increase in the number of addicts. These people, nodding on heroin or living in the delusion-ridden high of cocaine, would hardly be ideal employees. Many would steal simply to support themselves, since snatch-and-grab, opportunistic crime can be managed even by people unable to hold a regular job or plan an elaborate crime.

Proponents of legalization claim that the costs of having more addicts around would be largely if not entirely offset by having more money available with which to treat and care for them. The money would come from taxes levied on the sale of heroin and cocaine.

To obtain this fiscal dividend, however, legalization's supporters must first solve an economic dilemma. If they want to raise a lot of money to pay for welfare and treatment, the tax rate on the drugs will have to be quite high. Even if they themselves do not want a high rate, the politicians' love of "sin taxes" would probably guarantee that it would be high anyway. But the higher the tax, the higher the price of the drug, and the higher the price the greater the likelihood that addicts will turn to crime to find the money for it and that criminal organizations will be formed to sell tax-free drugs at below-market rates. If we managed to keep taxes (and thus prices) low, we would get that much less money to pay for welfare and treatment and more people could afford to become addicts. There may be an optimal tax rate for drugs that maximizes revenue while minimizing crime, bootlegging, and the recruitment of new addicts, but our experience with alcohol does not suggest that we know how to find it.

The advocates of legalization find nothing to be said in favor of the current system except, possibly, that it keeps the number of addicts smaller than it would otherwise be. In fact, the benefits are more substantial than that.

We are now investing substantially in drug-education programs in the schools. Though we do not yet know for certain what will work, there are some promising leads. But I wonder how credible such programs would be if they were aimed at dissuading children from doing something perfectly legal. We could, of course, treat drug education like smoking education: Inhaling crack and inhaling tobacco are both legal, but you should not do it because it is bad for you. That tobacco is bad for you is easily shown; the Surgeon General has seen to that. But what do we say about crack? It is pleasurable, but devoting yourself to so much pleasure is not a good idea (though perfectly legal)? Unlike tobacco, cocaine will not give you cancer or emphysema, but it will lead you to neglect your duties to family, job, and neighborhood? Everybody is doing cocaine, but you should not?

Again, it might be possible under a legalized regime to have effective drug-prevention programs, but their effectiveness would depend heavily, I think, on first having decided that cocaine use, like tobacco use, is purely a matter of practical consequences; no fundamental moral significance attaches to either. But if we believe—as I do—that dependency on certain mind-altering drugs is a moral issue and that their illegality rests in part on their immorality, then legalizing them undercuts, if it does not eliminate altogether, the moral message.

That message is at the root of the distinction we now make between nicotine and cocaine. Both are highly addictive; both have harmful physical effects. But we treat the two drugs differently, not simply because nicotine is so widely used as to be beyond the reach of effective prohibition, but because its use does not destroy the user's essential humanity. Tobacco shortens one's life, cocaine debases it. Nicotine alters one's habits, cocaine alters one's soul. The heavy use of crack, unlike the heavy use of tobacco, corrodes those natural sentiments of sympathy and duty that constitute our human nature and make possible our social life. To say, as does Nadelmann, that distinguishing morally between tobacco and cocaine is "little more than a transient prejudice" is close to saying that morality itself is but a prejudice.

Now we have arrived where many arguments about legalizing drugs begin: Is there any reason to treat heroin and cocaine differently from the way we treat alcohol?

There is no easy answer to that question because, as with so many human problems, one cannot decide simply on the basis either of moral principles or of individual consequences; one has to temper any policy by a commonsense judgment of what is possible. Alcohol, like heroin, cocaine, PCP, and marijuana, is a drug—that is, a mood-altering substance—and consumed to excess it certainly has harmful consequences: auto accidents, barroom fights, bedroom shootings. It is also, for some people, addictive. We cannot confidently compare the addictive powers of these drugs, but the best evidence suggests that crack and heroin are much more addictive than alcohol.

Many people, Nadelmann included, argue that since the health and financial costs of alcohol abuse are so much higher than those of cocaine or heroin abuse, it is hypocritical folly to devote our efforts to preventing cocaine or drug use. But as Mark Kleiman of Harvard has pointed out, this comparison is quite misleading. What Nadelmann is doing is showing that a *legalized* drug (alcohol) produces greater social harm than *illegal* ones (cocaine and heroin). But of course. Suppose that in the 1920s we had made heroin and cocaine legal and alcohol illegal. Can anyone doubt that Nadelmann would now be writing that it is folly to continue our ban on alcohol because cocaine and heroin are so much more harmful?

Perform the following mental experiment: Suppose we legalized heroin and cocaine in this country. In what proportion of auto fatalities would the state police report that the driver was nodding off on heroin or recklessly driving on a coke high? In what proportion of spouse-assault and child-abuse cases would the local police report that crack was involved? In what proportion of industrial accidents would safety investigators report that the forklift or drill-press operator was in a drug-induced stupor or frenzy? We do not know exactly what the proportion would be, but anyone who asserts that it would not be much higher than it is now would have to believe that these drugs have little appeal except when they are illegal. And that is nonsense.

Suppose that today we had, not fifteen million alcohol abusers, but half a million. Suppose that we already knew what we have learned from our long experience with the widespread use of alcohol. Would we make whiskey legal? I do not know, but I suspect there would be a lively debate. The Surgeon General would remind us of the risks alcohol poses to pregnant women. The National Highway Traffic Safety Administration would point to the likelihood of more highway fatalities caused by drunk drivers. The Food and Drug Administration might find that there is a nontrivial increase in cancer associated with alcohol consumption. At the same time the police would report great difficulty in keeping illegal whiskey out of our cities, officers being corrupted by bootleggers, and alcohol addicts often resorting to crime to feed their habit. Libertarians, for their part, would argue that every citizen has a right to drink anything he wishes and that drinking is, in any event, a "victimless crime."

However the debate might turn out, the central fact would be that the problem was still, at that point, a small one. The government cannot legislate away the addictive tendencies in all of us, nor can it remove completely even the most dangerous addictive substances. But it can cope with harms when the harms are still manageable.

No one can know what our society would be like if we changed the law to make access to cocaine, heroin, and PCP easier. I believe, for reasons given, that the result would be a sharp increase in use, a more widespread degradation of the human personality, and a greater rate of accidents and violence.

I may be wrong. If I am, then we will needlessly have incurred heavy costs in law enforcement and some forms of criminality. But if I am right, and the legalizers prevail anyway, then we will have consigned millions of people . . . and hundreds of neighborhoods to a life of oblivion and disease. To the lives and families destroyed by alcohol we will have added countless more destroyed by cocaine, heroin, PCP, and whatever else a basement scientist can invent.

Human character is formed by society; indeed, human character is inconceivable without society, and good character is less likely in a bad society. Will we, in the name of an abstract doctrine of radical individualism, and with the false comfort of suspect predictions, decide to take the chance that somehow individual decency can survive amid a more general level of degradation?

I think not. The American people are too wise for that, whatever the academic essayists and cocktail-party pundits may say. But if Americans today are less wise than I suppose, then Americans at some future time will look back on us now and wonder, what kind of people were they that they could have done such a thing?

Drug Legalization: The Importance of Asking the Right Question
Mark A.R. Kleiman and Aaron J. Saiger

18 Hofstra Law Review 527 (1990)

Ethan Nadelmann, a prominent advocate of legalization, asks his readers to compare today's commerce in licit tobacco to the state of the world if the production, sale and possession of tobacco were made illegal. As millions of newly criminal nicotine addicts searched for ways to feed their addiction, black-market dealers would take over. Revenue which now flows to the states as cigarette excise taxes would, instead, feed the coffers of criminal organizations. A large, expensive and corruptible "Tobacco Enforcement Administration" would need to be created. Courts would be clogged with users caught with tobacco, and with dealers caught selling it to them. The nation would suddenly confront a daunting, dangerous, and expensive "tobacco problem."

Nadelmann, and other proponents of drug legalization, contend that this allegory of illicit tobacco closely resembles the reality of illicit drugs. Their argument rests on the proposition that the social costs of prohibiting some drugs, and enforcing that prohibition, exceeds the value of the goals which that prohibition achieves (i.e., the social cost it avoids). Such arguments maintain that making psychoactive drugs illegal simply creates a dangerous and menacing black market without significantly diminishing the quantity consumed. On this view, legalization would make the streets safer, put the black-market dealers out of business, and focus attention on the medical problem of addiction rather than the legal problem of drug dealing.

In reply, supporters of existing prohibitions contend that the benefits of prohibition justify its costs. Some of these supporters claim that safer neighborhoods and lower law enforcement budgets would not balance the damage to the public health and well-being that increased consumption of legal drugs would create. Others hold that the damage done by prohibition is not as significant as legalization advocates assert.

On this level, the argument between advocates and opponents of legalization involves different predictions about the results of alternative policies and different value weightings of those results. For example, legalizers are likely to stress crime reduction, whereas prohibitionists would emphasize the protection of users' health. But both sides can agree that policies are to be judged by their predictable consequences, and that the balance of advantage ought to determine the choice. Drugs ought to be prohibited if, and to the extent that, the benefits of prohibition outweigh its costs.

This sort of argument requires both analysis and evaluation. It must both identify the probable consequences of a range of possible policies, and suggest which bundles are "better" and which are "worse."

Neither the analysis nor the evaluation is straightforward. Like other major social problems, the drug problem has costs that resist quantification and even description. Costs range from the obvious and the assignable—lung cancer deaths, dealer violence—to problems to which drugs may or may not contribute, such as the weakening of the traditional family structure or the undermining of the work ethic. Comparing these costs is even more difficult. How much liberty is worth sacrificing to prevent how many drug-related deaths? How much drug intoxication would be accepted to empty ten percent of the prison cells?

A central accomplishment of the consequentialist proponents of legalization has been to stress the vital distinction between the costs of drug abuse and the costs of drug control. Drug use is one problem. It makes some users sicker, poorer, more dangerous, and less responsible. On the other hand, state control of drug use creates different problems: crowded prisons, unsafe neighborhoods, wealthy criminal consortia, corrupt officials. These problems should not be confused; prison overcrowding should not be treated as if it were a pharmacological result of cocaine use.

Equally important, legalization advocates have refused to treat currently legal drugs as conceptually distinct from currently illegal ones. Alcohol and tobacco, like marijuana and heroin, are drugs with significant costs of abuse and costs of control. Tobacco is an important special case: addictive and health damaging. But the rhetoric of the "war on drugs" attempts to obscure this fact, as if there were chemical categories of "legal" and "illegal" drugs. Reminding us to treat alcohol and tobacco as drugs, in both explanatory and comparative contexts, is therefore an important service.

Current consequentialist arguments for legalization, however, suffer from grave weaknesses.

Legalization advocates have pointed out that some costs that appear to be the costs of drug abuse are in fact costs of its control. However, the discovery that prohibition has significant costs appears to have obscured, for these advocates, its possible benefits. Some advocates of legalization simply argue that prohibition has no effect on consumption, and, thus, that legalization can shrink the drug problem at a stroke by legislating away a whole category of costs. In short, while illegal drugs have costs of abuse and costs of control, legal ones would have only costs of abuse. Other, more sophisticated accounts simply minimize prohibition's effects.

The problem legalization advocates face in accounting for the effects of prohibition is illustrated by their treatment of alcohol and tobacco. Correctly, they use the heavy load of damage associated with the currently licit drugs to point up the arbitrariness, perhaps irrationality, of the current categorization of drugs into forbidden and permitted. But unless one thinks that drug policies are made under Murphy's Law, the fact that the licit substances cause more health damage than the currently forbidden ones suggests that prohibition tends, on balance, to protect health. From a public health standpoint, creating a cocaine problem the size of the current alcohol problem or the current tobacco problem would be a major disaster. Yet it is far from clear that legal cocaine would be less attractive, or do less damage to users' health, than alcohol or tobacco. Alcohol and tobacco are indeed instructive, but they make a point quite opposite to the one legalization's advocates intend: they demonstrate that legal availability can carry costs at least as significant as those of prohibition.

Drugs that are currently legal provide a convenient set of models for the legalization debate. Examining licit drug control allows us to consider real-life, working, regulatory regimes, rather than the artists' sketches now passing as legalization proposals. Alcohol provides a superb example of legalization gone awry. Regulations governing alcohol, the nation's premier recreational psychoactive, are fantastically permissive, measured against either the rules for other drugs or benefit-cost criteria.

Alcohol is a very dangerous drug. Had Congress failed to specifically exempt it from the provisions of the Controlled Substances Act, it could be placed along with marijuana and heroin in Schedule I, as a psychoactive drug with no accepted medical use and great potential for harm. Indeed, as a product unsafe in its intended use, it could perhaps be vulnerable to challenge under the Consumer Product Safety Act.

When compared with other drugs, casual or experimental alcohol users are at significant risk of progressing to heavy, chronic use or to alcoholic bingeing. An estimated eighteen million Americans, out of 140 million total current drinkers, have significant drinking problems. Many of these "problem" drinkers find that their alcohol use is no longer fully under their deliberate control, and some of them are the victims of a physical dependency that makes them actively ill if they do not get a daily ration of their drug—they are alcohol addicts, alcoholics. Heavy chronic alcohol use is associated with a wide variety of diseases, and alcohol has been estimated to cause approximately twenty thousand excess disease deaths per year. More than one-third of all crime leading to state prison sentences is committed under the influence of alcohol, as is an even greater proportion of domestic assault, sexual assault, and the physical and sexual abuse of children, all of which are under-reported and under-punished. Tens of thousands die annually and many more are maimed in alcohol-related traffic accidents, drownings, and fires, including thousands of people who were not drinking themselves. Alcohol's contribution to industrial accidents and decreased economic productivity is unknown.

One possible conclusion to be drawn from this catalogue of catastrophes would be that alcohol should be assigned its rightful place in Schedule I of the Controlled Substances Act. This is a conclusion with some appeal. But just as the costs of controlling illicit drugs do not of themselves justify legalization, the extensive damage caused by alcohol abuse is not, in and of itself, sufficient to justify re-Prohibition. The costs of criminalizing alcohol would be high; there are other means of reducing alcohol-related damage; and not all alcohol users incur, or cause, harm related to their drug use. Many users testify that they derive pleasure and relaxation from drinking, that it contributes to sociability, and that they drink responsibly and behave responsibly while drinking, doing no harm to others and suffering nothing worse than an occasional hangover.

This testimony need not be taken at face value. Drug users can and do deceive themselves about the damage they incur and the damage they do to others. However, neither should such testimony be ignored. Benefits are an essential part of a cost-benefit calculation, and consumers—even drug consumers—have information about benefits. However, an explanation and analysis of the purported benefits of drug use is notably absent from the debate over legalization.

Even if it turned out that the total benefits of alcohol availability—the sum of consumers' and producers' surpluses from its use and sale—were exceeded by its total costs, that alone would not establish the case for its re-prohibition. It would still have to be shown that the excess of costs (including black market and enforcement costs) over benefits would be less under some practicable form of prohibition than it is now. The larger the existing market, the higher those added costs of implementing prohibition are likely to be. One can regret Repeal without wishing to reverse it.

But consider those "other means" of reducing the costs alcohol imposes on drinkers and others. What are they? To what extent can they reduce costs while preserving benefits?

The only regulatory institution now in force which has significant potential as a mechanism for controlling alcohol abuse is alcohol taxation. Such taxation discourages consumption by making the drug more expensive, but American alcohol taxes have been declining in real terms since the Korean War. Even if the social costs of crime and costs to the drinkers are excluded, alcohol taxes fall markedly short of the costs to society of alcohol consumption. It has been estimated by one study that there is an external social cost, excluding tax, of forty-eight cents per ounce of alcohol, while the average sale and excise taxes (federal and state) add up to only twenty-three cents per ounce. Beer, the alcohol product most widely used by adolescents, is particularly undertaxed, with the result that cheap beer is less expensive at the retail level than many name-brand soft drinks.

Alcohol taxes ought to be significantly higher and alcohol in beer should be taxed as heavily as alcohol in liquor. Fixing the magnitude of an increase, however, is complex. The costs of raising taxes include lost consumers' surplus, some redistribution of the total tax burden toward the poor, and further impoverishment of those who cannot or do not quit heavy drinking. A very steep tax increase might also lead to the development of a black market in untaxed alcohol with attendant costs of enforcement and likely injury caused by adulterated products.

The central problem with taxation is that it is by nature nondiscriminating. In theory, every drink should be taxed according to its own social costs. Some drinks do no harm, and therefore ought not be taxed; other drinks impose extraordinary costs, and thus should be taxed heavily. However, the practical barriers to multiple levels of taxation are all but insurmountable. Taxation set to cover average social cost is sure to put too high a price on most use and not enough on some. Another mechanism is therefore required.

The obvious solution is to prohibit drinking entirely by persons whose drinking carries social costs above the level set by taxation. Youthful drinking is not the only type of drinking which causes disproportionate harm. Heavy drinking by anyone, drinking by "compulsive" users (i.e., those whose drinking is no longer under their deliberate self-control) and drinking by those who commit crimes or act recklessly while intoxicated all fall into this category.

All of these types of use could be prohibited. Children and those whose use has led to crime or recklessness could be forbidden from purchasing alcohol entirely, and there could be an absolute limit as to the maximum quantity of alcohol anyone could purchase in a given period. A central database of ineligible purchasers could be maintained, or, if that proved costly or infeasible, all persons could be licensed to purchase alcohol as they are to drive, with licenses revocable for alcohol-related offenses, including resale to unlicensed individuals.

Such "positive" licensure is an attractive strategy. It could be conditioned on passing a written test on drinking safety, as is now done for driving. The drinkers' licenses might be issued in conjunction with drivers' licenses, and might in fact be the same documents with different colors. Licensure could allow relatively easy enforcement of personal quantity limits by a system similar to the system used to keep credit card holders within their credit limits. It could allow "teetotalers" to identify themselves—and thus, perhaps, to make themselves eligible for lower auto, life and health insurance premiums—and it could allow those who wish to become teetotalers the crutch of tearing up their drinkers' licenses.

But licensure would have its costs as well. A number of practical problems, some more difficult than others, suggest themselves immediately. State licensing would interfere with interstate travel and, therefore, a national system might be required. Everyone, not just young adults, would need to be "carded" in bars, in liquor stores, and at social functions where alcohol was distributed without charge.

Finally, licensure would involve significant enforcement costs, especially because access to alcohol is made, in some cases, inversely proportional to the motivation for obtaining it. Leakage is sure to be significant, though its specific features depend on regulatory details. For example, if personal alcohol limits were high, light drinkers would have a strong incentive to sell their excess to others at a profit; if the limits were low, much harmless drinking would be curtailed, and a black market encouraged.

Despite these problems, a regime consisting of taxation and licensure has strong potential to control the costs of alcohol use, including the costs of its own enforcement, while maintaining most of the benefits of legal availability.

This regime departs from the dichotomy which currently governs American drug control: prohibition or free commerce. It concedes that the social costs of a flat ban are too great to justify prohibition, but does not replace it with free drug commerce and offers a middle way, one that might be called "grudging toleration," with strict controls to decrease consumption and minimize harms.

If the category of "grudgingly tolerated vice" could be successfully institutionalized, over time it might provide a framework for the control of some other licit and illicit drugs. With a working alcohol control regime in place, the alcohol problem would be considerably smaller, at which time a proposal to make our marijuana problem more like our alcohol problem might sound attractive, or at least more attractive than it does now.

But at the moment, there is no socially recognized category of "grudgingly tolerated vice," nor are there working models. In the absence of such models, new legalization regimes are likely to tend towards the relatively unrestricted availability which characterizes alcohol. The costs of such availability suggest that those who advocate the legalization of now-illicit drugs might best begin the process of drug control reform by proposing and testing reforms of current alcohol policy.

If one of the currently illicit drugs had to be chosen for legalization, marijuana would be the most obvious candidate. Indeed, those who argue in favor of legalizing "drugs" often argue as if marijuana is the typical case, while opponents of legalization concentrate their fire on heroin and cocaine. Several facts combine to make marijuana prohibition look like a questionable bargain:

- Marijuana is the most widely used of the illicit drugs.
- Despite its prohibited status, marijuana is very easy to obtain. Thus, a substantial fraction of those who would use marijuana if it were legal are probably using it currently.
- Government expenditures on marijuana enforcement are quite high. It is estimated that the Federal Government alone has spent $636 million on marijuana enforcement in 1986. Similar calculations suggest that expenditures in 1988 were $968 million. Thus, prohibition is expensive.
- Marijuana has by far the lowest ratio of measured harm to total use of all the illicit drugs. A substantial fraction of all regular marijuana users become at least daily users for some period of time, but this becomes a chronic condition for relatively few. The most frightening fact about marijuana is that the number of heavy daily users, people who spend most of their waking hours under the influence, is quite large: a few million Americans at any given time. But even the existence of this rather obvious "problem" population must be inferred

> from data about the drug market rather than being directly observed in the form of deaths, injuries, crimes or skid-row personal collapse. Thus, even if prohibition and enforcement were very successful in reducing marijuana consumption, questions could still be raised about the benefits of that reduction.

Marijuana prohibition, then, seems like an expensive, largely ineffective effort to control a relatively modest problem. It is no wonder that legalization of marijuana is offered as an obvious and relatively risk-free "first step" in the deployment of legalization. Nevertheless our experience with alcohol should make us skeptical of claims that any drug legalization is "risk-free." Even the best control regimes have significant costs, and the control regime that actually emerges from a legalization process might not be the best one.

Such a regime could tax marijuana, license users, limit quantity and potency and so on. It is plausible that such a regime, constructed on the model of grudging toleration, would have the effect of vastly reducing the enforcement problem, even though this potential benefit is reduced by the fact that marijuana use is so great among age groups for whom it would presumably remain illegal under a regulatory regime. Several billion dollars in annual revenue would become available to various levels of government, most of it transferred from the revenues of illicit businesses.

However, legalization could, at the same time, lead to dramatic increases in consumption. Under prohibition, marijuana is available to a determined buyer but still far less easy to find and of a less consistent quality than most legal commodities. Under a regulatory regime, it would become vastly more available. Buying marijuana would be as quick and easy as buying a chocolate bar.

Some proponents are likely to reply that any resulting consumption increase would be of little significance. Like occasional and moderate drinking, occasional and moderate marijuana use is without evident harm. However, there are two sorts of use which have significant social costs: use by children and very heavy use. Preventing growth of either of these user populations must be a design criterion for any legalization strategy.

Effective prevention of such growth would require taxation, licensing, and quantity restrictions similar to those described for alcohol, with all their associated problems. In particular, there would be laws proscribing sale to minors, who now make up a large minority of marijuana users. If enforcement of this law were lax, consumption would grow; if it were severe, enforcement levels might not decrease much from the current regime. Because marijuana legalization involves a change in legal status, it would also have important social effects, including the effects of use by role models. It may be that such acceptability would make marijuana use no worse a problem than cigarette smoking; but making the marijuana problem more like the cigarette problem is not a desideratum.

Setting tax rates itself poses a difficult problem. Untaxed or lightly taxed marijuana would be significantly cheaper than it is on the current black market; a pre-rolled "joint" might cost a few cents, like a tobacco cigarette or a tea bag. Significant increases in consumption could be expected to result from such a sharp decline in price.

Heavy taxation, however, risks the possibility that the black market would continue to profit from selling untaxed marijuana. Some heavy users who now pay for their marijuana from their earnings as marijuana dealers might turn to property crime instead. At best, heavy taxation would require serious enforcement efforts.

Marijuana legalization, then, has the potential to make some things better and others worse. The magnitude of these changes under any specific regulatory regime is a matter for further conjecture and analysis; whether they add up to a good or bad trade depends on what is likely to happen and on what weights are assigned to different aspects of the problem. But the spectrum of the possible results of marijuana legalization is much broader than some of its proponents seem to believe. Low-tax, high-potency legal marijuana could lead to severe social costs within user populations of the greatest concern; high-tax, low-potency marijuana could sustain black markets and their associated costs while increasing consumption more modestly.

If legalizing marijuana were to lead to modest increases in heavy drug use and drug use by minors (say ten percent), it could reasonably be counted a success. If, instead, those levels were to triple, and marijuana potency were to rise, it would have to be counted as an expensive and difficult-to-reverse failure. In the absence of any quantitative estimate of the probabilities of these two outcomes, legalizing marijuana has to be rated as a gamble, and a high-stakes gamble at that.

The pragmatic question about drug control policy is how to manage the availability of a wide range of existing and potential psychoactives to get the best mix of cost and benefits. Changing drugs' legal status is only one of many possible interventions which can effect that mix. Less dramatic proposals, which offer the potential of real progress with minimal risks, deserve at least equal attention.

Without changing the legal status of alcohol, we could create a new regulatory regime to make it less widely abused and responsible for less crime. Without changing the legal status of marijuana, we could reduce enforcement costs greatly with little or no increase in abuse.

The challenge of drug policy is to find least-cost solutions to the problems created by the age-old fact that some human beings take more of various mind-altering substances than is good for them or their neighbors, and by the modern fact that the variety of available psychoactives is rapidly increasing. To concentrate on changing labels from "legal" to "illegal" is to miss all of the hard work and most of the social importance that accompanies that challenge.

2. Alternatives to Prohibition

Any discussion about whether or not drug criminalization works must also take the available alternatives into account. It is possible, for example, to think that drug criminalization produces only modest benefits at a high cost while nevertheless supporting criminalization on the grounds that the other policy options would be even worse.

The trio of articles in the previous section focused on the most familiar alternative to drug prohibition—legalization. Alcohol and tobacco are drugs that are legal to buy and sell for non-medical use. As of June 2019, ten states have passed laws legalizing the sale of non-medical marijuana, although the drug remains illegal federally. (Marijuana legalization is examined in detail in Chapter 8.)

Of course, there are alternatives to drug prohibition that stop short of legalization. This section focuses on two policy options adopted in some other countries but that, to date, have not been tried in the United States: drug decriminalization and heroin-assisted treatment. Both of these policies are rooted in the theory of harm reduction, which focuses on reducing the harms associated with substance use.

a. Decriminalization

As federal Judge Juan Torruella has observed, "legalization" and "decriminalization," "although technically distinct, are often used almost interchangeably." Juan R. Torruella, *One Judge's Attempt at a Rational Discussion of the So-Called War on Drugs*, 6 B.U. Pub. Int'l L. J. 1, 12–13 (1996). This is especially true in news coverage of drug policy. But the line between decriminalization and legalization is not always clear even among policy wonks. Consider, for example, Washington, D.C.'s marijuana law, which makes it legal to grow, possess, and share small amounts of marijuana for personal use, while continuing to prohibit commercial sale and manufacture. Some people describe D.C.'s marijuana law as a form of legalization, since personal possession and cultivation are legal. But others refer to it as a form of decriminalization, since the drug cannot be sold legally. Adding to the confusion, the term decriminalization is sometimes used to refer to laws that merely remove the possibility of a jail sentence, while still classifying the offense as a crime.

This section focuses on a particular form of drug decriminalization. In 2001, Portugal decriminalized the possession of personal use amounts of all drugs. Instead of making drug possession a crime, Portugal's law sends drug users to a civil panel that is designed to determine whether the user has a substance use disorder. The excerpt below compares Portugal's decriminalization law to the United States model of criminal drug courts. Which approach do you prefer and why? Do you think Portugal's decriminalization law could work in the United States?

The Decriminalization Option: Should States Consider Moving from a Criminal to a Civil Drug Court Model?

Alex Kreit

2010 University of Chicago Legal Forum 299

Today, we have over two thousand drug courts in the United States, a number that . . . is likely to increase in the coming years along with the expanding budget.

Drug courts vary widely in the details of their operations, but in essence they allow some drug offenders to obtain treatment under the close supervision of a drug court in place of a traditional sentence. Drug courts are designed to be non-adversarial, with the prosecutor, defense attorney, and judge working together for the goal of promoting public safety. Drug court judges typically monitor and evaluate defendants through regular status hearings, frequent drug and alcohol testing, and other methods. If a drug court participant fails to comply with program requirements—by, for example, testing positive for drugs—the judge may impose sanctions. These sanctions are generally imposed on a graduated basis and can range from the imposition of work detail or community service to brief jail sentences to termination from the program. Judges can likewise reward participants who are on track with intermediate benefits, such as complimentary public transportation passes.

In 1997, the National Association of Drug Court Professionals, in partnership with the U.S. Department of Justice, formalized this basic structure by publishing a report with "ten key components" for drug courts and requiring state and local drug courts to abide by them in order to be eligible for federal funding. Beyond these ten components, however, there is a wide diversity in the operation of drug courts. In terms of procedural posture drug courts can be grouped into three basic models: (1) pre-plea/pre-adjudication, (2) post-plea/pre-adjudication, and (3) post-adjudication. In the first category, prosecution is deferred while the defendant goes through the drug court process. A defendant will typically be required to waive certain procedural rights (such as the right to a speedy trial), but will retain her right to challenge the charge against her should she fail to complete the program and be returned to a traditional court. In the "post-plea/pre-adjudication" scenario, a guilty plea is part of the price of admission into the drug court, but the plea is held in abeyance during the defendant's participation in the program. If the defendant succeeds in the drug court, the charge will be dismissed, but if she fails, the plea is entered and a sentence is imposed. Finally, in the post-adjudication model, a defendant pleads guilty and is convicted. The sentence is then suspended pending the successful completion of the drug court program. Some post-adjudication programs provide a method for a successful defendant to have her record expunged. In others, however, a successful defendant will escape imposition of the suspended sentence but will still have a conviction on her record.

Eligibility requirements also vary significantly from court to court, though typically a defendant who wishes to gain entry into a drug court program must be charged with drug possession or another nonviolent offense and must demonstrate that she has a substance abuse problem.

For all their differences, perhaps the most important quality that unites American drug courts is that they are uniformly a part of the criminal system. Drug possession remains criminalized and those caught with drugs are arrested and processed by the police as usual. Drug court programs only enter the picture at this stage, offering a way out for individuals who are facing a prison sentence or who would simply prefer not to have a criminal record. In every instance—whether pre-plea or post-adjudication—the threat of a criminal sanction hangs over the treatment process, and judges are responsible for meting out graduated sanctions. As a result, within the drug court system, "the court, rather than treatment center, becomes the focal point of the treatment process." Similarly, though drug courts operate on the premise that drug addiction is a disease that should be treated and not punished, criminal sanctions ultimately await those who fail the program and those who either choose not to participate or are excluded from participating.

[U.S. d]rug courts appear to have been born primarily out of necessity. As drug war arrests and prosecutions reached a crescendo in the late 1980s, many urban court and prison systems were having a hard time keeping pace. Drug courts were conceived as a method for helping to control rapidly increasing court caseloads and prison populations. But as the courts spread during the early 1990s, drug court advocates began to look beyond the immediate benefits in managing caseloads and jail populations and focused their attention on drugs courts as a potentially more effective and therapeutic alternative to the status quo.

Today, most drug court advocates view them as both a less expensive method for processing low-level drug offenders through the criminal justice system and a more humane and effective approach to addressing the problem of substance abuse than conventional options. Whatever faults that drug courts may have, there does appear to be a fairly broad consensus for the proposition that drug courts produce better results than incarceration and at a reduced cost. Various studies have found that drug courts reduce criminal justice and victimization costs as compared to incarceration or even simple probation, and others have found long-term savings have been achieved in counties where drug court programs have been instituted. An analysis in California, for example, found that the drug courts studied cost only $3,000 on average per client while generating an average savings of $11,000 per client in reductions in recidivism and costs to victims. A systemic review of drug court research by the Government Accountability Office (GAO) in 2005 found that the studies showed net benefits ranging from $1,000 to $15,000 per drug court participant. As the 2009 National Drug Control Strategy put it when summarizing the research into the efficacy of drug courts, "Over a decade of drug court research shows that drug courts work better than jail or prison."

[In sum], there is a great deal of evidence that when it comes to dealing with low-level drug offenders, drug courts are less expensive and far more effective than incarceration. And yet, drug courts that operate within the criminal system are still a very cumbersome way to address the underlying concerns in this area: drug demand, drug abuse, and drug addiction.

The criminal prohibition of the possession and distribution of small quantities of controlled substances turns all drug users into criminals, whether or not they are addicted, violent, or otherwise law abiding. A substantial percentage of drug users, however, do not have a drug abuse problem and will never develop one. Indeed, the available evidence shows that most people who use an illegal drug will stop using entirely within five years. Many more will continue to use drugs regularly or sporadically without any negative impact on their lives. And, even among users who do go on to abuse drugs (including alcohol), many will simply outgrow the problem without treatment. Of course, someone who is arrested for drug possession or sale is more likely than the average user to suffer from an abuse or addiction problem. A person who has an addiction or abuse problem may be more likely to engage in risky behavior that would lead them to encounter the police and be arrested for drug possession. And a drug abuser is more likely to be in possession of a controlled substance at any given time than a casual user simply because someone who abuses or is addicted to drugs will use and carry them more frequently. Nevertheless, in any system that criminalizes the possession, cultivation, and distribution of small quantities of controlled substances, a substantial percentage of those who are arrested and prosecuted will inevitably be nonaddicts and nonabusers.

For these reasons, drug courts that operate within the criminal justice system run into the problem of overinclusiveness and run the risk of funneling nonaddicts into treatment that they don't need. Not surprisingly, then, drug courts often require would-be participants to have either tested positive for drugs or to demonstrate that they suffer from an abuse problem in order to gain entry. These requirements are undermined, however, by the relative ease with which an individual can fake an abuse or addiction problem and by incentives that tend to result in the admission of nonaddicts into drug court programs.

Nonaddicted defendants will often have a very strong motivation to embellish the extent of their use in order to prove that they have an abuse problem and become eligible to participate in a drug court. This is because, for an individual without addiction or abuse problems, a drug court will often be a far more preferable alternative to a drug conviction. Even if the punishment a person is facing is relatively minimal, an otherwise law-abiding recreational drug user will generally have an especially strong interest in avoiding a drug conviction. A drug conviction carries with it a wide array of collateral legal consequences (in addition to the social stigma associated with a criminal conviction), including the loss of a range of federal benefits and professional licenses. A nonaddict, who may be a student or have a regular job, is likely to be more concerned with these types of consequences than someone who is suffering from an abuse or addiction problem and living on the margins of society. At the same time, participating in a drug court program is a low-risk endeavor for a nonaddict because he will not have much difficulty passing drug tests and adhering to other program requirements. As one commentator put it: "Defendants understand that they have to play the treatment game to pass through the criminal hoops." And, because addiction and abuse are imprecise disorders the diagnosis of which will typically depend on an individual's self-reported behavior, it would be difficult to stop a determined defendant from entering a drug court program under false pretenses even in a system that was firmly dedicated to weeding out nonaddicts.

At the same time, despite the letter of their eligibility requirements, drug courts generally have a very strong interest in admitting nonaddicted clients. This is because drug courts rely on funding that is contingent, implicitly or explicitly, upon demonstrating results and treating a sufficient number of defendants. Indeed, a substantial amount of anecdotal evidence indicates that many drug courts actively seek out "low-risk" nonaddicted clients and do their best to "skim" high-risk clients away from their programs in order to boost their success rate. Many drug court gatekeepers may also have less self-interested reasons for admitting nonaddicts. [A National Association of Criminal Defense Lawyers] report recounted the testimony of a drug court judge who "favors opening the door 'as wide as we can' because 'treatment court is the best game in town.'"

Few studies have attempted to quantify the prevalence of drug court participants who do not have addiction or abuse problems within drug court programs. Drug court studies that have attempted to assess rates of drug dependency among participants, however, indicate that a substantial number of drug court clients do not have a substance use disorder. One team of researchers that has measured drug dependency in drug court found that "nearly one half of misdemeanor drug court clients, one third of felony drug court clients, and two thirds of pretrial clients in a drug treatment and monitoring program produced 'sub-threshold' drug composite scores on the Addiction Severity Index."

An examination of past-month use rates of individuals entering treatment from the Substance Abuse and Mental Health's Treatment Episode Data Set suggests that the findings in the handful of individual studies to address the issue are not anomalous. The data set includes the frequency of a treatment client's drug use prior to entering treatment for his or her primary drug substance of abuse, as well as the person or entity responsible for referring the client to the program. Looking at the frequency of use by referral type from the most recent available year (2007) reveals that an unusually large number of individuals referred to treatment by the criminal justice system had used their primary substance of supposed abuse either not at all or only rarely within the month before entering treatment. Specifically, 38 percent of individuals who entered treatment because of a referral from a state or federal court had not used drugs at all within the past month. Another 17 percent had only used their primary substance of abuse one to three times in the one month prior to entering treatment. That means 55 percent of all individuals who were referred to treatment by a court program had used their primary drug of abuse less than three times in the month before they entered into treatment. By comparison, only 21 percent of individuals who referred themselves to treatment had used their primary drug of abuse less than three times in the past month.

These statistics are, of course, inherently limited in their ability to tell us the total number of drug court participants who do not have a genuine abuse or addiction problem. It is certainly possible, for example, for a person to suffer from a substance abuse or addiction problem without having used (or having used only infrequently) within the month prior to their admission into treatment. Similarly, some criminal justice treatment clients might be motivated to conceal their use or to scale back their use before entering treatment in order to demonstrate their compliance to the court. While these statistics cannot tell us the scope of the overinclusiveness problem with specificity, however, the abnormally large number of criminal justice treatment clients who had used three times or fewer prior to entering treatment seems to provide strong corroboration for the general proposition that a not-insubstantial number of drug court participants do not have a substance abuse or addiction problem. Rather, these individuals are gaming the system and entering treatment not because they have any need for it but because it is a preferable alternative to the punishment they would otherwise receive.

It is self-evident, of course, that sending an individual who does not have a drug abuse or addiction problem to receive drug treatment is not an efficient use of scarce and costly drug treatment resources. Processing nonaddicts through the machinery of drug courts—including regular drug testing, drug court appearances, and other requirements—is also unlikely to provide significant benefits in return for the investment. Indeed, participation in drug court programs may be counterproductive for nonaddicted defendants since meeting program requirements are likely to interfere with their work and family responsibilities. Because drug courts generally attempt to tailor their treatment regimens to the participant, it is worth noting that low-risk offenders without abuse problems may cost drug courts less than the average drug court participant. And drug courts are still less expensive than incarceration. This fact, however, is precisely why there is unlikely to be a solution to the overinclusiveness problem within criminal drug courts. As long as treatment or typical criminal justice solutions like incarceration are the only options, drug courts will be seen as the most cost-effective option for low-risk defendants, even those who do not have substance abuse problems.

Even if criminal drug courts may have their shortcomings, it does not necessarily mean that they are not our best option. Drug use—along with abuse and addiction—has existed in almost every society in recorded history. There is no silver bullet that will solve the problem of drug abuse and addiction, and any system that we design is going to involve trade-offs.

The inefficiencies discussed above, however, seem to be preventable problems that flow primarily from a single source: the criminalization of drug use and abuse. Because drug courts are located within the criminal system, they put individuals who are caught in possession of drugs to a choice between a drug court treatment program and the (more costly and less effective) traditional criminal penalty. In some cases, this choice will lead defendants who do not have a drug abuse problem and are unlikely to develop one to obtain treatment they do not need to avoid the punishment they would otherwise face. In others, defendants who might benefit from a detailed course of treatment or a brief medical consultation about their substance use are counseled by their attorneys not to enter drug court programs because the punishment they face does not justify the risks or burdens of drug court. As a result, drug courts can, in some instances, waste scarce treatment resources on those without drug problems while allowing others who truly need treatment to pass through the system without so much as speaking with a treatment or addiction specialist.

That criminal drug courts retain these inefficiencies is not surprising. Criminal laws against possession of small quantities of drugs for personal use are not really concerned with possession itself or even with drug use generally. They exist in order to address the problems of drug abuse and drug addiction—problems that are medical in nature and that only affect a small percentage of those in possession of drugs. As a result, criminal laws against possession of small drug quantities are a very imprecise method for addressing the chief problem with which they are concerned.

[Recent experience in Portugal suggests that a civil drug court system may offer advantages over criminal drug courts.]

Under Portugal's law, passed nearly a decade ago, simple possession of small amounts of drugs is no longer a crime. And yet, the possession and use of drugs remains subject to close scrutiny by the Portuguese government.

A brief overview of Portugal's system is instructive. Beginning in July of 2001, Portugal implemented a "decriminalization model" for drug users. The law removes criminal penalties for the purchase, possession, and cultivation of all drugs for personal-use quantities, which the law defines as an amount sufficient for ten days' usage for one person. The sale of drugs in any quantity, meanwhile, remains illegal in Portugal.

What distinguishes Portugal's approach from the traditional decriminalization model is what happens to users who are caught with drugs in personal-use amounts. Rather than receiving no penalty or being given a fine, individuals who are found in possession of personal-use quantities of drugs are referred into what we might think of as a civil drug court system. Because drug possession has been decriminalized, when a police officer in Portugal encounters a person under the quantity limit, she is not permitted to make an arrest. Instead, she issues a citation for the person in possession of drugs to appear before what the law calls a "dissuasion panel." Typically, a person will appear before the commission within seventy-two hours of receiving the citation.

Dissuasion panels are organized to be as nonadversarial in nature as possible. They are made up of three members—typically two people from the medical or social services fields and one attorney. The panels meet with the individuals who appear before them in order to try to assess their treatment needs and to assist them in addressing any abuse or addiction problems. The "offender" is not represented by counsel when he appears before the commission, though he does have the right to request a therapist of his choice to take part in the proceedings or to have a medical examination conducted to aid in the panel's review.

One of the primary objectives of the dissuasion panel structure is to try to foster a supportive atmosphere that is focused exclusively on the health of the offender. Every effort is made to guard against creating an impression that the panels are there to assess guilt or that drug usage is morally blameworthy conduct. So, for example, the commission members sit at a table with the offender, as opposed to behind an elevated bench as in a courtroom.

Consistent with this approach, the dissuasion panel has a good deal of flexibility in terms of how it will handle cases where an individual appears to have an abuse or addiction problem. If, however, the panel determines that an offender is a non-addicted consumer of drugs with no prior offenses, the law requires it to suspend proceedings and impose no sanction. This is the result in approximately 80 percent of all proceedings. Of course, in these cases the panel still has the opportunity to talk with and advise the individual about drug addiction and abuse issues as part of the meeting.

For offenders who do not fall into the dismissal category, the panels can take a range of action, including issuing a warning to the offender, requiring the offender to check in with the panel at specified times, ordering the offender to enter into a treatment program, and even banning the offender from visiting certain places or associating with certain people. The panels can also impose a fine, but the law provides that fines are to be imposed as a last resort. The more common course with regard to a fine is that a panel may order treatment or some other sanction along with a fine, but suspend the fine contingent upon meeting the required treatment. Because drug possession has been decriminalized, the panels cannot, under any circumstances, impose prison sentences or even send someone to treatment through civil commitment—instead fines are the only mechanism for enforcing compliance with orders to seek treatment.

Portugal's decriminalization law was, perhaps unsurprisingly, strongly criticized by United States and United Nations drug enforcement officials and in the international press. Critics worried that the country would become a destination for "drug tourism." Nearly ten years later, however, these fears have not been realized and Portugal's program appears to have been quite successful at reducing the harms associated with drug use in a cost-effective manner. A 2009 CATO Institute Report on Portugal's decriminalization policy by Glenn Greenwald concluded that "usage has declined in many key categories and drug-related social ills have been far more contained in a decriminalized regime." There has, for example, been a substantial decline in HIV infections among drug users, with instances of new cases dropping from 1,400 to 400. Likewise, drug overdose deaths dropped from 400 to 290. Meanwhile, the reforms have helped to alleviate some of the burdens on Portugal's criminal justice system and contributed to progress in addressing prison overcrowding. The savings in criminal justice spending has allowed Portugal to increase its treatment capacity and helped lead to a 147 percent increase in the number of people in substitution treatment from 1999 to 2003.

Joao Castel-Branco Goulao, the director of Portugal's principal drug policy agency—the Instituto da Droga e da Toxicodependencia—is careful to emphasize that he does not believe decriminalization by itself has been the driving force behind the successes of Portugal's model. Rather, in his view, decriminalization has provided Portugal with a framework for the noncriminal dissuasion commission system to operate and to treat drug supply and demand as distinct problems. By detaching drug use from the criminal justice system and treating the issue through a civil system, Portugal was able to create an atmosphere in which addiction is viewed purely as a medical and public health problem.

While the available studies indicate that Portugal's decriminalization law has been successful on its own terms, there has been little discussion of what the benefits and drawbacks of such a system might be in comparison to other approaches. [There is good reason to believe that a] civil drug court system similar to Portugal's, in which possession of personal-use quantities of drugs has been decriminalized and those found in possession are given medical consultations before civil panels, is likely to be more cost effective than [the] criminal drug court model.

A civil drug court like Portugal's model would remedy the overinclusiveness problem of spending treatment resources on those who do not need them. When drug courts are incorporated within the criminal justice system, drug court treatment programs exist only as an alternative to the traditional penalty the offender would otherwise face. As a result, drug defendants who do not have an abuse or addiction problem often have a strong incentive to enter into treatment through drug courts whether or not they truly need it. Moving drug courts from the criminal to civil system would squarely address this problem by allowing the court or treatment panel to base the outcome in each case entirely on the individual's treatment needs. Those without abuse or addiction problems—who constitute a substantial majority of offenders—could be sent on their way with nothing more than a warning and a consultation, accompanied by information about the benefits of cessation and how to recognize the early signs of addiction in their own behavior. Nonaddicted defendants, in turn, would no longer have an incentive to exaggerate their drug use. Because there are few, if any, conceivable benefits from treating or punishing individuals in this category of offenders, this would yield substantial cost savings over criminal drug courts while incurring minimal additional costs.

While the flexibility of a decriminalized drug court system may provide some substantial benefits over the rigidity of our current criminal drug court model, critics may counter that any benefits . . . would be outweighed by losses from removing the deterrent value of the criminal justice system. Deterrence-based objections to a civil drug court system might proceed on two fronts. First, some might argue that removing criminal penalties for possession of small amounts of drugs would lead to an increase in new and casual drug users who may presently be dissuaded by the possibility of criminal punishment. Second, some might argue that treatment courts will not be as effective if judges are unable to deter bad behavior through the use of short jail stints to punish those who slip up or the threat of a prison sentence for those who fail the programs entirely.

The fear that decriminalization may lead to an increase in use, particularly by new users, while understandable in theory, is belied by the experience in Portugal. In the decade since Portugal enacted its decriminalization policy, drug use rates in the country have largely remained stable or declined. Use rates among the key demographics of thirteen to fifteen-year-olds and sixteen to eighteen-year-olds fell by approximately 4 and 6 percent respectively in the years following decriminalization in Portugal.

The argument that removing drug courts' access to criminal sanctions will diminish their ability to incentivize treatment is a more serious and realistic concern. For example, in his insightful book *When Brute Force Fails*, Mark Kleiman points to the successes of an innovative probation program in Hawaii as evidence that a regime with increased drug testing and criminal sanctions may be more effective that current models that focus on treatment at the outset. In the program, named Hawaii's Opportunity Probation with Enforcement (HOPE), a state judge tired of probation violations put problem probationers on a strict program in which any violation—from a failed drug test to a missed appointment—would result in an immediate but short jail sentence. The results were impressive, with a decrease of over 90 percent in the violation rates of program participants and rearrest rates less than half than the comparison group. Kleiman argues that the lesson to be learned from Project HOPE is that successful diversion programs should include "frequent drug tests and quick and consistent sanctions for failure to comply."

Although the HOPE program persuasively demonstrates that sanctions can be a successful tool for problem probationers, evidence on the effectiveness of sanctions in drug court programs remains inconsistent. While some studies have shown sanctions to be effective, others have found that they have little, if any, effect. A study in Clark County, Nevada, for example, even indicated that imposing sanctions was associated with higher rearrest rates and lower graduation rates.

The inconsistent evidence may be due, in part, to differences in the make-up of offenders in the studies. Specifically, sanctions for failed drug tests might be expected to be more effective in deterring use in programs that include large percentages of individuals without drug abuse or addiction problems. This is because those without addiction or abuse problems are better able to abstain from drug use and more likely to respond more rationally to threats of punishment than are addicts. In assessing the implications of the HOPE program and the usefulness of sanctions, then, it is important to consider that HOPE's participants were not primarily drug offenders, but rather felony probationers who had been convicted of a wide range of offenses—from sexual assault and burglary to drug dealing—and were facing five- to ten-year prison terms. Likewise, the program's aim was to reduce probation violations, not address substance abuse or addiction problems. Accordingly, while HOPE provides strong evidence that incorporating swift and certain sanctions for probation violations is an effective method for deterring such violations and recidivism among serious felony offenders, it does not necessarily mean that the availability of sanctions provides better outcomes among drug court populations. This is not to say that sanctions may not be an effective method for persuading some drug addicts to stay on track in drug court programs, only that we should be careful not to overstate their importance.

Even if we grant that the deterrent effect of sanctions is likely to help some drug court participants stay on track, civil drug courts may offer other benefits that would counter the loss of a deterrent effect and leave treatment success rates unchanged. In particular, a civil drug court system modeled after Portugal's might be able to achieve better outcomes for some participants than a coercion-based system. There is a wealth of evidence that indicates internal motivation to be a strong predictor of treatment success and reveals that voluntary treatment is more successful than compulsory treatment. There is good reason to believe that a decriminalized civil drug court system, in which addicts meet with a treatment panel to determine the outcome in their cases, would be better positioned to convince participants that they need treatment than a criminal system in which their participation is based entirely on external coercion. Rather than facing a judge who is mandating sobriety as evidenced by clean drug tests, an offender would meet with treatment professionals who would have the opportunity to discuss his use and convince him that he is in need of treatment. If civil drug courts are successful at inspiring internal motivation among participants, the benefits from that effect may balance any possible negative consequences from the loss of criminal sanctions as a deterrent tool. And, while a civil system would remove the availability of jail sanctions, sanctions in the form of fines or other civil remedies would remain an option in the event of noncompliance. Finally, we must keep in mind that jail sanctions are not cost free. Indeed, they are quite expensive, both in terms of the direct costs of incarceration and the collateral costs of disrupting the treatment client's social bonds and ability to maintain employment.

Even if those who argue that eliminating criminal sanctions would decrease the overall rate of success among treatment participants are correct, the benefits of addressing the over- and under-inclusiveness problems inherent in a criminal drug court system might still make a civil drug court system more efficient overall. Solving those problems would result in substantial cost savings by ensuring treatment resources are not wasted on those who do not need treatment. It would also dramatically expand the net of drug users who have the opportunity to consult with treatment professionals [because all users found with drugs would be sent to a dissuasion panel, rather than the current system in which many users found in possession of drugs are given a fine or probation without any treatment opportunity]. By sending all users directly to a treatment panel, we could expect to see dramatic long-term savings through "brief interventions" that reach casual users before they have become addicted, as well as treatment of addicts who may not have a sufficient incentive to enter a drug court in a criminal system. Thus, even if the success rate for treatment in a civil drug court system were lower than in a criminal drug court system, the significantly larger pool of individuals receiving treatment consultations in a civil system, in combination with the savings achieved by removing nonaddicts from costly treatment programs, make a compelling case for the proposition that civil drug courts are likely be more cost effective than criminal drug courts.

b. Heroin-Assisted Treatment and Supervised Injection Facilities

Heroin-assisted treatment, also sometimes called heroin maintenance, has been employed in a number of countries outside of the United States, including

Switzerland and Canada. Under heroin maintenance policies, heroin-dependent people are given medical prescriptions for the drug and allowed to use it in a safe, controlled environment. The paper below, published in 2009, provides an overview of Switzerland's experience with heroin maintenance.

Can Heroin Maintenance Help Baltimore?
Peter Reuter

The Abell Foundation 2009

Baltimore City in particular has been adversely affected by the problem of heroin addiction. Whether measured by the number of heroin-related deaths per capita, heroin treatment admissions, or HIV related to heroin injecting, Baltimore City has for decades been the leading or close to the leading city in the United States. Even the massive expansion of Baltimore City's treatment programs that has occurred since 1995 has failed to rid the city of the problem.

Given that tougher enforcement and greater treatment provisions have not managed to make a large dent in the harm that heroin causes Baltimore City, there is a continuing desire to consider more radical solutions. In November 2007, the Baltimore City Council once again considered a bill proposing the legalization of drugs, hardly a realistic option given the federal government's views on, and role in, drug policy.

There is, however, a less radical, though still bold, innovation that has received attention from time to time in Baltimore City: heroin maintenance. Under this option, heroin users who have tried and failed in other kinds of treatment, including methadone maintenance, are provided heroin in the context of a medically supervised facility. The assumption is that if an addict has cheap access to heroin in safe conditions, many of the harms of the drug will disappear; the risk of overdose will become minimal, and the addict will no longer have to commit numerous property crimes, or sell to other users, in order to finance an extremely expensive habit.

There are many arguments against this assumption, involving both principle and pragmatic considerations. For example, in the heroin maintenance program, the government appears simply to be providing addicts with what they want rather than curing them of a dependence that prevents them from leading productive and socially engaged lives. Others assert that these programs lead to an increase in heroin initiation because they make the consequences less harmful. Nonetheless, a small but growing number of Western nations are experimenting with heroin maintenance. In two European countries, the Netherlands and Switzerland, heroin maintenance is now a routine treatment option, available to most heroin addicts, though taken up by few. Germany, the United Kingdom, and Spain are seriously considering the option. Canada has experimented with heroin maintenance in two cities, Vancouver and Montreal. The treatment evaluations, which are of varying quality, generally show positive results; none show negative results.

There are now 23 facilities in Switzerland providing heroin-assisted treatment (HAT); two are located in prisons. The total number of clients in treatment has stabilized at about 1200, constituting less than 5 percent of the estimated heroin-addict population. The total number of places available for treatment has been capped, but there is no indication of substantial waiting lines.

A decision to allow addicts to choose their own dose was critical. It removed any incentive to supplement the clinic provision with black-market purchases. A patient could receive heroin three times daily, 365 days of the year; very few now receive it more than twice daily. The average daily dose stabilized at 500 to 600 milligrams of pure heroin, a massive amount by the standards of U.S. street addicts.

The programs, by design, offer a very sterile, indeed clinical, environment. Operators make every effort to reduce this experience to medicine rather than recreation. Patients must turn up on time, take the drug promptly, and leave the premises. There is to be no congregating and socializing. For example, in one facility there are few chairs in the waiting room; the aim is to move patients in and out as soon as they have recovered from their dose. They are expected, here and elsewhere, to leave within 20 minutes of taking their heroin.

The patient population is aging and, mostly, very troubled. They have longstanding problems in all aspects of their personal lives and little prospect of being able to improve their conditions.

Perhaps the most significant evaluation of the Swiss experience appeared in a 2001 issue of *The Lancet*, a leading British medical research journal. The study followed 2,000 addicts admitted to HAT over a six-year period. One thousand were discharged for some reason but the retention rate was high; even at the six-year mark nearly 30 percent remained in the program.

Of particular note was the analysis of reasons for discharge; more than 60 percent of those who left HAT did so in order to take up another treatment option. Most of those seeking other treatment went into a methadone maintenance program (60 percent) but almost 40 percent went into an abstinence program.

What these data suggest is that heroin maintenance is not a terminal state, as most critics have (plausibly) alleged, but that it is mostly a transitional state. The Swiss experience suggests that the transition might take a few years and that some will stay in heroin assisted therapy. Nonetheless, it does potentially change assessments of the desirability of the program if perhaps one-third of those who enter have transitioned to other treatment within a few years.

[There have been a total of three major studies of HAT programs to date.] All evaluations so far have been positive. Retention in treatment has been high and drop-out has often been into other treatment modalities. Reductions in crime and improvements in health and social functioning are somewhat, but not greatly, better than the results to be expected for a good methadone program. However, the clients in HAT have a record of repeated failure in methadone maintenance treatment (MMT) so that crude comparison may be misleading. It is difficult to find any evidence that HAT has caused additional harms either to users or to the broader population. There is no indication that heroin has leaked from the facilities, dispensing the drug into the black market. Though it is difficult to develop a research design that would assess changes in initiation, no one has claimed that the availability of HAT has led to an increase in the number of persons experimenting with heroin.

One concern is that heroin assisted treatment is substantially more expensive than MMT. That has been the experience in both Switzerland and the Netherlands. The heroin patients costs were much higher not because of the cost of the heroin itself but primarily because of all the associated program costs. However, studies in both countries found that the additional benefits outweighed the additional costs. For example, adding the social costs to the costs of provision of services, a patient in treatment for a given period of time in the heroin arm of the Dutch trials cost 37,000 Euros compared to 50,000 Euros for the methadone arm of the trial. Reductions in crime were a large part of the gains, as was true in the Swiss studies. This comparison points to a chronic problem of substance abuse treatment funding; the expenditures are borne by the health-care sector, while the benefits are primarily reaped by the criminal justice sector and the community.

Heroin assisted therapy is clearly a supplement to methadone maintenance rather than a substitute for it. In no site where the HAT has been available has it attracted a substantial share of the heroin users who seek treatment; 10 percent is a high estimate of the potential share of treatment slots that might be occupied by HAT clients. Given the political and programmatic challenges that confront HAT in Baltimore, the question for the community is: Is the undertaking worth the effort for such a small share of clients?

At best there is a case only for an experiment. There are too many potential differences between Baltimore City and the other sites in which HAT has been tried to allow confident predictions of the outcomes. Visits to facilities in other countries hardly provide an inspiring model. The client population in Baltimore City is highly troubled so even if HAT leads to better outcomes for the group as a whole, many of the clients will remain unemployed, marginalized, and in poor health conditions. There will be some poster children but not many.

The potential for gain, however, is substantial. Even in the aging heroin-addict population, there are many who are heavily involved in crime and return frequently to the criminal justice system. Their continued involvement in street markets imposes a large burden on the community in the form of civil disorder that helps keep investment and jobs out. If heroin maintenance could remove 10 percent of Baltimore's most troubled heroin addicts from the streets, the result could be substantial reductions in crime and various other problems that greatly trouble the city. That is enough to make a debate on the matter worthwhile.

In the United States, heroin-assisted treatment has been a politically charged topic, in part because many politicians describe it as a form of "legalization." In the early 1970s, for example, New York City Mayor John Lindsay suggested investigating the implementation of a heroin maintenance program. In response, New York Congressman Charles Rangel attacked Lindsay's proposal as a plan to "legalize heroin." *See* JOSEPH A. CALIFANO, JR., HIGH SOCIETY: HOW SUBSTANCE ABUSE RAVAGES AMERICA AND WHAT TO DO ABOUT IT 130 (2007). Is heroin maintenance a form of heroin "legalization" or a harm reduction measure? Or both? How important do you think the characterization of a program like this as "legalization" would be to its political viability?

Sharp increases in heroin use and overdoses in recent years have led officials in some cities to voice tentative support for heroin-assisted treatment programs. In 2016, for example, Ithaca, New York, Mayor Svante Myrick's office issued a report on drug abuse that recommended the city "request the New York Academy of Medicine or another objective research institute to study the efficacy and feasibility of heroin maintenance therapy for people who do not respond effectively to other forms of opioid replacement therapies." THE ITHACA PLAN: A PUBLIC HEALTH AND SAFETY APPROACH TO DRUGS AND DRUG POLICY 7 (2016), http://www.cityofithaca.org/DocumentCenter/View/4224.

Local officials interested in establishing a heroin-assisted treatment program face an obstacle beyond politics, however: federal law. Federal drug laws would likely make it impossible for a city or state to adopt a heroin maintenance policy, even on a trial basis. This is because distributing heroin, whether on the streets or as part of a local-government run treatment program, is a federal crime. As a result, the federal Controlled Substances Act would almost certainly preempt a local or state-run heroin-assisted treatment program. (Although heroin-assisted treatment is illegal under federal law, as discussed in Chapter 7, the Controlled Substances Act does permit the medication-assisted treatment of opioid addiction using other substances—namely methadone, buprenorphine, and naltrexone.)

Some cities and states have also begun to examine the idea of opening supervised injection facilities (which are also sometimes called safe injection sites, drug consumption rooms, or overdose prevention sites). Indeed, as of 2019, five cities—Denver, New York, Philadelphia, San Francisco, and Seattle—had gone so far as to announce plans to open a safe injection site. A safe injection site is a place where injection drug users can self-administer drugs in a controlled environment under medical supervision. They have been operating in other countries, including Canada, for decades, and a wealth of evidence suggests that they can help to reduce overdose deaths. A 2014 review of 75 studies into safe injection facilities found that they have been effective at "promoting safer injecting conditions, enhancing access to primary health care, and reducing the overdose frequency" of users, all without "increase[ing] drug injecting, drug trafficking or crime in the surrounding environments." Chloé Potier et al., *Supervised Injection Services: What Has Been*

Demonstrated? A Systemic Literature Review, 145 DRUG & ALCOHOL DEPENDENCE 48, 48 (2014).

As with heroin-assisted treatment programs, however, federal law may stand in the way of efforts to establish supervised injection facilities in the United States. Under the federal "crack house" statute, it is illegal to "knowingly open, lease, rent, use, or maintain any place, whether permanently or temporarily, for the purpose of manufacturing, distributing, or using any controlled substance." 21 U.S.C. § 856. In February 2019, the United States Attorney for the Eastern District of Pennsylvania filed a lawsuit against a nonprofit named Safehouse that has been working with the city of Philadelphia to open a safe injection site. Citing the crack house statute, the lawsuit seeks a declaratory judgment to stop Safehouse from going through with its plans. For more on this issue, see Alex Kreit, *Safe Injection Sites and the Federal "Crack House" Statute*, 60 B.C. L. REV. 413 (2019).

Should Congress amend federal law to let states and cities experiment with heroin-assisted treatment programs and/or safe injection facilities? What federal concerns, if any, are implicated by these programs?

C. The Opioid Crisis

Shifting substance use patterns can present unique public health and safety challenges. Sometimes these challenges are so considerable that they rise to the level of a crisis or epidemic, whether in fact or in hyperbole. In the 1980s, there was the crack cocaine epidemic. In the early 2000s, the methamphetamine epidemic. Today, there is the opioid crisis, arguably the most damaging drug epidemic in at least the last 100 years. This section introduces some of the central legal and policy questions related to the opioid crisis, but materials throughout the book touch on this subject—from the impact of drug paraphernalia laws on syringe access (covered in Chapter 3) to controls on pharmacies and physicians (covered in Chapter 7) to the question of heroin-assisted treatment discussed in the previous section.

Today's Fentanyl Crisis: Prohibition's Iron Law, Revisited
Leo Beletsky and Corey S. Davis

46 International Journal of Drug Policy 156 (2017)

The United States is in the midst of the worst drug-related crisis in its history. Over 52,000 Americans were killed by drug overdose in 2015, an increase of more than 300% since the turn of the century. Driven primarily by opioids that kill an average of nearly 100 Americans every day, the grim toll of overdose-related death and disability has reached levels of devastation unseen since the height of the AIDS epidemic.

Like that terrible pandemic and many other public health emergencies, the opioid overdose crisis has multiple, overlapping causes. Initially, one primary cause of the crisis was the over-prescription of opioid analgesics (OA). Most of these prescriptions were issued in good faith, but some providers prescribed (and sometimes dispensed) large amounts of opioids without regard for the patients' medical need.

In an effort to address opioid overprescribing, policymakers have mounted a series of supply-side interventions. These have included crackdowns on unscrupulous providers and facilities, prescription limits and guidelines, bolstering prescription monitoring systems, reformulation of some OAs to make them more difficult to misuse, and nudging (or threatening) prescribers to curtail the quantity and dosage of opioid prescriptions. These efforts have seen some effectiveness in reducing the volume of opioids prescribed, and some have been associated with reductions in prescription opioid overdose mortality.

These supply-side strategies have seldom been balanced with concerted efforts to engage and retain people with opioid use disorder . . . or poorly-managed pain in a comprehensive spectrum of care. Unfortunately, opioid dependence and addiction do not simply dissipate with the contraction in the availability of OA pills or the introduction of "abuse deterrent" formulations. Instead, individuals who lost access have turned to cheaper, more accessible, and more potent black market opioid alternatives—including heroin—in unprecedented numbers. In concert, prevalence of injection drug use, and its infectious disease sequelae also saw substantial increases.

Unintended but foreseeable, this transition exposed users to drastically higher risk of overdose because of the lack of regulation over the contents, quality, and dosage in black market opioid products. Many people with untreated pain and addiction also became shut out from the health care system and the risk-reduction interventions that it potentiated. As a result, after remaining largely stable for years, overdose deaths involving heroin spiked rapidly, tripling between 2010 and 2015.

As heroin began to devastate suburban and rural communities, renewed emphasis was placed on interdiction and enforcement efforts. This included major scale-up in the staffing and funding of federal agents along the US-Mexico Border, where the amount of heroin seized quintupled between 2008 and 2015. On the domestic front, prosecutors and police reached for their toolkit of harsh criminal penalties, including high-profile prosecutions of overdose victims' dealers and fellow users. These efforts are increasingly drawing on hitherto seldom-used drug-induced homicide provisions that carry harsh mandatory minimum sentences—an intervention modality that had fuelled mass incarceration, but failed to prevent the worst drug-related crisis in US history.

Starting in 2014, the crisis began another transformation. Black market drug products—both heroin and counterfeit pills—became increasingly adulterated with illicitly-manufactured synthetic opioids, mainly fentanyl analogues. Fentanyl can be synthesised cheaply and with relative ease, and synthesised it has been: In the US, its availability has rapidly grown sourced primarily from China and distributed by Internet cryptomarkets and Mexican drug trafficking organizations. In the span of a single year, from 2014 to 2015, deaths attributed to fentanyl analogues in America spiked by over 72% to almost 10,000. In an increasing number of locales, these clandestinely-manufactured synthetics now constitute the primary drivers of fatal opioid poisoning. Emerging year-over-year figures and episodic outbreaks of fentanyl-related deaths paint a grim picture of an uncontained, plague-like contagion.

These increases in harm were as predictable as they are disastrous. Opioids can be effective in treating acute pain, but they produce dependence when used beyond a limited time period, and can cause addiction in some patients. Simply removing access to OAs without replacing this therapy with other pain management modalities and delivering evidence-based opiate substitution treatment could lead to only two outcomes: increases in untreated pain, unmanaged withdrawal or substitution with other, likely more potent, opioids. One need only look to the country's most well-known experience with massive supply reduction to see this mechanism in action.

During the period of national alcohol prohibition between 1920 and 1933, the production and sale of alcoholic beverages was outlawed, save for industrial or limited medical use. The economic, social, and health effects of national prohibition are disputed; drawing overarching conclusions about those outcomes is complicated by inconsistent and sometimes unreliable historical data.

Some facts are beyond dispute, however. The resourcing of alcohol interdiction and law enforcement during Prohibition reached unprecedented levels: The Bureau of Prohibition saw its budget increase four-fold over the 1920s; the US Coast Guard saw similar scale-up in federal investment to deter smuggled alcohol from entering US ports. While physicians were permitted to prescribe alcohol for medicinal use, this ability was limited by regulatory barriers and high prices.

The effect of this intensive effort to decrease supply, including to those who were dependent on alcohol, should not be surprising in light of the recent opioid epidemic: soon after national Prohibition came into effect, America saw a massive shift towards black market production, supply, and distribution of alcohol. The application of this restrictive regime generated a rapid transition from less potent forms of alcoholic beverages to highly-distilled spirits like gin and moonshine. Specifically, Americans' expenditure on distilled spirits as a share of total alcohol sales skyrocketed from around 40% pre-Prohibition to almost 90% directly following, as the consumption of spirits and fortified wines quintupled.

Described as the "Iron Law of Prohibition", this phenomenon follows fundamental economic logic. Imposing substantial barriers and costs to the illicit drug supply chain creates direct pressure to minimise volume while maximising profit. More bulky products become more expensive relative to less bulky ones, incentivising increases in potency. Indeed, relative to products with lower alcohol content like beer (Prohibition-era cost increase: over 700%), the price of spirits rose much more slowly (Prohibition-era cost increase: 270%). While the full causal pathway behind these trends is a matter of speculation, it principally relates to the risk of more voluminous contraband being seized and destroyed.

While the overall *volume* of alcohol consumption initially decreased, Americans were consuming less of far more intoxicating products. The potency of alcohol products during Prohibition is estimated to have risen by more than 150% relative to pre-Prohibition and post-Prohibition periods. At the same time, the ability of black market traffickers to get the "biggest bang for their buck" is catalysed by reduced consumer ability to exercise preferences; in the context of scarcity, legal risk, and opacity, customers may not be able to afford their preferred libation and are less able to act on informed choices.

The Iron Law of Prohibition helps to elucidate the folly of interdiction targeting a product with inelastic demand. During the Prohibition Era, increased effort and investment in interdiction did lead to initial sharp reductions in the volume of alcohol consumed. These interventions also resulted in market-driven changes in the potency of products that were made available through clandestine supply chains.

Over the course of the national alcohol prohibition experiment, the lack of quality control and regulation of these more potent black market products resulted in outbreaks of poisoning that came to characterise the era: tens of thousands were poisoned, and thousands died after drinking adulterated contraband liquor. In just one such episode, 60 people became ill and 16 died in New York City on Christmas Eve 1926. Ultimately, the American people decided that the aggregate negative economic, social, and public security consequences of Prohibition could not be justified by dwindling returns in terms of reduced consumption, and the policy was repealed barely more than a decade after it was enacted.

History repeats itself, Marx wrote, "first as tragedy and then as farce." The continued emphasis on supply-side interventions to suppress non-medical opioid use is both. As this crisis has evolved, the iatrogenic risk to the health of people who use drugs was not just foreseeable, but in some cases directly foreseen by policy-makers. One of the most shocking articulations of this came from Pennsylvania's former Physician General, who recently remarked, "We knew that [drug user transition to the black market] was going to be an issue, that we were going to push addicts in a direction that was going to be more deadly. But . . . you have to start somewhere." This statement is emblematic of the belief that decisive action is more important than reducing overall societal harm. While seemingly widespread, this sentiment is inimical to both public health scientific and ethical norms.

In contrast to the early years of HIV/AIDS, the drivers of opioid use disorder are well-understood, and efficacious treatment already exists. Substitution therapy using methadone and buprenorphine is decisively protective against overdose and proven to reduce many of the health and societal harms associated with [opioid use disorder]. Naloxone is extremely effective at preventing opioid overdoses from turning fatal. Yet, these medications are often not available to those who need them. The Affordable Care Act (ACA), and the recently passed Comprehensive Addiction and Recovery Act (CARA) took major steps to improve access. But these and other reforms have done little to assure that naloxone distribution is well-targeted, or that drug treatment moves away from being dominated by non-evidence-based modalities and unethical business practices. Efforts to undermine or repeal the ACA and short-sighted budgetary austerity measures threaten to further undermine access to evidence-based treatment and prevention.

Overall, little of the energy and resources dedicated to the crisis has focused on evidence-driven policies and programs. In health care settings, prescription drug monitoring programs have figured as one of the key answers to the opioid crisis. These programs can potentially help identify individuals with [opioid use disorder], untreated pain, and known overdose risk factors, connecting patients with appropriate treatment resources and other care. They are generally neither designed nor equipped to serve these clinical decision support or care coordination functions, however. Similarly, health care provider education on opioid therapy and addiction management are dramatically underutilised and often compromised by industry bias.

In place of these and other common-sense efforts to improve care and prevention, the modal programmatic and policy response has had an almost singular focus on suppression of opioid access. In pursuit of that focus, the criminal justice sector has readily intensified its emphasis on arresting, prosecuting, and incarcerating drug dealers and users. These interventions are problematic not only because they are often counter-productive, but also because, under the semblance of decisive action, they crowd out evidence-driven measures. Every dollar spent on enforcement is a dollar not spent on treatment, harm reduction, or prevention. As we failed to invest in what works, the crisis has mutated into something far more deadly.

Alcohol prohibition, while well-intentioned, was undertaken without sufficient consideration of potential unintended consequences, with disastrous results. Under the Iron Law of Prohibition, the current approach to illicit opioids is likewise doomed to failure. Without serious, sustained efforts to address the direct and root causes non-medical opioid use, intensive supply suppression efforts that brought us fentanyl will continue to push the market towards deadlier alternatives. We must shift the focus from supply reduction to demand and harm reduction.

In the short term, focusing on overdose fatality prevention and education, including expanding access to naloxone is critical, especially following periods of forced abstinence or other times of special vulnerability. Broad scale-up in access to high-quality, low cost drug treatment and other physical and mental health services is also urgently needed. Ultimately, however, we must re-examine our policies through the lens of the social determinants of the opioid crisis, such as unemployment, concentrated disadvantage, isolation, and inadequate access to physical and mental health care. Though difficult and multifaceted, structural solutions are the only way to significantly move the needle on the most formidable drug-related public health crisis of our time.

In contrast to other modern drug epidemics, the rise in opioid use and abuse is closely linked to the pharmaceutical industry. Cocaine and methamphetamine exist almost entirely within the illegal market. While the same is true of certain opioids like heroin (a Schedule I substance with no legally recognized medical use), others are widely prescribed as pain medications. The article that follows describes the role of the pharmaceutical industry in the opioid crisis.

The Opioid Epidemic: Fixing a Broken Pharmaceutical Market
Ameet Sarpatwari, Michael S. Sinha, and Aaron S. Kesselheim

11 Harvard Law and Policy Review 463 (2017)

It is difficult to overstate the extent of opioid overuse and misuse in the United States. Over four million Americans misuse opioids each month. Between 2005 and 2014, the annual number of opioid-related emergency department visits doubled. Almost as many people now die from an opioid-related overdose each day as die in automobile accidents.

A fundamental cause of the epidemic was—and continues to be—an over-prescription of opioids. From 2000 to 2010, the number of prescriptions for oral opioid analgesics rose 104%. Greater use occurred among men and women, and across all age groups. In 2015, U.S. clinicians wrote approximately three hundred million opioid prescriptions, more than one for every adult in the country. The societal cost of such overuse and misuse is rapidly approaching eighty billion dollars annually.

The origins of the surge in prescription opioid use can be traced to increased awareness of the widespread prevalence and under-treatment of pain. In a 1986 article, for example, Marilee Donovan and colleagues found that forty-five percent of patients in medical and surgical units of a large Midwestern medical center reported experiencing excruciating pain. Of those who reported any pain, less than half recalled being asked about it by their health care team. These findings prompted Russell Portenoy, a leading pain specialist, to decry the lack of pain treatment in hospitals as "absolutely medieval."

Of particular concern was chronic, non-malignant pain. In Donovan et al.'s survey, twenty-one percent of patients reported pain that started months or years earlier. Another study found that eight percent of adult enrollees in a large health maintenance organization suffered from severe and persistent pain, which "was strongly associated with ... frequent use of ambulatory health care, unfavorable self-appraisal of health status, and psychological impairment."

Such findings were harnessed to promote more aggressive pain management. In 1996, James Campbell introduced the concept of pain as the fifth vital sign in his presidential address to the American Pain Society. The Joint Commission on Accreditation of Healthcare Organizations took up the idea in 1999, issuing pain management standards that hospitals and outpatient centers would have to meet for certification. So too did the Department of Veterans Affairs, developing a "Pain as the 5th Vital Sign Toolkit" as part of a national pain management strategy in 2000.

For chronic, non-malignant pain, prominent medical figures urged physicians to make greater use of opioids. Summarizing their review of thirty-eight patients who had been maintained on opioids for such pain, Portenoy and neurologist Kathleen Foley wrote in 1986 that long-term opioid use could be safe and effective. Four years later, the psychologist Ronald Melzack favorably cited this view in a widely read *Scientific American* article, lamenting: "Many people suffer not because their discomfort is untreatable but because physicians are often reluctant to prescribe morphine."

Many experts—in retrospect, often erroneously—downplayed the potential for opioid misuse and addiction. Portenoy referred to the risk as a medical myth, while Melzack commented that development of addiction from treatment with morphine was rare. Seminal to their arguments was a study by the Boston Collaborative Drug Surveillance Program, published as a one-paragraph correspondence in the *New England Journal of Medicine* in 1980. In reviewing the cases of 11,882 hospitalized patients who received an opioid, program investigators found only four reported cases of addiction.

In time, several influential organizations came to adopt the view that opioids posed limited danger when used for chronic, non-malignant pain. A consensus statement from the American Pain Society and the American Academy of Pain Medicine in 1997 and best practice guidance from the American Medical Association's Council on Scientific Affairs in 2000 noted that the risk of opioid addiction among patients without a history of misuse or abuse was low. The Federation of State Medical Boards went further, concluding that "controlled substances, including opioid analgesics, may be essential in the treatment of . . . chronic pain, whether due to cancer or non-cancer origins."

Purdue Pharma successfully contributed to and capitalized on the medical establishment's changing view of pain management. Procured in 1952 by the Sacklers—three brothers, all psychiatrists—the company set its sights on developing an improved synthetic opioid. This effort culminated in Food and Drug Administration (FDA) approval of extended-release oxycodone (OxyContin) "for the management of moderate to severe pain where use of an opioid analgesic is appropriate for more than a few days" in 1995.

Using aggressive marketing tactics, Purdue successfully turned extended-release oxycodone into a blockbuster. Between 1996 and 2000, the company more than doubled its U.S. marketing team and created lucrative incentives and powerful tools to bolster sales. In 2001, Purdue paid forty million dollars in bonuses tied to extended-release oxycodone. Average bonuses among sales representatives exceeded average salaries by thirty percent. Purdue also invested heavily in analytics, developing a database to identify high-volume prescribers and pharmacies to help focus their marketing resources. Patients were offered starter coupons for a free initial supply of extended-release oxycodone, 34,000 of which were redeemed by 2001. Finally, Purdue hosted forty all-expenses-paid pain management and speaker training conferences at lavish resorts. Over five thousand clinicians attended, receiving toys, fishing hats, and compact discs while listening to sales representatives tout the alleged benefits of extended-release oxycodone over more affordable, non-extended release generic opioids for malignant and non-malignant chronic pain. A degree of such activity typically accompanied new product launches. However, Purdue elevated the stakes, spending an estimated six to twelve times more promoting extended-release oxycodone than its competitor Janssen spent marketing a rival opioid. Purdue's efforts paid off. Between 1996 and 2001, extended-release oxycodone generated $2.8 billion in sales. From 2008 to 2014, annual sales exceeded $2 billion.

Purdue's success was attributable in part to low patenting standards that enabled the company to secure and extend market exclusivity for extended-release oxycodone, providing motivation for its aggressive marketing. A history of tepid enforcement against pharmaceutical companies engaging in illegal marketing further incentivized Purdue to make false claims about the safety and effectiveness of the drug. Both practices helped drive opioid overuse and misuse, with tragic public health consequences.

Purdue was able to patent extended-release oxycodone in the United States despite the fact that its constituent elements—the active ingredient oxycodone and the controlled-release system Contin—had been developed decades earlier. German scientists Martin Freund and Edmund Speyer first synthesized oxycodone in 1916 in an effort to create a less addictive analgesic than either morphine or heroin, which Bayer had been forced to pull from worldwide markets three years earlier. Oxycodone was used in clinical practice in Germany as early as 1917, and was first introduced in the United States in 1939.

Use of oxycodone increased gradually during the twentieth century. However, like all then-available opioids, oxycodone was generally considered contraindicated for treating chronic pain. In a 1957 bulletin on synthetic opioids, the World Health Organization concluded that oxycodone's "respiratory depressant effect and addiction liability" were "not materially different" from those of morphine." Six years later, the California Attorney General estimated that up to one quarter of cases of addiction in the states were attributable to the combination product oxycodone/aspirin (Percodan). This news prompted the California Medical Association to recommend that oxycodone-containing drugs require a triplicate prescription.

It was against this backdrop that Purdue entered the field of pain medicine. In 1972, the company developed Contin, a method to control the release of the active ingredient of a drug from a tablet. Purdue subsequently applied Contin to morphine. The resulting product—extended-release morphine (MS Contin)—quickly became the company's highest grossing drug, generating annual sales of approximately $170 million in the early 1990s.

As expiration of market exclusivity for extended-release morphine approached, Purdue grew increasingly concerned over sustaining its revenues. An internal debate ensued, with the company's vice president for research advocating for the development of other controlled-release opioids:

> While we are "going laterally" with MS Contin to non-cancer pain indications, it would be unwise to "put all of our eggs into the MS Contin basket" in the face of the prospect of generic MS Contin competition that would "crush all of the analgesic eggs." It has also been said that [we] should market in controlled-release formulation every major opioid analgesic and combination analgesic.

Purdue ultimately adopted the recommendation, combining Contin and oxycodone to form extended-release oxycodone. The United States Patent and Trademark Office (USPTO) granted Purdue a patent for the invention on November 30, 1993.

Patents are government-issued rights that enable their holders to exclude others from making, using, or offering to sell the subject matter covered by the patents. In the United States, utility patents last twenty years from their date of filing and can protect "anything under the sun that is made by man," provided it is novel, useful, and non-obvious. The primary patent on a pharmaceutical product usually covers its active chemical ingredient. So-called secondary patents can also cover other aspects of a drug, such as its method of manufacturing or use in clinical care.

Determinations as to whether inventions are obvious must be made from the perspective of a person possessing ordinary skill in the relevant field. [Under Supreme Court precedent, "i]f a technique has been used to improve one device, and a person of ordinary skill in the art would recognize that it would improve similar devices in the same way, using the technique is obvious unless its actual application is beyond his or her skill."

In the case of extended-release oxycodone, the combination of Contin and oxycodone would have been obvious to any pharmaceutical chemist. One need only substitute "one device" with "morphine" and "similar devices" with "oxycodone" in the Court's opinion in *Teleflex*. Methods disclosed in the original patent for extended-release morphine additionally provided a reasonable guide on how to apply Contin to oxycodone. In fact, the USPTO initially rejected Purdue's patent as obvious. However, the company's response that a person of ordinary skill would not have sought to use a narrower dosage range for extended-release oxycodone than for other extended-release opioid analgesics prevailed. Purdue's claim that extended-release oxycodone provided pain relief for ninety percent of patients within this narrower dosage range was false, and it would later emerge that Purdue was aware of this falsehood. By failing to reject Purdue's patent application on obviousness grounds, the USPTO provided the company with a lengthy period of market exclusivity for extended-release oxycodone, incentivizing its aggressive marketing of the drug.

Non-rigorous patenting standards also enabled Purdue to extend its market exclusivity for extended-release oxycodone. As expiration of the primary patent for extended-release oxycodone approached, Purdue secured secondary patents on an abuse-deterrent formulation of the drug. The FDA approved the formulation in 2010, and Purdue ceased manufacturing the original formulation soon thereafter. This action forced patients who had been taking the original formulation onto the newer one—a so-called hard switch. The company additionally filed a citizen petition asking the FDA to refuse to accept generic versions of the original extended-release oxycodone formulation on safety grounds. To the surprise of some commentators, the FDA acquiesced, effectively preventing the marketing of low-cost, therapeutically equivalent products that might undercut Purdue's incentive to continue to widely promote its new abuse-deterrent formulation.

Generic drug manufacturers challenged the secondary patents. A federal district court ruled that one was non-infringed and invalidated the other as obvious. In declaring the patent invalid as both anticipated and obvious, the court noted that "the prior art included the motivation and capability to create the [patent] with a reasonable expectation of success." Upon appeal, the Federal Circuit affirmed the ruling. Although the generic manufacturers were thus successful, generic versions of extended-release oxycodone remained off the market over the course of the litigation, providing Purdue with an extended window in which to promote the drug and reap windfall profits.

Ineffectual penalties for illegal marketing additionally incentivized Purdue to make misleading claims. In 1995, the year Purdue launched extended-release oxycodone Johnson & Johnson demonstrated the benefits of aggressive promotion. A federal court fined them $7.5 million that year for shredding thousands of documents pertaining to its involvement in marketing the acne medication tretinoin (Retin-A) as an anti-wrinkle agent. This was a non-FDA-approved use of the product, which the agency prohibited manufacturers from directly promoting. The fine, however, stood in stark contrast to revenue tied to the media campaign: a three-fold increase in tretinoin sales that generated one hundred million dollars in 1989 alone.

In following suit with its aggressive marketing of extended-release oxycodone, Purdue made numerous problematic assertions. For example, the company heavily touted the convenience of its drug over other non-extended release opioids. As Purdue noted in its press release announcing FDA approval of extended-release oxycodone:

> Unlike short-acting pain medications, which must be taken every 3 to 6 hours—often on an "as needed" basis—OxyContin Tablets are taken every 12 hours, providing smooth and sustained pain control all day and all night. Dosing with OxyContin Tablets on a regular schedule spare patients from anxious "clock-watching" when pain must be controlled over long periods.

Yet Purdue was aware of the inadequacy of the twelve-hour dosing regimen for many patients. Clinical trial data and follow-up reports from patients who received the drug indicated that the drug often wore off after six to eight hours. Senior management at Purdue nevertheless instructed sales representatives to press prescribers not to prescribe extended-release oxycodone at shorter intervals, fearing that the drug would lose its competitive advantage over alternative opioid medications. As one sales manager commented, shorter-interval prescribing needed to be "nipped in the bud. NOW!!" Instead, prescribers were pressured to write prescriptions for stronger doses.

Although civil claims and criminal charges were brought against Purdue and its executives, the resulting penalties paled in comparison to extended-release oxycodone profits. In May 2007, the company and its president, chief counsel, and former chief medical officer pled guilty to falsely marketing extended-release oxycodone as "less addictive, less subject to abuse and diversion, and less likely to cause tolerance and withdrawal than other pain medications." As part of the plea bargain, Purdue agreed to pay the federal government $600 million and 27 states $20 million. The three executives agreed to $34.5 million in fines but avoided jail-time. By contrast, Purdue has earned an estimated $31 billion in total revenues from extended-release oxycodone since its launch. Rather than deterring fraudulent marketing, the penalties simply became a cost of doing business.

What is the best strategy for reducing opioid abuse and overdose?

With respect to non-medical users and the black market, the debate plays out in broadly familiar territory. Some favor a zero tolerance approach, with aggressive enforcement of possession laws against users and supply-side measures like increased interdiction efforts and lengthy mandatory minimum sentences. Others argue for a public health strategy, focused on treatment and harm reduction measures in order to prevent overdoses and reduce demand.

Elements of both of these visions are present in current policy. Consider the response to overdoses, for example. The past few years have seen a rise in prosecutions under drug-induced homicide statutes, which let prosecutors charge "people who provide the drugs that ultimately contribute to an overdose death with homicide," usually on a strict liability basis. DRUG POLICY ALLIANCE, DRUG-INDUCED HOMICIDE LAWS: A MISGUIDED RESPONSE TO OVERDOSE DEATHS 1 (2016). (These laws are covered in more depth in Chapter 3.) On the other hand, over "the past decade, states have begun to adopt 911 immunity laws," also sometimes called "Good Samaritan" statutes, which give individuals who call 911 in response to a drug overdose legal protection from prosecution for specified offenses like drug possession. Kelsey Bissonnette, *Anti-Death Legislation: Fighting Overdose Mortality from a Public Health Perspective,* 23 TEMP. POL. & CIV. RTS. L. REV. 451, 459 (2014).

In addition to the traditional divide between zero tolerance and harm reduction, opioid policy presents unique questions surrounding the legal market for pain medication. After all, even among unyielding drug warriors, there is little support for banning all opioid pain medications. The legal and regulatory problems that arise when trying to balance the availability of pain medication with concerns about abuse and addiction are examined in Chapter 7.

D. The War on Drugs

The United States has pursued a particularly forceful brand of drug prohibition, known as the war on drugs. Although the drug war has differentiated U.S. drug policy from drug prohibition in many other countries, it is not easily defined. The article that follows describes the development of the war on drugs and considers what separates it from non-war prohibition.

Drug Truce
Alex Kreit

77 Ohio State Law Journal 1323 (2016)

The war on drugs is one of the most familiar public policy ideas of the past four decades but it is also one of the most difficult to define. The guiding tenets of the drug war strategy have been the vision of a "drug free" society and the belief that vigorous enforcement of uncompromising criminal justice measures is the most effective method for realizing it. This philosophy has manifested itself in a focus on supply-side initiatives, on the theory that these efforts will suppress the market for drugs. Policies directly aimed at demand reduction have largely followed a similar rationale by addressing drug use and addiction problems primarily within the criminal justice system.

This sort of description still does not tell us much about what differentiates the drug war from pre-war prohibition, however. After all, laws criminalizing drug possession and distribution pre-date the modern war on drugs by at least half a century. Indeed, there is not even universal agreement about when the war began. Though federal drug prohibition has existed for nearly a century, it was not until forty-five years ago that President Richard Nixon used the phrase "war on drugs" to describe America's drug strategy. There is a debate, however, about whether to mark the start date for the drug war at Nixon's statement or by some later development.

Those who believe it is a mistake to label Nixon the author of the modern war on drugs point out that federal drug funding was heavily weighted toward demand reduction during his administration. In the same speech where he described drug abuse as "public enemy number one," Nixon also proposed a federal drug budget that allocated $105 million of $155 million to treatment and rehabilitation. As Michael Massing argued in his book, *The Fix*, although Nixon "had declared war on drugs," he made "treatment his principal weapon." Noted drug and alcohol historian David T. Courtwright has even referred to 1971 to 1973 as a "therapeutic golden age" for U.S. drug policy.

Progressive federal drug policy reforms in the early 1970s were not limited to drug treatment. Even as "Nixon's legislative message gave rhetorical priority to law enforcement," strict federal mandatory minimum drug penalties that had been enacted in the 1950s were repealed under his watch. Interestingly, among the legislators who spoke in favor of eliminating mandatory minimum drug sentences was then-Congressman George H.W. Bush, who argued that the change would "result in better justice and more appropriate sentences."

On the other hand, the law that continues to serve as the foundation for federal drug policy was signed into law by Nixon. The Comprehensive Drug Abuse Prevention and Control Act of 1970—the same bill that repealed mandatory minimum sentences—also instituted a comprehensive regulatory scheme for federal drug control in the form of the Controlled Substances Act. In the decades following the Harrison Narcotics Tax Act of 1914, Congress had enacted "[a] patchwork of regulatory, revenue, and criminal measures" that featured "contorted presumptions and other awkward devices" (an approach necessitated by the narrow interpretation of the interstate commerce power that held sway at the time). As a result, by the late 1960s, opiates and cocaine were controlled by one law (the 1914 Harrison Act), marijuana by another (the 1937 Marihuana Tax Act), and hallucinogens, stimulants and depressants by yet a third (the Food, Drug and Cosmetic Act, under amendments passed in 1965). Still more federal drug statutes filled other regulatory gaps.

The 1970 Controlled Substances Act (CSA) cleared away nearly all then-existing federal drug laws in favor of a single comprehensive statutory scheme to criminalize the possession, distribution, and manufacture of all drugs for recreational use. The CSA was designed to prevent the need for piecemeal legislation in the future by granting the U.S. Attorney General rule-making authority to ban new substances administratively. None of the substances regulated by the CSA can be manufactured, possessed, or distributed for recreational purposes. As a result, the CSA established, for the first time, a standing federal policy of prohibition of the recreational market for all mind-altering substances (with the exception of alcohol and tobacco, which Congress specifically exempted from the CSA).

Nixon also restructured the bureaucracy charged with enforcing federal drug laws by creating the Drug Enforcement Administration (DEA) via Executive Order in 1973. When Nixon took office, federal drug agencies were—much like the drug laws themselves—in a state of disarray. Nixon designed the DEA to be a "super-agency to provide the momentum needed to coordinate all federal efforts related to drug enforcement" and to stop ongoing inter- and intra-agency disputes.

As part of this bureaucratic transformation, the federal drug control budget ballooned. In 1967, the primary federal agency tasked with drug control had a budget of only $3 million. By 1973, the DEA's primary predecessor agency, the Bureau of Narcotics and Dangerous Drugs (BNDD), was operating on a $74 million budget. This money was put toward significantly expanding the ranks of drug enforcement agents and their footprint overseas. When Nixon came into office, the 300 federal drug "agents spread over the nation and ten foreign countries . . . [was] not much higher than [the number of federal drug agents] in the 1930s." Between 1969 and 1973 alone, the federal government opened twenty-six new foreign drug enforcement offices and by the time the DEA was established, it inherited 1,470 special agents. During this expansion, the BNDD formed the first multijurisdictional law enforcement task force that pooled federal, state, and local resources in order to encourage increased involvement in drug enforcement at the local level.

It was not until the 1980s, however, that many of the laws and criminal justice outcomes that are most closely associated with the drug war really took shape. During the first few years of Ronald Reagan's presidency, federal funding for drug treatment programs was slashed to less than one-fourth of what it had been under Nixon. Journalist Dan Baum described the impact in stark terms: "With the 1982 budget came the beginning of the end of the federally funded drug treatment network that four drug czars had worked a decade to build." Meanwhile, the federal drug enforcement budget enjoyed a substantial increase. By the time President George H.W. Bush left office, the DEA's budget was more than ten times what it was when Reagan arrived in 1981.

The increase in drug enforcement funding was accompanied by changes to federal drug laws, including the reintroduction of mandatory minimum sentencing. Beginning in 1984, and continuing for the rest of the decade, Congress passed a series of new mandatory minimum sentences for drug offenses. Unlike the mandatory drug sentences of the 1950s, which had been "based upon the type of controlled substance and number of prior drug convictions," the new provisions mostly pegged minimum sentences to drug quantity. In 1988, Congress expanded the reach of the mandatory minimum provisions to include attempts and conspiracies. The new mandatory minimum statutes led the U.S. Sentencing Commission to "jettison[] its data entirely and ma[k]e the quantity-based sentences . . . proportionately applicable to *every* drug trafficking offense." In a 2004 report, the Sentencing Commission observed that "no other decision of the Commission has had such a profound impact on the federal prison population." The result was a dramatic rise in the length of federal drug sentences, particularly for low-level offenders. People involved at the periphery of drug operations—like lookouts, couriers, and street dealers—now faced steep sentences based on the type and amount of drugs involved in the offense.

The 1980s also saw the federal government develop incentives to enlist state and local law enforcement agencies in the drug war. As part of the Anti-Drug Abuse Act of 1986, Congress created a new federal grant program to fund state and local drug enforcement efforts, with a significant expansion in 1988. The funds led to the proliferation of the multijurisdictional drug task forces first developed under Nixon. The number of task forces nearly doubled between 1988 and 1991 alone and they accounted for between 220,000 and 280,000 arrests annually during that same period. Similarly, in 1984, the federal government revised its asset forfeiture laws to give "state and local police agencies the lion's share of seized assets even when federal agents were involved in the arrest." Because state and local police are responsible for the vast majority of drug arrests, these policies were critical to developing the foot soldiers of the drug war.

As a political issue, enthusiasm for the drug war probably hit its peak in the late 1980s. In 1989, a Gallup poll showed that more than six in ten Americans believed drug abuse to be "the most important problem facing this country today." As the

Los Angeles Times observed in connection with the poll, "[o]nly wars and economic disasters have registered such a large consensus in the past." (The *Times* was referring to actual—not metaphorical—wars, of course.) In this environment, politicians were eager to constantly try to one-up each other in their commitment to getting tough on drugs. This led to a host of new war-era drug laws and programs, including the provision of military equipment to local police, the denial of public benefits based on drug convictions, and the widespread adoption of employee drug testing. The one notable exception to the steady stream of increasingly punitive drug policies during this period was the 1994 "safety valve" law, which created an exception to mandatory minimum drug penalties for offenders with very minimal criminal history who also meet a handful of other requirements.

During the mid-to-late-1990s and early 2000s, the war on drugs mostly faded into the political background, continuing to run on its own momentum under the already-established conceptual and legal framework. To be sure, Congress did not stop expanding the reach of federal drug penalties. But these new initiatives were focused at the margins, on issues like denying federal financial aid to students with drug convictions[.]

An understanding of how the drug war developed over time is only a small step in trying to disentangle the drug war from non-war prohibition. Any attempt to define the drug war must inevitably focus on identifying its distinguishing characteristics[, which include ideology, arrests, and incarceration.]

The war on drugs has been held together by rhetoric and ideology as much as anything else. Labeling our drug policy a war has signaled that it is something more than just prohibition for the sake of public health. War is a life and death struggle against an enemy. The only acceptable outcome is defeating the enemy, in this case drugs and drug use. And, because the stakes of war are so high, we must pursue that goal at almost any cost. The war has been waged with a single-minded focus on reducing all illegal drug use, sometimes articulated as an idealized vision of a drug free society. This outlook concerns itself with "the consumption of the prohibited substance rather than any secondary consequences that might" result. Unlike, for example, Britain's 1980s drug strategies, which focused on goals like reducing the health risks and consequences of drug use, the U.S. drug war always had "one overarching goal—the reduction of drug use."

Over time, the rhetoric and ideology of war permeated nearly all of our drug laws and enforcement strategies. It drove the adoption of harsh and inflexible policies, like mandatory minimum sentencing laws. But just as important, policy ideas thought to be inconsistent with the drug war's use reduction goal—like needle exchange or medical marijuana—came to be considered "treason" because they might amount to a sort of concession to the enemy.

Former drug czar William J. Bennett, for example, described the placement of ballot measures "to decrease penalties for possession of marijuana" in early 2000s in Arizona, Nevada, and Ohio as "the drug legalization movement's advance on the[] home fronts" of those states. "We should not capitulate in our war on drugs any more than we should surrender in our war on terrorism," Bennett argued.

And according to Bennett, "[t]he forms of surrender are manifold." They include "[b]uzzwords like 'harm reduction' [which] crowd[] out clear no-use messages," allowing for the medicinal use of marijuana, and even the release of the film *Traffic* for having "portrayed the war on drugs as a futile effort."

If we are fighting a war against drugs, the only acceptable policies are those that further the goal of a drug free society. While it is possible to have drug *prohibition* alongside programs like heroin maintenance or needle exchange, these ideas are incompatible with the drug *war*. This is because the drug war requires a uniformity of purpose that a non-war form of prohibition does not. As Reagan's Attorney General Edwin Meese told a group of newspaper editors in the 1980s, in the war against drugs "there are no neutrals."

The war metaphor also signifies the intensity with which we should pursue the goal of reducing all drug use and the sorts of sacrifices or "collateral damage" we should accept. Drug *prohibition* is agnostic on questions like how much punishment drug offenders should receive or how we should rank drug investigations relative to other law enforcement priorities. But in a drug *war*, drug crime is an offense "of the highest order"—"a threat worse than any nuclear warfare or any chemical warfare waged on any battlefield."

Drug trafficking was officially declared "a threat to national security" by the Reagan Administration in 1986. Cities became drug war "battlefield[s]" to be policed by militaristic equipment and tactics. Exceptions to constitutional protections could be justified on the theory that "all bets are off and government may do whatever is necessary to ensure the nation's continued prosperity."

President George H.W. Bush's first drug czar even went so far as to question the idea of due process for drug offenders, remarking that "[i]t's a funny war when the 'enemy' is entitled to due process of law and a fair trial." And who is the enemy? "Let me tell you straight out," Bush said in 1989. "Everyone who uses drugs. Everyone who sells drugs. And everyone who looks the other way." This is the sort of atmosphere that led Congress to vote to double crack cocaine sentences "simply to symbolize redoubled Congressional seriousness."

There is perhaps no clearer manifestation of the drug war ideology than the strategy of "seek[ing] out and punish[ing] casual, nonaddicted drug users." In 1970, when the Controlled Substances Act was passed, there were a little more than 400,000 drug arrests nationwide. This number climbed quickly during the Nixon administration, to over 600,000 by 1974, followed by a period of relative stability until 1980. Then, beginning in 1980, drug arrests rose fairly steadily and dramatically, from 581,000 to a height of almost 1.9 million in 2005. Drug arrests have declined somewhat since, with just over 1.5 million in 2013. But there are still two and a half times as many drug arrests annually today as in 1980.

Drug arrests did not just increase on their own terms but relative to overall arrest numbers. Drug offenses were 5.9% of all arrests in the United States in 1980 and 11.1% of all arrests by 1990. In 2013, 13.3% of all arrests in the United States were for drugs. Some years saw more arrests for drugs than for any other single category of crime—in 2006, for example, arrests for drugs topped all categories at 1,889,810 arrests, with the next closest group, property offenses, at 1,540,297 arrests.

Also notable is that arrests for simple possession—particularly marijuana possession—were chiefly responsible for the rise in drug arrests after 1990. Indeed, arrests for drug sale or manufacture actually *declined* at a slow but fairly steady pace between 1990 and 2010. There were 13% fewer trafficking arrests in 2010 (302,300 arrests) than there were in 1990 (347,900 arrests). In stark contrast, drug possession arrests were about 80% higher during that same period (1,336,530 arrests in 2010 versus 741,600 arrests in 1990). In terms of drug type, marijuana was the main focus. Between 1990 and 2002, marijuana possession was responsible for 78.7% of the 450,000 additional drug arrests. While arrests for all offenses decreased by 3% during that period, marijuana arrests rose by 113%.

As John Pfaff has persuasively argued, the impact of drug enforcement on the U.S. prison population is often overstated. But it is hard to exaggerate the importance of incarceration in distinguishing the drug war era from pre-war prohibition. Indeed, the post-1980 increase in drug prisoners is in many ways even more striking than the rise in drug arrests. Between 1980 and 2005, drug arrests tripled. During that same period, the number of drug offenders in prisons and jails increased by 1100%, from 41,100 in 1980 to 493,800 in 2005. By the time President Obama took office, the number of Americans incarcerated for drug offenses was larger than the entire United States prison and jail population had been in 1980.

A number of factors appear to have contributed to the rise in drug incarcerations. In addition to the increase in drug arrests, the drug war saw a greater proportion of people convicted of drug offenses receive prison sentences. The average sentence for drug offenders also increased by 17% between 1988 and 2004. Meanwhile, "the expansion of mandatory minimum sentencing and the abolition of parole" meant that people ended up serving a longer portion of those sentences than they might have in the past.

Looking outside the United States helps to highlight the difference between our drug war and non-war drug prohibition when it comes to imprisonment. While drugs are prohibited in nearly every country in the world, "[t]he United States stands out relative to other developed countries for the intensity with which it enforces drug laws." A 2011 study comparing the criminal justice policies of the United States to five other countries, for example, showed that we have a much higher drug imprisonment rate than the others. At the time of the study, drug offenders accounted for 24% of the United States prison population, compared to 16.8% in England and Wales, 15.2% in Finland, 10% in Australia, and 5.6% in Canada. And, of course, the slice of drug offenders in the United States comes from a bigger pie than in the other nations. At the time of the study, the overall incarceration rate in the United States was five times as high as in England and Wales and eleven times as high as in Finland.

Support for the drug war has declined significantly in recent years. President Obama's first Director of the Office of National Drug Control Policy (a position often referred to as "drug czar"), Gil Kerlikowske, said in in his first interview after taking office that he thought it was time to retire the phrase "war on drugs". In 2011, Kerlikowske described his outlook in even bolder terms, telling a reporter, "We certainly ended the drug war now almost two years ago."

In the 1980s or 1990s, Kerlikowske's comments would have received a swift and strong reaction from drug war supporters. But the early 2010s saw prominent politicians from across the political spectrum call for an end to the drug war. In his second inaugural address, in 2014, New Jersey's Republican Governor Chris Christie declared: "We will end the failed war on drugs that believes that incarceration is the cure of every ill caused by drug abuse." A few months later Kentucky Senator Rand Paul said he will "do everything to end the war on drugs." On the left, New Jersey Senator Cory Booker has called the war on drugs a "tremendous failure." And California Governor Gavin Newsom's 2018 campaign website featured an issues page that began: "The war on drugs has failed." With so many elected officials loudly abandoning the drug war, it is hard to believe that as recently as 2008, former Virginia Senator Jim Webb was lamenting the fact that "to be viewed as 'soft on crime' is one of the surest career-killers in American politics."

To date, growing opposition to the drug war has not translated into much legislative action, at least at the federal level. With the exception of a 2010 law that reduced the sentencing disparity between crack and powder cocaine from 100-to-1 to 18-to-1, discussed more in Chapter 4, federal drug laws were essentially unchanged during Obama's presidency. In 2015, "Congress seemed on the brink of enacting significant limitations on the use of mandatory minimum sentences and of providing the beginnings of a more flexible, generous mechanism for back-end release of federal prisoners." Frank O. Bowman III, *Good Enough to Be Getting on With? The State of Federal Sentencing Legislation, December 2015*, 28 Fed. Sent'g. Rep. 105, 105 (2015). There were a number of sentencing reform proposals with significant bipartisan support. But none made it through the legislative process. President Obama's administration did see some noteworthy non-legislative action, however. Under former Attorney General Eric Holder, the Department of Justice (DOJ) issued a few important enforcement policies concerning drug laws. In August 2013, the DOJ issued a memorandum advising federal prosecutors not to interfere with state marijuana laws, effectively allowing states to implement marijuana legalization laws. Also in 2013, the DOJ released a memo advising federal prosecutors not to seek mandatory minimum drug sentences in certain cases.

The Trump administration has reversed some of these Obama-era policies, in what many observers see as a return to the war on drugs strategy. In May 2017, former Attorney General Jeff Sessions rescinded the DOJ memo that had advised federal prosecutors not to seek mandatory minimum sentences against lower-level drug offenders. Under the DOJ's new policy, federal prosecutors are instructed to "charge and pursue the most serious, readily provable offense," including in low-level drug cases. *See* Joseph Tanfani and Evan Halper, *Sessions Restores Tough Drug War Policies That Trigger Mandatory Minimum Sentences*, L.A. Times (May 12, 2017). In January 2018, Sessions withdrew the DOJ policy that had advised federal prosecutors not to prosecute people who comply with state marijuana legalization laws. The Trump administration has also returned to the rhetoric of the war on drugs. Trump himself has proposed the death penalty for "drug dealers" and praised Rodrigo Duterte, President of the Philippines, for carrying out a drug war in which there have been thousands of extrajudicial killings of suspected drug sellers and users. And yet, in December 2018, Trump signed into law the FIRST STEP Act, a criminal justice reform bill (covered in Chapter 4) that reduces federal drug sentences in some cases.

States, which are responsible for most drug enforcement, have been quicker than the federal government to reform their drug laws. A Pew Research Center analysis found that "40 states took some action to ease their drug laws" between 2009 and 2013. Drew DeSilver, *Feds May Be Rethinking the Drug War, but States Have Been Leading the Way*, Pew Res. Ctr. (Apr. 2, 2014). These reforms ranged from ameliorating the collateral consequences of a drug conviction to repealing mandatory minimum drug sentencing laws. And, of course, as of 2019, ten states have passed laws legalizing the commercial manufacture and retail sale of marijuana. Still, a number of harm reduction policies that have been embraced by other countries, such as safe injection facilities, have yet to be adopted by any U.S. state or locality.

Do you believe the U.S. would be better off renewing its commitment to the war on drugs or trying a different approach? How would you define an "end" to the drug war? Does an end to the drug war mean the legalization of some or even all drugs? Or is it possible to end the war against drugs while retaining drug prohibition?

E. Race, Class, and the Drug War

In *From Chocolate to Morphine*, Andrew Weil and Winifred Rosen observe that "[e]verybody is willing to call certain drugs bad, but there is little agreement from one culture to the next as to which these are." If opinions about drugs are largely cultural, do cultural considerations also influence drug laws?

There is a good deal of evidence that many early U.S. drug laws were enacted, at least in part, because of racial and cultural animus. In *Ex parte Yung Jon*, 28 F. 308 (D. Ore. 1886), for example, the court considered the constitutionality of a law outlawing "opium dens." In upholding the law, Judge Deady explained: "Smoking opium is not our vice, and therefore it may be that this legislation proceeds more from a desire to vex and annoy the 'Heathen Chinee' in this respect, than to protect the people from the evil habit. But the motives of legislators cannot be the subject of judicial investigation for the purposes of affecting the validity of their acts." *Id.* at 312.

Similarly, in *The Forbidden Fruit and the Tree of Knowledge: An Inquiry into the Legal History of American Marijuana Prohibition*, 56 Va. L. Rev. 971 (1970), Richard J. Bonnie and Charles H. Whitebread conclude that "racial prejudice" was the "most prominent" factor in the passage of the first marijuana prohibition laws. As they explain it, at the time these early marijuana prohibition laws were passed, "not only did few middle-class Americans know about marijuana and its use, but what little 'information' was available provided an automatic association of the drug with Mexican immigration, crime and the deviant life style in the Black ghettos. Naturally, the impending drug legislation . . . became entangled with society's views of these minority groups." Among the examples cited by Bonnie and Whitebread is a *Montana Standard* newspaper article about a 1929 marijuana prohibition bill, which reported: "There was fun in the House Committee during the week when the Marihuana bill came up for consideration. Marihuana is Mexican opium, a plant used by Mexicans and cultivated for sale by Indians. 'When some beet field peon takes a few rares of this stuff,' explained Dr. Fred Fulsher of Mineral County, 'He thinks he has just been elected president of Mexico so he starts out to execute all his political enemies. I understand that over in Butte where the Mexicans often go for the winter they stage imaginary bullfights in the "Bower of Roses" or put on tournaments for the favor of "Spanish Rose" after a couple of whiffs of Marijuana. The Silver Bow and Yellowstone delegations both deplore these international complications.' Everybody laughed and the bill was recommended for passage."

It is rare (although not unheard of) to see this sort of overt racism in the public dialogue about drug laws today. Nevertheless, drug law enforcement continues to have a disproportionate impact on people of color.

Race, Drugs, and Law Enforcement in the United States
Jamie Fellner

20 Stan. L. & Pol'y Rev 257 (2009)

Race has been and remains inextricably involved in drug law enforcement, shaping the public perception of and response to the drug problem. A recent study in Seattle is illustrative. Although the majority of those who shared, sold, or transferred serious drugs in Seattle are white (indeed seventy percent of the general Seattle population is white), almost two-thirds (64.2%) of drug arrestees are black. The racially disproportionate drug arrests result from the police department's emphasis on the outdoor drug market in the racially diverse downtown area of the city, its lack of attention to other outdoor markets that are predominantly white, and its emphasis on crack. Three-quarters of the drug arrests were crack-related even though only an estimated one-third of the city's drug transactions involved crack. Whites constitute the majority of those who deliver methamphetamine, ecstasy, powder cocaine, and heroin in Seattle; blacks are the majority of those who deliver crack.

Not surprisingly then, seventy-nine percent of those arrested on crack charges were black. The researchers could not find a "racially neutral" explanation for the police prioritization of the downtown drug markets and crack. The focus on crack offenders, for example, did not appear to be a function of the frequency of crack transactions compared to other drugs, public safety or public health concerns, crime rates, or citizen complaints. The researchers ultimately concluded that the Seattle Police Department's drug law enforcement efforts "reflect implicit racial bias: the unconscious impact of race on official perceptions of who and what constitutes Seattle's drug problem.... Indeed, the widespread racial typification of drug offenders as racialized 'others' has deep historical roots and was intensified by the diffusion of potent cultural images of dangerous black crack offenders. These images appear to have had a powerful impact on popular perceptions of potential drug offenders, and, as a result, law enforcement practices in Seattle."

The racial dynamics reflected in Seattle's current drug law enforcement priorities are long-standing and can be found across the country. Indeed, they provided the impetus for the "war on drugs" that began in the mid-1980s. Spearheaded by federal drug policy initiatives that significantly increased federal penalties for drug offenses and markedly increased federal funds for state anti-drug efforts, the drug war reflected the popularity of "tough on crime" policies emphasizing harsh punishments as the key to curbing drugs and restoring law and order in America. The drug of principal concern was crack cocaine, erroneously believed to be a drug used primarily by black Americans. The use of cocaine, primarily powder cocaine, had increased in the late 1970s and early 1980s, particularly among whites, but powder cocaine use did not provoke the "orgy of media and political attention" that occurred in the mid-1980s when a cheaper, smokable cocaine in the form of crack appeared.

Crack was the latest in a series of drugs that since the late nineteenth century have preoccupied policy makers in the United States. In each case, "the drug of primary concern was strongly associated in the white public mind with a particular racial minority." Race was the lens through which drug problems in the United States were viewed, coloring both the definition of the problem and the proposed solutions. As the case of Seattle exemplifies, race continues today to influence the perceptions of the danger posed by those who use and sell illicit drugs, the choice of drugs that warrant the most public attention, and the choice of communities in which to concentrate drug law enforcement resources.

Although the use of crack was by no means limited to low-income, urban, minority neighborhoods, it was those neighborhoods which more visibly suffered from crack addiction, and the nuisance and violence that accompanied the struggle of different drug-dealing groups to establish control over its distribution in the 1980s and 1990s. The dismay of local residents, however, was exceeded by the censure and outrage from outsiders fanned by sensationalist media stories and by politicians eager to seek electoral advantage. With politicians and the media focused on the putative effects of crack in inner-city neighborhoods—although many of those effects were subsequently proven to have been greatly exaggerated or just plain wrong—those neighborhoods became and remain the principal "fronts" in the war on drugs.

Crack in black neighborhoods was a lightning rod for a complicated and deep-rooted set of racial, class, political, social, and moral dynamics. Politicians were able to woo a white electorate anxious about its declining status through the race-coded language of "drugs" and "crime." "Public discourse focused on addiction and violence but the subtext was understood as that of race. Crack cocaine was perceived as a drug of the Black inner-city urban poor, while powder cocaine, with its higher costs, was a drug of wealthy whites. . . . This framing of the drug in class and race-based terms provides important context when evaluating the legislative response." That response, most notoriously, included the federal Anti-Drug Abuse Act of 1986 and the Anti-Drug Abuse Act of 1988, which imposed far higher penalties for possession or sale of crack cocaine than powder cocaine, as well as state laws that required prison sentences even for low level drug offenses.

The legislative and law enforcement responses to crack "cannot be attributed solely to objective levels of criminal danger, but [also reflect] the way in which minority behaviors are symbolically constructed and subjected to official social control." Law enforcement efforts against crack in poor minority neighborhoods reinforced control of the urban "underclass," a group deemed by the political and white majority to be particularly "dangerous, offensive and undesirable." The conflation of the underclass with crack offenders meant the perceived dangerousness of one increased the perceived threat of the other. Urban blacks, the population most burdened by concentrated socio-economic disadvantage, became the population at which the war on drugs was targeted.

When asked to close their eyes and envision a drug offender, Americans did not picture a white middle class man snorting powder cocaine or college students smoking marijuana. They pictured unkempt African-American men and women slouched in alleyways or young blacks hanging around urban street corners. At least for the last twenty years, however, whites have engaged in drug offenses at rates higher than blacks.

According to the 2006 surveys conducted by the federal Substance Abuse and Mental Health Services Administration (SAMHSA), an estimated 49% of whites and 42.9% of blacks age twelve or older have used illicit drugs in their lifetimes; 14.5% of whites and 16% of blacks have used them in the past year; and 8.5% of whites and 9.8% of blacks have used them in the past month. Because the white population is more than six times greater than the black population, the absolute number of white drug offenders is far greater than that of black drug offenders. SAMHSA estimates that 111,774,000 people in the United States age twelve or older have used illicit drugs during their lifetime, of whom 82,587,000 are white and 12,477,000 are black. Even among powder and crack cocaine users—which remain a principal focus of law enforcement—there are more whites than blacks. According to SAMHSA's calculations, there are 27,083,000 whites who have used cocaine during their lifetime, compared to 2,618,000 blacks and, indeed, 5,553,000 whites who have used crack cocaine, compared to 1,537,000 blacks.

According to the most recent SAMHSA survey, if black and white drug users are combined, blacks account for 13% of the total who have ever used an illicit drug, 8% of those who have ever used cocaine, and 21% of those who have ever used crack cocaine.

By definition, drug users violate laws against drug possession. They also frequently engage in illegal drug distribution activities—e.g., selling drugs for cash or providing them to friends. If blacks constitute a relatively small proportion of those who use drugs (between 13% and 20% depending on the drug), they likely constitute a comparable proportion of those who engage in other illegal drug-related activities. Although there is little direct research on the race of drug sellers, for example, that which exists suggests a racial breakdown among sellers similar to that among users. National surveys of drug abuse conducted by the federal Substance Abuse and Mental Health Services Administration have sometimes included questions on drug selling. In 1991, 0.7% of adult whites and 1.4% of adult blacks reported selling drugs in the past twelve months. Although the proportion of sellers was twice that among blacks than among whites, in absolute numbers far more whites (939,345) reported drug selling than blacks (268,170). Black sellers constituted 12% of the combined number of self-reported black and white sellers. Fifteen years later, 1.6% of whites and 2.8% of blacks surveyed in 2006 reported they had sold drugs in the past twelve months, or an estimated 2,461,797 whites, and 712,044 blacks. Blacks thus represented 14% of the combined black and white sellers.

Evidence regarding the race of drug sellers also emerges from research in specific urban drug markets. For example, the study of Seattle's drug market, discussed above, indicates that the majority of the drug sellers are white (as are a majority of the users). In fact, research suggests that drug users tend to obtain their drugs from people of the same race as themselves. As one researcher addressing racial congruity in drug activities concluded, "Dealers with direct contact with their customers . . . are likely to look like the customers . . ."

Some might question whether blacks constitute a higher percentage than whites of persons occupying higher ranks in the drug business, e.g., major traffickers. Empirical research addressing this question is not available, but experts suggest that higher positions in the drug trade are not likely to be held by black individuals. The race of persons in the upper echelons of the drug trade is also not particularly relevant, because the overwhelming preponderance of drug offenders entering the criminal justice system are low-level non-violent offenders. For example, between 1980 and the present, arrests for drug sales, possession with intent to sell, manufacturing, transportation, or importing have never constituted more than 36% of all drug arrests. Drug offenders who are incarcerated are mostly street-level dealers, couriers, and other bit players in the drug trade.

All other things being equal, if blacks constitute an estimated 13% to 20% of the total of black and white drug offenders, they, should constitute a roughly similar proportion of the total number of blacks and whites who are arrested, convicted, and sent to prison for drug law violations. But all other things are not equal. The data demonstrate clearly and consistently that blacks have been and remain more likely to be arrested for drug offending behavior relative to their percentage among drug offenders than whites who engage in the same behavior. There are many reasons for the racial disparities in drug arrests, including demographics, the extent of community complaints, police allocation of resources, racial profiling, and the relative ease of making drug arrests in minority urban areas compared to white areas. One analyst has observed that in the war on drugs: "Racial profiling is almost inevitable. Race becomes one of the readily observable visual clues to help identify drug suspects, along with age, gender and location. There is a certain rationality to this—if you are in poor black neighborhoods, drug dealers are more likely to be black. Local distribution networks are often monoracial; downscale markets are often neighborhood-based; and downscale urban neighborhoods are often segregated.... The law and practice of drug enforcement is market-specific, and the markets are divided by race and class."

Former New York Police Commissioner Lee Brown explained the police concentration in certain neighborhoods and the consequent racial impact as follows: "In most large cities, the police focus their attention on where they see conspicuous drug use—street-corner drug sales—and where they get the most complaints. Conspicuous drug use is generally in your low-income neighborhoods that generally turn out to be your minority neighborhoods.... It's easier for police to make an arrest when you have people selling drugs on the street corner than those who are [selling or buying drugs] in the suburbs or in office buildings. The end result is that more blacks are arrested than whites because of the relative ease in making those arrests."

Between 1980 and 2007, there were more than twenty-five million adult drug arrests in the United States. The percentage of arrests that involved black men and women increased from 27% in 1980 to a high ranging from 40% to 42% between 1989 and 1993, and then declined more or less steadily to the current percentage of 35%. Relative to population, blacks have been arrested on drug charges at consistently higher rates than whites. In 1980 blacks were arrested at rates almost three (2.9) times the rate of whites. In the years with the worst disparities, between 1988 and 1993, blacks were arrested at rates more than five times the rate of whites. In the last six years, the ratio of black to white drug arrest rates has ranged between 3.5 and 3.9.

Although the ratio of black to white arrests has decreased somewhat since the mid-1990s when it was at its highest, racial disparity in drug arrests has continued despite changes in drug use and law enforcement priorities. As the crack cocaine market began to constrict in urban areas and the use of cocaine stabilized, "Law enforcement shifted its emphasis toward marijuana." Methamphetamine manufacture and use emerged as law enforcement concerns in the late 1990s. Yet although marijuana use is prevalent across races, and methamphetamine is used primarily by whites, blacks continue to be disproportionately arrested.

The difference between the black proportion of drug offenders and the black proportion of drug arrests reflects the ongoing salience of urban drug law enforcement, or, more specifically, drug law enforcement in black urban neighborhoods. In 2007, for example, 77% of drug arrests occurred in cities. Although urban blacks account for approximately 6% of the national population, they constituted 29.8% of all drug arrests in 2007. A longitudinal analysis of urban drug arrests by race shows that in the largest American cities, drug arrests for African Americans rose at three times the rate for whites between 1980 and 2003, 225% compared to 70%. In eleven cities, black drug arrests rose by more than 500%. In the seventy-five largest counties in the United States, blacks in 2002 accounted for 46% of drug offense arrests, even though they represented only 15.6% of the population. New York State provides a particularly striking example: blacks in New York City represent 10.7% of the state population, yet accounted for 42.1% of drug arrests statewide.

The racial disparities evident in drug arrests grow larger as cases wind their way through the criminal justice system. Blacks constitute 43% and whites 55% of persons convicted of drug felonies in state courts, and blacks account for 53.5% and whites for 33.3% of persons admitted to state prison with new convictions for drug offenses. In 2007, blacks accounted for 33.2% of people entering federal prison for drug offenses.

A comparison of the rates, relative to population, at which blacks and whites are sent to state prison for drug offenses offers what may be the most compelling evidence of the diste racial impact of drug control policies: the black rate (256.2 per 100,000 black adults) is ten times greater than the white rate (25.3 per 100,000 white adults). Disaggregating these rates by gender reveals that black men were sent to prison on drug charges at 11.8 times the rate of white men and black women are sent to prison on drug charges at 4.8 times the rate of white women.

Just as conscious and unconscious racial notions helped define the drug problem, they have also helped shape political and policy responses to that problem. The legislative history of federal crack sentencing laws, for example, provides reason "to suspect that regardless of the objectives Congress was pursuing, it would have shown more restraint in fashioning the crack penalties or more interest in amending them in ensuing years, if the penalties did not apply almost exclusively to blacks." To the extent that the white majority in the United States identified both crime and drugs with racialized "others," it has no doubt been easier to endorse or at least acquiesce to punitive penal policies that might have been rejected if applied at equivalent rates to members of their own families and communities. Politicians have been able to reap the electoral rewards of endorsing harsh drug policies because the group that suffered most from those policies—black Americans—lacked the numbers to use the political process to secure a different strategy.

Throughout the modern war on drugs, measures to battle the use and sale of drugs have emphasized arrest and incarceration rather than prevention and treatment. The emphasis on harsh penal sanctions cannot be divorced from the widespread and deeply rooted public association of racial minorities with crime and drugs, just as the choice of crack as an ongoing priority for law enforcement cannot be divorced from public association of crack with blacks.

Faced with concerns about crack, the United States could have emphasized a public health and harm reduction approach prioritizing drug education, substance abuse treatment, and increased access to medical assistance. It could have sought to stem the spread of drug use and the temptations of the drug trade in deteriorating inner cities by making investments to reduce poverty, build social infrastructure, improve education, increase medical and mental health treatment, combat homelessness, increase employment, and provide more support to vulnerable families. It could have restricted prison to only the most serious drug offenders (e.g., major traffickers).

Instead, federal and state governments embraced harsh penal sanctions to battle the use of drugs and their sale to consumers. They adopted policies that increased the arrest rates of low-level drug offenders, the likelihood of a prison sentence upon conviction of a drug offense, and the length of such prison sentences.

Defenders of anti-drug efforts claim they want to protect poor minority neighborhoods from addiction and violence. But the choice of arrest and imprisonment as the primary anti-drug strategy evokes the infamous phrase from the Vietnam War: "It became necessary to destroy the town in order to save it." Noted criminologist Michael Tonry has pointed out that unless and until drug control policies are less destructive, the life prospects for many disadvantaged blacks and their communities will remain bleak.

In a fair, equitable, and non-discriminatory criminal justice system, sanctions should be imposed equally on offending populations. Yet the racial patterns of persons arrested and incarcerated on drug charges are distantly related, at best, to racial patterns of drug offending.

The Pathological Politics of Criminal Law
William J. Stuntz

100 Michigan Law Review 505 (2001)

Relative to other Western legal systems, America's criminal justice system has long had a strong focus on vice—prostitution and gambling a century ago, alcohol in the 1920s, and drugs more recently. That focus is usually attributed to America's moralism. It is also a consequence of the interacting incentives of law enforcers and legislators.

Most criminal litigation deals with crimes that nearly all non-offenders believe should be crimes. Prosecutors may make sorting errors in burglary cases, and criminalizing the possession of burglars' tools may make those sorting errors more likely.

But there will be no dispute about whether burglars should be punished. The huge majority of the population thinks the relevant behavior wrong and, importantly, the huge majority of the population has no desire to engage in the relevant behavior themselves. For crimes like these, the lawmaking dynamic yields broader liability rules but does not change the nature of the behavior the system is seeking to punish.

With vice, the story is different. Gambling, sex for hire, and intoxicants are all things that a large portion of the public wants, and these goods and services are sufficiently cheap, at least in some forms, that people of all social classes can afford them. At the same time, these things generate both intense disapproval among another large slice of the population, and substantial social costs that tend to concentrate in poor communities. The result is complicated: anti-vice crusades tend to have strong public support, but only so long as the crusades are targeted at a fairly small subset of the population. Our tradition of giving police and prosecutors basically unregulated enforcement discretion makes that targeting easy. Which in turn permits legislatures to define criminal liability in ways that might otherwise be politically impossible.

One sees hints of this dynamic with each of the major vice crimes that have occupied the criminal justice system over the past century. Begin with prostitution. Before the late nineteenth century, most jurisdictions had no prostitution statutes; the relevant crime was running a "disorderly house," a more circumscribed offense. The period after about 1880 saw the growth of a powerful urban reform movement that led first to prostitution statutes, and then to broader solicitation and procurement statutes. But when some urban police forces tried to enforce those laws generally—when they actually tried to shut down prostitution, across neighborhoods and classes—they generated a significant backlash, in Lawrence Friedman's words, from the "silent army" of middle-class customers who frequented the more upscale houses. There were two typical results: non-enforcement coupled with graft, with the police using the prostitution laws as devices for extracting payoffs, or enforcement targeted mostly at poor immigrant neighborhoods.

The story with respect to gambling is similar. For a long time the market for illegal games tended to segment by class, with numbers businesses dominating the downscale market, and bookmaking and illegal casinos playing the same role in the upscale market. Throughout this time, in most jurisdictions the criminal law of gambling was all-encompassing. Enforcement was not. In those times and places when police and prosecutors took gambling seriously, they almost always targeted numbers operations, which were in turn concentrated in poor urban neighborhoods.

Prohibition was likewise legally all-encompassing, banning manufacture and sale of beer and wine as well as hard liquors. There, too, the illegal market tended to segment by class (there is some evidence that Prohibition made beer the working-class drink of choice, as liquor was priced out of reach for urban factory workers). And there, too, enforcement was largely class-based: contemporaneous accounts report that blacks were the prime focus of alcohol enforcement and prosecution in the South; in Northern cities, it was working-class white ethnics.

Notice the pattern. For each of these three classic vice crimes, a majority of the population seems to have supported the ban, but a sizeable minority, cutting across classes and ethnic groups, wished to participate in the illegal market. Given the size of that minority—and, consequently, the sheer number of illegal transactions—across-the-board enforcement of the ban was unsustainable. The solution was enforcement aimed primarily at lower-class markets: street prostitutes, numbers operations, and working-class beer distribution networks. That tended to be a relatively popular solution, at least for a time, for two reasons. First, the social harms associated with these transactions—violence, impoverishment, disease—tended to correlate not only with the illegal transactions but with class as well. Second, lower-class neighborhoods were often politically convenient targets. Hostility to blacks in the South and to working-class immigrants in Northern cities were strong themes of turn-of-the-century American politics.

Notice, too, how hard that solution would be to define legislatively. Had legislatures sought to capture the difference between downscale and upscale gambling, they probably would have banned some kinds of games but not others. But that strategy would have had limited effect, for the downscale market could simply have shifted from illegal games to legal ones. Had street solicitation but not prostitution been criminalized, prostitutes in poor neighborhoods could have retreated to fixed houses—as they did in most American cities through much of the nineteenth century. Had beer but not liquor been banned, working-class consumption would have moved, perversely, toward products with a higher alcohol content. That kind of flexibility is probably in the nature of markets for pleasurable-but-sometimes-harmful goods and services. As a consequence, serious criminal enforcement of vice may depend on broad criminalization, coupled with equally broad law enforcement power to target particular neighborhoods and, inevitably, particular racial or ethnic groups. Without enforcement discretion, criminalization might be impossible.

Contemporary drug law and drug enforcement paint a complex picture, but one sees elements of the same pattern there as well. Not only are classically "hard" drugs like cocaine and heroin banned, but so are a wide variety of "softer" drugs like marijuana. Enforcement tends to be more aggressive than with past anti-vice crusades. Drug sentences are more severe than were sentences for gambling or illegal alcohol earlier this century, and the policing of upscale drug markets appears to be more persistent than policing of other upscale illegal markets over the course of the past hundred years. To that extent, the pattern breaks down; support for drug criminalization is probably both broader and deeper than support for earlier crusades against prostitutes, gamblers, or saloonkeepers. Yet class-based, and hence to some degree race-based, enforcement remains common. Thus, crack markets in urban black neighborhoods are targeted, while more upscale, and whiter, drug markets receive less law enforcement attention.

Once again, that type of enforcement strategy, and that type of criminal law, would be much harder in a regime with limited police and prosecutorial discretion. Perhaps one reason support for drug criminalization remains so high—and surely one reason why the scope of drug criminalization remains so broad—lies in legislatures' ability to prohibit without fear that the prohibition will be applied equally everywhere.

The New Jim Crow
Michelle Alexander

9 Ohio State Journal of Criminal Law 7 (2011)

I find that when I tell people that mass incarceration amounts to a New Jim Crow, I am frequently met with shocked disbelief. The standard reply is: "How can you say that a racial caste system exists? Just look at Barack Obama! Just look at Oprah Winfrey! Just look at the black middle class!"

The reaction is understandable. But we ought to question our emotional reflexes. The mere fact that some African Americans have experienced great success in recent years does not mean that something akin to a caste system no longer exists. No caste system in the United States has ever governed all black people. There have always been "free blacks" and black success stories, even during slavery and Jim Crow. During slavery, there were some black slave owners—not many, but some. And during Jim Crow, there were some black lawyers and doctors—not many, but some. The unprecedented nature of black achievement in formerly white domains today certainly suggests that the old Jim Crow is dead, but it does not necessarily mean the end of racial caste. If history is any guide, it may have simply taken a different form.

Any honest observer of American racial history must acknowledge that racism is highly adaptable. The rules and reasons the legal system employs to enforce status relations of any kind evolve and change as they are challenged. Since our nation's founding, African Americans have been repeatedly controlled through institutions, such as slavery and Jim Crow, which appear to die, but then are reborn in new form-tailored to the needs and constraints of the time.

For example, following the collapse of slavery, the system of convict leasing was instituted—a system many historians believe was worse than slavery. After the Civil War, black men were arrested by the thousands for minor crimes, such as loitering and vagrancy, and sent to prison. They were then leased to plantations. It was our nation's first prison boom. The idea was that prisoners leased to plantations were supposed to earn their freedom. But the catch was they could never earn enough to pay back the plantation owner the cost of their food, clothing and shelter to the owner's satisfaction, and thus they were effectively re-enslaved, sometimes for the rest of their lives. It was a system more brutal in many respects than slavery, because plantation owners had no economic incentive to keep convicts healthy or even alive. They could always get another one.

Today, I believe the criminal justice system has been used once again in a manner that effectively re-creates caste in America. Our criminal justice system functions more like a caste system than a system of crime control.

For those who find that claim difficult to swallow, consider the facts. Our prison system has quintupled for reasons that have stunningly little to do with crime. In less than 30 years, the U.S. penal population exploded from around 300,000 to more than 2 million. The United States now has the highest rate of incarceration in the world, dwarfing the rates of nearly every developed country, including highly repressive regimes like China and Iran.

In fact, if our nation were to return to the incarceration rates of the 1970s—a time, by the way, when civil rights activists thought that imprisonment rates were egregiously high—we would have to release four out of five people who are in prison today. More than a million people employed by the criminal justice system could lose their jobs. That is how enormous and deeply entrenched the new system has become in a very short period of time.

As staggering as those figures are, they actually obscure the severity of the crisis in poor communities of color. Professor Loïc Wacquant has argued that the term "mass incarceration" itself is a misnomer, since it implies that nearly everyone has been subject to the new system of control. But, of course that is not the case. The overwhelming majority of the increase in imprisonment has been poor people of color, with the most astonishing rates of incarceration found among black men. It was estimated several years ago that, in Washington, D.C.—our nation's capital-three out of four young black men (and nearly all those in the poorest neighborhoods) could expect to serve time in prison. Rates of incarceration nearly as shocking can be found in other communities of color across America.

So what accounts for this vast new system of control? Crime rates? That is the common answer. But no, crime rates have remarkably little to do with skyrocketing incarceration rates. Crime rates have fluctuated over the past thirty years, and are currently at historical lows, but incarceration rates have consistently soared. Most criminologists and sociologists today acknowledge that crime rates and incarceration rates have, for the most part, moved independently of one another. Rates of imprisonment—especially black imprisonment—have soared regardless of whether crime has been rising or falling in any given community or the nation as a whole.

So what does explain this vast new system of control, if not crime rates? The War on Drugs. The War on Drugs and the "get tough" movement explain the explosion in incarceration in the United States and the emergence of a vast, new racial undercaste. In fact, drug convictions alone accounted for about two-thirds of the increase in the federal system, and more than half of the increase in the state prison population between 1985 and 2000. Drug convictions have increased more than 1000% since the drug war began, an increase that bears no relationship to patterns of drug use or sales.

People of all races use and sell drugs at remarkably similar rates, but the enemy in this war has been racially defined. The drug war has been waged almost exclusively in poor communities of color, despite the fact that studies consistently indicate that people of all races use and sell drugs at remarkably similar rates. This evidence defies our basic stereotype of a drug dealer, as a black kid standing on a street corner, with his pants hanging down. Drug dealing happens in the ghetto, to be sure, but it happens everywhere else in America as well. Illegal drug markets, it turns out—like American society generally—are relatively segregated by race. Blacks tend to sell to blacks, whites to whites, Latinos sell to each other. University students sell to each other. People of all races use and sell drugs. A kid in rural Kansas does not drive to the 'hood to get his pot, or meth, or cocaine, he buys it from somebody down the road. In fact, the research suggests that where significant differences by race can be found, white youth are more likely to commit drug crimes than youth of color.

But that is not what you would guess when entering our nation's prisons and jails, overflowing as they are with black and brown drug offenders. In the United States, those who do time for drug crime are overwhelmingly black and brown. In some states, African Americans constitute 80 to 90% of all drug offenders sent to prison.

I find that many people are willing to concede these racial disparities once they see the data. Even so, they tend to insist that the drug war is motivated by concern over violent crime. They say: just look at our prisons. Nearly half of the people behind bars are violent offenders. Typically this is where the discussion ends.

The problem with this abbreviated analysis is that violent crime is not responsible for the prison boom. Violent offenders tend to get longer sentences than nonviolent offenders, which is why they comprise such a large share of the prison population. One study suggests that the entire increase in imprisonment can be explained by sentence length, not increases in crime. To get a sense of how large a contribution the drug war has made to mass incarceration, consider this: there are more people in prison today just for drug offenses than were incarcerated in 1980 for all reasons. The reality is that the overwhelming majority of people who are swept into this system are non-violent offenders.

In this regard, it is important to keep in mind that most people who are under correctional control are not in prison or jail. As of 2008, there were approximately 2.3 million people in prisons and jails, and a staggering 5.1 million people under "community correctional supervision"—i.e., on probation or parole. Millions more have felony records and spend their lives cycling in and out of prison, unable to find work or shelter, unable to vote or to serve on juries. This system depends on the prison label, not prison time. It does not matter whether you have actually spent time in prison; your second-class citizenship begins the moment you are branded a felon. It is this badge of inferiority—the criminal record—that ushers you into a parallel social universe in which discrimination is, once again, perfectly legal.

How did this extraordinary system of control, unprecedented in world history, come to pass? Most people insist upon a benign motive. They seem to believe that the War on Drugs was launched in response to rising drug crime and the emergence of crack cocaine in inner city communities. For a long time, I believed that too. But that is not the case. Drug crime was actually declining, not rising, when President Ronald Reagan officially declared the drug war in 1982. President Richard Nixon was the first to coin the term a "war on drugs," but President Reagan turned the rhetorical war into a literal one. From the outset, the war had little to do with drug crime and much to do with racial politics.

The drug war was part of a grand and highly successful Republican Party strategy—often known as the Southern Strategy—of using racially coded political appeals on issues of crime and welfare to attract poor and working class white voters who were resentful of, and threatened by, desegregation, busing, and affirmative action. Poor and working class whites had their world rocked by the Civil Rights Movement. White elites could send their kids to private schools and give them all of the advantages wealth has to offer. But poor and working class whites were faced with a social demotion. It was their kids who might be bused across town, and forced to compete for the first time with a new group of people they had long believed to be inferior for decent jobs and educational opportunities. Affirmative action, busing, and desegregation created an understandable feeling of vulnerability, fear, and anxiety among a group already struggling for survival.

Republican party strategists found that thinly veiled promises to "get tough" on "them"—the racially defined others—could be highly successful in persuading poor and working class whites to defect from the Democratic New Deal Coalition and join the Republican Party. H.R. Haldeman, President Richard Nixon's former Chief of Staff, reportedly summed up the strategy: "[T]he whole problem is really the blacks. The key is to devise a system that recognizes this while not appearing to."

A couple years after the drug war was announced, crack cocaine hit the streets of inner-city communities. The Reagan administration seized on this development with glee, hiring staff who were responsible for publicizing inner-city crack babies, crack mothers, the so-called "crack whores," and drug-related violence. The goal was to make inner-city crack abuse and violence a media sensation that, it was hoped, would bolster public support for the drug war and would lead Congress to devote millions of dollars in additional funding to it.

The plan worked like a charm. For more than a decade, black drug dealers and users became regulars in newspaper stories and saturated the evening TV news-forever changing our conception of who the drug users and dealers are. Once the enemy in the war was racially defined, a wave of punitiveness took over. Congress and state legislatures nationwide devoted billions of dollars to the drug war and passed harsh mandatory minimum sentences for drug crimes-sentences longer than murderers receive in many countries. Many black politicians joined the "get tough" bandwagon, apparently oblivious to their complicity with the emergence of a system of social control that would, in less than two decades, become unprecedented in world history.

Almost immediately, Democrats began competing with Republicans to prove that they could be even tougher on "them." In President Bill Clinton's boastful words, "I can be nicked on a lot, but no one can say I'm soft on crime." The facts bear him out. Clinton's "'tough on crime' policies resulted in the largest increases in federal and state prison inmates of any president in American history." But Clinton was not satisfied with exploding prison populations. In an effort to appeal to the "white swing voters," he and the so-called "new Democrats" championed legislation banning drug felons from public housing (no matter how minor the offense) and denying them basic public benefits, including food stamps, for life. Discrimination in virtually every aspect of political, economic, and social life is now perfectly legal, once you're labeled a felon.

All of this has been justified on the grounds that getting brutally tough on "them" is the only way to root out violent offenders or drug kingpins. The media images of violence in ghetto communities—particularly when crack first hit the street—led many to believe that the drug war was focused on the most serious offenders. Yet nothing could be further from the truth. Federal funding has flowed to those state and local law enforcement agencies that increase dramatically the volume of drug arrests, not the agencies most successful in bringing down the bosses. What has been rewarded in this war is sheer numbers—the sheer volume of drug arrests.

The results are predictable. People of color have been rounded up en masse for relatively minor, non-violent drug offenses. In 2005, for example, four out of five drug arrests were for possession, only one out of five for sales. Most people in state prison for drug offenses have no history of violence or even of significant selling activity. In fact, during the 1990s—the period of the most dramatic expansion of the drug war—nearly 80% of the increase in drug arrests was for marijuana possession, a drug generally considered less harmful than alcohol or tobacco and at least as prevalent in middle-class white communities as in the inner city.

In this way, a new racial undercaste has been created in an astonishingly short period of time. Millions of people of color are now saddled with criminal records and legally denied the very rights that were supposedly won in the Civil Rights Movement.

None of this is to say, of course, that mass incarceration and Jim Crow are the "same." There are significant differences between mass incarceration and earlier forms of racial control, to be sure. Just as there were vast differences between slavery and Jim Crow, there are important differences between Jim Crow and mass incarceration. Yet all three (slavery, Jim Crow, and mass incarceration) have operated as tightly networked systems of laws, policies, customs, and institutions that operate collectively to ensure the subordinate status of a group defined largely by race. When we step back and view the system of mass incarceration as a whole, there is a profound sense of deja vu. There is a familiar stigma and shame. There is an elaborate system of control, complete with political disenfranchisement and legalized discrimination in every major realm of economic and social life. And there is the production of racial meaning and racial boundaries.

If someone were to visit the United States from another country (or another planet) and ask: "Is the U.S. criminal justice system some kind of tool of racial control?", most Americans would swiftly deny it. Numerous reasons would leap to mind why that could not possibly be the case. The visitor would be told that crime rates, black culture, or bad schools were to blame. "The system is not run by a bunch of racists," the apologist would explain. They would say, "It is run by people who are trying to fight crime." Because mass incarceration is officially colorblind, and because most people today do not think of themselves as racist, it seems inconceivable that the system could function much like a racial caste system.

But more than forty-five years ago, Martin Luther King Jr. warned of the danger of precisely this kind of thinking. He insisted that blindness and indifference to racial groups is actually more important than racial hostility to the creation and maintenance of systems of racial control. Those who supported slavery and Jim Crow, he argued, typically were not bad or evil people; they were just blind. Many segregationists were kind to their black shoe shiners and maids and genuinely wished them well. Even the Justices who decided the infamous Dred Scott case, which ruled "that the Negro had no rights which the white man was bound to respect," were not wicked men, he said. On the whole, they were decent and dedicated men. But, he hastened to add, "They were victims of spiritual and intellectual blindness. They knew not what they did. The whole system of slavery was largely perpetuated by sincere though spiritually ignorant persons."

The same is true today. People of good will—and bad—have been unwilling to see black and brown men, in their humanness, as entitled to the same care, compassion, and concern that would be extended to one's friends, neighbors, or loved ones.

After all, who among us would want a loved one struggling with drug abuse to be put in a cage, labeled a felon, and then subjected to a lifetime of discrimination, scorn and social exclusion? Most Americans would not wish that fate on anyone they cared about. But whom do we care about? In America, the answer to that question is still linked to race. Dr. King recognized that it was this indifference to the plight of African Americans that supported the institutions of slavery and Jim Crow. And this callous racial indifference supports mass incarceration today.

Chapter 3

Drug Crimes

A. Drug Possession

The United States addresses drug use and abuse primarily through laws against simple drug possession. In 2017, there were just under 1.4 million arrests for drug possession offenses in the United States, according to the FBI's Uniform Crime Report. With 10.6 million arrests for all offenses in 2017, arrests for simple drug possession made up 13% of *all* arrests nationwide (excluding any arrests for traffic infractions, which are not included in the FBI's report). These figures tell us drug possession as measured by its impact on the criminal justice system is undeniably one of the most important crimes in the United States today. But what legal issues arise in the context of drug possession offenses?

On the surface, drug possession might seem to be a fairly straightforward crime that is unlikely to raise interesting or difficult questions of law. After all, someone who is found with drugs on their person or in their car or home would seem to present a classic "open and shut" case. To be sure, if the police discovered the drugs as the result of an illegal search or seizure, the defendant could seek to exclude them from evidence. But, in the absence of a Fourth Amendment claim, what defense could a drug possession defendant possibly have?

While it is true that some drug possession cases are clear-cut, others can present surprisingly complicated and fascinating problems. Consider, for example, the following scenarios:

<u>Scenario 1:</u> Dave, a youth soccer coach, arrives at Bushrod Park early to get everything set up for his team's weekly practice. As Dave is putting down some cones for a drill, he notices a little baggie lying on the ground. He picks it up and sees that the small bag contains marijuana. Dave walks over to a garbage can across the field to throw it away. Just as Dave is about to reach the garbage can, however, Officer Walters approaches him. Walters notices the baggie in Dave's hand and arrests him for possession of marijuana.

<u>Scenario 2:</u> Pam and Paul are a couple in their mid-40s raising three children. Tammy, their oldest, just turned 16 and has begun experimenting with drugs and alcohol. Pam and Paul have done everything they can to convince Tammy to stop her substance use but to no avail. One night, Tammy tells her parents that she is going out to see a movie and does not return. In response to text messages from Paul and Pam, Tammy tells them: "Stop treating me like a baby. I'm having fun and will come home tomorrow morning." Frustrated, Pam and Paul decide to search

through Tammy's room. Inside one of the dresser drawers, they discover what appears to be a bag of 20 "ecstasy" (MDMA) pills. Paul puts the pills in his pocket so that he and Pam can confront Tammy with them when she comes home. An hour later, Paul experiences chest pains and calls 911. When the medical crew responds, they discover the ecstasy pills in Paul's pocket and notify the police, who arrest Paul for possession of ecstasy.

Scenario 3: Southgate is in charge of a small cocaine operation in Indianapolis, Indiana. Southgate has devised a method to try to avoid arrest and prosecution. Instead of selling the cocaine himself, Southgate employs two lieutenants: Victor, who collects money from the customers and Beatrice, who gives the customers their cocaine. Victor, Beatrice and Southgate operate on a corner in front of an abandoned building. After Victor takes a customer's money, he sends the customer to Beatrice and flashes her a hand signal to let her know how much cocaine the customer has purchased. Beatrice usually carries no more than enough cocaine on her person to supply five customers. The group keeps the rest of the product in a little spot underneath the steps of the abandoned building. Southgate sits on the stoop to guard the cocaine and watch over Victor and Beatrice. Southgate is careful never to touch the cocaine or the money in public and only collects his share of the money from Victor at the end of each day. After receiving complaints from neighbors, the police go to observe Southgate's operations from within an unmarked vehicle. The police quickly identify the activity as a drug operation and they would like to arrest Southgate for possession of cocaine. But, after three hours of observation, they have not seen Southgate so much as lay a finger on the cocaine.

* * *

Based on your intuitions, which (if any) of the individuals in these problems do you think has committed a drug possession crime? On the one hand, Southgate seems to be more culpable either than Paul or Dave. On the other hand, Paul and Dave were both found with illegal drugs on their person and Southgate was not. Keep these scenarios in mind as you read through the cases in this section and consider how the criminal law should define "possession."

1. An Introduction to Drug Possession

"[N]either a status offense nor a conduct offense," possession criminalizes a relationship between a person and contraband. Markus Dirk Dubber, *Policing Possession: The War on Crime and the End of Criminal Law*, 91 J. Crim. L. & Criminology 829 (2001). Conceptually, possession cases usually fall into one of two categories: "actual" possession or "constructive" possession. These categories do not represent separate offenses. Rather, they describe two different scenarios in which a person may be shown to have committed the crime of possession. Actual possession refers to situations in which an individual has drugs on their person. Constructive possession, by contrast, involves circumstances where illegal drugs are found *near* a person—such as in a person's car or home.

Although possession is an age-old concept in property law, courts first began to seriously grapple with the idea of possession in the criminal context during alcohol prohibition. These Prohibition-era possession cases employed a somewhat narrow definition of the term, in which possession was almost synonymous with ownership. Courts consistently found, for example, that holding a bottle of liquor in one's hand to take a drink from it did not constitute "possession" of the liquor, at least where the person taking the drink did not own the liquor. As Judge Samford of the Alabama Court of Appeals put it: "Possession of whisky within the meaning of the prohibition law contemplates a control over the whisky, whereas when the whisky is in the man the whisky controls the man." *Evans v. State*, 24 Ala. App. 196, 197 (1931).

The Prohibition-era understanding of possession was abandoned, however, during the 1960s and 1970s as courts began to redefine the term in the context of drug laws. The following case provides an example of the contrasting views.

Hawaii v. Hogue

Supreme Court of Hawaii
52 Haw. 660 (1971)

Marumoto, J.

Defendant was convicted after a jury trial in the circuit court of knowingly possessing marihuana in violation of H[awaii] R[evised] S[tatute] § 329-5. The portion of the statute relevant to this case reads as follows:

> "No person shall knowingly plant, cultivate, produce, manufacture, possess, have under his control, prescribe, administer, or compound any narcotic drug as defined by section 329-1 except as provided in this chapter."

The case was submitted to the jury upon the following stipulation of facts:

> "That the State is able to prove by the testimony of the three arresting officers, upon the trial of Gregory Dale Hogue, that the defendant Gregory Dale Hogue on or about the 5th day of March, 1970, in the County of Kauai, State of Hawaii, did then and there at the invitation of a friend, one Charles Glagolich, who was the owner of a pipe containing marihuana in hashish form while sitted at a picnic table at Lydgate Park with Mr. Glagolich and three other friends, Stephanie Kay Stearns, Johnny Ray Griffith and Georgia Marie Shannon, did knowingly take two puffs from a pipe containing marihuana in hashish form.
>
> "That the three officers will testify that, prior to the arrest, they observed Charles Glagolich turn over a pipe containing marihuana in hashish form to one Stephanie Kay Stearns, who after a couple of puffs turned it over to one Johnny Ray Griffith, who after a couple of puffs turned it over to defendant Gregory Dale Hogue. That defendant Gregory Dale Hogue was observed by the three arresting officers with a hashish pipe in his hands, no one else was holding it, and did take two puffs from said pipe knowing it to

> contain marihuana in hashish form. That after the pipe had been passed and the actions were observed by the three arresting officers, defendant together with his friends were placed under arrest for unlawful possession or control of marihuana. Defendants were properly advised of their constitutional rights.
>
> "That the State's contention is that the offense committed by defendant Gregory Dale Hogue is the knowingly taking of two puffs from a pipe containing marihuana in hashish form owned by one Charles Glagolich. Defendant, if called, will testify that he took only one puff from said pipe.
>
> "That the residue within the pipe was analyzed by Dr. Quentin Belles. Said analysis revealed an oily residue which a chemical test showed was charred marihuana."
>
> Among the instructions given by the circuit court to the jury were the following:
>
> "Hawaii statutes do not state that smoking marihuana, per se, is legal or illegal. It does state that possession or control of marihuana, in its various forms, is illegal.
>
> "Considering the totality of the circumstances, a person may smoke marihuana *without* 'possessing' or 'controlling' it, or he may smoke marihuana in such a way that he *does* have possession or control over it.
>
> "To 'possess' means to have the actual control, care and management of the marihuana (hashish), and not a passing control fleeting and shadowy in its nature."

[This] appeal is based on the denial by the circuit court of [a] motion to dismiss made before the trial.

The motion for dismissal was made on the ground that the mere passing and puffing from a marihuana pipe owned and supplied by another was insufficient as a matter of law to constitute a possession of marihuana proscribed in HRS § 329-5. The stipulation quoted above provided the factual basis for the motion.

The stipulation stated that the defendant was observed by three police officers "with a hashish pipe in his hands, no one else was holding it, and did take two puffs from said pipe knowing it to contain marihuana in hashish form", after two other persons sitting at the same table took two puffs each from the same pipe. The facts stipulated, as having been observed by the officers, show conscious and substantial possession, not a mere involuntary or superficial possession, and much more than a passing control, fleeting and shadowy in nature.

Thus, the circuit court did not err in denying the motion to dismiss.

The defense argues that the legislature has not expressly outlawed the smoking of marihuana, that its silence in this regard suggests that it was more concerned with curbing the dealer and supplier than with the user at the end of the supply chain, and that in an area where the legislature has remained silent it appears to be a proper judicial function "to dilute the number of marihuana defendants down to only the owner-user while freeing the non-owner user."

The answer to the argument is that the question before us is in an area where the legislature has spoken, not where it has remained silent. In an area where the legislature has spoken, our function is to give effect to the legislative will.

The acts proscribed in HRS § 329-5 are basically those which are prohibited in § 2 of the Uniform Narcotic Drug Act. Contention has frequently been advanced that the word "possess," as used in § 2 of the uniform act, does not refer to possession of a narcotic drug for the personal use of the possessor. Courts have rejected such contention. It is stated in *State* v. *Reed* as follows, as one of the reasons for rejection:

> "[S]ection 4 of the Drug Act provides that 'it shall be unlawful for any person to possess any narcotic drug, *except as authorized by this chapter.*' There follows a number of sections which permit possession under certain conditions by physicians, pharmacists, and others who must handle narcotics in the regular course of business. Section 36 expressly permits possession for the possessor's personal consumption or use if he has obtained the drug from an authorized dispenser for medical treatment and if he keeps the unused drug in the container in which he received it. This exception shows that the Legislature considered the problem of possession by a user." [34 N.J. 554 (1961).]

Furthermore, the concern of the legislature with dealers and suppliers of narcotic drugs is shown specifically in its enactment of HRS § 329-3, which reads: "It shall be unlawful for any person to possess *with the intent to sell or to sell or dispense* any narcotic drug, except as provided in this chapter." (Emphasis supplied) The legislature would have had no reason to enact [HRS § 329-3] if [HRS § 329-5] were directed solely against dealers and suppliers.

Affirmed.

Levinson, J., dissenting.

I would reverse the appellant's conviction on the ground that a person who receives from another a pipe containing marihuana for the sole purpose of inhaling therefrom and subsequently returning it does not, as a matter of law, unlawfully "possess" or "have under his control" a narcotic drug, within the meaning of HRS § 329-5. That statute provides in relevant part:

> No person shall knowingly plant, cultivate, produce, manufacture, possess, have under his control, prescribe, administer, or compound any narcotic drug as defined by section 329-1 except as provided in this chapter.

The Narcotics Act, of which the above provision is a part, does not define the words "possess" or "control." It falls upon this court, therefore, to give these words a sensible and reasonable meaning within the context of the Act. To do so it is first necessary, I believe, to determine the regulatory purposes of the Narcotics Act.

Specifically, does the Act disclose any discernible pattern of legislative concern which would throw light on whether the appellant's brief dominion over the pipe containing marihuana amounted to possession or control as proscribed by HRS § 329-5? My analysis of the Narcotics Act and the case law relevant to illegal possession leads me to conclude that the possession and control contemplated by the legislature is of a more substantial character than the momentary possession necessary to take one or two puffs.

I do not believe that the possession or control contemplated by the legislature was meant to encompass the mere taking in hand of a pipe or cigarette for the immediate purpose of smoking marihuana. Instead I think that the possession and control prohibited by the statute is the *power to distribute* the drugs as the possessor sees fit. In the instant case this status belonged to the owner of the marihuana who offered it to the appellant for the latter's immediate consumption. At all times control over distribution remained in the offeror. He is the one, not the mere user, who falls within the prohibition of the Act.

The majority does not agree with this analysis. It does concede, however, that mere "superficial possession" and "passing control" are exempt from the operation of the statute. Nevertheless it holds that the present conduct is not "superficial" or "passing." I am at a loss to conceive what these phrases import if they do not describe the appellant's acts in the present case. What possession could be more superficial, or what control more passing, than the fleeting act of holding and puffing on a marihuana pipe and "passing" it to another? A sensible construction of HRS § 329-5, consistent with the statutory scheme of regulating the marketing and distribution of narcotic drugs, requires that possession be equated with ownership, and control be defined as such management or dominion over the prohibited substance as gives to the controller the power to dispose of it to others. Such an interpretation sweeps broad enough to encompass those in a position to dispense the prohibited drugs, while passing over persons whose only contact is immediate consumption. In addition, this construction of the Narcotics Act is supported by the case law dealing with fact situations closely analogous to the instant case.

During the "Great Experiment" of the Prohibition era numerous cases arose where a group of persons would be arrested for passing and drinking from a bottle of illegal liquor owned and distributed by one member of the group. The defendants in such cases were charged with unlawful possession of liquor, under statutes worded similarly to our own. The courts were called upon to construe the meaning of possession within the context of a statute aimed at controlling the traffic in intoxicating liquor. Adopting a statutory analysis which parallels the one asserted above, these courts concluded that possession did not include the mere taking in hand for drinking purposes. What was prohibited was ownership or control of such a degree as to give the controller the power of distribution to others.

> [In] *State v. Jones,* 114 Wash. 144, 148 (1921), the Washington Supreme Court held that:

> [P]ossession, as the word is used in the statute, means something more than the mere taking in the hand for the purpose of immediately drinking the thing thus possessed upon the express invitation of the owner so to do ... the court should at least have defined possession as including control of the thing possessed with the right to dispose of it in any manner the possessor saw fit. As we understand the laws of hospitality, when one is offered a glass of liquor, he has a right to accept and drink it, or refuse it, and his possession, if he accepts it, is not broader than the invitation upon which he acts.

Similarly, one who is offered a pipe of marihuana for immediate consumption obtains only the dominion necessary for that act. Actual possession and control lies at all times in the offeror. It is he, as the distributor of the prohibited substance, who falls within the regulatory purposes of the Act.

In effect, the majority opinion's definition of possession extends the coverage of the Narcotics Act to penalize the smoking or use of marihuana. This result is, I believe, clearly beyond that contemplated by the legislature. This belief is supported by the Narcotics Act itself because the provisions of the Act indicate that at the time the legislature acted it was familiar with the specific limiting language necessary to deal with the consumption of marihuana. Yet it chose not to employ this language to prohibit the use of narcotic drugs.

HRS § 329-4 of the Narcotics Act prohibits the sale of narcotic drugs to minors. This provision also makes it a crime to induce "any person under the age of twenty years to buy, traffic in, receive, *take, inject, inhale, or smoke* any narcotic drug. . . ." (emphasis added). This is the language the legislature would have used had it desired to prohibit the acts of the appellant. The legislature chose, however, not to proscribe the "taking," "inhaling," "injecting," or "smoking" of marihuana because it was not concerned with penalizing the user of drugs. Therefore, if the legislature did not intend to prohibit the use of marihuana directly, this court should not indirectly do so by broadly defining possession so as to include the superficial custody required for the immediate inhalation of marihuana.

In deciding this case it is important to recognize what is not in issue. The appellant does not contend that possession as used in HRS § 329-5 is limited only to dealers and suppliers of narcotic drugs. Nor is it argued that a person falls outside the statute if he possesses narcotic drugs for his personal consumption. The motive for possession as the word is used in this section is irrelevant. What is important is the power to dispense narcotic drugs to others. This is what is meant by unlawful possession. Thus one who buys a single marihuana cigarette, even for his own immediate consumption, violates the statute because he has acquired the power to dispense, not necessarily by sale, to others. Similarly one who lacks this power does not have unlawful possession, even though he takes a puff on a marihuana pipe. What this case puts in issue is not whether possession for personal use violates the statute but whether personal use without possession has been made a crime.

The majority opinion attempts to answer this question by arguing that all contact with marihuana is prohibited unless specifically authorized by HRS ch. 329. The cases cited in support of this position are based upon different factual situations since they deal only with the question whether ownership for personal use constitutes unlawful possession. Nevertheless, the decision in *State v. Reed*, one of the cases cited by my Brother Marumoto, is enlightening for its analysis of the reasons behind defining unlawful possession so as to include possession for personal use.

> [T]he inclusion of unauthorized possession for personal consumption within the proscriptions of the Drug Act seems necessary to fulfill the legislative goal of suppressing illegal narcotics traffic. Every possessor of narcotics has the power to dispense them to another. That power in the hands of any person is a potential source of illegal traffic.

As we have seen, by holding in his hand and puffing on the marihuana pipe in the presence, at the invitation, and under the control of the owner, the appellant did not acquire this statutorily proscribed power to dispense to another. Therefore, as the New Jersey Supreme Court points out, he does not fall within the class of persons whom the legislature desired to penalize for unlawful possession.

Currently the wisdom of dealing with the problem of marihuana use through the criminal process is being assiduously questioned. There may even exist a serious question as to the constitutionality of marihuana laws.[11] At the very least, scholars who have studied the problem raise grave doubts as to the social utility of criminalizing marihuana use. As Professor John Kaplan of the Stanford University Law School concludes, in his excellent book, *Marijuana: The New Prohibition* (1970), "the social and financial costs directly and indirectly attributable to the criminalization of marijuana far outweigh the benefits of this policy." In addition, Professor Kaplan warns in his book, "[t]he most serious cost of the criminalization of marijuana is probably that it make felons of a large portion of our population, especially our youth."[14]

This court need not be blind to the practical consequences of its interpretations of law. As the above analysis indicates the purposes of the Narcotics Act will not be undermined if the temptation is resisted to extend the coverage of the Act so as to penalize persons who, perhaps through social pressures, accept an invitation to

11. M. Town, "*Privacy and the Marijuana Laws*," reprinted in The New Social Drug (1970); Wallenstein, *Marijuana Possession as an Aspect of the Right to Privacy*, 5 Crim. L. Bull. 59 (1969), Note *Marijuana and the Law: The Constitutional Challenge to Marijuana Laws in Light of the Social Aspects of Marijuana Use*, 13 Vill. L. Rev. 851 (1968).

14. Professor Kaplan reports that recent studies indicate that approximately thirty percent of California's high school students and sixty-nine percent of the students at Stanford University have used marihuana at least once. J. Kaplan, *supra* note 10, at 23. Studies have not yet been conducted in Hawaii. Nevertheless, extrapolating from the available information, I do not believe that in enacting HRS ch. 329 the legislature contemplated that it would be used to label as criminals one-third of today's high school students and two-thirds of today's college students.

puff on a marihuana pipe or cigarette. I see little social value in the majority opinion's rigid interpretation of existing drug laws. As Professor Michael P. Rosenthal cogently noted, *A Plea for Amelioration of the Marihuana Laws*, 47 Tex. L. Rev. 1359, 1372 (1969):

> Certainly, the consequences of criminalization would seem to be least warranted in the case of the experimenter. A small transgression or even a small number of transgressions, especially—but not exclusively—when committed by the young and developing, should not be the basis for permanently scarring a person's life. This is part of the rehabilitative ideal. While that ideal is usually spoken of in connection with sentencing after conviction of a crime, it should be given weight in formulating definitions of criminality also.

Based on the above statutory analysis, case law and policy considerations, I would reverse the appellant's conviction.

Taking "two puffs" of marijuana from a pipe may constitute possession, according to *Hawaii v. Hogue*, but is evidence of use, standing alone, enough to sustain a possession conviction? Specifically, is a positive drug test sufficient evidence of possession? Most courts to consider the question have held that more is required to convict. *See, e.g., North Carolina v. Harris*, 178 N.C. App. 723, 725–26 (2006) (collecting cases). As the Kansas Supreme Court explained in *Kansas v. Flinchpaugh*, 232 Kan. 831 (1983):

> Discovery of a drug in a person's blood is circumstantial evidence tending to prove prior possession of the drug, but it is not sufficient evidence to establish guilt beyond a reasonable doubt. The absence of proof to evince knowledgeable possession is the key. The drug might have been injected involuntarily, or introduced by artifice, into the defendant's system. In the narrow holding of this case, we find that evidence of a controlled substance assimilated in one's blood does not establish possession of that substance, nor is it adequate circumstantial evidence to show prior possession by that person.

Though *Flinchpaugh* represents the majority view, a few states have adopted laws that directly criminalize internal possession of a controlled substance. South Dakota, for example, amended its drug laws in 2001 to provide that "the term [controlled substances] includes an altered state of a drug or substance . . . absorbed into the human body." *See South Dakota v. Schroeder*, 2004 S.D. 21 (holding that the 2001 amendment "permits a defendant to be convicted of 'unauthorized possession' of a controlled drug or substance when the only evidence is from the ingested or absorbed unauthorized substance in the defendant's body"). Utah makes it a crime for a person to "knowingly and intentionally" have "any measurable amount of a controlled substance in [his or her] body." *See Utah v. Robinson*, 2011 UT 30 (rejecting a constitutional challenge to the "measurable quantity" law).

Jurisdictions are more closely divided on the questions of whether a person found with less than a "usable quantity" of a drug—for example, a small amount of drug residue—is guilty of drug possession. In some jurisdictions, possession of any amount is sufficient to support a conviction for possession. Others, however, provide that a usable amount is required, at least in some circumstances. *Compare, e.g., Richardson v. Colorado*, 25 P.3d 54, 58 (Colo. 2001) ("[W]e reject the defendant's argument that evidence of less than a usable amount creates an inference against knowing possession by the defendant.") *with Harbison v. Arkansas*, 302 Ark. 315, 322 (1990) ("The intent of the legislation prohibiting possession of a controlled substance is to prevent use of and trafficking in those substances. Possession of a trace amount or residue which cannot be used and which the accused may not even know is on his person or within his control contributes to neither evil.") *and Arizona v. Cheramie*, 218 Ariz. 447, 451 (2008) ("A 'usable quantity' is neither an element of the possession offense nor necessary to sustain a conviction for it. Rather, it is simply evidence from which a factfinder may infer intent.").

2. Possession for Disposal

Under *Hogue*'s interpretation of possession, a person need not own or have lasting authority over an item to possess it. It is enough that she holds the object in her hand, even if only for an instant. The dissent in *Hogue* argues that this definition of possession is flawed because it criminalizes casual drug users who do not exert any lasting control over the drugs that they use.

The first two scenarios from the beginning of this section indicate that this view of possession has the potential to sweep even further than the *Hogue* dissent envisions, however, by making criminals out of people like our hypothetical good Samaritan soccer coach or concerned parents. After all, if knowingly holding drugs in one's hand is all that is required to commit the crime of drug possession, then the person who takes a bag of marijuana from the ground in order to throw it in the trash would seem to be just as guilty as the person who takes a marijuana cigarette from their friend in order to smoke it.

To address this problem, courts have developed the "possession for disposal" doctrine (also sometimes referred to as the "fleeting" or "temporary" possession doctrine). This doctrine provides a defense to individuals who possess a controlled substance for the sole purpose of disposing of it, at least in some circumstances.

a. Overview

Stanton v. Florida provides an introduction to the "possession for disposal" rule. In reading *Stanton*, it is useful to consider what distinguishes Stanton's case from Hogue's. If the answer is that Stanton possessed drugs for an admirable purpose, does that mean the definition of possession turns entirely on the defendant's motive? If so, what is the basis for incorporating motive into the definition of criminal possession?

Stanton v. Florida

Court of Appeal of Florida, Third District
746 So. 2d 1229 (1999)

Cope, J.

David Stanton appeals his conviction for possession of cocaine. We conclude that the evidence was legally insufficient to support the conviction, and reverse it.

The very unusual facts of the case are that defendant Stanton was in an area of Key West during the Goombay Festival. He encountered a drug dealer who asked what defendant was looking for, meaning what drugs the defendant was looking for. After repeatedly saying that he was not looking for any drugs, the drug dealer handed defendant a rock of crack cocaine, saying that it was "on the house," and if defendant wanted more, he should come back.

Defendant, who testified that he had a long-standing cocaine problem but had managed to stay clear of cocaine for some time, decided to turn the drug dealer in. He accepted the cocaine rock and walked to the first police officer he could find. He put the cocaine rock down on a barricade by which the police officer was standing. There is some disagreement about the details of the conversation, but the defendant indicated that he wanted to assist the police in apprehending the drug dealer, such as by acting as an undercover buyer.

The police arrested the defendant for possession of cocaine and did not take up the offer of assistance in arresting the drug dealer. The State took the position at trial that since the defendant was in physical possession of a cocaine rock, it followed that he had committed the crime of possession of cocaine, regardless of the circumstances.

We do not think that a person who takes temporary possession of contraband for the sole purpose of turning it into the authorities, and promptly does so, is guilty of a crime. If a person finds contraband washed up on the beach, or floating in the sea, and takes the contraband forthwith to the authorities, we do not think that the law does, or is intended to, criminalize temporary possession for that purpose. Likewise if a parent discovers contraband in possession of his or her child, and disposes of it, we do not think the law criminalizes the parent's temporary possession.

In the trial court, the State's position was that if defendant had physical possession of the contraband, he was guilty; that the circumstances did not matter; and that his motive for turning the cocaine over to the police were not relevant and could not be considered by the jury.

On this appeal, the State concedes, correctly, that it is not a crime for a citizen to take temporary possession of contraband in order to turn it over to the police. The State argues, however, that there are some factual differences in the testimony of the arresting officer and the defendant, which created issues for consideration by the jury. We find that argument unpersuasive.

The undisputed fact is that the defendant voluntarily approached a uniformed police officer and turned over a cocaine rock. We are unable to see any plausible explanation for this act, other than, as defendant said, to turn it over to proper authorities and offer to assist in the apprehension of the drug dealer.

We conclude that the evidence is legally insufficient to support the conviction.

Reversed.

Many readers will find themselves agreeing with the result in *Stanton*. But does the possession for disposal concept have any basis in law or is it something judges invented from thin air in order to avoid reaching results they would personally consider to be unjust? Whatever the answer, most courts that have considered the possession for disposal rule in the context of drug possession have decided to adopt it. *But see Kansas v. Calvert,* 27 Kan. App. 2d 390, 392 (Kan. Ct. App. 2000) (declining to adopt "the so-called innocent possession defense" but stating "[o]ur ruling does not prevent a defendant from presenting a common-sense defense to a charge of a possessory crime").

While *Stanton* presents a straightforward example of the possession for disposal rule, cases in which a defendant seeks to raise the defense can often pose difficult line-drawing problems for courts. These problems are arguably exacerbated by the fact that the possession for disposal rule is judge-made and so there is no statutory definition of the concept that might help to resolve tough cases.

b. Length of Possession

Perhaps the most common problem that courts wrestle with in possession for disposal cases concerns the length of time that one may possess an item and still benefit from the defense. Courts that recognize the possession for disposal defense have answered the length of possession question in different ways.

In *People v. Cole,* a California appeals court held that the length of time a defendant has physical control over the drugs should be, at most, one factor for the jury to consider in assessing a possession for disposal claim. In *Cole*, the police found a bag containing .651 grams of cocaine in a safe in defendant Richard Andrew Cole's home along with a small amount of cocaine in the purse of Cole's 18-year-old daughter Jennifer. At trial, Jennifer testified that the cocaine in the safe was also hers. "She said that her father confiscated it the day before the search when he caught her using it in the bathroom. According to Jennifer, appellant took the cocaine, stormed out of the bathroom, and threatened to call the police. She was already on juvenile court probation for drug use." Andrew Cole testified that "[h]e told his wife, when he seized the baggies from Jennifer, that he was going to call the police, but his wife urged him not to do so. She wanted to dispose of the drugs immediately but later agreed to discuss the matter with him over the weekend and then to decide whether to discard the cocaine or turn it over to the police." Cole's wife also corroborated this version of events and testified "she had asked appellant not to call the police because she feared Jennifer would be removed from their home since she was already on probation." The police found the cocaine in the safe the day after Andrew's confrontation with Jennifer. The trial court instructed the jury that the possession for disposal theory required acquittal if Cole "handl[ed] the controlled substance for only brief moments for the purpose of disposal[.]" The appellate court reversed, finding that the defense "is not limited to possession for 'brief moments' only," but encompasses any "possession of illegal drugs *solely for the purpose of disposal*[.]" 202 Cal. App. 3d (1988) (emphasis in original).

Thirteen years later, in *People v. Martin*, the California Supreme Court overruled *Cole* and adopted a length-based limitation on the possession for disposal rule.

California v. Martin

Supreme Court of California
25 Cal. 4th 1180 (2001)

Baxter, J.

In *People v. Mijares* (1971), this court held that, under limited circumstances, momentary or transitory possession of an unlawful narcotic for the sole purpose of disposing of it can constitute a defense to a charge of criminal possession of the controlled substance. Nearly two decades later, [a lower California appellate] court in *People v. Cole* (1988) read our decision in *Mijares* as holding that "possession of illegal drugs *solely for the purpose of disposal* does not constitute unlawful possession," and further concluded the defense "is not limited to possession for 'brief moments' only."

To date, with the exception of one published decision that, in dicta, seemingly accepted the rationale and holding of *Cole*, every court that has considered the issue has rejected *Cole*'s expansive reading of *Mijares*'s transitory possession defense. We granted review to clarify the nature and scope of the affirmative defense of transitory possession for disposal first announced in *Mijares*. We conclude the rationale and holding of *Cole* misconstrues the defense as devised in *Mijares*, and that *Cole* should therefore be disapproved. Accordingly, the judgment of the Court of Appeal will be affirmed.

On June 3, 1997, defendant Robert Louis Martin was living with his girlfriend, Janelle Davis, and her 19-year-old son, Guy Davis, in Hemet, California. Sometime in the late afternoon a family altercation commenced at the home during a visit by Janelle's nephew, Charles Trip, and his wife, Nicole Trip. Defendant returned home with his three young children shortly after Charles and Nicole arrived. According to Janelle, who testified for the defense, when defendant entered the house she called him into the kitchen, handed him a small packet of white powder she had just discovered in Guy's room, which she suspected to be drugs, and asked defendant to "[g]et rid of it." The two then returned to the living room and began arguing with the visitors.

The melee escalated. Guy Davis entered the argument and, according to his mother's testimony, hit defendant with a pipe, accidentally hitting her as well. Nicole Trip testified Guy was wielding a small "bat" and defendant had picked up a chair and was holding it over his head in a threatening manner. As the visitors and a neighbor, Kenneth Biggs, became involved in the fracas, defendant yelled for everyone to get out of the house. Defendant's children ran from the house, and most of the adults also exited, including defendant. Ultimately, defendant wound up outside in the alley behind the house, facing a group of adults comprised of family members and neighbors as he screamed and swung a metal pipe around himself in an arc, as one would swing a baseball bat. Defendant also picked up and threw rocks at the group, hitting a neighbor, Naomi Biggs, in the leg. Nicole Trip testified that as she tried to go past defendant to enter the house to call police,[2] defendant stepped in her direction and took a "full swing" at her with the pipe. She "jump[ed] back" and the pipe missed her by three or four feet. Defendant did not actually hit anyone with the pipe during the episode.

Police officers Randy Jahn and Scott Jernagan arrived on the scene at 7:00 p.m. They found defendant and a neighbor, Kenneth Biggs, in a fighting stance with others standing around. A three-foot length of pipe was recovered from the ground six inches from where defendant was standing. After questioning defendant and the others at the scene for approximately 30 minutes, Officer Jahn handcuffed defendant and took him into custody, and Officer Jernagan transported him to the Hemet police station. At the station Officer Jernagan searched defendant's pants pockets and discovered a "bindle" containing .12 grams of methamphetamine. When Officer Jahn questioned defendant about the methamphetamine, he responded, "I don't know how I got it, and it's not mine. I don't know how it got there."

Defendant was charged with two felonies and two misdemeanors: assault with a deadly weapon (swinging the pipe at victim Nicole Trip); possession of methamphetamine; misdemeanor battery (hitting Naomi Biggs with rocks); and misdemeanor fighting in public. The misdemeanor charge of fighting in public was dismissed pursuant to section 1385 prior to the start of trial. Defendant was found guilty by a jury of the three remaining charges.

The Court of Appeal . . . rejected defendant's claim that the trial court erred in refusing to give a defense-requested [jury instruction] pertaining to the possession of methamphetamine charge (the standard version was given) and affirmed the judgment and sentence in all other respects.

The essential elements of unlawful possession of a controlled substance are "dominion and control of the substance in a quantity usable for consumption or sale, with knowledge of its presence and of its restricted dangerous drug character. Each of these elements may be established circumstantially." It has been observed that the statute proscribing the unlawful possession of controlled substances "makes possession illegal without regard to the specific intent in possessing the substance." *People v. Sullivan* 215 Cal. App. 3d 1446, 1452 (1989). Although the possessor's

---

2. There was also evidence that defendant himself, at Janelle's request, had called the police when the argument first erupted.

knowledge of the presence of the controlled substance and its nature as a restricted dangerous drug must be shown, no further showing of a subjective mental state is required.

Intent to possess the controlled substance for a minimally prescribed period of time has never been an element of the statutes criminalizing simple possession. Nonetheless, in *Mijares,* we held that, under limited circumstances, facts showing only a "brief," "transitory" or "momentary" possession could constitute a complete defense to the crime.[5]

In *Mijares* the principal question presented was whether the act of momentarily handling a narcotic for the sole purpose of disposal constituted unlawful "possession" within the meaning of Health and Safety Code former section 11500. Defendant Mijares was observed by a woman bystander as he leaned inside a parked car and slapped the passenger (his friend) across the face. Moments later he was seen removing an object from the passenger compartment of the car, which he threw into a nearby field. He then drove his friend, who was suffering from a heroin overdose, to a fire station. The friend, who was not breathing, was revived and taken away by ambulance while Mijares waited at the station for the police. The authorities recovered the object tossed into the field and determined it contained heroin and related paraphernalia, whereupon Mijares was arrested for possession of narcotics. At trial Mijares claimed he believed his friend was overdosing and needed medical help. Suspecting the friend might still have narcotics on his person if he had recently taken drugs, Mijares looked inside the friend's pockets, found the narcotics outfit, and threw it out of the car before driving to the fire station for help.

We explained in *Mijares* that "in throwing the heroin out of the car, defendant Mijares maintained momentary possession for the sole purpose of putting an end to the unlawful possession of [his friend]." We concluded that the physical control inherent "during the brief moment involved in abandoning the narcotic" was not possession for purposes of the statute. We reasoned that if such transitory control were to constitute possession, "manifest injustice to admittedly innocent individuals" could result. As an example, we referred to the witness who saw the defendant throw the object. Had she "briefly picked up the package and identified the substance as heroin and then placed the outfit back on the ground, during the time after which she had realized its narcotic character she, too, would have been guilty of possession under an unduly strict reading of [the statute], notwithstanding the fact that her transitory handling of the contraband might have been motivated solely by curiosity." We refused to "read the possession statutes to authorize convictions under such guileless circumstances." We further relied on certain federal court decisions that had rejected the notion that criminal possession under federal statutes includes such transitory activity as the momentary handling of drugs. We

5. The *Mijares* theory has been alternately described as the "temporary possession defense," the "momentary possession defense," the "transitory possession defense," and the "disposal defense."

noted that the Seventh Circuit Court of Appeals had reversed a federal narcotics conviction, declaring, "To 'possess' means to have actual control, care and management of, and not a passing control, fleeting and shadowy in its nature."[6]

Our decision in *Mijares* gave rise to the initial version of [California Jury Instruction No. 12.06], entitled Momentary Possession as Not Unlawful.[7] Nearly two decades later, the court in *Cole* concluded the core holding of our decision in *Mijares* was that "possession of illegal drugs *solely for the purpose of disposal* does not constitute unlawful possession," and that the defense recognized in *Mijares* "is not limited to possession for 'brief moments' only." Defendant Cole claimed he had seized cocaine from his teenage daughter and placed it in his safe while he and his wife decided how to dispose of it. The cocaine was found in the safe by police the following day during a search pursuant to a warrant. The *Cole* court concluded the trial court had erred in defining constructive possession for the jury followed by an instruction based on *Mijares* because the jury might have accepted Cole's claim—that he had only "momentarily handled the cocaine for purposes of disposal or abandonment"—but nevertheless felt it had to convict him because the drugs remained "in his constructive possession in the safe for more than 'brief moments.' . . ."

The court held: "For guidance on retrial, we suggest the instruction could be tailored as follows: If the defendant physically controlled the substance solely for the purpose of its disposal, such possession would not be unlawful even though he knew its nature as a controlled substance. Length of time of possession is one of the factors which may be considered when deciding whether the defendant physically handled the substance solely for disposal."

Accordingly, [California Jury Instruction No. 12.06] was revised in the wake of *Cole*. The instruction was renamed Possession—Not Unlawful, reference to "momentary possession" was deleted, and a paragraph was added pursuant to the suggested language in *Cole* stating that, "Length of time of possession is one of the factors that may be considered in deciding whether the defendant physically handled the substance solely for abandonment, disposal, or destruction."

---

6. We also found support for defendant Mijares's position in a Prohibition era case, *Garland v. State* (1933) 165 Miss. 136, in which the Mississippi Supreme Court declared that a wife who had been arrested for throwing out a jug of illegal alcohol had possessed it for the sole purpose of putting an end to the unlawful possession of the liquor by her husband. Paraphrasing *Garland*, we observed that "in throwing the heroin out of the car, defendant Mijares maintained momentary possession for the sole purpose of putting an end to the unlawful possession of [his passenger]", and that Mijares's jury therefore should have been instructed that the possession prohibited by Health and Safety Code former section 11500 "does not include mere[] handling for only brief moments prior to abandoning the narcotic."

7. The instruction provided that possession of an item is not unlawful where (1) possession is "momentary" and "based on neither ownership nor the right to exercise control over" the item; (2) the item is "possessed in furtherance of its abandonment or destruction"; (3) the item is possessed "for the purpose of terminating the unlawful possession of it by another person or preventing another person from acquiring possession of it"; and (4) "control is not exercised over the [item] for the purpose of preventing its imminent seizure by law enforcement."

[W]ithin one year after *Cole* was decided a different [California] appellate court disagreed with *Cole*'s expansive reading of the *Mijares* defense [in *People v. Sullivan*]. The defendant in *Sullivan* was stopped for Vehicle Code violations, whereupon it was quickly discovered that his Land Cruiser contained chemicals, a gram scale, plastic baggies and other items commonly associated with the manufacture of methamphetamine. He was searched and found in possession of a quantity of methamphetamine. The police proceeded to Sullivan's house and searched a locked shed in which they found more chemicals and paraphernalia associated with methamphetamine labs. Sullivan's defense was that all the chemicals, paraphernalia and quantities of methamphetamine belonged to a person who rented the shed behind his house. Since he (Sullivan) was on probation for a drug offense, he was afraid to call the police. Knowing the methamphetamine materials were dangerous, and fearful for his children, Sullivan loaded them into his Land Cruiser and was heading to an industrial park to dispose of them in a dumpster when he was stopped by police a quarter-mile from his house.

Sullivan contended on appeal that the trial court had erred in refusing his requested instruction, purportedly derived from the holding of *Mijares*, that "'Limited handling of contraband, such as for the purpose of abandonment, will not support a conviction for possession.'" The trial court had rejected the requested instruction because the facts did not indicate a "fleeting possession" such as occurred in *Mijares*. Sullivan therefore sought to invoke the holding of *Cole* which, he urged, held that "fleeting possession" was not a necessary prerequisite for the *Mijares* instruction.

The *Sullivan* court disagreed, reasoning as follows: "We think the *Cole* court, by abandoning the requirement the possession be 'fleeting,' has unreasonably expanded the *Mijares* rule. *Mijares*'s rule arose from a situation involving a fleeting, de minimis possession and a reflexive act of abandonment. The Supreme Court's holding was that this de minimis possession and reflexive response was not a criminal possession[.] [T]his rule is one which is an understandable and simple rule. *Cole* complicates the rule by bringing in inquiries into the defendant's subjective intent in possessing the contraband. These inquiries are not suggested by *Mijares* or supported by the language of the statute. *Mijares*'s focus was on the fleeting nature of the possession (during the instant of abandonment), not on the subjective mental state of the defendant. The statute makes possession illegal without regard to the specific intent in possessing the substance. We conclude the *Cole* court misinterpreted the *Mijares* decision and erred in deleting the 'momentary' possession requirement. We therefore decline to follow *Cole*, preferring instead to apply pure *Mijares*."

We agree with the decision[] in *Sullivan* that reject[ed] *Cole*'s expansive reading of our opinion in *Mijares*. As noted, the statutes (past and present) at issue in the cases we have reviewed all make unlawful the possession of enumerated controlled substances "without regard to the [possessor's] specific intent in possessing the substance." As aptly explained in *People v. Spry*[:] "When a defendant relies on the *Mijares* defense, he or she essentially admits the commission of the offense of simple possession of narcotics: The defendant exercised control over the narcotics, he or she knew of its nature and presence, and possessed a usable amount. However, the defendant additionally asserts that he or she possessed the narcotics for the limited purpose of disposal, abandonment, or destruction. *Mijares* does not serve to negate an element of the offense of possession of narcotics. Instead, it offers a judicially created exception of lawful possession under certain specific circumstances as a matter of public policy, similar to the defenses of entrapment and necessity."

We agree that recognition of a "momentary possession" defense serves the salutary purpose and sound public policy of encouraging disposal and discouraging retention of dangerous items such as controlled substances and firearms. The theory of defense to unlawful possession of narcotics announced in *Mijares* "arose from a situation involving a fleeting, de minimis possession and a reflexive act of abandonment. [Our] holding was that this de minimis possession and reflexive response was not a criminal possession." Throughout our opinion we repeatedly focused on the fleeting and transitory nature of Mijares's possession of his passenger's "narcotics outfit" during the instant he removed it from the latter's person and threw it into the nearby field. We concluded in *Mijares* that such momentary or transitory handling or possession, coupled with intent to dispose, could establish a defense to the crime of unlawful possession of narcotics. *Cole*'s expansion of the momentary possession defense to lengthier possession incidental to the defendant's intent to dispose of controlled substances effectively rewrites the statutory requirements of unlawful possession by introducing a new element of "specific intent to retain."[9]

We conclude that the defense of transitory possession devised in *Mijares* applies only to momentary or transitory possession of contraband for the purpose of disposal, and that the trial court did not err in refusing defendant's requested instruction based on the holding in *Cole*. To the extent *People v. Cole* [is] inconsistent with the views expressed herein, [it is] disapproved.

Returning to the facts of this case, even assuming arguendo the jury fully credited Janelle Davis's testimony that she found the methamphetamine bindle in her son Guy's room and handed it over to defendant with a request that he dispose of it, defendant was still not entitled to even the pre-*Cole* version of the *Mijares* transitory possession instruction that he received. The Court of Appeal concluded as much as four hours had elapsed between the time Davis first gave the narcotics to defendant (when he first returned to the home at approximately 3:00 p.m., 20 minutes after the Tripps had arrived) and the time of the arrival of the officers on the scene of the altercation at 7:00 p.m. Defendant vigorously contested the Court of Appeal's conclusion that the time of possession was as long as four hours. We agree that the testimony in the record upon which that conclusion was based is equivocal. We note, however, that at the instruction-settling conference, defense counsel conceded the relevant time of

9. We reiterate: although there is no such specific intent element in the crime of simple possession of controlled substances, brief or transitory possession of narcotics *with the intent to dispose of the contraband* can establish the *Mijares* defense of transitory possession.

possession was "not a fleeting instantaneous possession, such as in *Sullivan*."[11] In any event, according to the officers' testimony, an additional 30 minutes elapsed between the time they arrived and questioned defendant and others, and the time defendant was placed under arrest. At least another 10 minutes elapsed from the time defendant was arrested and transported to the police station until the point he was searched, leading to discovery of the narcotics in his pants pocket. There is no indication in the record that during these periods defendant made any attempt, or took any physical action, to dispose of the methamphetamine bindle, much less enlist the assistance of the officers in doing so. Indeed, there is nothing in the record from which to infer that defendant would have voluntarily relinquished possession of the drugs were it not for the search conducted incident to his arrest and booking that led to recovery of the methamphetamine bindle. On these facts, defendant was not entitled to a *Mijares* instruction on transitory possession for the purpose of disposal.

The judgment of the Court of Appeal is affirmed.

Kennard, J., concurring.

I concur in the result.

In *People v. Mijares* this court held that momentary handling of a controlled substance for the sole purpose of disposal is not possession. Although the majority repeatedly states that in *Mijares* this court held that momentary handling of a controlled substance is a "defense" to a charge of possessing that substance, this court did not there create or recognize any affirmative defense to such a charge. Rather, this court in *Mijares* simply noted that the issue of momentary handling "goes to the very essence of the offense." Thus, unlike the majority, I would reaffirm *Mijares* without modification.

The *Martin* court concluded that "*Cole*'s expansion of the momentary possession defense to lengthier possession incidental to the defendant's intent to dispose of controlled substances effectively rewrites the statutory requirements of unlawful possession by introducing a new element of 'specific intent to retain.'" In footnote 9, however, *Martin* emphasizes that "although there is no such specific intent element in the crime of simple possession of controlled substances, brief or transitory possession of narcotics *with the intent to dispose of the contraband* can establish the *Mijares* defense of transitory possession." Do you agree that there is a principled distinction between the use of intent in *Martin*'s test and *Cole's*? Or do both tests interject a defendant's "specific intent" into the crime of possession?

While the *Martin* court clearly disapproves of the rule adopted in *Cole*, does the decision articulate a clear standard to govern future cases? The court holds that the

11. In oral argument before this court, appellate counsel likewise acknowledged that as far as *Mijares*'s brief or momentary time requirement, the facts of this case do not meet the *Mijares* test. Appellate counsel urged that we instead follow *Cole* and conclude "it all boils down to an issue of intent."

possession for disposal defense "applies only to momentary or transitory possession of contraband." But what constitutes "momentary or transitory" possession? The court does not provide a direct answer, though its analysis indicates that possession for just a few hours may be too long as a matter of law.

Utah v. Miller presents another take on the possession for disposal rule.

Utah v. Miller

Supreme Court of Utah
2008 UT 61

Durrant, J.

Following a jury trial, Curtis Miller ("Miller") was convicted of two counts of felony possession of a controlled substance in violation of Utah Code section 58-37-8(2)(a)(I) (the "possession statute"). Miller seeks to have his conviction reversed and his case remanded for a new trial. He claims that the trial court erred in failing to instruct the jury on his proposed defense of innocent possession. For the reasons detailed below, we remand for a new trial in which Miller will be entitled to an instruction on the defense of innocent possession.

The material facts are not in dispute. Miller works as a general contractor, and in April 2004, he had a crew of about ten men working for him on a basement remodel project. Among the crew were Jason Lemon and Vincent Henderson. On April 10, the crew finished the project and had a party at Miller's house to celebrate. About twenty people, including Lemon and Henderson, came to Miller's home that night.

According to Miller, by 2:00 a.m., only one of Miller's friends, who was asleep on Miller's sofa, remained at his home. Then, at 2:30 a.m., a woman arrived at Miller's door asking if he had called an escort.[1] Miller said, "no," but the woman demanded that he pay her $85.00 for "showing up." Miller refused.

After the woman left, Miller started cleaning up his apartment in preparation for a visit from his grandchildren the next day. Fifteen minutes later, the same woman returned with "two other guys," who were yelling and "kicking the door." After Miller opened the door and told the group he was calling 911, they left. Miller did not call 911 at that time. The men returned shortly thereafter and "were even louder[,]. . . . [were] kicking [Miller's] door[,]" and "were very threatening, saying that they were going to beat [him] and make him pay." In response to this, Miller called 911 for the first of four times that night.

Sergeant John Beener responded to Miller's first call, checked around the home's exterior, but found no one. Sergeant Beener then entered Miller's home and talked with Miller, who appeared to be "extremely intoxicated, [with] bloodshot, watery eyes, slurred[,] interrupted speech, a lack of comprehension, [and] a loss of balance."

---

1. Jason Lemon testified that while at the party, Vincent Henderson was "really wasted . . . [and] excited that he had called this escort service." He also testified that Henderson "announced it to everybody," but left the party before anyone from the escort service arrived.

Miller told Sergeant Beener about the threats he had received from the escort service. When Sergeant Beener attempted to get more information from Miller, Miller accused Sergeant Beener of being "on the take" from the escort service. Sergeant Beener left Miller's home because he did not consider the issue to be a police matter. He got into his police car and pulled into a parking lot across the street from Miller's home to complete paperwork.

After Sergeant Beener left, Miller began cleaning up again and found a glass pipe and a pill bottle on his coffee table. He recognized the pill bottle as one containing a prescription medication, so he put it in his pants pocket with the intention of later putting it in his medicine cabinet—out of the reach of his grandchildren—and then returning it to its owner. Although Miller did not look at the name on the bottle before placing it in his pocket, he learned after his arrest that it belonged to Henderson. Miller also put the glass pipe in his pants pocket. As Miller was cleaning, the escort service called Miller's home one or two times to demand payment. In response, Miller called 911 the second and third times. Sergeant Beener did not respond to Miller's second and third calls because he "was sitting there staring at the residence" and could see that no one was at Miller's home. When Miller called the fourth time, Sergeant Beener returned to Miller's home and arrested him for abuse of the 911 system and for intoxication.

In a search incident to Miller's arrest, Sergeant Beener found the glass pipe and the prescription bottle with Vincent Henderson's name on it in Miller's pants pocket. The bottle contained four pills of oxycodone, four pills of hydrocodone, and one pill for gastro-intestinal problems.

Sergeant Beener prepared to take Miller to jail and, at Miller's request, went to Miller's bedroom to get Miller's shoes and keys. While Sergeant Beener was in the bedroom, he found "a mirror and a pipe laying out."

Miller was charged with two counts of possession of a controlled substance, both third degree felonies; one count of possession of drug paraphernalia, a class B misdemeanor; emergency reporting abuse, a class B misdemeanor; and intoxication, a class C misdemeanor. In November 2004, Miller was bound over on all charges and was tried to a jury in June 2006.

At the close of Miller's jury trial, the trial court excused the jury, and Miller's counsel proposed that the court give the jury an instruction on the defense of innocent possession. The proposed instruction, which was based on a weapons charge defense, provided that possession was innocent if "(1) the firearm was attained innocently and held with no illicit or illegal purpose, and (2) . . . the possession of the firearm was transitory; that is that the defendant took adequate measures to rid himself of possession of the firearm as promptly as reasonably possible."

The trial court rejected the proposed instruction. The jury found Miller guilty of two counts of possession of a controlled substance and possession of drug paraphernalia but acquitted him of abusing the reporting system and intoxication. The court sentenced Miller to two terms of zero to five years, suspended the terms, and ordered Miller to report to jail to serve 365 days followed by thirty-six months probation.

Miller timely appealed, claiming that the court erred in refusing to instruct the jury on his proposed defense of innocent possession of the controlled substances.[2] Miller claims that he was entitled to an instruction on this defense because the evidence supported his claim that "his possession of the drugs was innocent, where he did not take control of the drugs for any illegal purpose; rather, he took possession of the bottle in order to return it to its lawful owner."

"Whether a jury instruction correctly states the law presents a question of law which we review for correctness."

Our analysis focuses on Utah Code section 58-37-8(2)(a)(I), the possession statute under which Miller was charged.

Miller was charged under a statute that prohibits possession of certain controlled substances, including oxycodone and hydrocodone. Utah Code section 58-37-8(2)(a)(I) provides that a defendant is guilty of the crime of possession if he (1) knowingly and intentionally, (2) possesses, (3) a controlled substance.

Utah's criminal law is statutory. Thus, all criminal defenses "must be grounded in the specific code sections" under which the defendant is charged. The possession statute under which Miller was charged provides an affirmative defense to the crime of possession in only one instance—if the controlled substance "was obtained under a valid prescription or order, directly from a practitioner." Because this possession statute does not provide an explicit affirmative defense of innocent possession, the defense exists only if the statute implicitly includes it. And the State concedes that—at least in some measure—the statute does.

During oral argument, the State was asked how Miller, or any homeowner, could avoid criminal liability if a house guest inadvertently leaves a bottle of controlled substance prescription pills in the homeowner's home. The State responded that a homeowner would not violate the possession statute if he or she immediately called the police or the owner of the medication. But during either call, the homeowner would clearly "possess" the medication.[9] By admitting that certain types of possession do not violate the statute, the State conceded that some form of innocent possession defense exists. We agree.

The plain language of the possession statute provides that a defendant is guilty of the crime of possession if he (1) knowingly and intentionally, (2) possesses, (3)

2. Miller has not appealed his conviction for possession of drug paraphernalia; therefore, we limit our discussion and application of the innocent possession defense to Miller's possession of the controlled substances.

9. Under the theory of constructive possession, a person may be found guilty of possession where drugs or contraband are in the person's home even if not on his or her person. *See e.g.*, State v. Layman, 1999 UT 79 (2000), 985 P.2d 911.

a controlled substance. The Controlled Substance Act defines "possession" using terms such as "retaining" and "maintaining," and it provides that possession may be inferred if the person charged has "the ability and the intent to exercise dominion and control over" the item. This definition does not, however, clarify whether the term "possess," as it is used in the possession statute, includes the type of innocent possession at issue here—temporary possession for the purpose of returning a controlled substance to its lawful owner. And when we "find a provision that causes doubt or uncertainty in its application, we must analyze the act in its entirety and harmonize its provisions in accordance with the legislative intent and purpose."

In this case, the legislature has clearly evinced its intent regarding how courts are to interpret the penal code. Most important is the legislature's directive that the penal code shall not "be strictly construed." Rather, courts are to construe the code's provisions "according to the fair import of their terms *to promote justice* and to effect the objects of the law and the general purposes of Section 76-1-104." Section 76-1-104 further advises courts to construe the code to "[d]efine adequately the conduct and mental state which constitute each offense and *safeguard conduct that is without fault from condemnation.*"

Strictly construing the term "possess" to include every type of possession, whether culpable or innocent, contradicts the legislature's directive to avoid strictly construing the code, and it is contrary to the policy goals of safeguarding faultless conduct and promoting justice. This is most apparent in the many examples of injustices that may result from strictly construing the term "possess." A daughter who no longer lives at home but who picks up her sick mother's prescription medication and drives it to her mother's home, for example, could be guilty of felony possession under a strict construction of the term "possess."[19] And, as this case demonstrates, a house guest who inadvertently leaves a prescription bottle of pills at a homeowner's home creates an impossible situation for the homeowner wherein she could do nothing short of immediately fleeing her home to avoid "possessing" the pills. Because construing the term "possess" to include brief, innocent possession contradicts the legislature's interpretative guidelines and creates a myriad of absurd prosecutorial possibilities, we hold that the term "possess," as it is used in section 58-37-8(2)(a)(I), excludes transitory possession of a controlled substance for the purpose of returning it to its lawful owner. That is, we hold that the possession

19. Universally, courts that recognize an innocent possession defense cite public policy reasons for doing so, chiefly to "prevent a conviction for an innocent act." *People v. E.C.*, 761 N.Y.S.2d 443, 445 (Sup. Ct. 2003). In *People v. E.C.*, the New York appellate court recognized an innocent possession defense and hypothesized that a juror who handles illegal drugs as part of a review of the evidence would be guilty of possession under a strict interpretation of the possession statute. *Id.* California also recognizes the innocent possession defense and applies it to "fleeting and transitory" possession of illegal drugs "for the purpose of disposal." *People v. Martin*, 25 P.3d 1081, 1088–89, n.9 (Cal. 2001).

statute implicitly includes the defense of innocent possession.[20] We next address the parameters of that defense.

Miller proposed an instruction for the innocent possession of drugs based on an instruction that the Court of Appeals for the District of Columbia recognizes for the innocent possession of firearms. Tailoring the innocent possession of firearms defense to a controlled substance possession charge, the defense applies if (1) the controlled substance was attained innocently and held with no illicit or illegal purpose, and (2) the possession of the controlled substance was transitory; that is, that the defendant took adequate measures to rid himself of possession of the controlled substance as promptly as reasonably possible.

This is an appropriate instruction. It requires that a standard of reasonableness be applied to the innocent possession of a controlled substance, and in so doing, does not impose an obligation on individuals to focus their efforts exclusively on returning a controlled substance to its lawful owner once it comes into their possession. Nor does this instruction impose an arbitrary time limit for return of a controlled substance or require only fleeting or momentary possession that may not be practical given the circumstance. If a possessor of a controlled substance takes reasonable action to return that substance to its lawful owner, possession may be longer than momentary, yet the possessor would still be entitled to an instruction on the defense of innocent possession. The instruction leaves to the jury the question of whether a defendant took adequate measures to rid himself of a controlled substance as promptly as reasonably possible.

Because the trial court refused Miller's proposed instruction, we remand for a new trial at which Miller is entitled to the following innocent possession defense instruction: the defendant's possession of the controlled substances found in his pocket did not violate Utah Code subsection 58-37-8(2)(a)(i) if (1) the controlled substance was obtained innocently and held with no illicit or illegal purpose, and (2) the possession of the controlled substance was transitory; that is, the defendant took adequate measures to rid himself of possession of the controlled substance as promptly as reasonably possible. It will be for the jury to decide whether, given this instruction along with the facts Miller presents, his possession was innocent.

c. What Qualifies as Disposal?

In *Miller*, the Utah Supreme Court applied the possession for disposal defense where the defendant sought to return a lawfully prescribed controlled substance to its owner. Should the defense apply to transitory possession of an illegal drug for purposes of returning it to its "owner"? Or, for illegal drugs, should the defense be

20. We also note that the legislature has provided the statutory defense of justification. The justification defense protects from prosecution conduct that is "justified for *any* . . . *reason* under the laws of this state." Utah Code Ann. § 76-2-401(1)(e). This is a broad catchall provision that allows courts to ensure that justice is done. In this case, we believe that justice requires interpreting the possession statute to include the defense of innocent possession.

limited to cases where an individual plans to throw the substance away or turn it over to the police? In the next case, *Adams v. Alaska*, the Court of Appeals of Alaska adopts an unusually forgiving interpretation of what counts as "disposal." Though other jurisdictions have not followed the *Adams* court's approach, the case is useful for thinking more about the crime of possession and about what sort of purpose a defendant ought to have in order to qualify for the innocent possession defense.

Adams v. Alaska

Court of Appeals of Alaska
706 P.2d 1183 (1985)

Coats, J.

Daniel Adams was convicted, following a jury trial, of one count of misconduct involving a controlled substance in the third degree, and two counts of misconduct involving a controlled substance in the fourth degree. The misconduct involving a controlled substance in the third degree count consisted of a charge that on August 3, 1983 Adams possessed approximately three and one-half ounces of cocaine with the intent to deliver that substance. The two counts of misconduct involving a controlled substance in the fourth degree involved charges that Adams possessed approximately one-fourth of an ounce of cocaine on August 23, 1983, and that Adams possessed approximately one-eighth of an ounce of cocaine on August 25, 1983. Judge Victor Carlson imposed a sentence of seven years with three years suspended on the possession with intent to deliver count, and sentences of three years with one year suspended on the possession of cocaine counts. The sentences were all concurrent. Adams appeals his convictions and sentences. We reverse Adams' conviction for possession of cocaine with intent to deliver but affirm his convictions and sentences for possession of cocaine.

The trial in this case focused mainly on the charge that, on August 3, 1983, Adams possessed approximately three and one-half ounces of cocaine with the intent to deliver that substance. Adams testified that he was a user of cocaine, and admitted possessing cocaine on August 25, 1983. Adams additionally indicated that he could have had the one-quarter ounce of cocaine on August 23, 1983. However, Adams testified that his possession of the three and one-half ounces of cocaine on August 3, 1983 was involuntary.

In support of his contention that he involuntarily possessed the cocaine Adams testified that Alex Resek was a cocaine dealer and that he got his cocaine from Resek. On August 3, 1983 both Alex Resek and his family and Adams and his family were in Campbell Creek Park. Daniel Adams' car, a Corvette, was parked in the lot; the top was down and the windows were open. According to Adams, Alex Resek borrowed his keys so he could listen to the radio in the Corvette. After going to the car, Resek came back to Adams and told Adams to watch the car because there was something in it. Adams testified that he concluded that Resek had left cocaine in the car, and that he told Resek to get it out. Resek refused and said he would be back. Alex Resek then left the park and did not return. Adams discovered that Resek had left a brown bag in Adams' car. Adams testified that he did not look inside the bag.

Approximately forty-five minutes after Alex Resek placed the bag in the car Mark Flechsing arrived. Flechsing was one of Alex Resek's closest collaborators in the cocaine selling operation and, unknown to Adams or Resek, was also operating as a police informant. Flechsing testified that when he arrived at the park, Alex Resek was gone. Adams gave Flechsing the brown paper bag from the car and told him to get the package out of there. Additionally, Adams instructed Flechsing to meet him at the Hall Closet, a business that Adams owned which sold drug paraphernalia. Flechsing drove off and secretly met with a police officer who took a sample of the contents of the brown package. The sample was tested. It was cocaine. Flechsing then drove to meet Adams. After Flechsing reached the Hall Closet, Alex Resek arrived and had Flechsing place the brown package in his car. The package was not taken into the Hall Closet.

Adams' defense at trial was that he had never voluntarily possessed the cocaine found in his car. He contended that Resek placed the cocaine in his car without his permission, and that when he found out it was in his car he attempted to have Resek take the cocaine out of the car. When that failed he gave the cocaine to Flechsing to return to Resek. On the other hand, the state argued that Adams was deeply involved in Resek's cocaine selling business and that Adams' possession of the cocaine had been entirely voluntary. The state presented evidence that during the time the cocaine was in Adams' car an off-duty police officer coincidently happened to come into the park and talk to another police officer in a marked police car. The state argued that Adams had panicked and had the cocaine removed from his car because of the presence of the police, not because he involuntarily possessed the cocaine.

Judge Carlson instructed the jury on what constituted possession: "'possess' means having physical possession or the exercise of dominion or control over property. A passing control, fleeting and shadowy in nature does not constitute possession." After some deliberation the jury asked for an explanation of "passing control." The court gave the following supplemental instruction, which defense counsel objected to:

> SUPPLEMENTAL INSTRUCTION NO. 1
>
> "Passing control" of a controlled substance is control for only such a period of time as is reasonably necessary for the possessor to learn of the nature of the substance and to make a *legal disposition of it by throwing it away, destroying it, or by giving it to police.*
>
> If you find that the defendant had control of a controlled substance only for the purpose of putting to an end another's illegal possession, you may not find him guilty of a crime. For example, if a person finds a heroin addict unconscious on the street, empties the addict's pockets of heroin and throws the heroin away before taking the heroin addict to the hospital, that

> person may not be convicted for that brief control of the heroin. Similarly, if a person finds a package on the street, opens it, finds cocaine and then puts the package back down and walks away, that person may not be convicted for that brief control of the cocaine.
>
> If you find that the defendant had control of a controlled substance only because another forced it upon him, *you may find the defendant guilty only if you find he did not act reasonably in disposing of it.*
>
> "Passing control" is not a defense for the person who, having possession of a substance he knows is a controlled substance and fearing that he is about to be apprehended by police, removes the controlled substance from his immediate possession.
>
> If you find beyond a reasonable doubt that the defendant possessed a controlled substance long enough after knowing it was a controlled substance to have had a reasonable opportunity to dispose of it through legal channels (be throwing it away or giving it to police, for example), then you may find the defendant guilty; if this has not been proved beyond a reasonable doubt, you must find the defendant not guilty.

Adams argued at trial, and now argues on appeal, that the supplemental instruction was erroneous because it unduly restricted ways in which a person could have "passing control." Adams argues that if the jury believed him that Resek forced the cocaine on him by placing it in his car, the jury could have read the supplemental instruction as requiring him to get rid of the cocaine by "throwing it away, destroying it, or by giving it to the police." He argues that the jury therefore could have believed him that he got rid of the cocaine by returning it to Resek through Flechsing, and yet have convicted him under the supplemental instruction because he did not dispose of the cocaine as the instruction required.

We agree with Adams that it is a reasonable interpretation of the jury instruction that a person who has cocaine forced upon him must throw it away, destroy it, or give it to the police. Therefore, we agree that under the given jury instruction the jury could have believed Adams' version that he came into possession of the cocaine involuntarily and that he got rid of it as soon as possible by giving it to Flechsing to return to Resek, and still have convicted him under the supplemental instruction. The next question is whether Adams' version of events, if believed, constitutes possession of cocaine with intent to distribute. Alaska case authority on this issue appears to be sparse. In *Moreau v. State,* 588 P.2d 275 (Alaska 1978), the supreme court dealt with a case where the defendant momentarily possessed a napkin which contained heroin residue. Moreau was staying in a house which the police entered under a search warrant. When her co-defendant, Stone, spit out the napkin, Moreau picked the napkin up and may have attempted to move towards the bathroom. The police grabbed her and took the napkin. The supreme court held that there was insufficient evidence to convict Moreau of possession of heroin. The court held that momentary possession for purposes of disposing of a controlled substance did not constitute possession. In its holding, the court approved of the definition of possession in *United States v. Landry*, 257 F.2d 425, 431 (7th Cir. 1958):

> To "possess" means to have actual control, care and management of, and not a passing control, fleeting and shadowy in nature. (Citation omitted.)

The *Moreau* court also relied on *People v. Mijares*, 6 Cal. 3d 415 (1971). In that case the defendant testified that in attempting to help a friend who had overdosed on drugs, he discovered a handkerchief which contained heroin. He threw the heroin out of the window of a car. The *Mijares* court held that the defendant's version, if believed, was not possession of heroin in violation of the statute.

In addition to the authority that the defendant cites, we have also considered the Model Penal Code. Section 201(4) of the Model Penal Code states, "possession is an act, within the meaning of this section, if the possessor knowingly procured or received the thing possessed or was aware of his control thereof for a sufficient period to have been able to terminate his possession."

The authorities to which the parties have cited us and our own research have not clearly resolved the problem. However, it is clear that more is required than momentary or fleeting possession of a controlled substance; some sort of dominion or control of the substance is required. We note that the state has not cited any cases standing for the proposition that a person who has drugs forced upon him is required to dispose of the drugs by throwing them away or giving them to the police.

It appears to us that if the jury believed Adams' version of the events, Adams was not in possession of cocaine because he was not aware of his control of the cocaine "for a sufficient period to have been able to terminate his possession[.]" Under Adams' version the cocaine belonged to Alex Resek. Adams came into possession involuntarily and terminated his possession as soon as reasonably possible by returning it to Alex Resek through Flechsing. This appears to us to be the sort of fleeting possession which the cases allow. We do not believe that he was required to turn the cocaine over to the police or destroy it in order to not be in possession. His returning it promptly to Resek through Flechsing would be sufficient to terminate his possession.

Since the jury could have understood the trial court's instructions to require Adams to terminate his possession of the cocaine by "throwing it away, destroying it, or by giving it to the police," we reverse Adams' conviction for possession of cocaine with intent to distribute. However, we affirm Adams' two convictions for possession of cocaine since he essentially admitted the incidents on which those convictions were based. Those convictions could not have been affected by the supplemental instruction.

The conviction for misconduct involving a controlled substance in the third degree is REVERSED. The convictions and sentences for misconduct involving a controlled substance in the fourth degree are AFFIRMED.

The possession for disposal doctrine can sometimes work its way into a criminal defense attorney's practice in unexpected ways. How should a criminal defense attorney respond to a client who asks him to take possession of contraband? A Connecticut case presented this problem in the context of possession of child pornography. A church found pornographic pictures of children on its choirmaster's laptop. The church took the laptop to its attorney, Phillip Russell, and told him that it did not want to report the crime. "So Russell chose what he likely saw as the only remaining option to protect the church from illegal possession of the images—he destroyed the hard drive. Federal prosecutors indicted Russell on two counts of obstruction of justice, each carrying a twenty-year prison term." Stephen Gillers, *Guns, Fruits, Drugs, and Documents: A Criminal Defense Lawyer's Responsibility for Real Evidence*, 63 Stan. L. Rev. 813 (2011) (discussing the legal and ethical problems that criminal attorneys face when asked by a client to take possession of contraband, stolen property, or evidence of a crime).

3. Constructive Possession

a. Introduction to Constructive Possession

Constructive possession cases can present particularly vexing problems. In a typical constructive possession case, authorities find a controlled substance in an area that more than one person has access to, such as a shared home or a car. Imagine, for example, that the police pull over a vehicle for a traffic violation and see marijuana in plain view sitting on the console between the passenger and the driver. If one of the parties admits the marijuana is theirs, the case might be an easy one. But what if both deny owning the marijuana or stay silent? The marijuana almost surely belongs to either the driver or the passenger (or both) and the police have probable cause to place them both under arrest. See *Maryland v. Pringle*, 540 U.S. 366 (2003). Is this evidence, standing alone, sufficient to prove one or both of them guilty of possession *beyond a reasonable doubt*?

Courts have struggled to craft a constructive possession doctrine capable of protecting the innocent from being convicted simply for being found near someone else's drugs without making it overly difficult to convict the guilty. The result is a body of case law that can be hard to make sense of. In 1971, Judge Edward Tamm of the U.S. Court of Appeals for the District of Columbia Circuit did not pull punches in critiquing constructive possession precedent. "The more cases one reads on constructive possession the deeper is he plunged into a thicket of subjectivity," Tamm wrote. "Successive cases enumerate a continuing re-interpretation which can only be described as judicial whimsy.... Both prosecutor and defendant's attorney present their cases with the unfortunate knowledge that the law of constructive possession is what we will say it is in our next opinion." *United States v. Holland*, 445 F.2d 701, 703–04 (D.C. Cir. 1971) (Tamm, J., concurring). Unfortunately, the law of constructive possession has not become much clearer with time.

Though constructive possession cases remain filled with conflicts, most jurisdictions today have coalesced around at least one basic principle: proximity to contraband, standing alone, is insufficient to prove possession. In *Taylor v. Maryland*, for example, Richard Jamison Taylor had been convicted of marijuana possession after he and four friends were found inside a hotel room with marijuana. The appellate court reversed Taylor's conviction, finding that the evidence was sufficient to prove only that "Taylor was present in a room where marijuana had been smoked recently, that he was aware that it had been smoked, and that Taylor was in proximity to the contraband that was concealed in a container belonging to another." The court explained that "[p]ossession requires more than being in the presence of other persons having possession; it requires the exercise of dominion or control over the thing possessed." 346 Md. 452 (1997).

The basic concept articulated in *Taylor* is straightforward: if a defendant is found in a location (such as a car, a home, or a street corner) with contraband and others have access to that location as well, the defendant's proximity to the contraband or his control over the location are not sufficient to prove he was in possession of the contraband. This principle makes a great deal of sense. If the rule were otherwise, a person would be guilty of possession simply because she was at a party where others were using illegal drugs in her presence or because she was in a car with another passenger who had placed drugs on the vehicle's floor.

But, if proximity to a controlled substance along with knowledge of its presence is insufficient to sustain a conviction for possession, what more is needed? On this issue, courts have continued to have difficulty settling on a consistent set of rules or principles. The materials that follow consider constructive possession cases in three settings: vehicles, open-air drug markets, and go-betweens. As you read each case, consider whether you believe courts have been able to create an objective set of standards to govern constructive possession cases or whether you agree with Judge Tamm's view that "[t]he more cases one reads on constructive possession the deeper [he or she] is plunged into a thicket of subjectivity."

b. Constructive Possession in Vehicles

Regan v. Wyoming

Supreme Court of Wyoming
2015 WY 62

Davis, J.

On October 26, 2012, Regan and his roommate[1] Shayne Trujillo drove from Denver[, Colorado] to Gillette[, Wyoming]. A six-year veteran of the Gillette Police Department, Officer Troy Cyr, pulled them over after they stopped at a yield sign

1. There was a female passenger in the rear of the vehicle but the record tells us nothing more about her.

because there was no traffic on the roadway to yield to, and because the officer could not tell whether the vehicle had a rear license plate. Regan was the driver and owner. When Officer Cyr approached his window, he immediately smelled raw marijuana and requested that a drug dog be dispatched. Officer Vos arrived on the scene, spoke to Officer Cyr, and explained to Regan and Trujillo why he was there. He also smelled marijuana before retrieving his dog, Jordy, from his patrol vehicle. Jordy alerted at the front passenger door, signaling that it had detected the odor of a controlled substance in the car.

Officer Vos then directed Trujillo to get out of the car, looked inside, and saw two glass jars containing what he recognized as marijuana on the passenger floorboard. After further inspection of the vehicle's interior, he discovered a plastic grocery bag, Ziploc sandwich bags, and a large white plastic bin in the passenger and cargo portions of the vehicle. Each contained clumps of a green leafy substance that he recognized as marijuana. The total weight of the marijuana was approximately one and a half pounds. Vos also found paraphernalia commonly associated with the sale of marijuana and $1,000 in cash in the glove box.

The officers arrested Regan and Trujillo and took them to the Gillette police station, where Regan voluntarily consented to an interview. Officer Greg Brothers interviewed Regan, and he testified at trial to Regan's account of the journey to Gillette with Trujillo. While still in Denver, Regan saw Trujillo load marijuana into his vehicle. He told Officer Brothers that he had expressly rejected Trujillo's offer to join in Trujillo's plan to make money distributing marijuana because "it wasn't worth the risk."

When they arrived in Gillette, Trujillo directed Regan to three different locations, and at each one Trujillo got out of the car and delivered marijuana. Regan remained in the vehicle at each stop. He gave the interviewing officer detailed descriptions of each location and the amount of marijuana Trujillo delivered at each stop. He showed him the locations on a map, and then helped officers identify them in an unmarked police car. Regan admitted that a quarter-ounce of the marijuana found in the car was his, but maintained that the rest of the marijuana in the vehicle belonged solely to Trujillo.

Trujillo testified at Regan's trial and corroborated Regan's claim. He confirmed his admission to officers that over a pound of marijuana in the car belonged exclusively to him, and that no one else had anything to do with it. He also confirmed that in the course of entering a guilty plea to felony possession of the marijuana found in Regan's car, he had admitted to the court that more than a pound of marijuana was his.

The jury found Regan guilty of felony possession of marijuana under Wyo. Stat. Ann. § 35-7-1031(c)(iii). He was sentenced to not less than four nor more than five years of incarceration and a $10,000 fine, which were suspended in favor of five years of supervised probation and a $5,000 fine. This appeal was timely perfected.

Our standard for reviewing challenges to the sufficiency of the evidence is well-established. We recently restated it as follows:

> We examine and accept as true the State's evidence and all reasonable inferences which can be drawn from it. We do not consider conflicting evidence presented by the defendant. We do not substitute our judgment for that of the jury; rather, we determine whether a jury could have reasonably concluded each of the elements of the crime was proven beyond a reasonable doubt.

Wyo. Stat. Ann. § 35-7-1031(c)(iii) makes it a felony "for any person knowingly or intentionally to possess [more than three ounces of] a controlled substance [in plant form.]" Regan argues that . . . the State failed to prove that he "possessed" enough marijuana to support a felony conviction.

Wyoming recognizes two kinds of possession of a controlled substance, actual and constructive. Actual possession obviously occurs when an individual has direct physical custody over the substance.

Two scholars have observed that "the courts have constructed a terminology purportedly designed to focus factual inquiries on factors likely to reveal whether the defendant had the ability or capacity to possess the item." Charles H. Whitebread and Ronald Stevens, *Constructive Possession in Narcotics Cases: To Have and Have Not,* 58 Va. L. Rev. 751 (1972). Stated more simply, courts have "extended the concept of possession . . . to include constructive as well as actual possession." *Id.* The State does not argue that Regan's actions amounted to actual possession, at least of a felony quantity of marijuana. Rather, it asserts only that Regan constructively possessed all of the marijuana found in his car.

"The word 'possession' is often used in the criminal law without definition, which perhaps reflects only the fact that it is 'a common term used in everyday conversation that has not acquired any artful meaning.'" 1 Wayne R. LaFave, *Substantive Criminal Law,* § 6.1(e), at 432 (2d ed. 2003) (citing *Kramer v. United States,* 408 F.2d 837 (8th Cir.1969)). However, "[t]he word 'possession,' though frequently used in both ordinary speech and at law, remains one of the most elusive and ambiguous of legal constructs. . . . Currently, the most controversial use of possession is the doctrine of constructive possession in narcotics cases." Whitebread and Stevens, *supra,* at 751.

It is well established that in order to convict for possession of illegal drugs, the prosecution must prove beyond a reasonable doubt that the accused: (1) either individually or jointly with another exercised dominion and control over the substance; (2) had knowledge of its presence; and (3) had knowledge that the substance was a controlled substance. The parties disagree as to whether the State proved the first element beyond a reasonable doubt, and specifically whether it showed that Regan exercised the requisite dominion and control over a sufficient quantity of the marijuana to support a felony conviction.

Our case law defines the terms "dominion and control" in a somewhat vague and circular manner, reciting the requirement that the accused must have the "requisite control" without offering much guidance as to the proof required to establish it. Wyoming's Criminal Pattern Jury Instruction regarding constructive possession provides in part that "[a] person who, although is not in actual possession, knowingly has both the power and the intention, at a given time, to exercise dominion or control over a thing either directly or through another person or persons, is in constructive possession of it." This Court has approved the use of this instruction in cases decided subsequent to its adoption. The pattern instruction continues to be an accurate statement of Wyoming law. We also note that the Wyoming pattern instruction was given without objection in this case.

We therefore focus specifically on the requirement that the accused must have "both the power and the intention" to control the substance. Our prior holdings have only generally defined what it means to have dominion and control because the facts in those cases fell within the common meaning of the term "control."

We have said "if a defendant is sufficiently associated with the persons having physical custody so that he is able, without difficulty to cause the drug to be produced for a customer, he can also be found by a jury to have dominion and control over the drug, and therefore, possession." Something akin to that sort of power was what the Court of Appeals for the Tenth Circuit characterized in *United States v. King,* when it said "what matters is whether the defendant has an 'appreciable ability' (i.e. the power) to exercise dominion or control over the contraband." In *Al-Rekabi,* the court even more helpfully addressed what is meant by the "power to control" by discussing constructive possession as evincing "an appreciable ability to guide the destiny of the contraband."

However, this is only one element of constructive possession. Even if we assume that a jury could reasonably find beyond a reasonable doubt that Regan could have controlled the marijuana because it was in his vehicle and he could have driven away with it while Trujillo was making deliveries, the State also had to show that Regan intended to control the marijuana. Intent is frequently incorporated into the definition of constructive possession. Whitebread and Stevens, *supra,* at 759 ("[P]ossession consists of two elements: a particular physical relationship that exists among an object, the possessor, and the world at large, . . . and the possessor's manifested intent to exercise such control over the object."). In fact, that definition prevails in the federal courts.

Although it is not always clearly articulated, an element of intention is inherent in our prior decisions relating to constructive possession. Our precedent allows an inference of constructive possession when the accused has exclusive possession over the premises where drugs are found. The State seems to rely on this principle by emphasizing that Regan "actually owned and drove the car containing the marijuana" and that "he knew that the marijuana was present in the car that he owned and was driving."

However, this Court has also noted that, "if possession is not shown to be exclusive, there must be other evidence to warrant such inference."

The facts in *Wise* illustrate the type of additional evidence needed to allow an inference of constructive possession in cases in which the accused does not have exclusive control of the place where the drugs are located. Wise contacted a female friend in Cheyenne for assistance in selling marijuana and along with a male companion traveled from Fort Collins, Colorado, to Cheyenne to meet a potential buyer. When they arrived, Wise and the female friend got out of the car and negotiated the sale of marijuana with undercover narcotics agents. He inquired about how much the agents wanted to buy, indicated how much marijuana was for sale, discussed the price (with input from the male companion), and pointed out the location of the marijuana in the back of his companion's car. We found that these facts showed that Wise had dominion and control over the marijuana, and that he therefore constructively possessed it.

The evidence in this case shows that Regan and Trujillo drove from Denver to Gillette where Trujillo directed Regan to his requested stops. To show that Regan had "complete access to the marijuana," the State emphasizes that "[w]hile Trujillo was inside three different homes, Regan stayed in his car." However, that evidence does not prove that he intended to access the marijuana. It only shows that Regan waited for his passenger to return, and that he did not actually do anything which might support a conclusion that he intended to control the drugs. "Mere presence in a vehicle belonging to another where contraband is discovered does not amount to possession of a controlled substance." *Rodarte,* 552 P.2d at 1257.

The rule of *Rodarte* could be read narrowly to say that mere presence without knowledge that contraband is present does not amount to possession. However, it must be read more broadly in light of the principle noted above, i.e., that having knowledge that drugs are in one's presence cannot be equated with proof of the power and intent to control. The fact that Regan was in his own car therefore does not show that he had both the power and intention to exercise control over the substance.

The facts of *Wise* bear a superficial similarity to this case, but they are distinguishable. The marijuana in each case admittedly belonged to the appellants' companion, and there is no evidence that either appellant ever physically touched the marijuana. In both cases, the appellants and their respective companions drove from Colorado to Wyoming, where the transactions were executed. In *Wise,* however, the State presented the following evidence of Wise's intent and power to control the marijuana: 1) he initiated the trip from Fort Collins to Cheyenne; 2) he directly enlisted the assistance of his female friend to sell the marijuana and requested she call the buyer and arrange the meeting; 3) he personally got out of the vehicle and negotiated the sale of marijuana; and 4) he directed the buyer to the marijuana on the floor of the vehicle and gave the buyer permission to examine it for quality and quantity.

These facts are substantially different from those in the instant case. Regan did not initiate the illegal activity. Trujillo directed Regan to specific locations at which he delivered the marijuana and collected money himself. Regan did not get out of the vehicle. There was no evidence indicating that Regan arranged any of the interactions, took any part in any negotiations, or made any attempt at all to associate himself with or influence the destiny of the marijuana. In fact, Officer Brothers testified that Regan told him that he refused to become involved in the transactions "because it wasn't worth the risk[.]" Regan's complete and purposeful noninvolvement in these activities does nothing to meet the State's burden to prove that he had the intent and power to exercise dominion and control over the drugs.

We therefore conclude that the evidence presented was insufficient, even when viewed in the light most favorable to the State and after giving it the benefit of all favorable inferences, to support a conviction of felony possession of marijuana. We note that Regan was not charged with being an accessory before the fact (aiding and abetting) to the distribution of marijuana, or with conspiracy to distribute, which the evidence might have supported.[5]

We find the evidence insufficient as a matter of law to support a conviction of constructive felony possession, and we reverse that conviction. However, [t]he evidence was . . . sufficient to support a conviction of the lesser included offense of actual misdemeanor possession, since Regan admitted to possessing a quarter-ounce of the marijuana found in the vehicle.

We reverse Regan's conviction of felony possession, reduce it to misdemeanor possession of marijuana under Wyo. Stat. Ann. § 35-7-1031(c)(i), and remand to the district court for resentencing.

Rivas v. United States

District of Columbia Court of Appeals
783 A.2d 125 (2001)

Glickman, J.

Applying principles of constructive possession, a jury convicted appellant Baltazar Rivas and his codefendant Jose Melgar of possessing, with intent to distribute, cocaine found in plastic bags that lay between them in the console of a car in which Melgar was the driver and Rivas the front seat passenger. A division of this court affirmed both convictions in *Rivas v. United States*, 734 A.2d 655 (D.C. 1999) *(Rivas I)*. We granted Rivas's petition for rehearing en banc in order to reconsider a rule followed in *Rivas I* and other recent cases that appears to ease the government's burden of proving constructive possession when drugs are found in the "close confines" of an automobile, as distinct from, say, a dwelling. The division relied upon this special "automobile" rule in rejecting Rivas's challenge to the sufficiency of the evidence that he intended to exercise dominion or control over the cocaine in Melgar's car, stating that "our decisions leave no doubt that the requisite intent may be

5. The penalties for that offense would be considerably more severe than those for felony possession. Distribution-related charges carry a maximum penalty of ten years of imprisonment and/or a $10,000 fine. Being an accessory before the fact carries the same penalty as the underlying offense, as does conspiracy. Felony possession carries a five-year maximum term of imprisonment and/or a $10,000 fine. Nonetheless, we deal with the offense charged.

inferred from the presence of contraband in an automobile, in plain view, conveniently accessible to the defendant."

We agree with Rivas that no categorical distinction based on where drugs are found—and certainly no lessening of the government's burden of proving constructive possession on that basis—is justified. A defendant's close proximity to drugs in plain view is certainly probative in determining not only whether he knew of the drugs and had the ability to exert control over them, but also whether he had the necessary intent to control (individually or with others) their use or destiny. Nevertheless, we make clear today that there is no "automobile" exception to the settled general rule that knowledge and proximity alone are insufficient to prove constructive possession of drugs beyond a reasonable doubt. A passenger in someone else's car, who is not the driver and who does not have exclusive control over the vehicle or its contents, may not be convicted *solely* on the basis that drugs were in plain view and conveniently accessible in the passenger compartment. As in all other constructive possession cases, there must be something more in the totality of the circumstances—a word or deed, a relationship or other probative factor—that, considered in conjunction with the evidence of proximity and knowledge, proves beyond a reasonable doubt that the passenger *intended* to exercise dominion or control over the drugs, and was not a mere bystander.

Viewed in the light most favorable to the government, the evidence showed that two police officers in uniform, in a marked police cruiser, were patrolling on Hyatt Place, N.W., at around 1:00 a.m. when they saw an automobile stopped in the middle of the street. The officers pulled up behind the car, a two-door Honda occupied by the driver (Melgar, who was also the registered owner of the vehicle), a front seat passenger (Rivas), and two rear seat passengers. Seconds later the passenger-side door opened and Rivas stepped out; leaving the door open, he walked to the sidewalk where he engaged another man in conversation. Soon afterwards the Honda pulled over to the curb. The police officers activated their overhead emergency lights and moved in behind the parked car. As they did so, Rivas, who evidently saw the officers approach, left the man he was speaking with and walked a short distance around the corner onto Park Road. There he remained to talk with someone else, out of sight of the police until he was apprehended a few minutes later.

In the meantime, as the officers approached the car on foot, Officer Mitchell looked in on the passenger side and saw an open container of alcohol on the rear floorboard. The occupants were ordered out of the car, and as Mitchell reached in to retrieve the container, he saw two plastic bags containing a visible white rock substance in the console between the two front seats. Mitchell, who could see the bags because a streetlight illuminated the interior of the car, told his partner to secure the other occupants while he went looking for Rivas. He found him in the midst of conversation some twenty to thirty feet from the corner of Hyatt Place and Park Road.

The plastic bags taken from the console of the car were later determined to contain twelve and six rocks of crack cocaine, respectively, weighing in the aggregate 1,951 milligrams. This was enough, according to a police expert, to furnish 195 separate "hits" or uses of the cocaine. The expert opined, hypothetically, that if the eighteen rocks weighed the same they would sell individually for about twenty dollars on the street; in other words, that the cocaine had a total street value of a few hundred dollars. In the expert's opinion, the amount and configuration of the drugs (in small rocks) were inconsistent with possession for personal consumption.

There was no evidence to show how long Rivas had been in Melgar's car when the police arrived on the scene, or what he or anyone else in the car had been doing. No evidence was presented that Rivas's fingerprints were found on the bags of cocaine seized from the car, or that Rivas had ever handled the bags or engaged in a drug transaction. No incriminating evidence was taken from Rivas's person,[2] and he said nothing to inculpate himself.

To prove constructive possession, the prosecution was required to show that Rivas knew that the cocaine was present in the car and that he had both the ability and the intent to exercise dominion or control over it. Constructive possession may be sole or joint and may be proven by direct or circumstantial evidence.

No one disputes that the jury permissibly could find that Rivas *knew* the cocaine was in the console (given that it was in plain view), and that he had the *ability* to exercise dominion and control over it (given his proximity to it).[4] The question before us is whether the jury rationally could find beyond a reasonable doubt that Rivas *intended* to exercise that power, in other words that he in fact "had a substantial voice vis-a-vis the drug[s]." In general, the settled rule in constructive possession cases is that "mere presence of the accused on the premises, or simply his proximity to the drug, does not itself enable . . . a deduction" beyond a reasonable doubt that he had the requisite intent. "Nor is mere association with another, standing alone, enough even when the other is known to possess the drug." Rather, there must be something more in the totality of the circumstances that—together with proximity and knowledge—establishes that the accused meant to exercise dominion or control over the narcotics:

> There must be some action, some word, or some conduct that links the individual to the narcotics and indicates that he had some stake in them, some power over them. There must be something to prove that the individual was not merely an incidental bystander. It may be foolish to stand by when others are acting illegally, or to associate with those who have committed a crime. Such conduct or association, however, *without more*, does not establish the offenses here charged. *United States v. Pardo*, 636 F.2d 535, 549 (1980) (emphasis in the original).

---

2. Melgar had $236 in small denominations of bills on his person.

4. Nor is it disputed that, if Rivas constructively possessed the cocaine, he did so with the intent to distribute it. *See, e.g., Earle v. United States*, 612 A.2d 1258, 1270 (D.C. 1992) (packaging of drugs "in ziplock bags, in amounts regularly sold and purchased on the street," sufficient to establish intent to distribute).

In recent years, decisions of this court have attempted to distill at least one principle from constructive possession cases, which, when compared to one another, can sometimes seem "a thicket of subjectivity." *United States v. Holland,* 445 F.2d 701, 703 (1971) (Tamm, J., concurring). Recognizing the normal difference in size between a room in a house or other building and the interior of an automobile, our decisions have stated that "the requisite inferences [of dominion or control] may be drawn from the location of weapons [or other contraband] in plain view and substantially within a defendant's reach in the closer confines of an automobile." In *In re F.T.J.,* 578 A.2d 1161, 1163 (D.C. 1990), we declared that "our decisions . . . leave no doubt that the requisite intent may be inferred from the presence of contraband in an automobile, in plain view, conveniently accessible to the defendant"—a declaration that the division echoed in *Rivas I,* as mentioned earlier. We have suggested that "it is reasonable to expect the law to require a somewhat higher degree of proof [of intent] where an apartment visitor is alleged to have possessed contraband located somewhere within the large space of an apartment, as opposed to that required for an automobile occupant who knows a pistol [or other contraband] is within easy reach under or behind the seat."

Rivas criticizes these statements, contending that they amount to an unjustified relaxation of the proof requirements when persons are found near drugs in automobiles. Rivas observes that there is nothing "about the nature of a car, except its limited size, that would necessitate a different standard [of proof] in constructive possession cases." Limited size, however, is of questionable significance in this context. Rivas persuasively argues that physical proximity to drugs in the "close confines" of a car, at least one occupied jointly with other persons, may be *less* probative of possession than proximity in some larger enclosure because a passenger "is greatly restricted in her ability to distance herself from contraband in plain view. There is simply nowhere to go," especially when the car is in motion. Moreover, Rivas points out, "the relationship of a 'visitor' in a car may be far more attenuated than a visitor to a house or apartment":

> People offer or accept rides from colleagues or acquaintances solely because they are travelling to a common destination. We might pick someone up in bad weather, merely recognizing them as a neighbor. We arrange car pools, and drive people home from parties knowing only that we have friends in common. In all these circumstances, we find ourselves in cars with people whom we might never have occasion to invite into the privacy of our own homes. There is no reason to conclude that a "visitor" in a car, as a general rule, has any greater relationship to its contents than a visitor to a home.

We agree with these reasons why any categorical distinction between cars and other enclosed places in deciding issues of constructive possession is untenable. Whether constructive possession has been proven beyond a reasonable doubt in any given case depends, as the parties before us agree, on a fact-specific inquiry into all of the circumstances. A special exception for automobiles does not stand up to scrutiny. Thus, to the extent that language in our decisions may have implied from the normal size of a passenger compartment that proximity to exposed drugs in a car, without more, is sufficient to prove (beyond a reasonable doubt) the requisite intention to exercise dominion or control, we disavow that language.

Lest our holding be misconstrued, we do not mean to suggest that close proximity to exposed contraband—whether in a car or in a room—has no bearing on the issue of control. It plainly does. Nor do we mean to say that inferences of possession may not be drawn more readily from a person's presence in a car with contraband in plain sight, particularly if that presence is more than momentary, than in other circumstances. To acknowledge no such distinction between a car and other surroundings would ignore the judgment and common experience[.]

Acknowledging, then, the relevance of the evidence that Rivas was seen in close proximity to exposed drugs in the confined space of an automobile, we turn to the remaining issue. Was the evidence adduced in this case sufficient to prove possession by Rivas beyond a reasonable doubt? We hold that it was not.

Before discussing the sufficiency of that evidence, we think it useful to review the principles that must guide our evaluation; for this truly is a case that turns not on the absence of proof, but on the difference between the reasonable doubt standard and less stringent standards of proof.

The reasonable doubt standard of proof requires the factfinder "to reach a subjective state of near certitude of the guilt of the accused." *Jackson v. Virginia*, 443 U.S. 307, 315 (1979). Proof of a fact beyond a reasonable doubt is thus "more powerful" than proof that the fact is "more likely true than not;" more powerful, even, than proof "that its truth is highly probable." This requirement, a component of due process, "'plays a vital role in the American scheme of criminal procedure,' because it operates to give 'concrete substance' to the presumption of innocence, to ensure against unjust convictions, and to reduce the risk of factual error in a criminal proceeding." *Jackson*, 443 U.S. at 315 (quoting *In re Winship*, 397 U.S. 358, 363 (1970)).

Proof beyond a reasonable doubt is not merely a guideline for the trier of fact; it also furnishes a standard for judicial review of the sufficiency of the evidence. We have an obligation to take seriously the requirement that the evidence in a criminal prosecution must be strong enough that a jury behaving rationally really could find it persuasive beyond a reasonable doubt.

Turning now to the evidence in this case, it has the quality of a snapshot—a frozen instant in time and space, crystallized but devoid of explanatory context. The police discovered two bags of cocaine, worth a few hundred dollars on the street, lying exposed to view in the front console of Melgar's vehicle. Rivas had just been seen sitting for a few moments in the front passenger seat, in the company of Melgar himself and two other passengers. But there was no evidence as to how long Rivas had been in the car, how he had come to be there, or what he had been doing. There was no evidence that the occupants of the car were actively engaged in distributing drugs or preparing them for distribution when Rivas was present. When the police arrived, Rivas made no gestures toward the drugs and did not signal in any other way an intent to hide or dispose of them. No other evidence was presented that linked Rivas to the cocaine.

There is no serious doubt that at least one of the car's occupants was in possession of the drugs, and the jury could reasonably infer that Melgar, who was the owner and driver of the automobile and who was found with $236 in cash on his person, had control over its contents. But that does not mean that any of the other occupants shared possession of the cocaine with Melgar (indeed, the government did not charge the two rear seat passengers with possession), nor that Rivas in particular had a stake in it.

The government argues that the jury could find that Rivas jointly possessed the cocaine with Melgar in light of three factors. First and foremost, the government points to Rivas's proximity to drugs lying unconcealed next to him as one factor the jury could rely on to conclude, that he possessed them. Second, the government argues that the jury could infer that Rivas was Melgar's ally in distributing drugs from his car from the fact that Melgar apparently entrusted Rivas with immediate access to the drugs. And third, the government argues that Rivas's actions after the police arrived suggested a person distancing himself from drugs in his possession; for having left the car door open, Rivas evidently intended to return to the car, but he changed his mind and took evasive action when the police signaled their intent to investigate.

Could a reasonable jury find that these factors add up to proof beyond a reasonable doubt that Rivas knowingly had the ability and the intention to exercise control over the cocaine? Knowledge of the cocaine, yes; ability, yes; but intention to exercise control over the cocaine, no—not beyond a reasonable doubt. A reasonable jury perhaps could find it *more likely than not* that Rivas jointly possessed the cocaine with Melgar. But that is where we think any reasonable jury would have to draw the line. In the record before us there is no *substantial* evidence of "some action, some word, or some conduct that links [Rivas] to the narcotics and indicates that he had some stake in them, some power over them." If the standard of proof beyond a reasonable doubt means anything, the factors on which the government relies are not compelling enough to permit a reasonable jury to find Rivas guilty.

The first factor, Rivas's immediate proximity to unconcealed drugs in an automobile, certainly does make it more probable that he possessed the drugs. If the standard of proof were less rigorous, this evidence alone might have been enough to support Rivas's conviction. But the evidence that Rivas knowingly sat next to the cocaine in Jose Melgar's car did not by itself prove beyond a reasonable doubt that he "was not merely an incidental bystander." Perhaps, for example, Rivas accepted a ride with Melgar not knowing there were drugs present until some time after he got in the car. Or Rivas may have been aware that Melgar had cocaine in his vehicle, but rode in the car anyway, intending to do nothing more than (foolishly) ride around with a friend who was also a drug dealer.[10] The critical question is whether the other factors cited by the government add anything substantial to the mix, i.e., whether they reasonably combine with knowing presence to permit an inference of joint possession *beyond a reasonable doubt.*

The second factor on which the government relies is not about Rivas's state of mind; it is about Melgar's. The argument is that Melgar would not have been likely to let Rivas sit in the car next to the cocaine unless Rivas was part of his criminal operations. But whatever assumptions a jury might reasonably make about the usual operating procedures of drug dealers in general, and particularly those displaying large quantities of drugs, it is pure speculation that in this particular case Melgar—about whom we know nothing—was cautious rather than careless. Indeed, even if Melgar was cautious, he could have had many reasons to trust Rivas without Rivas having been part of his drug trafficking operation or having joint possession of his drugs. If knowing proximity to drugs is insufficient to prove guilt, being permitted to be in proximity adds virtually nothing unless the evidence also divulges *why* permission was granted. Melgar's unexplained willingness to let Rivas near his drugs in the circumstances of this case does not illuminate the intent of Rivas.

The government's third factor is Rivas's conduct after the police arrived: exiting the car when he (presumably) saw them drive up, leaving the door open behind him, and walking around the corner and out of sight when the officers approached the car on foot. We find these facts to be too equivocal to be informative on the central question of Rivas's intentions vis-a-vis the drugs. Rivas's behavior may have been evasive (though hardly stealthy or precipitous), but "in our cases, we have looked for more than 'walking away' to find manifestation of a consciousness of guilt." We have appreciated that even "leaving a scene hastily may be inspired by innocent fear, or by a legitimate desire to avoid contact with the police." "Headlong flight" may be "the consummate act of evasion: . . . not necessarily indicative of wrongdoing, but . . . certainly suggestive of such." *Illinois v. Wardlow,* 528 U.S. 119, 124 (2000).

10. As Judge Farrell ruefully observed in his concurrence in *Rivas I,* "perhaps, especially in today's culture, the fact that a passenger has taken no steps to distance himself from drugs visibly meant for sale lying inches from him in a car driven by a friend says nothing, or too little, about whether he personally has 'some stake in [the drugs], some power over them.'" 734 A.2d at 659 (citation omitted). In this vein, Rivas complains that the government's position improperly "imposes on innocent citizens an affirmative obligation to distance themselves from contraband" that they are aware is at hand. The government counters that a jury *should* be able to draw guilty inferences from a person's failure to utilize readily available means of separating himself from marketable drugs, and that our cases have recognized as much. *See Brown,* 546 A.2d at 397 ("in full knowledge that [his codefendant] was carrying the pistol, appellant knowingly and voluntarily continued his association with him"); *Parker,* 601 A.2d at 52 ("each [defendant] had control of whether to be present with the other at all"). We need not enter this debate in this case. Assuming that a passenger might remain in a vehicle containing contraband for so long a time and in such distinctive circumstances that his constructive possession of the contraband could be inferred, no such inference can be drawn in this case, given the total absence of evidence as to how long Rivas had been in Melgar's car and as to what he and the car had been doing before the police arrived.

But Rivas did not engage in headlong flight or anything close. Assuming that the jury could conclude that Rivas did mean to distance himself while the police were around, that might reinforce the implication that he knew there was cocaine in the car and did not want to be connected with it,[11] but it does not show also that he "had some stake in" the drugs himself. The additional fact that Rivas left the car door open, while perhaps suggesting that he planned to re-enter the car and hence that he may have been more than a momentary or casual occupant, is marginally significant at best. If Rivas's guilt cannot be inferred from the fact that he was in Melgar's car for an unknown length of time, it cannot be inferred from the fact that he expected to continue to be in Melgar's car.

In short, an innocent person in Rivas's shoes might have acted exactly as he did when the police arrived. On the issue of whether he exercised control over the cocaine, Rivas's actions were insolubly ambiguous. *Cf. Speight v. United States,* 599 A.2d 794, 798 (D.C. 1991).[12]

When the government proves the presence of contraband in an automobile, in plain view, conveniently accessible to a passenger defendant, the additional evidence necessary to prove constructive possession is comparatively minimal. As Rivas acknowledges in his brief,

> it could be a furtive gesture indicating an attempt to access, hide or dispose of the object, flight or other evidence of consciousness of guilt, evidence of participation in an ongoing criminal venture involving the contraband, an inculpatory statement, evidence of prior possession of the item, actual possession of paraphernalia relating to the use or sale of the contraband, control of the area or container in which the contraband is found, or the like.[13]

---

11. Although we indulge this interpretation of Rivas's behavior under our deferential standard of review, an alternative interpretation, also reasonable but favorable to Rivas rather than to the government, is that he left the car door open (knowingly exposing its interior to police inspection) and did not run away when he had the chance because he had no idea there were drugs in the vehicle.

12. In *Speight,* this court deemed the evidence of constructive possession insufficient even though the appellant, who was found with others in a private apartment standing a few feet away from drugs and drug paraphernalia in plain view, gave a false name in order to conceal his identity at the time of his arrest. While we fully appreciated that engaging in elusive behavior to avoid detection can "indicate" consciousness of guilt, we held that appellant's use of an alias, combined with his proximity to drugs in plain view, "falls short . . . in establishing that appellant intended to exercise any dominion and control over the contraband in question or to guide its destiny." 599 A.2d at 796, 798. In words that might be applied almost verbatim to the present case, this court concluded:

> Based on what the government has presented, there are at least three plausible explanations for appellant's presence: (1) he was innocently visiting a neighbor who happened to be engaged in illegal drug trafficking; (2) he was present in order to purchase drugs; or, (3) he was actively involved in the drug trafficking. The jury could only speculate as to appellant's actual role. We conclude that no reasonable juror could find that appellant's role was as a participant in drug trafficking in light of other plausible reasons for his presence. *Id.* at 798.

13. Needless to say, Rivas's listing of additional evidence that would, together with proximity to contraband in plain view, support a conviction for constructive possession is not exhaustive.

In this case, however, such additional probative evidence was lacking. The jury could only speculate about whether Rivas possessed the critical intent to exercise dominion or control over the cocaine in Melgar's car, or just happened to be present in the wrong place at the wrong time. The circumstances were suspicious, and perhaps Rivas is *probably* guilty; but on the thin record of this case, a reasonable doubt about his guilt ineluctably remains. The risk that an innocent man was convicted is therefore unacceptably large under our system of justice. Fidelity to the requirement of proof beyond a reasonable doubt in criminal cases requires that we reverse Rivas's conviction for insufficiency of the evidence.

So ordered.

Ruiz, J., concurring.

The doctrine of constructive possession is a judicially developed theory of liability designed to be a "proxy" for actual possession. *Burnette v. United States,* 600 A.2d 1082, 1084 (D.C. 1991). As early as fifteen years ago we noted that our case law on "the question of who may be held responsible when the police find an illegal item in a location together with more than one individual demonstrates some inconsistency." Cases decided since then have likewise failed to craft a coherent methodology in approaching this question. This case presents a good opportunity to review and clarify our constructive possession jurisprudence.

I write separately to explain how the decision we reach today fits in our jurisprudence on constructive possession, and why I think it correctly confines us to our judicial role, and away from policy-making in an area properly left to the legislature.

This court has had numerous opportunities to consider what evidence is necessary to sustain a conviction under a constructive possession theory. For example, recognizing that innocent presence or even guilty knowledge are insufficient to sustain a conviction for constructive possession, we regularly have stated that "mere presence at the scene, association with one in possession, or proximity to the drugs do not in themselves substantiate a finding of constructive possession." We have noted the particular ambiguity of situations where more than one person is in the presence, but not in actual possession, of drugs, and that "any legitimate inference which can be drawn from such presence, proximity, or association is considerably weakened where the accused is one of several people gathered in the place where the contraband is found." We have also demonstrated an unwillingness to impute possession of an illegal item to a visitor or even to "a resident of premises to which others have access . . . without proof that the accused is actually involved in some criminal enterprise of which the contraband is a part."

We think it appropriate to add, as has already been intimated, that a claim of innocent presence becomes decidedly less plausible in an environment (vehicular or otherwise) that is rife with evidence of ongoing drug production or distribution, such as a manufacturing or cutting facility, a warehouse, or a staging or preparation area where a large quantity of drugs or drug paraphernalia is exposed to view.

Even though we continuously stressed that proximity to contraband in plain view in an apartment or house fails to support an inference of intent, our case law developed, without much explanation, to allow proximity to contraband in plain view to support an inference of intent when the contraband was "substantially within, a defendant's reach in the closer confines of an automobile." In *In re F.T.J.*, the court explicitly recognized that "our decisions . . . leave no doubt that the requisite intent may be inferred from the presence of contraband in an automobile, in plain view, conveniently accessible to the defendant."

Having reconsidered the issue, we now abandon the standard announced in *In re F.T.J.* and hold today that there is no special rule for automobiles that allows a sufficient inference of intent to control or exercise dominion over contraband to be derived merely from the fact of presence and proximity to that contraband in plain view. We are right to do so.

Although proximity to drugs can be probative of intent to control the drugs, proximity is a relative concept that must be evaluated in the context of the totality of the circumstances in a particular case. As the majority notes, a categorical distinction between knowing proximity to drugs in a car, as opposed to a house or apartment, does not withstand scrutiny. The closer proximity to drugs (or any item) in an automobile, where a passenger's ability to remove him or herself from the presence of contraband is limited by the car's close space and mobility, may be less probative of intent than proximity in a house or an apartment, where an individual has greater freedom of movement and may therefore choose where to be in relation to the item in question. Therefore, just as caution is in order before possession of an illegal item is imputed to a visitor in a house or apartment without some further proof, at least a like caution should operate before imputing possession to one of several passengers in an automobile. Absent additional evidence that proximity is probative of intent in the totality of the circumstances of a defendant's situation, in the ambiguous situation involving more than one person with access to contraband, physical proximity alone is insufficient to establish the intent element of constructive possession beyond a reasonable doubt.[22] There is no distinction in the quantum of proof required to prove the element of intent under a theory of constructive possession whether the contraband be found in a house, apartment or automobile.

Finally, an important consideration for me is that a less demanding standard has too great a potential to impose criminal liability on a person who simply fails to disassociate from, or has mere knowledge of, the presence of contraband. This would ignore the reality that there is a broad range of what may be considered tolerable exposure to criminal activity. *See Rivas*, 734 A.2d at 659 (Farrell, J., concurring)

22. In situations where there is only one person in possible constructive possession, the ambiguity is lessened, although not necessarily eliminated. It then also becomes relevant to know the period of time during which the person has been in "exclusive" proximity, and evidence that others may have been responsible for the contraband's presence may render the situation just as ambiguous as when more than one person is present.

("Perhaps, especially in today's culture, the fact that a passenger has taken no steps to distance himself from drugs visibly meant for sale lying inches from him in a car driven by a friend says nothing, or too little, about whether he personally has some stake in the drugs."). Moreover, a person's living conditions, relatives and friends may not permit the luxury of safe distance from criminal behavior in a crowded, harsh and sometimes inescapable urban environment. If we permit too low an evidentiary threshold for constructive possession, we would in essence be setting a heightened standard of behavior, on pain of criminal sanction, for individuals faced with close proximity to contraband in plain view. If knowing proximity to contraband is to be a crime, it is for the legislature to declare it. What we must do is ensure that in setting the evidentiary minimum to establish the judge-made elements of constructive possession as a proxy for actual possession, the jury does not stray from the offense of drug *possession* that the legislature has criminalized, as possession is normally understood.[24]

I agree with the majority's analysis that the evidence in this case is insufficient to meet the demanding standard of guilt beyond a reasonable doubt because the jurors must have had a reasonable doubt about Rivas' guilt. I add some comments about evidence and arguments not discussed by the majority, and to respond to the dissent.

The dissent argues that the manner in which Rivas distanced himself from the car shows a guilty conscience, particularly because Rivas exited the car right after the police pulled up behind, while the car was still in the middle of the street. The evidence taken as a whole significantly weakens the inference the dissent would permit the jury to draw, that Rivas left the car because he was aware of the police presence. Co-defendant Melgar testified that he was out driving that night with three friends when his car "died out" in the middle of the street. After attending to the carburetor for one minute, Melgar was able to restart the car. With the car running again, Melgar was just about to drive on to Park Road when he noticed the police cruiser behind him with its emergency lights on. Upon seeing the police, he pulled his car over to the curb. The evidence was therefore undisputed from Officer Mitchell's and Melgar's testimony that the police did not turn on their lights and make their presence known until *after* Rivas had exited the car where it was stopped in the middle of the road. Although the jury could discount Melgar's testimony that the car had stalled and not draw the inference that the car's stalling prompted Rivas to exit the car where he did, there was scant evidence from which the jury could infer that Rivas left the car in the middle of the road in order to distance himself from the drugs once the presence of the police became known. To infer that Rivas exhibited a guilty conscience because he left the vehicle within a "couple of seconds" of the

24. The majority states it does not need to "enter the debate in this case" about whether criminal intent may be inferred from failure to separate from contraband. My position is that it is not for the court—in this case or in any other—to decide whether a person's failure to distance himself or herself from contraband constitutes a criminal act. As the statute is currently worded in terms of "possession," it will not allow such an attenuated proof.

unannounced arrival of a police cruiser behind the car in which he was a passenger is too slim a reed to support an inference of intent beyond a reasonable doubt.

In this case, the reason for Rivas' action of leaving the passenger door open when he exited the car is particularly opaque. Although the government argues that it evidences Rivas' intent to return, not only to the car, but to the drugs, it is equally possible that, although Rivas might well have intended to return to the car, he left momentarily not to avoid trouble with the police, but to seek help moving the car, which had stalled in the middle of the road. Further, to the extent that the government's argument is premised on the assumption that Rivas acted once he was aware of the police's presence, it would be anomalous for a person who knows he has drugs in the car to leave the door open, making it easier for police to spot the contraband, as happened here, where Officer Mitchell testified that he was able to see the drugs because of the light from street lamps, no doubt aided by the car's open door. An inference that Rivas intended to maintain dominion and control over the drugs from the fact that he left the passenger door open also requires speculation because it assumes a fact as to which there was no direct evidence, that the drugs were on the console before Rivas left the vehicle a full five minutes prior to their discovery—time during which any of the three other passengers in the car who by then had a better basis than Rivas to be aware of the police's presence might have tried to dispossess themselves of the drugs.

The government's expert testified that drug dealers "sometimes" work together with other people; that they do not always personally carry the drugs they intend to sell or the money they make from distribution, but instead use a "stash or hiding place"; and that drug dealers working together "sometimes" have different responsibilities, "somebody might hold the narcotics, somebody might hold the money." The generalized expert testimony presented in this case can meet only part of the government's burden to prove intent to possess beyond a reasonable doubt; the government must prove also that Rivas was acting pursuant to such shared division of labor with Melgar.

Our prior cases have recognized, and we reaffirm today, that "presence, proximity or association may establish a prima facie case of . . . possession when colored by evidence linking the accused to an ongoing criminal operation of which that possession is a part." "The proof of such an ongoing criminal operation need not be explicit or strong," but there must be evidence "linking the accused to [the] ongoing criminal operation." We have cautioned, however, of the risk "that the patina of expert testimony will endow purely innocent activity with criminal attributes merely because that activity is 'consistent' with actions of criminals"

The evidence presented in this case is readily distinguishable from that presented in *Carpenter v. United States,* 475 A.2d 369 (D.C. 1984), in which an expert on drug transactions testified that "a common arrangement in drug transactions is for one man . . . , to have control of the drugs, and for another man . . . to have control of the money, while one or more additional persons ("runners") act as go-betweens. . . ." In addition to the expert testimony, evidence was presented that the appellant's movements "were fully consistent with the role of 'runner.'" The appellant was observed approaching vehicles, receiving money, going to another party making "hand-to-hand contact," then to another from which he received "a small white object" that he in turn gave to the driver of the vehicle. Likewise, in *Bullock v. United States,* 709 A.2d 87, 90 (D.C. 1998), expert testimony that "explained how open-air drug enterprises tend to operate," was related to the case at hand by eyewitness testimony that the appellant "physically gave a bundle of cellophane packets" later found to contain heroin and "periodically emerged from [an] alley to check" on the distribution. In each of these cases, the expert testimony described the appellant's affirmative actions as part of an overall ongoing criminal enterprise consistent with expert testimony.

Apart from Rivas' presence in the car, there is no evidence in this case that links Rivas to an ongoing criminal operation of which possession of the rock cocaine is a part. Notably, in this case there was no evidence presented of the relationship between Rivas and the driver of the vehicle; nor was there evidence that the car was stopped in an area known for drug trafficking, that the car in which Rivas was a passenger had any of the characteristics of those driven by drug dealers as the expert testified in *Parker,* or that Rivas' movements were consistent with the roles described by the government expert, that "somebody might hold the narcotics, somebody might hold the money." Although Melgar was found with $236 on his person, suggesting that he could be the "money" man, the facts do not indicate that Rivas was "holding" the drugs; the drugs were neither in a "stash or hiding place" nor in Rivas' personal possession. Indeed, the facts are at least equally consistent, if not more consistent, with the possibility that Melgar, in whose car the drugs were found in a location under his control as driver, was in charge of both the money and the drugs.

In sum, the factors relied upon by the government, neither singly or in combination, permitted the jury reasonably to infer beyond a reasonable doubt that Rivas intended to possess the drugs found some five minutes after he exited the car where he had been a passenger. Although the jury is allowed leeway to weigh the evidence and make inferences, to be beyond a reasonable doubt, its findings must be based on the evidence or lack of evidence. In this case, the jury did not have sufficient evidence from which it could, without engaging in impermissible speculation, dispel a reasonable doubt that Rivas may have been an innocent bystander to the drugs found on the brake console.

Steadman, J., with whom Wagner, CJ. and Terry, J. join, concurring in part and dissenting in part.

I concur in [the legal principles set forth in the majority opinion.] My disagreement is with the application of those principles to the specific facts of this case in order to determine the sufficiency issue.[1]

1. This issue standing alone would hardly justify review by the en banc court. See D.C. App. R. 40(e) (rehearing en banc will not ordinarily be ordered except where necessary to maintain

The task of ruling on constitutional sufficiency "does not require a court to ask itself whether *it* believes that the evidence at trial established guilt beyond a reasonable doubt. Instead, the relevant question is whether, after viewing the evidence in the light most favorable to the prosecution, *any* rational trier of fact could have found the essential elements of the crime beyond a reasonable doubt." *Jackson v. Virginia*, 443 U.S. 307, 318–19 (1979).

Applying that test, I am unable to conclude on the record here that *no* rational trier of fact could have found appellant guilty under the requisite standard. The majority opinion lays out the factual elements, and I note most particularly the actions of appellant in exiting the automobile and departing the scene in the presence of police. This behavior, in the context of the entire circumstances, admitted of a reasonable conclusion and inference that the actions were those of a person increasingly disassociating himself from drugs in his possession with the growing involvement of the police; that is, an initial act of distancing himself—but not too far—from the car followed by his abrupt departure from sight when he saw that the police were serious about investigating. Furthermore, the nature of the exit itself from the car bears note: the Honda was stopped in the middle of the street late at night, the police car pulled up behind it, and at that point, presumably having observed the police car, the appellant left the car still parked in the middle of the street, leaving the door open in a manner suggesting an intention to return and maintain ready access to the inside of that vehicle where the drugs were in plain view next to where he had been sitting,

As the Supreme Court reasserted in the above-cited case, in which it ultimately concluded that the evidence was constitutionally sufficient, the prosecutor is not under an affirmative duty to rule out every hypothesis except that of guilt.

No claim is made that the jury here was not fully and correctly instructed on the meaning of the concept of "proof beyond a reasonable doubt." While I do not doubt the duty of this court to strike down convictions that fail to meet the constitutional standard of proof, I cannot say that the twelve members of the jury who heard all the evidence first-hand acted irrationally in finding the appellant guilty beyond a reasonable doubt or that the trial court twice erred in coming to a like conclusion in denying the repeated motions for a judgment of acquittal.

Rivas demonstrates the difficulty of crafting a consistent and principled set of factors for analyzing constructive possession cases. The majority, concurrence, and dissent all agree on the basic premise that proximity and knowledge alone are not sufficient to sustain a conviction for drug possession. Likewise, all of the judges in

uniformity of decisions or where proceeding involves a question of exceptional importance). The en banc opinion having resolved the possible conflict in our prior decisions, I would have been quite willing to remand the case to the panel for application of the relevant principles to this specific case. However, since the en banc court has determined to deal with the appeal as a whole, I will do likewise.

Rivas appear to agree that in *some* instances evidence of proximity and knowledge combined with evasive action may be enough to prove drug possession. Under what circumstances are a defendant's evasive actions sufficient to demonstrate he intended to exercise control over nearby drugs? It is at this point that the judges part ways.

The majority and concurrence find the fact that Rivas left the car when the police approached it to be insufficient to sustain his conviction. Would the result have been different if Rivas had engaged in "headlong flight" from the vehicle? The majority opinion implies that it would. But, the majority also explains, even "[a]ssuming that the jury could conclude that Rivas did mean to distance himself while the police were around, that might reinforce the implication that he knew there was cocaine in the car and did not want to be connected with it." Couldn't the same be said of headlong flight?

Though the sufficiency of the evidence for the driver, Jose Melgar, was not at issue in this appeal, the court distinguishes Melgar's situation from Rivas's by explaining that "the jury could reasonably infer that Melgar, who was the owner and driver of the automobile and who was found with $236 in cash on his person, had control over its contents." What evidence was there, however, to indicate that the drugs belonged to Melgar and not Rivas (or, for that matter, one of the passengers in the back seat)? If the presence of money on Melgar's person is what differentiates his case from Rivas's, why is Melgar's $236 in cash any more inculpatory than Rivas's open-door exit from the vehicle? If the distinction is that Melgar was the driver and owner of the vehicle, does that put the *Rivas* court's decision at odds with *Regan* (above)?

c. Constructive Possession in Open-Air Drug Markets

Bullock v. United States

District of Columbia Court of Appeals
709 A.2d 87 (1998)

Steadman, J.

Appellant Jay Bullock was convicted by a jury of one count of unlawful distribution of a controlled substance and one count of unlawful possession with intent to distribute a controlled substance ("PWID"). At the same trial, appellant Kenneth V. Rawlinson was convicted of one count of PWID. All charges relate to a quantity of heroin that was stashed beside a tree near the corner of Georgia Avenue and Otis Place, N.W.

On the morning of March 12, 1994, Officer Richard Fitzgerald of the Metropolitan Police Department manned an observation post near the "high drug area" of Georgia Avenue and Otis Place, N.W. From approximately 10:20 a.m. until 11:10 a.m., Fitzgerald observed the two appellants and a third person, Cynthia Davis,[2] through binoculars.

---

2. Davis was indicted with Bullock and Rawlinson for PWID, but she pled guilty before trial.

At around 10:20 a.m., appellant Bullock emerged from an alley known for drug trafficking, engaged Davis in conversation, and gave her a bundle of objects wrapped in a plastic band. Fitzgerald believed the objects were cellophane ziplock bags. Through his binoculars, Fitzgerald watched Davis count out ten objects by "flipping through" the bundle. Davis stashed the bundle at the base of a nearby tree. Davis remained near the tree while Bullock wandered up and down the street, often looking back toward the tree.

Shortly after Bullock gave the bundle to Davis, appellant Rawlinson entered the scene. Rawlinson approached Davis and struck up a conversation. Fitzgerald could not hear what was said, but he observed Davis gesture toward the base of the tree with her head. Rawlinson nodded in response to this gesture, and he and Davis walked a short distance together. Rawlinson continued to associate with Davis throughout the surveillance period. Fitzgerald testified that Rawlinson once "motioned and directed" a passerby to Davis, who then appeared to sell drugs from the stash to the passerby.

During the fifty minutes of Fitzgerald's surveillance, a total of five or six pedestrians appeared to buy drugs from Davis. After every one or two sales, Davis would approach Bullock, appear to give him money, and then return to the tree while Bullock disappeared into the alley. Fitzgerald testified that Bullock appeared to be "more or less overlooking what [was] going on, supervising his troops." Fitzgerald also saw Rawlinson appear to make two or three drug sales to different passersby, although his testimony was unclear as to whether these sales were linked to the stash by the tree or to a different source. At one point during the observation, all three suspects conferred in a group.

At 11:10 a.m., two arrest teams moved into the area and apprehended Bullock, Rawlinson, and Davis. After Bullock's arrest, police found $115 in one of his pockets. Police found no drugs on Bullock's person, and they did not find drugs or money in the alley. Police recovered neither drugs nor money from Rawlinson after his arrest. A police officer searched the base of the tree and found two small cellophane ziplock bags hidden inside a bottle-cap. There were no other items of significance beneath the tree. The contents of the ziplock bags were identified as heroin in a field test.

At trial, an expert explained how open-air drug enterprises tend to operate. The expert identified a common pattern in which one individual, designated a "runner," would solicit potential customers and direct them to the "holder," who supervised the supply of drugs. A holder in an enterprise rarely keeps the drugs on his or her person for fear of being caught with incriminating evidence. Instead, the holder might stash the drugs in a vehicle, near a tree, or in a bag amongst litter. For the same reason, the participants in an open-air drug enterprise might arrange to have incoming cash stashed separately. Finally, the expert identified "an executive lieutenant or captain who will pass [the drugs] out to the street lieutenants for selling on the street."

Neither defendant presented any evidence.

Bullock claims the evidence was insufficient to convict him of distribution and PWID, and, for that reason, contends that the trial court erred in denying his motion for judgment of acquittal ("MJOA"). In reviewing the denial of an MJOA, we view the evidence "in the light most favorable to the government, with due regard for the jury's right to weigh the evidence and assess credibility."

As for the distribution, the government presented eyewitness testimony that Bullock physically gave Davis a bundle of cellophane packets, which she deposited by the tree. Davis exchanged some of these packets with various passersby over the course of fifty minutes, but two packets remained when the police moved in. The contents of these two packets field-tested positive for heroin. The delivery of a controlled substance between two participants in a drug enterprise, whether or not an agency relationship exists, is a distribution. The identification testimony of even a single eyewitness is sufficient to sustain a conviction for distribution, "coupled, of course, with other evidence identifying the substance itself." A reasonable factfinder could conclude that Bullock distributed heroin to Davis.

Bullock's PWID conviction was based on a theory of constructive possession of the stash after it was distributed to Davis. "To establish constructive possession, the government must prove that the accused (1) knew the location of the drugs, (2) had the ability to exercise dominion and control over them, and (3) intended to exercise such dominion and control." "Constructive possession may be established by circumstantial as well as direct evidence, and may be sole or joint possession."

There was eyewitness testimony from which a jury could infer all three elements of constructive possession. Bullock appeared to know the location of the drugs because he saw Davis place them by the tree and he periodically emerged from the alley to check on Davis and Rawlinson. There was expert testimony that a drug enterprise often includes an "executive lieutenant or captain" who keeps an eye on the runner and holder. Moreover, the packaging of the drugs, the operation of the enterprise, and the fact that he periodically accepted incoming cash from Davis would allow the inference that Bullock intended to distribute the remainder of the stash. From the government's evidence, a reasonable factfinder could conclude that Bullock continued to have both the ability and the intent to exercise dominion and control over the stash.

Having established that the evidence was sufficient as to each offense, we now address Bullock's more novel contention that he cannot remain convicted of both. Bullock argues that logically he cannot continue to possess the same heroin he already distributed to Davis; alternatively, he cannot be said to have distributed the heroin to Davis if, as the government alleged, he retained dominion and control over the stash during the fifty minutes of surveillance. To remain convicted of both distribution and PWID with respect to the same drugs, he claims, is a "legal impossibility."

We rejected a similar claim in *Allen v. United States*, 580 A.2d 653 (D.C. 1990), where we affirmed convictions for both PWID and distribution even when they concerned the same contraband. The appellant in *Allen* had offered a tinfoil packet of cocaine to a passerby, but changed his mind and withdrew the packet when he saw a police car approach. He tried to resume, but did not complete, the transaction after he thought the police car had passed. The police had not left but remained and caught him with a total of three tinfoil packets of cocaine. He was convicted of distribution as to the first incident[4] and PWID as to the second.

Not unlike Bullock, the appellant in *Allen* contended that he could not remain convicted of PWID and distribution of "the same drugs in the same place to the same person at approximately the same time." We disagreed and held that the offenses arose from separate acts. The key factor in *Allen* was the passage of time between the first incident and the second, which were interrupted by the passing of a police car.

> Sometime during that interval, appellant reached the "fork in the road". . . . After the [police] car disappeared around the corner, appellant could have chosen to put his drugs away and go home. Instead, however, he decided to try again to distribute his drugs to a prospective customer. This decision, made after the first attempt was completed, was the product of a new criminal impulse and thus was punishable separately from the earlier act. . . .

We find the *Allen* analysis appropriate to Bullock's case. Bullock gave a bundle of heroin packets to Davis, thus completing the distribution offense. At that point, Bullock reached the "fork in the road." He could have ended his participation in the enterprise and gone home, but instead, for over fifty minutes, he continued to supervise the others and periodically receive money from Davis. These acts reflected a renewed criminal impulse with respect to the heroin stash and are thus punishable separately from the earlier offense.

There is nothing "legally impossible" about holding an individual responsible for both distribution and PWID of the same drugs on these facts. Distribution is a physical act. Possession with intent to distribute, particularly under a theory of constructive possession, is a conceptual act. An individual commits the offense of distribution upon transferring physical control of the drugs. But he or she may continue to "possess" the drugs because constructive possession may encompass joint possession. Thus in certain circumstances our law would permit convictions of both offenses, even with respect to the same quantity of drugs.[6]

We repeat our admonition in *Allen* that "we would not look kindly upon a prosecution that attempted to subdivide [a single transaction] into two parts, focusing first on the period before the sale (and charging PWID) and then on the sale itself

4. The statutory definition of distribution includes attempted distribution.

6. No claim has been made in this case that at the time Bullock physically handed the drugs to Davis, she was already in joint constructive possession of them. We express no view as to whether the transfer of contraband into the physical possession of a party can constitute distribution if, prior to the transfer, the recipient possessed the contraband constructively.

(and charging distribution)." However, given the particular circumstances here, we conclude that the passage of time between Bullock's distribution of the heroin to Davis and his continuing exercise of dominion and control over the stash was enough to render the PWID a separate offense.

Finally, we address appellant Rawlinson's single contention that the trial court should have granted his MJOA because the evidence was insufficient to convict him of PWID.

Rawlinson's case was submitted to the jury under two alternative theories, as a principal and as an aider and abettor. We conclude that the evidence was sufficient to support a conviction under either theory.

First, a reasonable jury could find Rawlinson guilty as a principal offender under a theory of constructive possession. The eyewitness testimony showed that Rawlinson (1) approached Davis soon after she stashed the heroin by the tree, (2) engaged her in conversation and nodded in response to her gesture to the stash, (3) associated with Davis throughout the fifty-minute surveillance, (4) conferred with both Davis and Bullock, and (5) "motioned and directed" a pedestrian to Davis, who then appeared to sell drugs to the pedestrian from the stash. The government's expert explained the role of a runner, who refers potential customers to the holder in an open-air drug enterprise.

From this evidence, the jury could infer that Rawlinson knew the location of the stash and that he shared both the ability and the intent to exercise dominion and control over the stash by the tree. Rawlinson's referral of a customer to Davis is further proof of his intent to distribute the remaining heroin. In short, Rawlinson's activities fit the expert's description of a runner. "The failure of police to find any money or drugs on [appellant] at the time of his arrest in no way detracts from the strength of that evidence," particularly where there was expert testimony as to the reluctance of open-air drug dealers to keep their product and its proceeds on their person.

Second, the same evidence also would have been sufficient to support Rawlinson's PWID conviction as an aider and abettor. To establish that Rawlinson aided and abetted possession with intent to distribute heroin, the government must prove that (1) someone committed the PWID offense as a principal and (2) appellant knowingly assisted or participated in the principal's offense.

The government's evidence was sufficient to permit a reasonable juror to find both prongs of aiding and abetting PWID. First, there was evidence that *someone* possessed the stash by the tree with the intent to distribute it, whether that someone was Davis, whose participation in the enterprise was known to the jury, or Bullock, whom the jury had convicted of PWID before it reached a decision as to Rawlinson. The trial court instructed the jurors that if they considered the aiding and abetting theory, they must agree on the identity of the principal that Rawlinson aided and abetted, whether Davis or Bullock. Second, the jury could infer from the government's evidence that Rawlinson knowingly assisted or participated in the PWID offense by acting as a runner. Davis showed Rawlinson the stash, Rawlinson nodded, and Rawlinson referred at least one buyer to Davis during the surveillance.

In *Lowman v. United States*, 632 A.2d 88, 90–92 (D.C. 1993), we held that a runner aids and abets the offense of distribution when she directs a potential buyer to the holder.[9] Rawlinson's case is somewhat different because his PWID conviction is based on the quantity of heroin that remained in the stash *after* his participation in that particular sale. Nevertheless, in light of both the eyewitness and expert testimony, a reasonable juror could infer that Rawlinson intended to assist in further sales of heroin from the stash.

For the foregoing reasons, the convictions of both appellants are

Affirmed.

d. Constructive Possession by Go-Betweens

United States v. Manzella

United States Court of Appeals for the Seventh Circuit
791 F.2d 1263 (1986)

Posner, J.

A jury convicted Louis Manzella of one count of possession of cocaine with intent to distribute it, in violation of 21 U.S.C. § 841(a)(1), and one count of conspiracy to distribute cocaine and to possess it with intent to distribute it, in violation of 21 U.S.C. § 846. Manzella appeals, arguing that there was insufficient evidence to convict him on either count.

Lopez, an undercover agent of the Drug Enforcement Administration, began negotiating with Ernest Rizzo to buy a kilogram of cocaine. At a meeting with Tom Apuzzo, Manzella told Apuzzo that Rizzo would need a new source for the cocaine that he wanted to sell to Lopez. Later the same day, Rizzo told Lopez on the phone that Manzella "has to bring the guy [with the cocaine] to me." Lopez and Rizzo agreed to meet the next day at a restaurant to complete the sale. When Lopez arrived at the appointed time, Manzella was there with Rizzo. Manzella told Lopez that he would make a phone call and the cocaine would arrive in 15 minutes. Manzella went to make the call and came back and said the cocaine was en route. When it did not arrive Manzella became angry. Eventually he received a phone call at the restaurant and was overheard saying, "The package won't be ready?" Manzella then told Lopez that the people who had the cocaine couldn't do the deal. Another meeting was set up—this time in a conversation between Lopez and Manzella—but

9. The concerns expressed by the dissenting judge in *Lowman* are absent from Rawlinson's case. The dissent was concerned that the runner in that case was acting more as an agent of the buyer than as an agent of the seller. Here, however, the evidence collected during the fifty minutes of surveillance more clearly established links between the runner and the others in the enterprise than the evidence in *Lowman*.

was later postponed because Manzella was unable to procure the cocaine. During this period Manzella was negotiating with Apuzzo, who had found a possible source for the cocaine, Richard Weiss. Eventually Manzella told Lopez that the deal was set for the next day and that he should call Rizzo. Rizzo and Lopez then arranged another restaurant meeting. At the meeting Apuzzo showed up at last with cocaine that Weiss had supplied him, and Apuzzo and Rizzo were then arrested. At trial Manzella testified that he had sought a source for the cocaine out of friendship for Rizzo, and not for money.

The evidence was ample to show that Manzella conspired with Rizzo and Apuzzo to sell cocaine to Lopez. Manzella's role as broker probably was essential and certainly was helpful to the consummation of the transaction. He was as much a part of the conspiracy as a real estate broker is a part of the deal to sell a house. It makes no difference that Manzella was not present at the sale; he had played a significant role, through his negotiations with Apuzzo, in bringing about Weiss's sale to Lopez.

But in the analogy to the real estate broker we encounter the greatest weakness in the government's case—the lack of evidence that Manzella possessed cocaine; for remember that he was convicted for possession as well as conspiracy. A real estate broker does not possess the house he is trying to sell, or a loan broker the money of the bank whose funds he is trying to get for his customer; and while a stock broker often will have custody of his customer's stocks, rarely will he possess the stocks before buying them for the customer. Manzella knew where the cocaine was. He arranged (at first unsuccessfully) for it to be transported to the place of sale. But he never had control over it.

There is, it is true, a doctrine of constructive possession, under which a person can be convicted for possessing cocaine though he does not possess it in a literal sense. The doctrine creates a legal fiction to take care of such cases as that of a drug dealer who operates through hirelings who have physical possession of the drugs. It would be odd if a dealer could not be guilty of possession, merely because he had the resources to hire a flunky to have custody of the drugs. Of course he might be guilty of many other things, not only conspiracy but also violation of the drug "kingpin" statute, 21 U.S.C. § 848, which carries the heaviest noncapital penalties in the federal criminal code; but he would also be guilty of possession with intent to distribute. See, e.g., *United States v. Caspers,* 736 F.2d 1246, 1249 (8th Cir. 1984); *United States v. Caballero,* 712 F.2d 126, 130–31 (5th Cir. 1983).

But as this example suggests, the essential point is that the defendant have the ultimate control over the drugs. He need not have them literally in his hands or on premises that he occupies but he must have the right (not the legal right, but the recognized authority in his criminal milieu) to possess them, as the owner of a safe deposit box has legal possession of the contents even though the bank has actual custody. Mere association with those who possess the drugs is not good enough. There is no evidence that Manzella had possession in this sense. His was the role of a finder, a broker, a bringer together of seller and buyer. Manzella was furious when his principals in the first transaction pooped out but there is no suggestion that he thought that by failing to show up with the drugs as arranged the people who had the drugs had stolen them from him, as would have been the case if he had been the possessor and they the custodians. He had no right to control Weiss's cocaine. Weiss, and later Apuzzo, had the possessory interest in that cocaine. Manzella was again just a broker, a finder working for Rizzo.

The line between broker and seller in the murky depths of the underworld is of course a fine one, and many cases have upheld convictions of middlemen for possession in circumstances superficially like those in the present case. But we can find no case in which the evidence was so weak. In *United States v. Esdaille,* 769 F.2d 104 (2d Cir. 1985), the defendant was identified to the buyer of the cocaine as a supplier, led the buyer to an apartment, and emerged a short time later with the cocaine; this was held to be enough evidence that he constructively possessed the cocaine in the apartment. *United States v. Davis,* 679 F.2d 845 (11th Cir. 1982), is similar; the evidence supported an inference that the defendant was part of a group of conspirators who jointly controlled the cocaine. There is no indication that Manzella had any control, individually or jointly, over the cocaine that he tried to obtain for Rizzo. In *United States v. White,* 660 F.2d 1178 (7th Cir. 1981), where we acknowledged that the evidence of defendant Rogers' constructive possession was much weaker than that relating to his codefendant White, Rogers was present in White's apartment when the sale of heroin was made and accompanied the buyer to her car to get the money for it, so again the evidence pointed to a conspiracy in which the coconspirators jointly controlled the drugs. In *United States v. Virciglio,* 441 F.2d 1295 (5th Cir. 1971), the defendant collected, and retained half of, the purchase price of the machine gun that he was accused of constructively possessing. He had actual possession of many other illegal guns. The court said that, jointly with others, he had "the intention and the power to exercise dominion and control over the machine gun." The same cannot be said about Manzella in regard to Weiss's cocaine.

Admittedly there is language in some cases which if taken literally would allow Manzella to be convicted of constructive possession; for he "instigated the sale, negotiated the price, and caused the drug to be produced for the customer," *United States v. Felts,* 497 F.2d 80, 82 (5th Cir. 1974), and he "likely had some appreciable ability to guide the destiny of the drug," *United States v. Staten,* 581 F.2d 878, 883 (D.C. Cir. 1978). But in each of these cases the evidence of constructive possession was stronger than in this case. If the quoted language were taken literally, every broker would be guilty of constructive possession, a result inconsistent with the fundamental proposition that constructive possession requires the right or power to control. Some cases hold that ability to assure delivery is enough, in combination with association with the actual possessors, to convict of constructive possession. See, e.g., *United States v. Weisser,* 737 F.2d 729, 732 (8th Cir. 1984). We have no quarrel with this formulation; he who can *assure* the delivery of a good controls it. But given the difficulties Manzella had in arranging delivery, it can hardly be inferred that he could assure delivery at the time and place of his choosing; the extent of his association with the actual possessors was also more limited (so far as the record shows) than in the cases we have cited.

[W]e affirm Manzella's conviction for conspiracy but reverse his conviction for possession.

4. When Does a Drug Buyer Acquire Possession?

One particularly difficult possession problem is how to determine whether a would-be buyer has acquired possession from a seller. This scenario often straddles the line between "actual" and "constructive" possession and is especially useful for considering the difference between the two theories of possession. It also adds a new twist to the constructive possession inquiry. The disputed issue in most of the constructive possession cases above was the defendant's intent to exercise control over the contraband. In *Epps v. Georgia*, by contrast, there is no question the defendants intended to exercise control over the cocaine, but it is not clear that they had the *power* to do so.

Epps v. Georgia

Court of Appeals of Georgia

251 Ga. App. 645 (2001)

Phipps, J.

William Epps, Rogelio Angulo, Dwayne Brayboy, and Fondel Barr were arrested by a drug task force conducting a reverse sting (wherein undercover police officers pose as drug dealers, sell drugs to purchasers, and then arrest the purchasers for possession of the drugs). The arrestees were charged with trafficking in cocaine and other offenses. Epps, Angulo, and Brayboy appeal their convictions of trafficking in cocaine. Because possession of cocaine is an essential element of trafficking in cocaine, and because law enforcement authorities arrested appellants before they acquired possession of the cocaine, we must reverse their convictions based on an insufficiency of supporting evidence.

Construed in a light most favorable to support the verdict, the evidence showed that a City of Doraville police sergeant was told by a confidential informant that a man later identified as Angulo wanted to purchase a kilogram of cocaine. The sergeant decided to conduct a reverse sting with the assistance of a DeKalb County drug task force. The sting was conducted at an apartment complex in Doraville where Brayboy resided. The informant met Angulo at the apartment complex entrance. They were driving their respective cars. The informant was in possession of a block of cocaine weighing almost 998 grams.

Epps and Barr later arrived in Epps's truck with the purchase money. After going to Brayboy's apartment, Epps and Angulo returned with Brayboy to the informant's car. Epps and Angulo went to the rear of the vehicle and asked to see the cocaine. The informant had put the cocaine on the backseat of his car, and he took it out and showed it to Epps and Angulo. At Epps's request, the informant unsealed the cocaine. The informant also cut a piece out of it. Epps then bent down, smelled the cocaine, and took a piece of it to test at Brayboy's apartment.

After Epps, Angulo, and Brayboy went back to Brayboy's apartment and tested the cocaine, they returned to the area of the informant's car to make the purchase. Epps and Angulo approached the car while Brayboy remained in the background. Angulo placed the money in the backseat of the car. The informant, however, had put the cocaine in the trunk of his car at the direction of the police sergeant who wanted to hide the cocaine from the appellants because he was concerned they might try to steal it. Observing that the cocaine had been moved from its prior location, Angulo asked where it was. The informant asked where the money was. When Angulo told the informant the whereabouts of the money, the informant alerted task force officers by prearranged signal that the buy had been completed. The informant continued giving the signal while telling the appellants that the cocaine was in his trunk. When the informant opened the trunk, the officers converged on the scene and arrested Epps, Angulo, and Brayboy. As the trunk was opened, Epps and Angulo stood approximately three feet from the informant's car.

The relevant element of trafficking in cocaine is knowing possession of 28 grams or more of cocaine. Possession may be joint or exclusive and actual or constructive. A person who knowingly has direct physical control over a thing at a given time is in actual possession of it. A person who, though not in actual possession, knowingly has both the power and the intention at a given time to exercise dominion or control over a thing is then in constructive possession of it. If one person alone has actual or constructive possession of a thing, possession is sole. If two or more persons share actual or constructive possession of a thing, possession is joint. Spatial proximity alone is insufficient to prove joint constructive possession of contraband.

The State argues that the evidence in this case supports a finding that when Epps inspected the cocaine and acquired actual possession of a piece of it, he and the other appellants, along with the informant, were in joint constructive possession of the entire block of cocaine. Alternatively, the State argues that once the appellants paid the purchase price for the cocaine, they obtained constructive possession of it as a result of their apparent ability to overpower the informant and take the cocaine from him.

We cannot agree with either of these arguments. The appellants could not have been in constructive possession of the entire kilogram of cocaine when Epps conducted his inspection, because they indisputably lacked the intention to exercise dominion or control over it until they had tested the sample. Upon tendering the purchase price to the informant, the appellants clearly possessed the intent to exercise control over all of the cocaine, but the evidence is insufficient to show that they ever acquired the power of control so as to give them constructive possession, as the informant hid the cocaine from them by placing it in his closed trunk until the police arrived to make the arrests. This is simply a case in which authorities conducting a sting arrested the subjects before they acquired possession of the drug and then obtained convictions against them for an offense which has possession of the drug as an element. Applying the law to the facts as established by the evidence, we must reverse the convictions for trafficking in cocaine.

Judgments reversed.

Smith, J., dissenting.

I respectfully dissent. Whether sufficient evidence was presented from which the jury could have convicted the defendants of the crime charged is a close question. But given the circumstances of this case, I believe the issue of whether the defendants had the ability to exercise control over the contraband, even though it was in the trunk of the informant's vehicle, was properly submitted to the jury and that evidence existed from which a rational trier of fact could have concluded that the defendants were in constructive possession of the cocaine.

United States v. Kitchen

United States Court of Appeals for the Seventh Circuit
57 F.3d 516 (1995)

Cudahy, J.

Isiah Kitchen was associated with the El Rukn street gang. For activities arising out of that association, a grand jury charged Kitchen with the possession of cocaine with intent to distribute and with the possession of firearms by a felon. A jury convicted Kitchen of both offenses. Kitchen appeals, suggesting that the evidence is insufficient to support either conviction. We accept the jury verdict as to the conviction for the possession of the firearm. We believe, however, that the evidence was insufficient to support the conviction for the possession of cocaine. We therefore affirm in part and reverse in part.

The police arrested Isiah Kitchen as part of an undercover narcotics operation. In March, 1989, undercover agents posing as drug dealers apprehended him during the course of a sale—also termed a "reverse buy"—of cocaine. Later that day, federal agents recovered two firearms from the house that Kitchen shared with his girlfriend. These events form the basis for Kitchen's convictions.

The specifics of the reverse buy are largely undisputed. The government engineered the setup by contacting Lawrence Griffin, a long-time acquaintance of Kitchen and an associate of the El Rukn street gang. Griffin was, at that time, incarcerated at the Cook County Jail. Griffin and Kitchen had several discussions over a three-month period. A number of these discussions proved to be fruitless, ultimately failing to result in a scheduled transaction. Griffin and Kitchen stayed in touch, however, with Kitchen able to page Griffin (actually federal agents) at a number Griffin had provided. Finally, Griffin and Kitchen agreed to a sale. Griffin told Kitchen that he would be released from prison soon, and that at that time, he would be able to deal narcotics. After further negotiations, Kitchen agreed to purchase two kilograms of cocaine from Griffin. The parties decided to transact the deal the next day for a total price of $28,000. Kitchen was to bring $14,000 to the deal, with Griffin "fronting" him the remainder of the cocaine for payment at a later date.

The next day, authorities removed Griffin from prison for the purpose of conducting the transaction. Griffin telephoned Kitchen. The two men agreed to meet at Montrose Harbor at 3:00 p.m. that afternoon. At the scheduled time, Griffin traveled to the Harbor with Special Agent Michael Casali, who was posing as a drug trafficker. Griffin and Casali waited for Kitchen to arrive. Kitchen arrived with an individual named Kenneth Dowdell and parked his car behind the undercover vehicle. Griffin and Casali entered Kitchen's vehicle. At that point, Kitchen and Dowdell produced $14,000 in cash in a series of envelopes. Kitchen left the cash with Dowdell and accompanied Casali to the location of the cocaine in order to "check the merchandise." Griffin and Dowdell stayed with the cash in Kitchen's vehicle. Another special agent, Eduardo Fernandez (Fernandez), was waiting at a different location with two kilograms of cocaine in the trunk of his car.

Casali and Kitchen pulled up to the right of Fernandez's car. The three men then met at the rear of that car, where Fernandez had popped the hatchback. A white garbage bag containing two kilograms of cocaine sat in the trunk. One of the agents opened the bag to reveal two packages of cocaine. The parties dispute exactly what happened next. Kitchen contends that he never touched the cocaine. The government suggests that Kitchen picked up one of the kilograms of cocaine for "two or three seconds." All agree that Kitchen made a comment expressing concern about the drug's purity—that he was worried about "slabs" (apparently one of the most desirable forms of cocaine). At that point, Casali and Fernandez placed Kitchen under arrest.

Following the arrest, agents served a search warrant on Mary Williams's residence in Chicago. The search uncovered a fully loaded .357 magnum revolver and a .9 millimeter semiautomatic handgun. Both weapons were found in a bedroom on the first floor of the residence. The .357 magnum was discovered in the bed area, leaning up against the back of the headboard. The .9 millimeter was recovered from a dresser drawer along with an additional magazine of ammunition.

In the same bedroom, agents found both men's and women's clothing, shoes and toiletries. They also found miscellaneous papers and invoices bearing the name "Ike Kitchen." Among these papers were some containing handwritten numerical figures like those on papers seized from Dowdell at the scene of the arrest. In addition, agents located a gold bracelet with Kitchen's El Rukn nickname lying on the dresser.

Whether Kitchen actually lived with Williams is the subject of some dispute. Kitchen claims to have been residing with his mother in Robbins, Illinois. He denies living with Williams and suggests that he only stayed overnight with her occasionally. The government points to evidence of Kitchen's presence at Williams's house. Kitchen apparently gave Williams's telephone number to Griffin, and was observed at Williams's address on a number of occasions. In addition, the government suggests that Kitchen was responsible for $10,000 worth of repairs on Williams's basement.

The jury ultimately found the government's version of events credible. They found Kitchen guilty of possession of cocaine with intent to distribute in violation of 21 U.S.C. § 841(a)(1), and of possession of a firearm by a felon in violation of 18 U.S.C. § 922(g)(1). Kitchen appeals, suggesting that the evidence was insufficient to support both determinations.

A defendant challenging the sufficiency of the evidence supporting a jury's verdict bears a "heavy burden." Both the evidence and all of the reasonable inferences that can be drawn from the evidence are viewed in the light most favorable to the government. After applying this standard, we must uphold the verdict if a rational trier of fact could have found the existence of each element of the crime beyond a reasonable doubt. Here, Kitchen mounts challenges to both counts of his conviction—that for possession of cocaine and that for possession of a firearm. He suggests, particularly, that the element of possession was not established in either case.

To convict Kitchen of the unlawful possession of a firearm by a felon, the government had the burden of proving: (1) that he had a previous felony conviction, (2) that he possessed a firearm and (3) that the firearm had traveled in or affected interstate commerce. Kitchen does not contest the first and third elements of his conviction, but he does contend that evidence supporting the second element is lacking.

Under the doctrine of constructive possession, the jury could have determined that Kitchen possessed the weapons. The evidence adduced at trial suggested that Kitchen was something more than a casual visitor at Williams's home. In many of the recorded drug conversations with Kitchen, agents had reached him by calling the telephone number at that address. According to the government, Kitchen had stated that he lived at that address. Agents in fact saw Kitchen at that address on numerous occasions. The search revealed, in addition to the firearms, a number of Kitchen's possessions—his El Rukn bracelet, bills and papers bearing his name and various articles of men's clothing. Finally, the government also came forward with evidence suggesting that Kitchen had spent about $10,000 on repairs to Williams's basement. Kitchen argues that he in fact lived with his mother in Robbins, Illinois, and only visited Williams occasionally. But the jury was under no obligation to accept his testimony on this point. It could have instead concluded that Kitchen shared the residence with Williams.

Such a conclusion supports the determination that Kitchen constructively possessed the handguns found at the residence. "Constructive possession can be established by a showing that the firearm was seized at the defendant's residence." It is not material, contrary to Kitchen's assertions, that he was incarcerated at the time the agents actually seized the guns. The jury might nevertheless have determined that he constructively possessed the guns before he was incarcerated, despite the fact that the guns were seized later. If he in fact resided at Williams's home, then he had the power to exercise control over the two firearms.

Neither is it material that other adults had access to the residence and may have had the same power to exercise control over the firearms that Kitchen had.

Constructive possession may be either sole or joint. The fact that Williams, too, had access to the firearms fails to negate the inference that Kitchen did as well. The law recognizes the possibility of joint possession.

The evidence is therefore sufficient to support Kitchen's conviction for a felon's possession of a firearm under Section 922(g)(1). The jury might have determined that he lived at the residence and occupied the bedroom where the guns were located. Under these circumstances, we believe that Kitchen constructively possessed the guns in question.

The sufficiency of the evidence supporting Kitchen's conviction for the possession of cocaine under 21 U.S.C. § 841(a)(1) gives us more pause, however. In order to sustain a conviction under 21 U.S.C. § 841(a)(1), the government must show that: (1) the defendant knowingly or intentionally possessed cocaine, (2) he possessed cocaine with the intent to distribute it and (3) he knew that the material was a controlled substance. Here, again, the only element that Kitchen contests is possession, and the issue is a close one.

As the foregoing discussion demonstrates, the doctrine of "possession" contains concepts that can become almost metaphysical. Few would suggest that "possession" of an object should be confined to instances of physical holding. The second part of this case raises the opposite, yet related, question: is any physical holding—no matter the circumstances—sufficient to establish possession? It is the government's position that Kitchen actually possessed the cocaine because he picked up one of the kilograms for 2 or 3 seconds.[1]

Possession, again, may be either "actual" or "constructive." It is the government's position that actual possession is established if a defendant picks a controlled substance up for "one fleeting moment"—or 2 or 3 seconds, as seems to have occurred here. This position, the government asserts, is supported by cases such as *United States v. Toro,* 840 F.2d 1221 (5th Cir. 1988), *United States v. Jones,* 676 F.2d 327 (8th Cir.) and *United States v. Posner,* 868 F.2d 720 (5th Cir. 1989).

These cases do discuss actual possession, each ultimately suggesting that the government need not risk a defendant's escape in order to produce evidence for a later charge of possession. The common theme in each case is the court's refusal to define possession in "a manner that affords [a defendant] an opportunity to escape with the contraband." And in each case, the court rejects the argument that a defendant cannot have possessed the controlled substance in light of the presence of federal agents. But these cases hardly establish that Kitchen's "fleeting moment" of contact

1. Kitchen contends that he never actually touched the cocaine and points to an expert's inability to locate his fingerprints on the bags containing the substance. Given the standard for our review of a jury's verdict, we are constrained to accept the government's version of events on this point. Assuming Kitchen did pick up the cocaine for two or three seconds, therefore, we will examine whether the requirements of possession have been satisfied.

with the narcotics demonstrates actual possession. The record here in no way suggests that Kitchen was preparing to leave with the drugs. And Kitchen does not argue that the presence and authority of federal agents alone should stand in the way of a possession conviction.

Toro and *Jones* and *Posner* do not otherwise support the government's position, which we understand to be some extraordinarily literal application of the definition of "possession." The government suggests that any time a defendant has an object in his hands, the law should recognize his "possession" of it. Yet none of the cases upon which the government relies embraces such an application of the doctrine. Instead, in each, the defendant engaged in some act that was clearly consistent with transporting the narcotics away from the scene of the transaction. In *Toro,* the defendant took the cocaine from the government agent and put it in a briefcase which he then locked. In *Jones,* the defendant loaded bales of marijuana into his van. And in *Posner,* the defendant's coconspirator accepted keys to a van containing marijuana, got into the van and attempted to start it. These cases all involve conduct over and above a defendant's momentary handling of a controlled substance.

This conduct—all acts indicating that transportation of narcotics is imminent—is important precisely because it is unequivocal. By taking delivery of the drug and loading it into a briefcase or a van, a defendant clearly demonstrates his assent to the drug transaction. Here, however, we have no indication of assent. The record is devoid of evidence that Kitchen intended to walk away with the narcotics or otherwise transport them. This factual distinction might not be dispositive if the record revealed *any* evidence that Kitchen had completed the sale or indicated some sort of unequivocal agreement to complete the drug transaction. Given that sort of clear evidence, perhaps a momentary holding, without more, would be sufficient to demonstrate actual possession. But that is not the case before us now.

The undisputed evidence in Kitchen's case tells a strikingly different story—different, ultimately, because here, the sale of the drugs remained incomplete at the time of arrest, and the record reveals no other indication that Kitchen would have proceeded with the drug sale. On the day of the proposed transaction, Kitchen and his coconspirator Dowdell met the government informant Griffin and the undercover agent Casali at a predetermined location. There, the four men got into Kitchen's car. The stated plan was for Kitchen to pay for one kilogram of cocaine and have the remaining kilogram "fronted" to him for payment at a later date. Kitchen showed Casali the money and then handed it to his coconspirator, Dowdell. Casali admitted that at no point did either Kitchen or Dowdell offer Griffin or him the money or attempt to hand the money over. Instead, Kitchen left the money with Dowdell and proceeded to another location with Casali to examine the drugs.

Both at the initial meeting and en route to the second location, Casali repeatedly urged Kitchen to "check out the merchandise" or otherwise inspect the narcotics. Griffin, too, suggested that Kitchen should satisfy himself by inspecting the drugs. It is clear that Kitchen proceeded to the second location with Casali to do just this.

It is also clear, however, that at the second location, no transaction occurred. Casali admitted that Kitchen never stated that he would complete the transaction or made a similar affirmative comment to that effect. Instead, Kitchen made a statement expressing doubt about the quality of the cocaine. These factors indicate that the transaction simply had not been completed at the time of Kitchen's arrest. Absent evidence suggesting that the transaction was in any sense final or certain, we are quite uncomfortable with the notion that momentary contact with narcotics establishes actual possession.

Our discomfort stems from a number of sources. First, the cases upholding convictions for possession do so only in the context of some sort of unequivocal conduct on the part of the defendants. Often, as in *Toro, Jones* and *Posner,* that conduct will consist of actions consistent with transporting the drug away from the site of the deal. In other circumstances, however, the conduct may be more idiosyncratic. In *United States v. Santiago,* 889 F.2d 371 (1st Cir. 1989), for instance, the court fastened upon the fact that one of the defendants was leaving to purchase a pair of shoes to replace the government informant's shoes, which secreted illegal drugs. "The informant had unequivocally given up his shoes, and petitioner was about to go buy him new shoes. Delivery was complete." *See also O'Connor,* 737 F.2d at 818 (performance of tests on each of thirty one-kilo bags of cocaine over a two-hour period established possession).

We do not attempt to use the present case to formulate a rule workable for all circumstances. Nor, by focusing on the incomplete nature of the narcotics deal here, do we wish to suggest that all drug transactions must be "complete" in order to later establish possession at trial. Of necessity, the particulars of a given drug transaction will drive the determination that a certain aspect of the defendant's conduct is unequivocal enough to establish possession. But here, nothing in the record convinces us that Kitchen's momentary holding constitutes possession of the drugs. Money had not yet changed hands, and Kitchen had not otherwise assented to the deal. Instead, Kitchen's momentary holding was in the context of inspection, not delivery.

[H]ere, the essential proof of possession that we require is *some factor* indicating that Kitchen had the authority or the ability to exercise control over the contraband. This demand is hardly foreign to the doctrine of possession. Constructive possession, as developed in this circuit, expressly demands this sort of showing. The government suggests that this factor is not relevant in light of Kitchen's momentary holding of the narcotics. Yet the cases discussing actual possession do not support this argument; in each, as demonstrated, some sort of unequivocal conduct indicating acceptance of the drug or assent to the transaction was present. We suspect, in any event, that the notion of control is not absent from the concept of actual possession.[2] In most cases of

2. Implicit in a common-sense understanding of possession—both actual and constructive—is the notion that a defendant has some right or ability to control the disposition of an object. An approved jury instruction on actual possession, for instance, states that a "person who knowingly has direct physical control over a thing, at a given time, is then in actual possession of it."

actual possession, because the defendant physically holds or carries the narcotics, his control over them is presumed. But to state that control is presumed is not to suggest that actual possession can be established when it is completely absent.

The facts suggest that it was absent in this case. The constructive possession cases teach that a defendant must have ultimate control over the drugs. This requirement translates into the right, or the recognized authority within the "criminal milieu," to possess the drugs in question. *Manzella,* 791 F.2d at 1266. This authority is not necessarily established when a defendant acts as a broker in a drug transaction. As we noted in *Manzella,* "a stock broker often will have custody of his customer's stocks, [but] rarely will he possess the stocks before buying them for the customer." Neither is this authority established merely because a defendant has the power or the opportunity to make off with another's property, because "the power to make off with someone else's property is not equivalent to a right to the property." *United States v. Ortega,* 44 F.3d 505 (7th Cir. 1995).

The government does, however, point to evidence of Kitchen's *intent* to transact a drug deal. And it suggests that the jury concluded that Kitchen *intended* to purchase the cocaine. It further suggests that various indicia of Kitchen's intent should be sufficient to establish possession of the narcotics. In support of this conclusion, the government highlights the repeated phone conversations between Kitchen and Griffin discussing potential transactions; Kitchen's various admissions about unrelated drug dealings; and Kitchen's arrival at the scene with the required cash in hand. Yet these factors establish only that Kitchen intended to purchase cocaine, and Kitchen's intent to purchase, without more, is insufficient to establish possession because it overlooks the required element of dominion or control.

By reading the element of control out of the equation, we risk confusing possession with attempted possession. It is well-established that intent is a key element of the doctrine of attempted possession. *United States v. Weaver,* 8 F.3d 1240 (7th Cir. 1993) ("Because attempt to possess a controlled substance is an inchoate crime, it does not require completion of the act of possession.").

The intent to engage in a drug transaction, without more, cannot support a conviction for possession. The missing link in this case is the ability to control the contraband. Had the evidence indicated some sort of unequivocal assent to the transaction, then a momentary holding might have been sufficient to establish the required element of control. But the momentary holding upon which the government relies here simply is not adequate to overcome our concerns. There simply is no evidence—such as payment of the purchase price or verbal agreement—that the drug transaction was in any sense certain or complete. We believe that although Kitchen held the drugs for a moment, he neither controlled them nor had recognized authority over them. His conduct was consistent with inspection—but nothing more. Lack of control is dispositive under both the doctrines of actual and constructive possession. We therefore find the evidence insufficient to support Kitchen's conviction for possession of cocaine.

Because the evidence established that Kitchen resided in the home in which the police located the firearms, it was sufficient to support Kitchen's conviction for the possession of a firearm. We therefore AFFIRM in part. We are not, however, persuaded that the momentary holding that occurred here established Kitchen's possession—either actual or constructive—of the cocaine. Kitchen's conviction for possession of cocaine is therefore REVERSED.

B. Trafficking Offenses

1. Distribution and Possession with the Intent to Distribute

a. Proving an Intent to Distribute

The most frequently prosecuted drug trafficking offense is possession with the intent to distribute.* As an initial matter, it is worth asking why the law divides "possession with the intent to distribute" and "distribution" into separate offenses in the first place. Why isn't the crime of distribution (or sale) a sufficient mechanism for distinguishing between users and sellers? What does the offense of "possession with the intent to distribute" offer that "distribution" does not? One answer might be that criminalizing possession with the intent to distribute allows the government to reach would-be sellers before a sale has occurred (although wouldn't "attempted distribution" also meet this goal?). The most important advantage that possession with the intent to distribute has—at least from the government's perspective—is that it is generally much easier to prove than distribution or attempted distribution. The government does not need to show that the defendant sold drugs or took a substantial step toward selling drugs; a mere intent to distribute the drugs possessed is enough.

But, if a defendant hasn't distributed or attempted to distribute drugs, how can we be sure what her intention is in possessing them? Consider the following scenario: The police execute a search warrant on Denise's home and uncover a large quantity of an intoxicating substance—enough for one year of daily use by an addict, according to the government's expert. In addition, the police find $500 in small bills and a passport belonging to Denise in a safe. In the garage, they discover a gun registered to Denise and bags that are commonly used to package the substance. Is this evidence sufficient to prove that Denise intended to distribute the substance? If you believe that it is, what fact(s) are determinative for you? Would the quantity of the substance alone be sufficient to prove her intent to distribute? Would your answer change if you learned that the intoxicating substance the police

* Though federal law and most states use the term "distribution" in their statutes, some states criminalize "sale" rather than "distribution." This distinction can carry important legal consequences in some factual settings. In most cases, however, the terms are essentially interchangeable. For the sake of simplicity, this section uses the term "distribution" to refer to both "sale" and "distribution" statutes unless otherwise noted.

found at Denise's home was alcohol? (Of course, it is perfectly legal to possess alcohol today. Our concern for present purposes is not the substance's legal status but what the circumstances surrounding Denise's possession might tell us about her *intent* in possessing the substance.) Isn't it as likely Denise is an alcoholic, or a wine collector, or preparing to throw a big party—though, as we'll soon see, serving a controlled substance to social guests constitutes distribution under today's drug laws—as it is that she is planning to sell the alcohol?

As this hypothetical suggests, trying to determine what a person intends to do with an item in her possession can sometimes be a difficult and uncertain endeavor. Of course, in other cases, intent to distribute may be perfectly clear, as *California v. Peck* demonstrates.

California v. Peck

Court of Appeal of California 52 Cal. App. 4th 351 (1996)

Richli, J.

Defendant is a member of a church which uses marijuana as a sacrament. He was convicted of transportation of more than 28.5 grams of marijuana in violation of Health and Safety Code section 11360, subdivision (a), and of possession of marijuana for sale in violation of section 11359 of that code.

Defendant was apprehended at the border patrol checkpoint in Temecula driving a car with 40 pounds of marijuana in the trunk. The marijuana was divided into bags of about one pound each. Cash in the amount of $2,350 was found under the dash cover. The wholesale value of the marijuana was about $40,000.

Defendant is president and a priest of the Israel Zion Coptic Church (IZCC). The IZCC has about 200 or 250 members. The IZCC is an offshoot of the Ethiopian Zion Coptic Church, commonly known as the Rastafarians.

The IZCC uses marijuana as a sacrament. The purpose of using the marijuana is to make the users aware of their sins. Typically, marijuana would be used approximately three times a day.

Defendant had grown marijuana for use in the IZCC, but had been criminally prosecuted and convicted for it. (See *State v. Peck* (1988) 143 Wis.2d 624.) Defendant and the other members of the IZCC then began buying small amounts of marijuana in Wisconsin for church use, but considered it too expensive. Therefore, defendant and two other members contributed a total of about $30,000, so that defendant could buy a large quantity of marijuana in San Diego, where defendant had grown up. Defendant was returning to Wisconsin when he was stopped.

The court, sitting without a jury, found defendant guilty of transportation of and possession for sale of marijuana.

Possession of illegal drugs for sale requires that the defendant have the intent to sell the drugs. During grand jury proceedings, which the parties stipulated the court could consider at trial, a sheriff's investigator gave the opinion that defendant possessed the marijuana for sale, based on the quantity. Such an opinion is sufficient to support a conviction of possession for sale.

Defendant argues the evidence of intent to sell was insufficient, despite the officer's opinion, because defendant testified without contradiction he intended only to give the marijuana away, not to sell it. We find the evidence sufficient, for at least two reasons. First, defendant testified that when he provided marijuana for use in the church, members were "free and welcomed to put some money in" towards the cost of the marijuana, and that they did so from time to time. A sale of an illegal drug is "a transfer of possession of such a drug to another for cash." At least with respect to the members who contributed money, defendant made such a transfer. The court reasonably could infer defendant intended to follow the same practice with respect to the marijuana he bought in California.

Second, a "sale" of drugs "includes transfers other than for money." The record shows defendant received a quantity of marijuana himself, over and above the amount he paid for with his own money, in return for providing it to the other members. Defendant testified that if he had not been apprehended, he would have received more than one-quarter of the marijuana, despite the fact he paid less than one-quarter of the total price, for getting the marijuana. Receiving a valuable commodity—here, the additional marijuana beyond the amount defendant paid for—in return for providing the commodity to another qualifies as a sale.

The judgment is affirmed.

Peck introduces two important and widely followed principles. First, most courts have held that a law enforcement officer's opinion that the quantity of drugs possessed is clearly inconsistent with personal use can be sufficient evidence to support a conviction for possession with intent to distribute, at least in some circumstances. Second, in most jurisdictions, the terms "sale" and "distribution" encompass a broader range of activity than the exchange of drugs for money.

Beyond these basic principles, however, things become more difficult. The next two cases raise the problem of drug quantity and expert testimony in more nuanced settings.

Missouri v. McLeod

Missouri Court of Appeals
186 S.W.3d 439 (2006)

Ellis, J.

Jarrod R. McCleod appeals from his conviction of one count of possession of a controlled substance with the intent to deliver. For the following reasons, we reverse the trial court's judgment and remand for further proceedings.

On June 25, 2004, a Federal Express employee, Franky Vanderpool, was working at the Federal Express office in Sedalia, Missouri, when he discovered a package that was missing some paperwork and did not have an address for the intended recipient aside from the zip code. In accordance with commonly accepted practices at Federal Express, Vanderpool opened the package to see if it contained information on the address of the intended recipient. Inside, Vanderpool found some plant material packaged in shrink-wrap plastic that he thought might be marijuana. Vanderpool notified the Sedalia Police Department of this discovery.

While waiting for the police to arrive, Vanderpool placed an entry on the Federal Express web-site under the package's tracking number indicating that the package was undeliverable due to an incorrect address. Shortly thereafter, Federal Express received a telephone call indicating that Appellant was the intended recipient and providing them with a phone number at which he could be reached to arrange delivery.

Subsequently, Officers Phil Stewart and Daniel Keltner arrived at the Federal Express office to investigate the package. After examining the plant material and determining that it was indeed marijuana, the officers decided to have Federal Express attempt to deliver the package. The officers repackaged the marijuana and asked Vanderpool to call Appellant at the number that had been provided. Vanderpool called and left a message indicating that Federal Express had a package that it believed was intended for Appellant and that they needed for Appellant to pick up the package or provide them with an address for delivery.

About three or four hours later, Vanderpool received a call indicating that Appellant was coming by to pick up the package. Vanderpool called Officer Keltner, who had left the Federal Express office with the package about an hour before, and notified him that Appellant was on his way to pick up the package.

When Appellant arrived at the Federal Express office, one of the employees told Appellant that the package was still on a delivery truck and that they were waiting for it to arrive. Soon thereafter, Officer Keltner arrived through the back door to the office and gave Vanderpool the package. Vanderpool took the package up front and gave it to Appellant after he signed for it.

Appellant walked out to the parking lot and climbed into the driver's seat of a parked car. As Officer Keltner followed Appellant to the car, a woman with a small child approached the passenger side door of the car. Officer Keltner opened the driver's side door of the car and asked Appellant to step out of the car. Appellant quickly climbed over the center console, climbed out through the passenger door, and fled. While chasing Appellant, Officer Keltner repeatedly identified himself as a police officer and ordered Appellant to stop. After about five minutes, Appellant finally stopped running, and Officer Keltner caught and handcuffed him.

Officer Keltner searched Appellant and found a small plastic bag containing marijuana and rolling papers in one of Appellant's pockets. Upon searching Appellant's vehicle, Officer Keltner recovered the unopened Federal Express package, rolling papers, and some marijuana "roaches".

Subsequent testing confirmed that the material in the Federal Express package, the small plastic bag, and the roaches were indeed marijuana. The marijuana in the package weighed 222.74 grams, approximately 7 ½ ounces. The plastic bag contained 6.72 grams of marijuana.[2]

Appellant was subsequently charged by information with one count of possession of a controlled substance with intent to deliver and one count of possession of drug paraphernalia with intent to use. Appellant was tried by jury and found guilty as charged. The trial court sentenced appellant as a prior offender to a term of five years on the first count to be served concurrently with a thirty-day term on the second count.

In his sole point on appeal, Appellant challenges the sufficiency of the evidence to support his conviction for possession of a controlled substance with intent to distribute.

Appellant . . . contends that . . . the evidence did not support a finding that he intended to deliver the marijuana to anyone else. Appellant points out that he was not found with any of the evidence usually relied upon to establish intent to deliver like the division of the marijuana into several small packages or possession of plastic bags, scales, or a large amount of cash.

In response, the State contends that the amount of marijuana in Appellant's possession, about 7 ½ ounces, was, in and of itself, sufficient to support a finding that Appellant had the intent to deliver the marijuana. The State argues that the amount of marijuana, along with testimony from officers offering their opinion that the amount was a sales amount, sufficiently supports Appellant's conviction.

[I]n order for Appellant to be convicted of possession with intent to deliver, the State was required to prove beyond a reasonable doubt that Appellant intended to deliver the marijuana contained in the package. The State claims that this burden was sufficiently met by showing that Appellant possessed the 7 ½ ounces or so of marijuana but fails to cite to any case law actually supporting that assertion.

In its brief, the State relies upon *State v. Gonzalez*, 108 S.W.3d 209 (Mo.App. S.D.2003), contending that *Gonzalez* held that the sheer quantity of marijuana recovered from the defendant's bedroom in that case, 159 grams or about 5 ½ ounces, was sufficient to prove the defendant's intent to distribute. The State quotes *Gonzalez* as stating that "[t]he 'sheer quantity of the marijuana' was 'sufficient to sustain the conviction and sentence per [the intent to deliver] element.'" But the State takes this language out of context. The State selectively fails to mention the fact that *Gonzalez* also relied upon the fact that "[s]ome of the marijuana in Defendant's room was individually wrapped as ounces in Ziploc-type bags" and that those bags of marijuana were similar to those found in a car stopped shortly after leaving the apartment where the defendant lived. In fact, the sentence quoted by the State reads, in full, "The sheer quantity of the marijuana in his room *and the baggies used*

2. The marijuana in the "roaches" weighed 1.33 grams.

to package a portion thereof were sufficient to sustain the conviction and sentence per that element." (emphasis added).

The State also claims that *United States v. Glenn,* 667 F.2d 1269 (9th Cir.1982), held that the defendant's possession of 185 grams, about 6 ½ ounces, of marijuana alone was "sufficient to prove intent when fortified by expert testimony that the amount was considerably greater than a person would ordinarily possess for personal use." In so doing, the State wholly misrepresents the holding in *Glenn,* which offered no opinion as to whether the amount of marijuana and the expert testimony alone would support a finding of intent to deliver. Instead, the court noted that the following evidence, viewed as a whole, was sufficient to support a finding of intent:

> The evidence introduced at trial showed that Glenn possessed approximately 185 grams (between five and six ounces)[5] of marijuana. An expert witness testified that this was considerably more than a person would ordinarily possess for personal use. The marijuana was divided into small packages, as if for sale. Glenn was carrying a 100-gram scale, and a box of plastic sandwich bags suitable for packaging marijuana. In addition, the evidence showed that Glenn had several hundred dollars on his person when he was arrested, although he was unemployed; that he was arrested on payday for Yosemite employees; and that he had written on a Yosemite map several columns of figures which could have been calculations of profit.

Thus, *Glenn* offered no opinion as to whether the amount of marijuana in the defendant's possession could support a finding of intent to distribute, in and of itself.

Certainly, at some point, the amount of a controlled substance in a defendant's possession can establish, beyond a reasonable doubt, that the defendant intended to deliver or distribute that substance to others. Conversely, "'[p]roof of possession of a small amount of a controlled substance, standing alone, is an insufficient basis from which an intent to distribute may be inferred.'"

"Intent to distribute may be inferred solely from the possession of an amount of controlled substance too large to be used by the possessor alone." *United States v. Hunt,* 129 F.3d 739, 742 (5th Cir.1997). "On the other hand, a quantity that is consistent with personal use does not raise such an inference in the absence of other evidence." For the quantity alone to sufficiently support a finding, beyond a reasonable doubt, of intent to deliver or distribute the controlled substance, the amount must be inconsistent with personal use. Thus, the amount of the controlled substance found in the defendant's possession must be sufficiently large that a jury could find beyond a reasonable doubt that the drugs are not for the defendant's personal use and are intended for distribution. *See State v. Williams,* 464 So.2d 822,

5. The opinion does not indicate whether this evaluation of the amount came from testimony in the record or the court's calculation. However, we note that "[u]nder avoirdupois weight, commonly used in this country, one ounce equals 28.349 grams." Thus, 185 grams would equal 6.53 ounces.

823 (La.Ct.App.1985) ("[M]ere possession of marijuana is not evidence of intent to distribute unless the quantity is so large that no other reasonable inference can be concluded from the mere possession of the quantity.").

With regard to Missouri cases that have relied solely upon the amount of marijuana found in the defendant's possession to support a finding of an intent to deliver, we note that in *State v. Sanderson,* 169 S.W.3d 158, 163, 164 n. 3 (Mo.App. S.D.2005), the court stated that ten pounds of marijuana found in ten vacuum-sealed bags was a distribution amount and that "if Defendant is found to have constructively possessed the 10 pounds of marijuana found in the trunk, intent to distribute may be inferred from the amount of the drug that was seized." In *State v. Belton,* 108 S.W.3d 171, 176 (Mo.App. W.D.2003), the court held that possession of 820 grams (28.93 ounces, almost 2 pounds) of marijuana in a form unsuitable for consumption supported a finding of intent to distribute.

The amount of marijuana involved in the case at bar is significantly less than the amounts involved in *Sanderson* or *Belton.*

Appellant was found in possession of approximately 7 ½ ounces of marijuana. The State has failed to cite to any case in which marijuana in a quantity this small was deemed sufficient, based solely upon the quantity present, to infer the defendant's intent to deliver. While there is certainly a point at which a defendant is in possession of so much marijuana that there is no reasonable doubt that he intends to sell or otherwise share the marijuana, that point has not been reached in this case. The fact that Appellant was found in possession of approximately 7 ½ ounces of marijuana is not sufficient, in and of itself, to establish beyond a reasonable doubt that he intended to deliver the marijuana to others. *See United States v. Meshack,* 225 F.3d 556, 568 (5th Cir.2000) ("[T]he amount of marijuana found, slightly over one pound, can be consistent with personal use and, therefore, does not in and of itself raise an inference of intent to distribute."); *Williams,* 464 So.2d at 824 (holding that possession of two pounds of marijuana, without more, was insufficient to support a finding of intent to distribute); *State v. Williams,* 656 A.2d 975, 978 (R.I.1995) ("Although one and two-thirds pounds is a substantial amount of marijuana, possession of that amount in and of itself would be insufficient to prove defendant's intent to deliver it to others."). While the State also presented testimony from law enforcement officers stating their opinion that this was a "sales amount", the officers did not testify that this amount was wholly inconsistent with personal use. And the State has not cited, nor have we found, a case where the officer's opinion testimony, without more, added enough to sustain a conviction based on this small a quantity of marijuana. All such cases involved much larger amounts of marijuana. *See United States v. Zuniga-Perez,* 69 Fed. Appx. 906, 2003 WL 21386434 (10th Cir.2003) (2,600 pounds of marijuana plus agents testimony that it was more than a personal use amount held sufficient); *Blissett v. State,* 754 So.2d 1242, 1244–45 (Miss.2000) (40–50 pounds of marijuana plus agents' testimony that it was more than one would keep for personal consumption sufficient).

Because the evidence was insufficient to support Appellant's conviction of possession of a controlled substance with the intent to distribute, that conviction must be reversed. Since the jury found Appellant guilty of possession of a controlled substance with the intent to deliver under § 195.211 it did not reach a decision on the alternate instruction asking the jury to consider whether Appellant was guilty of possession of over 35 grams of marijuana in violation of § 195.202.2. While the evidence was certainly sufficient to support a conviction of possession of over 35 grams of marijuana, because § 195.202 is not a lesser included offense of § 195.211 and because the jury only needed to find Appellant in possession of 5 grams or more of marijuana to support his conviction under § 195.211.3, the case must be remanded for a new trial to determine if Appellant is guilty of that offense.

United States v. Hunt

United States Court of Appeals for the Fifth Circuit
129 F.3d 739 (1997)

Garza, J.

Latarsha Hunt appeals her conviction for possession of cocaine base with intent to distribute in violation of 21 U.S.C. § 841(a)(1). Finding insufficient evidence to support the verdict, we reverse, vacate the sentence, and remand for sentencing on the lesser included offense of simple possession.

A confidential informant told police that marijuana was being sold out of 832 Arthur Walk, which police identified as property leased to Hunt. Executing a search warrant on those premises, police officers discovered a brown paper bag containing marijuana on a coffee table in the living room along with loose tobacco and cigar labels on the floor. In addition, they found a loaded handgun under the couch. In Hunt's bedroom, they discovered 7.998 grams of cocaine base (or "crack") and a razor blade on a plate on the top of a dresser. The cocaine was broken into one large rock and several smaller pieces. Hunt, Dashanta Burton, who is a friend of Hunt's, and an unidentified male juvenile were present when the police entered the house. Hunt was standing near the front door when police entered, and, according to the testimony of the officers, did not appear to be expecting the police.

Detective Ruben Rodriguez testified that the cocaine was worth about $200, an amount that could be doubled depending on how it was cut, and that it was a distributable amount. Furthermore, he stated that each of the smaller rocks would be "a lot of crack for a crack head" and that the rocks are available in sizes smaller than that size. Brian Cho, a forensic drug analyst, stated that the amount of cocaine base he usually receives for testing is around 100 to 200 mg per submission, usually in the form of one small rock.

Detective Rodriguez also stated, however, that a cocaine base addict may smoke close to $500 worth in one day. He explained that although a junkie who had a rock as big as the largest one "would be in heaven," it would produce only a three-second high. When questioned about the razor blade that was found with the cocaine, he testified that a razor blade is necessary to cut the cocaine base, either for distribution or, as he conceded on cross-examination, for personal use (i.e., to fit in a smoking device).

When questioned about drug paraphernalia, Detective Rodriguez testified that crack users will smoke from homemade crack pipes, which can be made from objects such as broken car antennas, aluminum cans, and aluminum foil. The officers did not find any smoking devices, such as a smoke pipe, and, according to Detective Rodriguez, this indicated that no crack cocaine smokers were present. Furthermore, in his opinion, the tobacco and cigar wrappings they found were evidence of "blunts" being sold out of Hunt's house. He explained that blunts are made by taking the tobacco out of cigars and replacing it with marijuana and that "primos" are made by adding crack cocaine to the marijuana. He stated that in the area of town where Hunt's house was located, marijuana and crack are usually sold hand in hand, "like a little drug store." On recross, however, he stated that "primos" are one way that cocaine users smoke cocaine.

Hunt testified that she arrived at home just before the police officers and that she had not yet entered her bedroom, where the police officers found the cocaine. She admitted that she used marijuana, but claimed she did not "indulge" in crack cocaine. She said she knew the marijuana was in the house, but denied knowledge of the cocaine being there. She also denied allegations that she had ever sold drugs. She said she had given a key to the house to Burton, who was also living in the house, and that Burton had obtained the marijuana for a "get-together" they were going to have with a few friends that night. She also admitted she owned the gun, but denied owning the tobacco. Wendy Wilson, Hunt's neighbor and friend, testified that she had never seen Hunt use or deal crack cocaine.

Hunt was indicted under § 841(a)(1) for possession of cocaine base with intent to distribute. The first trial resulted in a hung jury. During the first and second trials, neither the government nor the defendant requested that the lesser included offense of possession be submitted to the jury. Moreover, neither the government nor Hunt challenged the instructions at trial or on appeal. In the second trial, the jury returned a verdict of guilty.

On appeal, Hunt contends that the evidence is insufficient to support the jury's verdict regarding the element of intent to distribute. She does not contend that the evidence was insufficient to support possession. In reviewing a challenge to the sufficiency of the evidence in a criminal case, we will affirm a conviction if a rational trier of fact could have found that the evidence established the essential elements of the offense beyond a reasonable doubt.

To establish a violation of 21 U.S.C. § 841(a)(1), the government must prove the knowing possession of a controlled substance with the intent to distribute. The elements of the offense may be proved either by direct or circumstantial evidence.

Intent to distribute may be inferred solely from the possession of an amount of controlled substance too large to be used by the possessor alone. On the other hand, a quantity that is consistent with personal use does not raise such an inference in the absence of other evidence. *See Skipper,* 74 F.3d at 611 (holding as a matter of law that 2.89 grams of crack cocaine alone was insufficient to prove intent, despite testimony indicating that amount could suggest drug dealing, because it was "not clearly inconsistent with personal use"); *see also Turner v. United States,* 396 U.S. 398, 423 (1970) (holding that a small quantity of cocaine, which could be for the defendant's personal use as well as for sale, does not support an inference of distribution).

Hunt contends that the 7.998 grams of crack cocaine that the police discovered in her house is insufficient as a matter of law to infer intent, and we agree. Although the government introduced testimony that this amount is a distributable amount and that the individual rocks may be larger than those that Detective Rodriguez believes are usually smoked or that Cho, the forensic analyst, usually tests, the testimony also indicated, as in *Skipper,* that this amount was also consistent with personal use. In particular, Detective Rodriguez testified that a crack cocaine user may smoke, in one day alone, close to $500 worth, an amount that exceeds even the highest value he assigned to the cocaine found in Hunt's house. Furthermore, at oral argument, the government conceded that "the amount alone, by itself, is not sufficient" to support an inference of intent to distribute.[1]

We must therefore examine the other evidence to determine whether it, in conjunction with the quantity of cocaine found, suffices to establish the requisite intent to distribute. *See United States v. Munoz,* 957 F.2d 171, 174 (5th Cir. 1992) (noting that even a small quantity of cocaine is sufficient to infer intent when augmented by the presence of evidence such as distribution paraphernalia or large quantities of cash). As with the quantity of drugs, however, "paraphernalia that could be

1. In considering the quantity of crack cocaine found in Hunt's house, we note that, in a few cases, other circuit courts rested their decisions that the evidence was sufficient to support an inference of intent in large part on quantities comparable to this amount. In *United States v. Lamarr,* 75 F.3d 964, 973 (4th Cir. 1996), the court quoted a letter to the editor of the Washington Post (regarding sentencing), which stated that "'five grams of crack cocaine is the equivalent of 50 street doses'" and that "'anybody holding that much crack is dealing.'" The court concluded that the 5.72 grams the defendant possessed was roughly the amount a strong user would use in two months and held that, combined with testimony that the defendant was dealing, the evidence was sufficient to infer intent. *See also United States v. Haney,* 23 F.3d 1413 (8th Cir. 1994) (emphasizing the testimony of a criminologist that if an addict ingested 6.57 grams of crack in one or two days he would probably die; but also relying on confidential informant's information that defendant would be selling crack in exchange for food stamps, the $371 cash and $97 in food stamps found on defendant, and the fact that cocaine was cut into $20 pieces). Here, however, the only testimony the jury heard regarding the quantity of drugs was that a crack cocaine user can consume in one day, a value of crack greater than that found in Hunt's house and that the size of the individual rocks may be larger than those usually smoked by crack users or those tested by Brian Cho. Furthermore, we note again the government's concession at oral argument that this amount, by itself, is not sufficient to support an inference of intent. Therefore, although we recognize the import of the quantity in determining the intent to distribute controlled substances, we conclude that the quantity of cocaine base at issue here, as evaluated by the testimony presented, does not support an inference of intent to distribute.

consistent with personal use does not provide a sound basis for inferring intent to distribute." As evidence of intent to distribute, the government points to the razor blade, the absence of smoking pipes or other such instruments, the evidence of blunts, the gun, and Hunt's testimony. In *Skipper*, the government similarly argued that a straight-edged razor and the absence of smoking paraphernalia suggested the intent to distribute. We held that, even viewed in the light most favorable to the government, the evidence was insufficient to prove intent beyond a reasonable doubt. The same conclusion is warranted here. Detective Rodriguez testified that although a razor blade is needed to cut crack cocaine for distribution, it is also needed to cut the cocaine for personal use. Furthermore, even though Rodriguez testified that the evidence of blunts indicated drug sales, he also said that the evidence indicated use, namely, the smoking of cocaine in the form of primos. Because this evidence is also consistent with personal use, we do not believe it provides a sound basis for inferring that Hunt intended to distribute the cocaine.

The government also points to the gun found under her couch as evidence of Hunt's intent to distribute. We have often recognized that guns are tools of the trade in the drug business. In *United States v. Lucien,* 61 F.3d 366, 375 (5th Cir. 1995), the government argued that three guns that were found in the defendant's apartment were evidence that he was distributing cocaine base. In response, we noted that "although we do not discount the prevalence of guns in drug trafficking, we do not place undue weight on the presence of the guns in this case because [the defendants] could have untold reasons, nefarious and otherwise, for keeping guns in the apartment." The reasoning in *Lucien* applies with equal force to this case. Hunt's gun was found in her residence, under a couch, and not with the cocaine. Furthermore, Hunt made no move toward the gun when the police entered, and she admitted when asked that she did have a gun in the house. This evidence can be contrasted with cases in which a weapon was found in a more incriminating context. *See, e.g., United States v. Harrison,* 55 F.3d 163, 165 (5th Cir.) (noting that loaded .22 caliber pistol and ammunition were found next to 49.32 grams of cocaine base in dresser drawer); *United States v. Perez,* 648 F.2d 219, 220–21 (5th Cir. Unit B June 1981) (noting that when defendant noticed police observing him feeding bales of marijuana on conveyor belt to boat, he ran into house and was apprehended as he reached toward a shelf on which there were two loaded weapons). Unconnected with any such circumstances, however, the gun is no more probative of distribution of drugs than of other, non-nefarious purposes for which one may keep a gun. We therefore cannot affirm Hunt's conviction based on the presence of the gun.

The government also argues that the jury could have rejected Hunt's testimony that she had no knowledge of the cocaine and that Hunt's denial of use of cocaine necessitates a conclusion that the cocaine was kept on the premises for distribution. On appeal, however, Hunt does not challenge the jury's finding that she possessed the cocaine. Furthermore, although denial of personal consumption may be a factor in inferring intent to distribute in certain circumstances, we have stated that a defendant's "denial of guilt itself should not be permitted to become evidence of guilt." *United States v. Sutherland,* 428 F.2d 1152, 1157 (5th Cir. 1970). Accordingly, we reject the government's argument that Hunt's denial of use leads to the inference that she intended to distribute the crack.

When we have concluded that the evidence presented at trial was sufficient to support an inference of intent to distribute, we have pointed to evidence that is not as equally probative of possession as of distribution. *See, e.g., Lucien,* 61 F.3d at 376 (over $1200 cash, three weapons, and a plastic bag with several aluminum foil packets); *United States v. Pigrum,* 922 F.2d 249, 251 (5th Cir. 1991) (two sets of scales, coffee cup containing a test tube, cutting agent); *United States v. Onick,* 889 F.2d 1425, 1430–31 (5th 1989) (drug paraphernalia, particularly 4,063 empty gelcaps, and testimony that dealers package drugs in these gelcaps for street distribution); *United States v. Prieto-Tejas,* 779 F.2d 1098, 1101 (5th Cir. 1986) (value of cocaine between $2,200 and $9,000). We do not, however, see any evidence in this case, viewed individually or collectively, that is more probative of distribution than of possession. We therefore hold that a reasonable jury could not conclude beyond a reasonable doubt that Hunt intended to distribute the cocaine. We accordingly reverse Hunt's conviction for possession with intent to distribute.

The government asked us to remand for entry of judgment and for sentencing on the lesser included offense of simple possession if we found the evidence insufficient to support the element of intent to distribute.

In certain limited circumstances, we may exercise our power under 28 U.S.C. § 2106 and reduce a conviction to a lesser included offense.

Hunt has conceded the element of possession on appeal, challenging only the element of intent. We therefore find that reducing Hunt's conviction to possession will occasion her no undue prejudice.

For the foregoing reasons, Hunt's conviction is REVERSED, the sentence is VACATED, and the cause is REMANDED with instructions.

The *Hunt* court concluded that 7.998 grams of cocaine base was insufficient to demonstrate an intent to distribute. But in *United States v. Lamarr* (cited by *Hunt* in footnote 1), the Fourth Circuit found sufficient evidence to prove an intent to distribute where the defendant was found with 5.72 grams of crack. In *Lamarr,* the court found that 5.72 grams was enough to last a "strong user" two months. In *Hunt,* however, the officer testified that a crack user might smoke more than 7.998 grams "in one day alone."

The contrast between *Lamarr* and *Hunt* highlights two important and interrelated issues in this area. The first is the use of law enforcement officers as expert witnesses on drug use and drug sales. Critics argue that members of law enforcement are likely to be biased against defendants and that this bias might color their testimony. In a similar vein, juries may be too quick to defer to an officer's testimony that a given drug quantity or a certain piece of evidence is indicative of an intent to sell. Finally, while some police officers may have expert knowledge about aspects of the drug *trade*, their familiarity with issues like the amount of drugs an average user consumes or possesses is arguably more tenuous and the reliability of their estimates on these issues is uncertain. Perhaps as a result of these issues, it is not uncommon to see the same drug quantity described as a two-month supply in one case and a one-day supply in another, as in *Lamarr* and *Hunt*. Despite these concerns, the use of police officers as experts in "intent to distribute" cases remains widespread. While evidentiary rules place limits on the scope of police officer testimony in these cases, most courts have rejected arguments that officers should not be allowed to give their opinion about whether circumstances are consistent with an intent to distribute drugs. *See, e.g.*, Dana R. Hassin, *How Much is Too Much? Rule 704(b) Opinions on Personal Use vs. Intent to Distribute*, 55 U. Miami L. Rev. 667 (2001) (discussing the federal evidentiary rule against "ultimate issue" testimony and its impact on police officer testimony in drug cases). For a forceful argument that courts have been too lenient in permitting police officers to testify as experts in drug cases, see Brian R. Gallini, *To Serve and Protect? Officers as Expert Witnesses in Federal Drug Prosecutions*, 19 Geo. Mason L. Rev. 363(2012) (arguing that "courts should limit officers' expert testimony in federal drug prosecutions to law enforcement members who did not also participate in the underlying criminal investigation").

The second issue highlighted by *Lamarr* and *Hunt* is the extent to which judgments about a defendant's intent to distribute should be based on the quantity of drugs involved. The inconsistencies that can arise from a case-by-case approach to the relationship between drug quantity and intent to distribute might suggest that legislatures should adopt numerical limits to govern intent to distribute cases. Some legislatures have done just that. But statutorily enshrined presumptions that tie a defendant's intent to a fixed drug quantity raise their own set of problems. A number of defendants have brought constitutional challenges to intent-to-distribute-presumption laws. These challenges have generally been unsuccessful, however. *See, e.g., Stone v. Arkansas*, 254 Ark. 1011 (1973) (upholding a state law that created a rebuttable presumption of an intent to deliver for anyone found with a quantity of heroin in excess of 100 milligrams).

At least one state responded to difficulties posed by the crime of possession with the intent to distribute by abandoning it in favor of an alternative approach. In 1989, Minnesota adopted a scheme in which "[t]he crime of possession with intent to sell . . . vanished, except in cases where small amounts of drugs are involved." Philip Leavenworth, Note, *Illegal Drugs, New Laws, and Justice: An Examination of Five Recently Enacted Minnesota Statutes*, 16 Wm. Mitchell L. Rev. 523, 521 (1990). In its place, the legislature separated the offense of drug possession into five degrees based on the amount and type of drug possessed. *Id.* at 523 (noting that the law was developed because "police and prosecutors were frustrated with the burden of proving the intent element of the crime of possession with intent to sell").

b. Is Sharing between Users Distribution?

Hunt addresses the question of how to determine whether a person found in possession of drugs intended to distribute them. But what actions qualify as "distribution"? Clearly, the exchange of drugs for money amounts to distribution. But does passing a marijuana cigarette to a friend at a party constitute distribution of the cigarette? In *New Jersey v. Morrison* the Supreme Court of New Jersey considered the meaning of the term distribute in a tragic factual setting.

New Jersey v. Morrison

Supreme Court of New Jersey
902 A.2d 860 (2006)

Albin, J.

In the early morning hours of September 27, 2002, Daniel Shore and his friend defendant Lewis B. Morrison trolled the streets of Plainfield for drugs. When they found a dealer, defendant took their pooled money and bought four decks of heroin—little glassine packets containing the powdery substance. Afterwards, defendant gave two of the decks to Shore. Later that day, Shore died of a heroin overdose.

A grand jury returned an indictment charging defendant with distributing the heroin to Shore and, as such, with causing Shore's drug-induced death. Based on the grand jury record, the trial court concluded that the evidence could not support a finding that defendant distributed the heroin to Shore, but only that defendant and Shore jointly purchased and possessed the drugs for their personal use. For that reason, the court dismissed the distribution and drug-induced death charges. The Appellate Division overruled the trial court, finding that the evidence raised a jury issue, and reinstated the charges. We now reverse. We agree with the trial court that the evidence revealed only that defendant and Shore were joint purchasers and possessors of the heroin and therefore no act of distribution occurred between the two. Accordingly, we hold that the trial court did not abuse its discretion in dismissing the distribution and strict liability for drug-induced death charges.

On the evening of September 26, 2002, Shore and defendant Morrison, both twenty-four years old, were playing in a band together. After band practice, which ended between 1:00 and 2:00 a.m., they went to defendant's home in Raritan Township. Defendant lived there with his parents, who apparently were not home at the time. At approximately 3:00 a.m., with defendant behind the wheel, defendant and Shore drove to Plainfield to buy heroin. Defendant was a heroin addict, and Shore had experimented with the drug on an infrequent basis. To make the purchase, they pooled their money, Shore contributing thirty dollars and defendant ten dollars. Seemingly familiar with the area, defendant drove around Plainfield until an unknown man appeared on a bicycle. They honked the horn and, in return, the man whistled. In exchange for forty dollars, the man gave defendant four decks of heroin. Defendant placed the decks in his pocket and, after driving out of the city, gave one to Shore. While still in the car, Shore snorted half of the deck. When they returned to defendant's home, defendant handed Shore a second deck of heroin. Shore entered a downstairs bathroom and shut the door, where he presumably ingested the remainder of the heroin. At the same time, defendant walked upstairs where he injected his two bags of heroin. When defendant returned downstairs, he and Shore "talked about how messed up they both were." The two young men then went to sleep. Sometime that afternoon, defendant injected another dose of heroin from the remnants of two bags he had purchased earlier and fell back asleep.

At about 6:00 p.m., defendant went outside to feed his horses. On his return, he found Shore lying on the couch, blue and not breathing. [D]efendant dialed 911, and shortly afterwards, Raritan Township Police Department officers and paramedics responded to the scene. When Patrolmen David Carson and Gary Brewer arrived, they observed defendant attempting to perform CPR on Shore, who was lying face up in the driveway. Patrolmen Carson and Brewer, both trained Emergency Medical Technicians, took over the CPR efforts. In response to questioning from Patrolman Carson, defendant repeatedly denied that Shore had taken an "illegal drug," mentioning only that Shore was on some prescription medications. Significantly, an off-duty paramedic on the scene had with him a drug called Narcan, which is administered to counter the effects of a heroin overdose. Because of defendant's deceptive responses, the Narcan was not immediately given to Shore.

Upon his arrival, Raritan Township Police Detective Benedict Donaruma, Jr., also questioned defendant, who again "denied any knowledge of any type of illegal narcotics." Based on defendant's constricted pupils and slow speech, it was obvious to Detective Donaruma that defendant was on drugs and not being truthful. Despite defendant's misleading responses, paramedics by that time had administered the Narcan.

Police officers next took defendant to headquarters, where he was advised of his *Miranda* rights. After a brief line of questioning by Detective Donaruma, defendant broke down crying. Defendant explained that he had a heroin addiction, had been dishonest in his earlier answers, and wanted to tell the truth. Defendant next provided a narrative of the trip that he and Shore took to Plainfield and the events that unfolded.

In the meantime, Shore had been transported to a hospital, where he was pronounced dead. Dr. Daksha Shah of the Hunterdon County Medical Examiner's Office conducted an autopsy and determined that Shore had died of a heroin overdose.

Defendant was charged with both distribution of a controlled dangerous substance (heroin) to Shore, in violation of N.J.S.A. 2C:35-5(a)(1) and N.J.S.A. 2C:35-5(b)(3), and strict liability for Shore's drug-induced death on the basis of the alleged heroin distribution, in violation of N.J.S.A. 2C:35-9. Both crimes require proof of an act of drug distribution. The distribution statute provides that "it shall be unlawful for any person knowingly or purposely . . . [to] distribute or dispense . . . a controlled dangerous substance." The drug-induced death statute provides that "[a]ny person who . . . distributes or dispenses [heroin or other classified controlled dangerous substances], in violation of [the distribution statute], is strictly liable for a death which results from the injection, inhalation or ingestion of that substance."

The key issue here is whether defendant distributed the heroin to Shore or whether both jointly possessed the heroin at the time defendant purchased the drug from the street dealer. To address that issue, we must understand the meaning of the concepts of distribution, possession, and joint possession of a controlled dangerous substance under the Comprehensive Drug Reform Act. Under the Act, distribution is defined as "the actual, constructive, or attempted transfer from one person to another of a controlled dangerous substance" for other than lawful medical or research purposes. It hardly requires stating that the "transfer" of a controlled dangerous substance cannot occur under N.J.S.A. 2C:35-2 if the intended recipient already possesses that substance.

The law recognizes three distinct forms of possession, actual, constructive, and joint. A person has actual possession of "an object when he has physical or manual control of it." Alternatively, a person has constructive possession of "an object when, although he lacks 'physical or manual control,' the circumstances permit a reasonable inference that he has knowledge of its presence, and intends and has the capacity to exercise physical control or dominion over it during a span of time." Two persons have joint possession of an object when they "share actual or constructive knowing possession of" that object.

Relying on those basic concepts, a number of jurisdictions have concluded that when "two individuals simultaneously and jointly acquire possession of a drug for their own use, intending only to share it together, their only crime is personal drug abuse—simple joint possession, without any intent to distribute the drug further." *United States v. Swiderski,* 548 F.2d 445, 450 (2d Cir. 1977); *accord Commonwealth v. Johnson,* 413 Mass. 598, 602, 602 (Mass. 1992); *People v. Schultz,* 246 Mich. App. 695 (Mich. Ct. App. 2001).

In the seminal case of *United States v. Swiderski,* the defendant and his codefendant fiancee, accompanied by a government informant, went to a studio apartment in New York City to purchase cocaine. There, a drug supplier gave the defendant a package containing cocaine, which both he and his fiancee sampled. The defendant purchased the package for $1,250, put it in his pocket, and left with his fiancee and the informant. Shortly afterwards, government agents stopped the van in which they were traveling and arrested them. The codefendant fiancee had the cocaine in her purse along with a substantial amount of cash. The defendant had in his possession only $529. Both were charged with possession with intent to distribute cocaine in violation of 21 U.S.C.A. § 841(a). At trial, the government and the defendants disputed whether the defendants intended to sell the cocaine to third parties.

In summation, the Assistant United States Attorney argued that "even if the defendants bought the cocaine with a view to sharing it between themselves as users, ... this proof would be sufficient to establish possession 'with intent to distribute.'" In instructing the jury, the court "made it clear over defense objections that distribution could be satisfied solely by a transfer between [the defendant] and [his fiancee]." Both defendants were found guilty by the jury of possession with intent to distribute. The Second Circuit Court of Appeals reversed the convictions, concluding that, in enacting the Comprehensive Drug Abuse Prevention and Control Act, Congress did not intend to make "the exchange of physical possession between two persons who jointly acquired and hold the drug for their own use" an act of distribution under 21 U.S.C.A. § 841(a).

The Second Circuit limited its holding to "the passing of a drug between joint possessors who simultaneously acquired possession at the outset for their own use."[4] The Second Circuit distinguished its decision from *United States v. Branch*, 483 F.2d 955 (9th Cir. 1973), in which the Ninth Circuit Court of Appeals held that an act of distribution under 21 U.S.C.A. § 841(a) occurred when "the defendant had handed over a small amount of marijuana to an informer for smoking purposes." The Second Circuit did not "quarrel" with the result in *Branch* because in that case "there was no evidence that the informer-friend had jointly and simultaneously acquired possession of the drug at the outset." Unlike in *Swiderski*, "sole possession in *Branch* rested with the defendant" and therefore the transfer of the drug to the informer, whether a "friend or not," constituted an act of distribution.

Our Appellate Division applied "the *Swiderski* principle" in *State v. Lopez* and held that "the sharing of drugs by individuals in joint possession . . . does not constitute 'intent to distribute' within the meaning of N.J.S.A. 2C:35-5 and N.J.S.A. 2C:35-7." In that case, in executing a warrant to search an apartment shared by Lopez and Garcia, the police discovered, in all, 7.37 grams of marijuana, 0.41 grams of cocaine, and drug paraphernalia. In particular, the police found remnants of three hand-rolled marijuana cigarettes in the living room, a few grams of loose marijuana and a marijuana cigarette in Lopez's bedroom, and the cocaine in the kitchen. Lopez and Garcia were charged with and convicted of a number of crimes, including possession and possession with intent to distribute cocaine and marijuana.

The appellate panel noted that "[t]he prosecution's theory of culpability as to the element of 'possession' was based on joint possession by both defendants of the marijuana and the cocaine." Nevertheless, the prosecutor argued in summation

---

4. A number of jurisdictions have limited *Swiderski* to its precise holding. *See, e.g., United States v. Speer,* 30 F.3d 605, 609 (5th Cir. 1994) (stating that court "need not pass on the validity of the *Swiderski* doctrine" because it was "undisputed that at least some of the cocaine was intended . . . to be subsequently distributed to [a person] who was not at or near the scene of the transaction"); *Long v. United States,* 623 A.2d 1144, 1150–51 (D.C. 1993) (declining government's "invitation to reject *Swiderski* as incorrectly decided" but agreeing with government that *Swiderski* did not apply because defendant brought drugs home to his friends and thus served "'as a link in the chain of distribution'" (quoting *Swiderski, supra, 548 F.2d at 450*)); *State v. Moore,* 529 N.W.2d 264, 266–67 (Iowa 1995) (declining to apply *Swiderski* where both participants did not "actively participate[] in the drug purchase" but rather one "purchase[d] drugs and later share[d] them with others," noting that in those circumstances delivery has occurred "even if joint funds have been used to finance the purchase").

that "'the sharing of this marijuana by the two of them is possession with the intent to distribute.'" The panel found the prosecutor's remarks, suggesting that distribution occurs when two persons in joint possession of drugs share those same drugs with each other, to be a misstatement of law. The panel explained:

> The legal concept of "joint possession" is premised upon a metaphysical event in which two or more persons simultaneously possess an entire object, without leaving any piece of it outside the joint possessors' control. A corollary of this proposition is that one cannot acquire something one already possesses. Having an object with the intent to distribute presumes that the intended recipient does not have possession of it. Therefore, as a matter of law, two or more defendants cannot intend to distribute to each other drugs they jointly possess. Stated differently, the element of "intent to distribute" under either N.J.S.A. 2C:35-5 or N.J.S.A. 2C:35-7 cannot be established on the basis of the sharing of drugs between or among joint possessors.

Because the prosecutor's statement conflicted with those principles of law and was clearly capable of producing an unjust result, the Appellate Division reversed the possession with intent to distribute convictions.

We accept the self-evident precept in *Lopez* that "one cannot acquire something one already possesses" and thus two or more persons cannot "distribute to each other drugs they jointly possess." We also accept the limited *Swiderski* principle that when "two individuals simultaneously and jointly acquire possession of a drug for their own use, intending only to share it together," they have not committed the crime of distribution, in violation of N.J.S.A. 2C:35-5. We note that the appellate panel in this case, although sustaining the indictment, accepted the basic principles enunciated in *Swiderski* and *Lopez* as discussed above.

We also note that in enacting New Jersey's Comprehensive Drug Reform Act, the Legislature made findings and declarations that shed some light on how distinctions should be made concerning culpability. The Legislature stated that "it is the policy of this State to distinguish between drug offenders based on the seriousness of the offense, considering principally the nature, quantity and purity of the controlled substance involved, and the role of the actor in the overall drug distribution network." In passing the Act, the Legislature deemed the sentencing guidelines under the old drug laws inadequate in "identify[ing] the most serious offenders and offenses and [in] guard[ing] against sentencing disparity." The consequences of a finding of distribution are significantly greater than that of possession. Whereas the maximum term of imprisonment for distributing heroin that causes a person's drug-induced death is twenty years, the maximum term for possession of heroin is only five years. The Legislature expected the criminal culpability of parties to bear some proportion to their conduct. We are mindful, as well, that criminal statutes are to be strictly construed.

We now apply the concepts and principles discussed to the facts of this case. In determining whether there are any facts to support the indictment charging defendant with distributing two decks of heroin to Shore, we must engage in a fact-sensitive analysis based on the totality of the circumstances. Among the factors to be considered are whether the relationship of the parties is commercial or personal, the statements and conduct of the parties, the degree of control exercised by one over the other, whether the parties traveled and purchased the drugs together, the quantity of the drugs involved, and whether one party had sole possession of the controlled dangerous substance for any significant length of time. *Cf. Swiderski*, 548 F.2d at 450 (discussing factors to consider in determining whether fair inference can be drawn that party possessed drugs with intent to distribute).

The grand jury testimony revealed that defendant and Shore played in a band together and enjoyed a friendly relationship. After band practice, in the early morning hours of September 27, 2002, they traveled to defendant's home and from there to Plainfield in search of heroin. Defendant had a heroin addiction, and Shore had dabbled with the drug in the past. They drove together and pooled their money, Shore contributing thirty dollars and defendant ten dollars. Despite the Appellate Division's speculation that the division of proceeds "could be interpreted as compensation for defendant finding the drug seller and making the purchase," nothing in the grand jury record even remotely suggests that defendant and Shore's relationship was commercial in nature. Considering that defendant provided the transportation and the place for the evening, the difference in their monetary contributions is not an overriding factor, transforming a case of simple joint possession into distribution. Here were two friends on a misguided and ill-fated venture. They found the street dealer together, but as a practical matter only one could actually conduct the purchase for the two of them.

In reality, defendant was nothing more than Shore's designee, making the buy for both. Typically, when two persons jointly purchase drugs, the one who gives the money for the drugs will necessarily have the drugs in his possession before he hands a portion over to his companion. To accept the State's strained view would lead to the absurd result that an act of distribution between defendant and Shore depended solely on the fortuity of who first took in hand the drugs from the dealer. Both defendant and Shore acted for a common purpose, and both were simultaneously present at the time of the drug purchase. Shore had the intent and capacity to take control of his share of the heroin. The evidence clearly implies that when defendant bought the four decks both were in joint possession of the drugs—that is, defendant had actual possession and Shore constructive possession of the heroin. Viewing the evidence in the light most favorable to the State, we agree with the trial court that because defendant and Shore simultaneously and jointly acquired possession of the drugs for their own use, intending only to share it together, defendant cannot be charged with the crime of distribution.

To summarize, we agree with the trial court that there is insufficient evidence in the grand jury record to support count one charging defendant with strict liability for Shore's drug-induced death and count three charging distribution of a controlled dangerous substance. We therefore find that the trial court did not abuse its discretion in dismissing those counts of the indictment. We reverse the judgment of the Appellate Division and remand to the trial court for entry of an order consistent with this opinion.

Justice RIVERA-SOTO, dissenting.

I am entirely in accord with *Swiderski's, Lopez's,* the majority's and the panel's legal reasoning that the joint possession of controlled substances is inconsistent with the intent to distribute statutorily required for the crimes for which defendant stands charged. However, I part company with the majority's conclusion because, as the Appellate Division correctly acknowledged, great deference is due to our constitutionally mandated grand jury process. Unless the basic protective guidelines applied to that process are violated, and there is no intimation here that they were violated in any way, the adversary process started by an indictment must be allowed to proceed. Viewed differently, the issue of whether defendant's and his victim's possession of the heroin that claimed that victim's life was joint is a matter of defense at trial, and was not an element of the charges returned against defendant. Therefore, the resolution of this issue should not be addressed prematurely via a motion to dismiss the indictment, but at the ripe time for the determination of defenses: at trial.

I respectfully dissent.

New Jersey's strict liability drug-induced death statute, and the prosecutor's decision to charge Morrison under it, represents one possible legal response to heroin overdoses. As noted by Leo Beletsky and Corey Davis in their article excerpted in Chapter 2, the opioid crisis has led to a rise in prosecutions under these statutes in some jurisdictions. Do you think this is an effective approach? Drug-induced death laws are examined in greater depth later in this chapter.

United States v. Wallace

U.S. Court of Appeals for the Second Circuit
532 F.3d 126 (2008)

Jacobs, J.

In May, 2003, a confidential informant made two controlled purchases of cocaine base at an apartment in Rochester, New York. Each time, the seller took the cash, went into a bedroom, and came back with one or two small ziplock bags containing cocaine base. A week later, Rochester police executed a search warrant at the apartment, in which Wallace lived with his father. During the search, Wallace advised the officers that he lived in the apartment, that he was unemployed, and that he had a shotgun in his bedroom. From his bedroom, the police recovered ziplock bags containing a total of 1.5 grams of cocaine base, a quantity of new unused ziplock bags, 91.22 grams of marijuana, an AK-47 semi-automatic assault weapon and ammunition compatible with it, and $460 in cash.

After his arrest, Wallace waived his *Miranda* rights and made several statements to the police: that he had cocaine base and marijuana to use and share with his friends, but was not a drug dealer; that he used the ziplock bags to store the drugs for his own use; that he kept the AK-47 to protect himself and his bed-ridden father; and that he knew the weapon was illegal, but made sure to keep it unloaded. These statements were admitted at trial.[1]

Wallace testified to the following at trial. He was unemployed; however, his father received disability and Social Security checks, which Wallace (who had power of attorney) would cash to pay the monthly $400 rent and utilities for the apartment. The narcotics and ziplock bags belonged to him, while the gun belonged to his father. He purchased $50 worth of cocaine base every month or so. He had purchased about $600 worth of marijuana two or three years earlier, the remains of which were seized by the police. He had the drugs for his personal use and, on occasion, to share with friends. He purchased ziplock bags in bulk. It was his practice to break the cocaine base into smaller pieces and place them in the ziplock bags so that his visitors would not know how much he had and try to "use it all up." Wallace's girlfriend and his father got the AK-47 from "a boss" and brought it to the apartment. To prevent it from hurting anyone, he "put it up for safety," keeping it under his mattress and putting the ammunition in an empty baby wipes container.

On April 9, 2004, the jury convicted Wallace of possession of cocaine base with intent to distribute, possession of a firearm as a convicted felon and possession of marijuana.

Wallace argues that the evidence was insufficient to support his conviction for possession with the intent to distribute cocaine because the government failed to prove that he held (or shared) drugs with a commercial purpose.

On the same legal theory, Wallace challenges the district court's supplemental jury instruction that "[s]haring drugs with another constitutes distribution."

This Circuit has not yet decided whether the social sharing of a small quantity of drugs, without consideration, constitutes the distribution of drugs within the meaning of 21 U.S.C. § 841(a). *See United States v. Williams,* 247 F.3d 353, 358 n.6 (2d Cir. 2001) ("Drugs intended for personal use are not for distribution. It may be, however, that drugs held to be shared gratis with family and friends, though not for personal use, are also not for 'distribution,' pursuant to 21 U.S.C. § 841. On this point, we take no position whatsoever.").

Several of our sister circuits, however, have concluded that distribution within the meaning of 21 U.S.C. § 841(a) can take place without a sale. *See, e.g., United States v. Cormier,* 468 F.3d 63, 70 n.3 (1st Cir. 2006) ("It is well accepted that drugs may be distributed by giving them away for free; 21 U.S.C. § 841(a)(1) imposes no requirement that a sale take place."); *United States v. Fregoso,* 60 F.3d 1314, 1325 (8th Cir.

1. No evidence of the confidential informant's controlled purchases was admitted at trial.

1995) ("No 'sale' is required to violate the statute."); *United States v. Vincent,* 20 F.3d 229, 233 (6th Cir. 1994) ("In order to establish the knowing or intentional distribution of a controlled substance, the government needed only to show that defendant knowingly or intentionally delivered a controlled substance. It was irrelevant for the government to also show that defendant was paid for the delivery."); *United States v. Washington,* 41 F.3d 917, 919 (4th Cir. 1994) (holding that the defendant's "intent to share the cocaine with others is sufficient for a court to find that he possessed drugs with intent to distribute"); *United States Ramirez,* 608 F.2d 1261, 1264 (9th Cir. 1979) ("[T]here is direct evidence that appellant engaged in the 'distribution' of cocaine; although apparently no commercial scheme is involved, his sharing the cocaine . . . constitutes 'distribution' for purposes of 21 U.S.C. § 841(a)(1).").

We now join this sound majority and hold that the sharing of drugs, without a sale, constitutes distribution for purposes of 21 U.S.C. § 841(a), which makes it illegal to "possess with intent to manufacture, distribute, or dispense, a controlled substance." The word "distribute" means "to deliver," and "deliver" means "the actual, constructive, or attempted transfer of a controlled substance[.]" These definitions, which take no account of consideration, bespeak a congressional intent "to proscribe a range of conduct broader than the mere sale of narcotics."

This reading respects the line between "possession" and "distribution." Simple possession, in violation of 21 U.S.C. § 844, refers to "possession for one's own use," *United States v. Dovalina,* 525 F.2d 952, 958 (5th Cir. 1976), whereas distribution, in violation of 21 U.S.C. § 841(a), "can only be ultimately accomplished by 'delivery' to a distributee," *United States v. Binkley,* 903 F.2d 1130, 1138 (7th Cir. 1990). Thus a defendant who holds narcotics solely for personal use is in possession; one who delivers or transfers narcotics to another—for consideration or gratis—is distributing.

Wallace testified that he purchased cocaine base and marijuana for his own personal use, and also shared the drugs with friends[:] "Most of the time I used it by myself . . . but if a lady friend come by we use it together, you know, have some and relax. . . ." This testimony is direct evidence that Wallace engaged in the distribution of cocaine base.

Accordingly, we reject Wallace's sufficiency challenge. We likewise reject his challenge to the supplemental jury charge that "[s]haring drugs with another constitutes distribution"—the charge is sound.

Wallace contends that *United States v. Swiderski,* 548 F.2d 445 (2d Cir. 1977), indicates that a felony drug offense must be commercial in nature. *Swiderski* held that "where two individuals simultaneously and jointly acquire possession of a drug for their own use, intending only to share it together, their only crime is personal drug abuse—simple joint possession, without any intent to distribute the drug further." Since neither one of the joint possessors "serves as a link in the chain of distribution," we concluded that "simple joint possession does not pose any of the evils which Congress sought to deter and punish through the more severe penalties provided for those engaged in a 'continuing criminal enterprise' or in drug distribution."

Wallace never testified that he shared his drugs with anyone as "joint possessors" within the meaning of *Swiderski*. The rule announced in *Swiderski* is expressly limited "to the passing of a drug between joint possessors who simultaneously acquired possession at the outset for their own use." We advised that the rule would not apply where the evidence showed that the defendant "handed over a small amount of marijuana . . . for smoking purposes" to another individual without proof that the other individual "had jointly and simultaneously acquired possession of the drug at the outset." Rather, since "sole possession" in such a case would rest with the defendant, "his transfer of the drug to a third person, friend or not," would violate the prohibition on drug distribution. Wallace had "sole possession" of the drugs, even if he "handed over a small amount" to his occasional visitor.

Nor can Wallace find refuge in cases in which convictions under 21 U.S.C. § 841(a) were reversed for want of evidence that the possession of narcotics was with the intent to distribute. In *United States v. Boissoneault*, 926 F.2d 230 (2d Cir. 1991), we reversed a conviction on sufficiency grounds where "the quantity of cocaine at issue, 5.31 grams (.19 oz.), was not inconsistent with personal use." But in that case, and other similar cases, it mattered that defendant had none of the tools of the trade. Thus there was no proof that Boissoneault had "scales, beepers, and other devices," or the "materials needed to process cocaine or to package it in druggist folds," or "a gun or other weapon, which would have helped sustain an inference that he was engaged in the dangerous business of drug trafficking."

This is not the *Boissoneault* case. When the Rochester police searched Wallace's bedroom, they found (among other things) 1.5 grams of cocaine base parceled out in more than a dozen small ziplock bags; a dinner plate holding numerous new and unused small ziplock bags; a ziplock bag containing numerous new and unused small ziplock bags bearing green dollar signs; a dresser drawer full of empty and unused glassine ziplock bags; and a semi-automatic assault weapon and ammunition for it. Viewed in the light most favorable to the government, this evidence supports the inference that Wallace had the intent to distribute narcotics. *See United States v. Gamble*, 388 F.3d 74, 77 (2d Cir. 2004) (affirming finding of intent to distribute where "[l]aw enforcement officers found 1.7 grams of cocaine base (with a purity of 79 percent), packaged in twenty-six zip-lock bags, . . . along with hundreds of empty zip-lock bags," and evidence showed "an unusually high volume of pedestrian traffic at [the defendant's] apartment in the weeks preceding the search"); *United States v. Garrett*, 903 F.2d 1105, 1113 (7th Cir. 1990) ("Intent to distribute has been inferred in cases where small amounts of drugs have been packaged in a manner consistent with distribution or have been possessed in conjunction with other indicia of drug distribution, such as a weapon." (footnote omitted)).

Also seized was $460 in cash. Wallace testified that he was unemployed, and that he relied on his father's disability checks to pay the $400 monthly rent, the utility bills and medical expenses. These facts made it permissible to infer that Wallace lacked any legitimate income to purchase the cocaine base for his personal use and for sharing with friends.

For the reasons stated in this opinion, the judgment is AFFIRMED.

If two or more people acquire drugs together then they are considered to be "joint users" and sharing between them does not constitute distribution. *Wallace*, however, demonstrates the narrow construction many courts have given to the "joint user" doctrine. Most federal courts have held that if one friend shares a controlled substance socially with another, it constitutes "distribution" unless the users acquired the drugs together at the same time. In *United States v. Wright*, for example, the Ninth Circuit held the defendant was not entitled to the "joint user" defense to possession with intent to distribute where a friend "asked him to procure heroin so that they might use it together; she gave him $20 with which to buy the heroin but did not tell him where to buy it; he left her dwelling and procured the heroin; then he brought the heroin back and they 'snorted' it together." 593 F.2d 105, 108 (1979). Because Wright and his friend had not acquired the heroin "simultaneously," the court found Wright's conduct constituted "distribution." The *Wallace* court reasoned that this interpretation of the term distribution "respects the line between 'possession' and 'distribution'" because "a defendant who holds narcotics solely for personal use is in possession; one who delivers or transfers narcotics to another—for consideration or gratis—is distributing."

In light of the fact that many drug users (including users of alcohol) share the substance with friends, however, doesn't *Wallace*'s approach to distribution have the potential to turn most users into distributors in the eyes of the law? If so, is such a result consistent with the policy objectives underlying the distinction between users and distributors?

Some states take a more forgiving approach than federal courts to the joint user defense. *See, e.g., Minnesota v. Carithers*, 490 N.W.2d 620 (1992) ("That the absent spouse did not exercise physical control over the substance at the moment of acquisition is an irrelevancy when there is no question that the absent spouse was *entitled* to exercise joint physical possession."). Similarly, in some jurisdictions sharing between users is not considered to be distribution. In *Massachusetts v. Jackson*, for example, the Supreme Judicial Court of Massachusetts held that "the social sharing of marijuana is akin to simple possession" and so "does not violate the distribution statute." 464 Mass. 758, 764–65 (2013). In support of this interpretation, the court reasoned that the distribution statute was enacted in order "to target those 'in the drug business,'" not users sharing small amounts of marijuana. *Id.*

2. Manufacture

Though possession with intent to distribute is the predominant drug trafficking offense, before a drug can be sold it must first be produced. Most states target the production of illegal drugs by criminalizing their "manufacture." The same is true of federal law.

There are far fewer prosecutions for manufacture than for possession with intent to distribute. In part this is because, as discussed in Chapter 9, drugs are often produced in other countries and then smuggled into the United States. In addition, drug manufacturers are better positioned to avoid detection and arrest than sellers—especially couriers and retail level sellers—since they are less susceptible to undercover buyers or getting busted as a result of a traffic stop. Nevertheless, the offense of manufacture is an important component of drug criminalization.

a. Manufacture of Naturally Occurring Substances

The term "manufacture" can be awkward to apply to a plant and in some states "cultivation" is specifically prohibited alongside "manufacture." But even where only "manufacture" is illegal, growing marijuana (or another naturally occurring controlled substances, like hallucinogenic mushrooms) almost always qualifies. This is so whether the marijuana was being grown for sale or for personal use.

North Carolina v. Childers

Court of Appeals of North Carolina
41 N.C. App. 729 (1979)

Martin, J.

Defendant first assigns as error the failure of the trial court to instruct the jury that defendant could not be found guilty of manufacturing marijuana if it were found that she was growing the plants for her personal use. She contends that in order for her to be found guilty of the offense of manufacturing marijuana, it must be proved beyond a reasonable doubt by the State that she was manufacturing it with intent to distribute.

N.C. Gen. Stats. § 90-95(a) provides that "it is unlawful for any person: (1) To manufacture . . . a controlled substance." Marijuana is a controlled substance under Schedule VI of the North Carolina Controlled Substances Act, pursuant to the provisions of N.C. Gen. Stats. § 90-94. N.C. Gen. Stats. § 90-87(15) defines "manufacture" as:

> . . . the production, preparation, propagation, compounding, conversion or processing of a controlled substance by any means, whether directly or indirectly, artificially or naturally, or by extraction from substances of a natural origin, or independently by means of chemical synthesis, or by a combination of extraction and chemical synthesis; and "manufacture" further includes any packaging or repackaging of the substance or labeling or relabeling of its container except that this term does not include the preparation or compounding of a controlled substance by an individual for his own use . . .

N.C. Gen. Stats. § 90-87(24) defines "production" as including "the manufacture, planting, cultivation, growing, or harvesting of a controlled substance."

"Preparation" is defined by *Webster's Third New International Dictionary* as being "the action or process of making something ready for use or service." The same source provides, in addition, definitions as stated for the following terms: (1) propagation: causing to continue or increase by natural reproduction; (2) compounding: the putting together of elements, ingredients or parts to form a whole; (3) conversion: changing [of a substance] from one form, state or character into another; (4) processing: to subject [something] to a particular method, system or technique of preparation, handling or other treatment designed to effect a particular result.

N.C. Gen. Stats. § 90-87(15), in defining the term "manufacture" used six specific terms to illustrate what activity was being proscribed. It excepts "preparation or compounding of a controlled substance by an individual for his own use." Defendant argues that, because these two activities are excepted, any manufacture of a controlled substance for personal use would not be "manufacturing" within the contemplation of the statute. With this contention we cannot agree. The plain meaning of the exception is to avoid making an individual liable for the felony of manufacturing controlled substance in the situation where, being already in possession of a controlled substance, he makes it ready for use (*i.e.*, rolling marijuana into cigarettes for smoking) or combines it with other ingredients for use (*i.e.*, making the so-called "Alice B. Toklas" brownies containing marijuana). The four activities not excepted by this proviso contemplate a significantly higher degree of activity involving the controlled substance (*i.e.*, planting, growing, cultivating or harvesting a controlled substance or creating it by any synthetic process or mixture of processes, or taking a controlled substance and, by any process or conversion, changing the form of the controlled substance or concentrating it) and thus are more appropriately made felonies without regard to the intent of the person charged with the offense as to whether the controlled substance so "manufactured" was for personal use or for distribution.

We are aware that our interpretation of the statute may lead to some apparently anomalous results, where a person cultivating one marijuana plant weighing less than one ounce would be subject to conviction for a felony, while possessing less than one ounce of the final product of the plant would constitute only a misdemeanor. However, the Legislature has chosen, in its wisdom, to impose a higher penalty for manufacturing even small quantities of controlled substances than for merely possessing them. We may not presume to contravene that legislative intent. Should a revision of the present manufacturing statute be deemed advisable such an action must be done by the Legislature itself.

Like North Carolina, federal law and the law in nearly every state includes the production of naturally occurring substances like marijuana under the crime of "manufacture." In New Mexico, however, the legislature appears to have consciously decided to exclude the production of naturally occurring substances from its manufacture statute. Can you think of reasons why the New Mexico legislature would have made this choice?

New Mexico v. Pratt

Court of Appeals of New Mexico
138 N.M. 161 (2005)

Wechsler, J.

Defendant appeals his conviction of trafficking psilocybin mushrooms by manufacture contrary to NMSA 1978, § 30-31-20(A)(1) (1990) of the Controlled Substances Act (CSA). He argues that his conviction should be reversed because the legislature did not intend to punish the act of growing mushrooms as "manufacturing" when it enacted Section 30-31-20(A)(1). We agree and reverse Defendant's conviction.

The facts are not in dispute. On June 6, 2002, police, on information obtained from a confidential informant, obtained and executed a search warrant on Defendant's home. Throughout the house, they found glass mason jars containing psilocybin mushrooms at varying stages of maturity. Some of the jars had psilocybin spores growing on top of a rice cake mixture. The officers also found syringes filled with spores, which were allegedly used to inoculate the rice cake mixture. In the kitchen, the officers found a white styrofoam cooler containing a "bubbling apparatus," which was apparently used by Defendant as a humidifier for growing the psilocybin mushrooms. The machine was "turned on and pumping" when the officers found it. The officers also found "recipes" with instructions on growing psilocybin mushrooms. A message was written on the cooler stating "Remember to be patient!!!! Pinning might take a few weeks."

After a jury trial, Defendant was convicted of trafficking psilocybin mushrooms by manufacture and possession of drug paraphernalia. Defendant does not appeal the possession conviction. We will address the remaining facts as they pertain to the issue on appeal.

The State argues that Defendant "manufactured" psilocybin mushrooms by growing them artificially using special equipment. Defendant, relying primarily on our holding in *State v. Shaulis-Powell,* 127 N.M. 667 argues that the mushrooms "were in a natural state of mushroomness" when they were seized by police and that "assisting a growing plant or a fungus by providing [a] growing medium and water" is not "manufacture" as proscribed by Section 30-31-20(A)(1).

The question of whether Defendant's conduct of artificially growing psilocybin mushrooms falls within the ambit of Section 30-31-20(A)(1) is a legal question subject to de novo review. When we interpret a statute, our goal is to give effect to the intent of the legislature. "We do this by giving effect to the plain meaning of the words of [the] statute, unless this leads to an absurd or unreasonable result."

The CSA prohibits, as intentional trafficking, the "manufacture of any controlled substance enumerated in Schedules I through V or any controlled substance analog as defined in Subsection W of Section 30-31-2." Section 30-31-20(A)(1). "Manufacture" is defined in Section 30-31-2(M) in relevant part as:

> the production, preparation, compounding, conversion or processing of a controlled substance or controlled substance analog by extraction from substances of natural origin or independently by means of chemical synthesis or by a combination of extraction and chemical synthesis and includes any packaging or repackaging of the substance or labeling or relabeling of its container.

Section 30-31-20(A)(1) is silent as to its applicability to the act of artificially growing psilocybin mushrooms. However, *Shaulis-Powell* is instructive in deciding this issue. In *Shaulis-Powell*, one defendant was convicted of violating Section 30-31-20(A)(1) by growing eight marijuana plants in his yard. In reversing that defendant's conviction for trafficking by manufacture, we stated that "the plain meaning of 'manufacture' does not include simply growing marijuana. Without more, growing marijuana does not constitute manufacture."

The State seeks to distinguish *Shaulis-Powell* on its facts by arguing that: (1) mushrooms are different from marijuana plants, which were at issue in *Shaulis-Powell*, and (2) the mushrooms found in Defendant's possession were not in their natural state. In making these arguments, the State relies primarily on the testimony at trial of its expert witness.

The witness, a forensic scientist with the Minnesota Bureau of Criminal Apprehension Forensic Science Laboratory, testified that "Mushrooms are fungi, and so they are different from plants [in] that they don't have seeds; they have spores that they start out with. . . . Spores are . . . the seeds of the mushroom; they're the reproductive cells." The witness also stated that the four stages that make up the life cycle of the mushroom are the spores, the mycelium, the primordia, and the mature fruit. The witness detailed an experiment she conducted in an attempt to duplicate the process Defendant used to grow psilocybin mushrooms. She prepared a substrate using distilled water, brown rice powder, and vermiculite. She placed this mixture into glass jars and inoculated the substrate with psilocybin mushroom spores she purchased legally from an advertisement in High Times Magazine. The witness stated that the mushroom spores were legal because they did not contain psilocybin. However, she detected psilocybin at the "mycelium knot" stage of mushroom development during her experiment. The witness also stated that the process is labor intensive, and, if not followed carefully, the mushrooms will not grow. Based on this evidence, the State argues that Defendant "manufactured" mushrooms as defined by Section 30-31-20(A)(1) and Section 30-31-2(M).

Although *Shaulis-Powell* noted that the marijuana plants at issue "were growing in their natural state when the officers seized them," we based our holding in the case on the statutory definition of "manufacture." We stated that "even if growing marijuana could be considered 'production' under the statute, 'production' is modified by the phrase 'by extraction from substances of natural origin or independently by means of chemical synthesis.'" The same statutory analysis applies in this case.

We do not agree with the State that Defendant's actions met the chemical synthesis requirement of "manufacture" by "using a specialized process [thereby manufacturing] illegal . . . mushrooms from the legal spores . . . received in the mail." This argument is controverted by the State's own expert witness who testified that "spores are . . . the seeds of the mushroom" and that the drug was produced naturally in the mushrooms at the mycelium knot stage. Because there is no evidence that Defendant engaged in "extraction from substances of natural origin or . . . chemical synthesis" as defined by Section 30-31-2(M), his acts of cultivating or growing mushrooms, even if by artificial means, are not prohibited by Section 30-31-20(A)(1). To interpret Section 30-31-20(A)(1) otherwise, as the State suggests, would require us to read language into the statute that is not there. See *Marshall,* 2004 NMCA 104, PP 10, 13 (refusing to read a personal use exception into the CSA, reasoning that to do so "would impermissibly read language into a statute that makes sense as written").

Our holding is also supported by an analysis of the federal counterpart to Section 30-31-20(A)(1), 21 U.S.C. § 841(a)(1) of the Federal Drug Abuse Prevention and Control Act (federal act). See *State v. Carr,* 95 N.M. 755, 760 (Ct. App. 1981) (recognizing that the [New Mexico] CSA is patterned after the federal act and relying on federal interpretation to the extent that the statutes are similar). The federal act, in pertinent part, proscribes any person from knowingly or intentionally manufacturing, distributing, dispensing, or possessing "with intent to manufacture, distribute, or dispense, a controlled substance." Its definitional section, which is virtually identical to Section 30-31-2(M), defines "manufacture" in pertinent part as:

> the production, preparation, propagation, compounding, or processing of a drug or other substance, either directly or indirectly or by extraction from substances of natural origin, or independently by means of chemical synthesis or by a combination of extraction and chemical synthesis, and includes any packaging or repackaging of such substance or labeling or relabeling of its container. 21 U.S.C. § 802(15).

However, the federal act specifically includes a separate definition of "production" as the "planting, cultivation, growing, or harvesting of a controlled substance." 21 U.S.C. § 802(22); see also *United States v. Klein,* 850 F.2d 404, 405 (8th Cir. 1988) (affirming the defendant's conviction of the "manufacture" of marijuana when the defendant grew ninety-four marijuana plants in the basement of his home using fluorescent lights, light fixtures, a heater, planting pots, and soil testing equipment). Because the CSA is patterned after the federal act, we believe the legislature acted intentionally when it omitted a similar definition of "production," criminalizing as manufacture the "planting, cultivation, growing, or harvesting of a controlled substance," from the CSA. [S]ee also *State v. Bennett,* 134 N.M. 705 ("We presume that the legislature knows the law when enacting a statute.").

Because Defendant's conduct did not fall within the ambit of Section 30-31-20(A)(1), we reverse his conviction. We remand for proceedings consistent with this opinion.

b. Proof of Manufacture

Saul v. Arkansas

Supreme Court of Arkansas
365 Ark. 77 (2006)

Brown, J.

On February 13, 2002, Officer Andy Lee of the Bentonville Police Department stopped Saul for speeding in a white van in Bentonville. After running a warrants check on Saul, he discovered that Saul had an outstanding misdemeanor warrant for forging checks. Officer Lee arrested Saul based on the warrant, searched the van, and found a blue plastic container in the rear of the vehicle. He opened the container and found items and substances he associated with a methamphetamine lab. After that discovery, Officer Lee backed away from the van and secured the scene. He also called in another investigator to assist him with the processing of the found items. Evidence was collected, following which some of the items from the blue container were sent to the crime lab and other items were sent to an environmental agency for disposal. When Officer Lee later questioned Saul at the jail about the blue container, Saul denied ever having seen it before. Officer Lee described Saul's denial in his affidavit of probable cause dated February 20, 2002. Saul was charged with manufacturing methamphetamine, based on the contents of the blue container, and also as a habitual offender with two prior convictions for possession of drug paraphernalia.

On November 3, 2003, Saul was tried before a jury on the charge of manufacturing methamphetamine which derived from the February 13, 2002 traffic stop. The State introduced, as part of its case-in-chief, the testimony of Officer Lee, Detective Woodruff, and Officer Allen, as well as testimony from a representative of the Arkansas State Crime Lab, Matthew Sarver. Saul testified in his defense that he had been at work all day on February 13, 2002, and that he was on his way to have dinner with his ex-wife and children at the time he was stopped by Officer Lee. Saul denied any ownership or knowledge of the blue container that was found in his vehicle. The jury found Saul guilty of manufacturing methamphetamine and sentenced him to thirty years.

Saul appealed his judgment of conviction to the court of appeals, and that court reversed. We subsequently granted review.

Saul first claims that his motion for a directed verdict should have been granted because the evidence at trial was insufficient to prove that he had actually engaged in the manufacture of methamphetamine. Saul cites this court to *Chapman v. State*, 343 Ark. 643 (2001), where he claims that this court held the evidence sufficient to prove manufacture of methamphetamine after the state had presented evidence that all of the ingredients, solvents, chemicals, and hardware necessary to manufacture methamphetamine had been found, together with the additional factor of the defendant's attempted flight from the scene. Saul also relies on *Ford v. State*, 75 Ark. App. 126 (2001), where the court of appeals found the evidence insufficient that the defendant was an accomplice to manufacturing methamphetamine, when the State was unable to prove that the process had actually taken place.

Saul also argues that there was no direct evidence that he actually had manufactured methamphetamine. In this regard, he explains that there was no heat source found among the items in the blue container and that Officer Lee testified that a heat source was necessary for the type of manufacturing process that was alleged in this case (the red phosphorus method). Additionally, Saul notes that there were other items necessary for the manufacturing process that were not found in the blue container, including no empty or used bottles of hydrogen peroxide; no used striker plates; no baggies for packaging the unfinished product; no clean coffee filters to filter the unfinished product; and no powder methamphetamine (the finished product). He further emphasizes that no objects were sent to the crime lab for fingerprinting. As a final point, he contends that the blue container did not belong to him. In sum, Saul claims that the circumstantial evidence presented at trial clearly allows for other reasonable explanations consistent with innocence, and that the jury had to resort to surmise and conjecture to find him guilty of manufacturing methamphetamine.

Saul was convicted of manufacturing methamphetamine, in violation of Ark. Code Ann. 5-64-401(a). Section 5-64-101(m) of the Arkansas Code Annotated defines "manufacture":

> "Manufacture" means the production, preparation, propagation, compounding, conversion, or processing of a controlled substance, either directly or indirectly by extraction from substances of natural origin, or independently by means of chemical synthesis, or by a combination of extraction and chemical synthesis, and includes any packaging or repackaging of the substance or labeling or relabeling of its container[.]

We agree with the State that the evidence supporting Saul's conviction is more than sufficient. The arresting officer, Officer Lee, was extensively trained, certified, and experienced in the identification of methamphetamine labs and the production of methamphetamine. Officer Lee testified that he smelled a strong chemical odor coming from Saul's van after he stopped Saul. Inside the van, Officer Lee found a blue plastic container that contained what he recognized as a methamphetamine lab. The State lists dozens of items found in the blue plastic container which are associated with producing methamphetamine by the red phosphorus method, including jars, tubing, funnels, lye, filters stained with red sludge, filters containing iodine crystals, hydrogen peroxide, camping fuel, acetone, hand scales, materials used as a hydrogen chloride gas generator, and items for cutting such as scissors, knives, and razor blades.

In addition, Matthew Sarver, a chemist for the crime lab who was trained and certified in the testing of methamphetamine labs, testified that the evidence in this case indicated that the lab discovered by Officer Lee was used for the red phosphorous method of producing methamphetamine. Mr. Sarver testified that the results of his tests showed iodine and phosphorous on the coffee filters, and he explained that the sludge left on the filters was what is left after methamphetamine has been "cooked." He also stated that tests of the samples taken from the liquid in a plastic bottle showed pseudoephedrine and methanol, and that the liquid appeared to be a "pill soak," which is used in the first stage of manufacturing methamphetamine by combining pills with alcohol. Sarver went on to describe the liquid found in other plastic bottles as organic solvent and acid, both of which are used throughout the process of manufacturing methamphetamine. According to Sarver, tests of samples taken from still another jar showed methamphetamine with an organic solvent. He pointed out that the liquid contained in this jar was actually methamphetamine and that the substance found in the jar is the result of one of the final stages of the manufacturing process.

We do not view the fact that Saul was not apprehended in the process of "cooking meth" as being determinative. In *Stone v. State*, 348 Ark. 661 (2002), police officers found ingredients for making methamphetamine as well as containers the officers suspected to be involved in the manufacture of methamphetamine at the defendant's home. The defendant was later convicted of manufacturing methamphetamine. He appealed and in a challenge to the sufficiency of the evidence, this court found that the State had "produced sufficient evidence that Stone was indeed manufacturing methamphetamine by means of the necessary ingredients and required apparatus." We held that this was so even though the defendant was not caught in the actual act of manufacturing methamphetamine.

We further note that the case of *Chapman v. State* is not helpful to Saul. In that case, this court found the evidence to be sufficient to support the defendant's conviction for manufacturing methamphetamine where the state had presented evidence that all of the ingredients, solvents, chemicals, and hardware necessary to manufacture methamphetamine were found on defendant's property, and where the defendant's attempted flight at the scene of the search provided additional evidence of guilt. Saul now contends that the proof introduced in *Chapman* is the standard against which the proof in the instant case must be weighed. We disagree. As already stated, the multiple ingredients and devices used in methamphetamine production which were found together with the by-products of such production and the actual methamphetamine discovered as well as the testimony of the police officers more than suffices as substantial evidence.

Although Saul concludes that the fact no heat source was found in the blue container is significant, the items found in Saul's van could well have been used with a heat source at a different location to produce the methamphetamine. Simply because a heat source was not present in Saul's van does not lead ineluctably to the conclusion that no heat source had been previously used to manufacture methamphetamine.

Affirmed. Court of appeals reversed.

The items in Saul's possession were certainly suspicious, but did they really prove that Saul had *already* manufactured methamphetamine or only that Saul *planned* to manufacture methamphetamine? Wouldn't the evidence in this case be more consistent with proof of attempted manufacture of methamphetamine rather than manufacture?

3. Accomplice Liability and Conspiracy

As you may recall from your criminal law class, accomplice liability is a doctrine by which a person who helps someone else commit a crime can be convicted of that crime. So, for example, the getaway driver to a bank robbery can be convicted of robbery (as an accomplice) without ever setting foot inside the bank. Conspiracy is a stand-alone offense that criminalizes the agreement to commit some other crime. If A and B agree to rob a bank together and take some action in furtherance of their plan, they are both guilty of the crime of conspiracy (whether or not the robbery ever actually occurs).

Though accomplice liability and conspiracy apply to virtually all crimes, they play an especially important role in drug enforcement. Because drug crimes occur within a marketplace, drug conspiracies are often much more sprawling than bank robbery conspiracies. Selling drugs is an ongoing business enterprise, not a discrete crime or series of crimes. As a result, people engaged in the illegal drug business collaborate with one another in a different way than people who are planning to rob a bank. This fact, in combination with the practice of sentencing offenders based primarily on drug type and quantity (discussed in Chapter 4), can sometimes result in relatively lengthy sentences for peripheral participants in drug conspiracies. It can also make it difficult to decide what conspiratorial group a particular defendant belongs to. For example, is the mid-level drug dealer a co-conspirator of the drug wholesaler or is he a co-conspirator of the street-level dealer?

For similar reasons, an act that might seem like a social courtesy to the person doing it could make them a drug trafficking accomplice or conspirator in the eyes of the law. Few people would drive a friend to rob a bank as a friendly favor. But a person whose friend is a drug user might be willing to drive them to make a purchase on the way to dinner or a movie without a second thought. In *Regan v. Wyoming* (presented above in the section on constructive possession), for example, the court overturned the marijuana possession conviction of a defendant who had driven his friend to a few marijuana sales. The court concluded there was insufficient evidence to prove Regan intended to exercise dominion and control over the marijuana. In footnote 5 and the accompanying text, however, the court observed that the evidence "might have supported" a conviction for "conspiracy to distribute" or distribution as an accomplice, if the prosecution had charged Regan with either offense.

As you read the cases that follow, consider whether you think conspiracy and accomplice liability principles should apply the same way to market-based crimes, like drug offenses, as they do to traditional offenses. If not, what additional limits would you place on conspiracy and accomplice liability for drug crimes?

a. Drug Conspiracies and Minimally Involved Participants

United States v. Brigham

United States Court of Appeals for the Seventh Circuit
977 F.2d 317 (1992)

Easterbrook, J.

Steep penalties await those who deal in drugs. Buying or selling 10 kilograms of cocaine—even agreeing to do so, without carrying through—means a minimum penalty of 10 years' imprisonment, without possibility of parole.

The "mandatory" minimum is mandatory only from the perspective of judges. To the parties, the sentence is negotiable. Did a marginal participant in a conspiracy really understand that a 10-kilo deal lay in store? A prosecutor may charge a lesser crime, if he offers something in return. Let's make a deal. Does the participant have valuable information; can he offer other assistance? Congress authorized prosecutors to pay for aid with sentences below the "floor." Let's make a deal.

Bold dealers may turn on their former comrades, setting up phony sales and testifying at the ensuing trials. Timorous dealers may provide information about their sources and customers. Drones of the organization—the runners, mules, drivers, and lookouts—have nothing comparable to offer. They lack the contacts and trust necessary to set up big deals, and they know little information of value. Whatever tales they have to tell, their bosses will have related. Defendants unlucky enough to be innocent have no information at all and are more likely to want vindication at trial, losing not only the opportunity to make a deal but also the 2-level reduction the sentencing guidelines provide for accepting responsibility.

Mandatory minimum penalties, combined with a power to grant exceptions, create a prospect of inverted sentencing. The more serious the defendant's crimes, the lower the sentence—because the greater his wrongs, the more information and assistance he has to offer to a prosecutor. Discounts for the top dogs have the virtue of necessity, because rewards for assistance are essential to the business of detecting and punishing crime. But what makes the post-discount sentencing structure topsy-turvy is the mandatory minimum, binding only for the hangers on. What is to be said for such terms, which can visit draconian penalties on the small fry without increasing prosecutors' ability to wring information from their bosses?

Our case illustrates a sentencing inversion. Such an outcome is neither illegal nor unconstitutional, because offenders have no right to be sentenced in proportion to their wrongs. Still, meting out the harshest penalties to those least culpable is troubling, because it accords with no one's theory of appropriate punishments.

Agents of the Drug Enforcement Agency* learned from an informant that Craig Thompson was in the market to buy 10 kilograms of cocaine. The DEA's undercover agents feigned willingness to supply him. During negotiations, Thompson said that he had just sold 17 kilograms and needed 10 more that very day to tide his organization over until the arrival of a shipment that he was expecting. Thompson and the agents did not trust one another. Jeffrey Carter, one of Thompson's goons, searched an agent; the agent's gun, normal in the business, did not trouble Carter, but a transmitter or recorder would mean big trouble. Carter was not very good at his job; he didn't find the concealed recorder. Thompson ultimately agreed to pay $30,000 per kilogram, a premium price for quick service. After the agents let on that they didn't trust Thompson any more than Thompson trusted them, Thompson agreed to let the agents hold his Rolls Royce as collateral until payment. In the agents' presence, Thompson called Tyrone Amos and told him to pick up "ten of those things today" at a suburban motel. Thompson and Carter would hand over the Rolls in a different suburb.

At the appointed time, less than five hours after the agents first met Thompson, one team descended on a restaurant to receive the Rolls Royce and another decamped to the motel to "deliver" the cocaine. Amos arrived at the motel in a car driven by Anthony Brigham. Amos and the agents at the motel had a conversation; Brigham stayed in the car. Carter had not appeared at the restaurant with the Rolls Royce, so everyone settled down to wait. Brigham looked around the parking lot but scrunched down in his seat when the agents' Corvette drove slowly by. At the restaurant Thompson and the agents discussed future deals of 50–100 kilograms per month. At the motel Brigham paced nervously in the lobby. After touring the parking lot again, lingering over the Corvette, Brigham joined Amos at a nearby gas station, where Amos placed a phone call. The two had a conversation and returned to the motel, where Amos told the agents that Carter and the Rolls were still missing. While Amos and one agent were dining together some distance from the motel, Thompson paged Amos with news that the Rolls had arrived.

Back at the motel, the agents went through the motions of delivering cocaine. As Amos headed for the agents' car to retrieve the drug from the trunk, Brigham moved his car to a location from which he could keep the delivery in sight. But there was no cocaine. Before Amos could open the trunk other agents moved in, arresting Amos and Brigham, just as they pinched Thompson and Carter at the restaurant.

All but Brigham pleaded guilty and provided valuable assistance to prosecutors. All but Brigham were sentenced to less than the "mandatory" minimum. Thompson received 84 months' imprisonment and Amos 75 months', after the prosecutor made motions under § 3553(e). Carter, who was allowed to plead to a charge that did not carry a minimum term, received 4 years' probation, 4 months of which were

* The court's opinion mistakenly referred to the DEA as the "Drug Enforcement Agency." Its true name is the Drug Enforcement Administration. [*Footnote by casebook author.*]

to be in a work-release program run by the Salvation Army. That left Brigham, who went to trial, was convicted, and received the "mandatory" term of 120 months' imprisonment.

Was the evidence sufficient? Appellate judges do not serve as additional jurors. After a jury convicts, the question becomes whether any sensible person could find, beyond a reasonable doubt, that the defendant committed the crime.

Brigham emphasizes that "mere" presence at the scene of a crime does not implicate the bystander in that offense. Conspiracy is agreement and what proof of agreement did the prosecutor present? Brigham arrived with Amos, conferred with Amos, and was in position to watch an exchange occur. No one testified that Brigham had any role in the exchange or Thompson's organization. Although the prosecutor portrayed Brigham as a lookout, he asks: What kind of lookout would be unarmed, without radio, pager, cellular phone, or any other way to give or receive alerts? What countersurveillance operative would hunker down in the car rather than keep a hawk-eyed watch? Thompson, Carter, and Amos, who reaped rewards for their assistance, were conspicuously absent at Brigham's trial. Had they no evidence to offer against him?

No one questions the rule that "mere presence" at the scene of a crime does not prove conspiracy. "Mere" presence differs from, say, "revealing" presence. Like many a weasel word, "mere" summarizes a conclusion rather than assisting in analysis. When the evidence does not permit an inference that the defendant was part of the criminal organization, the court applies the label "mere presence." So we must examine the evidence, taking inferences in the light most favorable to the jury's verdict, rather than resting content with slogans.

Brigham shows up on short notice with Amos, who the jury could conclude was there to receive 10 kilograms of cocaine from strangers whom Thompson and Amos do not trust. Is Amos likely to come alone? Is a companion apt to be ignorant of the nature and risks of the transaction? For almost three hours Brigham remains at the motel, generally observant and generally nervous; he follows Amos to a pay phone where a telephone call and conversation ensue. Amos reveals the contents of this conversation to the agents; the jury could conclude that he revealed it to Brigham too. While Amos and an agent go to dinner, Brigham keeps watch. After Amos returns, eye contact and a nod from Amos lead Brigham to take up position where he can watch the trunk of the agents' car. Just what *was* Brigham doing for three hours in the lobby and parking lot of the motel, if not assisting Amos? He was not exactly passing through while a drug deal went down around him. Brigham did not testify, and his lawyer offered no hypothesis at trial. At oral argument of this appeal the best his counsel could do was to suggest that Brigham might have believed that Amos was picking up counterfeit money rather than drugs. Tell us another! The jury was entitled to conclude that Brigham knew about, and joined, a conspiracy to distribute cocaine.

Thin the evidence was, but it was also sufficient.

Wise exercise of prosecutorial discretion can prevent egregious sentencing inversions. How that discretion is to be exercised is a subject for the political branches. Brigham joined the conspiracy and received a sentence authorized by Congress. His judicial remedies are at a close.

AFFIRMED.

Bauer, J., dissenting.

I respectfully dissent. Taking all the evidence as described in the majority opinion as absolutely true, and viewing it in the light most favorable to the government, I still do not find that any sensible juror could find Brigham guilty of the crime of conspiracy beyond a reasonable doubt. At oral argument, counsel for Brigham could only suggest, in answer to a question from the bench as to what explanation he could give for Brigham's actions on the day in question, "that Brigham might have believed that Amos was picking up counterfeit money rather than drugs." An unbelievable scenario. The fact is, no one testified as to what exactly Brigham was doing or why he was doing it; no one, in spite of the marvelous totally cooperating witnesses who, if the government's theory is correct, could have nailed Brigham's hide to the jailhouse wall. But they didn't. And it is not Brigham's missing explanation that is fatal; it is the government's inability to explain that creates the problem.

Tell us another, indeed, but only if it is the government tale; the accused has absolutely no burden to explain anything. The government accuses, the defendant says "prove it," and the government says the suspicious activity is enough to convince and convict.

And so it proved.

I would have directed a verdict of "not guilty" had I been the trial judge and I construe my role in review to be the same. I do not believe the evidence sufficient to convince a sensible juror of proof beyond a reasonable doubt. The existence of cooperating witnesses who knew all and told nothing virtually implies the missing witness analysis: you had the control, you didn't produce, I infer the testimony would have been adverse to you.

I would reverse.

Accomplice liability and conspiracy charges can sometimes ensnare people from legitimate lines of business. Consider the case of Alfred Anaya, who ran a stereo installation business, Valley Customs Audio Fanatics, and ended up convicted of conspiracy to distribute cocaine, methamphetamine, and marijuana. Anaya's case, which is presented below, drew the attention of *Wired* magazine. *See* Brendan I. Koerner, *Alfred Anaya Put Secret Compartments in Cars. So the DEA Put Him in Prison*, Wired (March 19, 2013).

According to the story in *Wired*, "[b]y 2002, Anaya had become one of the most sought-after installers in Southern California, with a client list that included rappers, pro basketball players, and porn stars. *Mobile Electronics* honored him as one of the top 100 installers in the nation, and his systems were later featured in the bikini-laden pages of magazines like *Lowrider* and *Lug*." To capitalize on his success, Anaya opened up Valley Custom Audio Fanatics in San Fernando. But, "[l]ike many people blessed with formidable creative talent, Anaya was a horrendous manager of both time and money. He took on too many projects and failed to keep track of expenditures." This led to financial troubles and, in 2007, Anaya "was forced to move the failing business to his home."

Not long after that, Anaya took a job that would ultimately lead to his arrest and prosecution:

> Anaya . . . offered all of his clients a lifetime warranty: If there was ever any problem with his handiwork, he would fix it for the cost of parts alone—no questions asked.
>
> Anaya's customers typically took advantage of this deal when their fiendishly loud subwoofers blew out or their fiberglass speaker boxes developed hairline cracks. But in late January 2009, a man whom Anaya knew only as Esteban called for help with a more exotic product: a hidden compartment that Anaya had installed in his Ford F-150 pickup truck. Over the years, these secret stash spots—or traps, as they're known in automotive slang—have become a popular luxury item among the wealthy and shady alike. This particular compartment was located behind the truck's backseat, which Anaya had rigged with a set of hydraulic cylinders linked to the vehicle's electrical system. The only way to make the seat slide forward and reveal its secret was by pressing and holding four switches simultaneously: two for the power door locks and two for the windows.
>
> Esteban said the seat was no longer responding to the switch combination and that no amount of jiggling could make it budge. He pleaded with Anaya to take a look.
>
> Anaya was unsettled by this request, for he had suspicions about the nature of Esteban's work. There is nothing intrinsically illegal about building traps, which are commonly used to hide everything from pricey jewelry to legal handguns. But the activity runs afoul of California law if an installer knows for certain that his compartment will be used to transport drugs. The maximum penalty is three years in prison. Anaya thus thought it wise to deviate from his standard no-questions-asked policy before agreeing to honor his warranty. "There's nothing in there I shouldn't know about, is there?" he asked. Esteban assured him that he needn't worry.
>
> Esteban drove the F-150 to Anaya's modest ranch-style house and parked by the back porch. A friend of his, who introduced himself as Cesar, followed right behind in a black Honda Ridgeline truck. The 37-year-old Anaya, a boyishly handsome man whose neck and arms are covered with

tattoos of dice and Japanese art, tested the switches that controlled the truck's trap. He heard the hydraulics whirr to life, but the seat stayed firmly in place. He would have to use brute force.

Anaya punched a precise hole through the upholstery with his 24-volt Makita drill, probing for the screws that anchored the seat to the hydraulics. After a few moments he heard a loud pop as the drill seemed to puncture something soft. When he finally managed to remove the backseat, he saw what he had hit: a wad of cash about 4 inches thick. The whole compartment was overflowing with such bundles, several of which spilled onto the truck's floor. Esteban had jammed the trap by stuffing it with too much cash—over $800,000 in total.

Anaya stumbled back from the truck's cab, livid. "Get it out of here," he growled at Esteban. "I don't want to know about this. I don't want any problems."

Esteban Magallon Maldanado and Cesar Bonilla Montiel scrambled to haul armfuls of money from the F-150 to the Ridgeline's trunk. They wanted to stay in Anaya's good graces, because men with his skills are extremely valuable in the narcotics trade. To distribute product from wholesalers to retailers, drug-trafficking organizations need vehicles equipped with well-disguised traps so that loads aren't routinely seized while in transit. The word in the California underworld was that no one built more elegant traps than Anaya, a perfectionist who made sure his hiding spots were invisible to even the most expert eyes. Maldanado and Montiel, key players in a smuggling ring that was sending large quantities of cocaine and methamphetamine to the Midwest, were eager to use his services again.

Once all of the money had been moved to the Ridgeline, Anaya, now feeling calmer, agreed to fix the F-150's trap for $1,500—a third of what he had originally charged to install it. He even offered to improve the compartment by adding another switch—the one that reclined the driver's seat—to the unlocking sequence.

A grateful Maldanado then asked Anaya if he could install a trap in the Ridgeline too. The Honda truck already had one, but it was the work of a rank amateur—just a crude hole sawed into the base of the trunk. Maldanado wanted an electronic trap like the F-150's, and he offered to leave a cash deposit so Anaya could buy the necessary hydraulics.

Anaya, who was deeply in debt to numerous creditors, decided to accept the job. He hadn't totally forgiven Maldanado for failing to warn him about the money jammed in the trap, but he figured that he was still adhering to the letter of the law. The fact was that he hadn't seen any drugs, and there had been no discussion of how Maldanado had earned his small fortune. Given those circumstances, Anaya assumed that he was immune from legal trouble in connection with his meticulous creations. He was, after all, just an installer.

Just a few years after installing the trap for Maldanado, Anaya was sentenced to 292 months (or a little over 24 years) in federal prison. The Tenth Circuit upheld Anaya's conviction and sentence in the opinion that follows.

United States v. Anaya

United States Court of Appeals for the Tenth Circuit
727 F.3d 1043 (2013)

Matheson, J.

Alfred Anaya was indicted on one count of conspiracy to distribute and possess with intent to distribute cocaine, methamphetamine ("meth"), and marijuana[.] A jury convicted him on the conspiracy charges related to cocaine and meth[.] The district court sentenced him to 292 months in prison for the conspiracy count[.][1]

Count One of the indictment charged Mr. Anaya with conspiracy to distribute and possess with intent to distribute more than 5 kilograms of cocaine, more than 50 grams of meth, and marijuana, in violation of 21 U.S.C. § 841(a)(1), (b)(1)(A)(ii)(II), (b)(1)(A)(viii) and (b)(1)(D). Count One also charged him with aiding and abetting the conspiracy under 18 U.S.C. § 2.

Evidence at trial revealed an extensive drug trafficking organization ("DTO") that bought marijuana, cocaine, and meth in California and transported the drugs for sale in Kansas. Californians Esteban Magallon-Maldanado and Cesar Bonilla-Montiel headed the DTO, which included around twenty individuals. Curtis Crow ran the DTO operations in Kansas. The evidence included intercepted calls and records of hotel, airline, and car rental costs incurred by the DTO for drug transportation. The DTO used several vehicles that had been modified to include hidden compartments to transport drugs. Mr. Anaya built the hidden compartments. He lived in California during this time.

Mr. Bonilla-Montiel learned from a friend that Mr. Anaya installed compartments in cars that were difficult for police to discover and open. The DTO employed Mr. Anaya to build compartments in their vehicles. Mr. Bonilla-Montiel credited Mr. Anaya with enabling the DTO's drug loads to travel without detection from California to Kansas.

In late 2008, a secret compartment that Mr. Anaya had installed in the DTO's Ford F150 truck jammed after being stuffed with $800,000. Mr. Bonilla-Montiel and Mr. Magallon-Maldanado testified that they took the vehicle to Mr. Anaya's residence in California, where he worked on cars. Mr. Bonilla-Montiel also brought

1. Because Mr. Anaya challenges the sufficiency of the evidence for his conviction, we recite the facts in the light most favorable to the Government.

the DTO's Honda Ridgeline truck to determine whether Mr. Anaya could install a compartment in it.

Mr. Anaya could not open the compartment in the F150 using the series of buttons that he had programmed to open it, so he took it apart. When the compartment opened and Mr. Anaya could see large amounts of money inside, he said, "I don't want to see this; I don't want any problems." He immediately got out of the car. He accepted $1,500 as payment for opening and repairing the F150 compartment. He continued to build compartments for the DTO, including the compartment in the Ridgeline.

Mr. Bonilla-Montiel asked Mr. Anaya to install a compartment in the Ridgeline that was large enough to hold "at least 10 kilos" and showed him a red brick to indicate the approximate size of a kilo. While Mr. Anaya was building the compartment in the Ridgeline, the DTO used the compartment he installed in the F150 to transport six kilos of cocaine and five pounds of meth. Police stopped the F150 during this time as it was travelling with drugs from California to Kansas, but they could not find or open Mr. Anaya's compartment and released the F150 and its drivers. Mr. Crow sold the drugs from the F150 to two of the DTO's top distributors for approximately $70,000–$80,000.

In 2009, officers began surveillance of DTO operations, including a wiretap that intercepted calls to and from Mr. Anaya between January 30, 2009, and November 29, 2009. During this time, the officers witnessed DTO members dropping off and picking up many vehicles from Mr. Anaya's residence and Mr. Anaya meeting with known drug dealers.

On February 19, 2009, officers saw a white Toyota Sequoia arrive at Mr. Anaya's home. Mr. Bonilla-Montiel testified that he and Mr. Magallon-Maldanado drove the Sequoia to Mr. Anaya's home to pick up the Ridgeline. After Mr. Anaya showed them how to work the Ridgeline's hidden compartment, they paid him $5,000 in $10 and $20 bills and took the Ridgeline. Mr. Crow and other DTO members loaded the Ridgeline's compartment with 100 pounds of marijuana. Another DTO member, Jaime Rodriguez, drove it from California to Kansas. Mr. Crow then left the Ridgeline, still loaded with marijuana, at DTO member Noah Adams's house in Kansas for safekeeping.

On another occasion, Mr. Rodriguez transported cocaine and meth in the Ridgeline's compartment from California to Kansas. On that trip, Mr. Rodriguez was pulled over and given a speeding ticket, but no drugs were detected. After the trip, Mr. Crow kept the Ridgeline at his house in Kansas and used it as a safe for drugs and money. Mr. Rodriguez also made later trips in the Ridgeline to transport marijuana.

Mr. Bonilla-Montiel, Mr. Magallon-Maldanado, and Mr. Crow arranged for Mr. Anaya to install a hidden compartment between the back seats of the Toyota Sequoia for "4 kilos or to store money." Mr. Anaya charged them $4,500 for the work on the Sequoia. Mr. Anaya warned Mr. Crow not to show anyone how to open the compartment or where it was located because the police had apprehended previous cars with his compartments. Mr. Crow later unloaded cocaine from the compartment in the Sequoia. Mr. Bonilla-Montiel and other DTO members transported cocaine and proceeds from marijuana sales between California and Kansas in the Sequoia.

On March 30, 2009, Mr. Bonilla-Montiel went to Mr. Anaya's house to pick up the Sequoia and drop off a Toyota Camry so that Mr. Anaya could figure out where to put a compartment. Mr. Bonilla-Montiel testified that the compartment in the Camry was to hold drugs or money, and that it was Mr. Crow's car at the time.

On April 5, 2009, police officers stopped several DTO members during a return trip to California. Officers found $106,000 in heat-sealed packets in the Sequoia's hidden compartment and noted that someone had insulated the "sophisticated" compartment to mask the smell of drugs.

On April 4–6, 2009, officers intercepted calls between Mr. Bonilla-Montiel and Mr. Anaya, during which Mr. Anaya said that he could put "three speakers" in the Camry for $2,500. Mr. Bonilla-Montiel testified "three speakers" was their code term for three kilos or three pounds of meth. Once Mr. Anaya completed the compartment in the Camry, DTO members used the car to transport two pounds of meth from California to Kansas in the hidden compartment.

On April 24, 2009, officers stopped the Camry and found the two pounds of meth concealed in the compartment. Mr. Crow and Mr. Bonilla-Montiel then began to fear that Mr. Anaya was involved with the police. They traded the Ridgeline for an Altima and did no further business with Mr. Anaya.

On November 18, 2009, police executed a search warrant at Mr. Anaya's home and shop. Officers found more than 15 removed airbags, insulation, electrical devices required to build the hidden compartments, rifles, shotguns, pistols, bulletproof vests, and various ammunition. They found stereo wires but no speakers. Mr. Anaya confessed that he had built hidden compartments in cars for more than ten years.

After the Government presented its case, Mr. Anaya moved for a judgment of acquittal under Rule 29. The district court denied the motion, finding there was sufficient evidence for a reasonable jury to find him guilty. The jury found Mr. Anaya guilty of the single count of conspiracy[.] But using a special verdict form, the jury found him responsible for conspiring to distribute and possess with intent to distribute only cocaine and meth and not marijuana. Mr. Anaya then moved again for acquittal and for a new trial. The district court denied those motions. The court sentenced him to 292 months of imprisonment for the conspiracy count[.] Mr. Anaya filed a timely appeal.

Mr. Anaya ... argues ... the evidence was insufficient for the jury to convict him of conspiracy[.]

To prove a conspiracy, the Government must show "(1) that two or more persons agreed to violate the law, (2) that the defendant knew at least the essential objects of the conspiracy, (3) that the defendant knowingly and voluntarily became a part of it, and (4) that the alleged coconspirators were interdependent." *United States v.*

Caldwell, 589 F.3d 1323, 1329 (10th Cir.2009). In a drug conspiracy case, the Government is not required to prove that the defendant possessed the drugs or played a major role in the conspiracy.

Mr. Anaya's sufficiency of the evidence arguments contest only whether the Government proved his knowledge of "the essential objects of the conspiracy" (second element) and knowledge that he "became a part of it" (third element). He does not deny that he voluntarily joined the conspiracy. Instead, he argues that he did not *knowingly* join the conspiracy because he did not know its scope and objectives. Although he concedes knowing that the DTO used his compartments for illegal activity, he contends the Government failed to prove that he knew the DTO used his compartments for drug trafficking and what types of drugs the DTO trafficked. Mr. Anaya's arguments combine the second and third elements of conspiracy and overstate what the Government was required to show.

The Government needed to prove that Mr. Anaya had "a general awareness of both the scope and the objectives of the conspiracy." Evidence that he knew all of the details of the DTO's operations was not necessary, only that he "shared a common purpose or design with his alleged coconspirators."

The government did not need to prove that Mr. Anaya knew of every type or amount of drug trafficked by the conspiracy. In *United States v. De La Torre*, 599 F.3d 1198 (10th Cir.2010), we explained that 21 U.S.C. § 841(a)(1) "does not require the Government to prove a defendant knew the precise nature of the controlled substance he possessed, so long as he knew he did in fact possess a controlled substance." Although Mr. De La Torre was charged with possessing controlled substances and not with conspiracy, the same reasoning applies to defendants charged with conspiracy. The knowledge element of conspiracy was satisfied if the Government proved that Mr. Anaya knew that conspiracy members "knowingly or intentionally" possessed a "controlled substance" with the intent to distribute it. 21 U.S.C. § 841(a).

"[K]nowledge [of illegal activity] and presence [at the crime scene] coupled with knowing participation in the illegal drug activities are sufficient to sustain a drug conspiracy." Evidence of a defendant's actions can be used to establish the defendant's knowledge "in the context of a conspiracy prosecution."

At trial, the Government presented evidence that Mr. Anaya

- built multiple hidden compartments in vehicles for the DTO that were insulated to mask the smell of drugs;
- witnessed $800,000 in one of his compartments in a DTO vehicle;
- used "kilos" as a unit of measurement for building compartments;
- communicated by phone with the DTO through a secret code to discuss compartment sizes; and
- warned Mr. Crow not to discuss the compartments or how they worked with anyone to avoid police detection.

Evidence of Mr. Anaya's actions—installing secure, hidden compartments, which furthered the conspiracy's goals—pointed to his knowing participation in the conspiracy. A reasonable jury could infer from the evidence that Mr. Anaya knew the conspiracy's general drug-trafficking goals and knew that he helped the DTO to transport drugs without detection. The conspiracy's objective was to transport drugs, and the compartments that Mr. Anaya custom made for the conspiracy were instrumental to fulfilling that goal. The evidence was therefore sufficient to establish the second and third elements of conspiracy.

Mr. Anaya relies on *United States v. Lovern,* 590 F.3d 1095 (10th Cir.2009), in which we reversed the conspiracy conviction of a computer technician at an Internet pharmacy. Although evidence showed it was likely he "knew something was wrong," the evidence was insufficient that he knew he was helping fill prescriptions "outside the usual course of professional medical practice or without a legitimate medical purpose." Unlike Mr. Lovern, who performed routine tasks and never had contact with the prescribing doctors, Mr. Anaya performed a specialized task that was integral to the DTO's goals, and he interacted directly with the conspiracy's leaders.

Based on the foregoing, Mr. Anaya's challenge to the sufficiency of the evidence on his conspiracy conviction fails.

We therefore affirm Mr. Anaya's conviction.

One of the most striking examples of the potential for people on the periphery of the drug trade to find themselves facing stiff criminal penalties is the so-called "girlfriend" drug conspiracy cases. In these cases, significant others of drug dealers (often wives or girlfriends) have been convicted of conspiracy and received lengthy prison sentences for arguably minor involvement in the drug operations of their boyfriends or husbands.

Single Moms, Battered Women, and Other Sex-Based Anomalies in the Gender-Free World of the Federal Sentencing Guidelines
Myrna S. Reader

20 Pepperdine Law Review 905 (1993)

The most troubling gender questions concerning female offenders are raised by simply reading the published facts of many drug cases, which identify women by their relationships with men. Such females are typically married to, living with, or intimately involved with males who are described as being central to the conspiracies in question. In contrast, the women often have relatively minor roles in the conspiracies: facilitating drug deals by answering the telephone, opening the door, or acting as couriers for their male intimates. While the mate of a white-collar criminal may be shielded from his crime in the suites, the live-in companion of a drug dealer who sells his wares on the streets or at home is not equally sheltered. Mere presence is easily converted to membership in a conspiracy by the number of ways in which women have been socialized to further their relationships with men. Thus, indigent women can become active participants in crime by permitting drugs in the home, answering the door or the telephone, and by giving or bringing contraband to buyers.

Given the nature of such women's relationships, unless a female leaves her mate who is dealing drugs, it may be difficult for her to totally disassociate herself from the conspiracy. In other words, she is likely to be aware of his criminal endeavors and familial actions on her part often promote his criminal activities. Undoubtedly, such females do receive the benefit of drug money, and have enough involvement with illicit activity to be charged and convicted of crime. However, while the mates of drug dealers and mates of men accused of white-collar crime equally receive the benefits of tainted money, mates of drug dealers usually live at the scene of criminal activity. Therefore, some women who are poor may be sucked into crime, whereas richer women who associate with white-collar felons do not face sacrificing their relationships in order to remain crime-free.

The interrelationship of gender to crime and sentencing is fairly complex in such situations and raises a number of policy questions. When charging conspiracies, how do prosecutors determine which women to arrest? Are some women really arrested to provide leverage for plea bargaining with the more culpable male, either to provide information and testimony in exchange for immunity, or to be dismissed in exchange for the male's plea? Since decisions concerning the nature of the charge and plea bargaining rest with the prosecutor, gender questions concerning a woman's culpability are often not raised at the appellate level because evidence supporting the verdict will always exist. For example, one female defendant who moved to Minneapolis to marry her male codefendant claimed she had no criminal intent to join the conspiracy, but found herself counting money and writing messages for him. Large quantities of drugs and money were found in their residence and she admitted to maintaining ledgers. Needless to say, the jury convicted her. Similarly, another women who pleaded guilty to a drug conspiracy agreed to accompany her boyfriend of five years on a drug buy and carry the purchase money. While she claimed it was the first time she had actively participated in his drug dealing, she admitted that for two years she suspected his illegal earnings were drug-related.

It is obvious that such women are not really innocent. However, unless the prosecutor permits them to plead to lesser offenses, they become subject to long mandatory minimums which are disproportionate to their culpability as a member of the conspiracy. Men can similarly show circumstances in which they are given sentences that have no relationship to their activities in a conspiracy, but such arguments will depend on the facts in a given case rather than on gender-based role patterns.

b. Recommending a Source from Which to Buy Drugs

United States v. Tyler

United States Court of Appeals for the Second Circuit
758 F.2d 66 (1985)

Meskill, J.

Warren Tyler appeals from a judgment of conviction entered in the United States District Court for the Southern District of New York on a jury verdict. Following a two day trial, the jury found Tyler guilty of conspiracy to distribute heroin in violation of 21 U.S.C. § 846 and of aiding and abetting the distribution of heroin in violation of 18 U.S.C. § 2 and 21 U.S.C. § 841. Tyler was sentenced to concurrent terms of two years imprisonment on each of the two counts, to be followed by a five year special parole term on the aiding and abetting count. He is currently serving his sentence.

Tyler's arrest, indictment and conviction stemmed from a purchase of heroin by New York City Police Detective Cleveland Baxter. Baxter made the actual purchase of heroin from James Bennett. Tyler was arrested because Baxter identified Tyler as the man who had introduced him to Bennett. Tyler was charged in two counts of a four count indictment. Count one charged conspiracy to distribute heroin and count two charged aiding and abetting the distribution of heroin.

At trial, Baxter was the government's main witness. He testified that on May 10, 1984, he went over to Harlem as part of an undercover narcotics operation. His goal was to make at least two purchases of drugs. As he was walking along the street he encountered Tyler. After an exchange of greetings, Tyler asked Baxter "if everything was all right." Baxter told Tyler that he "was looking for some good dope." (Dope is the street name for heroin.) Tyler told Baxter that "he would take care of [him]."

The two began to walk down the street. They stopped and Tyler went off to the side and spoke briefly to an unidentified individual. Tyler returned to Baxter and told him that "he was trying to get [him] something that was good, because there was a lot of dope on the street that was not good." The two then continued to walk down the street.

They next encountered Bennett. Tyler and Bennett stepped off to the side and had a brief conversation, after which Bennett walked over to Baxter and asked "how many did [he] want." Baxter told him three. Baxter and Bennett then began to walk down the street. As they were walking, they exchanged three glassine envelopes containing heroin for thirty dollars.

After completing the transaction with Bennett, Baxter turned around and walked back up the street. As he was walking away, Tyler approached him and asked him for some change. Baxter told him that he was low on cash and "that maybe he could check with [Bennett] and [Bennett would] take care of him." Baxter testified that Tyler replied "yes, but he just wanted to have more change, he was trying to get something." Baxter gave Tyler seventy-five cents and the two parted company. Baxter reported the buy to his back-up team and they arrested Tyler approximately twenty minutes later. At the time of his arrest, Tyler was carrying two dollars and seventy-five cents.

Tyler was the only witness called by the defense. He testified that although Baxter asked him about drugs, he did not take Baxter to Bennett nor did he have any role in the sale. He did testify, however, that he saw the sale take place and that after it was completed he approached Baxter to ask him for some money.

After two days of deliberations the jury found Tyler guilty on both the conspiracy count and the aiding and abetting count. Tyler's motion for entry of judgment of acquittal notwithstanding the verdict or for a new trial was denied. The appeal before us ensued.

Tyler's first argument is that there was insufficient evidence of an agreement between himself and Baxter to establish the existence of a conspiracy to distribute heroin.

[W]e have recognized that "'[a] conspiracy by its very nature is a secretive operation.'" Thus, we have held that the existence of "a conspiracy . . . may be established . . . through circumstantial evidence." Moreover, to be sufficient "the evidence need not have excluded every possible hypothesis of innocence."

Our narrow standard of review, however, does not require us to affirm all conspiracy convictions. On the contrary, we have found the evidence insufficient to sustain a conspiracy conviction in a number of cases. Likewise, we find the evidence in the instant case insufficient to sustain Tyler's conspiracy conviction.

The government's evidence against Tyler consisted mainly of Baxter's testimony. According to Baxter's version of the transaction, Tyler told Baxter that he would get him some good dope. After making some type of inquiry of an unidentified individual, Tyler encountered Bennett. Tyler had a brief side conversation with Bennett and Bennett then approached Baxter. Bennett and Baxter walked away from Tyler and consummated their deal. The two then separated and Tyler walked up to Baxter and asked him for some change. Conspicuously absent from this scenario is any evidence that Tyler asked Baxter how much heroin he sought to purchase, that Tyler indicated that he had a specific source of heroin in mind for Baxter, that Tyler knew where to find Bennett or expected him to be in the area, or that Tyler had made any previous deals with Bennett.[1]

The evidence adduced by the government merely shows that Tyler helped a willing buyer locate a willing seller. As we have stated in the past, such evidence, standing

1. The government argues that the jury could have concluded that two dollars of the two dollars and seventy-five cents Tyler was carrying at the time of his arrest came from Bennett. From this, the government claims that the jury could have inferred that Tyler had a stake in the outcome of Bennett's sale. The evidentiary support for these inferences along with the other evidence in this case is simply not substantial enough to establish a conspiracy between Tyler and Bennett.

alone, is insufficient to establish the existence of an agreement between the facilitator and the seller. *United States v. Hysohion,* 448 F.2d 343, 347 (2d Cir. 1971) ("The fact that Rimbaud told Everett, a willing buyer, how to make contact with a willing seller does not necessarily imply that there was an agreement between that seller . . . and Rimbaud."); *United States v. Torres,* 519 F.2d 723, 726 (2d Cir.) ("membership in a conspiracy is not established . . . by the fact that a defendant told a willing buyer how to make contact with a willing seller").

In an attempt to fill in the holes in its case, the government relies on the jury's obvious disbelief of Tyler's testimony to support the conspiracy conviction. We also agree that the jury has a right to consider the defendant's lack of credibility in reaching its verdict.

Th[is] proposition[], however, [is] not helpful to the government's case here. In each of the cases in which the jury's disbelief was relied on as a factor supporting affirmance, the evidence apart from the incredibility of the defendant's testimony was sufficient or very close to sufficient. We merely added that the defendant's incredible story was another circumstance that the jury was entitled to consider. Here, on the other hand, the evidence of an agreement between Tyler and Bennett was nonexistent. Thus, although the jury's disbelief of a defendant's testimony may supplement already existing evidence and help make the evidence in a borderline case sufficient, in the instant case there was simply no existing evidence to supplement.

In sum, even viewing the evidence in the light most favorable to the government, the evidence shows no more than that Tyler helped a willing buyer find a willing seller. Under the law of this Circuit, such evidence is insufficient to prove the existence of a conspiratorial agreement between Tyler and the seller. Thus, Tyler's conspiracy conviction must be reversed.

Tyler also urges us to reverse his aiding and abetting conviction. He argues that because the government failed to prove that he had a stake in the outcome of Bennett's sale the evidence was insufficient to establish aiding and abetting. We do not find this argument compelling.

[T]he requirements for the offense of aiding and abetting are "'that [a defendant] in some sort associate himself with the venture, that he participate in it as in something that he wishes to bring about, [and] that he seek by his action to make it succeed.'"

Looking at the evidence in the light most favorable to the government, we concluded that these requirements have been satisfied. Tyler told Baxter that he would find him some good dope; he approached the unidentified individual, apparently in an effort to locate drugs; he continued to assist Baxter until they encountered Bennett; he apparently told Bennett what Baxter was seeking; and after Baxter and Bennett made their deal he asked Baxter for some change, apparently seeking a reward for his making good on his claim that he would find Baxter some good dope. From this evidence the jury was entitled to conclude that Tyler associated himself with the criminal venture, participated in it as something he wished to bring about and sought by his actions to make it succeed. Therefore, "there was enough evidence here to support the conclusion that [Tyler] was an aider and abettor. He had sufficient ability, influence and control here to bring about a sale that, without his participation, would not have been made."

Finally, we note that there is nothing inconsistent in our determination that the evidence was insufficient with respect to the conspiracy count but sufficient with respect to the aiding and abetting count. The two offenses are separate and distinct.

The essence of conspiracy is proof of a conspiratorial agreement while aiding and abetting requires there be a "community of unlawful intent" between the aider and abettor and the principal. While a community of unlawful intent is similar to an agreement, it is not the same. Thus, a defendant may wittingly aid a criminal act and be liable as an aider and abettor . . . but not be liable for conspiracy, which requires knowledge of and voluntary participation in an agreement to do an illegal act.

For the foregoing reasons, Tyler's conviction on the conspiracy count is reversed and his conviction on the aiding and abetting count is affirmed.

The court upheld Tyler's conviction for aiding and abetting heroin distribution. But wouldn't it be more accurate to say that Tyler aided and abetted the undercover officer's heroin *possession*? After all, Tyler was trying to help the undercover officer buy heroin. There was no evidence that Tyler was working for the seller.

Prior to passage of the Controlled Substances Act in 1970, a substantial number—perhaps a majority—of jurisdictions recognized a partial defense in exactly these circumstances. The "purchasing agent" (or "procuring agent") defense provided that someone who acts as a buyer's agent has not committed a distribution offense. Under this doctrine, a purchasing agent was considered to be an accomplice of the buyer—and, therefore, an accomplice to the crime of possession—rather than an accomplice of the seller. Today, only a handful of jurisdictions continue to recognize the defense. *See* Scott W. Parker, Note: *An Argument for Preserving the Agency Defense As Applied to Prosecutions for Unlawful Sale, Delivery, and Possession of Drugs*, 66 Fordham L. Rev. 2649 (1998) (detailing the history of the defense and its demise); New York v. Roche, 45 N.Y.2d 78 (1978) (examining the defense in depth); Yuval Simchi-Levi, *The Agency Defense: Can the Legislature Help?*, 59 Buffalo L. Rev. 1109 (2011) (arguing that "[c]ourts in New York are struggling to consistently apply the agency defense").

Elaine M. Chiu has argued that the agency defense raises intriguing questions about the role of motive in the criminal law because "its litmus test is expressed directly in terms of a defendant's motive." As Chiu describes the defense, "[i]n order to be treated as an agent, a jury must conclude that the defendant is motivated" by a desire to help the purchaser, rather than a desire to help the seller. *See* Elaine M. Chiu, *The Challenge of Motive in the Criminal Law*, 8 Buff. Crim. L. Rev. 653 (2005).

Is the agency defense's reliance on motive unusual in the criminal law? If so, might that help to explain why most jurisdictions no longer recognize the defense?

c. When Do Purchasers Become Co-Conspirators with Sellers?

In *Brigham* and *Anaya*, defendants with relatively slight connections to the drug trade were found guilty of conspiracy to distribute large amounts of drugs. The convictions were upheld on appeal in both cases. In the next two cases, courts take a more skeptical view of conspiracy convictions for defendants whose involvement in the drug trade was much greater than that of Anthony Brigham or Alfred Anaya. In both cases, the question is how far a drug distributor's conspiracy liability extends. Is a defendant who sells drugs at a retail level to end-users guilty of conspiracy with the wholesaler who supplied her? What about other retail-level dealers who get their drugs from the same supplier? The seller can be convicted of distribution and conspiracy either way. But her sentence could increase by months, years, or even decades based on exactly who it is the law considers to be her co-conspirator(s).

United States v. Colon

United States Court of Appeals for the Seventh Circuit
549 F.3d 565 (2008)

Posner, J.

The defendant was convicted by a jury of possessing cocaine with intent to sell it, conspiring to possess cocaine with intent to sell it, and aiding and abetting the conspiracy, and he was sentenced to 135 months in prison. The principal ground of his appeal is that he was not a conspirator or an aider and abettor of a conspiracy, but was merely a purchaser from a conspirator, and that the jury's contrary finding lacked sufficient basis in the evidence to stand.

The evidence of his guilt of these offenses, as summarized in the government's brief, is that the "defendant regularly obtained distribution quantities of cocaine from Saucedo and Rodriguez.... The dealings between ... [the defendant and Saucedo, with whom alone the defendant dealt] were standardized and exhibited mutual trust. Saucedo and Rodriguez had a stake in defendant's distribution activities as well as their ongoing arrangement, given that their profits depended on the success of defendant's distribution efforts.... [The defendant and Saucedo] conducted regular, standardized transactions through which defendant obtained cocaine in quantities of either 4.5 or 9 ounces at consistent prices, and distributed it to customers. Defendant and Saucedo regularly arranged deliveries by telephone," with defendant being the caller, using Saucedo's cellphone number.

The government's summary describes a routine buyer/seller relationship, as in *United States v. Mercer*, 165 F.3d 1331, 1336 (11th Cir. 1999), where the court remarked that "the evidence shows simply that his co-defendant Miller knew that Mercer sold drugs and that he had sources from which he could get drugs, that Mercer had a source for drugs and if that source failed he would 'go somewhere else,' that he bought quantities of cocaine from some unknown source and sold it to police agents presumably at a profit." The relationship in the present case was "standardized" only in the sense that because seller and buyer dealt regularly with each other, the sales formed a regular pattern, as one would expect in any repeat purchase, legal or illegal. The length of the sales relationship is unclear; it may have been as long as six weeks, but the total number of sales was no more than six or seven, involving a total of 30 to 35 ounces of cocaine.

In any event, how "regular" purchases on "standard" terms can transform a customer into a co-conspirator mystifies us. "[A]greement—the crime of conspiracy—cannot be equated with repeated transactions." *United States v. Thomas*, 150 F.3d 743, 745 (7th Cir. 1998). The government either is confusing buying with conspiring or believes that a seller and buyer who fail to wrangle over each sale aren't dealing at arms' length and therefore lack mutual trust. But "mutual trust" is already a factor in the conventional analysis of conspiracy; an act that is merely evidence of mutual trust cannot be a separate factor. And anyway repeat transactions need not imply greater mutual trust than is required in any buyer-seller relationship. If you buy from Wal-Mart your transactions will be highly regular and utterly standardized, but there will be no mutual trust suggestive of a relationship other than that of buyer and seller.

It is different if, as in *United States. v. Sax*, 39 F.3d 1380, 1385–86 (7th Cir. 1994), a seller assists his customers in establishing the methods by which they will take delivery from him, for then he is more than just a seller; he is helping to create a distribution system for his illegal product. But the defendant in our case (a buyer, not a seller) did nothing to help Saucedo and Rodriguez establish a delivery system that would enable them to serve him, or serve him better.

The fact that in his conversations with Rodriguez, Saucedo referred to Colon as "Dude" or "Old Boy," rather than calling him by his name, is not, as the government believes, indicative of intimacy or a pre-existing relationship; it is for obvious reasons a convention in the drug trade not to refer to a customer by his real name. There were no sales on credit to the defendant, or other evidence of mutual trust or dependence, and he had no dealings with—indeed, he never met or spoke to—Rodriguez, Saucedo's unquestioned co-conspirator, although the defendant knew that they worked together. There is no suggestion that the defendant could expect to receive any part of the income that Saucedo obtained from selling cocaine to other customers. There was no "stimulation, instigation," or "encouragement" by the defendant of Saucedo and Rodriguez's business, no "informed and interested cooperation" between that business and the defendant's retail drug business. In his conversations with Rodriguez, Saucedo referred to the defendant only as a "customer," not as an associate, colleague, pal, or "one of us." The prosecutor in closing argument described the defendant as the conspirators' customer, and its own witnesses denied that Saucedo had ever asked the defendant to sell cocaine for him or Rodriguez.

Of course Saucedo and Rodriguez had, as the government says, "a stake in defendant's distribution activities." Every seller to a distributor has a stake in the distributor's activities; a person who buys for resale will not enrich his seller if his resale business dries up. Saucedo and Rodriguez had other customers; we do not know how many, or what the defendant's volume of purchases was relative to that of other customers.

Cases in this and other circuits list factors such as we have discussed, along with others, as indicative of participation in a conspiracy. But in every case such factors have to be placed in context before an inference of participation in a conspiracy can be drawn. In *United States v. Hicks,* 368 F.3d 801, 805 (7th Cir. 2004), for example, we listed a number of these factors but added "prolonged cooperation" between the parties (a quotation from *Direct Sales Co. v. United States,* 319 U.S. at 713, the Supreme Court's leading case on the difference between a conspiracy and a mere buyer-seller relationship) and "sales on credit," factors that strengthen an inference of participation drawn from observing circumstances also found in a routine buyer-seller relationship.

So the government's theory of conspiracy, when stripped of its redundancies and irrelevancies, reduces to an assertion that a wholesale customer of a conspiracy is a coconspirator per se. The implication is that during Prohibition a speakeasy was a co-conspirator of the smuggler who provided it with its supply of booze. And the logic of the government's position does not stop with the customer who is a wholesale purchaser rather than a retail one. Had the defendant been purchasing for his personal consumption, he would still have had "regular, standardized" transactions with Saucedo, as in our Wal-Mart example, and Saucedo would have had a stake in whatever activity the defendant engaged in to obtain the money to buy cocaine. There would have been the same level of "mutual trust" as required in any illegal sale because either buyer or seller might be a government informant or turn violent. The mutual trust in this case was less than it would have been had Saucedo "fronted" cocaine to the defendant (a factor mentioned in almost all the cases) rather than being paid in cash at the time of sale. With fronting, the seller becomes the buyer's creditor, adding a dimension to the relationship that goes beyond a spot sale for cash.

There are practical reasons for not conflating sale with conspiracy. "A sale, by definition, requires two parties; their combination for that limited purpose does not increase the likelihood that the sale will take place, so conspiracy liability would be inappropriate." *United States v. Townsend,* 924 F.2d 1385, 1394 (7th Cir. 1991). As we put it in *United States v. Manzella,* 791 F.2d 1263, 1265 (7th Cir. 1986), "A conspiracy involves more people and can therefore commit more crimes; and it can do so more efficiently, by exploiting the division of labor and by arranging concealment more effectively—sometimes through suborning law enforcers." There is nothing like that here, so far as the defendant's involvement was concerned. And the situation is not altered just because he was a buyer for resale rather than for his personal consumption. As the plurality opinion in *United States v. Lechuga,* 994 F.2d 346 (7th Cir. 1993) (en banc), explains, "before today, it was widely assumed that a conviction for participation in a drug conspiracy could be affirmed with no more evidence than that the defendant had sold in a quantity too large to be intended for his buyer's personal consumption, though some of our cases . . . tugged the other way. Today we resolve the conflict in our cases by holding that 'large quantities of controlled substances, without more, cannot sustain a conspiracy conviction.' What is necessary and sufficient is proof of an agreement to commit a crime other than the crime that consists of the sale itself."

The Eleventh Circuit pointed out in *United States v. Dekle* that "what distinguishes a conspiracy from its substantive predicate offense is not just the presence of any agreement, but an agreement with the same joint criminal objective—here the joint objective of distributing drugs. This joint objective is missing where the conspiracy is based simply on an agreement between a buyer and a seller for the sale of drugs. Although the parties to the sales agreement may both agree to commit a crime, they do not have the joint criminal objective of distributing drugs." This would be a different case, therefore, had the defendant agreed to look for other customers for Saucedo and Rodriguez, had received a commission on sales to those customers, had advised Saucedo and Rodriguez on the conduct of their business, or had agreed to warn them of threats to their business from competing dealers or from law-enforcement authorities. It would be a different case if "Lechuga [the seller] had told Pinto [the buyer] that he needed a good distributor on the south side of Chicago and wanted to enter into a long-term relationship with Pinto to that end. Then it would be as if Lechuga had hired Pinto to assist him in reaching his market." *United States v. Lechuga*, 994 F.2d at 349.

All these would be settings in which, in the Eleventh Circuit's terminology, Saucedo, Rodriguez, and the defendant would have had "the same joint criminal objective . . . of distributing drugs." But in our case there is no evidence of a relationship other than a conventional sales relationship between the defendant and the conspiracy from which he bought drugs. It is true that after discarding, in his flight from the police, the cocaine he had just bought from Saucedo, the defendant called Saucedo and told him what had happened. But there is no suggestion that he was warning Saucedo, in order to help the latter evade capture, rather than merely reporting an incident that might affect the defendant's future purchases. A drug runner employed by Saucedo phoned the defendant and told him he'd been stopped by the police after delivering cocaine to him, but that is not evidence of the defendant's participation in a conspiracy either.

The muddle that was the government's theory of the case was mirrored in the jury instructions, which after correctly noting that the defendant's purchase of drugs from another person for resale was insufficient evidence that the defendant had conspired with that person, told the jury to consider whether "the parties had an understanding that the cocaine would be sold" and whether "the transaction involved large quantities of cocaine." If the defendant was a middleman, as he was, the parties would understand that he would be reselling the cocaine; and as a middleman he would be likely to buy in quantities greater than one would buy for one's personal consumption, and therefore "large." The jury was also asked to consider whether the parties had "a standardized way of doing business over time," whether they had "a continuing relationship," "whether the sales were on credit or on consignment," and whether the seller had a "financial steak [*sic*] in a resale by the buyer." Only the question about credit or consignment was germane, for reasons that we've indicated, and that question could only have confused the jury, since all the transactions with the defendant were cash transactions. And the judge made no effort to relate the factors that she told the jury to consider to the difference between a customer and a conspirator. It is no surprise that the jury convicted; given the warped instructions, the conviction does nothing to advance the government's argument that the evidence of conspiracy was sufficient for a reasonable jury to convict.

Nor was the defendant proved to be an aider or abettor of the Saucedo-Rodriguez conspiracy. An aider and abettor is conventionally defined as one who knowingly assists an illegal activity, wanting it to succeed. This is a general definition, however, and like most legal generalizations requires qualification in particular cases. Suppose you own and operate a store that sells women's clothing. Every month the same young woman buys a red dress from your store. You happen to know that she's a prostitute and wears the dress to signal her occupation to prospective customers. By selling her the dress at your normal price you assist her illegal activity, and probably you want the activity to succeed since if it fails she'll stop buying the dress and your income will be less. But you are not an aider and abettor of prostitution because if you refused to sell to her she would buy her red dress from another clothing store, one whose proprietor and staff didn't know her profession. So you're not *really* helping her or promoting prostitution, as you would be if you recommended customers to her in exchange for a commission.

It is the same here, so far as the record reveals. By buying from Saucedo, the defendant was assisting an illegal activity, which he doubtless wanted to be successful as otherwise he would have to find another seller. If that is enough to establish aiding and abetting, every buyer from a drug conspiracy is an aider and abettor of a conspiracy and is therefore to be treated by the law exactly as a member of the conspiracy would be treated. Yet as with the sale of the red dress, there is no basis for thinking that the defendant really helped Saucedo and Rodriguez's drug conspiracy—that he made a difference—because so far as appears they could have found another customer for the modest amount of cocaine that they sold to him.

The government relies on *United States v. Kasvin,* 757 F.2d 887 (7th Cir. 1985), but omits mention of the part of the opinion that shows how different that case is from this one. Kasvin, the buyer defendant, "for several years ... had visited the headquarters of the conspiracy several times weekly, had been assigned a number just as some of the admitted members of the conspiracy had been assigned, his telephone number had been encoded, on occasion he provided the organization with marijuana for use in its business, his transactions with the conspiracy ran into hundreds of thousands of dollars annually but unlike an ordinary customer of a business, he simply picked up quantities of marijuana from headquarters, presumably disposed of it through a distribution network, and brought the money back from time to time in amounts which, so far as the records show, bore no definite relationship to the amounts of marijuana carried away at any particular time." There is nothing like that here.

Even the government has its doubts whether the defendant was a member or an aider and abettor of the Saucedo-Rodriguez conspiracy. A conspirator is liable for the foreseeable crimes that his co-conspirators commit in furtherance of the conspiracy, *Pinkerton v. United States,* 328 U.S. 640, 646–47 (1946), yet the only drug quantity on which the government sought to base the defendant's sentence was the quantity that Saucedo sold him, though he knew that Saucedo and Rodriguez were selling cocaine to others as well as to him. One is led to wonder why the government added charges of conspiracy and of aiding and abetting to the charge of possession with intent to distribute. The guideline ranges were the same and the additional charges were likely to confuse the jury by making the defendant's conduct seem more ominous than it was.

So probably the additional charges added nothing to the charge of possession with intent to distribute. But maybe the government was concerned that in the (unlikely) event that the evidence obtained when the defendant was caught at Saucedo's house was suppressed, the jury might acquit the defendant of possession or the sentence for possession might be based on a smaller quantity of cocaine and therefore be shorter.

Since the defendant was given concurrent sentences on the two counts, it may seem that reversing the conspiracy and aiding and abetting count could not alter his sentence. But the district judge sentenced him very near the top of the applicable guideline range, and in doing so may have been influenced by the fact that the jury had found the defendant guilty of conspiracy and aiding and abetting as well as of possession. So while the defendant's conviction of possession stands, he is entitled to be acquitted on the other count and he must therefore be resentenced.

United States v. Caldwell

United States Court of Appeals for the Tenth Circuit
589 F.3d 1323 (2009)

Lucero, J.

This case is before us on direct appeal of a criminal conviction and sentence. Among other dispositions,[1] Michael Caldwell was convicted by a jury of participating in a three-party conspiracy to distribute marijuana. The government alleged the conspiracy consisted of Caldwell, the defendant; David Anderson, a street dealer of marijuana; and Samuel Herrera, the drug supplier for both Anderson and Caldwell. In its verdict, the jury concluded the three men entered into a single conspiracy—a

1. Caldwell was also convicted of two counts of using a telephone in furtherance of a drug trafficking crime. Caldwell does not appeal those convictions or sentences.

tripartite conspiracy—to distribute at least 100 kilograms of marijuana over a two-year period. Although Caldwell admits that he conspired with Herrera, he argues that insufficient evidence supports the theory of a tripartite conspiracy. Caldwell maintains that both the jury and the sentencing judge attributed an improper quantity of marijuana to him.

On our review of the record on appeal, we conclude that the evidence presented at Caldwell's trial was indeed sufficient to establish conspiracies between Caldwell and Herrera and between Caldwell and Anderson, but that it was insufficient to establish a tripartite conspiracy among all three. Both the jury and the sentencing court erroneously attributed quantities of marijuana to Caldwell based on the existence of a tripartite conspiracy. Exercising jurisdiction under 28 U.S.C. § 1291 and 18 U.S.C. § 3742(a)(1), we affirm Caldwell's conviction, but vacate his sentence and remand the case to the district court for resentencing.

Beginning in 1995, the United States Drug Enforcement Administration ("DEA") began investigating a drug ring headed by the Rosales family of El Paso, Texas. The family's main contact in Oklahoma was Robert Williams, who distributed marijuana to a number of intermediary suppliers in the state. These suppliers distributed the marijuana, mostly on consignment, to street-level dealers.

Herrera was one such intermediary supplier. He sold marijuana to a number of street-level dealers in Oklahoma City, including Caldwell. The first transaction between Herrera and Caldwell took place in 2004. During that transaction, Caldwell received between two to four kilograms of marijuana on consignment. For approximately two years thereafter, Herrera distributed two to seven kilograms of marijuana once every several weeks to Caldwell. Caldwell then resold the marijuana to users.

Anderson, a friend of Caldwell's since early 2005, eventually became another one of Herrera's main customers. Early in their friendship, Anderson dealt drugs to Caldwell: On two or three occasions shortly after they met, Anderson sold Caldwell approximately one kilogram of marijuana on consignment. For roughly one year after these sales occurred, Anderson and Caldwell had no drug-related interaction. Then in early 2006, Anderson's regular supplier was "running short" on marijuana, and Anderson asked Caldwell if he knew of a reliable drug supplier. Caldwell arranged a meeting between Anderson and Herrera. Even though Caldwell was present at the initial meeting, during which Herrera sold approximately 4.5 kilograms of marijuana to Anderson on consignment, Caldwell received no economic benefit from the introduction. From that point on, Anderson and Herrera dealt with one another "one-on-one"—that is, no subsequent drug transactions between Anderson and Herrera involved Caldwell. Anderson received monthly supplies of approximately four to nine kilograms of marijuana from Herrera, generally on consignment.

During the course of its investigation, the DEA intercepted several incriminating calls regarding the distribution of marijuana between Herrera and Caldwell, and a number of similar calls between Herrera and Anderson. It did not intercept any drug-related telephone conversations between Caldwell and Anderson.

In October 2007, a grand jury indicted Caldwell for conspiracy to distribute 100 kilograms or more of marijuana in violation of 21 U.S.C. § 841(a)(1). The indictment listed Caldwell, Herrera, and Anderson as members of the same conspiracy. In exchange for reduced sentences, both Herrera and Anderson testified at trial. A DEA agent also testified that, during the course of the conspiracy, Herrera sold 54 to 163 kilograms of marijuana to Caldwell and 163 to 327 kilograms of marijuana to Anderson.

Caldwell was convicted of conspiracy to distribute marijuana, and the jury returned a special verdict finding that the conspiracy involved 100 kilograms or more of marijuana. During sentencing, the court relied on the special verdict and a presentence investigation report ("PSR"). The PSR attributed 188 kilograms of marijuana to Caldwell. Caldwell objected to the drug quantity determinations of the jury and the PSR, but the court overruled Caldwell's objection. Based on its finding that over 100 kilograms of marijuana was attributable to Caldwell, the court sentenced Caldwell to 130 months' imprisonment.

We must first consider whether the government produced sufficient evidence for a reasonable jury to conclude that Herrera, Caldwell, and Anderson were engaged in a tripartite conspiracy to distribute marijuana. Where "an indictment charges a single conspiracy, but the evidence presented at trial proves only the existence of multiple conspiracies," a variance occurs. In considering a claimed variance, "we view the evidence and draw all reasonable inferences therefrom in the light most favorable to the government, asking whether a reasonable jury could have found [the defendant] guilty of the charged conspirac[y] beyond a reasonable doubt." The existence of a variance that would support acquittal is a matter of law that we review de novo.

As noted, we conclude that Herrera's role as a common supplier, Caldwell's earlier purchase of marijuana from Anderson, and Caldwell's introduction of Anderson to Herrera do not constitute sufficient evidence of a single conspiracy among the three drug dealers. Instead, the evidence presented at trial demonstrates the existence of separate conspiracies between Caldwell and Anderson, and between Caldwell and Herrera. Assuredly, each of the three conspired to distribute marijuana, but a conspiracy did not exist among Herrera, Caldwell, and Anderson as a group.

Distinguishing between a single, large conspiracy and several smaller conspiracies is often difficult; we will generally defer to the jury's determination of the matter. Nonetheless, "we may not uphold a conviction obtained by piling inference upon inference. . . . The evidence supporting the conviction must be substantial and do more than raise a suspicion of guilt."

To prove a conspiracy, the government must demonstrate: "(1) that two or more persons agreed to violate the law, (2) that the defendant knew at least the essential objectives of the conspiracy, (3) that the defendant knowingly and voluntarily became a part of it, and (4) that the alleged coconspirators were interdependent." In reviewing a jury's determination that a single conspiracy existed, "a focal point of the analysis is whether the alleged coconspirators' conduct exhibited interdependence." Interdependence exists where coconspirators "inten[d] to act together for their shared mutual benefit within the scope of the conspiracy charged." Circumstantial evidence alone is often sufficient to demonstrate interdependence; indeed, it is often the only evidence available to the government. Further, a single act can be sufficient to demonstrate interdependence. *See, e.g., United States v. Hamilton*, 587 F.3d 1199 (10th Cir. 2009) (determining that a single instance of traveling to collect another drug dealer's debts was sufficient to show defendant became a part of a large and wide-reaching conspiracy).

We are told by the government that the relationship between Caldwell, Anderson, and Herrera was a "vertical conspiracy." A vertical conspiracy, or "chain-and-link" conspiracy, involves a series of consecutive buyer-seller relationships. The classic vertical conspiracy involves Supplier A selling contraband to Supplier B, who then sells the contraband to Supplier C. But drug distribution organizations often do not fit neatly into the concept of vertical conspiracy.

In the present case, Caldwell and Anderson were equal-level purchasers rather than links in a vertical chain. After Herrera became their joint supplier, neither Caldwell nor Anderson bought or sold marijuana to the other. Instead, each independently sold marijuana to third parties. Thus, their relationship does not evince the characteristics of a vertical conspiracy. Were we to categorize this alleged conspiracy, it would fit more neatly into the concept of a "hub-and-spoke" conspiracy, in which several separate players all interact with a common central actor, here Herrera. However, because *any* conspiracy requires a showing of interdependence, we prefer to eschew rigid labels and instead engage in the general, yet fact-specific, inquiry of whether there is evidence of interdependence among all alleged coconspirators.

When multiple individuals are involved in the sale of illegal drugs, they are engaged in an inherently illicit enterprise. Consequently, the degree of specificity with which the government must prove interdependence among them may be lower in the drug context than in the context of other types of conspiracies. But even in the drug context, we must "scrupulously safeguard each defendant individually, as far as possible, from loss of identity in the mass."

It is essential that the evidence demonstrate a mutual benefit before we proceed to determine that several drug dealers who interact with one another are involved in a single conspiracy:

> It is not enough that a group of people separately intend to distribute drugs in a single area, nor even that their activities occasionally or sporadically place them in contact with each other. People in the same industry in the same locale (even competitors) can occasionally be expected to interact with each other without thereby becoming coconspirators. What is needed

> is proof that they intended to act *together* for their *shared mutual benefit* within the scope of the conspiracy charged.

For example, we determined in *Powell* that several drug dealers who shared a common supplier and sold to the same customers and wholesalers in a cooperative matter could be found to have engaged in a single conspiracy. However, sharing a common supplier, without more, does not demonstrate that two drug dealers are acting together for their shared mutual benefit. Accordingly, in the case at bar, the fact that Caldwell and Anderson both bought from Herrera is insufficient to establish interdependence among the three.

The government argues that Anderson's sale of a relatively small amount of marijuana to Caldwell, approximately one year before Anderson met Herrera, supports the jury's finding of a tripartite conspiracy. Undoubtedly, the government presented sufficient evidence for a jury to conclude that Caldwell and Anderson were involved in a conspiracy to distribute marijuana in early 2005: Anderson provided Caldwell with two or three kilograms of marijuana on consignment in early 2005. Our court has previously held that providing drugs on credit can be sufficient to demonstrate a conspiracy to distribute drugs. But the question is whether Caldwell's introduction of Anderson to Herrera constituted a continuation of the earlier Caldwell-Anderson conspiracy. If Caldwell and Anderson were still involved in a conspiracy to distribute marijuana when the introduction occurred, that conspiracy (and thus Caldwell as a member) would have benefitted from Anderson being introduced to Herrera.

"[A] conspiracy, once instituted, continues to exist until it is abandoned, succeeds, or is otherwise terminated by some affirmative act, such as withdrawal by the defendant." Although a lapse in time does not necessarily convert a single conspiracy into multiple conspiracies, time in combination with other factors can "sever the single continuous conspiracy alleged in the indictment into two separate conspiracies."

Under the totality of the circumstances present here, a reasonable jury could not have concluded that the introduction of Anderson to Herrera constituted a continuation of the earlier Caldwell-Anderson conspiracy. Approximately one year passed between Anderson's last sale of drugs to Caldwell and the introduction. A relatively small quantity of drugs passed between Anderson and Caldwell, indicating the objectives of their conspiracy were achieved through a discrete sale of marijuana. Unlike the coconspirators in *Williamson*, Anderson and Caldwell did not spend their year apart merely "enjoying the fruits of their proceeds," and Anderson did not stop selling drugs to Caldwell in order to cover up their crimes. To the contrary, Anderson and Caldwell used the year to build separate illicit businesses, wherein each obtained marijuana and sold it to customers. Because this arrangement demonstrates that the two were competing rather than cooperating, the government failed to meet its burden of proving that the earlier Caldwell-Anderson conspiracy "still functioned as a single ongoing entity" when Caldwell introduced Anderson to Herrera.

We now address a question of first impression for the Tenth Circuit: Is the mere introduction of a common supplier, made by one drug dealer to another, sufficient to create a single conspiracy among all the dealers? We conclude that it is not.

The government attempts to equate this case with *United States v. Ivy*, 83 F.3d 1266 (10th Cir. 1996), in which we held that a single conspiracy existed among three drug dealers. There, a jury convicted Kenny Taylor, a street-level drug dealer, of conspiring with Samuel Norwood and Raymond Hickman to distribute crack cocaine. Norwood sold crack cocaine to Hickman, who in turn sold it to Taylor. We upheld the jury's finding of a single conspiracy in part because Taylor referred a customer to Hickman. In that situation, however, the government used the introduction to demonstrate that Taylor, Norwood, and Hickman were interdependent, not that Taylor and the man he introduced to Hickman were interdependent.[3] By contrast, the government is attempting to use an introduction to show that Caldwell was interdependent with Anderson, the man Caldwell introduced to his supplier.

Having established that *Ivy* does not govern this case, we look to the type of evidence required to uphold a conspiracy conviction. Under our case law, "mere presence is not sufficient in and of itself [to establish a conspiracy], nor is it sufficient for the government to show only mere association with conspirators known to be involved in crime." Likewise, "the government must do more than show there were casual transactions between the defendant and the conspirators." To distinguish a "casual transaction" from an act demonstrating interdependence, we consider the circumstances surrounding the transaction.

Evidence showing that an alleged coconspirator has an economic stake in the outcome of a drug transaction can demonstrate that a transaction is not merely casual. Of course, direct economic benefit for all individuals involved is not necessarily a prerequisite for a jury to find a single conspiracy. But in the profit-driven world of illicit drugs, the fact that several individuals are in an economically symbiotic relationship may demonstrate that transactions among them are in pursuit of mutual benefit. For example, in *Edwards*, we determined that a reasonable jury could have found a single conspiracy existed when multiple defendants pooled their money to negotiate a lower drug price from a supplier.

On the other hand, an act that merely facilitates the distribution of drugs may be insufficient to show that two individuals intend to act together for their mutual benefit. For example, loaning scales to a drug dealer knowing he would use them to weigh crack cocaine is, in isolation, insufficient to establish a conspiracy between the person who loans the scales and the person who uses them. Without more, loaning of scales "could have been merely a gratuitous favor or isolated act among friends."

3. The government also presented more evidence than just the introduction: It demonstrated that Hickman sold Taylor large quantities of crack cocaine, the vast majority of which Hickman had obtained from Norwood.

United States v. Pressler, 256 F.3d 144 (3d Cir. 2001), is instructive in determining whether Caldwell's introduction of Anderson to Herrera was merely a casual favor among friends, or evidence of interdependence among coconspirators. In that case, a jury convicted Scott Shreffler of conspiracy to distribute heroin. Shreffler introduced two other drug dealers, Anthony and Aaron Forshey, to his heroin supplier, Pete Caban. As in the present case, Shreffler did not receive a discount on his own drug purchases or any other economic benefit from Caban or the Forsheys as a result of this introduction. The Third Circuit held that evidence showing "Shreffler introduced the Forsheys to another, superior source of supply from which Shreffler himself had purchased a large amount of heroin" was insufficient to establish that Shreffler had entered into any sort of agreement to distribute heroin to the Forsheys. In a somewhat insouciant comparison, the court stated:

> It is common for people to tell their friends about a good store or restaurant. Though the Government proved that Shreffler was a very good customer to Caban, that he had recommended Caban to others, and that Caban benefitted from Shreffler's patronage, *it did not show that Shreffler and Caban ever agreed to work together on anything.*

Similarly, Caldwell's introduction of Anderson to Herrera undoubtedly broadened Herrera's customer base. But the facts surrounding the introduction demonstrate that it was friendly rather than conspiratorial. As in *Pressler*, the government offered no evidence that Caldwell received any economic benefit from the introduction, and Anderson testified that Caldwell received no such benefit. After the introduction, Caldwell was not involved with any drug transaction between Herrera and Anderson. On the facts of this case, Caldwell's introduction alone cannot demonstrate beyond a reasonable doubt that a single conspiracy existed among Caldwell, Anderson, and Herrera. Although the government established that Caldwell was involved in two separate conspiracies, it failed to prove the tripartite conspiracy alleged in the indictment. As a result, a variance occurred.

Not every variance, however, requires reversal. A variance becomes fatal, and thus reversible error, "only if it affects the substantial rights of the accused." We review de novo the question of whether a particular variance constitutes reversible error.

A variance is not fatal "merely because the defendant is convicted upon evidence which tends to show a narrower scheme than that contained in the indictment, provided that the narrower scheme is fully included within the indictment." The primary purpose of the prohibition against variances is "to insure notice of the charges." When an indictment charges a conspiracy among multiple individuals, it generally provides sufficient notice to a defendant that she must defend against the smaller conspiracies. By comparison, a variance may be substantially prejudicial "if the evidence adduced against co-conspirators involved in separate conspiracies was more likely than not imputed to the defendant by the jury in its determination of the defendant's guilt."

Caldwell contends he was substantially prejudiced because the jury must have relied on the amount of marijuana Herrera sold to Anderson in assessing drug quantity. Caldwell's argument fails, however, because "when asking what facts the jury had to find in order to convict, we look to the elements of the crime as defined by law." Moreover, Caldwell admits that the government presented sufficient evidence to prove Caldwell was involved in two separate drug conspiracies. As a result [h]is conviction stands.

Even though Caldwell's conviction is valid, his sentence is not.

In the present case, the jury's determination of drug quantity was clearly erroneous because it was based on an unsupported tripartite conspiracy. The government proved at trial that Herrera sold Caldwell between 54 and 163 kilograms of marijuana, and that Anderson sold Caldwell between 2 and 4 kilograms of marijuana. While these ranges demonstrate that Caldwell could have been responsible for over 100 kilograms of marijuana, they do not demonstrate beyond a reasonable doubt that Caldwell was responsible for that quantity.

Moreover, the PSR attributed approximately 188 kilograms to Caldwell, a quantity that could not have been reached without taking into account the marijuana Herrera sold to Anderson. The sentencing court relied both on this amount and the jury's special verdict in calculating Caldwell's sentence. Consequently, the factual basis for Caldwell's sentence was clearly erroneous, and we remand the matter to the district court for resentencing. In doing so, the district court should not consider the amount of marijuana Herrera sold to Anderson.

4. Continuing Criminal Enterprise and "Drug Kingpin" Laws

In 1970, Congress created a crime targeted at managers of drug conspiracies, the "continuing criminal enterprise" (or "CCE") offense. 21 U.S.C. § 848. The CCE offense requires proof that the defendant engaged in a "continuing series" of federal drug crimes "which are undertaken by such person in concert with five or more other persons with respect to whom such person occupies a position of organizer, a supervisory position, or any other position of management and from which such person obtains substantial income or resources." Though the CCE crime is occasionally referred to as a federal "drug kingpin" law, courts have held that "[a] defendant need not be the dominant organizer or manager of a criminal enterprise; the statute requires only that he occupy some managerial position." *United States v. Becton*, 751 F.2d 250, 255 (8th Cir. 1984).

CCE is rarely prosecuted today. Of the 19,750 defendants sentenced for drug offenses under the federal sentencing guidelines in 2017, just *three* were sentenced under the CCE sentencing guideline. Sourcebook of Federal Sentencing Primary Drug Type of Offenders Sentenced Under Drug Guidelines, S-104 tbl. 33 (2018). Nevertheless, the offense raises interesting questions about vicarious and group criminality. Moreover, the fact that the offense has fallen into disuse may itself be a sign of just how much federal drug enforcement has changed since 1970. When Congress enacted CCE, it provided for much longer terms of imprisonment than were typically available for other federal drug offenses. As discussed more in Chapter 4, however, sentences for federal drug offenses like conspiracy and possession with intent to distribute are much longer today than they were in 1970.

United States v. Witek

United States Court of Appeals for the Eleventh Circuit
61 F.3d 819 (1995)

Black, J.

Appellant Ralston Wright was convicted of engaging in a continuing criminal enterprise (CCE) under 21 U.S.C.A. § 848. We must decide whether the Government presented sufficient evidence to prove Wright's guilt beyond a reasonable doubt. We conclude that it did not, and vacate Wright's CCE conviction.

In late 1991 and early 1992, Ralston Wright and his girlfriend, Appellant Claudette Hubbard, sold narcotics from their residence in Cocoa, Florida. Wright and Hubbard would obtain powdered cocaine and marijuana in Dallas, Texas, process most of the cocaine into cocaine base (crack), and then sell the drugs to customers in and around the Cocoa area. Wright and Hubbard's initial supplier was Thomas Semple, but they switched their source to Paul Ohaegbu in March 1992. Ohaegbu entered into a plea agreement with the Government and testified against Wright and Hubbard.

Wright and Hubbard's primary customers were street dealers who operated in and around Cocoa. They included Appellants Alfred Bain, George Calhoun, John Dixon, Tommie Dixon, Earl Green, Reginal Hardy, and Edward Witek; and cooperating witnesses Barbara Chelewski, Siricia Mitchell, and Charles Williams. Generally, sales were negotiated over the phone using code words common to the drug trade. Wright or Hubbard usually delivered the drugs to their buyers at the customer's residence or at some mutually arranged location. Sales were at the going market price and often involved "fronting"—allowing the customer to pay for the drugs after delivery.

In 1992, Wright was arrested and charged with: (1) conspiracy to possess with intent to distribute five kilograms or more of cocaine base in violation of 21 U.S.C. § 846; (2) engaging in a continuing criminal enterprise in violation of 21 U.S.C. § 848; (3) possession with intent to distribute cocaine hydrochloride in violation of 18 U.S.C. § 2 and 21 U.S.C. § 841(a)(1), (b)(1)(C); (4) unlawful use of a communication facility in the commission of a felony in violation of 21 U.S.C. § 843(b); and (5) use of firearms during and in relation to drug trafficking crimes in violation of 18 U.S.C. §§ 2 and 924(c). At trial, Wright's motion for judgment of acquittal was denied and the jury found him guilty on all counts. The district court sentenced

Wright to life for the conspiracy and CCE convictions, concurrent twenty and four-year terms for possession and unlawful use of a communication facility, and consecutive five-year enhancements for use of a firearm. This appeal follows.

In order to convict a defendant for engaging in a continuing criminal enterprise, the government must show:

(1) a felony violation of the federal narcotics laws

(2) as part of a continuing series of violations

(3) in concert with five or more persons

(4) for whom the defendant is an organizer or supervisor

(5) from which he derives substantial income or resources.

Wright argues that the Government did not adequately demonstrate that he organized or supervised five or more persons as required by the statute. The Government responds that Wright organized or supervised (1) Hubbard, (2) Ohaegbu, and (3) his street-dealing customers, most notably Bain, John Dixon, Tommie Dixon, and Witek.

Section 848(c), which defines a continuing criminal enterprise, requires the government to demonstrate that the defendant "occupies a position of organizer, a supervisory position, or any other position of management" with respect to five other persons engaged in the illegal drug trade. 21 U.S.C.A. § 848(c)(2)(A). This management requirement is disjunctive, allowing the government to meet its burden by showing the defendant functioned "as an organizer *or* a supervisor *or* any other type of manager." Three broad considerations influence our interpretation of the management requirement. First, we must give § 848 a "common-sense reading." Second, we must recall that the statute "is designed to reach the "top brass" in the drug rings, not the lieutenants and foot soldiers." Third, where it is unclear whether particular conduct is prohibited by ambiguous terms in a criminal statute, the rule of lenity requires us to construe that statute narrowly.

It is unnecessary to restate every rule this Court applies when examining § 848's management requirement. At the outset, however, we must make clear what should be obvious from the statute's text: A mere buyer-seller relationship does not satisfy § 848's management requirement. We thereby join with every circuit to consider the issue. A contrary interpretation would do violence to the common-sense meaning of the words "organizer" and "supervisor" and extend § 848's reach beyond the scope Congress intended. Congress knew how to proscribe the mere selling of narcotics when they adopted § 848, *see* 21 U.S.C.A. § 841(a) ("it shall be unlawful . . . to . . . *distribute, or dispense*"), but did not do so in § 848. We must assume that the use of different language in § 848 was the result of a deliberate choice by Congress.

With these principles in mind, we examine the record to determine whether Wright served as an organizer or supervisor of five or more persons connected to the drug conspiracy in this case.

1. Hubbard.

Wright insists that Hubbard was at least his equal, and therefore could not be managed or supervised within the meaning of § 848. Although much of the evidence suggests an equal partnership between Wright and Hubbard, that would not prevent the jury from inferring that, at least on some occasions, Wright organized or supervised Hubbard. Section 848 does not require the Government to prove that Wright was the only, or even the dominant, organizer of the Wright-Hubbard operation. Nor does it require the Government to prove that Wright *controlled* Hubbard, because an organizer does not necessarily control those people he organizes, but simply arranges their activities into an orderly operation.

The Government presented enough evidence for the jury to conclude that Wright organized Hubbard's activities within the meaning of § 848. While on a drug-buying trip to Dallas, Wright called Hubbard with instructions to collect money from Tommie Dixon. Hubbard agreed and placed two calls to Dixon asking for payment. Hubbard made other calls for Wright to tell Ohaegbu when to expect Wright in Dallas. Finally, when Charles Williams could not find Wright at an agreed meeting place, Hubbard assisted Wright by directing Williams to the correct location. The evidence is not overwhelming, and could support a conclusion that Wright and Hubbard were equal partners. Nevertheless, viewing the evidence in the light most favorable to the Government, the jury could have believed that this evidence demonstrated that Wright sometimes organized Hubbard's illegal activities.

2. Ohaegbu.

Wright contends that Ohaegbu's role as a narcotics broker does not support a finding that Wright organized or supervised him in any way. We agree. Although there may be cases where a narcotics buyer organizes or supervises his supplier within the meaning of § 848, this is not such a case.

> Every legitimate retail store makes arrangements with its regular suppliers. In one sense it may be said to organize its supply, but does it organize its suppliers? Surely not in the sense of being a manager of its suppliers. To be an organizer within the sense of the statute more is required than simply being a steady customer. *United States v. Jerome*, 942 F.2d 1328, 1331 (9th Cir.1991).

Wright's steady purchases of Ohaegbu's drugs, standing alone, does not satisfy the management requirement of § 848.

A review of the record uncovers no additional evidence from which to infer that Wright organized Ohaegbu's activities. Although Ohaegbu picked up and dropped off Hubbard at the airport on her request,[4] a reasonable factfinder could not interpret this act as evidence of organization or supervision. Buyers and sellers often

---

4. Our conclusion that Wright organized Hubbard's activities allows us to treat her actions on behalf of the Wright-Hubbard enterprise as attributable to Wright for § 848 purposes.

need to accommodate one another when meeting and arranging for delivery. Such conduct is simply incidental to the buyer-seller relationship. In sum, a reasonable jury could not conclude that Wright, alone or acting through Hubbard, organized or supervised the activities of Ohaegbu.

3. The Street Dealers.

Wright argues that the Government cannot rely on his relationship with customers to sustain the CCE conviction. The Government replies that evidence of Wright and Hubbard's fronting drugs to the street dealers satisfies the management requirement of § 848 and brings the number of persons organized above the five required by the statute.[5] Although evidence of fronting is certainly relevant to the question of organization or supervision under § 848, this Court has never sustained a CCE conviction based solely on fronting. We now join the circuits which have held that evidence of fronting, *without more,* is insufficient to satisfy the management requirement of § 848.

The Government's reliance on *United States v. Aguilar,* 843 F.2d 155 (3rd Cir.), *United States v. Cruz,* 785 F.2d 399 (2nd Cir.1986), and *United States v. Adamo,* 742 F.2d 927 (6th Cir.1984), is misplaced. In these cases, the defendants' arrangement with their dealers went beyond simple fronting and constituted a consignment or franchise type of operation, with the defendants retaining ultimate control and authority over the drugs. In *Aguilar,* for example, the evidence showed that when a dealer was unable to repay on time, the defendant would reclaim the drugs. Wright and Hubbard never operated at such a level of sophistication.

Just as importantly, in *Aguilar, Cruz,* and *Adamo,* other substantial evidence helped satisfy § 848's management requirement. As the Sixth Circuit noted in distinguishing *Adamo* from a case where fronting was the sole evidence, "the government proved many other facts about the organization's activities in *Adamo.*" Finally, to the extent that these cases can be interpreted to sustain a conviction based on fronting alone, we must disagree. Such an expansive reading of § 848 does not comport with the plain meaning of the terms "organize" or "supervise," goes beyond the scope intended by Congress, and violates the rule of lenity. Thus, the evidence of fronting relied on by the Government does not satisfy § 848's management requirement.

In sum, the Government did not produce enough evidence for a reasonable jury to conclude that Wright organized or supervised the street dealers. The record, viewed in the light most favorable to the Government, only supports a conclusion that Wright organized or supervised Hubbard, four short of the minimum number required by § 848.

We hold that the record does not contain sufficient evidence for a reasonable jury to conclude, beyond a reasonable doubt, that Wright was guilty of engaging in a

5. Viewed in a light most favorable to the Government, Wright and Hubbard fronted cocaine to Bain, Chelewski, John Dixon, Tommie Dixon, and Witek.

continuing criminal enterprise. Consequently, we vacate Wright's CCE conviction.[8] We affirm the other convictions and sentences involved in this appeal.

A frequent criticism of the war on drugs strategy is that it has led to a large number of lengthy prison sentences for low-level offenders. In theory, offenses like CCE could allow legislatures to address this problem by reserving long sentences for defendants convicted of those offenses and dramatically reducing statutory sentencing ranges for crimes like distribution and possession with intent to distribute. *Witek* suggests one possible reason legislatures have not adopted this approach: proving a crime like CCE is difficult and resource-intensive. (And remember, the CCE offense is *not* limited to so-called "drug kingpins." It can apply to mid- or low-level managers as well.) Another barrier to focusing enforcement resources and mandatory minimum sentences on the ringleaders of drug organizations is that, as the case that follows demonstrates, translating the idea of a drug kingpin into the elements of a criminal offense is quite difficult.

New Jersey v. Alexander

Supreme Court of New Jersey
136 N.J. 563 (1994)

Handler, J.

A jury convicted defendant of several drug-related offenses, including a charge of violating N.J.S.A. 2C:35-3, commonly known as the "drug kingpin" statute. The Appellate Division reversed the "drug kingpin" conviction because it found error in the trial court's instructions to the jury. Specifically, the court below held that in a prosecution for violation of N.J.S.A. 2C:35-3, the trial court must instruct the jury that the State bears the burden of proving that "the defendant functioned as an 'upper echelon member' of an organized 'drug trafficking network' ..." and must define for the jury certain other terms contained in the statute. We granted the State's petition for certification to review that determination.

Defendant, Ryan Lee Alexander, hired Anthony Harewood to sell crack cocaine in Hackensack, introduced Harewood to his customers, and supplied Harewood daily with thirty to seventy baggies of crack. Harewood sold the baggies at $10 each and gave seventy percent of his gross receipts to defendant or to Chris Kittrell, defendant's cousin and an unindicted coconspirator. Harewood's paramour, Sandra Palmer, assisted him by carrying the crack and by delivering the drugs to buyers after they had paid Harewood. Making between $300 and $1,500 per day, Harewood gave up to $5,000 per week to Alexander, and kept up to $2,000.

---

8. As we affirm Wright's other convictions, the only collateral consequence of vacating his CCE conviction is eliminating the $250 special assessment imposed for that count. Nevertheless, the presence of a special assessment required us to review Wright's CCE conviction.

A confidential informant identified Harewood to an undercover narcotics officer as a drug seller. The officer gave $100 to Harewood, who directed him to Palmer for completion of the drug transaction. Palmer gave the officer nine baggies containing what was later identified as crack cocaine. When Harewood and Palmer were arrested, they had 7.34 grams of cocaine contained in nine $100 baggies and $341.02 in cash. They identified defendant as their supplier, described the commission arrangement, and said that they had sold crack five to six days per week. A search of defendant's apartment yielded 11.08 grams of cocaine contained in forty-two baggies that matched those sold by Harewood and Palmer. The State charged Alexander with possession of cocaine; with possession of cocaine with intent to distribute; and with being a leader of a drug-trafficking network in violation of N.J.S.A. 2C:35-3. The State also charged Harewood and Palmer with various counts of possession of cocaine and of possession of cocaine with intent to distribute.

At trial, Harewood and Palmer testified against defendant, and the jury convicted him on all counts. The trial court sentenced defendant to the mandatory term of life imprisonment with a twenty-five-year parole disqualifier on his conviction for being a leader of a narcotics-trafficking network, and to two five-year sentences on the charges of possession of cocaine and possession of cocaine with intent to distribute, to run concurrently with the life sentence.

The Appellate Division affirmed in part and reversed and remanded in part. Other than merging defendant's conviction for possession of cocaine into his conviction for possession of cocaine with intent to distribute, the court below rejected all defendant's arguments except those directed at the N.J.S.A. 2C:35-3 charge. That statute provides in pertinent part as follows:

> A person is a leader of a narcotics trafficking network if he conspires with others as an organizer, supervisor, financier or manager, to engage for profit in a scheme or course of conduct to unlawfully manufacture, distribute, dispense, bring into or transport in this State methamphetamine, lysergic acid diethylamide, phencyclidine or any controlled dangerous substance classified in Schedule I or II, or any controlled substance analog thereof. Leader of narcotics trafficking network is a crime of the first degree and upon conviction thereof * * * a person shall be sentenced to an ordinary term of life imprisonment during which the person must serve 25 years before being eligible for parole. * * *
>
> Notwithstanding the provisions of N.J.S.A. 2C:1-8, a conviction of leader of a narcotics trafficking network shall not merge with the conviction for any offense [that] is the object of the conspiracy. * * *
>
> It shall not be necessary in any prosecution under this section for the State to prove that any intended profit was actually realized. The trier of fact may infer that a particular scheme or course of conduct was undertaken for profit from all of the attendant circumstances, including but not limited

> to the number of persons involved in the scheme or course of conduct, the actor's net worth and his expenditures in relation to his legitimate sources of income, the amount or purity of the specified controlled dangerous substance or controlled dangerous substance analog involved, or the amount of cash or currency involved.

According to the Appellate Division, a correct jury instruction should define "'[o]rganized "drug trafficking net-work"' ... as a group of individuals who, by reason of their number and interrelationships, constitute a structured organization or system engaged in the manufacture or distribution of illegal drugs," and should define "'[u]pper echelon member' ... as someone who stands on an upper level of the chain of command of a drug trafficking network, exercising command authority over members of that organization whose status is subordinate to his." Finally, the Appellate Division held that the jury charge should define an "upper" level as "a level [that] is superior to street-level distributors and to their immediate supervisors or suppliers."

On its appeal to this Court from the Appellate Division's reversal of the N.J.S.A. 2C:35-3 conviction, the State argues that the court below erred by "engraft[ing] a declaration of legislative policy onto the drug kingpin statute so as to redefine the elements of the offense," and by requiring that the jury find beyond a reasonable doubt that the State had established each of those newly-defined elements.

N.J.S.A. 2C:35-3 is an unusually-constructed criminal statute. It describes the offense by giving a label to the offender: leader of a narcotics-trafficking network. It then lists the activities that will result in one being branded with that label, namely, (1) that the defendant conspired with at least two others; (2) that the defendant was an organizer, supervisor, financier, or manager; (3) that the defendant engaged in the conspiracy for profit; and (4) that the conspiracy included a scheme or course of conduct unlawfully to manufacture, distribute, dispense, or transport a controlled dangerous substance or analog. Those enumerated activities constitute the material elements of the crime.

When the Legislature enacted the "Comprehensive Drug Reform Act of 1986," it included a statement of policy that is set forth at N.J.S.A. 2C:35-1.1. That statement declares in part that

> to be effective, the battle against drug abuse and drug-related crime must be waged aggressively at every level along the drug distribution chain, but in particular, our criminal laws must target for expedited prosecution and enhanced punishment those repeat drug offenders and upper echelon members of organized narcotics trafficking networks who pose the greatest danger to society.... [T]o ensure the most efficient and effective dedication of limited investigative, prosecutorial, judicial and correctional resources, it is the policy of this State to distinguish between drug offenders based on the seriousness of the offense, considering principally the nature, quantum and purity of the controlled substance involved and the role of the actor in

> the overall drug distribution network. It is the intention of the Legislature to provide for the strict punishment, deterrence and incapacitation of the most culpable and dangerous drug offenders.

The State argues that in a prosecution for violating N.J.S.A. 2C:35-3, to include as part of the basic definition and as a specific element of the crime in the jury instructions any reference to the role of the defendant as an "upper echelon member" in the overall drug-distribution network improperly redefines the statutory crime. It reasons that the inclusion of that element is at odds with the elements of the offense that are set forth in N.J.S.A. 2C:35-3. Thus, the State contends that the Appellate Division's proposed instruction rewrites the drug-kingpin statute by requiring the State to prove beyond a reasonable doubt a material element that the Legislature did not include in its definition of the offense.

N.J.S.A. 2C:35-3 does not include some of the important factors used in the statutory statement of purpose to describe the drug-kingpin crime, and, to that extent, does not completely convey the full legislative understanding in creating this crime. The statement of purpose expressly makes the defendant's "upper-level" role in a drug network central to the activity criminalized by the Legislature. The prominence of the upper-level status of the defendant in the description and explanation of the purpose of the crime clearly evidences the Legislature's intent that the status or the position of the defendant in the drug trafficking network is a substantive part of the crime. Consistent with that intent, the status or position of the defendant should be considered a material element of the crime. Accordingly, we conclude that a trial court, in a prosecution pursuant to N.J.S.A. 2C:35-3, should instruct the jury that it must find that the defendant occupies a high-level position, that is, a position of superior authority or control over other persons, in a scheme or organization of drug distribution (or manufacture or dispensing or transporting), and that in that position the defendant exercised supervisory power or control over others engaged in an organized drug-trafficking network.

That conclusion is based largely on the fact that the words of the statute alone under N.J.S.A. 2C:35-3, whether their meaning is "plain" or "clear" for constitutional purposes, without any further explanation would not fully convey to the jury the nature of the actual elements of the conduct that the Legislature intended to criminalize. Those elements, in addition to the activities enumerated in N.J.S.A. 2C:35-3, such as supervision, management, financing, and the like, include the role of the defendant as an "upper-level member" of a drug operation.

The recognition of the upper-level position of the defendant as an essential element of the crime under the drug-kingpin statute does not, as the State believes, entail a rewriting of the statute.

This Court has made abundantly clear that correct jury instructions are at the heart of the proper execution of the jury function in a criminal trial: "'[a]ppropriate and proper charges to a jury are essential for a fair trial.'" A court's obligation properly to instruct and to guide a jury includes the duty to clarify statutory language that prescribes the elements of a crime when clarification is essential to ensure that the jury will fully understand and actually find those elements in determining the defendant's guilt.

For the purpose of instructing and guiding juries, courts regularly explain and define statutory language consistent with legislative intent. Courts commonly clarify statutory language to give more precise meaning to statutory terms to effect the legislative intent and to make sure that juries carry out that intent in determining criminal culpability.

Courts follow that approach even when statutory terms have common or well-understood meanings based on ordinary experience. In a prosecution under N.J.S.A. 2C:35-5 for possession of a controlled dangerous substance (C.D.S.) with the intent to distribute, for example, the model jury instruction includes a long definition of a relatively common term—"possession." That definition of possession does not appear anywhere in N.J.S.A. 2C:35-5. Rather, the definition reflects this Court's numerous expositions of the meaning of "possession." The model jury instruction's definition of "possession" includes the situation in which a person "is aware of the presence of the [C.D.S.] and is able to exercise intentional control or dominion over it." The language of "intentional control or dominion" comes not from the literal language of N.J.S.A. 2C:35-5 but from this Court's interpretation of that statute.

Further, statutes containing words whose meanings are ordinary and understandable often require a judicial determination with respect to their intended scope of application. *State v. Thomas,* 132 N.J. 247, 254 (1993) (defining use of school property for school purposes as "essential element" of school-zone drug offense); *State v. Ivory,* 124 N.J. 582, 587–92, 592 A.2d 205 (1991) (defining property that constitutes "school property used for school purposes" for purposes of school-zone drug offense); *see also State ex rel. M.T.S.,* 129 N.J. 422, 609 A.2d 1266 (1992) (finding that legislative history was relevant to under-standing of legislative intent that principles of criminal assault were relevant in defining element of force and role of consent for crime of second-degree sexual assault).

An instruction that makes explicit the implicit elements of the crime does not involve rewriting the statute or redefining, modifying, amending, or adding to the substantive elements prescribed by the statute because that instructional definition conforms to the legislative intent and carries out that intent. Thus, a proper instruction should, in addition to reciting the statutory language of N.J.S.A. 2C:35-3, at least inform the jury that it must find that the defendant occupies a high-level position of authority in the scheme of distribution (or manufacture or dispensing or transporting, as the evidence may permit). A court should instruct the jury that a defendant's position and status must be at a superior or high level in relation to other persons in the drug trafficking network and that the defendant's role must be that of a "leader" in the drug organization or system and, in that capacity, the defendant exercised supervisory power or control over others engaged in the organized drug-trafficking network.

Under the statute a drug-trafficking network need not have any specific configuration or chain of command. Such a network is not to be understood primarily or exclusively as a vertical, in contrast to a horizontal, organization. Rather, it is to be considered as an organization of persons who are collectively engaged in drug activities. A "high-level" or "upper-echelon" "leader" of such an organization is one who occupies a significant or important position in the organization and exercises substantial authority and control over its operations. Neither the specific elements enumerated in the provisions of N.J.S.A. 2C:35-3 nor the additional requirements extrapolated from the statute's statement of purpose indicate that a drug operator exercising authority and controlling other people in an organization or network, even at the street level, could not be a "leader" or "drug kingpin" within the contemplation of the Legislature. Rather, the role of a defendant as a leader or drug kingpin turns more on the nature of that person's authority, the magnitude or extent of control, and the number of persons over whom that power is exercised.

An appropriate instruction should also amplify the other statutory terms that are expressed as material elements of the crime under N.J.S.A. 2C:35-3. Thus, the statutory terms "organizer, supervisor, financier or manager" should be explained so that the meaning of those terms is more fully understood by the jury. For example, the court might define an "organizer" as a person who arranges, devises, or plans a drug-trafficking network; a "supervisor" as one who oversees the operation of a drug-trafficking network; a "financier" as one who is responsible for providing the funds or resources necessary to operate a drug-trafficking network; and a "manager" as one who directs the operations of a drug-trafficking network.

We affirm so much of the judgment of the Appellate Division as reverses defendant's conviction and remands for a new trial. We modify the terms of the remand with respect to the proper jury charge.

Clifford, J., dissenting.

This Court does not have to love a statute, but we do have to apply it unless it is invalid. I fear that the majority's hostility to the enactment that the Legislature has given us has caused the Court to rewrite the "drug kingpin" statute—an illicit exercise bad enough in itself, made worse by the Court's botching of a job for which it is demonstrably ill-suited.

I would apply the statute as written and would reinstate the conviction of this \$1500-to-\$9000-per-week drug entrepreneur as a "leader of a drug trafficking network."

We are told that "without any further explanation" the words of section 35-3 alone "would not fully convey to the jury the nature of the actual elements of the conduct that the Legislature intended to criminalize." And so, relying on a separate statutory section, N.J.S.A. 2C:35-1.1 (section 35-1.1), the court has added to section 35-3's list of criminal elements yet another "essential element of the crime under the drug-kingpin statute," characterized variously as a defendant's "high-level position" in the nefarious scheme, or a defendant's "role * * * as an 'upper-level member' of a drug operation."

Reliance on section 35-1.1 as justification for the court's stunning addition of a defendant's "upper-level position" as "an *essential element* of the crime under the drug-kingpin statute," is badly misplaced. Section 35-1.1c, quoted in essential part in the majority opinion does nothing more than set forth the Legislature's findings and its declaration of public policy. Section 35-1.1c does not criminalize any conduct, define any elements of any offense, provide for any penalties, or otherwise display any of the identifying features of a criminal statute. Those functions are left to N.J.S.A. 2C:35-2 to -16, in which the Legislature got down to the business of defining and grading the related criminal offenses. Section 35-1, which precedes those sections, is only what it purports to be, nothing more: a statement, an announcement of the Legislature's intent in creating certain crimes and prescribing the penalties therefor, an identification of the targets at which the Comprehensive Drug Reform Act of 1986 is aimed.

Facing the dilemma created when the Legislature writes a statute whose operative provisions are crystal clear but whose operative provisions may not conform with the Legislature's explicit statement of legislative purpose, the Court attempts to remedy the situation by rewriting the operative provisions. We will never know why the Legislature, having so clearly indicated its intention that the statute should apply only to high-level drug dealers, went on to define the crime in a way that would permit conviction of drug dealers at a lower level. What we do know, however, is that one part of the statute is a declaration of legislative intent and purpose, not a definition of a crime, and that another section of the statute is unmistakably the definition of the crime. The crime defined is "leader of narcotics trafficking network." The Legislature says so: "leader of narcotics trafficking network is a crime of the first degree and upon conviction thereof * * * a person shall be sentenced to an ordinary term of life imprisonment during which the person must serve 25 years before being eligible for parole." That is the crime. The Legislature also left no doubt about the elements of that crime:

> A person is a leader of a narcotics trafficking network if he conspires with others as an organizer, supervisor, financier or manager, to engage for profit in a scheme or course of conduct to unlawfully manufacture, distribute, dispense, bring into or transport in this State methamphetamine, lysergic acid diethylamide, phencyclidine or any controlled dangerous substance classified in Schedule I or II, or any controlled substance analog thereof.

One need not twist and turn to figure out what the Legislature meant by "leader of a narcotics trafficking network." It is there in black and white. The crime is named by the Legislature "leader of a narcotics trafficking network," and the crime is defined by the Legislature. As much as section 35-3 may not conform to section 35-1.1c's statement of legislative purpose and intent, that circumstance is for the Legislature, not for this Court, to remedy; for when this Court attempts to remedy it, as no case better shows than this, the Court drafts a new statute. Whether that new statute comes closer to the legislative intent or wanders farther from it is immaterial. The important point is that the Court's gratuitous and painfully inept amendment now becomes the law—not of the people of New Jersey, not of the Legislature, but of this Court.

But, says the Court, a jury is left in the dark by a charge that simply instructs in the language of the criminal statute as dutifully delivered by the trial court in this case. And so, to pierce the newly-developed fog of language, the Court declares that in addition to reciting the statutory language of section 35-3, the trial court must "at least inform the jury that it must find that the defendant occupies a high-level position of authority in the scheme of distribution * * *." Presumably as a definition of what it means by "a high-level position of authority," the Court, in the very next sentence, rules that a trial court should instruct the jury that a "defendant's role must be that of a 'leader' in the drug organization or system and, in that capacity, the defendant exercised supervisory power or control over others engaged in the organized drug-trafficking network," an almost verbatim repetition of the definition provided earlier, in the Court's explanation of why a defendant's "upper-level" role in a drug network is "a substantive part of the crime."

Stop right there. Either the court has added a new element—high-level position of authority—to the criminal offense, or it has introduced a requirement for a "clarifying" jury instruction whose most conspicuous attribute is a limitless potential for jury confusion and for production of inconsistent verdicts on similar facts. Either result is assiduously to be avoided.

I tend to think that the majority rewrites the statute and redefines the elements of the offense by engrafting a declaration of legislative policy onto the operative or criminalizing section. Most of the discussion thus far seeks to support that conclusion. But assuming that the Court's endeavor is only to give more complete definition to the Legislature's terms, without adding any essential elements to the offense itself, that effort has, I suggest, produced more chaos than clarification. The majority unearths no novel concept, clarifies nothing, illuminates no shadowy corners of the "drug-kingpin" statute by declaring that in a prosecution under that statute the State must demonstrate that the defendant occupies "a position of superior authority or control over other persons * * * and that in that position the defendant exercised supervisory power or control over others engaged in an organized drug-trafficking network."

What, then, are we to make of the Court's holding that the trial court here committed plain error in failing to instruct the jury that defendant occupied a "high-level" or "upper-echelon" position? Furnishing no definition of those terms, the Court leaves jurors at sea, with no judicial guidance on how they should determine whether the defendants in the cases before them are "high-level" or "upper-echelon" players in the drug-trafficking scheme. Those terms, unlike the language of section 35-3, are not terms of the street, not in common usage. Including them as elements of a criminal statute in which they nowhere appear represents judicial mucking about in an area in which we have neither authority nor competence.

I would reverse and remand to the Law Division for reinstatement of defendant's conviction for violation of the "drug kingpin" statute.

C. *Mens Rea*: Knowledge in Drug Offenses

Most drug offenses include knowledge as a mental state. Federal law makes it a crime to "knowingly or intentionally" manufacture a controlled substance or possess it with the intent to distribute, for example. 21 U.S.C. § 841(a)(1). Likewise, it is only unlawful to possess a controlled substance if done "knowingly or intentionally." 21 U.S.C. § 844(a). This makes sense. A defendant who thought she was in possession of a bag full of oregano should not be convicted of a drug crime if it turns out the bag contained marijuana.

But proving knowledge in drug cases can sometimes be tricky. And the question of exactly what it is the government should have to prove the defendant "knew" can pose its own problems.

To get a sense of the problems that can arise in this area, consider the case of Lisette Lee, a 28-year-old California woman, who was arrested at an airport in Ohio on marijuana charges. Lee was traveling on a chartered private plane with a bodyguard and two personal assistants. She also had 506 pounds of marijuana in 13 suitcases. Lee told Drug Enforcement Administration agents that a friend had paid her $60,000 to transport the suitcases from Los Angeles and leave them in a hotel room in Columbus. Lee said she had been told the suitcases contained equipment for a horse farm but that she knew that story was false. Instead, she suspected the people paying her were involved with "weapons and money laundering or something." *See*, Jeannie Nuss, *Lissette Lee Arrested for 506 Pounds of Pot on Private Jet*, Associated Press, June 16, 2010.

Assuming that a jury believed Lee's story, should she be guilty of a crime? If so, what crime should she be convicted of? Even if one were to conclude that Lee "knew" she was transporting contraband of some kind, she did not know *what* or exactly *how much* contraband was in her possession. (Lee was ultimately sentenced to six years in prison pursuant to a plea agreement. *See Lee v. United States*, 2013 WL 5521874.)

1. Knowledge of Drug Type and Quantity

What happens if a defendant admits to possessing drugs but is mistaken about the type and quantity? Because drug sentences are primarily driven by drug type and quantity in most jurisdictions, the answer can dramatically affect a defendant's punishment.

Federal precedent holds that a defendant who is mistaken about the amount of drugs she possesses should be convicted and sentenced based on what she actually has. Not everyone agrees with this rule, however, as the concurring opinion in the case that follows shows.

United States v. Jefferson

United States Court of Appeals for the Ninth Circuit
791 F.3d 1013 (2015)

Wardlaw, J.

George Jefferson appeals his ten-year mandatory minimum sentence for knowingly and intentionally importing a controlled substance into the United States in violation of 21 U.S.C. §§ 952 and 960. We reject Jefferson's argument that recent Supreme Court authority requires the government to prove that the defendant knew the specific type and quantity of the drugs he imported in order to trigger the ten-year mandatory minimum under 21 U.S.C. § 960(b)(1)(H). Accordingly, we affirm.

Jefferson entered a guilty plea to one count of knowingly and intentionally importing 4.65 kilograms of a mixture containing methamphetamine into the United States. Jefferson claims that, at the time he crossed the border, he thought the substance he was transporting was marijuana, not methamphetamine, and that he did not know how much of the illegal substance was in his truck. At sentencing he contended, among other things, that under the Supreme Court's decision[] in *Alleyne v. United States,* 133 S.Ct. 2151 (2013), knowledge of drug type and quantity were elements of the offense, and that, therefore, the government had to prove he knew the exact drug type and quantity he was transporting for the 10-year mandatory minimum under 21 U.S.C. § 960(b)(1)(H) to apply. The district court concluded that *Alleyne* . . . did not abrogate long-established Ninth Circuit precedent that the government is not required to prove that a defendant knew the type or quantity of the controlled substance he imported to be found guilty under § 960. The district court imposed a sentence of 144 months of incarceration, followed by 10 years of supervised release.

It is "unlawful . . . to import into the United States from any place outside thereof, any controlled substance in schedule I or II of subchapter I" of the Controlled Substances Act. 21 U.S.C. § 952(a). Methamphetamine is a schedule II controlled substance. 21 C.F.R. § 1308.12(a), (d)(2). "Any person who . . . knowingly or intentionally imports or exports a controlled substance . . . shall be punished as provided in [21 U.S.C. § 960(b)]." 21 U.S.C. § 960(a) (citing 21 U.S.C. § 952).

21 U.S.C. § 960(b), entitled "Penalties," prescribes varying minimum and maximum terms of imprisonment and fines depending on the type and quantity of controlled substance a person imports. For example, a person convicted of importing 500 grams or more of a mixture containing methamphetamine shall be sentenced to a minimum of 10 years imprisonment and a maximum of life imprisonment. *Id.* § 960(b)(1)(H). A person convicted of importing less than 50 kilograms of marijuana faces no mandatory minimum, and shall be sentenced to a maximum of 5 years imprisonment, a fine not exceeding $250,000, or both. *Id.* § 960(b)(4).

We have consistently held that a defendant can be convicted under § 960 if he believed he imported or exported *some* controlled substance. *See United States v.*

Carranza, 289 F.3d 634, 644 (9th Cir.2002). The government is not required to prove that the defendant knew the type or quantity of the controlled substance he imported to obtain a conviction under § 960(a) or for the penalties under § 960(b) to apply. Section 960(a) requires a person to "knowingly or intentionally" import a controlled substance; § 960(b) refers to different types and amounts of controlled substances for sentencing purposes.

Jefferson first argues that this long established precedent was abrogated[2] by the Supreme Court's decision in *Alleyne v. United States*, which held that any fact that increases the mandatory minimum sentence is an "element" of the offense that must be submitted to the jury and found beyond a reasonable doubt. The decision extended the rule of *Apprendi v. New Jersey*, 530 U.S. 466, 490 (2000), in which the Court established that, "[o]ther than the fact of a prior conviction, any fact that increases the penalty for a crime beyond the prescribed statutory maximum must be submitted to a jury, and proved beyond a reasonable doubt." The *Alleyne* Court reasoned that "there is no basis in principle or logic to distinguish facts that raise the maximum from those that increase the minimum."

Jefferson correctly notes that *Alleyne* renders the type and quantity of a controlled substance "elements" of a § 960 offense. Both drug type and quantity can trigger, or increase, a mandatory minimum sentence under § 960(b), and therefore both facts must be proved to a jury beyond a reasonable doubt—or, as here, admitted by the defendant.

This does not mean, however, as Jefferson urges, that the "knowingly or intentionally" mens rea standard found in § 960(a) applies to the elements found in § 960(b). *Alleyne* provides no guidance as to which facts increase mandatory minimum sentences under a given statute. It addressed only who must determine such facts, and which burden of proof applies. *See United States v. Montalvo*, 331 F.3d 1052, 1061 (9th Cir.2003) (Kozinski, J., concurring) ("*Apprendi* affects only the identity of the decisionmaker and the burden of proof. . . ."). Determining which facts increase the mandatory minimum sentence is instead a statute specific inquiry—and *Alleyne* does not alter our precedent that a defendant's knowledge of the type and quantity of the controlled substance he imports is not such a fact, and, therefore, not an element of the offense.

Nor do two decisions that postdate the district court's ruling—*Burrage v. United States*, 134 S.Ct. 881 (2014), and *Rosemond v. United States*, 134 S.Ct. 1240 (2014)—require § 960(a)'s "knowingly or intentionally" standard to be applied to drug type and quantity. The *Burrage* Court examined a twenty-year mandatory minimum that applies when a defendant "knowingly or intentionally . . . distribute[s] . . . a controlled substance" and its use results in "death or serious bodily injury." In

2. We may overrule our precedent only if it is clearly irreconcilable with an intervening higher authority. Absent such an intervening higher authority, "a later three-judge panel . . . has no choice but to apply the earlier-adopted rule.".

summarizing the charged offense, the Court stated that an element was the "knowing or intentional distribution of heroin." The Court's use of the word "heroin" instead of "controlled substance" does not clearly signal that a defendant must know the type of drug he imports or distributes. The statute's mens rea standard was not at issue, and the Court's analysis was devoted entirely to the question of causation: whether § 841(b)(1)(C) "applies when use of a covered drug supplied by the defendant contributes to, but is not a but-for cause of, the victim's death or injury."

In *Rosemond,* the Court concluded that a defendant charged with aiding and abetting an armed drug sale under 18 U.S.C. §§ 2 and 924(c) must have had "advance knowledge" that one of his confederates would use or carry a gun as part of the crime's commission, because "a state of mind extending to the entire crime" is necessary for conviction. The federal aiding and abetting statute, unlike § 960, derives from common law standards of accomplice liability, a fact which was critical to the Court's decision. *Rosemond* says nothing about the mens rea required for the crime of importing a controlled substance, or about mens rea requirements generally.

Our conclusion that *Alleyne* did not change the mens rea requirement for § 960 is further supported by the Sixth Circuit's decision in *United States v. Dado,* 759 F.3d 550, 570 (6th Cir.). 510 (2014). [T]he Sixth Circuit rejected Dado's argument that *Alleyne* effectively overruled its precedent that "the government need not prove *mens rea* as to the type and quantity of the drugs in order to establish a violation of § 841(b)." We agree with the Sixth Circuit that this contention confuses the requisite burden of proof with the mens rea standard, and that *Alleyne* did not—and could not—change the statutory text.

Relying on *United States v. X-Citement Video, Inc.,* 513 U.S. 64 (1994), . . . Jefferson further contends that the presumption that scienter is generally implied in a criminal statute, even when it is not expressed, requires us to read a mens rea element into § 960(b). In *X-Citement Video,* the Court interpreted a child pornography statute, 18 U.S.C. § 2252 (1988 ed. and Supp. V), that . . . had different textual and structural features than § 960, and that, if interpreted in its most natural manner would criminalize a significant amount of innocent behavior. The Court there held that the "knowingly" mens rea in § 2252(a)(1) applied to the terms "use of a minor" and "sexually explicit conduct" in § 2252(a)(1)(A). The Court's imputation of knowledge to the use of a minor, i.e., requiring the government to prove that the defendant knew that the person depicted in the sexually explicit material was in fact underage, also avoided a potential First Amendment problem.

Here, there is no potential for the penalization of innocent conduct nor do we face constitutional avoidance concerns. If the government must prove that the defendant knew he was importing some amount of a controlled substance, that is sufficient to ensure the statute penalizes only culpable conduct.

Our precedent holding that the government need not prove that the defendant knew the precise type or quantity of the drug he imported is not clearly irreconcilable with any of the Supreme Court decisions cited by Jefferson. Because Jefferson knew that he imported a controlled substance into the United States, and because he in fact imported 4.65 kilograms of a mixture containing methamphetamine, the district court did not err in concluding that § 960(b)(1)(H)'s ten-year mandatory minimum term of imprisonment applied.

AFFIRMED.

W. Fletcher, J., concurring.

I concur in Judge Wardlaw's careful opinion, which faithfully applies our circuit's law regarding the *mens rea* required to sentence a defendant convicted of illegally importing drugs. But I do so only because we are bound by *United States v. Carranza*, 289 F.3d 634 (9th Cir.2002). Under the rule of *Carranza* and its predecessors, a defendant who reasonably believes that he is importing a relatively small quantity of marijuana into the country must be sentenced to the ten-year mandatory minimum prison term that applies to a defendant who knowingly imports the same quantity of methamphetamine. I do not believe that Congress intended this result. I write to explain why, in my view, *Carranza* should be overruled.

Jefferson was convicted of violating 21 U.S.C. §§ 952 and 960, which together criminalize the importation of narcotic drugs into the United States. Section 960, under which Jefferson's penalty was determined, is an omnibus narcotics statute that prescribes penalties for a variety of trafficking crimes. Section 960(a) sets out "[u]nlawful acts." 21 U.S.C. § 960(a). As relevant here, it provides that "[a]ny person who ... knowingly or intentionally imports ... a controlled substance ... shall be punished as provided in subsection (b) of this section."

Section 960(b) sets out separate and increasingly severe penalties corresponding to different types and quantities of drugs. Defendants who import up to 50 kilograms of marijuana, for example, are not subject to a mandatory minimum sentence; instead, they face a maximum prison sentence of five years. By contrast, defendants who import as little as 500 grams of cocaine are subject to a five-year mandatory minimum sentence. Defendants who import as little as 50 grams of methamphetamine are subject to a ten-year mandatory minimum sentence.

These escalating penalties, which depend on the particular drug a defendant imported, were established by the Anti-Drug Abuse Act of 1986. *See* U.S. Sentencing Comm'n, *Special Report to Congress: Cocaine and Federal Sentencing Policy* 116 (1995). Under the Act, a defendant who manufactures, distributes, or imports certain quantities of dangerous illegal drugs faces significantly more severe sentences than a person who traffics in the same quantities of less dangerous drugs. The increasingly severe penalties correspond to the culpability of the defendant, as well as the danger to the public posed by the importation of the particular drugs.

The question presented in this appeal is whether a defendant who reasonably believed he was illegally importing several kilograms of marijuana, but in fact illegally imported several kilograms of methamphetamine, must be sentenced to the ten-year minimum term that corresponds to methamphetamine. As Judge

Wardlaw's opinion explains, we have confronted this question on several occasions. Each time, we have concluded that "the government need not prove that the defendant knew the *type* and *amount* of a controlled substance that he imported or possessed; the government need only show that the defendant knew that he imported or possessed *some* controlled substance." *Carranza,* 289 F.3d at 644 (emphasis in original).

The *Carranza* rule has devastating consequences for a defendant who reasonably believes that he is carrying a controlled substance but is mistaken about what that substance is. This case makes those consequences clear. The government does not dispute Jefferson's claim that he believed he was importing marijuana into the United States. If Jefferson had in fact been carrying only the four kilograms of marijuana that he believed he was carrying, he would have faced a maximum sentence of five years, with no mandatory minimum. Under *Carranza,* however, he must be sentenced to a minimum of ten years in prison because he was, in fact, carrying methamphetamine.

If I were writing on a clean slate, I would hold that Jefferson, who reasonably believed he was importing marijuana, may not be punished by the mandatory minimum that attaches to the importation of methamphetamine. I reach this conclusion for three reasons.

First, it is a cardinal rule of the interpretation of criminal statutes that "the existence of a *mens rea* is the rule of, rather than the exception to, the principles of Anglo-American criminal jurisprudence." *United States v. U.S. Gypsum Co.,* 438 U.S. 422, 436 (1978). That is, we generally interpret criminal statutes to require the government to prove beyond a reasonable doubt that "the defendant kn[e]w the facts that ma[d]e his conduct illegal." *Staples v. United States,* 511 U.S. 600, 605 (1994). Absent this background rule, the terms of many federal statutes "would sweep out . . . , except when expressly preserved, the ancient requirement of a culpable state of mind"—a result "inconsistent with our philosophy of criminal law." *Morissette v. United States,* 342 U.S. 246, 250 (1952). Subjecting a defendant to a decade in prison based on a fact that he did not know—indeed, in this case, a fact that Jefferson reasonably believed not to be true—is inconsistent with "fundamental and far-reaching" principles of criminal liability.

Second, I find nothing in the Anti-Drug Abuse Act that overcomes the presumption of a *mens rea.* An important purpose of the escalating mandatory minimums established by the Act, as noted above, is to approximate the culpability of the defendant and the dangerousness of his act. Whether or not these mandatory minimums are reliable approximations, they reflect the basic insight that someone who imports a kilogram of methamphetamine is more culpable than someone who imports a kilogram of marijuana.

The Supreme Court has recognized an exception to the presumption of a *mens rea* for so-called "public welfare" offenses. *See [C]f. United States v. Balint,* 258 U.S. 250 (1922). This exception originated in *Balint,* which considered whether a predecessor to the Anti-Drug Abuse Act, the Narcotic Act of 1914, required the government to prove only that a defendant knew that the items he sold were "narcotics" criminalized by the statute. But the sentencing scheme established by the Anti-Drug Abuse Act looks nothing like the scheme considered in *Balint.* Under the 1914 Act, a convicted defendant faced only the imposition of a discretionary fine or a short term in prison. The purpose of the "criminal penalty," as the Court explained, was simply "to secure recorded evidence" of transactions in narcotics, and thereby to promote compliance.

By contrast, the Anti-Drug Abuse Act sets up a sentencing scheme that—at least as applied absent a *mens rea* requirement—is indiscriminately punitive in nature. It is considerably more punitive than the statutes considered in *Staples, U.S. Gypsum,* and *Morissette.* As Judge Kavanaugh has pointed out:

> The "harsh penalties" in *Staples* and [*United States v. X-Citement Video, Inc.,* 513 U.S. 64 (1994)] were statutory *maximums* of 10 years' imprisonment. The "sever[e]" sanction in *U.S. Gypsum* was a statutory *maximum* of 3 years' imprisonment. And the "high" penalty in *Morissette* was a statutory *maximum* of one year in prison. The Supreme Court deemed those penalties sufficiently stringent to support a requirement of mens rea.

United States v. Burwell, 690 F.3d 500, 548 (D.C.Cir.2012) (en banc) (Kavanaugh, J., dissenting) (citations omitted). The penalties considered in these cases were "harsh." The mandatory minimum sentences imposed under § 960(b) are even more so. Anyone convinced that he is importing marijuana but convicted of importing methamphetamine faces a mandatory minimum of ten years. The presumption of a mens rea is designed to avoid precisely this injustice.

Third, my conclusion is underscored by the Supreme Court's increasing attention to the Sixth Amendment consequences of statutory sentencing schemes. *See Alleyne v. United States,* 133 S.Ct. 2151 (2013). Although I agree with Judge Wardlaw that *Alleyne,* the most recent in this line of cases, is not "clearly irreconcilable" with *Carranza, Alleyne* reflects a broader concern with the unfairness of sentencing schemes in which the facts that are "'legally essential to the punishment to be inflicted'" need not be found beyond a reasonable doubt.

Alleyne held that any "facts that increase mandatory minimum sentences must be submitted to the jury." The government agrees that in a case brought under 21 U.S.C. § 960, such facts include the type and quantity of drug. After *Alleyne,* "the core crime and the fact triggering the mandatory minimum sentence"—here, the drug type and quantity—"together constitute a new, aggravated crime, each element of which must be submitted to the jury." There is no reason, in light of *Alleyne,* why it should be enough for the government to prove that a defendant knew that he was carrying a controlled substance, irrespective of what that substance was, in order to subject him to the mandatory minimum sentences set out at § 960(b). If the government must prove that Jefferson "knowingly" imported four kilograms of methamphetamine into the United States—that is, if both the fact of importation and the type of drug are "elements" of the crime—it should be required to prove not only that Jefferson knew he was importing an illegal drug, but also that he knew what that drug was.

I have no quarrel with the proposition that the government can prove a violation of §960(a) by proving only that a defendant knew he violated the narcotics laws by importing "some unspecified substance listed on the federal drug schedules." But I do not believe the government can subject that defendant to the escalating mandatory minimums set out at §960(b)(1) and (2) without proving that he knew which illegal drug he was importing. Our longstanding presumption of a *mens rea* requirement, the history and purpose of the Anti-Drug Abuse Act, and the lessons of *Alleyne* and *Apprendi* teach us otherwise.

Imposing ten years of mandatory imprisonment on this defendant is fundamentally "inconsistent with our philosophy of criminal law." *Morissette,* 342 U.S. at 250. While I join Judge Wardlaw's careful opinion, I do so only because we are bound by *Carranza.* The government does not dispute that Jefferson reasonably believed that he was illegally importing marijuana. In the absence of *Carranza,* I would hold that Jefferson is not subject to the ten-year mandatory minimum applicable to the illegal importation of methamphetamine.

In his concurring opinion in *Jefferson,* Judge Fletcher suggests that the majority's rule can result in sentences that are "indiscriminately punitive" and divorced from the defendant's true culpability. Those who favor the current approach often argue that it is justified by the "enhanced threat to society" posed by the drug type and quantity involved in the offense. *See* United States v. Gomez, 905 F.2d 1513 (1990). On this view, a person who agrees to carry a controlled substance without determining its "true identity" might be said to "assume the risk" that the type and quantity involved "will subject them to enhanced criminal liability." *Id.* Which position do you find more persuasive? *See also,* United States v. Cordoba-Hincapie, 825 F. Supp. 485 (E.D.N.Y. 1993) (arguing that drug defendants should not be held strictly liable for drug type and quantity).

2. Willful Blindness

Jefferson reveals that a defendant who thinks she is importing marijuana that is actually methamphetamine is subjected to penalties based on the methamphetamine. But what about a defendant who does not have positive knowledge that she is carrying drugs at all, but is suspicious? In this scenario, the government may be able to prove knowledge by relying on the controversial willful blindness (or deliberate ignorance) doctrine.

In *United States v. Heredia,* the Ninth Circuit considered the legitimacy of the willful blindness rule. The majority concluded that the doctrine exists because, "when Congress made it a crime to 'knowingly . . . possess'" drugs, "it meant to punish not only those who know they possess a controlled substance, but also those who don't know because they don't want to know." As you read the court's decision, the concurrence, and the dissent, consider whether you find this reasoning convincing.

United States v. Heredia

United States Court of Appeals for the Ninth Circuit
483 F.3d 913 (2007)

Kozinski, J.

We revisit *United States v. Jewell,* 532 F.2d 697 (9th Cir. 1976) [in which the Ninth Circuit adopted the willful blindness doctrine], and the body of caselaw applying it.

Defendant Carmen Heredia was stopped at an inland Border Patrol checkpoint while driving from Nogales to Tucson, Arizona. Heredia was at the wheel and her two children, mother and one of her aunts were passengers. The border agent at the scene noticed what he described as a "very strong perfume odor" emanating from the car. A second agent searched the trunk and found 349.2 pounds of marijuana surrounded by dryer sheets, apparently used to mask the odor. Heredia was arrested and charged with possessing a controlled substance with intent to distribute under 21 U.S.C. § 841(a)(1).

At trial, Heredia testified that on the day of her arrest she had accompanied her mother on a bus trip from Tucson to Nogales, where her mother had a dentist's appointment. After the appointment, she borrowed her Aunt Belia's car to transport her mother back to Tucson.[1] Heredia told DEA Agent Travis Birney at the time of her arrest that, while still in Nogales, she had noticed a "detergent" smell in the car as she prepared for the trip and asked Belia to explain. Belia told her that she had spilled Downey fabric softener in the car a few days earlier, but Heredia found this explanation incredible.

Heredia admitted on the stand that she suspected there might be drugs in the car, based on the fact that her mother was visibly nervous during the trip and carried a large amount of cash, even though she wasn't working at the time. However, Heredia claimed that her suspicions were not aroused until she had passed the last freeway exit before the checkpoint, by which time it was too dangerous to pull over and investigate.

The government requested a deliberate ignorance instruction, and the judge obliged, overruling Heredia's objection. The instruction read as follows:

> You may find that the defendant acted knowingly if you find beyond a reasonable doubt that the defendant was aware of a high probability that drugs were in the vehicle driven by the defendant and deliberately avoided learning the truth. You may not find such knowledge, however, if you find that

1. Belia was not the aunt in the car with Heredia at the time she was stopped at the checkpoint. Belia was traveling on the same interstate at about the same time, but in a separate car.

> the defendant actually believed that no drugs were in the vehicle driven by the defendant, or if you find that the defendant was simply careless.

On appeal, defendant asks us to overrule *Jewell* and hold that section 841(a)(1) extends liability only to individuals who act with actual knowledge. Should *Jewell* remain good law, she asks us to reverse her conviction because the instruction given to the jury was defective and because there was an insufficient factual basis for issuing the instruction in the first place.

While *Jewell* has spawned a great deal of commentary and a somewhat perplexing body of caselaw, its core holding was a rather straightforward matter of statutory interpretation: "'[K]nowingly' in criminal statutes is not limited to positive knowledge, but includes the state of mind of one who does not possess positive knowledge only because he consciously avoided it." In other words, when Congress made it a crime to "knowingly . . . possess with intent to manufacture, distribute, or dispense, a controlled substance," it meant to punish not only those who know they possess a controlled substance, but also those who don't know because they don't want to know.[4]

Overturning a long-standing precedent is never to be done lightly, and particularly not "in the area of statutory construction, where Congress is free to change [an] interpretation of its legislation." Even in the criminal context, where private reliance interests are less compelling, stare decisis concerns still carry great weight, particularly when a precedent is as deeply entrenched as *Jewell*. Since *Jewell* was decided in 1976, every regional circuit—with the exception of the D.C. Circuit—has adopted its central holding. Indeed, many colloquially refer to the deliberate ignorance instruction as the "*Jewell* instruction." Congress has amended section 841 many times since *Jewell* was handed down, but not in a way that would cast doubt on our ruling. Given the widespread acceptance of *Jewell* across the federal judiciary, of which Congress must surely have been aware, we construe Congress's inaction as acquiescence.[6]

---

4. As our cases have recognized, deliberate ignorance, otherwise known as willful blindness, is categorically different from negligence or recklessness. A willfully blind defendant is one who took *deliberate* actions to avoid confirming suspicions of criminality. A reckless defendant is one who merely knew of a substantial and unjustifiable risk that his conduct was criminal; a negligent defendant is one who should have had similar suspicions but, in fact, did not.

6. Our dissenting colleague seeks support for her position from the fact that Congress has, on occasion, defined the scienter requirement in some criminal statutes as "knows, or has reasonable grounds to believe." But "has reasonable grounds to believe" defines a mental state that is less than actual knowledge. By contrast, *Jewell* defines willful blindness as knowledge—and sets a much higher standard for satisfying it. Thus, under *Jewell*, the prosecution must prove that defendant was aware of a "high probability" that he is in the possession of contraband, and that he "deliberately avoided learning the truth." This standard focuses on defendant's actual beliefs and actions, whereas "has reasonable grounds to believe" is an objective standard that could be satisfied by showing what a reasonable person would believe, regardless of defendant's actual beliefs. That Congress chose to set a lower scienter requirement in some criminal statutes tells us nothing about our interpretation of "knowledge" in *Jewell*. It certainly provides an insufficient basis for rejecting

That said, there are circumstances when a precedent becomes so unworkable that keeping it on the books actually undermines the values of evenhandedness and predictability that the doctrine of stare decisis aims to advance. Here, we recognize that many of our post-*Jewell* cases have created a vexing thicket of precedent that has been difficult for litigants to follow and for district courts—and ourselves—to apply with consistency. But, rather than overturn *Jewell*, we conclude that the better course is to clear away the underbrush that surrounds it.

The parties have pointed out one area where our cases have not been consistent: Whether the jury must be instructed that defendant's motive in deliberately failing to learn the truth was to give himself a defense in case he should be charged with the crime.[8] *Jewell* itself speculated that defendant's motive for failing to learn the truth in that case was to "avoid responsibility in the event of discovery." Yet the opinion did not define motive as a separate prong of the deliberate ignorance instruction. And we affirmed, even though the instruction given at Jewell's trial made no mention of motive. Since then, we've upheld two-pronged instructions, similar to the one given here, in at least four other published opinions.

The first mention of the motive prong came in a dissent by then-Judge Kennedy, who also authored the dissent in *Jewell*. *See United States v. Murrieta-Bejarano,* 552 F.2d 1323, 1326 (9th Cir. 1977) (Kennedy, J., dissenting). Judge Kennedy's chief concern was with what he viewed as the absence of *deliberate* avoidance on the part of the defendant in that case. At any rate, he was not writing for the court. Yet some of our opinions seem to have adopted the motive prong, providing little justification for doing so other than citation to Judge Kennedy's dissent. Three other federal circuits have followed suit. *See United States v. Puche,* 350 F.3d 1137, 1149 (11th Cir. 2003); *United States v. Willis,* 277 F.3d 1026, 1032 (8th Cir. 2002); *United States v. Delreal-Ordones,* 213 F.3d 1263, 1268–69 (10th Cir. 2000).

Heredia argues that the motive prong is necessary to avoid punishing individuals who fail to investigate because circumstances render it unsafe or impractical to do so. She claims that she is within this group, because her suspicions did not arise until she was driving on an open highway where it would have been too dangerous to pull over. She thus claims that she had a motive *other* than avoiding criminal culpability for failing to discover the contraband concealed in the trunk.

We believe, however, that the second prong of the instruction, the requirement that defendant have *deliberately* avoided learning the truth, provides sufficient protections for defendants in these situations. A deliberate action is one that is "[i]ntentional; premeditated; fully considered." *Black's Law Dictionary* 459 (8th ed. 2004). A decision influenced by coercion, exigent circumstances or lack of meaningful choice

---

an interpretation that Congress has left undisturbed for three decades and that has since been adopted by ten of our sister circuits.

8. The motive prong usually requires the jury to find that defendant was deliberately ignorant "in order to provide himself with a defense in the event of prosecution."

is, perforce, not deliberate. A defendant who fails to investigate for these reasons has not deliberately chosen to avoid learning the truth.[10]

We conclude, therefore, that the two-pronged instruction given at defendant's trial met the requirements of *Jewell* and, to the extent some of our cases have suggested more is required they are overruled. A district judge, in the exercise of his discretion, may say more to tailor the instruction to the particular facts of the case. Here, for example, the judge might have instructed the jury that it could find Heredia did not act deliberately if it believed that her failure to investigate was motivated by safety concerns. Heredia did not ask for such an instruction and the district judge had no obligation to give it sua sponte. Even when defendant asks for such a supplemental instruction, it is within the district court's broad discretion whether to comply.

Defendant also claims there was insufficient foundation to give the *Jewell* instruction.

In deciding whether to give a particular instruction, the district court must view the evidence in the light most favorable to the party requesting it. When knowledge is at issue in a criminal case, the court must first determine whether the evidence of defendant's mental state, if viewed in the light most favorable to the government, will support a finding of actual knowledge.[13] If so, the court must instruct the jury on this theory. Actual knowledge, of course, is inconsistent with willful blindness. The deliberate ignorance instruction only comes into play, therefore, if the jury rejects the government's case as to actual knowledge. In deciding whether to give a willful blindness instruction, in addition to an actual knowledge instruction, the district court must determine whether the jury could rationally find willful blindness even though it has rejected the government's evidence of actual knowledge. If so, the court may also give a *Jewell* instruction.

This case well illustrates the point. Taking the evidence in the light most favorable to the government, a reasonable jury could certainly have found that Heredia

10. The concurrence would add the third prong to the *Jewell* instruction in order to protect defendants who have "innocent" motives for deliberately avoiding the truth. But the deliberate ignorance instruction defines when an individual has sufficient information so that he can be deemed to "know" something, even though he does not take the final step to confirm that knowledge. The *reason* the individual fails to take that final step has no bearing on whether he has sufficient information so he can properly be deemed to "know" the fact. An innocent motive for being deliberately ignorant no more vitiates the knowledge element of a crime than does an innocent motive vitiate any other element.

Equally misplaced is the concurrence's concern about FedEx and similar package carriers. The fact that a tiny percentage of the tens of thousands of packages FedEx transports every day may contain contraband hardly establishes a high probability that any particular package contains contraband. Of course, if a particular package leaks a white powder or gives any other particularized and unmistakable indication that it contains contraband, and the carrier fails to investigate, it may be held liable—and properly so.

13. As previously noted, willful blindness is tantamount to knowledge. We use the phrase "actual knowledge" to describe the state of mind when defendant, in fact, knows of the existence of the contraband rather than being willfully blind to its existence.

actually knew about the drugs. Not only was she driving a car with several hundred pounds of marijuana in the trunk, but everyone else who might have put the drugs there—her mother, her aunt, her husband—had a close personal relationship with Heredia. Moreover, there was evidence that Heredia and her husband had sole possession of the car for about an hour prior to setting out on the trip to Tucson. Based on this evidence, a jury could easily have inferred that Heredia actually knew about the drugs in the car because she was involved in putting them there.

The analysis in the foregoing paragraph presupposes that the jury believed the government's case in its entirety, and disbelieved all of Heredia's exculpatory statements. While this would have been *a* rational course for the jury to take, it was not the only one. For example, a rational jury might have bought Heredia's basic claim that she didn't know about the drugs in the trunk, yet disbelieved other aspects of her story. The jury could, for example, have disbelieved Heredia's story about *when* she first began to suspect she was transporting drugs. The jury could have found that her suspicions were aroused when Belia gave her the unsatisfactory explanation for the "detergent" scent,[15] or while she drove to Tucson but before the last exit preceding the checkpoint. Or, the jury might have believed Heredia that she became suspicious only after she had passed the last exit before the checkpoint but disbelieved that concerns about safety motivated her failure to stop.

All of these are scenarios the jury could rationally have drawn from the evidence presented, depending on how credible they deemed Heredia's testimony in relation to the other evidence presented. The government has no way of knowing which version of the facts the jury will believe, and it is entitled (like any other litigant) to have the jury instructed in conformity with each of these rational possibilities. That these possibilities are mutually exclusive is of no consequence. A party may present alternative factual theories, and is entitled to instructions supporting all rational inferences the jury might draw from the evidence.

We do not share the worry that giving both an actual knowledge and a deliberate ignorance instruction is likely to confuse the jury. A jury is presumed to follow the instructions given to it and we see no reason to fear that juries will be less able to do so when trying to sort out a criminal defendant's state of mind than any other issue. Nor do we agree that the *Jewell* instruction risks lessening the state of mind that a jury must find to something akin to recklessness or negligence. The instruction requires the jury to find beyond a reasonable doubt that defendant "was aware of a high probability" of criminality and "deliberately avoided learning the truth." Indeed, the instruction actually given in this case told the jurors to acquit if they

15. Some of our cases have suggested that irregular or strong scents are not enough to support the inference that defendant suspected he might be transporting drugs. This rule is a byproduct of the hands-on approach to reviewing *Jewell* cases we eschew today and does not survive our opinion. Whether an irregular scent provides a sufficient foundation for the first prong of the *Jewell* instruction depends on the evidence in each case. It is a matter committed to the sound discretion of the district court. Contrary statements in our opinions are disapproved.

believed defendant was "simply careless." Recklessness or negligence never comes into play, and there is little reason to suspect that juries will import these concepts, as to which they are not instructed, into their deliberations.

Even if the factual predicates of the instruction are present, the district judge has discretion to refuse it. In cases where the government does not present a deliberate ignorance theory, the judge might conclude that the instruction will confuse the jury. Concerns of this nature are best dealt with by the district judge, whose familiarity with the evidence and the events at trial is necessarily superior to our own. We will second guess his decision only in those rare cases where we find an abuse of discretion. For the reasons explained, the district court did not abuse its discretion by giving the *Jewell* instruction here.

We decline the invitation to overrule *Jewell*, and further hold that district judges are owed the usual degree of deference in deciding when a deliberate ignorance instruction is warranted. While the particular form of the instruction can vary, it must, at a minimum, contain the two prongs of suspicion and deliberate avoidance. The district judge may say more, if he deems it advisable to do so, or deny the instruction altogether. We review such decisions for abuse of discretion. The instruction given at defendant's trial met these requirements, and the district judge did not abuse his discretion in issuing it.

Kleinfeld, J., concurring in the result.

Suppose Heredia were a witness rather than defendant, perhaps because the government had charged her aunt who owned the car instead of her. If Heredia were asked "was there marijuana in the car," counsel would have objected for lack of foundation, and the objection would have been sustained.[1] Heredia's suspicion would not be enough to let her testify to knowledge. Yet she can be convicted under a statute that requires her to have knowledge. This is not impossible, but it is a troubling paradox for criminal knowledge to require *less* than evidentiary knowledge. To avoid injustice, the jury needs to be instructed that they must find a motivation to avoid criminal responsibility to be the reason for lack of knowledge.

In our en banc decision in *United States v. Jewell*, a man offered to sell marijuana to the defendant and his friend in a Tijuana bar, and then to pay defendant $100 to drive a car across the border. The friend refused, saying that "it didn't sound right," and he "wanted no part of driving the vehicle." But the defendant accepted the offer, even though he "thought there was probably something illegal in the vehicle." The defendant determined that there was no contraband in the glove compartment, under the front seat, or in the trunk, so he concluded that "the people at the border wouldn't find anything either." He admitted to seeing a secret compartment in the trunk (where 110 pounds of marijuana was later found), but did not attempt to open it.

1. *See* F.R.E. 602 ("A witness may not testify to a matter unless evidence is introduced sufficient to support a finding that the witness has personal knowledge of the matter.").

We held that, in these circumstances, the knowledge element in the applicable drug statutes could be satisfied without positive, confirmed personal knowledge that the marijuana was in the trunk. We took particular note of the motive in such deliberate avoidance of knowledge cases "to avoid responsibility in the event of discovery":

> [T]he jury could conclude that . . . although appellant knew of the presence of the secret compartment and had knowledge of facts indicating that it contained marijuana, he deliberately avoided positive knowledge of the presence of the contraband *to avoid responsibility in the event of discovery.* If . . . positive knowledge is required to convict, the jury would have no choice consistent with its oath but to find appellant not guilty even though he deliberately contrived his lack of positive knowledge.

We described such blindness as "wilful" and not merely negligence, foolishness or recklessness, differing from positive knowledge "only so far as necessary to encompass a calculated effort to avoid the sanctions of the statute while violating its substance."

> A court can properly find wilful blindness only where it can almost be said that the defendant actually knew. He suspected the fact; he realised its probability; but he refrained from obtaining the final confirmation because he wanted in the event to be able to deny knowledge. This, and this alone, is wilful blindness. It requires in effect a finding that the defendant intended to cheat the administration of justice. Any wider definition would make the doctrine of wilful blindness indistinguishable from the civil doctrine of negligence in not obtaining knowledge.

Then-judge Kennedy, joined by Judges Ely, Hufstedler and Wallace, vigorously dissented. They presciently warned that the majority opened the door too wide to suspicion as a substitute for scienter.

"Wilfulness" requires a "purpose of violating a known legal duty," or, at the very least, "a bad purpose." That is why wilful blindness is "equally culpable" to, and may be substituted for, positive knowledge. But to allow conviction without positive knowledge or wilful avoidance of such knowledge is to erase the scienter requirement from the statute. And we do not have the authority to do this: "The definition of the elements of a criminal offense is entrusted to the legislature, particularly in the case of federal crimes, which are solely creatures of statute." The statute made it a crime for Heredia to "knowingly or intentionally" possess the marijuana in the trunk of her aunt's car with an intent to distribute it (that is, give the car back to her aunt or to someone else). If she did not act "knowingly or intentionally," then she did not commit the crime.

The majority converts the statutory element that the possession be "knowing" into something much less—a requirement that the defendant be suspicious and deliberately avoid investigating. The imposition on people who intend no crime of a duty to investigate has no statutory basis. The majority says that its requirement is enough to protect defendants who cannot investigate because of "coercion, exigent circumstances or lack of meaningful choice." I am not sure what the latter two novelties mean (especially the term "meaningful" choice) or how a jury would be instructed to give them concrete meaning. The majority's statement that "[a]n innocent motive for being deliberately ignorant" does not bar conviction under its rule seems to contradict its proposition that coercion or exigent circumstances excuse failure to investigate. The majority seems to mean that if someone can investigate, they must. A criminal duty to investigate the wrongdoing of others to avoid wrongdoing of one's own is a novelty in the criminal law.

The majority's "coercion, exigent circumstances or lack of meaningful choice" justifications for failure to investigate are too few. The government has not conscripted the citizenry as investigators, and the statute does not impose that unpleasant and sometimes risky obligation on people. Shall someone who thinks his mother is carrying a stash of marijuana in her suitcase be obligated, when he helps her with it, to rummage through her things? Should Heredia have carried tools with her, so that (if her story was true) she could open the trunk for which she had no key? Shall all of us who give a ride to child's friend search her purse or his backpack?

No "coercion, exigent circumstances, or lack of meaningful choice" prevents FedEx from opening packages before accepting them, or prevents bus companies from going through the luggage of suspicious looking passengers. But these businesses are not "knowingly" transporting drugs in any particular package, even though they know that in a volume business in all likelihood they sometimes must be. They forego inspection to save time, or money, or offense to customers, not to avoid criminal responsibility. But these reasons for not inspecting are not the ones acceptable to the majority ("coercion, exigent circumstances, or lack of meaningful choice"). The majority opinion apparently makes these businesses felons despite the fact that Congress did not. For that matter, someone driving his mother, a child of the sixties, to Thanksgiving weekend, and putting her suitcase in the trunk, should not have to open it and go through her clothes.

A *Jewell* instruction ought to incorporate what our case law has developed, that the wilful blindness doctrine is meant to punish a defendant who "all but knew" the truth—a defendant who "suspects a fact, realizes its [high] probability, but refrains from obtaining final confirmation in order to be able to deny knowledge if apprehended." "This, and this alone, is wilful blindness." The jury instruction in this case told the jury that Heredia had "knowing" possession of the marijuana in the trunk if she "was aware of a high probability" that drugs were in the car and "deliberately avoided learning the truth." That mental state would fit FedEx and the child of an aging hippy, as well as a drug mule. A *Jewell* instruction ought to require (1) a belief that drugs are present, (2) avoidance of confirmation of the belief, and (3) wilfulness in that avoidance—that is, choosing not to confirm the belief in order to "be able to deny knowledge if apprehended." The instruction should expressly exclude recklessness, negligence and mistake (the one given only excluded "simpl[e] careless[ness]" and an "actual[] belie[f] that no drugs were in the vehicle"). Anything less supports convictions of persons whom Congress excluded from statutory coverage with the word "knowingly." People who possess drugs, but do not do so "knowingly," are what we traditionally refer to as "innocent."

The reason that I concur instead of dissenting is that defendant did not object to these deficiencies in the instruction, and the deficiencies were not "plain." To constitute plain error, "[a]n error . . . must be . . . obvious or readily apparent."

Our previous cases did not make clear that the instruction had to say these things (they only made clear that the judge must decide there was some evidence of wilfulness before giving the instruction). For that reason, it is not surprising that the instruction given tracked the language of our own form. Defendant's objection was to giving a *Jewell* instruction at all, rather than to the language in the *Jewell* instruction. She argued that "the instruction is not appropriate in this particular case" because "there is no evidence that she did anything . . . to deliberately avoid [learning the truth]. . . ." She did not argue in the district court, as she now does on appeal, that the wilful blindness instruction, if given, should include a requirement that a defendant's wilful blindness be motivated by a desire to avoid criminal responsibility.

Graber, J., dissenting.

Assuming the *Jewell* instruction to be proper, I agree with the majority that the standard by which to review a district court's decision to give one is "abuse of discretion" in the light of the evidence presented at trial. But as a matter of statutory construction, I believe that the *Jewell* instruction is not proper because it misconstrues, and misleads the jury about, the mens rea required by 21 U.S.C. § 841(a)(1). Because the legal error of giving a *Jewell* instruction in this case was not harmless beyond a reasonable doubt, I respectfully dissent.

Under 21 U.S.C. § 841(a)(1), it is a crime to "*knowingly or intentionally* . . . manufacture, distribute, or dispense, or possess with intent to manufacture, distribute, or dispense, a controlled substance." (Emphasis added.) The plain text of the statute does not make it a crime to have a high probability of awareness of possession—knowledge or intention is required.

The majority recognizes that willful blindness is a mens rea separate and distinct from knowledge. *See* Majority op. ("Actual knowledge, of course, is inconsistent with willful blindness."); *see also United States v. Jewell,* 532 F.2d 697, 705–06 (9th Cir. 1976) (en banc) (Kennedy, J., dissenting) ("The majority opinion justifies the conscious purpose jury instruction as an application of the wilful blindness doctrine recognized primarily by English authorities. . . . [T]he English authorities seem to consider wilful blindness a state of mind *distinct from, but equally culpable as,* 'actual' knowledge."). Similarly, if not even more obviously, willful blindness is at least one step removed from intention.

Instead of justifying its sleight-of-hand directly, the majority points to the fact that *Jewell* has been on the books for 30 years and that Congress has not amended the statute in a way that repudiates *Jewell* expressly. I find this reasoning unpersuasive.

"[C]ongressional inaction lacks persuasive significance because several equally tenable inferences may be drawn from such inaction. . . ."

Whatever relevance congressional *inaction* holds in this case is outweighed by actual congressional *action*. Under 21 U.S.C. § 841(a)(1), a person is guilty of a crime only if the requisite act is performed "knowingly or intentionally." By contrast, both before and after *Jewell*, Congress has defined several other crimes in which the mens rea involves a high probability of awareness—but it has done so in phrases dramatically different than the one here, which lists only knowledge and intent. *See, e.g.*, 18 U.S.C. §§ 175b(b)(1) ("knows or has reasonable cause to believe"), 792 ("knows, or has reasonable grounds to believe or suspect"), 842(h) ("knowing or having reasonable cause to believe"), 2332d(a) ("knowing or having reasonable cause to know"), 2339(a) ("knows, or has reasonable grounds to believe"), 2424(a) ("knowing or in reckless disregard of the fact"). Most importantly, Congress has done so in adjacent sections of the same statute, the Controlled Substances Act, 21 U.S.C. §§ 801–971, and even within the same section of the same statute. *See* 21 U.S.C. §§ 841(c)(2) ("knowing, or having reasonable cause to believe"), 843(a)(6) ("knowing, intending, or having reasonable cause to believe"), 843(a)(7) (same). "It is axiomatic that when Congress uses different text in 'adjacent' statutes it intends that the different terms carry a different meaning." Thus, "[i]f we do our job of reading the statute whole, we have to give effect to [its] plain command, even if doing that will reverse the longstanding practice under the statute and the rule."

The majority recognizes that the *Jewell* instruction embodies a substantive decision that those who possess a controlled substance and "don't know because they don't want to know" are just as culpable as those who knowingly or intentionally possess a controlled substance. But Congress never made this substantive decision about levels of culpability—the *Jewell* court did. By "clear[ing] away the underbrush that surrounds" the instruction, the majority chooses to reaffirm this judge-made substantive decision. In so doing, the majority directly contravenes the principle that "[i]t is the legislature, not the Court, which is to define a crime, and ordain its punishment." *United States v. Wiltberger*, 18 U.S. (5 Wheat.) 76, 95 (1820). "'The spirit of the doctrine which denies to the federal judiciary power to create crimes forthrightly admonishes that we should not enlarge the reach of enacted crimes by constituting them from anything less than the incriminating components contemplated by the words used in the statute.'" *Jewell*, 532 F.2d at 706 n.7 (Kennedy, J., dissenting). The majority creates a duty to investigate for drugs that appears nowhere in the text of the statute, transforming knowledge into a mens rea more closely akin to negligence or recklessness.

I agree with the *Jewell* court that "one 'knows' facts of which he is less than absolutely certain." That being so, the mens rea-reducing *Jewell* instruction not only is wrong, it also is unnecessary in the face of the kind of proof that a prosecutor is likely to produce. For example, if your husband comes home at 1:00 a.m. every Friday (after having left work at 5:00 p.m. the day before as usual), never reveals where he has been, won't look you in the eye on Fridays, and puts Thursday's shirts in the hamper bearing lipstick stains, your friends will agree that you "know" he is having an affair even if you refuse to seek confirmation. The role of a jury is to apply common sense to the facts of a given case. A sensible jury will be persuaded that a drug mule "knows" what she is carrying when confronted with evidence of how mules typically operate and how this mule acted—all without reference to a *Jewell* instruction.

Thus, I would overrule *Jewell* and interpret 21 U.S.C. § 841(a) to require exactly what its text requires—a knowing or intentional mens rea. If Congress wants to criminalize willful ignorance, it is free to amend the statute to say so and, in view of the several examples quoted above, it clearly knows how.

As the *Heredia* court explains, in a willful blindness case, the courier is suspicious that there are drugs in her possession but "refrain[s] from obtaining the final confirmation" in order "to be able to deny knowledge." In other drug courier cases—so-called "blind mule" cases—the defendant may deny knowledge or suspicion of the contraband entirely.

In cases where the defendant advances a blind mule argument, prosecutors have often sought to introduce "expert" testimony by drug agents, who claim that "a blind mule is a 'mythical character.'" *California v. Covarrubias,* 202 Cal. App. 4th 1 (2012). In one blind mule case, for example, Immigration Customs Enforcement Special Agent Andrew Flood testified "he had never been involved with, nor heard of, a case involving a blind mule." Agent Flood explained: "You have to look at it not as 193 pounds of marijuana in the car, but say, . . . $185,000 of cash in the car. It's a business. You don't—the idea of putting drugs . . . on someone and hope to retrieve it somewhere north of the border is—it's guesswork." *Id.*

In 2012, however, the federal government revealed that the use of blind mules near the San Diego border had in fact become somewhat widespread. According to a news report of the U.S. Immigrations and Customs Enforcement announcement, "[s]mugglers have long advertised work as security guards, housecleaners and cashiers, telling applicants they must drive company cars to the United States. They aren't told the cars are loaded with drugs." Elliot Spagat, *Drug Smugglers Placing Job Ads In Mexican Newspapers*, Associated Press, April 11, 2012. "For drug traffickers, the tactic lowers expenses and, they hope, makes drivers appear less nervous when questioned by border inspectors, said Millie Jones, an assistant special agent in charge of investigations for ICE in San Diego." *Id.* With respect to expenses, the cost savings appears to be substantial. According to the report, "blind mules" are paid $50 to $200 per-trip compared to $1,500 to $5,000 for a courier who knows she is carrying contraband.

In addition to addressing the willful blindness doctrine, *Heredia* involved a question about the relationship in time between knowledge and possession. The defendant argued that she only became suspicious there might be drugs in the car after she "had passed the last freeway exit before the [border] checkpoint, by which time it was too dangerous to pull over and investigate." Can a person who realizes mid trip that the car they are driving contains drugs be convicted of drug possession? The court's decision in *Heredia* indicates that, at least on the facts of that case, she can. Is it possible to reconcile that outcome with the constructive possession cases that require proof of an intent to exercise dominion and control over the substance in addition to knowledge of its existence?

In a 2011 San Francisco case, a man charged with drug possession raised a time-based *mens rea* defense of a much different nature. Eric Meoli was acquitted of possessing magic mushrooms "after his lawyer argued that he forgot they were in his backpack, so he could not have knowingly possessed them." Margaret Baum, *San Francisco Jury Acquits Man who Forgot Mushrooms Were in his Backpack*, S.F. EXAMINER, July 15, 2011. Meoli, an employee at a medical marijuana dispensary, claimed that he "had given $10 of legally-obtained medical marijuana to 'a hippy in Golden Gate Park' suffering from insomnia" and the hippy gave Meoli the mushrooms in return. Meoli then put the mushrooms in a backpack and "forgot all about them" until he was stopped by the police six months later for riding his bicycle on the platform of a subway station and consented to a search of his backpack. Meoli's lawyer, public defender Kimberly Lutes-Koths, told the *Examiner*: "One of the elements of the law requires that the defendant know of the presence of the substance. Some people think my argument was unique, but it just seemed logical to me." Did the jury faithfully apply the law by acquitting Meoli based on this defense? Or is jury nullification a better explanation for the verdict?

3. Knowledge in Khat and Analogue Cases

Drug statutes do not make it a crime to sell every substance that produces a high (if they did, alcohol would be illegal). Instead, drug statutes list by name specific plants and chemicals that are against the law to possess, sell, and manufacture. In addition to commonly used drugs like marijuana and cocaine, the Controlled Substances Act criminalizes hundreds of other drugs. *See* 21 C.F.R. § 1308 (providing a current list of substances scheduled under the CSA).

How should the law deal with proof of knowledge where a plant or consumer product contains a relatively obscure controlled substance?

Consider the case of khat, for example. Khat is an East African plant than contains the stimulant cathinone. Although cathinone is a controlled substance under federal law, the khat plant itself is *not* listed as a controlled substance. As a result of this odd state of affairs, courts have been left to decide whether a defendant can be convicted of a controlled substances offense based upon proof that he knew he was in possession of khat or whether the government must also prove the defendant knew that khat contains the controlled substance cathinone. The khat cases raise perplexing due process, knowledge, and mistake of law questions and courts have yet to reach consensus on exactly how to answer them. *United States v. Caseer* provides one of the more detailed discussions of the khat issue.

United States v. Caseer

United States Court of Appeals for the Sixth Circuit
399 F. 3d 828 (2005)

Moore, J.

For centuries, persons in East African and Arabian Peninsular countries such as Somalia, Kenya, and Yemen have chewed or made tea from the stems of the native khat shrub (*Catha edulis*), which is known to have stimulant properties. Khat is often consumed in social settings, and many men in the East African/Arabian Peninsular region use khat. Khat is legal in many parts of East Africa, the Middle East, and Europe; however, khat is illegal in the United States because it contains cathinone, a Schedule I controlled substance, and cathine, a Schedule IV controlled substance. *See* 21 C.F.R. § 1308.11(f) (listing cathinone as a Schedule I stimulant); 21 C.F.R. § 1308.14(e) (listing cathine as a Schedule IV stimulant). State and federal prosecutions relating to khat seem to be a recent phenomenon, with the first reported cases appearing in the mid-1990s.

At the time of his trial in 2001, Daahir Caseer had lived in the United States for approximately three years, having spent the first sixteen years of his life in Somalia and seven years in Kenya. The events in question began in the spring of 2000, when Caseer approached John Eldridge, a bookkeeper at the Nashville, Tennessee taxicab company where Caseer worked, about the possibility of Eldridge traveling to Amsterdam, the Netherlands, to transport about fifty pieces of khat to the United States. Caseer explained to Eldridge that he could not make the trip himself because of visa issues. Caseer assured Eldridge that khat was an agricultural product and, at worst, customs might confiscate the khat and assess a fine.[2] At trial, Eldridge testified that taxicab drivers in Nashville (80% to 90% of whom he believed to be of Somali or East African descent) frequently chewed khat and that, from his observations, khat was no stronger than caffeine.

Eldridge agreed to go to Amsterdam along with his girlfriend, Shannon Adams. Eldridge would receive $200.00 to compensate him for a day of missed work, and Eldridge and Adams's travel expenses would be covered by Caseer and several other taxicab drivers who would be dividing the khat. Caseer also admitted during trial that three weeks before Eldridge's trip, $1,500.00 had been sent to Amsterdam via Western Union. However, Caseer explained that the money wired to Amsterdam was unrelated to the khat and was bound for Somalia and that the khat was a gift from a Mr. Awale and three or four other people.

After arriving in Amsterdam on June 3, 2000, Eldridge and Adams met with Awale, who removed the contents of their luggage and left with the empty bags.

2. Douglas Panning, an agent with the United States Customs Service, testified that the U.S. Customs Service's practice at that time was to levy $500.00 fines for small amounts of khat intended for personal use if federal or local authorities decided not to prosecute.

The morning that Eldridge and Adams were to fly back to the United States, Awale returned with the three bags, now containing approximately 285 bundles of khat, or roughly 14,250 stems.

Eldridge and Adams returned to the United States on June 5, 2000, landing at the airport in Detroit, Michigan. A drug-detection dog at the Detroit airport alerted on one of the bags filled with khat, and a Drug Enforcement Agency ("DEA")[*] agent approached Eldridge and Adams. The pair agreed to cooperate with the investigation, and Eldridge placed a recorded telephone call to Caseer informing him that he had arrived and had cleared customs. At trial, Eldridge testified that during the telephone call, he complained about the amount of khat being greater than Caseer had indicated and reiterated his understanding that Caseer would pay his travel and related expenses. Caseer told Eldridge to trust him and that Eldridge did not need to discuss the matter with anyone else. Eldridge also testified that he met with Caseer after returning to Nashville and that Caseer told him they had not done anything illegal and would not be prosecuted, that he would take care of it, and that Eldridge should just stay quiet and not say anything about Caseer's involvement.

Agent Panning then traveled to Nashville and arrested Caseer. During questioning, Caseer admitted knowing Eldridge, Adams, and Awale. Caseer initially stated that Eldridge had purchased the airplane tickets; however, Caseer later said that a Hussein Abugar had made the purchase. At trial, Caseer stated that he may have lied to Agent Panning, but that he only did so because he was shaky and scared.

A sample of the khat seized by the DEA was sent to the Michigan State Police for analysis. Jurgen Switalski, a chemist employed by the Michigan State Police, tested the khat and concluded that it contained cathinone and cathine, but did not determine in what amounts. Switalski testified that, once khat has been harvested, the cathinone begins to dissipate and the cathine level rises; however, Switalski stated that he did not know how long it would take for the cathinone to degrade.

Eldridge, Adams, and Caseer were indicted on two counts: (1) conspiracy to import cathinone; and (2) importation of cathinone, and aiding and abetting the importation of cathinone. Eldridge agreed to testify against Caseer and pleaded guilty to misdemeanor possession of cathinone pursuant to a plea agreement recommending six months' probation. Caseer waived his right to trial by jury and was tried before a district judge for the Eastern District of Michigan.

At the conclusion of the prosecution's case-in-chief, Caseer filed a motion for judgment of acquittal pursuant to Federal Rule of Criminal Procedure 29, claiming: (1) that his constitutional right to due process had been violated because he had not been fairly warned of the criminality of his actions; (2) that khat qualified as a food item not subject to regulation by the Controlled Substances Act; and (3) that the evidence presented at trial was insufficient to prove beyond a reasonable doubt that

* The court's opinion mistakenly refers to the DEA as the "Drug Enforcement Agency." Its true name is the Drug Enforcement Administration. [*Footnote by casebook author.*]

Caseer intended to import cathinone. The district court took Caseer's motion under advisement, later denying the motion and finding Caseer guilty on both counts. The district court sentenced Caseer to two years' probation. Caseer now appeals his conviction, asserting the fair warning and insufficiency-of-the-evidence claims first raised in his motion for judgment of acquittal.

A. Fair Warning

Caseer first appeals his conviction on the basis that, because the schedule of controlled substances in 21 C.F.R. § 1308.11(f) lists cathinone as a controlled substance without making explicit reference to "khat," he was not fairly warned that importing khat into the United States was illegal and thus his conviction violates due process. Whether a criminal statute is unconstitutionally vague is a legal question which we review de novo.

1. Establishment of Cathinone as a Controlled Substance

Section 812 of the Controlled Substances Act, 21 U.S.C. § 812, sets forth five schedules of controlled substances which are revised annually by rules promulgated by the Administrator of the DEA and published in 21 C.F.R. § 1308.01 *et seq.* Cathinone was not listed in the original Controlled Substances Act schedules but was added by agency rule as a Schedule I controlled substance in 1993:

> (f) *Stimulants.* Unless specifically excepted or unless listed in another schedule, any material, compound, mixture, or preparation which contains any quantity of the following substances having a stimulant effect on the central nervous system, including its salts, isomers, and salts of isomers:
>
> * * *
>
> (3) Cathinone . . . 1235 Some trade or other names: 2-amino-1-phenyl-1-propanone, alphaaminopropiophenone, 2-aminopropiophenone, and norephedrone

Although 21 C.F.R. § 1308.11(f) makes clear that cathinone is a controlled substance, neither the U.S. Code nor the Code of Federal Regulations controlled substances schedules refers to the plant from which cathinone is derived, *Catha edulis*, commonly known as "khat." In contrast, several other chemicals classified as controlled substances are listed in the schedules along with their botanical sources. *See, e.g.*, 21 C.F.R. § 1308.11(d)(23) (listing "peyote" as a controlled hallucinogenic substance and explaining that this listing refers to "all parts of the plant presently classified botanically as *Lophophora williamsii Lemaire*, whether growing or not, the seeds thereof, any extract from any part of such plant, and every compound, manufacture, salts, derivative, mixture, or preparation of such plant, its seeds or extracts"); 21 C.F.R. § 1308.11(d)(28) (stating that the term "tetrahydrocannabinols" means "tetrahydrocannabinols naturally contained in a plant of the genus Cannabis (cannabis plant), as well as synthetic equivalents of the substances contained in the cannabis plant or in the resinous extractives of such plant, and/or synthetic substances, derivatives, and their isomers with similar chemical structure and pharmacological activity to those substances contained in the plant"); 21 C.F.R. § 1308.12(b)(4) (listing in Schedule II "coca leaves (9040) and any salt, compound, derivative or preparation of coca leaves (including cocaine (9041) and ecgonine (9180) and their salts, isomers, derivatives and salts of isomers and derivatives), and any salt, compound, derivative, or preparation thereof which is chemically equivalent or identical with any of these substances, except that the substances shall not include decocainized coca leaves or extraction of coca leaves, which extractions do not contain cocaine or ecgonine.").

However, the Supplementary Information published in the Federal Register along with the text of the rule adding cathinone as a Schedule I substance does explain the connection between khat and cathinone. 58 Fed. Reg. at 4,317 ("Cathinone is the major psychoactive component of the plant Catha edulis (khat). The young leaves of khat are chewed for a stimulant effect. Enactment of this rule results in the placement of any material which contains cathinone into Schedule I. When khat contains cathinone, khat is a Schedule I substance. During either the maturation or the decomposition of the plant material, cathinone is converted to cathine, a Schedule IV substance. In a previously published final rule, the Administrator stated that khat will be subject to the same Schedule IV controls as cathine. When khat does not contain cathinone, but does contain cathine, khat is a Schedule IV substance."). The U.S. Sentencing Guidelines also provide for marijuana equivalency with respect to khat-related offenses, but do not reference the chemical "cathinone." United States Sentencing Guidelines Manual § 2D1.1 (Commentary) (2003) (listing one gram of khat as equivalent to 0.01 grams of marijuana).

2. Application of Fair-Warning Doctrine to Khat-Related Offenses

At the heart of the fair-warning doctrine is one of the central tenets of American legal jurisprudence, that "living under a rule of law entails various suppositions, one of which is that '(all persons) are entitled to be informed as to what the State commands or forbids.'" *Papachristou v. City of Jacksonville,* 405 U.S. 156, 162 (1972).

Although the doctrine of fair warning emphasizes the importance of citizens understanding what conduct is and is not prohibited, courts also frequently invoke the maxim that ignorance of the law is no defense. *See Lambert v. California,* 355 U.S. 225, 228 (1957) (noting that the "the rule that 'ignorance of the law will not excuse' is deep in our law. . . .").

The case at bar differs from most fair-warning cases in that the criminal provision at issue here is not ambiguous in the traditional sense. Neither party has challenged the fact that 21 C.F.R. § 1308.11(f)(3) on its face explicitly establishes cathinone as a Schedule I controlled substance. Rather, the asserted constitutional defect of this provision is that through the definition of prohibited conduct by the use of an obscure scientific term, i.e., "cathinone," persons of ordinary intelligence, even after reading the statutory text, would be unaware that khat is a controlled substance. In other words, the controlled substances schedule's vagueness derives not from the language's imprecision but rather from the schedule essentially being written in a language foreign to persons of ordinary intelligence. When a statute is precise on its face yet latently vague, the danger of persons being caught unaware of the criminality of their conduct is high. *Cf. Bouie v. City of Columbia,* 378 U.S. 347, 352 (1964) ("When a statute on its face is vague or overbroad, it at least gives a potential defendant some notice, by virtue of this very characteristic, that a question may arise as to its coverage, and that it may be held to cover his contemplated conduct. When a statute on its face is narrow and precise, however, it lulls the potential defendant into a false sense of security, giving him no reason even to suspect that conduct clearly outside the scope of the statute as written will be retroactively brought within it by an act of judicial construction.").

We have previously noted that the "general rule that citizens are presumed to know the requirements of the law . . . is not absolute, and may be abrogated when a law is 'so technical or obscure that it threatens to ensnare individuals engaged in apparently innocent conduct,' because to presume knowledge of such a law would violate a core due process principle, namely that citizens are entitled to fair warning that their conduct may be criminal."

The use of scientific or technical terminology or terms of art common in a regulated field does not automatically render a statute unconstitutionally vague. However, when we evaluate a provision, like the one at issue here, that regulates the conduct of the public at large and not a particular industry or subgroup, we do not impute specialized knowledge to the "person of ordinary intelligence" by whom we judge the statute's vagueness. As the Supreme Court explained in *Connally*:

> The precise point of differentiation in some instances is not easy of statement; but . . . generally . . . the decisions of the court, upholding statutes as sufficiently certain, rested upon the conclusion that they employed words or phrases having a technical or other special meaning, well enough known to enable those within their reach to correctly apply them, or a well-settled common law meaning, notwithstanding an element of degree in the definition as to which estimates might differ, or . . . that, for reasons found to result either from the text of the statutes involved or the subjects with which they dealt, a standard of some sort was afforded.

Here, the term "cathinone" is sufficiently obscure that persons of ordinary intelligence reading the controlled substances schedules probably would not discern that possession of khat containing cathinone and/or cathine constitutes possession of a controlled substance. Persons seeking clarification of 21 C.F.R. § 1308.11(f) would be unaided by many mainstream dictionaries, as they contain no definitions for "cathinone" and make no reference to the chemical in their definitions of "khat." *See* American Heritage Dictionary of the English Language 294, 961 (4th ed. 2000) (including no definition for "cathinone" and defining "khat" as "1. An evergreen shrub (*Catha edulis*) native to tropical East Africa, having dark green opposite leaves that are chewed fresh for their stimulating effects. 2. A tea like beverage prepared from the leaves of this plant.").[5]

Despite these concerns, we are mindful of the fact that "the classification of a federal statute as void for vagueness is a significant matter. The Supreme Court has held that every reasonable construction must be resorted to, in order to save a statute from unconstitutionality." Crimes arising out of the importation of controlled substances require proof that the defendant "knowingly or intentionally imported . . . a controlled substance. . . ." 21 U.S.C. § 960(a)(1). Thus, the concern that a person of ordinary intelligence could unwittingly expose himself or herself to criminal penalties due to the vagueness of the controlled substances schedules with respect to khat is overcome here because, as discussed below, conviction requires a showing of actual knowledge that khat contains a controlled substance. Although the requirement of specific intent in this case mitigates any constitutional infirmity resulting from the vagueness of the controlled substances schedules, we caution against the drafting of criminal statutes, targeted at the general populace, that rely on obscure technical or scientific terms foreign to ordinary persons, lest we "sanction[] the practice of Caligula who 'published the law, but it was written in a very small hand, and posted up in a corner, so that no one could make a copy of it.'" *Screws,* 325 U.S. at 96.

B. Sufficiency of the Evidence

Caseer also asserts that his conviction cannot stand because the district court erred in denying his motion for judgment of acquittal and convicting him on the basis that he had sufficient notice and knowledge to satisfy the scienter requirement. Where, as here, the district court has conducted a bench trial, this court reviews the district court's findings of fact for clear error and its conclusions of law de novo.

As we concluded above in our analysis of Caseer's fair-warning claim, the criminal provisions at issue here are saved from potential unconstitutionality because 21 U.S.C. § 960 establishes as an element of the offenses that the accused knowingly or intentionally imported a controlled substance. Thus, to convict Caseer properly of the charged offenses, the district court would need to have found beyond a reasonable doubt that Caseer actually knew that khat contained a controlled substance.[8] *See*

5. We also note that the failure to include a reference to the khat shrub in the controlled substances schedule is not, as the government contends, akin to omitting street names or slang terms. In *United States v. Levy,* we rejected a challenge to the use of the term "cocaine base" in lieu of "crack cocaine," stating that, "The fact that a type of contraband may have various nicknames on the street does not render a statute punishing possession of that contraband invalid simply because it fails to list all of the then-current nicknames." 904 F.2d 1026, 1033 n.1 (6th Cir. 1990). Here, in contrast, referring to the botanical source of cathinone as "khat" is not a passing fad that would require repeated amendment of the controlled substances schedules, but rather is the commonly accepted method of referencing the plant *Catha edulis.*

8. This is not to suggest that in all Controlled Substances Act prosecutions the government must prove beyond a reasonable doubt that the defendant had actual knowledge that the substance

United States v. Restrepo-Granda, 575 F.2d 524, 527 (5th Cir.) ("Although knowledge that the substance imported is a particular narcotic need not be proven, 21 U.S.C. 952(a) is a 'specific intent' statute and requires knowledge that such substance is a controlled substance."). Keeping in mind that the government must prove beyond a reasonable doubt that Caseer knew khat contained a controlled substance, we now turn to the facts identified by the district court as supporting its finding of scienter, considering whether the district court clearly erred in making any individual fact findings and whether the evidence taken as a whole is sufficient that a reasonable trial judge could conclude beyond a reasonable doubt that Caseer had the requisite intent for conviction.

First, the district court points to the 1971 United Nations Convention on Psychotropic Substances and several Federal Register publications that explain that khat contains cathine and cathinone, that establish marijuana equivalency for sentencing of khat-related crimes, and that indicate that khat may be subject to FDA regulation. Although Caseer might be charged with constructive knowledge of the contents of these documents, the mere existence of these documents does not speak to whether Caseer had actual knowledge of their contents. The district court made no finding, and the record furnishes no evidence, that Caseer read or was otherwise familiar with any of these publications. Thus, the existence of the United Nations and Federal Register publications provides no support for a finding of scienter in this case.

Second, the district court cites this court's decision in *Hofstatter* and several state prosecutions for khat-related offenses as evidence that Caseer knew khat was a controlled substance. In *Hofstatter*, we affirmed the convictions of two defendants charged with possessing and conspiring to possess listed precursor chemicals with the intent to manufacture controlled substance analogues. We noted in passing that during a search of one of the defendants' automobiles, DEA agents:

> found two bags containing personal papers, notebooks, and envelopes in the name of [the codefendant]. The documents described "khat" (an East African plant containing cathinone) and methylaminorex.... Formulae for the manufacture of methylcathinone were found in the car, as was a Federal Register notice indicating that methylaminorex was to be scheduled as a controlled substance by the DEA.

In the absence of proof that Caseer read or was otherwise aware of our decision in *Hofstatter*, concluding that this single reference in *Hofstatter* to khat furnished the

---

at issue is controlled. For substances such as cocaine that are controlled per se under the controlled substances schedules and for which there are no due process fair-warning concerns, constructive knowledge inferred from the listing of the substance in the controlled substances schedules may suffice. However, when a targeted item, such as khat, is not itself listed in the controlled substances schedules, due process requires that the government prove beyond a reasonable doubt that the defendant had actual knowledge that the targeted item contained a controlled substance regulated under federal drug abuse laws. *See United States v. Hussein*, 351 F.3d 9, 17–19 (1st Cir. 2003).

actual notice to Caseer required for conviction in the present case would be clear error. Moreover, the state cases referenced by the district court, all pertain to state, not federal, controlled substances statutes, and there is no evidence to suggest that Caseer had ever been subject to the laws of these three states. Hence, it cannot be inferred from the existence of these four cases that Caseer knew that khat contains controlled substances regulated by the federal government.

Third, the district court found that Caseer was "aware of the stimulant effect of khat" based on Caseer's trial testimony that "khat is a stimulant and gives energy like tea or coffee." Although actual knowledge that a substance is controlled might in some cases be inferred from the physical effects caused by the substance, in this case the stimulant effect of khat is too mild to permit a reasonable inference that Caseer knew that khat contained a controlled substance. The district court's opinion indicates that Caseer knew only that khat had a mild stimulant effect and indeed seems to suggest that chewing khat is the Somali equivalent of drinking coffee or tea in the United States. The seeming ubiquity of coffee houses in the United States attests to the fact that consuming products with stimulating effects is common custom in the United States, and the average American coffee drinker most likely does not pause to consider while drinking his or her morning "cup of Joe" whether he or she may be subject to criminal sanction for possession of a controlled substance. *See Lambert v. California,* 355 U.S. 225, 229–30 (1957) (reversing conviction for failure to comply with felon-registration ordinance, explaining that, "As Holmes wrote in The Common Law, 'A law which punished conduct which would not be blameworthy in the average member of the community would be too severe for that community to bear.' Its severity lies in the absence of an opportunity either to avoid the consequences of the law or to defend any prosecution brought under it. Where a person did not know of the duty to register and where there was no proof of the probability of such knowledge, he may not be convicted consistently with due process. Were it otherwise, the evil would be as great as it is when the law is written in print too fine to read or in a language foreign to the community."). Thus, Caseer's awareness of the mild stimulant effect of khat provides little support for the conclusion that Caseer actually knew that the khat he was importing was a controlled substance.

Finally, the district court found that, although Caseer "testified that he did not know that khat or cathinone was illegal, he was aware that khat could be seized or confiscated at Customs." Not all items that may be seized by the U.S. Customs Service, however, are classified as controlled substances pursuant to 21 U.S.C. § 812 and 21 C.F.R. § 1308.11. Thus, while the district court could reasonably infer from Caseer's testimony that Caseer knew importation of khat violated U.S. customs laws, it is less reasonable to infer that Caseer knew he would be violating U.S. drug laws by importing a controlled substance.[10]

10. The government also contends that it is reasonable to infer from Caseer's behavior in arranging for the importation of khat and his subsequent conduct during the government's investigation

In sum, the evidence cited by the district court in its determination of whether Caseer had the requisite scienter for conviction lends, at best, only tenuous support for the conclusion that Caseer knew that he was participating in the importation of a controlled substance. Even drawing all inferences in the light most favorable to the government, a rational trier of fact would have reasonable doubt that Caseer knew that khat was a controlled substance. Thus, Caseer's conviction cannot stand.

For the reasons set forth above, we conclude that, although the criminal provisions at issue are not unconstitutional for failure to furnish fair warning, we must REVERSE the judgment of conviction because of the insufficiency of the evidence and REMAND the case to the district court for further proceedings consistent with this decision.

Boggs, J., concurring in part and dissenting in part.

I concur in Judge Moore's well-reasoned opinion with respect to the interpretation and constitutionality of the language of the federal drug laws, as they apply to the substance khat. Since the application of the drug laws to Mr. Caseer is constitutional so long as the statutory requirement of *scienter* is met, the question of *scienter* is crucial. I dissent, however, from the court's conclusion that there was insufficient evidence of *scienter.*

In this case the government had presented evidence that:

> 1. Caseer had been in this country for three years, and had been immersed in an employment and ethnic culture in which consumption of khat was widespread.
>
> 2. Even though Caseer himself had recently gone to Europe, he recruited and paid apparently unwitting persons to go to Europe and courier a large quantity of khat back to him.
>
> 3. Immediately before the trip, he had wired $1,500 to an acquaintance in Amsterdam, who was the person who supplied the khat to the couriers.

---

that Caseer knew khat was a controlled substance. The district court did not make any findings regarding Caseer's state of mind based on such behavior, and arguably such conduct is consistent with that of a recent immigrant concerned with violating U.S. customs laws. Any inference from this evidence that Caseer knew he would be importing a controlled substance, and not simply an agricultural product regulated by customs laws, would be weak at best and insufficient to permit a rational trier of fact to conclude beyond a reasonable doubt that Caseer had actual knowledge that the khat he imported was a controlled substance. *See Hussein,* 351 F.3d at 20–21 (finding "very close" the question of whether sufficient evidence of scienter had been presented to sustain conviction, notwithstanding that the defendant: (1) "was a knowledgeable individual; he was not a recent immigrant, but a successful businessman who had been in the United States for a number of years;" (2) knew that khat was a stimulant; (3) had made prior trips to pick up khat for a local distributor; and (4) knew that the methods for sending and receiving packages, including mislabeling, use of fake addresses, and recruitment of multiple couriers, were "elaborately contrived to avoid detection").

> Although Caseer later provided an explanation for the sending of this money, that explanation was uncorroborated and the court was under no obligation to accept it.
>
> 4. Caseer coached the couriers in silence with respect to law enforcement officers, and took steps to prevent his name from being connected with the khat, both before and after the couriers were apprehended. Even when Caseer thought the couriers had successfully cleared customs and delivered the khat, he continued to counsel them to silence.

As seen in a variety of other cases, evidence of evasion and consciousness of guilt can support a finding of *scienter.* In this case, such evidence is present in abundance. Caseer's best argument to the contrary is that his questionable actions were all because he feared simple confiscation of his cargo under the agricultural laws, not because he had any idea that he was trafficking in controlled substances, of whatever variety. Indeed, his brief argues that "many things people bring in from other countries, such as apples or bottles of liquor, can be confiscated at customs without being controlled substances."

However, his attempts at insulating himself from connection with the khat went far beyond what would be consistent with bringing in illicit apples, or at least the district judge, as finder of fact, was entitled to make such a judgment. And in denying the Rule 29 motion, the judge, as determiner of law, was entitled, contrary to this panel, to determine that she was rational in so doing.

While Caseer's explanation is ingenious, the judge was not obliged to believe it, any more than the judge in *Barnes* was required to believe that the person who arranged for a "swallower" to import a substance in ingested condoms actually thought he was dealing in gold rather than in heroin.

In addition, at the time of the Rule 29 motion, there was evidence that the "street value" of the khat imported was upward of $100,000. This would be strong additional support for the *scienter* that there was something considerably more sinister involved than illegal fruit importation. The judge could take that testimony at face value at the time of the initial submission of the Rule 29 motion.

The value figure was contradicted, though not demolished, in Caseer's own testimony, but when judging the final verdict of guilt we may, as did the district judge, take into account Caseer's own testimony, and the unbelievability of some parts of it, such as his explanations of why he recently went to Germany, but just didn't have time to pick up khat, and couldn't go to Amsterdam himself, but had to use a courier, as well as his explanation that the money wired to the khat supplier, just before the importation, had nothing to do with the almost contemporaneous supplying of the khat.

Under these circumstances *some* rational finder of fact could determine that Caseer's clandestine efforts to avoid detection and thwart law enforcement, coupled with his knowledge of the khat culture, constitutes adequate circumstantial evidence that he knew that he was importing a controlled substance. I do not believe Judge Hood erred in being such a rational fact finder.

In a relatively comparable case, albeit involving a person who was only a courier, the First Circuit found, in *Hussein*, that the finder of fact could find sufficient evidence of *scienter* based on

> four key facts. First, the appellant was a knowledgeable individual; he was not a recent immigrant, but a successful businessman who had been in the United States for a number of years. Second, he knew that what he possessed was khat and that khat was used as a stimulant. Third, this was not his first trip for Mohamed. Last—but far from least—he knew that the arrangements for shipping and retrieving the packages were elaborately contrived to avoid detection.

Hussein, 351 F.3d at 20. Although the First Circuit found the case to be a close one, as I find this case, I would come to the same conclusion. In our case, there are several factors that are even stronger than in *Hussein*, primarily that Caseer was not a mere courier, but was the organizer, recipient, and paymaster for the operation and that Caseer here testified, permitting the finder of fact to assess the credibility of his explanations. Although in the *Hussein* case the court also noted the repeat nature of Hussein's involvement, that factor, when weighed against the other similarities (including knowledge of the nature of khat as a stimulant and elaborate measures to evade detection) lead me to the same conclusion.

On balance, the case against Caseer is at least as strong, and the *Hussein* case would therefore counsel toward an affirmance of the district court judgment. I would so hold, and I therefore respectfully dissent.

Holschuh, J., concurring in part and dissenting in part.

Judge Moore's opinion is not only a thorough and well-written recitation of the facts and a careful analysis of the law, it also is very balanced in its consideration of the two major issues in this appeal, the constitutionality of the regulations that make the possession of cathinone and cathine criminal offenses and the sufficiency of the evidence in this case to support appellant's conviction for the importation of cathinone. I totally agree with Judge Moore that there was insufficient evidence to show that the appellant knew that the khat plant contained a controlled substance. My dissent is based on my firm belief that the due process requirement of fair warning has not been met, and that this constitutional failure is not overcome by the fact that conviction of a defendant violating the regulation at issue requires a showing of actual knowledge that the khat plant contains a controlled substance.

Whether a law does or does not give fair warning to a person of ordinary intelligence requires, in my opinion, a consideration of not just the text of the law, but also the nature of the subject of the law and the persons who are subjected to it.

Cathinone is a psychoactive substance that is produced naturally in the khat plant. The khat plant is unique in that it produces naturally two different chemical components relevant to this case. When it is cut, the khat plant contains a substance identified as cathinone, which begins to degrade after the plant is cut. What remains in the plant is a substance identified as cathine, which has a lesser stimulant effect than cathinone. The Controlled Substances Act ("CSA") does not list cathinone or cathine as a controlled substance, but subsequent regulations place these two substances, emanating from the same plant, in different controlled substances schedules.

The regulations that place cathinone and cathine in different schedules do not mention the khat plant and do not give growers or users of the khat plant even a hint that the khat plant contains *any* controlled substance, much less two different types of controlled substances. Anyone looking at the regulations, however, would readily see that *some plants* that contain controlled substances *are themselves* listed in the schedules by their commonly known names.

Marihuana,[5] the common name for a plant of the genus Cannabis, is specifically listed in the statute as a Schedule I controlled substance. In addition to listing the plant itself, both the statute and the regulations specifically list Tetrahydrocannabinols ("THC"), which is the main psychoactive substance produced naturally by the marihuana plant.

Peyote, a small spineless cactus, is specifically listed in the statute. In addition to listing the plant itself, the regulations specifically list mescaline, the main psychoactive substance produced naturally by the peyote cactus plant, as a controlled substance.

The poppy plant is specifically listed in the statute as a Schedule II controlled substance. In addition to listing the plant itself, the regulations list specific psychoactive substances produced naturally by the opium poppy plant, *e.g.*, morphine, and codeine, as well as opium derivatives, *e.g.*, heroin, and opiates.

The leaves of the coca plant are specifically listed in the statute. In addition to listing the leaves of the coca plant themselves, both the statute and the regulations specifically list cocaine and ecgonine (products of the cocaine alkaloid, a psychoactive substance produced naturally by the coca plant) as controlled substances.

The regulations, therefore, list a number of specific plants as being themselves controlled substances, giving clear warning that possession of these plants is illegal, regardless of whether the person is aware that the plant contains a particular chemical substance that has a psychoactive effect. Remarkably—and in my opinion, fatally—absent from the regulations is the khat plant. Any person who wants to know whether it is illegal to make a cup of tea from the khat plant would find that, in contrast to other plants such as the marihuana plant, the peyote cactus plant, the poppy plant, and the coca plant, there is no reference of any kind to the khat plant any place in the law of the United States, *i.e.*, either in statutes or in

5. Although the more common spelling is "marijuana," the spelling found in the CSA and the regulations is used in this opinion.

regulations. I totally agree with the majority's statement that "the term 'cathinone' is sufficiently obscure that persons of ordinary intelligence reading the controlled substances schedules probably would not discern that possession of khat constitutes possession of a controlled substance."[9] I would go further, however, because it is my opinion that persons of ordinary intelligence reading the controlled substances schedules could reasonably conclude that possession of the khat plant is clearly *not illegal* because, unlike other plants containing naturally-produced psychoactive substances, the khat plant is not listed.

The failure to include in the regulations the khat plant as a controlled substance itself (a seemingly logical inclusion) may stem from the fact that the Convention on Psychotropic Substances listed only cathinone and cathine as controlled substances. But whatever the reason for the omission, the result is a failure to give fair warning to a person of ordinary intelligence that possession of the khat plant is unlawful, and hence a denial of the due process guaranteed by the Constitution.

There is absolutely no evidence that the khat plant with its cathinone and cathine ingredients presented a significant problem to the population of the United States when the regulations in question were promulgated by the Drug Enforcement Administration ("DEA") of the Department of Justice. In 1986, the United Nations Commission on Narcotic Drugs included cathinone and cathine in the schedules of the Convention on Psychotropic Substances ("Convention"), to which the United States is a signatory. In 1987, the DEA Administrator found that cathinone and cathine "must be controlled under the CSA in order to meet the requirements imposed by the Convention on Psychotropic Substances."

According to the DEA, khat has been used since antiquity as a recreational and religious drug by natives of Eastern Africa, the Arabian Peninsula, and the Middle East. Khat is legal in many countries, and has long been an acceptable substitute for alcohol among Muslims. During the period of Ramadan, the use of khat is popular to alleviate fatigue and reduce hunger. Although khat can be abused, it is often used in a social context similar to the manner in which coffee is consumed in other parts of the world. While the amount of khat seized in the United States has been steadily increasing, the increase appears to be related to the increasing number of immigrants from Somalia, Ethiopia, Yemen, Eritrea, and other countries where khat use is common. It does not seem likely that khat use will expand beyond the ethnic Somalian, Ethiopian, Yemeni, and Eritrea communities. According to the DEA, there is no indication that khat is marketed outside these ethnic communities, although it appears to be readily available.

---

9. The Government's expert witness, a forensic chemist with a PhD in chemistry, had been employed by the Michigan State Police scientific laboratory for 22 years. He had never heard the word "cathinone" until five years before his testimony in May, 2001. Other than forensic chemists, he knew of no one outside his area of expertise who "would have the faintest idea what cathinone would be."

While every person, regardless of nationality and ethnic background, is obviously subject to the controlled substances regulations, I believe it is nevertheless a relevant factor, when considering the due process requirement of fair notice, that the khat plant has had widespread acceptance as a recreational and religious drug by millions of people in a number of nations, primarily in Africa, the Arabian Peninsula and the Middle East, where its use has been an important part of the cultures of those areas for centuries. Immigrants understandably bring that culture with them when they enter the United States. While the regulations at issue present the same fair warning problem for everyone, they unquestionably severely impact those ethnic groups who traditionally use khat in the same manner as others in the United States use legal stimulants such as coffee and tobacco. The regulations, however, do not mention khat or serve in the slightest way to warn anyone that it is illegal to chew khat, make tea from khat, or possess khat for any purpose whatsoever, including recreational and religious purposes. They truly, in my opinion, constitute a trap for the innocent.

I respectfully disagree with the majority's conclusion that the lack of fair warning is overcome by the requirement to prove scienter, *i.e.*, in this case, that the defendant knew that the khat plant contained a controlled substance.

It is, of course, true that certain statutes have been saved from a finding of unconstitutionality, due to a failure to give fair warning, by the fact that the statute in question required a specific intent to do the prohibited act.

The present case, however, does not fall in the group of cases in which the statute or regulation is subject to a void-for-vagueness attack. There is nothing vague in the listing of cathinone as a controlled substance. The due process problem with this regulation is not a vagueness problem, but the *manner* in which the DEA has chosen to list controlled substances in the schedules. While it has chosen to list some specific plants by their commonly known names as well as their psychoactive substances, it has chosen to list only the psychoactive substances found in the khat plant—substances that are not found in any mainstream dictionaries—and failed to include or mention in any way the khat plant. A person of ordinary intelligence desiring to know whether it is illegal to chew khat during Ramadan or to join friends for a cup of khat tea would not find khat mentioned any place in the laws of the United States. Worse yet, that person, examining the DEA's regulations could reasonably conclude that possession of khat—by reason of its omission from schedules that contain other plants—is *not* a crime.

In my view, it is not enough to excuse this omission by the familiar recitation that while the drafters might have chosen clearer and more precise language, this does not mean that the poorly drafted regulation is unconstitutionally vague. The regulation in the present case is aimed at groups of immigrants from Somalia, Ethiopia, Yemen, Eritrea and other countries where use of the khat plant is an accepted and important part of the lifestyles of the people in those regions. This regulation is not just poorly drafted. It is placed in the context of regulations that would make persons of ordinary intelligence reasonably believe that they can lawfully possess the khat plant.

[I]n the present case, because the regulation on its face is narrow and precise, it lulls a potential defendant into a false sense of security. The fact that the khat plant contains listed illegal psychoactive substances is not revealed to a person of ordinary intelligence until that person is arrested, indicted and endures a criminal prosecution based on the expert testimony of a DEA chemist.

While I appreciate the fact that "a scienter requirement may *mitigate* a law's *vagueness,* especially with respect to the adequacy of notice to the complainant that his conduct is proscribed," I don't believe that a scienter requirement serves to save any and all criminal statutes and regulations from being in violation of the Due Process Clause of the Fifth and Fourteenth Amendments. Otherwise, the "constitutional vice" referred to in *Screws,* "the essential injustice to the accused of placing him on trial for an offense, the nature of which the statute does not define and hence of which it gives him no warning," 325 U.S. at 101, becomes virtually non-existent. I believe that due process issues require that each case be considered on its own unique facts, including not just the text of a regulation, but also the subject matter of that regulation and the persons who are targeted by its enactment. In this case, I seriously doubt that Mr. Caseer, who was indicted and burdened with the cost, both emotionally and financially, of a criminal trial and the fear of possibly being imprisoned, would appreciate the argument that his due process rights under the Constitution of the United States can be satisfied by requiring the government to prove at trial that he knew that the khat plant contained a controlled substance.

For the reasons stated, I believe that 21 C.F.R. § 1308.11(f)(3), listing cathinone as a Schedule I stimulant, and 21 C.F.R. § 1308.14(e)(1) listing cathine as a Schedule IV stimulant, do not provide fair notice to persons of ordinary intelligence that possession of the khat plant is a criminal offense. In my opinion, these regulations do not meet the due process requirements of the Fifth and Fourteenth Amendments, and I therefore respectfully dissent from the majority's conclusion to the contrary. I join Judge Moore, however, in finding that there was insufficient evidence to show that the defendant knew that the khat plant contained a controlled substance, and that the judgment of conviction consequently must be vacated.

Controlled substances analogues can present challenges similar to khat. As outlined in Chapter 6, the Drug Enforcement Administration has the power to administratively ban newly created chemicals by adding them to the Controlled Substances Act's schedules. But the agency is not always able to keep pace with underground chemists. For this reason, Congress has also criminalized so-called controlled substances analogues. What sort of knowledge must a defendant have to be convicted of selling a controlled substances analogue?

The Supreme Court considered the issue in *McFadden v. United States.*

McFadden v. United States

Supreme Court of the United States
135 S. Ct. 2298 (2015)

Justice Thomas delivered the opinion of the Court.

The Controlled Substance Analogue Enforcement Act of 1986 (Analogue Act) identifies a category of substances substantially similar to those listed on the federal controlled substance schedules, 21 U.S.C. § 802(32)(A), and then instructs courts to treat those analogues, if intended for human consumption, as controlled substances listed on schedule I for purposes of federal law, § 813. The Controlled Substances Act (CSA) in turn makes it unlawful knowingly to manufacture, distribute, or possess with intent to distribute controlled substances. § 841(a)(1). The question presented in this case concerns the knowledge necessary for conviction under § 841(a)(1) when the controlled substance at issue is in fact an analogue.

We hold that § 841(a)(1) requires the Government to establish that the defendant knew he was dealing with "a controlled substance." When the substance is an analogue, that knowledge requirement is met if the defendant knew that the substance was controlled under the CSA or the Analogue Act, even if he did not know its identity. The knowledge requirement is also met if the defendant knew the specific features of the substance that make it a "'controlled substance analogue.'" § 802(32)(A). Because the U.S. Court of Appeals for the Fourth Circuit approved a jury instruction that did not accurately convey this knowledge requirement, we vacate its judgment and remand for that court to determine whether the error was harmless.

In 2011, law enforcement officials in Charlottesville, Virginia, began investigating individuals at a Charlottesville video store for suspected distribution of "bath salts"—various recreational drugs used to produce effects similar to those of cocaine, methamphetamine, and other controlled substances. The owner of the store, Lois McDaniel, had been purchasing bath salts from petitioner Stephen McFadden for several months. McFadden had marketed the substances to her as "Alpha," "No Speed," "Speed," "Up," and "The New Up," and had compared them to cocaine and crystal meth. He had often sold those products with labels borrowing language from the Analogue Act, asserting that the contents were "not for human consumption" or stating that a particular product "does not contain any of the following compounds or analogues of the following compounds" and listing controlled substances. McDaniel purchased the bath salts for $15 per gram and resold them for $30 to $70 per gram.

After investigators had conducted two controlled buys from the store and confronted McDaniel, she agreed to cooperate in their investigation by making five controlled buys from McFadden. The Government intercepted the substances McFadden sent when they arrived at the local FedEx store. Like the substances sold in the video store, these substances were white and off-white powders packaged in small plastic bags. Chemical analysis identified the powders as containing, among other substances, 3,4-Methylenedioxypyrovalerone, also known as MDPV;

3,4-Methylenedioxy-N-methylcathinone, also known as Methylone or MDMC; and 4-Methyl-N-ethylcathinone, also known as 4-MEC. When ingested, each of these substances is capable of producing effects on the central nervous system similar to those that controlled substances (such as cocaine, methamphetamine, and methcathinone) produce.

A federal grand jury indicted McFadden on eight counts of distribution of controlled substance analogues and one count of conspiracy. At trial, McFadden argued that he did not know the substances he was distributing were regulated as controlled substances under the Analogue Act. He and the Government also disagreed about what knowledge was required for a conviction. The Government sought an instruction requiring only "[t]hat the defendant knowingly and intentionally distributed a mixture or substance . . . [t]hat . . . was a controlled substance analogue . . . with the intent that it be consumed by humans." McFadden sought a more demanding instruction requiring that he "knew that the substances that he was distributing possessed the characteristics of controlled substance analogues," including their chemical structures and effects on the central nervous system. The District Court compromised, instructing the jury that the statute required that "the defendant knowingly and intentionally distributed a mixture or substance that has" substantially similar effects on the nervous system as a controlled substance and "[t]hat the defendant intended for the mixture or substance to be consumed by humans."

The jury convicted McFadden on all nine counts. On appeal, McFadden insisted that the District Court "erred in refusing to instruct the jury that the government was required to prove that he knew, had a strong suspicion, or deliberately avoided knowledge that the [substances] possessed the characteristics of controlled substance analogues." Rejecting that argument, the Court of Appeals affirmed. Stating that it was bound by Circuit precedent, the court concluded that the "intent element [in the Act] requires [only] that the government prove that the defendant meant for the substance at issue to be consumed by humans."

We granted a writ of certiorari and now vacate the judgment of the Court of Appeals and remand.

The Analogue Act requires a controlled substance analogue, if intended for human consumption, to be treated "as a controlled substance in schedule I" for purposes of federal law. We therefore must turn first to the statute that addresses controlled substances, the CSA. The CSA makes it "unlawful for any person knowingly or intentionally . . . to manufacture, distribute, or dispense, or possess with intent to manufacture, distribute, or dispense, a controlled substance." 21 U.S.C. § 841(a)(1). Under the most natural reading of this provision, the word "knowingly" applies not just to the statute's verbs but also to the object of those verbs—"*a* controlled substance." When used as an indefinite article, "a" means "[s]ome undetermined or unspecified particular." Webster's New International Dictionary 1 (2d ed. 1954). And the CSA defines "controlled substance" as "a drug or other substance, or immediate precursor, included in schedule I, II, III, IV, or V." § 802(6) (internal quotation marks omitted). The ordinary meaning of § 841(a)(1) thus requires a defendant to know only that the substance he is dealing with is some unspecified substance listed on the federal drug schedules. The Courts of Appeals have recognized as much.

That knowledge requirement may be met by showing that the defendant knew he possessed a substance listed on the schedules, even if he did not know which substance it was. Take, for example, a defendant whose role in a larger drug organization is to distribute a white powder to customers. The defendant may know that the white powder is listed on the schedules even if he does not know precisely what substance it is. And if so, he would be guilty of knowingly distributing "a controlled substance."

The knowledge requirement may also be met by showing that the defendant knew the identity of the substance he possessed. Take, for example, a defendant who knows he is distributing heroin but does not know that heroin is listed on the schedules. Because ignorance of the law is typically no defense to criminal prosecution, this defendant would also be guilty of knowingly distributing "a controlled substance."[1]

The Analogue Act extends the framework of the CSA to analogous substances. The Act defines a "controlled substance analogue" as a substance:

> "(i) the chemical structure of which is substantially similar to the chemical structure of a controlled substance in schedule I or II;
>
> "(ii) which has a stimulant, depressant, or hallucinogenic effect on the central nervous system that is substantially similar to or greater than the stimulant, depressant, or hallucinogenic effect on the central nervous system of a controlled substance in schedule I or II; or
>
> "(iii) with respect to a particular person, which such person represents or intends to have a stimulant, depressant, or hallucinogenic effect on the central nervous system that is substantially similar to or greater than the stimulant, depressant, or hallucinogenic effect on the central nervous system of a controlled substance in schedule I or II."

It further provides, "A controlled substance analogue shall, to the extent intended for human consumption, be treated, for the purposes of any Federal law as a controlled substance in schedule I."

The question in this case is how the mental state requirement under the CSA for knowingly manufacturing, distributing, or possessing with intent to distribute "a controlled substance" applies when the controlled substance is in fact an analogue. The answer begins with § 841(a)(1), which expressly requires the Government to

1. The Courts of Appeals have held that, as with most *mens rea* requirements, the Government can prove the requisite mental state through either direct evidence or circumstantial evidence. Direct evidence could include, for example, past arrests that put a defendant on notice of the controlled status of a substance. Circumstantial evidence could include, for example, a defendant's concealment of his activities, evasive behavior with respect to law enforcement, knowledge that a particular substance produces a "high" similar to that produced by controlled substances, and knowledge that a particular substance is subject to seizure at customs. The Government presented such circumstantial evidence in this case, and neither party disputes that this was proper.

prove that a defendant knew he was dealing with "a controlled substance." The Analogue Act does not alter that provision, but rather instructs courts to treat controlled substance analogues "as . . . controlled substance[s] in schedule I." Applying this statutory command, it follows that the Government must prove that a defendant knew that the substance with which he was dealing was "a controlled substance," even in prosecutions involving an analogue.

That knowledge requirement can be established in two ways. First, it can be established by evidence that a defendant knew that the substance with which he was dealing is some controlled substance—that is, one actually listed on the federal drug schedules or treated as such by operation of the Analogue Act—regardless of whether he knew the particular identity of the substance. Second, it can be established by evidence that the defendant knew the specific analogue he was dealing with, even if he did not know its legal status as an analogue. The Analogue Act defines a controlled substance analogue by its features, as a substance "the chemical structure of which is substantially similar to the chemical structure of a controlled substance in schedule I or II"; "which has a stimulant, depressant, or hallucinogenic effect on the central nervous system that is substantially similar to or greater than" the effect of a controlled substance in schedule I or II; or which is represented or intended to have that effect with respect to a particular person. A defendant who possesses a substance with knowledge of those features knows all of the facts that make his conduct illegal, just as a defendant who knows he possesses heroin knows all of the facts that make his conduct illegal. A defendant need not know of the existence of the Analogue Act to know that he was dealing with "a controlled substance."

The Court of Appeals did not adhere to [the Analogue Act]'s command to treat a controlled substance analogue "as a controlled substance in schedule I," and, accordingly, it did not apply the mental-state requirement in § 841(a)(1). Instead, it concluded that the only mental state requirement for prosecutions involving controlled substance analogues is the one in § 813—that the analogues be "intended for human consumption." Because that interpretation is inconsistent with the text and structure of the statutes, we decline to adopt it.

Unsurprisingly, neither the Government nor McFadden defends the Court of Appeals' position. But their alternative interpretations fare no better. The Government agrees that the knowledge requirement in § 841(a)(1) applies to prosecutions involving controlled substance analogues, yet contends that it is met if the "defendant knew he was dealing with an illegal or regulated substance" under some law. Section 841(a)(1), however, requires that a defendant knew he was dealing with "a controlled substance." That term includes only those drugs listed on the federal drug schedules or treated as such by operation of the Analogue Act. It is not broad enough to include all substances regulated by any law.[3]

---

3. Although the Government must prove that a defendant knew that the substance in question was "a controlled substance" under federal law, the Government need not introduce direct evidence of such knowledge. As with prosecutions involving substances actually listed on the drug

For his part, McFadden contends that, in the context of analogues, knowledge of "a controlled substance" can *only* be established by knowledge of the characteristics that make a substance an "analogue" under the Act. In support of that argument, he relies heavily on our conclusion in *Staples v. United States,* 511 U.S. 600 (1994), that a statute making it "'unlawful for any person . . . to receive or possess a firearm which is not registered to him in the National Firearms Registration and Transfer Record'" required proof that a defendant "knew of the features of his AR-15 that brought it within the scope of the Act." McFadden reasons by analogy that a defendant convicted under § 841(a)(1) must also know the features of the substance that brought it within the scope of the Analogue Act. But that position ignores an important textual distinction between § 841(a)(1) and the statute at issue in *Staples.* The statute at issue in *Staples* defined "a firearm" by its physical features such as the length of its barrel and its capacity to shoot more than one shot with a single function of the trigger. Unlike those physical features that brought the firearm "within the scope of" that statute, the feature of a substance "that br[ings] it within the scope of" § 841(a)(1) is the fact that it is "'controlled.'" Knowledge of *that* fact can be established in the two ways previously discussed: either by knowledge that a substance is listed or treated as listed by operation of the Analogue Act or by knowledge of the physical characteristics that give rise to that treatment.

McFadden also invokes the canon of constitutional avoidance, arguing that we must adopt his interpretation of the statute lest it be rendered unconstitutionally vague. But that argument fails on two grounds. Under our precedents, this canon "is a tool for choosing between competing plausible interpretations of a provision." It "has no application" in the interpretation of an unambiguous statute such as this one. Even if this statute were ambiguous, McFadden's argument would falter. Under our precedents, a scienter requirement in a statute "alleviate [s] vagueness concerns," "narrow[s] the scope of the [its] prohibition[,] and limit[s] prosecutorial discretion." The scienter requirement in this statute does not, as McFadden suggests, render the statute vague. Moreover, to the extent McFadden suggests that the substantial similarity test for defining analogues is itself indeterminate, his proposed alternative scienter requirement would do nothing to cure that infirmity.

The District Court's instructions to the jury did not fully convey the mental state required by the Analogue Act. The jury was instructed only that McFadden had to "knowingly and intentionally distribut[e] a mixture or substance that has an actual, intended, or claimed stimulant, depressant, or hallucinogenic effect on the central nervous system" substantially similar to that of a controlled substance.

The Government contends that any error in the jury instructions was harmless because no rational jury could have concluded that McFadden was unaware that

schedules, the Government may offer circumstantial evidence of that knowledge. In such cases, it will be left to the trier of fact to determine whether the circumstantial evidence proves that the defendant knew that the substance was a controlled substance under the CSA or Analogue Act, as opposed to under any other federal or state laws.

the substances he was distributing were controlled. We have recognized that even the omission of an element from a jury charge is subject to harmless-error analysis. Because the Court of Appeals did not address that issue, we remand for that court to consider it in the first instance.

For the foregoing reasons, we vacate the judgment of the Court of Appeals and remand the case for further proceedings consistent with this opinion.

It is so ordered.

Chief Justice Roberts, concurring in part and concurring in the judgment.

I join the Court's opinion, except to the extent that it says the Government can satisfy the mental state requirement of Section 841(a)(1) "by showing that the defendant knew the identity of the substance he possessed." Section 841(a)(1) makes it "unlawful for any person knowingly . . . to manufacture, distribute, or dispense . . . a controlled substance." As the Court points out, the word "knowingly" applies "not just to the statute's verbs, but also to the object of those verbs—'a controlled substance.'" That suggests that a defendant needs to know more than the identity of the substance; he needs to know that the substance is *controlled*.

In cases involving well-known drugs such as heroin, a defendant's knowledge of the identity of the substance can be compelling evidence that he knows the substance is controlled. But that is not necessarily true for lesser known drugs. A pop quiz for any reader who doubts the point: Two drugs—dextromethorphan and hydrocodone—are both used as cough suppressants. They are also both used as recreational drugs. Which one is a controlled substance?[1]

The Court says that knowledge of the substance's identity suffices because "ignorance of the law is typically no defense to criminal prosecution." I agree that is "typically" true. But when "there is a legal element in the definition of the offense," a person's lack of knowledge regarding that legal element *can* be a defense. *Liparota v. United States,* 471 U.S. 419, 425, n. 9 (1985). And here, there is arguably a legal element in Section 841(a)(1)—that the substance be "controlled."

The analogy the Court drew in *Liparota* was to a charge of receipt of stolen property: It is no defense that the defendant did not know such receipt was illegal, but it is a defense that he did not know the property was stolen. Here, the argument goes, it is no defense that a defendant did not know it was illegal to possess a controlled substance, but it is a defense that he did not know the substance was controlled.

Ultimately, the Court's statements on this issue are not necessary to its conclusion that the District Court's jury instructions "did not fully convey the mental state required by the Analogue Act." Those statements should therefore not be regarded as controlling if the issue arises in a future case.

1. The answer is hydrocodone.

D. Proof of the Identity of a Substance

In most drug cases, the government will conduct a chemical analysis to prove the identity of a controlled substance. What happens, however, if the government does not have physical possession of the alleged drug? Should courts accept a police officer's visual identification of a substance as proof that it is a controlled substance?

Surely, one might think, a police officer can tell the difference between an illegal drug and an innocuous look-alike substance. But just how reliable is an officer's on-the-scene assessment of a suspected controlled substance? Consider this news story. In Corpus Christi, Texas, what authorities "initially thought to be one of the largest marijuana plant seizures in the police department's history turned into what amounted to a city park cleanup" after tests revealed that the plants were not marijuana. Law enforcement was alerted to the suspected marijuana by a teen who noticed the plants while riding his bike through a park. Police officers then spent "more than an hour removing and tagging" 300–400 plants. They stopped their search after nightfall with plans to return the next morning "to look around for more." Before the officers could resume their efforts, however, "testing revealed that none of it was marijuana at all." *See* Bart Bedsole, *Marijuana Seizure Turns Into Yardwork*, KRISTV.COM, May 20, 2010, *available at* http://www.kristv.com/news/marijuana-seizure-turns-into-yardwork/.

Historically, "most courts agreed that proof of the identity of a suspected controlled substance could not rest on an opinion based solely on visual inspection. Courts reasoned that it was impossible to ascertain the chemical composition of a substance just by looking at it." Michael D. Blanchard and Gabriel J. Chin, *Identifying The Enemy in the War on Drugs: A Critique of the Developing Rule Permitting Visual Identification of Indescript White Powder in Narcotics Prosecutions,* 47 Am. U. L. Rev. 557 (1998). During the 1990s, however, a number of courts held "that an opinion based on visual inspection is admissible and sufficient to prove the identity of the substance." *Id.*

Today, different jurisdictions take different approaches when it comes to the sort of evidence (short of chemical analysis) the government may use to prove that a substance is, indeed, an illegal drug. The issue can arise as a question of evidence law: what foundation is necessary for a witness to give her opinion about the identity of a substance? In other cases, it is dealt with as a sufficiency of the evidence question. Often, it touches on both issues. *Ohio v. McKee* provides an example.

Ohio v. McKee

Supreme Court of Ohio
91 Ohio St. 3d 292 (2001)

Sweeney, J.

Defendant-appellee, Cassandra N. McKee, was indicted on two counts of corrupting another with drugs, in violation of R.C. 2925.02. At her trial, two girls, Tiffany Friar and Melissa Austin, ages thirteen and fourteen at the time of the alleged crime, testified that appellee, the girlfriend of Tiffany's father, shared a marijuana joint with them while they were traveling in appellee's car.

The incident was discovered when Tiffany wrote a note to another friend, Stacy Cole, and mentioned that she might obtain marijuana from appellee. Stacy's mother found this note in Stacy's bookbag and gave it to Tiffany's mother. Tiffany's mother contacted the sheriff's department. An investigation ensued, and these charges were brought against appellee. Based upon this evidence, the jury convicted appellee as charged.

Upon appeal, the court of appeals reversed appellee's convictions, finding no evidence that the substance involved was marijuana after excluding the girls' testimony identifying it. However, finding its judgment in conflict with that of the Fifth District Court of Appeals in *State v. Coffey,* 1995 Ohio App. LEXIS 5908 (Oct. 16, 1995), (where the court upheld the use of lay testimony to prove that a substance furnished to minors was marijuana), the appellate court entered an order certifying a conflict. The cause is now before this court upon our determination that a conflict exists and pursuant to the allowance of a discretionary appeal.

The appellate court certified the following issue for our review and resolution: "Is there insufficient evidence as a matter of law to convict a defendant for corrupting another with drugs in violation of R.C. 2925.02, when the alleged drug in question is marihuana, and at trial there is no expert witness or laboratory analysis presented to identify the substance alleged to be marihuana, and the only identification of the substance is the testimony of the juveniles who allegedly smoked the substance?" While we affirm the court of appeals' decision reversing appellee's convictions, we do not believe the issue as framed is dispositive of the case. Because we believe that lay opinion testimony, if properly qualified, may be sufficient to sustain a conviction, we necessarily answer the certified question in the negative.

Appellee was convicted of two counts of corrupting another with drugs in violation of R.C. 2925.02(A)(4)(a), which provides, "No person shall knowingly * * * furnish or administer a controlled substance to a juvenile who is at least two years the offender's junior, when the offender knows the age of the juvenile or is reckless in that regard." Of these elements, the only one in dispute is that the substance in issue was marijuana, a controlled substance according to R.C. 3719.41 Schedule I, (C) (17). The state offered the testimony of the girls to prove this element of the offense.

[W]e must decide whether a person can be convicted for corrupting another with drugs based on identification of the controlled substance solely by the person to whom the substance was given.

The state argues that under either Evid.R. 701 or Evid.R. 702, the girls' testimony was properly admitted. Appellee, however, maintains that according to *State v. Maupin* (1975), 42 Ohio St. 2d 473, 71, Ohio law requires either laboratory analysis or other expert testimony to prove the identity of the drug. Since the record does not establish that the girls were more than novice users, they could not be considered experts. Thus, in the absence of laboratory testing or expert testimony, appellee argues, the state failed to prove its case.

Maupin does not fully answer the issue here. In *Maupin,* the court was asked to decide whether scientific analysis is required for the identification of the substance. In concluding that it is not, the court first determined that a drug may be identified by circumstantial evidence. Yet the court recognized that the identity of a controlled substance is beyond the common experience and knowledge of juries. At the time *Maupin* was decided, the Rules of Evidence, which govern lay and expert testimony, had yet to be adopted. Therefore, the court followed the established common law and held that expert testimony in some form is required. In this regard, the court considered cases where experienced police officers or drug addicts had been found to be experts and cases where casual drug use was found insufficient for qualification. Based upon these cases, the court concluded that the police officer's testimony in question was properly admitted as expert testimony.

However, since the adoption of the Rules of Evidence, both on the state and federal levels, many courts have used an Evid.R. 701 analysis and have allowed lay witnesses to testify about the identity of a drug. For example, in *United States v. Westbrook* (C.A.8, 1990), 896 F.2d 330, the court permitted lay testimony from two witnesses who used the substance at issue and had extensive experience with that type of drug. Courts have considered familiarity with effects of a drug coupled with similar effects from the substance at issue. All these cases, however, recognize the importance of a foundation of sufficient familiarity with the substance to support the opinion. To understand why a foundation is necessary before this testimony is admitted, it is important to consider the language of Evid.R. 701 and its jurisprudence.

Evid.R. 701 provides:

"If the witness is not testifying as an expert, his testimony in the form of opinions or inferences is limited to those opinions or inferences which are (1) rationally based on the perception of the witness and (2) helpful to a clear understanding of his testimony or the determination of a fact in issue."

At common law, lay witnesses were required to testify to facts rather than opinions. However, the practical possibility of distinguishing between fact and opinion proved to be elusive, if not impossible to draw, and led to extensive litigation and pervasive criticism by commentators. Consequently, former Fed.Evid.R. 701, upon which Ohio Evid.R. 701 is based, was adopted, and it "obviated the common law requirement for rigid compartmentalization of lay witness testimony into fact or opinion." Although at first Evid.R. 701 contemplated testimony about such ordinary things as the color, speed, type of vehicle, identity of a person, a person's health, age, or appearance, or even testimony regarding a person's sanity or intoxication under controlled situations, as case law developed, the rule was interpreted to allow for "'"shorthand renditions" of a total situation, or [for] statements of collective facts.'" Although the line between fact and opinion began to blur, all these situations met the core requirements—that the opinion is rationally based upon personal knowledge and is helpful to the trier of fact. Moving further from this core of "shorthand statements," courts began to permit witnesses with firsthand knowledge to offer lay opinion testimony "where they have a reasonable basis—grounded either in experience or specialized knowledge—for arriving at the opinion expressed." Before this type of opinion testimony has been allowed, however, the trial court has made an initial determination that the witness possessed sufficient experience or specialized knowledge, thus satisfying the rule's requirements that the opinion be both "helpful to a clear understanding * * * of a fact in issue" and "rationally based" upon the witness's perception.

It is consistent with this emerging view of Evid.R. 701 that courts have permitted lay witnesses to express their opinions in areas in which it would ordinarily be expected that an expert must be qualified under Evid.R. 702. The situation presented in this case fits into this classification. Although these cases are of a technical nature in that they allow lay opinion testimony on a subject outside the realm of common knowledge, they still fall within the ambit of the rule's requirement that a lay witness's opinion be rationally based on firsthand observations and helpful in determining a fact in issue. These cases are not based on specialized knowledge within the scope of Evid.R. 702,[2] but rather are based upon a layperson's personal knowledge and experience.

We follow this line of cases and hold that the experience and knowledge of a drug user lay witness can establish his or her competence to express an opinion on the identity of a controlled substance if a foundation for this testimony is first established. This meets the requirements of Evid.R. 701. It is testimony rationally based on a person's perceptions and helpful to a clear understanding of a fact in issue.

Applying our holding to the facts of this case, we find that the evidence was insufficient to show that the girls were qualified to testify as lay witnesses. Their testimony was sketchy and conclusory. Melissa testified that she "assumed it was" marijuana without explaining in detail how she arrived at this conclusion. There was no evidence as to how many prior experiences the girls had had with the drug. While the girls testified that the marijuana was in a "joint" form, neither girl testified as to the actual appearance of the drug itself. Moreover, while Melissa testified in general terms as to the effects of marijuana, she did not explicitly say whether she experienced those effects this time. We conclude that there was an insufficient foundation of experience or knowledge to support their opinions. Without a proper foundation, this evidence should have been excluded. The trial court abused its discretion in permitting this lay opinion testimony. Once the evidence is excluded, there is no

---

2. In contrast to Evid.R. 701, Evid.R. 702 authorizes expert testimony. The distinction between lay and expert witness opinion testimony is that lay testimony "results from a process of reasoning familiar in everyday life," while expert testimony "results from a process of reasoning which can be mastered only by specialists in the field."

remaining evidence of this element of the crime. When evidence of an element of the crime is deemed insufficient on appeal, the conviction must be reversed.

Even where the government has subjected a substance to chemical analysis, this does not necessarily end the matter. The testing method itself may be flawed. Or the government agent administering it may improperly conduct the test or even intentionally falsify evidence.

One study on false positives in drug identification, for example, recounts the story of Don Bolles, drummer for the punk band, *The Germs*. In the spring of 2007, Bolles "was arrested and jailed for three and a half days because the bottle of Dr. Bronner's Magic Soap found in his possession tested positive for the drug GHB. Police tested the soap at the scene using the NarcoPouch 928 field drug kit. Subsequent testing found that a wide variety of natural soaps as well as soy milk tested positive for GBH [using the kit.]" John Kelly, False Positives Equal False Justice at 3 (2008). *See also*, Alan Harris, Comment: *A Test of a Different Color: The Limited Value of Presumptive Field Drug Tests and Why That Value Demands Their Exclusion from Trial*, 40 Sw. L. Rev. 531 (2011) (discussing field drug tests and arguing that "courts should exclude the results of such tests for the purpose of establishing positive identification and further exclude such results altogether because of the risk of undue prejudice to criminal defendants"); Tim Evans, *Indiana Lacks Answers on Toxicology Lab Tests Used in Criminal Cases*, Indianapolis Star, March 30, 2012 (reporting that an independent check of blood tests in Indiana found no trace of drugs in 30% of the samples that had been "reported to prosecutors as positive for marijuana or cocaine").

In *State v. Roche*, the Washington Court of Appeals reversed a methamphetamine conviction after it was discovered that the state chemist who testified at Roche's trial had routinely tampered with evidence in order to hide his own heroin addiction. 114 Wash. App. 424 (2002). The chemist had been "self-medicating with heroin sent to the crime lab for testing purposes" and had "reduc[ed] his workload by testing a single purified sample and applying the results across a number of cases, a practice known as 'dry labbing.'" 114 Wash. App. 424 (2002). In a similar story, prosecutors in San Francisco had to "drop hundreds of narcotics cases" after it was discovered that a police drug analyst had been skimming cocaine and possibly other drugs for her own use from the crime lab. *See* Jason Van Derbeken, *Drug Lab Scandal Could Undermine Murder Case*, S.F. Chron., April 6, 2010. Likewise, in Massachusetts, a state chemist name Annie Dookhan admitted to improperly handling drug samples for a significant period, with misconduct ranging from "not properly calibrating equipment, to intentionally contaminating evidence in order to ensure a positive drug test." Sean K. Driscoll, *"I Messed Up Bad": Lessons on the Confrontation Clause from the Annie Dookhan Scandal*, 56 Ariz. L. Rev. 707 (2014). Over 21,000 cases were ultimately dismissed as a result of the Dookhan scandal.

In 2009, the United States Supreme Court held defendants have a constitutional right under the Sixth Amendment to confront government agents about their chemical analysis of drugs at trial. *See* Melendez-Diaz v. Massachusetts, 557 U.S. 305 (2009). A familiarity with hearsay and Confrontation Clause principles is necessary to fully appreciate the Supreme Court's decision in *Melendez-Diaz*, which is typically covered in Evidence courses. For this reason, this book does not include either *Melendez-Diaz* or the Supreme Court's subsequent decision applying the Sixth Amendment to blood alcohol tests in *Bullcoming v. New Mexico*, 546 U.S. 647 (2011).

Although this book leaves coverage of *Melendez-Diaz* and *Bullcoming* to Evidence courses, stories like those of Massachusetts chemist Annie Dookhan highlight the practical importance, and challenges, of cross-examining drug chemists. On the one hand, the right to cross-examine may help uncover wrongdoing in cases like Dookhan's. On the other hand, this may be easier said than done. Indeed, Annie Dookhan's misdeeds were discovered "only after supervisors caught her removing 90 samples from the evidence vault without signing them out." Driscoll, *supra*, at 717. At that point, Dookhan was suspended from conducting new tests but she continued to testify about tests she had already performed. During this period, "not one defense attorney uncovered her falsified lab work on cross-examination," or even that "she had been suspended from laboratory work." *Id.* at 718.

E. Additional Controlled Substances Offenses

Fueled in part by the war on drugs, legislatures have created a range of additional drug crimes to supplement the more frequently prosecuted offenses. The number and variety of additional offenses is too large to permit a survey of them all in this book. They range from serious offenses like drug-induced homicide to possession of drug paraphernalia to more obscure crimes like unlawful use of a communication facility (e.g., a telephone) to further a drug crime. Some laws, such as money laundering and the Racketeer Influenced and Corrupt Organizations Act, can be used to target drug offenders, though they apply in other contexts as well. This section introduces a sampling of these additional offenses. When reading the material, consider what (if anything) each offense adds to the foundational drug offenses of possession, possession for sale, and manufacture, addressed above.

1. Firearms and Controlled Substances

A number of different federal and state offenses criminalize the use or possession of guns in relation to drugs. For example, 18 U.S.C. § 922(g)(3) focuses on drug users, making it a crime for anyone "who is an unlawful user of or addicted to any controlled substance ... to possess in or affecting commerce, any firearm or ammunition." Similarly, a Virginia statute provides that "[i]t shall be unlawful for any person unlawfully in possession of a controlled substance classified in Schedule

I or II . . . to simultaneously with knowledge and intent possess any firearm," Va. Code Ann. § 18.2-308.4(a).

Perhaps the most significant gun-and-drug offense is 18 U.S.C. § 924(c), which makes it a crime to "during and in relation to any crime of violence or drug trafficking crime . . . use[] or carr[y] a firearm" or to possess a firearm "in furtherance" of a drug trafficking crime. This crime is an especially important one in part because it can result in lengthy mandatory minimum penalties, as we will see in Chapter 4 in *United States v. Angelos*. The next case, *United States v. Doody*, considers the "in furtherance of" prong of the statute.

United States v. Doody

United States Court of Appeals for the Seventh Circuit
600 F.3d 752 (2010)

Flaum, J.

The defendant, Alduff Doody, was charged with possessing a firearm in furtherance of a drug trafficking crime, in violation of 18 U.S.C. § 924(c). Unlike the defendants most commonly charged under § 924(c), Doody did not possess the firearm for protection. Instead, he accepted the gun as collateral to secure a drug debt. Thus, he argues, his conduct did not violate § 924(c). Because Doody took possession of a firearm in manner that facilitated a drug transaction, we affirm.

On March 11, 2009, Doody was indicted by a grand jury on one count of possessing a firearm in furtherance of a drug trafficking crime in violation of 18 U.S.C. § 924(c) and one count of distributing cocaine in violation of 21 U.S.C. § 841(a)(1). Although he originally pleaded not guilty to both counts, on May 20, 2009, Doody agreed to plead guilty to Count 2 of the indictment, distributing a controlled substance. The parties also agreed that Count 1 would be submitted to the district court in a bench trial on stipulated facts. Doody waived his right to appeal, except for the right to appeal an adverse decision as to guilt or innocence as a result of the bench trial on Count 1. On May 27, 2009, the district court approved the plea agreement.

According to the stipulated facts, Doody distributed powder cocaine from about April 2008 through February 2009 in Marshall County, Indiana. He distributed a little over a kilogram of powder cocaine during that ten-month period. On August 5, 2008 and February 24, 2009, Doody distributed cocaine to two confidential informants working with the Bureau of Alcohol, Tobacco, and Firearms. In a separate transaction in the fall of 2008, Doody distributed one-sixteenth of an ounce of cocaine to Gil Rodriguez, who did not at that time have the money to pay for it. Rodriguez instead offered his nine-millimeter pistol as collateral to secure the drug debt. Doody took possession of the firearm and held it for four or five days until Rodriguez paid him $60 for the cocaine. Doody then returned the firearm to Rodriguez. When agents searched Doody's residence on February 24, 2009, they found nine-millimeter ammunition and a nine-millimeter magazine.

The district court conducted the bench trial on June 8, 2009. Based exclusively on the stipulated facts, the district court denied Doody's motion for an acquittal and found Doody guilty of Count 1 of the indictment. On August 20, 2009, the district court sentenced Doody to 60 months of imprisonment on Count 1 of the indictment and 51 months of imprisonment on Count 2 of the indictment, with the terms to run consecutively. Doody appeals his conviction on Count 1.

Here, because the facts were stipulated before trial, [this case] turn[s] on the legal question of whether a defendant who accepts a firearm as collateral to secure a drug debt can be said to possess that firearm "in furtherance" of a drug trafficking crime and thus be convicted under 18 U.S.C. § 924(c).

Section 924(c) provides for a mandatory minimum sentence of five years for any person "who, during and in relation to any . . . drug trafficking crime . . . uses or carries a firearm, or who in furtherance of any such crime, possesses a firearm. . . ." 18 U.S.C. § 924(c)(1)(A). The "uses" prong of § 924(c) has been the subject of a line of Supreme Court cases, culminating in a case addressing the receipt of a firearm in exchange for drugs. First, in *Smith v. United States*, 508 U.S. 223 (1993), the Supreme Court held that a person who trades his firearm for drugs "uses" the firearm "during and in relation to . . . [a] drug trafficking crime." Two years later, in *Bailey v. United States*, 516 U.S. 137 (1995), the Court suggested it would follow a more restrictive interpretation of "use," holding that a defendant who had a loaded firearm locked in a bag in the trunk of his car and a defendant who had an unloaded pistol locked in a trunk in her bedroom closet did not "use" the firearms during and in relation to their drug-dealing activities because they did not "actively employ" them. Finally, in *Watson v. United States,* 552 U.S. 74 (2004), a unanimous Court held that a defendant who receives a gun as payment for drugs does not "use" a gun for the purposes of § 924(c). By the time the Court decided *Watson*, Congress had responded to *Bailey* by amending § 924(c) to its present form, adding the prohibition on possessing a firearm in furtherance of a drug trafficking crime. Because the defendant in *Watson* was charged under only the "use" prong of § 924(c), the Court reserved the question of whether he could have been found guilty of possessing a gun "in furtherance of" his drug trafficking.

Since *Watson*, six courts of appeals have considered whether a defendant who receives a firearm in exchange for drugs possesses that firearm in furtherance of a drug trafficking crime, and all six have decided or assumed without deciding that such a defendant does violate § 924(c).

We have not previously addressed this question, but we have considered the "in furtherance of" prong of § 924(c) in other situations. In *United States v. Castillo*, 406 F.3d 806 (7th Cir. 2005), we considered what might be the archetypical possession of a gun in furtherance of drug trafficking: possessing a gun to protect the drugs and the dealer and to serve as a warning to those who might attempt to steal the drugs. We interpreted the phrase "in furtherance of" to mean "furthering, advancing, or helping forward." *Castillo* places the burden on the government to "present a viable theory as to how the gun furthered the [drug distribution] . . . and it must present specific, non-theoretical evidence to tie that gun and the drug crime together under that theory." Applying this standard, we concluded that the government had established that the defendant had possessed a gun for protection during a drug offense and thus violated § 924(c).

In *United States v. Vaughn*, 585 F.3d 1024 (7th Cir. 2009), we applied the standard articulated in *Castillo* to a more unusual scenario. In *Vaughn*, the defendant had previously acquired a rifle from a man named Gee, who often bought drugs from him. Gee later became a confidential informant and asked if he could buy back the rifle. Vaughn declined to sell him the rifle, but said he would give the rifle back to Gee if Gee sold six pounds of marijuana for him. Gee agreed, and Vaughn gave him the rifle after Gee paid him for the marijuana. We held that by offering the rifle as an incentive for selling marijuana, Vaughn possessed it in furtherance of a drug trafficking crime. We acknowledged that this was a "novel" use of § 924(c) but held that Vaughn's possession of the rifle "helped forward" the sale of six pounds of marijuana by acting as an incentive to sell the marijuana, speeding payment for the marijuana, and assuring the full payment of the marijuana's purchase price.

Castillo and *Vaughn* lead us to the same interpretation of § 924(c) as our sister circuits: when a defendant receives a gun for drugs, he takes possession of the firearm in a way that "further[s], advance[s], or help[s] forward" the distribution of drugs. As the Sixth Circuit observed, "If the defendant did not accept possession of the gun, and instead insisted on being paid fully in cash for his drugs, some drug sales—and therefore some drug trafficking crimes—would not take place." The same is true when the defendant holds the gun only as collateral, rather than taking permanent ownership of it. Without the gun serving as security for the drug debt, some drug dealers would refuse to extend credit to their customers, and some drug transactions would not take place. Receiving a gun in exchange for drugs—whether as payment or collateral—facilitates the drug transaction.

Doody makes two closely related arguments against this interpretation of § 924(c). First, he relies on the holding in *Watson* that mere "receipt" is not "use" and on 18 U.S.C. §§ 922(g) & (h), both of which make it a crime to "receive" a firearm or ammunition under certain circumstances. This, Doody suggests, means that Congress must use the word "receipt," not "possession," to criminalize accepting a gun for drugs. Second, he argues that he did not possess the pistol "during and in relation to" the drug trafficking crime, because he did not possess the gun during the drug distribution or possessed it only momentarily (the record is silent on whether the gun or the contraband was handed over first), after which he possessed the gun only "'in furtherance of' a secured debt."

Doody's reliance on *Watson* is misplaced. *Watson* rested on the plain meaning of the word "use"—one who receives something in a bartering transaction is not ordinarily said to use the object he received in relation to trade. Here, Doody "possessed" the pistol in the ordinary meaning of the word: he held it and controlled it. Whatever the merits in another context of Doody's argument that Congress intended to distinguish "possession" from "receipt," the distinction makes no difference here. After receiving the gun, Doody possessed it. And unless Doody had been willing to take possession of the gun in exchange for drugs, the transaction could not have taken place. Thus, Doody's eventual possession furthered his drug trafficking crime.

Finally, we must address Doody's argument that he did not violate § 924(c) because he did not take possession of the gun until after he distributed the drugs. This argument rests on a misreading of the text of § 924(c). The mandatory minimum applies to a defendant "*who*, during and in relation to any . . . drug trafficking crime . . . , uses or carries a firearm, *or who*, in furtherance of any such crime, possesses a firearm. . . ." 18 U.S.C. § 924(c)(1)(A) (emphasis added). The repetition of the subject "who" in this parallel construction makes clear that "during and in relation to" applies only to those defendants accused of using or carrying a firearm. For those who are charged with possessing a firearm, the only limit is that the possession be "in furtherance of" the drug trafficking crime. Thus, Doody cannot rely on the fact that his possession of the firearm may not have come until after the drugs were distributed. Even if it did not come until after the drugs were distributed, Doody's possession of the pistol made the drug transaction possible, and thus furthered it, and § 924(c) requires no more.

The district court's judgment of conviction is AFFIRMED.

2. Drug-Induced Homicide

As discussed briefly in Chapter 2, the past decade has seen a rise in prosecutions under drug-induced homicide statutes. *Morrison v. New Jersey*, presented earlier in this chapter in the section on distribution, involved a prosecution under New Jersey's drug-induced death statute. In *Morrison*, the court held that because the defendant and the decedent had "simultaneously and jointly acquired possession of the drugs for their own use," the defendant could not be charged with distribution. As a result, he also could not be prosecuted for drug-induced homicide.

This section focuses on drug-induced homicide laws. In *Burrage v. United States*, presented below, the Supreme Court considered the federal drug-induced homicide statute, which provides for a 20-year mandatory minimum sentence for drug distribution offenders "if death or serious bodily injury results from the use of such substance." Like most drug-induced homicide laws, the federal statute does not include a *mens rea* requirement, making drug distributors strictly liable for overdoses. The Court in *Burrage* imposed a modest limitation on the scope of the law based on but-for causation, but it declined to reach the question of whether the law also incorporates a proximate cause (or foreseeability) requirement.

Burrage v. United States

Supreme Court of the United States
134 S. Ct. 881 (2014)

Justice Scalia delivered the opinion of the Court.*

The Controlled Substances Act imposes a 20-year mandatory minimum sentence on a defendant who unlawfully distributes a Schedule I or II drug, when "death or serious bodily injury results from the use of such substance." 21 U.S.C. § 841(a)(1), (b)(1)(A)–(C) (2012 ed.). We consider whether the mandatory-minimum provision applies when use of a covered drug supplied by the defendant contributes to, but is not a but-for cause of, the victim's death or injury.

I

Joshua Banka, a long-time drug user, died on April 15, 2010, following an extended drug binge. The episode began on the morning of April 14, when Banka smoked marijuana at a former roommate's home. Banka stole oxycodone pills from the roommate before departing and later crushed, cooked, and injected the oxycodone. Banka and his wife, Tammy Noragon Banka (Noragon), then met with petitioner Marcus Burrage and purchased one gram of heroin from him. Banka immediately cooked and injected some of the heroin and, after returning home, injected more heroin between midnight and 1 a.m. on April 15. Noragon went to sleep at around 5 a.m., shortly after witnessing Banka prepare another batch of heroin. When Noragon woke up a few hours later, she found Banka dead in the bathroom and called 911. A search of the couple's home and car turned up syringes, 0.59 grams of heroin, alprazolam and clonazepam tablets, oxycodone pills, a bottle of hydrocodone, and other drugs.

Burrage pleaded not guilty to a superseding indictment alleging two counts of distributing heroin in violation of § 841(a)(1). Only one of those offenses, count 2, is at issue here. (Count 1 related to an alleged distribution of heroin five months earlier than the sale to Banka.) Count 2 alleged that Burrage unlawfully distributed heroin on April 14, 2010, and that "death . . . resulted from the use of th[at] substance"—thus subjecting Burrage to the 20-year mandatory minimum of § 841(b)(1)(C).

Two medical experts testified at trial regarding the cause of Banka's death. Dr. Eugene Schwilke, a forensic toxicologist, determined that multiple drugs were present in Banka's system at the time of his death, including heroin metabolites, codeine, alprazolam, clonazepam metabolites, and oxycodone. (A metabolite is a "product of metabolism," Webster's New International Dictionary 1544 (2d ed. 1950), or, as the Court of Appeals put it, "what a drug breaks down into in the body.") Although morphine, a heroin metabolite, was the only drug present at a level above the therapeutic range—*i.e.*, the concentration normally present when

* Justice Alito joins all but Part III-B of this opinion.

a person takes a drug as prescribed—Dr. Schwilke could not say whether Banka would have lived had he not taken the heroin. Dr. Schwilke nonetheless concluded that heroin "was a contributing factor" in Banka's death, since it interacted with the other drugs to cause "respiratory and/or central nervous system depression." The heroin, in other words, contributed to an overall effect that caused Banka to stop breathing. Dr. Jerri McLemore, an Iowa state medical examiner, came to similar conclusions. She described the cause of death as "mixed drug intoxication" with heroin, oxycodone, alprazolam, and clonazepam all playing a "contributing" role. Dr. McLemore could not say whether Banka would have lived had he not taken the heroin, but observed that Banka's death would have been "[v]ery less likely."

The District Court denied Burrage's motion for a judgment of acquittal, which argued that Banka's death did not "result from" heroin use because there was no evidence that heroin was a but-for cause of death. The court also declined to give Burrage's proposed jury instructions regarding causation. One of those instructions would have required the Government to prove that heroin use "was the proximate cause of [Banka's] death." Another would have defined proximate cause as "a cause of death that played a substantial part in bringing about the death," meaning that "[t]he death must have been either a direct result of or a reasonably probable consequence of the cause and except for the cause the death would not have occurred." The court instead gave an instruction requiring the Government to prove "that the heroin distributed by the Defendant was a contributing cause of Joshua Banka's death." The jury convicted Burrage on both counts, and the court sentenced him to 20 years' imprisonment, consistent with § 841(b)(1)(C)'s prescribed minimum.

The Court of Appeals for the Eighth Circuit affirmed Burrage's convictions.

We granted certiorari on two questions: Whether the defendant may be convicted under the "death results" provision (1) when the use of the controlled substance was a "contributing cause" of the death, and (2) without separately instructing the jury that it must decide whether the victim's death by drug overdose was a foreseeable result of the defendant's drug-trafficking offense.

II

As originally enacted, the Controlled Substances Act "tied the penalties for drug offenses to both the type of drug and the quantity involved, with no provision for mandatory minimum sentences." That changed in 1986 when Congress enacted the Anti-Drug Abuse Act, which redefined the offense categories, increased the maximum penalties and set minimum penalties for many offenders, including the "death results" enhancement at issue here. With respect to violations involving distribution of a Schedule I or II substance (the types of drugs defined as the most dangerous and addictive[1]) the Act imposes sentences ranging from 10 years

1. Schedule I drugs, such as heroin, have "a high potential for abuse," "no currently accepted medical use in treatment in the United States," and "a lack of accepted safety" even "under medical supervision." § 812(b)(1). Schedule II drugs, such as methamphetamine, likewise have "a high

to life imprisonment for large-scale distributions, from 5 to 40 years for medium-scale distributions, and not more than 20 years for smaller distributions, the type of offense at issue here. These default sentencing rules do not apply, however, when "death or serious bodily injury results from the use of [the distributed] substance." In those instances, the defendant "shall be sentenced to a term of imprisonment which . . . shall be not less than twenty years or more than life," a substantial fine, "or both."[2]

Because the "death results" enhancement increased the minimum and maximum sentences to which Burrage was exposed, it is an element that must be submitted to the jury and found beyond a reasonable doubt. See *Alleyne v. United States,* 133 S.Ct. 2151, 2162–2163 (2013). Thus, the crime charged in count 2 of Burrage's superseding indictment has two principal elements: (i) knowing or intentional distribution of heroin, § 841(a)(1),[3] and (ii) death caused by ("resulting from") the use of that drug, § 841(b)(1)(C).

III

A

The law has long considered causation a hybrid concept, consisting of two constituent parts: actual cause and legal cause. When a crime requires "not merely conduct but also a specified result of conduct," a defendant generally may not be convicted unless his conduct is "both (1) the actual cause, and (2) the 'legal' cause (often called the 'proximate cause') of the result." 1 W. LaFave, Substantive Criminal Law § 6.4(a), pp. 464–466 (2d ed. 2003) (hereinafter LaFave); see also ALI, Model Penal Code § 2.03, p. 25 (1985). Those two categories roughly coincide with the two questions on which we granted certiorari. We find it necessary to decide only the first: whether the use of heroin was the actual cause of Banka's death in the sense that § 841(b)(1)(C) requires.

The Controlled Substances Act does not define the phrase "results from," so we give it its ordinary meaning. A thing "results" when it "[a]rise[s] as an effect, issue, or outcome *from* some action, process or design." 2 The New Shorter Oxford English Dictionary 2570 (1993). "Results from" imposes, in other words, a requirement of actual causality. "In the usual course," this requires proof "'that the harm would not have occurred' in the absence of—that is, but for—the defendant's conduct." The Model Penal Code reflects this traditional understanding; it states that "[c]onduct is the cause of a result" if "it is an antecedent but for which the result in question would not have occurred." § 2.03(1)(a). That formulation represents "*the*

---

potential for abuse" and a propensity to cause "severe psychological or physical dependence" if misused. 21 U.S.C. § 812(b)(2).

2. Although this language, read literally, suggests that courts may impose a fine *or* a prison term, it is undisputed here that the "death results" provision mandates a prison sentence. Courts of Appeals have concluded, in effect, that the "or" is a scrivener's error.

3. Violation of § 841(a)(1) is thus a lesser included offense of the crime charged in count 2. It is undisputed that Burrage is guilty of that lesser included offense.

minimum requirement for a finding of causation when a crime is defined in terms of conduct causing a particular result." *Id.*, Explanatory Note (emphasis added).

Thus, "where A shoots B, who is hit and dies, we can say that A [actually] caused B's death, since but for A's conduct B would not have died." LaFave 467–468 (italics omitted). The same conclusion follows if the predicate act combines with other factors to produce the result, so long as the other factors alone would not have done so—if, so to speak, it was the straw that broke the camel's back. Thus, if poison is administered to a man debilitated by multiple diseases, it is a but-for cause of his death even if those diseases played a part in his demise, so long as, without the incremental effect of the poison, he would have lived.

This but-for requirement is part of the common understanding of cause. Consider a baseball game in which the visiting team's leadoff batter hits a home run in the top of the first inning. If the visiting team goes on to win by a score of 1 to 0, every person competent in the English language and familiar with the American pastime would agree that the victory resulted from the home run. This is so because it is natural to say that one event is the outcome or consequence of another when the former would not have occurred but for the latter. It is beside the point that the victory also resulted from a host of *other* necessary causes, such as skillful pitching, the coach's decision to put the leadoff batter in the lineup, and the league's decision to schedule the game. By contrast, it makes little sense to say that an event resulted from or was the outcome of some earlier action if the action merely played a nonessential contributing role in producing the event. If the visiting team wound up winning 5 to 2 rather than 1 to 0, one would be surprised to read in the sports page that the victory resulted from the leadoff batter's early, non-dispositive home run.

Where there is no textual or contextual indication to the contrary, courts regularly read phrases like "results from" to require but-for causality.

Our insistence on but-for causality has not been restricted to statutes using the term "because of." We have, for instance, observed that "[i]n common talk, the phrase 'based on' indicates a but-for causal relationship" and that "the phrase, 'by reason of,' requires at least a showing of 'but for' causation,"

In sum, it is one of the traditional background principles "against which Congress legislate[s]" that a phrase such as "results from" imposes a requirement of but-for causation. The Government argues, however, that distinctive problems associated with drug overdoses counsel in favor of dispensing with the usual but-for causation requirement. Addicts often take drugs in combination, as Banka did in this case, and according to the National Center for Injury Prevention and Control, at least 46 percent of overdose deaths in 2010 involved more than one drug. This consideration leads the Government to urge an interpretation of "results from" under which use of a drug distributed by the defendant need not be a but-for cause of death, nor even independently sufficient to cause death, so long as it contributes to an aggregate force (such as mixed-drug intoxication) that is itself a but-for cause of death.

In support of its argument, the Government can point to the undoubted reality that courts have not *always* required strict but-for causality, even where criminal liability is at issue. The most common (though still rare) instance of this occurs when multiple sufficient causes independently, but concurrently, produce a result. See LaFave 467 (describing these cases as "unusual" and "numerically in the minority"). To illustrate, if "A stabs B, inflicting a fatal wound; while at the same moment X, acting independently, shoots B in the head . . . also inflicting [a fatal] wound; and B dies from the combined effects of the two wounds," A will generally be liable for homicide even though his conduct was not a but-for cause of B's death (since B would have died from X's actions in any event). *Id.*, at 468 (italics omitted). We need not accept or reject the special rule developed for these cases, since there was no evidence here that Banka's heroin use was an independently sufficient cause of his death. No expert was prepared to say that Banka would have died from the heroin use alone.

Thus, the Government must appeal to a second, less demanding (but also less well established) line of authority, under which an act or omission is considered a cause-in-fact if it was a "substantial" or "contributing" factor in producing a given result. Several state courts have adopted such a rule but the American Law Institute declined to do so in its Model Penal Code.

We decline to adopt the Government's permissive interpretation of § 841(b)(1). The language Congress enacted requires death to "result from" use of the unlawfully distributed drug, not from a combination of factors to which drug use merely contributed. Congress could have written § 841(b)(1)(C) to impose a mandatory minimum when the underlying crime "contributes to" death or serious bodily injury, or adopted a modified causation test tailored to cases involving concurrent causes, as five States have done, see Ala.Code § 13A-2-5(a) (2005); Ark .Code Ann. § 5-2-205 (2006); Me.Rev.Stat. Ann., Tit. 17-A, § 33 (2006); N.D. Cent. Code Ann. § 12.1-02-05 (Lexis 2012); Tex. Penal Code Ann. § 6.04 (West 2011). It chose instead to use language that imports but-for causality. Especially in the interpretation of a criminal statute subject to the rule of lenity, we cannot give the text a meaning that is different from its ordinary, accepted meaning, and that disfavors the defendant.

B

The Government objects that the ordinary meaning of "results from" will "unduly limi[t] criminal responsibility" and "cannot be reconciled with sound policy." We doubt that the requirement of but-for causation for this incremental punishment will prove a policy disaster. A cursory search of the Federal Reporter reveals that but-for causation is not nearly the insuperable barrier the Government makes it out to be. See, *e.g., United States v. Krieger,* 628 F.3d 857, 870–871 (C.A.7 2010) (affirming "death results" conviction based on expert testimony that, although the victim had several drugs in her system, the drug distributed by the defendant was a but-for cause of death). Moreover, even when the prosecution is unable to prove but-for causation, the defendant will still be liable for violating § 841(a)(1) and subject to a substantial default sentence under § 841(b)(1).

Indeed, it is more likely the Government's proposal that "cannot be reconciled with sound policy," given the need for clarity and certainty in the criminal law. Here the Government is uncertain about the precise application of the test that it proposes. Taken literally, its "contributing-cause" test would treat as a cause-in-fact every act or omission that makes a positive incremental contribution, however small, to a particular result. But at oral argument the Government insisted that its test excludes causes that are "not important enough" or "too insubstantial." Unsurprisingly, it could not specify how important or how substantial a cause must be to qualify. Presumably the lower courts would be left to guess. That task would be particularly vexing since the evidence in § 841(b)(1) cases is often expressed in terms of probabilities and percentages. One of the experts in this case, for example, testified that Banka's death would have been "[v]ery less likely" had he not used the heroin that Burrage provided. Is it sufficient that use of a drug made the victim's death 50 percent more likely? Fifteen percent? Five? Who knows. Uncertainty of that kind cannot be squared with the beyond-a-reasonable-doubt standard applicable in criminal trials or with the need to express criminal laws in terms ordinary persons can comprehend. See *United States v. L. Cohen Grocery Co.*, 255 U.S. 81, 89–90 (1921).

But in the last analysis, these always-fascinating policy discussions are beside the point. The role of this Court is to apply the statute as it is written—even if we think some other approach might "'accor[d] with good policy.'" As we have discussed, it is written to require but-for cause.

* * *

We hold that, at least where use of the drug distributed by the defendant is not an independently sufficient cause of the victim's death or serious bodily injury, a defendant cannot be liable under the penalty enhancement provision of 21 U.S.C. § 841(b)(1)(C) unless such use is a but-for cause of the death or injury. The Eighth Circuit affirmed Burrage's conviction based on a markedly different understanding of the statute and the Government concedes that there is no "evidence that Banka would have lived but for his heroin use." Burrage's conviction with respect to count 2 of the superseding indictment is therefore reversed, and the case is remanded for further proceedings consistent with this opinion.

It is so ordered.

In *Burrage*, the government argued that requiring proof of but-for causation to convict a defendant of drug-induced homicide would be at odds "with sound policy" by "unduly limi[ting] criminal responsibility." But others argue the opposite is true—that strict liability drug-induced homicide statutes cannot be justified under the traditional theories of punishment. The paper that follows, published by the Drug Policy Alliance, critiques drug-induced homicide statutes and cites "Good Samaritan" laws as a better alternative. Do you agree with the Drug Policy Alliance's arguments? Or do you think drug-induced homicide statutes help further worthy public policy goals?

Drug-Induced Homicide Laws: A Misguided Response to Overdose Deaths

Drug Policy Alliance (2016)

Overdose death rates in the United States have more than doubled over the past decade, surpassing motor vehicle accidents as the leading cause of injury-related death in the country. According to the Centers for Disease Control and Prevention, 47,055 people—an average of 128 people a day—died from drug overdoses in 2014. More than 18,000 overdose deaths in 2014 involved prescription opioids, such as hydrocodone (VicodinTM) and oxycodone (OxyContinTM), while an additional 10,000 fatalities were attributed to heroin. Synthetic opioids, such as fentanyl, claimed nearly 5,550 lives.

Policymakers are understandably alarmed at the overdose crisis with which they are now confronted. The public is calling for help and solutions. Elected officials unfamiliar with, or resistant to, harm reduction, prevention, and treatment interventions, however, are introducing punitive, counter-productive legislative measures in a misguided effort to reduce overdose fatalities. In particular, some states, including New York, Ohio, and Virginia are considering bills that would allow prosecutors to charge people who provide the drugs that ultimately contribute to an overdose death with homicide.

More than 20 other states already have laws allowing similar charges. Known as "drug-induced homicide," these laws range from capital one offenses that impose the death penalty or a life sentence to lesser prison sentence terms under various felony-murder, depraved heart, or involuntary or voluntary manslaughter statutes. Though many of these laws have sat idle on the books since their enactment decades ago during the height of the war on drugs, prosecutors are now reinvigorating them with a rash of drug-induced homicide charges in the wake of increasing overdose deaths.

There is no existing evidence, however, that indicates that further criminalizing opioid sales by allowing a charge of murder or manslaughter will achieve the goal of reducing overdose fatalities. Rather, drug-induced homicide laws are actually more likely to harm the very people they are seeking to protect, and to further reduce access to the critical services that do have the potential to save lives.

The importance and efficacy of providing limited criminal immunity to those who seek medical assistance in the event of an overdose is evidenced by the 35 states that have passed some form of "Good Samaritan" law [which provides immunity or an affirmative defense to certain charges to those who call 911 to report an overdose]. The most common reason people cite for not calling 911 is fear of police involvement. It is accordingly widely recognized that reducing barriers to calling 911 has the potential to save victims of overdose from severe injury and death.

Drug-induced homicide laws, on the other hand, discourage people from seeking help for fear of prosecution for manslaughter or murder. In [one study in] Illinois, [for example,] in the majority of drug-induced homicide cases there was an opportunity to save the overdose victim but the defendants chose inaction because of fear of prosecution. This is unsurprising—most states do not provide immunity from drug-induced homicide even if they have a Good Samaritan law, or, in the case of new legislation, are introducing harsh new criminal penalties that undermine Good Samaritan laws already in place. Rather than reducing the potential for mortality, as supposedly intended, drug-induced homicide laws will only result in additional overdose deaths due to fear of prosecution.

Presumably, the intent of punishing people who supply drugs with incredibly harsh sentences like murder or manslaughter is to deter others from also supplying drugs that could lead to an overdose. But, it is widely understood, both in the general population as well as the academic and scientific communities, that increased arrests or increased severity of criminal punishment for drug-related offenses do not, in fact, result in less use (demand) or sales (supply). In other words, punitive sentences for drug offenses have no deterrent effect.

The supply chain for controlled substances is not ameliorated because a single seller is incarcerated, whether for drug-induced homicide or otherwise. Supply follows demand; not the other way around. Indeed, numerous studies have found that incarceration of drug dealers simply results in a "replacement effect," meaning that the market responds to the demand for drugs by replacing drug sellers sent to prison with either new recruits or by the increased drug selling of dealers already in the market. One such study concluded that the main effect of imprisoning drug sellers "is merely to open the market for another seller."

Drug-induced homicide laws, then, might fulfill an instinct for retribution, but they do nothing to reduce demand and necessarily implicate additional people in sustaining the supply chain that fulfills continuing demand. Neither of these approaches does anything to prevent future deadly drug overdoses.

Drug-induced homicide laws assume that the seller can play some role in reducing overdose deaths—presumably by not supplying the drug in the first place. But, as already noted, as long as the demand exists, there will be supply to meet it. There are a host of factors that contribute to an overdose death, including tolerance, poly-drug use, circumstances of consumption, and familiarity with the substance—none of which can be controlled by the person who supplied the drugs. Indeed, 77% of prescription opioid overdose deaths and 67% of heroin overdose deaths are the result of mixing opioids with other drugs or alcohol. As a result, cases of drug-induced homicide are difficult to prove and win, primarily because of questions of . . . causation, and therefore require a significant outpouring of legal and other resources that could be better utilized. Were the resources focused on a different intervention point, such as education on the dangers of mixing substances or reducing demand, for example, the chances of reducing overdose death would correspondingly improve.

Many of the drug-induced homicide laws already in existence as well as those being proposed as new legislation are touted as intended to punish so-called "professional" drug sellers who profit from their user clients' addictions. But, the distinction between "seller" and "user" is artificial. Though data evaluating the drug use history of people who sell drugs is scant, a 2004 Bureau of Justice report found that an astonishing 70% of people incarcerated for drug trafficking in state prison used drugs themselves in the month prior to the offense. It is widely understood among experts who have studied drug markets that many sellers are people who are addicted and selling to support their own drug use. Moreover, the drug-induced homicide laws are often drafted so broadly that they, in many cases, encompass drug delivery or aiding and abetting drug use (even if between friends or people who are using drugs together). As a result, more often than not, the people being punished are the very people that the drug-induced homicide laws are actually intended to protect—people who are at risk of death due to a substance use disorder.

New Jersey's law proves illustrative. [O]ut of the 32 drug-induced homicide prosecutions identified by the New Jersey Law Journal in the early 2000s, 25 involved prosecutions of friends of the decedent who did not deal drugs in any significant manner. Accordingly, people who use drugs and are in the most desperate need of services are, instead, facing significant amounts of time behind bars as a result of their addiction.

Many of the drug-induced homicide cases recently prosecuted have involved defendants that have sold some form of fentanyl, a synthetic, rapid-acting opiate analgesic often added to heroin to increase its potency. Fentanyl has been widely reported in the media as one reason overdose fatalities are increasing. However, in the vast majority of cases, street-level sellers who are supplying heroin likely do not know it has had fentanyl added to it. Rather, fentanyl is generally manufactured in labs in Mexico and mixed with heroin before shipment. Even though the Drug Enforcement Administration has confirmed that they have found little evidence that fentanyl is added to heroin in the United States, low-level sellers who are unaware of the makeup of their product and its potency, and who are likely users themselves, have increasingly faced murder and manslaughter chargers rather than being offered the assistance and treatment necessary to move beyond their addiction and their need to support it through selling opioids.

Rather than diminishing the harms of drug misuse, criminalizing people who sell and use drugs amplifies the risk of fatal overdoses and diseases, increases stigma and marginalization, and drives people away from needed treatment, health, and harm reduction services. Reducing the role of the criminal justice system is therefore critical to ensuring that people who use drugs are able to access vital treatment and harm reduction services.

There is no evidence that drug-induced homicide charges are effective at reducing overdose deaths or curtailing the use or sale of controlled substances. On the other hand, proven strategies are available to reduce the harms associated with drug misuse, treat dependence and addiction, improve immediate overdose responses, enhance public safety, and prevent fatalities.

These strategies include expanding access to the life- saving medicine naloxone and its associated training; improving fact-based drug education for young people that includes an overdose prevention and response component; enacting legal protections that encourage people to call for help for overdose victims; training people how to prevent, recognize and respond to an overdose; increasing access to medication-assisted treatment, including methadone and buprenorphine; and implementing safe injection facilities.

3. Maintaining a Drug-Involved Premises

Federal law makes it a crime to maintain a drug-involved premises. Although formally titled "maintaining drug-involved premises," the statute is often referred to as the crack house statute because it was passed in response to concerns about "so-called 'crack-houses,' where 'crack', cocaine and other drugs are manufactured or used." 132 Cong. Rec. 26,474 (1986) (excerpt of Senate Amendment No. 3034 to H.R. 5484). Like conspiracy and accomplice liability, this offense can sometimes apply to people whose personal involvement with drug distribution is minimal.

United States v. Tebeau

United States Court of Appeals for the Eighth Circuit
713 F.3d 955 (2013)

Murphy, J.

James Tebeau owns more than 300 acres of land in southern Missouri where he has held weekend music festivals at which drug use was widespread. After undercover officers investigated the festivals, Tebeau was charged with having maintained a property from 2004 to 2011 for the purpose of manufacturing, storing, and distributing controlled substances in violation of 21 U.S.C. § 856(a)(2). Tebeau moved to dismiss the indictment, arguing that it was deficient because it alleged only that he had allowed others to distribute controlled substances on his property. The district court denied Tebeau's motion, concluding that a defendant may be indicted under § 856(a)(2) for making a property available for drug distribution without any further illegal purpose. Tebeau pled guilty but reserved his right to appeal the denial of his motion to dismiss. The district court sentenced Tebeau to 30 months imprisonment, two years of supervised release, and a $50,000 fine. Tebeau now appeals, and we affirm.

Tebeau owns more than 300 acres of land in Shannon County, Missouri known as "Camp Zoe." From 2004 to 2010, Camp Zoe was the site of 24 weekend festivals known variously as "Spring Jam," "Schwagstock," or "Spookstock." The festivals were held on a monthly basis from April to October. Tebeau invited various bands to perform at the festivals, and he also performed with his own Grateful Dead tribute band, The Schwag. Attendees paid $60 to enter Camp Zoe for a three day festival, and the number of attendees at each festival ranged from approximately 3,600 to nearly 8,000.

After government officials had arrested several individuals near Tebeau's property for using or selling drugs, they conducted an undercover investigation into illegal drug sales at Camp Zoe. Between April 2009 and August 2010, undercover officers attended ten music festivals and made more than 150 controlled purchases of illegal drugs including marijuana, psychedelic mushrooms, ecstasy, cocaine, LSD, MDMA, opium, and moonshine liquor. The officers observed 100 to 200 drug sellers at each festival and estimated that approximately $500,000 in illegal drugs were sold at each event. Officers also witnessed many campers using controlled substances, and saw that the sale and use of drugs was open and obvious. Some sellers congregated along a gravel road known as "Lovers Lane" where they displayed the drugs they were selling and shouted to passing campers that they had "Nuggets" (marijuana), "Doses" (LSD), or "Molly" (ecstasy) for sale. Other sellers walked through camp advertising marijuana stalks with large buds of marijuana attached.

Tebeau was present at almost every Camp Zoe festival and admits that he was aware of drug sales at the festivals. He operated a medical facility on the campground known as "Safestock," where campers who had overdosed were treated during each festival. Campers who were combative or violent were handcuffed or tied down with nylon straps. Investigative reports indicated that instances of drug overdose occurred at every festival, and Tebeau met with his employees after each festival to discuss drug overdoses and other problems which had arisen during the event. During interviews with Camp Zoe employees, officers learned that Tebeau had instructed them that certain types of drugs were permissible at the camp, such as marijuana, LSD, and mushrooms, but that anyone selling crack cocaine, methamphetamine, heroin, or nitrous oxide gas should be ejected. According to employees, Tebeau instructed security guards in the camp to move sellers away from the front gates to avoid detection by officers.

In November 2010 a federal search warrant was executed at Camp Zoe, and Tebeau was thereafter indicted on one count of managing a drug involved premises in violation of 21 U.S.C. § 856(a)(2). In [Tebeau's] plea agreement, the government stipulated that Tebeau had not participated in any drug sales or received any funds from their sale. Tebeau admitted, however, that he had "intended that Camp Zoe be made available" for individuals who "had the intent to sell and use controlled substances," and that he was responsible "for the distribution by others of the equivalent of at least 700 kilograms of marijuana." The district court required Tebeau to pay a $50,000 fine, and it sentenced him to 30 months in prison and two years of supervised release.

We review a district court's interpretation and application of a statute de novo. The statute at issue, 21 U.S.C. § 856, contains two subsections making it a crime to:

> (a)(1) knowingly *open or maintain any place for the purpose of* manufacturing, distributing, or using any controlled substance;
>
> (a)(2) manage or control any place whether permanently or temporarily, either as an owner, lessee, agent, employee, occupant, or mortgagee, and *knowingly and intentionally rent, lease, profit from, or make available* for use, with or without compensation, *the place for the purpose of* unlawfully manufacturing, storing, distributing, or using a controlled substance.

(emphasis added). Tebeau was charged with violating subsection (a)(2). The district court concluded that § 856(a)(2) did not require proof that Tebeau had the specific intent to manufacture, store, distribute, or use a controlled substance. Rather, § 856(a)(2) only required that the government show that Tebeau intended to make the property available for others who had that purpose.

Tebeau first argues that the district court's reading of § 856(a)(2) conflicts with the statute's text and legislative history, and that the statute should be interpreted to require proof that he specifically intended illegal drugs to be manufactured, stored, distributed, or used on his property. We have not before considered whether § 856(a)(2) criminalizes a defendant's knowing and intentional making available such a place even if he himself does not have the purpose to manufacture, store, distribute, or use a controlled substance there. The "starting point in interpreting a statute is always [its] language."

Several circuit courts have considered the meaning of § 856(a)(2)'s plain language, and their analysis is useful in interpreting the statute. In *United States v. Chen*, 913 F.2d 183 (5th Cir.1990), the Fifth Circuit concluded that the government need not show that a property owner had the illegal purpose of storing, distributing, using, or manufacturing a controlled substance to convict her under § 856(a)(2). In *Chen*, the owner of a motel which had become "an area for drug traffickers" was charged with violating both § 856(a)(1) and (a)(2). The district court instructed the jury that it could convict her under either subsection if it found she had been deliberately ignorant to the drug use at her hotel.

On appeal, the Fifth Circuit considered whether the phrase "for the purpose of" in both subsections of § 856(a) precluded a deliberate ignorance instruction. In reviewing § 856(a)(1), the court concluded that "the phrase *for the purpose of* applies to the person who opens or maintains the place for the illegal activity." A deliberate indifference instruction would therefore be improper under subsection (a)(1) which requires proof of "specific purpose to engage in drug activities." Section 856(a)(2), by contrast, applies "to the person who may not have actually opened or maintained the place for the purpose of drug activity, but who has knowingly allowed others to engage in those activities" by making the place available for unlawful use. The Fifth Circuit concluded that under § 856(a)(2) "the person who manages or controls the [property] and then rents to others[ ] need not have the express purpose in doing so that drug related activity take place," as long as "others have the purpose."

Other circuits have agreed that § 856(a)(2) only requires that a defendant has the purpose of maintaining property where drug use takes place, and not that the defendant intends the drug use to occur. In *United States v. Tamez,* 941 F.2d 770 (9th Cir.1991), the Ninth Circuit concluded that the "plain meaning and interrelation of the two § 856 provisions" suggest that § 856(a)(2) does not require proof that the defendant intended to use a property for a prohibited purpose. The *Tamez* court reasoned that § 856(a)(1) applies "to purposeful activity," and that interpreting § 856(a)(2) to require an illegal purpose would cause the subsections to overlap "entirely" and carry "no separate meaning." The Second Circuit has followed *Chen* and *Tamez,* observing that any other reading of § 856(a)(1) and § 856(a)(2) would "conflate these two subsections, rendering one superfluous." *United States v. Wilson,* 503 F.3d 195, 198 (2d Cir.2007). The First and Seventh Circuits have reached similar conclusions.

We agree with the other circuits that the "bare meaning" of the purpose requirement in § 856(a)(2) indicates that the government was not required to prove that Tebeau had the intent to manufacture, distribute, or use a controlled substance to convict him under the statute. Tebeau's reading of § 856(a)(2) to require proof of specific intent to manufacture, distribute or use controlled substances would render it redundant with § 856(a)(1). Such an interpretation would conflict with the "cardinal principle of statutory construction that [we] must give effect, if possible, to every clause and word of a statute."

We conclude that § 856(a)(2) does not require proof that Tebeau had the illegal purpose to use, manufacture, sell, or distribute controlled substances; it is sufficient that Tebeau intended to make his property available to others who had that purpose. This conclusion is mandated by the text and structure of § 856(a)(1) and (a)(2), and it is consistent with the case law and jury instructions in our circuit and others.

Tebeau next argues that interpreting § 856(a)(2) to lack a specific intent requirement renders the statute unconstitutionally vague in violation of the Fifth Amendment due process clause. A statute is unconstitutional for vagueness if it fails to "provide adequate notice of the proscribed conduct" or "lend[s] itself to arbitrary enforcement." Tebeau contends that such an interpretation of § 856(a)(2) would allow law enforcement to enforce it selectively and would give festival promoters no guidance as to what level of precautions could lawfully be made available to treat those who use drugs at festivals.

The Sixth Circuit in *United States v. Rosa,* 50 Fed.Appx. 226 (6th Cir.2008) (unpublished), rejected Tebeau's vagueness argument and explained that § 856(a)(2) "furnishes fair notice that it is illegal for a homeowner to knowingly and intentionally allow her house to be used in the distribution of drugs." We agree that § 856(a)(2) is not unconstitutionally vague because it prohibits a person from knowingly and intentionally making his property available for others to use or sell controlled substances. The inclusion of a specific mens rea element provides fair notice to Tebeau and others that certain conduct is prohibited. Tebeau also supplies no evidence to support his argument that § 856(a)(2) has lent itself to arbitrary enforcement. Moreover, Tebeau has admitted that he was aware of the large amount of drug sales at Camp Zoe and that he knew the camp would be used for other people to sell drugs during festivals. Drug sellers marketed their products openly on his Lover's Lane, and campers who had overdosed were handcuffed and tied down in Safestock. Such open and obvious drug use is precisely the conduct prohibited by § 856(a)(2)'s plain language, and the statute therefore was not unconstitutionally vague as applied to Tebeau.

Tebeau also argues that our interpretation of § 856(a)(2) violates his First Amendment rights by effectively preventing him from organizing music festivals. He contends that both speech (music) and nonspeech (making Camp Zoe available as a concert venue) activities are regulated by § 856(a)(2). Where "'speech' and 'nonspeech' elements are combined in the same course of conduct," the government regulation is justified if (1) "it is within the constitutional power of the Government," (2) "it furthers an important or substantial governmental interest," (3) "the governmental interest is unrelated to the suppression of free expression," and (4) "the incidental restriction on alleged First Amendment freedoms is no greater than is essential to the furtherance of that interest." *United States v. O'Brien,* 391 U.S. 367, 376–77 (1968). Only the third and fourth of these elements are at issue here. As to the third element, Tebeau argues that § 856(a)(2) fails because it was originally aimed at eliminating music festivals with high drug use which is a form of protected speech. He contends that § 856(a)(2) also fails to satisfy the fourth element because it too broadly punishes organizers and promoters of music festivals.

We conclude that § 856(a)(2) satisfies the *O'Brien* test and therefore does not violate the First Amendment. As to the third element, the government interest in regulating drug use is unrelated to any incidental impact the law has on music festivals. Similarly with respect to the fourth element, a prohibition on knowingly making premises available for drug use imposes only an incidental restriction on music festival hosts which does not "significantly compromise" their First Amendment rights. Tebeau's concern about the "chilling effect" of § 856(a)(2) on music festivals is also overstated. He cites no case in which the government has charged another music festival organizer under the statute, and Tebeau's own involvement in the drug activities at Camp Zoe was extensive. We conclude that § 856(a)(2) does not violate the First Amendment.

Accordingly, we affirm the judgment of the district court.

Although *Tebeau* has not led to a wave of criminal prosecutions of concert promoters, its reasoning arguably might allow for it. After all, as a *Riverfront Times* reporter wrote in a story about Tebeau, "[a]nybody who has ever attended

Bonnaroo, Lollapalooza, Coachella, Sasquatch or other major summer music festivals understands that drugs are an inescapable part of the experience." Keegan Hamilton, *He's Gone: As Schwagstock Founder Jimmy Tebeau Enters Federal Prison, Should Other Music-Festival Organizers Worry About On-site Drug Use?*, RIVERFRONT TIMES (June 13, 2013).

Imagine you are an attorney representing the promoter of an annual music festival. At last year's festival, a total of 100 attendees were caught by festival security selling illegal drugs on festival grounds. Your client plans to increase security this year but he knows that some attendees will slip into the venue with illegal drugs and that some will sell drugs on festival grounds. Do you think this fact alone could subject your client to potential liability for maintaining a drug-involved premises under the reasoning of *Tebeau*? If so, what steps (if any) could the promoters take to reduce or eliminate the risk?

One particularly noteworthy fact in *Tebeau* is that James Tebeau "operated a medical facility on the campground known as 'Safestock,' where campers who had overdosed were treated during each festival." The court cited this as evidence of Tebeau's knowledge of "open and obvious drug use" at his events. But a medical facility like "Safestrock" is a harm reduction strategy that many would argue has significant public health benefits. In a similar vein, an organization called DanceSafe volunteers to set up booths at concerts where they test drugs like MDMA (also known as ecstasy or Molly) to determine whether the drugs are what they claim to be or if they contain dangerous adulterants. Advocates of these programs, which are more common in Europe than the United States, "say people are more likely to reject taking drugs to get high if the substances do not contain what they think they do, which reduces the risk of overdose and other harmful effects." Ariana Eunjung Cha, *Real-time Testing of Drugs at Music Festivals Shows 'Molly' Often Isn't 'Molly,'* WASH. POST. (July 11, 2017). A study of DanceSafe's data published in *Journal of Psychopharmacology* provides some support for this position, finding "that pill-testing services are a legitimate harm-reduction service that decreases intent to consume potentially dangerous substances and may warrant consideration by legislators for legal protection." Sarah Saleemi et al., *Who is 'Molly'? MDMA Adulterants by Product Name and the Impact of Harm-Reduction Services at Raves*, 8 J. PSYCHOPHARMACOLOGY 1056 (2017). If you were an attorney for a concert promoter, would you advise the promoter to permit DanceSafe to set up a booth at their event in light of the holding in *Tebeau*?

As noted in Chapter 2, the crack house statute could also stand in the way of efforts to open safe injection sites in the United States. Safe injection sites are places where people can use drugs they have purchased elsewhere under the supervision of trained professionals. The sites aim to reduce some of the harms associated with injection drug use by providing a range of services, including having medical personnel on site to administer the overdose reversal drug Naloxone. As of early 2019, officials in five U.S. cities had announced plans to open a safe injection site. But federal opposition has effectively blocked them from opening. In February 2019, citing the crack house statute, the United States Attorney for the Eastern District of Pennsylvania filed a lawsuit against a nonprofit named Safehouse that has been working with the city of Philadelphia to open a safe injection site. In light of the holding in *Tebeau*, do you think a safe injection site would violate the crack house statute?

In addition to frustrating efforts to open safe injection sites in the United States and putting concert promoters at legal risk, the maintaining a drug-involved premises statute also has the potential to put the roommates of drug sellers in legal jeopardy, as the next case demonstrates.

United States v. Wilson

United States Court of Appeals for the Second Circuit
503 F.3d 195 (2007)

Per Curiam:

Defendant-Appellant Maletha Wilson appeals from a judgment of conviction entered in the United States District Court for the Western District of New York, convicting her after a jury trial of two counts of knowingly and intentionally making her residence available for use for the purpose of unlawfully manufacturing, storing, distributing, or using a controlled substance, in violation of 21 U.S.C. § 856(a)(2). She shared two apartments with a drug dealer, and acknowledges that there were drugs, along with drug-related paraphernalia, at both premises; but she argues that the evidence was insufficient chiefly on the ground that the government failed to prove that she herself intended that the premises would be used for the unlawful purpose.

On October 3, 2002, Rochester police officers arrested one Yusef Blocker outside 323 Arnett Boulevard, where he was living with Wilson. Wilson allowed the police to enter her apartment, told them that she wanted to check on her baby in a back bedroom, and was followed there by the police. There, they saw—in plain view—two plastic bags containing a white rock substance. At trial, Wilson stipulated that the substance was 12.836 grams of cocaine base. Also in the bedroom were unused Ziploc bags and a razor blade in the baby's coat, as well as a second razor blade and a plate inside the top drawer of a dresser.

On May 7, 2004, Rochester police officers executed a search warrant at 35 Jackson Street, where Wilson was then living. No one was present when the officers entered and found a digital scale and unused Ziploc bags in the master bedroom closet. In another bedroom, the officers found a cigar box containing a substance which they suspected was cocaine. At trial, Wilson stipulated that the substance consisted of 61.690 grams of powder cocaine and 31.648 grams of cocaine base.

On February 23, 2005, Wilson was interviewed by a special agent of the Bureau of Alcohol, Tobacco and Firearms. She said that she was living with Yusef Blocker in the apartment on Arnett Boulevard when it was searched in October 2002, and that she was living with Blocker at 35 Jackson Street when it was searched in May 2004. Evidence at trial also indicated that her name was on both leases. The

Department of Social Services paid half the rent (and her mother the other half) at each location.

Wilson argues that the evidence against her was insufficient to support her conviction.

In the main, Wilson contends that under 21 U.S.C. § 856(a)(2), the government had to prove that, in making her home available to others, it was Wilson's own purpose to allow them to engage in narcotics trafficking there. This is a fundamental misreading of subsection (a)(2).

Section 856(a)(2) makes it unlawful for a person to:

> manage or control any place, whether permanently or temporarily, either as an owner, lessee, agent, employee, occupant, or mortgagee, and knowingly and intentionally rent, lease, profit from, or make available for use, with or without compensation, the place for the purpose of unlawfully manufacturing, storing, distributing, or using a controlled substance.

The law thus prohibits a person with a premises from knowingly and intentionally allowing its use for the purpose of manufacturing, storing or distributing drugs. The intent of the prohibition is "to prohibit an owner from providing a place for illegal conduct, and yet to escape liability on the basis either of lack of illegal purpose, or of deliberate ignorance". *United States v. Tamez,* 941 F.2d 770, 774 (9th Cir. 1991). Accordingly, "under § 856(a)(2), the person who manages or controls the building and then rents to others, need not have the express purpose in doing so that drug related activity take place; rather such activity is engaged in by others (*i.e.*, others have the purpose)." *United States v. Chen,* 913 F.2d 183, 190 (5th Cir. 1990). The phrase "for the purpose," as used in this provision, references the purpose and design *not* of the person with the premises, but rather of those who are permitted to engage in drug-related activities there.

This interpretation is compelled by the preceding subsection, 856(a)(1), in which the phrase "for the purpose" applies to the intent of the person with an interest in the premises. That is, subsection 856(a)(1) makes it illegal to:

> knowingly open, lease, rent, use, or maintain any place, whether permanently or temporarily, for the purpose of manufacturing, distributing, or using any controlled substance.

Under Wilson's reading, both *subsections*— (a)(1) and (a)(2)—would proscribe the same conduct. But it would be impermissible to conflate these two subsections, rendering one superfluous. *See Williams v. Taylor,* 529 U.S. 362, 404, (2000) ("It is . . . a cardinal principle of statutory construction that we must give effect, if possible, to every clause and word of a statute.").

Wilson also challenges the sufficiency of the evidence to prove that she knew her residence was being used for drug trafficking. Our review of the trial record discloses sufficient evidence to support Wilson's conviction. A cooperating witness testified that on numerous occasions, he and Blocker engaged in drug manufacturing activities at both of Wilson's residences, and that he overheard Blocker ask Wilson for Ziploc bags and a Pyrex dish, two items used for those activities. Wilson admitted to the police that she knew Blocker sold drugs. And crack cocaine, cocaine powder and drug paraphernalia were found in her residences, including a razor and Ziploc bags in baby clothes in her bedroom. Given this evidence, a reasonable jury could—and did—conclude that Wilson knowingly allowed others to use those residences for the manufacture, storage and distribution of narcotics.

For the foregoing reasons, the judgment of the district court is affirmed.

4. Drug Free School Zones

A Moving Violation? Hypercriminalized Spaces and Fortuitous Presence in Drug Free School Zones
L. Buckner Inniss

8 Texas Forum on Civil Liberties and Civil Rights 51 (2003)

Over the last thirty years, both the federal government and a majority of states have enacted statutes that prohibit certain types of conduct involving illicit drugs in or near schools, school buses, or other youth or family-related facilities and locales. These statutes vary from jurisdiction to jurisdiction in terms of whether they stand alone as separate offenses or serve as a sentencing enhancement and in terms of the defenses available. The net effect of such statutes in either case is to "hyper-criminalize" certain areas or spaces where drug activity takes place by increasing the length of incarceration after conviction. Such statutes have been subject to a number of challenges over the years. Chief among them are constitutional claims that such statutes are an invalid exercise of legislative or police power, violate due process and equal protection guarantees, violate the Eighth Amendment's prohibition on punishment that is grossly disproportionate to the crime, violate double jeopardy provisions, or are overbroad. A number of other claims have been based upon the allegedly vague and arbitrary nature of statutes that punish persons who were found with drugs in their vehicles while passing through school zones. A third set of claims point to the lack of a requirement that the offender intended to be present in the drug-prohibited zone. To date, virtually none of these challenges have succeeded, and both federal and state schoolyard statutes are widely hailed as major weaponry in the war against drugs.

Both federal and state [drug] schoolyard statutes take to high art form the notion of criminalizing spaces. Indeed, the ambit of federal and state schoolyard statutes usually includes both public and private spaces, as the creation of perimeters around schools or other facilities does not make allowances for activities which occur in private homes and some provisions criminalize certain drug activities around publicly funded housing projects.

The federal schoolyard statute was enacted its original form in 1984. It provided for an enhanced penalty for the distribution of drugs within 1,000 feet of a school.

The 1984 statute, introduced by Senator Paula Hawkins of Florida, was intended to reduce the presence of drugs in the schools by threatening those who distributed drugs near schools with heavy penalties. In 1986, the statute was amended to prohibit both manufacturing and distributing within 1,000 feet of a school. The 1986 amendment also broadened the scope of educational institutions where such penalties applied. A particular concern of the drafters of the 1986 amendments was the threat of crack cocaine near schools. In 1988, the statute again underwent changes, this time to prohibit possession with intent to distribute within 1,000 feet of a school. The impetus of Congress seems to have again been the fear of having large quantities of drugs near schools.

Several cases at both the federal and state level, which raise equal protection or substantive due process claims, involve defendants who argue that their living conditions are such that they cannot reasonably live outside of a drug prohibited zone. Their presence is, to a great degree, merely happenstance. Thus, they argue, they are treated differently than persons who are able to live elsewhere. For example, in *United States v. White*, the defendant raised substantive due process and equal protection claims based upon a portion of an indictment charging him with violation of 21 U.S.C. Section 845a. This statute provides for sentence enhancement for a conviction of narcotics distribution within 1,000 feet of a school. The alleged narcotics distribution took place in the city of New Haven, Connecticut, where almost all the city falls within the protected 1,000 foot school zone. The defendant argued that the existence of such widespread prohibited zones failed to comport with the intent of the legislation, which was to create drug free zones around schools in particular. The court disagreed with the defendant, finding that application of the statute met with legislative intent, and that there was no reason to "carve out an exception" for New Haven even given its numerous schools throughout the city.

A similar happenstance or fortuitous presence claim was raised in *United States v. Nieves*. There, a defendant argued that the schoolyard statute denied him equal protection of the laws because the statute's enhanced penalties had a greater impact upon racial minorities who, he argued, were more likely to live in high density inner city areas where there are likely to be more schools than in other places. The court, however, rejected this argument, finding that even assuming there to be some statistical validity to defendant's claim, this disparate impact alone would not be the basis of an equal protection claim.

United States v. Agilar

United States Court of Appeals for the Second Circuit

779 F.2d 123 (1985)

Newman, J.

Anthony Agilar appeals from a judgment of the District Court for the Southern District of New York convicting him, after a bench trial, of distributing heroin within 1,000 feet of a public elementary school in violation of 21 U.S.C. §§ 812,

841(a)(1), and 841(b)(1)(B) (1982) and 21 U.S.C. § 845a. Appellant primarily challenges the constitutionality of section 845a, the so-called "schoolyard" provision, which increases penalties for distribution of narcotics within 1,000 feet of a public or private elementary or secondary school. We affirm.

The evidence disclosed that Agilar sold three glassine envelopes containing heroin for $30 to Maritza Ortiz, an undercover New York City police officer. Ortiz had first approached Agilar's co-defendant, Edwin Jimenez, at the corner of Second Avenue and 118th Street in Manhattan and asked for heroin, specifically requesting the brand name "Checkmate," which is sold at that location. Jimenez said, "I will take you to the man." He led Ortiz only 25 feet along 118th Street to a location where Agilar was selling heroin to customers waiting in line. Agilar told Jimenez that Ortiz would have to wait her turn at the end of the line. While she was waiting, Agilar asked her how many glassine envelopes she wanted. She said she wanted three, and he replied, "I am going to take care of you." When Ortiz reached the head of the line, she purchased three envelopes for $30, using money that had been photocopied to record the serial numbers.

Promptly after the sale, Ortiz radioed a backup police officer and gave a description of the seller. The officer arrived on the scene a minute later, arrested Jiminez, and stopped three men, including Agilar, who met the description given by Ortiz. When the three were brought to the undercover officer's presence, she immediately identified Agilar as the seller. Agilar was arrested and searched; he had $140 in cash, but none of the bills that Ortiz had used in the heroin purchase. The evidence also revealed that Agilar, while waiting outside the office of a United States Magistrate the following day, was overheard admonishing Jimenez for bringing an "undercover" to him.

Though the case was developed by New York City police officers, concerns readily visible criminal conduct requiring no special investigatory resources or equipment, and involves a $30 transaction, the matter became the subject of a federal criminal prosecution because it occurred on "federal day,"* the day of the week when federal law enforcement authorities have decided to convert garden-variety state law drug offenses into federal offenses. Though we are urged in other contexts to tolerate missed deadlines because of the enormous burdens placed upon limited numbers of federal law enforcement personnel, on "federal day" there are apparently enough federal prosecutors available with sufficient time to devote to $30 drug cases that have been developed solely by state law enforcement officers. Be that as it may, the case is lawfully within the jurisdiction of the federal courts and must be decided.

---

* "Federal day" was a charging policy instituted by Rudy Giuliani when he was the United States Attorney for the Southern District of New York. Under the policy "a day [was] chosen occasionally, without notice, when street drug dealers answer[ed] charges in Federal, instead of state, court." William Glaberson, *Giuliani's Powerful Imagine Under Campaign Scrutiny,* N.Y. TIMES at A!, July 11, 1989. [*Footnote by casebook author.*]

It poses issues concerning the constitutionality of the federal "schoolyard" statute because Agilar had the double misfortune to sell to a customer who happened to be an undercover police officer and to make the sale at a location that happened to be within 1,000 feet of a public elementary school.

We have thus far encountered the schoolyard statute on two occasions, ruling in *United States v. Falu*, 776 F.2d 46 (2d Cir. 1985), that the statute does not require knowledge of the proximity of a school and in *United States v. Jones*, 779 F.2d 121 (2d Cir. 1985), that the statute does not require evidence that the specific location of the sale, within the 1,000-foot zone, is one where school children are present or likely to congregate. Agilar's constitutional challenge is no more substantial than the statutory arguments rejected in *Falu* and *Jones*.

Agilar contends that the statute offends the Due Process Clause by creating an unwarranted irrebuttable presumption that every sale of narcotics within 1,000 feet of a school has the detrimental effects upon school children that Congress sought to avoid by enacting section 845a. The cases condemning irrebuttable presumptions that lack rationality do not require that the means chosen by Congress to deal with a problem score a notable success in every application of the statute. Congress wanted to lessen the risk that drugs would be readily available to school children. It is surely rational to achieve that goal by increasing penalties for those who sell drugs near schools. Whether or not each sale within the 1,000-foot zone, if not deterred, would have led to acquisition of drugs by school children, the proscription of sales within the environs of schools is a rational means of reducing the risk of easy availability that can lead to such acquisition.

Nor is the statute constitutionally vulnerable because of appellant's doubt that the increased penalties will in practice add any incremental deterrence to that arising from the already substantial penalties Congress has provided for selling narcotics. Congress is entitled to add higher penalties in the hope of providing further deterrence, whether or not much success is thereby achieved. Appellant's final due process challenge alleges that the 1,000-foot demarcation line is not sufficiently ascertainable by the average person. Since the statute is violated whether or not the seller knows he is within the prohibited zone, this argument has no force. And since there is no protected right to sell narcotics anywhere, there need be no concern for the person who removes his selling activity a considerable distance from a school in order to avoid the risk of being within the 1,000-foot zone.

Agilar also challenges section 845a on equal protection grounds on the strained theory that the statute has a disproportionate impact on members of racial minorities, more of whom live, it is asserted, within 1,000 feet of schools than do non-minority residents, a smaller proportion of whom live in densely populated urban areas. The argument fails, among other reasons, for lack of any claim, much less showing, of a discriminatory purpose.

The judgment of the District Court is affirmed.

5. Driving Under the Influence

The crime of driving under the influence (or, in some states, driving while intoxicated) presents a variety of legal issues. Many private criminal defense attorneys specialize in handling DUI cases, with some devoting their entire practice to it. This section introduces DUI laws, with a particular focus on the application of DUI laws to marijuana, a question that has been receiving increased attention in connection with state legalization laws. Before turning to drugged driving, the California Supreme Court case of *Burg v. Municipal Court* provides a useful history of drunk-driving statutes as well as a glimpse at the blood-alcohol-content-based approach employed in modern DUI laws.

Burg v. Municipal Court

Supreme Court of California
35 Cal. 3d 257 (1983)

Mosk, J.

Richard Joseph Burg, hereafter defendant, appeals from a judgment denying his petition for a writ of prohibition. He contends that Vehicle Code section 23152, subdivision (b),[1] fails to give constitutionally adequate notice of the conduct it prohibits, and that the municipal court erred in overruling his demurrer to that effect. We conclude that section 23152, subdivision (b), is constitutional, and therefore affirm the judgment.

Defendant was arrested at 2:25 in the morning of March 27, 1982, for violation of section 23152, subdivision (a) (driving while under the influence of alcohol). A chemical test administered 50 minutes later revealed a blood-alcohol content of 0.23 percent. He was charged with violating section 23152, subdivision (b), i.e., driving a vehicle while having 0.10 percent or more, by weight, of alcohol in one's body. The complaint also alleged a prior conviction of former section 23102, subdivision (a) (driving while under the influence of alcohol).

Defendant demurred on the ground that section 23152, subdivision (b), gives constitutionally inadequate notice of the conduct proscribed. The municipal court overruled his demurrer, and defendant sought a writ of prohibition in the superior court. The petition was denied on the merits, and this appeal followed.

Eighty years ago an editorialist complained, "Inebriates and moderate drinkers are the most incapable of all persons to drive motor wagons. The general palsy and diminished power of control of both the reason and the senses are certain to invite disaster in every attempt to guide such wagons." In the ensuing decades motor vehicles have become faster, heavier, and ubiquitous, with proportionately tragic consequences to the victims of drinking drivers. Nearly half of the traffic deaths in California between 1976–1980 involved drinking drivers. Nearly one-quarter of all

---

1. All statutory references are to the [California] Vehicle Code unless otherwise indicated.

traffic accidents resulting in injury involved the use of alcohol. Traffic deaths in the United States exceed 50,000 annually, and approximately one-half of those fatalities are alcohol-related.

The drunk driver cuts a wide swath of death, pain, grief, and untold physical and emotional injury across the roads of California and the nation. The monstrous proportions of the problem have often been lamented in graphic terms by this court and the United States Supreme Court. As observed in *Breithaupt v. Abram* (1957) 352 U.S. 432, "[the] increasing slaughter on our highways, most of which should be avoidable, now reaches the astounding figures only heard of on the battlefield." Indeed, in the years 1976 to 1980 there were many more injuries to California residents in alcohol-related traffic accidents than were suffered by the entire Union Army during the Civil War, and more were killed than in the bloodiest year of the Vietnam War. Given this setting, our observation that "[drunken] drivers are extremely dangerous people" seems almost to understate the horrific risk posed by those who drink and drive.

Recognizing the effect of alcohol on drivers, state legislatures early in the century attempted to regulate such conduct. Because "both popular and legal views of the problem centered on the grossly intoxicated driver", the laws also reflected that conception. Thus, California's first statute on the topic read simply, "No *intoxicated* person shall operate or drive a motor vehicle or other vehicle upon any public highway within this state." (Italics added.)

A more satisfactory means of defining the problem of drinking and driving emerged in the middle decades of this century, with the development of scientific measurement of blood-alcohol levels. Research on alcohol's effect on both motor skills and judgment revealed that impairment occurred at alcohol concentrations as low as 0.05 percent, considerably below the point at which typical clinical symptoms of intoxication appear in most persons. Thus, in 1969, after a number of intervening amendments that attempted to refine definitions and specified penalties, California's "driving under the influence" statute was fortified by the addition of former section 23126, which created a presumption of being under the influence if a driver had 0.10 percent or more by weight of alcohol in his blood. By 1972, 47 states had similar statutes. (Murray and Aitken, *The Constitutionality of California's Under-the-Influence-of-Alcohol Presumption* (1972) 45 So. Cal. L. Rev. 955, 958, fn. 8.)

Even these laws, which considerably assisted the prosecution of "driving under the influence" cases, proved inadequate in many respects. Under them, the ultimate question was defined in terms of the defendant's subjective behavior and condition: "Was the defendant under the influence at the time he drove?" Celerity and certainty of punishment were frustrated by the ambiguity of the legal criteria; no matter what his blood-alcohol level, a defendant could escape conviction merely by raising a doubt as to his intoxication.

In response to this continuing problem, in the past decade most states enacted additional legislation supplementing existing "driving under the influence" statutes and fashioned after what has been termed the "Scandinavian model." These statutes—which are most frequently subdivisions of a general "driving and alcohol" statute—define the substantive offense not by the subjective term "driving under the influence," but instead as the act of driving with a specified blood-alcohol level. Under these laws, proof of being "under the influence" is unnecessary. The statutes represent a legislative determination that public safety is endangered when a person drives a motor vehicle while having a specified percentage (typically 0.10) or more by weight of alcohol in his blood.

As noted, former section 23102 made it illegal to drive while under the influence of alcohol. Conviction required a showing that alcohol had "so far affected the nervous system, the brain, or muscles as to impair to an appreciable degree the ability to operate a vehicle in a manner like that of an ordinarily prudent and cautious person in full possession of his faculties." As explained above, prosecution under this section was facilitated by former section 23126, which established a presumption that a person with a blood alcohol level of 0.10 or more was under the influence of alcohol.

In an attempt to address the continuing threat to public safety posed by drinking drivers, in 1981 the Legislature retained the "driving under the influence" statute, renumbered it section 23152, subdivision (a), and added the statute at issue here, section 23152, subdivision (b), which provides: "It is unlawful for any person who has 0.10 percent or more, by weight, of alcohol in his or her blood to drive a vehicle. For purposes of this subdivision, percent, by weight, of alcohol shall be based upon grams of alcohol per 100 milliliters of blood."

At the urging of Congress,[3] statutes of this kind have recently been enacted in 28 states and the District of Columbia. Depending on the statutory scheme, these enactments create either a new offense, or an alternative definition of "driving under the influence," or a lesser included offense within driving under the influence. Our statute establishes a new and separate offense.

Contrary to assertions by amici curiae, some commentators, and one court, section 23152, subdivision (b), does not create a conclusive presumption of intoxication, nor does it "eliminate[] the prosecutor's burden of proof when the accused is found to have [0.10] percent, by weight, of alcohol in [his] blood." Instead, the statute defines, in precise terms, the conduct proscribed. In other states that have enacted a statute similar to section 23152, subdivision (b), the courts have drawn the same conclusion, notably the Washington Supreme Court which declared, "The statute does not presume, it defines."

Although under section 23152, subdivision (b), it is no longer necessary to prove that the defendant was in fact under the influence, the People still must prove

---

3. 23 United States Code Annotated, section 408(e)(1)(C) (making enactment of a 0.10 percent blood-alcohol law mandatory for any state wishing to receive federal highway funds to support alcohol traffic safety programs).

beyond a reasonable doubt that at the time he was driving his blood alcohol exceeded 0.10 percent.[10]

Scientific evidence and sad experience demonstrate that any driver with 0.10 percent blood alcohol is a threat to the safety of the public and to himself. At least two states and several foreign countries have established standards between 0.05 percent and 0.08 percent. We have no difficulty concluding that the 0.10 percent figure fixed by section 23152, subdivision (b), is rationally related to exercise of the state's legitimate police power.

Five of our sister states have addressed claims of unconstitutional indefiniteness with respect to analogous 0.10 percent statutes, and all have found the contentions meritless. Defendant asserts, however, that we should not be persuaded by these decisions, because they fail to sufficiently analyze the issues and justify the results. We proceed to review defendant's claim that section 23152, subdivision (b), is void for vagueness.

Both article I, section 7, of the California Constitution and the Fourteenth Amendment to the United States Constitution declare that no person shall be deprived of life, liberty or property without due process of law. It has been recognized for over 80 years that due process requires inter alia some level of definiteness in criminal statutes. (Note, *Due Process Requirements of Definiteness in Statutes* (1948) 62 Harv. L. Rev. 77, 77, fn. 2.) Today it is established that due process requires a statute to be definite enough to provide (1) a standard of conduct for those whose activities are proscribed and (2) a standard for police enforcement and for ascertainment of guilt. *Connally v. General Const. Co.* (1926) 269 U.S. 385, 391.

To begin with the second component, the statute could not be more precise as a standard for law enforcement. (Freund, *The Use of Indefinite Terms in Statutes* (1921) 30 Yale L.J. 437, 437.) It gives no discretion whatever to the police, and thus is not susceptible of arbitrary enforcement. Indeed, the very precision of the standard assures the statute's validity in this respect.

Turning now to the "fair notice" component of the void-for-vagueness doctrine, we observe that the real thrust of defendant's argument is that the statute is in effect "void for preciseness." His complaint is not that the language of the statute is vague or ambiguous, but that it is too exact. His novel theory is that the statute fails to notify potential violators of the condition it proscribes, because it is impossible for

---

10. Section 23152, subdivision (b), prohibits driving a vehicle with a blood-alcohol level of 0.10 percent or higher; it does not prohibit driving a vehicle when a subsequent test shows a level of 0.10 percent or more. Circumstantial evidence will generally be necessary to establish the requisite blood-alcohol level called for by the statute. A test for the proportion of alcohol in the blood will, obviously, be the usual type of circumstantial evidence, but of course the test is not conclusive: the defendant remains free to challenge the accuracy of the test result, the manner in which it was administered, and by whom. Of course, both parties may also adduce other circumstantial evidence tending to establish that the defendant did or did not have a 0.10 percent blood-alcohol level while driving.

a person to determine by means of his senses whether his blood-alcohol level is a "legal" 0.09 percent or an "illegal" 0.10 percent. The latter observation is probably true as a matter of fact, but it does not affect the constitutionality of the statute.

Defendant's theory would render the void-for-vagueness doctrine internally inconsistent: the notice requirement would compete with the need to provide precise standards for law enforcement. When, as in the present case, a statutory standard requires scientific measurement, the very factor that assures due process under the "standards" component would violate due process under the "notice" component.

It is apparently defendant's contention that due process requires notice that is subjectively verifiable, according to the terms of the statute, at the instant before the alleged violation. He claims the statute is invalid because it is impossible for ordinary persons actually to know when their blood alcohol reaches the proscribed point. No court, however, has interpreted the notice requirement so strictly; indeed, such a view would invalidate many other criminal laws, violations of which depend on an after-the-fact determination by a judge or jury as to the defendant's state of mind or the reasonableness of his behavior.

"Fair notice" requires only that a violation be described with a "'reasonable degree of certainty'" so that "ordinary people can understand what conduct is prohibited." The notice provided must be such that prosecution does not "trap the innocent" without "fair warning."

One who drives a vehicle after having ingested sufficient alcohol to approach or exceed the level proscribed is neither "innocent" within the meaning of *Grayned*, nor is he without "fair warning." His behavior is not "innocent" because one who drives with a blood-alcohol content above 0.05 percent is in jeopardy of violating section 23152, subdivision (a), i.e., driving while under the influence. Indeed, in a number of states such a driver would be prima facie impaired well before he reached 0.10 percent. It is difficult to sympathize with an "unsuspecting" defendant who did not know if he could take a last sip without crossing the line, but who decided to do so anyway.

The very fact that he has consumed a quantity of alcohol should notify a person of ordinary intelligence that he is in jeopardy of violating the statute. Those who drink a substantial amount of alcohol within a relatively short period of time are given clear warning that to avoid possible criminal behavior they must refrain from driving. Although this factor alone sustains our determination that the statute provides adequate warning to potential violators, we find some further support in this regard from the existence for over 15 years of an analogous "0.10 percent" rebuttable presumption of being under the influence of alcohol pursuant to section 23155 and its predecessor, section 23126. Considering also today's heightened level of public awareness regarding the problem, we cannot believe that any person who drives after drinking would be unaware of the possibility that his blood-alcohol level might equal or exceed the statutory standard.

We decline to frustrate the Legislature's clear and legitimate purpose in enacting the statute involved here. We conclude that under both the federal and state Constitutions, section 23152, subdivision (b), provides adequate notice of the conduct proscribed, and is not void for vagueness.[21]

The judgment is affirmed.

Driving under the influence laws fall into one of two broad categories: "effect-based" and "per se." Effect-based laws require proof of the driver's actual impairment, based on evidence like a field sobriety test. By contrast, per se DUI laws criminalize driving with a certain amount of a drug or drug metabolite in the driver's system. Per se laws are based on the rationale that anyone driving at or above the specified level is impaired to the point that they pose a significant public safety risk. In the case of alcohol, every state has made it a crime to drive with a blood alcohol content of .08% (BAC) or higher. (This uniform standard came about in the early 2000s, after the federal government decided to require states to enact .08% BAC statutes in order to receive federal highway funds.)

The enforcement of effect-based laws relies in large part on "training and certifying police officers to conduct drug recognition evaluations (DREs) in suspected drugged driving cases. The DRE consists of a 12-step process that includes: a breath alcohol test, an interview of the arresting officer, preliminary examination and pulse rate, an eye examination, divided attention psychophysical testing, vital sign testing, dark room examinations, muscle tone examinations, injection site examinations, questioning regarding drug use, analysis of the total circumstances, and finally, a conclusion as to whether the suspect should undergo a toxicology exam." Zack G. Goldberg, *Potholes: DUI Law in the Budding Marijuana Industry*, 82 Brooklyn L. Rev. 241, 272–73 (2016). Training police officers as drug recognition experts and administering these tests is both time-consuming and costly. It is also reliant on police discretion, which can both increase the risk of false positives and make it more difficult to convince juries to convict. The challenge of enforcing effect-based laws is one of the reasons for the widespread adoption of per se laws for alcohol.

As states have legalized marijuana, marijuana DUI laws have increasingly become a point of debate. But the issue is really only tangentially related to marijuana's legal status. It is not yet clear whether legalization will result in a significant increase in the number of regular marijuana users, let alone the number of users that drive while under the influence. Whether marijuana is legal or illegal, millions of Americans use it every year. This means the question of how to deal with

---

21. We also reject the contentions of amici curiae that section 23152, subdivision (b), constitutes an impermissible discrimination against "those adult drivers who consume alcohol," or that it has an impermissible "chilling effect" on the right to travel. Equally untenable are assertions that the statute "invests the police with unlimited discretion to randomly stop and detain drivers," or that it somehow denies equal protection of the laws, or that it is invalid because mixed drinks from different bartenders may contain different amounts of alcohol.

marijuana-impaired drivers is an important one, regardless of whether marijuana is legal or illegal. The same is true for other drugs, including prescription medications. *See, e.g.*, Tina Wescott Cafaro, *Slipping Through the Cracks: Why Can't We Stop Drugged Driving?*, 32 W. New Eng. L. Rev. 33 (2010).

Though legislators would probably like to be able to mirror the alcohol DUI laws when it comes to illegal drugs, currently available technology does not make that possible for most commonly used substances. The problem is that it is not possible to measure impairment as easily for marijuana and other drugs as it is for alcohol. Marijuana can be detected in a user's blood days or weeks after use. And the levels that are in the blood do not neatly correspond to impairment.

Andrea Roth described the problem in *The Uneasy Case for Marijuana as Chemical Impairment Under a Science-Based Jurisprudence of Dangerousness*, 103 Cal. L. Rev. 841, 884–87 (2015):

> One unique property of alcohol, not shared by marijuana, is the manner in which its concentration in the blood so uniformly and predictably reflects proximity of use. Ethyl alcohol is the only psychoactive compound in the alcohol we drink. Ethyl alcohol is both fat soluble and entirely water soluble, creates no long-lived metabolites, and quickly dissipates from the body. One's BAC has a predictable relationship with rates of absorption, distribution, and elimination that are similar among humans. Because of these qualities, breath test results can indicate with relatively high precision how long ago a person drank alcohol and in what quantity.
>
> The problem with marijuana's detectability is, one might say, that it is an embarrassment of riches; . . . it can be detected quickly, effectively, and for a long time. These characteristics confound the ability to infer recency or extent of use from blood levels, which in turn makes the inference between consumption and dangerousness difficult to draw. Cannabis, the plant with marijuana as a derivative, has over 421 chemicals, and when one smokes it, the human body breaks down more than two thousand compounds. The most psychoactive of these compounds is delta9-tetrahydrocannabinol (THC), on which most studies of the effects of marijuana impairment focus. THC from smoked cannabis is "detectable in plasma within seconds after the first puff," with peak plasma concentration generally happening within three to ten minutes. But THC also produces two additional compounds when it is metabolized in the liver: a psychoactive compound, 11-OH-THC [also called hydroxy THC], and a non-impairing, inactive compound, THCCOOH [also called carboxy THC].
>
> After cannabis consumption, THC and its metabolites may remain in the body for a time period that varies among humans. While THC and its metabolites reach their *peak* concentrations within three to ninety minutes, and the metabolites are excreted from the body through feces and urine, the compounds linger in low levels in the body for much longer. Even THC itself

can be found for several hours or even days after consumption, depending on the frequency and amount of usage; a 2014 study from Norway concluded that THC can remain in the saliva of frequent cannabis users for over eight days. THC's metabolites linger even longer, and can be found in one's blood for days, weeks, or even over a month in chronic users. For example, the level and timing of concentrations change not only with tolerance, but with ingestion method. For those who orally ingest marijuana by swallowing an extract or applying a tincture to the bottom of the tongue (practices used by most medical marijuana patients), the efficiency of THC's effect decreases compared to smoking. Because THC (unlike alcohol) is "barely soluble in water, the body absorbs only a small fraction of the available [THC] when it is swallowed," causing THC blood levels and impairment effect to be delayed. In sum, marijuana's unpredictable qualities render nearly impossible any determination from THC blood levels alone whether a person is actually under the influence of marijuana at the time of driving or has simply ingested marijuana in the somewhat recent past.

A second distinction between the measurability of impairment from alcohol and from marijuana is that the properties of alcohol render its dose-related psychoactive effects predictable and uniform among humans. Ethyl alcohol's fat and water solubility, as well as its effectiveness at only high concentrations, cause it to affect the entire body and to "equilibrate[] readily" between levels in the brain, blood, and other tissue. Its water solubility and volatility at body temperature also render BAC and BrAC levels constant and proportional. These properties together make BAC highly correlated to the level of alcohol intoxication in the brain, and therefore to alcohol's psychoactive effects.

THC's psychoactive effect, in contrast, is much more complex and more disconnected to its levels in bodily fluids. When a person smokes marijuana, highly fat soluble THC gets rapidly absorbed through the lungs and distributed quickly into lung tissue, fat tissue, the liver, and the spleen. But because it is "barely soluble in water," it does not—like alcohol—reach a uniform concentration throughout bodily tissues at a rate similar among humans. Thus, unlike brain alcohol intoxication and BAC, the level of THC in the brain is not predictable from the level of THC in the blood. Further, while THC's active metabolite, 11-OH-THC [hydroxy THC], also has some psychoactive effect, though much smaller than THC (though it might be responsible for users feeling the "munchies"), it is just as unconnected from levels in bodily fluids. THC's inactive compound, THC-COOH [carboxy THC], has no psychoactive effect, regardless of its level in bodily fluids.

Moreover, while the pharmacodynamics of alcohol are decently well understood, scientists are not in agreement on exactly how and why THC affects the brain. We do know that THC interacts with specific cannabinoid receptors in the brain that are in regions associated with "cognition,

> memory, reward, anxiety, pain sensory perception, motor co-ordination and endocrine function." We also know that THC can affect a range of other targets in diffuse and unpredictable ways, including opioid receptors, enzyme systems, hormones, and neurotransmitters. But unlike with ethyl alcohol, the extent of THC's effects is a function of several variables that interact in complex ways, including dosage and tolerance. And with respect to dosage, because of THC's pharmacokinetic qualities, there is simply no predictable or uniform connection between specific blood levels of THC and its metabolites and these psychoactive effects. Thus, even if . . . scientists could straightforwardly infer proximity of use from THC blood levels, marijuana's unpredictable properties render nearly impossible any inference about the likely psychoactive effect on the brain of a specific THC blood level.

All of this has prevented scientists from establishing a measurement for marijuana comparable to BAC. "Because BAC, unlike THC blood level, corresponds so predictably to proximity of use, brain concentration, and level and type of psychoactive effect, BAC's effects on driving can be well studied and generalized to the adult population." By contrast, "as a recent consensus report on drugged driving concluded, '[i]nterpreting the meaning of either drug/metabolite concentration in a single biological specimen with reference to impaired driver performance is . . . an extremely difficult task for a scientist and even more difficult for a prosecutor.'" *Id.* at 888.

Roth argues that in the absence of a scientifically valid standard, policymakers should avoid the temptation to enact per se marijuana DUI laws. Instead, she suggests they focus on data collection and facilitating better enforcement of effects-based laws. "With better detection methods and more comprehensive data collection on crash involved drivers and dose-specific drug prevalence in the overall driving population, it might be that we will find a scientific way to measure marijuana as chemical impairment," Roth notes. "But if marijuana is truly impossible to measure in a way that allows for a coherent per se DUI law in the foreseeable future based on THC blood levels, then the answer should not be to settle for incoherency in our criminal law in the name of securing more convictions. The answer should be to settle for an imperfect subjective impairment standard for criminal DUI marijuana laws and to use numerical thresholds, if at all, to trigger nonpunitive regulatory sanctions. In any event, we should be guided by science in tackling the issue of drugged driving, whether our goal is to achieve justice, to promote public safety, or to have the audacity to try to do both." *Id.* at 916–17.

Notwithstanding criticisms of per se drugged driving laws, the Office of National Drug Control Policy has encouraged states to enact them. Between 1990 and 2010, 13 states enacted "zero tolerance" per se drugged driving laws, making it a crime to drive with *any* detectable amount of specified substances. Another four enacted per se laws with "nonzero thresholds for controlled substances (or their metabolites) above which a driver is automatically considered impaired." D. Mark Anderson and

Daniel I. Rees, *Per Se Drugged Driving Laws and Traffic Fatalities*, 42 INT'L REV. L. & ECON. 122 (2015).

Are states better off setting a legal limit that imperfectly measures impairment? Or should states rely on effect-based laws until it is possible to more accurately gauge impairment through blood or breath testing?

In states that have already enacted "zero tolerance" per se drugged driving laws, how broadly should courts interpret the prohibition against driving with drug "metabolites" in one's body? Specifically, should these laws prohibit driving with non-impairing drug metabolites in the body? Or should they be limited to driving with metabolites that are capable of causing impairment?

In the case that follows, the Arizona Supreme Court tackled this question. The majority concluded that "[a]lthough the legislature could rationally choose to penalize the presence of any amount of an impairing metabolite, we do not believe that the legislature contemplated penalizing the presence of a metabolite that is not impairing." As a result, the court held that Arizona's zero tolerance law does not apply to non-impairing drug metabolites. It is still illegal under Arizona's law, however, to drive with *any* amount of a drug metabolite that is capable of causing impairment—even if the driver is not actually impaired and has only a trace amount of an impairment-causing metabolite in her body.

As you read the decision, consider whether you find the Arizona Supreme Court's distinction to be a convincing one.

Arizona ex rel. Montgomery v. Harris

Supreme Court of Arizona
234 Ariz. 343 (2014)

Brutinel, J.

Arizona Revised Statutes § 28-1381(A)(3) makes it unlawful for a driver to be in actual physical control of a vehicle if there is "any drug defined in [A.R.S.] § 13-3401 or its metabolite in the person's body." We are asked to determine whether the phrase "its metabolite" includes Carboxy-Tetrahydrocannabinol ("Carboxy-THC"), a non-impairing metabolite of Cannabis,[1] a proscribed drug listed in § 13-3401. We conclude that it does not.

Police stopped a vehicle driven by Hrach Shilgevorkyan for speeding and making unsafe lane changes. Suspecting that he was impaired, officers administered field sobriety tests. After participating in the tests, Shilgevorkyan admitted that he had smoked some "weed" the night before and voluntarily submitted to a blood test that revealed Carboxy-THC in his blood.

1. Cannabis is commonly referred to as marijuana and as defined in A.R.S. § 13-3401(4)(b) includes tetrahydrocannabinol ("THC"), its primary psychoactive component.

The State charged Shilgevorkyan with two counts of driving under the influence. Count one alleged a violation of A.R.S. § 28-1381(A)(1) ("the (A)(1) charge"), which prohibits a person from driving a vehicle in Arizona "[w]hile under the influence of . . . any drug . . . if the person is impaired to the slightest degree." Count two alleged a violation of A.R.S. § 28-1381(A)(3) ("the (A)(3) charge"), which prohibits driving a vehicle "[w]hile there is any drug defined in § 13-3401 or its metabolite in the person's body."

Shilgevorkyan moved to dismiss the (A)(3) charge, arguing that the blood test revealed neither the presence of THC nor "its metabolite" Hydroxy-Tetrahydrocannabinol ("Hydroxy-THC"). At an evidentiary hearing, the State presented expert witness testimony that: (1) marijuana has "many, many metabolites," (2) Hydroxy-THC and Carboxy-THC are the two major marijuana metabolites, (3) although it is possible to test for Hydroxy-THC in the blood, the Arizona Department of Public Safety chooses not to do so because Hydroxy-THC does not "exist in the blood for very long" and is quickly converted to Carboxy-THC, (4) Carboxy-THC is inactive and does not cause impairment, and (5) Carboxy-THC can remain in a person's body for as many as twenty-eight to thirty days after the ingestion of marijuana.

At the conclusion of the hearing, the justice court dismissed the (A)(3) charge, and the State voluntarily dismissed the (A)(1) charge. The State appealed to the superior court, which affirmed. That court reasoned that the word "metabolite" in § 28-1381(A)(3) is ambiguous because it is unclear whether it should be read as singular or plural. Although the court acknowledged that Carboxy-THC is a marijuana metabolite, it was unconvinced that the legislature intended to include all possible byproducts—particularly those that are inactive and cannot impair the driver.

The State then filed a petition for special action with the court of appeals, which accepted jurisdiction and granted relief. The court held that "§ 28-1381(A)(3)'s language prohibiting driving with a proscribed drug or 'its metabolite' includes the metabolite Carboxy-THC" based on the reasoning in *State v. Hammonds,* 192 Ariz. 528 (App.1998), and *State v. Phillips,* 178 Ariz. 368 (App.1994). The court in *Hammonds* held that the (A)(3) offense was not "irrationally overinclusive" and the court in *Phillips* determined that it was not unconstitutionally vague or overbroad. The court of appeals noted that although neither case considered the meaning of "metabolite," they demonstrated that A.R.S. § 28-1381(A)(3) "must be interpreted broadly to appropriately effectuate the legislative purpose and intent underpinning the statutory language."

We granted review because whether § 28-1381(A)(3) applies to non-impairing metabolites presents a recurring issue of statewide importance.

We review questions of statutory interpretation de novo. When interpreting a statute, our goal is to "fulfill the intent of the legislature that wrote it."

The term "metabolite" is not defined by statute. When statutory terms are undefined, courts may reference dictionaries. A standard medical dictionary defines metabolite as "[a]ny product of metabolism." Taber's Cyclopedic Medical Dictionary 1349 (20th ed.2005). It defines metabolism in pertinent part, as "the sum of all physical and chemical changes that take place within an organism." *Id.* These definitions comport with the State's expert's testimony, which defined "metabolite" as "any chemical compound that is produced during the process of metabolism, the breakdown process of getting rid of a drug or substance."

Shilgevorkyan argues that the meaning of "its metabolite" in § 28-1381(A)(3) is clear. He asserts that because the statute uses the possessive singular, it prohibits only Hydroxy-THC, the initial product of the metabolism of THC. Labeling Hydroxy-THC the "primary" metabolite, he contends the statute does not include the products of the further breakdown of Hydroxy-THC into subsequent or "secondary" metabolites such as Carboxy-THC. He further argues that interpreting "metabolite" in the plural expands the statutory definition to include a "secondary non-psychoactive metabolite . . . [that] does not cause impairment," which is inconsistent with the legislature's intent to criminalize driving under the influence of an intoxicating substance. The State, on the other hand, argues we should construe "metabolite" in the plural in accordance with A.R.S. § 1-214(B), which generally provides that statutory "[w]ords in the singular . . . include the plural. . . ."

There is more than one plausible meaning for the phrase "its metabolite," whether read as singular or plural. The argument that "its metabolite," although phrased in the singular, includes all of a proscribed drug's byproducts is reasonable based on § 1-214(B). Conversely, the argument that the statutory language reflects the legislature's intent to only penalize drivers with primary or impairment-causing metabolites in their system is equally reasonable. Additionally, even if read in the plural, "metabolites" could reasonably mean multiple primary metabolites for drugs having more than one rather than both primary and secondary metabolites.

Because the term "its metabolite" is reasonably susceptible to differing interpretations, the statute is ambiguous and we cannot determine from the term alone whether the legislature intended to penalize the presence of any byproduct, including Carboxy-THC, in a driver's blood. *[S]ee also* Joshua C. Snow, *The Unconstitutional Prosecution of Controlled Substance Metabolites Under Utah Code § 41-6A-517,* 2013 Utah L.Rev. OnLaw 195, 198 (2013) ("Although [per se DUI] statutes are purportedly designed to make prosecution simpler and more effective by removing the necessity to prove impairment or quantifiable levels of drugs in the system, the statutes are rife with ambiguity and complexity, which weaken their legitimacy and validity."). Accordingly, we look to secondary rules of statutory construction to determine § 28-1381(A)(3)'s meaning.

Statutes should be construed sensibly to avoid reaching an absurd conclusion. When a statute's meaning cannot be discerned from its language alone, "we attempt to determine legislative intent by interpreting the statute as a whole, and consider 'the statute's context, subject matter, historical background, effects and consequences, and spirit and purpose.'" Courts also consider "the policy behind the statute and the evil it was designed to remedy." Furthermore, we consider a statute "in light of its place in the statutory scheme," and although statutory title headings are not part of the law, they can aid in its interpretation.

The State's interpretation that "its metabolite" includes *any* byproduct of a drug listed in § 13-3401 found in a driver's system leads to absurd results.

Most notably, this interpretation would create criminal liability regardless of how long the metabolite remains in the driver's system or whether it has any impairing effect. For example, at oral argument the State acknowledged that, under its reading of the statute, if a metabolite could be detected five years after ingesting a proscribed drug, a driver who tested positive for trace elements of a non-impairing substance could be prosecuted.

Additionally, this interpretation would criminalize otherwise legal conduct. In 2010, Arizona voters passed the Arizona Medical Marijuana Act ("AMMA"), legalizing marijuana for medicinal purposes. Despite the legality of such use, and because § 28-1381(A)(3) does not require the State to prove that the marijuana was illegally ingested, prosecutors can charge legal users under the (A)(3) provision. Because Carboxy-THC can remain in the body for as many as twenty-eight to thirty days after ingestion, the State's position suggests that a medical-marijuana user could face prosecution for driving any time nearly a month after they had legally ingested marijuana. Such a prohibition would apply even when the driver had no impairing substance in his or her body and notwithstanding the State's ability to test both for THC, the primary substance that causes impairment, and Hydroxy-THC, the metabolite capable of causing impairment.

Finally, this interpretation would allow the prosecution of an individual who drives after ingesting a legal substance that shares a non-impairing metabolite with a proscribed substance. For example, serotonin, a legal substance, and the proscribed drug bufotenine share a common metabolite, 5-hydroxindoleactic acid ("5-HIAA").[2] Under the State's interpretation of "metabolite," it could prosecute a driver who had 5-HIAA in his or her system after ingesting a legal serotonin supplement or, for that matter, whose blood contains 5-HIAA as a byproduct of naturally produced serotonin. Because § 28-1381(A)(3) does not require the State to prove that a substance discovered in a driver's body is actually metabolized from a proscribed drug, the State's interpretation would permit prosecution if the discovered substance is a metabolite of a proscribed drug even if the proscribed drug was never ingested. These results are absurd and make the State's argument untenable.[3]

---

2. Bufotenine, proscribed by A.R.S. § 13-3401(6)(a)(v), is a hallucinogenic drug generally ingested by licking the backs of cane toads. *See* Christen Conger, *Are there really hallucinogenic frogs?*, How Stuff Works (August 12, 2008), http://www.science.howstuffworks. com/zoology /reptiles-amphibians/hallucinogenic-frog1.htm

3. The Dissent notes that under its plain language interpretation, § 28-1381(A)(3) might be constitutionally challenged as applied to a driver who had ingested a legal (or naturally occurring) substance that shares a metabolite with an illegal drug or who legally ingested marijuana. In

The legislative history behind § 28-1381(A)(3) reflects that the legislature sought to prevent impaired driving. The statute was added in 1990 by House Bill ("H.B.") 2433. A Senate fact sheet explained that H.B. 2433's purpose was to "make numerous substantive and conforming changes to the provisions relating to the offense of driving under the influence of liquor or drugs."

Section 28-1381(A)(3)'s placement within the statutory scheme also demonstrates a legislative intent to prevent and punish impaired driving, not simply driving while having a non-impairing metabolite in one's system. The "its metabolite" language appears in the "Driving Under the Influence" section of Arizona's statutes. And the statute's title begins "Driving or actual physical control *while under the influence*. . . ." A.R.S. § 28-1381 (emphasis added).

Consistent with this legislative history, the court of appeals has noted that "[t]he state has a compelling legitimate interest in protecting the public from drivers whose ability may be impaired by the consumption of controlled substances. . . ." The court further explained that the (A)(3) charge was enacted as a part of comprehensive DUI legislation "designed to protect the public by 'reducing the terrible toll of life and limb' on our roads."

This legislative intent is further evidenced by A.R.S. § 28-1381(A)(2), which provides that "[i]t is unlawful for a person to drive or be in actual physical control of a vehicle . . . [i]f the person has an alcohol concentration of 0.08 or more within two hours of driving or being in actual physical control of the vehicle. . . ." Neither the (A)(2) nor (A)(3) charge requires that the State prove impairment. The (A)(2) charge creates a per se threshold at which a driver is presumed to be under the influence. *See State v. Cooperman*, 232 Ariz. 347, 350 (2013) (explaining that under § 28-1381(A)(2), whether the driver was impaired does not matter—the only pertinent questions are whether the alcohol concentration exceeded 0.08 and the reading was taken within two hours of driving or being in actual physical control of the vehicle).

Similarly, in enacting the (A)(3) charge, the legislature sought to proscribe driving by those who could be impaired from the presence of illegal drugs in their body. However, unlike alcohol, there is no generally applicable concentration that can be identified as an indicator of impairment for illegal drugs. *Phillips*, 178 Ariz. at 372 (explaining that drugs' potency cannot be accurately predicted); *see also* Gary M. Reisfield et al., *The Mirage of Impairing Drug Concentration Thresholds: A Rationale for Zero Tolerance* Per Se *Driving under the Influence of Drugs Laws*, 36 J. Analytical Toxicology 353 (2012) (explaining that multiple phenomena make the task of establishing impairing concentrations impossible). The (A)(3) charge establishes that a driver who tests positive for any amount of an impairing drug is legally and irrefutably presumed to be under the influence. Although the legislature could rationally

---

support of this assertion the Dissent cites *State v. Boyd*, 201 Ariz. 27, 29–30 (App.2001), which held § 28-1381(A)(3), as applied, void for vagueness. That § 28-1381(A)(3) is subject to more than one reasonable interpretation, one of which might render it unconstitutional, highlights its ambiguity. Furthermore, we "construe statutes, when possible, to avoid constitutional difficulties."

choose to penalize the presence of any amount of an impairing metabolite, we do not believe that the legislature contemplated penalizing the presence of a metabolite that is not impairing.

We find that the legislature intended to prohibit driving with any amount of an impairing substance resulting from a drug proscribed in § 13-3401 in the body. The State, however, essentially contends that the legislature intended a law that punishes *driving under the influence* to also punish drivers who it cannot prove were under the influence or had any impairing substance in their system at the time of driving. We are not persuaded and reject the State's argument that § 28-1381(A)(3) "creates a flat ban on the presence of any drug or its metabolite in a person's body while driving or in actual physical control of a vehicle," even when the only metabolite found is not impairing. But we likewise reject Shilgevorkyan's argument that "its metabolite" means only the primary metabolite, because there are drugs proscribed under § 13-3401 that have multiple primary or secondary impairing metabolites.

Because the legislature intended to prevent impaired driving, we hold that the "metabolite" reference in § 28-1381(A)(3) is limited to any of a proscribed substance's metabolites that are capable of causing impairment. Accordingly, marijuana users violate § 28-1381(A)(1) if they drive while "impaired to the slightest degree," and, regardless of impairment, violate (A)(3) if they are discovered with any amount of THC or an impairing metabolite in their body. Drivers cannot be convicted of the (A)(3) offense based merely on the presence of a non-impairing metabolite that may reflect the prior usage of marijuana.

The record establishes that Carboxy-THC, the only metabolite found in Shilgevorkyan's blood, does not cause impairment. Accordingly, we vacate the court of appeals' opinion and affirm the trial court's dismissal of the (A)(3) charge.

Timmer, J., dissenting.

Arizona is one of at least seven states that combats drugged driving with a zero-tolerance, per se ban on driving with any controlled substance or its metabolite in the body. Joshua C. Snow, *The Unconstitutional Prosecution of Controlled Substance Metabolites Under Utah Code § 41-6A-517,* 2013 Utah L.Rev. OnLaw 195, 197–98 & n. 14 (2013). One of these states, Delaware, explicitly excludes inactive metabolites from its per se ban. Del.Code Ann. tit. 21, § 4177(c)(10) (West 2014). The Majority aligns Arizona with Delaware by construing A.R.S. § 28-1381(A)(3) in a manner that contradicts its plain meaning. I respectfully dissent.

The Majority holds that § 28-1381(A)(3) is ambiguous because the phrase "its metabolite" can mean all of a proscribed drug's metabolites, some of its metabolites, or only those that can cause impairment. But "metabolite" has an accepted meaning, *see* Taber's Cyclopedic Medical Dictionary 1349 (20th ed.2005), and nothing in the language of § 28-1381 suggests that the legislature intended to exclude certain types of metabolites from the statutory prohibition. Because § 28-1381(A)(3) "admits of only one meaning," it is not ambiguous.

I also disagree with the Majority that the legislature must have intended something different from what it plainly stated in § 28-1381(A)(3) because imposing a flat ban on driving with any metabolite of an illegal drug in the body is absurd. The legislature reasonably could have concluded that a zero-tolerance provision would most effectively enhance detection and prosecution of drugged driving.

First, the difficulty of detecting drug impairment justifies a flat ban. *See Phillips*, 178 Ariz. at 372 (noting that, unlike the case with alcohol impairment, "there is no useful indicator of impairment from . . . drugs because they are fundamentally different from alcohol"). For example, an expert witness in this case testified that Hydroxy-THC converts quickly to Carboxy-THC, which is why law enforcement typically does not test blood for Hydroxy-THC. Thus, a driver with Carboxy-THC in the blood at the time of testing may or may not have had Hydroxy-THC in the blood while driving. The flat ban ensures that a driver who had an impairing substance in the body while driving is prosecuted even though that substance may have quickly metabolized into a non-impairing substance.

Second, the flat ban permits law enforcement to detect drugged driving by testing urine as well as blood. "[W]hile a urine test detecting metabolites does not conclusively establish the presence of the active proscribed parent drug in the bloodstream, neither does it rule it out, because the metabolite and the active parent will often be present in the body simultaneously." *State v. Hammonds*, 192 Ariz. 528, 531 (App.1998). Imposing a flat ban on driving with a metabolite of a controlled substance in the body enhances law enforcement's ability to detect drugged driving. *Cf. id.* ("In seeking to protect the life and health of its citizenry, the legislature cannot be required to forego an effective prophylactic measure simply because it may be somewhat imprecise.").

The Majority contends that a flat ban is absurd because it permits prosecution if the non-impairing metabolite in the driver's body derives from ingesting either medically authorized marijuana or a legal substance that shares a metabolite with a controlled substance. These isolated examples do not make the flat ban on the presence in the body of hundreds of proscribed drugs or their metabolites absurd. Either scenario described by the Majority would unquestionably trigger constitutional scrutiny that might invalidate § 28-1381(A)(3) as applied in particular circumstances. *Cf. State v. Boyd*, 201 Ariz. 27, 29–30 (App.2001) (holding that although "A.R.S. § 28-1381(A)(3) is not facially vague," applying it to a defendant who consumed a legal product, GBL, that metabolized into GHB, a proscribed substance, was unconstitutional as applied to the defendant because it "fail[ed] to give him adequate notice that his actions were illegal"). And § 28-1381(A)(3) might not apply if the detected metabolites—active or inactive—emanated from medically authorized marijuana use. *See* A.R.S. § 28-1381(D) ("A person using a drug as prescribed by a medical practitioner licensed pursuant to title 32, chapter 7, 11, 13 or 17 is not guilty of violating subsection A, paragraph 3 of this section."). This case does not present either situation.

I share some of the Majority's concerns about imposing a zero-tolerance, per se ban on driving with the presence of non-impairing metabolites in the body. But because §28-1381(A)(3) clearly and unambiguously reflects that the legislature intended this result, it is not appropriate to employ secondary canons of statutory construction to find a different meaning. Any constitutional challenges to this provision should be addressed on a case-by-case basis. I would affirm the court of appeals' opinion.

6. Drug Paraphernalia

South Dakota v. Holway

Supreme Court of South Dakota
644 N.W. 2d 624 (2002)

Gilbertson, CJ.

Thomas Holway is a co-owner of Video Blue, an adult bookstore in Rapid City, South Dakota. Ellie Holway is an employee at Video Blue. The Holways attended a trade show in Las Vegas and determined that it would be "very lucrative" to carry certain smoking devices for sale in the store. Thomas Holway contacted the Pennington County State's Attorney, Glenn Brenner (Brenner), to determine if selling the devices would be legal. Brenner read the statute to him and informed him that if it could be proven that the devices could be used for smoking marijuana, law enforcement would be involved.

When Thomas contacted Brenner a second time and showed him a "sample" pipe, Brenner referred him to Todd Love, the drug prosecutor for the Attorney General's Office. One of the Holways did contact Love with the same questions presented to Brenner. Love informed the Video Blue representative that it is illegal to deliver, or to possess with the intent to deliver, any drug paraphernalia. He also informed him that he would not be able to claim immunity based upon anything Brenner had said to them. Love explained that the State Attorney General's Office could prosecute Video Blue's owners and employees for drug violations even if the Pennington County State's Attorney did not.

In April 2000, the devices were put out for sale in two display cases at Video Blue. The display cases contained various items used for smoking including: pipes, water pipes, bongs, wood dugouts, and carburetors. They also contained roach clips and pipes disguised to look like cigarette lighters, lipstick containers, and hi-liter felt tip markers. Each display case had a sign stating "All paraphernalia sales are only sold with the understanding that the purchaser has only legal intent for its use." Yet, no cigarette or pipe tobacco was sold in the store.

On April 14, 2000, the South Dakota Division of Criminal Investigation (DCI) began investigating Video Blue based on allegations that drug paraphernalia was being sold there. Four officers were involved in the investigation: Deputy Sheriff Jeff Whittle (Whittle), Deputy Sheriff Martin Graves (Graves), Detective Dale McCabe (McCabe), and DCI Supervising Agent Robert Overturf (Overturf).

Whittle entered the store on April 14, 2000, and purchased a "one-hitter," a small water pipe, and a wood "dug-out" pipe from Ellie. Ellie gave him a free package of screens, which are commonly used to prevent a marijuana smoker from inhaling the seeds and stems. When Whittle made a comment about how a friend of his got caught selling items like these, Ellie pointed to the sign. Whittle mockingly replied that he, of course, had only legal intent. Ellie raised her hands and said, "Well, I don't want to know about it." She also acknowledged Whittle's comment about a wood dug-out being an "old standard."

Graves entered the store on April 18, 2000, and purchased a red bong and a metal pipe from Ellie. McCabe also entered the store on April 18. He purchased a school bus pipe and a blue hi-liter pipe from Ellie. McCabe asked Ellie if they made a pipe that looked like a police car. She replied "They would probably frown upon that." McCabe also inquired whether he could get a discount. Ellie spoke with Thomas, who agreed to the discount. She also gave McCabe a free package of screens.

Thomas and Ellie were each charged with seven counts of delivery of drug paraphernalia in violation of SDCL 22-42A-4 and SDCL 22-3-3. The two were tried together before a jury on June 5–6, 2001. Thomas and Ellie were each convicted on three of the seven counts and sentenced to 90 days in jail on count I, and two years in prison on counts III and VII. The terms were to run consecutively, with execution of the prison sentences suspended.

SDCL 22-42A-4 sets forth the elements for the crime of delivering drug paraphernalia:

> No person, knowing the drug[-]related nature of the object, may deliver, possess with intent to deliver, or manufacture with intent to deliver, drug paraphernalia, knowing, or under circumstances where one reasonably should know, that it will be used to . . . contain, conceal, inject, ingest, inhale, or otherwise introduce into the human body a controlled substance or marijuana in violation of this chapter. Any person who violates any provision of this section is guilty of a Class 6 felony.

The term "drug paraphernalia" means any equipment, products and materials of any kind which are primarily used, intended for use or designed for use by the person in possession of them, . . . containing, concealing, injecting, ingesting, inhaling or otherwise introducing into the human body any controlled substance or marijuana in violation of the provisions of this chapter. It includes, but is not limited to:

* * *

(10) Objects used, intended for use or designed for use in ingesting, inhaling or otherwise introducing marijuana, cocaine, hashish or hashish oil into the human body, such as:

(a) Metal, wooden, acrylic, glass, stone, plastic or ceramic pipes with or without screens, permanent screens, hashish heads or punctured metal bowls;

(b) Water pipes;

(c) Carburetion tubes and devices;

(d) Smoking and carburetion masks;

(e) Roach clips: meaning objects used to hold burning material, such as a marijuana cigarette, that has become too small or too short to be held in the hand;

(f) Miniature cocaine spoons and cocaine vials;

(g) Chamber pipes;

(h) Carburetor pipes;

(i) Electric pipes;

(j) Air-driven pipes;

(k) Chillums;

(l) Bongs; and

(m) Ice pipes or chillers.

Therefore, to sustain a conviction, the State is required to prove that: (1) the defendant delivered or possessed with the intent to deliver an object; (2) that object is drug paraphernalia; (3) the defendant knew of the drug-related nature of the object; and (4) the defendant knew or reasonably should have known that the object would be used to introduce illegal drugs into the human body.

The Holways claim that they cannot be guilty because SDCL 22-42A-1 requires those in possession to intend the objects for drug use. They claim that because they did not intend the items for drug use and the undercover officers to whom they sold the objects did not intend or actually use them for drugs, the conviction cannot be sustained. We disagree. The statute identifies drug paraphernalia in the disjunctive. It includes objects "primarily used" for drug use, objects intended for drug use by the person in possession of them, or objects designed for drug use by the person in possession of them. The Holways cannot escape liability by pretending to ignore the most common use of such objects.

While the Holways claim that the objects could have been used to smoke tobacco, we agree with the trial court's characterization of the items herein as being "primarily used" to introduce illegal drugs into the human body. The Holways also assert that they did not know of the objects' drug-related nature. But the jury was justifiably incredulous. It is difficult to believe that those who chose to sell such items because they would be "very lucrative," but who first made inquiries to the State's Attorney and the Attorney General to determine how they could escape liability, did not have a clue as to the drug-related and *illegal* nature of such items.

Ellie actually sold the items at issue. She gave both Whittle and McCabe the free packages of screens, which are commonly used for smoking marijuana, when they purchased the pipes. She indicated that she recognized a wood dug-out as being an "old standard." Yet, an expert witness testified that it certainly is not an "old standard" for smoking tobacco. When Whittle commented on the possible illegality of selling the items, she pointed to the sign and informed him that she did not want to know about his supposedly "legal intent." Her reply to McCabe's question of whether she had any pipes shaped like police cars indicates that she knew law enforcement would "frown upon" having a pipe, used for smoking marijuana, designed in such a shape.

Thomas not only owned the store that the items were sold in, but he was also intricately involved in stocking the items for sale. His statements to Brenner are indicative of his knowledge that the items he wished to sell were legally questionable, at best. The fact that he approved the discount to McCabe indicates he supervised the sales of the items. There was evidence that he displayed the items at issue with many others specifically enumerated within SDCL 22-42A-1(10) as constituting drug paraphernalia. Copies of *Cannabis Culture* and *High Times*, magazines advocating drug use, show photographs advertising the very same objects.

The facts laid out above give sufficient reason for a jury to believe, beyond a reasonable doubt, that not only were the objects drug paraphernalia, but that Thomas and Ellie knew or reasonably should have known of the objects' drug-related nature. Accepting, as we must, the evidence and the most favorable inferences to be drawn therefrom in favor of the verdict, we do not see that the judgment was in error. Therefore, we affirm the decision of the trial court.

Village of Hoffman Estates v. The Flipside

Supreme Court of the United States
455 U.S. 489 (1982)

Justice Marshall delivered the opinion of the Court.

For more than three years prior to May 1, 1978, appellee The Flipside sold a variety of merchandise, including phonographic records, smoking accessories, novelty devices, and jewelry, in its store located in the village of Hoffman Estates, Ill. On February 20, 1978, the village enacted an ordinance regulating drug paraphernalia, to be effective May 1, 1978. The ordinance makes it unlawful for any person "to sell any items, effect, paraphernalia, accessory or thing which is designed or marketed for use with illegal cannabis or drugs, as defined by Illinois Revised Statutes, without obtaining a license therefor." The license fee is $150. A business must also file affidavits that the licensee and its employees have not been convicted of a drug-related offense. Moreover, the business must keep a record of each sale of a regulated item, including the name and address of the purchaser, to be open to police inspection. No regulated item may be sold to a minor. A violation is subject to a fine of not less than $10 and not more than $500, and each day that a violation continues gives rise to a separate offense. A series of licensing guidelines prepared by the Village Attorney define "Paper," "Roach Clips," "Pipes," and "Paraphernalia," the sale of which is required to be licensed.

After an administrative inquiry, the village determined that Flipside and one other store appeared to be in violation of the ordinance. The Village Attorney notified Flipside of the existence of the ordinance, and made a copy of the ordinance and guidelines available to Flipside. Flipside's owner asked for guidance concerning which items were covered by the ordinance; the Village Attorney advised him to remove items in a certain section of the store "for his protection," and he did so. The items included, according to Flipside's description, a clamp, chain ornaments, an "alligator" clip, key chains, necklaces, earrings, cigarette holders, glove stretchers, scales, strainers, a pulverizer, squeeze bottles, pipes, water pipes, pins, an herb sifter, mirrors, vials, cigarette rolling papers, and tobacco snuff. On May 30, 1978, instead of applying for a license or seeking clarification via the administrative procedures that the village had established for its licensing ordinances, Flipside filed this lawsuit in the United States District Court for the Northern District of Illinois.

The complaint alleged, *inter alia*, that the ordinance is unconstitutionally vague and overbroad, and requested injunctive and declaratory relief and damages. The District Court . . . issued an opinion upholding the constitutionality of the ordinance, and awarded judgment to the village defendants.

The Court of Appeals reversed on the ground that the ordinance is unconstitutionally vague on its face. The court reviewed the language of the ordinance and guidelines and found it vague with respect to certain conceivable applications, such as ordinary pipes or "paper clips sold next to *Rolling Stone* magazine." It also suggested that the "subjective" nature of the "marketing" test creates a danger of arbitrary and discriminatory enforcement against those with alternative lifestyles. Finally, the court determined that the availability of administrative review or guidelines cannot cure the defect. Thus, it concluded that the ordinance is impermissibly vague on its face.

In a facial challenge to the overbreadth and vagueness of a law,[5] a court's first task is to determine whether the enactment reaches a substantial amount of constitutionally protected conduct. If it does not, then the overbreadth challenge must fail. A plaintiff who engages in some conduct that is clearly proscribed cannot complain of the vagueness of the law as applied to the conduct of others. A court should therefore examine the complainant's conduct before analyzing other hypothetical applications of the law.

We first examine whether the ordinance infringes Flipside's First Amendment rights or is overbroad because it inhibits the First Amendment rights of other parties. Flipside makes the exorbitant claim that the village has imposed a "prior restraint" on speech because the guidelines treat the proximity of drug-related literature as an indicium that paraphernalia are "marketed for use with illegal cannabis or drugs." Flipside also argues that because the presence of drug-related designs, logos, or slogans on paraphernalia may trigger enforcement, the ordinance infringes "protected symbolic speech."

5. A "facial" challenge, in this context, means a claim that the law is "invalid *in toto*—and therefore incapable of any valid application." *Steffel v. Thompson*, 415 U.S. 452, 474 (1974).

These arguments do not long detain us. First, the village has not directly infringed the noncommercial speech of Flipside or other parties. The ordinance licenses and regulates the sale of items displayed "with" or "within proximity of" "literature encouraging illegal use of cannabis or illegal drugs," but does not prohibit or otherwise regulate the sale of literature itself. Although drug-related designs or names on cigarette papers may subject those items to regulation, the village does not restrict speech as such, but simply regulates the commercial marketing of items that the labels reveal may be used for an illicit purpose. The scope of the ordinance therefore does not embrace noncommercial speech.

Second, insofar as any *commercial* speech interest is implicated here, it is only the attenuated interest in displaying and marketing merchandise in the manner that the retailer desires. We doubt that the village's restriction on the manner of marketing appreciably limits Flipside's communication of information—with one obvious and telling exception. The ordinance is expressly directed at commercial activity promoting or encouraging illegal drug use. If that activity is deemed "speech," then it is speech proposing an illegal transaction, which a government may regulate or ban entirely.

A law that does not reach constitutionally protected conduct and therefore satisfies the overbreadth test may nevertheless be challenged on its face as unduly vague, in violation of due process. To succeed, however, the complainant must demonstrate that the law is impermissibly vague in all of its applications. Flipside makes no such showing.

Flipside's facial challenge fails because, under the test appropriate to either a quasi-criminal or a criminal law, the ordinance is sufficiently clear as applied to Flipside.

The ordinance requires Flipside to obtain a license if it sells "any items, effect, paraphernalia, accessory or thing which is designed or marketed for use with illegal cannabis or drugs, as defined by the Illinois Revised Statutes." Flipside expresses no uncertainty about which drugs this description encompasses; as the District Court noted, Illinois law clearly defines cannabis and numerous other controlled drugs, including cocaine. On the other hand, the words "items, effect, paraphernalia, accessory or thing" do not identify the type of merchandise that the village desires to regulate. Flipside's challenge thus appropriately focuses on the language "designed or marketed for use." Under either the "designed for use" or "marketed for use" standard, we conclude that at least some of the items sold by Flipside are covered. Thus, Flipside's facial challenge is unavailing.

The Court of Appeals objected that "designed . . . for use" is ambiguous with respect to whether items must be inherently suited only for drug use; whether the retailer's intent or manner of display is relevant; and whether the intent of a third party, the manufacturer, is critical, since the manufacturer is the "designer." For the reasons that follow, we conclude that this language is not unconstitutionally vague on its face.

The Court of Appeals' speculation about the meaning of "design" is largely unfounded. The guidelines refer to "paper of colorful design" and to other specific items as conclusively "designed" or not "designed" for illegal use. A principal meaning of "design" is "[to] fashion according to a plan." It is therefore plain that the standard encompasses at least an item that is principally used with illegal drugs by virtue of its objective features, *i.e.*, features designed by the manufacturer. A business person of ordinary intelligence would understand that this term refers to the design of the manufacturer, not the intent of the retailer or customer. It is also sufficiently clear that items which are principally used for nondrug purposes, such as ordinary pipes, are not "designed for use" with illegal drugs. Moreover, no issue of fair warning is present in this case, since Flipside concedes that the phrase refers to structural characteristics of an item.

The ordinance and guidelines do contain ambiguities. Nevertheless, the "designed for use" standard is sufficiently clear to cover at least some of the items that Flipside sold. The ordinance, through the guidelines, explicitly regulates "roach clips." Flipside's co-operator admitted that the store sold such items and the village Chief of Police testified that he had never seen a "roach clip" used for any purpose other than to smoke cannabis. The Chief also testified that a specially designed pipe that Flipside marketed is typically used to smoke marihuana. Whether further guidelines, administrative rules, or enforcement policy will clarify the more ambiguous scope of the standard in other respects is of no concern in this facial challenge.

Whatever ambiguities the "designed . . . for use" standard may engender, the alternative "marketed for use" standard is transparently clear: it describes a retailer's intentional display and marketing of merchandise. The guidelines refer to the display of paraphernalia, and to the proximity of covered items to otherwise uncovered items. A retail store therefore must obtain a license if it deliberately displays its wares in a manner that appeals to or encourages illegal drug use. The standard requires scienter, since a retailer could scarcely "market" items "for" a particular use without intending that use.

Under this test, Flipside had ample warning that its marketing activities required a license. Flipside displayed the magazine *High Times* and books entitled *Marijuana Grower's Guide*, *Children's Garden of Grass*, and *The Pleasures of Cocaine*, physically close to pipes and colored rolling papers, in clear violation of the guidelines. As noted above, Flipside's co-operator admitted that his store sold "roach clips," which are principally used for illegal purposes. Finally, in the same section of the store, Flipside had posted the sign, "You must be 18 or older to purchase any head supplies."[20]

The Court of Appeals also held that the ordinance provides insufficient standards for enforcement. Specifically, the court feared that the ordinance might be used to harass individuals with alternative lifestyles and views. In reviewing a business

---

20. The American Heritage Dictionary of the English Language 606 (1980) gives the following alternative definition of "head": "Slang. One who is a frequent user of drugs."

regulation for facial vagueness, however, the principal inquiry is whether the law affords fair warning of what is proscribed. Moreover, this emphasis is almost inescapable in reviewing a pre-enforcement challenge to a law. Here, no evidence has been, or could be, introduced to indicate whether the ordinance has been enforced in a discriminatory manner or with the aim of inhibiting unpopular speech. The language of the ordinance is sufficiently clear that the speculative danger of arbitrary enforcement does not render the ordinance void for vagueness.

We do not suggest that the risk of discriminatory enforcement is insignificant here. Testimony of the Village Attorney who drafted the ordinance, the village President, and the Police Chief revealed confusion over whether the ordinance applies to certain items, as well as extensive reliance on the "judgment" of police officers to give meaning to the ordinance and to enforce it fairly. At this stage, however, we are not prepared to hold that this risk jeopardizes the entire ordinance.[21]

"Although it is possible that specific future applications . . . may engender concrete problems of constitutional dimension, it will be time enough to consider any such problems when they arise." *Joseph E. Seagram & Sons, Inc.* v. *Hostetter,* 384 U.S. 35, 52 (1966).

Many American communities have recently enacted laws regulating or prohibiting the sale of drug paraphernalia. To determine whether these laws are wise or effective is not, of course, the province of this Court. We hold only that such legislation is not facially overbroad or vague if it does not reach constitutionally protected conduct and is reasonably clear in its application to the complainant.

The application of drug paraphernalia laws to syringes has been particularly controversial. While syringes, when used to inject illegal drugs, would easily meet the definition of many drug paraphernalia statutes, there is a great deal of evidence that suggests giving injection drug users access to clean syringes helps reduce the spread of blood-borne infections such as HIV. The following excerpt provides an overview of some of the legal and policy issues related to the distribution of syringes to injection drug users.

Lethal Injections: The Law, Science, and Politics of Syringe Access for Injection Drug Users
Scott Burris, Steffanie A. Strathdee, and Jon S. Vernick

37 University of San Francisco Law Review 813 (2003)

Access to sterile syringes through syringe exchange programs (SEPs) has been associated with decreased rates of needle sharing, decreased prevalence and incidence

21. The theoretical possibility that the village will enforce its ordinance against a paper clip placed next to *Rolling Stone* magazine is of no due process significance unless the possibility ripens into a prosecution.

of blood borne infections such as HIV and hepatitis B and C, and increased rates of entry into drug treatment among injection drug users (IDUs). There is no evidence that such programs increase crime, drug use or the number of discarded needles on the street. Pharmacies, syringe vending machines, and deregulating syringe access can further expand sterile syringe coverage to IDUs, thereby increasing the potential to achieve these positive public health outcomes.

Despite its public health value, however, syringe access has been politically controversial in the United States. In our political culture, driven by symbols and perceptions, improved syringe access has been painted as "soft on drugs," a retreat from zero tolerance that will be seen as an endorsement of drug use. Polls continue to show that only a little more than half of respondents support enhanced syringe access—a majority, but evidently one that is too narrow or uncommitted to counterbalance the intense symbolic force of the syringe access issue in policy-making. Syringe access, then, is quite a familiar public health policy dilemma: science and professional judgment point to an intervention that is unsettling, if not absolutely unacceptable, to a significant part of the United States public and its political leaders.

Syringe access is regulated by state law. The legal regulation of syringe access varies from state to state but takes one or more of three forms: syringe prescription laws and regulations; other pharmacy regulations or miscellaneous statutes imposing a variety of restrictions on the sale of syringes by pharmacists or others; and drug paraphernalia laws prohibiting the sale or possession of items intended to be used to consume illegal drugs. Laws on drug possession also may be applied in a manner that in practical terms regulate the possession of syringes and so must also be considered for their possible effects on syringe access.

Access to injection equipment has been regulated at the state level for many years. The hypodermic syringe came into common usage in the latter half of the nineteenth century, often as a means for injecting opiates such as morphine and heroin. As rates of opiate addiction began to increase, states responded with legislation making it more difficult for drug users to obtain syringes. New York State enacted the first such law in 1911. Among other provisions, New York's law required a written order from a physician before a syringe could be obtained. Beginning in 1915, several other states, mostly in the east, followed New York's lead and enacted their own laws limiting the availability of syringes.

Legislative efforts to restrict access to injection equipment were not limited to the early part of the past century, however. Another important flurry of activity occurred in the 1970s with the rapid adoption of state laws criminalizing the possession of certain devices, including syringes, used to inject illegal drugs. These so-called "drug paraphernalia" laws were often patterned after a Model Drug Paraphernalia Act (MDPA) written by the Drug Enforcement [Administration] in 1979 at the request of President Carter. They were originally intended to provide a means of prosecuting operators of "head shops"—stores specializing in equipment for drug users. By 1976, it was estimated that between fifteen and thirty thousand of these stores were doing an annual three billion dollar business in such items as cigarette rolling papers, bongs, and freebasing kits. Syringes were not generally mentioned in the legislative debates or court challenges to these laws, nor is it even clear that syringes were being sold in head shops. Debate about the laws usually focused on their breadth and the danger that innocent sellers of items with both legal and illegal uses (such as rolling papers or scales) might be prosecuted. In a few states, the model law was amended to explicitly exclude pharmacists, but in most states the possibility that pharmacists would be covered through the laws' reference to needles was apparently not considered. Until the emergence of HIV, these laws were seen exclusively in the context of the control of drug abuse.

HIV changed that as transmission through drug injection was recognized as a serious threat to public health. The first syringe exchange program (SEP) was introduced in Amsterdam, the Netherlands, in 1984. The program, initiated by a drug user organization whose name may loosely be translated as the Junkies' Union, was soon adopted by the Municipal Health Department of Amsterdam, where it became a fundamental component of HIV prevention activities among IDUs. In the late 1980s, SEPs were introduced in the United Kingdom, Australia, Canada, and several other European countries. Global expansion of SEPs has occurred in both developed and developing countries, including China, Russia, the Ukraine, Kyrgyzstan, Nepal, Bangladesh, India, Pakistan, and Colombia. "As of December 2000, there were at least 46 regions, countries and territories that reported having at least one SEP."

In the United States, the first SEP was introduced in 1988, in Tacoma, Washington, and spread with the help of non-governmental organizations such as the National AIDS Brigade, the North American Syringe Exchange Network, and Act-Up. Expert reviews of the science supported syringe exchange, but early commentators generally assumed that syringe exchange was illegal in the United States unless explicitly authorized by state law. By 1995, there were at least 60 SEPs operating in 46 cities in 21 states. A review of the legal strategies used to implement these SEPs found that 27 programs in ten jurisdictions had been authorized by law or court decision, or were in a state without a syringe-related law. Thirteen programs were operating without any change in law, backed by local governments exercising their legal authority to protect public health. At least nine SEPs were operating without any claim to legal authorization.

Since the beginning of the HIV epidemic, twelve states (Connecticut, Hawaii, Illinois, Maine, Minnesota, New Hampshire, New Mexico, New York, Oregon, Rhode Island, Washington, and Wisconsin) have deregulated the sale or possession of at least some number of syringes. In others, notably California, efforts at deregulation have been unsuccessful. To date, no state that has liberalized syringe access in response to HIV has rescinded the change, but change continues to be a controversial matter in states that maintain restrictive access policies.

Public health authorities recommend that injection drug users use a new, sterile syringe for every injection. Despite the continued growth of syringe exchange, and the deregulation of syringes in one-fifth of the states, the United States has consistently fallen far short of this public health goal. In the third decade of its HIV epidemic, the United States continues to debate whether and how to make syringes available to injection drug users.

Thirteen states and the Virgin Islands impose some form of syringe prescription requirement by statute. Pennsylvania requires a prescription by pharmacy board regulation, not by statute. The prescription requirement stands as a substantial barrier to syringe access in only six of these jurisdictions: California, Delaware, Massachusetts, New Jersey, Pennsylvania, and the Virgin Islands. In Florida and Virginia, a prescription is required only for minors. In Nevada, a prescription is not required for syringes to be used for asthma, diabetes, or other medical conditions; these exceptions, in combination with a favorable view of syringe sales from the pharmacy board, have reportedly led to reasonably liberal syringe access in the state. The remaining five prescription-law states—Connecticut, Illinois, New Hampshire, New York, and Maine—have partially deregulated syringes and now allow non-prescription sale and possession of syringes in limited numbers. Illinois, like Florida and Virginia, does not permit non-prescription sale to minors.

Four other types of restriction on the sale of syringes appear in state law, usually but not always within the Pharmacy Code. Twenty-two states allow only pharmacies to sell syringes. Nine require the seller to determine, or the buyer to produce information about, how the syringe will be used. Fourteen require records of some type to be kept. Eleven require the buyer to show identification. Finally, twelve states specify limits on the display of syringes in retail establishments, normally requiring that they be kept behind the counter.

The District of Columbia and every jurisdiction studied except Alaska and Puerto Rico have drug paraphernalia laws. Most of these laws were passed in the 1970s and 1980s to regulate an increasing retail trade in drug-use equipment, and closely followed a model paraphernalia law drafted by the United States Department of Justice. The typical statute defines drug paraphernalia to include all equipment, products, and materials of any kind which are used, intended for use, or designed for use to "manufacture, inject, ingest, inhale, or otherwise introduce into the human body a controlled substance" in violation of law. It then provides an exemplary list of items that could be considered drug paraphernalia in some intended uses. In the majority of states, this list includes "hypodermic syringes, needles, and other objects used, intended for use, and designed for use in parenterally injecting controlled substances into the human body." Under this definition, the status of any item as paraphernalia depends not just on the characteristics of the item itself but also on the intention or acts of the defendant. To commit a crime, the seller must not only transfer possession of the syringe, but must do so knowing of the intended drug-related use. Paraphernalia laws usually create two basic offenses:

manufacturing or distributing and possessing paraphernalia. Not every state has created both offenses. The crime is typically a misdemeanor.

Nearly all state paraphernalia laws follow the same pattern, though there are small but important differences in many states that influence the applicability of paraphernalia laws to syringes. In addition to the states . . . that have fully or partially deregulated syringes as a public health measure, a significant minority of states have provisions that, at least on paper, make it legal under some circumstances for a seller knowingly to dispense a syringe to an IDU. These exemptions . . . take several forms. Ten state paraphernalia laws explicitly or implicitly exempt the possession of syringes in at least some quantity. Indiana's statute, for example, exempts items "historically and customarily used in connection with the . . . injecting . . . of . . . lawful substances," thus, at least in theory, legalizing over-the-counter pharmacy sales of syringes. In nine states, pharmacists and in some instances other health care providers are exempt from the law. In four states with laws based on the Justice Department's model act, the drafters of the paraphernalia law chose to depart from the model and did not refer to injection or syringes in the text of the law. Although the broad definition of paraphernalia reasonably could be deemed to include syringes even without explicit reference, the decision to omit the references while otherwise adopting the Justice Department model could be read by a judge as evidence of a legislative decision not to prohibit syringe sale and possession. In a fifth state, South Carolina, the statute was not based on the model act: it does not allude to injection or syringes, and more importantly does not apply to items to be used in the consumption of heroin. In states that have both paraphernalia and prescription laws, the interaction of the two must be assessed individually.

Paraphernalia laws were broadly written to criminalize sale or possession of any item intended to be used to facilitate illegal drug use. In theory, items that are used in drug injection—like cotton and small vessels used to dissolve drugs ("cookers") and even bleach kits—are legally indistinguishable from syringes. Because items used in drug preparation have also been implicated in the spread of blood borne diseases, especially hepatitis C virus, public health agencies and syringe exchange programs have routinely distributed them along with syringes. In areas where syringe exchange has not been authorized, some agencies distribute bleach kits as an alternative harm reduction measure. With the political focus on syringe access, the potential legal ambiguity of these other activities was largely ignored. In recent years, however, there have been anecdotal reports of SEPs being deterred from offering, and IDUs being arrested for possessing, sterile cookers and cotton. Efforts to import specially designed sterile cookers that have been used in other countries' public health efforts have been affected by concern about the potential application of paraphernalia laws. The problem does not appear to be widespread, but does illustrate the potential scope of drug paraphernalia laws.

7. Pregnancy and Substance Use

Criminalizing Pregnancy
Cortney E. Lollar

92 Indiana Law Journal 947 (2017)

In July 2014, Jamillah Washington, a thirty-year-old African American woman, was arrested under a new Tennessee law allowing prosecution of a woman for assault for using illegal narcotic drugs while pregnant. Ms. Washington gave birth to a daughter who "tested positive" for marijuana and heroin. She sought treatment for her opioid addiction on three occasions during the course of her pregnancy but was turned away each time due to her pregnancy. Police reported that she admitted using heroin two days before the birth. At least ninety-five other women were prosecuted under this law prior to its sunset in June 2016.

Although Tennessee's statute was the first to explicitly criminalize the use of drugs by a pregnant woman, the law is only the most recent incarnation in a long history of states using criminal laws to punish primarily poor, often minority mothers for their behavior while pregnant. Four additional states have contemplated similar legislation since Tennessee's law went into effect. Prior to the statute's enactment, numerous states relied on generally applicable criminal statutes—criminal neglect, delivery of drugs to a minor, chemical endangerment of a child, involuntary manslaughter, and other similar statutes—to pursue prosecutions of women for using drugs during pregnancy. In the federal system, judges rely on sentencing enhancements to accomplish a similar end. For example, one federal judge recently enhanced a woman's sentence under the federal sentencing guidelines, doubling her sentence from six to twelve years, based on her use of drugs while pregnant. The judge granted the enhancement based on the prosecution's argument that a substantial risk of harm arose when "this defendant [gave] birth to a drug addicted baby."

The articulated motivation for pursuing these prosecutions is the risk of harm to the fetus, with the focus being on the short-term harms to the fetus and the long-term harms to the future child. Preventing a mother from hurting either her fetus or her child is a compelling and intuitive desire. And most of us probably feel fairly confident in our assumption that a pregnant woman's use of illegal drugs *will* cause damage, certainly to the developing fetus but likely to the child once born as well. As a result, few question the judgment of punishing a woman who engages in such behavior. After all, fetuses and newborn children are among the most vulnerable of our population. A clear message of "accountability" and moral condemnation must be sent.

Over the past thirty years, several prominent legal scholars have suggested, based on preliminary data, that the science might not support our intuitions and assumptions. However, until recently, scientists did not have the strong long-term data to support the scholars' assertions. The results of national longitudinal studies were not yet available.

As a result, the legal scholarship has not considered in depth the scientific evidence regarding the fetal and postnatal consequences of substance use by a woman during pregnancy. Counter to most of our intuitions, the science challenges the purported ill effects offered to justify the use of the criminal law to punish a pregnant woman who uses, and often is addicted to, illegal drugs.

In the vast majority of cases, exposure to drugs in utero does not result in the negative long-term effects legislators, and most of us, presume.

In fact, many behaviors in which pregnant women engage have been documented and shown to be far more damaging to a developing fetus than using illegal drugs. For example, the lawful behaviors of smoking cigarettes, taking certain prescription drugs under the supervision of a physician, and in some women, drinking alcohol, each have an equal or greater negative effect on a developing fetus than illegal drugs. Likewise, environmental factors such as household violence have a more significant impact than any drug, legal or illegal, on the health and development of a fetus and child.

The collateral consequences attributable to criminalizing a mother's use of illegal drugs are substantial. The prosecution of a woman for her behavior while pregnant tends to result in greater harm to the child, rather than less. If a pregnant woman using illegal drugs comes to the attention of law enforcement and prosecutorial authorities, odds are great that immediately after birth, her child will be taken away from her, in the name of the safety and protection of the child. Ample scientific and social science studies indicate that this removal of the child, without any evidence of actual harm, consistently results in poorer outcomes for that child, tending to cause greater long-term damage. To the extent a newborn experiences short-term withdrawal symptoms, taking her from her mother only cements the potential harmful effects of the drug.

In light of criminalization's ineffectiveness in addressing the potential harms from in utero maternal drug use, one has to question why states that use criminal statutes to prosecute pregnant women continue to pursue this course of action. At first blush, one might conclude that legislators, prosecutors, and courts are simply misguided. Perhaps they are unaware of the science and the potential negative impacts of prosecuting pregnant women and new mothers, despite the repeated entreaties of prominent doctors and medical organizations against this path.

Having reviewed the science, the demographics of pregnant drug, alcohol, and tobacco users, and the history of these prosecutions, this author concludes prosecutions of women for using drugs while pregnant are really about socioeconomics, gender, and fundamentally, race. Only when one includes and explores these factors does the narrative make sense. For example, if our society were truly concerned about harms caused by a woman's activities while pregnant, we would expect to see middle- and upper-class white women charged with child endangerment for lawfully taking prescription drugs, drinking alcohol, or smoking cigarettes while pregnant. Yet such prosecutions are rare to nonexistent. When anyone is prosecuted for their activities while pregnant, they are primarily, if not only, poor and African American women.

Almost twenty-five years ago, in the wake of the crack cocaine epidemic, troubling stories circulated about babies born "addicted to crack." Reports alleged "so-called crack babies . . . had small heads and were easily agitated and prone to tremors and bad muscle tone." Others claimed the babies were "aloof and avoided eye contact." "Crack babies" became the prototypical symbol of bad mothering. A billboard in Los Angeles in 1991 depicted a tiny African American baby, lying in a hospital incubator with tubes coming from his nostrils, limbs, and head. The caption read: "He couldn't take the hit . . . If you're pregnant, don't take drugs."

The fears of a generation of troubled children—children born with learning, emotional, and behavioral deficits who would overwhelm the school system and jails, be unable to hold a job, or form meaningful relationships—turned out to be unfounded. In fact, scientists and physicians have long suspected that the effects of cocaine use by pregnant mothers on their children are relatively small and short-term, and certainly not the "catastrophic effects" predicted. A recent large-scale longitudinal study confirmed early scientific findings. Additionally, prominent physicians and medical advocacy groups have been outspoken in asserting that babies born with these illegal drugs in their system do not tend to have lasting problems.

Despite this generally accepted professional understanding, legislatures have continued to endorse and propagate a flawed myth of maternal harm, largely based on race- and class-based ideas of motherhood, leading to laws that have little to no anchoring in medical realities.

Although Tennessee's 2014 statute was the first in the nation to explicitly criminalize the use of illegal drugs by a pregnant woman, Tennessee is certainly not the first state to prosecute a woman for this behavior. As of April 1992, approximately 167 women had been arrested on criminal charges because they used illegal drugs while pregnant. These women came from twenty-four states, although a disproportionate number of them came from four particular counties in Florida and South Carolina. None of the twenty-four states had criminal statutes aimed at punishing drug-using pregnant women; rather, prosecutors extended generally applicable criminal statutes to this group of women. Prosecutors relied on a wide range of preexisting statutes, including criminal child support laws, contributing to the delinquency of a minor, child endangerment, delivery of drugs to a minor, assault with a deadly weapon, manslaughter, and homicide. In the cases where the race of the woman could be identified, approximately 70% involved women of color.

A more recent study, analyzing data from 1973 until 2005, was published in 2011. Lynn Paltrow and Jeanne Flavin reviewed data from legal, medical, news, and other periodical databases and obtained additional information through their own involvement with cases as well as through conversations with lawyers, judges, and health care providers. Paltrow and Flavin identified 413 women against whom state action had been taken due to their behavior during pregnancy. Not all of these cases involved allegations of drug use, but the majority did—approximately 84%. Approximately 71% of the women were economically disadvantaged, and approximately 59% were women of color. African American women constituted 52% of those subject to state intervention in their pregnancies, whereas they constitute approximately 6–7% of the general population.

Strikingly, in the majority of cases, no evidence of harm to the fetus or newborn was present. Rather, in many cases, the criminal charges relied on a positive drug test or an identified "risk of harm." Often, that "risk of harm" never evolved into an actual harm. Even in cases where harm was alleged, the causal link between the pregnant woman's action or inaction and the identified harm often could not be established.

Tennessee's bill brought a new dimension to the legal landscape. Tennessee's law permitted, "prosecution of a woman for assault . . . for the illegal use of a narcotic drug . . . while pregnant, if her child is born addicted to or harmed by the narcotic drug and the addiction or harm is a result of her illegal use of a narcotic drug taken while pregnant." The statute did not define "harm," and it disregarded the medical definition of "addiction." The law allowed for an affirmative defense if "the woman actively enrolled in an addiction recovery program before the child is born, remained in the program after delivery, and successfully completed the program, regardless of whether the child was born addicted to or harmed by the narcotic drug." Although other states had tried to pass similar statutes over the past several decades, those statutes never made it through the legislative process, or they morphed into other, noncriminal laws.

Prosecutors spearheaded the legislative effort in Tennessee, telling legislators "they needed stronger penalties to control addicted women's behavior." One district attorney told a House committee the goal was to balance "deterrence with accountability and with treatment." [One] prosecutor in favor of the bill asserted that if the legislature passed the bill, it would hopefully "save the state money because these women, if they get cured of that addiction, are not going to be breaking into cars to feed that habit and then have to be housed out at the penal farm or at the Tennessee Department of Corrections or whatever the situation might warrant."

Similarly, the bill's legislative sponsor, State Representative Terri Lynn Weaver, expressed an interest in holding addicts "accountable" for their use of drugs while pregnant. According to Representative Weaver, her bill was needed in order to reach "ladies . . . who would [not] consider prenatal care. These are ladies who are strung out on heroin and cocaine, and their only next decision is how to get their next fix. . . . What they're thinking about . . . is just money for the next high."

Tennessee's bill passed convincingly in the state Senate and House with bipartisan support and backing from both white and Black lawmakers, despite a range of objections from conservatives and liberals alike. The law that passed in 2014 included a sunset provision to allow for legislators to review how the statute was working after a two-year period.

After several days of hearings in March 2016, the House Subcommittee on Criminal Justice voted, in a three-three tie, to let the law expire. The three members rejecting the law—the one Black Committee member, joined by two lawyer colleagues—expressed concern about the "unintended consequences" of the statute, primarily that the law discouraged women from seeking drug treatment early in their pregnancies. The law was allowed to sunset on June 30, 2016.

Because Tennessee's law is the only one to have explicitly criminalized the use of drugs by pregnant women, it remained under close scrutiny throughout the two years it was in force. The number of infants born with [Neonatal Abstinence Syndrome] remained about the same over the two years the law was in effect—approximately 1000 infants annually were born with NAS at the time the law went into force as well as two years later. No evidence suggested that the law itself, or the threat of being arrested under the law, prevented opioid use by pregnant women. Notably, even after the bill's passage, approximately 80% of newborns experiencing withdrawal from NAS in Tennessee were exposed to lawfully prescribed drugs, not heroin or other illegal substances. The statute did not contemplate ingestion of lawfully obtained prescriptions by a pregnant woman.

Since Tennessee passed its 2014 bill into law, four other states contemplated similar legislation. As of this writing, none of these bills has been passed into law.

Underlying the actions of the state courts, legislators, and prosecutors in their decisions to allow the pursuit of criminal charges against women for using drugs while pregnant is the intuitive belief that such drug use causes harm, or at the very least, a serious risk of harm, to both the developing fetus and the child subsequently born.

Typically, maternal prenatal substance abuse has been defined in relation to three types of addictive substances: alcohol, tobacco, and illegal drugs. According to a recent national study, approximately 5.4% of pregnant women nationwide use illicit drugs, 9.4% consume alcohol, and 15.4% smoke tobacco cigarettes. These rates have remained fairly consistent over the past decade. However, substantial overlap exists. "Approximately 32% of women who use illicit drugs during pregnancy also use alcohol and cigarettes."

Recent longitudinal studies have begun to explore pregnant women's use of legally authorized prescription drugs. Yet medications vary in their prenatal effects and scientists are only beginning to look comprehensively and comparatively at the effects of various prescriptions on fetal and childhood development. As a result, most conversations about prenatal substance abuse focus on the three substances listed in the preceding paragraph, despite increasing evidence of prescription drug use and abuse by pregnant women.

Illicit drugs constitute the smallest percentage of addictive substances pregnant women ingest. Yet, over a thirty-two-year period between 1973 and 2005, pregnant women were arrested or subjected to restrictions on physical liberty at least 348 times due to an allegation that they had used an illegal drug. Between 2005 and

December 2014, another 380 cases arose, marking a rapid acceleration in the criminalization of drug use by pregnant mothers.

Arrests and prosecutions disproportionately affect poor women and women of color, even though wealthier women and white women are as likely to use substances—including alcohol and tobacco—and far more likely than others to voluntarily report substance use during pregnancy. White pregnant women are "less likely to be screened for substance abuse compared to Black women" and are less likely to have substance use documented in their charts than both Black and Latina women. Women who seek care in public clinics and hospitals, usually women of lower socioeconomic status, also are much more likely to be screened than those of greater means who tend to visit private doctors' offices or hospitals.

Despite illicit drug use being relatively rare among pregnant women, criminal laws focus on this behavior, overlooking other maternal, paternal, and external factors that play a greater role in a fetus and child's development. Rather than rely on scientific research, our laws assess harm based on the social meaning of different drugs. As several notable scientists observed, "Illicit drugs are the most often targeted drugs in the fight against maternal substance abuse, because they are perceived to produce the most harmful side effects in both the mothers and the children." These perceptions do not always match up with reality, however.

Cocaine was the first major illegal drug to inspire the expansive and aggressive use of criminal laws to punish pregnant women for its use. Cocaine remains the drug most used by women subject to arrest or court intervention. Although initial studies suggested that children exposed to cocaine in utero were "irreparably doomed and damaged," numerous subsequent studies, including a national large-scale, longitudinal study, debunked those findings.

Now, scientists generally acknowledge that their initial suppositions and studies were incorrect. Children exposed in utero to cocaine do not end up with developmental or behavioral differences markedly distinct from similarly situated children who did not receive such exposure. Rather, studies have documented that prenatal exposure to cocaine does not have a negative effect on a child's weight, length, or head circumference, has little impact on "children's scores on nationally normed assessments of cognitive development," has not shown consistent negative effects on cognitive or psychomotor development, inhibitory control, memory, or receptive language, revealed no association with a reduction in receptive or expressive language skills, and has shown no effect on motor development. Cocaine exposure in utero has not been shown to affect toddler play or problem-solving abilities, or to cause behavioral disturbances, although there is some evidence that prenatal exposure to cocaine may contribute to difficulties with sustained attention and behavioral self-regulation starting during adolescence.

The second most commonly used drug by pregnant women who have come into contact with the justice system is methamphetamine/amphetamines. The number of pregnant women using methamphetamine while pregnant tripled between 1994 and 2006, although several studies indicate that fewer than one percent of women use methamphetamine while pregnant. The prenatal effects of methamphetamine are only beginning to be studied, and are complicated by the fact that women who use methamphetamine frequently use tobacco, alcohol, and other drugs as well, skewing the outcomes of the studies.

The National Institute of Drug Abuse is currently in the midst of a population-based longitudinal study to evaluate developmental outcomes in mothers who used amphetamines while pregnant. Early results suggest findings slightly more troubling than those found with prenatal exposure to cocaine. Although the multi-center longitudinal study indicates no cognitive differences in children exposed to methamphetamine in utero, it has revealed increased emotional reactivity, anxiety, and depression in children ages three and five. At age five, attention problems also began to manifest. By age seven-and-a-half, some of the children exhibited more aggressive, rule-breaking behavior.

However, several other indications make it less clear that methamphetamine is the source of these deficits. The study found that children prenatally exposed to methamphetamines faced other significant adversity in their early years, such as extreme poverty or a change in caregiver before the age of three, which were "strong determina[nts] of adverse behavioral outcomes in methamphetamine exposed children" and associated with behavioral and emotional control issues. Additionally, many of the women who gave birth to children with these deficits also drank alcohol and smoked cigarettes, making the specific effects of methamphetamine less certain.

Opioids come in both legal and illegal forms. They include morphine, codeine, Vicodin, Demerol, oxycodone, heroin, and methadone. Only a very small number of women nationally use opioids while pregnant, and more women abuse prescription pain relievers than illegal opiates. According to a 2008 study, 0.1% of pregnant women were estimated to have used heroin in the past thirty days, and 1% reported "nonmedical use of opioid-containing pain medication." Another study suggests the numbers are slightly higher.

One of the primary conditions associated with the use of opioids by pregnant women is Neonatal Abstinence Syndrome (NAS). Some babies exposed to opioids in utero are born with NAS, a group of treatable side effects of prenatal exposure to prescription medications and heroin. Some of the most prominent side effects include excessive and high-pitched crying, irritability, and poor sucking reflexes, among other symptoms. The condition itself has not been associated with any long-term adverse effects.

Conversely, reducing a pregnant woman's opiate intake, or forcing/encouraging her to cease the use of opioids altogether while pregnant, is much more dangerous to the fetus. In the first trimester, withdrawal can cause miscarriage. In the third trimester, premature labor or stillbirth may result. As a result, for many years, the preferred method of addressing a pregnant woman's opioid use has been maintenance of opioid intake, preferably through the use of methadone as opposed to other opioids. According to [the American Congress of Obstetricians and Gynecologists], methadone maintenance during pregnancy is "part of a comprehensive package of prenatal care." Buprenorphine, another opioid, is increasingly recommended and used in a manner similar to methadone.

Studies have not found significant differences in cognitive development between children up to five years of age exposed to methadone and those who are not, controlling for age, race, and socioeconomic status. In fact, children exposed to heroin or methadone in utero function in the normal range of mental and motor development through ages five to six. Most opioids do not carry an increased risk of birth defects, with the exception of codeine, and even those risks are fairly small.

Although tobacco and alcohol are the most common addictive substances pregnant women ingest, marijuana is the leading illegal drug. A recent study found that 3.7% of pregnant women use marijuana.

The evidence from numerous well-controlled studies concludes there are "minimal to no effects" of prenatal exposure [to marijuana]. Some evidence suggests this is because the placenta acts as a barrier, limiting exposure to THC, although the evidence is not conclusive. In utero marijuana exposure is not associated with any major fetal growth or physical abnormalities. Numerous studies have shown no association with low birth weight, gestational age, or preterm birth. Likewise, school-aged children exposed to marijuana in utero did not show any lower IQs, although some showed deficits in problem solving, memory, and attention up to the age of sixteen. This may be due to the fact that smoking marijuana produces five times the amount of carbon monoxide as tobacco smoking.

In contrast to findings indicating relatively few harmful effects to a fetus from most illegal drugs, the negative effects of excessive alcohol consumption during pregnancy are well documented and established, yet not criminalized. Medical experts continue to assert that both alcohol and tobacco are the most dangerous addictive drugs to a developing fetus. Fetal Alcohol Syndrome (FAS) has been recognized in medical literature since 1968, and it contributes to slow growth, damage to the nervous system, facial abnormalities, and developmental delays. Although "high levels" of alcohol consumption are the undisputed cause of FAS, what constitutes a "high level" is unclear. Fetal Alcohol Spectrum Disorder (FASD), which is much more prevalent than FAS, "encompasses all patients displaying some of the clinical features of fetal alcohol exposure." The syndromes falling under the FASD umbrella include cognitive deficits, growth retardation, memory deficits, poor motor skills, facial abnormalities, and behavioral problems.

Despite the well-documented effects and presence of FAS and FASD, only 5–10% of women who drink during pregnancy give birth to children manifesting these syndromes. Numerous factors contribute to the presence or absence of FAS/FASD, including poor nutrition and health, the quantity of alcohol consumed over the course of the pregnancy, frequency and duration of alcohol exposure, and the developmental stage of the fetus at the time of consumption. Additionally, recent genetic studies have revealed that certain genes are more susceptible to the negative effects of alcohol than others.

Notwithstanding the commonly known and identifiable effects of FAS and FASD, to this author's knowledge, no state has prosecuted a woman for consuming alcohol while pregnant, nor has any legislature criminalized the intake of alcohol by pregnant women. In forty-one of 348, or about 11%, of identifiable cases of arrest or forced legal intervention between 1973 and 2005, alcohol consumption was mentioned, but only in addition to other illegal drug use.

Of the three categories of addictive substances outlined above, tobacco use is the most prevalent among pregnant women, and, research would suggest, the most dangerous. Tobacco is one of the more harmful addictive substances on the fetus. As one expert noted, "[I]f substances were ranked in terms of the severity of their devastating consequences to fetal and maternal health, the two legal substances of alcohol and tobacco would likely decidedly trump the negative consequences associated with illicit substances such as cocaine, heroin, and marijuana."

Cigarette smoke contains approximately 4000 chemical compounds, including carbon monoxide, approximately thirty of which are dangerous to the fetus. Cigarette smoke reduces uterine blood flow by up to 38%, results in low birth weight, and interferes with normal placental function and fetal development, particularly the developing nervous system and brain. Some studies have linked prenatal nicotine exposure to sudden infant death syndrome (SIDS) as well as short- and longer-term behavioral and cognitive problems and effects on IQ and attention deficits.

Despite its known dangers, tobacco use is not illegal for pregnant women, and, as with alcohol, neither legislators nor prosecutors have sought to criminalize or prosecute women for using tobacco while pregnant. In a review of cases involving forced legal intervention of pregnant women, the fact that a woman smoked cigarettes was mentioned in only 3% of cases.

Proponents of Tennessee's law argued that it would "save the state money because these women, if they get cured of that addiction" would no longer be committing crimes. In a similar vein, the statute provided for an affirmative defense for women who participated in an addiction recovery program. The threat of criminal punishment under Tennessee's law might theoretically provide an incentive for pregnant women to seek treatment. But for the threat to be effective, quality treatment programs would need to be easily accessible. In most parts of the country, however, there is a shortage of drug treatment programs. A 2016 Democratic Senate staff report described the problem:

> This country is the midst of an epidemic, yet there is a devastating lack of capacity to treat those seeking help. Several recent studies have revealed that upwards of 80 percent of people in need of treatment are unable to access services—with many put on waiting lists for weeks or even months before

> there is capacity to care for them. More than 30 million people live in counties that do not have a single provider of medication assisted treatment. The vast majority of these are rural counties, where mental and behavioral health professionals are also scarce, leaving people in many regions of the U.S. without options for treatment.

Democratic Staff of the Senate Committee on Finance, *Dying Waiting for Treatment: The Opioid Use Disorder Treatment Gap and the Need for Funding* 1 (2016).

F. Constitutional Limitations on the Criminalization of Drug Use and Addiction

From the Fourth Amendment to the scope of Congress' Commerce power, drug laws and their enforcement have impacted a range of constitutional provisions. Constitutional cases involving drug laws appear throughout this book. This section focuses on the constitutional boundaries of the criminalization of drug use and addiction. With well over one million drug possession arrests every year, the constitutionality of making drug possession a crime might seem self-evident. But in the 1968 case *Powell v. Texas*, four members of the United States Supreme Court argued in dissent that punishing a person addicted to drugs for conduct which is "part of the pattern of his disease" is inconsistent with the Eighth Amendment. If just one more Justice had adopted the dissent's view in *Powell*, the constitutionality of prosecuting persons with substance use disorder for possession would have been in serious doubt. Six years before *Powell*, in *Robinson v. California*, a majority of the Court struck down a law that made it a crime to "be addicted to the use of narcotics."

1. The Prohibition Against "Status" Crimes

Robinson v. California

United State Supreme Court
370 U.S. 660 (1962)

Mr. Justice Stewart delivered the opinion of the Court.

A California statute makes it a criminal offense for a person to "be addicted to the use of narcotics." This appeal draws into question the constitutionality of that provision of the state law, as construed by the California courts in the present case.

The appellant was convicted after a jury trial in the Municipal Court of Los Angeles. The evidence against him was given by two Los Angeles police officers. Officer Brown testified that he had had occasion to examine the appellant's arms one evening on a street in Los Angeles some four months before the trial. The officer testified that at that time he had observed "scar tissue and discoloration on the inside" of the appellant's right arm, and "what appeared to be numerous needle marks and a scab which was approximately three inches below the crook of the elbow" on the appellant's left arm. The officer also testified that the appellant under questioning had admitted to the occasional use of narcotics.

Officer Lindquist testified that he had examined the appellant the following morning in the Central Jail in Los Angeles. The officer stated that at that time he had observed discolorations and scabs on the appellant's arms, and he identified photographs which had been taken of the appellant's arms shortly after his arrest the night before. Based upon more than ten years of experience as a member of the Narcotic Division of the Los Angeles Police Department, the witness gave his opinion that "these marks and the discoloration were the result of the injection of hypodermic needles into the tissue into the vein that was not sterile." He stated that the scabs were several days old at the time of his examination, and that the appellant was neither under the influence of narcotics nor suffering withdrawal symptoms at the time he saw him. This witness also testified that the appellant had admitted using narcotics in the past.

The appellant testified in his own behalf, denying the alleged conversations with the police officers and denying that he had ever used narcotics or been addicted to their use. He explained the marks on his arms as resulting from an allergic condition contracted during his military service. His testimony was corroborated by two witnesses.

The jury returned a verdict finding the appellant "guilty of the offense charged." An appeal was taken to the Appellate Department of the Los Angeles County Superior Court, "the highest court of a State in which a decision could be had" in this case. Although expressing some doubt as to the constitutionality of "the crime of being a narcotic addict," the reviewing court in an unreported opinion affirmed the judgment of conviction, citing two of its own previous unreported decisions which had upheld the constitutionality of the statute. We noted probable jurisdiction of this appeal because it squarely presents the issue whether the statute as construed by the California courts in this case is repugnant to the Fourteenth Amendment of the Constitution.

The broad power of a State to regulate the narcotic drugs traffic within its borders is not here in issue. More than forty years ago, in *Whipple v. Martinson,* 256 U.S. 41, this Court explicitly recognized the validity of that power: "There can be no question of the authority of the State in the exercise of its police power to regulate the administration, sale, prescription and use of dangerous and habit-forming drugs. . . . The right to exercise this power is so manifest in the interest of the public health and welfare, that it is unnecessary to enter upon a discussion of it beyond saying that it is too firmly established to be successfully called in question."

Such regulation, it can be assumed, could take a variety of valid forms. A State might impose criminal sanctions, for example, against the unauthorized manufacture, prescription, sale, purchase, or possession of narcotics within its borders. In the interest of discouraging the violation of such laws, or in the interest of the general health or welfare of its inhabitants, a State might establish a program of compulsory treatment for those addicted to narcotics.[7] Such a program of treatment might require periods of involuntary confinement. And penal sanctions might be imposed for failure to comply with established compulsory treatment procedures. Cf. *Jacobson v. Massachusetts*, 197 U.S. 11. Or a State might choose to attack the evils of narcotics traffic on broader fronts also—through public health education, for example, or by efforts to ameliorate the economic and social conditions under which those evils might be thought to flourish. In short, the range of valid choice which a State might make in this area is undoubtedly a wide one, and the wisdom of any particular choice within the allowable spectrum is not for us to decide. Upon that premise we turn to the California law in issue here.

It would be possible to construe the statute under which the appellant was convicted as one which is operative only upon proof of the actual use of narcotics within the State's jurisdiction. But the California courts have not so construed this law. Although there was evidence in the present case that the appellant had used narcotics in Los Angeles, the jury were instructed that they could convict him even if they disbelieved that evidence. The appellant could be convicted, they were told, if they found simply that the appellant's "status" or "chronic condition" was that of being "addicted to the use of narcotics." And it is impossible to know from the jury's verdict that the defendant was not convicted upon precisely such a finding.

This statute, therefore, is not one which punishes a person for the use of narcotics, for their purchase, sale or possession, or for antisocial or disorderly behavior resulting from their administration. It is not a law which even purports to provide or require medical treatment. Rather, we deal with a statute which makes the "status" of narcotic addiction a criminal offense, for which the offender may be prosecuted "at any time before he reforms." California has said that a person can be continuously guilty of this offense, whether or not he has ever used or possessed any narcotics within the State, and whether or not he has been guilty of any antisocial behavior there.

It is unlikely that any State at this moment in history would attempt to make it a criminal offense for a person to be mentally ill, or a leper, or to be afflicted with a venereal disease. A State might determine that the general health and welfare require that the victims of these and other human afflictions be dealt with by compulsory treatment, involving quarantine, confinement, or sequestration. But, in the light of contemporary human knowledge, a law which made a criminal offense of such a disease would doubtless be universally thought to be an infliction of cruel and unusual punishment in violation of the Eighth and Fourteenth Amendments.

We cannot but consider the statute before us as of the same category. In this Court counsel for the State recognized that narcotic addiction is an illness.[8] Indeed,

---

7. California appears to have established just such a program in §§ 5350–5361 of its Welfare and Institutions Code. The record contains no explanation of why the civil procedures authorized by this legislation were not utilized in the present case.

8. In its brief the appellee stated: "Of course it is generally conceded that a narcotic addict, particularly one addicted to the use of heroin, is in a state of mental and physical illness. So is an

it is apparently an illness which may be contracted innocently or involuntarily.[9] We hold that a state law which imprisons a person thus afflicted as a criminal, even though he has never touched any narcotic drug within the State or been guilty of any irregular behavior there, inflicts a cruel and unusual punishment in violation of the Fourteenth Amendment. To be sure, imprisonment for ninety days is not, in the abstract, a punishment which is either cruel or unusual. But the question cannot be considered in the abstract. Even one day in prison would be a cruel and unusual punishment for the "crime" of having a common cold.

We are not unmindful that the vicious evils of the narcotics traffic have occasioned the grave concern of government. There are, as we have said, countless fronts on which those evils may be legitimately attacked. We deal in this case only with an individual provision of a particularized local law as it has so far been interpreted by the California courts.

Reversed.

Mr. Justice Harlan, concurring.

I am not prepared to hold that on the present state of medical knowledge it is completely irrational and hence unconstitutional for a State to conclude that narcotics addiction is something other than an illness nor that it amounts to cruel and unusual punishment for the State to subject narcotics addicts to its criminal law. Insofar as addiction may be identified with the use or possession of narcotics within the State (or, I would suppose, without the State), in violation of local statutes prohibiting such acts, it may surely be reached by the State's criminal law. But in this case the trial court's instructions permitted the jury to find the appellant guilty on no more proof than that he was present in California while he was addicted to narcotics. Since addiction alone cannot reasonably be thought to amount to more than a compelling propensity to use narcotics, the effect of this instruction was to authorize criminal punishment for a bare desire to commit a criminal act.

If the California statute reaches this type of conduct, and for present purposes we must accept the trial court's construction as binding, it is an arbitrary imposition which exceeds the power that a State may exercise in enacting its criminal law. Accordingly, I agree that the application of the California statute was unconstitutional in this case and join the judgment of reversal.

Mr. Justice Clark, dissenting.

The Court finds § 11721 of California's Health and Safety Code, making it an offense to "be addicted to the use of narcotics," violative of due process as "a cruel and unusual punishment." I cannot agree.

---

alcoholic." Thirty-seven years ago this Court recognized that persons addicted to narcotics "are diseased and proper subjects for [medical] treatment." *Linder v. United States,* 268 U.S. 5, 18.

9. Not only may addiction innocently result from the use of medically prescribed narcotics, but a person may even be a narcotics addict from the moment of his birth. See Schneck, Narcotic Withdrawal Symptoms in the Newborn Infant Resulting from Maternal Addiction, 52 Journal of Pediatrics 584 (1958).

The statute must first be placed in perspective. California has a comprehensive and enlightened program for the control of narcotism based on the overriding policy of prevention and cure. It is the product of an extensive investigation made in the mid-Fifties by a committee of distinguished scientists, doctors, law enforcement officers and laymen appointed by the then Attorney General, now Governor, of California. The committee filed a detailed study entitled "Report on Narcotic Addiction" which was given considerable attention. No recommendation was made therein for the repeal of § 11721, and the State Legislature in its discretion continued the policy of that section.

Apart from prohibiting specific acts such as the purchase, possession and sale of narcotics, California has taken certain legislative steps in regard to the status of being a narcotic addict—a condition commonly recognized as a threat to the State and to the individual. The Code deals with this problem in realistic stages. At its incipiency narcotic addiction is handled under § 11721 of the Health and Safety Code which is at issue here. It provides that a person found to be addicted to the use of narcotics shall serve a term in the county jail of not less than 90 days nor more than one year, with the minimum 90-day confinement applying in all cases without exception. Provision is made for parole with periodic tests to detect readdiction.

Where narcotic addiction has progressed beyond the incipient, volitional stage, California provides for commitment of three months to two years in a state hospital. For the purposes of this provision, a narcotic addict is defined as "any person who habitually takes or otherwise uses *to the extent of having lost the power of self-control* any opium, morphine, cocaine, or other narcotic drug as defined in Article 1 of Chapter 1 of Division 10 of the Health and Safety Code."

This proceeding is clearly civil in nature with a purpose of rehabilitation and cure. Significantly, if it is found that a person committed under § 5355 will not receive substantial benefit from further hospital treatment and is not dangerous to society, he may be discharged—but only after a minimum confinement of three months.

The majority strikes down the conviction primarily on the grounds that petitioner was denied due process by the imposition of criminal penalties for nothing more than being in a status. This viewpoint is premised upon the theme that § 11721 is a "criminal" provision authorizing a punishment, for the majority admits that "a State might establish a program of compulsory treatment for those addicted to narcotics" which "might require periods of involuntary confinement." I submit that California has done exactly that. The majority's error is in instructing the California Legislature that hospitalization is the *only treatment* for narcotics addiction—that anything less is a punishment denying due process. California has found otherwise after a study which I suggest was more extensive than that conducted by the Court. Even in California's program for hospital commitment of nonvolitional narcotic addicts—which the majority approves—it is recognized that some addicts will not respond to or do not need hospital treatment. As to these persons its provisions are identical to those of § 11721—confinement for a period of not less than 90 days. Section 11721 provides this confinement as treatment for the volitional addicts to whom its provisions apply, in addition to parole with frequent tests to detect and prevent further use of drugs. The fact that § 11721 might be labeled "criminal" seems irrelevant,[1] not only to the majority's own "treatment" test but to the "concept of ordered liberty" to which the States must attain under the Fourteenth Amendment. The test is the overall purpose and effect of a State's act, and I submit that California's program relative to narcotic addicts—including both the "criminal" and "civil" provisions—is inherently one of treatment and lies well within the power of a State.

However, the case in support of the judgment below need not rest solely on this reading of California law. For even if the overall statutory scheme is ignored and a purpose and effect of punishment is attached to § 11721, that provision still does not violate the Fourteenth Amendment. The majority acknowledges, as it must, that a State can punish persons who purchase, possess or use narcotics. Although none of these acts are harmful to society *in themselves*, the State constitutionally may attempt to deter and prevent them through punishment because of the grave threat of future harmful conduct which they pose. Narcotics addiction—including the incipient, volitional addiction to which this provision speaks—is no different. California courts have taken judicial notice that "the inordinate use of a narcotic drug tends to create an irresistible craving and forms a habit for its continued use until one becomes an addict, and he respects no convention or obligation and will lie, steal, or use any other base means to gratify his passion for the drug, being lost to all considerations of duty or social position." Can this Court deny the legislative and judicial judgment of California that incipient, volitional narcotic addiction poses a threat of serious crime similar to the threat inherent in the purchase or possession of narcotics? And if such a threat is inherent in addiction, can this Court say that California is powerless to deter it by punishment?

The argument that the statute constitutes a cruel and unusual punishment is governed by the discussion above. Properly construed, the statute provides a treatment rather than a punishment. But even if interpreted as penal, the sanction of incarceration for 3 to 12 months is not unreasonable when applied to a person who has voluntarily placed himself in a condition posing a serious threat to the State. Under either theory, its provisions for 3 to 12 months' confinement can hardly be deemed unreasonable when compared to the provisions for 3 to 24 months' confinement under § 5355 which the majority approves.

I would affirm the judgment.

Mr. Justice White, dissenting.

If appellant's conviction rested upon sheer status, condition or illness or if he was convicted for being an addict who had lost his power of self-control, I would have other thoughts about this case. But this record presents neither situation. And

1. Any reliance upon the "stigma" of a misdemeanor conviction in this context is misplaced, as it would hardly be different from the stigma of a civil commitment for narcotics addiction.

I believe the Court has departed from its wise rule of not deciding constitutional questions except where necessary and from its equally sound practice of construing state statutes, where possible, in a manner saving their constitutionality.

I am not at all ready to place the use of narcotics beyond the reach of the States' criminal laws. I do not consider appellant's conviction to be a punishment for having an illness or for simply being in some status or condition, but rather a conviction for the regular, repeated or habitual use of narcotics immediately prior to his arrest and in violation of the California law. As defined by the trial court,[2] addiction *is* the regular use of narcotics and can be proved only by evidence of such use. To find addiction in this case the jury had to believe that appellant had frequently used narcotics in the recent past.[3]

The Court has not merely tidied up California's law by removing some irritating vestige of an outmoded approach to the control of narcotics. At the very least, it has effectively removed California's power to deal effectively with the recurring case under the statute where there is ample evidence of use but no evidence of the precise location of use. Beyond this it has cast serious doubt upon the power of any State to forbid the use of narcotics under threat of criminal punishment. I cannot believe that the Court would forbid the application of the criminal laws to the use of narcotics under any circumstances. But the States, as well as the Federal Government, are now on notice. They will have to await a final answer in another case.

I respectfully dissent.

Powell v. Texas

Supreme Court of the United States
392 U.S. 514 (1968)

Mr. Justice Marshall announced the judgment of the Court and delivered an opinion in which The Chief Justice, Mr. Justice Black, and Mr. Justice Harlan join.

In late December 1966, appellant was arrested and charged with being found in a state of intoxication in a public place, in violation of Texas Penal Code, Art. 477, which reads as follows:

---

2. The court instructed the jury that, "The word 'addicted' means, strongly disposed to some taste or practice or habituated, especially to drugs. In order to inquire as to whether a person is addicted to the use of narcotics is in effect an inquiry as to his habit in that regard. . . . To use them often or daily is, according to the ordinary acceptance of those words, to use them habitually."

3. This is not a case where a defendant is convicted "even though he has never touched any narcotic drug within the State or been guilty of any irregular behavior there." The evidence was that appellant lived and worked in Los Angeles. He admitted before trial that he had used narcotics for three or four months, three or four times a week, usually at his place with his friends. He stated to the police that he had last used narcotics at 54th and Central in the City of Los Angeles on January 27, 8 days before his arrest. According to the State's expert, no needle mark or scab found on appellant's arms was newer than 3 days old and the most recent mark might have been as old as 10 days, which was consistent with appellant's own pretrial admissions. The State's evidence was that appellant had used narcotics at least 7 times in the 15 days immediately preceding his arrest.

"Whoever shall get drunk or be found in a state of intoxication in any public place, or at any private house except his own, shall be fined not exceeding one hundred dollars."

Appellant was tried in the Corporation Court of Austin, Texas, found guilty, and fined $20. He appealed to the County Court at Law No. 1 of Travis County, Texas, where a trial *de novo* was held. His counsel urged that appellant was "afflicted with the disease of chronic alcoholism," that "his appearance in public [while drunk was] . . . not of his own volition," and therefore that to punish him criminally for that conduct would be cruel and unusual, in violation of the Eighth and Fourteenth Amendments to the United States Constitution.

The trial judge in the county court, sitting without a jury ruled as a matter of law that chronic alcoholism was not a defense to the charge. He found appellant guilty, and fined him $50. There being no further right to appeal within the Texas judicial system, appellant appealed to this Court.

Despite the comparatively primitive state of our knowledge on the subject, it cannot be denied that the destructive use of alcoholic beverages is one of our principal social and public health problems. The lowest current informed estimate places the number of "alcoholics" in America (definitional problems aside) at 4,000,000, and most authorities are inclined to put the figure considerably higher. The problem is compounded by the fact that a very large percentage of the alcoholics in this country are "invisible" — they possess the means to keep their drinking problems secret, and the traditionally uncharitable attitude of our society toward alcoholics causes many of them to refrain from seeking treatment from any source. Nor can it be gainsaid that the legislative response to this enormous problem has in general been inadequate.

There is as yet no known generally effective method for treating the vast number of alcoholics in our society. Some individual alcoholics have responded to particular forms of therapy with remissions of their symptomatic dependence upon the drug. But just as there is no agreement among doctors and social workers with respect to the causes of alcoholism, there is no consensus as to why particular treatments have been effective in particular cases and there is no generally agreed-upon approach to the problem of treatment on a large scale. Most psychiatrists are apparently of the opinion that alcoholism is far more difficult to treat than other forms of behavioral disorders, and some believe it is impossible to cure by means of psychotherapy; indeed, the medical profession as a whole, and psychiatrists in particular, have been severely criticized for the prevailing reluctance to undertake the treatment of drinking problems. Thus it is entirely possible that, even were the manpower and facilities available for a full-scale attack upon chronic alcoholism, we would find ourselves unable to help the vast bulk of our "visible" — let alone our "invisible" — alcoholic population.

However, facilities for the attempted treatment of indigent alcoholics are woefully lacking throughout the country. It would be tragic to return large numbers of helpless, sometimes dangerous and frequently unsanitary inebriates to the streets of our cities without even the opportunity to sober up adequately which a brief jail term provides. Presumably no State or city will tolerate such a state of affairs. Yet the medical profession cannot, and does not, tell us with any assurance that, even if the buildings, equipment and trained personnel were made available, it could provide anything more than slightly higher-class jails for our indigent habitual inebriates. Thus we run the grave risk that nothing will be accomplished beyond the hanging of a new sign—reading "hospital"—over one wing of the jailhouse.

One virtue of the criminal process is, at least, that the duration of penal incarceration typically has some outside statutory limit; this is universally true in the case of petty offenses, such as public drunkenness, where jail terms are quite short on the whole. "Therapeutic civil commitment" lacks this feature; one is typically committed until one is "cured." Thus, to do otherwise than affirm might subject indigent alcoholics to the risk that they may be locked up for an indefinite period of time under the same conditions as before, with no more hope than before of receiving effective treatment and no prospect of periodic "freedom."[24]

Faced with this unpleasant reality, we are unable to assert that the use of the criminal process as a means of dealing with the public aspects of problem drinking can never be defended as rational. The picture of the penniless drunk propelled aimlessly and endlessly through the law's "revolving door" of arrest, incarceration, release and re-arrest is not a pretty one. But before we condemn the present practice across-the-board, perhaps we ought to be able to point to some clear promise of a better world for these unfortunate people. Unfortunately, no such promise has yet been forthcoming. If, in addition to the absence of a coherent approach to the problem of treatment, we consider the almost complete absence of facilities and manpower for the implementation of a rehabilitation program, it is difficult to say in the present context that the criminal process is utterly lacking in social value. This Court has never held that anything in the Constitution requires that penal sanctions be designed solely to achieve therapeutic or rehabilitative effects, and it can hardly be said with assurance that incarceration serves such purposes any better for the general run of criminals than it does for public drunks.

Appellant claims that his conviction on the facts of this case would violate the Cruel and Unusual Punishment Clause of the Eighth Amendment as applied to the States through the Fourteenth Amendment. The primary purpose of that clause

---

24. Counsel for *amici curiae* ACLU et al., who has been extremely active in the recent spate of litigation dealing with public intoxication statutes and the chronic inebriate, recently told an annual meeting of the National Council on Alcoholism:

"We have not fought for two years to extract DeWitt Easter, Joe Driver, and their colleagues from jail, only to have them involuntarily committed for an even longer period of time, with no assurance of appropriate rehabilitative help and treatment.... The euphemistic name 'civil commitment' can easily hide nothing more than permanent incarceration.... I would caution those who might rush headlong to adopt civil commitment procedures and remind them that just as difficult legal problems exist there as with the ordinary jail sentence."

has always been considered, and properly so, to be directed at the method or kind of punishment imposed for the violation of criminal statutes; the nature of the conduct made criminal is ordinarily relevant only to the fitness of the punishment imposed.

Appellant, however, seeks to come within the application of the Cruel and Unusual Punishment Clause announced in *Robinson v. California,* 370 U.S. 660 (1962), which involved a state statute making it a crime to "be addicted to the use of narcotics." This Court held there that "a state law which imprisons a person thus afflicted [with narcotic addiction] as a criminal, even though he has never touched any narcotic drug within the State or been guilty of any irregular behavior there, inflicts a cruel and unusual punishment. . . ."

On its face the present case does not fall within that holding, since appellant was convicted, not for being a chronic alcoholic, but for being in public while drunk on a particular occasion. The State of Texas thus has not sought to punish a mere status, as California did in *Robinson;* nor has it attempted to regulate appellant's behavior in the privacy of his own home. Rather, it has imposed upon appellant a criminal sanction for public behavior which may create substantial health and safety hazards, both for appellant and for members of the general public, and which offends the moral and esthetic sensibilities of a large segment of the community. This seems a far cry from convicting one for being an addict, being a chronic alcoholic, being "mentally ill, or a leper. . . ."

Robinson so viewed brings this Court but a very small way into the substantive criminal law. And unless *Robinson* is so viewed it is difficult to see any limiting principle that would serve to prevent this Court from becoming, under the aegis of the Cruel and Unusual Punishment Clause, the ultimate arbiter of the standards of criminal responsibility, in diverse areas of the criminal law, throughout the country.

It is suggested in dissent that *Robinson* stands for the "simple" but "subtle" principle that "[criminal] penalties may not be inflicted upon a person for being in a condition he is powerless to change." In that view, appellant's "condition" of public intoxication was "occasioned by a compulsion symptomatic of the disease" of chronic alcoholism, and thus, apparently, his behavior lacked the critical element of *mens rea.* Whatever may be the merits of such a doctrine of criminal responsibility, it surely cannot be said to follow from *Robinson.* The entire thrust of *Robinson*'s interpretation of the Cruel and Unusual Punishment Clause is that criminal penalties may be inflicted only if the accused has committed some act, has engaged in some behavior, which society has an interest in preventing, or perhaps in historical common law terms, has committed some *actus reus.* It thus does not deal with the question of whether certain conduct cannot constitutionally be punished because it is, in some sense, "involuntary" or "occasioned by a compulsion."

Likewise, as the dissent acknowledges, there is a substantial definitional distinction between a "status," as in *Robinson,* and a "condition," which is said to be involved in this case. Whatever may be the merits of an attempt to distinguish between behavior and a condition, it is perfectly clear that the crucial element in this case, so far as the dissent is concerned, is whether or not appellant can legally be held responsible for his appearance in public in a state of intoxication. The only relevance of *Robinson* to this issue is that because the Court interpreted the statute there involved as making a "status" criminal, it was able to suggest that the statute would cover even a situation in which addiction had been acquired involuntarily. That this factor was not determinative in the case is shown by the fact that there was no indication of how Robinson himself had become an addict.

Ultimately, then, the most troubling aspects of this case, were *Robinson* to be extended to meet it, would be the scope and content of what could only be a constitutional doctrine of criminal responsibility. In dissent it is urged that the decision could be limited to conduct which is "a characteristic and involuntary part of the pattern of the disease as it afflicts" the particular individual, and that "[it] is not foreseeable" that it would be applied "in the case of offenses such as driving a car while intoxicated, assault, theft, or robbery." That is limitation by fiat. In the first place, nothing in the logic of the dissent would limit its application to chronic alcoholics. If Leroy Powell cannot be convicted of public intoxication, it is difficult to see how a State can convict an individual for murder, if that individual, while exhibiting normal behavior in all other respects, suffers from a "compulsion" to kill, which is an "exceedingly strong influence," but "not completely overpowering." Even if we limit our consideration to chronic alcoholics, it would seem impossible to confine the principle within the arbitrary bounds which the dissent seems to envision.

Affirmed.

Mr. Justice Black, whom Mr. Justice Harlan joins, concurring.

While I agree that the grounds set forth in Mr. Justice Marshall's opinion are sufficient to require affirmance of the judgment here, I wish to amplify my reasons for concurring.

The rule of constitutional law urged by appellant is not required by *Robinson v. California*, 370 U.S. 660 (1962). In that case we held that a person could not be punished for the mere status of being a narcotics addict. We explicitly limited our holding to the situation where no conduct of any kind is involved, stating:

"We hold that a state law which imprisons a person thus afflicted as a criminal, *even though he has never touched any narcotic drug within the State or been guilty of any irregular behavior there,* inflicts a cruel and unusual punishment in violation of the Fourteenth Amendment." (Emphasis added.)

The argument is made that appellant comes within the terms of our holding in *Robinson* because being drunk in public is a mere status or "condition." Despite this many-faceted use of the concept of "condition," this argument would require converting *Robinson* into a case protecting actual behavior, a step we explicitly refused to take in that decision.

A different question, I admit, is whether our attempt in *Robinson* to limit our holding to pure status crimes, involving no conduct whatever, was a sound one. I believe it was. Although some of our objections to the statute in *Robinson* are equally applicable to statutes that punish conduct "symptomatic" of a disease, any attempt to explain *Robinson* as based solely on the lack of voluntariness encounters a number of logical difficulties.[3] Other problems raised by status crimes are in no way involved when the State attempts to punish for conduct, and these other problems were, in my view, the controlling aspects of our decision.

Punishment for a status is particularly obnoxious, and in many instances can reasonably be called cruel and unusual, because it involves punishment for a mere propensity, a desire to commit an offense; the mental element is not simply one part of the crime but may constitute all of it. This is a situation universally sought to be avoided in our criminal law; the fundamental requirement that some action be proved is solidly established even for offenses most heavily based on propensity, such as attempt, conspiracy, and recidivist crimes. In fact, one eminent authority has found only one isolated instance, in all of Anglo-American jurisprudence, in which criminal responsibility was imposed in the absence of any act at all.

The reasons for this refusal to permit conviction without proof of an act are difficult to spell out, but they are nonetheless perceived and universally expressed in our criminal law. Evidence of propensity can be considered relatively unreliable and more difficult for a defendant to rebut; the requirement of a specific act thus provides some protection against false charges. See 4 Blackstone, Commentaries 21. Perhaps more fundamental is the difficulty of distinguishing, in the absence of any conduct, between desires of the day-dream variety and fixed intentions that may pose a real threat to society; extending the criminal law to cover both types of desire would be unthinkable, since "[there] can hardly be anyone who has never thought evil. When a desire is inhibited it may find expression in fantasy; but it would be absurd to condemn this natural psychological mechanism as illegal."

In contrast, crimes that require the State to prove that the defendant actually committed some proscribed act involve none of these special problems. In addition, the question whether an act is "involuntary" is, as I have already indicated, an inherently elusive question, and one which the State may, for good reasons, wish to regard as irrelevant. In light of all these considerations, our limitation of our *Robinson* holding to pure status crimes seems to me entirely proper.

The rule of constitutional law urged upon us by appellant would have a revolutionary impact on the criminal law, and any possible limits proposed for the rule would be wholly illusory. If the original boundaries of *Robinson* are to be discarded,

3. Although we noted in *Robinson* that narcotics addiction apparently is an illness that can be contracted innocently or involuntarily, we barred punishment for addiction even when it could be proved that the defendant had voluntarily become addicted. And we compared addiction to the status of having a common cold, a condition that most people can either avoid or quickly cure when it is important enough for them to do so.

any new limits too would soon fall by the wayside and the Court would be forced to hold the States powerless to punish any conduct that could be shown to result from a "compulsion," in the complex, psychological meaning of that term.

[E]ven if we were to limit any holding in this field to "compulsions" that are "symptomatic" of a "disease," in the words of the findings of the trial court, the sweep of that holding would still be startling. Such a ruling would make it clear beyond any doubt that a narcotics addict could not be punished for "being" in possession of drugs or, for that matter, for "being" guilty of using them.

I would confess the limits of my own ability to answer the age-old questions of the criminal law's ethical foundations and practical effectiveness. I would hold that *Robinson* v. *California* establishes a firm and impenetrable barrier to the punishment of persons who, whatever their bare desires and propensities, have committed no proscribed wrongful act. But I would refuse to plunge from the concrete and almost universally recognized premises of *Robinson* into the murky problems raised by the insistence that chronic alcoholics cannot be punished for public drunkenness, problems that no person, whether layman or expert, can claim to understand, and with consequences that no one can safely predict. I join in affirmance of this conviction.

Mr. Justice White, concurring in the result.

If it cannot be a crime to have an irresistible compulsion to use narcotics, *Robinson v. California,* 370 U.S. 660, I do not see how it can constitutionally be a crime to yield to such a compulsion. Punishing an addict for using drugs convicts for addiction under a different name. Distinguishing between the two crimes is like forbidding criminal conviction for being sick with flu or epilepsy but permitting punishment for running a fever or having a convulsion. Unless *Robinson* is to be abandoned, the use of narcotics by an addict must be beyond the reach of the criminal law. Similarly, the chronic alcoholic with an irresistible urge to consume alcohol should not be punishable for drinking or for being drunk.

Powell's conviction was for the different crime of being drunk in a public place. Thus even if Powell was compelled to drink, and so could not constitutionally be convicted for drinking, his conviction in this case can be invalidated only if there is a constitutional basis for saying that he may not be punished for being in public while drunk. The statute involved here, which aims at keeping drunks off the street for their own welfare and that of others, is not challenged on the ground that it interferes unconstitutionally with the right to frequent public places. No question is raised about applying this statute to the nonchronic drunk, who has no compulsion to drink, who need not drink to excess, and who could have arranged to do his drinking in private or, if he began drinking in public, could have removed himself at an appropriate point on the path toward complete inebriation.

Whether or not Powell established that he could not have resisted becoming drunk on December 19, 1966, nothing in the record indicates that he could not have done his drinking in private or that he was so inebriated at the time that he had lost control of his movements and wandered into the public street. Indeed, the evidence in the record strongly suggests that Powell could have drunk at home and made plans while sober to prevent ending up in a public place. Powell had a home and wife, and if there were reasons why he had to drink in public or be drunk there, they do not appear in the record.

It is unnecessary to pursue at this point the further definition of the circumstances or the state of intoxication which might bar conviction of a chronic alcoholic for being drunk in a public place. For the purposes of this case, it is necessary to say only that Powell showed nothing more than that he was to some degree compelled to drink and that he was drunk at the time of his arrest. He made no showing that he was unable to stay off the streets on the night in question.[5]

Because Powell did not show that his conviction offended the Constitution, I concur in the judgment affirming the Travis County court.

Mr. Justice Fortas, with whom Mr. Justice Douglas, Mr. Justice Brennan, and Mr. Justice Stewart join, dissenting.

The issue posed in this case is a narrow one. There is no challenge here to the validity of public intoxication statutes in general or to the Texas public intoxication statute in particular. This case does not concern the infliction of punishment upon the "social" drinker—or upon anyone other than a "chronic alcoholic" who, as the trier of fact here found, cannot "resist the constant, excessive consumption of alcohol." Nor does it relate to any offense other than the crime of public intoxication.

The sole question presented is whether a criminal penalty may be imposed upon a person suffering the disease of "chronic alcoholism" for a condition—being "in a state of intoxication" in public—which is a characteristic part of the pattern of his disease and which, the trial court found, was not the consequence of appellant's volition but of "a compulsion symptomatic of the disease of chronic alcoholism." We must consider whether the Eighth Amendment, made applicable to the States through the Fourteenth Amendment, prohibits the imposition of this penalty in these rather special circumstances as "cruel and unusual punishment." This case does not raise any question as to the right of the police to stop and detain those who are intoxicated in public, whether as a result of the disease or otherwise; or as to the State's power to commit chronic alcoholics for treatment. Nor does it concern the responsibility of an alcoholic for criminal *acts*. We deal here with the mere *condition* of being intoxicated in public.[2]

---

5. I do not question the power of the State to remove a helplessly intoxicated person from a public street, although against his will, and to hold him until he has regained his powers. The person's own safety and the public interest require this much. A statute such as the one challenged in this case is constitutional insofar as it authorizes a police officer to arrest any seriously intoxicated person when he is encountered in a public place. Whether such a person may be charged and convicted for violating the statute will depend upon whether he is entitled to the protection of the Eighth Amendment.

2. It is not foreseeable that findings such as those which are decisive here—namely that the appellant's being intoxicated in public was a part of the pattern of his disease and due to a

It is true, of course, that there is a great deal that remains to be discovered about chronic alcoholism. Although many aspects of the disease remain obscure, there are some hard facts—medical and, especially, legal facts—that are accessible to us and that provide a context in which the instant case may be analyzed. We are similarly woefully deficient in our medical, diagnostic, and therapeutic knowledge of mental disease and the problem of insanity; but few would urge that, because of this, we should totally reject the legal significance of what we do know about these phenomena.

The manifestations of alcoholism are reasonably well identified. It is well established that alcohol may be habituative and "can be physically addicting." It has been said that "the main point for the nonprofessional is that alcoholism is not within the control of the person involved. He is not willfully drinking."

It is entirely clear that the jailing of chronic alcoholics is punishment. It is not defended as therapeutic, nor is there any basis for claiming that it is therapeutic (or indeed a deterrent). The alcoholic offender is caught in a "revolving door"—leading from arrest on the street through a brief, unprofitable sojourn in jail, back to the street and, eventually, another arrest. The jails, overcrowded and put to a use for which they are not suitable, have a destructive effect upon alcoholic inmates.

It bears emphasis that these data provide only a context for consideration of the instant case. They should not dictate our conclusion. The questions for this Court are not settled by reference to medicine or penology. Our task is to determine whether the principles embodied in the Constitution of the United States place any limitations upon the circumstances under which punishment may be inflicted, and, if so, whether, in the case now before us, those principles preclude the imposition of such punishment.

It is settled that the Federal Constitution places some substantive limitation upon the power of state legislatures to define crimes for which the imposition of punishment is ordered. In *Robinson v. California*, 370 U.S. 660 (1962), the Court considered a conviction under a California statute making it a criminal offense for a person to "be addicted to the use of narcotics." At Robinson's trial, it was developed that the defendant had been a user of narcotics. The trial court instructed the jury that "[to] be addicted to the use of narcotics is said to be a status or condition and not an act. It is a continuing offense and differs from most other offenses in the fact that [it] is chronic rather than acute; that it continues after it is complete and subjects the offender to arrest at any time before he reforms."

---

compulsion symptomatic of that disease—could or would be made in the case of offenses such as driving a car while intoxicated, assault, theft, or robbery. Such offenses require independent acts or conduct and do not typically flow from and are not part of the syndrome of the disease of chronic alcoholism. If an alcoholic should be convicted for criminal conduct which is not a characteristic and involuntary part of the pattern of the disease as it afflicts him, nothing herein would prevent his punishment.

This Court reversed Robinson's conviction on the ground that punishment under the law in question was cruel and unusual, in violation of the Eighth Amendment of the Constitution as applied to the States through the Fourteenth Amendment. The Court noted that narcotic addiction is considered to be an illness and that California had recognized it as such. It held that the State could not make it a crime for a person to be ill. Although Robinson had been sentenced to only 90 days in prison for his offense, it was beyond the power of the State to prescribe such punishment. As Mr. Justice Stewart, speaking for the Court, said: "[even] one day in prison would be a cruel and unusual punishment for the 'crime' of having a common cold."

Robinson stands upon a principle which, despite its subtlety, must be simply stated and respectfully applied because it is the foundation of individual liberty and the cornerstone of the relations between a civilized state and its citizens: Criminal penalties may not be inflicted upon a person for being in a condition he is powerless to change. In all probability, Robinson at some time before his conviction elected to take narcotics. But the crime as defined did not punish this conduct.[29] The statute imposed a penalty for the offense of "addiction"—a condition which Robinson could not control. Once Robinson had become an addict, he was utterly powerless to avoid criminal guilt. He was powerless to choose not to violate the law.

In the present case, appellant is charged with a crime composed of two elements—being intoxicated and being found in a public place while in that condition. The crime, so defined, differs from that in *Robinson.* The statute covers more than a mere status. But the essential constitutional defect here is the same as in *Robinson,* for in both cases the particular defendant was accused of being in a condition which he had no capacity to change or avoid. The trial judge sitting as trier of fact found, upon the medical and other relevant testimony, that Powell is a "chronic alcoholic." He defined appellant's "chronic alcoholism" as "a disease which destroys the afflicted person's will power to resist the constant, excessive consumption of alcohol." He also found that "a chronic alcoholic does not appear in public by his own volition but under a compulsion symptomatic of the disease of chronic alcoholism." I read these findings to mean that appellant was powerless to avoid drinking; that having taken his first drink, he had "an uncontrollable compulsion to drink" to the point of intoxication; and that, once intoxicated, he could not prevent himself from appearing in public places.

Article 477 of the Texas Penal Code is specifically directed to the accused's presence while in a state of intoxication, "in any public place, or at any private house

29. The Court noted in *Robinson* that narcotic addiction "is apparently an illness which may be contracted innocently or involuntarily." In the case of alcoholism it is even more likely that the disease may be innocently contracted, since the drinking of alcoholic beverages is a common activity, generally accepted in our society, while the purchasing and taking of drugs are crimes. As in *Robinson,* the State has not argued here that Powell's conviction may be supported by his "voluntary" action in becoming afflicted.

except his own." This is the essence of the crime. Ordinarily when the State proves such presence in a state of intoxication, this will be sufficient for conviction, and the punishment prescribed by the State may, of course, be validly imposed. But here the findings of the trial judge call into play the principle that a person may not be punished if the condition essential to constitute the defined crime is part of the pattern of his disease and is occasioned by a compulsion symptomatic of the disease. This principle, narrow in scope and applicability, is implemented by the Eighth Amendment's prohibition of "cruel and unusual punishment," as we construed that command in *Robinson.*

The findings in this case, read against the background of the medical and sociological data to which I have referred, compel the conclusion that the infliction upon appellant of a criminal penalty for being intoxicated in a public place would be "cruel and inhuman punishment" within the prohibition of the Eighth Amendment. This conclusion follows because appellant is a "chronic alcoholic" who, according to the trier of fact, cannot resist the "constant excessive consumption of alcohol" and does not appear in public by his own volition but under a "compulsion" which is part of his condition.

I would reverse the judgment below.

Although *Robinson* provides that the State may not make addiction itself a crime, civil commitment based on addiction alone is permissible. Most states have civil commitment statutes for people addicted to drugs but they are rarely used. *See, e.g.,* M. Susan Ridgely and Martin Y. Iguchi, *Coercive Use of Vaccines Against Drug Addiction: Is It Permissible and Is It Good Public Policy?*, 12 VA. J. SOC. POL'Y & L. 260 (2004) (describing the history of laws permitting the civil commitment of alcohol and drug abusers in the United States). In recent years, however, one state—Massachusetts—has engaged in "extensive[]" civil commitment of opioid users, leading legislators in at least three other states to show a renewed interest in the idea. Christine Vestal, *Support Grows for Civil Commitment of Opioid Users*, THE PEW CHARITABLE TRUSTS: STATELINE (June 15, 2017).

Civil commitment carries its own set of concerns regarding issues like due process and whether treatment is masquerading as punishment. In 2017, for example, 11 Massachusetts residents who had been civilly committed sued the state. The group claimed that they had been placed in the same institution as "the state's most dangerous sex offenders," where they receive "little to no treatment." Instead of treatment, the complaint alleged that "Counselors have . . . offered the patients word-search puzzles with themes like 'Famous American Football Players' to pass the time." The mother of one of the committees described the conditions as "[t]he worst jail there is." Maria Cramer, *State is Sued by 11 Over Civil Commitments*, BOSTON GLOBE (Jul. 14, 2017). The lack of treatment in civil commitment programs is not a new phenomenon. *See* John C. Kramer, *The State Versus The Addict: Uncivil Commitment,* 50 B.U. L. REV. 1 (1970) (arguing that California's post-*Robinson* civil commitment scheme "entirely resembles prison programs and has almost no elements which resemble hospital programs").

2. The Right to Privacy

Throughout the years, laws criminalizing drug possession—particularly in the home—have faced a number of challenges based on a substantive due process "right to privacy" theory. In the United States, courts have nearly universally rejected these challenges. *See* Eric Blumenson and Eva Nilsen, *Liberty Lost: The Moral Case for Marijuana Law Reform*, 85 Ind. L.J. 279, 282 at n. 8 (2010) (describing courts' rejection of constitutional challenges to marijuana laws). In Alaska, however, the State Supreme Court held in 1970 that the right to privacy contained in Alaska's Constitution protects marijuana possession in the home. In 2014, Alaskans voted to legalize the possession and commercial sale of marijuana. In the aftermath of Alaska's legalization vote, the Alaska Supreme Court's 1970 opinion is of less practical significance. But it continues to raise important questions about the extent to which the government should be permitted to regulate and punish private conduct.

Ravin v. Alaska

Supreme Court of Alaska
537 P.2d 494 (1975)

Rabinowitz, J.

The constitutionality of Alaska's statute prohibiting possession of marijuana is put in issue in this case. Petitioner Ravin was arrested in 1972 and charged with violating AS 17.12.010. Before trial Ravin attacked the constitutionality of AS 17.12.010 by a motion to dismiss in which he asserted that the State had violated his right of privacy under both the federal and Alaska constitutions.

Ravin's basic thesis is that there exists under the federal and Alaska constitutions a fundamental right to privacy, the scope of which is sufficiently broad to encompass and protect the possession of marijuana for personal use. Given this fundamental constitutional right, the State would then have the burden of demonstrating a compelling state interest in prohibiting possession of marijuana. In light of these controlling principles, petitioner argues that the evidence submitted below by both sides demonstrates that marijuana is a relatively innocuous substance, at least as compared with other less-restricted substances, and that nothing even approaching a compelling state interest was proven by the State.

Ravin's arguments necessitate a close examination of the contours of the asserted right to privacy and the scope of this court's review of the legislature's determination to criminalize possession of marijuana.

We have previously stated the tests to be applied when a claim is made that state action encroaches upon an individual's constitutional rights. In *Breese v. Smith*, 501 P.2d 159 (Alaska 1972), we had before us a school hair length regulation which encroached on what we determined to be the individual's fundamental right to determine his own personal appearance. There we stated:

> Once a fundamental right under the constitution of Alaska has been shown to be involved and it has been further shown that this constitutionally protected right has been impaired by governmental action, then the government must come forward and meet its substantial burden of establishing that the abridgement in question was justified by a compelling governmental interest.

When, on the other hand, governmental action interferes with an individual's freedom in an area which is not characterized as fundamental, a less stringent test is ordinarily applied. In such cases our task is to determine whether the legislative enactment has a reasonable relationship to a legitimate governmental purpose. Under this latter test, which is sometimes referred to as the "rational basis" test, the State need only demonstrate the existence of facts which can serve as a rational basis for belief that the measure would properly serve the public interest.

Thus, our undertaking is two-fold: we must first determine the nature of Ravin's rights, if any, abridged by AS 17.12.010, and, if any rights have been infringed upon, then resolve the further question as to whether the statutory impingement is justified.

As we have mentioned, Ravin's argument that he has a fundamental right to possess marijuana for personal use rests on both federal and state law, and centers on what may broadly be called the right to privacy. This "right" is increasingly the subject of litigation and commentary and is still a developing legal concept.

In Ravin's view, the right to privacy involved here is an autonomous right which gains special significance when its situs is found in a specially protected area, such as the home. Ravin begins his privacy argument by citation of and reliance upon *Griswold v. Connecticut,* in which the Supreme Court of the United States struck down as unconstitutional a state statute effectively barring the dispensation of birth control information to married persons. Writing for five members of the Court, Mr. Justice Douglas noted that rights protected by the Constitution are not limited to those specifically enumerated in the Constitution. In order to secure the enumerated rights, certain peripheral rights must be recognized. In other words, the "specific guarantees in the Bill of Rights have penumbras, formed by emanations from those guarantees that help give them life and substance." Certain of these penumbral rights create "zones of privacy", for example, First Amendment rights of association, Third and Fourth Amendment rights pertaining to the security of the home, and the Fifth Amendment right against self-incrimination. The Supreme Court of the United States then proceeded to find a right to privacy in marriage which antedates the Bill of Rights and yet lies within the zone of privacy created by several fundamental constitutional guarantees. It was left unclear whether this particular right to privacy exists independently, or comes into being only because of its connection with fundamental enumerated rights.

The next important Supreme Court opinion regarding privacy is *Stanley v. Georgia,* in which a state conviction for possession of obscene matter was overturned as violative of the First and Fourteenth Amendments. The Supreme Court had previously held that obscenity is not protected by the First Amendment. But in *Stanley* the Count made a distinction between commercial distribution of obscene matter and the private enjoyment of it at home. The Constitution, it said, protects the fundamental right to receive information and ideas, regardless of their worth. Moreover, the Supreme Court said,

> .... in the context of this case—a prosecution for mere possession of printed or filmed matter in the privacy of a person's own home—that right takes on an added dimension. For also fundamental is the right to be free, except in very limited circumstances, from unwanted governmental intrusions into one's privacy.

The Supreme Court concluded that the First Amendment means a state has no business telling a man, sitting alone in his own home, what books he may read or what films he may watch. The Court took care to limit its holding to mere possession of obscene materials by the individual in his own home. It noted that it did not intend to restrict the power of the state or federal government to make illegal the possession of items such as narcotics, firearms, or stolen goods.

In Alaska this court has dealt with the concept of privacy on only a few occasions. One of the most significant decisions in this area is *Breese v. Smith,* where we considered the applicability of the guarantee of "life, liberty, the pursuit of happiness" found in the Alaska Constitution, to a school hair length regulation. Noting that hairstyles are a highly personal matter in which the individual is traditionally autonomous, we concluded that governmental control of personal appearance would be antithetical to the concept of personal liberty under Alaska's constitution. Since the student would be forced to choose between controlling his own personal appearance and asserting his right to an education if the regulations were upheld, we concluded that the constitutional language quoted above embodied an affirmative grant of liberty to public school students to choose their own hairstyles, for "at the core of [the concept of liberty] is the notion of total personal immunity from government control: the right 'to be let alone.'" That right is not absolute, however; we also noted that this "liberty" must yield where it "intrude[s] upon the freedom of others."

Subsequent to our decision in *Breese,* a right to privacy amendment was added to the Alaska Constitution. Article I, section 22 reads:

> The right of the people to privacy is recognized and shall not be infringed. The legislature shall implement this section.

The effect of this amendment is to place privacy among the specifically enumerated rights in Alaska's constitution. But this fact alone does not, in and of itself, yield answers concerning what scope should be accorded to this right of privacy. We have suggested that the right to privacy may afford less than absolute protection to "the ingestion of food, beverages or other substances." For any such protection must be limited by the legitimate needs of the State to protect the health and welfare of its citizens.[25]

Although a number of other jurisdictions have considered the privacy issue as it applies to marijuana prosecutions, they provide little help in defining the scope of article I, section 22 of Alaska's constitution. In Hawaii, whose constitution also contains an express guarantee of the right to privacy, the supreme court has faced a similar issue. In *State v. Kantner,* the Supreme Court of Hawaii upheld a conviction for possession of marijuana by a 3–2 vote, with one member of the majority concurring only because he thought the constitutional issue had not been properly raised. A majority rejected the claim that application of the statute violated guarantees of equal protection and due process, and two members of the court rejected the claim of violation of "fundamental liberty" based on *Griswold.* In dissent, Justice Levinson emphasized the guarantees of privacy and personal autonomy which he found in both the Hawaii Constitution and the due process clause of the Fourteenth Amendment to the United States Constitution. He found that the right to privacy "guarantees to the individual the full measure of control over his own personality consistent with the security of himself and others." The experiences generated by use of marijuana are mental in nature, he wrote, and thus among the most personal and private experiences possible. So long as conduct does not produce detrimental results, the right of privacy protects the individual's conduct designed to affect these inner areas of the personality. The state failed to show, he found, any harm to the user or others from the private, personal use of marijuana, and so the statute infringed on the right to personal autonomy.

In a Michigan case the same year, a conviction for possession of marijuana was overturned by a unanimous court, though for a variety of reasons. One of the justices in *People v. Sinclair,* Justice T. G. Kavanagh, rested his opinion squarely on the basic right of the individual to be free from government intrusions. He found the marijuana possession statute to be "an impermissible intrusion on the fundamental rights to liberty and the pursuit of happiness, and is an unwarranted interference with the right to possess and use private property." He noted the basic freedom of the individual to be free to do as he pleases so long as his actions do not interfere with the rights of his neighbor or of society. ". . . . 'Big Brother' cannot, in the name of *Public* health, dictate to anyone what he can eat or drink or smoke in the *privacy* of his own home."

Generally, however, privacy as a constitutional defense in marijuana cases has not met with much favor. It was rejected, for instance, by the Massachusetts Supreme Judicial Court in *Commonwealth v. Leis,* where the court held that there

25. If the State were required, for instance, to carry the extremely heavy burden of showing a compelling state interest before it could regulate the purity of foodstuffs and medicines, the result would be a practical inability to protect the public from health threats which consumers could neither know about nor protect themselves against.

was no constitutional right to smoke marijuana, that smoking marijuana was not fundamental to the American scheme of justice or necessary to a regime of ordered liberty, and that smoking marijuana was not locatable in any "zone of privacy." Furthermore, the court said, there is no constitutional right to become intoxicated.

Assuming this court were to continue to utilize the fundamental right-compelling state interest test in resolving privacy issues under article I, section 22 of Alaska's constitution, we would conclude that there is not a fundamental constitutional right to possess or ingest marijuana in Alaska. For in our view, the right to privacy amendment to the Alaska Constitution cannot be read so as to make the possession or ingestion of marijuana itself a fundamental right. Nor can we conclude that such a fundamental right is shown by virtue of the analysis we employed in *Breese*. In that case, the student's traditional liberty pertaining to autonomy in personal appearance was threatened in such a way that his constitutionally guaranteed right to an education was jeopardized. Hairstyle, as emphasized in *Breese*, is a highly personal matter involving the individual and his body. In this sense this aspect of liberty-privacy is akin to the significantly personal areas at stake in *Griswold* and *Eisenstadt v. Baird*. Few would believe they have been deprived of something of critical importance if deprived of marijuana, though they would if stripped of control over their personal appearance. And, as mentioned previously, a discrete federal right of privacy separate from the penumbras of specifically enumerated constitutional rights has not as yet been articulated by the Supreme Court of the United States. Therefore, if we were employing our former test, we would hold that there is no fundamental right, either under the Alaska or federal constitutions, either to possess or ingest marijuana.

The foregoing does not complete our analysis of the right to privacy issues. For in *Gray* we stated that the right of privacy amendment of the Alaska Constitution "clearly it shields the ingestion of food, beverages or other substances," but that this right may be held to be subordinate to public health and welfare measures. Thus, Ravin's right to privacy contentions are not susceptible to disposition solely in terms of answering the question whether there is a general fundamental constitutional right to possess or smoke marijuana. This leads us to a more detailed examination of the right to privacy and the relevancy of where the right is exercised.

At one end of the scale of the scope of the right to privacy is possession or ingestion in the individual's home. If there is any area of human activity to which a right to privacy pertains more than any other, it is the home. The importance of the home has been amply demonstrated in constitutional law. Among the enumerated rights in the federal Bill of Rights are the guarantee against quartering of troops in a private house in peacetime (Third Amendment) and the right to be "secure in their.... houses.... against unreasonable searches and seizures...." (Fourth Amendment). The First Amendment has been held to protect the right to "privacy and freedom of association in the home." The Fifth Amendment has been described as providing protection against all governmental invasions "of the sanctity of a man's home and the privacies of life." The protection of the right to receive birth control information in *Griswold* was predicated on the sanctity of the marriage relationship and the harm to this fundamental area of privacy if police were allowed to "search the sacred precincts of marital bedrooms." And in *Stanley v. Georgia,* the Court emphasized the home as the situs of protected "private activities." The right to receive information and ideas was found in *Stanley* to take on an added dimension precisely because it was a prosecution for possession in the home: "For also fundamental is the right to be free, except in very limited circumstances, from unwanted governmental intrusions into one's privacy." In a later case, the Supreme Court noted that *Stanley* was not based on the notion that the obscene matter was itself protected by a constitutional penumbra of privacy, but rather was a "reaffirmation that 'a man's home is his castle.'"

In Alaska we have also recognized the distinctive nature of the home as a place where the individual's privacy receives special protection. This court has consistently recognized that the home is constitutionally protected from unreasonable searches and seizures, reasoning that the home itself retains a protected status under the Fourth Amendment and Alaska's constitution distinct from that of the occupant's person. The privacy amendment to the Alaska Constitution was intended to give recognition and protection to the home. Such a reading is consonant with the character of life in Alaska. Our territory and now state has traditionally been the home of people who prize their individuality and who have chosen to settle or to continue living here in order to achieve a measure of control over their own lifestyles which is now virtually unattainable in many of our sister states.

The home, then, carries with it associations and meanings which make it particularly important as the situs of privacy. Privacy in the home is a fundamental right, under both the federal and Alaska constitutions. We do not mean by this that a person may do anything at anytime as long as the activity takes place within a person's home. There are two important limitations on this facet of the right to privacy. First, we agree with the Supreme Court of the United States, which has strictly limited the *Stanley* guarantee to possession for purely private, noncommercial use in the home. And secondly, we think this right must yield when it interferes in a serious manner with the health, safety, rights and privileges of others or with the public welfare. No one has an absolute right to do things in the privacy of his own home which will affect himself or others adversely. Indeed, one aspect of a private matter is that it *is* private, that is, that it does not adversely affect persons beyond the actor, and hence is none of their business. When a matter does affect the public, directly or indirectly, it loses its wholly private character, and can be made to yield when an appropriate public need is demonstrated.

Thus, we conclude that citizens of the State of Alaska have a basic right to privacy in their homes under Alaska's constitution. This right to privacy would encompass the possession and ingestion of substances such as marijuana in a purely personal, non-commercial context in the home unless the state can meet its substantial burden and show that proscription of possession of marijuana in the home is supportable by achievement of a legitimate state interest.

This leads us to the second facet of our inquiry, namely, whether the State has demonstrated sufficient justification for the prohibition of possession of marijuana in general in the interest of public welfare; and further, whether the State has met the greater burden of showing a close and substantial relationship between the public welfare and control of ingestion or possession of marijuana in the home for personal use.

The evidence which was presented at the hearing before the district court consisted primarily of several expert witnesses familiar with various medical and social aspects of marijuana use. Numerous written reports and books were also introduced into evidence.

According to figures published by the National Commission on Marihuana and Drug Abuse in 1973, an estimated 26 million Americans have used marijuana at least once. The incidence generally cuts across social and economic classes, though use is greatest among young persons (55% of 18–21 year-olds have used it). Only about 2% of the adults who have used it were classified by the National Commission as "heavy users" (more than once daily). The experience in Alaska seems to be similar. A report published in the Journal of the American Medical Association in 1971 indicated that 24% of Anchorage school children in grades six through twelve had used marijuana, as had 46% in grades eleven and twelve.

Scientific testimony on the physiological and psychological effects of marijuana on humans generally stresses the variability of effects upon different individuals and on any one individual at different times. The setting and psychological state of the user can affect his responses. Responses also vary with the amount of marijuana one has used in the past. A new user, for instance, often feels no effects at all.

The short-term physiological effects are relatively undisputed. An immediate slight increase in the pulse, decrease in salivation, and a slight reddening of the eyes are usually noted. There is also impairment of psychomotor control. These effects generally end within two to three hours of the end of smoking.

Long-term physiological effects raise more controversy among the experts. The National Commission on Marihuana and Drug Abuse reported that among users "no significant physical, biochemical, or mental abnormalities could be attributed solely to their marijuana smoking." Certain researchers have pointed to possible deleterious effects on the body's immune defenses, on the chromosomal structures of users, and on testosterone levels in the body. The methodology of certain of these studies has been extensively criticized by other qualified medical scientists, however. It should be noted that most of the damage suggested by these studies comes in the context of intensive use of concentrated forms of THC. It appears that the use of marijuana, as it is presently used in the United States today, does not constitute a public health problem of any significant dimensions. It is, for instance, far more innocuous in terms of physiological and social damage than alcohol or tobacco. But the studies suggesting dangers in intensive cannabis use do raise valid doubts which cannot be dismissed or discounted.

The experts generally agree that the early widely-held belief that marijuana use directly causes criminal behavior, and particularly violent, aggressive behavior, has no validity. On the contrary, the National Commission found indications that marijuana inhibits "the expression of aggressive impulses by pacifying the user, interfering with muscle coordination, reducing psychomotor activities and generally producing states of drowsiness, lethargy, timidity and passivity." Moreover, the Commission and most other authorities agree that there is little validity to the theory that marijuana use leads to use of more potent and dangerous drugs. Although it has been stated that the more heavily a user smokes marijuana, the greater the probability that he has used or will use other drugs, "it has been suggested that such use is related to 'drug use proneness' and involvement in drug subcultures rather than to the characteristics of cannabis, *per se*."

While there is no confirmed report of a human ever having died from an overdose of cannabis, the toxic levels of THC have been determined from tests on animals. The lethal dose for marijuana is approximately 40,000 times the dose needed to achieve intoxication. The equivalent ratio of intoxicating to lethal doses for alcohol is 4/10 and for barbiturates is 3/50.

The number of persons arrested for marijuana possession has climbed steeply in recent years. In 1973, over 400,000 marijuana arrests occurred, a 43% rise over the previous year. It should also be noted that 81% of persons arrested for marijuana-related crimes have never been convicted of any crime in the past, and 91% have never been convicted of a drug-related crime.

The justifications offered by the State to uphold AS 17.12.010 are generally that marijuana is a psychoactive drug; that it is not a harmless substance; that heavy use has concomitant risk; that it is capable of precipitating a psychotic reaction in at least individuals who are predisposed towards such reaction; and that its use adversely affects the user's ability to operate an automobile. The State relies upon a number of medical researchers who have raised questions as to the substance's effect on the body's immune system, on chromosomal structure, and on the functioning of the brain. On the other hand, in almost every instance of reports of potential danger arising from marijuana use, reports can be found reaching contradictory results. It appears that there is no firm evidence that marijuana, as presently used in this country, is generally a danger to the user or to others. But neither is there conclusive evidence to the effect that it is harmless. The one significant risk in use of marijuana which we do find established to a reasonable degree of certainty is the effect of marijuana intoxication on driving.

Possibly implicit in the State's catalogue of possible dangers of marijuana use is the assumption that the State has the authority to protect the individual from his own folly, that is, that the State can control activities which present no harm to anyone except those enjoying them. Although some courts have found the "public interest" to be broad enough to justify protecting the individual against himself, most have found inherent limitations on the police power of the state. An apposite example is the litigation regarding the constitutionality of laws requiring motorcyclists to wear helmets. Most of the courts addressing the issue, including this one, have resolved it by finding a connection between the helmet requirement and the safety of other motorists, but a significant number of courts have explicitly rejected such restrictive measures as beyond the police power of the state because they do not benefit the public.

We glean from these cases the general proposition that the authority of the state to exert control over the individual extends only to activities of the individual which affect others or the public at large as it relates to matters of public health or safety, or to provide for the general welfare. We believe this tenet to be basic to a free society. The state cannot impose its own notions of morality, propriety, or fashion on individuals when the public has no legitimate interest in the affairs of those individuals. The right of the individual to do as he pleases is not absolute, of course: it can be made to yield when it begins to infringe on the rights and welfare of others.

Further, the authority of the state to control the activities of its citizens is not limited to activities which have a present and immediate impact on the public health or welfare. It is conceivable, for example, that a drug could so seriously develop in its user a withdrawal or amotivational syndrome, that widespread use of the drug could significantly debilitate the fabric of our society. Faced with a substantial possibility of such a result, the state could take measures to combat the possibility. The state is under no obligation to allow otherwise "private" activity which will result in numbers of people becoming public charges or otherwise burdening the public welfare. But we do not find that such a situation exists today regarding marijuana. It appears that effects of marijuana on the individual are not serious enough to justify widespread concern, at least as compared with the far more dangerous effects of alcohol, barbiturates and amphetamines. Moreover, the current patterns of use in the United States are not such as would warrant concern that in the future consumption patterns are likely to change.

But one way in which use of marijuana most clearly does affect the general public is in regard to its effect on driving. All of which brings us to the opposite (from the home) end of the scale of the right to privacy in the context of ingestion or possession of marijuana, namely, when the individual is operating a motor vehicle. Recent research has produced increasing evidence of significant impairment of the driving ability of persons under the influence of cannabis. Distortion of time perception, impairment of psychomotor function, and increased selectivity in attentiveness to surroundings apparently can combine to lower driver ability. In this regard, Ravin points out that marijuana usually produces passivity and inactivity, in contrast to alcohol, which increases aggressiveness and is likely to result in overconfidence in one's driving ability. Although a person under the influence of marijuana may be less likely to attempt to drive than a person under the influence of alcohol, there exists the potential for serious harm to the health and safety of the general public.

In view of the foregoing, we believe that at present, the need for control of drivers under the influence of marijuana and the existing doubts as to the safety of marijuana, demonstrate a sufficient justification for the prohibition found in AS

17.12.010 as an exercise of the state's police power for the public welfare. Given the evidence of the effect of marijuana on driving an individual's right to possess or ingest marijuana while driving would be subject to the prohibition provided for in AS 17.12.010. However, given the relative insignificance of marijuana consumption as a health problem in our society at present, we do not believe that the potential harm generated by drivers under the influence of marijuana, standing alone, creates a close and substantial relationship between the public welfare and control of ingestion of marijuana or possession of it in the home for personal use. Thus we conclude that no adequate justification for the state's intrusion into the citizen's right to privacy by its prohibition of possession of marijuana by an adult for personal consumption in the home has been shown. The privacy of the individual's home cannot be breached absent a persuasive showing of a close and substantial relationship of the intrusion to a legitimate governmental interest. Here, mere scientific doubts will not suffice. The state must demonstrate a need based on proof that the public health or welfare will in fact suffer if the controls are not applied.

The state has a legitimate concern with avoiding the spread of marijuana use to adolescents who may not be equipped with the maturity to handle the experience prudently, as well as a legitimate concern with the problem of driving under the influence of marijuana. Yet these interests are insufficient to justify intrusions into the rights of adults in the privacy of their own homes. Further, neither the federal or Alaska constitution affords protection for the buying or selling of marijuana, nor absolute protection for its use or possession in public. Possession at home of amounts of marijuana indicative of intent to sell rather than possession for personal use is likewise unprotected.

In view of our holding that possession of marijuana by adults at home for personal use is constitutionally protected, we wish to make clear that we do not mean to condone the use of marijuana. The experts who testified below, including petitioner's witnesses, were unanimously opposed to the use of any psychoactive drugs. We agree completely. It is the responsibility of every individual to consider carefully the ramifications for himself and for those around him of using such substances. With the freedom which our society offers to each of us to order our lives as we see fit goes the duty to live responsibly, for our own sakes and for society's. This result can best be achieved, we believe, without the use of psychoactive substances.

For an analysis of the relationship between *Ravin* and Alaska's marijuana legalization law, see Jason Brandeis, *Ravin Revisited: Alaska's Historic Common Law Marijuana Rule at the Dawn of Legalization,* 32 ALASKA L. REV. 309 (2015).

Chapter 4

Sentencing and Civil Sanctions

A. An Introduction to Sentencing

Speech at the American Bar Association Annual Meeting

An Address by Anthony M. Kennedy,
Associate Justice, Supreme Court of the United States
August 9, 2003

Were we to enter the hidden world of punishment, we should be startled by what we see. Consider its remarkable scale. The nationwide inmate population today is about 2.1 million people. In California, even as we meet, this State alone keeps over 160,000 persons behind bars. In countries such as England, Italy, France and Germany, the incarceration rate is about 1 in 1,000 persons. In the United States it is about 1 in 143.

We must confront another reality. Nationwide, more than 40% of the prison population consists of African-American inmates. About 10% of African-American men in their mid-to-late 20s are behind bars. In some cities more than 50% of young African-American men are under the supervision of the criminal justice system.

While economic costs, defined in simple dollar terms, are secondary to human costs, they do illustrate the scale of the criminal justice system. The cost of housing, feeding and caring for the inmate population in the United States is more than $40 billion per year. In the State of California alone, the cost of maintaining each inmate in the correctional system is about $26,000 per year. And despite the high expenditures in prison, there remain urgent, unmet needs in the prison system.

To compare prison costs with the cost of educating school children is, to some extent, to compare apples with oranges, because the State must assume the full burden of housing, subsistence, and medical care for prisoners, yet the statistics are troubling. When it costs so much more to incarcerate a prisoner than to educate a child, we should take special care to ensure that we are not incarcerating too many persons for too long.

It requires one with more expertise in the area than I possess to offer a complete analysis, but it does seem justified to say this: Our resources are misspent, our punishments too severe, our sentences too long.

In the federal system the sentencing guidelines are responsible in part for the increase in prison terms. In my view the guidelines were, and are, necessary. Before they were in place, a wide disparity existed among the sentences given by different judges, and even among sentences given by a single judge. As my colleague Justice Breyer has pointed out, however, the compromise that led to the guidelines led also to an increase in the length of prison terms. We should revisit this compromise. The Federal Sentencing Guidelines should be revised downward.

By contrast to the guidelines, I can accept neither the necessity nor the wisdom of federal mandatory minimum sentences. In too many cases, mandatory minimum sentences are unwise and unjust.

Consider this case: A young man with no previous serious offense is stopped on the George Washington Memorial Parkway near Washington D.C. by United States Park Police. He is stopped for not wearing a seatbelt. A search of the car follows and leads to the discovery of just over five grams of crack cocaine in the trunk. The young man is indicted in federal court. He faces a mandatory minimum sentence of five years. If he had taken an exit and left the federal road, his sentence likely would have been measured in terms of months, not years.

United States Marshals can recount the experience of leading a young man away from his family to begin serving his term. His mother says, "How long will my boy be gone?" They say "Ten years" or "15 years." Ladies and gentlemen, I submit to you that a 20-year-old does not know how long ten or fifteen years is. One day in prison is longer than almost any day you and I have had to endure.

Because every jurisdiction has a different sentencing regime, there is not a single body of drug sentencing law. There are, however, some legal and policy issues that are common to drug sentencing. Before turning to these issues, this section begins with an introduction to sentencing law and federal drug sentencing.

Until the late 1970s, sentencing in the United States was a "highly discretionary system" in which federal and state trial judges "had nearly unfettered discretion to impose upon defendants any sentence from within the broad statutory ranges provided for criminal offenses; parole officials likewise possessed unfettered discretion to decide precisely when offenders were to be allowed to leave prison." Doug Berman, *Reconceptualizing Sentencing*, 2005 U. Chi. Legal. F. 1, 3 (2005). This open-ended approach to sentencing was based in large part on the idea that judges and parole boards were in the best position to tailor punishments to the specifics of the offense and the offender.

In the 1960s and 1970s, a series of studies revealed this system sometimes resulted in troubling sentencing disparities for similarly situated defendants based on factors like race and socioeconomic status. During the same period, there was also a growing concern among law-and-order politicians and activists that some judges were too lenient when it came to punishing criminals. In combination, these two schools of thought generated bipartisan interest in proposals to bring more uniformity to criminal sentencing by taking the kind of considerations judges had previously weighed case-by-case (the defendant's criminal history, his degree of involvement in the offense, etc.) and translating them into a set of guidelines that could be applied to all cases. As a result of this effort, the federal government and many states adopted sentencing guidelines systems in some form or fashion.

Today, federal sentencing is rooted in a comprehensive set of advisory guidelines, called the Federal Sentencing Guidelines. These guidelines look at a defendant's "offense level" and "criminal history" to set an initial sentencing range, which might then be adjusted up or down based on a variety of factors, such as whether the defendant accepted responsibility for her crime. State sentencing schemes vary as far as how much guidance they give to courts. In some states, sentencing operates very much like it does at the federal level. Other states leave it to the judge to weigh various factors at sentencing, with only relatively minimal constraints. Complicating matters even more, policies that provide an opportunity for early release—for example, parole and good-time credits—have been abolished in some states but remain important components of sentencing law in others.

Because the federal government plays an important role in drug enforcement, and because many state sentencing schemes share some of the federal sentencing system's key features, federal sentencing is a useful lens for beginning to think about sentencing in drug cases. The remainder of this section outlines the core rules that govern federal drug sentencing.

Two considerations drive most federal drug sentences: the federal sentencing guidelines, and mandatory minimum penalties.

The Federal Sentencing Guidelines

The federal sentencing guidelines date back to the Sentencing Reform Act of 1984 ("SRA"), passed as part of the Comprehensive Crime Control Act of 1984. The SRA created a standing body—the United States Sentencing Commission—to draft the guidelines and oversee and refine them on an ongoing basis. Together, the guidelines and the Sentencing Commission were intended "to provide certainty and fairness at sentencing" by ensuring that "similarly situated federal defendants convicted of similar offenses [would be] sentenced within the same, relatively narrow range[.]" William W. Wilkins et al., *Competing Sentencing Policies in a 'War on Drugs' Era*, 28 Wake Forest L. Rev. 305, 305–06 (1993).

The guidelines apply to all federal felony and serious misdemeanor convictions, from air piracy to treason. The foundation of the guidelines is a grid—the sentencing table—that provides sentencing ranges based on the seriousness of the offense ("offense level") and the defendant's criminal record ("criminal history category").

SENTENCING TABLE
(in months of imprisonment)

		Criminal History Category (Criminal History Points)					
	Offense Level	**I (0 or 1)**	**II (2 or 3)**	**III (4, 5, 6)**	**IV (7, 8, 9)**	**V (10, 11, 12)**	**VI (13 or more)**
	1	0-6	0-6	0-6	0-6	0-6	0-6
	2	0-6	0-6	0-6	0-6	0-6	1-7
	3	0-6	0-6	0-6	0-6	2-8	3-9
	4	0-6	0-6	0-6	2-8	4-10	6-12
Zone A	**5**	0-6	0-6	1-7	4-10	6-12	9-15
	6	0-6	1-7	2-8	6-12	9-15	12-18
	7	0-6	2-8	4-10	8-14	12-18	15-21
	8	0-6	4-10	6-12	10-16	15-21	18-24
Zone B	**9**	4-10	6-12	8-14	12-18	18-24	21-27
	10	6-12	8-14	10-16	15-21	21-27	24-30
	11	8-14	10-16	12-18	18-24	24-30	27-33
Zone C	**12**	10-16	12-18	15-21	21-27	27-33	30-37
	13	12-18	15-21	18-24	24-30	30-37	33-41
	14	15-21	18-24	21-27	27-33	33-41	37-46
	15	18-24	21-27	24-30	30-37	37-46	41-51
	16	21-27	24-30	27-33	33-41	41-51	46-57
	17	24-30	27-33	30-37	37-46	46-57	51-63
	18	27-33	30-37	33-41	41-51	51-63	57-71
	19	30-37	33-41	37-46	46-57	57-71	63-78
	20	33-41	37-46	41-51	51-63	63-78	70-87
	21	37-46	41-51	46-57	57-71	70-87	77-96
	22	41-51	46-57	51-63	63-78	77-96	84-105
	23	46-57	51-63	57-71	70-87	84-105	92-115
	24	51-63	57-71	63-78	77-96	92-115	100-125
	25	57-71	63-78	70-87	84-105	100-125	110-137
	26	63-78	70-87	78-97	92-115	110-137	120-150
	27	70-87	78-97	87-108	100-125	120-150	130-162
Zone D	**28**	78-97	87-108	97-121	110-137	130-162	140-175
	29	87-108	97-121	108-135	121-151	140-175	151-188
	30	97-121	108-135	121-151	135-168	151-188	168-210
	31	108-135	121-151	135-168	151-188	168-210	188-235
	32	121-151	135-168	151-188	168-210	188-235	210-262
	33	135-168	151-188	168-210	188-235	210-262	235-293
	34	151-188	168-210	188-235	210-262	235-293	262-327
	35	168-210	188-235	210-262	235-293	262-327	292-365
	36	188-235	210-262	235-293	262-327	292-365	324-405
	37	210-262	235-293	262-327	292-365	324-405	360-life
	38	235-293	262-327	292-365	324-405	360-life	360-life
	39	262-327	292-365	324-405	360-life	360-life	360-life
	40	292-365	324-405	360-life	360-life	360-life	360-life
	41	324-405	360-life	360-life	360-life	360-life	360-life
	42	360-life	360-life	360-life	360-life	360-life	360-life
	43	life	life	life	life	life	life

Applying the sentencing guidelines can sometimes be a difficult undertaking. The 2018 United States Sentencing Commission's Guidelines Manual, which contains all of the guidelines provisions and related commentary, is 600 pages long. The description that follows is an oversimplification. But it suffices for purposes of illustrating the major steps to calculating an offender's sentencing range under the guidelines in a typical drug case.

Determine the base offense level: The first step to applying the guidelines is to identify the applicable base offense level. For most drug cases, this means consulting guideline § 2D1.1(c), which contains the "drug quantity table." This table ties the offense level in almost every federal drug case to the type and quantity of drug involved in the crime. Below is an abridged version of the drug quantity table (set out in two parts due to space) that shows the relevant offense levels for some of the most common controlled substances. The table only lists the minimum drug quantity for each offense level. The maximum quantity for each range is the minimum for the next offense level—for example, the range for heroin in offense level 34 is "[a]t least 10 KG but less than 30 KG." U.S.S.G. § 2D1.1(c)(2).

Drug Quantity Table, U.S.S.G. § 2D1.1(c)—Offense Levels 38–24

	Offense Level	38	36	34	32	30	28	26	24
Substance & Quantity	Heroin	90 kg	30 kg	10 kg	3 kg	1 kg	700 g	400 g	100 g
	Cocaine	450 kg	150 kg	50 kg	15 kg	5 kg	3.5 kg	2 kg	500 g
	Cocaine base	25.2 kg	8.4 kg	2.8 kg	840 g	280 g	196 g	112 g	28 g
	Methamphetamine	45 kg	15 kg	5 kg	1.5 kg	500 g	350 g	200 g	50 g
	Methamphetamine (actual)	4.5 kg	1.5 kg	500 g	150 g	50 g	35 g	20 g	5 g
	LSD	900 g	300 g	100 g	30 g	10 g	7 g	4 g	1 g
	Marihuana*	90,000 kg	30,000 kg	10,000 kg	3,000 kg	1,000 kg	700 kg	400 kg	100 kg
	Hashish	18,000 kg	6,000 kg	2,000 kg	600 kg	200 kg	140 kg	80 kg	20 kg
	Hashish oil	1,800 kg	600 kg	200 kg	60 kg	20 kg	14 kg	8 kg	2 kg

* In cases involving marijuana plants, the guidelines instruct courts to "treat each plant, regardless of sex, as equivalent to 100 G of marihuana. *Provided*, however, that if the actual weight of the marihuana is greater, use the actual weight of the marihuana." U.S.S.G. § D21.1(c) n.(E).

Drug Quantity Table, U.S.S.G. § 2D1.1(c)—Offense Levels 22–6

	Offense Level	22	20	18	16	14	12	10	8	6
Substance & Quantity	Heroin	80 g	60 g	40 g	20 g	10 g	<10 g	X	X	X
	Cocaine	400 g	300 g	200 g	100 g	50 g	<50 g	X	X	X
	Cocaine base	22.4 g	16.8 g	11.2 g	5.6 g	2.8 g	<2.8 g	X	X	X
	Methamphetamine	40 g	30 g	20 g	10 g	5 g	<5 g	X	X	X
	Methamphetamine (actual)	4 g	3 g	2 g	1 g	500 mg	<500 mg	X	X	X
	LSD	800 mg	600 mg	400 mg	200 mg	100 mg	<100 mg	X	X	X
	Marihuana	80 kg	60 kg	40 kg	20 kg	10 kg	5 kg	2.5 kg	1 kg	<1 kg
	Hashish	16 kg	12 kg	8 kg	5 kg	2 kg	1 kg	500 g	200 g	<200 g
	Hashish oil	1.6 kg	1.2 kg	800 g	500 g	200 g	100 g	50 g	20 g	<20 g

Adjust the offense level: The base offense level set by the amount of drugs involved in the offense is only the starting point for determining the offense level in a particular case. The offense level can increase or decrease as a result of rules meant to factor in other considerations.

For example, a drug defendant's offense level increases by 2 "[i]f a dangerous weapon (including firearm) was possessed" or "[i]f the defendant maintained a premises for the purpose of manufacturing or distributing a controlled substance[.]" U.S.S.C. §§ 2D1.1(b)(1),(12). On the other hand, the offense level decreases by 2 "[i]f the defendant clearly demonstrates acceptance of responsibility for his offense" or "[i]f the defendant was a minor participant" in the crime ("minimal" participation results in a 4 level reduction). U.S.S.G. §§ 3E1.1, 3B1.2. These are just a few examples. Not surprisingly, a body of law has developed on questions like whether a drug courier is a "minor" or a "minimal" participant. In the next section, which focuses on drug quantity, *United States v. Rodriguez De Varon* provides an example of how one federal circuit approaches that issue.

Although these adjustments can have a significant impact on the offense level in any particular case, in most cases the amount of drugs involved in the crime is the predominant factor that drives the offense level.

Calculate the offender's criminal history: Once the offense level has been determined, the offender's criminal history will fix the applicable sentencing range. As the sentencing table above shows, there are six criminal history categories. The number of criminal history "points" a defendant has will dictate which category applies. A defendant with zero or one point is in category one, a defendant with two or three points is in category two, and so on.

The table below provides a simplified version of the major criminal history provisions contained in U.S.S.G. § 4A1.1:

Points	Triggering event
3	Each prior sentence of imprisonment exceeding one year and one month
2	Each prior sentence of imprisonment between 60 days and one year and one month
1	Each prior sentence of less than 60 days of imprisonment
2	If the defendant committed the instant offense while under any criminal justice sentence—e.g., while on probation or parole

An example case: To put all of this together, try calculating the sentencing range under the guidelines for this example case. Derrick is convicted of possession of marijuana with the intent to distribute. The offense involved 150 kg of marijuana and Derrick received a 2 level "minor role" reduction.

Derrick has one prior conviction that resulted in a sentence of one year of probation. Derrick committed the instant offense (possession of marijuana with the intent to distribute) while he was on probation.

What is Derrick's sentencing range?

The federal sentencing guidelines and the right to a trial by jury: When first enacted, the sentencing guidelines were mandatory. This meant that if the sentencing range in a particular case was 46–57 months, the judge was *required* to impose a sentence within that range. The only exception was if there was a statutory basis for a "departure," which the guidelines permitted in "specific, limited cases." *United States v. Booker*, 543, U.S. 220, 234 (2005).

Today, the guidelines are advisory, not mandatory. But most judges still continue to adhere to them in most cases.

The switch from a mandatory to an advisory system came as the result of litigation, not legislation. Beginning in the late 1990s, the Supreme Court decided a series of cases that called the constitutionality of the guidelines into question. In these decisions, the court held that the Sixth Amendment's guarantee of the right to a trial by jury meant that "any fact that increases the penalty for a crime beyond the prescribed statutory maximum must be submitted to a jury, and proved beyond a reasonable doubt." *Apprendi v. New Jersey*, 530 U.S. 466 (2000). The theory was that allowing judges to engage in fact-finding to increase a defendant's punishment in these circumstances undermined the role of the jury and the defendant's constitutional right to a jury trial.

This line of cases ultimately doomed the sentencing guidelines in their original mandatory incarnation. This is because the guidelines operate by calling on judges to engage in post-trial (or post-plea) fact-finding—by, for example, deciding if the defendant possessed a weapon or if he played an aggravating role in the crime. In the 2005 case of *United States v. Booker*, the Supreme Court found this system violated the Sixth Amendment's jury trial guarantee, at least so long as judges were *required* to follow the guidelines. Instead of striking down the guidelines in their entirety, however, the Court simply excised the statutory language that made the guidelines mandatory.

The practical effect of the *Booker* decision was to leave the sentencing guidelines intact while rendering them advisory. The fact that the guidelines are advisory does not mean that courts are free to disregard them completely, however. Sentencing judges are still required to "begin all sentencing proceedings by correctly calculating the applicable Guidelines range." *Gall v. United States*, 552 U.S. 38, 49 (2007). At that point, the *Booker* decision grants the trial court the power to impose a sentence outside of the applicable guidelines range. But this authority is not unlimited. Federal sentencing decisions are still subject to appellate review for reasonableness under an abuse of discretion standard.

Despite the power given to trial courts by *Booker*, most judges continue to impose "within range" sentences—meaning a sentence within the range provided for by the sentencing guidelines—in most cases.

Mandatory minimum penalties

In addition to the guidelines, federal drug cases are sometimes subject to mandatory minimum penalties. Mandatory minimum penalties do not exist for many federal crimes. This is in contrast to the sentencing guidelines, which apply in all federal criminal cases, except for very minor ones. Mandatory minimum penalties are most common in three categories of offenses: drugs, firearms, and child-sex offenses. The policy reasons behind Congress's decision to provide for mandatory minimum penalties for certain offenses but not others has been the subject of a great deal of criticism and debate, especially when it comes to mandatory minimum drug penalties.

While federal criminal law has included mandatory minimum penalties since 1790, "they remained rare . . . until the passage of the Narcotic Control Act of 1956, which imposed stiff mandatory sentences for drug importation and distribution[.]" Stephen J. Schulhofer, *Rethinking Mandatory Minimums*, 28 WAKE FOREST L. REV. 199, 200–01 (1993). The Narcotic Control Act's mandatory minimum penalties were harsher than today's penalties in some respects and more forgiving in others. The 1956 law set "a mandatory sentence of five years . . . for first offenses of sale of narcotic drugs [or] marihuana" along with a minimum of 10 years for subsequent offenses. Ross B. Ellis, *A General Outline of Federal Narcotics Statutes*, 18 FOOD DRUG COSM. L.J. 372, 374 (1963). The 1956 law was heavily criticized and even led some federal prosecutors to become reluctant to pursue drug cases. In response, Congress repealed the Narcotic Control Act's mandatory minimums in 1970.

During the drug war in the 1980s, Congress revived mandatory minimums for drug cases. In 1986, Congress "set up a new regime of non-parolable, mandatory minimum sentences for drug trafficking offenses that tied the minimum penalty to the amount of drugs involved in the offense." UNITED STATES SENTENCING COMMISSION, MANDATORY MINIMUM PENALTIES IN THE FEDERAL CRIMINAL JUSTICE SYSTEM: A SPECIAL REPORT TO CONGRESS 10 (1991). Two years later, in 1988, Congress extended drug quantity-based mandatory minimum penalties to apply to convictions for attempts and conspiracies.

Today, drug cases make up the lion's share of federal prosecutions that involve a mandatory minimum sentence. In fiscal year 2016, drug offenses accounted for more than two-thirds (67.3%) of the federal convictions that carried a mandatory minimum sentence, "significantly higher than the next closest category of offenses." U.S. SEN'G COMM'N, OVERVIEW OF MANDATORY MINIMUM PENALTIES IN THE FEDERAL CRIMINAL JUSTICE SYSTEM 34 (2017).

Mandatory minimum penalties based on drug quantity: Mandatory minimum penalties based on drug type and quantity are the most common. Drug quantity-based mandatory minimum penalties can come into play for the main drug trafficking offenses—manufacture, distribution, possession with intent to distribute, and importation—and extend to conspirators and accomplices to those crimes. *See* 21 U.S.C. §§ 841(b) and 960(b).

The penalties are as follows:

Drug Quantities Triggering a Mandatory Minimum Sentence*

	5 year mandatory minimum	10 year mandatory minimum
Cocaine (powder)	500 grams	5 kilograms
Cocaine base (crack)	28 grams (Prior to enactment of the Fair Sentencing Act on August 3, 2010, 5 grams)	280 grams (Prior to enactment of the Fair Sentencing Act on August 3, 2010, 50 grams)
Heroin	100 grams	1 kilogram
Lysergic acid diethylamide (LSD)	1 gram	10 grams
Marijuana	100 kilograms or 100 plants	1,000 kilograms or 1,000 plants
Methamphetamine	5 grams of methamphetamine or 50 grams of a mixture or substance containing a detectable amount of methamphetamine	50 grams of methamphetamine or 500 grams of a mixture or substance containing a detectable amount of methamphetamine
Fentanyl	40 grams or 10 grams if an analogue	400 grams or 100 grams if an analogue
Phencyclidine (PCP)	10 grams of PCP or 100 grams of a mixture or substance containing a detectable amount of PCP	100 grams of PCP or 1 kilogram or more of a mixture or substance containing a detectable amount of PCP

To trigger these penalties, the amount of drugs involved in the offense must be charged in the indictment and proven to the jury beyond a reasonable doubt (or admitted to by the defendant as part of a plea). *Alleyne v. United States*, 133 S. Ct. 2151 (2013). As a result, prosecutors have a great deal of control over whether a mandatory minimum penalty will apply in any given case through their charging decisions.

Mandatory minimum enhancements for recidivists: Drug quantity-based mandatory minimum penalties can increase for offenders who have a prior conviction for a "serious drug felony" or a "serious violent felony." A single prior conviction can double a five-year drug quantity-based mandatory minimum sentence; 10-year quantity-based penalties increase to 15 years. If the defendant has two prior applicable convictions, a 10-year mandatory minimum can become a mandatory 25 years. Before passage of the FIRST STEP Act in late 2018 (discussed later in this chapter), these penalties were even longer.

* Unless otherwise noted, all quantities refer to a "mixture or substance containing a detectable amount of" the relevant drug. 21 U.S.C. § 841(b).

The recidivist enhancements do not apply automatically, however. Instead, to trigger a recidivist enhancement, the prosecutor must affirmatively seek the higher penalties before a defendant is convicted. *See* 21 U.S.C. § 851. This allows prosecutors to rely on the threat of filing a recidivist enhancement for leverage in plea negotiations.

Substantial assistance and the safety valve: Where applicable, the mandatory minimum penalty sets a sentencing floor for the judge. If the applicable mandatory minimum penalty exceeds the penalty called for by the sentencing guidelines, the mandatory minimum controls. There are two situations where a federal judge may impose a sentence below that minimum, however: if the defendant has provided "substantial assistance" to the government or if he qualifies for relief under what is called the "safety valve" provision. Both the safety valve and substantial assistance are covered later in this chapter.

B. Drug Quantity

Formulating criteria for sentencing drug offenders is complicated by the ambiguous nature of many drug offenses. For crimes like murder, burglary or rape, the essence of what makes the offense wrongful is easy to grasp. As a result, though there is surely disagreement about how to differentiate more serious from less serious offenses in these areas, the contours of the debate tend to present themselves naturally. Take homicide offenses as an example. Few would disagree that a person who kills "recklessly" should generally receive a lower sentence than a person who kills "intentionally" because the reckless killer is typically less culpable and dangerous than the intentional killer. We may debate how much more severely intentional killings should be punished, or whether certain types of intentional killings such as those that are "willful, deliberate, and premeditated" should be considered more culpable than other types of intentional killings. But there is broad consensus that a primary factor in determining a homicide offender's blameworthiness (and hence her sentence) is her mental state.

By contrast, because drug offenses lack a direct victim and often involve conduct that is more extensive than a discrete act like a homicide or a burglary, there is greater room for disagreement about what makes them fundamentally wrongful. Consider the following scenario: Kingpin is an illegal marijuana distributor based in San Diego. He purchases 39 kilos of marijuana from Mexico and pays Addict $1,000 to drive the marijuana across the border in a hidden compartment in Addict's car. Addict makes it across the border successfully and arrives at Kingpin's warehouse. At the warehouse, Addict pays Day Laborer $100 to help her unload the marijuana. Acting on a tip, the police go to the warehouse while Addict and Day Laborer are unloading the marijuana and arrest them both. Kingpin, Addict, and Day Laborer have all committed the crimes of conspiracy and possession with intent to distribute. Should each of them receive the same sentence for their crimes? If not, why not? What objective factors could we use to distinguish each offender's sentence?

1. The Importance of Drug Type and Quantity in Sentencing

As discussed in the introduction to sentencing above, drug quantity is usually the single most important factor in a federal drug offender's sentence. The same is true in many states. Is linking drug sentences to quantity an accurate measure of culpability? If not, why does the law place so much importance on drug quantity in sentencing?

United States v. Dossie

United States District Court for the Eastern District of New York
851 F.Supp.2d 478 (2012)

Gleeson, J.

This case illustrates how mandatory minimum sentences in drug cases distort the sentencing process and mandate unjust sentences. In the substantial percentage of cases in which they apply, they produce a sentencing regime that is worse than the one the Sentencing Reform Act of 1984 was enacted to replace. They make opaque what that law was intended to make transparent. They strip criminal defendants of the due process rights we consider fundamental to our justice system. Most importantly, too many nonviolent, low-level, substance-abusing defendants like Jamel Dossie "lose their claim to a future"—to borrow a phrase from Attorney General Eric H. Holder, Jr.—because lengthy mandatory prison terms sweep reasonable, innovative, and promising alternatives to incarceration off the table at sentencing.

A. The Mandatory Minimum Sentences in Drug Cases

1. Why They Were Enacted

Already engaged in a fervent war on drugs, Congress was galvanized by the tragic death by overdose of University of Maryland basketball star Len Bias on June 19, 1986, and it promptly enacted the Anti-Drug Abuse Act of 1986 ("ADAA"). The ADAA created mandatory minimum sentences and enhanced maximum sentences that have now become central features of our federal sentencing landscape. Despite the speed with which the ADAA was enacted, there is ample evidence from related congressional reports of the purpose of the new enhanced minimum and maximum penalties. The ADAA's five-year minimum sentence, with a maximum enlarged from 20 to 40 years (the "5-to-40 sentence enhancement" or the "five-year mandatory minimum"), was specifically intended for the managers of drug enterprises, while the Act's ten-year minimum sentence with life as the maximum (the "ten-to-life sentence enhancement" or the "ten-year mandatory minimum") was intended for the organizers and leaders. The Sentencing Commission's recent report to the Congress on Mandatory Minimum Penalties in the Federal Criminal Justice System provided the following useful summary of that evidence:

> Floor statements delivered by members in support of the [ADAA] and a committee report on a predecessor bill suggest that Congress intended to create a two-tiered penalty structure for discrete categories of drug

> traffickers. Specifically, Congress intended to link the five-year mandatory minimum penalties to what some called "serious" traffickers and the ten-year mandatory minimum penalties to "major" traffickers. Drug quantity would serve as a proxy for identifying the type of trafficker.
>
> Senator Robert Byrd, then the Senate Minority Leader, summarized the intent behind the legislation:
>
>> For the kingpins—the masterminds who are really running these operations—and they can be identified by the amount of drugs with which they are involved—we require a jail term upon conviction. If it is their first conviction, the minimum term is 10 years. . . . Our proposal would also provide mandatory minimum penalties for the middle-level dealers as well. Those criminals would also have to serve time in jail. The minimum sentences would be slightly less than those for the kingpins, but they nevertheless would have to go to jail—a minimum of 5 years for the first offense.
>>
>> A report issued by the House Judiciary Subcommittee on Crime following its consideration of a predecessor bill also provides evidence of Congress's intent to establish two tiered mandatory minimum penalties for serious and major traffickers. The Subcommittee determined that the five and ten-year mandatory minimum sentencing structure would encourage the Department of Justice to direct its "most intense focus" on "major traffickers" and "serious traffickers." "One of the major goals of this bill is to give greater direction to the DEA and the U.S. Attorneys on how to focus scarce law enforcement resources."

U.S. Sent'g Comm'n, *Report to the Congress: Mandatory Minimum Penalties in the Federal Criminal Justice System* 24 (2011) [hereinafter *Mandatory Minimum Report*] (second alteration in original) (quoting 132 Cong. Rec. 27, 193–94 (Sept. 30, 1986); H.R. Rep. No. 99-845, pt. 1, at 11–12 (1986)) (internal footnotes omitted).

2. The Mistake: Using Drug Quantity as a Proxy for Role

Most people would agree that the people who lead or manage drug-trafficking businesses deserve severe punishment. But right from the start Congress made a mistake, which is apparent in the statement of Senator Byrd quoted above: The severe sentences it mandated to punish specified *roles* in drug-trafficking offenses were triggered not by role but by drug type and quantity instead. If it wanted the statute to serve its explicitly stated purpose, Congress should have said that an offense gets the 5-to-40 sentence enhancement when the defendant is proved to be a manager of a drug business. Instead, the 5-to-40 sentence enhancement is triggered by offenses involving 28 grams of crack, 100 grams of heroin, or 500 grams of cocaine. 21 U.S.C. § 841(b)(1)(B). And instead of hinging the ten-to-life sentence enhancement on the government's proof of "kingpin" or leadership status, Congress simply used larger drug quantities: 280 grams of crack, 1,000 grams of heroin, or 5,000 grams of cocaine. 21 U.S.C. § 841(b)(1)(A). So if an offense happens to involve a drug type and quantity that triggers an enhancement, every defendant involved in that crime, whatever his or her actual role, can be treated as a leader or manager at the option of the United States Attorney.[3]

Drug quantity is a poor proxy for culpability generally and for a defendant's role in a drug business in particular. Senator Byrd's statement that the leaders and managers of drug operations "can be identified by the amount of drugs with which they are involved" was incorrect. Compare Defendant A, who organizes a dozen teenagers into a business to distribute cocaine in a New York City housing project and adjacent high school, with Defendant B, an addict who is paid $300 to stand at the entrance to a pier and watch for the police while a boatload of cocaine is offloaded. Defendant A is more culpable, and he is the sort of defendant Congress had in mind when it enacted the ten-to-life sentence enhancement, but he will not face even the 5-to-40 sentence enhancement if the conspiracy is nipped in the bud, before it deals more than half a kilogram of cocaine. Defendant B, on the other hand, qualifies for kingpin treatment and a ten-year mandatory minimum if the prosecutor so chooses, based solely on the amount of cocaine on the boat.

Congress's mistake of equating drug quantity with a defendant's role in the offense need not continue to have the devastating consequences on display in this case. If DOJ [the Department of Justice] invokes the harsh sentence enhancements only in cases in which the defendants have supervisory roles—always fewer than 10% of federal drug cases—such unintended and unjust results can be avoided in the future. However, . . . in deploying the mandatory minimum penalties, DOJ has disregarded their purpose. It has turned a law that sought to impose enhanced penalties on a select few into a sentencing regime that imposes them on a great many, producing unfairly harsh consequences that Congress did not intend.

3. How DOJ Uses the Mandatory Minimum Provisions

DOJ uses mandatory minimum sentences without regard to their purpose. In fiscal year ("FY") 2011, over 74% of crack defendants faced a mandatory minimum, *see* U.S. Sent'g Comm'n, 2011 Sourcebook of Federal Sentencing Statistics tbl.44 (2011) [hereinafter 2011 Sourcebook], yet only 5.4% of them occupied an aggravating role of leader or manager of a drug business, *see id.* tbl.40. Thus, the overwhelming majority of crack defendants who feel the pain of mandatory prison terms are not the criminals Congress had in mind in creating those penalties. The "safety valve" provision that was supposed to save minor defendants from the two-by-four that a mandatory minimum becomes on sentencing day has too many conditions to be effective. Even though more than 94% of crack defendants have no leadership

3. A defendant is subject to the mandatory minimum only if the charging instrument puts him on formal notice of it by alleging the requisite type and quantity of drug and citing the relevant penalty provision. *E.g., United States v. Thomas,* 274 F.3d 655, 663 (2d Cir. 2001). Thus, whether a defendant faces a mandatory minimum at all is a matter left to prosecutorial discretion. At any time during a prosecution the government can withdraw its invocation of the mandatory minimum provision, allowing the court to sentence without being bound by it.

or managerial role, fewer than 10% of such defendants qualify for the safety valve, *see id.* tbl.44.

B. Jamel Dossie and His Offense of Conviction

Jamel Dossie is a young, small-time, street-level drug dealer's assistant. No one could reasonably characterize him as a leader or manager of anything, let alone of a drug business. Like many young men in our community, he was in the drug business because he is a drug user.

Dossie was born in the Brownsville section of Brooklyn. His father's illegal drug use caused a split with his mother before Dossie was even born; Dossie saw his father only three times per year before his father died in 2009. Dossie's mother was (and still is) a bus driver, and she raised Dossie and his two siblings by herself.

By the time Dossie began high school, he was already abusing drugs and alcohol, which got him into trouble regularly. Finally, at age 16, a family court judge ordered him out of his home and into a residential substance abuse treatment program at Phoenix House in the Bronx. Phoenix House reports that Dossie "displayed a poor attitude and unwillingness to engage in treatment" and that he made little academic or clinical progress before his discharge a year later. He never returned to school.

Dossie has a typical criminal history for a young man with his background. A car stop in 2008 led to a simple possession (of marijuana) conviction, and in 2010 he was convicted of a misdemeanor for possessing heroin and crack. His sentences for those misdemeanors were only seven days in custody and probation, respectively, but each conviction nevertheless earned Dossie a criminal history point, terminating any chance he had for safety-valve relief even without considering the two additional points he got for committing his offense while on probation. See 18 U.S.C. § 3553(f).[5] Dossie has no history of violence except as a victim; he was hit in the leg by a stray bullet while walking down the street in 2008.

Dossie on four occasions was a go-between in hand-to-hand crack sales. On April 15, 2010, when Dossie was 20 years old, a confidential informant made a recorded phone call to him and asked about buying crack. Later that day, the informant met Dossie in Brooklyn. Dossie called an unidentified supplier, who arrived by Mercedes Benz ten minutes later. The informant gave $440 to Dossie—$420 for the person in the Mercedes and $20 for Dossie. Dossie took the money into the car. When he got out, the car left, and then Dossie handed the informant 9.4 grams of crack. On April 29, 2010, they did the same thing, except this time it was $860 ($820 for the supplier, $40 for Dossie) for 15.6 grams. This was less crack than the

5. The Sentencing Commission has recommended that Congress "consider marginally expanding the safety valve at 18 U.S.C. § 3553(f) to include certain non-violent offenders who receive two, or perhaps three, criminal history points." *Mandatory Minimum Report* at xxxi; *accord id.* at 355–56. This recommendation is too tepid, given how easy it is for nonviolent offenders to rack up criminal history points, especially while under supervision, *see* U.S.S.G. § 4A1.1(d).

informant had asked for; Dossie explained that the supplier didn't have enough crack and returned $120 to the informant.

On June 10, 2010, they did it again, except this time the supplier of the crack stayed in a nearby store instead of a car, and it was $1,140 ($1,100 for the supplier and $40 for Dossie) for 29.6 grams. Finally, on November 9, 2010, Dossie transferred to the informant 33.5 grams of crack for $1,225. Dossie was arrested three and one-half months later, and he subsequently pled guilty to conspiring to distribute crack.

In sum, Dossie sold a total of 88.1 grams, or 3.1 ounces, of crack. His sole function was to ferry money to the supplier and crack to the informant on four occasions for a total gain to himself of $140.[6]

Dossie's advisory Guidelines range was 57–71 months. That range is too severe for a low-level addict selling drugs on the street. [T]he drug-offense Guidelines ranges are excessively severe. In formulating those ranges, the Commission decided to jettison its pre-Guidelines data and instead chose to make the sentencing range in every single drug case proportional to the onerous mandatory sentences meant only for leaders and managers.

Despite the harsh Guidelines range, Dossie would have had access to justice if he had not been charged with the five-year mandatory minimum enacted for drug business managers. But he caught two bad breaks. First, as the prosecutor pointed out at his sentencing, two of his four crack sales happened to exceed the threshold quantity of 28 grams that can trigger the five-year mandatory minimum. They only barely exceeded it—sales three and four put Dossie in mandatory minimum territory by only 1.6 and 5.5 grams, respectively—but just as baseball is a game of inches, our drug-offense mandatory minimum provisions create a deadly serious game of grams. The conspiracy charge to which Dossie pled guilty also aggregates all 88.1 grams, rendering him eligible for the mandatory minimum on that basis as well.

Dossie's second bad break occurred when the government chose to cite the mandatory minimum provision in the indictment. If it hadn't, I would have been permitted, indeed obligated, to consider, among others, the facts that (1) Dossie had a very minor role in the offense; (2) the drugs he helped to sell weren't his, and he got hardly any money for his involvement; (3) Dossie got off to a very rocky start in life—there's no surer sign of a dysfunctional childhood than a family court judge ordering a 16-year-old out of his home and into a residential drug treatment program; (4) Dossie's criminal record and unsuccessful drug treatment suggest strongly that his legal problems all arose from a drug problem he developed as a child; (5) Dossie is from a very supportive family—his family made all of his court

6. The amounts paid to Dossie are detailed in the Complaint, ECF No. 1. Since the Complaint does not describe the last of the four transactions, I am assuming here that Dossie received $40 for that transaction as well, as it is comparable to the second and third sales, from which he received $40 each.

appearances—which could very well have provided the support he needs to get and remain drug-free; and (6) Dossie is genuinely remorseful. I would have considered all of these factors in sentencing Dossie, and there is no way I would have sentenced him to a prison term within the severe advisory range. I might even have given him the chance to enter our Court's Pretrial Opportunity Program, which would have given Dossie the chance to both conquer his substance abuse problem and avoid prison altogether.[8]

Instead, we had a "sentencing proceeding" that involved no written submissions, no oral advocacy, and no judging. The defense lawyer stated the obvious: The five-year mandatory minimum was more than necessary to properly punish Dossie. The prosecutor agreed that the mandatory minimum of five years should be the sentence. So that was the sentence. The proceeding had all the solemnity of a driver's license renewal and took a small fraction of the time.

C. The Evils of Mandatory Minimum Sentencing

When I observed at Dossie's sentencing that the five-year mandatory minimum was being used by the government to overly punish a defendant for whom it was not intended, the prosecutor assured me that there were "other factors" that justified the mandatory five-year penalty. Specifically, the colloquy went as follows:

> The Court: He's not a kingpin or a manager, he's a street-level dealer, and one would think that if a 60-month sentence were appropriate you'd talk the judge into it rather than bind the judge into it. I think it's an inappropriate exercise of discretion given the purpose of these laws.
>
> The Prosecutor: Well, I think in terms of the exercise of discretion, I don't think that the only question from the office's perspective is what the quantity involved is. I think there are a lot of other factors and information that go into it. And because we're not relying on any of that at sentencing I wouldn't necessarily belabor it, but I think there are other factors that go into a charging decision and I can represent to the Court that there are besides just mere quantity.

As this dialogue exemplifies, the use of these mandatory minimum provisions—which were utilized in over 74% of all crack cases in FY 2011, *see* 2011 Sourcebook tbl.44—results in a sentencing process that is far more objectionable and dangerous than the regime the Guidelines were created to replace. It is true that the

8. The Pretrial Opportunity Program is designed for nonviolent defendants with documented substance abuse problems. Participating defendants have their sentences postponed to engage in drug treatment that involves monthly meetings with the sentencing judge and the Chief Magistrate Judge of the district. The program relies on drug court methodologies that have been proven successful in many state criminal justice systems. If the defendant successfully completes the program by, *inter alia*, staying drug-free for at least one year, the post-arrest rehabilitation is considered by the sentencing judge. For a description of the program, see U.S. Pretrial Servs. Agency, E.D.N.Y., Pretrial Opportunity Program (2012), *available at* http://www.nyed.uscourts.gov/pub/docs/local/POPDescription01112012.pdf.

pre-Guidelines regime was a "wasteland" characterized by unexplained, unguided, and unreviewed sentencing discretion, Marvin E. Frankel, *Lawlessness in Sentencing*, 41 U. Cin. L. Rev. 1, 54 (1972); *see also* Kate Stith and José A. Cabranes, *Fear of Judging: Sentencing Guidelines in the Federal Courts* 172 (1998) ("What made sentencing authority truly extraordinary . . . was not the broad discretion the judge exercised, but rather, the fact that his decision was virtually unreviewable on appeal."), but at least the discretion was exercised by a *judge*, whose mission was to impose a just sentence. The sentencing discretion in Dossie's case was exercised by one of the parties to the case, in furtherance of the undisclosed interests of law enforcement.

Moreover, even the harshest critics of the Guidelines acknowledge that one of their greatest accomplishments is transparency. Judges now must follow established procedures and explain the reasons for their sentences. Those procedures, together with the reasons for the sentence and the sentence itself, are all subject to appellate review. This case reveals how mandatory-minimum provisions create the ultimate opaque sentencing regime: No explanation is required for why Dossie must do five years, none of the "factors" that went into the selection of that sentence was offered, and appellate review is impossible.

When I pressed the government further, the prosecutor reluctantly implied that the decision to charge Dossie with the mandatory minimum might have related to "information that . . . link[s] him to a gang." I agree that if Dossie were dealing drugs as his way of participating in a gang, that would be a relevant, aggravating sentencing consideration. I think any judge would want to know facts like what sort of gang it was, what Dossie's alleged link to it was, how long any such link lasted, and how Dossie's actions as a middleman in street-level drug deals were related to the gang. But in this respect as well, Dossie's case places in clear relief the insidious consequences of mandatory sentencing provisions. If not for the mandatory minimum, Dossie would have had the opportunity to contest the government's suggestion that his offense was gang-related, and the government would have had the obligation to prove it.

That's how our system is supposed to work; if facts material to the sentencing are in dispute, they get resolved after both sides have notice of them and an appropriate opportunity to be heard. Where the fact in dispute would aggravate the sentence, the government bears the burden of persuasion. These are basic tenets of due process.

Mandatory minimum sentencing strips all of this away. In Dossie's case, the government's unreviewable decision to invoke the mandatory sentencing provision made the actual facts irrelevant. Dossie might have denied a gang affiliation or that any such affiliation had anything to do with his offense. The government might not have been able to prove its suggestion that Dossie was linked to a gang. Dossie, for all we know, might even have been able to affirmatively disprove the link. But because a mandatory minimum was involved and everyone agreed that Dossie should not be sentenced above that minimum, none of these facts mattered. The government simply dictated a five-year sentence without even having to allege, let alone prove, the aggravating fact that it implied warranted the sentence. There is no fairness in a system that allows that to happen.

In *Dossie*, Judge Gleeson writes that Congress intended to punish leaders and managers of drug operations when it enacted mandatory minimum penalties in 1986, but that it "made a mistake" by linking punishment to drug type and quantity instead of to role. "If it wanted the statute to serve its explicitly stated purpose," Gleeson argues, "Congress should have said that an offense gets the 5-to-40 sentence enhancement when the defendant is proved to be a manager of a drug business. Instead, the 5-to-40 sentence enhancement is triggered by offenses involving 28 grams of crack, 100 grams of heroin, or 500 grams of cocaine."

If Congress truly meant to reserve mandatory minimum penalties for organizers and leaders, why do you think it chose to tie the penalties to drug type and quantity? One answer might be that drug quantity is a much easier metric for lawmakers to define and for courts to apply than more open-ended concepts like whether a person is a leader in a drug organization. Drug type and quantity can be "easily reduced to quantifiable and therefore readily compared scales," making them a natural fit for minimum penalties and guidelines sentencing. Ian Weinstein, *Fifteen Years after the Federal Sentencing Revolution: How Mandatory Minimums Have Undermined Effective and Just Narcotics Sentencing*, 40 Am. Crim. L. Rev. 87 (2003). Simply put, "objective factors, such as drug weight or dollar amount" result in a more "workable system" than "subjective [factors], such as the offender's role or state of mind[.]" Paul J. Hofer and Mark H. Allenbaugh, *The Reason Behind the Rules: Finding and Using the Philosophy of the Federal Sentencing Guidelines*, 40 Am. Crim. L. Rev. 19 (2003).

The use of drug type and quantity in sentencing is especially controversial in drug courier cases because couriers often possess significant quantities of drugs even though they are on the periphery of the drug trade. Critics argue that this can result in punishments that are only minimally related to the defendant's culpability. Imagine, for example, two drug couriers who are each paid $1,500 to drive vehicles across the border. Neither courier is told the drug type or quantity in his vehicle. They are both caught at the border and arrested. Courier A's car turns out to have a moderate amount of marijuana inside of it. In Courier B's car, the agents find a large amount of methamphetamine. In this hypothetical, Courier B is likely to receive a significantly longer sentence than Courier A, even though their cases are arguably indistinguishable from the perspective of moral blameworthiness.

Supporters of the current system typically point to utilitarian considerations. They argue that calibrating drug courier sentences to the drug type and quantity involved in the offense is necessary to deter drug importation and distribution. If couriers were to receive the same or very similar sentences regardless of what they were carrying, the argument goes, drug cartels would have a strong incentive to give couriers as large a quantity of drugs as logistically possible.

For those who object to current drug courier sentencing practices on retributivist grounds, utilitarian justifications are unlikely to be persuasive. Putting retributivist objections to one side, however, the effectiveness of the current system is also debatable. A study by Caleb Mason and David Bjerk shined some light on this issue by analyzing data from probable cause statements for every federal drug smuggling case along the Southwest border of the United States between 2006 and 2010. The pair found that "the data shows the cartels do compensate [couriers] for differential sentencing risk [based on drug type and quantity], but that doing so is actually quite cheap. As a fraction of the cargo value, it is a drop in the bucket." Caleb Mason, *International Cooperation, Drug Mule Sentences, and Deterrence: Preliminary Thoughts From the Cross-Border Drug Mule Survey*, 18 Sw. J. Int'l L 189 (2011). *See also, e.g.*, Jonathan P. Caulkins, C. Peter Rydell, William L. Schwabe, and James Chiesa, *Mandatory Minimum Drug Sentences: Throwing Away the Key or the Taxpayers' Money?*, RAND (1997) (estimating that arresting, prosecuting, and sentencing more dealers to standard prison terms would be more cost effective than sentencing fewer dealers to longer, mandatory terms).

Though drug sentences are largely driven by drug type and quantity, most sentencing schemes allow for additional factors to influence the final sentence. As discussed in the introduction to sentencing above, the federal sentencing guidelines take offender characteristics like role in the offense or acceptance of responsibility into account for sentencing. In federal drug courier cases, a frequently litigated issue is the extent to which a courier may receive a sentencing reduction under the Guidelines for having played a "minimal" or "minor" role in the offense. Under the Guidelines, minimal participants may receive a "four-level" reduction while minor participation yields a "two-level" reduction. Drug couriers who hope to receive these reductions can face an uphill battle in front of some judges, however.

United States v. Rodriguez De Varon

United States Court of Appeals for the Eleventh Circuit
175 F.3d 930 (1999)

Marcus, J.

The central issue presented in this appeal is whether the district court clearly erred in denying a drug courier who imported 512.4 grams of 85 percent pure heroin from Colombia into the United States a two-point downward adjustment for her minor role in the offense under § 3B1.2 of the United States Sentencing Guidelines. U.S. Sentencing Guidelines Manual § 3B1.2 (1996) [hereinafter U.S.S.G.]. We hold that the district court did not commit clear error, that there was in fact ample evidence in the record to support its determination that the defendant did not play a minor role in the offense. Accordingly, we affirm the judgment of the district court.

On June 12, 1996, Isabelle Rodriguez De Varon ("De Varon") smuggled 70 heroin-filled pellets into the United States. She had ingested the pellets and smuggled them from Colombia into the United States inside her body. Upon arrival,

De Varon reported to United States Customs. Suspecting that she was an internal carrier of narcotics, the customs officials confronted De Varon and she confessed. The government then accompanied De Varon to a hospital and ultimately recovered 512.4 grams of 85 percent pure heroin. At the time of her arrest, De Varon was carrying $2,350. De Varon admitted that a woman identified only as "Nancy" provided her with $1,350 of travel advance money and instructed her to bring an additional $1,000 of her own money to cover her expenses. De Varon said that upon delivery of the drugs in Miami she had expected to receive $6,000.

A federal grand jury returned a two-count indictment against De Varon, charging her with importing heroin into the United States and with possessing heroin with the intent to distribute it. Pursuant to a plea agreement with the government, De Varon pled guilty to the allegations in Count I and agreed to forfeit the $2,350 she was carrying at the time of her arrest in return for the government agreeing to dismiss Count II. The government also agreed that it would not oppose De Varon's request for a three-level sentence reduction for timely acceptance of responsibility, *see* U.S.S.G. § 3E1.1, or her application for the "safety valve" protection provided in the Guidelines if she met all of the requirements.

The district court accepted the plea and ordered a probation officer to prepare a Presentence Investigation Report ("PSI"). The PSI set De Varon's base offense level under the Guidelines at 28. The officer then deducted two levels because De Varon qualified for the "safety valve" provision and three more levels for De Varon's timely acceptance of responsibility for her conduct. After these adjustments, De Varon's resulting offense level was 23. The probation officer then assigned De Varon a criminal history category of I because she had no prior criminal convictions. The sentencing guideline range for an offense level of 23 with a criminal history of I is 46 to 57 months.

De Varon objected to the PSI's assessment and claimed, *inter alia,* that she should be granted a downward adjustment for her minor role in the offense under U.S.S.G. § 3B1.2. In support of her claim, De Varon argued that she was an internal carrier of narcotics and that she was recruited by another, more culpable participant. Specifically, De Varon relied on the oral statement that she had given to the probation officer who prepared her PSI. That statement is recounted in De Varon's PSI as follows:

> [De Varon] reports that she met a lady by the name of Nancy at the office where she works in Colombia. Nancy inquired about moving some items with the trucking company [that employed De Varon]. After several visits to the company, Nancy asked [De Varon] if she possessed a visa. [De Varon] reports that Nancy knew that [De Varon] was having financial problems. [De Varon] reports that her son is mentally retarded and requires medical attention. Nancy asked [De Varon] if she would bring drugs to the United States. [De Varon] was told that she would have to swallow some pills and that [she] would be paid $6,000. [De Varon] relates that she agreed to swallow the drugs because she needed the money for her ill child. [De Varon] states that she knew what she did was wrong and regrets her actions.

At sentencing, De Varon's counsel further said that De Varon was "prepared to testify to that statement before the Court today, if the Court so chooses." De Varon did not present any other information or evidence in support of her claim.

The district court then denied De Varon's request for a minor role reduction[.]

The district court subsequently sentenced De Varon to 46 months of imprisonment, three years of supervised release, and a $100 assessment. The district court also ordered that De Varon be deported as a condition of her supervised release. De Varon appealed her sentence on the ground that the district court erred in failing to reduce her sentence based on her minor role as a heroin courier.

On appeal, a panel of this Court vacated De Varon's sentence and remanded the case to the district court for resentencing. Following the issuance of the panel's opinion, the government filed a suggestion of rehearing *en banc* with this Court. On May 29, 1998, this Court granted the government's petition, entered an order vacating the panel's decision, and set the case for *en banc* rehearing.

This Court has long and repeatedly held that a district court's determination of a defendant's role in the offense is a finding of fact to be reviewed only for clear error.

The sentence imposed for a particular offense is based upon the applicable sentencing offense levels set forth in Chapter Two (Offense Conduct) of the Sentencing Guidelines. A sentence adjustment for "the role the defendant played in committing the offense" (either mitigating or aggravating) may also be available. Specifically, a defendant may receive a two to four level reduction in her base offense level where her role in the offense can be described as minimal, minor, or somewhere in between. *See* U.S.S.G. § 3B1.2. Minimal participants may receive a four-level reduction, minor participants may receive a two-level reduction, and those whose participation falls in between may receive a three-level reduction. The commentary to the Guidelines instructs that a four-level reduction "is intended to cover defendants who are plainly among the least culpable of those involved in the conduct of a group.... [and their] lack of knowledge or understanding of the scope and structure of the enterprise and of the activities of others is indicative of a role as minimal participant." The application note provides, for example, that a four-level reduction would be appropriate "for someone who played no other role in a very large drug smuggling operation than to off-load part of a single marihuana shipment, or in a case where an individual was recruited as a courier for a single smuggling transaction involving a small amount of drugs." In contrast, a minor role in the offense "means any participant who is less culpable than most other participants, but whose role could not be described as minimal." U.S.S.G. § 3B1.2, comment. (n.3).

The proponent of the downward adjustment—here the defendant—always bears the burden of proving a mitigating role in the offense by a preponderance of the evidence.

Notwithstanding our deference to the district court's discretion in this uniquely fact-intensive inquiry, the district court's ultimate determination of the defendant's role in the offense should be informed by two principles discerned from the

Guidelines: first, the defendant's role in the relevant conduct for which she has been held accountable at sentencing, and, second, her role as compared to that of other participants in her relevant conduct. We address each of these principles in turn.

First and foremost, the district court must measure the defendant's role against the relevant conduct for which she has been held accountable. This measurement is compelled by both the Guidelines and our case precedent. The Guidelines provide that the district court should evaluate the defendant's role in the offense "on the basis of all conduct within the scope of § 1B1.3 (Relevant Conduct), *i.e.*, all conduct included under § 1B1.3(a)(1)–(4), and not solely on the basis of elements and acts cited in the count of conviction." In other words, the district court must assess whether the defendant is a minor or minimal participant in relation to the relevant conduct attributed to the defendant in calculating her base offense level.

We believe that this principle of symmetry of relevant conduct is analytically sound. One main purpose of the Guidelines is to punish similarly situated defendants in a like-minded way. However, given the relatively broad definition of relevant conduct under § 1B1.3, some defendants may be held accountable for conduct that is much broader than their specific acts. A conspiracy conviction is the classic example of this phenomenon. In such cases, a defendant's relevant conduct may be coextensive with the entire conspiracy even though her role in that conspiracy was relatively minor. Under these circumstances, a district court may adjust the defendant's sentence for her mitigating role in this broad criminal conspiracy. This adjustment allows a district court to impose a sentence that more closely mirrors the defendant's actual conduct, furthering the Guidelines' goal of imposing comparable sentences for similar acts. However, such an adjustment only makes sense analytically if the defendant can establish that her role was minor as compared to the relevant conduct *attributed to her.* Otherwise, a defendant could argue that her relevant conduct was narrow for the purpose of calculating base offense level, but was broad for determining her role in the offense. A defendant cannot have it both ways. Application note four illustrates this principle by analogy: "If a defendant has received a lower offense level by virtue of being convicted of an offense significantly less serious than warranted by his actual criminal conduct, a reduction for a mitigating role under this section ordinarily is not warranted because such defendant is not substantially less culpable than a defendant whose only conduct involved the less serious offense." According to this example, a defendant must prove that she played a minor role in the relevant conduct attributed to her. Where her actual conduct is more serious than her base offense level suggests, a defendant will not be able to meet this burden. Similarly, where the relevant conduct attributed to a defendant is identical to her actual conduct, she cannot prove that she is entitled to a minor role adjustment simply by pointing to some broader criminal scheme in which she was a minor participant but for which she was not held accountable.

Moreover, a defendant's status as a drug courier does not alter the principle that the district court must assess the defendant's role in light of the relevant conduct attributed to her. In [a prior case], we recognized that courier status in and of itself is not dispositive of whether a defendant is entitled to or precluded from receiving a downward adjustment for role in the offense. Simply put, the drug courier may or may not qualify for a minor role reduction. Having posited this unremarkable proposition, however, it is perfectly legitimate for a district court to consider *any* fact related to a defendant's conduct as a courier in an importation scheme, including her status and assigned tasks in that scheme. Indeed, in many drug courier cases these are the *only* discernable facts. Therefore, when a drug courier's relevant conduct is limited to her own act of importation, a district court may legitimately conclude that the courier played an important or essential role in the importation of those drugs. This is permissible even though facts related to the defendant's status as a drug courier form the basis for this determination. We do not create a presumption that drug couriers are never minor or minimal participants, any more than that they are always minor or minimal. Rather, we hold only that the district court must assess all of the facts probative of the defendant's role in her relevant conduct in evaluating the defendant's role in the offense.

We further note, in the drug courier context, that the amount of drugs imported is a material consideration in assessing a defendant's role in her relevant conduct. Indeed, because the amount of drugs in a courier's possession—whether very large or very small—may be the best indication of the magnitude of the courier's participation in the criminal enterprise, we do not foreclose the possibility that amount of drugs may be dispositive—in and of itself—in the extreme case.

Indeed, the Guidelines explicitly recognize that amount of drugs may be determinative in the context of minimal participants. Application note two states that an adjustment for minimal participation "would be appropriate, for example, for someone who played no other role in a very large drug smuggling operation than to off-load part of a single marihuana shipment, or in a case where an individual was recruited as a courier for a single smuggling transaction involving a small amount of drugs." U.S.S.G. § 3B1.2, comment. (n.2). We do not believe that the Guidelines intended to preclude a district court from considering the amount of drugs as a factor in the context of minor participants.

To reiterate, in determining a defendant's role in the offense, a district court must measure the defendant's role against the relevant conduct attributed to her in calculating her base offense level. This methodology is essential to any evaluation of mitigating role. Only if the defendant can establish that she played a relatively minor role in the conduct for which she has already been held accountable—not a minor role in any larger criminal conspiracy—should the district court grant a downward adjustment for minor role in the offense.

The second principle we derive from the text of the Guidelines is that the district court may also measure the defendant's culpability in comparison to that of other participants in the relevant conduct. We draw this principle from two application notes. Application note one states that minimal participants are those "who are plainly among the least culpable of those involved in the conduct of a group." U.S.S.G. § 3B1.2, comment. (n.1). Application note three says that "a minor participant means any participant who is less culpable than most other participants, but whose role could not be described as minimal." U.S.S.G. § 3B1.2, comment. (n.3). These definitions clearly contemplate some assessment of relative culpability. However, not all participants may be relevant to this inquiry. First, the district court should look to other participants only to the extent that they are identifiable or discernable from the evidence. This is a fact-intensive inquiry. Second, the district court may consider only those participants who were involved in the relevant conduct attributed to the defendant. The conduct of participants in any larger criminal conspiracy is irrelevant.

Relative culpability does not end the inquiry, however. The fact that a defendant's role may be less than that of other participants engaged in the relevant conduct may not be dispositive of role in the offense, since it is possible that none are minor or minimal participants.

In sum, we believe that a district court's determination of a defendant's mitigating role in the offense should be informed by two modes of analysis: First, and most importantly, the district court must measure the defendant's role against the relevant conduct for which she was held accountable at sentencing; we recognize that in many cases this method of analysis will be dispositive. Second, the district court may also measure the defendant's role against the other participants, to the extent that they are discernable, in that relevant conduct.

In making the ultimate finding as to role in the offense, the district court should look to each of these principles and measure the discernable facts against them. In the drug courier context, examples of some relevant factual considerations include: amount of drugs, fair market value of drugs, amount of money to be paid to the courier, equity interest in the drugs, role in planning the criminal scheme, and role in the distribution. This is not an exhaustive list, nor does it suggest that any one factor is more important than another. In the final analysis, this decision falls within the sound discretion of the trial court. Indeed, we acknowledge that a similar fact pattern may on occasion give rise to two reasonable and different constructions. This is inherent in the fact-intensive inquiry specifically contemplated by the Guidelines. As the Supreme Court has recognized, a trial court's choice between "two permissible views of the evidence" is the very essence of the clear error standard of review. So long as the basis of the trial court's decision is supported by the record *and* does not involve a misapplication of a rule of law, we believe that it will be rare for an appellate court to conclude that the sentencing court's determination is clearly erroneous.

Applying the aforementioned analysis to the instant case, the district court's determination that De Varon did not play a minor role in the relevant conduct of heroin importation was not clearly erroneous.

The record amply supports the district court's finding that De Varon did not play a minor role in her offense of heroin importation. First, De Varon played an important or essential role in her relevant conduct of importing 512.4 grams of 85 percent pure heroin from Colombia into the United States. De Varon knowingly and intentionally entered the United States with the entire amount of drugs in her possession. Although De Varon claims that she did not supply the heroin, we believe that it was within the trial court's discretion to conclude that her participation was central to the importation scheme. Second, De Varon's relevant conduct involved carrying a substantial amount of heroin of high purity. Third, although De Varon was, by one construction of the evidence, arguably less culpable than the only other known participant, Nancy, it is altogether possible on this abbreviated record for the trial court to have concluded that Nancy was no more than a messenger and of relatively equal culpability to De Varon. The facts, as recounted by De Varon, even if fully credited by the trial court, establish no more than that she was hired by someone (Nancy) to smuggle one-half kilogram of heroin into the United States, and to deliver the drugs to someone else—albeit unidentified—in Miami. This bare record does not compel the conclusion that Nancy was sufficiently more culpable than De Varon. At all events, these choices fell within the district court's discretion under U.S.S.G. § 3B1.2. Fourth, De Varon's admission that she furnished $1000 of her own money to finance the smuggling enterprise may likewise be taken as support for the district court's conclusion, notwithstanding De Varon's claim that she became involved in the enterprise because of financial problems.

We reiterate that the burden of establishing a minor role in the offense rests with the proponent. De Varon was free to put on evidence in support of her position, and the district court was free to find, as it plainly did, that De Varon failed to meet this burden.

Moreover, the defendant's alternate suggestion that the district court was obligated to investigate and make detailed findings concerning the relative roles of all who may participate in a far-flung narcotics enterprise—that may stretch from the grower, to the manufacturer in a foreign land, through the distribution mechanism, to the final street-level distributor in the United States—is similarly without merit.

On the basis of this record and consonant with this Circuit's longstanding view affording substantial deference to the district court, we conclude that the district court's determination that De Varon was not entitled to a downward adjustment for her minor role in the offense was not clearly erroneous. Accordingly, De Varon's sentence must be, and is, AFFIRMED.

Barkett, J., dissenting.

In applying the law to the facts to determine whether a § 3B1.2 minor role reduction is warranted, a district court should be guided by the spirit and the letter of the Sentencing Guidelines. The "guidance" offered by the majority in this regard is not supported by either, and in fact, conflicts with both.

The majority offers two "principles" which should guide the inquiry: "first, the defendant's role in the relevant conduct for which she has been held accountable at sentencing, and second, her role as compared to that of other participants in her relevant conduct." As the Guidelines make clear, a defendant's "relevant conduct" for purposes of § 3B1.2 includes not just the defendant's *own* acts but also, in the case of jointly undertaken criminal activity, the acts of any other participants in the offense of conviction taken "during the commission of the offense of conviction, [or] in preparation for that offense," whether or not the case is charged as a conspiracy.

This broad understanding of a defendant's "relevant conduct" as expressed in the Guidelines reflects an awareness of two factors of significance here: (1) many criminal endeavors, even those not charged as conspiracies, are joint undertakings involving several participants; and (2) different levels of culpability may be appropriately ascribed to participants in a joint criminal enterprise when those participants perform different tasks in furtherance of the crime charged.

Perhaps no crime illustrates these considerations as effectively as that of importing narcotics through the use of swallowers like De Varon. It is of course true that the completion of this crime requires the participation of a courier, but the actions of a courier are hardly the only components of the crime. Rather, several other significant tasks must be undertaken to complete even the simple crime of importation. Someone must, for example, formulate the plan, recruit the participants, coordinate their actions, locate suppliers, procure the drugs, purchase the tickets, arrange for a drop-off on the other side, and finance the whole venture. All of these activities, which may or may not involve only one person, constitute "relevant conduct" with respect to the crime of importation, "whether or not charged as a conspiracy." U.S.S.G. § 1B1.3 comment. (n.2).

The task of district courts in cases like De Varon's is therefore to determine the relative culpability of the courier as compared to those other participants, if any, who performed the additional tasks necessary to the importation scheme. In a given case, the same person may be found to have performed all the many tasks necessary to complete the crime of drug importation—the masterminding, financing, recruiting, coordinating, procuring, etc. In such a case, that person would plainly not be entitled to a § 3B1.2 role reduction as a minor participant. In other cases, however, the tasks necessary to carry out the crime of importing narcotics will be undertaken by several different participants. Here, if the court finds the defendant "less culpable than most other participants" although her "role could not be described as minimal," it must likewise conclude that a § 3B1.2 minor role reduction is appropriate. Indeed, it is precisely for such cases that § 3B1.2 was intended.

In this case, the district court reasoned that but for the acts of couriers like De Varon there would be no crime of importation, thus essentially rejecting the suggestion that a courier could ever be a minor participant in this crime. Yet this "but for" analysis could be applied to most criminal acts prosecuted, treating all those defendants performing acts necessary to accomplish the crime as equally culpable. The Guidelines, however, reject this categorical approach and instead support the principle of relative culpability by enhancing the punishment for those with greater responsibility in the criminal enterprise and reducing the punishment for those less culpable. Specifically, the commentary to § 3B1.1 identifies characteristics which would make a participant "integral and essential" to the enterprise and therefore more culpable, including the exercise of decision making authority, the nature of participation in the commission of the offense, the recruitment of accomplices, the claimed right to a larger share of the fruits of the crime, the degree of participation in planning or organizing the offense, the nature and scope of the illegal activity, and the degree of control and authority exercised over others.

These same factors also help distinguish those individuals who play only a minor role in the criminal activity from the leaders and other mid-level criminal actors, clearly indicating the Sentencing Commission's view that foot soldiers who actually carry out the crime are less culpable than the "organizers, leaders, managers or supervisors." Under the facts of a given case, a foot soldier may well not receive a § 3B1.2 reduction, but it is wrong to assume that by virtue of his or her participation he or she is automatically to be considered "integral or essential" to the crime.

It is important to recognize what this Guidelines scheme does *not* entail. The majority fears that a defendant could "argue that her relevant conduct was narrow for the purpose of calculating base offense level, but was broad for determining her role in the offense." I agree with the majority that our opinion in *United States v. Fernandez*, 92 F.3d 1121 (11th Cir.1996), in which we reject the defendant's suggestion that his role in the offense could be determined on the basis of an *uncharged conspiracy*, forecloses such an argument. However, under the definition of "relevant conduct" established in the Guidelines, a defendant whose *charged crime* required the performance of several different tasks and whose own actions toward the common goal were minor in relation to the other participants could well be found to be *a minor participant in the conduct on which her base offense level was calculated.* This is directly acknowledged in the Guidelines, which broadly defines an individual defendant's "relevant conduct" for purposes of establishing the base offense level to include "all reasonably foreseeable acts and omissions of others in furtherance of the jointly undertaken criminal activity." U.S.S.G. § 1B1.3(a)(1)(B). *See also* U.S.S.G. § 1B1.3 comment. (n.2) (defining a "jointly undertaken criminal activity" as a criminal plan "undertaken by the defendant in concert with others, whether or not charged as a conspiracy").

Therefore, it seems clear that, under the Guidelines, if a drug courier is found to have acted in concert with others, his or her acts in furtherance of the charged conduct are to be measured against the acts of those others, regardless of whether the offense was charged as a conspiracy or a simple count of importation.

I am also troubled by the suggestion that *in and of itself* the amount of drugs attributed to a defendant has any bearing on whether that defendant is entitled to a minor role reduction. The amount involved may be taken into account, but always as part of the inquiry into relative culpability. The majority asserts that "the amount of drugs in a courier's possession ... may be the best indication of the magnitude of the courier's participation in the criminal enterprise." This may or may not be the case, however, depending on how the amount informs the evidence, viewed in light of § 3B1.2's emphasis on the relative culpability of the defendant to be sentenced. The majority does not explain how it is that the culpability of a drug courier *as compared with "most other participants"* in the offense, U.S.S.G. § 3B1.2 comment. (n.3) (emphasis added), would be affected by the amount of drugs with which she was caught. Whatever amount the courier sought to smuggle will be the same amount that defines the offense, and the same amount that must therefore be attributed to the other participants in the scheme. De Varon, for example, was convicted of importing 512.4 grams of 85 percent pure heroin. This is the same amount given to her by "Nancy" and organized by Nancy or others for her to carry. The amount, in other words, remains constant throughout the court's assessment of De Varon's role in the relevant conduct relative to the other participants in the offense. For this reason, when assessing the relative culpability of the participants—the guiding consideration for courts considering requests for minor role reductions—the amount of drugs may well be beside the point.

Finally, I must also dissent from the reasoning used by the majority to uphold the district court's conclusion that De Varon was not entitled to a minor role reduction. First, the district court made no credibility determination regarding De Varon's testimony, and we are in no position to do so here. The most generous interpretation of the district court's ruling on this record is that it provided no indication as to the court's view of the defendant's credibility.

Moreover, assuming that there was such a "finding," which I believe the record refutes, I cannot agree with the majority's analysis concluding that the record in this case "amply supports the district court's finding that De Varon did not play a minor role in her offense of heroin importation." The majority explains that "[t]he facts, as recounted by De Varon, even if fully credited by the trial court, establish no more than that she was hired by someone (Nancy) to smuggle one-half kilogram of heroin into the United States, and to deliver the drugs to someone else—albeit unidentified—in Miami. This bare record does not compel the conclusion that Nancy was sufficiently more culpable than De Varon."

I find this logic flawed. According to De Varon's testimony, if De Varon were to be believed, we know that someone else—maybe Nancy,[6] maybe one or more other participants—masterminded and financed the operation, called the shots, recruited and coordinated the several players, procured the drugs, bought the tickets, and arranged for a drop-off in Miami. In light of this knowledge, De Varon's inability to provide the names of the other participants should not be allowed to render her ineligible for a minor role reduction. Yet rather than assessing De Varon's role in the offense in light of all the relevant conduct suggested by both the law and common sense, the majority implicitly crafts a rule to the effect that, for purposes of § 3B1.2, an unnamed participant to the crime is no participant at all.

---

6. If "Nancy was no more than a messenger and of relatively equal culpability as De Varon," this may only go to show merely that both Nancy *and* De Varon were minor participants in the relevant conduct.

The majority's implicit requirement that a defendant must provide the names of all the participants to the crime has the paradoxical and troubling effect of rendering defendants with little inside knowledge or understanding of the larger scheme less likely to receive a minor participant reduction, while allowing those defendants with sufficient knowledge to name all the players and the tasks performed by each to widen the range of participants against whose actions theirs will be judged, thus making them more likely to receive the reduction. Yet as the Guidelines explicitly recognize, a "defendant's lack of knowledge or understanding of the scope and structure of the enterprise and of the activities of others is indicative of a role as minimal participant." U.S.S.G. § 3B1.2 comment. (n.1). This is not to say that where the concerted criminal act involves a single leader and many actors with small roles, the minor players would necessarily be entitled to reductions as "less culpable than most other participants." At the same time, however, minimal knowledge of the larger scheme should not automatically defeat the very defendants who might be most entitled to a § 3B1.2 reduction.

Either a witness who professes to possess limited information about the larger scheme is telling the truth, or she is not. If the judge finds it to be the latter, the judge is free to deny the reduction. But if the judge finds the witness credible and the testimony consistent, the judge may on the basis of the testimony alone determine that the defendant is entitled to a reduction. The judge would, in that instance, consider all of those factors which we know to impact upon the concept of relative culpability, including the defendant's level of education and sophistication, prior involvement in criminal activity, and manner of involvement in the concerted criminal activity relative to other participants.

With regard to the manner in which De Varon participated in the crime at issue, I am troubled by the complete exclusion from the majority's discussion of any consideration of what, exactly, De Varon *did*, and what is done by an unfortunately high number of the men and women apprehended as drug smugglers at our nation's borders. She swallowed and carried in her intestinal tract 512.4 grams of 85 percent pure heroin, risking not just an extended stay in an American prison, but her very life.[9] This is not a reason that De Varon should not be held responsible for the act she undertook. But the Guidelines direct courts to determine a defendant's relative culpability, and no one can debate the position of a courier like De Varon in the hierarchy of the criminal enterprise. If De Varon was part of a larger enterprise, it is clear that, as a swallower, she was considered by definition as expendable to that organization, for no organization, illicit or otherwise, would risk the lives of

9. *See United States v. Purchess*, 107 F.3d 1261, 1263–64, 1270–71 (7th Cir.1997) (affirming a § 5K2.1 upward departure for conduct resulting in death, where the defendant was convicted of organizing the importation of drugs through the use of swallowers and one of his couriers died en route of "body packer syndrome" after a "deadly amount of cocaine [] leaked from the [ingested drug-filled] pellets"); *Huguez v. United States*, 406 F.2d 366, 391 (9th Cir.1968) (explaining that "the acidic nature of the gastric juices in the [stomach] makes the swallowing of almost any flexible container of narcotics quite dangerous").

its central or valuable members in this way. The fact that De Varon filled the role of swallower in the importation scheme cannot be totally ignored in considering whether she was a minor player.

For all the foregoing reasons, I would reverse the district court's denial of De Varon's request for a § 3B1.2 minor participant reduction, and remand for the court to consider whether De Varon met her burden of demonstrating that she was less culpable than most other participants in the offense.

Because sentencing schemes vary from state to state, the extent to which factors other than drug type and quantity are considered at sentencing is different in every state. In general, however, the type and quantity of drugs involved in the offense plays a central role in state drug sentencing laws.

The United States is not alone in emphasizing drug type and quantity in sentencing. In the United Kingdom, for example, "the weight and class of drug captured [also] largely determine the sentence." Jennifer Fleetwood, *Five Kilos*, 51 Brit. J. Criminology 375 (2011). Although drug type and quantity may play a similar role for sentencing in other countries, the United States often imposes longer sentences than other countries for comparable drug amounts. *See, e.g.*, MaryBeth Lipp, *A New Perspective on the "War on Drugs": Comparing the Consequences of Sentencing Policies in the United States and England*, 37 Loy. L.A. L. Rev. 979 (2004).

2. Measuring Drug Quantity

a. Carrier Mediums and Cutting Agents

Chapman v. United States

Supreme Court of the United States
500 U.S. 453 (1991)

Chief Justice Rehnquist delivered the opinion of the Court.

Section 841(b)(1)(B)(v) of Title 21 of the United States Code calls for a mandatory minimum sentence of five years for the offense of distributing more than one gram of a "mixture or substance containing a detectable amount of lysergic acid diethylamide (LSD)." We hold that it is the weight of the blotter paper containing LSD, and not the weight of the pure LSD, which determines eligibility for the minimum sentence.

Petitioners Richard L. Chapman, John M. Schoenecker, and Patrick Brumm were convicted of selling 10 sheets (1,000 doses) of blotter paper containing LSD, in violation of § 841(a). The District Court included the total weight of the paper and LSD in determining the weight of the drug to be used in calculating petitioners' sentences. Accordingly, although the weight of the LSD alone was approximately 50 milligrams, the 5.7 grams combined weight of LSD and blotter paper resulted in the imposition of the mandatory minimum sentence of five years required by § 841(b)(1)(B)(v) for distributing more than 1 gram of a mixture or substance containing a detectable amount of LSD. The entire 5.7 grams was also used to determine the base offense level under the United States Sentencing Commission, Guidelines Manual (1990) (Sentencing Guidelines). Petitioners appealed, claiming that the blotter paper is only a carrier medium, and that its weight should not be included in the weight of the drug for sentencing purposes. Alternatively, they argued that if the statute and Sentencing Guidelines were construed so as to require inclusion of the blotter paper or other carrier medium when calculating the weight of the drug, this would violate the right to equal protection incorporated in the Due Process Clause of the Fifth Amendment.

Title 21 U. S. C. § 841(b)(1)(B) provides that

> "any person who violates subsection (a) of this section [making it unlawful to knowingly or intentionally manufacture, distribute, dispense, or possess with intent to manufacture, distribute, or dispense, a controlled substance] shall be sentenced as follows:
>
> . . . .
>
> "(1)(B) In the case of a violation of subsection (a) of this section involving—
>
> . . . .
>
> "(v) 1 gram or more of a mixture or substance containing a detectable amount of lysergic acid diethylamide (LSD);
>
> . . . .
>
> "such person shall be sentenced to a term of imprisonment which may not be less than 5 years. . . ."

Section 841(b)(1)(A)(v) provides for a mandatory minimum of 10 years' imprisonment for a violation of subsection (a) involving "10 grams or more of a mixture or substance containing a detectable amount of [LSD]." Section 2D1.1(c) of the United States Sentencing Commission, Guidelines Manual parallels the statutory language and requires the base offense level to be determined based upon the weight of a "mixture or substance containing a detectable amount of" LSD.

According to the Sentencing Commission, the LSD in an average dose weighs 0.05 milligrams; there are therefore 20,000 pure doses in a gram. The pure dose is such an infinitesimal amount that it must be sold to retail customers in a "carrier." Pure LSD is dissolved in a solvent such as alcohol, and either the solution is sprayed on paper or gelatin, or paper is dipped in the solution. The solvent evaporates, leaving minute amounts of LSD trapped in the paper or gel. Then the paper or gel is cut into "one-dose" squares and sold by the dose. Users either swallow the squares, lick them until the drug is released, or drop them into a beverage, thereby releasing the drug. Although gelatin and paper are light, they weigh much more than the LSD. The ten sheets of blotter paper carrying the 1,000 doses sold by petitioners weighed 5.7 grams; the LSD by itself weighed only about 50 milligrams, not even close to the one gram necessary to trigger the 5-year mandatory minimum of § 841(b)(1)(B)(v).

Petitioners argue that § 841(b) should not require that the weight of the carrier be included when computing the appropriate sentence for LSD distribution, for the words "mixture or substance" are ambiguous and should not be construed to reach an illogical result. Because LSD is sold by dose, rather than by weight, the weight of the LSD carrier should not be included when determining a defendant's sentence because it is irrelevant to culpability. They argue that including the weight of the carrier leads to anomalous results, viz: a major wholesaler caught with 19,999 doses of pure LSD would not be subject to the 5-year mandatory minimum sentence, while a minor pusher with 200 doses on blotter paper, or even one dose on a sugar cube, would be subject to the mandatory minimum sentence.[2] Thus, they contend, the weight of the carrier should be excluded, the weight of the pure LSD should be determined, and that weight should be used to set the appropriate sentence.

We think that petitioners' reading of the statute—a reading that makes the penalty turn on the net weight of the drug rather than the gross weight of the carrier and drug together—is not a plausible one. The statute refers to a "mixture or substance containing a detectable amount." So long as it contains a detectable amount, the entire mixture or substance is to be weighed when calculating the sentence.

This reading is confirmed by the structure of the statute. With respect to various drugs, including heroin, cocaine, and LSD, it provides for mandatory minimum sentences for crimes involving certain weights of a "mixture or substance containing a detectable amount" of the drugs. With respect to other drugs, however, namely phencyclidine (PCP) or methamphetamine, it provides for a mandatory minimum sentence based *either* on the weight of a *mixture or substance* containing a detectable amount of the drug, *or* on lower weights of *pure* PCP or methamphetamine. For example, § 841(b)(1)(A)(iv) provides for a mandatory 10-year minimum sentence for any person who distributes "100 grams or more of . . . PCP . . . or 1 kilogram or more of a mixture or substance containing a detectable amount of . . . PCP. . . ." Thus, with respect to these two drugs, Congress clearly distinguished between the pure drug and a "mixture or substance containing a detectable amount of" the pure drug. But with respect to drugs such as LSD, which petitioners distributed,

2. Likewise, under the Sentencing Guidelines, those selling the same number of doses would be subject to widely varying sentences depending upon which carrier medium was used. For example, those selling 100 doses would receive the following disparate sentences:

Carrier	Weight of 100 doses	Base offense level	Guidelines range (months)
Sugar cube	227 gr.	36	188–235
Blotter paper	1.4 gr.	26	63–78
Gelatin capsule	225 mg.	18	27–33
[Pure LSD]	5 mg.	12	10–16

Congress declared that sentences should be based exclusively on the weight of the "mixture or substance." Congress knew how to indicate that the weight of the pure drug was to be used to determine the sentence, and did not make that distinction with respect to LSD.

Petitioners maintain that Congress could not have intended to include the weight of an LSD carrier for sentencing purposes because the carrier will constitute nearly all of the weight of the entire unit, and the sentence will, therefore, be based on the weight of the carrier, rather than the drug. The same point can be made about drugs like heroin and cocaine, however, and Congress clearly intended the dilutant, cutting agent, or carrier medium to be included in the weight of those drugs for sentencing purposes. Inactive ingredients are combined with pure heroin or cocaine, and the mixture is then sold to consumers as a heavily diluted form of the drug. In some cases, the concentration of the drug in the mixture is very low. *E.g., United States v. Buggs*, 904 F.2d 1070 (CA7 1990) (1.2% heroin); *United States v. Dorsey*, 192 U.S. App. D.C. 313, 591 F.2d 922 (1978) (2% heroin); *United States v. Smith*, 601 F.2d 972 (CA8) (2.7% and 8.5% heroin) (1979). But, if the carrier is a "mixture or substance containing a detectable amount of the drug," then under the language of the statute the weight of the mixture or substance, and not the weight of the pure drug, is controlling.

The history of Congress' attempts to control illegal drug distribution shows why Congress chose the course that it did with respect to sentencing. The Comprehensive Drug Abuse Prevention and Control Act of 1970 divided drugs by schedules according to potential for abuse. LSD was listed in schedule I(c), which listed "any material, compound, mixture, or preparation, which contains any quantity of the following hallucinogenic substances," including LSD. That law did not link penalties to the quantity of the drug possessed; penalties instead depended upon whether the drug was classified as a narcotic or not.

The Controlled Substances Penalties Amendments Act of 1984, which was a chapter of the Comprehensive Crime Control Act of 1984, first made punishment dependent upon the quantity of the controlled substance involved. The maximum sentence for distribution of five grams or more of LSD was set at 20 years. The 1984 amendments were intended "to provide a more rational penalty structure for the major drug trafficking offenses" by eliminating sentencing disparities caused by classifying drugs as narcotic and nonnarcotic. Penalties were based instead upon the weight of the pure drug involved.

The current penalties for LSD distribution originated in the Anti-Drug Abuse Act of 1986, Congress adopted a "market-oriented" approach to punishing drug trafficking, under which the total quantity of what is distributed, rather than the amount of pure drug involved, is used to determine the length of the sentence. To implement that principle, Congress set mandatory minimum sentences corresponding to the weight of a "mixture or substance containing a detectable amount of" the various controlled substances, including LSD. It intended the penalties for drug trafficking to be graduated according to the weight of the drugs in whatever form they were found—cut or uncut, pure or impure, ready for wholesale or ready for distribution at the retail level. Congress did not want to punish retail traffickers less severely, even though they deal in smaller quantities of the pure drug, because such traffickers keep the street markets going.

We think that the blotter paper used in this case, and blotter paper customarily used to distribute LSD, is a "mixture or substance containing a detectable amount" of LSD. Neither the statute nor the Sentencing Guidelines define the terms "mixture" and "substance," nor do they have any established common law meaning. Those terms, therefore, must be given their ordinary meaning. A "mixture" is defined to include "a portion of matter consisting of two or more components that do not bear a fixed proportion to one another and that however thoroughly commingled are regarded as retaining a separate existence." Webster's Third New International Dictionary 1449 (1986). A "mixture" may also consist of two substances blended together so that the particles of one are diffused among the particles of the other. 9 Oxford English Dictionary 921 (2d ed. 1989). LSD is applied to blotter paper in a solvent, which is absorbed into the paper and ultimately evaporates. After the solvent evaporates, the LSD is left behind in a form that can be said to "mix" with the paper. The LSD crystals are inside of the paper, so that they are commingled with it, but the LSD does not chemically combine with the paper. Thus, it retains a separate existence and can be released by dropping the paper into a liquid or by swallowing the paper itself. The LSD is diffused among the fibers of the paper. Like heroin or cocaine mixed with cutting agents, the LSD cannot be distinguished from the blotter paper, nor easily separated from it. Like cutting agents used with other drugs that are ingested, the blotter paper, gel, or sugar cube carrying LSD can be and often is ingested with the drug.

Petitioners argue that the terms "mixture" or "substance" cannot be given their dictionary meaning because then the clause could be interpreted to include carriers like a glass vial or an automobile in which the drugs are being transported, thus making the phrase nonsensical. But such nonsense is not the necessary result of giving the term "mixture" its dictionary meaning. The term does not include LSD in a bottle, or LSD in a car, because the drug is easily distinguished from, and separated from, such a "container." The drug is clearly not mixed with a glass vial or automobile; nor has the drug chemically bonded with the vial or car. It may be true that the weights of containers and packaging materials generally are not included in determining a sentence for drug distribution, but that is because those items are also clearly not mixed or otherwise combined with the drug.

Petitioners argue that the due process of law guaranteed them by the Fifth Amendment is violated by determining the lengths of their sentences in accordance with the weight of the LSD "carrier," a factor which they insist is arbitrary. They argue preliminarily that the right to be free from deprivations of liberty as a result of arbitrary sentences is fundamental, and therefore the statutory provision at issue may be upheld only if the Government has a compelling interest in the classification in question. But we have never subjected the criminal process to this sort of truncated analysis, and we decline to do so now. Every person has a fundamental right to liberty in the sense that the Government may not punish him unless and until it proves his guilt beyond a reasonable doubt at a criminal trial conducted in accordance with the relevant constitutional guarantees. But a person who *has* been so convicted is eligible for, and the court may impose, whatever punishment is authorized by statute for his offense, so long as that penalty is not cruel and unusual and so long as the penalty is not based on an arbitrary distinction that would violate the Due Process Clause of the Fifth Amendment.

We find that Congress had a rational basis for its choice of penalties for LSD distribution. The penalty scheme set out in the Anti-Drug Abuse Act of 1986 is intended to punish severely large-volume drug traffickers at any level. It assigns more severe penalties to the distribution of larger quantities of drugs. By measuring the quantity of the drugs according to the "street weight" of the drugs in the diluted form in which they are sold, rather than according to the net weight of the active component, the statute and the Sentencing Guidelines increase the penalty for persons who possess large quantities of drugs, regardless of their purity. That is a rational sentencing scheme.

This is as true with respect to LSD as it is with respect to other drugs. Although LSD is not sold by weight, but by dose, and a carrier medium is not, strictly speaking, used to "dilute" the drug, that medium is used to facilitate the distribution of the drug. Blotter paper makes LSD easier to transport, store, conceal, and sell. It is a tool of the trade for those who traffic in the drug, and therefore it was rational for Congress to set penalties based on this chosen tool. Congress was also justified in seeking to avoid arguments about the accurate weight of pure drugs which might have been extracted from blotter paper had it chosen to calibrate sentences according to that weight.

Petitioners do not claim that the sentencing scheme at issue here has actually produced an arbitrary array of sentences, nor did their motions in District Court contain any proof of actual disparities in sentencing. Rather, they challenge the Act on its face on the ground that it will inevitably lead to arbitrary punishments. While hypothetical cases can be imagined involving very heavy carriers and very little LSD, those cases are of no import in considering a claim by persons such as petitioners, who used a standard LSD carrier. Blotter paper seems to be the carrier of choice, and the vast majority of cases will therefore do exactly what the sentencing scheme was designed to do—punish more heavily those who deal in larger amounts of drugs.

Petitioners argue that those selling different numbers of doses, and, therefore, with different degrees of culpability, will be subject to the same minimum sentence because of choosing different carriers.[6] The same objection could be made to a stat-

6. We note that distributors of LSD make their own choice of carrier and could act to minimize their potential sentences. As it is, almost all distributors choose blotter paper, rather than the heavier and bulkier sugar cubes.

ute that imposed a fixed sentence for distributing any quantity of LSD, in any form, with any carrier. Such a sentencing scheme—not considering individual degrees of culpability—would clearly be constitutional. Congress has the power to define criminal punishments without giving the courts any sentencing discretion. Determinate sentences were found in this country's penal codes from its inception and some have remained until the present. A sentencing scheme providing for "individualized sentences rests not on constitutional commands, but on public policy enacted into statutes." That distributors of varying degrees of culpability might be subject to the same sentence does not mean that the penalty system for LSD distribution is unconstitutional.

We hold that the statute requires the weight of the carrier medium to be included when determining the appropriate sentence for trafficking in LSD. Accordingly, the judgment of the Court of Appeals is

Affirmed.

Justice Stevens, with whom Justice Marshall joins, dissenting.

The consequences of the majority's construction of 21 U. S. C. § 841 are so bizarre that I cannot believe they were intended by Congress. Neither the ambiguous language of the statute nor its sparse legislative history supports the interpretation reached by the majority today. Indeed, the majority's construction of the statute will necessarily produce sentences that are so anomalous that they will undermine the very uniformity that Congress sought to achieve when it authorized the Sentencing Guidelines.

This was the conclusion reached by five Circuit Judges in their two opinions dissenting from the holding of the majority of the Court of Appeals for the Seventh Circuit sitting en banc in this case. In one of the dissenting opinions, Judge Cummings pointed out that there is no evidence that Congress intended the weight of the carrier to be considered in the sentence determination in LSD cases, and that there is good reason to believe Congress was unaware of the inequitable consequences of the Court's interpretation of the statute. *United States v. Marshall,* 908 F.2d 1312, 1327–1328 (CA7 1990). As Judge Posner noted in the other dissenting opinion, the severity of the sentences in LSD cases would be comparable to those in other drug cases only if the weight of the LSD carrier were disregarded.

If we begin with the language of the statute, as did those judges who dissented from the Seventh Circuit's en banc decision, it becomes immediately apparent that the phrase "mixture or substance" is far from clear. As the majority notes, neither the statute nor the Sentencing Guidelines define the terms "mixture" or "substance." The majority initially resists identifying the LSD and carrier as either a mixture or a substance; instead, it simply refers to the combination, using the language of the statute, as a "mixture or substance containing a detectable amount" of the drug. Eventually, however, the majority does identify the combination as a mixture: "After the solvent evaporates, the LSD is left behind in a form that can be said to 'mix' with the paper. The LSD crystals are inside of the paper, so that they are commingled with it, but the LSD does not chemically combine with the paper." Although it is true that ink which is absorbed by a blotter "can be said to 'mix' with the paper," I would not describe a used blotter as a "mixture" of ink and paper. So here, I do not believe the word "mixture" comfortably describes the relatively large blotter which carries the grains of LSD that adhere to its surface.

Because I do not believe that the term "mixture" encompasses the LSD and carrier at issue here, and because I, like the majority, do not think that the term "substance" describes the combination any more accurately, I turn to the legislative history to see if it provides any guidance as to congressional intent or purpose. As the Seventh Circuit observed, the legislative history is sparse, and the only reference to LSD in the debates preceding the passage of the 1986 amendments to § 841 was a reference that addresses neither quantities nor weights of drugs.

Perhaps more telling in this case is the subsequent legislative history. In a letter to Senator Joseph R. Biden, Jr., dated April 26, 1989, the Chairman of the Sentencing Commission, William W. Wilkens, Jr., commented on the ambiguity of the statute:

> "'With respect to LSD, it is unclear whether Congress intended the carrier to be considered as a packaging material, or, since it is commonly consumed along with the illicit drug, as a dilutant ingredient in the drug mixture.... The Commission suggests that Congress may wish to further consider the LSD carrier issue in order to clarify legislative intent as to whether the weight of the carrier should or should not be considered in determining the quantity of LSD mixture for punishment purposes.'"

Presumably in response, Senator Biden offered a technical amendment, the purpose of which was to correct an inequity that had become apparent from several recent court decisions. According to Senator Biden: "The amendment remedies this inequity by removing the weight of the carrier from the calculation of the weight of the mixture or substance." Although Senator Biden's amendment was adopted as part of Amendment No. 976 to S. 1711, the bill never passed the House of Representatives. Senator Kennedy also tried to clarify the language of 21 U.S.C. § 841. He proposed the following amendment:

> "CLARIFICATION OF 'MIXTURE OR SUBSTANCE.'
>
> "Section 841(b)(1) of title 21, United States Code, is amended by inserting the following new subsection at the end thereof:
>
> "'(E) In determining the weight of a "mixture or substance" under this section, the court shall not include the weight of the carrier upon which the controlled substance is placed, or by which it is transported.'" 136 Cong. Rec. 12454 (1990).

Although such subsequent legislation must be approached with circumspection because it can neither clarify what the enacting Congress had contemplated nor speak to whether the clarifications will ever be passed, the amendments, at the very least, indicate that the language of the statute is far from clear or plain.

In light of the ambiguity of the phrase "mixture or substance" and the lack of legislative history to guide us, it is necessary to examine the congressional purpose behind the statute and to determine whether the majority's reading of the statute leads to results that Congress clearly could not have intended. The figures [contained] in [the table in footnote 2] of the Court's opinion are sufficient to show that the majority's construction will lead to anomalous sentences that are contrary to one of the central purposes of the Sentencing Guidelines, which was to eliminate disparity in sentencing. As the majority's chart makes clear, widely divergent sentences may be imposed for the sale of identical amounts of a controlled substance simply because of the nature of the carrier. If 100 doses of LSD were sold on sugar cubes, the sentence would range from 188–235 months, whereas if the same dosage were sold in its pure liquid form, the sentence would range only from 10–16 months. The absurdity and inequity of this result is emphasized in Judge Posner's dissent:

> "A person who sells LSD on blotter paper is not a worse criminal than one who sells the same number of doses on gelatin cubes, but he is subject to a heavier punishment. A person who sells five doses of LSD on sugar cubes is not a worse person than a manufacturer of LSD who is caught with 19,999 doses in pure form, but the former is subject to a ten-year mandatory minimum no-parole sentence while the latter is not even subject to the five-year minimum. If defendant Chapman, who received five years for selling a thousand doses of LSD on blotter paper, had sold the same number of doses in pure form, his Guidelines sentence would have been fourteen months. And defendant Marshall's sentence for selling almost 12,000 doses would have been four years rather than twenty. The defendant in *United States v. Rose*, 881 F.2d 386, 387 (7th Cir. 1989), must have bought an unusually heavy blotter paper, for he sold only 472 doses, yet his blotter paper weighed 7.3 grams—more than Chapman's, although Chapman sold more than twice as many doses. Depending on the weight of the carrier medium (zero when the stuff is sold in pure form), and excluding the orange juice case, the Guidelines range for selling 198 doses (the amount in *Dean*) or 472 doses (the amount in *Rose*) stretches from ten months to 365 months; for selling a thousand doses (*Chapman*), from fifteen to 365 months; and for selling 11,751 doses (*Marshall*), from 33 months to life. In none of these computations, by the way, does the weight of the LSD itself make a difference—so slight is its weight relative to that of the carrier—except of course when it is sold in pure form. Congress might as well have said: if there is a carrier, weigh the carrier and forget the LSD.
>
> "This is a quilt the pattern whereof no one has been able to discern. The legislative history is silent, and since even the Justice Department cannot explain the why of the punishment scheme that it is defending, the most plausible inference is that Congress simply did not realize how LSD is sold."

Sentencing disparities that have been described as "crazy," and "loony" could well be avoided if the majority did not insist upon stretching the definition of "mixture" to include the carrier along with the LSD. It does not make sense to include a carrier in calculating the weight of the LSD because LSD, unlike drugs such as cocaine or marijuana, is sold by dosage rather than by weight. Thus, whether one dose of LSD is added to a glass of orange juice or to a pitcher of orange juice, it is still only one dose that has been added. But if the weight of the orange juice is to be added to the calculation, then the person who sells the single dose of LSD in a pitcher rather than in a glass will receive a substantially higher sentence. If the weight of the carrier is included in the calculation not only does it lead to huge disparities in sentences among LSD offenders, but also it leads to disparities when LSD sentences are compared to sentences for other drugs.

There is nothing in our jurisprudence that compels us to interpret an ambiguous statute to reach such an absurd result. In construing a statute, Learned Hand wisely counseled us to look first to the words of the statute, but "not to make a fortress out of the dictionary; but to remember that statutes always have some purpose or object to accomplish, whose sympathetic and imaginative discovery is the surest guide to their meaning." In the past, we have recognized that "frequently words of general meaning are used in a statute, words broad enough to include an act in question, and yet a consideration of . . . the absurd results which follow from giving such broad meaning to the words, makes it unreasonable to believe that the legislator intended to include the particular act."

Undoubtedly, Congress intended to punish drug traffickers severely, and in particular, Congress intended to punish those who sell large quantities of drugs more severely than those who sell small quantities. But it did not express any intention to treat those who sell LSD differently from those who sell other dangerous drugs. The majority's construction of the statute fails to embody these legitimate goals of Congress. Instead of punishing more severely those who sell large quantities of LSD, the Court would punish more severely those who sell small quantities of LSD in weighty carriers, and instead of sentencing in comparable ways those who sell different types of drugs, the Court would sentence those who sell LSD to longer terms than those who sell proportionately equivalent quantities of other equally dangerous drugs. The Court today shows little respect for Congress' handiwork when it construes a statute to undermine the very goals that Congress sought to achieve.

I respectfully dissent.

Most states follow the federal approach and measure quantity based on the weight of the total "mixture or substance" rather than the pure controlled substance alone. *Chapman* presents a hard question about how far to extend this principle. Where "cutting agents" are used (such as in the sale of heroin or cocaine), however, application of the rule is straightforward and relatively uncontroversial. In dissent in *Chapman*, Justice Stevens argues that "[t]he consequences of the majority's construction of 21 U.S.C. § 841 are so bizarre that I cannot believe they were intended by Congress." But if cutting agents are included in the measurement of heroin or cocaine, what makes including the weight of the carrier paper (or sugar cube) when weighing LSD bizarre? If the weight of the carrier relative to the weight of the LSD is the answer, what is the response to the case referenced by Justice Rehnquist where the amount of heroin in the overall mixture was only 1.2%? Is the difference between carrier paper and cutting agents simply one of degree?

Not all are in agreement with *Chapman*'s application of "mixture or substance" in the context of carrier mediums. Most notably, the federal Sentencing Commission has taken a different approach, instructing that "[i]n the case of LSD on a carrier medium (e.g., a sheet of blotter paper), do not use the weight of the LSD/carrier medium. Instead, treat each dose of LSD on the carrier medium as equal to 0.4 mg of LSD for the purposes of the [Guidelines'] Drug Quantity Table." U.S.S.G. § 2D1.1(c) note g. *Chapman* remains good law, however, for purposes of mandatory minimum sentencing. The result is somewhat peculiar and cumbersome: the weight of an LSD carrier medium is included when applying federal mandatory minimum sentencing provisions but not when applying the federal sentencing guidelines. *See* United States v. Morgan, 292 F.3d 460, 465 (5th Cir. 2002) (explaining that the "[a]mendments to the Guidelines do not override *Chapman* for the purpose of statutory mandatory minimums").

How far should the definition of "mixture or substance" extend? In *Minnesota v. Peck*, 773 N.W.2d 768 (2009), the Minnesota Supreme Court held that bong water that contains a controlled substance should be included in drug quantity calculations. In *Peck*, the police searched the defendant's home and found a "glass water bong" with 37.17 grams of liquid inside of it that "tested positive for the presence of methamphetamine." In a strident dissent, Justice Paul H. Anderson argued that "permit[ting] bong water to be used to support a first-degree felony controlled-substance charge runs counter to the legislative structure of our drug laws, does not make common sense, and borders on the absurd." The Minnesota legislature partially abrogated the decision in *Peck* by amending its drug laws to provide that "the weight of fluid used in a water pipe may not be considered in measuring the weight of a mixture except in cases where the mixture contains four or more fluid ounces of fluid." Minn. Stat. §§ 152.021, subd. 2(b).

b. Counting Marijuana Plants

Counting the number of plants involved in a marijuana case can be an important, and surprisingly difficult, task. Federal law ties marijuana sentences to either weight or the number of plants involved in an offense. Many states follow this same approach. In non-manufacture cases, sentences are usually based on the weight of marijuana, whereas manufacture cases more often rely on the number of plants. In addition, some states that have legalized marijuana allow residents to cultivate marijuana for personal use but cap the number of plants they may legally grow. As a result, the number of marijuana plants a person is growing can matter a great deal in the eyes of the law.

So, what qualifies as a marijuana "plant"?

Kansas v. Holsted

Court of Appeals of Kansas
52 Kan. App. 2d 655 (2016)

Hill, J.

There is a difference between what might be and what is. In this appeal, we must decide whether marijuana clippings are plants as the term is used in Kansas' statute defining the crime of cultivation of marijuana. Because the clippings here had no roots, we hold the 29 cuttings found by the police were not plants and, therefore, the State failed to prove Steven Holsted was cultivating 5 or more marijuana plants as required by law.

The State charged Holsted with cultivation of marijuana, possession of drug paraphernalia, and possession of marijuana. After the court denied his motion to suppress the evidence based on his allegations of coerced consent to search, Holsted pled guilty to all counts but later withdrew his plea to the cultivation of marijuana charge. The court took up the matter on stipulated facts. We summarize the parties' stipulations:

The Narcotics Unit of the Kansas City, Kansas, Police Department received an anonymous tip advising that there was a strong odor of marijuana coming from a house on 39th Street in Kansas City, Wyandotte County, Kansas. The anonymous tip also described the color of the house and stated that it had a chain link fence.

On March 1, 2013, Kansas City, Kansas, police officers responded to the area and discovered the description of the house actually matched the house next door. Officers knocked on the front door of the house and showed police identification and badges to Holsted. The officers told Holsted that there was a drug complaint regarding his residence. Holsted invited officers inside the residence. Once they were inside, the officers noticed a strong odor of raw marijuana. Holsted admitted to having 2.1 grams of marijuana for personal use, which officers found on the stove in the kitchen.

The officers asked Holsted for permission to search the residence. After that, Holsted signed a consent to search form. Holsted was not under arrest at this time, and he walked around freely and cared for his 3-year-old son.

In the attic of the residence, officers found an apparent marijuana-growing operation. The police found:

- 29 small marijuana plants (marijuana cuttings) with no visible roots in an aeroponic/hydroponic growing system;
- one large marijuana plant with a complete root system;
- one white horticultural 100-watt lighting ballast;
- one four-bulb grow light; and
- one white Sun Leaves grow light.

Additionally, the officers found the 2.1 grams of marijuana in a box on the kitchen stove that Holsted had told them about.

The parties agreed that a marijuana cutting will grow roots in approximately 1 to 3 weeks if kept properly in an aeroponic/hydroponic grow system. Because the 29 smaller marijuana cuttings or clippings came from the larger mother plant, the small marijuana cuttings or clippings would become almost a perfect clone of the mother plant.

In making its ruling, the district court spoke of intent and expectations but not about the cuttings themselves:

> "I suppose if the defendant had snipped these pieces of marijuana from the healthy mother plant and tossed them aside, we wouldn't be here. . . . There's no question the defendant intended and was in the process of cultivating the clippings, the cuttings, from the main plant so that they would propagate and grow stronger: The lights, the water. . . . When you take a clipping from a mature healthy plant and you put it in an environment to propagate and cultivate, then that is indeed a plant, smaller plant, but you have the same expectations."

Thus, the issue is framed. Are 29 marijuana clippings with no roots sitting in a growing medium marijuana plants as contemplated in our cultivation of marijuana law?

We turn first to the charging statute. "Cultivate" means "the planting or promotion of growth of five or more plants which contain or can produce controlled substances." K.S.A. 2015 Supp. 21–5701(c). The term "plants" is not defined. The parties take opposing positions on the issue.

Holsted contends that cuttings or clippings taken from a mother plant are not plants until there is visible root formation. The State contends that clippings or cuttings constitute plants at least when they have been transplanted into an aeroponic/hydroponic grow system, as here.

The Cambridge English Dictionary defines "plant" as "a living thing that usually produces seeds and typically has a stem, leaves, roots, and sometimes flowers." Merriam-Webster defines "plant" as "a living thing that grows in the ground, usually has leaves or flowers, and needs sun and water to survive." A plant includes "a young tree, vine, shrub, or herb planted or suitable for planting." Merriam-Webster The Oxford English dictionary defines "plant" as "[a] living organism of the kind exemplified by trees, shrubs, herbs, grasses, ferns, and mosses, typically growing in a permanent site, absorbing water and inorganic substances through its roots, and synthesizing nutrients in its leaves by photosynthesis using the green pigment chlorophyll." These definitions contemplate that a plant is marked by leaves and roots, growth, and the taking in of sun and water.

The clippings found by the police here were just that—clippings. They may have been on the way to becoming plants, but with no roots they could not sustain life by absorbing water and inorganic substances through their roots. The test thus becomes manifest. Does the cutting have some visible root formation? There is a utility to this test. If the clippings have roots, they are plants. If they have no roots, they are not plants and cannot be the basis for a criminal charge of cultivating marijuana under the statute as it is now written.

After all, the statute speaks to what *is* five or more plants, not what the accused *intends* to grow. We have no doubt that Holsted went to all of this trouble of clipping portions of the mother plant and putting them into the growing medium in the hope that they would develop roots. But Holsted's intent does not make a useful definition of what a plant is.

We have found no Kansas cases on the subject. But at least seven federal circuit courts have defined "plant" in the context of the federal sentencing guidelines. Under the guidelines, the number of plants determines the mandatory minimum sentence for the manufacture, distribution, or possession with intent to manufacture or distribute marijuana when the marijuana is seized in plant form.

The federal circuit courts have uniformly held that a marijuana cutting is not a plant until there is "'some readily observable evidence of root formation.'" *United States v. Foree,* 43 F.3d 1572, 1574, 1581 (11th Cir.1995) (marijuana plants have three characteristics: roots, stems, and leaves); *United States v. Delaporte,* 42 F.3d 1118, 1120–21 (7th Cir.1994) (a cutting that has sprouted roots, even if only rudimentary ones, is a plant); *United States v. Robinson,* 35 F.3d 442, 446 (9th Cir.1994) ("Until a cutting develops roots of its own, it is not a plant itself but a mere piece of some other plant."); *United States v. Burke,* 999 F.2d 596, 600–01 (1st Cir.1993) (a plant exists "at the first sign of roots"); *United States v. Edge,* 989 F.2d 871, 877–79 (6th Cir.1993) (a cutting with callus tissue that formed after the cutting was taken from a mature plant, without more, is not a plant); *United States v. Bechtol,* 939 F.2d 603, 604–05 (8th Cir.1991) (a cutting that has developed root hairs is a plant); *United States v. Eves,* 932 F.2d 856, 859–60 (10th Cir.) (a cutting that has developed a root ball is a plant), *cert. denied* 502 U.S. 884, 112 S.Ct. 236, 116 L.Ed.2d 192 (1991). Later, the federal Sentencing Commission adopted that definition. U.S.S.G. § 2D1.1, cmt. 2 (2015); see *United States v. Fletcher,* 74 F.3d 49, 55 (4th Cir.1996).

Additionally, two state appellate courts have adopted the root requirement in the context of their state's marijuana laws. The Idaho Court of Appeals said it best. "In common parlance, one plant does not immediately become many plants as soon as it is cut into pieces, even if those pieces have been placed in soil or a growing medium." *State v. Schumacher,* 136 Idaho 509, 519–20, 37 P.3d 6 (Ct.App.2001), *rev. denied* December 19, 2001; see *Com. v. Burnsworth,* 543 Pa. 18, 25–27, 669 A.2d 883 (1995). The State cited no cases that have defined the term "plant" differently.

The State contends that Holsted's reliance on the 10th Circuit's holding in *Eves* is misplaced because while the court held that root formation is an indication that a cutting is a plant, it did not hold that root formation is necessary for a cutting to be a plant. To the contrary, in *Eves,* the 10th Circuit was clear that "plant" meant there was some visible root formation, rejecting a more involved scientific inquiry. 932 F.2d at 858, 860. The 10th Circuit affirmed the district court's definition:

> "[A] marijuana 'plant' includes those cuttings accompanied by root balls. Whether the plant could survive on its own would not be an issue; if it looks like a 'plant'—that is, if it has a reasonable root system—it will be considered a 'plant.' No expert need testify, no experiments with instrumentation to monitor whether gaseous exchange is occurring need be conducted, no elaborate trimester or viability system need be established. If a cutting has a root ball attached it will be considered a plant." 932 F.2d at 860.

Additionally, other circuits have squarely held that a cutting without some visible root formation is not a plant. A root must be "readily apparent to the unaided layperson's eye." This root test is a "clear, easily[ ]implemented standard rather than one requiring extensive litigation and expert botanical testimony."

The 10th Circuit reasoned that "[t]o distinguish [two] plants from one plant cut into two pieces, there must be evidence of individual growth after the severance, such as growing of roots, from a cutting." *Eves,* 932 F.2d at 859. A cutting or clipping without roots is not a plant because there is no evidence of individual growth on its own. Once a cutting/clipping has become a plant, *i.e.,* developed roots, then we count it. It does not make a difference whether the plant has newly formed roots or is a fully grown "mother" plant—in other words, it counts at "any level of growth."

The State does not offer any compelling reason to rule in a fashion that differs from the federal courts. Holsted did not possess 29 individual marijuana plants—he possessed 29 freshly cut pieces of his mother plant.

The State contends that the "clear legislative intent is to punish the cultivation of marijuana, and there is no question in this case that the defendant intended for these cuttings to be cultivated and intended and expected these cuttings to become almost exact replicas of the mother plant from which they came." We have no doubt that Holsted's clippings were not only cut from the mother plant but had already been transplanted into an aeroponic/hydroponic grow system such that he was certainly promoting the growth of the clippings into distinct plants.

Indeed, the parties stipulated that *the clippings would grow* roots in approximately 1 to 3 weeks' time if kept properly. We note the future tense of that statement. The clippings here did not yet constitute plants when they were seized by the police.

And, even though Holsted had placed his clippings into a growing medium, that fact does not make his case unlike other cases. For example, in *Edge,* marijuana cuttings were found in a growing medium, saturated with a rooting hormone. Some of the cuttings had developed callus tissue, which is formed after a cutting is clipped from a mature plant and is the marker of the beginning of the development of a root. It is from this callus tissue that roots will come. But, the cuttings did not yet have any visible roots or root hairs. The court adopted the commonly accepted root test and held that those cuttings were not plants.

The legislature set the minimum plant requirement at five. If defendants have only cultivated four plants, they can be punished for the possession of the plants under, but they would not have a sufficiently large enough operation for a cultivation charge. The legislature emphasized the importance of properly counting the plants; the number of plants determines the severity of the crime.

By not defining the term "plants," it is presumed that the common, widely used definition was contemplated. There is a consensus among other courts that the common meaning of "plant" contemplates observable root formation. We share their view.

Here, the parties stipulated that Holsted's clippings had no root formation. Therefore, there was insufficient evidence that Holsted cultivated five marijuana plants in violation of K.S.A. 2012 Supp. 21–5705(c).

Reversed.

c. Calculating Drug Quantity in Conspiracy Cases

As discussed in Chapter 3, federal drug conspiracy convictions can sometimes result in lengthy sentences for peripheral participants in drug operations (such as in the so-called "girlfriend cases"). Part of the reason for this is the method for determining drug quantity in a conspiracy, under which a drug conspirator is sentenced based on the drug quantity that was reasonably foreseeable and in furtherance of the conspiracy rather than the amount of drugs with which she was directly involved.

Weighing the Evidence: Drug Quantity Issues in Mandatory Minimum Cases

Kyle O'Dowd

24 Champion 43 (2000)

Federal drug offenders sentenced in 1998 will spend almost three times as much time in prison as did offenders in 1984. There are three conspicuous causes for this threefold increase in sentence severity: (1) the Anti-Drug Abuse Act of 1986, which established most of the mandatory minimum penalties for drug trafficking; (2) the Omnibus Anti-Drug Abuse Act of 1988, which extended the mandatory minimums to conspiracy cases; and (3) the U.S. Sentencing Guidelines, which incorporate the mandatory minimums for drug offenses. Because the federal sentencing guideline for drug trafficking is invariably applied in roughly 40 percent of all cases the last 15 years have witnessed a sea change in the composition of the federal prison population. In 1984, drug law violators constituted 30 percent of the federal prisoner population—a figure which swelled to 60 percent by the end of 1998. This translates to approximately 60,000 federal prisoners who are confined for drug law violations—many of whom are low-level, first-time offenders.

For all their structural and functional differences, federal mandatory minimums and the Sentencing Guidelines have one thing in common: under both schemes, drug quantity is the most significant determinant of sentences for drug trafficking.

The Omnibus Anti-Drug Abuse Act of 1988 amended 21 U.S.C. § 846 to provide that "any person who attempts or conspires to commit any offense defined in this subchapter shall be subject to the same penalties as those" set forth for the object offenses.[28] Prescribing mandatory minimums for drug offenses charged as conspiracies—"that elastic, sprawling and pervasive offense"—greatly increased the risk of low-level defendants receiving the same sentences as defendants with greater roles.

Exacerbating this risk and carrying the new language to its untenable extreme, prosecutors argued that all the defendants in a drug conspiracy should be held accountable for the entire weight distributed by the conspiracy as a whole. According to this interpretation, which no circuit abided, a defendant who helps a large-volume dealer in completing a single, small sale of drugs is liable for the dealer's prior and subsequent activities. The first published decision on point was *Jones v. United States*, in which the Eighth Circuit held that, with respect to a conviction for conspiracy, a mandatory minimum is triggered by the amount of drugs that was reasonably foreseeable to the defendant and within the scope of the defendant's agreement with the other conspirators.

This two-pronged analysis is also employed by the Sentencing Guidelines, a fact which some courts of appeals have claimed is the basis for adopting the approach. A better rationale—one that does not overstate the influence of the guidelines on interpretation of the mandatory minimum statutes—is that "there is nothing to indicate that Congress intended to abandon the theory of conspiratorial liability that has descended from *Pinkerton*." Regardless of which source the decisions identify, all the circuits to have decided the issue require an assessment of each defendant's level of responsibility.

Drug quantity calculations for defendants who are convicted of conspiracy charges often present particularly difficult challenges for courts. In cases where the conspiracy was still in the planning stages at the time of arrest, the amount of drugs that were actually involved may be zero. At the opposite end of the spectrum, a large-scale ongoing drug operation may involve significant quantities of drugs but it is likely that most members of the group are personally involved with only a small portion of the total amount. *United States v. Hickman* provides one example of some of the issues that can arise when calculating drug quantity in a conspiracy prosecution.

United States v. Hickman

United States Court of Appeals for the Fourth Circuit 626 F.3d 756 (2010)

Davis, J.

The evidence offered by the Government in this prosecution resulted from the confluence of two distinct investigations by federal and local law enforcement

28. Prior to this change, § 846 provided that the sentence "may not exceed the maximum punishment prescribed for the . . . object of the attempt or conspiracy." 21 U.S.C.A. § 846 (West 1981).

agencies into heroin distribution activities in Baltimore. In the course of the federal component of the investigation, agents of the Drug Enforcement Administration obtained wiretaps on the phones of Hickman's co-defendants James Jones (also known as "Fat Cat") and James Henderson, among others, and instituted surveillance of an inner-city store known as Fat Cat's Variety Store, run by Jones.

The wiretaps intercepted calls between Tony Caldwell (who was also a co-defendant) and Jones on April 24, 2007, in which Caldwell informed Jones he had found a buyer for him, whom he called "Hookie" (Hickman). Agents then set up surveillance at Fat Cat's Variety Store. Special Agent Bennet Strickland observed Hickman's car arrive at Fat Cat's Variety Store, and the wiretap confirmed that Hickman and Henderson spoke by phone only minutes before.

A few minutes after Hickman's arrival, Jones called Caldwell to ask if the person named "Kevin" at his store was, in fact, "Hookie," and was told that he was. Jones also told Caldwell that he had five more grams of heroin than Hickman could pay for, and asked whether he should give Hickman the extra five; Caldwell instructed him to deliver only "what he [was] supposed to get". Shortly afterward, Caldwell asked Jones, "You all know each other?" and Jones confirmed, "Yeah, yeah, yeah, I know him, I know him. Definitely yeah." Caldwell then told Jones that Hickman was "my co-defendant," (apparently alluding to an earlier drug prosecution in state court). Just after leaving the store, Hickman spoke with Henderson by phone; Henderson asked if he "ever ma[d]e it to the store" and Hickman confirmed that he had.

The investigators directed city police to stop Hickman, and after allowing Hickman to drive a few blocks away from the store so as not to raise suspicion, Baltimore Police Officer Keith Sokolowski stopped Hickman's vehicle for a traffic violation. Hickman was driving and his girlfriend, Claudia Lake, was in the front passenger seat. Officer Sokolowski testified that he discovered and seized 32.14 grams of heroin in the passenger area of the car, which Lake had tried to hide. Subsequent analysis revealed that the heroin was 38% pure. Sokolowski also found 17 gold-topped vials of heroin hidden under the gas cap of the vehicle, though the heroin in the vials was never weighed.

Hickman was arrested and then released on bail. The day of his release, he called Henderson about arranging an additional purchase from Jones. Over the next few days, the two spoke several times about it; though Hickman told Henderson that he had spoken with Jones and was simply waiting on him, the Government produced no evidence that this plan was ever consummated.

Meanwhile, in a search of Caldwell's house on May 8, 2007 arising from a separate investigation, local law enforcement officers seized 139 grams of heroin, later found to be 29% pure. In a subsequent search of Fat Cat's Variety Store on June 7, 2007, federal agents seized more than 25,000 vials and a variety of colored tops, packaged by the hundred. The evidence showed that the vials were of the sort customarily employed to package street-level quantities of heroin (one-tenth of a gram).

Hickman was charged with seven others in an 11-count superseding indictment. He was named in two counts; count one alleged a "conspir[acy] . . . to distribute, and possess with intent to distribute, one kilogram or more of . . . heroin," and count six alleged "possess[ion] with the intent to distribute a quantity . . . of heroin." Although all of Hickman's co-defendants pled guilty, none of them testified at trial, nor did the Government call as a witness any other participant in the overall conspiracy. Rather, the Government adduced the testimony of the following witnesses: Special Agent Strickland, who was conducting surveillance outside of Fat Cat's Variety Store at the time of Hickman's purchase; Officers Sokolowski and Michael Woodlon, who took part in the traffic stop of Hickman; Detective Constantine Passamichalis, who assisted in the raid on Caldwell's residence; and criminologists Anthony Rumber and Theodis Warnick, Jr., who tested the narcotics seized from Hickman and Caldwell.

Perhaps most significant for purposes of this appeal was extensive testimony from Special Agent Brendan O'Meara, who monitored the Jones wiretap and who was accepted by the court as an expert in narcotics investigations. The Government relied heavily on the content of the wiretap recordings, and it was Agent O'Meara who interpreted them for the jury, explaining the vague and coded terminology used by drug dealers. In its effort to prove that the conspiracy (which the indictment alleged subsisted for only four months, from February 2007 through May 2007) involved more than one kilogram of heroin, the Government asked Agent O'Meara to explain how heroin is typically cut down from its raw, high-purity state to user-strength level of approximately 8% via mixture with mannite and quinine. Critical to the Government's theory of the case was O'Meara's opinion that the 25,000 vials seized from Fat Cat's Variety Store would be enough to hold one kilogram of user-strength heroin.

After the Government rested, the defense moved for a judgment of acquittal, which the district court denied. The defense at no time specifically argued that the Government's proof established only a conspiracy involving a lesser amount than one kilogram, and the defense never requested a lesser included offense instruction. Nor did the defense call any witnesses.

The jury found Hickman guilty on both the conspiracy and possession with intent to distribute counts. The jury was asked on the verdict form to determine whether the amount of heroin involved in the conspiracy and reasonably foreseeable to Hickman was (1) one kilogram or more, (2) less than one kilogram but greater than or equal to one hundred grams, or (3) less than one hundred grams. It found the conspiracy involved one kilogram or more and that such amount was foreseeable to Hickman. Because Hickman had two predicate felony drug convictions which the Government had noticed pursuant to 21 U.S.C. § 851, he was sentenced to life imprisonment on the conspiracy count and to a concurrent sentence of 360 months for possession with intent to distribute.

Overwhelming evidence supports the jury's finding that Hickman was a knowing member of the basic conspiracy alleged in Count I of the superseding indictment.

Conviction for conspiracy to distribute narcotics under 21 U.S.C. § 846 requires proof beyond a reasonable doubt of three elements: (1) "an agreement between two or more persons to engage in conduct that violates a federal drug law"—here, to distribute or possess narcotics with intent to distribute; "(2) the defendant's knowledge of the conspiracy; and (3) the defendant's knowing and voluntary participation in the conspiracy." Proof of a conspiratorial agreement need not be by direct evidence, and rather may "be proven inferentially and by circumstantial evidence."

Given the plethora of direct evidence, including but not limited to the content of the telephone communications and the circumstances surrounding the traffic stop of Hickman, only very modest inferences, if any, were required here to show the existence of a conspiratorial agreement and Hickman's knowing membership in a heroin conspiracy. The damning wiretap recordings reveal Hickman and Henderson's coordination before and after Hickman purchased 32 grams of heroin from Jones; Henderson discussing his stake in the transaction;[3] and later exchanges between Hickman and Henderson concerning the possibility of a subsequent transaction after the police seized the heroin initially purchased. Moreover, agents observed Hickman entering and exiting Jones's store; in the interim, wiretaps record Jones discussing the Hickman sale with Caldwell; and a police stop some minutes later found Hickman in possession of those 32 grams. In the face of this mountain of evidence of Hickman's knowing participation in a heroin distribution conspiracy, Hickman's broader challenge to the sufficiency of the evidence is plainly unavailing.[8]

Although there is overwhelming evidence of Hickman's knowing membership in a heroin distribution conspiracy, his challenge to the jury's finding that the conspiracy of which he became a member involved at least one kilogram of heroin has merit. Sufficient evidence supported a finding that Hickman knowingly became a member of a large-scale heroin distribution conspiracy which involved, at the least Jones, Henderson, and Caldwell, and that many of the acts of the co-conspirators were reasonably foreseeable to Hickman. Yet, no matter how generously we indulge the available *reasonable* inferences in favor of the Government, adding the post-dilution weight of heroin from all known and reasonably inferable transactions—whether completed, attempted, or merely agreed upon by any of Hickman's co-conspirators—to reach a sum of one kilogram, if not a mathematical

3. *See* J.A. 426–27 (an hour after the buy, having just learned of Hickman's arrest, Henderson telling an unidentified man that Hickman "had my fucking bread yo" and complains "I ain't even get to get that [i.e., retrieve the narcotics] from him yo").

8. We pause to acknowledge the practical conundrum faced by counsel for Hickman. Rare is the lawyer who wants to make an argument to a jury that, "My client was not involved in a conspiracy, but if you disagree, it was at most a conspiracy involving less than one kilogram of heroin." Thus, in his arguments on the motion for judgment of acquittal, in his request for jury instructions, and in his closing argument to the jury, counsel largely sought to cast Hickman as involved merely in one or more buy-sell transactions rather than in a conspiracy, and that argument is pressed on us in this appeal. Nonetheless, we have no doubt that Hickman's argument on the motion for judgment of acquittal was adequate to alert the district court to the deficiency in the Government's proof of *drug quantity* and to preserve the sufficiency of evidence issue for purposes of this appeal.

impossibility, would require reasoning so attenuated as to provide insufficient support for the jury's verdict on the one-kilogram verdict.

The jury heard evidence of the amounts and purity of heroin seized during the traffic stop of Hickman and the raid on Caldwell's home; evidence of discussion between Hickman and Henderson of an attempt in the days after Hickman's initial arrest to "do the same thing [transaction] again," presumably with Jones; and a vague statement the defense itself elicited on recross-examination of a Government witness concerning the "recover[y] [of] heroin . . . the week prior" from someone exiting Jones's store.

The indictment alleged a four-month conspiracy. The only definite amounts of heroin established by the Government were the 32.14 grams of 38% pure heroin recovered during the stop of Hickman's vehicle; 17 gold-topped vials also recovered during the traffic stop, the contents of which were never weighed; the 5 grams of heroin Jones kept from Hickman; and 139 grams of 29% pure heroin seized from the raid on Caldwell's apartment. Expert testimony from Agent O'Meara provided a basis for inferring that the coconspirators intended that the heroin be substantially diluted before reaching end-users. To "step on" or "cut down" the heroin, a dealer would mix one part raw heroin with one, two, or three parts of "cut"—the solvent used to dilute the heroin, often mannite or quinine—to reach a concentration fit for most users, which Agent O'Meara estimated to be 8%.

Agent O'Meara's discussion of the dilution process was the jury's only basis for inflating the weight of the recovered heroin, and as such the method of dilution he described must constrain the trier of fact's reasonable inferences. As Agent O'Meara described, raw heroin is said, in the "slang vernacular," to "take[ ] a one, two, or a three" depending on how many parts of solvent are mixed with each part of heroin; because "the drug dealers on the street don't have a laboratory" they are limited to this simple mixing process. Agent O'Meara's lengthy discussion, and the vernacular terms he cites, indicate that this mixing of heroin with "cut" is always in the ratio of 1:n, where n is a natural number. This, of course, would bound the maximum dilution of heroin of a given purity: without "a laboratory" capable of more precise measurements and mixtures, dilution to precisely 8% will ordinarily be impossible. Thus the 38% pure heroin recovered from Hickman would only "take a four"—be mixed 1:4 with solvent—since a 1:5 mixture would decrease the purity below 8%; similarly, the heroin seized from Caldwell, 29% pure, would "take a three."[9] These

9. We note that 8%, though Agent O'Meara gave it as a "rough" estimate of the "average" for lowest-purity "scramble" heroin in Baltimore City, was the lowest purity discussed at trial. The Government's criminologist, who had worked for the Baltimore City Police Department for eleven years and tested "thousands" of samples for the presence of controlled dangerous substances put the weakest heroin submitted to the crime lab for testing at "around 9 to about 11" percent. (In fact, Government counsel pegged "[w]hat's on the street" at "10%" during a colloquy with the district judge and defense counsel, in which he went on to explain to the judge that the Government's theory was that the seized heroin would have been "cut down further . . . [d]own to 10%.") As we view the facts in the light most favorable to the Government, we assume 8% purity was the conspiracy's

dilutions would result in 128.56 grams of 9.5% purity and 417 grams of 9 2/3% purity—together, approximately 546 grams of heroin. But we will assume, *arguendo*, that the Hickman conspiracy would have diluted this heroin precisely to 8% purity, generating 153 grams and 504 grams for Hickman and Caldwell, respectively. Together with the 5 grams Jones kept from Hickman—which, assuming it was of the same purity as the 32 grams Jones sold him, would add another 23.75 grams—the Government would have established a total of 681 grams.

As for the 17 gold-top vials recovered during the traffic stop of Hickman, their contents were never weighed. Rumber, one of the Government's two criminologists at trial, testified that the gross weight of the vials was 24.30 grams, and confirmed that the net weight—the weight of the heroin itself—was never measured. The only testimony on point is from Agent O'Meara, who explained that a vial of heroin typically contains 0.1 grams. Thus the 17 vials support an additional 1.7 grams of heroin. Added to the 681 grams assumed above, this would support a finding of no more than 683 grams.

Evidence concerning the remaining two potential transactions is scant, to say the least. During the week after Hickman's initial arrest and release, he and Henderson spoke about attempting to "do the *same thing again*" and Hickman claimed he had made several telephone calls to a potential narcotics supplier, apparently Jones. Though Hickman remained free until his arrest in August 2007, no evidence of this transaction was offered. Aside from Henderson's reference to "do[ing] the *same thing again*," there is no evidence concerning the amount of heroin Hickman and Henderson sought. Attributing any more than another 32.14 grams to this potential transaction—like the earlier purchase from Jones—would be purely speculative; thus, at a maximum, the jury could find that the conspiracy involved another 153 grams of "cut" heroin, giving them a hypothetical sum of 836 grams.

Evidence of the final alleged transaction—a brief statement on recross-examination by Agent O'Meara about the seizure of some amount of heroin from some individual exiting Jones's store a week before Hickman's purchase—is extremely vague:

> Q. How many people did you stop coming out of Fat Cat's and recover heroin from?
>
> A. We recovered heroin out of—the week prior. I think it was April 17th.
>
> Q. And you recovered it in terms of the stop of Hickman; is that right?
>
> A. Yes, sir.

There is no evidence that this seizure had anything to do with Hickman, Henderson, or Caldwell. Moreover, given that Jones was in the business of selling drug paraphernalia and so would likely be visited by those who had recently bought (or

---

intended target. But finding, beyond a reasonable doubt, even higher weights via speculation as to a lower purity target would be wholly unreasonable on this record.

intended to buy) narcotics elsewhere, there is little reason to believe that the seized heroin had just been sold through Jones's store. That the month-long surveillance of Jones's store bore no more fruit than this single drug seizure further undermines the circumstantial evidence of drug quantity implicating Jones. Even if, squinting our eyes, it were to appear nonspeculative to attach an amount to this earlier seizure and link it to the Count I conspiracy, the evidence could by no means bear any more than the "stepped on" amount of Hickman's purchase from Jones, 153 grams. And even with this final amount, the sum would fall short of one kilogram.

To reach its finding that the Count I conspiracy involved at least one kilogram, the jury would have had to rely on either or both of two grounds: (1) that Hickman was criminally liable for the distribution of heroin by buyers of paraphernalia from Jones—a theory that fails as a matter of law; or that, (2) on account of the conspirators' apparent familiarity with the drug trade, they must have undertaken to distribute some amount beyond the amounts involved in the evidenced transactions. Neither theory can sustain Hickman's conviction on the one-kilogram conspiracy.

The Government told jurors during closing argument that Jones "basically runs a one-stop shop[ ] for heroin," with "thousands and thousands of vials that heroin goes in." Indeed, the evidence well supports the inference that Jones was in the business of selling drug paraphernalia. As Agent O'Meara testified, a raid on Jones's store produced bins containing more than 25,000 glass vials of the sort used to distribute heroin, packaged in groups of one hundred, in various sizes and with variously colored tops, also packaged in groups of one hundred; customers were apprised of the merchandise by a three-ring binder on the counter.

Yet there is absolutely no evidence to support a finding that Hickman is liable for heroin distributions by those who had purchased empty vials from Jones. Indeed, it strains credulity even to think that, on the evidence in the record, Jones himself could be convicted of a widespread conspiracy to distribute heroin on the mere fact that he sells drug paraphernalia and had such packaged merchandise at his store. Finding such conspiracy liability for Jones would have required the trier of fact to find beyond a reasonable doubt that Jones's purchase of paraphernalia for resale evidenced a conspiracy to conspire with future paraphernalia buyers concerning subsequent distribution. While paraphernalia vendors can certainly become parties to the distribution conspiracies of their buyers, such cases present substantial evidence of the vendor's involvement in and/or knowing facilitation of, a distributor's operations.

Tellingly, Agent O'Meara testified that law enforcement "did not stop a lot of people coming out of [Jones's store]" because they knew that Jones was "also selling paraphernalia, like vials, and . . . we're not going to go out and arrest a particular person just for having the actual vials . . . empty vials." "Unless there is a specific reason, [and] we know that a drug deal is taking place," he testified, "we're not just stopping everybody that's coming out of there and . . . trying to pull a bunch of empty vials off the street." In fact, the jury was told that in more than a month of surveillance of Jones's store, only a single patron other than Hickman was found with narcotics on his person. Where the Government failed to present evidence about even a single buyer of the paraphernalia or any plans on the part of Jones to involve himself in the distribution activities of his paraphernalia customers, it would be mere speculation to find that Jones's own distribution activities were coextensive with his paraphernalia business.[11] On this paltry evidence, no reasonable inference as to the scope of Jones's conspiracy to distribute narcotics could be drawn from the amount of paraphernalia merchandise he hoped to sell.

Furthermore, even if the evidence had supported widespread conspiracy liability for Jones on the basis of his trafficking in drug paraphernalia, this liability could not be transferred to Hickman on this record. As an initial matter, while we have assumed that Hickman and Jones conspired together with respect to the distribution chain that included Henderson and Caldwell, no evidence was presented to suggest that the selling of paraphernalia entered into this agreement. Moreover, as there was no evidence that Hickman had or planned to have any involvement with (or even any knowledge of) Jones's paraphernalia buyers, such a conspiracy (having Jones at the center) would have been a classic "rimless," "hub-and-spokes" conspiracy, which has long been held to make out multiple, distinct conspiracies and not a single, large one. Thus evidence of the number of packaged, empty vials in Jones's store is not a sufficient basis for further inflating the amount of heroin ascribable to the Count I conspiracy.

Nor could the jury properly convict Hickman of the one-kilogram conspiracy in reliance on the Government's repeated assertions during closing argument that the four-month Count I conspiracy encompassed far more drug distribution activity (and that Hickman could reasonably foresee such quantity) than that of which the Government could produce competent evidence. The Government strenuously urged jurors to draw such an inference, claiming that the evidence presented was only "a window into the conspiracy," merely "part of something larger"; that the evidenced transactions were simply "two brief episodes . . . in the life of this conspiracy" or "a few days in the life of a heroin conspiracy"; that "this [was] an ongoing course of business," an "ongoing thing." "[I]t's clear," said the prosecutor, "that this is a regular course of business for these gentlemen. It's clear that this isn't the first time they've done this before [sic]. It's clear that this wasn't going to be the last time. . . . [Hickman] would have continued to [seek out drug transactions]."

This line of argument is troubling, not just because it seems to urge jurors to convict the defendant for what he "would have continued to do" which, to the extent

11. Even where co-conspirators have had no connection to paraphernalia sales, and thus any packaging materials would presumably be used for their own distribution, some circuit courts have been skeptical of relying on unused drug packaging materials to increase drug amounts charged to a conspiracy. *See United States v. Henderson*, 58 F.3d 1145 (7th Cir. 1995) (explaining that the court "question[ed] whether multiple boxes of unused baggies present the same degree of reliability [as the used baggies relied on in an earlier case]" and declining to rely upon them to support lower court's finding as to amount of narcotics within the scope of the conspiracy, where lower court's methodology appeared to lack sufficient indicia of reliability).

these hypothesized future bad acts were not captured by an agreement within the charged period, is clearly improper, but also because it invites the jury to speculate as to the amount of heroin involved in the conspiracy.

Where no evidence exists to guide the trier of fact in determining the outer scope of a conspiracy, the trier may not simply guess at the magnitude or frequency of unknown criminal activity. Unbridled speculation is an impermissible basis for conviction beyond a reasonable doubt.

Under more than two decades of federal law, it is impermissible to enhance drug amounts without particularized evidence of narcotics transactions. Federal district courts have long struggled with extrapolating drug amounts under the U.S. Sentencing Guidelines, which instruct that, "[w]here . . . the amount [of narcotics] seized does not reflect the scale of the offense, the court shall approximate the quantity of the controlled substance." U.S.S.G. § 2D1.1 n.12. In reviewing district courts' findings, the courts of appeals have developed a sizable body of case law narrowing the range of permissible inferences. Its teachings are instructive here.

As the First Circuit has explained, "[w]here drug-quantity extrapolations have been upheld, the Government managed to demonstrate an adequate basis in fact and that the drug quantities were determined in a manner consistent with the accepted standards of reasonable reliability." Concerned about the methodologies district courts employ to calculate their extrapolations, courts have cautioned against using small sample sizes.

To be sure, where courts have evidence of a number of transactions, they have been permitted to multiply that number by an average weight-per-transaction to reach an estimate, *see, e.g., United States v. Correa-Alicea,* 585 F.3d 484 (1st Cir. 2009) (upholding such a calculation using "highly conservative" estimates), though the circuit courts have urged district courts to "make conservative approximations," *United States v. Sklar,* 920 F.2d 107 (1st Cir. 1990) ("[W]hen choosing between a number of plausible estimates of drug quantity . . . a court must err on the side of caution.").

Such conservative extrapolation as to the amount sold in *evidenced* transactions is perfectly proper; but the courts of appeals have refused to allow a trier of fact to extend this extrapolation so far as to fabricate transactions of which there is no evidence. Thus the First Circuit has held that evidence that a drug conspiracy "did a substantial amount of narcotics business" was insufficient, "[i]n the absence of *particularized findings,*" to support a determination by a preponderance of the evidence of an amount of narcotics that "seem[ed] attainable given the appellant's role in the conspiracy," explaining that a court "cannot uphold a drug quantity calculation on the basis of hunch or intuition."

Here the Government contends, unpersuasively, that Hickman's use of "vague and coded language" establishes "familiar[ity] with drug trafficking" and that "only someone heavily involved in repeated drug trafficking would be so brazen and unrepentant to return almost immediately to trying to find more heroin to sell." In a case like Hickman's, where a lack of evidence would make particularized findings impossible, courts would have reversed a sentencing court's finding—made by a mere preponderance of the evidence—that Hickman's conspiracy involved one kilogram or more of heroin. And if such an inference would have been too speculative to satisfy the Sentencing Guidelines, which merely require an "approximat[ion]," U.S.S.G. § 2D1.1 n.12, based on evidence with "sufficient indicia of reliability to support a conclusion that they are probably accurate," U.S.S.G. § 6A1.3, then a *fortiori* it would fail to satisfy a rational trier of fact tasked with making findings beyond a reasonable doubt.

In this case, where evidence of unknown transactions was meager and offered virtually no guide as to the amounts that may have been involved, we hold that the jury verdict finding the heroin conspiracy involved one kilogram or more was not supported by sufficient evidence.

Yet it is within our power to direct entry of judgment on a lesser included offense when vacating a greater offense for insufficient evidence.

Because we conclude that the record contains sufficient evidence to persuade a rational fact finder beyond a reasonable doubt of Hickman's guilt on the lesser included offense of conspiracy to distribute one hundred grams or more of heroin, we direct entry of judgment against Hickman under Count I of the indictment for conspiracy to distribute and to possess with intent to distribute heroin in the amount of one hundred grams or more.[12]

Hickman's second contention, that the trial judge erred in rejecting his proposed instructions regarding the amount of heroin attributable to him, is without merit.

At trial, defense counsel requested that the judge instruct the jury that Hickman could only be held responsible for the "amount of drugs that were foreseeable to the Defendant and within the scope of his agreement."

The trial court repeatedly instructed the jury that coconspirators' actual or intended distribution of narcotics could only be charged to Hickman "so long as it was reasonably foreseeable to [him] that such a type and quantity of drugs would be involved in the conspiracy which he joined."

These instructions accord with the principles of *Pinkerton v. United States,* 328 U.S. 640, 66 S. Ct. 1180, 90 L. Ed. 1489 (1946).

To the extent that defendant's proposed instruction differs from the instructions given, it misstates the law. It is true that Hickman is responsible only for the amount of drugs "within the scope of his agreement," if this "scope" is properly understood as encompassing any co-conspirators' conduct in furtherance of the conspiracy and reasonably foreseeable to him; but the trial court instructions adequately covered

12. Because Hickman had been convicted of two prior felony drug offenses, the Government filed a notice of enhanced punishment mandating a minimum mandatory sentence for the one-kilogram conspiracy of life imprisonment. We of course express no view as to what might be an appropriate sentence after further proceedings.

this. If the requested instruction is taken to mean that Hickman is responsible only for an amount of drugs he personally knew of and explicitly agreed to distribute or have distributed, then it mistakes a basic tenet of our conspiracy law, *see Pinkerton*, 328 U.S. at 647. There was no abuse of discretion in the district court's rejection of Hickman's proposed instruction.

For the reasons explained, we conclude that the evidence was insufficient to establish beyond a reasonable doubt that Hickman knowingly became a member of a conspiracy to distribute or to possess with the intent to distribute more than one kilogram of heroin. On the other hand, there is overwhelming evidence in the record to show, beyond a reasonable doubt, that Hickman knowingly became a member of a lesser included conspiracy involving 100 grams or more of heroin, and that such amount was reasonably foreseeable to Hickman. Accordingly, we vacate the conviction for conspiracy to distribute heroin in the amount of one kilogram or more and the life sentence imposed thereon, and we remand the case to the district court with directions to enter a judgment of sentence as to the lesser offense and to resentence accordingly. In all other respects, the judgment is affirmed.

AFFIRMED IN PART, VACATED IN PART, AND REMANDED WITH INSTRUCTIONS

C. Issues in Federal Drug Sentencing

1. Mandatory Minimum Penalties

Competing Sentencing Policies in a "War on Drugs" Era
Hon. William W. Wilkins, Jr., Phyllis J. Newton and John R. Steer

28 Wake Forest Law Review 305 (1993)

In the 1970s, members of the public and Congress denounced the ineffectiveness of the "revolving-door" criminal justice system. Offenders often were incarcerated, deemed rehabilitated, and released only to start the cycle anew. At the same time, the combination of unwarranted disparity in the sentencing of similarly situated offenders and deficiencies in the parole process caused many to question the system's certainty and fairness. Still other critics argued that the disparity problem had an even uglier side, with some defendants being treated by the criminal justice system in a discriminatory manner for reasons unrelated to their offense or offender characteristics properly bearing upon punishment.

In response to these concerns and after more than a decade of study and debate, a bipartisan Congress enacted the most far-reaching reform of federal sentencing in this country's history—the Sentencing Reform Act of 1984 (SRA). This legislation directed the creation of a permanent, bipartisan commission to develop and, over time, refine sentencing guidelines to further the basic purposes of criminal sentencing. In response to concerns that similar defendants convicted of similar offenses were being sentenced dissimilarly, the sentencing guidelines were to provide certainty and fairness at sentencing and reduce the unwarranted disparity in sentencing that Congress found "shameful." Within specific criteria established by the sentencing guidelines, similarly situated federal defendants convicted of similar offenses were to be sentenced within the same, relatively narrow sentencing range which, in the case of imprisonment, could not exceed the greater of twenty-five percent or six months.

As Congress put its finishing touches on the sentencing reform package that abolished parole and mandated sentencing guidelines, problems associated with drug abuse took on increasing national prominence. Opinion polls showed that drug abuse far surpassed economic problems as the number one public concern. Glaring headlines, dramatic footage on nightly news programs, and regular reports in all forms of mass media chronicled various battles in the war on drugs.

Heightened public concern raised congressional awareness of the devastating effects of illicit drugs. Frustrated by the alarming, apparently increasing, flow of drugs into the country, Congress sought a broad solution that involved curbing both the supply and demand for drugs. Moreover, because Congress believed that too often major drug traffickers were arrested, prosecuted, and convicted only to reappear quickly on the streets as a result of unduly lenient sentencing practices by the judiciary, Congress turned to statutorily mandated sentencing provisions for drug offenses in an effort to stop this "revolving door process" in the federal criminal justice system. More than simply a message to the federal judiciary, these swift and certain mandatory provisions were viewed as a statement that society would no longer tolerate the illegal drug epidemic. By enacting mandatory penalty provisions, Congress believed serious drug offenders would have no escape from lengthy terms of imprisonment.

As part of this strategy, Congress passed the Anti-Drug Abuse Act of 1986, which contained a number of mandatory minimum statutory provisions for drug-related offenses. These new mandatory provisions were tied to the quantity of drugs involved in the offense. For example, trafficking in one kilogram or more of a mixture or substance containing a detectable amount of heroin triggers a mandatory minimum sentence of ten years' imprisonment without parole, as does five kilograms or more of a mixture or substance containing a detectable amount of cocaine. For those involved in trafficking somewhat smaller quantities, Congress provided five-year mandatory minimum penalties. For example, the five-year mandatory minimums were triggered by trafficking in 100 grams or more of a mixture or substance containing a detectable amount of heroin, or 500 grams or more of a mixture or substance containing a detectable amount of cocaine.

For defendants with a prior conviction for a felony drug offense, the applicable mandatory minimum sentence was set at twice that otherwise applicable. Also, a mandatory minimum sentence of twenty years would apply if death or serious bodily injury resulted from use of the controlled substance. In addition, the 1986 Act provided an increased mandatory minimum penalty if the drug distribution was to a person under age twenty-one or to a pregnant female, occurred near a school or college, or involved a person under age eighteen in the distribution process.

By 1988, drug-related violence was still on the rise, and many major urban areas experienced record increases in homicide rates and gang violence, often prompted by drug trafficking. Looking to areas not specifically highlighted by the Anti-Drug Abuse Act of 1986, Congress focused on the increased violence associated with the drug trade and the growing involvement of youth. Out of concern for public safety, Congress again considered enacting a number of new mandatory penalties and strengthening some that were already in place.

By the time congressional debate began on the 1988 Anti-Drug Abuse Act, however, a number of congressional members had begun to question the wisdom of the mandatory minimum penalty structures, especially in light of the Sentencing Reform Act of 1984. The record of Senate debate regarding the omnibus drug bill reflects the following statement of Senator Kennedy, pointing to the apparent inconsistencies between mandatory minimum penalties and the SRA:

> As the principal author of the Sentencing Reform Act of 1984, . . . I am concerned about the effect these mandatory sentencing provisions and others in existing law will have on the Sentencing Commission concept and its central role in formulating the details of sentencing policy.
>
> . . . .
>
> For example, mandatory minimum penalty statutes appear to be inconsistent with the guidelines system. Such statutes mandate sentences without regard for either the particular circumstances of the offense or important offender characteristics. As a result, similarly situated defendants may receive different sentences and dissimilarly situated defendants may receive the same sentence. This is precisely the injustice we sought to eliminate in 1984.

Nevertheless, Congress ultimately did include several mandatory minimum provisions in the Anti-Drug Abuse Act of 1988. Perhaps the most far-reaching was a provision making the mandatory minimum sentences for drug distribution and importation/exportation offenses also applicable to convictions for attempts and conspiracies to commit those offenses.

Rethinking Mandatory Minimums
Stephen J. Schulhofer

28 Wake Forest Law Review 199 (1993)

Mandatory minimum penalties have been a feature of federal criminal law since 1790. The first Congress mandated capital punishment for a number of offenses, and statutes mandating prison terms for various offenses were enacted from time to time during the nineteenth century. Mandatories remained rare in the federal system, however, until the passage of the Narcotic Control Act of 1956, which imposed stiff mandatory minimum sentences for drug importation and distribution in an effort to more effectively deter those offenses. In 1970, Congress concluded that its effort to deter through mandatory minimum sentences had been a failure, and it repealed virtually all of the drug mandatories. Congress found that these mandatories actually tended to reduce deterrence because in many instances prosecutors viewed them as too severe and accordingly declined to prosecute violators. Among those who supported the 1970 repeal of drug mandatories was Congressman George Bush, who urged that mandatories were ineffective and unjust.

Fourteen years later the pendulum swung again. In 1984, Congress enacted mandatory penalties for a number of drug offenses and directed that any offender who used or carried a gun during a crime of violence serve a mandatory five-year term, consecutive to the sentence on the underlying offense. Every two years thereafter, from 1986 through 1990, Congress enacted additional mandatories and stiffened some of those already on the books.

The Sentencing Commission [has] identified six objectives of mandatory minimum sentences: assuring "just" (i.e., appropriately severe) punishment, more effective deterrence, more effective incapacitation of the serious offender, elimination of sentence disparities, stronger inducements for knowledgeable offenders to cooperate in the investigation of others, and judicial economies resulting from increased pressure on defendants to plead guilty. Of these objectives, just punishment, effective deterrence and disparity reduction have probably been the goals most prominently and openly cited by legislators. Prosecutors who support mandatories tend to share these goals but often also stress the value of mandatories as a tool for inducing cooperation. The goal of facilitating guilty pleas is less often cited, at least overtly, and recent Justice Department policy has sought to discourage the tactic of bargaining away mandatories to induce a plea. Nonetheless, this last goal remains prominently in the background, an objective that may be primary for prosecutors charged with the day-to-day implementation of mandatories, but which stands in tension with the ostensibly dominant objectives of just punishment, effective deterrence and disparity reduction.

Mandatories require the judge to impose a given minimum sentence upon conviction under a specified charge, but they do not necessarily obligate prosecutors to bring such a charge just because the facts support it. Therefore, the most important question in any mandatory minimum statute concerns the prosecutor's role: Does the statute entail a *mandate to prosecute* or merely an *option to bargain*? Legislatures rarely address this crucial threshold issue explicitly. Rather, they in effect delegate to prosecutors the power to decide whether the statute is really a mandate to impose a minimum sentence or instead is only a source of discretion. Prosecutors, in turn, often assume that the statute imposes no mandate *on them*. Mandatories then become little more than a bargaining chip, a "hammer" which the prosecutor can invoke at her option, to obtain more guilty pleas under more favorable terms. Bargaining-chip mandatories help avoid the high process costs of the additional trials that real mandatories can generate, and they may even *reduce* process costs because potentially severe penalties can induce pleas that would not otherwise be forthcoming. Bargaining-chip mandatories also have two important crime-control benefits. Though they do not constrain prosecutors, they do constrain judges, who are sometimes perceived as more likely than prosecutors to be "soft" on crime. Even when bargained away, the mandatories have crime-control value because they tend to increase the severity of sentences that guilty plea defendants will accept. Yet, the deterrence value of both severity effects is undercut by the uncertainty that mandatories will be applied and by the perception among offenders that the mandatory can be manipulated. Moreover, bargaining-chip mandatories tend to increase rather than reduce disparity because their application depends so much on low-visibility prosecutorial choices and because their most severe effects fall not on flagrantly guilty repeat offenders (who avoid the mandatory by their guilty pleas), but rather on first offenders in borderline situations (who may have plausible defenses and are more likely to insist upon trial).

These potential effects of the bargaining-chip approach are dramatically illustrated by recent experience in the Arizona state courts. Prosecutors there have treated mandatories primarily as a bargaining tool and have made clear their willingness, in return for a guilty plea, to drop counts carrying stiff minimum penalties. As a result, the trial rate in Arizona has fallen dramatically, from ten percent in the period just before introduction of mandatories to only four percent currently. Average sentences, prison populations, and, of course, the correctional budget have all risen substantially, but the deterrence pay-off from these effects remains speculative because of the perception that anyone willing to "cop a plea" can avoid the mandatory sentence. At the same time, mandatories have produced severe punishments for offenders of marginal culpability who showed the poor judgment to insist on trial.

When mandatories are actually applied to all fact situations falling within their scope, predictable and severe sentences are achieved. The results are longer prison terms, increased correctional costs, and enhanced deterrence.

The consequences of inflexibility are difficult to categorize because they are inherently unpatterned and unpredictable. But there are four common effects of inattention to context: cliffs, mistakes, misplaced equality, and the cooperation paradox.

Cliffs result when an offender's conduct just barely brings him within the terms of a mandatory minimum. For example, a first offender who helps sell 495 grams of cocaine might be thought to deserve anywhere from two to four years of imprisonment. Under the sentencing guidelines, his presumptive sentence (after allowance for his acceptance of responsibility and minimal role in the offense) would fall in the range of twenty-seven to thirty-three months, or about two and one-half years. For an identical offender who sold just five grams more, the sentence would double, because the five-year mandatory minimum applicable to sales of 500 grams would kick in. Conversely, an offender facing the five-year minimum can obtain a dramatic decrease in his sentence if he can establish a very small reduction in the quantity for which he is held responsible. The cliff effect means that small drug quantities have enormous importance, while all other factors bearing on culpability and dangerousness have no importance at all.

Misplaced equality occurs even if all outright mistakes can be eliminated. Ensuring equal treatment of like offenders prevents one form of disparity, but the resulting equal treatment of *unlike* offenders creates another serious problem—*excessive uniformity.* Excessive uniformity is inevitable under mandatories because the statutes necessarily single out just one or a very small number of factors to determine the minimum sentence. Offenders who differ in a host of crucial respects receive inappropriately equal treatment.

For example, a common problem associated with mandatories is the equal treatment of offenders who played sharply different roles in the offense. The ringleader faces the same sentence as a moderately important underling, who in turn gets the same sentence as a young messenger or secretary who had little responsibility or control over the events. Parties who were pressured to provide minor assistance face the same sentence as the most violent and abusive leaders. Since mandatories are usually stated as minimums, they could, in theory, incorporate such factors by permitting an offender's role in the offense to aggravate the applicable sentence. However, this approach would require setting the mandatory penalty at the level appropriate for the least culpable offender, and such a statute would hardly "send a message" in the way that legislators intend. Instead, mandatories are invariably pegged at a level that the legislature considers appropriate for a highly culpable participant. In fact, in some of the federal mandatories, the "minimum" sentence is life imprisonment without parole. Just punishment for lesser roles is inevitably precluded.

The cooperation paradox provides a final example of the serious distortions that result from inattention to context. One universally recognized exception to a mandatory minimum requirement is the situation in which a defendant offers to testify against confederates or to provide leads in other investigations. Informal mechanisms for avoiding mandatories, in federal courts and elsewhere, insure that sentence concessions will be available to those defendants who provide the most information at the earliest possible point in an investigation, thus guaranteeing that mandatories will not choke the flow of cooperation. Indeed, mandatories coupled with an exception for cooperation provide powerful inducements for assistance that might not otherwise be forthcoming. This practice is formalized in 18 U.S.C. § 3553(e), which renders all federal mandatories inoperable and authorizes the judge to impose a sentence below the mandatory minimum, if the government makes a motion for a lower sentence on the basis of a defendant's substantial assistance in the investigation or prosecution of others.

Yet, the escape hatch for cooperation creates a paradox. Defendants who are most in the know, and thus have the most "substantial assistance" to offer, are often those who are most centrally involved in conspiratorial crimes. The highly culpable offender may be the best placed to negotiate a big sentencing break. Minor players, peripherally involved and with little knowledge or responsibility, have little to offer and thus can wind up with far more severe sentences than the boss.

Of course, sentence concessions for helping the government have always been part of American sentencing systems and always will be. The vice of an escape hatch for "substantial assistance" stems from its interaction with the unqualified rigidity that mandatories otherwise impose. The quantity-driven drug mandatories pose this problem in its most acute form. Normal principles holding defendants accountable for the acts of their co-conspirators, even if carefully applied, can leave low-level dealers, middlemen and more important distributors responsible for the same quantity of drugs flowing through the conspiratorial network. On a theory of aiding and abetting liability, the "go-fer" who occasionally helps a drug enterprise may be subject to the same penalty as the kingpin, and in some of these cases, the "minimum" can be life imprisonment. Thus, the inflexibility of mandatories means that all participants tend to face the same high sentence, regardless of their limited role in the offense or any mitigating personal circumstances. The "big fish" and the "minnows" wind up in the same sentencing boat. Enter the statutory escape hatch, with sentence concessions that tend to increase with the knowledge and responsibility of the offender. The big fish get the big breaks, while the minnows are left to face severe and sometimes draconian penalties.

This result makes nonsense of the intuitively plausible scale of punishments that Congress and the ordinary person envisage when they think of sentences linked to drug quantity or other hallmarks of the most serious criminal responsibility. Instead of a pyramid of liability with long sentences for leaders at the top of the organizational ladder, the mandatory system can become an inverted pyramid with stiff sentences for minor players and modest punishments for knowledgeable insiders who can cut favorable deals.

2. The "Safety Valve"

In response to the "cooperation paradox" phenomenon discussed above, Congress enacted a "safety valve" law in 1994. The safety valve establishes an exception from mandatory minimum sentences for certain federal drug offenders who meet five statutory requirements. In fiscal year 2016, just under 20 percent of federal drug offenders received relief from mandatory minimum sentences under the safety valve. U.S. Sen'g Comm'n, Overview of Mandatory Minimum Penalties in the Federal Criminal Justice System 39 (2017).

To be eligible for the safety valve, a defendant must meet the following requirements: (1) not have a disqualifying number of criminal history points as determined under the sentencing guidelines; (2) not have used violence or possessed a dangerous weapon in connection with the offense; (3) the offense cannot have resulted in death or serious bodily injury to any person; (4) not have played a managerial or supervisory role, as determined by the sentencing guidelines; (5) truthfully provide the government with all information and evidence concerning the offense. 18 U.S.C. § 3553(f)(1)–(5).

a. The Requirement to Truthfully Provide Information

Of the five safety valve conditions, the requirement to truthfully provide information to the government is "overwhelmingly [the] most frequent area of dispute." George H. Newman, *Fighting for the Safety Valve Reduction (Without Cooperation)*, 33 CHAMPION 24 (2009). In order to meet the requirement, defendants must provide information "whether or not it is relevant or useful to the government's investigation." *United States v. Shrestha*, 86 F.3d 935, 939 (9th Cir. 1996). Why do you think Congress would make a defendant's safety valve eligibility contingent on giving the government information that has no value?

The next case, *United States v. Reynoso*, involved a somewhat unusual set of facts. The defendant provided information that was objectively false. She argued, however, that she subjectively believed the information to be true and attributed the discrepancy to memory impairment. The case required the court to consider whether to apply an objective or a subjective standard to the safety valve's truthful provision of information condition.

United States v. Reynoso

United States Court of Appeals for the Second Circuit
239 F.3d 143 (2000)

Jose A. Cabranes, J.

The facts relevant to this appeal are essentially undisputed. On July 8, 1998, officers and agents of the High Intensity Drug Task Force, a joint task force of the New York City Police Department ("NYPD") and the United States Drug Enforcement Administration, were conducting an investigation in the area of Broadway and 151st Street in Manhattan. As part of that investigation, a confidential informant ("CI") approached an unidentified male and arranged for Ricky Nesmith, an undercover NYPD detective, to purchase 62 grams of crack cocaine. The CI and Detective Nesmith then took a livery taxi to 605 West 151st Street, where the unidentified male had indicated to the CI that the crack cocaine would be delivered.

Soon after the CI and Detective Nesmith arrived at 605 West 151st Street, Reynoso approached the car. Following a conversation with the CI, Reynoso then left. A short time later, however, she returned carrying a brown bag, and handed the bag, which turned out to contain approximately 44 grams of crack cocaine, to the CI. Reynoso told the CI that there were only 45 grams of crack cocaine in the bag, and instructed the CI and Detective Nesmith that because of police activity in the area they should return later for the remaining 17 grams. Reynoso was arrested almost five months later, on December 7, 1998, and charged in a two-count indictment with conspiracy to distribute and possess with intent to distribute more than fifty grams of crack cocaine, in violation of 21 U.S.C. § 846; and distribution and possession with intent to distribute more than five grams of crack cocaine, in violation of 21 U.S.C. § 812, 841(a)(1), and 841(b)(1)(B).

On August 13, 1999, Reynoso met with prosecutors for a so-called "safety valve proffer." At the meeting, Reynoso informed the Government that she had been addicted to drugs at the time she distributed the crack cocaine to Detective Nesmith. Although she acknowledged distributing the crack cocaine, Reynoso nevertheless denied having served—on July 8, 1998 or on any other date—as a courier or deliverer of drugs for a Washington Heights drug dealer. Instead, Reynoso steadfastly maintained that she had stolen the crack cocaine at issue from a nearby billiards parlor and that she then had approached the first car she saw to sell the drugs. As Reynoso's counsel concedes, "The objective facts known to the parties did not support Ms. Reynoso's story. . . . The only logical inference [from the known facts] is that Ms. Reynoso was working for a drug dealer as a courier, not that she had stolen the crack and sold it herself."

Because Reynoso continued to deny having served as a courier or distributor, despite the known facts to the contrary, defense counsel retained Dr. Mark Mills, a forensic psychiatrist, to examine Reynoso. After Dr. Mills briefly examined Reynoso in jail and reviewed the case materials, he reported his findings to defense counsel in September 1999. Dr. Mills concluded that Reynoso had no "psychiatric illness," nor any "major psychiatric issues." Nevertheless, after reviewing Reynoso's accounts of neglect and drug use during her childhood and adolescence, Dr. Mills opined:

> [Reynoso's] history of intoxication, impaired memory and neglect accounts for her behavior at her proffer session. While she was ready to accept responsibility for her criminal behavior, she unconsciously elaborated, the technical term is "confabulated[,]" a story that would account for her behavior given the highly incomplete recollection that she had. Expressed differently, Ms. Reynoso told something that was untrue, *but did not appreciate that it was untrue* because of her organic memory impairment, secondary to cocaine intoxication. Such a pattern of confabulation is common in those with significant organic memory impairment.

On October 6, 1999, Reynoso pleaded guilty to Count Two of the indictment—for distribution and possession with intent to distribute more than five grams of crack cocaine. Thereafter, armed with Dr. Mills's report, Reynoso's counsel made a motion pursuant to the safety valve provision of § 3553(f) for relief from the mandatory minimum sentence of 60 months' imprisonment. Defense counsel conceded that Reynoso had not been "objectively" truthful at her safety valve proffer, but argued that she nevertheless satisfied § 3553(f)(5)—which, as noted, requires that "the defendant has truthfully provided to the Government all information and evidence the defendant has concerning the offense"—because "she did not appreciate the fact that her information was untrue [as a result] 'of organic memory impairment, secondary to cocaine intoxication.'" In opposing the motion, the Government did not contest that Reynoso satisfied the other four requirements for relief under the safety valve provision[1] or challenge the findings of Dr. Mills. Instead, the Government argued that Dr. Mills's findings were irrelevant as a matter of law and that Reynoso could not satisfy § 3553(f)(5) because the information she had provided was "objectively untruthful."

Following oral argument, the District Court denied Reynoso's motion for relief from the mandatory minimum sentence in a ruling from the bench. The District Court agreed to assume *arguendo* that Dr. Mills's findings were valid and that Reynoso "genuinely believes that she was telling the truth." Nevertheless, the District Court concluded, primarily as a matter of plain language and of "policy," that Reynoso did not satisfy the requirement of § 3553(f)(5) because she had provided objectively false information to the Government. Accordingly, the District Court sentenced Reynoso to the statutory minimum of 60 months' imprisonment, followed by four years' supervised release, and imposed a mandatory special assessment of $100. This appeal followed.

The sole question on this appeal is whether Reynoso qualifies for relief under the safety valve statute. The parties agree that this question turns on whether Reynoso satisfies the fifth requirement of the statute, which provides that

> not later than the time of the sentencing hearing, the defendant has truthfully provided to the Government all information and evidence the defendant has concerning the offense or offenses that were part of the same course of conduct or of a common scheme or plan, but the fact that the defendant has no relevant or useful other information to provide or that the Government is already aware of the information shall not preclude a determination by the court that the defendant has complied with this requirement.

Reynoso, who bears the burden of proving that she qualifies for safety valve relief, argues that § 3553(f)(5) requires only that a defendant "subjectively believe[]" information provided to the Government is true. In response, the Government contends that the provision requires a defendant to show that the information he or she provided was objectively true. The proper construction of the statute is a question of law, subject to *de novo* review.

We conclude that Reynoso and the Government are both partially correct—that is, that a defendant seeking to qualify for relief under the safety valve provision must prove *both* that the information he or she provided to the Government was objectively true *and* that he or she subjectively believed that such information

1. The other four requirements for relief under the safety valve provision are as follows: (1) the defendant does not have more than 1 criminal history point, as determined under the sentencing guidelines; (2) the defendant did not use violence or credible threats of violence or possess a firearm or other dangerous weapon (or induce another participant to do so) in connection with the offense; (3) the offense did not result in death or serious bodily injury to any person; (4) the defendant was not an organizer, leader, manager, or supervisor of others in the offense, as determined under the sentencing guidelines and was not engaged in a continuing criminal enterprise . . .

was true. This conclusion is supported, first and foremost, by the plain language of § 3553(f)(5). As noted, § 3553(f)(5) states that a defendant qualifies for relief only by "*truthfully* providing to the Government all information and evidence [he or she] has concerning the offense." One authority defines "truthful" as both "telling or disposed to tell the truth" and "accurate and sincere in describing reality." Other dictionaries similarly define the word to encompass both a subjective belief in the truth of information conveyed *and* the conveyance of true information. We see no reason to believe that Congress did not intend for the word "truthfully" in § 3553(f)(5) to encompass both these meanings. Accordingly, we hold that in order to qualify for safety valve relief, a defendant must prove both that the information he or she provided to the Government was objectively true and that he or she subjectively believed that such information was true.

Reynoso and our dissenting colleague emphasize that the statutory language is "truthfully provided" rather than "truthful information," and would have us infer from Congress's use of an adverb that "the emphasis in the statute is on the defendant's state of mind," but we are unpersuaded. In previous cases concerning § 3553(f)(5), we have, except when quoting the statute itself, almost without fail used the adjective "truthful" when articulating the standard to be applied. *See United States v. Schreiber*, 191 F.3d 103, 106 (2d Cir. 1999) (holding that § 3553(f)(5) requires that a defendant provide "to the government complete and truthful information no later than the time of sentencing"). This consistent usage, considered in conjunction with both the dictionary definitions of the term "truthful" quoted above and the ordinary, common-sense meaning of the word, leads ineluctably to the conclusion that Congress intended no legal significance to attach to its use of the words "truthfully provided" rather than "truthful information."

Our conclusion, that § 3553(f)(5) requires both that information provided to the Government be objectively truthful and that a defendant subjectively believe that such information is truthful, is further supported by the legislative history and purposes of the safety valve provision. The legislative history of the Mandatory Minimum Sentencing Reform Act of 1994 ("MMSRA"), which contained the safety valve provision, indicates that one of the principal purposes of the statute was to reform the then "current operation of mandatory minimums [under which] mitigating factors that are recognized in the [sentencing] guidelines and generally are considered in drug cases do not apply to the least culpable offenders except in rare instances." As we have explained, Congress intended "to remedy an inequity in the old system, which allowed relief from statutory minimum sentences" to those defendants who rendered "substantial assistance" to the Government—usually higher-level offenders, "whose greater involvement in criminal activity resulted in their having more information"—but effectively denied such relief to the least culpable offenders, who often "had no new or useful information to trade."

The critical point to draw from this legislative history is that Congress, in enacting the MMSRA, was concerned about the low-level figure in a drug conspiracy who sought to provide the Government with substantial assistance but, by virtue of his or her minor involvement in the criminal activity, "had no new or useful information to trade." Thus, Congress intended to provide relief from statutory minimum sentences to those defendants who, *but for their minor roles in criminal activity*, could (and would) have provided the Government with substantial assistance. To be sure, because a defendant may get safety valve relief even when the information provided is neither "new" nor "useful," the Government cannot legitimately claim an entitlement under § 3553(f)(5) to information of value. However, aided by the legislative history, we read the statute to mean that the Government is entitled under § 3553(f)(5) *not* to be provided with objectively false information, which may well be harmful to the Government. Indeed, we are confident that, in enacting the MMSRA, Congress did not intend to reward the defendant who, for whatever reason, tries "to trade" on objectively false information. Similarly, because Congress was concerned primarily with "the least culpable offenders," we conclude that a defendant must subjectively believe he or she is providing truthful information in order to qualify for safety valve relief.

In sum, we hold that a defendant may not qualify for safety valve relief under 18 U.S.C. § 3553(f) without proving both that information he or she provided to the Government was objectively true and that he or she subjectively believed that such information was true. Because Reynoso concedes that the information she provided to the Government was objectively false, she is not entitled to relief under the safety valve provision. Accordingly, the judgment of the District Court is affirmed.

Calabresi, J, dissenting.

This case presents the question of whether 18 U.S.C. § 3553(f)(5)—which requires a defendant to prove that she has "truthfully provided to the Government all information and evidence [she] has" in order to obtain "safety valve" relief from a statutory minimum sentence—employs an objective or a subjective standard of truthfulness. Put otherwise, we are called upon to determine whether a defendant who provides information that she believes to be true has met the requirements of § 3553(f)(5) and is eligible for safety valve relief, even though the data she gives is objectively false. The majority has determined that she is not. Because I believe that the majority's reading of the safety valve provision finds no support (a) in its language when read according to the most elementary rules of grammar, (b) in prior cases interpreting that language, or (c) in the provision's legislative history, I respectfully dissent.

As with all matters of statutory interpretation, we begin with the language of the statute. Although the majority claims to have analyzed what § 3553(f)(5) says, it does not actually respect the provision's plain language. Section 3553(f)(5) requires that a defendant who has otherwise met the "safety valve" criteria "truthfully provide[] to the Government all the information and evidence the defendant has." The majority interprets this sentence to mean that a defendant must prove *both* "that the information he or she provided to the Government was objectively true and that he or she subjectively believed that such information was true." But § 3553(f)(5) in fact says nothing about the veracity of the information a defendant gives; it requires only that the defendant provide information that she believes to be true.

The majority's interpretation treats the provision as if it stated that the defendant must "truthfully provide[] to the Government all the *truthful information* . . . the defendant has." The majority attempts to avoid the problem that the statutory language creates for its interpretation by treating the word "truthfully" both as an *adverb* modifying the verb "provide[]" (which it is) and as an *adjective* modifying the noun "information" (which it is not and grammatically cannot be).

It is, in other words, obvious that the provision as it is written (not as the majority might wish it to be) contains no requirement that the information provided comport with the facts of the case as the court finds them to be. Rather, the provision requires that the defendant "truthfully provide[] all the information . . . [she] has." She must, that is, make "*a good faith attempt* to cooperate with the authorities." And the placement and form of the word "truthfully" unmistakably indicates that it is the defendant's state of mind rather than the quality of the information that is at issue.

Further evidence that this is the proper reading of the statute can be found in the remainder of the provision: A defendant must truthfully provide "all the information *the defendant has.*" 18 U.S.C. § 3553(f)(5) (emphasis added). I cannot see how someone *has* information that she does not know about. As a result, when the government, remarkably, conceded that Reynoso genuinely believed what she said, it also necessarily conceded that she had *truthfully provided the evidence she had.* And this remains so even though the evidence she gave is not true.

The majority's opinion is thus doubly wrong linguistically: Not only does the grammatical structure of the statute make it clear that the relevant issue is the defendant's state of mind, but so too does the language requiring her to provide all the information she has. One need not be a philologist to conclude that a person *has* no information that for whatever reason, mental or otherwise, she is *conceded not to have.*

Moreover, neither the majority's lengthy citation of cases that have mentioned "truthful information," nor its reliance on the provision's legislative history, support—and certainly do not justify—its misreading of the plain language of the statute.

In none of the cases the majority cites was the courts' rewriting of the sentence in any way relevant, let alone necessary, to their results, and so such judicial rewriting is of no significance. There is, in fact, not a shred of evidence that the question now before us was even subconsciously in the minds of the courts deciding the cases cited above. It follows that their modifications of the statutory language have no bearing on our decision here.

More important, the only appellate cases that have directly focused on the issue before us have rejected the majority's position. *See United States v. Thompson,* 76 F.3d 166 (7th Cir. 1996) and *United States v. Sherpa,* 110 F.3d 656 (9th Cir. 1997). Of the two cases, *Thompson* is more directly germane. In both *Thompson,* and the instant case, the question is the same: What information did the defendant actually have, given the "limitations on [her] perceptual and analytical abilities." Thompson received safety valve relief when she provided objectively false information that the court found she subjectively believed. As in the case before us, a psychologist evaluated the defendant. The expert found "a diminished capacity to understand complex situations." The court stated that Thompson "gave the government information as she knew it and as she understood it." The Seventh Circuit accepted the district court's reliance "on expert testimony presented at the sentencing hearing concerning limitations on Thompson's perceptual and analytical abilities and conclusion that Thompson was forthright within the range of her ability."

The same is true of this case. Reynoso was convicted of distributing and possessing with intent to distribute crack cocaine to an undercover police detective. Throughout her safety valve proffer, she consistently maintained that she believed she had stolen the drugs that she gave to the undercover detective. Dr. Mark Mills, a forensic psychiatrist retained by Reynoso's counsel, testified that Reynoso's

> history of intoxication, impaired memory and neglect accounts for her behavior at her proffer session. While she was ready to accept responsibility for her criminal behavior, she unconsciously elaborated, the technical term is "confabulated" a story that would account for her behavior given the highly incomplete recollection that she had. Expressed differently, Ms. Reynoso told something that was untrue, but *did not appreciate that it was untrue* because of her organic memory impairment, secondary to cocaine intoxication. Such a pattern of confabulation is common in those with significant memory impairment.

Like Thompson, then, Reynoso "was forthright within the range of her ability." As a result, she provided the government all of the information she possessed. (Indeed, the government has *conceded* as much.) That is all the plain language of § 3553(f)(5) requires.

The majority attempts to justify its deviation from the plain meaning of the statute by reference to the legislative history of § 3553(f). It argues that that history provides only one legitimate justification for a defendant's failure to have (and hence to be able to give) information about the offense: the defendant's limited role. The majority also reads into the legislative history a government entitlement "*not* to be provided with objectively false information."

In fact, the legislative history indicates neither such entitlement, nor any other support for the majority's interpretation. Rather, that history, as is often the case, is inconclusive. Most likely, all it shows is that Congress did not really think about the issue. But, if anything, it cuts against the majority view.

The principal goal behind the safety valve provision was undoubtedly to remedy the irony that "for the very offenders who most warrant proportionally lower sentences—offenders that by guideline definitions are the least culpable—mandatory minimums generally operate to block the sentence from reflecting mitigating factors." H.R. Rep. No. 103-460, at 3 (1994). Ordinarily, downward departures that are grounded in cooperation with the police, because they are based on *substantial* assistance being given to the Government, require that the defendant provide useful information that the Government does not already possess, 18 U.S.C. § 3553(e), U.S.S.G. § 5K1.1. The safety valve provision was enacted to benefit defendants even if they "had no new or useful information to trade." It would seem to follow that defendants may be eligible for safety valve relief regardless of whether they have useful knowledge, useless knowledge, wrong knowledge, or no knowledge at all.

This object of the provision—to ensure proportionality in sentencing for "the least culpable offenders" and provide incentives for them to tell all they know—does not militate in favor of any particular interpretation of the language at issue in the instant case. On the one hand, it is not out of the question that the Government might also hope to gain useful information as a result of safety valve proffers by minor participants. To that extent, the provision of true information might be desirable. On the other hand, the obtaining of information, and hence its quality—whether it is true or false, helpful to future prosecutions or not—is beside the point of the statute.

Underlying the majority's refusal to read § 3553(f)(5) as it is written is a prediction that, under a subjective interpretation, defendants will be "rewarded" for "'trading on' objectively false information". This reflects a fear that allowing those like Reynoso, who profess to believe false information, to benefit from safety valve relief will lead to a mare's nest. As the Government states in its brief: "Permitting such a class of persons to receive the safety valve's benefit could mire district courts in a search for the intent behind a defendant's proffer of information when such information is not in fact truthful but the defendant contends his or her perception is sincerely held." Thus far, the Government continues, courts "'have found it fairly easy to cull serious efforts at full disclosure from mere pretense.'" "Permitting the result advocated by Reynoso would drastically change the courts' abilities in this regard, inviting frequent battles between experts, and rendering a court's fact finding mission exponentially more difficult." The majority, like the Government, is understandably worried about defendants who might take advantage of a reversal in this case to gain safety valve relief without providing truthful information. Lying, the majority warns, "may well be harmful to the Government."

[T]hese fears are misguided. [T]he district courts are already involved in determinations of the credibility of defendants' proffers. *See Gambino,* 106 F.3d at 1111 (describing how the district court based its denial of the safety valve motion on "the detailed representations in the government's letter, which the court credited over [defendant's] implausible arguments in rebuttal"). As a result, allowing defendants who provide subjectively believed but objectively false information to receive safety valve relief does not suddenly inject credibility determinations where they have never been required in the past. The fact is, moreover, that defendants willing to lie can, under the majority's own holding, readily take advantage of the safety valve by credibly denying that they have any knowledge at all. This is so since, as all seem to concede, under the safety valve (a) a defendant can say that she thought that she had gotten the drugs in a particular way but frankly couldn't remember, and (b) her lack of memory, if truthfully held, would be a defense. Hence, rather than avoiding credibility fights, all the majority does is to create a perverse incentive to deny knowledge of uncomfortable facts.

Nor are the credibility determinations that must be made in such cases any easier than those to be made in the case before us. To the contrary, they present much the same problems as those the majority fears. As a result, the principle effect of the majority's interpretation is to create the need for Ptolemaic cycles and epicycles to enable courts to distinguish cases of lack of information due specifically to the minor role played by the defendant in the offense, from those due to lack of memory of the offense, and finally from those that, as in the instant case, are due to self-deluding false information.

What makes this case odd, and so raises the problem, is the absurdity of the government's concession, which both the district court and the majority of this panel accept *arguendo*. Let me be absolutely clear. My position in no way suggests that the evidence Reynoso proffered was sufficient to carry her burden of proof. Because, however, the government *conceded* that Reynoso believed she was telling the truth, I have no choice but respectfully to dissent.

United States v. Brownlee

United States Court of Appeals for the Eleventh Circuit
204 F.3d 1302 (2000)

Strom, J.

Appellant, Elliott Brownlee, entered a plea of guilty on August 14, 1997, to six counts involving conspiracy to possess with intent to distribute cocaine base and cocaine under 21 U.S.C. § 846, possession of those substances with intent to distribute under 21 U.S.C. § 841(a)(1), and distribution of those substances under 21 U.S.C. § 841(a)(1). Upon his arrest in January 1997, Brownlee gave a proffer regarding his drug activity to a Drug Enforcement Administration task force agent. In this proffer, Brownlee admitted to his involvement in the sale of cocaine, but he did not truthfully disclose the source of the cocaine at this time, nor on later occasions.

On January 8, 1998, the day before Brownlee's sentencing hearing, Brownlee's trial counsel contacted the prosecutor, telling him that Brownlee would meet with him before the sentencing hearing to disclose information. On the morning of Brownlee's sentencing hearing, Brownlee met with the prosecutor and case agent and disclosed that co-defendant Alfred Wright, Jr. was the source of the cocaine. The district court then conducted the sentencing hearing for co-defendant Alfred Wright, Jr., at which the government called Brownlee as a witness. On the witness stand, Brownlee testified that Alfred Wright was the source of the cocaine. After the district court sentenced Wright, it conducted Brownlee's sentencing hearing. Finding that Brownlee's base offense level was 32, the district court added a two-level enhancement pursuant to U.S.S.G. § 3C1.1 for obstruction of justice, and reduced that level by three offense levels for acceptance of responsibility pursuant to U.S.S.G. § 3E1.1, resulting in a total offense level of 31. The district court sentenced Brownlee to 120 months imprisonment, the mandatory minimum for his offenses. Had the district court applied safety-valve relief for Brownlee, he would have been entitled to a two-level reduction pursuant to U.S.S.G. § 2D1.1(b)(6), resulting in an offense level of 29 and a sentencing range of 87–108 months.

In 1994 Congress enacted a provision allowing district courts to sentence less-culpable defendants without regard to the mandatory minimum sentences in certain cases. This Guideline has been nicknamed the "safety-valve" provision. The safety valve provision requires a district court to sentence a defendant in certain drug-possession cases "without regard to any statutory minimum sentence" if the defendant meets five criteria. If the Court determines that all five criteria are met, "'the court shall impose a sentence pursuant to [the Guidelines] without regard to any statutory minimum sentence.'" There is no dispute in this case that the first four criteria of § 5C1.2 are satisfied. The sole issue on appeal is whether Brownlee satisfied U.S.S.G. § 5C1.2(5), which provides:

> Not later than the time of the sentencing hearing, the defendant has truthfully provided to the Government all information and evidence the defendant had concerning the offense or offenses that were part of the same course of conduct or of a common scheme or plan, but the fact that the defendant has no relevant or useful other information to provide or that the Government is already aware of the information shall not preclude a determination by the court that the defendant has complied with this requirement.

The government argues that the Court should read § 5C1.2(5) as requiring a defendant to disclose all information in good faith. The government further contends that defendant's previous lies about his knowledge do not constitute disclosing information in good faith. *See United States v. Ramunno,* 133 F.3d 476 (7th Cir.1998) (stating that § 5C1.2 benefits only those defendants who have made a good faith attempt to cooperate with the authorities) (citations omitted). We decline to adopt the government's view.

The plain language of 18 U.S.C. § 3553(f) and U.S.S.G. § 5C1.2 provides only one deadline for compliance, "not later than the time of the sentencing hearing." It is undisputed that Brownlee met this deadline. Nothing in the statute suggests that a defendant who previously lied or withheld information from the government is automatically disqualified from safety-valve relief. A similar situation to Brownlee's occurred in *United States v. Tournier,* 171 F.3d 645 (8th Cir.1999). In *Tournier,* the defendant gave three interviews prior to sentencing, each time disclosing information that was untruthful. The defendant later gave a fourth interview prior to sentencing, where she completely and truthfully disclosed the relevant information. Upon such disclosure, the district court granted the defendant safety-valve relief. In affirming that decision, the Eighth Circuit declined to adopt the government's view that safety-valve relief should not apply to defendants who wait until the last minute to fully cooperate. The court held that since the defendant had finally provided truthful and complete information before the sentencing hearing, although the court admitted that obtaining truthful information from that defendant had been "grudging and fitful," like "pulling teeth," she was entitled to safety-valve relief. *See also United States v. Gama-Bastidas,* 142 F.3d 1233 (10th Cir.1998) (holding that defendant's attempt to furnish information to the court and the government in the Judge's chambers prior to the sentencing hearing was not "too late" to be entitled to safety-valve relief). "Moreover, to the extent that the government's interest in disclosure could justify penalizing defendants who lie or withhold information during proffer sessions, a similar scheme already exists independent of the safety valve." *See Schreiber,* 191 F.3d at 108 (citing U.S.S.G. § 3C1.1 (obstruction of justice)). We follow those circuits who have held that lies and omissions do not, as a matter of law, disqualify a defendant from safety-valve relief so long as the defendant makes a complete and truthful proffer not later than the commencement of the sentencing hearing.

This does not mean that the defendant's prior lies are completely irrelevant. In making this determination, the evidence of his lies becomes "part of the total mix of evidence for the district court to consider in evaluating the completeness and truthfulness of the defendant's proffer."

The question of whether the information Brownlee supplied to the government the morning of his sentencing was truthful and complete, however, is a factual finding for the district court. Because the district court disqualified Brownlee from safety-valve relief at the threshold, the district court never considered the factual question of whether his final proffer was complete and truthful.

We therefore VACATE Brownlee's sentence and REMAND with instructions that the district court resentence Brownlee in accordance with this opinion.

b. The Criminal History Limitation

The safety valve's criminal history limitation is seldom litigated because the rules for calculating criminal history points are generally clear-cut. It is arguably the most important of the safety valve requirements, however, because it can disqualify many defendants from eligibility.

The criminal history limitation was originally quite strict. Until December 2018, a defendant who had more than one criminal history point as determined by the federal sentencing guidelines was ineligible for safety valve relief. This aspect of the safety valve was widely criticized as unduly harsh. Because people with a substance use disorder often have more than one criminal history point, the requirement disqualified many offenders from eligibility.

The FIRST STEP Act, which was passed in late 2018, relaxed the criminal history limitation somewhat. To satisfy the criminal history requirement today, the defendant cannot have "(A) more than 4 criminal history points, excluding any criminal history points resulting from a 1-point offense, as determined under the sentencing guidelines; (B) a prior 3-point offense, as determined under the sentencing guidelines; [or] (C) a prior 2-point violent offense, as determined under the sentencing guidelines." 18 U.S.C. § 3553(f)(1).

The following table (which also appeared in the introduction to sentencing at the beginning of this chapter) provides a simplified version of the key criminal history provisions contained in U.S.S.G. § 4A1.1:

Points	Triggering event
3	Each prior sentence of imprisonment exceeding one year and one month
2	Each prior sentence of imprisonment between 60 days and one year and one month
1	Each prior sentence of less than 60 days of imprisonment
2	If the defendant committed the instant offense while under any criminal justice sentence—e.g., while on probation or parole

As the table reveals, a single prior sentence of imprisonment of 60 days or more results in two criminal history points. This would have been enough to place an offender above the original one-point limit, although it would not necessarily be disqualifying under the new limit. The next case illustrates the mechanical and unforgiving nature of the safety valve's original criminal history cut-off. Although the criminal history limitation is now more forgiving, the FIRST STEP Act did not make its safety valve expansion retroactive. As a result, defendants who were convicted before the FIRST STEP Act took effect cannot seek resentencing on the grounds that they would be eligible for safety valve relief under the new rule.

United States v. Boddie

United States Court of Appeals for the Third Circuit
318 F.3d 491 (2003)

Sloviter, J.

The issue presented in this case is whether a district court has the authority under the Sentencing Guidelines to apply the safety valve to a defendant whose criminal history category of II overstated the seriousness of the defendant's prior record. This court has not previously spoken to this issue. Seven other courts of appeals have considered the issue, and each has held that the statutory language limiting the availability of the safety valve to defendants with one criminal history point must govern. We turn to the facts of this case before considering the legal issue.

From the late summer of 1999 until March of 2001, Appellant Jermaine Boddie and Saunders Mabrey supplied cocaine to Gregory Armstrong, who distributed about 15 kilograms of the drug in the Western District of Pennsylvania. Boddie and Mabrey, who were located in San Francisco, initially met with Armstrong in California, and later shipped cocaine to him in food cans sent to a store in McKeesport, Pennsylvania. Armstrong repackaged and distributed the cocaine. He paid Boddie and Mabrey approximately $17,000 per kilogram of cocaine.

Armstrong was arrested in March 2001. He told authorities that he was still in touch with his suppliers and that he owed them about $75,000 for the last shipment of cocaine. In August 2001, the Drug Enforcement Administration ("DEA") recorded telephone conversations between Armstrong and Mabrey about their cocaine dealings and the debt that Armstrong owed. On October 3, 2001, one of Armstrong's associates who was working as a confidential informant with the DEA had a recorded conversation with Mabrey, in which the confidential informant told Mabrey that the money to repay the debt had been gathered. On October 4, 2001, DEA agents arrested Boddie and Mabrey, who had arrived in Pittsburgh, Pennsylvania, to collect the $75,000.

On October 31, 2001, a grand jury indicted Boddie and Mabrey, charging them with conspiracy to distribute and possess with intent to distribute in excess of five kilograms of cocaine, in violation of 21 U.S.C. § 846. On February 8, 2002, Boddie and Mabrey pled guilty to the charge pursuant to a plea agreement in which it was agreed, among other things, that the quantity of cocaine attributable to each of them was at least five but less than 15 kilograms. The Government agreed that if Boddie and Mabrey satisfied statutory requirements, it would recommend at sentencing that the District Court apply the safety valve provision and sentence them without regard to the statutory mandatory minimum penalty.

In Boddie's Presentence Investigation Report ("PSR"), the United States Probation Office determined that Boddie has a criminal history category of II based upon three criminal history points, including one point for a 1999 conviction for driving with a suspended license and two points because the present offense occurred during the period of probation imposed for the driving violation. The Probation Office also stated that it appeared that Boddie did not qualify for the safety valve provision and that he was subject to the statutory mandatory minimum sentence of 120 months.

Boddie objected to the PSR, claiming that his criminal history category was overstated based upon the absence of any involvement with the criminal justice system other than driving violations, and that he qualifies for the application of the safety valve provision. The District Court agreed with Boddie that his criminal history category overstates the seriousness of his past criminal conduct and that a criminal history category of I applies. It ruled, however, that Boddie does not qualify for the safety valve provision because he has more than one criminal history point. The District Court sentenced Boddie to the statutory mandatory minimum of 120 months imprisonment and 60 months supervised release, and ordered him to pay a $100.00 special assessment. This appeal followed.[19]

Boddie argues that the Sentencing Guidelines do not prohibit the application of the safety valve provision of U.S.S.G. § 5C1.2 to an individual whose criminal history is found to be overstated pursuant to § 4A1.3. He contends that the determination of

---

19. The District Court sentenced Mabrey to 70 months imprisonment and 60 months supervised release, and ordered him to pay a $100.00 special assessment. Mabrey did not appeal his sentence.

whether a defendant has more than one criminal history point should be made after a downward departure has been applied.

Under 18 U.S.C. § 3553(f), in cases involving certain drug offenses, the sentencing court shall impose a sentence pursuant to the Sentencing Guidelines without regard to any statutory minimum sentence if the court finds that five criteria are satisfied.

This provision, known as the safety valve, is also set forth in the Sentencing Guidelines at § 5C1.2. It is the first criterion that is at issue in this appeal, as it requires that for Boddie to have the benefit of the safety valve, he must "not have more than 1 criminal history point, as determined under the sentencing guidelines." 18 U.S.C. § 3553(f)(1); U.S.S.G. § 5C1.2(a)(1).

The commentary to U.S.S.G. § 5C1.2 defines "more than 1 criminal history point, as determined under the sentencing guidelines" to mean "more than one criminal history point as determined under § 4A1.1 (Criminal History Category)." Under U.S.S.G. § 4A1.1, criminal history points are assigned for prior criminal convictions and the total number of points determines a defendant's criminal history category. A defendant's criminal history category is used, along with his/her offense level, to determine the applicable sentencing guideline range. Under U.S.S.G. § 4A1.3, a court may depart from the otherwise applicable guideline range and use as a reference the range for a defendant with a lower criminal history category if a defendant's criminal history category significantly over-represents the seriousness of a defendant's criminal history.

Boddie argues that because the District Court had determined that his criminal history category of II overstated the seriousness of his past criminal conduct and that his proper criminal history category was I, he should be deemed eligible for application of the safety valve. However, the safety valve provision is written in terms of criminal history points, not criminal history category.

This issue was most recently considered by the Court of Appeals for the Sixth Circuit in *United States v. Penn,* 282 F.3d 879 (6th Cir. 2002). The district court had granted the defendant a downward departure under U.S.S.G. § 4A1.3, finding that his criminal history category of II, based upon two criminal history points, did not accurately reflect the seriousness of his past criminal conduct. The district court found that the defendant should only receive one criminal history point for his prior conviction based upon the amount of time he spent in prison, and that a criminal history category of I applied. The court then applied the safety valve and sentenced the defendant below the statutory mandatory minimum.

On appeal, the court held that the district court did not have authority to alter the defendant's criminal history points based upon its conclusion that his criminal history category overstated the seriousness of his past criminal conduct. Similarly, the district court was not free to sentence the defendant below the statutory mandatory minimum where he had more than one criminal history point. The court explained that the commentary to § 5C1.2, quoted above, limits the district court's authority to apply the safety valve "to cases where a defendant has not more than one criminal history point as calculated under § 4A1.1, regardless of whether the district court determines that a downward departure in the defendant's sentence is warranted by § 4A1.3." The court further explained that the effect of a departure under § 4A1.3 is not to change the defendant's actual criminal history category or the calculation of a defendant's criminal history points.

Similarly, in *United States v. Robinson*, 158 F.3d 1291 (D.C. Cir. 1998) (per curiam), the district court had adjusted the defendant's criminal history category downward from category II (based on three criminal history points) to category I on the ground that defendant's criminal history category over-represented the seriousness of his criminal history. The court then found the defendant eligible for the safety valve provision based upon the downward departure. The Court of Appeals for the District of Columbia Circuit remanded the case for re-sentencing, explaining that

> while U.S.S.G. § 4A1.3 affords a sentencing court discretion to determine whether a criminal history category accurately reflects a defendant's criminal history, nothing in U.S.S.G. § 4A1.1 suggests that the sentencing court has any discretion with respect to the calculation of a defendant's criminal history score: Section 4A1.1 is a mechanistic provision which merely instructs the sentencing court to add points for various carefully-defined criminal history occurrences.

These cases rely on the commentary to U.S.S.G. § 5C1.2. Although Boddie recognizes that federal courts are bound by the commentary to the Sentencing Guidelines, he argues that the commentary to § 5C1.2 does not limit the courts with respect to consideration of downward departures as authorized in § 4A1.3. Rather, he contends, the commentary is silent concerning the effect of a downward departure. Boddie is correct that the commentary to § 5C1.2 does not address § 4A1.3. However, it specifically defines "more than 1 criminal history point, as determined under the sentencing guidelines" to mean "more than one criminal history point as determined under § 4A1.1."

We agree with the other courts of appeals that have addressed this issue that this definition precludes a court from applying the safety valve provision where a defendant has more than one criminal history point as determined under § 4A1.1, notwithstanding the fact that the court granted a downward departure after finding that the criminal history category is overstated.

It is no secret that the Sentencing Guidelines have been the subject of substantial controversy since their promulgation, often because of what appears to be their inflexibility in situations where equitable considerations might suggest a different outcome. In this case, for example, Boddie is sentenced to serve ten years imprisonment whereas Mabrey, his codefendant, who engaged in the same conduct and pled guilty to the same offense was sentenced to serve less than six years imprisonment, with the differential being that Boddie had more criminal history points because he committed the drug offense while on probation for driving with a suspended license. In other circumstances, the sentencing court's ability to depart downward (or upward) tempers what may be a special circumstance. Here, however, we face not only the Sentencing Guidelines but a congressional statute that is framed in terms of criminal history points. If there is to be any change in this respect, it must be by congressional action. After all, the crime that Boddie committed was a serious drug offense and if Congress chose to ameliorate the effect of some sentences in drug cases by providing a safety valve, it clearly had the option to choose the conditions for eligibility for that safety valve. Boddie is not eligible, Mabrey was.

For the reasons discussed above, we will affirm the judgment of sentence of the District Court.

3. Providing Substantial Assistance

Defendants who are able to offer "substantial assistance" to the government may be eligible to receive a sentence below an applicable mandatory minimum. As the name implies, the substantial assistance exception applies where a defendant has helped out the government by providing it with useful information, testimony against another defendant, or assistance in some other form. The law provides that, "*[u]pon a motion by the Government*, the court shall have the authority to impose a sentence below a level established by statute as a minimum sentence so as to reflect a defendant's substantial assistance in the investigation or prosecution of another person who has committed an offense." 18 U.S.C. § 355(e) (emphasis added).

Because the substantial assistance reduction requires a motion by the government, it is up to the prosecutor to decide whether or not a defendant qualifies. In *Wade v. United States*, the Supreme Court held that the decision of whether to file a substantial assistance motion is within the sole discretion of the prosecutor, except if there is a plea agreement to the contrary or unconstitutional action (such as racial discrimination) on the part of the prosecutor. 504 U.S. 181 (1992). As a result, a defendant who cooperates may nevertheless receive a mandatory minimum sentence, particularly if she cooperated before entering a plea agreement. In *United States v. Crickon*, for example, 66-year-old defendant Jerry Crickon was stopped by the police and confessed to transporting methamphetamine. Crickon "agreed to make a controlled delivery, thus helping the police catch Juan Carlos Delatorre, the man to whom Crickon was bringing his shipment of methamphetamine." After making the controlled delivery, the government indicted Crickon who entered a guilty plea. At sentencing, the government declined to file a substantial assistance motion and Crickon received a 151-month sentence. The United States Court of Appeals for the Seventh Circuit held this decision was within the sole discretion of the prosecutor. "Although we are understanding of [Crickon's] plight," the Court wrote, "we are constrained to affirm." 240 F.3d 652 (7th Cir. 2001).

Even in cases where the defendant provides assistance as part of plea negotiations, the government often has nearly boundless discretion with respect to substantial assistance motions. *See, e.g.*, Ian Weinstein, *Regulating the Market for Snitches*, 47 BUFFALO L. REV. 563, 591 (1999) (observing that "the overall trend is to leave even the cooperator who complies fully with his or her agreement subject to the government's evaluation of his or her cooperation"). A handful of courts, however, have sought to provide limits on the government's decision not to file a substantial assistance motion in plea agreement cases. Some of these courts have relied on principles of contract law to impose a duty of good faith dealing on the government while others have held that the government's action should be subject to a rationality review.

United States v. Rounsavall

United States Court of Appeals for the Eighth Circuit
128 F.3d 665 (1997)

Heaney, J.

On November 9, 1995, Mary Ann Rounsavall entered into a plea agreement with the government. As part of her agreement, she pled guilty to drug and money laundering charges. Absent such an agreement, she would have faced 360 months to life with a statutory minimum of twenty years. Her agreement with the government provided that if she cooperated in the prosecution of her brother, the government would consider filing motions allowing her to receive a sentence at or below the statutory mandatory minimum. According to an affidavit submitted by Rounsavall to the district court, Assistant United States Attorney Bruce Gillan told Rounsavall that he did not want or believe that she should go to prison for the twenty years required by the statutory mandatory minimum sentence if she complied with the terms of the plea agreement. Gillan indicated Rounsavall should expect to receive somewhere between seven to ten years for her cooperation, although the decision as to the length of her sentence would be entirely up to the judge. In his affidavit, United States Attorney Thomas Monaghan stated that the government initially sought Rounsavall's assistance because the government believed that once she helped in the prosecution, Rounsavall's brother would also cooperate.

Rounsavall testified against her brother in two separate criminal proceedings. First, she testified against her brother at his drug and money laundering trial. During his trial, she testified for four days. She also testified against her brother for an additional day at a forfeiture proceeding. All told, she testified for five days, longer than any other witness, in helping the government convict her brother and secure a life sentence against him. Ultimately, the government [did not file] an 18 U.S.C. § 3553(e) motion [mandatory minimum substantial assistance motion]. Rounsavall was sentenced to twenty years, the lowest possible sentence the district court could order under the statutory mandatory minimum. Because the government withheld filing a § 3553(e) motion, the district court could not further lower Rounsavall's sentence.

According to an affidavit from United States Attorney Thomas Monaghan, the government considered but decided against filing a § 3553(e) motion for the following reasons:

> (a) the failure of the defendant to cooperate with the government until her second trial; (b) the fact that a portion of her testimony regarding money

> laundering given during a trial against a codefendant was not accurate or complete; (c) the fact that no other persons can be prosecuted as a result of her cooperation; and (d) the fact that she violated her plea agreement by not giving reliable and complete testimony regarding money laundering.

The district court judge strongly disagreed with the decision of the prosecutor not to file a § 3553(e) motion:

> In my opinion, Ms. Rounsavall's testimony against her brother was extremely helpful to the Government, was, in large measure, truthful and was provided to the Government at great personal cost to Ms. Rounsavall. In some ways, she's going to have to live the rest of her life knowing she contributed to her brother probably dying in prison. If the Government had filed a motion under the statute, I would likely have substantially departed below the sentence that I now must impose under the law.

Despite disagreeing with the government's decision, the district court found that there was no reason to hold an evidentiary hearing regarding Rounsavall's claim of a breach of her agreement because the government had simply agreed to consider her cooperation and nothing more. Rounsavall appeals the district court's denial of her motion to compel the government to file a § 3553(e) motion.

"A sentencing court may not grant a downward departure for substantial assistance absent a motion by the government." There are, however, limited exceptions to this rule. "Relief may be granted absent a government substantial assistance motion if a defendant shows that the government's refusal to make the motion was based on an unconstitutional motive, that the refusal was irrational, or that the motion was withheld in bad faith." A defendant is entitled to an evidentiary hearing to determine whether the government acted improperly if she is able to make a substantial threshold showing that the government acted irrationally, in bad faith, or in violation of one's constitutional rights.

We agree with the district court that United States Attorney Monaghan should have made the § 3553(e) motion for a statutory downward departure. We go a step further, however, and hold that Rounsavall made a sufficient threshold showing to require that an evidentiary hearing be held to determine whether the United States Attorney's reasons for not granting the motion were irrational and/or were made in bad faith.

No credence can be given to the United States Attorney's first reason, that the defendant failed to cooperate until her second trial. The fact is that the plea agreement was not entered into until the second trial. Thus, if the United States Attorney was going to take into consideration that Rounsavall was late in entering a plea, he should have said so at that time rather than after the fact.

Nor do we find merit in the United States Attorney's view that the testimony regarding money laundering given during the trial against a codefendant was not accurate or complete. It appears from the record that the codefendant was her brother. She testified against him for the better part of five days and he was convicted, the district court found, largely because of her testimony.

The third reason for failing to file a statutory motion, that no other person can be prosecuted as a result of her cooperation, is equally specious. If this, in fact, were a condition of her agreement, then the prosecutor should have made it clear before he accepted her plea agreement. He failed to do so.

On the basis of this record, we are unable to divine the rationale behind the [prosecutor's claim that the] money laundering [testimony] was not reliable or complete. Again, her brother was not only convicted of money laundering because of her testimony, but the district court found that she had completely cooperated post-trial in terms of her own money laundering and had voluntarily agreed to the entry of a money judgment against her in the sum of $200,000. It is difficult to imagine a higher degree of cooperation.

We then come to appellant's contention that Assistant United States Attorney Gillan told Rounsavall that she could expect to receive between seven to ten years for substantially assisting the government. At oral argument, Gillan contended that whether he made such representations to Rounsavall is outside the record. In its memorandum and order, however, the district court acknowledged that it reviewed Rounsavall's affidavit as part of the entire record before making its final determination.

Based on the alleged representations made to Rounsavall, as set forth in her affidavit, the government may have violated the plea agreement in failing to file the § 3553(e) motion. In *Wade*, the Supreme Court suggested that the decision to forego filing a § 3553(e) motion could be "superseded" by another agreement made by the prosecutor.

In this case, Gillan's representations to Rounsavall may have superseded the broad discretion prosecutors generally enjoy in determining whether to file a substantial assistance motion under § 3553(e). In her affidavit before the district court, Rounsavall alleged that Gillan said that he did not believe she deserved to go to prison for twenty years if she fully cooperated; and although it was entirely up to the judge, she should expect a seven- to ten-year sentence. As the district court found, Rounsavall clearly cooperated in providing substantial assistance to the government. The twenty-year sentence, therefore, may well have been a violation of the plea agreement between Rounsavall and the Assistant United States Attorney who prosecuted the case. This court attempted unsuccessfully to get the Assistant United States Attorney's view on this matter at oral argument. The question will have to be thoroughly addressed on remand.

The government argues that its only agreement was to consider whether Rounsavall had cooperated in determining whether it would file a § 3553(e) motion. The district court appears to have accepted this view. We do not believe the district court's authority is so limited. Notwithstanding the language of an agreement, if the government's refusal to file a § 3553(e) motion is irrational and/or in bad faith, particularly in light of representations made to a defendant, a district court may require the government to make a downward departure motion.

Additionally, it appears that the government may have based its decision to enter into a plea agreement with Rounsavall on factors other than her substantial assistance.

In this case, United States Attorney Monaghan admitted in his affidavit that the government had sought Rounsavall's "assistance because we believed that her brother would cooperate with the government once he realized that she was helping" the government. The record indicates that Rounsavall was never informed that the government wanted her assistance to get her brother to cooperate. As it turned out, Rounsavall's brother did not cooperate with the government. It appears, therefore, that when Rounsavall's brother decided not to enter into a plea agreement, the government may have acted irrationally and/or in bad faith by withholding the § 3553(e) motion.

Consistent with this opinion, we reverse and remand to the district court for an evidentiary hearing to determine whether the government acted irrationally and/or in bad faith in failing to file a § 3553(e) motion in light of Rounsavall's substantial assistance and the government's conduct, and whether the government considered factors outside of Rounsavall's substantial assistance in declining to file the § 3553(e) downward departure motion.

4. The Crack and Powder Cocaine Sentencing Disparity

The disparity between crack and powder cocaine sentences has been one of the most hotly debated aspects of federal drug laws.

When Congress revived federal mandatory minimum drug penalties in 1986, it included a 100-to-1 differential between the amount of powder and crack cocaine needed to trigger a mandatory minimum sentence. To maintain consistency, the Sentencing Commission adopted the same ratio in the federal sentencing guidelines. Under this scheme, it took 100 times the amount of powder cocaine as cocaine base (better known as crack) to result in the same mandatory minimum sentence.

In 2010, Congress passed the Fair Sentencing Act, which reduced the disparity from 100-to-1 to 18-to-1. To appreciate both the impact of the Fair Sentencing Act and the case presented below, *United States v. Blewett*, it is important to recall the relationship between federal mandatory minimum penalties and the federal sentencing guidelines. Mandatory minimum penalties are established by Congress and courts are not free to disregard them (unless, of course, a defendant satisfies the safety valve or qualifies for substantial assistance). It takes an act of Congress to change a mandatory minimum penalty. By contrast, the federal sentencing guidelines are overseen by the United States Sentencing Commission, which has the power to adjust the guidelines without congressional action.

The Fair Sentencing Act reduced the disparity for mandatory minimum penalties from 100-to-1 to 18-to-1. The Sentencing Commission also adjusted the quantity levels for crack and powder cocaine in its drug quantity table to follow the new 18-to-1 ratio. But the Sentencing Commission went one step further. The Commission decided to apply *its* reduction in crack penalties *under the guidelines* retroactively. This meant that federal prisoners who had been sentenced under the old 100-to-1 ratio could seek to have their sentences reduced based on the new ratio under sentencing guidelines. "As of December 2014, 6,880 crack cocaine offenders had received reduced sentences," resulting in an estimated "savings of 14,333 bed-years to the Bureau of Prisons." U.S. SEN'G COMM'N, REPORT TO THE CONGRESS: FAIR SENTENCING ACT OF 2010 26 (2015).

Although the Sentencing Commission had the authority to make its reduction to crack sentences under the guidelines retroactive, there was disagreement over whether the reduced mandatory minimum penalties for crack also applied retroactively.

To better understand the importance of this distinction in concrete terms, consider two hypothetical prisoners who were originally sentenced in 2007 under the old 100-to-1 ratio. First, Dave, who did not have enough crack cocaine to trigger a mandatory minimum penalty under the 100-to-1 ratio. Dave was sentenced to four years and eight months. Because Dave's offense did not involve a mandatory minimum penalty, he would have been eligible to have his sentence reduced pursuant to the Commission's retroactive 18-to-1 sentencing guidelines ratio. Second, Erin, who had enough crack to trigger a five-year mandatory minimum penalty under the 100-to-1 ratio. The Sentencing Commission's decision to retroactively reduce sentences under the guidelines would not be enough to help Erin. For Erin to have her five-year sentence reduced pursuant to the new 18-to-1 ratio, the mandatory minimum penalties would need to apply retroactively.

In *United States v. Blewett*, a divided Sixth Circuit sitting *en banc* considered whether the Fair Sentencing Act's mandatory minimum penalties for crack cocaine applied retroactively to prisoners who had been sentenced under the old penalty structure. The majority held that the law did not apply retroactively. That holding was consistent with the outcome in other circuits. In December 2018, Congress finally made the Fair Sentencing Act of 2010 retroactive as part of the FIRST STEP Act. As a result, the central holding in *Blewett*—that the Fair Sentencing Act's reduced mandatory minimum penalties do not apply retroactively—is no longer good law.

Although the Fair Sentencing Act's mandatory minimum penalties for crack cocaine are now retroactive, the decision in *Blewett* is still well worth reading. In the process of addressing the question of retroactivity, the judges in *Blewett* engaged in a thought-provoking exchange about the disparity between crack and powder cocaine sentences, Congress's reasons for treating the two substances differently, and whether the disparity poses constitutional problems. In addition, the FIRST STEP Act came too late to be helpful to defendants, like the Blewetts, who had already served their full sentences by December 2018.

United States v. Blewett

United States Court of Appeals for the Sixth Circuit
746 F.3d 647 (2013)

Sutton, J.

The Anti-Drug Abuse Act of 1986 established mandatory minimum sentences for possessing crack cocaine with the intent to distribute it: 5 years for possessing 5 grams, 10 years for possessing 50 grams. The Fair Sentencing Act of 2010 increased the amount of crack cocaine needed to activate the same mandatory minimums. It now takes 28 grams to trigger the 5-year penalty and 280 grams to trigger the 10-year penalty. Through these changes, the Fair Sentencing Act significantly reduced, but did not eliminate, a sentencing disparity between offenses involving crack and powder cocaine. What used to be a 100:1 ratio between the amount of powder and crack needed to trigger the mandatory minimums has become an 18:1 ratio.

At issue in this case is whether the changes created by the Act apply to defendants sentenced five years before the new law took effect.

In 2005, a federal court convicted cousins Cornelius Blewett and Jarreous Blewitt (the Blewetts) of possessing crack cocaine with the intent to distribute it. Neither side contests that Cornelius had 19.65 grams and Jarreous 26.92 grams. Under the Anti-Drug Abuse Act, those amounts normally would have produced a 5-year minimum sentence. But because the Blewetts each had a prior felony drug conviction, the Act doubled the minimum. The court sentenced each cousin to 10 years, the lowest sentence possible under the law.

After Congress enacted the Fair Sentencing Act, the Blewetts moved for a sentence reduction. The Blewetts' 19.65 and 26.92 grams of crack cocaine fall short of the 28 grams required for the Fair Sentencing Act's new mandatory minimums to kick in. As a result, the Blewetts claimed that, even though they were sentenced before the Fair Sentencing Act took effect, they should benefit from Congress's reduction of the statutory penalties. The district court denied their request.

In our view: . . . the Fair Sentencing Act's new mandatory minimums do not apply to defendants sentenced before it took effect [and . . .] the Constitution does not provide a basis for blocking it.

Under the general saving statute, enacted in 1871, a law that reduces statutory penalties for an offense presumptively does not alter penalties incurred before the new law took effect. 1 U.S.C. § 109. A statute may overcome this default rule but only expressly or by clear implication. The Fair Sentencing Act nowhere provides that it covers offenders sentenced before it became effective. Nor do the Act's clear implications show a desire to apply the new law to offenders already sentenced. To the contrary, no feature of the Act is backward looking and many are forward looking. Congress, to be sure, disapproved of the old mandatory minimums; that is why it changed them. But if rejection of the old penalty were all it took to make a new penalty retroactive to all individuals previously sentenced, every new penalty would be fully retroactive, shearing the general saving statute of meaning.

Precedents from [three-judge panels of] our circuit have ... held ... that the Fair Sentencing Act does not apply to individuals sentenced before its effective date. Every other federal court of appeals—except the Federal Circuit, which does not hear criminal cases—has followed this path. Notwithstanding hundreds if not thousands of opportunities, no other appellate court in the country has held to the contrary.

Swimming against this tide, the Blewetts target an alleged anomaly that arises from our conclusion. Suppose, the Blewetts point out, that the district court had sentenced Cornelius to the minimum of 120 months but Jarreous to 125 months because Jarreous possessed more cocaine. In this scenario, the Blewetts correctly observe, Jarreous could get a five-month sentence reduction (down to the mandatory minimum), but Cornelius, already at the minimum, would get nothing.*

Yet this result says nothing about the forward-looking or backward-looking nature of the Fair Sentencing Act.

[T]he whole point of *any* retroactivity debate is whether to apply more lenient penalties to everyone or to apply them only to those sentenced after the new law takes effect. And the whole point of § 109 is to *create a presumption in favor of a disparity* between people who offended before a decrease in statutory penalties and people who offended after. The lead dissent authored by Judge Rogers mentions the saving statute once ..., and it is fair to ask whether the dissent has flipped the § 109 presumption against retroactivity into a presumption in favor of it.

The Fair Sentencing Act, for what it is worth, offers little guidance on [the question of retroactivity]. The Act ... affirmatively instructs the Sentencing Commission to use the new ratios for all *future* sentences [under the sentencing guidelines]. The Act does not tell the Commission to use the new ratios for all *past* sentences—that is, to make the new ratios retroactive. At first, indeed, the Commission adopted the new ratios only prospectively. Months later, the Commission solicited public comments about whether to make the new ratios retroactive. Later still, almost a year after the Fair Sentencing Act became law, the Commission finally voted for retroactivity.

In the last analysis, all indicators of meaning—the default rule that reductions in criminal penalties are not retroactive, the absence of any language in the Fair Sentencing Act that overcomes this presumption, ... a cascade of authority from our court and every other court of appeals, and the Sentencing Commission's own interpretation—show that the Act does not apply to defendants sentenced before its effective date.

---

* This is because the Sentencing Commission made its reduction to crack cocaine penalties under the sentencing guidelines retroactive. [*Footnote by casebook author.*]

Even if the Fair Sentencing Act applies only to individuals sentenced after its effective date . . . , the Blewetts claim that the Constitution's equal-protection and cruel-and-unusual-punishment principles give them relief. Long before the passage of the Fair Sentencing Act, our court and others repeatedly rejected similar constitutional challenges to the crack and powder cocaine sentencing disparities. Congress's *mitigation* of the crack and powder disparities does not weaken these precedents; it strengthens them. Besides, the Blewetts cite no cases that call these conclusions into question.

Observing that users of crack cocaine are predominantly black but users of powder are predominantly white, the Blewetts insist (along with the dissents authored by Judges Merritt, Cole, Clay and White, and with support from the concurrence in the judgment authored by Judge Moore) that a congressional failure to make the Fair Sentencing Act fully retroactive would violate the equal protection component of the Fifth Amendment's Due Process Clause. But this guarantee forbids only *intentional* discrimination. A law that lacks a "racially discriminatory purpose" does not become unconstitutional "solely because it has a racially disproportionate impact." No evidence shows that Congress acted with the purpose to discriminate when it refused to apply the Fair Sentencing Act to defendants—*all* defendants, white or black—sentenced before the Act took effect.

The Blewetts and Judge Clay add that Congress must have *foreseen* that its failure to make the Fair Sentencing Act fully retroactive would have a racially disproportionate impact. But . . . that makes no difference. A disproportionate effect does not violate the Equal Protection Clause, even if it was foreseen. The Supreme Court has instructed us that the "intent" in "intentional discrimination" means more than "intent as awareness of consequences." A violation arises only when a public official takes an action "'because of,' not merely 'in spite of,' its adverse effects upon an identifiable group." No evidence exists that Congress refused to make the Fair Sentencing Act retroactive *because* this refusal would disproportionately harm black defendants.

This theory of discrimination also makes little sense. Is it really possible that the same Congress that was deeply concerned about racial justice when looking at future sentences suddenly became racist when contemplating past sentences? That is a heavy lift. A more basic explanation exists for what Congress did, and for what it failed to do, in the Fair Sentencing Act. The government has a powerful interest in avoiding the disruption of final sentences. Congress did nothing extraordinary or for that matter discriminatory when it respected this interest.

The Blewetts, joined by several of the dissents, insist that Congress acted "irrationally" by failing to make the Fair Sentencing Act fully retroactive. But the government has a strong interest in the finality of sentences, and the Fair Sentencing Act advances that interest.

[In dissent, Judge Cole argues] that, because Congress did not insist on the finality of sentences based on the old *guidelines,* it acted irrationally by insisting on the finality of sentences based on the old statutory *minimums*. That does not follow. Congress created the minimums, and the Commission created the guidelines. It is eminently rational for Congress to decide the retroactivity of its creations and to allow the Commission to decide the retroactivity of *its* creations.

Turning to another part of the Constitution, the Blewetts . . . (with support from Judge Moore's opinion) contend that the Eighth Amendment prohibits the continued imprisonment of a defendant sentenced under the old mandatory minimum laws. Yet they cannot contend that their 10-year sentences were cruel and unusual when imposed. After all, the Supreme Court has upheld a mandatory minimum of *life without parole* for possession of 672 grams of cocaine *without intent to distribute. Harmelin v. Michigan,* 501 U.S. 957 (1991). The Blewetts' crimes are less serious in one respect (they possessed less cocaine), but more serious in two others (they possessed with intent to distribute and they had prior felony drug convictions). *Harmelin* precludes the conclusion that the Blewetts' much shorter mandatory minimum sentences were cruel and unusual.

The Blewetts persist that their sentences *became* cruel and unusual when Congress passed the Fair Sentencing Act. But the Eighth Amendment is not a ratchet that makes a harsher system of penalties unconstitutional the moment a more lenient one is (prospectively) adopted, a theory that would have the perverse effect of discouraging lawmakers from *ever* lowering criminal sentences. Withholding the benefits of a change from previously sentenced defendants at any rate is not "unusual"; it is the general practice in federal sentencing[.]

At the end of the day, this is a case about who, not what—about who has authority to lower the Blewetts' sentences, not what should be done with that authority. In holding that the courts lack authority to give the Blewetts a sentence reduction, we do not mean to discount the policy arguments for granting that reduction. Although the various opinions in this case draw different conclusions about the law, they all agree that Congress should think seriously about making the new minimums retroactive. Indeed, the Fair Sentencing Act, prospective though it is, dignifies much of what the Blewetts are saying as a matter of legislative reform and may well be a powerful ground for seeking relief from Congress. Yet the language of the relevant statutes . . . and the language of the relevant [Supreme Court] decisions . . . leave us no room to grant that relief here. Any request for a sentence reduction must be addressed to a higher tribunal (the Supreme Court) or to a different forum altogether (the Congress and the President).

Karen Nelson Moore, J., concurring in the judgment.

Each of our sister circuits has held that the Fair Sentencing Act does not apply to prisoners sentenced to the statutory minimum before the Act's effective date. The Sentencing Commission shares this view, though it has repeatedly asked Congress to extend the Act's benefits to all prisoners serving sentences for crack-cocaine violations. Nothing in the statute's text leads me to conclude that these positions are in error. Petitioners' arguments to the contrary are unconvincing, and therefore, I must concur in the majority's judgment to affirm the district court. I write separately, however, to express several reservations.

[In my view, t]he constitutionality of Cornelius Blewett's and Jarreous Blewitt's sentences is not before us today. But let there be no mistake: if a prisoner, who is serving a sentence based on the old mandatory minimums, challenged his sentence [in a petition for writ of habeas corpus], we could address the constitutional question directly.[3] Two decades ago, we held that sentences imposed pursuant to the 100-to-1 ratio did not violate the Fifth or the Eighth Amendments. For the reasons stated below, I lack faith in the soundness of those decisions.

The federal government may not "deny to any person within its jurisdiction the equal protection of the laws." U.S. Const. amend. XIV, § 1. At one point, these blunt words meant "'that equal protection and security should be given to all under like circumstances in the enjoyment of their personal and civil rights; . . . that no greater burdens should be laid upon one than are laid upon others in the same calling and condition; and that in the administration of criminal justice no different or higher punishment should be imposed upon one than such as is prescribed to all for like offenses.'" *Yick Wo v. Hopkins*, 118 U.S. 356, 367–68 (1886) (quoting *Barbier v. Connolly*, 113 U.S. 27 (1884)). Today, this fundamental protection prevents the federal government from enforcing its laws in a racially discriminatory manner or maintaining statutes that are no longer rationally related to a legitimate end.

In 2012, 82.6 percent of convicted federal crack-cocaine defendants were African American, yet African Americans represent only one-third of crack-cocaine users in the United States. In the same time-frame, only 6.7 percent of convicted federal crack-cocaine defendants were Caucasian, despite the fact that the majority of users is white. No conception of equality, no decent government, can long tolerate a criminal-justice system in which its citizens are treated so differently if such treatment is based on the color of their skin.

On its face, the 100-to-1 ratio is not a racial classification, and thus, proof of disparate impact is not enough. The Supreme Court also requires a demonstration that the discriminatory enforcement of the law is motivated by a discriminatory purpose, that the government "selected or reaffirmed a particular course of action at least in part 'because of,' not merely 'in spite of,' its adverse effects upon an identifiable group[.]" In most cases, satisfying this standard requires particularized proof of motive, yet "[s]ometimes a clear pattern, unexplainable on grounds other than race, emerges from the effect of the state action even when the governing legislation appears neutral on its face." In those rare situations, "[t]he evidentiary inquiry is then relatively easy."

3. The petitioners neither ask us to construe their . . . motions [for sentence modification] as applications for habeas relief nor challenge the constitutionality of their sentences. Thus, we cannot rule on the question now.

The federal government's enforcement of the crack-cocaine laws is stark and wildly disproportionate in its effects. Since Congress created the 100-to-1 ratio in 1986, African Americans have constituted eighty to ninety-five percent of federal crack-cocaine defendants while continuing to be a minority of crack-cocaine users. While the 100-to-1 ratio was in effect, the average federal drug sentence for African Americans was forty-nine percent longer than the average federal drug sentence for Caucasians. The impact of this policy was, and is, felt beyond the prison walls. At minimum, these statistics begin to suggest a criminal-justice system that treats one race much harsher than others. If true, this cannot stand. "Our Constitution is color-blind, and neither knows nor tolerates classes among citizens." *Plessy v. Ferguson,* 163 U.S. 537, 559 (Harlan, J., dissenting). By burdening one race above all others, the enforcement of the 100-to-1 ratio has potentially offended the Constitution's basic guarantee of equal treatment.

The Eighth Amendment provides that "[e]xcessive bail shall not be required, nor excessive fines imposed, nor cruel and unusual punishments inflicted." While these words may be imprecise, the Supreme Court has held that the "Amendment contains a 'narrow proportionality principle,' that 'does not require strict proportionality between crime and sentence' but rather 'forbids only extreme sentences that are grossly disproportionate to the crime.'" When considering whether a sentence is grossly disproportionate, we are largely "guided by objective criteria, including (i) the gravity of the offense and the harshness of the penalty; (ii) the sentences imposed on other criminals in the same jurisdiction; and (iii) the sentences imposed for commission of the same crime in other jurisdictions." But in addition, we must remember that "[t]he Amendment . . . draw[s] its meaning from the evolving standards of decency that mark the progress of a maturing society."

In *Levy, United States v. Avant*, 907 F.2d 623 (6th Cir. 1990), and *United States v. Pickett*, 941 F.2d 411 (6th Cir. 1991), we upheld the 100-to-1 ratio against Eighth Amendment challenges. A panel noted in *Levy*—without much explanation—that "[a] ten-year sentence for drug possession simply does not approach the same level of gross inequity" that had previously been held unconstitutional. In *Avant,* a panel stated that a ten-year sentence for possessing 7.3 grams of crack cocaine was "severe," but nonetheless constitutional.

In the past two decades, however, new information and events have cast doubt upon the continued validity of those decisions. Congress has passed the Fair Sentencing Act, lowering the disparity between crack and powder cocaine. The Sentencing Commission has, in turn, lowered the guidelines for crack cocaine. As of 2007, "[o]nly 13 states ha[d] some form of distinction between crack cocaine and powder cocaine," none of which employed a 100-to-1 ratio or worse. Since then, Missouri has lowered its ratio from 75-to-1 down to 18.75-to-1. Now, only Missouri, Arizona (12-to-1), and New Hampshire (28-to-1) have ratios above 10-to-1. In short, no American jurisdiction today treats crack-cocaine offenders in such a disproportionate way as the federal government did prior to the Fair Sentencing Act.

These changes, particularly when considered in conjunction with the new information discussed above . . . and in the dissents, suggest that the mandatory minimums in force before the enactment of the Fair Sentencing Act now constitute grossly disproportionate punishment. At the very least, we should reconsider whether *Levy* and its progeny still remain good law.

Rogers, J., dissenting.

We should not interpret the Fair Sentencing Act to create an anomaly unless the words of the statute compel it. They do not.

[In my view], Congress wanted the new minimums to apply whenever, after the statutory effective date, the sentence had to be calculated by the trial court. In that sense, . . . when a post-Fair Sentencing Act sentence is properly calculated . . . because a guideline has been retroactively changed, the new statutory minimums should be applied as well. In other words, when a post-Fair Sentencing Act sentencing court properly has before it the calculation of a sentence, the court should use the Fair Sentencing Act minimums.

The result of the majority's analysis is, in contrast, entirely anomalous. This is not the simple anomaly created by giving Fair Sentencing Act relief to criminals whose guideline range is far above the applicable statutory minimum, but not giving any relief to the less culpable criminals whose guideline range is affected by the minimum (although that discrepancy is unfortunate enough). The anomaly instead is that Congress directed the Sentencing Commission to promulgate sentencing guidelines incorporating the 18-1 ratio, and authorized the Commission to make the guidelines changes retroactive, such that the changed ratio would apply retroactively to all sentenced criminals when their sentence resulted from a guideline, but somehow did not want the 18-1 ratio to apply retroactively if incorporated in a statutory minimum, even though the sentencing minimums were changed for post-enactment sentencing.

The issue thus is not whether the Fair Sentencing Act applies the 18-1 ratio retroactively so as to open the prison doors. The Fair Sentencing Act clearly provides for this when the 18-1 ratio is implemented through a guideline rather than through a statutory minimum. The question in this case is whether the Fair Sentencing Act contemplates retroactivity when it provides for the 18-1 ratio through a guideline, but does not contemplate retroactivity when it provides for the 18-1 ratio through a revised statutory minimum. There is no coherent rationale for this distinction. It is an anomaly.

First, "the 1871 saving statute permits Congress to apply a new Act's more lenient penalties to pre-Act offenders without expressly saying so in the new Act." As the Supreme Court instructs . . . , in order to apply the Fair Sentencing Act to a new set of pre-Act offenders, we are to "assure ourselves that ordinary interpretive considerations point clearly in that direction." They . . . do here.

The default rule of [the savings] statute applies under neither the majority's analysis nor ours. Under the majority's analysis, the 18-1 statutory minimums apply to defendants sentenced after the effective date, but not to [sentence modification] proceedings initiated after the effective date. Under our dissenting analysis, the 18-1 statutory minimums apply to sentencing after the effective date and to [sentence modification] proceedings properly brought after the effective date. Under *neither* analysis does the applicability of the 18-1 statutory minimums depend on when the offense was committed—the default rule created by the saving statute. In other words, there are three possible relevant times for applying the 18-1 statutory minimums: (A) the time of the offense, (B) the time of sentencing, or (C) the time of sentencing or the time of a properly brought [sentence modification] motion. It makes no sense to say that because (A) is the default under the saving statute, (B) rather than (C) is the law. This questionably-based assumption, however, is the cornerstone of the other arguments for the anomalous interpretation of the applicability of the Fair Sentencing Act. Without it, such arguments essentially collapse.

Second, . . . Congress . . . enacted the Fair Sentencing Act against the backdrop of § 3582—a statute that permits retroactive modification of sentences after the Sentencing Commission amends guideline ranges downward. Congress' grant of the power to make guideline amendments retroactive to the Commission in 28 U.S.C. § 994(u) shaped the enactment of the Fair Sentencing Act because Congress knew that the Fair Sentencing Act's enactment would lead to modification proceedings under § 3582(c)(2). Congress can hardly have intended to give retroactive reductions of sentences with one hand, but to take that relief away with the other when it simultaneously amended the very statutory minimums that the majority says limit the Blewetts' access to relief under § 3582(c)(2).

Section 3582(c)(2) permits a modification when a defendant "has been sentenced to a term of imprisonment based on a sentencing range that has subsequently been lowered by the Sentencing Commission . . . if such reduction is consistent with applicable policy statements issued by the Sentencing Commission." It is true that the statute, which was of course passed before the Fair Sentencing Act, does not refer to reduced statutory minimums. But it does refer to guidelines reduced by the Commission, and the Blewetts have reduced sentencing ranges because of the Commission's changes to the § 2D1.1 drug quantity table. It is also true that the words can be parsed not to apply to mandatory minimum-driven sentences, on the theory that a reduction of the sentence was not "based on" a reduced guideline. But the language can just as well be read to say that, for purposes of the later-enacted Fair Sentencing Act, § 3582 applies where a guideline, even one restricted by a statutory minimum, is reduced. In that sense, the sentences in the Blewetts' cases were based on since-reduced guidelines.

This analysis does not mean that the Sentencing Commission is trumping the statute. The revised statutory minimums are, after all, created by statute. The Sentencing Commission, acting properly under 28 U.S.C. § 994(u), made the Fair Sentencing Act-driven guidelines retroactive. Doing so provided the statutory key to making the statutory minimum changes applicable under § 3582. This is a reasonable statutory interpretation, and it is particularly reasonable to avoid an incoherent anomaly.

It is true that the Sentencing Commission was not required to make the 18-1 guideline change retroactive, regardless of how expected such a move was. And if the Commission had not made the guideline change retroactive, the anomalies emphasized above would not have occurred. It made sense, therefore, for the retroactivity of the 18-1 ratio to be applied in § 3582 only if the Commission made the guidelines changes retroactive. Tying the retroactivity of the revised statutory minimums to the retroactivity of the revised guidelines, which a fair reading of the statutory provisions would do, creates a system that is fair and coherent overall. It gives the Commission the responsibility for making the 18-1 ratio retroactive, works fairness, and avoids anomalies that are an embarrassment to the law. Sticking persistently to the 100-1 ratio for the sole purpose of statutory minimums applied prior to the effective date of the Fair Sentencing Act, while in other respects permitting the 18-1 ratio to be applied retroactively, attributes to Congress the creation of a strange deformed one-winged bird. I would not attribute such an intent to Congress.

The purpose of the Fair Sentencing Act was to increase fairness in sentencing, and it is entirely incoherent to provide for retroactive fairness in some cases but not in others on a formalistic distinction not compelled by the language of the statute.

Cole, J., dissenting.

There is no question now that the 100-to-1 ratio is unjustified. The Sentencing Commission issued four separate reports telling Congress that the ratio was too high and unjustified because, in part, the "current quantity-based penalties overstate the relative harmfulness of crack cocaine compared to powder cocaine" and the "current severity of crack cocaine penalties mostly impacts minorities." Congress enacted the Fair Sentencing Act in response to these concerns.

Why, then, are [offenders who are] otherwise eligible for sentence modifications still imprisoned by a racially discriminatory, unjustified, repealed law? "Finality," the majority and the government reply. They argue that Congress intended to keep these sentences final.

Judge Rogers's analysis cogently explains that Congress did not, in fact, intend to keep these sentences final when it passed the Fair Sentencing Act. Instead, the Act's 18-to-1 ratio applies retroactively to reduce sentences driven by the 100-to-1 guidelines *and* those driven by the 100-to-1 minimums. But the bigger problem, to my mind, is that this claim of finality cannot withstand even rational basis scrutiny under equal protection principles.

Take those everyone agrees are eligible for [sentencing reductions under the new 18-to-1 ratio]: crack convicts sentenced above the 100-to-1 minimums. The majority and the government concede that an individual in this category could receive a sentence reduction. In other words, a district court could hold a hearing and recalculate the inmate's sentence, thereby disrupting its finality and incurring the time and costs of doing so. But then the majority says something odd: a district court still must apply the racially discriminatory, unjustified, repealed minimums to deny a full reduction to the new guidelines, all in the name of finality—finality that *already* has been set aside. This approach is irrational; it does not rationally further finality. Applying the minimums in this way would fail basic rational basis scrutiny.

Finality is easily used as a post-hoc explanation that makes past unjustified discrimination permanent. But . . . [t]he Fair Sentencing Act cannot be said to further finality interests rationally when it permits modification of sentences above, but not at, the racially discriminatory, unjustified, repealed 100-to-1 minimums.

I respectfully dissent.

Clay, J., dissenting.

The Fair Sentencing Act ("FSA") was passed by Congress in 2010 to reinstill some semblance of fairness and equality to a system plagued by inequality and injustice. Under the majority's interpretation of this statute, however, thousands of individuals, predominately African Americans from low-income communities like Cornelius Blewett and Jarreous Blewitt ("the Blewetts"), are foreclosed from obtaining the benefits of the FSA. Instead, the majority reads the FSA to further the injustice that has existed in the crack cocaine sentencing system for over twenty years. Under this reading, individuals like the Blewetts will continue to be incarcerated in a disproportionate, unjustified manner, in violation of their rights under the Equal Protection Clause. Because I disagree with the majority's characterization of the FSA's retroactivity and believe this Court's opinion furthers the injustice that has resulted from such an unequal sentencing regime, I respectfully dissent.

With the Anti-Drug Abuse Act of 1986 ("1986 Drug Act"), Congress created an unequal sentencing regime designed to punish drug offenders more heavily "depending primarily upon the kind and amount of drugs involved in the[ir] offense." Because this regime established a 100-to-1 sentencing ratio between crack and powder cocaine, a crack cocaine offender possessing five grams of crack with intent to distribute received a five-year mandatory minimum sentence while such a sentence was only applied to a powder cocaine offender in possession of 500 grams of powder cocaine with intent to distribute. Under this regime, the mean sentence for crack cocaine offenders was 133.4 months, while powder cocaine offenders "receive[d] a mean sentence of approximately [90] months."

Although, at that time, this ratio may have been deemed necessary in some quarters to confront the troubling rise of crack cocaine, the rationale behind such a sentencing disparity has since been debunked and has been abandoned by most of the parties originally in favor of the 1986 statute. *See* 155 CONG. REC. S10491 (daily ed. Oct. 15, 2009) (statement of Sen. Durbin) ("Vice President Joe Biden, one of the authors of the legislation creating this disparity in sentencing, has said: 'Each of the myths upon which we based the disparity has since been dispelled or altered.'").

In 2010, after years of reports from the United States Sentencing Commission ("Sentencing Commission") and criticism from parties on all sides of the American legal system, including the law enforcement community, Congress finally heeded the loud call for reform by enacting the FSA. Among other things, this statute greatly reduced the ratio for mandatory minimum sentencing between crack and powder cocaine from 100-to-1 to 18-to-1 and instructed the Sentencing Commission to create sentencing guidelines consistent with those new mandatory minimums. The Sentencing Commission did as instructed by designing sentencing guidelines in tandem with Congress' new mandatory minimums and explicitly making the guidelines retroactive.

Each of the justifications originally presented in support of the 1986 Drug Act's disparity between crack and powder cocaine sentencing has since been debunked. The original disparity was justified by what appeared to be an important pharmacological difference between crack and powder cocaine as well as a fear of greater violence surrounding dealings and use of crack cocaine versus powder cocaine. However, as Republican Representative, Daniel Lungren, stated in support of the FSA, "We initially came out of committee with a 20-to-1 ratio. By the time we finished on the floor, it was 100-to-1. We didn't really have an evidentiary basis for it, but that's what we did, thinking we were doing the right thing at the time." Mr. Elmore Briggs, Director of Clinical Services at the District of Columbia Department of Health, Addiction, Recovery, and Prevention Administration, has concluded that despite differences in mechanisms for delivery of crack and powder cocaine into the body, "trafficking sentencing should be equalized for cocaine regardless of the form of drug."[2] Members of Congress have similarly acknowledged that there is no pharmacological basis for the large disparity in sentencing between crack and powder cocaine.

Additionally, members of Congress and the legal and criminal justice communities, including the "bipartisan U.S. Sentencing Commission, the Judicial Conference of the United States, the National District Attorneys Association, the National Association of Police Organizations, the Federal Law Enforcement Officers Association, the International Union of Police Associations, and dozens of former Federal judges and prosecutors ..." have recognized that there is no penological evidence supporting the continued application of the old mandatory minimums that created such huge disparities in sentencing. Dr. Bruce Johnson, Director of the Institute for Special Populations Research at the National Development and Research Institutes echoed this perspective when he suggested replacing the 100-to-1 drug quantity ratio with either a 10-to-1 or a 2-to-1 drug quantity ratio to more appropriately capture the respective safety concerns surrounding crack and powder cocaine.

Even more disconcerting than the lack of evidence to support the great disparity in cocaine offense sentencing is the disparate impact such sentences have had on low-income, African American communities. Representative Bobby Scott, speaking on the floor of the House of Representatives, stated that "[the] disparity is particularly

---

2. Dr. Nora Volkow, Director of the National Institute on Drug Abuse, also testified before the Sentencing Commission that "all forms of cocaine, regardless of the route of administration, result in a similar blockage of dopamine transporters ... which is why repeated use of any form of cocaine can lead to addiction and other health consequences." Despite acknowledging that route of administration can cause different effects in the body, "she emphasized that the excess risk [of addiction] is not attributable to crack cocaine smoking or injecting [powder] cocaine."

egregious when you consider that the Sentencing Commission has concluded that there is no pharmacological difference between the two forms of cocaine, and that 80 percent of the crack defendants are black, whereas only 30 percent of the powder cocaine defendants are black."

Members of Congress were emphatic in suggesting that these racial disparities in cocaine sentencing produced equal protection problems. Representative Ron Paul stated on the floor of the House of Representatives that "[the FSA] makes an attempt to correct a very, very serious problem in equal justice in our systems. . . ." Senator Patrick Leahy also stated that "[t]he racial imbalance that has resulted from the cocaine sentencing disparity disparages the Constitution's promise of equal treatment for all Americans. . . . [The FSA] reduces the disparities that leave some in jail for years while their more privileged counterparts go home after relatively brief sentences." The racial disparities inherent in the old sentencing regime create an equal protection issue and a human rights issue, which could be resolved by retroactive application of the FSA's new sentencing ratio.

The Equal Protection Clause stipulates that "[n]o state shall . . . deny to any person within its jurisdiction the equal protection of the laws" and these protections apply equally against acts of state governments and the federal government.

The concerns leading to the passage of the Thirteenth, Fourteenth, and Fifteenth Amendments are particularly relevant in the context of legislation that draws distinctions based on race and disproportionately impacts African Americans. *Bell v. Maryland,* 378 U.S. 226, 289 (1964) (Goldberg, J., concurring). At the heart of equal protection is an intent to eradicate racial disparity in treatment under the law. "Such opinions immediately following the adoption of the Amendments clearly reflect the contemporary understanding that they were 'to secure to the colored race, thereby invested with the rights, privileges, and responsibilities of citizenship, the enjoyment of all the civil rights that, under the law, are enjoyed by white persons. . . .'" *Id.* (quoting *Neal v. Delaware,* 103 U.S. 370, 386 (1880)).

Although the FSA is not facially discriminatory, an interpretation of the FSA foreclosing the retroactive application of its new mandatory minimums would present an equal protection problem inasmuch as it would subject a group that is overwhelmingly predominately African American to starkly different treatment under the law. Such an interpretation can meet neither strict scrutiny nor rational basis review and should therefore be avoided by this Court.

Although the FSA is neutral on its face and a decision regarding the retroactivity of the mandatory minimums would also be facially neutral, the majority's interpretation of the FSA's retroactivity poses serious constitutional concerns. A law presents an equal protection violation and must therefore be struck down or read differently if it is motivated by a racially discriminatory purpose and has a disparate impact on an identifiable group. The Supreme Court explained in *Vill. of Arlington Heights v. Metro. Hous. Dev. Corp.* that "[t]he impact of the official action whether it 'bears more heavily on one race than another,' may provide an important starting point. Sometimes a clear pattern, unexplainable on grounds other than race, emerges from the effect of the state action even when the governing legislation appears neutral on its face."

The 100-to-1 ratio under the 1986 Drug Act clearly disproportionately impacts African Americans without any evidentiary basis in science or criminal justice theory. In 1993, for example, black and Hispanic individuals accounted for over 95% of the offenders who were convicted for crack distribution. Although the proportion of crack cocaine offenders who are African American has declined since 1992, the proportion still remained at 81.8% of the total crack cocaine offender population in 2006. In 2010, Congress acted, in large part, to rectify this injustice and to equalize the crack and powder cocaine sentencing regime that had been criticized on all fronts. In fact, "African Americans serve almost as much time in Federal prison for a drug offense (58.7 months) as whites do for a violent offense (61.7 months), largely due to sentencing laws such as the 100-to-1 crack-powder cocaine disparity."

Of course, this information was known to Congress prior to the FSA's enactment. In fact, on a number of occasions, this Court and other circuits considered this information and ultimately held that the disparities in sentencing alone were not sufficient to amount to an equal protection violation. However, the legislative enactment of the FSA [has] rendered the old case law obsolete.

In his concurring opinion in [*United States v.*] *Then,* [56 F.3d 464, 467 (2d Cir. 1995)], Judge Calabresi recognized that the disproportionate sentencing ratio was seemingly justified at the time it was adopted, and "the link between foreseeable discriminatory impact and motive was insufficient to establish the kind of discriminatory intent on the part of Congress or the Commission that is needed to support [an] equal protection claim." However, he also suggested that "what is known today about the effects of crack and cocaine, and about the impact that the crack/cocaine sentencing rules have on minority groups, is significantly different from what was known when the 100-to-1 ratio was adopted." Therefore, Judge Calabresi opined that "[i]f Congress . . . though it was made aware of both the dramatically disparate impact among minority groups of enhanced crack penalties and of the limited evidence supporting such enhanced penalties, were nevertheless to act affirmatively and negate the Commission's proposed amendments to the Sentencing Guidelines (or perhaps were even just to allow the 100-to-1 ratio to persist in mandatory minimum sentences), subsequent equal protection challenges based on claims of discriminatory purpose might well lie. . . . As the Supreme Court has pointed out, facially-neutral legislation violates equal protection if there is evidence that the legislature has "selected *or reaffirmed* a particular course of action at least in part 'because of,' not merely 'in spite of,' its adverse effects upon an identifiable group." *Then,* 56 F.3d at 468 (Calabresi, J., concurring) (quoting *Pers. Adm'r of Mass. v. Feeney,* 442 U.S. 256, 279 (1979)).

To interpret [the FSA] in a manner that does not extend this equalizing mechanism to the thousands of individuals sentenced under the old mandatory minimums would create a "clear pattern, unexplainable on grounds other than race. . . ."

Arlington Heights, 429 U.S. at 266. In fact, such a reading of the FSA creates the exact equal protection concerns raised by Judge[] Calabresi . . . in [his] concurring opinion[]. Adopting new mandatory minimums for the purpose of righting the racially discriminatory wrongs of the past and not extending the benefits of the new enactment to the thousands of predominately African American individuals serving disproportionate sentences under a now-rejected statute violates equal protection because Congress has recognized and reaffirmed "its adverse effects" upon the African American community.

The constitutional avoidance principle demands that we interpret a statute in a way that avoids any violation of the Constitution. Therefore, we must interpret the FSA's new mandatory minimums to apply retroactively; otherwise, thousands of incarcerated individuals, most of whom are impoverished African Americans, will remain incarcerated under unequal, unjust, and unconstitutional prison sentences. Had Congress intended the new mandatory minimums to be only prospective, then Congress would have reaffirmed the inequalities that have now been acknowledged as lacking in any evidentiary basis and creating deep racial disparities. The majority's reading of the FSA would assign to Congress an improper discriminatory purpose, which must be avoided under the Constitutional avoidance doctrine.[5]

On the other hand, even absent Congressional discriminatory intent, the FSA's mandatory minimums must still be interpreted to apply retroactively under rational basis review. Where the government's action "neither burdens a fundamental right nor targets a suspect class, [this Court] will uphold the legislative classification so long as it bears a rational relation to some legitimate end."

Under the rational basis test, a petitioner generally carries a heavy burden to show that a statute is arbitrary and unsupported by any rational basis. This principle, however, has broken down when "[a] protesting group was historically disadvantaged or unpopular, and the statutory justification seemed thin, unsupported or impermissible." *Massachusetts v. U.S. Dept. of Health & Human Servs.,* 682 F.3d 1, 10 (1st Cir.2012). The Supreme Court has applied this more rigid version of rational basis review to strike down group classifications that are not traditionally entitled to heightened scrutiny. *See, e.g., Cleburne,* 473 U.S. at 447–50 (applying a more rigorous rational basis review to a zoning law impacting the mentally retarded); *Romer,*

5. According to Judge Sutton's opinion, to demonstrate an equal protection violation based on a disparate impact theory, we must find that the same Congress responsible for addressing the racial inequality in cocaine sentencing was also "racist" with respect to the FSA's retroactivity. To the contrary, Congress' lack of clear expression on the issue can be interpreted in at least two different ways: either Congress chose to apply the new mandatory minimums retroactively, finally rectifying a racial disparity that is unsupported by any penological or pharmacological justification, or Congress deliberately chose to deny relief to those individuals currently incarcerated under what is now recognized as an unjust, unequal, and unconstitutional sentencing scheme. The constitutional avoidance principle requires us to adopt the former interpretation and interpret Congress' lack of explicitness in harmony with its intent to diminish the racial disparity in crack and powder cocaine sentencing.

517 U.S. at 631–35 (applying a heightened rational basis standard to a classification subjecting gays and lesbians to different treatment).

Congress has made a distinction between crack cocaine offenders and powder cocaine offenders, the former being overwhelmingly impoverished African Americans. There may be no more abject, disparaged, powerless minority group than those sentenced under the old crack cocaine mandatory minimums. This is where the democratic process breaks down and traditional rational basis review is insufficient to protect the group of individuals convicted under federal crack cocaine mandatory minimums, more than 82% of whom were African American in 2005. Courts should not be as deferential to government enactments under circumstances where an irrational classification based on the *form* of cocaine, which has real-world consequences in terms of sentencing disparities, tracks so closely with race.

The State cannot proffer any legitimate penological or pharmacological reason for the continued incarceration of those who were subjected to extended sentences under the unjust 100-to-1 ratio. Instead, in the face of this more rigorous rational basis standard, the government can only offer *finality* as its legitimate interest in support of the continued application of the old mandatory minimums. Although finality has previously been recognized as a legitimate state interest, no one has cited a single case that says finality can support criminal convictions and overly onerous sentences based upon a premise that Congress has overwhelmingly and demonstrably acknowledged to be false as of the day it was passed. This crack versus powder cocaine sentencing scheme has institutionalized young black men at a rate entirely disproportionate to the facts on the ground. Here, where Congress is silent on the retroactive application of mandatory minimums, finality cannot serve as a legitimate interest in the face of such abhorrent inequality.

[A] judicial determination that the FSA should apply retroactively would comport with Congress' legislative objectives, as substantiated by the statute's legislative history, and would permit the statute to be construed in a manner that satisfies rather than violates the requirements of the Constitution's Equal Protection Clause.

[Dissenting opinions by Judges Merritt and White have been omitted.]

In 2014, the Department of Justice announced a clemency project that was motivated in part by the "prospective-only nature of the Fair Sentencing Act[.]" Paul J. Larkin, Jr., *Revitalizing the Clemency Process* 39 Harv. J.L. & Pub. Pol'y 833, 886 (2016). The clemency project was designed to facilitate the use of the pardon power to reduce sentences for federal prisoners who would have likely received shorter sentences if sentenced under current laws and policies—including, of course, crack cocaine offenders. The initiative resulted in a total of 1,715 commutations and 212 pardons granted by President Obama, along with 25,000 denials of petitions. Mark Osler, *Fewer Hands, More Mercy: A Plea For a Better Federal Clemency System*, 41 Vt. L. Rev. 465, 487 (2017). The effort did not benefit all federal prisoners who would have received shorter sentences under current laws, however. The criteria for eligibility for consideration under the clemency project included requirements beyond whether an offender would have received a shorter sentence today, such as demonstrated good conduct in prison. In addition, President Obama "failed to rule on ... 9,400 [petitions] received during his presidency" as the project was plagued by a number of bureaucratic problems. *Id.* at 485–489 (2017).

As already noted above, Congress finally made the Fair Sentencing Act retroactive in December 2018 with passage of the FIRST STEP Act of 2018.

5. The FIRST STEP Act

Advocates for reducing federal drug sentences achieved a surprise victory in late 2018, with passage of the Formerly Incarcerated Reenter Society Transformed Safely Transitioning Every Person Act (the FIRST STEP Act).

The FIRST STEP Act was the culmination of years of activism and advocacy. During President Obama's second term, Congress came very close to passing sentencing reform, but the effort "stalled in the Senate." Shon Hopwood, *The Effort to Reform the Federal Criminal Justice System*, 128 YALE L.J. FORUM 791, 794 (2019). Immediately after Trump took office, "it would have been hard to convince anyone ... that any federal criminal justice reform was possible." *Id.* at 798. But a number of factors—including support from Trump's son-in-law Jared Kushner, "whose father was incarcerated in the federal system in 2002 and who has thus been directly affected by the system"—led Trump to support the FIRST STEP Act. *Id.* at 799. As a result of Trump's support, Senate Majority Leader Mitch McConnell allowed the bill to get a vote in the Senate. *See also* Jonathan Feniak, *The FIRST STEP Act: Criminal Justice Reform at a Bipartisan Tipping Point*, 96 DENV. L. REV. ONLINE 166, 171–72 (2019) (describing the events that resulted in passage of the FIRST STEP Act).

The FIRST STEP Act focuses primarily on reentry and prison conditions by, among other things, requiring the Bureau of Prisons "to provide meaningful rehabilitation programs for federal prisoners and t[ying] those programs to earned time that federal prisoners can use to serve out some of their prison sentence in a halfway house or in home confinement." Hopwood, *supra*, at 795. But the law also included a number of important, if relatively modest, reforms to federal drug sentencing laws. Specifically, the law reduced some mandatory minimum penalties for drug offenses committed by people with prior convictions, expanded eligibility for the safety valve, reduced mandatory minimums based on the "stacking" of charges for using or carrying a firearm in furtherance of a drug crime, and made retroactive the Fair Sentencing Act of 2010 (which reduced the disparity between crack and powder cocaine sentences). Each of these reforms is briefly described below.

Mandatory minimum penalty reductions: The FIRST STEP Act reduced some of the harshest mandatory minimum drug penalties—those based on a prior drug conviction. It did this in two ways. First, it limited the types of offenses that can trigger a recidivist enhancement-based mandatory minimum penalty. Second, it reduced the length of the mandatory term for certain categories of offenders.

To better understand this aspect of the FIRST STEP Act, a quick review of some federal drug sentencing basics is helpful. Recall that most mandatory minimum drug penalties are based on the type and quantity of the drug involved in the offense. For example, distributing more than 28 grams of crack cocaine triggers a five-year mandatory minimum sentence; more than 280 grams triggers a 10-year mandatory sentence. These mandatory minimum penalties can increase even more for defendants who were previously convicted of certain offenses. It is this aspect of the law—sometimes referred to as the recidivist enhancement provision—that the FIRST STEP Act reformed.

Before passage of the FIRST STEP Act, drug quantity-based mandatory minimum penalties could increase for offenders who have a "prior drug felony" conviction. The Controlled Substances Act defines a "felony drug offense" as "an offense that is punishable by imprisonment for more than one year under any law of the United States or of a State or foreign country that prohibits or restricts conduct relating to narcotic drugs, marihuana, anabolic steroids, or depressant or stimulant substances." 21 U.S.C. § 802(44). Under this definition, crimes that are classified as misdemeanors under state law could be considered felonies for purposes of the federal recidivist enhancement provision. This is because the enhancement applied to "all defendants whose prior drug crimes were punishable by more than one year in prison . . . regardless of the punishing jurisdiction's classification of the offense." *Burgess v. United States,* 553 U.S. 124, 129 (2008).

Before passage of the FIRST STEP Act, a single prior drug felony conviction could double the drug quantity-based mandatory minimum sentence that would otherwise apply, turning a five-year mandatory sentence into 10 years and a 10-year mandatory sentence into 20 years. If the defendant had two prior drug felony convictions, a 10-year mandatory minimum could become a *mandatory life sentence.* (Notably, the enhancements are not automatic. They only apply if charged by the prosecutor.)

Because it is not uncommon for people with a substance use disorder to have a state conviction or two that meets the definition of a "felony drug offense," the recidivist enhancement provision had the potential to dramatically impact many federal drug cases. Consider the case of Paul E. Free, who was convicted of conspiracy to distribute and possess with intent to distribute 1,756 kilograms of marijuana in 1995. Without the recidivist enhancement, Free would have been subjected to a 10-year mandatory minimum penalty. Because Free had two prior drug felony convictions, however—a 1974 conviction for possession with intent to distribute marijuana and a 1975 conviction for conspiracy to distribute marijuana—he received a mandatory life sentence. ACLU FOUNDATION, A LIVING DEATH: LIFE WITHOUT PAROLE FOR NONVIOLENT OFFENSES 162–32 (2013). (In 2016, President Obama commuted Free's sentence to 30 years.)

The FIRST STEP Act limited the scope of these recidivist enhancements. Now, a felony drug offense is no longer sufficient to trigger a recidivist enhancement. Instead, the recidivist enhancement is triggered by a "serious drug felony" or a "serious violent felony." Both serious drug felony and serious violent felony have somewhat technical definitions. Broadly speaking, however, a serious drug felony is defined as a drug trafficking offense punishable by a term of imprisonment of 10 years or more, and for which the defendant served a term of imprisonment of more than 12 months and was released from prison within the last 15 years. A serious violent felony is a crime of force, attempted force, or threatened force against another person that is punishable by 10 years or more in prison and for which the defendant served a term of imprisonment of more than 12 months. 21 U.S.C. § 802(57), (58).

The FIRST STEP Act also reduced the length of some of the enhanced mandatory minimum penalties. Specifically, mandatory 20-year penalties were reduced to 15 years and mandatory life sentences were reduced to 25 years.

The FIRST STEP Act's Changes to Recidivist Enhancement Penalties

Quantity-based penalty	Enhanced penalty *before* the FIRST STEP Act	Enhanced penalty *after* the FIRST STEP Act
5-year mandatory minimum (21 U.S.C. § 841(b)(1)(B) and 21 U.S.C. § 960(b)(2))	10-year mandatory minimum after one prior *drug felony* conviction	10-year mandatory minimum after one prior *serious drug felony or serious violent felony* conviction
10-year mandatory minimum (21 U.S.C. § 841(b)(1)(A) and 21 U.S.C. § 960(b)(1))	*20-year* mandatory minimum after one prior *drug felony* conviction	*15-year* mandatory minimum after one prior *serious drug felony or serious violent felony* conviction
	Mandatory *life* sentence after two or more prior *drug felony* convictions*	*25-year* mandatory minimum after two or more prior *serious drug felony or serious violent felony* convictions*

Note: The enhanced penalties only apply if the prior convictions are charged by the prosecutor.

* These penalties do not apply to violations of 21 U.S.C. § 960(b)(1) because that statute does not include an enhancement for two or more prior convictions.

The United States Sentencing Commission estimated in early 2019 that this reform will benefit approximately 56 offenders annually and will result in an average sentence reduction of 21% for these offenders.

Safety valve expansion: The FIRST STEP Act expanded eligibility for the safety valve—the law that grants an exception to mandatory minimum drug penalties for certain drug defendants. Before passage of the FIRST STEP Act, defendants who had more than one criminal history point as determined under the sentencing guidelines were ineligible for the safety valve. This criminal history requirement has been relaxed. Now, for a defendant to be disqualified from safety valve relief as a result of her criminal history, she must have either "(A) more than 4 criminal history points, excluding any criminal history points resulting from a 1-point offense, as determined under the sentencing guidelines; (B) a prior 3-point offense, as determined under the sentencing guidelines; [or] (C) a prior 2-point violent offense, as determined under the sentencing guidelines." 18 U.S.C. § 3553(f)(1).

To appreciate what these changes mean in practical terms, consider a few hypothetical examples that the Sentencing Commission provided in its overview of the FIRST STEP Act:

> [Example 1] Defendant has four 1-point convictions and two 2-point convictions for possession of cocaine, for a total of eight criminal history points (Criminal History Category IV). Is this defendant eligible for relief from a mandatory minimum under [the safety valve,] 18 U.S.C. § 3553(f)?
>
> [Answer 1] Yes. He has no more than four criminal history points excluding the 1-point convictions, no prior 3-point offenses, and no prior 2-point violent offenses. However, the defendant would not meet the criteria for the 2-level reduction at § 2D1.1(b)(18), which only allows for reduction where the defendant has no more than one criminal history point.
>
> [Example 2] Defendant's instant offense is Possession with Intent to Distribute Cocaine. The defendant is a Career Offender under § 4B1.1 because he has a prior conviction for sale of a controlled substance and another separate prior conviction for distribution of crack. The defendant received a sentence of three years' probation on the first conviction and 30 days imprisonment on the second conviction for a total of two criminal history points. However, the defendant is a Career Offender and his Criminal History Category is VI. Is this defendant eligible for relief under 18 U.S.C. § 3553(f)?
>
> [Answer 2] Yes. Although the defendant is a Career Offender, this defendant's prior record does not disqualify him from being eligible for relief under the revised statutory safety valve.
>
> [Example 3] A defendant has a total of six criminal history points. The defendant has two prior 2-point convictions (for non-violent offenses) and he also received two criminal history points for "status" under § 4A1.1(d) for being under a criminal justice sentence for one of the prior 2-point convictions. Is this defendant eligible for relief from a mandatory minimum penalty under 18 U.S.C. § 3553(f)?
>
> [Answer 3] No. This defendant has more than four criminal history points (excluding any criminal history points resulting from a 1-point offense), and is therefore not eligible for the statutory safety valve.

The United States Sentencing Commission estimated in early 2019 that this reform will benefit approximately 2,000 offenders annually and will result in an average sentence reduction of 22% for these offenders.

"Stacking" charges under 18 U.S.C. § 924(c): 18 U.S.C. § 924(c) makes it a crime to use, carry, or possess a firearm in furtherance of a drug trafficking crime. The statute also provides for a mandatory minimum penalty of five years for the first offense and 25 years for subsequent offenses.

Before passage of the FIRST STEP Act, if a defendant was convicted of more than one section 924(c) count in a single case, the 25-year penalty applied to the second count of conviction. So, for example, a defendant who was convicted of two marijuana sales and of carrying a gun during each sale (i.e., two section 924(c) counts) was subject to a total mandatory minimum penalty of 30 years for the section 924(c) counts alone—five years for the first count and 25 years for the second count. (This "stacking" of section 924(c) counts was responsible for the 55-year prison sentence in the case presented in the next section on drug sentencing and the Eighth Amendment, *United States v. Angelos.*)

Under the FIRST STEP Act, the 25-year mandatory minimum penalty for a second section 924(c) offense does not apply unless the defendant has a prior section 924(c) conviction that has already become final. In other words, the enhanced 25-year mandatory minimum penalty only applies if the defendant was already convicted of violating section 924(c), served his sentence for the conviction, and then committed a new section 924(c) offense.

The FIRST STEP Act did not eliminate the stacking of 924(c) charges entirely, however. The defendant in the hypothetical above (who was convicted of two section 924(c) counts in a single case) would now receive a mandatory five years for each section 924(c) conviction, for a total mandatory term of 10 years.

The United States Sentencing Commission estimated in early 2019 that this reform will benefit approximately 57 offenders annually and will result in an average sentence reduction of 53% for these offenders.

Retroactive application of the Fair Sentencing Act of 2010: The Fair Sentencing Act of 2010 increased the amount of crack cocaine that triggers a five-year mandatory minimum penalty from 5 grams to 28 grams and the amount that triggers a 10-year mandatory minimum penalty from 50 grams to 280 grams. The Fair Sentencing Act did not make its mandatory minimum penalty changes retroactive, however. As a result, crack cocaine defendants who were subject to a mandatory minimum penalty before the Fair Sentencing Act took effect were stuck with that mandatory minimum penalty. (A number of defendants unsuccessfully challenged this aspect of the Fair Sentencing Act, including the defendants in *United States v. Blewett*, presented in the section immediately above.)

The FIRST STEP Act made the Fair Sentencing Act of 2010 retroactive.

The United States Sentencing Commission estimated in early 2019 that as many as 2,660 offenders may be eligible for resentencing based on the retroactive application of the Fair Sentencing Act.

Retroactive application?: Although the FIRST STEP Act made the Fair Sentencing Act of 2010 retroactive, its other sentencing reforms—the mandatory minimum penalty reductions, the safety valve expansion, and the limitation on stacking section 924(c) counts—were *not* made retroactive.

D. Drug Sentencing and the Eighth Amendment

Some drug defendants have attempted to challenge long mandatory minimum sentences based on the Eighth Amendment's prohibition against cruel and unusual punishment. The following case, *United States v. Angelos*, exemplifies the extraordinary burden that a drug defendant who attempts to challenge his sentence as cruel and unusual will face.

Angelos involved a prosecution under a statute—18 U.S.C. § 924(c)—that provides an additional mandatory minimum penalty in the case of "any person who, during and in relation to any crime of violence or drug trafficking crime . . . uses or carries a firearm, or who, in furtherance of any such crime, possesses a firearm." 18 U.S.C. § 924(c). The law defines a drug trafficking crime as "any felony punishable under the Controlled Substances Act[.]" 18 U.S.C. § 924(c)(2). Charges brought under this statute are often referred to as section 924(c) charges.

The mandatory minimum penalty for violating section 924(c) is five years for the first offense and 25 years for subsequent offenses. At the time Weldon Angelos was prosecuted, the 25-year mandatory penalty for a "second or subsequent conviction" under 18 U.S.C. § 924(c) applied to multiple convictions in a *single* prosecution. This meant that a defendant who sold marijuana three times to an undercover agent three days in a row, and possessed a gun during each sale, could face a mandatory 55 years in prison (five for the first offense, and a total of 50 for the second and third offenses). Prosecutors were required to charge each offense separately for these penalties to be triggered, giving them significant power over sentencing and plea negotiations in cases of multiple drug sales involving guns.

As discussed in the section immediately above, this aspect of section 924(c) was amended in late 2018 as part of the FIRST STEP Act. Today, the 25-year mandatory minimum penalty for a second section 924(c) conviction only applies if the defendant has an already-final section 924(c) conviction. In other words, the enhanced 25-year mandatory minimum penalty does not apply unless the defendant was already convicted of violating section 924(c), served his sentence for the conviction, and then committed a new section 924(c) offense. The FIRST STEP Act did not make this amendment retroactive. As a result, defendants who were sentenced under the old scheme are not eligible to receive reduced sentences.

Although the sentencing scheme that led to the 55-year mandatory minimum sentence at issue in *Angelos* has since been amended, the court's treatment of Angelos's Eighth Amendment claim remains good law.

United States v. Angelos

United States District Court for the District of Utah
345 F. Supp. 2d 1227 (2004)

Cassell, J.

Defendant Weldon Angelos stands now before the court for sentencing. He is a twenty-four-year-old first offender who is a successful music executive with two young children. Because he was convicted of dealing marijuana and related offenses, both the government and the defense agree that Mr. Angelos should serve about six to eight years in prison. But there are three additional firearms offenses for which the court must also impose sentence. Two of those offenses occurred when Mr. Angelos carried a handgun to two $350 marijuana deals; the third when police found several additional handguns at his home when they executed a search warrant. For these three acts of possessing (not using or even displaying) these guns, the government insists that Mr. Angelos should essentially spend the rest of his life in prison. Specifically, the government urges the court to sentence Mr. Angelos to a prison term of no less than 61 1/2 years—six years and a half (or more) for drug dealing followed by 55 years for three counts of possessing a firearm in connection with a drug offense. In support of its position, the government relies on a statute—18 U.S.C. § 924(c)—which requires the court to impose a sentence of five years in prison the first time a drug dealer carries a gun and twenty-five years for each subsequent time. Under § 924(c), the three counts produce 55 years of additional punishment for carrying a firearm.

The court's role in evaluating § 924(c) is quite limited. The court can set aside the statute only if it is irrational punishment without any conceivable justification or is so excessive as to constitute cruel and unusual punishment in violation of the Eighth Amendment. After careful deliberation, the court reluctantly concludes that it has no choice but to impose the 55 year sentence. While the sentence appears to be cruel, unjust, and irrational, in our system of separated powers Congress makes the final decisions as to appropriate criminal penalties. Under the controlling case law, the court must find either that a statute has no conceivable justification or is so grossly disproportionate to the crime that no reasonable argument can be made its behalf. If the court is to fairly apply these precedents in this case, it must reject Mr. Angelos' constitutional challenges. Accordingly, the court sentences Mr. Angelos to a prison term of 55 years and one day, the minimum that the law allows.

Weldon Angelos is twenty-four years old. He was born on July 16, 1979, in Salt Lake City, Utah. He was raised in the Salt Lake City area by his father, Mr. James B. Angelos, with only minimal contact with his mother. Mr. Angelos has two young children by Ms. Zandrah Uyan: six-year-old Anthony and five-year-old Jessie. Before his arrest Mr. Angelos had achieved some success in the music industry. He started Extravagant Records, a label that produces rap and hip hop music. He had worked with prominent hip hop musicians, including Snoop Dogg, on the "beats" to various songs and was preparing to record his own album.

The critical events in this case are three "controlled buys" of marijuana by a government informant from Mr. Angelos. On May 10, 2002, Mr. Angelos met with the informant, Ronnie Lazalde, and arranged a sale of marijuana. On May 21, 2002, Mr. Angelos completed a sale of eight ounces of marijuana to Lazalde for $350. Lazalde observed Mr. Angelos' Glock pistol by the center console of his car. This drug deal formed the basis for the first § 924(c) count.

During a second controlled buy with Lazalde, on June 4, 2002, Mr. Angelos lifted his pant leg to show him the Glock in an ankle holster. Lazalde again purchased approximately eight ounces of marijuana for $350. This deal formed the basis for the second § 924(c) count.

A third controlled buy occurred on June 18, 2002, with Mr. Angelos again selling Lazalde eight ounces of marijuana for $350. There was no direct evidence of a gun at this transaction, so no § 924(c) count was charged.

On November 15, 2003, police officers arrested Mr. Angelos at his apartment pursuant to a warrant. Mr. Angelos consented to a search. The search revealed a briefcase which contained $18,040, a handgun, and two opiate suckers. Officers also discovered two bags which contained approximately three pounds of marijuana. Officers also recovered two other guns in a locked safe, one of which was confirmed as stolen. Searches at other locations, including the apartment of Mr. Angelos' girlfriend, turned up several duffle bags with marijuana residue, two more guns, and additional cash.

The original indictment issued against Mr. Angelos contained three counts of distribution of marijuana, one § 924(c) count for the firearm at the first controlled buy, and two other lesser charges. Plea negotiations began between the government and Mr. Angelos. On January 20, 2003, the government told Mr. Angelos, through counsel, that if he pled guilty to the drug distribution count and the § 924(c) count, the government would agree to drop all other charges, not supersede the indictment with additional counts, and recommend a prison sentence of 15 years. The government made clear to Mr. Angelos that if he rejected the offer, the government would obtain a new superseding indictment adding several § 924(c) counts that could lead to Mr. Angelos facing more than 100 years of mandatory prison time. In short, Mr. Angelos faced the choice of accepting 15 years in prison or insisting on a trial by jury at the risk of a life sentence. Ultimately, Mr. Angelos rejected the offer and decided to go to trial. The government then obtained two superseding indictments, eventually charging twenty total counts, including five § 924(c) counts which alone carried a potential minimum mandatory sentence of 105 years. The five § 924(c) counts consisted of two counts for the Glock seen at the two controlled buys, one count for three handguns found at his home, and two more counts for the two guns found at the home of Mr. Angelos' girlfriend.

Perhaps recognizing the gravity of the situation, Mr. Angelos tried to reopen plea negotiations, offering to plea to one count of drug distribution, one § 924(c) count, and one money laundering count. The government refused his offer, and the case proceeded to trial. The jury found Mr. Angelos guilty on sixteen counts, including three § 924(c) counts: two counts for the Glock seen at the two controlled buys and a third count for the three handguns at Mr. Angelos' home. The jury found him not guilty on three counts—including the two additional § 924(c) counts for the two guns at his girlfriends' home. (The court dismissed one other minor count.)

Mr. Angelos' sentence is presumptively governed by the Federal Sentencing Guidelines. Under governing Guideline provisions, the bottom line is that all counts but the three § 924(c) counts combine to create a total offense level of 28. Because Mr. Angelos has no significant prior criminal history, he is treated as first-time offender (a criminal history category I) under the Guidelines. The prescribed Guidelines' sentence for Mr. Angelos for everything but the § 924(c) counts is 78 to 97 months.

After the Guideline sentence is imposed, however, the court must then add the § 924(c) counts. Section 924(c) prescribes a five-year mandatory minimum for a first conviction, and 25 years for each subsequent conviction. This means that Mr. Angelos is facing 55 years (660 months) of mandatory time for the § 924(c) convictions. In addition, § 924(c) mandates that these 55 years run consecutively to any other time imposed. As a consequence, the minimum sentence that the court can impose on Mr. Angelos is 61 1/2 years–6 1/2 years (78 months) for the 13 counts under the Guidelines and 55 consecutive years for the three § 924 convictions. The federal system does not provide the possibility of parole, but instead provides only a modest "good behavior" credit of approximately 15 percent of the sentence. Assuming good behavior, Mr. Angelos' sentence will be reduced to "only" 55 years, meaning he could be released when he is 78 years old.

Mr. Angelos challenges this presumptive sentence [and argues] that § 924(c) is unconstitutional as applied to him because the additional 55-year sentence is cruel and unusual punishment that violates the Cruel and Unusual Punishment Clause.

Before turning to the merits of Mr. Angelos' claims, it is important to understand the length of the sentence that the government is asking the court to impose. If Angelos serves his full 61 1/2-year sentence, he will be 85 years old upon release. Assuming the 15 percent credit for good behavior, Mr. Angelos sentence will be reduced to "only" 55 years, leading to the earliest possible release date for Mr. Angelos at 77 years of age. The average life expectancy for males in the United States is about 74 years of age. Therefore, under the best case scenario, Angelos *might* live long enough to be released from prison (assuming that the harshness of prison life does not decrease his life expectancy). Put another way, if the court imposes the sentence sought by the government, Mr. Angelos will effectively receive a sentence of life.

[T]he enhancement provided for under § 924(c) increases his sentence by 55 years, whereas were the Guidelines alone to be applied, his sentence would be enhanced by only two years. There is, of course, the possibility that the Sentencing Guidelines are too low in this case and that mandatory minimums specify the proper sentence. The more the court investigates, however, the more the court finds evidence that the § 924(c) counts here lead to unjust punishment. For starters, the court asked the twelve jurors in this case what they believed was the appropriate punishment for Mr. Angelos. Following the trial, the court sent—over the government's objection—each of the jurors the relevant information about Mr. Angelos' limited criminal history, described the abolition of parole in the federal system, and asked the jurors what they believed was the appropriate penalty for Mr. Angelos. Nine jurors responded and gave the following recommendations: (1) 5 years; (2) 5–7 years; (3) 10 years; (4) 10 years; (5) 15 years; (6) 15 years; (7) 15–20 years; (8) 32 years; and (9) 50 years. Averaging these answers, the jurors recommended a mean sentence of about 18 years and a median sentence of 15 years. Not one of the jurors recommended a sentence closely approaching the 611/2 year sentence created by § 924(c).

At oral argument, the court asked the government what it thought about the jurors' recommendations and whether it was appropriate to impose a sentence so much higher than what the jurors thought appropriate. The government's response was quite curious: "Judge, we don't know if that jury is a random representative sample of the citizens of the United States. . . ." Of course, the whole point of the elaborate jury selection procedures used in this case was to assure that the jury was, indeed, such a fair cross section of the population so that the verdict would be accepted with confidence. It is hard to understand why the government would be willing to accept the decision of the jury as to the guilt of the defendant but not as to the length of sentence that might be imposed.

More important, the jurors' answers appear to reflect a representative of what people across the country believe. The crimes committed by Mr. Angelos are not uniquely federal crimes. They could have been prosecuted in state court in Utah or elsewhere across the country. The court asked the Probation Office to determine what the penalty would have been in Utah state court had Mr. Angelos been prosecuted there. The Probation Office reported that Mr. Angelos would likely have been paroled after serving about two to three years in prison. The government gives a substantially similar estimate, reporting that on its understanding of Utah sentencing practices Mr. Angelos would have served about five to seven years in prison. Even taking the higher figure from the government, the § 924(c) counts in this case result in punishment far beyond what Utah's citizens, through its state criminal justice system, provides as just punishment for such crimes.

The same conclusion obtains if the comparison is to the sentence that would be imposed in other states. Indeed, the government conceded that Mr. Angelos' federal sentence after application of the § 924(c) counts is more than he would have received in any of the fifty states.

In evaluating the § 924(c) counts, the court starts from the premise that Mr. Angelos committed serious crimes. Trafficking in illegal drugs runs the risk of ruining lives through addiction and the violence that the drug trade spawns. As the government properly argued, when a defendant engages in a drug-trafficking operation and "carries and possesses firearms to aid in that venture, as was the case here, the actual threat of violence always exists, even it if does not actually occur." But do any of these general rationales provide a rational basis for punishing the *potential* violence which §924(c) is meant to deter more harshly than *actual* violence that harms a victim in its wake? In other words, is it rational to punish a person who *might* shoot someone with a gun he carried far more harshly than the person who actually *does* shoot or harm someone?

Section 924(c) imposes on Mr. Angelos a sentence 55 years or 660 months. Added to the minimum 78-month Guidelines sentence for a total sentence of 738 months, Mr. Angelos is facing a prison term which more than doubles the sentence of, for example, an aircraft hijacker (293 months), a terrorist who detonates a bomb in a public place (235 months), a racist who attacks a minority with the intent to kill and inflicts permanent or life-threatening injuries (210 months), a second-degree murderer, or a rapist.

At oral argument, to its credit, the government conceded that at least some of the[se crimes are] more serious than those committed by Mr. Angelos. Thus, the government agreed (after extensive questioning from the court) that Mr. Angelos has committed less serious crimes than a second-degree murderer, a marijuana dealer who shoots someone, or a rapist. The government maintained, however, that the court was not making the proper comparison. Because Mr. Angelos was convicted of three counts of violating §924(c), the government argued, the proper comparison is between Mr. Angelos and a three-time hijacker, a three-time rapist, or a three-time second degree murderer. The government maintains that "the hijacker and kidnapper would serve much longer sentences if they were sentenced for committing those crimes three separate times."

The government's argument misses the whole point of the comparison. All of Mr. Angelos' crimes taken together are less serious than, for example, even a single aircraft hijacking, a single second-degree murder, or a single rape. But even adopting the government's approach, the irrationality of the scheme only becomes more apparent. Amazingly, Mr. Angelos' sentence under §924(c) is still far more severe than criminals who committed, for example, three aircraft hijackings, three second-degree murders, three kidnappings, or three rapes. Mr. Angelos will receive a longer sentence than any three-time criminal, with the sole exception of a marijuana dealer who shoots three people. (Mr. Angelos still receives a longer sentence than a marijuana dealer who shoots two people.)

To some, this may seem like a law professor's argument—one that may have some validity in the classroom but little salience in the real world. After all, the only issue in this case is the extent of punishment for a man justly convicted of serious drug trafficking offenses. So what, some may say, if he spends more years in prison than might be theoretically justified? It is common wisdom that "if you can't do the time, don't do the crime."

The problem with this simplistic position is that it overlooks other interests that are inevitably involved in the imposition of a criminal sentence. For example, crime victims expect that the penalties the court imposes will fairly reflect the harms that they have suffered. When the sentence for actual violence inflicted on a victim is dwarfed by a sentence for carrying guns to several drug deals, the implicit message to victims is that their pain and suffering counts for less than some abstract "war on drugs."

This is no mere academic point, as a case from this court's docket will illustrate. Earlier today, shortly before Mr. Angelos' hearing, the court imposed sentence in *United States v. Visinaiz,* a second-degree murder case. There, a jury convicted Cruz Joaquin Visinaiz of second-degree murder in the death of 68-year-old Clara Jenkins. On one evening, while drinking together, the two got into an argument. Ms. Jenkins threw an empty bottle at Mr. Visinaiz, who then proceeded to beat her to death by striking her in the head at least three times with a log. Mr. Visinaiz then hid the body in a crawl space of his home, later dumping the body in a river weighted down with cement blocks. Following his conviction for second-degree murder, Mr. Visinaiz came before the court as a first-time offender for sentencing. The Sentencing Guidelines require a sentence for this brutal second-degree murder of between 210 to 262 months. The government called this an "aggravated second-degree murder" and recommended a sentence of 262 months. The court followed that recommendation. Yet on the same day, the court is to impose a sentence of 738 months for a first-time drug dealer who carried a gun to several drug deals!? The victim's family in the Visinaiz case—not to mention victims of a vast array of other violent crimes—can be forgiven if they think that the federal criminal justice system minimizes their losses. No doubt § 924(c) is motivated by the best of intentions—to prevent criminal victimization. But the statute pursues that goal in a way that effectively sends a message to victims of actual criminal violence that their suffering is not fully considered by the system.

Another reason for concern is that the unjust penalties imposed by § 924(c) can be expected to attract public notice. As shown earlier, applying § 924(c) to cases such as this one leads to sentences far in excess of what the public believes is appropriate. Perhaps in the short term, no ill effects will come from the difference between public expectations and actual sentences. But in the longer term, the federal criminal justice system will suffer. Most seriously, jurors may stop voting to convict drug dealers in federal criminal prosecutions if they are aware that unjust punishment may follow. It only takes a single juror who is worried about unjust sentencing to "hang" a jury and prevent a conviction. This is not an abstract concern. In the case of *United States v. Molina*, the jury failed to reach a verdict on a § 924(c) count which would have added 30 years to the defendant's sentence. Judge Weinstein, commenting on "the dubious state of our criminal sentencing law" noted that "jury nullification of sentences deemed too harsh is increasingly reflected in refusals to convict." In the last several drug trials before this court, jurors have privately expressed considerable concern after their verdicts about what sentences might be imposed. If federal juries are to continue to convict the guilty, those juries must have confidence that just punishment will follow from their verdicts.

Mr. Angelos argues that his 55-year sentence under § 924(c) violates the Eighth Amendment's prohibition of cruel and unusual punishment. In this argument, he is joined in an *amicus* brief filed by a distinguished group of 29 former United States District Judges, United States Circuit Court Judges, and United States Attorneys, who draw on their expertise in federal criminal law and federal sentencing issues to urge that the sentence is unconstitutional as disproportionate to the offenses at hand.

Mr. Angelos and his supporting *amici* are correct in urging that controlling Eighth Amendment case law places an outer limit on punishments that can be imposed for criminal offenses, forbidding penalties that are grossly disproportionate to any offense. This principle traces its roots to the Supreme Court's 1983 decision in *Solem v. Helm,* in which the Supreme Court seemed to modify its earlier holding in *Rummel v. Estelle* and "held as a matter of principle that a criminal sentence must be proportionate to the crime for which the defendant has been convicted." The principles of *Solem* were themselves seemingly modified by the Court's fractured 1991 decision in *Harmelin v. Michigan,* in which the Court held that imposition of a life sentence without possibility of parole for possession of 650 grams of cocaine did not violate the Eighth Amendment. Then, last year, the Supreme Court confirmed that the gross disproportionality principle—"the precise contours of which are unclear"—is applicable to sentences for terms of years; that there was a "lack of clarity" in its precedents; that it had "not established a clear or consistent path for courts to follow;" and that the proportionality principles from Justice Kennedy's *Harmelin* concurrence "guide our application of the Eighth Amendment." The Tenth Circuit, too, has instructed that "Justice Kennedy's opinion controls because it both retains proportionality and narrows *Solem.*"

In light of these controlling holdings, the court must engage in a proportionality analysis guided by factors outlined in Justice Kennedy's *Harmelin* concurrence. In particular, the court must examine (1) the nature of the crime and its relation to the punishment imposed, (2) the punishment for other offenses in this jurisdiction, and (3) the punishment for similar offenses in other jurisdictions.

The first *Harmelin* factor requires the court to compare the seriousness of the three § 924(c) offenses to the harshness of the contemplated penalty to determine if the penalty would be grossly disproportionate to such offenses. In weighing the gravity of the offenses, the court should consider the offenses of conviction and the defendant's criminal history, as well as "the harm caused or threatened to the victim or society, and the culpability of the offender." Simply put, "disproportionality analysis measures the relationship between the nature and number of offenses committed and the severity of the punishment inflicted upon the offender."

The criminal history in this case is easy to describe. Mr. Angelos has no prior adult criminal convictions and is treated as a first-time offender under the Sentencing Guidelines.

The sentence-triggering criminal conduct in this case is also modest. Here, on two occasions while selling small amounts of marijuana, Mr. Angelos possessed a handgun under his clothing, but he never brandished or used the handgun. The third relevant crime occurred when the police searched his home and found handguns in his residence. These handguns had multiple purposes—including recreational activities—but because Mr. Angelos also used the gun to protect himself while dealing drugs, the possession of these handguns is also covered by § 924(c).

Mr. Angelos did not engage in force or violence, or threats of force or violence, in furtherance of or in connection with the offenses for which he has been convicted. No offense involved injury to any person or the threat of injury to any person. It is well-established that crimes marked by violence or threat of violence are more serious and that the absence of direct violence affects the strength of society's interest in punishing a particular criminal.

It is relevant on this point that the Sentencing Commission has reviewed crimes like Mr. Angelos' and concluded that an appropriate penalty for all of Mr. Angelos' crimes is no more than about ten years (121 months). With respect to the firearms conduct specifically, the Commission has concluded that about 24 months is the appropriate penalty. The views of the Commission are entitled to special weight, because it is a congressionally-established expert agency which can draw on significant data and other resources in determining appropriate sentences. Comparing a recommended sentence of two years to the 55-year enhancement the court must impose strongly suggests not merely disproportionality, but gross disproportionality.

The next *Harmelin* factor requires comparing Mr. Angelos' sentence with the sentences imposed on other criminals in the federal system. Generally, "if more serious crimes are subject to the same penalty, or to less serious penalties, that is some indication that the punishment at issue may be excessive." This factor points strongly in favor of finding that the sentence in this case is excessive. As [discussed] earlier in this opinion, Mr. Angelos will receive a far longer sentence than those imposed in the federal system for such major crimes as aircraft hijacking, second-degree murder, racial beating inflicting life-threatening injuries, kidnapping, and rape. Indeed, Mr. Angelos will receive a far longer sentence than those imposed for three aircraft hijackings, three second-degree murders, three racial beatings inflicting life-threatening injuries, three kidnappings, and three rapes. Because Mr. Angelos is "treated in the same manner as, or more severely than, criminals who have committed far more serious crimes," it appears that the second factor is satisfied.

The final *Harmelin* factor requires the court to examine "sentences imposed for the same crime in other jurisdictions." Evaluating this factor is also straightforward. Mr. Angelos sentence is longer than he would receive in any of the fifty states. The government commendably concedes this point in its brief, pointing out that in Washington State Mr. Angelos would serve about nine years and in Utah would serve about five to seven years. Accordingly, the court finds that the third factor is satisfied.

Having analyzed the three *Harmelin* factors, the court believes that they lead to the conclusion that Mr. Angelos' sentence violates the Eighth Amendment. But before the court declares the sentence unconstitutional, there is one last obstacle to overcome. The court is keenly aware of its obligation to follow precedent from superior courts—specifically the Tenth Circuit and, of course, the Supreme Court. The Supreme Court has considered one case that might be regarded as quite similar to this one. In *Hutto v. Davis,* the Supreme Court held that two consecutive twenty-year sentences—totaling forty years—for possession of nine ounces of marijuana said to be worth $200 did not violate the Eighth Amendment. If *Davis* remains good law, it is hard see how the sentence in this case violates the Eighth Amendment. Here, Mr. Angelos was involved in at least two marijuana deals involving $700 and approximately sixteen ounces (one pound) of marijuana. Perhaps currency inflation could equate $700 today with $200 in the 1980s. But as a simple matter of arithmetic, if 40 years in prison for possessing nine ounces marijuana does not violate the Eighth Amendment, it is hard to see how 61 years for distributing sixteen ounces (or more) would do so.

The court is aware of an argument that the 1982 *Davis* decision has been implicitly overruled or narrowed by the 1983 *Solem* decision and other more recent pronouncements. For example, Justice Kennedy's concurring opinion in *Harmelin,* explained that "our most recent pronouncement on the subject in *Solem* appeared to apply a different analysis than in . . . *Davis.*" But the Court apparently continues to view *Davis* as part of the fabric of the law. Thus, Justice Kennedy's concurrence in *Harmelin,* after noting the seeming overruling of *Davis,* went on to discuss *Davis* along with other cases in distilling various "common principles" that control Eighth Amendment analysis. More recently, in reviewing California's "three strikes" legislation last year, the plurality opinion reviewed *Davis* as one of a string of cases that guide analysis of Eighth Amendment challenges.

In light of these continued references to *Davis,* the court believes it is it obligated to follow its holding here. Indeed, in *Davis* the Supreme Court pointedly reminded district court judges that "unless we wish anarchy to prevail within the federal judicial system, a precedent of this Court must be followed by the lower federal courts. . . ." Under *Davis,* Mr. Angelos' sentence is not cruel and unusual punishment. Therefore, his Eighth Amendment challenge must be rejected.

Having disposed of the legal arguments in this case, it seems appropriate to make some concluding, personal observations. I have been on the bench for nearly two-and-half years now. During that time, I have sentenced several hundred offenders under the Sentencing Guidelines and federal mandatory minimum statutes. By and large, the sentences I have been required to impose have been tough but fair. In a few cases, to be sure, I have felt that either the Guidelines or the mandatory minimums produced excessive punishment. But even in those cases, the sentences seemed to be within the realm of reason.

This case is different. It involves a first offender who will receive a life sentence for crimes far less serious than those committed by many other offenders—including violent offenders and even a murderer—who have been before me. For the reasons explained in my opinion, I am legally obligated to impose this sentence. But I feel ethically obligated to bring this injustice to the attention of those who are in a position to do something about it.

For all the reasons previously given, an additional 55-year sentence for Mr. Angelos under § 924(c) is unjust, disproportionate to his offense, demeaning to victims of actual criminal violence—but nonetheless constitutional. While I must impose the unjust sentence, our system of separated powers provides a means of redress. The Framers were well aware that "the administration of justice . . . is not necessarily always wise or certainly considerate of circumstances which may properly mitigate guilt." In my mind, this is one of those rare cases where the system has malfunctioned. "To afford a remedy, it has always been thought essential in popular governments, as well as in monarchies, to vest in some other authority than the courts power to ameliorate or avoid particular criminal judgments." Under our Constitution, the President has "the Power to grant Reprieves and Pardons for Offenses against the United States. . . ." One of the purposes of executive clemency is "to afford relief from undue harshness."

I therefore believe that it is appropriate for me to communicate to the President, through the Office of the Pardon Attorney, my views regarding Mr. Angelos' sentence. I recommend that the President commute Mr. Angelos' sentence to a prison term of no more than 18 years, the average sentence recommended by the jury that heard this case. The court agrees with the jury that this is an appropriate sentence in this matter in light of all of the other facts discussed in this opinion. The Clerk's Office is directed to forward a copy of this opinion with its commutation recommendation to the Office of Pardon Attorney.

The 55-year sentence mandated by § 924(c) in this case appears to be unjust, cruel, and irrational. But our constitutional system of government requires the court to follow the law, not its own personal views about what the law ought to be. Perhaps the court has overlooked some legal point, and that the appellate courts will find Mr. Angelos' sentence invalid. But applying the law as the court understands it, the court sentences Mr. Angelos to serve a term of imprisonment of 55 years and one day.

As *Angelos* demonstrates, it is virtually impossible for a drug defendant to successfully challenge his sentence based on the Eighth Amendment to the federal Constitution. The same is not necessarily true when it comes to state sentences, however, as some states have adopted more robust interpretations of analogous provisions that prohibit cruel and unusual punishment in their constitutions. *See*, Julia Fong Sheketoff, Note: *State Innovations in Noncapital Proportionality Doctrine*, 85 N.Y.U. L. Rev. 2209 (2010) (surveying the noncapital proportionality jurisprudence of the states).

Following Judge Paul Cassell's 2004 decision, Weldon Angelos appealed his convictions and 55-year sentence to the U.S. Court of Appeals for the Tenth Circuit. A group of 163 former federal officials that included retired United States Circuit and District Court Judges, former United States Attorneys, and four former United States Attorneys General, among others, filed an amicus brief in support of Angelos' appeal. The Tenth Circuit upheld Angelos' convictions and 55-year sentence, in an opinion that was far more sympathetic to the government than Judge Cassell's.

Judge Mary Beck Briscoe, who authored the decision, maintained that "although it is true Angelos may have had no significant adult criminal history, that appears to have been the result of good fortune rather than Angelos's lack of involvement in criminal activity." The court found that Angelos' sentence was not grossly disproportionate to his crimes, explaining "Congress 'could with reason conclude that the threat posed to the individual and society' by possessing firearms in connection with serious felonies, in particular drug-trafficking crimes, was 'momentous enough to warrant the deterrence and retribution' of lengthy consecutive sentences, such as those imposed on Angelos in this case." *United States v. Angelos*, 433 F.3d 738, 752 (10th Cir. 2006). Angelos' petition for certiorari was denied in December 2006.

Angelos then pursued post-conviction relief under 28 U.S.C. § 2255, arguing that "his sentence was cruel and unusual, and that he was a victim of prosecutorial vindictiveness in charging and plea bargaining, prosecutorial misconduct at trial, and ineffective assistance of counsel before and at trial." *Angelos v. United States*, 2008 WL 5156602 (D. Utah). The District Court denied all of Angelos' claims outright with one exception, granting him an evidentiary hearing on his claim of ineffective assistance of counsel during the plea negotiations. Following the evidentiary hearing, however, the court denied Angelos' ineffective assistance claim. Unsuccessful appeals to the Tenth Circuit and the Supreme Court followed, with the Supreme Court denying Angelos' petition for certiorari in October, 2011. Melinda Rogers, *High Court Won't Hear Case of Music Producer Sentenced to 55-Year Minimum*, SALT LAKE TRIB., Oct. 4, 2011.

Although Angelos did not succeed in getting his sentence reversed through the appeals process, he was released early, in 2016, after serving 12½ years in prison. Over time, Angelos' case generated a good deal of publicity. More than 250,000 people signed an online petition calling for his release. The precise legal justification for his release remains unclear, however. When the news of Angelos' release was first announced, many assumed he had been granted clemency by President Obama. But this was not the case. Instead, "Angelos unexpectedly was released . . . after receiving an immediate sentence reduction. The records of how all this came about are sealed, but Angelos' lawyer, Mark Osler, a law professor at the University of St. Thomas in Minnesota, told *The Washington Post* his client is free 'because of the fair and good action of a prosecutor.'" Pamela Mason, *Freed Early From a 55-year Prison Term, a 'Changed' Weldon Angelos is Rebuilding His Life One Brick At a Time*, SALT LAKE TRIBUNE (June 24, 2016).

E. Prosecutorial Discretion

Charging decisions made by prosecutors played a central role in the sentencing outcomes in many of the cases included in this chapter. Consider *Angelos*, for example, where the prosecutor originally offered a deal in which the government would recommend a 15-year sentence. When Angelos refused this offer, the prosecutor "obtained two superseding indictments, eventually charging 20 total counts, including five §924(c) counts which alone carried a potential minimum mandatory sentence of 105 years." In a portion of the opinion that was not included in the edited version of *Angelos* above, Judge Cassell highlighted the importance of the prosecutor's decisions to Angelos' sentence. With respect to the effect of plea bargaining, Cassell commented that "[s]o far as the court can determine, the superseding indictment rested not on any newly-discovered evidence but rather solely on the defendant's unwillingness to plead guilty."

Judge Cassell also examined the prosecutor's decision to charge the multiple §924(c) counts that resulted in the 55-year mandatory minimum. He concluded that the prosecutor's approach in this regard was unusual and because of it "Mr. Angelos is probably receiving a sentence far in excess of what many other identically-situated offenders will receive for identical crimes in other federal districts. The court has been advised by judges from other parts of the country that, in their districts, an offender like Mr. Angelos would not have been charged with multiple §924(c) counts."

Last but not least, the decision to charge Angelos in federal and not state court also significantly impacted his sentence. Angelos committed his crimes in Utah. If Angelos had been charged and convicted under Utah law, the federal government estimated he would have served only about five to seven years in prison. In federal court, he was subject to a 55-year mandatory minimum sentence.

The importance of prosecutorial discretion is, of course, not unique to drug offenses. Indeed, in his book *Locked In*, John Pfaff argues that "[t]he primary driver of incarceration is increased prosecutorial toughness when it comes to charging people, not longer sentences." John F. Pfaff, Locked In: The True Causes of Mass Incarceration and how to Achieve Real Reform 6 (2017). There are a few characteristics of modern drug sentencing laws that can give prosecutors unusual power to guide outcomes in drug cases through their charging decisions. As *Angelos* demonstrates, the emergence of lengthy federal mandatory minimum drug sentences in combination with concurrent federal and state jurisdiction over drug crimes means that a prosecutor's decision to bring federal—rather than state—charges, or to bring charges that carry a mandatory minimum sentence, will often have much greater influence on a defendant's sentence than any decisions made by the judge who imposes it.

This section considers the relationship between prosecutorial discretion and drug sentences.

Unequal Justice: The Federalization of Criminal Law
Steven D. Clymer

70 Southern California Law Review 643 (1997)

As a result of the growth of federal criminal law, much criminal conduct is now subject to federal as well as state prosecution. Although the states prosecute the majority of offenders whose conduct violates both state and federal law, federal prosecution is not uncommon. Because of differences between federal and state criminal justice systems, an offender will often fare worse if prosecuted in federal court rather than state court. He may be detained pending trial when he would have been released if charged in state court, denied discovery allowable in state court, and confronted with evidence that would have been suppressed in state court. If convicted, a federally prosecuted defendant is likely to receive a longer sentence and to serve far more of that sentence than he would if sentenced in state court.

United States v. Palmer provides a stark example of such federal/state court disparity. Palmer and Roberts were partners in a marijuana-growing operation at Palmer's residence. After police arrested the men, the federal prosecutor assigned to the case chose not to bring charges against Roberts, who, as a result, was prosecuted in state court. The state court sentenced him to a fine of $1,000—which was waived because Roberts was indigent—and assessed court costs and fees of $176. Palmer was considerably less fortunate. The federal prosecutor brought charges against him. After Palmer was convicted, the federal court sentenced him to a nonparolable ten-year term of imprisonment and an eight-year supervised release term, the most lenient sentence that federal law allowed.

Cases like *Palmer*, in which partners in crime receive different treatment because one is prosecuted in state court and the other in federal court, are atypical. However, comparably dramatic sentencing differentials and other disparities routinely occur when some offenders are prosecuted in state court and others, who may not be their partners but have engaged in the same criminal conduct and are otherwise similarly situated, are instead selected for federal prosecution and the often harsher treatment that it entails. Such disparate treatment occurs nationwide on a daily basis when some defendants, engaged in drug transactions, weapons offenses, or other crimes over which there is overlapping federal and state criminal jurisdiction, happen to be among the unlucky ones selected for federal prosecution.

Despite the significant ramifications of the forum selection decision, there is little administrative direction or judicial oversight to guide federal prosecutors in exercising their discretion to choose among offenders eligible for federal prosecution. Although there were valid reasons for the federal prosecutor to seek harsher treatment for Palmer than for Roberts, the prosecutor could have made the same selection decision without good reason, perhaps selecting Roberts but not Palmer. Without fear of violating Department of Justice policy or risking judicial review, the federal prosecutor could have flipped a coin to select who to prosecute in federal court and, consequently, who to subject to the possibility of a vastly more severe federal sentence. Neither the United States Attorney's Office that chose to prosecute only Palmer nor the Department of Justice has a policy requiring prosecutors to have rational reasons for determining which eligible offenders to prosecute in federal court. Similarly, although its consideration of Palmer's equal protection and due process challenges prompted the Ninth Circuit to characterize the prosecutor's charging decision as "troubling" and to conclude that "there is something basically wrong with this type of exercise of prosecutorial discretion," the court refused to review the prosecutor's decision to select only Palmer. Consistent with approaches that other courts have taken, the *Palmer* court held that "separation of powers concerns prohibit us from reviewing a prosecutor's charging decisions absent a prima facie showing that it rested on an impermissible basis, such as gender, race or denial of a constitutional right."

United States v. Elliott

United States District Court for the District of Montana
351 F. Supp. 2d 1054 (2005)

Molloy, J.

This case is about bad judgment. Dustin Elliott exercised very bad judgment on December 12, 2003 when he was stopped at Garrison Junction because he was one of three people involved in selling two pounds of marijuana to a state undercover agent. When this sale took place, according to joint drug task force Agent Steven Spanogle, federal prosecution was not warranted for the small amounts of marijuana involved. Spanogle testified that he probably told Elliott on a number of occasions that such a small amount of marijuana would not be subject to federal prosecution under the referral rules in play at the time: The assurances were necessary because Elliott would not agree to cooperate with further investigation unless he had some assurance the case was not "federal."

Elliott then exercised what turns out to be more bad judgment. He believed law enforcement officers were telling the truth and that he would not be subject to federal prosecution. So, Elliott cooperated with the state investigators. His two cohorts immediately spilled their guts to save their respective hides but they had no useful information to help the agents climb the drug distribution food chain to the real culprits in the marijuana distribution scheme. Elliott did. Based on his knowledge, and after the assurances about federal referrals, confident that he would not be charged in federal court, he cooperated fully.

Because Elliott cooperated, the police were able to identify two or more distributors, and to obtain evidence of large enough quantities of marijuana that the case finally did satisfy federal prosecution minimums. So, despite Elliott's confidence that he would not be facing the ogre of federal prosecution, once enough marijuana had been discovered through the criminal investigation based on his disclosures and cooperation, the case was presented to the federal grand jury. Elliott was indicted in federal court as a direct result of his cooperation.

In this case Agent Spanogle was being truthful when he told Elliott that two pounds was not enough marijuana to warrant federal prosecution under existing referral standards. Furthermore, Spanogle had the courage to testify at the hearing in this case that he did not believe Elliott *would* be prosecuted in federal court, and, that he did not think Elliott *should* have been prosecuted in federal court. But, here we are.

The problem presented is whether the decision to refer the case to the grand jury, and to pursue Elliott's prosecution, is so fundamentally unfair that the case should be dismissed. See *United States vs. Williams,* 780 F.2d 802, 803 (9th Cir. 1986). I have struggled in seeking a just answer to this question. However, I am convinced that while this case is more properly a state prosecution, I have no legal basis to dismiss it.

Elliott argues that the indictment should be dismissed because he performed his end of the deal by participating in a sting operation that netted the government a large marijuana supplier. He argues that instead of getting what he bargained for, a deferred imposition of sentence in the state courts, he ended up being prosecuted in federal court. That reality is what he thought he bargained away when he agreed to cooperate with the state agents. He argues that had the government upheld the bargain by deferring a two pound marijuana case to the state, he would have been able to complete his undergraduate education and attend medical school.[1]

The United States argues that even if Agent Spanogle had promised a "particular sentence," Spanogle is without authority to bind the United States. Spanogle is a state agent working on state prosecutions and at the time of Elliott's cooperation Spanogle was not assigned to any task force that included federal agents. Thus the argument goes, he could not have bound the United States to "his 'agreement' with the defendant even if he had wanted to." The United States extends the argument by asserting that even if Spanogle was a federal agent, he could not bind the United States Attorney's Office. The prosecutor does acknowledge that an exception to the "non binding" rule exists, even where the United States Attorney was not a party to the cooperation agreement, if breach of the agreement renders the prosecution fundamentally unfair.

Here the uncontroverted testimony of Agent Spanogle is as follows: 1) before Elliott's cooperation took place, Elliott would not have been prosecuted in federal court because he was caught with so little marijuana the United States Attorney would not have taken the case for referred prosecution in federal court; 2) Elliott's two cohorts had no evidence to give the investigating agents that would have allowed them to go up the drug distribution food chain; 3) Spanogle did describe to Elliott scenarios he was aware of in state marijuana prosecutions that resulted in deferred state prosecutions though he carefully avoided making a "deal" he knew he could not make for the county attorney; 4) Elliott was very specific in his concern about avoiding federal prosecution; 5) without Elliott's cooperation the state investigation could not have gone forward and upward in identifying and prosecuting the marijuana distribution network; 6) Spanogle did not think Elliott would be prosecuted in federal court; 7) Spanogle does not think Elliott should be prosecuted in federal court; and, 8) Elliott cannot be held responsible for more than two pounds

1. Elliott is a chemistry major at Carroll College who maintains between a 3.9 and 4.0 GPA. A federal conviction will likely bar him from medical school matriculation.

of marijuana in the federal prosecution.[2] Elliott also signed an agreement stating he knew there were no binding promises regarding any state prosecution. The United States Attorney for the District of Montana considered, but refused dismissal or a deferred federal prosecution.

[In *United States v. Williams*,] Thomas Williams was convicted of theft and conspiring to sell government property. He worked as an administrator for the Veterans Administration. After his arrest, a personnel director of the VA promised him that if he resigned his job, the VA attorney would recommend dismissal of the charges to the United States Attorney. Williams resigned but the letter sent by the VA attorney did not recommend dismissal of the indictment, instead it suggested avenues of investigation to make the case. When the personnel director learned of these facts he spoke personally to the United States Attorney and recommended dismissal of the charges. The United States Attorney for the Southern District of California prosecuted anyway.

Like Elliott, Williams moved to dismiss the indictment because the VA had not honored the deal he made. The Williams court recognized that while the United States Attorney is generally not bound by a promise made by a government employee, there is an exception to the rule. When the "breach of the agreement rendered a prosecution fundamentally unfair," the district court has authority to dismiss the case.

In *Williams* the Ninth Circuit did not resolve the issue of whether the standard the district court applies is one of detrimental reliance and fundamental fairness, or whether the issue turns on the nature of the promisor. The crucial issue for the latter standard is whether the promise was made as a part of the criminal justice system of the sovereign prosecuting the case. The Williams court found under either standard the facts in Williams did not support dismissal of the case. Williams was not induced by the agreement to incriminate himself, to furnish information useful to the government in developing the case against him, or to plead guilty. Neither did he suffer any other prejudice that would render his conviction unfair.

2. Two pounds of marijuana sets an offense level of 8 according to the federal sentencing guidelines, §2D1.1 (At least 250 G but less than 1 KG of marijuana). With a criminal history of 1, that means the most Elliott would be looking at is 6 months of incarceration. One must question the futility of a federal felony conviction under the circumstances involved here. The question that needs to be answered is "Why is this a federal case?" If it is a federal case to deter, what will the felony conviction deter? It will deter a very bright student from becoming a doctor. It will deter an intelligent person from voting or from holding public office. It will deter a young man who made a stupid mistake from ever keeping or possessing firearms or ammunition and from ever hunting again. It will deter a smart person who made a mistaken judgment from ever being a juror or grand juror. It has a potential negative impact on Agent Spanogle's undercover law enforcement activities because his credibility is on the line. It will insert the federal government in what is clearly a state case. Ultimately, you have to ask "Why?" The fundamental issue here is "How has the federal sovereign been offended?" This prosecution is at odds with the idea that the state of Montana is a competent sovereign to prosecute drug offenses.

Elliott was induced by the state agent to believe that there was little or no risk of federal prosecution because the amount of marijuana was too small to make it a "federal case." Elliott would not have talked to the state authorities if he thought the case was federal. Likewise, without Elliott's cooperation the state would not have been able to develop the proof or gather the evidence to make the conspiracy case against his more culpable co-defendants and to take the case "federal." Elliott gave information that incriminated him in the larger conspiracy, though arguably there was enough to make a two pound conspiracy case in federal court against Elliott and his two companions that were arrested at Garrison. The conspiracy that led to federal charges against Elliott could not have been made without his cooperation. Thus, it is likely that had he not talked, he would be facing state charges for distribution of two pounds of marijuana. Had he gotten a deferred prosecution or a deferred sentence for a first offense in state court he would be eligible for clearing his record in its entirety on successful completion of the deferred prosecution or sentence. The state constitution and statutes, on petition or automatically, would allow a full restoration of all of his rights, including the right to vote, the right to hold public office, the right to be a juror or a grand juror, and the right to hunt.

Elliott will suffer other prejudice that, given the referral rules in place when he began cooperating[5] give credence to his claim that the prosecution is unfair. With a felony drug conviction, he is likely to lose any chance of ever entering medical school. He will be disqualified from many professions because of his lack of judgment resulting in a federal felony conviction. Given his age and culpability, he will pay a pretty price for his bad judgment.

Applying the fundamental fairness and detrimental reliance test, this federal prosecution makes no sense. It is facially unjust if what we are doing is seeking a fair and just resolution concerning federal criminal conduct. Depriving a bright young person of his future because of a federal conviction that is likely to get him probation is the harsh exercise of prosecutorial power and it seems to me to be at odds with the prosecutor's duty to seek justice, not to seek convictions. Prosecuting this case *in federal court as opposed to the Montana state courts,* raises the specter of judgment caused by the bad judgment that led to the wrongdoing in the first place. At some point the federal sovereign needs to defer to the state's interest in prosecuting minor drug offenses. Federalism is still important and should not be measured by the yardstick of severe sentences, especially when that concern has no application to the case at hand.

---

5. The only evidence in the record about the federal referral rules is the testimony of Agent Spanogle. His testimony is believable because one would think the federal prosecutor has bigger fish to fry than a two pound marijuana case. In other words, common sense tells us that this is not a "federal case," it is a state case. When deciding whether to initiate or to continue a prosecution "it is the duty of the United States Attorney not to simply prosecute, but to do justice. See *U.S. vs. Weber,* 721 F.2d 266, 268 (9th Cir. 1983).

Nonetheless, I am troubled by the idea that a court should exercise the power, except in the most egregious circumstances, to tell the prosecutor what cases to bring.[7] There is a [federal] statute that makes distributing two pounds of marijuana a federal crime. There is a [federal] statute that makes it a crime for two or more people to conspire to distribute two pounds of marijuana. So, if I impose my normative view on what cases *should* be prosecuted in federal court, I would dismiss this case and let the state prosecute it. But, such a holding would create a structural problem to say the least.

Therefore, IT IS ORDERED that Elliott's motion to dismiss is denied[.]

This case started with the bad judgment of a very bright college student who wants to be a doctor. His bad judgment continued when he believed an honest state agent who told him he would not likely be prosecuted in federal court because the amount of marijuana he had was too small for referral to make it a "federal case." The wraith of that judgment seems apparent when the case was taken to a federal grand jury against Elliott. The role of the court is to see that Elliott gets a fair trial and if he is found guilty, to fashion an appropriate sentence. Good judgment here would mean deference to the state or a deferred federal prosecution. But if there is an injustice it does not rise to the level of the "inherently unfair" standard for dismissal.

The *Elliott* court appeared to be troubled by the prosecutor's charging decision in part because of the defendant's personal background. But should the fact that Elliott was "a very bright college student who wants to be a doctor" impact his punishment? Some argue that prosecutors should not factor considerations like this into their charging decisions in drug cases because doing so contributes to racial disparities in drug enforcement. The sentiment recalls a quotation from Abraham Lincoln: "The best way to get a bad law repealed is to enforce it strictly." *See also*, Rehavi M. Marit and Sonja B. Starr, *Racial Disparity in Federal Criminal Charging and Its Sentencing Consequences*, 122 J. Political Econ. 1320, 1350 (2014) (analyzing federal data and determining that "more than half of the black-white sentence disparity that is unexplained by the arrest offense and offenders' prior traits can be explained by initial charge decisions, particularly the prosecutors' decision to file charges that carry 'mandatory minimum' sentences").

Perhaps one of the most famous (and most criticized) examples of the unrestrained power that federal prosecutors enjoy in exercising their discretion was New York's "federal day," mentioned by the court in *United States v. Agilar* in Chapter 3. Under the "federal day" scheme in the 1980s, "one random day a week all drug arrests [in Manhattan were] prosecuted in Federal court" where defendants faced

---

7. If federal judges in Montana could exercise such power or that choice, many of the cases charged in our federal court the past few years would properly be left to the state for prosecution. Not every crime is a "federal case." The doctrine of dual sovereignty is not a license to usurp the state criminal justice system. This is particularly so when the likely sentence in federal court is probation.

significantly longer sentences than they would have in state court. Stephen Labton, *Drugs and the Law; The Courts Overwhelmed*, N.Y. Times at A1, Dec. 29, 1989. *See also*, Ethan A. Brown, Snitch: Informants, Cooperators & the Corruption of Justice 19–22 (reporting on the history of "federal day").

Are critics of prosecutorial discretion in drug cases concerned about the existence of discretion or the way in which prosecutors have chosen to exercise it?

In the case that follows, *United States v. Dossie*, a federal trial judge suggested that the Department of Justice consider adopting a charging policy to limit the use of mandatory minimum sentences. A portion of the opinion in *Dossie* was presented toward the beginning of this chapter in the section on the importance of drug quantity in sentencing. As you may recall from that excerpt, Jamel Dossie was convicted for his role as a go-between in the sale of 88.1 grams of crack cocaine. As Judge Gleeson put it: "His sole function was to ferry money to the supplier and crack to the informant on four occasions for a total gain to himself of $140." Because of the quantity of drugs involved in the offense, and the federal prosecutor's decision to charge that quantity in the indictment, the court reluctantly imposed a five-year mandatory minimum sentence. In the excerpt of the decision presented above, Judge Gleeson argued that Congress intended for mandatory minimum drug penalties to apply only to "serious" or "major" drug traffickers, citing statements from then-Senate Majority Leader Robert Byrd. In this part of the opinion, Judge Gleeson recommends that the Department of Justice use its prosecutorial discretion to reserve charges that carry mandatory minimum penalties for "leaders and managers of drug enterprises."

United States v. Dossie

United States District Court for the Eastern District of New York
851 F. Supp. 2d 478 (2012)

Gleeson, J.

Congress should get rid of mandatory minimum sentences generally, but no one expects that to happen soon. In the meantime, DOJ can and must play the leading role in bringing about needed sentencing reform. DOJ should seek mandatory minimum sentences only in the cases for which Congress intended them: in cases against leaders and managers of drug enterprises, not the low-level drug offenders like Dossie who constitute the bulk of the federal drug docket. Federal prosecutors should exercise their discretion to bring mandatory minimum charges against only the small percentage of drug defendants (less than 6% in FY 2011) who deserve the aggravating role adjustments for being leaders or managers in a drug business. Specifically, they should charge the ten-year mandatory minimum only when they intend to prove that the defendant occupied a leadership role that warrants a four-level upward enhancement under U.S.S.G. § 3B1.1(a). They should charge the five-year mandatory minimum only when they intend to prove a managerial role worthy of a three- or two-level upward enhancement under § 3B1.1(b) or (c). And if the relevant aggravating role is not proved or admitted during the sentencing proceeding, prosecutors should withdraw (or reduce, as the case may be) the mandatory minimum.

Section 3B1.1 of the Sentencing Guidelines states:

> Based on the defendant's role in the offense, increase the offense level as follows:
>
> (a) If the defendant was an organizer or leader of a criminal activity that involved five or more participants or was otherwise extensive, increase by 4 levels.
>
> (b) If the defendant was a manager or supervisor (but not an organizer or leader) and the criminal activity involved five or more participants or was otherwise extensive, increase by 3 levels.
>
> (c) If the defendant was an organizer, leader, manager, or supervisor in any criminal activity other than described in (a) or (b), increase by 2 levels.

The four-level adjustment under subsection (a) for organizers and leaders of drug businesses that involve five or more people (including the defendant) or are "otherwise extensive" dovetails with Senator Byrd's description of the defendants who deserve the ten-year mandatory minimum as "kingpins" and "masterminds," as well as with the House committee report's description of them as "major traffickers." The three-level adjustment under subsection (b) for managers and supervisors in such organizations similarly parallels the "middle-level dealers" or "serious traffickers" at whom the five-year mandatory minimum was directed. Finally, the two-level adjustment under subsection (c) that applies to *all* management personnel (organizers, leaders, managers, and supervisors) when the drug business involves fewer than five people and is not otherwise extensive also captures the type of defendant for whom Congress intended the five-year mandatory minimum. Even the founder and leader of a drug business that involves fewer than five people and is not extensive is not the "kingpin" or "major trafficker" Congress had in mind. Thus by following my proposal, DOJ could ensure that its use of mandatory minimum charges hews closely to Congress's intentions.

My request is also consistent with the Attorney General Holder's policy on charging and sentencing. Under that policy, a prosecutor's charging decision "must always be made in the context of an individualized assessment of the extent to which particular charges fit the specific circumstances of the case." Memorandum from Eric H. Holder, Jr., U.S. Attorney Gen., to All Fed. Prosecutors 2 (May 19, 2010) (quoting U.S. Attorneys' Manual § 9-27.300) (internal quotation marks omitted). Furthermore, the policy provides that "[i]n all cases, the charges should fairly represent the defendant's criminal conduct." *Id.* And, most importantly, the policy requires that "the decision whether to seek a statutory sentencing enhancement should be guided by these same principles." *Id.* By utilizing mandatory minimum provisions only in cases involving managerial-type drug traffickers as I propose, prosecutors can better ensure that their charging decisions fit the specific circumstances of defendants' cases and that punishments defendants receive fairly represent their criminal conduct.

I am mindful of the fact that federal prosecutors find significant value in the way that charging mandatory minimum sentences helps them solicit the cooperation of defendants. *See* Lanny A. Breuer, *The Attorney General's Sentencing and Corrections Working Group: A Progress Report*, Fed. Sent'g Rep., Dec. 2010, at 110, 112 ("We favor mandatory minimum sentences because such sentences remove dangerous offenders from society, ensure just punishment, and are an essential tool in gaining cooperation from members of violent street gangs and drug distribution networks."). I have previously written about the "enormous boost" mandatory minimum sentences give to federal law enforcement in its effort to advance investigations and obtain convictions by enlisting cooperation. John C. Jeffries, Jr. and John Gleeson, *The Federalization of Organized Crime: Advantages of Federal Prosecution*, 46 HASTINGS L.J. 1095, 1120 (1995). Federal prosecutors have gotten so inured to using severe sentences to leverage cooperation that, "[t]o an increasing degree, the Department has come to justify its requests for tougher sentencing rules, not on the ground that offenders actually deserve the higher sentences, but simply because the threat of the higher sentence provides a greater inducement for defendant cooperation." Frank O. Bowman, *Mr. Madison Meets a Time Machine: The Political Science of Federal Sentencing Reform*, 58 STANFORD L. REV. 235, 252 (2005).

An interest in pursuing cooperation justifies charging leaders and managers of drug enterprises with the corresponding mandatory minimum drug offense. Though deserving of stiff sentences, such defendants may properly be rewarded with a sentence below the mandatory minimum for providing substantial assistance to the government. The flip side is that a decision not to cooperate may effectively result in a harsher sentence, but a harsh sentence is what Congress intended for that type of drug trafficker.

That same interest in pursuing cooperation cannot justify charging a mandatory minimum when the defendant is neither a leader nor a manager. It is one thing to lower an otherwise appropriate sentence to reward a defendant's cooperation but quite another to threaten to impose an otherwise unjust sentence if he decides not to cooperate or tries but produces no law enforcement results. The latter situation essentially converts a refusal or inability to cooperate into an aggravating sentencing factor, in violation of a basic principle of our sentencing regime. See U.S.S.G. § 5K1.2 ("A defendant's refusal to assist in the investigation of other persons may not be considered as an aggravating sentencing factor.").

I have reason to believe that Attorney General Holder will be receptive to my request. In 2009 he made the following remarks to the Vera Institute of Justice:

> One specific area where I think we can do a much better job by looking beyond incarceration is in the way we deal with non-violent drug offenses. We know that people convicted of drug possession or the sales of small amounts of drugs comprise a significant portion of the prison population. Indeed, in my thirty years in law enforcement, I have seen far too many young people lose their claim to a future by committing non-violent drug crimes.

> One promising, viable solution to the devastating effect of drugs on the criminal justice system and on American communities is the implementation of more drug treatment courts. Drug court programs provide an alternative to incarceration for non-violent offenders by focusing on treatment of their underlying addiction. Program participants are placed in treatment and routinely tested for drug use—with the imposition of immediate sanctions for positive tests balanced with suitable incentives to encourage abstinence from drug use. These programs give no one a free pass. They are strict and can be extraordinarily difficult to get through. But for those who succeed, there is the real prospect of a productive future.
>
> New York has been a leader in this area, diverting some non-violent offenders into drug court programs and away from prison, and extending early release to other non-violent offenders who participate in treatment programs. And while national prison populations have consistently increased, in New York the state prison population has dropped steadily and has 12,000 fewer inmates now than it did in 1999. And since 1999, the overall crime rate in New York has dropped 27%. Other states have followed New York's example. And most importantly, studies show significant reductions in re-arrests, from about 15 to 30 percentage points, for drug-court participants as compared to criminals simply incarcerated.

Those remarks preceded the crime in this case, but they may as well have been about Dossie, a young drug-user whose nonviolent drug offense now seriously threatens his "claim to a future" principally because the government forced me to impose a five-year jail term on him. The Attorney General was right to compliment the forward-looking approach of the state authorities here in New York. If Dossie had been prosecuted by them instead of by federal authorities he would have been given an opportunity to avoid not only time in jail but a conviction as well. The success of the Drug Treatment Alternative to Prison Program ("DTAP") in Brooklyn over the past twenty years proves the efficacy of treating defendants like Dossie rather than subjecting them to prison terms. Graduates of DTAP "have a five-year post-treatment recidivism rate that is almost half the rate for comparable offenders who served time in prison." Charles J. Hynes, Kings Cnty. Dist. Attorney, Drug Treatment Alternative-to-Prison Twentieth Annual Report at Exec. Summ. (2011).[10]

But the benefits of drug treatment and drug courts as alternatives to incarceration for nonviolent offenders are unavailable when DOJ itself *mandates* incarceration by invoking mandatory minimum sentences. Those provisions continue to be routinely invoked by DOJ against nonviolent, low-level offenders, even though it is

10. Ironically, Dossie is such a low-level drug defendant that he would not even be eligible for admission into the DTAP Program, which requires at least one prior felony drug conviction. However, he would be "eligible to be diverted into treatment through the court-run programs in Brooklyn's three drug court parts: Misdemeanor Brooklyn Treatment Court, Brooklyn Treatment Court, and the Screening and Treatment Enhancement Part."

crystal clear that Congress did not intend them to be used against such defendants. The result: Judges are removed from the sentencing process, along with transparency, appellate review, and, most importantly, justice. And young men like Jamel Dossie end up losing out on what may be their last chance to save their future.

The only reason for the five-year sentence imposed on Dossie is that the law invoked by the prosecutor required it. It was not a just sentence. To avoid similar injustices in other cases, I respectfully urge the Attorney General to lead the way forward by altering DOJ's charging policies in the manner described above.

In August 2013, then-Attorney General Eric Holder announced a new charging policy that was designed to limit the use of mandatory minimum sentences in certain drug cases. The prosecutorial guidelines were aimed at cases where punishment is tied to drug type and quantity in low-level cases. The policy instructed prosecutors not to include drug quantity when drafting indictments for certain drug defendants. As a result, in cases where prosecutors followed this guidance, sentencing judges were no longer bound by the mandatory minimum penalties in those cases.

The policy was much narrower than Judge Gleeson's proposal. It provided that prosecutors should "decline to charge the [drug] quantity necessary to trigger a mandatory minimum sentence" for defendants who met all of the following criteria:

- The defendant's relevant conduct does not involve the use of violence, the credible threat of violence, the possession of a weapon, the trafficking of drugs to or with minors, or the death or serious bodily injury of any person;
- The defendant is not an organizer, leader, manager or supervisor of others within a criminal organization;
- The defendant does not have significant ties to large-scale drug trafficking organizations, gangs, or cartels; and
- The defendant does not have a significant criminal history. A significant criminal history will normally be evidenced by three or more criminal history points but may involve fewer or greater depending on the nature of any prior convictions.

Memorandum from Eric Holder, Attorney General., to the U.S. Attorneys and Assistant Attorney General for the Criminal Division (Aug. 12, 2013). In addition, the charging policy instructed prosecutors not to file recidivist mandatory minimum penalty enhancements "unless the defendant is involved in conduct that makes the case appropriate for severe sanctions."

In May 2017, former Attorney General Jeff Sessions issued a memo rescinding Holder's mandatory minimum charging policy and replacing it with a new one. Attorney General Sessions' policy provides that "it is a core principle that prosecutors should charge and pursue the most serious, readily provable offense" and emphasizes that, "[b]y definition, the most serious offenses are those that carry the most substantial guidelines sentence, including mandatory minimum sentences."

Further, the Sessions memorandum states directly that "[a]ny inconsistent previous policy of the Department of Justice relating to these matters is rescinded, effective today." Finally, "any decision to vary from the [Sessions] policy must be approved by a United States Attorney or Assistant Attorney General, or a supervisor designated by the United States Attorney or Assistant Attorney General, and the reasons must be documented in the file." Memorandum from Jefferson Beauregard Sessions III, Attorney General., to All Federal Prosecutors (May 10, 2017).

In response to Attorney General Sessions' announcement of his charging policy, Eric Holder issued a statement calling the policy "dumb on crime" and an example of "an ideologically-motivated, cookie-cutter approach that has only been proven to generate unfairly long sentences that are often applied indiscriminately and do little to achieve long-term public safety." Sari Horwitz and Matt Zapotosky, *Sessions Issues Sweeping New Criminal Charging Policy*, Wash. Post (May 12, 2017).

While federal prosecutors enjoy nearly unfettered discretion over whether to charge a defendant in federal court and which charges to bring, at least one state court interpreted its laws to require judicial oversight of some charging decisions. In *New Jersey v. Lagares*, 127 N.J. 20 (1992), the Supreme Court of New Jersey held that aspects of the state's mandatory minimum drug sentencing scheme impermissibly delegated judicial sentencing powers to the prosecutor. To cure the defect, the court held that prosecutors' offices be required to adopt guidelines to govern the decision to seek enhanced sentences under the law; that prosecutors be required to state on the record the reasons for seeking an extended term; and that prosecutors' decisions be subject to judicial review under an arbitrary and capricious standard. For more on *Lagares* and court oversight over charging decisions in New Jersey, see Ronald F. Wright, *Prosecutorial Guidelines and the New Terrain in New Jersey*, 109 Penn. St. L. Rev. 1087 (2005).

F. Drug Courts

Criminal drug courts claim to provide treatment as an alternative to traditional sentences for drug defendants who meet certain criteria. Many public policy analysts have concluded that drug courts are more cost-effective than traditional modes of punishment. A systemic review of drug court research by the United States Government Accountability Office (GAO) in 2005, for example, found that the studies showed net benefits ranging from $1,000 to $15,000 per drug court participant. *See* Government Accountability Office, Report to Congressional Committees. No. GAO-05-219: Adult Drug Courts: Evidence Indicates Recidivism Reductions and Mixed Results for Other Outcomes 71 (2005), *available at* http://www.gao.gov/new.items/d05219.pdf.

Drug courts are not without their critics, however. This section provides an overview of modern criminal drug courts, including how they are structured and the debate over whether they are truly a cost-effective and humane alternative to traditional forms of punishment of drug defendants.

Embracing Addiction: Drug Courts and the False Promise of Judicial Intervention
Eric J. Miller

65 Ohio State Law Journal 1479 (2004)

Drug courts may be the most significant penal innovation in the last twenty years. Emerging as a direct response to the "severity revolution" in penal policy, they are an incredibly popular alternative to the War on Drugs. They present a vibrant counter to the stalled legislative and litigative strategies developed to stem the flow of drug users into the criminal justice system. Rather than targeting the scope or application of drug statutes, drug courts work at the level of court process and procedure to re-institutionalize the penological goals of diversion and rehabilitation.

Since its first appearance in the early 1990s, the drug court movement has sought to restructure court practice and procedure. Its goal is to use the court's sanctioning power to treat drug offenders rather than expedite the process of incarceration. Instead of challenging the drug laws, these courts operate within the current legislative framework but attempt to channel offenders away from prison and into treatment. Drug courts, therefore, constitute an alternative to the dominant liberal reaction to the War on Drugs—a reaction that either opposes the criminalization of drugs in general or seeks to end the disparate impact of drug laws on minority populations.

In 1989, the Florida Eleventh Judicial Circuit created the first drug court by administrative order of the Hon. Gerald Weatherington, the then-Chief Justice. The Miami program was set up as a diversion program, "combin[ing] treatment, including traditional treatment methods such as counseling, fellowship meetings, education, and rather non-traditional (at least then) methods like acupuncture and vocational services, with intense judicial review, including frequent reviews of urinalysis results."

The exponential growth in the numbers of drug courts is nothing short of astounding. From the first, in Dade County, there were more than eight hundred drug courts started or in the planning and implementation stages by 2000. All fifty states, as well as the District of Columbia, Guam, and Puerto Rico have founded drug courts. By now, drug courts have had a significant impact upon the lives of thousands of drug offenders. The courts' therapeutic problem-solving orientation is becoming commonplace in other areas of the legal system. Initially, however, the drug court movement developed without federal regulation or funding of the various courts. It developed as an ad hoc movement of like-minded judges and practitioners, loosely affiliated by 1993 into the National Association of Drug Court Professionals (NADCP).

A lack of uniform characteristics shared by all the courts complicates comprehensive analysis of drug court practice and procedure. In practice, there is no ideal or standard drug court; there are, rather, an immense number of local variations on the basic model.

Drug courts channel offenders into treatment at a variety of different stages of the criminal justice process. There are, however, two general channeling policies: deferred prosecution and post-adjudication diversion. Deferred prosecution drug courts require that the defendant waive his right to a speedy trial and enter treatment as soon after being charged as possible. Under the post-adjudication model, the defendant is, in fact, convicted, either after trial or after a plea bargain. In that event, an incarcerative sentence is deferred pending completion of a drug treatment program. Currently, thirty percent of drug courts divert offenders at the pretrial stage and before a plea agreement ("pretrial" and "preplea"); sixteen percent are pretrial and post-plea; twelve percent are post-conviction sentencing institutions; and the rest, forty-two percent, are some combination of the above.

Federal funding and general procedural standards ensure some degree of uniformity. These standards, promulgated initially by the NADCP, include a series of ten "key components" of the drug court and a set of guidelines governing the sanctions or rewards applicable to drug court defendants. These guidelines are tremendously influential. They embody the therapeutic practices of reward for compliance, limited tolerance of relapse, and graduated sanctions for non-compliance with the treatment program that are at the core of the drug court's methodology. In addition, the American Bar Association (ABA) has published a series of drug court standards to supplement the NADCP guidelines and ensure that defendants' procedural rights are protected.

Although neither set of standards is binding on any drug court unless adopted as the court's operating procedures, Congress has conditioned federal funding upon the adoption of the NADCP standards. Many state legislatures or judicial counsels, in formulating their local drug court procedures, clearly respond to the NADCP and ABA standards. Thus, although drug courts come in a variety of different models, in general they share certain common features.

Based on the NADCP model standards, Judge Peggy Hora has identified five features generally attributable to drug courts. First, drug courts use eligibility criteria to identify potential participants in the drug court program. These criteria generally require that the defendant be an addict who is either a nonviolent offender or an offender who poses no security risk to the community. Second, drug court procedure embodies a non-adversarial partnership among the criminal justice, correctional, and treatment systems. This partnership "work[s] together to find care for defendants and to ensure that they remain in treatment." The procedure is designed to maintain the courts' continuing jurisdiction over offenders by "delay[ing] the final disposition of cases [enabling] judges to maintain frequent ongoing contact with defendants." Third, the procedures effect a change in roles of judge, prosecutor, and defense counsel, each of whom participates as part of a treatment team. Fourth, the courts require offenders to attend a designated treatment program. Fifth, courts are able to accept and account for the potential of relapse by providing a range of prescribed and known sanctions for defendants who fail to comply with the program. Drug courts use a "system of graduated penalties.... [, which] may include more frequent contact with the court, increased urine testing, and short periods of so-called 'shock incarceration,'" to ensure compliance with their rehabilitation program.

The most striking feature of the drug court, and the feature most touted by its supporters, is its significantly reorganized court procedure premised upon therapeutic principles of justice.

Drug courts replace the predominantly punitive orientation of traditional approaches to crime control and rehabilitation with "an approach that seeks to confront and meliorate the problems associated with persons who appear in the criminal caseload." These courts eschew the due process accusatorial or adversarial model of courtroom practice. Under that form of procedure, the judge adopts a passive role that tasks the parties with investigating facts, interrogating witnesses, and developing proposals for treatment. The drug court judge no longer relies upon treatment proposals developed by a probation officer, subject to the prosecutor's and defense counsel's arguments over their propriety for the particular defendant. Instead, the drug court incorporates an invasive model of criminal procedure within the courtroom with the judge at the helm. "[J]ustice and therapy are no longer separate enterprises. Instead, they are fully merged into the common endeavor of therapeutic justice."

In drug court, the judge not only retains his authority to set the terms of treatment but now also assumes the role of regulating it. The court, rather than the treatment center, becomes the focal point of the treatment process. The other participants-prosecutor, defender, and defendant (or the drug court's "client")— are required to adopt non-traditional roles. They are supposed to form, along with the judge, a treatment team dedicated to the rehabilitation of the drug-addicted defendant. The team organization replaces the adversarial, adjudicative orientation of traditional courts with a therapeutic approach to drug addiction. The prosecutor and defender become partners collaborating in an effort to rehabilitate the addicted client. The defender must modify or mute her traditional role, "take a step back, [and] not intervene actively between the judge and the participant ... [to] allow that relationship to develop and do its work." Under the treatment team model, the offender's most direct relationships are, therefore, not with his or her counsel, but with the judge and the treatment officer.

Under the new, therapeutic orientation, the hallmarks of the drug court judge's role are, first, discretion in responding to the needs of her "clients" and, second, establishing "a personal 'on-going, working relationship' with the offender." Over the course of his or her participation in drug court, each offender engages in an intense and direct interaction with the judge directed towards "hold[ing] the defendant accountable for her actions during the course of treatment and reinforc[ing] one another in actions taken to ensure that the defendant stays in treatment whenever possible and appropriate."

The drug courts' methodology marks a dual attack on old-style criminal justice. Its strong emphasis on interventionist styles of interaction and authority reject the propriety of due process restrictions on the courts' therapeutic models. Drug courts also, however, dismiss the supposedly soft approach of prior rehabilitative regimes. They seek to bolster the safety net model of rehabilitation with tough love. Drug courts treat the addicted offender as in need of the shock and structure provided by sanctions, so long as those sanctions are consistently applied and so graduated as to recognize the role relapse plays in the therapeutic process. Rehabilitation in the drug court is not a process of "'referring, re-referring, and re-re-referring'" recalcitrant offenders to treatment regimes in hope of effecting a cure. Rather, drug courts envisage the consistent application of sanctions as part of the therapeutic process, one that imposes structure on the addicts' lives.

Generally, the court mandates supervision of drug offenders for one year and spreads treatment over a variety of phases, from intake, to counseling and drug education, to aftercare and transition issues. Each phase employs progressively less intensive supervision of the offender. The first phases are generally highly intensive and can require as much as four days per week of group and individual counseling and education or attendance at treatment providers as well as regular, often weekly, court appearances. Frequent urine testing is generally required throughout the program.

Matching offenders to particular treatment providers is central to the court's mission. In determining what treatment is appropriate, the drug court judge generally has a range of available treatment options from which to choose. Most require visits with a probation officer and a drug education component, along with the mandatory urine tests. In addition, some form of group or individual counseling is required.

Drug Courts: A Review of the Evidence
Ryan S. King and Jill Pasquarella

The Sentencing Project (2009)

The movement for an alternative court to sentence drug offenders emerged from the rapidly evolving reality that the nation's decision to address drug abuse through law enforcement mechanisms would continue to pose significant challenges for the criminal court system. In 2004, 53% of persons in state prison were identified with a drug dependence or abuse problem, but only 15% were receiving professional treatment. Drug-related crime continues to present a costly burden to American society, one that supply reduction efforts have failed to stem. In 2001, the Office of National Drug Control Policy estimated that in 1998 illegal drug use cost Americans $31.1

billion in criminal justice expenses, $30.1 billion in lost productivity and $2.9 billion in costs related to property damage and victimization.

Since 1989, drug courts have spread throughout the country; there are now over 1,600 such courts operating in all 50 states. The drug court movement reflects a desire to shift the emphasis from attempting to combat drug crimes by reducing the supply of drugs to addressing the demand for drugs through the treatment of addiction. Drug courts use the criminal justice system to address addiction through an integrated set of social and legal services instead of solely relying upon sanctions through incarceration or probation. This report surveys a range of research conducted on drug courts to date. Its aim is to outline general findings on the workings and efficacy of drug courts nationwide and to highlight potential concerns and areas where more research is needed.

Despite general indications of drug court efficacy, nearly two decades after their introduction a number of questions remain. Because drug courts are designed and operated at the local level, there are fundamental differences that make cross-jurisdictional comparisons difficult. While the general framework may be portable from program to program—a diversion program for certain categories of low-level defendants who have demonstrated a linkage between their drug abuse and criminal offending—specific selection criteria, protocols for adjudication, means of supervision and revocation procedures can differ dramatically. The localism that defines drug court design complicates efforts to identify best practices. However, we can identify specific elements from different drug courts that are critical ingredients for a successful program. The foundation of a vibrant and sustainable drug diversion program rests both on indicators of success and learning and adapting to emerging challenges.

Graduates of drug courts are, according to current evaluations, less likely to be rearrested than persons processed through traditional court mechanics. Findings from drug court evaluations show that participation in drug courts results in fewer rearrests and reconvictions, or longer periods between arrests.

A meta-analysis of 57 studies[, for example,] estimated that participation in a drug court program would produce an 8% decline in crime relative to no treatment. [And, a] Government Accountability Office report found that 13 of 17 courts reporting on post-program recidivism measured reductions between 4 and 25 percentage points in rearrests and reconvictions.

While it is generally accepted that drug courts effectively reduce rearrest rates relative to simple probation or incarceration, there is some reason to be cautious when interpreting these results. Some studies show little or no impact from drug court participation and it can be difficult to specify which components of the program or the research design may be contributing to these results.

For example, are the evaluation models appropriately specifying relevant factors that may impact outcomes, but are external to the treatment design? Gender, age, race, socioeconomic background, criminal history, and substance abuse history have all been shown to impact treatment outcomes. Many of these variables are not accounted for in analyses of drug court effectiveness. Operationalizing drug court variables can be difficult and outcome measures may be reflecting the interaction of these variables with the treatment modality.

Additionally, definitions of recidivism and the length of time that recidivism is measured differ among the studies, making an absolute comparison difficult. Some drug court evaluations have measured rearrest rates without distinguishing between participants currently under supervision and those who have completed the program. This is important because drug court participants who graduate tend to have much lower recidivism rates than drug court dropouts. Some studies suggest that among drug court dropouts, time spent in treatment had little if any effect on post-program recidivism.

Researchers have also noted that the composition of drug court participants needs to be addressed appropriately in developing a court model. For example, an evaluation of California's Proposition 36 diversion program for low-level drug offenders found that almost half of the persons who were receiving treatment for the first time had been using drugs for more than 10 years, and one in five had been using for more than 20 years.

Evaluations of the net costs and benefits of drug courts nationwide generally find that drug courts save taxpayer dollars compared to simple probation and/or incarceration, primarily due to reductions in arrests, case processing, jail occupancy and victimization costs. While not all persons diverted to drug court would have otherwise been sentenced to prison, for those individuals who are incarcerated, the average annual cost is estimated to be $23,000 per inmate, while the average annual cost of drug court participation is estimated to be $4,300 per person.

In 2005, the Government Accountability Office found that seven drug courts evaluated had net benefits of between $1,000 and $15,000 per participant due to reduced recidivism and avoided costs to potential victims.

Research to date has consistently reported that drug courts are achieving important benefits. Still largely unknown, however, are the practices which lead to success or failure of a drug court. Of great concern is the contention that drug courts could be increasing the number of people arrested for drug crimes, instead of decreasing in the long term the number of people processed in the criminal justice system. Research has not yet focused on determining whether drug court participants would have ended up in the criminal justice system if not for the drug court. Increased and uniform tracking of participants' criminal history may answer some concerns about the net-widening effects of the drug court. It would also be helpful for future research to look at the effects of a pre-plea versus a post-plea model and the use of sanctions. Research should continue to monitor the rearrest and reconviction rates of both graduates and dropouts, distinguishing between within program rates and post-program rates. It will continue to be useful to know the demographic of graduates along with the rates of recidivism in the years that follow their graduation.

Contraindicated Drug Courts
Josh Bowers

55 UCLA Law Review 783 (2008)

Drug courts have created a few enemies and a great many more supporters from all corners of political and institutional spectra. Supporters maintain that the courts effectively serve several goals: to provide second chances for nonviolent addicts, to preserve systemic resources, and to control crime by disrupting cycles of addiction and recidivism. The common refrain is that "what we were doing before simply was not working." Thus, drug courts are said to offer a necessary and fresh approach to combat drug use and drug crime. Conversely, critics principally raise institutional concerns: that these courts inappropriately convert traditional adversaries into "team players," subvert judicial function by turning historically impartial judges into therapists and interrogators, and even fail to reduce recidivism and save resources.

I wish to put to one side the broader debate over the effectiveness and institutional propriety of drug courts. My aim is to draw attention to two related, underappreciated, and troubling facets of these courts: first, that they provide the worst results to their target populations; and, second, that this inversion of intended effect produces particularly toxic consequences in the many drug courts that subject failing participants to alternative termination sentences that exceed customary plea prices. Put concretely, drug courts are "contraindicated" for genuine addicts and for other disadvantaged groups that have traditionally filled prisons as part of the war on drugs. The consequent adverse effects may be atypically long prison sentences for the very defendants that drug courts were supposed to keep out of prison and off of drugs.

Worse still, compulsive addicts are not the only ones who face comparatively bad results in drug courts. Studies have shown that other historically disadvantaged groups—for example minorities, the poor, the uneducated, and the socially disconnected—are also more likely to fail. Accordingly, drug courts may regressively tax communities already strained by the incarceration boom, and thereby exacerbate preexisting racial and socio-economic criminal-justice "tilts."

Conversely, drug offenders who are noncompulsive or less compulsive ultimately do much better in drug courts. Even if un-addicted offenders do not want to cease drug use, they possess sufficient self-control to modify rationally their behavior in response to external carrots and sticks. Faced with the choice between incarceration and manageable programs, these offenders have every incentive to be strategic and game entry into treatment that they do not, in fact, need, in order to receive favorable dispositions that (from a retributive-justice standpoint) they do not deserve.

The root cause of this contraindication problem is the lack of theoretical coherence in drug courts. On the one hand, drug courts follow the philosophy that addiction is a compulsive disease. On the other, the courts expect addicts to be receptive rationally to external coercion. More specifically, the courts subscribe, at least rhetorically, to the purported belief that addiction is a "brain disease"—a "chronic, progressive, relapsing disorder." Under this conception, addiction is unresponsive to traditional criminal punishment, because jails and prisons lack the tools to help addicts stop, and addicts lack the volition to stop on their own. Moreover, the courts view diversion from prison and the potential reduction or dismissal of charges as retributively justified, because addicts possess diminished self-control and therefore diminished responsibility. But drug courts have not—as advertised—abandoned the "traditional criminal justice paradigm, in which drug abuse is understood as a willful choice made by an offender capable of choosing between right and wrong." They have merely relocated the old paradigm to the background. Accordingly, drug courts see addicts as sick patients and their crimes as symptomatic of illness only as long as participants respond to care. When treatment results run thin, a switch is thrown and drug courts revert to economic conceptions of motivation and to conventional punishment. Pursuant to this mixed message, addiction controls addicts' behavior at the time of the crime (at least to a degree), and addicts therefore deserve less punishment and more rehabilitation; but addicts control their addictions at the time of treatment, and they therefore deserve greater punishment if they fail to exercise control.

Drug courts operate on faith that internal motivation will follow external motivation—that carrots and sticks will jumpstart inner desire. Put differently, drug courts meet addicts' inability to exercise self-control and reason not only with therapeutic opportunities to address these deficiencies, but also with concurrent external threats to respond to reason—or else. This confidence in addicts' abilities to discover reason once in drug courts runs counter to well-established therapeutic principles that treatment works better when addicts are internally motivated. Indeed, it would be somewhat surprising if it were otherwise. After all, addicts are people for whom the everyday negative external consequences of drug use—the social, economic, legal, and physical costs—have proven insufficient to modify behavior.

Ultimately, when drug courts imprison failing participants, they punish them not for their underlying crimes, but for their inability to get with the program. In this way, drug courts bear some resemblance to early medieval trials by ordeal. These trials—in which the accused performed some onerous task as a test of God's will—measured not culpability, but rather, say, calluses on hands that enabled the accused to carry safely hot iron. Likewise, drug courts measure not culpability, but strength of will and social support in the face of addiction. In both dispositional methods, final sentences are principally reflective of innate and preexisting advantages. In one sense, drug courts may be even more problematic than trials by ordeal: Drug-court results are not just haphazard, they are predictably worst for the most addicted, the least volitional, and the neediest. As such, the expected failure of addicts to respond to external stimuli seems an odd basis from which to subject them to alternative sentences that outstrip standard pleas.

Moreover, there is little reason to hope that treatment-resistant offenders might recognize their own fallibility and consequently opt-out of treatment. The most compulsive addicts are bound to reach the least sensible decisions; the enticements of drug court are dangled before the very individuals most easily tempted. When addicts cede to that temptation they exercise effectively the same cognitive limitations and bounded willpower that saddled them with drug dependencies in the first instance. They myopically undervalue the difficulties of recovery and the weight of the distant (but heavy) stick that awaits termination. And they optimistically grasp treatment's carrots, leaving for tomorrow the question of how to master their own defective rationalities and wills. Faced with the choice between conventional pleas, risky trials, or uncertain treatment, they are prone to see drug courts as the best means of remaining at, or recapturing, liberty, even when it often is not. Ultimately, then, external motivation may prove sufficient to convince addicts to take treatment, but it is less likely to keep them there.

Almost no studies have sought to compare the sentences of failing drug-court participants with the sentences of conventionally adjudicated defendants. Two limited exceptions are a pair of federally funded studies recently completed by the Center for Court Innovation in collaboration with the New York State Unified Court System. The chief study analyzed drug courts in several New York counties, including Queens, Brooklyn, Manhattan, and the Bronx. The other study looked exclusively at the drug court in Staten Island. Accordingly, the two studies collectively examined drug courts in all New York City counties.

The studies found that the sentences for failing participants in New York City drug courts were typically two-to-five times longer than the sentences for conventionally adjudicated defendants. At the outer margin, the sentences were well over five times the standard length in Staten Island and almost four times the standard length in the Bronx. Only in Brooklyn were termination sentences anywhere close to the length of customary sentences. Significantly, the Bronx and Staten Island drug-court participants did worse on average even when graduates were included. In fact, in the Bronx, the termination sentences approximated the literal worst-case scenario: The typical failing participant was sentenced to two-to-six years in prison, which was (at the time of the relevant studies) the maximum sentence on the maximum drug-court eligible charge.

Significantly, drug court proponents could spin rosy tales from even these data. Reading quite broadly, they could claim that diversion is working: in all counties, fewer drug offenders went to prison; and, in most counties, the collective population of offenders spent less time behind bars. But at the individualized level, the positive story does not hold. Take Queens County, for example. There, drug-court defendants were incarcerated at half the rate, but those who did go to jail or prison went away for more than twice as long. Such a result sits uncomfortably with defensible notions of distributive justice and cuts against drug-court advocates' professed aim of breaking the cycle of addiction and incarceration.

America's Problem-Solving Courts: The Criminal Costs of Treatment and the Case for Reform

National Association of Criminal Defense Lawyers (2009)

The debate over drug enforcement policy in the United States is almost always framed in stark terms premised on narrow options. Conventional thinking about criminal justice issues—prison, community corrections, probation, or possibly some sort of diversion program for minor offenses and first-time offenders—has not worked, nor has it abated the addiction problem. Drug courts have swept the nation without much debate or input from the criminal defense bar. That input is long overdue.

Policymakers, courts, and lawyers must take a step back and examine the problem being solved: drug addiction. Addiction is an illness. Illnesses should be treated through the public health system—not punished through the criminal justice system. Conditioning treatment on an arrest and entry in the criminal justice system sends a perverse message to the person who is ill and is an enormous waste of scarce public and court resources.

[The National Association of Criminal Defense Lawyers] has long believed that "addiction to any substance, whether legal or illegal, is really a health problem best treated by the medical community and others trained in the causes and treatments of addiction." Thoughtful policymakers from all points on the political spectrum have recommended the decriminalization of all drugs as the best way to combat drug addiction and make effective use of criminal justice resources. The experience of European nations provides powerful support for the soundness of this approach and belies concerns that drug use would increase. Although politicians have been unwilling to engage in a serious debate about legalizing drugs, the broader public has shown interest in the issue. It is time for a serious discussion of decriminalization.

Until decriminalization occurs, the conventional paradigm is likely to continue, and drug courts will have a role. Drug courts are largely well-intentioned efforts to offer substance abuse treatment as an alternative to lengthy prison terms and lifelong felony convictions. Much of the support for drug courts ultimately turns on their existence as the sole, or best, alternative to draconian punishment. Although drug courts may offer some positive benefits to some participants, they also cause problems and engender disparities in many areas, including the admission process, the role and ethical obligations of defense counsel, and the misguided use of limited public resources.

Most drug courts require a guilty plea as the price of admission. When guilty pleas are required before offering treatment, drug courts become little more than conviction mills. In post-adjudication courts, the defendant must plead guilty before entering drug court, and even if he or she is successful and completes the program, the conviction will never go away. In pre-adjudication courts, the defendant must plead guilty, but then, if he or she successfully completes the program there is a possibility that the plea can be withdrawn and the charge dismissed. Although procedures vary, the hoops through which participants must jump result in dismissals for relatively few defendants. Profound consequences flow from every failure.

A pre-plea, pre-adjudication program preserves due process rights, allows defendants an opportunity to seek treatment, and provides a strong incentive for successful completion. If the participant successfully completes the program, the charge is dismissed. If the participant does not succeed, the traditional court process can be pursued.

Pre-plea, pre-adjudication programs are also the only ones that permit informed, thoughtful decision-making by defendants and counsel. Conversely, in post-plea programs defendants often lack sufficient time to make informed decisions, do not have discovery, and are unable to litigate motions. This often creates impossible ethical quandaries for defense counsel.

Criteria for admission to drug court must be transparent and fully disclosed. Currently, many courts have no official criteria or have stated criteria that are backward or counterintuitive. For example, many drug courts exclude all violent offenders, including defendants charged with domestic violence. Excluding domestic violence offenses leads to the odd result of "the domestic violence offender who gets drunk and beats his wife up checking with his probation officer once every six weeks" while nonviolent offenders are appearing regularly for status hearings, giving random weekly urine samples, and attending 90 meetings in 90 days.

In many courts, whether a defendant is permitted to enter drug court is up to the prosecutor. Prosecutors are frequently hesitant to allow higher risk offenders, even those who desperately need and want the treatment and supervision, into drug court out of fear that they will be blamed for participant failure or recidivism. [W]hen prosecutors serve as gatekeepers they face the political risk of "a headline waiting to happen."

To avoid politics improperly affecting access to drug court programs, prosecutors should not be able to determine access. Admission criteria should be drafted by a panel or commission with broad representation from stakeholders in the criminal justice community, including judges, prosecutors, defense counsel, and social service providers. Admission criteria should be broad, allowing those who need and want treatment access to the program.

Drug courts seek to impose a team concept on defense lawyers, creating difficult ethical dilemmas and virtually no role for private counsel. In many situations, the current structure of drug courts requires defense attorneys to set aside their ethical obligations to further the purpose and framework of the drug court. That must change. When counsel says nothing in representing the interests of clients, defense lawyers appear headed "to an old Soviet Union model where your job as a lawyer is simply to hold your client's hand as they go off to the gallows—here's what's going to happen next."

Protecting defendants' Sixth Amendment right to competent counsel requires a process that allows defense attorneys to satisfy their ethical obligations of loyalty, confidentiality, and zealous advocacy. Doing so will not dismantle the drug court process or its objectives; rather, it will enhance the credibility of the process with both the participants and anyone who observes the court.

Too often, the criteria and process for admission into drug court are guided largely by tough-on-crime politics, focusing on first-time or nonviolent offenders, with little consideration of smart-on-crime approaches that target those most in need of intensive treatment who would otherwise spend a long time in prison.

Courts frequently select those most likely to succeed to participate in drug court—a process called skimming. [W]hen they engage in skimming, the drug courts are "sucking up all the resources that the community has to deal with this very thorny issue of addiction, and . . . using it on cream puffs." In fact, drug courts, with their program of intense supervision, should be utilized for high-risk offenders for whom everything else has failed. Courts should focus on those who are facing the longest sentences and most need treatment, "where we would get the biggest bang for our buck."

Other less intensive alternatives to drug courts must be developed for low-risk offenders, who perform better without intensive judicial intervention. Communities should not "invest all of their addiction resources into one program. You can't ignore the people who don't get into drug court who are drug- and alcohol-involved. They have the same needs, the same rights, and impose the same dangers as everyone else."

As the Sentencing Project's report *Drug Courts: A Review of the Evidence* discusses above, the available evidence appears to indicate that drug courts are generally a cost-effective alternative to traditional sentences for drug offenders. Even if criminal drug courts produce better results than traditional criminal sentences for drug offenders, however, it is possible that other alternatives would be even more cost-effective. The National Association of Criminal Defense Lawyers, for example, suggests "the decriminalization of all drugs as the best way to combat drug addiction and make effective use of criminal justice resources."

In 2001, Portugal decriminalized all drugs and developed a unique and innovative approach that might best be characterized as a civil drug court system. Portugal's program was discussed in the section on drug decriminalization in Chapter 2. Under Portugal's law, it is not a crime to possess small amounts of drugs for personal use. Instead, possession of drugs for personal use is a "purely administrative violation[], to be processed in a noncriminal proceeding." Glenn Greenwald, *Drug Decriminalization in Portugal: Lessons for Creating Far and Successful Drug Policies*, The Cato Institute (2009). Under this administrative system, a person who is found in possession of a small amount of drugs is given a citation and required to appear before what the law calls a "Dissuasion Commission." Portugal's Dissuasion Commissions are typically comprised of two members with an addiction treatment or medical background and one member with a legal background. If the Commission members determine that the offender does not have a substance use disorder, they will typically give him a warning. People who are addicted to drugs can be ordered into treatment, prohibited from associating with specific people, or banned from "visiting high-risk locales," among other options. Offenders who do not meet their obligations may be fined but—consistent with the administrative nature of the program—not imprisoned. Now that you have read more about criminal drug courts, how do you think they compare to Portugal's system?

G. Civil Sanctions and Controls

In addition to criminal punishment, drug-involved individuals face a wide range of civil sanctions and controls. Some civil penalties are collateral consequences of a criminal conviction. Others are wholly independent of criminal prosecution.

1. Collateral Consequences of a Drug Conviction

a. An Overview of Collateral Consequences

"Collateral Damage": No Re-Entry for Drug Offenders
Nora V. Demleitner

47 Villanova Law Review 1027 (2002)

"Punishment" for many drug offenders continues once they are released from prison. They are usually subject to so-called "collateral consequences." Many of these are virtually unknown outside the criminal justice community, and of some consequences, even judges, prosecutors and criminal defense attorneys are unaware. Federal legislation creating collateral consequences for drug offenses is frequently not part of crime legislation; it passes into law without being debated in relevant congressional committees, including the judiciary committee.

The so-called "collateral consequences" are legally classified as civil rather than criminal sanctions. For that reason they can be imposed without the protections and guarantees of the criminal justice system. This is particularly troubling since many of these "consequences" deny drug offenders fundamental social, economic and political rights. They impact the lives of ex-offenders dramatically and often also deprive their families of crucial governmental support.

Collateral consequences are justified either on punitive, deterrent or preventive grounds. The last rationale applies less to drug offenders because most collateral consequences imposed on them are not based on a risk model. On the other hand, punitive and deterrent grounds have played a dominant role in the congressional discourse surrounding drug offenders. The denial of governmental benefits to drug offenders has been justified as a measure of "user accountability." Drug users, often considered to have made a rational choice, should be held accountable and will be held out as an example.

Collateral sanctions befall all types of offenders. Although the public considers murder, rape and kidnapping more serious offenses than drug possession or distribution, the collateral consequences imposed on drug offenders tend to be more severe than those imposed on murderers, rapists and kidnappers. Drug offenders suffer from them disproportionately because many collateral consequences target them specifically. Next to sex offenders, drug felons and drug misdemeanants have borne the brunt of civil sanctions. Within the last fifteen years, the panoply of civil sanctions applicable to them has increased dramatically.

The civil sanctions most devastating to offenders are those that deprive them of the ability to reintegrate successfully. Re-entry and rehabilitation assistance are particularly crucial to offenders with two sets of characteristics, which may overlap. First, those who have served long prison terms need substantial reintegration assistance. They have lost the ability to operate as individual agents in a less structured environment, and often have difficulty adjusting to a society and job market very different than the ones in existence when they went to prison. Because of the long sentences imposed on drug traffickers, especially in the federal system, many of them fall into this category. Second, offenders who suffer from insufficient education and job training will become likely recidivists unless they receive reintegration assistance. However, it is precisely these offenders that are frequently excluded from the social safety net and from access to training and education because of collateral sanctions.

Federal law allows for the denial of a whole set of federal benefits to drug offenders. The Denial of Federal Benefits Program of 1988 empowers federal and state courts to prohibit drug offenders from accessing a broad range of benefits, excluding food stamps and other survival-type subsidies. A first drug trafficking conviction can lead to the denial of benefits for up to five years; a second conviction doubles the maximum possible ineligibility period; a third conviction mandates the court bar such benefits permanently.

Denial of survival-type welfare benefits takes collateral sanctions a step further by making critical assistance, particularly necessary after release, inaccessible. Any drug offender convicted after August 22, 1996, becomes permanently ineligible for food stamps and temporary assistance to needy families, unless the state of residence opts out. So far, twenty-four states have adopted the ban, eighteen have modified it, and eight have opted out. Modifications usually center around temporal ineligibility limitations and treatment or recovery as eligibility grounds.

Federal housing policies allow for the exclusion of drug offenders from federally subsidized or funded housing. Drug-related activity alone may result in eviction from public housing. The denial of public housing, therefore, does not result directly from a drug conviction. However, in the vast majority of cases, drug-related activity will come to the attention of housing authorities because of a conviction record. Unless an offender can demonstrate that she receives treatment, she will be banned from public housing. The public housing agency may consider proof of rehabilitation prior to issuing an eviction notice.

In many cases, the existence of an illegal drug user in a household will cause the entire household to be evicted and barred from public housing. As interpreted by the Supreme Court, the statute does not allow for an innocent owner defense. Evictions are ultimately discretionary decisions of housing agencies based on the threat drug activity constitutes.

Because private landlords often do not want to rent to ex-offenders, many of these ex-offenders find themselves on the street unless family members who do not reside in public housing are able to take them in. This creates a vicious circle for the drug offender. The lack of access to food and housing makes it frequently impossible for offenders to gain employment, and the lack of employment prevents access to food and housing.

Congress and the states have made it more difficult for ex-offenders to receive education and find employment after a drug conviction. Many of these provisions may not have been designed to limit an offender's employability, but rather were passed for punitive reasons. Only some are based on an assessment of the risk of re-offending. Nevertheless, the effect on employment is palpable while most of the restrictions are unlikely to impact public safety because they are drawn too broadly to accomplish that goal.

Some collateral consequences indirectly affect the employability of ex-offenders because they make it impossible for them to fulfill basic job requirements. [C]ongressional legislation demands the revocation or suspension of drivers' licenses for at least six months for persons convicted of drug felonies. Despite the lack of an apparent connection between drug felonies and the use of motor vehicles, Congress mandated the loss of this "privilege" as a punitive sanction. A state can avoid the imposition of this provision without penalty only if the state legislature and governor jointly express their opposition to the legislation. Unexplained noncompliance will lead to the loss of 10% of the state's highway funding.

Felony convictions lead to the automatic revocation of and bar on a wide variety of federal and state licenses. The denial of state employment licenses to felons has a long history. Throughout the 1980s many states restricted the employment opportunities of parolees and ex-offenders even further, largely to symbolize their sincerity in the "war" on crime. California, for example, prohibits parolees from working in real estate, nursing or physical therapy. Loss of such licenses means loss of employment, and in some cases a long-term, if not permanent, bar on re-employment in a profession in which the offender may have acquired certain skills and abilities. The same applies to public employment.

Federal restrictions on certain governmental programs and contracts also impact the employability of ex-offenders directly. Many of these bars, even those imposed by regulatory agencies, are virtually automatic. Drug offenders, especially, will find it difficult to obtain waivers of such bars and reinstatement of necessary licenses.

Even more problematic than the denial of specific employment opportunities are restrictions on training and education for drug offenders. Under the 1988 Denial of

Federal Benefits Program, convicted drug offenders may be denied access to government benefits, including funds to finance education and job training, upon conviction. While the bar is discretionary and the decision rests with the sentencing judge in cases of first convictions, it becomes mandatory when the offender faces his third conviction for drug sales.

Education grants, loans and work assistance are now being denied automatically to all those convicted of any drug offense—a felony or misdemeanor, trafficking, or simple possession. The length of such denial depends on the number and type of convictions. One conviction for drug possession triggers a one-year denial; two convictions lead to a two-year ineligibility period; three or more convictions make the ban permanent. For drug sales, a first conviction means a two-year ban; any subsequent conviction leads to a permanent denial of aid. Only a showing of drug rehabilitation can end an indefinite loss. The denial of aid does not affect individuals convicted of offenses other than drug crimes.

Lack of an education and of marketable skills combined with the stigma of a criminal conviction make it difficult for many ex-offenders to find employment. "One year after release, as many as sixty percent of former inmates are not employed in the legitimate labor market." How much of the difficulty in finding employment can be attributed to collateral sanctions is unclear. However, they effectively close a large number of employment opportunities, skilled and unskilled, to ex-offenders, and have made it more difficult for them to get additional skills training.

Some of the most dramatic sanctions that can befall a drug offender are immigration-related. Non-U.S. citizens are inadmissible if they admit to having committed or have been convicted of a drug-related offense. Federal law also allows the immigration service to deny admission to suspected drug traffickers and their family members, even if they are not criminally convicted.

Criminal convictions make non-citizens who are in the United States removable, even if they hold permanent residency status. Any conviction of a drug offense, other than possession of thirty grams or less of marijuana for one's own use, leads to deportation. Drug users and addicts are also deportable. Since under current law a conviction for drug trafficking constitutes an "aggravated felony," the offender is disqualified from relief from removal because he cannot establish "good moral character." Two misdemeanor drug possession convictions will be treated as "aggravated felonies" which make the non-citizen automatically deportable, irrespective of his or her background.

For new permanent residents the law is even less forgiving. A single drug possession conviction can lead to mandatory deportation even if the criminal court assessed only a probationary sentence. [L]ong-term permanent resident aliens who have led law-abiding lives for many years following a minor drug conviction may also be deported to their countries of citizenship. Unless personal, familial or societal considerations weigh in favor of keeping the ex-offender in the United States, deportation will occur, even though the ex-offender may have only very limited ties or no connection to his country of citizenship.

The denial of economic, social and political benefits and rights at best delays the reintegration of ex-drug offenders into society. At worst, it leads them back to prison. The difficulties these ex-offenders face also affect their families and communities negatively, often because they create greater instability, anomie and ultimately higher crime rates.

Civil sanctions turn all offenders, especially poor, female and minority offenders, their families and their communities, into "collateral damage." For drug offenders, collateral consequences come on top of already long prison sentences and often amount to a virtual life sentence. These restrictions frequently lead to re-offending and ultimately re-imprisonment.

Arguments of "user accountability" and deterrence traditionally supported collateral consequences. They, nevertheless, impact predominantly the worst off by denying them assistance upon release from prison and creating significant obstacles to their reintegration.

The denial of basic rights affects not only the offender and her family, but also her community. Many communities to which drug offenders return suffer disproportionately from lack of cohesion, unemployment, homelessness and family instability. By increasing the number of obstacles facing ex-offenders, their chances of succeeding in this environment are further reduced, with detrimental consequences for these communities.

b. Immigration

Drug convictions can subject noncitizens, including green card holders who have lived in the United States for a very long time, to deportation proceedings. A 2015 Human Rights Watch report found that "the US is deporting a significant number of both permanent residents and undocumented individuals with strong family and community ties to the US, often for minor or old drug offenses." HUMAN RIGHTS WATCH, A PRICE TOO HIGH: US FAMILIES TORN APART BY DEPORTATIONS FOR DRUG OFFENSES 5 (2015). The report continued:

> US immigration law began to dictate severe immigration consequences for non-citizens with drug offenses in the 1980s and 1990s, often as part of legislation passed in support of the US "War on Drugs."
>
> Lawful permanent residents—that is, people with legal immigrant status in the US—can be deported for any drug offense, with the sole exception of a conviction for possession of 30 grams or less of marijuana. Many lawful permanent residents with convictions for simple possession are eligible to apply for and receive "cancellation of removal" to remain in the US, but they must often fight their cases while being detained without bond. If the offense is considered "drug trafficking," even if it is a low-level sales

> offense involving small amounts of drugs—such as selling ten dollars-worth of cocaine—permanent residents face deportation as "aggravated felons," and are disqualified from almost every defense to deportation. In such cases, immigration judges, like judges forced to impose mandatory minimum sentences in criminal cases, are barred from considering each case individually and taking into account such factors as the circumstances of the offense, rehabilitation, length of residence in the US, and ties to US family.

Id. at 5–6. A 2016 analysis of Immigration and Customs Enforcement data found that of the 308,088 deportations between November 2014 and April 2016, approximately 11 percent (or 33,000) were for drug offenses, and nearly one-third of drug deportations were marijuana-related. Christie Thompson and Anna Flagg, *Who Is ICE Deporting?*, The Marshall Project (Sept. 26, 2016), https://www.themarshallproject.org/2016/09/26/who-is-ice-deporting.

The next case, *Moncrieffe v. Holder*, shows the impact drug convictions can have immigration status. In *Moncrieffe*, the Supreme Court considered the case of a man who was brought to the United States legally in 1984, when he was three years old. Although he had lived in the United States for more than two decades, Adrian Moncrieffe never became a citizen. In 2007, Moncrieffe pled guilty in Georgia to possession of 1.3 grams of marijuana with the intent to distribute. The issue before the Supreme Court was whether this conviction made Moncrieffe deportable *and* ineligible for discretionary relief (such as asylum or cancellation of removal), or whether the conviction merely made Moncrieffe deportable.

Moncrieffe v. Holder

Supreme Court of the United States
569 U.S. 184 (2013)

Justice Sotomayor delivered the opinion of the Court.

I. A

The Immigration and Nationality Act (INA) . . . allows the Government to deport various classes of noncitizens, such as those who overstay their visas, and those who are convicted of certain crimes while in the United States, including drug offenses. Ordinarily, when a noncitizen is found to be deportable on one of these grounds, he may ask the Attorney General for certain forms of discretionary relief from removal, like asylum (if he has a well-founded fear of persecution in his home country) and cancellation of removal (if, among other things, he has been lawfully present in the United States for a number of years). But if a noncitizen has been convicted of one of a narrower set of crimes classified as "aggravated felonies," then he is not only deportable but also ineligible for these discretionary forms of relief. See §§ 1158(b)(2)(A)(ii), (B)(i); §§ 1229b(a)(3), (b)(1)(C).

The INA defines "aggravated felony" to include a host of offenses. Among them is "illicit trafficking in a controlled substance." This general term is not defined, but the INA states that it "includ[es] a drug trafficking crime (as defined in section 924(c) of title 18)." In turn, 18 U.S.C. § 924(c)(2) defines "drug trafficking crime" to mean "any felony punishable under the Controlled Substances Act," or two other statutes not relevant here. The chain of definitions ends with § 3559(a)(5), which provides that a "felony" is an offense for which the "maximum term of imprisonment authorized" is "more than one year." The upshot is that a noncitizen's conviction of an offense that the Controlled Substances Act (CSA) makes punishable by more than one year's imprisonment will be counted as an "aggravated felony" for immigration purposes. A conviction under either state or federal law may qualify, but a "state offense constitutes a 'felony punishable under the Controlled Substances Act' only if it proscribes conduct punishable as a felony under that federal law." *Lopez v. Gonzales,* 549 U.S. 47, 60 (2006).

B

Petitioner Adrian Moncrieffe is a Jamaican citizen who came to the United States legally in 1984, when he was three. During a 2007 traffic stop, police found 1.3 grams of marijuana in his car. This is the equivalent of about two or three marijuana cigarettes. Moncrieffe pleaded guilty to possession of marijuana with intent to distribute, a violation of Ga.Code Ann. § 16-13-30(j)(1) (2007). Under a Georgia statute providing more lenient treatment to first-time offenders, the trial court withheld entering a judgment of conviction or imposing any term of imprisonment, and instead required that Moncrieffe complete five years of probation, after which his charge will be expunged altogether.[2]

Alleging that this Georgia conviction constituted an aggravated felony, the Federal Government sought to deport Moncrieffe. The Government reasoned that possession of marijuana with intent to distribute is an offense under the CSA punishable by up to five years' imprisonment and thus an aggravated felony. An Immigration Judge agreed and ordered Moncrieffe removed. The Board of Immigration Appeals (BIA) affirmed that conclusion on appeal.

The Court of Appeals denied Moncrieffe's petition for review. The court rejected Moncrieffe's reliance upon § 841(b)(4), a provision that, in effect, makes marijuana distribution punishable only as a misdemeanor if the offense involves a small amount of marijuana for no remuneration. It held that in a federal criminal prosecution, "the default sentencing range for a marijuana distribution offense is the CSA's felony provision, § 841(b)(1)(D), rather than the misdemeanor provision." 662 F.3d 387, 392 (C.A.5 2011). Because Moncrieffe's Georgia offense penalized possession of marijuana with intent to distribute, the court concluded that it was "equivalent to a federal felony."

We granted certiorari to resolve a conflict among the Courts of Appeals with respect to whether a conviction under a statute that criminalizes conduct described

2. The parties agree that this resolution of Moncrieffe's Georgia case is nevertheless a "conviction" as the INA defines that term.

by both §841's felony provision and its misdemeanor provision, such as a statute that punishes all marijuana distribution without regard to the amount or remuneration, is a conviction for an offense that "proscribes conduct punishable as a felony under" the CSA. We now reverse.

II. A

When the Government alleges that a state conviction qualifies as an "aggravated felony" under the INA, we generally employ a "categorical approach" to determine whether the state offense is comparable to an offense listed in the INA. Under this approach we look "not to the facts of the particular prior case," but instead to whether "the state statute defining the crime of conviction" categorically fits within the "generic" federal definition of a corresponding aggravated felony. By "generic," we mean the offenses must be viewed in the abstract, to see whether the state statute shares the nature of the federal offense that serves as a point of comparison. Accordingly, a state offense is a categorical match with a generic federal offense only if a conviction of the state offense "'necessarily' involved . . . facts equating to [the] generic [federal offense]." Whether the noncitizen's actual conduct involved such facts "is quite irrelevant."

Because we examine what the state conviction necessarily involved, not the facts underlying the case, we must presume that the conviction "rested upon [nothing] more than the least of th[e] acts" criminalized, and then determine whether even those acts are encompassed by the generic federal offense. But this rule is not without qualification. First, our cases have addressed state statutes that contain several different crimes, each described separately, and we have held that a court may determine which particular offense the noncitizen was convicted of by examining the charging document and jury instructions, or in the case of a guilty plea, the plea agreement, plea colloquy, or "'some comparable judicial record' of the factual basis for the plea." Second, our focus on the minimum conduct criminalized by the state statute is not an invitation to apply "legal imagination" to the state offense; there must be "a realistic probability, not a theoretical possibility, that the State would apply its statute to conduct that falls outside the generic definition of a crime."

This categorical approach has a long pedigree in our Nation's immigration law. See Das, The Immigration Penalties of Criminal Convictions: Resurrecting Categorical Analysis in Immigration Law, 86 N.Y.U.L.Rev. 1669, 1688–1702, 1749–1752 (2011) (tracing judicial decisions back to 1913). The reason is that the INA asks what offense the noncitizen was "convicted" of, not what acts he committed. "[C]onviction" is "the relevant statutory hook."

B

The aggravated felony at issue here, "illicit trafficking in a controlled substance," is a "generic crim[e]." So the categorical approach applies. As we have explained, this aggravated felony encompasses all state offenses that "proscrib[e] conduct punishable as a felony under [the CSA]." In other words, to satisfy the categorical approach, a state drug offense must meet two conditions: It must "necessarily" proscribe conduct that is an offense under the CSA, and the CSA must "necessarily" prescribe felony punishment for that conduct.

Moncrieffe was convicted under a Georgia statute that makes it a crime to "possess, have under [one's] control, manufacture, deliver, distribute, dispense, administer, purchase, sell, or possess with intent to distribute marijuana." We know from his plea agreement that Moncrieffe was convicted of the last of these offenses. We therefore must determine whether possession of marijuana with intent to distribute is "necessarily" conduct punishable as a felony under the CSA.

We begin with the relevant conduct criminalized by the CSA. There is no question that it is a federal crime to "possess with intent to . . . distribute . . . a controlled substance," 21 U.S.C. § 841(a)(1), one of which is marijuana, § 812(c). So far, the state and federal provisions correspond. But this is not enough, because the generically defined federal crime is "any felony punishable under the Controlled Substances Act," not just any "offense under the CSA." Thus we must look to what punishment the CSA imposes for this offense.

[21 U.S.C.] Section 841 is divided into two subsections that are relevant here: (a), titled "Unlawful acts," which includes the offense just described, and (b), titled "Penalties." Subsection (b) tells us how "any person who violates subsection (a)" shall be punished, depending on the circumstances of his crime (*e.g.*, the type and quantity of controlled substance involved, whether it is a repeat offense). Subsection (b)(1)(D) provides that if a person commits a violation of subsection (a) involving "less than 50 kilograms of marihuana," then "such person shall, except as provided in paragraphs (4) and (5) of this subsection, be sentenced to a term of imprisonment of not more than 5 years," *i.e.*, as a felon. But one of the exceptions is important here. Paragraph (4) provides, "Notwithstanding paragraph (1)(D) of this subsection, any person who violates subsection (a) of this section by distributing a small amount of marihuana for no remuneration shall be treated as" a simple drug possessor, 21 U.S.C. § 844, which for our purposes means as a misdemeanant.[7] These dovetailing provisions create two mutually exclusive categories of punishment for CSA marijuana distribution offenses: one a felony, and one not. The only way to know whether a marijuana distribution offense is "punishable as a felony" under the CSA is to know whether the conditions described in paragraph (4) are present or absent.

A conviction under the same Georgia statute for "sell[ing]" marijuana, for example, would seem to establish remuneration. The presence of remuneration would

---

7. Although paragraph (4) speaks only of "distributing" marijuana, the parties agree that it also applies to "the more inchoate offense of possession with intent to distribute that drug."

The CSA does not define "small amount." The BIA has suggested that 30 grams "serve[s] as a useful guidepost," noting that the INA exempts from deportable controlled substances offenses "a single offense involving possession for one's own use of 30 grams or less of marijuana," 8 U.S.C. § 1227(a)(2)(B)(i). The meaning of "small amount" is not at issue in this case, so we need not, and do not, define the term.

mean that paragraph (4) is not implicated, and thus that the conviction is necessarily for conduct punishable as a felony under the CSA (under paragraph (1)(D)). In contrast, the fact of a conviction for possession with intent to distribute marijuana, standing alone, does not reveal whether either remuneration or more than a small amount of marijuana was involved. It is possible neither was; we know that Georgia prosecutes this offense when a defendant possesses only a small amount of marijuana, see, *e.g., Taylor v. State,* 260 Ga.App. 890 (2003) (6.6 grams), and that "distribution" does not require remuneration, see, *e.g., Hadden v. State,* 181 Ga.App. 628 (1987). So Moncrieffe's conviction could correspond to either the CSA felony or the CSA misdemeanor. Ambiguity on this point means that the conviction did not "necessarily" involve facts that correspond to an offense punishable as a felony under the CSA. Under the categorical approach, then, Moncrieffe was not convicted of an aggravated felony.

III. A

The Government [argues that] §841(b)(4)'s misdemeanor provision is irrelevant to the categorical analysis because paragraph (4) is merely a "mitigating exception," to the CSA offense, not one of the "elements" of the offense. And because possession with intent to distribute marijuana is "presumptive[ly]" a felony under the CSA, the Government asserts, any state offense with the same elements is presumptively an aggravated felony. These two contentions are related, and we reject both of them.

Like the BIA and the Fifth Circuit, the Government believes the felony provision to be the default because, in practice, that is how federal criminal prosecutions for marijuana distribution operate. It is true that every Court of Appeals to have considered the question has held that a defendant is eligible for a 5-year sentence under §841(b)(1)(D) if the Government proves he possessed marijuana with the intent to distribute it, and that the Government need not negate the §841(b)(4) factors in each case. See, *e.g., United States v. Outen,* 286 F.3d 622, 636–639 (C.A.2 2002) (describing §841(b)(4) as a "mitigating exception"); *United States v. Hamlin,* 319 F.3d 666, 670–671 (C.A.4 2003) (collecting cases). Instead, the burden is on the defendant to show that he qualifies for the lesser sentence under §841(b) (4).

We cannot discount §841's text, however, which creates no default punishment, in favor of the procedural overlay or burdens of proof that would apply in a hypothetical federal criminal prosecution. In *Carachuri-Rosendo,* we rejected the Fifth Circuit's "'hypothetical approach,'" which examined whether conduct "'could have been punished as a felony' 'had [it] been prosecuted in federal court.'" The outcome in a hypothetical prosecution is not the relevant inquiry. Rather, our "more focused, categorical inquiry" is whether the record of conviction of the predicate offense necessarily establishes conduct that the CSA, on its own terms, makes punishable as a felony.

[T]here is a more fundamental flaw in the Government's approach: It would render even an undisputed misdemeanor an aggravated felony. This is "just what the English language tells us not to expect," and that leaves us "very wary of the

Government's position." Consider a conviction under a New York statute that provides, "A person is guilty of criminal sale of marihuana in the fifth degree when he knowingly and unlawfully sells, *without consideration,* [marihuana] of an aggregate weight of *two grams or less* ; or one cigarette containing marihuana." N.Y. Penal Law Ann. § 221.35 (West 2008) (emphasis added). This statute criminalizes only the distribution of a small amount of marijuana for no remuneration, and so all convictions under the statute would fit within the CSA misdemeanor provision, § 841(b)(4). But the Government would categorically deem a conviction under this statute to be an aggravated felony, because the statute contains the corresponding "elements" of (1) distributing (2) marijuana, and the Government believes all marijuana distribution offenses are punishable as felonies.

The same anomaly would result in the case of a noncitizen convicted of a misdemeanor in federal court under § 841(a) and (b)(4) directly. Even in that case, under the Government's logic, we would need to treat the federal misdemeanor conviction as an aggravated felony, because the conviction establishes elements of an offense that is presumptively a felony. This cannot be. "We cannot imagine that Congress took the trouble to incorporate its own statutory scheme of felonies and misdemeanors," only to have courts presume felony treatment and ignore the very factors that distinguish felonies from misdemeanors.

B

Recognizing that its approach leads to consequences Congress could not have intended, the Government hedges its argument by proposing a remedy: Noncitizens should be given an opportunity during immigration proceedings to demonstrate that their predicate marijuana distribution convictions involved only a small amount of marijuana and no remuneration, just as a federal criminal defendant could do at sentencing. This is the procedure adopted by the BIA in *Matter of Castro Rodriguez,* 25 I. & N. Dec. 698, 702 (2012), and endorsed by Justice Alito's dissent.

This solution is entirely inconsistent with both the INA's text and the categorical approach. As noted, the relevant INA provisions ask what the noncitizen was "convicted of," not what he did, and the inquiry in immigration proceedings is limited accordingly. The Government cites no statutory authority for such case-specific factfinding in immigration court, and none is apparent in the INA. Indeed, the Government's main categorical argument would seem to preclude this inquiry: If the Government were correct that "the fact of a marijuana-distribution conviction *alone* constitutes a CSA felony," then all marijuana distribution convictions would categorically be convictions of the drug trafficking aggravated felony, mandatory deportation would follow under the statute, and there would be no room for the Government's follow-on factfinding procedure. The Government cannot have it both ways.

Moreover, the procedure the Government envisions would require precisely the sort of *post hoc* investigation into the facts of predicate offenses that we have long deemed undesirable. The categorical approach serves "practical" purposes:

It promotes judicial and administrative efficiency by precluding the relitigation of past convictions in minitrials conducted long after the fact. Yet the Government's approach would have our Nation's overburdened immigration courts entertain and weigh testimony from, for example, the friend of a noncitizen who may have shared a marijuana cigarette with him at a party, or the local police officer who recalls to the contrary that cash traded hands. And, as a result, two noncitizens, each "convicted of" the same offense, might obtain different aggravated felony determinations depending on what evidence remains available or how it is perceived by an individual immigration judge. The categorical approach was designed to avoid this "potential unfairness."

Furthermore, the minitrials the Government proposes would be possible only if the noncitizen could locate witnesses years after the fact, notwithstanding that during removal proceedings noncitizens are not guaranteed legal representation and are often subject to mandatory detention where they have little ability to collect evidence.

Finally, the Government suggests that the immigration court's task would not be so daunting in some cases, such as those in which a noncitizen was convicted under the New York statute previously discussed or convicted directly under § 841(b)(4). True, in those cases, the record of conviction might reveal on its face that the predicate offense was punishable only as a misdemeanor. But most States do not have stand-alone offenses for the social sharing of marijuana, so minitrials concerning convictions from the other States, such as Georgia, would be inevitable.[10]

In short, to avoid the absurd consequences that would flow from the Government's narrow understanding of the categorical approach, the Government proposes a solution that largely undermines the categorical approach. That the only cure is worse than the disease suggests the Government is simply wrong.

C

The Government fears the consequences of our decision, but its concerns are exaggerated. The Government observes that, like Georgia, about half the States criminalize marijuana distribution through statutes that do not require remuneration or any minimum quantity of marijuana. As a result, the Government contends, noncitizens convicted of marijuana distribution offenses in those States will avoid "aggravated felony" determinations, purely because their convictions do not resolve whether their offenses involved federal felony conduct or misdemeanor conduct,

---

10. In addition to New York, it appears that 13 other States have separate offenses for § 841(b)(4) conduct. See Cal. Health & Safety Code Ann. § 11360(b) (West Supp.2013); Colo.Rev.Stat. Ann. § 18–18–406(5) (2012); Fla. Stat. § 893.13(2)(b)(3) (2010); Ill. Comp. Stat., ch. 20, §§ 550/3, 550/4, 550/6 (West 2010); Iowa Code § 124.410 (2009); Minn.Stat. § 152.027(4)(a) (2010); N.M. Stat. Ann. § 30–31–22(E) (Supp.2011); Ohio Rev.Code Ann. § 2925.03(C)(3)(h) (Lexis 2012 Cum.Supp.); Ore.Rev.Stat. § 475.860(3) (2011); Pa. Stat. Ann., Tit. 35, § 780–113(a)(31) (Purdon Supp.2012); S.D. Codified Laws § 22–42–7 (Supp.2012); Tex. Health & Safety Code Ann. § 481.120(b)(1) (West 2010); W. Va.Code Ann. § 60A–4–402(c) (Lexis 2010).

even though many (if not most) prosecutions involve either remuneration or larger amounts of marijuana (or both).

Escaping aggravated felony treatment does not mean escaping deportation, though. It means only avoiding mandatory removal. Any marijuana distribution offense, even a misdemeanor, will still render a noncitizen deportable as a controlled substances offender. At that point, having been found not to be an aggravated felon, the noncitizen may seek relief from removal such as asylum or cancellation of removal, assuming he satisfies the other eligibility criteria. But those forms of relief are discretionary. The Attorney General may, in his discretion, deny relief if he finds that the noncitizen is actually a member of one "of the world's most dangerous drug cartels," *post* (opinion of Alito, J.), just as he may deny relief if he concludes the negative equities outweigh the positive equities of the noncitizen's case for other reasons. As a result, "to the extent that our rejection of the Government's broad understanding of the scope of 'aggravated felony' may have any practical effect on policing our Nation's borders, it is a limited one."

In any event, serious drug traffickers may be adjudicated aggravated felons regardless, because they will likely be convicted under greater "trafficking" offenses that necessarily establish that more than a small amount of marijuana was involved. See, *e.g.*, Ga.Code Ann. § 16-13-31(c)(1) (Supp.2012) (separate provision for trafficking in more than 10 pounds of marijuana). Of course, some offenders' conduct will fall between § 841(b)(4) conduct and the more serious conduct required to trigger a "trafficking" statute. Those offenders may avoid aggravated felony status by operation of the categorical approach. But the Government's objection to that underinclusive result is little more than an attack on the categorical approach itself. We prefer this degree of imperfection to the heavy burden of relitigating old prosecutions. And we err on the side of underinclusiveness because ambiguity in criminal statutes referenced by the INA must be construed in the noncitizen's favor.

* * *

This is the third time in seven years that we have considered whether the Government has properly characterized a low-level drug offense as "illicit trafficking in a controlled substance," and thus an "aggravated felony." Once again we hold that the Government's approach defies "the 'commonsense conception'" of these terms. *Carachuri-Rosendo,* 130 S.Ct., at 2584–2585 (quoting *Lopez,* 549 U.S., at 53). Sharing a small amount of marijuana for no remuneration, let alone possession with intent to do so, "does not fit easily into the 'everyday understanding'" of "trafficking," which "'ordinarily . . . means some sort of commercial dealing.'" Nor is it sensible that a state statute that criminalizes conduct that the CSA treats as a misdemeanor should be designated an "aggravated felony." We hold that it may not be. If a noncitizen's conviction for a marijuana distribution offense fails to establish that the offense involved either remuneration or more than a small amount of marijuana, the conviction is not for an aggravated felony under the INA. The contrary judgment of the Court of Appeals is reversed, and the case is remanded for further proceedings consistent with this opinion.

It is so ordered.

[The dissenting opinions of Justices Thomas and Alito have been omitted.]

The Supreme Court ruled in Adrian Moncrieffe's favor, but his case also highlights the harsh immigration consequences of drug convictions. After all, Moncrieffe's court victory did not guarantee that he would be allowed to stay in the United States:

> Mr. Moncrieffe won a majority of the Court's sympathy. But what exactly did he win? Writing for the Court, Justice Sotomayor held that because the Georgia statute was broad enough to encompass conduct that could be considered either a federal drug felony or a misdemeanor, Mr. Moncrieffe's conviction should not be viewed categorically as an "aggravated felony." Federal law draws distinctions between drug traffickers and simple drug possessors, based in part on whether remuneration or more than a small amount of marijuana is involved. Because Georgia's statutory scheme draws no such distinctions, Mr. Moncrieffe could not have been categorically deemed a federal felon; he may well have only been a state misdemeanant.
>
> Although this ruling saved him from the "aggravated felony" grounds of removal, Mr. Moncrieffe was still deportable for having possessed a controlled substance. As Justice Sotomayor noted, "Escaping aggravated felony treatment does not mean escaping deportation, though. It means only avoiding mandatory removal." Mr. Moncrieffe is free to seek relief from the government, although such relief is discretionary.

Victor C. Romero, *A Meditation on Moncrieffe: On Marijuana, Misdemeanants, and Migration*, 49 GONZ. L. REV. 23, 32 (2014).

c. Public Housing

Department of Housing and Urban Development v. Rucker

Supreme Court of the United States
535 U.S. 125 (2002)

Chief Justice Rehnquist delivered the opinion of the Court.

With drug dealers "increasingly imposing a reign of terror on public and other federally assisted low-income housing tenants," Congress passed the Anti-Drug Abuse Act of 1988. The Act, as later amended, provides that each "public housing agency shall utilize leases which . . . provide that any criminal activity that threatens the health, safety, or right to peaceful enjoyment of the premises by other tenants or any drug-related criminal activity on or off such premises, engaged in by a public housing tenant, any member of the tenant's household, or any guest or other person under the tenant's control, shall be cause for termination of tenancy." 42 U.S.C. § 1437d (l)(6). Petitioners say that this statute requires lease terms that allow a local public housing authority to evict a tenant when a member of the tenant's household or a guest engages in drug-related criminal activity, regardless of whether the tenant knew, or had reason to know, of that activity. Respondents say it does not. We agree with petitioners.

Respondents are four public housing tenants of the Oakland Housing Authority (OHA). Paragraph 9(m) of respondents' leases, tracking the language of § 1437d(l)(6), obligates the tenants to "assure that the tenant, any member of the household, a guest, or another person under the tenant's control, shall not engage in . . . any drug-related criminal activity on or near the premises." Respondents also signed an agreement stating that the tenant "understands that if I or any member of my household or guests should violate this lease provision, my tenancy may be terminated and I may be evicted."

In late 1997 and early 1998, OHA instituted eviction proceedings in state court against respondents, alleging violations of this lease provision. The complaint alleged: (1) that the respective grandsons of respondents William Lee and Barbara Hill, both of whom were listed as residents on the leases, were caught in the apartment complex parking lot smoking marijuana; (2) that the daughter of respondent Pearlie Rucker, who resides with her and is listed on the lease as a resident, was found with cocaine and a crack cocaine pipe three blocks from Rucker's apartment; and (3) that on three instances within a 2-month period, respondent Herman Walker's caregiver and two others were found with cocaine in Walker's apartment. OHA had issued Walker notices of a lease violation on the first two occasions, before initiating the eviction action after the third violation.

United States Department of Housing and Urban Development (HUD) regulations administering § 1437d(l)(6) require lease terms authorizing evictions in these circumstances. The HUD regulations closely track the statutory language, and provide that "in deciding to evict for criminal activity, the [public housing authority] shall have discretion to consider all of the circumstances of the case. . . ." 24 CFR § 966.4(l)(5)(i) (2001). The agency made clear that local public housing authorities' discretion to evict for drug-related activity includes those situations in which "[the] tenant did not know, could not foresee, or could not control behavior by other occupants of the unit."

After OHA initiated the eviction proceedings in state court, respondents commenced actions against HUD, OHA, and OHA's director in United States District Court. They challenged HUD's interpretation of the statute under the Administrative Procedure Act, 5 U.S.C. § 706(2)(A), arguing that 42 U.S.C. § 1437d(l)(6) does not require lease terms authorizing the eviction of so-called "innocent" tenants, and, in the alternative, that if it does, then the statute is unconstitutional. The District Court issued a preliminary injunction, enjoining OHA from "terminating the leases of tenants pursuant to paragraph 9(m) of the 'Tenant Lease' for drug-related criminal activity that does not occur within the tenant's apartment unit when the tenant did not know of and had no reason to know of, the drug-related criminal activity."

A panel of the Court of Appeals reversed, holding that § 1437d(l)(6) unambiguously permits the eviction of tenants who violate the lease provision, regardless of whether the tenant was personally aware of the drug activity, and that the statute is constitutional. An en banc panel of the Court of Appeals reversed and affirmed the District Court's grant of the preliminary injunction. That court held that HUD's interpretation permitting the eviction of so-called "innocent" tenants "is inconsistent with Congressional intent and must be rejected" under the first step of *Chevron U.S.A. Inc. v. Natural Resources Defense Council, Inc.*, 467 U.S. 837, 842–843 (1984).

We granted certiorari and now reverse, holding that 42 U.S.C. § 1437d(l)(6) unambiguously requires lease terms that vest local public housing authorities with the discretion to evict tenants for the drug-related activity of household members and guests whether or not the tenant knew, or should have known, about the activity.

That this is so seems evident from the plain language of the statute. It provides that "each public housing authority shall utilize leases which . . . provide that . . . any drug-related criminal activity on or off such premises, engaged in by a public housing tenant, any member of the tenant's household, or any guest or other person under the tenant's control, shall be cause for termination of tenancy." 42 U.S.C. § 1437d(l)(6). The en banc Court of Appeals thought the statute did not address "the level of personal knowledge or fault that is required for eviction." Yet Congress' decision not to impose any qualification in the statute, combined with its use of the term "any" to modify "drug-related criminal activity," precludes any knowledge requirement. As we have explained, "the word 'any' has an expansive meaning, that is, 'one or some indiscriminately of whatever kind.'" Thus, *any* drug-related activity engaged in by the specified persons is grounds for termination, not just drug-related activity that the tenant knew, or should have known, about.

The en banc Court of Appeals also thought it possible that "under the tenant's control" modifies not just "other person," but also "member of the tenant's household" and "guest." The court ultimately adopted this reading, concluding that the statute prohibits eviction where the tenant "for a lack of knowledge or other reason, could not realistically exercise control over the conduct of a household member or guest." But this interpretation runs counter to basic rules of grammar. The disjunctive "or" means that the qualification applies only to "other person." Indeed, the view that "under the tenant's control" modifies everything coming before it in the sentence would result in the nonsensical reading that the statute applies to "a public housing tenant . . . under the tenant's control." HUD offers a convincing explanation for the grammatical imperative that "under the tenant's control" modifies only "other person": "by 'control,' the statute means control in the sense that the tenant has permitted access to the premises." Implicit in the terms "household member" or "guest" is that access to the premises has been granted by the tenant. Thus, the plain language of § 1437d(l)(6) requires leases that grant public housing authorities the discretion to terminate tenancy without regard to the tenant's knowledge of the drug-related criminal activity.

Comparing § 1437d(l)(6) to a related statutory provision reinforces the unambiguous text. The civil forfeiture statute that makes all leasehold interests subject to forfeiture when used to commit drug-related criminal activities expressly exempts tenants who had no knowledge of the activity: "No property shall be forfeited under this paragraph . . . by reason of any act or omission established by that owner to have been committed or omitted without the knowledge or consent of the owner." 21 U.S.C. § 881(a)(7). Because this forfeiture provision was amended in the same Anti-Drug Abuse Act of 1988 that created 42 U.S.C. § 1437d(l)(6), the en banc Court of Appeals thought Congress "meant them to be read consistently" so that the knowledge requirement should be read into the eviction provision. But the two sections deal with distinctly different matters. The "innocent owner" defense for drug forfeiture cases was already in existence prior to 1988 as part of 21 U.S.C. § 881(a)(7). All that Congress did in the 1988 Act was to add leasehold interests to the property interests that might be forfeited under the drug statute. And if such a forfeiture action were to be brought against a leasehold interest, it would be subject to the preexisting "innocent owner" defense. But 42 U.S.C. § 1437(d)(1)(6), with which we deal here, is a quite different measure. It is entirely reasonable to think that the Government, when seeking to transfer private property to itself in a forfeiture proceeding, should be subject to an "innocent owner defense," while it should not be when acting as a landlord in a public housing project. The forfeiture provision shows that Congress knew exactly how to provide an "innocent owner" defense. It did not provide one in § 1437d(l)(6).

The en banc Court of Appeals next resorted to legislative history. The Court of Appeals correctly recognized that reference to legislative history is inappropriate when the text of the statute is unambiguous. Given that the en banc Court of Appeals' finding of textual ambiguity is wrong there is no need to consult legislative history.

Nor was the en banc Court of Appeals correct in concluding that this plain reading of the statute leads to absurd results. The statute does not *require* the eviction of any tenant who violated the lease provision. Instead, it entrusts that decision to the local public housing authorities, who are in the best position to take account of, among other things, the degree to which the housing project suffers from "rampant drug-related or violent crime," "the seriousness of the offending action," and "the extent to which the leaseholder has . . . taken all reasonable steps to prevent or mitigate the offending action[.]" It is not "absurd" that a local housing authority may sometimes evict a tenant who had no knowledge of the drug-related activity. Such "no-fault" eviction is a common "incident of tenant responsibility under normal landlord-tenant law and practice." Strict liability maximizes deterrence and eases enforcement difficulties.

And, of course, there is an obvious reason why Congress would have permitted local public housing authorities to conduct no-fault evictions: Regardless of knowledge, a tenant who "cannot control drug crime, or other criminal activities by a household member which threaten health or safety of other residents, is a threat to other residents and the project." With drugs leading to "murders, muggings, and other forms of violence against tenants," and to the "deterioration of the physical environment that requires substantial governmental expenditures," it was reasonable for Congress to permit no-fault evictions in order to "provide public and other federally assisted low-income housing that is decent, safe, and free from illegal drugs[.]"

In another effort to avoid the plain meaning of the statute, the en banc Court of Appeals invoked the canon of constitutional avoidance. But that canon "has no application in the absence of statutory ambiguity." There are, moreover, no "serious constitutional doubts" about Congress' affording local public housing authorities the discretion to conduct no-fault evictions for drug-related crime.

The en banc Court of Appeals held that HUD's interpretation "raises serious questions under the Due Process Clause of the Fourteenth Amendment," because it permits "tenants to be deprived of their property interest without any relationship to individual wrongdoing." 237 F.3d at 1124–1125 (citing *Scales v. United States*, 367 U.S. 203, 224–225 (1961); *Southwestern Telegraph & Telephone Co. v. Danaher*, 238 U.S. 482 (1915)). But both of these cases deal with the acts of government as sovereign. In *Scales*, the United States criminally charged the defendant with knowing membership in an organization that advocated the overthrow of the United States Government. In *Danaher*, an Arkansas statute forbade discrimination among customers of a telephone company. The situation in the present cases is entirely different. The government is not attempting to criminally punish or civilly regulate respondents as members of the general populace. It is instead acting as a landlord of property that it owns, invoking a clause in a lease to which respondents have agreed and which Congress has expressly required. *Scales* and *Danaher* cast no constitutional doubt on such actions.

The Court of Appeals sought to bolster its discussion of constitutional doubt by pointing to the fact that respondents have a property interest in their leasehold interest, citing *Greene v. Lindsey*, 456 U.S. 444 (1982). This is undoubtedly true, and *Greene* held that an effort to deprive a tenant of such a right without proper notice violated the Due Process Clause of the Fourteenth Amendment. But, in the present cases, such deprivation will occur in the state court where OHA brought the unlawful detainer action against respondents. There is no indication that notice has not been given by OHA in the past, or that it will not be given in the future. Any individual factual disputes about whether the lease provision was actually violated can, of course, be resolved in these proceedings.

We hold that "Congress has directly spoken to the precise question at issue." *Chevron U.S.A. Inc. v. Natural Resources Defense Council, Inc.*, 467 U.S. at 842. Section 1437d(l)(6) requires lease terms that give local public housing authorities the discretion to terminate the lease of a tenant when a member of the household or a guest engages in drug-related activity, regardless of whether the tenant knew, or should have known, of the drug-related activity.

Accordingly, the judgment of the Court of Appeals is reversed, and the cases are remanded for further proceedings consistent with this opinion.

It is so ordered.

2. Asset Forfeiture

Asset forfeiture is hardly unique to drug enforcement, but it has played a central role in the drug war over the past few decades.

Congress established the basic structure for modern drug asset forfeiture law in 1970, with passage of the Comprehensive Drug Abuse Prevention and Control Act (which included the Controlled Substances Act). At first, forfeiture was limited to the raw materials and equipment used to manufacture controlled substances, vehicles used to distribute controlled substances, and the controlled substances themselves. In 1978, this list was expanded to include the forfeiture of drug business profits and assets purchased with drug profits.

The Comprehensive Crime Control Act of 1984 marked a turning point for civil asset forfeiture in drug cases. In it, Congress expanded forfeitable assets to include all real property used to facilitate a federal drug law violation, including "entire tracts of land and all improvements, regardless of what portion of the property facilitated the illegal activities." Marc B. Stahl, *Asset Forfeiture, Burdens of Proof and the War on Drugs*, 83 J. Crim. L. & Criminology 274, 277 (1992).

More importantly, the 1984 law gave state and federal law enforcement agencies new incentives to seize as many assets as possible. Before 1984, forfeiture proceeds went into the Treasury's General Fund. The Comprehensive Crime Control Act established an Asset Forfeiture Fund, which let law enforcement agencies keep proceeds from seizures. This Fund gives federal law enforcement agencies "a direct financial stake in generating forfeiture funds." Marian R. Williams et al., Policing for Profit: The Abuse of Civil Asset Forfeiture 11 (Institute for Justice, 2010).

To encourage state and local officials to seize more assets, the 1984 law also created the federal "equitable sharing" program. This program incentivizes increased state and local participation in asset forfeiture in two ways.

First, the program provides a formal method for sharing forfeitures in joint investigations, encouraging greater participation by state and local agencies in federal drug task forces.

Second, even if no federal agency was involved in the investigation, the equitable sharing program lets state and local agencies turn assets over to the federal government for seizure in a federal forfeiture proceeding through a process called "adoptive forfeiture." In adoptive forfeitures, the federal government receives 20% of the proceeds while state and local agencies receive the remaining 80%. Adoptive forfeitures have been especially controversial because they can allow state and local law enforcement agencies to circumvent state forfeiture restrictions. Many states limit the percentage of forfeiture proceeds that may go back to law enforcement agencies. Others require a higher burden of proof than federal law provides for in forfeiture proceedings. When a state or local agency transfers assets to the federal government for adoptive forfeiture, the federal burden of proof applies to the proceeding and state and local law enforcement agencies can retain their full 80% share, even if state law would have required some or all of the proceeds to go to other purposes (such as education or the general fund).

In the article that follows, Beth Colgan discusses how asset forfeiture can skew policing priorities.

Fines, Fees, and Forfeitures
Beth A. Colgan

4 Reforming Criminal Justice 205 (Erik Luna ed., 2017)

The revenue-generating capacity of fines, fees, and forfeitures risks perverting governmental incentives in two distinct ways. First, by promoting policing and adjudication methods that are most likely to increase revenue, governmental actors may fail to consider, or even implement policies that directly conflict with, public-safety needs. Second, systems that allow law enforcement and prosecutors to retain cash and property seized undermines the checks and balances otherwise afforded through normal budgeting practices.

There is . . . significant evidence that revenue rather than public safety drives policing decisions related to forfeitures. Eric Blumenson and Eva Nilsen have documented examples of how the thirst for cash has led to shifts in police practices. For example, a traditional drug buy-bust sting operation would involve the use of an undercover officer posing as a person interested in buying illegal drugs; following the exchange, the police would of course seize the drugs and therefore remove them from circulation. With the incentive of forfeiture laws, however, law enforcement has come to rely more heavily on the "reverse sting," under which the police pose as the dealer rather than the buyer, so that upon conclusion of the transaction, they can seize the cash used in the sale. Blumenson and Nilsen also cite to congressional testimony of former New York City Police Commissioner Patrick Murphy, who explained that financial incentives led to a policy whereby police would "impose roadblocks on the southbound lanes of I-95, which carry the cash to make drug buys, rather than the northbound lanes, which carry the drugs." While both reverse stings and forfeitures of cash arguably interrupt the illicit drug trade, the focus on obtaining cash rather than seizing drugs indicates that policing decisions are influenced by the revenue-generating power of forfeiture.

Further, forfeitures may be incentivizing policing of particular offenses where seizures of cash or property are most easily made, which would result in prioritizing the policing of drug crimes over violent offenses, which may in turn exacerbate problematic policing practices that disproportionately affect poor and minority communities. For example, one study testing the effects of allowing police to retain funds and assets seized in drug arrests found that it shifted the focus of police to activities that may produce forfeitures, and, in particular, increased arrests related to drug activity as compared to total arrests by nearly 20%. Further, in cities like Philadelphia and Washington, D.C., it appears that police may be going so far as to seize small amounts of cash—in many cases less than $20—during stop-and-frisk incidents. In other words, pressure to generate revenue may have significant implications for when and how policing occurs that may undermine public safety and intensify public concern regarding police-citizen encounters. The risk is that the focus on revenue generation will interfere with other policy considerations, including public safety.

A separate perversion of criminal justice priorities may occur where law enforcement entities or prosecutors are allowed to keep forfeited cash and property for their agency's own use, as is the case in many jurisdictions. Allowing law enforcement and prosecutors to retain funds removes the check set through budgeting processes, as it provides them the ability to set priorities that may contradict or interfere with crime-control aims of the legislative branch or the public at large. For example, under the federal "Equitable Sharing Program," the federal government "adopts" seizures of cash and property made by local and state law enforcement, thereby pulling the seized assets under federal forfeiture laws, which are at times more expansive than state laws in terms of what may be seized and more restrictive regarding the provision of procedural protections. This infusion of funds not only allows law enforcement to sidestep state restrictions on forfeiture, the retention of the profits of forfeiture insulates them from budgeting restrictions that would otherwise establish state and local control over policing overall.

Separate and distinct from the potential that inadequately designed systems for fines, fees, and forfeitures will distort criminal justice incentives, such systems can also undermine other governmental aims due to their inherently regressive nature. By entrenching or exacerbating the financial vulnerability of people and their families, fines, fees, and forfeitures can create long-term instability and familial disruption, increase criminal justice involvement, aggravate jail overcrowding, and—perhaps ironically—decrease net revenue.

Fines, fees, and forfeitures can have devastating consequences on those who are financially vulnerable, particularly in low-income communities and communities of color that are most likely to be heavily policed.

Though it does not result in ongoing debt, the forfeiture of funds or property may . . . leave people and their families in financially precarious circumstances. With, or more often without, a criminal conviction, people may lose funds they depend upon to meet basic needs, vehicles upon which they depend for transportation to work or school, or the homes in which they live.

United States v. $124,700, in U.S. Currency

United States Court of Appeals for the Eighth Circuit
458 F. 3d 822 (2006)

Colloton, J.

The United States initiated civil forfeiture proceedings against $124,700 in United States currency, alleging that the money was subject to forfeiture as the proceeds of a drug transaction or as property used to facilitate the possession, transportation, sale, concealment, receipt, or distribution of a controlled substance. Three individuals filed claims opposing the forfeiture, and after a bench trial, the district court entered judgment in favor of the claimants. The government appeals, and we reverse and remand for further proceedings.

The defendant currency was seized on May 28, 2003, from one of the claimants, Emiliano Gomez Gonzolez. According to testimony adduced at trial, Gonzolez was driving west on Interstate 80 in a rented Ford Taurus when a Nebraska State Patrol Trooper, Chris Bigsby, stopped Gonzolez for exceeding the posted speed limit. Trooper Bigsby testified that he asked Gonzolez to sit in the front passenger side of his patrol vehicle during the stop. At Bigsby's request, Gonzolez presented a Nevada driver's license and a rental contract for the car, but the rental contract was not in Gonzolez's name and did not list Gonzolez as an additional driver.

Trooper Bigsby did not speak fluent Spanish, but he testified that Gonzolez responded to his questions, which were mostly in English, in a combination of English and Spanish. Bigsby asked Gonzolez where he was going, and Gonzolez responded that he had been in Chicago for three days. Gonzolez indicated that a person named "Luis" had rented the car for him, but the name "Luis" did not match the name on the rental agreement that he presented to Trooper Bigsby. Trooper Bigsby also twice inquired whether Gonzolez had ever been arrested or placed on probation or parole, and Gonzolez said that he had not.

Before Trooper Bigsby had completed the traffic stop, another officer, Jason Brownell, stopped to ask if Bigsby needed any assistance. When Trooper Bigsby found out that Trooper Brownell had some Spanish-speaking ability, Bigsby asked if Brownell would stay and assist. Trooper Bigsby testified that with Brownell's assistance, he completed a warning citation and returned Gonzolez's license and paperwork. Having learned through his dispatcher that Gonzolez had been arrested in 2003 for driving while intoxicated, Bigsby then asked, through Trooper Brownell, if he could "ask a few more questions," and Gonzolez answered yes. Again through Trooper Brownell, Bigsby asked if Gonzolez had ever been arrested for driving while intoxicated, and Gonzolez answered that he had. Bigsby and Brownell also inquired whether any alcohol, guns, marijuana, methamphetamine, heroin, or large amounts of cash were in the car, and Gonzolez answered no. Brownell then asked for, and received, consent to search the car. Trooper Bigsby went directly to the rear passenger side of the vehicle and opened a cooler that was in the back seat, where he found a large plastic bag that contained seven bundles wrapped in rubber bands inside aluminum foil packaging. These bundles contained a total of $124,700 in currency. Gonzolez and the vehicle were then taken to the Nebraska State Patrol office in Lincoln.

In Lincoln, Trooper Bigsby continued his investigation with the help of another trooper, Sean Caradori, and Trooper Caradori's police canine, Rico. Rico was deployed to sniff the exterior of the car, and the dog alerted to the rear passenger side of the vehicle. Trooper Caradori testified that he conducted a test of the money that was found within the vehicle by hiding both the currency taken from Gonzolez's car and a separate stack of seven bills borrowed from other troopers in the troopers' break room. Caradori testified that Rico alerted to the defendant currency but not to the money borrowed from the troopers.

At trial, the government argued that the dog's alert, along with the large amount of cash that was seized, the circumstances of Gonzolez's travel, and Gonzolez's initial false denials that he was carrying cash or that he had a criminal history, showed that the currency was substantially connected to a drug transaction. The claimants, however, argued that the cash was acquired legitimately. Manuel Gomez testified that he had given Gonzolez $65,000 in cash, which was a combination of money that he had borrowed from his father-in-law and his own personal cash savings, with the expectation that Gonzolez would help him buy a refrigerated truck for the produce business. Gonzolez testified that he gave $40,000 of his own money, plus $20,000 from a friend, Andres Madrigal Morgan, as an investment in Gomez's truck. Consistent with Gonzolez's account, Andres Madrigal Morgan testified that he contributed $20,000 in proceeds from a vehicle sale to Gonzolez's investment in the truck.

Gonzolez testified that after he had pooled the cash from Madrigal Morgan and Gomez with his own cash, he heard from a friend in Chicago that a truck might be available there from a friend of the friend, and he set out for Chicago by plane, taking the cash with him in a small carry-on bag. Gonzolez said, however, that when he arrived in Chicago and his friend picked him up from the airport, he learned that the truck had been sold. In addition, the unidentified friend alerted Gonzolez that it was "bad" to carry more than $10,000 in cash on your person. Newly fearful of carrying his cash back to California by plane, Gonzolez testified that he decided to rent a car rather than fly, but because neither he nor his friend had a credit card, a third individual rented the car for him.

Gonzolez also testified that he hid the money in a cooler because he was afraid that he might be assaulted or have the money stolen if it was readily observable. He also explained that he was "scared" when the troopers began questioning him about whether he was carrying drugs or currency. He said that he lied about the money and about the names of other parties involved, because he believed that carrying large amounts of cash might be illegal, and he did not want to get his friends in trouble. With respect to Trooper Bigsby's question about whether he had ever been arrested, Gonzolez testified that Bigsby asked whether he "had any crimes" or "had been a prisoner." Gonzolez said he answered "no," despite his arrest for driving under the influence, because he "didn't think that that was a crime."

The district court concluded that the government had not established, by a preponderance of the evidence, that there was a substantial connection between the money and a drug trafficking offense. The court noted that large sums of unexplained currency can be evidence of drug trafficking, and that in this case the money was bundled in an unusual manner. The court also concluded, however, that the claimants had given a "plausible and consistent explanation for [the money's] origin and intended use," and that "the bundling is consistent with an attempt to sort the currency by contributor and conceal the currency from would-be thieves," and not just to evade law enforcement. In addition, the court observed that the government had not presented any expert testimony about "whether the manner the bundles were wrapped either increased or decreased the likelihood of the currency's use or connection with a drug trafficking offense."

With respect to the canine alert, the court agreed that the alert provided some, but only slight, evidence that the money was connected to drug trafficking. The court also considered the circumstances and route of Gonzolez's travel, and the fact that Gonzolez had lied about the names of his friends and other details, but did not believe that this evidence taken together with the other circumstances, including all the claimants' lack of significant criminal history, established a substantial connection to drug activity. Because the court determined that the money was not subject to forfeiture, it did not reach the question whether the claimants were innocent owners.

Since the enactment of the Civil Asset Forfeiture Reform Act of 2000, the burden is on the government to establish, by a preponderance of the evidence, that seized property is subject to forfeiture. Forfeiture is warranted under 21 U.S.C. § 881 when the government establishes a "'substantial connection' between the property" and a controlled substance offense. We review any predicate factual findings for clear error, but the ultimate conclusion as to whether those facts establish a "substantial connection" between seized currency and a narcotics transaction is a mixed question of law and fact that we review *de novo*.

The district court's opinion includes no finding as to the credibility of Gonzolez and the other two claimants. The court did observe that the explanations of the claimants were "plausible and consistent," but this is different from a finding that the court actually *believed* the testimony. "Plausible" means "apparently acceptable or trustworthy (sometimes with the implication of mere appearance)," and we thus read the district court's opinion to hold that given a "plausible and consistent" explanation from the claimants on one side of the balance, the government's countervailing proof was not strong enough to meet its burden of showing a substantial connection by a preponderance of the evidence.

On *de novo* review, we respectfully disagree and reach a different conclusion. We believe that the evidence as a whole demonstrates by a preponderance of the evidence that there was a substantial connection between the currency and a drug trafficking offense. Possession of a large sum of cash is "strong evidence" of a connection to drug activity and Gonzolez was carrying the very large sum of $124,700.

The currency was concealed in aluminum foil inside a cooler, and while an innocent traveler might theoretically carry more than $100,000 in cash across country and seek to conceal funds from would-be thieves on the highway, we have adopted the common-sense view that bundling and concealment of large amounts of currency, combined with other suspicious circumstances, supports a connection between money and drug trafficking. The canine alert also supports the connection.

The route and circumstances of Gonzolez's travel were highly suspicious. Gonzolez had flown on a one-way ticket, which we have previously acknowledged is evidence in favor of forfeiture and he gave a vague explanation, attributed to advice from an unidentified third person, about why he elected to return by car. Gonzolez purportedly carried $125,000 in cash with him on his flight, for the purpose of buying a truck that he had never seen, from a third party whom he had never met, with the help of a friend whose name he could not recall at trial. This testimony does not inspire confidence in the innocence of the conduct. When he was stopped by the Nebraska State Patrol, Gonzolez was driving a rental car that was leased in the name of another person who was not present, another circumstance that gives rise to suspicion. Then, when Gonzolez was questioned by officers, he lied about having money in the car and about the names of his friends, thus giving further reason to question the legitimacy of the currency's presence. The totality of these circumstances—the large amount of concealed currency, the strange travel pattern, the inability to identify a key party in the purported innocent transaction, the unusual rental car papers, the canine alert, and the false statements to law enforcement officers—leads most naturally to the inference that Gonzolez was involved in illegal drug activity, and that the currency was substantially connected to it.

While the claimants' explanation for these circumstances may be "plausible," we think it is unlikely. We therefore conclude that the government proved by a preponderance of the evidence that the defendant currency was substantially connected to a narcotics offense. Accordingly, we reverse the judgment of the district court and remand for further proceedings.

Lay, J., dissenting.

I respectfully dissent. Although the circumstantial evidence offered by the government provides some indication that the money seized in this case may be related to criminal activity, I cannot agree that the government has proven, by a preponderance of the evidence, the requisite *substantial* connection between the currency and a *controlled substance offense.*

Notwithstanding the fact that claimants seemingly suspicious activities were reasoned away with plausible, and thus presumptively trustworthy, explanations which the government failed to contradict or rebut, I note that no drugs, drug paraphernalia, or drug records were recovered in connection with the seized money. There is no evidence claimants were ever convicted of any drug-related crime, nor is there any indication the manner in which the currency was bundled was indicative of drug use or distribution. At most, the evidence presented suggests the money seized may have been involved in some illegal activity—activity that is incapable of being ascertained on the record before us.

The law of our circuit makes clear that the possession of a large amount of cash provides strong evidence of a connection between the *res* and illegal drug activity. Yet this fact is not dispositive. A faithful reading of the cases cited by the majority from our court reveal that we have required some additional nexus between the property seized and drug activity to support forfeiture. In *United States v. U.S. Currency, in the Amount of $150,660.00*, 980 F.2d 1200 (8th Cir. 1992), we recognized such a nexus where the investigating officer immediately smelled marijuana upon inspecting the currency. In *United States v. $84,615 in U.S. Currency*, 379 F.3d 496 (8th Cir. 2004), we concluded forfeiture was proper where the owner of the seized currency "undisputedly possessed illegal drugs at the time" the currency was discovered. Most recently, in *United States v. $117,920.00 in United States Currency*, 413 F.3d 826 (8th Cir. 2005), we determined that forfeiture was warranted where materials known to be used to package and conceal drugs were recovered in close physical proximity to the seized currency, and where the investigating officer detected the smell of marijuana on some of these materials.

Here, the only evidence linking the seized money to illegal drug activity is a canine sniff that alerted officers to the presence of narcotics on the currency itself and the exterior of the rear passenger side of the rental car where the currency was discovered. However, as Justice Souter recently recognized, a large percentage of currency presently in circulation contains trace amounts of narcotics. See *Illinois v. Caballes*, 543 U.S. 405, 410–12 (2005) (Souter, J. dissenting). As a result, this fact is virtually "meaningless and likely quite prejudicial." *United States v. Carr*, 25 F.3d 1194, 1216 (3d Cir. 1994) (Becker, J., concurring). Our decision in *$84,615 in U.S. Currency* to afford this evidence only "slight" weight is thus well-founded, and this factor, taken in conjunction with the large amount of currency seized, does not favor forfeiture. Finally, the mere fact that the canine alerted officers to the presence of drug residue in a *rental car*, no doubt driven by dozens, perhaps scores, of patrons during the course of a given year, coupled with the fact that the alert came from the same location where the currency was discovered, does little to connect the money to a controlled substance offense. Therefore, I respectfully dissent.

Chapter 5

Investigating Drug Crimes

A. Investigating Victimless Crimes

As discussed in Chapter 2, the question of whether drug crimes are "victimless" and undeserving of punishment is an important part of the drug policy debate. Some argue that drug users and distributors are engaged in consensual transactions and it is inappropriate to use the criminal law just to protect drug users from themselves. Others believe that drug users can be properly understood as victims in need of the criminal law's protection and that communities and families are also victimized by the negative consequences associated with drug addiction. We will not return to this debate here.

Instead, this chapter uses "victimless crime" in a much narrower sense related to the investigation of drug offenses: drug crimes lack a complaining witness. In the case of a robbery, the victim will generally report the crime to the police. The same is not true of the manufacture or sale of controlled substances where all of the parties to the transaction are willing participants who have an incentive to keep their activities hidden from the police. As one book designed as an investigative resource for drug enforcement officers puts it, "[f]requently . . . drug enforcement agents must initiate their own cases with few initial leads." Michael D. Lyman, Practical Drug Enforcement at 2 (3rd ed. 2007). Though many of the law enforcement techniques considered in this section are used in the policing of all crimes, the victimless nature of drug offenses makes these techniques uniquely important to drug investigations.

1. Police Participation in Drug Crimes

Undercover police operations are "a firmly entrenched aspect of contemporary American policing." Elizabeth E. Joh, *Breaking the Law to Enforce It: Undercover Police Participation in Crime*, 62 Stan. L. Rev. 155, 161 (2009). This is especially true for the policing of "secretive, complex, and consensual activities," like drug transactions. *Id.* at 162. Police participation in crime was not always so common, however. In the decision below, issued in 1899, a Missouri court considered whether a city council member could be convicted of gambling for placing a bet as part of an undercover sting.

Missouri v. Torphy

Court of Appeals of Missouri, Kansas City
78 Mo. App. 206 (1899)

Gill, J.

Defendant has appealed from a judgment of the lower court adjudging him guilty of the statutory crime of gambling. The case was submitted to the trial judge on an agreed statement of facts, the substance of which was, that while defendant was a member of the city council of Carthage and as such one of the committee on police, he undertook, under the instruction and direction of the mayor, to ferret out and secure evidence against certain parties suspected of violating the law relating to gambling. With this in view, and for this purpose only, the defendant visited the suspected room in Carthage; and there finding certain parties, he entered with them into a game of poker, betting a small sum of money on the result. The agreed case concedes that defendant's sole object and purpose in engaging in the game was to disarm suspicion and enable him to secure evidence to convict these habitual violators of the law.

On the facts above stated, it seems to me that defendant ought not to have been convicted; there was clearly no criminal intent. The general proposition is, that without a criminal intent there ought not to be criminal punishment. In the late work of McClain on Criminal Law, section 117, the learned author says:

"Another illustration of the doctrine that the intent determines criminality is found in the rule that a detective who joins with persons in the commission of a crime for the purpose of securing their arrest and conviction is not punishable, although he so far cooperates as to be guilty if his intention had been the same as theirs. Thus a detective who has cooperated with a criminal in committing an offense is not to be deemed an accomplice whose evidence must be corroborated." The cases cited in notes by the author fully sustain the text.

In view of the rule above stated and as announced in the foregoing authorities, the defendant ought not to be held. The other judges concurring the judgment will be reversed and defendant discharged.

Ellison, J., dissenting.

A detective, or a decoy, may seemingly take part with others in the commission of a crime or misdemeanor, for the purpose of bringing such others to justice. I think that is all the cases cited by Judge Gill will be found to sustain. But the detective can not actually commit the crime himself and escape punishment, on the ground that his object was to apprehend others. It was decided in Pennsylvania that a detective did not become the accomplice of those who murdered a man by reason of joining the conspiracy and urging the crime, his intention being to have them apprehended before the murder, though in this he failed. *Campbell v. Commonwealth*, 84 Pa. 187.

He may become a member of a band of murderers for the purpose of exposing them to justice, but he, himself, could not be excused for killing the man selected for assassination. For there he would do the act which makes up the whole crime. There are many instances where detectives, for the purpose of apprehending burglars or other thieves, join them in *their* perpetration of this offense, and such detectives, seemingly, do commit the offense, but in reality they do not convert the goods to their own use, and have no intention of doing so, and therefore the main ingredient of the crime does not attach to them. But if they joined such criminals, and though acting as detectives, they not only seemingly but did actually convert and secrete the property, they would be thieves of course, and would be punished as such.

So it has been decided that one may purchase liquor of another engaged in its illegal sale and he is not an accomplice; and this, whether he is acting as a detective or otherwise. But it would not be contended that for the purpose of discovering the illegal vendor of the liquor, a detective could engage as his clerk, or partner, and himself make the illegal sale and not be held guilty. In some jurisdictions it is a misdemeanor and in some, a felony, to commit adultery. It would scarcely be pretended that one could escape punishment when he actually committed the act, on the plea that he did it for the purpose of discovering the adulteress. The reason for all this is, that the detective has *purposely* committed *all* of the act which makes up the thing forbidden by law.

So in the case before us, the misdemeanor prohibited by law was playing at cards for money. Defendant did this: He did the thing prohibited by the statute, and he did it purposely, that is, intentionally. It will not do to say that he had no intention to gamble, for he *did* gamble, but said he did so with the view of detecting others. That was merely his motive, as distinguished from his intention. His intention was to do the act prohibited and his motive was to catch others. But one's motive, however sincere, will not excuse his violation of the penal statute. "That ultimate good was the transgressor's leading motive, while yet he intended to do what the law forbade, or that in fact good attended or followed the doing, will not avail him." 1 Bishop's Crim. Law, sec. 341. The motive to murder might be to rid the community of a bad man; or to theft or forgery, to obtain money for the payment of debts or to relieve necessities, yet these do not excuse. 1 Wharton's Crim. Law, sec. 119. In my opinion the defendant was properly convicted.

a. Entrapment

United States v. Russell

Supreme Court of the United States
411 U.S. 423 (1973)

Mr. Justice Rehnquist delivered the opinion of the Court.

Respondent Richard Russell was charged in three counts of a five-count indictment returned against him and codefendants John and Patrick Connolly. After a jury trial in the District Court, in which his sole defense was entrapment, respondent was convicted on all three counts of having unlawfully manufactured and processed methamphetamine ("speed") and of having unlawfully sold and delivered that drug. He was sentenced to concurrent terms of two years in prison for each offense, the terms to be suspended on the condition that he spend six months in prison and be placed on probation for the following three years. On appeal, the United States Court of Appeals for the Ninth Circuit, one judge dissenting, reversed the conviction solely for the reason that an undercover agent supplied an essential chemical for manufacturing the methamphetamine which formed the basis of respondent's conviction. The court concluded that as a matter of law "a defense to a criminal charge may be founded upon an intolerable degree of governmental participation in the criminal enterprise." We granted certiorari and now reverse that judgment.

There is little dispute concerning the essential facts in this case. On December 7, 1969, Joe Shapiro, an undercover agent for the Federal Bureau of Narcotics and Dangerous Drugs, went to respondent's home on Whidbey Island in the State of Washington where he met with respondent and his two codefendants, John and Patrick Connolly. Shapiro's assignment was to locate a laboratory where it was believed that methamphetamine was being manufactured illicitly. He told the respondent and the Connollys that he represented an organization in the Pacific Northwest that was interested in controlling the manufacture and distribution of methamphetamine. He then made an offer to supply the defendants with the chemical phenyl-2-propanone, an essential ingredient in the manufacture of methamphetamine, in return for one-half of the drug produced. This offer was made on the condition that Agent Shapiro be shown a sample of the drug which they were making and the laboratory where it was being produced.

During the conversation, Patrick Connolly revealed that he had been making the drug since May 1969 and since then had produced three pounds of it. John Connolly gave the agent a bag containing a quantity of methamphetamine that he represented as being from "the last batch that we made." Shortly thereafter, Shapiro and Patrick Connolly left respondent's house to view the laboratory which was located in the Connolly house on Whidbey Island. At the house, Shapiro observed an empty bottle bearing the chemical label phenyl-2-propanone.

By prearrangement, Shapiro returned to the Connolly house on December 9, 1969, to supply 100 grams of propanone and observe the manufacturing process. When he arrived he observed Patrick Connolly and the respondent cutting up pieces of aluminum foil and placing them in a large flask. There was testimony that some of the foil pieces accidentally fell on the floor and were picked up by the respondent and Shapiro and put into the flask.[3] Thereafter, Patrick Connolly added all of the necessary chemicals, including the propanone brought by Shapiro, to make two batches of methamphetamine. The manufacturing process having been completed the following morning, Shapiro was given one-half of the drug and respondent kept

3. Agent Shapiro did not otherwise participate in the manufacture of the drug or direct any of the work.

the remainder. Shapiro offered to buy, and the respondent agreed to sell, part of the remainder for $60.

About a month later, Shapiro returned to the Connolly house and met with Patrick Connolly to ask if he was still interested in their "business arrangement." Connolly replied that he was interested but that he had recently obtained two additional bottles of phenyl-2-propanone and would not be finished with them for a couple of days. He provided some additional methamphetamine to Shapiro at that time. Three days later Shapiro returned to the Connolly house with a search warrant and, among other items, seized an empty 500-gram bottle of propanone and a 100-gram bottle, not the one he had provided, that was partially filled with the chemical.

There was testimony at the trial of respondent and Patrick Connolly that phenyl-2-propanone was generally difficult to obtain. At the request of the Bureau of Narcotics and Dangerous Drugs, some chemical supply firms had voluntarily ceased selling the chemical.

At the close of the evidence, and after receiving the District Judge's standard entrapment instruction,[4] the jury found the respondent guilty on all counts charged. On appeal, the respondent conceded that the jury could have found him predisposed to commit the offenses but argued that on the facts presented there was entrapment as a matter of law. The Court of Appeals agreed, although it did not find the District Court had misconstrued or misapplied the traditional standards governing the entrapment defense. Rather, the court in effect expanded the traditional notion of entrapment, which focuses on the predisposition of the defendant, to mandate dismissal of a criminal prosecution whenever the court determines that there has been "an intolerable degree of governmental participation in the criminal enterprise." In this case the court decided that the conduct of the agent in supplying a scarce ingredient essential for the manufacture of a controlled substance established that defense.

This new defense was held to rest on either of two alternative theories. One theory is based on two lower court decisions which have found entrapment, regardless of predisposition, whenever the government supplies contraband to the defendants. The second theory, a nonentrapment rationale, is based on a recent Ninth Circuit decision that reversed a conviction because a government investigator was so enmeshed in the criminal activity that the prosecution of the defendants was held to be repugnant to the American criminal justice system. The court below held that these two rationales constitute the same defense, and that only the label distinguishes them. In any event, it held that "both theories are premised on fundamental

4. The District Judge stated the governing law on entrapment as follows: "Where a person already has the willingness and the readiness to break the law, the mere fact that the government agent provides what appears to be a favorable opportunity is not entrapment." He then instructed the jury to acquit respondent if it had a "reasonable doubt whether the defendant had the previous intent or purpose to commit the offense . . . and did so only because he was induced or persuaded by some officer or agent of the government." No exception was taken by respondent to this instruction.

concepts of due process and evince the reluctance of the judiciary to countenance 'overzealous law enforcement.'"

This Court first recognized and applied the entrapment defense in *Sorrells v. United States*, 287 U.S. 435 (1932). In *Sorrells*, a federal prohibition agent visited the defendant while posing as a tourist and engaged him in conversation about their common war experiences. After gaining the defendant's confidence, the agent asked for some liquor, was twice refused, but upon asking a third time the defendant finally capitulated, and was subsequently prosecuted for violating the National Prohibition Act.

Mr. Chief Justice Hughes, speaking for the Court, held that as a matter of statutory construction the defense of entrapment should have been available to the defendant. Under the theory propounded by the Chief Justice, the entrapment defense prohibits law enforcement officers from instigating a criminal act by persons "otherwise innocent in order to lure them to its commission and to punish them." Thus, the thrust of the entrapment defense was held to focus on the intent or predisposition of the defendant to commit the crime. "If the defendant seeks acquittal by reason of entrapment he cannot complain of an appropriate and searching inquiry into his own conduct and predisposition as bearing upon that issue."

Mr. Justice Roberts concurred but was of the view "that courts must be closed to the trial of a crime instigated by the government's own agents." The difference in the view of the majority and the concurring opinions is that in the former the inquiry focuses on the predisposition of the defendant, whereas in the latter the inquiry focuses on whether the government "instigated the crime."

In 1958[, in *Sherman v. United States*,] the Court again considered the theory underlying the entrapment defense and expressly reaffirmed the view expressed by the *Sorrells* majority. In *Sherman* the defendant was convicted of selling narcotics to a Government informer. As in *Sorrells*, it appears that the Government agent gained the confidence of the defendant and, despite initial reluctance, the defendant finally acceded to the repeated importunings of the agent to commit the criminal act. On the basis of *Sorrells*, this Court reversed the affirmance of the defendant's conviction.

In affirming the theory underlying *Sorrells*, Mr. Chief Justice Warren for the Court, held that "to determine whether entrapment has been established, a line must be drawn between the trap for the unwary innocent and the trap for the unwary criminal."

In the instant case, respondent asks us to reconsider the theory of the entrapment defense as it is set forth in the majority opinions in *Sorrells* and *Sherman*. His principal contention is that the defense should rest on constitutional grounds. He argues that the level of Shapiro's involvement in the manufacture of the methamphetamine was so high that a criminal prosecution for the drug's manufacture violates the fundamental principles of due process. The respondent contends that the same factors that led this Court to apply the exclusionary rule to illegal searches and seizures, *Weeks v. United States*, 232 U.S. 383 (1914); *Mapp v. Ohio*, 367 U.S. 643 (1961), and confessions, *Miranda v. Arizona,* 384 U.S. 436 (1966), should be considered here. But he would have the Court go further in deterring undesirable official conduct by requiring that any prosecution be barred absolutely because of the police involvement in criminal activity. The analogy is imperfect in any event, for the principal reason behind the adoption of the exclusionary rule was the Government's "failure to observe its own laws." *Mapp v. Ohio, supra,* at 659. Unlike the situations giving rise to the holdings in *Mapp* and *Miranda*, the Government's conduct here violated no independent constitutional right of the respondent. Nor did Shapiro violate any federal statute or rule or commit any crime in infiltrating the respondent's drug enterprise.

Respondent would overcome this basic weakness in his analogy to the exclusionary rule cases by having the Court adopt a rigid constitutional rule that would preclude any prosecution when it is shown that the criminal conduct would not have been possible had not an undercover agent "supplied an indispensable means to the commission of the crime that could not have been obtained otherwise, through legal or illegal channels." Even if we were to surmount the difficulties attending the notion that due process of law can be embodied in fixed rules, and those attending respondent's particular formulation, the rule he proposes would not appear to be of significant benefit to him. For, on the record presented, it appears that he cannot fit within the terms of the very rule he proposes.

The record discloses that although the propanone was difficult to obtain, it was by no means impossible. The defendants admitted making the drug both before and after those batches made with the propanone supplied by Shapiro. Shapiro testified that he saw an empty bottle labeled phenyl-2-propanone on his first visit to the laboratory on December 7, 1969. And when the laboratory was searched pursuant to a search warrant on January 10, 1970, two additional bottles labeled phenyl-2-propanone were seized. Thus, the facts in the record amply demonstrate that the propanone used in the illicit manufacture of methamphetamine not only *could* have been obtained without the intervention of Shapiro but was in fact obtained by these defendants.

While we may some day be presented with a situation in which the conduct of law enforcement agents is so outrageous that due process principles would absolutely bar the government from invoking judicial processes to obtain a conviction, the instant case is distinctly not of that breed. Shapiro's contribution of propanone to the criminal enterprise already in process was scarcely objectionable. The chemical is by itself a harmless substance and its possession is legal. While the Government may have been seeking to make it more difficult for drug rings, such as that of which respondent was a member, to obtain the chemical, the evidence described above shows that it nonetheless was obtainable. The law enforcement conduct here stops far short of violating that "fundamental fairness, shocking to the universal sense of justice," mandated by the Due Process Clause of the Fifth Amendment.

The illicit manufacture of drugs is not a sporadic, isolated criminal incident, but a continuing, though illegal, business enterprise. In order to obtain convictions for illegally manufacturing drugs, the gathering of evidence of past unlawful conduct frequently proves to be an all but impossible task. Thus in drug-related offenses law enforcement personnel have turned to one of the only practicable means of detection: the infiltration of drug rings and a limited participation in their unlawful present practices. Such infiltration is a recognized and permissible means of investigation; if that be so, then the supply of some item of value that the drug ring requires must, as a general rule, also be permissible. For an agent will not be taken into the confidence of the illegal entrepreneurs unless he has something of value to offer them. Law enforcement tactics such as this can hardly be said to violate "fundamental fairness" or "shocking to the universal sense of justice[.]"

Respondent also urges, as an alternative to his constitutional argument, that we broaden the nonconstitutional defense of entrapment in order to sustain the judgment of the Court of Appeals. This Court's opinions in *Sorrells v. United States* and *Sherman v. United States* held that the principal element in the defense of entrapment was the defendant's predisposition to commit the crime. Respondent conceded in the Court of Appeals, as well he might, "that he may have harbored a predisposition to commit the charged offenses." Yet he argues that the jury's refusal to find entrapment under the charge submitted to it by the trial court should be overturned and the view[] of Justice[] Roberts in *Sorrells*, which [would] make the essential element of the defense turn on the type and degree of governmental conduct, be adopted as the law.

We decline to overrule these cases. *Sorrells* is a precedent of long standing that has already been once reexamined in *Sherman* and implicitly there reaffirmed. Since the defense is not of a constitutional dimension, Congress may address itself to the question and adopt any substantive definition of the defense that it may find desirable.

Critics of the rule laid down in *Sorrells* and *Sherman* have suggested that its basis in the implied intent of Congress is largely fictitious, and have pointed to what they conceive to be the anomalous difference between the treatment of a defendant who is solicited by a private individual and one who is entrapped by a government agent. Questions have been likewise raised as to whether "predisposition" can be factually established with the requisite degree of certainty. Arguments such as these, while not devoid of appeal, have been twice previously made to this Court, and twice rejected by it, first in *Sorrells* and then in *Sherman*.

We believe that at least equally cogent criticism has been made of the concurring views in these cases. Commenting in *Sherman* on Mr. Justice Roberts' position in *Sorrells* that "although the defendant could claim that the Government had induced him to commit the crime, the Government could not reply by showing that the defendant's criminal conduct was due to his own readiness and not to the persuasion of government agents," Mr. Chief Justice Warren quoted the observation of Judge Learned Hand in an earlier stage of that proceeding: "'Indeed, it would seem probable that, if there were no reply [to the claim of inducement], it would be impossible ever to secure convictions of any offences which consist of transactions that are carried on in secret.'"

Nor does it seem particularly desirable for the law to grant complete immunity from prosecution to one who himself planned to commit a crime, and then committed it, simply because government undercover agents subjected him to inducements which might have seduced a hypothetical individual who was not so predisposed. We are content to leave the matter where it was left by the Court in *Sherman*:

> "The function of law enforcement is the prevention of crime and the apprehension of criminals. Manifestly, that function does not include the manufacturing of crime. Criminal activity is such that stealth and strategy are necessary weapons in the arsenal of the police officer. However, 'A different question is presented when the criminal design originates with the officials of the Government, and they implant in the mind of an innocent person the disposition to commit the alleged offense and induce its commission in order that they may prosecute.'"

Those cases establish that entrapment is a relatively limited defense. It is rooted, not in any authority of the Judicial Branch to dismiss prosecutions for what it feels to have been "overzealous law enforcement," but instead in the notion that Congress could not have intended criminal punishment for a defendant who has committed all the elements of a proscribed offense, but was induced to commit them by the Government.

Sorrells and *Sherman* both recognize "that the fact that officers or employees of the Government merely afford opportunities or facilities for the commission of the offense does not defeat the prosecution". Nor will the mere fact of deceit defeat a prosecution, for there are circumstances when the use of deceit is the only practicable law enforcement technique available. It is only when the Government's deception actually implants the criminal design in the mind of the defendant that the defense of entrapment comes into play.

Respondent's concession in the Court of Appeals that the jury finding as to predisposition was supported by the evidence is, therefore, fatal to his claim of entrapment. He was an active participant in an illegal drug manufacturing enterprise which began before the Government agent appeared on the scene, and continued after the Government agent had left the scene. He was, in the words of *Sherman*, not an "unwary innocent" but an "unwary criminal." The Court of Appeals was wrong, we believe, when it sought to broaden the principle laid down in *Sorrells* and *Sherman*. Its judgment is therefore

Reversed.

Mr. Justice Douglas, with whom Mr. Justice Brennan concurs, dissenting.

A federal agent supplied the accused with one chemical ingredient of the drug known as methamphetamine ("speed") which the accused manufactured and for which act he was sentenced to prison. His defense was entrapment, which the Court of Appeals sustained and which the Court today disallows. Since I have an opposed view of entrapment, I dissent.

In my view, the fact that the chemical ingredient supplied by the federal agent might have been obtained from other sources is quite irrelevant. Supplying the chemical ingredient used in the manufacture of this batch of "speed" made the United States an active participant in the unlawful activity. As stated by Mr. Justice Brandeis, dissenting in *Casey v. United States*:

> "I am aware that courts—mistaking relative social values and forgetting that a desirable end cannot justify foul means—have, in their zeal to punish, sanctioned the use of evidence obtained through criminal violation of property and personal rights or by other practices of detectives even more revolting. But the objection here is of a different nature. It does not rest merely upon the character of the evidence or upon the fact that the evidence was illegally obtained. The obstacle to the prosecution lies in the fact that the alleged crime was instigated by officers of the Government; that the act for which the Government seeks to punish the defendant is the fruit of their criminal conspiracy to induce its commission. The Government may set decoys to entrap criminals. But it may not provoke or create a crime and then punish the criminal, its creature."
>
> Mr. Justice Roberts in *Sorrells* put the idea in the following words:
>
> "The applicable principle is that courts must be closed to the trial of a crime instigated by the government's own agents. No other issue, no comparison of equities as between the guilty official and the guilty defendant, has any place in the enforcement of this overruling principle of public policy."

Federal agents play a debased role when they become the instigators of the crime, or partners in its commission, or the creative brain behind the illegal scheme. That is what the federal agent did here when he furnished the accused with one of the chemical ingredients needed to manufacture the unlawful drug.

Mr. Justice Stewart, with whom Mr. Justice Brennan and Mr. Justice Marshall join, dissenting.

In *Sorrells v. United States* and *Sherman v. United States* the Court took what might be called a "subjective" approach to the defense of entrapment. In that view, the defense is predicated on an unexpressed intent of Congress to exclude from its criminal statutes the prosecution and conviction of persons, "otherwise innocent," who have been lured to the commission of the prohibited act through the Government's instigation. The key phrase in this formulation is "otherwise innocent," for the entrapment defense is available under this approach only to those who would not have committed the crime but for the Government's inducements. Thus, the subjective approach focuses on the conduct and propensities of the particular defendant in each individual case: if he is "otherwise innocent," he may avail himself of the defense; but if he had the "predisposition" to commit the crime, or if the "criminal design" originated with him, then—regardless of the nature and extent of the Government's participation—there has been no entrapment. And, in the absence of a conclusive showing one way or the other, the question of the defendant's "predisposition" to the crime is a question of fact for the jury. The Court today adheres to this approach.

The concurring opinion of Mr. Justice Roberts in the *Sorrells* case, and that of Mr. Justice Frankfurter in the *Sherman* case, took a different view of the entrapment defense. In their concept, the defense is not grounded on some unexpressed intent of Congress to exclude from punishment under its statutes those otherwise innocent persons tempted into crime by the Government, but rather on the belief that "the methods employed on behalf of the Government to bring about conviction cannot be countenanced." Thus, the focus of this approach is not on the propensities and predisposition of a specific defendant, but on "whether the police conduct revealed in the particular case falls below standards, to which common feelings respond, for the proper use of governmental power." Phrased another way, the question is whether—regardless of the predisposition to crime of the particular defendant involved—the governmental agents have acted in such a way as is likely to instigate or create a criminal offense. Under this approach, the determination of the lawfulness of the Government's conduct must be made—as it is on all questions involving the legality of law enforcement methods—by the trial judge, not the jury.

In my view, this objective approach to entrapment advanced by the Roberts opinion in *Sorrells* and the Frankfurter opinion in *Sherman* is the only one truly consistent with the underlying rationale of the defense. Indeed, the very basis of the entrapment defense itself demands adherence to an approach that focuses on the conduct of the governmental agents, rather than on whether the defendant was "predisposed" or "otherwise innocent." I find it impossible to believe that the purpose of the defense is to effectuate some unexpressed congressional intent to exclude from its criminal statutes persons who committed a prohibited act, but would not have done so except for the Government's inducements. For, as Mr. Justice Frankfurter put it, "the only legislative intention that can with any show of reason be extracted from the statute is the intention to make criminal precisely the conduct in which the defendant has engaged." Since, by definition, the entrapment defense cannot arise unless the defendant actually committed the proscribed act, that defendant is manifestly covered by the terms of the criminal statute involved.

Furthermore, to say that such a defendant is "otherwise innocent" or not "predisposed" to commit the crime is misleading, at best. The very fact that he has committed an act that Congress has determined to be illegal demonstrates conclusively that he is not innocent of the offense. He may not have originated the precise plan or the precise details, but he was "predisposed" in the sense that he has proved to be quite capable of committing the crime. That he was induced, provoked, or tempted to do so by government agents does not make him any more innocent or any less predisposed than he would be if he had been induced, provoked, or tempted by a private person—which, of course, would not entitle him to cry "entrapment." Since the only difference between these situations is the identity of the tempter, it follows that the significant focus must be on the conduct of the government agents, and not on the predisposition of the defendant.

The purpose of the entrapment defense, then, cannot be to protect persons who are "otherwise innocent." Rather, it must be to prohibit unlawful governmental activity in instigating crime. As Mr. Justice Brandeis stated in *Casey v. United States*: "This prosecution should be stopped, not because some right of Casey's has been denied, but in order to protect the Government. To protect it from illegal conduct of its officers. To preserve the purity of its courts." If that is so, then whether the particular defendant was "predisposed" or "otherwise innocent" is irrelevant; and the important question becomes whether the Government's conduct in inducing the crime was beyond judicial toleration.

This does not mean, of course, that the Government's use of undercover activity, strategy, or deception is necessarily unlawful. Indeed, many crimes, especially so-called victimless crimes, could not otherwise be detected. Thus, government agents may engage in conduct that is likely, when objectively considered, to afford a person ready and willing to commit the crime an opportunity to do so.

But when the agents' involvement in criminal activities goes beyond the mere offering of such an opportunity, and when their conduct is of a kind that could induce or instigate the commission of a crime by one not ready and willing to commit it, then—regardless of the character or propensities of the particular person induced—I think entrapment has occurred. For in that situation, the Government has engaged in the impermissible manufacturing of crime, and the federal courts should bar the prosecution in order to preserve the institutional integrity of the system of federal criminal justice.

Since, in my view, it does not matter whether the respondent was predisposed to commit the offense of which he was convicted, the focus must be, rather, on the conduct of the undercover government agent. What the agent did here was to meet with a group of suspected producers of methamphetamine, including the respondent; to request the drug; to offer to supply the chemical phenyl-2-propanone in exchange for one-half of the methamphetamine to be manufactured therewith; and, when that offer was accepted, to provide the needed chemical ingredient, and to purchase some of the drug from the respondent.

It is undisputed that phenyl-2-propanone is an essential ingredient in the manufacture of methamphetamine; that it is not used for any other purpose; and that, while its sale is not illegal, it is difficult to obtain, because a manufacturer's license is needed to purchase it, and because many suppliers, at the request of the Federal Bureau of Narcotics and Dangerous Drugs, do not sell it at all. It is also undisputed that the methamphetamine which the respondent was prosecuted for manufacturing and selling was all produced on December 10, 1969, and that all the phenyl-2-propanone used in the manufacture of that batch of the drug was provided by the government agent. In these circumstances, the agent's undertaking to supply this ingredient to the respondent, thus making it possible for the Government to prosecute him for manufacturing an illicit drug with it, was, I think, precisely the type of governmental conduct that the entrapment defense is meant to prevent.

[A]ssuming in this case that the phenyl-2-propanone was obtainable through independent sources, the fact remains that that used for the particular batch of methamphetamine involved in all three counts of the indictment with which the respondent was charged—*i.e.*, that produced on December 10, 1969—was supplied by the Government. This essential ingredient was indisputably difficult to obtain, and yet what was used in committing the offenses of which the respondent was convicted was offered to the respondent by the Government agent, on the agent's own initiative, and was readily supplied to the respondent in needed amounts. If the chemical was so easily available elsewhere, then why did not the agent simply wait until the respondent had himself obtained the ingredients and produced the drug, and then buy it from him? The very fact that the agent felt it incumbent upon him to offer to supply phenyl-2-propanone in return for the drug casts considerable doubt on the theory that the chemical could easily have been procured without the agent's intervention, and that therefore the agent merely afforded an opportunity for the commission of a criminal offense.

In this case, the chemical ingredient was available only to licensed persons, and the Government itself had requested suppliers not to sell that ingredient even to people with a license. Yet the Government agent readily offered, and supplied, that ingredient to an unlicensed person and asked him to make a certain illegal drug with it. The Government then prosecuted that person for making the drug produced *with the very ingredient* which its agent had so helpfully supplied. This strikes me as the very pattern of conduct that should be held to constitute entrapment as a matter of law.

It is the Government's duty to prevent crime, not to promote it. Here, the Government's agent asked that the illegal drug be produced for him, solved his quarry's practical problems with the assurance that he could provide the one essential ingredient that was difficult to obtain, furnished that element as he had promised, and bought the finished product from the respondent—all so that the respondent could be prosecuted for producing and selling the very drug for which the agent had asked and for which he had provided the necessary component. Under the objective approach that I would follow, this respondent was entrapped, regardless of his predisposition or "innocence."

In the words of Mr. Justice Roberts:

"The applicable principle is that courts must be closed to the trial of a crime instigated by the government's own agents. No other issue, no comparison of equities as between the guilty official and the guilty defendant, has any place in the enforcement of this overruling principle of public policy."

I would affirm the judgment of the Court of Appeals.

Justice Rehnquist's opinion explains the rationale for the "subjective" test for entrapment. The subjective test considers the defendant's state of mind to determine whether he was "predisposed" to commit the offense. In dissent, Justice Stewart made the case for the "objective" test for entrapment, which focuses on the government's conduct rather than the defendant's predisposition and asks whether the government's actions were "of a kind that could induce or instigate the commission of a crime by one not ready and willing to commit it."

Though most states have followed the federal approach and adopted the subjective test, a sizeable minority employ the objective test. *See*, Derrick Augustus Carter, *To Catch the Lion, Tether the Goat: Entrapment, Conspiracy, and Sentencing Manipulation*, 42 Akron L. Rev. 135, 145–151 (2009) (providing an overview of the subjective, objective, and hybrid approaches to entrapment).

Utah v. J.D.W.

Court of Appeals of Utah
910 P.2d 1242 (1995)

Bench, J.

Appellant J.D.W., a seventeen-year-old minor, appeals from the trial court's determination that J.D.W. was not entrapped into committing a drug offense.

J.D.W. and a friend went to the Layton Hills Mall to buy a musical compact disc. While there, they were approached by officer Dave Wakefield of the Davis Metro Narcotics Strike Force. Wakefield asked if they were interested in a smoke. J.D.W.'s friend asked "smoke what?" and Wakefield made a gesture simulating smoking marijuana. Wakefield told them that he had some marijuana and hashish and that if they were interested they could go outside and look at it. J.D.W. and his friend thereupon followed Wakefield outside. Once outside, J.D.W.'s friend stopped while J.D.W. and Wakefield continued on a short distance further. Wakefield presented J.D.W. a baggy containing marijuana. J.D.W. took the baggy, "separated the buds from the shake" and smelled the contents. Wakefield also offered J.D.W. the hashish, but J.D.W. refused it. J.D.W. asked how much the marijuana cost. Wakefield told him that it was $35. J.D.W. only had a $100 bill and offered to go get change. Wakefield told J.D.W. that he could make change, whereupon J.D.W. paid Wakefield, who then gave J.D.W. the marijuana and the change. Wakefield then arrested J.D.W. for possession of a controlled substance.

J.D.W. was charged in a juvenile court petition with one count of possession of a controlled substance, a class B misdemeanor, in violation of Utah Code Ann. § 58-37-8(2)(a)(i). J.D.W. filed a motion to dismiss based on a claim of entrapment. After an evidentiary hearing on J.D.W.'s motion to dismiss, the trial court issued a memorandum decision in which it determined, based on the facts, that J.D.W. was not entrapped.

J.D.W. entered a conditional guilty plea in which he preserved his right to challenge the trial court's denial of his motion to dismiss. The issue on appeal is whether J.D.W. was entrapped, as a matter of law, when he purchased marijuana from an undercover police officer.

J.D.W. asks this court to adopt the entrapment per se rule, that is, anytime the police or their agents provide drugs for sale, then that action automatically constitutes entrapment. *See State v. Kummer*, 481 N.W.2d 437 (N.D. 1992). In Utah, however, the entrapment per se rule has never been adopted. Utah Code Ann. § 76-2-303(1) (1994) provides, in pertinent part:

> Entrapment occurs when a law enforcement officer or a person directed by or acting in cooperation with the officer induces the commission of an offense in order to obtain evidence of the commission . . . creating a substantial risk that the offense would be committed by one not otherwise ready to commit it. Conduct merely affording a person an opportunity to commit an offense does not constitute entrapment.

Several factors must be considered in determining whether government action induces criminal activity or, conversely, if it merely affords a person the opportunity to participate in criminal activity. "The transactions leading up to the offense, the interaction between the agent and the defendant, and the response to the inducements of the agent" must all be evaluated. Moreover, "extreme pleas of desperate illness or appeals based primarily on sympathy, pity, or close personal friendship, or offers of inordinate sums of money, are examples, depending on an evaluation of circumstances in each case, of what might constitute prohibited police conduct." Additionally, excessive pressure or goading by an undercover officer might constitute entrapment. Because entrapment is such a highly fact-intensive defense, we defer to the fact-finder's determination, unless we hold it to be erroneous, as a matter of law.

The facts in the record support the trial court's determination that, by merely providing the opportunity for a drug purchase, Wakefield did not engage in any activity that "would be effective to persuade an average person . . . to commit the offense."[2] Wakefield did not rely on any type of close, personal relationship to induce J.D.W. to buy the marijuana. Wakefield did not offer J.D.W. inordinate amounts of money, or large quantities of marijuana for an extremely low price. Rather, Wakefield used the market rate to determine the price of the marijuana. Furthermore, Wakefield did not make repeated requests or badger J.D.W. to buy the marijuana. J.D.W. immediately responded positively to Wakefield's offer. Despite the trial court's discomfort about some of Wakefield's actions, the trial court determined that Wakefield did not entrap J.D.W. under the standards set forth by the Utah Legislature.[3] We cannot say, as a matter of law, that J.D.W. was entrapped. We therefore defer to the trial court's resolution of the issue.

---

2. On the day of J.D.W.'s drug purchase, Wakefield approached over one hundred people in the mall. No one but J.D.W. made a purchase.

3. The trial court was concerned by the fact that Officer Wakefield sold drugs to a juvenile in a "drug-free zone." There is nothing, however, in the statute that precludes such activity as a matter of law. Officers are specifically exempted from the provisions of the statute establishing "drug-free zones" so long as the officers are acting within the scope of their employment. J.D.W. did not argue below, that Wakefield was acting outside the scope of his employment. J.D.W. also made no claim that Wakefield had entrapped J.D.W. because he sold drugs to a person that was not previously suspected of drug activity. Based on the facts and arguments presented at the evidentiary hearing, the trial court ruled that J.D.W. was not entrapped as the defense has been outlined by the legislature.

Affirmed.

Orme, J (concurring in the result).

Given clear and apparently controlling case law in Utah, I must reluctantly concur in this court's judgment affirming the trial court's ruling on this troublesome entrapment issue. In so doing, I must also note that, like the trial court, I am very concerned about the incident which led to charges in this case.

We have the situation in which an officer, newly assigned to drug enforcement responsibilities, takes marijuana from the police evidence room and goes to a nearby shopping mall where, for a period of some hours, he bothers innocent passers-by, many of whom are in the company of young children, and none of whom has been previously suspected of using drugs or has expressed to the officer any interest in procuring illegal drugs prior to his solicitation. Many of the shoppers were predictably annoyed that an apparent drug dealer would be openly purveying his wares in the common area of the local mall and several complained to mall management.

In what the Legislature has taken pains to characterize as a "drug-free zone," the drug-selling officer was not only making a nuisance of himself, but was—but for the cloak of statutory immunity—engaged in a course of trespass, soliciting illegal drug sales, and contributing to the delinquency of minors. It is reprehensible to me that someone charged with upholding the law would set about in this fashion to see if a randomly targeted minor, presented with adequate temptation, is willing to break the law.

I think what the officer did is indefensible. The overall societal cost of such methods is simply too great to justify the arrest of a single juvenile purchaser. I regret that the current state of the law is such that I can do nothing more than fuss about it. My hope is that the Supreme Court will grant certiorari in this case and consider the advisability of adopting some kind of per se entrapment doctrine, see, e.g., *State v. Kummer,* 481 N.W.2d 437, 441–44 (N.D. 1992), or consider whether "the conduct of the law enforcement agents is so outrageous that due process principles would absolutely bar the government from invoking judicial processes to obtain a conviction." *United States v. Russell,* 411 U.S. 423, 431–32 (1973). Alternatively, perhaps the Legislature will see fit to tighten up the "drug-free zone" concept so that such zones are completely drug free rather than only free of drugs except those introduced by the "good guys," or, at least, to limit police solicitations of this sort to individuals who have previously been identified as suspected drug users or traffickers.

Subjecting the general public to unwelcome and unsolicited offers to buy drugs is simply not a police method which our society should embrace as a tactic in the war on drugs.

It is not the prerogative of courts to modify the statutory scheme established by the legislature. The courts can only give construction to statutes as provided by the legislature. Any attempt to change the statutory scheme that allows law enforcement officers to sell drugs to a juvenile in a "drug-free zone" should therefore be addressed to the legislature.

In *J.D.W.*, the concurring judge laments the "cloak of statutory immunity" that allowed a police officer to sell marijuana to a minor in a school zone. What limitations should the law place on immunity for police participation in crime? If police officers can sell marijuana to a minor, as in *J.D.W.*, should they also be allowed to commit robbery or a violent crime while working undercover?

As Elizabeth Joh has explained, "the conditions under which undercover police officers may participate in crime have seldom been the subject of regulatory oversight" and are instead governed by a "patchwork of applicable state and federal constitutional law restraints that loosely regulates undercover operations[.]" Elizabeth E. Joh, *Breaking the Law to Enforce It: Undercover Police Participation in Crime*, 62 Stan. L. Rev. 155, 168 (2009). In the case of drug crimes, however, there is a federal statute that directly immunizes law enforcement officials who violate the Controlled Substances Act. 21 U.S.C. § 885(d) provides that "no civil or criminal liability shall be imposed ... upon any duly authorized Federal officer lawfully engaged in the enforcement of this title, or upon any duly authorized officer of any State, territory, political subdivision thereof, the District of Columbia, of any possession of the United States, who shall be lawfully engaged in the enforcement of any law or municipal ordinance relating to controlled substances." This immunity provision has been at issue in only a handful of published decisions. In one case that stands out for its unusual set of facts, Frank Fuller, the mayor of the small town Vance, South Carolina, was prosecuted after being videotaped selling crack cocaine outside of a convenience store on four separate occasions. "Fuller freely testified at trial and acknowledged his role in the transactions but rested his defense on his claim that he was conducting a police-style undercover investigation into employee misconduct at Angler's Mini-Mart. He asserted that he had the authority as mayor to engage in such activities." The jury, as well as the United States Court of Appeals for the Fourth Circuit, was not convinced, however. *United States v. Fuller*, 162 F.3d 256 (4th Cir. 1998) ("Since we conclude, however, that Fuller was not authorized under South Carolina law to engage in illegal drug transactions as part of his investigation, the immunity conferred by 21 U.S.C. § 885(d) does not apply.").

b. Stash House Strings and the Outrageous Government Conduct Defense

In addition to the entrapment defense, undercover drug operations can occasionally give rise to a defense based on outrageous government conduct. The outrageous government conduct defense was first suggested by the Supreme Court in *United States v. Russell*, excerpted above. There, the Court noted that "we may some day be presented with a situation in which the conduct of law enforcement agents is so outrageous that due process principles would absolutely bar the government from invoking judicial processes to obtain a conviction" but concluded Richard Russell's case was "distinctly not of that breed." 411 U.S. 423, 431–32 (1973).

Unlike traditional affirmative defenses, which are considered by the jury at trial, the outrageous government conduct defense bars the prosecution altogether. Motions to dismiss based on the outrageous government conduct defense are rarely successful, however. This is because "[t]he standard of police action that would warrant the judge dismissing the case is extremely high." Katherine Tinto, *Fighting the Stash House Sting*, Champion, October 2014 16, 17 (2014). Indeed, "[t]he Supreme Court has never affirmed the dismissal of an indictment based on a finding of outrageous government conduct, nor has the Court articulated a set of guidelines for lower courts to use in determining what government conduct would be sufficiently 'outrageous' to successfully invoke the defense." Marc D. Esterow, *Lead Us Not Into Temptation: Stash House Stings and the Outrageous Government Conduct Defense*, 8 Drexel L. Rev. Online 1, 6 (2016).

The outrageous government conduct defense has become increasingly relevant as a result of so-called "stash house sting" cases. In a stash house sting, an undercover agent creates a fictional drug stash house and then tries to recruit people to help rob it. The tactic has become a favorite of the Bureau of Alcohol, Tobacco, Firearms, and Explosives (ATF). "Since 2003, the ATF has more than quadrupled the use of these controversial sting operations as part of a crime-fighting strategy meant to target armed and violent criminals. Over 1,000 individuals have been prosecuted as a result of stash house stings, and operations have taken place in major metropolitan cities all across the United States." Esterow, *supra*, at 5.

In the typical stash house sting, "an undercover officer, or informant working at the police's direction, recruits one or more suspects to rob a location where drug dealers allegedly keep large amounts of drugs, money, or weapons. The undercover officer or informant frequently poses as a disgruntled drug dealer, with both inside knowledge of the stash house and the desire to 'rip off' former employers, competitors, or customers. After meeting with the suspects on one or more occasions, and after the suspects agree to commit the robbery, the suspects are arrested, often at an arranged meeting place or in a vehicle, supposedly on their way to commit the agreed upon crimes. Defendants caught in these operations are charged with a range of crimes, including conspiracy and firearms and narcotics offenses." Tinto, *supra*, at 16. Because the stash house is fictional, "the government has 'virtually unfettered ability' to guarantee a lengthy sentence" by telling targets that an amount of drugs that triggers a mandatory minimum sentence is inside the stash house. *Id.*

United States v. Black

United States Court of Appeals for the Ninth Circuit
733 F.3d 294 (2013)

Fisher, J.

Defendants Cordae Black, Kemford Alexander, Angel Mahon and Terrance Timmons were convicted of conspiracy to possess cocaine with intent to distribute and use of a firearm in furtherance of a drug trafficking offense. They were arrested as part of a reverse sting operation set up in Phoenix, Arizona by the Bureau of Alcohol, Tobacco, Firearms and Explosives (ATF).[1] An ATF undercover agent, working with a confidential informant, recruited the defendants to carry out an armed robbery of a (fictional) cocaine stash house. They were arrested as they were on their way to rob the supposed stash house.

Before trial, the defendants moved to dismiss the indictment, contending the fake robbery was the product of outrageous government conduct. After three days of hearings on the issue, the district court denied the motions. A jury convicted the defendants on both counts. Count one, for conspiracy [to possess cocaine], carried a statutory minimum sentence of 10 years.

We agree with the district court, and affirm the denial of the defendants' motions to dismiss for outrageous government conduct. Although the *initiation* of the reverse sting operation here raises questions about possible overreaching, as we shall explain, the defendants have not met the "extremely high standard" of demonstrating that the facts underlying their arrest and prosecution are so "extreme" as to "violate[] fundamental fairness" or are "so grossly shocking . . . as to violate the universal sense of justice."

Several years ago, the Bureau of Alcohol, Tobacco, Firearms and Explosives implemented Operation Gideon, conducting a series of undercover sting operations developed to find and arrest crews engaging in violent robberies of drug stash houses (which ATF denominates as "home invasions") in residential neighborhoods. As an alternative to planting fake drugs in a stash house and confronting the armed robbers once they broke into the house, ATF developed what it believed was a safer technique. ATF agents, working undercover, would describe a fictitious cocaine stash house to suspects, offering them the opportunity to plan and carry out an armed robbery of the stash house. Once the robbery plan was developed and the crew members were on their way to what they believed was a real armed home invasion, they were arrested. ATF decided to use this investigative technique in Phoenix, Arizona because of the level of violence and the number of kidnappings that had become associated with stash house robberies.

The investigation and arrest of the defendants here involved a confidential government informant (CI) and Agent Richard Zayas, an undercover ATF agent. ATF brought the CI from Miami to Phoenix (where he had never been) specifically to assist in reverse sting operations. This work was the CI's sole source of employment, for which the CI was paid $100 per day.

The CI's role was to "try and find some people that . . . are willing to go commit a home invasion." He was to talk to such individuals, tell them that a friend had all of the information about the home invasion and then set up a meeting between the individual and Agent Zayas. He testified that he found such individuals by "go[ing]

1. A "reverse sting" occurs when the government initiates the criminal conduct, setting up a fictitious crime and arresting the criminals as they begin to carry out what they believe is a real crime.

to the bars" and "meet[ing] people" who he then approached about possibly becoming involved in such crimes. In doing so, he targeted bars in "a bad part of town, a bad bar, you know . . . bars where you've got . . . a lot of criminal activity." He was not instructed to look only for particular individuals, such as those who were already involved in an ongoing criminal operation or that he knew were about to commit a crime. Zayas would then meet with interested individuals "to determine whether or not they are actually involved in that type of crime" and provide details on the fictitious home invasion.

In July 2009, the CI went to a bar in Glendale, Arizona to meet people as part of his work with ATF. He approached a man named Curtis at the bar to see if he would be interested in doing a home invasion. Curtis was not interested but said he knew somebody who would be—Shavor Simpson, aka "Bullet." Curtis introduced the CI to Simpson, and the CI told Simpson he had a friend who "has some information on a house possibly with some dope in it." He asked Simpson whether he would be "interested in putting a crew together" to rob the house. Simpson agreed that he would do it, and the CI set up a meeting between Zayas and Simpson.

On July 16, 2009, Zayas, Simpson and the CI met in a car outside Simpson's workplace. Zayas proceeded to tell Simpson his cover story: He was a cocaine courier who transported drugs for a group of Mexican drug dealers and was unhappy with the pay he was receiving. He was interested in robbing the Mexican drug dealers as retribution for his low pay. Describing the modus operandi, Zayas told Simpson that at the beginning or end of each month, he would receive a call informing him that the drugs were ready for transportation at a particular house, and that he would have only 15 minutes to pick up the drugs or they would be moved to a new location. When he would enter the house, he would see two individuals, at least one of whom would be armed. One individual would go to a back room, obtain 6 to 7 kilograms of cocaine, give the drugs to Zayas and tell him where to take the drugs. Zayas also told Simpson that each time he did this, he could see anywhere from 22 to 39 kilograms of cocaine in the living room alone and that he did not know what might be in the back room, which contained more cocaine.

Zayas emphasized several times that he wanted to make sure the people Simpson involved in the proposed robbery have the "balls to go do it because this ain't no easy lick." He testified that, in relating the details regarding the fictitious stash house, he purposely chose details that demonstrated a particularly high potential for danger and violence to ensure that only individuals who "are truly involved in this type of crime" would agree to it and those who were not would back out.

Simpson told Zayas that the day before, he had called his "goons" who wanted to know whether "we gonna murc"[5] the men inside the stash house or "we gonna rob" them, to which Zayas responded that he did not care. Simpson said that "real [men]

5. Zayas testified that "murc" means "murder."

shoot for kill he gotta be down with that shit homey" and that he and his "goons" are "ready" and "just waiting on the . . . say so."

Simpson said that he and one of his "goons" "did this shit already" but his friend "did ten years in prison" because "his home boy snitched." He told Zayas that he was "a four time felony dog" with "17 misdemeanors" consisting of "[d]rugs, guns, drugs, guns, drugs, guns, guns, drugs . . . that's all I been locked up for bro." He also said that if anyone snitched about the operation, whether it was one of his goons or someone on Zayas' side, "we'll have to murc [him]." He said that his "boy" had everything necessary to complete the robbery: "He got ski masks, he got a leather glove and he got his guns. He got a AK, he got a M16, he got a uh, a Desert Eagle, he got a Mac10, got a 45 Glock." Simpson suggested that they meet again soon, after he had a conversation with his "goons and whoever gonna ride."

The second meeting with Agent Zayas took place on Sunday, July 26. This time, Zayas, the CI and Simpson were joined by Cordae Black, whom Simpson introduced as his "right hand soldier." Zayas repeated his cover story about being a disgruntled drug courier and what he knew about the fictitious stash house. Black proposed several robbery plans. He suggested that once Zayas was let into the stash house, Black and Simpson would run in right afterwards to take the occupants by surprise. He also mentioned the possibility of taking an occupant to the back room as a hostage to obtain the drugs that were there. Toward the end of the conversation, he told Zayas, "I got this shit down to a science man."

Simpson told Zayas that he and Black needed guns for the robbery and that they did not have any. Zayas said he did not have any either and that if he did, he would do the robbery himself. Black eventually said that getting "burners" (guns) should not be a problem.

When Black and Simpson told Zayas they intended to perform the robbery without any other crew members, Zayas questioned that decision, asking if they would be able to handle it or would need more people. He said the men in the stash house "ain't just gonna hand it to you." Black insisted that having a small crew would be better for taking the stash house by surprise. He told Zayas he had "just done this—I just done it a few times." Black and Simpson eventually said they would probably bring one more crew member.

Zayas told Black and Simpson that he would receive the next call about transporting cocaine in two days, on Tuesday, July 28. The group decided to meet again on July 27, and Zayas told Simpson and Black to bring whoever would be participating in the robbery. Simpson testified at trial that after the July 26 meeting with Black and Agent Zayas, he met with Black, Angel Mahon, Kemford Alexander and Aaron Marsh (who is not involved in this appeal) to further discuss the robbery.[6]

6. As part of his plea agreement, Simpson cooperated with the government and testified against his codefendants at trial.

The third meeting with Agent Zayas took place on July 27; Black, Simpson, Alexander, Mahon and Marsh were all present. Zayas asked whether everyone would be doing the robbery, to which Alexander responded, "Yeah." Zayas again repeated his cover story and the information he had about the fictitious stash house. Alexander asked Zayas how he wanted the robbery done. Zayas responded, "You tell me dude I mean this is your gig, I mean I don't know about this shit." Alexander asked Zayas what he wanted out of the robbery, to which Agent Zayas responded, "[I]t's an even split, bro, even split." The group made plans to meet the next day at noon. Simpson testified at trial that after the meeting, he and the other individuals who had met with Zayas went to Alexander's house to discuss the robbery. They discussed such items as what each person would do with his portion of the drugs, who would carry a gun and how many people would enter the stash house.

The next day, the group did not show up to meet Agent Zayas at noon. Zayas testified that he felt he was being watched and that the crew was conducting a surveillance of him. However, at about 12:25 p.m., as Zayas was about to leave, Black, Alexander, Marsh and Mahon pulled up in two vehicles, along with Terrance Timmons. Simpson did not show up. Zayas briefly spoke with the individuals in each vehicle, and Alexander introduced Timmons as his driver. Zayas told the crew he had rented a warehouse unit nearby where they should deliver his portion of the cocaine from the stash house and asked them to follow him there. Once the group arrived at the warehouse location, federal agents arrested the robbery crew. A search of the vehicles uncovered four loaded weapons in a hidden compartment. Each of the defendants was charged with and convicted by a jury of conspiracy to possess cocaine with intent to distribute and use of a firearm in furtherance of a drug trafficking offense.

We review de novo the district court's denial of a motion to dismiss an indictment due to outrageous government conduct.

Outrageous government conduct occurs when the actions of law enforcement officers or informants are "so outrageous that due process principles would absolutely bar the government from invoking judicial processes to obtain a conviction." *United States v. Russell,* 411 U.S. 423, 431–32 (1973). Dismissing an indictment for outrageous government conduct, however, is "limited to extreme cases" in which the defendant can demonstrate that the government's conduct "violates fundamental fairness" and is "so grossly shocking and so outrageous as to violate the universal sense of justice." This is an "extremely high standard." Indeed, there are only two reported decisions in which federal appellate courts have reversed convictions under this doctrine. *See United States v. Twigg,* 588 F.2d 373 (3d Cir.1978); *Greene v. United States,* 454 F.2d 783 (9th Cir.1971). *See also State v. Lively,* 130 Wash.2d 1, 921 P.2d 1035 (1996) (reversing drug conviction under state law, but relying on federal cases in finding outrageous government conduct).

There is no bright line dictating when law enforcement conduct crosses the line between acceptable and outrageous, so "every case must be resolved on its own particular facts." In assessing the reasonableness of various law enforcement actions and tactics, however, we have set forth ground rules that provide some guidance. For example, it is outrageous for government agents to "engineer[] and direct[] a criminal enterprise from start to finish" or for the government to use "excessive physical or mental coercion" to convince an individual to commit a crime. It is also outrageous for the government to "generat[e] . . . new crimes merely for the sake of pressing criminal charges." It is not outrageous, however, to infiltrate a criminal organization, to approach individuals who are already involved in or contemplating a criminal act, or to provide necessary items to a conspiracy. Nor is it outrageous for the government to "use 'artifice and stratagem to ferret out criminal activity.'"

The reverse sting employed here largely falls within the bounds of law enforcement tactics that have been held reasonable. Once presented with the fictitious stash house robbery proposal, Simpson, Black (and, later, their cohorts) readily and actively acted as willing participants with a professed ability to carry out a dangerous armed robbery. Nonetheless, there are two troubling aspects about this fictional sting and how it came about in the first place.

First is the fiction itself. The crimes of conviction—conspiracy to possess cocaine with intent to distribute and the use of firearms in furtherance of drug trafficking—resulted from an operation created and staged by ATF. Most of the hard evidence against the defendants consisted of words used at meetings Zayas set up with help from the CI. Zayas invented the scenario, including the need for weapons and for a crew, and the amount of cocaine involved. The only overt actions by the defendants involved showing up at meetings, including arriving at the parking lot with four hidden, loaded weapons and then driving to the storage warehouse where they were arrested. Although those actions clearly corroborate the defendants' intent to carry out an armed robbery, defendants were responding to the government's script.

This leads to our second and major concern—how the government recruited these defendants. ATF was not infiltrating a suspected crew of home invasion robbers, or seducing persons known to have actually engaged in such criminal behavior. Rather, ATF found Simpson by "trolling for targets." The CI provocatively cast his bait in places defined only by economic and social conditions: "a bad part of town, a bad bar, you know . . . bars where you've got . . . a lot of criminal activity." The risk inherent in targeting such a generalized population is that the government could create a criminal enterprise that would not have come into being but for the temptation of a big payday, a work of fiction spun out by government agents to persons vulnerable to such a ploy who would not otherwise have thought of doing such a robbery. *See Bogart*, 783 F.2d at 1436 ("Criminal sanction is not justified when the state manufactures crimes that would otherwise not occur. Punishing a defendant who commits a crime under such circumstances is not needed to deter misconduct; absent the government's involvement, no crime would have been committed.").

For [these] reasons, the initiation of this sting warrants close scrutiny, and places a burden on the government to show that our concerns are not borne out in this case.

Previous outrageous government conduct cases, viewed collectively, have identified various factors as relevant to whether the government's conduct was outrageous: (1) known criminal characteristics of the defendants; (2) individualized suspicion of the defendants; (3) the government's role in creating the crime of conviction; (4) the government's encouragement of the defendants to commit the offense conduct; (5) the nature of the government's participation in the offense conduct; and (6) the nature of the crime being pursued and necessity for the actions taken in light of the nature of the criminal enterprise at issue. In this case, the first three are most relevant to the way in which the government set up the sting; the fourth and fifth look to the propriety of the government's ongoing role in the sting. The last focuses on the justification for the particular law enforcement strategy employed. These do not constitute a formalistic checklist, but help focus our analysis of the totality of circumstances.

Individualized suspicion. The government need not have individualized suspicion of a defendant's wrongdoing before conducting an undercover investigation. Whether the government had reason to suspect an individual or identifiable group before initiating a sting operation is an important consideration, however.

In some cases where the government did not suspect a particular individual, it has focused on a category of persons it had reason to believe were involved in the type of illegal conduct being investigated. An example is *Garza-Juarez,* 992 F.2d 896, involving an investigation of illegal firearm trafficking at swap meets. The government received a tip that a Hispanic male at a swap meet near Casa Grande, Arizona, had illegally sold an assault-type firearm. On that information alone, an undercover agent went to the Casa Grande swap meet looking for Hispanic males and came upon the defendant, who appeared to be selling firearms in numbers exceeding those of a professed "gun collector." The government then lured him into a faked sale of illegal weapons.

Known criminal characteristics of defendants. Closely related to the question of individualized suspicion is whether a defendant had a criminal background or propensity the government knew about when it initiated its sting operation. *See, e.g., Williams,* 547 F.3d at 1200 (noting that before the government suggested a stash house robbery, the defendant was introduced to the government "as a middleman drug dealer").

Government's role in creating the crime. Also relevant is whether the government approached the defendant initially or the defendant approached a government agent, and whether the government proposed the criminal enterprise or merely attached itself to one that was already established and ongoing. *See Williams,* 547 F.3d at 1200 (noting that government merely persuaded the defendant to substitute a stash house robbery for the planned bank robbery he had initially proposed to the government agent).

In the case before us, the government does not contend it had any individualized suspicion of any of the defendants as being involved in stash house robberies when it dispatched the CI into the field to find persons willing to do such a robbery. Rather, it knew nothing about them or their criminal inclinations or experiences until the CI surfaced Simpson through Curtis, a stranger at a bar. The only criterion the CI used to select the bar was that it was in a "bad" area where persons engaged in "criminal activity" were likely to gather. This is a much wider net than we have seen in previous cases. Moreover, the stash house robbery was entirely the ATF's creation, and it was Zayas who set the parameters for how it had to be carried out. Thus as to the inception stage of this sting, the argument for government overreaching has some force.

[T]he government created the proposed crime, initiated contact with the defendants through the CI's approach to Curtis at the Glendale bar, and set the bait—all without any previous individualized suspicion—or even knowledge—about the defendants' criminal history or activities. In these respects, the government's role in creating the crime of conviction was quite strong, raising concerns that it sought to manufacture a crime that would not have otherwise occurred.

Nonetheless, our concerns are mitigated to a large degree because Simpson—and, shortly after, Black—told Zayas very early and often that they had engaged in similar criminal activity in the past, in conversations that were recorded on tape. Simpson represented at the very first meeting with Zayas that he had both the experience and the connections necessary to carry out another such robbery with his "goons." He bragged that he had been convicted of four felonies and 17 misdemeanors, all involving drugs or guns, while Black said he had "just" performed a stash house robbery, had done so several times and had stash house robberies "down to a science."[10] Therefore, even though it weighs in the defendants' favor that the government had no knowledge of any past criminal conduct by any of the defendants when the CI brought Simpson to the first meeting with Zayas, Simpson's and Black's repeated representations that they had engaged in related criminal activity in the past quickly supplied reasons to suspect they were likely to get involved in stash house robberies.[11] Moreover, our review of the record persuades us that once Zayas set his bait, the defendants "responded *without further inducement by the government.*" Instead, they responded with enthusiasm. They were eager to commit the fictional

10. The defendants emphasize that by these statements they were merely "puffing," but the government was entitled to rely on the defendants' representations of their past criminal conduct.

11. We decline to examine the pertinent factors with respect to each individual defendant separately, as the defendants seem to advocate. The question before us is whether the *government's* conduct was outrageous in conducting this criminal investigation. As long as the government's investigation was initiated and performed tolerably with respect to the operation as a whole, it would undermine law enforcement's ability to investigate and apprehend criminals if its otherwise acceptable conduct became outrageous merely because an individual with no known criminal history whom the government did not suspect of criminal activity joined the criminal enterprise at the last minute at the behest of codefendants. If there were evidence that the government purposely and unnecessarily coerced additional individuals to join the operation (as opposed to those individuals joining at the behest of coconspirators), then an individualized approach may be warranted, but there is no evidence of that occurring here.

stash house robbery, and they joined the conspiracy without any great inducement or pressure from the government. Indeed, the defendants before us in this appeal were recruited by other defendants, not by Agent Zayas or the CI. We therefore turn to our review of the government's conduct once the sting got underway.

In reviewing the government's conduct once defendants agreed to the scheme and began its implementation, we are satisfied that there is no significant evidence of government overreaching or coercion—significant factors in determining whether the government acted outrageously.

Government's encouragement of defendants. The extent to which the government encouraged a defendant to participate in the charged conduct is important, with mere encouragement being of lesser concern than pressure or coercion.

There is little evidence of government coercion or pressure here. Simpson testified that he felt pressure from Agent Zayas urging him "to do something real quick" in putting a team together and planning the robbery; and the compressed time line of the operation and Zayas' comments implying that Black and Simpson should involve more individuals may have placed subtle pressure on defendants to put a team together and quickly plan the details of the robbery. But there is no evidence that the government engaged in inappropriate activity, threats or coercion to encourage defendants to engage in the robbery. Instead, the government proposed the stash house robbery, and the defendants eagerly jumped at the opportunity.

Government's participation in the crime. We have also considered various aspects of the government's participation in the offense conduct as relevant. The *duration* of the government's participation in a criminal enterprise is significant, with participation of longer duration being of greater concern than intermittent or short-term government involvement. We have also looked to the *nature* of the government's participation—whether the government acted as a partner in the criminal activity, or more as an observer of the defendant's criminal conduct—including any particularly offensive conduct taken by the government during the course of the operation. Finally, courts have examined the *necessity* of the government's participation in the criminal enterprise—whether the defendants would have had the technical expertise or resources necessary to commit such a crime without the government's intervention. *See, e.g., United States v. Twigg,* 588 F.2d 373, 380–81 (3d Cir.1978) (reversing conviction where the government "was completely in charge and furnished all of the laboratory expertise" and "[n]either defendant had the know-how with which to actually manufacture methamphetamine").

Here, although the government took the initiative of approaching the defendants and proposing the fictitious stash house robbery, thereafter it played a minimal role in the crime. Agent Zayas provided no weapons, plans, manpower or direction about how to perform the robbery, even when the defendants sought his advice. The nature of the government's involvement therefore is in stark contrast to the government's role in cases like *Twigg* and *Greene,* in which the government provided difficult-to-obtain and necessary materials for criminal activity. *See Twigg,* 588 F.2d at 380 ("The Government gratuitously supplied . . . the indispensable ingredient, phenyl-2-propanone. It is unclear whether the parties had the means or the money to obtain the chemical on their own."); *Greene,* 454 F.2d at 786 (noting that the government "offered to provide a still, a still site, still equipment, and an operator" and "provided two thousand pounds of sugar at wholesale").

Finally, we have considered the need for the investigative technique that was used in light of the challenges of investigating and prosecuting the type of crime being investigated.

As the district court noted, stash house robberies are largely unreported crimes that pose a great risk of violence in residential communities. The court permissibly credited Agent Zayas' testimony that many home invasions related to drug deals involve disputes between rival gangs, and trying to arrest one gang in the act of robbing another can lead to shoot-outs and hostage taking. The reverse sting tactic was designed to avoid these risks to the public and law enforcement officers by creating a controlled scenario that unfolds enough to capture persons willing to commit such an armed robbery without taking the final step of an actual home invasion. That said, the risks we have identified in such a government-created fictional operation are not to be taken lightly. The government does not have free license to forgo reasonable alternative investigative techniques of identifying and targeting potential suspects before approaching them. And because the operation is fake, we must remain vigilant that the government does more than set the "bait" and create criminal convictions by outrageous means. We emphasize that in this case, the existence of tape and video recordings to prove what was actually said and done has weighed heavily in our review of the record. We would be faced with a much different case if all we had to rely on was the credibility of the conflicting after-the-fact testimony of the government and defense witnesses.

* * *

"Law enforcement conduct becomes constitutionally unacceptable where government agents engineer and direct the criminal enterprise from *start to finish.* Generation of new crimes merely for the sake of pressing criminal charges against the defendant also constitutes outrageous government [conduct]," at least "where the government essentially *manufactured the crime.*" Nearly three decades ago, we acknowledged that it is difficult to discern "[t]he point of division at the margins between police conduct that is just acceptable and that which goes a fraction too far." That remains true today. We, however, are satisfied the government did not cross the line here. We cannot say that the government's conduct was "so grossly shocking and so outrageous as to violate the universal sense of justice."[13]

---

13. Our dissenting colleague raises compelling concerns about the risks of government overreaching inherent in fictitious stash house sting operations. We respectfully disagree that, in view of existing precedents and the record in this case, we can hold the government to have acted outrageously here.

We therefore affirm the defendants' convictions and sentences.

Noonan, J., dissenting.

"Lead us not into temptation" is part of a prayer familiar to many. But few, I believe, would think of this prayer as addressed to the government of the United States or would think it necessary to address the government with such a request. The present case creates a precedent and sets a framework in which such a prayer addressed to the government becomes comprehensible and probable. Today our court gives our approval to the government tempting persons in the population at large currently engaged in innocent activity and leading them into the commission of a serious crime, which the government will then prosecute.

The government of the United States paid a confidential informant (CI) $100 a day to recruit random persons willing to rob a cocaine stash house. Brought from Miami to Phoenix by Agent Richard Zayas of the Bureau of Alcohol, Tobacco, Firearms, and Explosives (ATF), the CI testified that he went to bars in "a bad part of town" and that he was not instructed to look for particular individuals who were already involved in an ongoing criminal operation, but simply to recruit anyone who showed an interest in his conversation.

The CI described his modus operandi in these words:

> Q. All right. And in your efforts to recruit these robbers, what instructions, what specific instructions were you given by Agent Zayas?
>
> A. What instructions? Just to go out and, you know, say—just trying to see what I can meet back—you know, meet people. Meet people, see if they know bad guys, you know.
>
> Q. Anyone off the street. Is that basically it?
>
> A. Pretty much. No, not—yeah. I mean, yeah, I go to the bars.
>
> Q. Right. Now, how do you determine if a person is a bad person without knowing them or without observing them being engaged in a crime?
>
> A. Well, it's hard to determine.
>
> Q. Does [Agent Zayas] tell you [to] look only for persons who you know are about to commit a crime?
>
> A. No.
>
> Q. No. And, in fact, you have approached people at restaurants randomly and have raised potential criminal activity, have you not?
>
> A. Yes.

These facts are not disputed. They establish that Zayas and the CI, acting for the ATF, recruited Simpson to rob the stash house and that Zayas encouraged Simpson to increase the number of robbers; that all of the defendants were informed of the plan to rob a stash house; that unknown to them, the stash house itself did not exist; and that Zayas proposed its robbery as the purpose of the plan. From the start when the CI contacted Simpson to the end when Zayas told the crew to follow him to the warehouse, the agents of the government wrote the crime-script and conducted the defendants in the execution of it.

The opinion of the majority does not hesitate to say, "Moreover, the stash house robbery was entirely the ATF's creation, and it was Zayas who set the parameters for how it had to be carried out." The crimes of conviction, the opinion states, "resulted from an operation created and staged by ATF.... Zayas invented the scenario, including the need for weapons and for a crew, and the amount of cocaine involved." As the majority acknowledges, the government had no particular information about the defendants that would have made them plausible targets of an investigation. There was a "risk inherent," the majority agrees, "that the government could create a criminal enterprise that would not have come into being but for the temptation of a big payday, a work of fiction spun out by government agents to persons vulnerable to such a ploy who would not otherwise have thought of doing such a robbery."

The majority opinion does not give full weight to Zayas's suggesting an increase in the numbers of the conspirators nor to Zayas's directing the conspirators to the location of the imaginary stash house. These omissions apart, the majority opinion lays out in convincing detail how, from beginning to end, the government wrote the script, found those who would act in it, and brought its dupes together so that they could be arrested.

The majority finds its concerns "mitigated to a large degree" by the claims of Simpson and Black that they had engaged in similar criminal activity in the past. With this argument, the majority opens a new ground for the government to justify setting up a defendant. Taking Black and Simpson's boasts as true, why do the boasts make the boasters fair game for a government ploy? In fact, the presentence reports on these defendants in this case show no stash house activity by either of them. In the population of this country, there is an indefinite number of persons who dream of clever and unlawful schemes to make money. Does their dreamy amorality cast them all as fit candidates for a sting by their government? Depraved as a person's imagination and hopes may be, what is imagined and hoped are not the subjects of criminal justice. The majority's rationale for permitting the government to tempt the general population to crime imposes no limits upon the imagination of agents of the government.

More than 600 persons have been prosecuted for attempting to rob stash houses which were fictitious. According to ATF's special operations chief, the sentence that the ATF seeks is fifteen years.

Our court has voiced concerns at least twice over the government's "unfettered ability" to set the sentence by inflating the fictitious amount of drugs in the fictitious drug house. In none of these cases have the courts disapproved the government's power.

Fictitious stash house stings "are a disreputable tactic," Judge Posner has written, because "[l]aw enforcement uses them to increase the amount of drugs that can be attributed to the persons stung, so as to jack up their sentences." *United States v. Kindle,* 698 F.3d 401, 414 (7th Cir.2012) (Posner, J., dissenting).

[I]t is a denial of due process for sentences to be at the arbitrary discretion of the ATF. The agency creating the fictitious stash house can place any amount of imaginary drugs within it. The amount must, no doubt, be plausible; this limit aside, the ATF may make the object of the robbery as large as it chooses, thereby effectively choosing the criminal penalties the defendants will incur. The ATF has free rein to amplify these penalties and influence the number of defendants by, as in our case, inventing armed guardians of the imaginary drugs.

The power exercised by the government is not only to orchestrate the crime but to control and expand those guilty of it. I do not see how this power can be rationally exercised. No standard exists to determine the limits of the government's discretion.

The four defendants were a portion of the population of Phoenix unknown by the government to harbor any specific criminal plans. Never in their past had they been convicted of a crime of such proportions or a federal crime of any kind. They were inveigled by the ATF to agree to commit a crime which in fact was impossible to commit because the stash house they agreed to rob did not exist. Besides providing this imaginary target for their crime, the ATF brought the CI from Miami to recruit them, fed them Zayas's cover story as to his own motivation, told them of the target to be robbed with detail as to its contents and guards, coached them as to the number of persons needed for the job, and directed them to where they would be arrested. The ATF wrote the script, cast the defendants as the actors, and directed the action to its denouement.

The United States has enormous resources that could be used to tempt and trap criminals. If these resources are deployed to bring an ongoing criminal enterprise to justice, the country is well served. If these resources are deployed to fire the imaginations of dreamers of easy wealth and turn them to conspiring to commit a crime, our government has been the oppressor of its people.

Massively involved in the manufacture of the crime, the ATF's actions constitute conduct disgraceful to the federal government. It is not a function of our government to entice into criminal activity unsuspecting people engaged in lawful conduct; not a function to invent a fiction in order to bait a trap for the innocent; not a function to collect conspirators to carry out a script written by the government. As the executive branch of our government has failed to disavow this conduct, it becomes the duty of the judicial branch to refuse to accept these actions as legitimate elements of a criminal case in a federal court.

The majority in *Black* cited the need for the investigative technique of stash house stings in support of its decision, observing that "stash house robberies are largely unreported crimes that pose a great risk of violence in residential communities." This, of course, is a consequence of prohibition. The "allure" of drug dealers as robbery "targets is not hard to fathom" when one considers that they "deal strictly in cash"; "cannot rely on bystanders to come to their aid"; and "have no recourse to the police." BRUCE A. JACOBS, ROBBING DRUG DEALERS: VIOLENCE BEYOND THE LAW 1 (2001). With that in mind, Judge Posner has argued that ATF's stash house sting program and drug prohibition are working at cross-purposes. "The effect of a fictitious stash house sting," according to Posner, is "to make stash houses more secure by reducing the likelihood of their being robbed." *United States v. Kindle*, 698 F.3d 401, 416 (7th Cir. 2012) (Posner, J., dissenting). This "reduces the[] cost of self-protection, which is a principal cost of the illegal-drug business. The lower the business's costs, the lower the prices charged consumers, and so the greater the demand for illegal drugs and the more sales and consumption of them. The operators of stash houses would *pay* law enforcement to sting potential stash house robbers." *Ibid.*

In addition to the outrageous government conduct defense, stash house sting cases often raise questions about selective prosecution and sentencing entrapment.

As *Black* suggests, ATF has not adopted any particular set of criteria for finding and selecting targets in its stash house sting investigations. Randomly approaching strangers at bars in "a bad part of town" raises the prospect of unconstitutional discriminatory enforcement. In *United States v. Davis*, 793 F.3d 712 (7th Cir. 2015), concerns about discriminatory enforcement led the Seventh Circuit to partially affirm a district court order granting the defendants in a stash house sting case discovery on the question of selective enforcement. In *Davis*, the defendants had presented evidence that "since 2006 the United States Attorney for the Northern District of Illinois has prosecuted 20 stash-house stings, and that of the defendants in these cases 75 were black and 19 white. According to defendants, 13 of the 19 white defendants were Hispanic." *Id.* at 715. The defendants argued that this data suggested that ATF had been "offer[ing] lucrative-seeming [stash house robbery] opportunities to black and Hispanic suspects, yet not to those similarly situated in criminal background and interests but of other ethnicity." *Id.* at 720. Noting that it would be unconstitutional for ATF to intentionally discriminate on the basis of race in its selection of stash house sting targets, the Seventh Circuit concluded that limited discovery was warranted. The discovery order did not extend to evidence regarding the exercise of prosecutorial discretion, however, because *United States v. Armstrong*, 517 U.S. 456 (1996) "forbids discovery into prosecutorial selectivity unless the defense first shows that similarly situated persons have not been prosecuted." *Id.* at 715. *See also United States v. Washington*, 869 F.3d 193, 219 (3d Cir. 2017) (agreeing with *Davis* and holding that "the special solicitude shown to prosecutorial discretion, which animated the Supreme Court's reasoning in *Armstrong* . . . does not inevitably flow to the actions of law enforcement, or even to prosecutors acting in an investigative capacity").

Because the government exercises so much control over the drug type and quantity involved in stash house stings, these cases also often give rise to claims of sentencing entrapment or sentencing manipulation. Although many federal and state courts recognize one or both doctrines, they "are widely divergent in both their definitions of the claim and their application of it in practice." Eda Katherine Tinto,

Undercover Policing, Overstated Culpability, 34 Cardozo L. Rev. 1401, 1404 (2013). The essence of the two closely related theories is that they "acknowledge[] the factual guilt of the defendant yet posit[] that a lower sentence may be warranted due to police conduct." *Ibid.* In *United States v. McLean*, 199 F. Supp. 3d 926, 928 (E.D. Pa. 2016), for example, the court declined to impose a mandatory minimum sentence in a stash house sting case, finding "imposing the sentence prescribed for the quantity of cocaine charged would violate [the defendant's] constitutional right to Due Process of Law on the facts of this case." As with the standard entrapment defense, however, sentencing manipulation and sentencing entrapment claims are not often successful.

c. Police Corruption

The Harmful Side Effects of Drug Prohibition
Randy Barnett

2009 Utah Law Review 11

To appreciate the hidden costs of drug law enforcement, it is not necessary to claim that the sale and use of drugs are "victimless" in the moral sense—that is, to claim that such activity harms only consenting parties and therefore that it violates no one's rights and may not justly be prohibited. For this limited purpose it is not necessary to question the contentions that drug users and sellers "harm society" or that drug use violates "the rights of society."

Nevertheless, to understand the hidden costs of drug laws, it is vitally important to note that drug laws attempt to prohibit conduct that is "victimless" in a strictly nonmoral or descriptive sense: there is no victim to complain to the police and to testify at trial.

When a person is robbed, the crime is usually reported to the police by the victim. When the robber is caught, the victim is the principal witness in any trial that might be held. As a practical matter, if the crime is never reported, there will normally not be a prosecution because the police will never pursue and catch the robber. From the perspective of the legal system, it will be as though the robbery never took place. So too, if the victim refuses to cooperate with the prosecution after a suspect has been charged, the prosecution of the robber will usually not go forward. What special law enforcement problems result from an attempt to prosecute crimes in the absence of a "complaining witness" who will assist law enforcement officials?

Because drug use takes place in private and drug users and sellers conspire to keep their activities away from the prying eyes of the police, law enforcement surveillance must be extremely intrusive to be effective. The police must somehow gain access to private areas to watch for this activity.

One way to accomplish this is for a police officer, or more likely an informant, to pose as a buyer or seller. This means that the police must initiate the illegal transaction and run the risk that the crime being prosecuted was one that would not have occurred but for the police instigation. And, since possession alone is also illegal, searches of persons without probable cause might also be necessary to find contraband.

Such illegal conduct by police is to be expected when one seeks to prohibit activity that is deliberately kept away from normal police scrutiny by the efforts of both parties to the transaction, thereby requiring police intrusion into private areas if they are to detect these acts. It is impossible for police to establish probable cause for every search for illicit drugs, no matter how small the quantity. Where no constitutional grounds exist for such an intrusion, a police department and its officers are forced to decide which is more important: the protection of constitutional rights or the political consequences of failing to get results.

The fact that such privacy-invading conduct by police may be unconstitutional and therefore illegal does not prevent it from occurring. Some of those who are most concerned about the harm caused by drug laws are lawyers who have confronted the massive violations of constitutional rights that drug laws have engendered. Such unconstitutional behavior is particularly likely, given our bizarre approach to policing the police.

At present we attempt to rectify police misconduct mainly by preventing the prosecution from using any illegally seized evidence at trial. In most instances, the success of a suppression motion depends on whether the police tell the truth about their constitutional mistake in their report and at trial. They may not do so if they think that their conduct is illegal. "There is substantial evidence to suggest that police often lie in order to bring their conduct within the limits of the practices sanctioned by judicial decisions." The only person who can usually contradict the police version of the incident is the defendant, and a defendant's credibility does not generally compare favorably with that of police officers.

Those who have committed no crime—who possess no contraband—will have no effective recourse at all. Because no evidence was seized, there is no evidence to exclude from a trial. As a practical matter, then, the police only have to worry about unconstitutional searches if something illicit turns up; but if they can confiscate whatever turns up and make an arrest, they may be better off than if they respect constitutional rights and do nothing at all. Moreover, by encouraging such frequent constitutional violations, the enforcement of drug laws desensitizes the police to constitutional safeguards in other areas as well.

The constitutional rights of the general public are therefore threatened in at least two ways. First, the burden placed on law enforcement officials to enforce possessory laws without complaining witnesses virtually compels them to engage in wholesale violations of constitutional prohibitions against unreasonable searches and seizures. For every search that produces contraband there are untold scores of searches that do not. Given our present method of deterring police misconduct by excluding evidence of guilt, there is little effective recourse against the police available to those who are innocent of any crime.

Second, the widespread efforts of police and prosecutors to stretch the outer boundaries of legal searches can be expected, over time, to contribute to the eventual loosening up of the rules by the courts. In drug prosecutions, the evidence being suppressed strongly supports the conclusion that the defendants are guilty. The more cases that police bring against obviously guilty defendants, the more opportunities and incentives appellate courts will have to find a small exception here or there. And instead of prosecuting the police for illegal conduct, the prosecutor's office becomes an insidious and publicly financed source of political and legal agitation in the defense of such illegal conduct. As I have said elsewhere, "the arm of the government whose function is to prosecute illegal conduct is called upon, in the name of law enforcement, systematically to justify police irregularities. If these arguments are successful, the definition of illegal conduct will be altered." Refusing to consider these long run effects on the stability of constitutional protections is both dangerous and unrealistic.

One point should be made clear. The police are not the heavies in this tale. They are only doing what drug-law advocates have asked them to do by the only means such a task can be done effectively.

While most people have read about corrupt law enforcement officials who are supposed to be enforcing drug laws, few people are fully aware how this corruption is caused by the type of laws being enforced. Drug laws allow the police to use force to prevent voluntary activities. Unavoidably, the power to prohibit also gives the police a de facto power to franchise the manufacture and sale of drugs, in return for a franchise fee.

The corruption caused by prohibiting consensual activity is increased still further by the ease with which law enforcement officers can assist criminals when there is no complaining witness. [W]ithout a victim to file an official complaint, it is easier for police to overlook a crime that they might see being committed. When there is no victim to contradict the police version of events, it is much easier for police to tailor their testimony to achieve the outcome they desire, for example by describing circumstances of a bad search that would lead to the evidence beings suppressed and the charges dropped. When it is the word of the police against the defendant's, the defendant usually loses. With no victim pressing for a successful prosecution, the police, prosecutor, or judge may scuttle a prosecution with little fear of public exposure.

When compared to a victim crime like robbery, the victimless character of drug offenses (in the descriptive sense discussed above), and the fact that drug users are willing to pay for drugs, creates perverse incentives. When robbery is made illegal, robbers who take anything but cash must sell their booty at a tremendous discount. In other words, laws against robbery reduce the profit that sellers of illegally obtained goods receive and thereby discourage both robbery and the potential for corruption.

Drug laws have the opposite effect. Drug law enforcement creates an artificial scarcity of a desired product resulting in sellers receiving a higher price than they would without such laws. While it is true that drug prohibition makes it more costly to engage in the activity, this cost is partially or wholly offset by an increased return in the form of higher prices and by attracting criminal types who are less risk-averse—that is, individuals who are less likely to discount their realized cash receipts by their risk of being caught. For such persons, the subjective costs of providing illicit drugs are actually less than they are for more honest persons.

The extremely lucrative nature of the illicit drug trade makes the increased corruption of police, prosecutors, and judges all but inevitable.

The fact that law enforcement personnel are corrupted by drug laws should be no more surprising than the fact that many people decide to get high by ingesting certain chemicals. Among the many tragic ironies of drug prohibition is that by attempting to prevent the latter, they make the former far more prevalent. Yet drug-law advocates typically avoid the question of whether the increased systemic corruption that their favored policies unavoidably cause is simply too high a price to pay for whatever reduction in the numbers of drug users is achieved.

United States v. Reese

United States Court of Appeals for the Ninth Circuit
2 F.3d 870 (1992)

O'Scannlain, J.

A jury convicted appellants of federal civil rights crimes stemming from their actions as Oakland Housing Authority police officers. Their appeals raise a number of difficult questions, among them certain matters of first impression. We are required to decide what the government must prove to convict a law enforcement officer of depriving an individual of his federal constitutional right to be free of excessive force during detention or arrest. We also must decide whether criminal liability may be imposed on a commanding police officer who fails to prevent the use of excessive force by officers under his command.

The Oakland Housing Authority (the "OHA") is a municipal agency that provides housing to low income residents in Oakland, California. The Oakland Housing Authority Police Department (the "OHAPD") provides security and police services to the residents of OHA properties. Prior to the events with which we are here concerned, the OHAPD consisted of some two dozen officers, including one chief, three sergeants, and one corporal.

Among the properties administered by the OHA were large public housing developments plagued by high levels of drug activity, much of it involving crack cocaine. In April 1989, a special drug suppression task force (the "Task Force") was created within the OHAPD using funds provided by a federal grant. Six new officers were hired to man the Task Force, among them appellants Reese, Dwyer, and Houston. Officers Garden, Barryer, and Yee were the remaining members. Appellant Broussard, already an OHAPD sergeant, was chosen to command them.

The Task Force operated as an independent unit within the department. The group was not assigned responsibility for patrolling any particular area, but was left free to deal with narcotics problems wherever they arose on OHA property. It held its daily group meetings apart from the regular OHAPD patrol officers. Its members worked on a single shift.

At Broussard's direction, the Task Force officers acted together virtually at all times while in the field. Typically, they would go out in two or three vehicles, drive up to an area on or near OHA property where they suspected drug activity, jump out of the vehicles, and, in the words of Officer Barryer, "just take anything and everything we saw on the street corner . . . more or less like a wolf pack."

Broussard offered guidance to the men under his command in a number of respects around the time when the Task Force was first assembled. He told them, for example, that a lot of "dirty" drug money would be passing through their hands, and that it would not really matter if they kept some of it for themselves. The suspects, he noted, would be in no position to complain if some of their money came up missing. He also regularly exhorted Task Force officers to keep their arrest numbers up. All the officers were aware that the federal grant that funded their unit, and on which their jobs depended, was good for only eighteen to twenty-four months. Broussard warned that they would need statistics to show that the federal money was well spent and thus to secure another grant. On more than one occasion, he sent the Task Force out to begin a shift with comments like, "Let's go out and kick ass," and "Everybody goes to jail tonight for everything, all right?"

We turn now to the various incidents that were part of the government's case at trial, whether charged as individual substantive violations or as overt acts in furtherance of appellants' alleged conspiracy.

On May 8, 1989, during the Task Force's first night on patrol, Dwyer and Garden chased and caught a fleeing suspect in a parking lot. The two officers had the suspect on the ground and were beating him when other Task Force members stepped in; he did not appear to be resisting. Dwyer then walked the suspect over to one of the patrol cars and slammed him against it abruptly, so that his face and chest came down on the hood, even though the suspect was under control and in handcuffs at the time. Yee then pulled the suspect away from Dwyer, and the suspect was arrested for loitering. At the Task Force's briefing the next day, Dwyer told Yee he did not appreciate having his "investigation" interfered with.

Garden received a cut on his face during this incident. In response, Broussard told his assembled officers that any suspect who injured a Task Force member had better end up going to the hospital himself. On other occasions, Broussard admonished his men that, if a suspect were to run from them, they should "catch him [and] whip his ass." "No one runs," Broussard told another OHAPD sergeant. "Those who run will pay."

On May 16, 1989, at about 2:00 p.m., Jackie Dailey was helping to fix the car of an OHA resident, across the street from his own residence. Task Force members arrived on the scene and ordered Dailey and the other individuals present to stand spread-eagled against the car while they were searched and their names checked for outstanding warrants. No such warrants were found, and the search revealed no contraband. Reese then approached Dailey and told him that he found the hat Dailey was wearing offensive. The hat had the words "One Pimp, six holes" written on it. Reese took the hat off Dailey's head, ripped it, and threw it on the ground. He then seized Dailey by the neck and the back of the pants and threw him against the police car, then lifted him and threw him to the ground twice in succession. Houston then arrested Dailey for loitering. Broussard, the supervisor in charge at the time, was present at this incident and watched it develop, but took no steps to intercede.

After his release from jail, Dailey went to a hospital emergency room, where an x-ray was taken. He was later diagnosed as having sustained a fracture of his right elbow. Pain medication was prescribed and his arm was placed in a sling, which prevented him from filling out the complaint form he wished to file with the OHA—a friend had to write out the complaint for him.

On May 19, 1989, Dwyer attempted to place a suspect in the back seat of a patrol car. He found himself unable to do so because another suspect, Bryan Kiel, already in custody and handcuffed, had fallen asleep there. Dwyer twice told Kiel to move, then, receiving no response, kicked him hard in the chest.

A meeting involving the members of the Task Force and the chief of the OHAPD was held in the wake of this incident. The chief told the officers that the use of unnecessary or excessive force would not be tolerated, that Dwyer had come close to being terminated, and that any officer guilty of using excessive force in the future would be. After the chief left, Dwyer confronted Yee, saying he would hold him directly responsible if he were fired. Houston then told Yee that he was not a team player and was not aggressive enough. Reese added that, while he had no problems with Yee personally, he "felt he had to watch his back and look over his shoulder when [Yee] was around, because he was afraid [Yee would] say something." Both Reese and Houston told Yee he should consider leaving the Task Force.

Broussard, who had said little to that point in the meeting, then stated that "team business should remain team business," that matters involving Task Force members were the Task Force's own affair, and that no one else need know about them. On this and other occasions, Broussard told his officers that "team business" was not to be discussed with OHA patrol officers. Any Task Force member who had a problem with this, he added, would be "severely dealt with" by Broussard himself.

On May 23, 1989, Barryer conducted a pat search of Demetrius Findley. Barryer found nothing, and was prepared to release the suspect, but Broussard told him to continue the search. Barryer eventually discovered a plastic baggie containing suspected rock cocaine underneath Findley's testicles.

Barryer believed, however, that he had not had probable cause to conduct such an extensive search. He and Broussard discussed the problem of how to write up the arrest report in such a way as to make the search appear valid. Barryer proposed saying that he had felt something like a weapon in Findley's pants, but Broussard rejected this idea on the grounds that it would not provide a strong enough case. Barryer then indicated that he would simply say that he had seen Findley throw the cocaine on the ground. "Yeah, that'll work," Broussard said. Barryer wrote up his report in these terms, and Broussard read and approved the report.

The following month, Barryer was subpoenaed to testify in court in connection with the Findley arrest. Upon meeting with the deputy district attorney, however, Barryer indicated that he would be unable to testify to what he had said in his arrest report because it was false. He was then released from his subpoena.

Barryer returned to the OHAPD where he related these events first to the chief and then to Broussard. Broussard insisted that Barryer should have testified to what he had written in the report, saying, "Who do you think they're going to believe, you or the dirt bag?" Barryer was fired two weeks later for having falsified his report.

On the night of June 1, 1989, a Task Force patrol car carrying Barryer, Dwyer, and Reese crashed into a backstop while pursuing David McClendon across a baseball field. Barryer, the driver of the car, chased McClendon on foot up an adjacent street, then caught him and threw him to the ground. Dwyer arrived promptly thereafter. Barryer had McClendon under control and was preparing to handcuff him when Garden's voice came through over his radio saying that Reese had been injured in the crash. Dwyer then hit McClendon on the top of the head with his flashlight, causing a wound that required twenty-five stitches to close.

McClendon was brought back to the ball field, where Broussard's attention was drawn to the bloody wound on his head. Broussard then stated that McClendon would have to be arrested for something in order to justify his injury and his trip to the hospital. Garden wrote a false report stating that he had seen McClendon discard rock cocaine while running from Task Force officers, and that he had dropped a package of narcotics while being transferred from one patrol car to another.

On June 2, 1989, Task Force members stopped Edward Jackson, a juvenile, walking across a parking lot. Reese searched Jackson, including his underwear, but found nothing and told him to go. Broussard then produced a plastic bag of rock cocaine from a nearby hole in the ground. Jackson denied the drugs were his, but was arrested anyway. Reese wrote a report stating that he and Garden had observed Jackson for some fifteen minutes, and had seen him return frequently to the hole in the ground, where he inspected a plastic bag and removed things from it. The report was false.

Later that month, Jackson came up for trial in juvenile court. Garden, reading the report Reese had written for the first time on the day of the trial, told Reese they were going to have to get their stories together. They met during breaks in the trial, and visited the scene of the arrest during the lunch recess, agreeing upon the content of their testimony. Jackson was found guilty of possessing cocaine for sale. On returning to OHAPD headquarters, Garden and Reese told Dwyer that they had "lied [their] asses off in court" that day.

On the evening of June 29, 1989, Glen Losh was sitting with his girlfriend in his pickup truck, parked near OHA property. The Task Force, with all appellants present, pulled up behind them. Reese removed Losh from the truck and frisked him, then directed him to cross the sidewalk and to place his hands above his head against a fence. Reese then asked Losh what he was doing in the area. When Losh replied that he was there to sell an extra car battery he had acquired, Reese accused him of lying, and struck him with the heel or palm of his hand in the ribs on both sides of his body, knocking the wind out of him and causing him to fall to his knees.

Reese then frisked Losh again and removed his billfold and $30 in cash. He asked again why Losh was in the area, and what he, a white person, was doing in a black neighborhood. Reese then held up Losh's money—a twenty-dollar bill and two five-dollar bills—and said, "It looks like you have ten dollars." Reese threw the two fives on the ground, and put the twenty in his pocket. Losh never received the money back.

Garden and Broussard searched Losh's truck. Garden found a mirror, a gold razor blade, and a gold straw, items that he considered to be cocaine paraphernalia, which he smashed in the street. Garden confronted Losh about these items, pulling his beard and backhanding him across the mouth to get his attention. Houston, meanwhile, came over and questioned Losh further regarding his presence in the area, striking him in the lower back near the kidneys more than once. Losh was not arrested.

During this same shift, early on the morning of June 30, 1989, the same Task Force officers encountered Rosie Verduzco and her husband Salvador. The two were sitting in their car, parked near OHA property in front of the home of Salvador's parents; Salvador was talking to his brother David Verduzco and his cousin Michael Guzman, who stood on the sidewalk. Arriving on the scene, the officers ordered Rosie and Salvador to get out of their car and to place their hands on the roof, which they did.

Rosie was searched and her identification was taken by one of the officers. She then asked Houston, who was standing to her left, what the problem was. He responded by saying, "Shut up, bitch." Rosie kept asking questions, and Houston repeatedly responded with the same phrase. Eventually, Houston grabbed Rosie's hair, then yanked her head back over her shoulder so that she was looking at him. He did this several times. At no time did Rosie take her hands off the roof of the car or make any moves toward Houston. Finally, Houston shoved Rosie against the side of the car and struck her on the head with his flashlight. The laceration bled profusely and later required two staples to close. Rosie was arrested for resisting arrest and for having an open container in her car. Broussard was standing five to ten feet behind Houston as this incident unfolded.

Meanwhile, Salvador stood spread-eagled on the opposite side of the car, his legs apart and his hands on the roof. When he protested against Houston's treatment of his wife, Dwyer kicked him in the testicles from behind, telling him to shut up, and adding, "How do you like that, wetback"? Salvador was not arrested.

The OHA received numerous citizen complaints regarding the conduct of OHAPD officers during the period between May and July 1989. On one occasion, OHAPD Sergeant Watson spoke to Broussard about complaints alleging the use of excessive force. Broussard said he was not aware of any such problems involving the members of the Task Force, but he would bring the matter to the attention of his men. Watson also spoke to Dwyer, Houston, and Reese about the complaints, and told them not to use more force than was necessary, and to document properly any incident in which they resorted to force.

When the other OHA sergeant, Sergeant Santiago, spoke to Broussard about the increased number of citizen complaints, he was told: "Don't worry about it. They're just dope dealers and . . . they don't have any complaint." Asked specifically about the complaints filed by Glen Losh and his girlfriend, Broussard said, "Oh, they were just out there to buy dope." On one occasion, when Broussard was delayed in arriving at work, Santiago convened a special joint briefing session of the Task Force and regular patrol officers. He discussed the influx of internal affairs complaints about excessive force and the theft of money and property, and warned the officers that such conduct would not be condoned, and could lead to an investigation by an outside agency.

On August 13, 1989, Task Force officers encountered a group of black males. Searching the area across the street from the group, Garden found a box containing baggies of marijuana. Reese and Broussard conferred, and Reese then asked whose box it was. When no one stepped forward, Reese announced that whoever was carrying the most money would go to jail. That person proved to be David Lyles, a juvenile, and he was promptly arrested. Reese wrote up an arrest report in which he stated that he and Garden had seen Lyles holding the box, and that Lyles had dropped the box and crossed the street when he saw the officers' vehicle pull up. This was untrue. Nonetheless, Reese and Garden both testified in court to what Reese had written, and Lyles was found guilty.

On August 25, 1989, acting on the basis of information received earlier that day, Reese and Houston stopped a car driven by Cliofus Soluno, a suspected drug supplier. Broussard, Garden, and Dwyer joined them, and Soluno's trunk was searched. A large amount of marijuana and $2000 in cash was found in the trunk. Observing that Soluno, an undocumented alien from Mexico, would not miss the money, the five officers divided the cash among themselves.

On or about September 23, 1989, Task Force members chased and caught a suspect in a field. No drugs were found on his person or anywhere near him. Dwyer went to the trunk of his patrol car, and retrieved a baggie containing three pieces of rock cocaine. Dwyer then wrote an arrest report stating that these drugs had been taken from the suspect. Houston and Garden, as well as Dwyer, maintained "stashes" of narcotics which they used against suspects at various times.

On the night of October 7, 1989, Jerry Watkins was walking down the street in a neighborhood known as a "heavy drug area," looking for his stepson. Dwyer jumped out of a civilian car, and, without identifying himself as a police officer, yelled at Watkins, "Come here, you son of a bitch, [or I'll] kill you." Frightened, Watkins attempted to escape through a backyard. Dwyer, however, caught up with him and struck him in the head with his flashlight as he attempted to climb through a hole in a fence. The wound Watkins received later required eight to ten stitches. Dwyer wrote a report stating that Watkins had dropped a piece of rock cocaine while attempting to flee; he submitted what he said was this cocaine into evidence. This report was false.

On October 26, 1989, the Task Force stopped Keith Rogers. Dwyer began to search him for drugs and found a small baggie of marijuana. Dwyer continued the search, but Rogers grew belligerent when Dwyer moved to search his underwear. In response, Dwyer tried to rip Rogers' underwear off him, then used a buck knife to cut it off, saying, "Fuck your rights. What about your rights now?" Broussard then directed the officers to drive Rogers to an area outside a closed OHA complex. Arriving there, the officers bent Rogers over the front of a patrol vehicle and held him there. Dwyer put on a pair rubber gloves and said, "The doctor is in," then proceeded to perform a rectal search on Rogers. Rogers was visible from the street during this search. No drugs were found.

On November 1, 1989, Task Force officers on patrol observed two black males looking into a brown paper bag. When the men saw the officers' vehicle, they fled. The bag turned out to contain a large amount of rock cocaine, and Sherman Gay was arrested for its possession by Task Force Officer Williamson. Broussard explained to Williamson and Garden that Gay was a big time drug dealer and that he "definitely" needed to go to jail in connection with the drugs. A discussion ensued among the three officers regarding what Williamson should write in his arrest report, and Williamson suggested that he could write up the arrest as an observed hand-to-hand drug transaction. Williamson wrote the report accordingly, even though he had observed no such transaction.

By November 1989, the activities of the Task Force had prompted an investigation by the Oakland Police Department and the Alameda County District Attorney's Office. As part of the investigation, several videotaped undercover operations were conducted. Generally these operations involved an undercover officer, carrying a pager and a predetermined sum of money, standing on the sidewalk near OHA property with drugs placed somewhere nearby. The investigating officers would then call the OHA dispatcher to complain about the "drug dealer" who was working in that area, giving the undercover agent's description. The jury viewed a number of these videotapes as evidence in appellants' trial.

On November 14, 1989, Officer Robert Pursley was working undercover in one of these operations. The drugs had been placed in a cigarette package; Pursley stood near the package, and once sat down next to it. Meanwhile, across the street from Pursley, genuine drug deals were being conducted by one Billy Cooley.

The Task Force was dispatched to the scene. Garden told Pursley to get on the ground, then went across the street to Cooley. Dwyer then approached Pursley, straddled him and told him to roll over onto his back. Pursley rolled over with his arms extended, whereupon Dwyer hit Pursley in the hands with his flashlight and told him never to raise his hands to him again. Dwyer then kicked Pursley in the ribs, and grabbed him by the throat and started choking him, without provocation.

On November 21, 1989, Officer George Elzie assumed the role of the undercover agent in this operation, and was arrested by Reese. Elzie had been given $630 prior to being placed in the field. Together, Reese and Houston removed all of this money from Elzie's pockets. However, Reese turned in just $280, and claimed in his arrest report that this was all that had been recovered from Elzie. The rest of the money was never accounted for.[14]

On the basis of these incidents among others, appellants were tried by jury under a nineteen count indictment. The first count charged all four appellants with a criminal conspiracy whose object was the deprivation of constitutional rights, in violation of 18 U.S.C. § 241. The jury returned a verdict of guilty on the conspiracy count. The other counts delineated the specific substantive violations of these rights committed by the individual officers, in violation of 18 U.S.C. § 242. The jury voted to convict on most of these counts. In particular, each appellant was convicted for his role in one or more episodes involving excessive force.

Appellants were sentenced under the Guidelines to terms ranging from thirty-six to ninety-six months. They filed timely notices of appeal. A panel of this court subsequently granted their motions for bail pending appeal.

[The Appellants raised various challenges to the district court's jury instructions and to its application of the Sentencing Guidelines. The Court of Appeals rejected each of Appellants' arguments and affirmed their convictions and sentences.]

2. Informants

a. The Importance of Informants in Drug Investigations

Deregulating Guilt: The Information Culture of the Criminal System

Alexandra Natapoff

30 Cardozo Law Review 965 (2008)

Nearly every drug case involves a snitch, and drug cases represent an ever larger proportion of both state and federal dockets. As U.S. District Judge Marvin Shoob once complained, "I can't tell you the last time I heard a drug case of any substance in which the government did not have at least one informant. . . . Most of the time, there are two or three informants, and sometimes they are worse criminals than

14. During the undercover operation staged on November 22, 1989, the Task Force learned that it was under surveillance when a suspect revealed the presence of video cameras at the surveillance location. The operation therefore had to be terminated.

the defendant on trial." As the use of informants becomes an increasingly common investigative and case management tool, the impact of the official practice of trading information for liability with criminals becomes of central importance for understanding the system's changing information culture.

Criminal informants—i.e., criminal offenders who receive lenient treatment because of their cooperation with the government—are a longstanding and important part of the criminal system. Certain kinds of cases—drug conspiracies, antitrust, corporate fraud, terrorism—are difficult to investigate or prosecute without them, as the government is in a poor position to obtain incriminating information without inside help. Some kinds of information, for example, are only possessed by participants. Moreover, informants are procedurally simple and cheap. For example, while the government can apply for a wiretap order under Title III, it needs to show probable cause, and the resulting order will include time and other limitations. Alternatively, the government can skip the warrant process altogether and get an informant to wear a wire, without having to show probable cause and without temporal or spatial restrictions. Their usefulness and ease have thus made informants a staple of drug and other investigations.

Notwithstanding their investigative value, informants pose significant challenges. The informant deal is the antithesis of the trial-centric, regulated, due process information model. It proceeds in secret, with almost no constraints on the parties' ability to use information or to bargain. Police have nearly unfettered discretion both to seek information from suspects and to decline to arrest them in exchange, while prosecutors have similarly unfettered discretion to trade charging and sentencing concessions for cooperation. The secrecy surrounding the practice enables the government to use almost any information it wants to pressure a deal, including illegal evidence, racial profiling, and personal information about the suspect or his/her intimate relationships.

One reason for these developments is that the use of criminal informants falls squarely between the gaps of informational doctrine. Street-corner interactions between police officer and informant are largely unaffected by search and seizure or self-incrimination law. Many seminal criminal procedure cases turn on the inapplicability of the Bill of Rights to interactions with informants. Even in more regulated settings, a defendant's decision to cooperate will eviscerate many constitutional restraints on governmental information gathering, not only against the informant himself but also against third parties. Perhaps the most dramatic consequence is the ability of the government to evade Fourth, Fifth and Sixth Amendment restrictions by persuading an informant to obtain information that government agents could not obtain on their own. The gaps in information doctrine thus create a zone of procedural permissiveness that naturally promotes the use of informants.

Once the deal is struck, the information obtained from informants is problematic in its own right. Not only is it famously unreliable, but it is colored by the choices made by informants themselves, who may identify others in order to further their own criminal or personal desires. For example, a suspected drug dealer who told Atlanta police that they would find a kilogram of cocaine at Kathryn Johnston's address was released in exchange for that tip, even though the tip was inaccurate and led to the death of the 92-year-old grandmother.

Despite these flaws and biases, informant information drives a great deal of official decision-making. Police design investigations and prosecutors select targets based on their informant sources. The kinds of information that informants tend to give become an important determinant shaping law enforcement. The symbiosis between source and handler, moreover, becomes an informational force to be reckoned with.

There are numerous examples of productive informant deals. From Sammy the Bull to Edward Partin to Jack Abramoff, using informants often produces important investigations and convictions. The fact that approximately fifteen percent of all federal defendants—and one-quarter of drug defendants—receive sentencing credit for "substantial assistance" indicates that federal prosecutors and courts believe that cooperating defendants provide valuable investigative resources.

The costs and dangers of informant use are more difficult to document, in part because there are few mechanisms for recording cases where informants give bad information, or commit new crimes, or lead to corruption. Anecdotal evidence, however, suggests the nature of some of the problems.

For example:

Ann Colomb and her three sons were federally indicted for allegedly running the largest crack ring in Louisiana out of their home. They were convicted in jury trials and served four months in prison before they were released and all charges dismissed. Their wrongful convictions were based on fabricated information obtained from a ring of jailhouse informants who bought and sold information about the Colomb family so that inmates could offer testimony and reduce their own sentences. The government identified 31 informants that it planned to use in this way, before the scheme was revealed. The presiding judge, U.S. District Judge Tucker Melancon, said afterwards: "It was like revolving-door inmate testimony. The allegation was that there was in the federal justice system a network of folks trying to get relief from long sentences by ginning up information on folks being tried in drug cases. I'd heard about it before. But it all culminated in the Colomb trial."

Amy Gepfert was suspected of participating in a conspiracy to deal cocaine. The police told her that she was facing a forty year sentence, although in fact her maximum sentence would have been ten years. Police also discouraged her from calling a lawyer. In exchange for avoiding prosecution, the police required her to engage in oral sex with another suspect and to ask him for money. That suspect was then charged with soliciting a prostitute.

In Dallas, police made an arrangement with a group of informants in which the informants planted fake drugs on Mexican immigrants. The police then arrested the immigrants and fabricated or failed to conduct the drug tests that would have revealed that the alleged cocaine was actually gypsum, the substance found in wallboard. The informants were paid thousands of dollars, while the police used the arrests to inflate their drug-bust statistics. Numerous immigrants pleaded guilty and were deported before the scheme was discovered.

In New York, Brooklyn police officers paid informants with drugs taken from dealers who were arrested after the informants pointed them out. One officer bragged about the practice on tape, explaining that officers would seize drugs but report a lesser amount, keeping the unreported drugs to give to informants later on.

Such examples—which represent just the tip of the iceberg—illustrate the myriad potential influences of informant use on the criminal process. They reveal not only the potential unreliability of the practice, but the often corrupting personal relationships established between police and snitches, particularly the power inequalities that characterize this method of gathering information. They demonstrate the reversal of means and ends implicit in the trading of information for liability, and the potential increase in crime and violence that can accompany it. Finally, they suggest the impact of the practice on the meaning of guilt itself.

The most infamous and best documented hallmark of snitching is its unreliability. Both in theory and practice, information obtained from criminal informants who are compensated for their information is often wrong. According to one recent report, nearly half of all wrongful capital convictions are a result of a lying informant witness. Numerous cases and media stories reveal the extent to which informants lie in exchange for lenience, and the extent to which police and prosecutors rely on their information knowing it to be problematic or outright false.

Informant unreliability is exacerbated by secrecy, making mistakes harder to discern and errors easier to conceal after the fact. Nevertheless, the pressure to keep informant identity and information secret has been a powerful force in criminal procedure

b. Reliability of Informants

One of the biggest challenges police and prosecutors face when dealing with informants is ensuring the information they provide is reliable. Most informants do not give information to the government out of the kindness of their hearts. They provide information in exchange for a benefit, such as a reduced sentence or money. Because of mandatory minimum sentencing, drug defendants can often have an especially strong incentive to cooperate with the police. Moreover, as discussed in Chapter 4, prosecutors may often have the final say over whether a defendant's information was useful enough to qualify as substantial assistance and yield a reduced sentence. These factors may, in some cases, give even scrupulous defendants a strong incentive to provide false information to the government if they come to view it as the only way to reduce a lengthy sentence.

Concern about the veracity of informants who are induced to testify against others by promises of leniency influenced one panel of the United States Court of Appeals for the Tenth Circuit in the late 1990s to issue a decision barring the practice. *United States v. Singleton*, 144 F.3d 1343 (10th Cir. 1998). The panel's decision was quickly overturned in the opinion below by the court sitting *en banc*.

United States v. Singleton

United States Court of Appeals for the Tenth Circuit
165 F.3d 1297 (1999)

Porfilio, J.

Sonya Singleton was convicted of money laundering and conspiring to distribute cocaine. A panel of this court reversed that conviction on the ground the prosecuting attorney violated 18 U.S.C. § 201(c)(2) when he offered leniency to a co-defendant in exchange for truthful testimony. The panel held the testimony of the co-defendant should have been suppressed and that the failure to do so was not harmless error. The en banc court vacated the panel decision and has now reheard the appeal. We now hold 18 U.S.C. § 201(c)(2) does not apply to the United States or an Assistant United States Attorney functioning within the official scope of the office.

The conspiracy forming the basis of Ms. Singleton's conviction required her to send and receive drug proceeds by Western Union wires. Her co-conspirator Napoleon Douglas entered into a plea agreement in which he agreed to testify truthfully in return for the government's promise not to prosecute him for related offenses, to advise the sentencing court of his cooperation, and to advise a state parole board of the "nature and extent" of his cooperation.

Before trial, Ms. Singleton moved to suppress the testimony of Mr. Douglas on the ground the government had violated 18 U.S.C. § 201(c)(2), the so-called "anti-gratuity statute," by promising him leniency in exchange for his testimony. The district court denied the motion and Mr. Douglas testified, acknowledging the benefits he would receive in exchange for his testimony and implicating Ms. Singleton in the charged offenses. Ms. Singleton asks us to review the court's denial of her motion.

The question before us is whether section 201(c)(2) applies to the government in the prosecution of criminal offenses. Ms. Singleton argues the plain language of the statute permits no answer but that it does. As expected, the government counters such a reading is beyond the intent of Congress and clearly wrong. We review this issue of law de novo and begin our analysis with the pertinent portions of 18 U.S.C. § 201(c)(2) itself:

> (c) Whoever—
>
> ....
>
> (2) directly or indirectly, gives, offers, or promises anything of value to any person, for or because of the testimony under oath or affirmation given or to be given by such person as a witness upon a trial ... before any court ... shall be fined under this title or imprisoned for not more than two years, or both.

Ms. Singleton takes the position that when Mr. Douglas testified after receiving the government's promise of lenient treatment in exchange for his truthful testimony, he became a "paid 'occurrence' witness," and testimony from those of such ilk is contrary to the fundamental precepts of American justice because the payment of something of value would give the witness a strong motivation to lie. She reasons section 201(c)(2) was enacted to deter that result, and we need only apply plain meaning to the word "whoever" contained in the statute to conclude it must apply broadly and encompass the government and its representatives.

In contrast, the United States argues to allow section 201(c)(2) to sweep so broadly would not only be a radical departure from the ingrained legal culture of our criminal justice system but would also result in criminalizing historic practice and established law. The government maintains Congress did not intend to hinder the sovereign's authority to prosecute violations against the United States in this fashion.

Viewing the statute on its face, it is apparent the dispute revolves about the word "whoever." Indeed, the significance of the remaining parts of the statute is not seriously controverted. However, like many words chosen by the legislative branch to convey its intent, this one word evokes more meaning than an innocent first reading of it would portend.

As correctly argued by Ms. Singleton, "whoever" is a broad term which by its ordinary definition would exclude no one. Indeed, if one were to take the word at face value, defendant's argument becomes colorable, at least. However, the defendant's approach, while facially logical, ignores a crucial point that must be considered in any attempt to apply the statute to the issues of this case. She argues the breadth of the word "'whoever' includes within its scope the assistant United States attorney who offered Douglas something of value in exchange for his testimony." To begin the parsing of the statute with this assumption, however, ignores a fundamental fact: the capacity in which the government's lawyer appears in the courts.

The prosecutor, functioning within the scope of his or her office, is not simply a lawyer advocating the government's perspective of the case. Indeed, the prosecutor's function is far more significant. Only officers of the Department of Justice or the United States Attorney can represent the United States in the prosecution of a criminal case. Indeed, a federal court cannot even assert jurisdiction over a criminal case unless it is filed and prosecuted by the United States Attorney or a properly appointed assistant. Therefore, the government's sovereign authority to prosecute and conduct a prosecution is vested solely in the United States Attorney and his or her properly appointed assistants. Of course, it cannot be otherwise because the government of the United States is not capable of exercising its powers on its own; the government functions only through its officers and agents. We thus infer in criminal cases that an Assistant United States Attorney, acting within the scope of authority conferred upon that office, is the alter ego of the United States exercising its sovereign power of prosecution. Hence, in the attempt to apply section 201(c)(2), the United States and the Assistant United States Attorney cannot be separated.

Indeed, the alter ego role of the prosecutor is not unusual, for in a similar case, the Sixth Circuit has noted:

> When an assistant United States Attorney (AUSA) enters into a plea agreement with a defendant, that plea agreement is between the United States government and the defendant. When an AUSA uses at trial testimony obtained through a plea agreement or an agreement not to prosecute, he does so as the government. An AUSA who, pursuant to the provisions of the United States Sentencing Guidelines, moves for a downward departure under § 5K1.1, does so as the government.

Put into proper context, then, the defendant's argument is: in a criminal prosecution, the word "whoever" in the statute includes within its scope the United States acting in its sovereign capacity. Extending that premise to its logical conclusion, the defendant implies Congress must have intended to subject the United States to the provisions of section 201(c)(2), and, consequently, like any other violator, to criminal prosecution. Reduced to this logical conclusion, the basic argument of the defendant is patently absurd.

There is even a more fundamental reason for arriving at the same conclusion, however. Although Congress may, by legislative act, add to or redefine the meaning of any word, it did not do so in the passage of section 201(c)(2). Therefore, we must presume it intended to employ the common meaning of the word. The word "whoever" connotes a being. The United States is an inanimate entity, not a being. Therefore, construing "whoever" to include the government is semantically anomalous. Looking beyond definitions, though, there are rules of statutory construction that will lead to the same conclusion.

Statutes of general purport do not apply to the United States unless Congress makes the application clear and indisputable. In *The Dollar Savings Bank v. United States,* 86 U.S. 227 (1873), the [United States Supreme] Court instructed:

> It is a familiar principle that the King is not bound by any act of Parliament unless he be named therein by special and particular words. The most general words that can be devised (for example, any person or persons, bodies politic or corporate) affect not him in the least, if they may tend to restrain or diminish any of his rights and interests. . . . The rule thus settled respecting the British Crown is equally applicable to this government, and it has been applied frequently in the different States, and practically in the Federal courts. It may be considered as settled that so much of the royal prerogatives as belonged to the King in his capacity of *parens patriae,* or universal trustee, enters as much into our political state as it does into the principles of the British constitution.

The Court revisited the concept in *Nardone v. United States,* 302 U.S. 379, 383–84 (1937), when it held this canon of construction generally applies when failure to limit the application of a statute would "deprive the sovereign of a recognized or established prerogative title or interest" or "where a reading which would include [the government] would work obvious absurdity."

The next question, then, is whether applying the statute to the government would deprive the sovereign of a recognized or established prerogative, title, or interest. The answer to that question is, inescapably yes.

From the common law, we have drawn a longstanding practice sanctioning the testimony of accomplices against their confederates in exchange for leniency. Indeed,

> no practice is more ingrained in our criminal justice system than the practice of the government calling a witness who is an accessory to the crime for which the defendant is charged and having that witness testify under a plea bargain that promises him a reduced sentence.

United States v. Cervantes-Pacheco, 826 F.2d 310, 315 (5th Cir. 1987).

This ingrained practice of granting lenience in exchange for testimony has created a vested sovereign prerogative in the government. It follows that if the practice can be traced to the common law, it has acquired stature akin to the special privilege of kings. However, in an American criminal prosecution, the granting of lenience is an authority that can only be exercised by the United States through its prosecutor; therefore, any reading of section 201(c)(2) that would restrict the exercise of this power is surely a diminution of sovereignty not countenanced in our jurisprudence.

Moreover, in light of the longstanding practice of leniency for testimony, we must presume if Congress had intended that section 201(c)(2) overturn this ingrained aspect of American legal culture, it would have done so in clear, unmistakable, and unarguable language.

Our conclusion in no way permits an agent of the government to step beyond the limits of his or her office to make an offer to a witness other than one traditionally exercised by the sovereign. A prosecutor who offers something other than a concession normally granted by the government in exchange for testimony is no longer the alter ego of the sovereign and is divested of the protective mantle of the government. Thus, fears our decision would permit improper use or abuse of prosecutorial authority simply have no foundation.[2] It is noteworthy, then, that defendant's premise relies upon the shibboleth "the government is not above the law." While we agree with that notion, we simply believe this particular statute does not exist for

2. The concurrence expresses a concern our disposition would "permit the conclusion that consistent with the provisions of § 201, a United States Attorney may pay a prosecution witness for false testimony." We believe the concern is misplaced. It is inconceivable that any court would hold that a prosecutor who pays for the *false* testimony of a witness is carrying out an official function of the government. Our disposition protects only those prosecutorial acts of the government which have been recognized in common law or authorized by statute. A prosecutor who goes beyond those limitations is clearly not performing a governmental function.

the government. Accordingly, we AFFIRM the district court's denial of the motion to suppress on 18 U.S.C. § 201(c)(2) grounds. We adopt the ruling of the panel that the evidence in the record was sufficient to sustain the judgment of conviction, notwithstanding the panel's conclusion the testimony of Mr. Douglas should have been suppressed.

Lucero, J., with whom Henry, J. joins, concurring.

I concur in the judgment that the United States and its agent, an Assistant United States Attorney, did not violate 18 U.S.C. § 201(c)(2) by offering in a plea agreement to exchange leniency for the testimony of Singleton's co-conspirator. But I write separately to state my disagreement with the majority's holding that the word "whoever" in 18 U.S.C. § 201(c)(2), as it is used to define the class of persons who can violate the statute, cannot include the government or its agents. The majority's interpretation would permit the conclusion that consistent with the provisions of § 201, a United States Attorney may pay a prosecution witness for false testimony.

I cannot join the dissent, however, because § 201(c)(2) operates in conjunction with other statutes to allow the government, upon proper disclosure and/or with court approval, to trade certain items of value for testimony. These statutes include 18 U.S.C. § 3553(e) and 28 U.S.C. § 994(n), passed as part of the Sentencing Reform Act of 1984, which allow courts, acting pursuant to the Sentencing Guidelines and upon motion of the government, to reduce sentences for individuals who provide "substantial assistance in the investigation or prosecution of another"; the federal immunity statutes, 18 U.S.C. §§ 6001–6005, passed as part of the Organized Crime Control Act of 1970, which require courts, upon the request of the government, to confer immunity upon witnesses for their testimony in aid of the prosecution; and the Witness Relocation and Protection Act, 18 U.S.C. §§ 3521–3528, passed as part of the Comprehensive Crime Control Act of 1974, which allows the government to bestow various benefits for the protection of cooperating witnesses. Because these specific statutes are in conflict with the general prohibitions of § 201(c)(2), the specific statutes control, and permit the prosecution's actions in this case.

Congress has developed an extensive and detailed statutory framework authorizing sentence reductions and recommendations, immunity, and other incentives for cooperating witnesses. Federal immunity statutes, for example, which authorize prosecutors to request immunity for cooperating witnesses "reflect[] the importance of testimony, and the fact that many offenses are of such a character that the only persons capable of giving useful testimony are those implicated in the crime." *Kastigar v. United States,* 406 U.S. 441, 446 (1972). The Supreme Court has characterized the immunity statutes as "essential to the effective enforcement of various criminal statutes" and "so familiar that they have become part of our 'constitutional fabric,'" *United States v. Mandujano,* 425 U.S. 564, 575–76 (1976).

Although, as the Singleton panel noted, the government moves the court to grant immunity rather than bestowing immunity directly upon a cooperating witness the government's role in the process is more important than that of the court.

See *United States v. Doe,* 465 U.S. 605 (1984) (noting that the immunity statutes grant government authorities "exclusive authority to grant immunities" and that the courts play "only a minor role in the immunizing process"). Indeed, the statutory language itself requires the court, "upon the request of the United States attorney," to "issue . . . an order requiring [a witness] to give testimony or provide other information which he refuses to give or provide on the basis of his privilege against self-incrimination."

When granted statutory immunity, the potential witness is given something of value by the government in that his immunized testimony cannot be used to prosecute him. By the same token, the government plainly gains something of value from immunizing the testimony—the testimony itself. The immunity statutes give the government leverage with which to obtain testimony from recalcitrant witnesses, and the power to grant immunity serves as one of the bargaining tools in the prosecutorial process.

Dispositive in this case is the Sentencing Reform Act of 1984, which, as amended, authorizes courts, upon motion of the government, to reduce sentences for individuals who provide "substantial assistance in the investigation or prosecution of another." There can be little doubt that Congress intended to include the provision of cooperative testimony under the rubric of "substantial assistance." Both 18 U.S.C. § 3553(e) and 28 U.S.C. § 994(n) define such assistance in terms of "the investigation or prosecution of another person who has committed an offense." Although there are some forms of assistance in prosecution that are neither testimonial nor duplicative of investigatory assistance, it stretches credulity to suppose that Congress intended to exclude cooperative testimony from "substantial assistance" as used in these statutes.

By allowing prosecutors to reward testimony with sentencing benefits, the statutes must also be read to authorize prosecutors to inform a defendant and potential witness of the possibility of such reward. Barring a prosecutor from discussing leniency prior to testimony would seriously inhibit the intended effect of these statutes by reducing the pool of defendants willing to testify against their co-conspirators to those informed by their counsel of the potential benefits of cooperation.

Pursuant to these grants of statutory authority, the Sentencing Commission has issued a policy statement entitled "Substantial Assistance to Authorities," *see* U.S.S.G. § 5K1.1, which allows a downward departure in consideration of "the truthfulness, completeness, and reliability of any information or testimony provided by the defendant." Courts have upheld the exchange of testimony for leniency under this authority.

In totality, these various statutes create both a substantive and procedural framework for bargaining between government agents and potential witnesses. They limit the "something of value" that the government may offer, and detail the roles of both the prosecution and the courts in determining sentences, providing immunity, and granting other forms of assistance. The result is a coherent, narrowly defined set of laws that operate in the same field as the more general prohibitions of § 201(c)(2). Under long-established principles of statutory construction, where specific statutes overlap with a general statute, the latter must give way, insofar as it would prohibit that which the narrow statutes would allow. It is for this reason that I concur with the majority's result.

This analysis has several advantages over that of the majority. It provides both a roadmap for the bargaining process and a clearly articulated criminal statute with which to punish straying prosecutors. The majority's reading of § 201(c)(2), on the other hand, creates a conceptually messy legal regime for handling the case of the errant United States Attorney "who offers something other than a concession normally granted by the government," such as bribing a witness to provide false testimony.

Kelly, J, with whom Seymour, CJ., and Ebel, J., join, dissenting.

The court holds that 18 U.S.C. § 201(c)(2) does not apply to the government because government prosecutors are inseparable from the sovereign, and that its application would deprive the sovereign of its power to grant leniency in exchange for testimony and would conflict with various statutory provisions. Because courts must apply unambiguous statutes as they are written and § 201(c) does not admit of an exception for the government or its prosecutors, I respectfully dissent.

As an initial observation, since the panel issued its opinion in this case, prosecutors from coast to coast have attempted to portray it as the death knell for the criminal justice system as we know it. These are the same grave forecasts made by prosecutors after the Supreme Court's decision in *Miranda v. Arizona,* 384 U.S. 436 (1966), and the advent of the exclusionary rule. But experience has proven that the government, just like the private citizens it regulates and prosecutes, can live within the rules. No one would suggest that the criminal justice system has ceased to function because the Court or Congress has effectuated constitutional or statutory guarantees designed to promote a more reliable outcome in criminal proceedings.

In holding that § 201(c)(2) simply does not apply to the government, the court does not hold that leniency in exchange for testimony does not constitute "anything of value." To be sure, the investigation and prosecution of criminal wrongdoing is an important societal function. Yet, largely missing from the debate since the panel opinion was issued is any concern for the other deeply held values that § 201(c) was intended to protect and which, I believe, the panel opinion honored by applying § 201(c) as Congress wrote it. Those concerns center on maintaining the integrity, fairness, and credibility of our system of criminal justice. Criminal judgments are accepted by society at large, and even by individual defendants, only because our system of justice is painstakingly fair. An additional core value honored by the panel opinion is the preservation of the separation of powers carefully articulated in the Constitution between the legislative and judicial branches, and the proper role of the judiciary as the law-interpreting, rather than lawmaking, branch of the federal government.

Contrary to the concerns expressed by some commentators and courts a straightforward interpretation of § 201(c), which encompasses a prohibition against the government buying witness testimony with leniency, actually aids the search for truth. In theory, the leniency is only in exchange for "truthful" testimony. But as the Supreme Court has recognized: "Common sense would suggest that [an accused accomplice] often has a greater interest in lying in favor of the prosecution rather than against it, especially if he is still awaiting his own trial or sentencing. To think that criminals will lie to save their fellows but not to obtain favors from the prosecution for themselves is indeed to clothe the criminal class with more nobility than one might expect to find in the public at large." *Washington v. Texas,* 388 U.S. 14, 22–23 (1967); see also Yvette A. Beeman, Note, Accomplice Testimony Under Contingent Plea Agreements, 72 Cornell L. Rev. 800, 802 (1987) ("Accomplice plea agreements tend to produce unreliable testimony because they create an incentive for the accomplice to shift blame to the defendant or other co-conspirators. Further, an accomplice may wish to please the prosecutor to ensure lenient prosecution in his own case."). To be sure, there are devices that partially ameliorate the problem. The government is required to disclose exculpatory information, including impeachment information, to a defendant. Testifying accomplices may be cross-examined. Their credibility may be impeached, and the jury is instructed that it may regard such testimony with caution. However, all of these devices have limitations. In the real world of trial and uncertain proof, and in view of § 201(c), a witness's demeanor and actual testimony are simply too important to hinge upon promises of leniency. Although the court notes that a prosecutor who procures false testimony could be prosecuted for subornation of perjury, such a remedy offers little practical advantage to a defendant facing trial. By barring an exchange of leniency for testimony, Congress in § 201(c) has sought to eliminate, at the source, the most obvious incentive for false testimony.

On the other side of the ledger is my concern for the institutional role of Article III courts. Much of this case has been about policy. I accept the government's position that accomplices can provide important information and interpreting § 201(c) to include prosecutors might require some changes to elicit testimony of some witnesses. While it would be up to the Department of Justice to devise ways of compliance, the government is not precluded from offering leniency in exchange for information and assistance short of actual testimony at trial. Likewise, the government could prosecute accomplices first, then compel their testimony by subpoena against co-conspirators. Finally, the government could request that the district court order an accomplice to testify under a grant of immunity. Surely the Department has the ability and resources to come up with effective and lawful means for procuring necessary accomplice testimony. However, I also accept the defense attorneys' position that government leniency in exchange for testimony can create a powerful incentive to lie and derail the truth-seeking purpose of the criminal justice system. The very nature and complexity of this policy debate reinforces my initial belief that this is an argument better left to Congress. This court must perform its constitutional duties and no more. Ours is not to explore the farthest meanings that the term "whoever" can bear so as to effectuate the policy we think best. Our duty is to interpret the plain meaning of the statute. I continue to believe that meaning is clear: § 201(c), as written, applies to prosecutors and criminal defendants alike. If the balance struck by § 201 is to be reweighed, that reweighing should be done by the policymaking branch of government—the Congress, and not the courts. In that regard, it bears repeating that the panel's original opinion was purely a matter of statutory construction, not constitutional analysis, and it remains completely open for Congress to reweigh the conflicting values sought to be addressed in § 201.

The government argues that construing the word "whoever" to include the government is semantically anomalous because "whoever" connotes a being. As a textual and contextual matter, this is wrong. Textually, "whoever" clearly connotes more than a being and in fact denotes inanimate entities. The Dictionary Act, 1 U.S.C. § 1, definition of "whoever" includes, but is not limited to, corporations, companies, associations, firms, partnerships, societies, and joint stock companies—all inanimate entities. Contextually, the government concedes that "whoever" in § 201(b) applies to the government and it acknowledges that § 201(c) applies to the government if the government pays an informant money to testify. It makes absolutely no sense to give "whoever" one meaning in § 201(b) (and in § 201(c) when the inducement offered by the government is money) and to give the very same word a completely different meaning in § 201(c) when the inducement offered is leniency or some other promise to improve the informant's position. Bought testimony is so fraught with the potential for perjury that Congress imposed a blanket prohibition that also applies to the government, just as hearsay testimony is so fraught with the potential for unreliability that the Federal Rules of Evidence generally prohibit its admission, whether offered by the government or private litigants.

Beyond Unreliable: How Snitches Contribute to Wrongful Convictions

Alexandra Natapoff

37 Golden Gate University Law Review 107 (2006)

[I]nformants do not generate wrongful convictions merely because they lie. After all, lying hardly distinguishes informants from other sorts of witnesses. Rather, it is how and why they lie, and how the government depends on lying informants, that makes snitching a troubling distortion of the truth-seeking process. Informants lie primarily in exchange for lenience for their own crimes, although sometimes they lie for money. In order to obtain the benefit of these lies, informants must persuade the government that their lies are true. Police and prosecutors, in turn, often do not and cannot check these lies because the snitch's information may be all the government has. Additionally, police and prosecutors are heavily invested in using informants to conduct investigations and to make their cases. As a result, they often lack the objectivity and the information that would permit them to discern when informants are lying. This gives rise to a disturbing marriage of convenience: both snitches and the government benefit from inculpatory information while neither has a strong incentive to challenge it. The usual protections against false evidence, particularly prosecutorial ethics and discovery, may thus be unavailing to protect the system from informant falsehoods precisely because prosecutors themselves have limited means and incentives to ferret out the truth.

In 2000, the groundbreaking book Actual Innocence estimated that twenty-one percent of wrongful capital convictions are influenced by snitch testimony. Four years later, a study by the Center on Wrongful Convictions doubled that number. Another recent report estimates that twenty percent of all California wrongful convictions, capital or otherwise, result from false snitch testimony.

Behind these general statistics lie numerous stories of informant crime, deceit, secret deals and government duplicity. In Los Angeles, DEA informant Essam Magid not only avoided jail for his many crimes but earned hundreds of thousands of dollars by serving as an informant. During this time, he framed dozens of innocent people before one person he targeted finally refused to plead guilty and revealed the arrangement.

Although such horror stories provoke outcry, little has been done to cabin the law enforcement discretion that makes such informant operations possible, or to impose greater transparency and oversight onto the process in order to curtail such abuses.

Informants have become law enforcement's investigative tool of choice, particularly in the ever-expanding world of drug enforcement. Informants are part of a thriving market for information. In this market, snitches trade information with police and prosecutors in exchange for lenience, the dismissal of charges, reduced sentences, or even the avoidance of arrest. It is a highly informal, robust market that is rarely scrutinized by courts or the public. And it is growing. While data is hard to come by, federal statistics indicate that sixty percent of drug defendants cooperate in some fashion. Informants permeate all aspects of law enforcement, from investigations to plea-bargaining to trial.

The growth in the sheer number of informants reflects the increasing dependence of police and prosecutors on informants. Professor Ellen Yaroshefsky describes prosecutors' own complaints: "These [drug] cases are not very well investigated.... Our cases are developed through cooperators and their recitation of the facts. Often, in DEA, you have agents who do little or no follow up so when a cooperator comes and begins to give you information outside of the particular incident, you have no clue if what he says is true."

Because investigations and cases rely so heavily on informants, protecting and rewarding informants has become an important part of law enforcement. Police and prosecutors are well known for protecting their snitches: all too often, when defendants or courts seek the identity of informants, cases are dismissed or warrant applications are dropped. More fundamentally, police and prosecutors become invested in their informants' stories, and therefore may lack the objectivity to know when their sources are lying.

Informants are thus punished for silence and rewarded for producing inculpatory information, even when that information is inaccurate. The system protects them from the consequences of their inaccuracies by guarding their identities and making their information the centerpiece of the government's cases. The front line officials who handle informants—police and prosecutors—are ill equipped to screen that information, and once they incorporate it into their cases, they acquire a stake in its validity. This phenomenon explains in part why snitch testimony generates so many wrongful convictions: it permeates the criminal system and there are few safeguards against it.

Although, as Alexandra Natapoff argues, police and prosecutors can "become invested in their informants' stories, and therefore may lack the objectivity to know when their sources are lying," defense attorneys have a strong incentive to challenge an informant's credibility. Because defense attorneys do not have the same investigative tools as the state, however, gathering information about an informant's credibility can sometimes be difficult. In one unusual case, an Indiana criminal defense attorney investigated an informant who had allegedly purchased methamphetamine from his client while working for the police. The attorney, David Schalk, came to believe that the informant was himself continuing to sell drugs while the police looked the other way. In an effort to confirm his suspicions, Schalk gave new meaning to the phrase zealous representation by attempting a private sting operation against the informant. The informant sold marijuana to Shalk's hired investigators and Shalk contacted the police to report the informant's crime. Unfortunately for Schalk, the police did not react to the news as he had expected.

Schalk v. Indiana

Court of Appeals of Indiana
943 N.E.2d 427 (2011)

Najam, J.

In June 2007, Schalk was representing Chad Pemberton, who had been charged with dealing in methamphetamine, as a Class A felony. Pemberton's charge stemmed from a sale of methamphetamine he had made to a confidential informant working with police. Schalk learned that Brandon Hyde was the confidential informant. Because Pemberton believed that Hyde continued to deal drugs while working with police, Schalk sought to obtain proof of his dealing in order to impeach his credibility at trial.

Schalk discussed with Pemberton's mother the idea of proving that Hyde was still dealing drugs. Schalk then asked Pemberton's sister, a minor, whether she or someone she knew might purchase marijuana from Hyde and record the transaction. Schalk recommended purchasing a large quantity of drugs to make the impeachment evidence more "reliable." When Pemberton's sister declined to help,

Pemberton suggested that his friends Lisa Edwards and Roger Grubb might be willing to participate in a drug buy with Hyde.

Leslie spoke with Edwards about the plan, and Pemberton spoke with Edwards and Grubb to convince them to talk with Schalk. Edwards then spoke with Schalk several times, and Schalk assured her that the plan for Edwards and Grubb to buy marijuana from Hyde was "legit" and that none of them would get into trouble. On June 25, Schalk telephoned Edwards and Grubb, and the three subsequently met at a restaurant in Ellettsville. Schalk gave Edwards a voice recorder to use during the buy, and he told her to buy a "felony amount" of marijuana from Hyde. Schalk wrote down the serial numbers from $200 in bills and gave the buy money to Edwards.

Shortly after the meeting in Ellettsville, Edwards left Schalk a voice mail message that the drug buy had been completed. However, instead of buying $200 worth of marijuana, Edwards and Grubb bought only $50 worth of marijuana from Hyde, and the pair spent the rest of the money on gas and food. And before Edwards and Grubb met with Schalk to deliver the marijuana and return the voice recorder, Grubb decided to keep the marijuana. Edwards also deleted the recording of the drug transaction with Hyde.

When Edwards and Grubb met with Schalk, they brought a rolled up newspaper and represented that the marijuana they had purchased from Hyde was inside the newspaper. Schalk refused to take possession of the newspaper alleged to contain marijuana, and he instructed Edwards and Grubb to keep it until he could find a law enforcement officer to take possession of it. Edwards and Grubb subsequently smoked all of the marijuana they had purchased from Hyde.

In the meantime, Schalk attempted to contact six or seven law enforcement officers in an effort to find someone who would take possession of the marijuana that Edwards and Grubb had purchased from Hyde. Schalk was unsuccessful in those attempts. He eventually reached Chief Deputy Prosecutor Robert Miller at home and reported that he had arranged the drug buy, had provided the buy money, and that the transaction was complete. Schalk asked Miller for "advice on how he should deal with the disposition" of the marijuana, and Miller advised Schalk to contact Sheriff's Deputy Jerry Reed "to make a report." But Schalk was unable to reach Deputy Reed by telephone.

The day following the drug buy, Schalk obtained reimbursement from Pemberton's mother for the buy money, which she thought was for the cost of depositions. The same day, Schalk also "petitioned the Court [in Pemberton's criminal proceeding] to take custody" of the marijuana Edwards and Grubb had purchased from Hyde for use "in the upcoming Pemberton trial."[1] Apparently, Schalk believed that if the contraband was turned over to law enforcement or to the court, a crime would

1. After a hearing, the trial court in Pemberton's criminal proceeding removed Schalk as Pemberton's counsel.

not have been committed. On June 26 or 27, Miller contacted the Monroe County Sheriff's Department to report Schalk's involvement in the scheme to buy marijuana from Hyde. After an investigation, Detective Shawn Karr filed an affidavit of probable cause, and the State charged Schalk with conspiracy to possess marijuana, a Class D felony.

Schalk filed various motions to dismiss the charge against him, which the trial court denied. The State ultimately amended the charge to attempted possession of marijuana, a Class A misdemeanor, after Schalk waived his right to a trial by jury. Following a bench trial, the trial court found Schalk guilty as charged, entered a judgment of conviction, and sentenced Schalk to three months, all suspended to non-supervised probation. This appeal ensued.

Schalk summarizes his argument on appeal as follows: "David Schalk's providing cash for the purchase of marijuana was never in dispute, and that is the basis of his conviction for attempted possession of marijuana. The issues presented pertain to the legality—or lack thereof—of Schalk's actions." Schalk's primary contention is that, as a defense attorney, he is "on the same legal footing as the prosecuting attorneys, other police officers, and confidential informants planning and executing controlled buys." Thus, he reasons that his conduct did not constitute a criminal offense. We think not.

To prove attempted possession of marijuana, as a Class A misdemeanor, the State was required to prove that Schalk knowingly or intentionally took a substantial step toward possessing marijuana. Schalk admitted to the trial court that he provided Edwards with money and a recording device to use in purchasing marijuana from Hyde. But Schalk asks that we recognize an exception to culpability under a criminal statute for a defense attorney who arranges a drug buy to discredit a witness against his client at trial. This we cannot do.

The Legislature has defined "law enforcement officer" as

> (1) a police officer (including a correctional police officer), sheriff, constable, marshal, prosecuting attorney, special prosecuting attorney, special deputy prosecuting attorney, the securities commissioner, or the inspector general;
>
> (2) a deputy of any of those persons;
>
> (3) an investigator for a prosecuting attorney or for the inspector general;
>
> (4) a conservation officer;
>
> (5) an enforcement officer of the alcohol and tobacco commission; or
>
> (6) an enforcement officer of the securities division of the office of the secretary of state.

The Legislature has not included defense attorneys in the definition of law enforcement officers.

Further, Schalk's assertion that . . . his conduct was legal given his intent to turn the marijuana from the drug buy over to police is not well taken. Intent is a mental state. Therefore, the trier of fact is entitled to make reasonable inferences based upon an examination of the surrounding circumstances and, here, the trial court did so adversely to Schalk. [W]e will not reweigh the evidence. The evidence supports the trial court's determination that Schalk knowingly or intentionally attempted to possess marijuana. While Schalk contends that his only intent was to deliver the marijuana to law enforcement or the court for use in defending his client at trial, such a purpose does not immunize him from prosecution.

Schalk next asks that we "hold that the Indiana State Legislature did not intend to prohibit Hoosiers from taking prohibited drugs away from dealers so the drugs' could be kept in police custody, used as evidence in court, and destroyed." In support of that contention, Schalk directs us to Indiana['s law authorizing a citizen arrest.] But no reasonable interpretation of the statute could support Schalk's contention on this issue. Schalk does not suggest, and there is no evidence, that he ever tried to "arrest" Hyde. Rather, Schalk arranged an illegal drug buy. Schalk's contention on this issue is without merit.

Schalk also alleges that "[t]he constitutional right of people accused of crimes to defend themselves is under attack. Chad Pemberton is not a party to this appeal, but David Schalk has standing to assert his right to defend his clients as part of the guarantees of the Sixth Amendment to the Constitution of the United States of America and Article I, Section 13 of the Constitution of Indiana."

We agree that Schalk's client has a right to legal representation guaranteed by both the federal and state constitutions. But we reject Schalk's contention that an attorney, an officer of the court, who has given an oath to support the Constitution of the United States and the Constitution of the State of Indiana is authorized to engage in criminal activity in defense of his client under either the Sixth Amendment or Article I, Section 13.

In sum, Schalk asks this court to grant him the same "legal footing" as law enforcement officers for the purpose of conducting an illegal drug buy in an effort to discredit a witness against his client. The legislature has clearly identified those persons legally authorized to engage in law enforcement, and defense attorneys are not included. An attorney is not exempt from the criminal law even if his only purpose is the defense of his client. "Under the Code of Professional Responsibility an attorney is charged with defending and advancing the interests of his clients within the framework of our legal system." *Matter of Mann*, 270 Ind. 358, 385 N.E.2d 1139, 1143 (1979). "It should be abundantly clear that an attorney cannot resort to illegal means in order to obtain a favorable disposition for his client." *Id.* This is not a close case. The material facts are undisputed and fully support the trial court's judgment of conviction. Schalk has not shown reversible error.

As the facts in *Schalk* suggest, a lack of oversight in the use of informants gives police and prosecutors the power to formally or informally sanction criminal behavior in exchange for information. In some cases, this might mean informants are allowed to continue committing relatively petty crimes without facing punishment. In other instances, law enforcement officials might become so focused on obtaining information that is helpful to their own investigation that they allow their informant to commit serious crimes whose costs outweigh any public safety benefit their cooperation could conceivably provide. In one case, a United States Attorney and the acting director of the Bureau of Alcohol, Tobacco, Firearms and Explosives (ATF) resigned their positions following a scandal in the gun control setting. In a program known as "Operation Fast and Furious," the ATF instructed "cooperating gun dealers to sell to people they suspected were straw purchasers [buying weapons on behalf of Mexican drug cartels] in the hopes of building cases against major arms smugglers." Susan Crabtree, *ATF Director 'Sick To His Stomach' When He Learned Details of Fast and Furious*, TPM MUCKRAKER, July 6, 2011. The ATF planned to monitor the weapons as they were taken across the border into Mexico, but the program "lacked adequate controls" and agents "lost track of hundreds" of weapons. "Many later turned up at crime scenes in Mexico, and two were revealed at a site in Arizona where a United States Border Patrol agent was killed." Charlie Savage, *Gun Inquiry Costs Officials Their Jobs*, N.Y. TIMES, Aug. 30, 2011. *See also, e.g.*, Evan Ratliff, *The Mark: The F.B.I. Needs Informants, But What Happens When They Go Too Far?*, THE NEW YORKER, May 2, 2011 ("In 1999, it was revealed that two F.B.I. agents had for many years helped the Boston gangster Whitey Bulger, who was working as an informant, cover up crimes and avoid arrest."); Ginger Thompson, *D.E.A. Launders Mexican Profits of Drug Cartels*, N.Y. TIMES, Dec. 3, 2011 (reporting that D.E.A. agents had "laundered or smuggled millions of dollars in drug proceeds" as part of undercover investigations and that "[a]s it launders drug money, the agency often allows cartels to continue their operations over months or even years before making seizures or arrests").

Although there are few legislative constraints on the power of police and prosecutors to informally immunize informants, a number of states have enacted laws to help address concerns about informant reliability by requiring corroboration of informant testimony for a conviction in certain circumstances. For example, California has adopted an informant corroboration law that provides: "A jury or judge may not convict a defendant, find a special circumstance true, or use a fact in aggravation based on uncorroborated testimony of an in-custody informant." The law defines an in-custody informant as "a person, other than a codefendant, percipient witness, accomplice, or coconspirator, whose testimony is based on statements allegedly made by the defendant while both the defendant and the informant were held within a city or county jail, state penal institution, or correctional institution." Cal. Pen. Code § 1111.5.

While many corroboration laws are aimed exclusively at jailhouse informants, Nebraska has a long-standing corroboration statute for controlled substances offenses specifically.

Nebraska v. Johnson

Supreme Court of Nebraska
261 Neb. 1001 (2001)

Miller-Lerman, J.

Johnson was convicted of two counts of distribution of a controlled substance, marijuana, in violation of Neb. Rev. Stat. § 28-416(1)(a). The charges arose out of incidents which were alleged to have occurred on January 14 and 15, 1999. Count I pertains to January 14, and count II pertains to January 15. The direct testimonial evidence against Johnson consisted primarily of the testimony of a confidential informant who assisted the city of Hastings and Adams County by participating in controlled drug transactions for which she was compensated by the drug task force. Johnson testified in his own defense. The confidential informant's and Johnson's versions of events differed.

The confidential informant's testimony regarding two alleged controlled buys on January 14 and 15, 1999, was as follows: As to the January 14 incident, the confidential informant testified that she contacted Johnson and arranged to meet him at the Olive Saloon in Hastings. Prior to the meeting, the confidential informant was searched by a police officer, given a transmitter disguised as a pager, and given "buy money." At the bar, the confidential informant told Johnson she needed to buy an ounce of marijuana. Johnson replied that he did not have that much with him, and the two arranged to meet later at the Reno Bar. The two met at the Reno Bar, then went outside to Johnson's car where Johnson gave the confidential informant two baggies of marijuana in exchange for $75. Four law enforcement personnel testified at trial that they had seen Johnson and the confidential informant leave the bar together and go to Johnson's car on January 14.

As to the January 15, 1999, incident, the confidential informant testified that she again contacted Johnson to make another purchase. As on January 14, she was searched and given a transmitter and "buy money" prior to the meeting. The confidential informant testified that she and Johnson met again at the Reno Bar where Johnson gave her three baggies of marijuana in exchange for $90. No law enforcement personnel or any other witness testified as to having seen Johnson at the Reno Bar or to having observed Johnson meeting with the confidential informant on January 15.

After each purchase, the confidential informant delivered the marijuana to the police officers with whom she was working. On cross-examination, the confidential informant testified that she was being compensated for each occasion. Johnson was ultimately arrested and charged with two counts of distribution on July 16, 1999. He pled not guilty, and the case went to trial.

In addition to the testimony of the confidential informant and law enforcement personnel as outlined above, Johnson testified at trial. Johnson denied having sold marijuana to the confidential informant on either January 14 or 15, 1999. Johnson, however, recalled an incident which he thought may have occurred on January 14. Johnson testified he met the confidential informant at the bar and went to his car with her at her invitation to smoke marijuana which she, rather than Johnson, provided. According to Johnson, the confidential informant handed him a small amount of marijuana which he placed in a pipe. Before he could light it, the confidential informant said she had to go and left the car. Johnson thought her behavior was strange because they had smoked marijuana together in the past. Johnson returned to the bar without smoking any marijuana.

With respect to the January 15, 1999, incident, Johnson testified that although he frequented the bar, he did not specifically recall being there on January 15 and did not recall any conversation or incident involving marijuana on that date.

During the course of the trial, Johnson requested that the jury be instructed on the lesser-included charge of possession. The request was denied by the district court. The jury convicted Johnson of two counts of distribution of a controlled substance.

Johnson appealed his convictions and sentences to the Court of Appeals. The Court of Appeals, in an unpublished decision, rejected Johnson's assignments of error and affirmed his convictions and sentences. Johnson petitioned this court for further review. We granted his petition.

Johnson . . . asserts that the Court of Appeals erred in affirming the district court's denial of Johnson's motion for directed verdict at the close of all the evidence and in concluding that his convictions were supported by sufficient evidence. In a criminal case, a court can direct a verdict only when there is a complete failure of evidence to establish an essential element of the crime charged or the evidence is so doubtful in character, lacking probative value, that a finding of guilt based on such evidence cannot be sustained. If there is any evidence which will sustain a finding for the party against whom a motion for directed verdict is made, the case may not be decided as a matter of law. We conclude that the evidence was sufficient to submit count I to the jury but that count II should not have been submitted to the jury due to the lack of evidence corroborating the cooperating individual's testimony.

In connection with our consideration of the sufficiency of evidence in this case, we note that Neb. Rev. Stat. § 28-1439.01 provides: "No conviction for an offense punishable under any provision of the Uniform Controlled Substances Act shall be based solely upon the uncorroborated testimony of a cooperating individual." We agree with the conclusion of the Court of Appeals that there was sufficient evidence to submit count I regarding the January 14, 1999, incident to the jury where properly instructed. However, with regard to count II involving the incident on January 15, we conclude that the testimony of the confidential informant regarding the critical events of January 15 is uncorroborated and, therefore, insufficient under § 28-1439.01. Johnson's motion for a directed verdict on count II should have been sustained, and such count should have been dismissed.

"Cooperating individual" is defined for purposes of the Uniform Controlled Substances Act as "any person, other than a commissioned law enforcement officer, who acts on behalf of, at the request of, or as agent for a law enforcement agency for the purpose of gathering or obtaining evidence of offenses punishable under the Uniform Controlled Substances Act." Neb. Rev. Stat. § 28-401(32). The confidential informant in this case is a "cooperating individual" under § 28-1439.01. We further note that Johnson was charged with two counts of distribution of a controlled substance, marijuana, in violation of § 28-416(1)(a), which is a provision of the Uniform Controlled Substances Act. Therefore, pursuant to § 28-1439.01, neither of Johnson's convictions in this case may be based solely upon the uncorroborated testimony of the confidential informant serving as a cooperating individual.

We have held that corroboration is sufficient to meet the requirement of § 28-1439.01 if the witness is corroborated as to material facts and circumstances which tend to support the testimony as to the principal fact in issue. We have further held that corroboration may be supplied by observation that a meeting between the subject and a cooperating individual actually took place, coupled with searches of the cooperating individual both before and within a reasonable time after the drug purchase took place. We have held, however, that the evidence is legally insufficient to sustain a conviction when the State has failed to corroborate the testimony of a cooperating individual which identifies the defendant as the person involved in a distribution.

Although the Court of Appeals did not directly address the corroboration issue, it did note that the confidential informant testified that she was searched for drugs prior to both her meetings with Johnson on January 14 and 15, 1999. Although not mentioned by the Court of Appeals, law enforcement personnel involved in the operation testified that the confidential informant had been searched prior to both meetings with Johnson; that the confidential informant was wired for both meetings; and that on January 14, they saw Johnson enter the bar and later exit the bar with the confidential informant and go to Johnson's vehicle, where according to the confidential informant, the actual distribution took place. However, aside from the confidential informant, no one testified as to having seen Johnson enter or exit the bar or meet with the confidential informant on January 15.

As to count I involving the incident on January 14, 1999, there is sufficient corroborating evidence because the police officers searched the confidential informant prior to and after the meeting with Johnson and because police officers observed Johnson going into the bar and later leaving the bar with the confidential informant and going to his car where, according to the confidential informant's testimony the distribution occurred. The fact of Johnson's having met with the confidential informant on January 14 is further corroborated by Johnson's testimony regarding the events of January 14, about which he testified that he met the confidential informant in the bar and that the two of them went to his car.

However, as to count II involving the January 15, 1999, incident, the record lacks sufficient evidence corroborating the testimony of the confidential informant serving as a cooperating individual. Although there was evidence that the confidential informant was searched by police prior to and after her alleged meeting with Johnson on January 15, the police officers did not testify that they observed Johnson on

January 15, nor did they testify that they observed the confidential informant and Johnson meet on January 15. There was no testimony by police officers or anyone other than the confidential informant that Johnson was actually at the bar on January 15 or that he met with the confidential informant on that date.

We have previously identified the objectives of the predecessor statute to § 28-1439.01 by referring to the legislative history. The introducer of the bill, Senator Fowler, indicated the concerns sought to be addressed by the legislation. Senator Fowler noted that cooperating individuals "often have ulterior motives in accusing others of drug offenses . . . such as monetary gain or relieving themselves of criminal liability from drug offenses they themselves have committed." Judiciary Committee Hearing, L.B. 276, 85th Leg., 1st Sess. 66 (Feb. 22, 1977). Senator Fowler also noted: "Arrests for delivery of controlled substances violations often do not occur until weeks and often months after the date upon which the violation was alleged to have occurred. This means that even . . . innocent persons charged with such . . . violations [have] little if any effective means of defending [themselves] against the unjust charges unless they can succeed in establishing their innocence by the often difficult if not impossible task of establishing that they could not have been in the place at that time the offense was alleged to have occurred."

Both concerns noted by Senator Fowler were present in the instant case because the confidential informant was paid for her work and because Johnson was not arrested until July 1999 for the violation alleged to have occurred on January 15, 1999. Regarding the January 15 incident, there was no evidence to corroborate the confidential informant's testimony that she met with Johnson at the Reno Bar or any evidence other than her testimony that Johnson was at the bar on that date. As noted by the introducer, testimony to corroborate a defendant's presence at the time and place of the alleged violation is especially vital when a period of months exists between the alleged violation and the defendant's arrest.

The State argues that the evidence is sufficient as to count II because the testimony by Johnson and the law enforcement officers specifically corroborating the confidential informant's testimony regarding the January 14, 1999, incident also corroborates her testimony regarding the January 15 incident. We reject this argument. Although both counts were charged in the same information, each count represents a separate offense. Because § 28-1439.01 requires that "no conviction for *an offense* punishable under any provision of the Uniform Controlled Substances Act shall be based solely upon the uncorroborated testimony of a cooperating individual," we conclude that each count represents a separate offense and that the evidence supporting each count must independently satisfy the requirements of § 28-1439.01.

We conclude that Johnson's conviction on count II was not based on sufficient evidence because it was based solely on the uncorroborated testimony of the confidential informant who was serving as a cooperating individual. In enacting § 28-1439.01, the Legislature has indicated that such uncorroborated testimony cannot be the sole basis for a conviction under the Uniform Controlled Substances Act. Accordingly,

Johnson's motion for directed verdict at the close of all the evidence should have been granted as to count II. The district court erred in denying this motion as to count II, and the Court of Appeals erred in affirming the district court's denial of Johnson's motion for a directed verdict as to count II made at the close of the evidence.

c. Informant Safety and Sanctioned Criminality

In some cases, the lack of judicial oversight over the use of informants can lead police and prosecutors to provide them with too many rewards, thereby increasing the risk informants will give inaccurate information. In other cases, however, the lack of judicial oversight can put informants themselves in danger.

Consider, for example, the case of Bianca Hervey, a 20-year-old college student from Attica, New York. In 2009, Hervey was driving home to her apartment one afternoon after her classes when she was stopped by the police and arrested for driving without a license, which had been suspended for failure to pay traffic tickets. At the police station, Hervey was handcuffed to a bench and told she would spend the night in jail unless she signed an agreement to become a confidential informant for the Wyoming County Drug Task Force. Hervey told the police she didn't use drugs and didn't know anyone who used or sold drugs. Even though Hervey's arrest had nothing to do with drugs and despite her insistence that she did not have any connections to the drug world, the police insisted she would spend the night in jail unless she signed up to become an informant for the drug task force. Hervey eventually agreed and signed the confidential informant contract. After she was released, Hervey told her father—an attorney who represents police unions—about the incident. Hervey's father complained to local officials that pressuring individuals without drug involvement to become drug informants might put them in danger. The Wyoming County Sheriff and District Attorney refused to release any information about the department's informant policy and said they stood by the effort to enlist Hervey as an informant. "'I think if you talk to people who have task forces anywhere,' the sheriff said, 'the policy would be similar.'" *See* Michael Beebe, *Would-be Informant Says Police Coerced Her Into Cooperation*, The Buffalo News, Nov. 8, 2009.

What problems, if any, do you think might arise from engaging individuals like Hervey to work as informants? What legal protections, if any, do you think should be established to regulate the use of informants?

Coerced Informants and Thirteenth Amendment Limitations on the Police-Informant Relationship

Michael L. Rich

50 Santa Clara Law Review 681 (2010)

On May 7, 2008, Rachel Morningstar Hoffman, a twenty-three-year-old Tallahassee resident and recent graduate of Florida State University, disappeared while trying to purchase 1500 pills of ecstasy, two-and-a-half ounces of cocaine, and a handgun for $13,000 from two suspected drug dealers. Two days later, the

Tallahassee Police Department ("TPD") arrested the dealers, Andrea Green and Deneilo Bradshaw, who led police to Hoffman's body. Hoffman had been shot and her body dumped in a rural area outside of the city.

The swift apprehension of Bradshaw and Green might, at first glance, appear to be an example of efficient police work. But in fact, the TPD were intimately involved in the events that led to her death, as Hoffman was a confidential informant who set up the deal at the TPD's express direction and under threat of criminal prosecution. Three weeks before her death, the TPD searched Hoffman's apartment and found approximately five ounces of marijuana, six ecstasy pills, and other drug paraphernalia. The next day, officers met with Hoffman and gave her a choice: she could help the TPD apprehend other drug dealers or face prosecution on multiple felony charges. The decision no doubt seemed simple to Hoffman. The TPD told her that she only had to provide "substantial assistance" or do "one big deal" to avoid charges and promised that they would keep her safe. But if she refused to cooperate, they threatened significant prison time on multiple felony charges, and these new charges would have made her ineligible for drug court disposition of earlier marijuana possession charges. Given her options, she agreed to cooperate with the TPD.

Hoffman's situation is typical of those faced by an increasing number of civilians who assist police in exchange for leniency. She decided to cooperate alone, without an opportunity to consult her attorney. She lacked a meaningful understanding of the charges she could face as a result of the drugs found in her apartment, or what she had to do in order to receive leniency. Once recruited, she risked injury and death to cooperate with the government and did so with no training in conducting undercover police operations or protecting herself from harm.

Given the importance of informants in many areas of law enforcement, police officers are encouraged to pursue all available avenues to grow their informant networks. At the state level, guidelines for determining whether a civilian is a good informant candidate are at best scattershot, and generally involve little oversight. At the federal level, the Department of Justice has established guidelines requiring that a case agent consider seventeen factors to determine a potential informant's suitability, including her age, motivation, relationship with the target of the investigation, reliability, and history of drug abuse. Though the guidelines provide no direction as to how these factors should be weighed or applied in making the ultimate suitability determination, they do require a supervisor's approval of the decision to recruit an informant. Nonetheless, even when guidelines do exist, they often give way to the government's constant need for more informants.

While informants can come from any walk of life, officers are encouraged to target those civilians who are engaged in criminal activity, live or work in close proximity to criminals or crime, or associate with criminals, because they are most likely to possess useful information and connections. Among law-abiding citizens, professions that place individuals in a position to interact with criminals and surreptitiously obtain information, such as barbers, bartenders, hotel clerks, postal workers, doormen, and waiters, are considered to be excellent sources of useful informants.

Non-criminals can be useful informants, but the most productive, long-term informants tend to be criminals themselves. Criminals rarely volunteer to become informants without any police encouragement, so efforts to "flip" a suspected criminal typically begin immediately following her arrest. A civilian's uncertainty about her future is highest in the hours after being arrested, thus making her most likely to agree to cooperate at that time. One former officer who trains police in informant recruitment recommends that "all individuals arrested should be interviewed for becoming potential informants," because "informants who have initiated significant cases or provided information for an investigation have been known to be developed following an arrest for a minor offense."

While the agreement to cooperate is superficially similar to a plea agreement, it lacks the safeguards that attach to a formal plea, including specificity, judicial review, and, in most cases, the participation of defense counsel. When promising leniency, police are instructed to avoid making specific promises about what amount of assistance will be sufficient to earn leniency or exactly what form that leniency will take. As a result, the police frequently tell an informant only that "substantial assistance" is expected of her, and promise nothing more than to share the fact of the informant's cooperation with the prosecutor or the court. Additionally, while a court must ensure that a defendant's waiver of his constitutional rights is knowing, voluntary, and intelligent before a plea is valid, the active informant agrees to cooperate without judicial oversight of, acquiescence in, or even awareness of the deal. Finally, the negotiation of the cooperation agreement often occurs outside the presence and without the knowledge of the informant's attorney.

Shortly after an arrest, police maximize the arrestee's fear of a long sentence by emphasizing the maximum penalties for the crimes with which she might be charged and suggesting that the only easy way out is for her to cooperate. At least one expert suggests that even when there is insufficient evidence to bring charges against an individual, police should claim that charges will soon be filed to encourage an arrestee to assist the police. Alternatively, he suggests filing criminal charges against uncooperative individuals for the sole purpose of encouraging them to become informants.

Following Rachel Hoffman's death, Florida enacted legislation known as "Rachel's Law" to regulate police interactions with informants in the state. The law was "the first of its kind to be passed by a state legislature" and "requires law enforcement agencies to establish policies and procedures, including recordkeeping rules, to guide police when they turn a suspect into an informant." Alexandra Natapoff, *Regulating Criminal Snitching*, L.A. DAILY JOURNAL (Sept. 15, 2009). Under the law, "[p]olice must consider an informant's suitability—including their age, maturity, and risk of physical harm—before entering into an agreement." *Id.*

The law does not, however, require that would-be informants consult with an attorney before agreeing to cooperate and "also leaves open what sort of information the police must collect and keep about their informants." *Id.* Alexandra Natapoff argues that "Rachel's Law illustrates just how secretive and unregulated law enforcement practices are. In any other legal context, it would be uncontroversial to require the government to have written procedures to guide and keep track of its important decisions. . . . Every year, thousands of drug suspects secretly become informants, and they do it without lawyers, judicial oversight, or documentation." *Id.*

d. The Public Authority and Innocent Intent Defenses

Because confidential informant agreements do not always precisely memorialize the work the informant will be performing for the government, there is a risk the informant might misunderstand the nature of his agreement and engage in criminal behavior in the mistaken belief that it is part of his work for the authorities. There are three closely related defenses that sometimes arise in cases where a defendant is prosecuted for crimes he committed while working as an informant: public authority, innocent intent, and entrapment by estoppel. Though the defenses are technically distinct, they are often confused for one another, even by courts. In the next case, the court considers the public authority and innocent intent defenses.

United States v. Fulcher

United States Court of Appeals for the Fourth Circuit
250 F.3d 244 (2001)

Luttig, J.

Defendants Ethel, Michael, and Rosanna Fulcher were convicted by a jury of various money laundering and drug violations. Following trial, a government agent wrote an *ex parte* letter to the district court explaining that he may have led the defendants to believe that they were authorized to conduct the entire operation on behalf of the government. The district court granted a new trial to the defendants pursuant to Fed. R. Crim. P. 33, holding that the newly discovered evidence satisfied every requisite element for a new trial. For the reasons that follow, we affirm.

This case arises out of the pervasive presence of drugs at Bland Correctional Center ("BCC"), an institution operated by the Virginia Department of Corrections. The network of drug distribution at BCC was extensive, involving inmates, prison officials, and even the relatives and girlfriends of inmates. The drug operation managed by Michael Fulcher ("Michael") was no exception.

Michael purchased his supply of marijuana from various prison officials, including prison guards and counselors. He would then divide the drugs he received into smaller quantities—most often teaspoon-sized servings—for distribution to inmates at BCC. Since his customers were prohibited from using cash while incarcerated, inmates purchased the drugs with money orders written on their inmate trust accounts, remitting payment to a number of individuals located outside the prison, including Rosanna Fulcher ("Rosanna"), Michael's wife, and Ethel Fulcher ("Ethel"), Michael's mother. The funds collected would then be used to purchase additional marijuana from prison officials, beginning the cycle anew.

The appellants, Michael and Rosanna, were charged in a 47-count indictment—along with 22 other defendants—with engaging in drug and money laundering conspiracies, as well as substantive counts of the same. The jury convicted Rosanna of a money laundering conspiracy and ten substantive counts of money laundering. Michael was convicted of drug and money laundering conspiracies, a continuing criminal enterprise offense ("CCE"), and 17 substantive money laundering counts.

On the eve of sentencing, the district court received an *ex parte* letter from Special Agent Donald O. Lincoln, Jr., of the Drug Enforcement Administration ("DEA"). In the letter, Lincoln explained that [Michael had contacted him with a] request to formally investigate the distribution of drugs at BCC [but that he had rejected the request] for two reasons: (1) it would be impossible to ensure his safety from other inmates and prison guards while he was incarcerated; and (2) the amount of marijuana was "so minuscule that I advised him that there was no way that we could justify a Federal investigation on what would at best be misdemeanor level quantities."

Although Lincoln never formally granted permission for Michael to initiate a formal drug investigation, Lincoln nonetheless stated his concern that he, along with state law enforcement officers working with the DEA, may have provided Michael with the mistaken impression that he had tacit approval to investigate drug dealing at BCC. Specifically, Lincoln explained:

> It has come to my attention that in my absence Mr. Fulcher would periodically talk to Deputy Kenny Parker of the Botetourt County Sheriff's Office, who was working in the DEA Office, serving as a DEA Task Force Officer at that time. In these conversations Mr. Fulcher told Deputy Parker what he was working on. Deputy Parker, believing that the operation had already been approved by me, discussed a number of options with Mr. Fulcher. One of these involved arranging for one or more of the guards who were involved to make an attempted pickup of marijuana from Deputy Parker, in an undercover capacity, in Botetourt County. Under those circumstances the case could have been taken to State Court in Botetourt or, if it developed into something interstate or substantial it could be brought to Federal Court. Deputy Parker discussed this potential operation with Sheriff Reed Kelly, and both of them recall the conversations. In addition Deputy Parker reminded me of a conversation he had with me concerning setting up a potential sting operation against a prison guard, to go down at a Botetourt County truck stop.

Lincoln also stated in the letter that during his numerous telephone conversations with Michael over a three-year period,

> there were indeed times when I was in a hurry to get him off the phone due to other commitments. If I said anything in haste which led him to believe

> he was "covered" it may be the proximate cause of all of this. I honestly do not recall ever saying anything to that effect, but if Task Force Agent Parker and Sheriff Kelly also believe that I did, then I must lend credibility to the possibility. I don't know what if any consideration can be given to all that I have related here, your Honor, but I felt it incumbent on me to state the facts as I now know them.

On the basis of the letter, appellants filed a motion, asserting that they were entitled to a new trial on the basis of newly discovered evidence pursuant to Fed. R. Crim. P. 33. The district court held an evidentiary hearing, in which both Lincoln and Deputy Parker testified. Lincoln stated that David Fulcher, Michael's father, told him that Michael and Parker had spoken on several occasions concerning a possible sting operation. According to Lincoln, Parker told him that he had talked with Michael several times regarding a possible drug operation, and that Parker had discussed a number of options with Michael about how to set up a sting operation involving prison officials. On redirect, Lincoln acknowledged that, since his testimony at the pretrial hearing, his opinion regarding whether the Fulchers may have believed that they were authorized to conduct the operation had changed:

> Q: All right. Now during your July testimony, June testimony (sic) in the courtroom, I asked you a question about, "Did you ever do anything that in your estimation could have been construed as permission to conduct this investigation?" And do you recollect your answer as being, "No"?
>
> A: I probably did say that, and I guess that's— . . .
>
> Q: Are you now of the opinion that you could have been communicating to him and his mother that if the case was bigger it would be prosecuted and he could get his sentence reduced?
>
> A: I don't know, but, yes, that's my primary concern at this point.
>
> Q: Do you believe you might have?
>
> A: Yes. And if not me, then the fact that he talked to the other people in my office or to other people in my office (sic) and he felt that they somehow blessed it, then there is the very real possibility, especially from the part of Mrs. Fulcher.

On the basis of the letter and the testimony adduced at the evidentiary hearing, the district court granted the motion for a new trial, holding that the newly discovered evidence was material because it was directly related to the public authority defense and to whether the defendants possessed the requisite *mens rea* for their crimes.

The government argues on appeal that the district court erred in granting a new trial to defendants on the basis of newly discovered evidence.

Under Fed. R. Crim. P. 33, "on a defendant's motion, the court may grant a new trial to that defendant if the interests of justice so require." In determining whether a new trial should be granted under Rule 33 for newly discovered evidence, this court utilizes a five-part test [articulated in *United States v. Custis*, 988 F.2d 1355, 1359 (4th Cir. 1989)]:

> (a) the evidence must be, in fact, newly discovered, i.e., discovered since the trial; (b) facts must be alleged from which the court may infer diligence on the part of the movant; (c) the evidence relied on must not be merely cumulative or impeaching; (d) it must be material to the issues involved; and (e) it must be such, and of such nature, as that, on a new trial, the newly discovered evidence would probably produce an acquittal.

5 part test

Without ruling out the possibility that a rare example might exist, we have never allowed a new trial unless all five elements were established.

The district court made extensive findings on each of the elements of the *Custis* test and, of course, we review for an abuse of discretion the district court's decision to grant a new trial based on those findings.

[The court then applied the first, second, and third elements of the five-part test and found that each had been met by the defendant.]

The fourth element of *Custis* is whether the newly discovered evidence is "material to the issues involved." The government's principal argument on appeal is that the district court misapplied the defenses of public authority and mistake of fact and, in doing so, granted a new trial when the newly discovered evidence is not material.

At the post-trial evidentiary hearing, the following colloquy took place between Lincoln and Assistant United States Attorney Mott regarding whether Lincoln had actual authority to authorize money laundering activities:

> Q: If you were conducting a money laundering investigation, would you expect to document where the money went?
>
> A: Yes. And first and foremost I would expect to have to get an attorney's general's exemption to do it.
>
> Q: *And in a money laundering case you've got to go to the AG to get an exemption?*
>
> A: *You have to go to the AG.* That's why I would never have authorized him to do that without permission.

Lincoln further testified to the following when asked about his authority to authorize a drug operation of the type managed by Michael:

> Q: And kind of a paramount rule in drug investigations is that you don't let the drugs walk?
>
> A: Correct.
>
> Q: And that means you would never allow Mr. Fulcher to sell marijuana to someone without recovering it very shortly thereafter?
>
> A: That's correct.

Q: *You would never authorize him to conduct drug sales on behalf of the DEA?*

A: *That's true, and he knows that.*

On the basis of Lincoln's testimony, the government argues that Lincoln and his colleagues possessed, at most, apparent authority to approve the operation undertaken by the Fulchers, and that such authority was insufficient to either negate intent or to support the defense of public authority. Though we agree with the legal arguments advanced by the government, we nonetheless conclude that there is insufficient evidence in the record regarding the extent of Lincoln's authority (or that of his colleagues at the DEA). Thus, we ultimately hold that the district court did not abuse its discretion when it concluded that the newly discovered evidence was material.

The defendants first seek to introduce Lincoln's testimony for the purpose of negating criminal intent. "The defendant may allege that he lacked criminal intent because he honestly believed he was performing the otherwise-criminal acts in cooperation with the government. Innocent intent is not a defense *per se*, but a defense strategy aimed at negating the *mens rea* for the crime, an essential element of the prosecution's case."

While an honest belief that a defendant is acting in cooperation with the government is a necessary element of establishing innocent intent, it is not alone sufficient. That is, evidence that defendants "honestly believed" that they acted in concert with a government official could abrogate the criminal intent necessary to prove the particular crimes with which the defendants were charged, but, as we have recognized previously, any such abrogation *also* depends upon the nature of that official's authority.

For instance, if a government official possessed *actual* authority to authorize the defendants' activity, then criminal intent certainly would be negated by the defendant's honest belief that he was cooperating with such an official. However, if the official possessed *neither* actual nor apparent authority to authorize the otherwise criminal activity, then criminal intent would not be negated.

The question most readily presented by Lincoln's testimony, and a question we have not heretofore addressed, is neither whether intent is negated when a defendant acts in concert with an official who does not possess either actual or apparent authority nor whether criminal intent is negated when a defendant acts in cooperation with an official with actual authority but, rather, whether the criminal intent for the crimes with which these defendants were charged is negated if they were acting in conjunction with an official who possesses only apparent authority. We hold, consistent with our sister circuits that have considered the question, that intent is not negated when a defendant cooperates with an official who possesses only *apparent* authority.

Essentially, defendants argue that, if they acted at the direction of an official who possessed apparent authority, they would lack the requisite *mens rea* for the crimes with which they were charged. According to defendants, under such a circumstance, they would have made only a mistake of fact—a cognizable defense negating intent when the *mens rea* requirement for a crime is at least knowledge—regarding whether DEA officials possessed actual authority to authorize their drug and money laundering activities.

Any such defense is foreclosed, however, by our reasoning in *Kelly.* There, the defendant relied on a government informant who enlisted his help to assist in a government operation. The defendant argued that if he acted at the invitation of the informant, he could not have possessed the requisite criminal intent for conspiracy to distribute drugs. We disagreed, explaining that defendant's mistake arose not from "a mistake of fact as to the informant's status, but resulted from a misconception of the legal prerogatives attached to that status." We thus held that if the defendant "indeed acted on the basis of a mistake . . . it was a mistake of law, not a mistake of fact." Of course, since defendant's error was a mistake of law, his belief did not constitute a defense to his criminal act.

Though we did not address in *Kelly* whether a defendant's intent may be negated when he acts pursuant to an official's apparent authority, the reasoning of that case compels us to now answer that question in the negative. For, reliance on the apparent authority of a government official is nothing more than a mistake about "the legal prerogatives attached" to such status and thus constitutes a mistake of law. *See United States v. Rosenthal,* 793 F.2d 1214, 1235–36 (11th Cir. 1986) (stating that a "defendant may only be exonerated on the basis of his reliance on real and not merely apparent authority."); *Duggan,* 743 F.2d at 83 ("The mistake that defendants advance here as an excuse for their criminal activities—their reliance on Hanratty's purported authority—is an error based upon a mistaken view of legal requirements and therefore constitutes a mistake of law.").

Therefore, we hold that criminal intent is negated if two elements are met: (1) the defendant honestly believed that he was acting in cooperation with the government, and (2) the government official or officials upon whose authority the defendant relied possessed actual authority to authorize his otherwise criminal acts.

Defendants also seek to introduce Lincoln's testimony to support their defense of public authority. The public authority defense allows "the defendant to seek exoneration based on the fact that he reasonably relied on the authority of a government official to engage him in a covert activity." Thus, in contrast to the innocent intent doctrine, this affirmative defense allows a defendant to seek exoneration based upon his *objectively reasonable reliance* on the authority of a government official.

We have never addressed the scope of the public authority defense, and, in particular, we have never explained whether such a defense entitles a defendant to rely on the apparent authority of a government official or whether actual authority is necessarily required. However, we again find *Kelly* persuasive in answering this question. As explained above, *Kelly* stands for the proposition that any mistake about "the legal prerogatives" attached to a person's status is not a defense to a criminal act.

Our recognition of an apparent public authority defense would contravene *Kelly* by creating an affirmative defense in precisely such circumstances.

Accordingly, we adopt the unanimous view of our sister circuits that the defense of public authority requires reasonable reliance upon the actual authority of a government official to engage him in a covert activity.

The government requests that we decide as a matter of law that the newly discovered evidence is not material despite the deferential standard of review we employ in reviewing a district court's decision to grant a new trial. We decline to reach that conclusion because neither party has been furnished with an opportunity to introduce any evidence regarding whether Lincoln or his colleagues at the DEA possessed actual authority to sanction defendants' money laundering and drug activities. Furthermore, while Lincoln's testimony certainly suggests that these officials did not possess such authority, his testimony does not conclusively establish that this is so, especially with regard to Michael's drug activities.

Therefore, if defendants can establish at a new trial that DEA officials authorized them to conduct the operation and that such officials had the actual authority to do so, defendants would be entitled to appropriate jury instructions on the defenses of public authority and innocent intent. Since the jury would then be entitled to acquit the defendants if it concluded that defendants' activities were legitimately authorized, we hold that the district court did not abuse its discretion in concluding that the newly discovered evidence is "material to the issues involved."

The fifth element of *Custis* is whether the evidence is "such, and of such nature, as that, on a new trial, the newly discovered evidence would probably produce an acquittal." Much of our analysis on the third and fourth elements of *Custis* is equally applicable here. In particular, we again note that the persuasive value of Lincoln's testimony cannot be underestimated due to his status as a DEA agent who participated in the investigation of this case. Furthermore, as the district court observed, if the jury credits Lincoln's testimony that DEA officials may have led defendants to believe that they were acting pursuant to governmental authority, "it would certainly create a record more favorable for the Fulchers." Therefore, we cannot say that the district court abused its discretion in concluding that the newly discovered evidence "would probably produce an acquittal."

For the foregoing reasons, the district court's decision to grant a new trial to defendants is affirmed and the case is remanded for further proceedings consistent with this opinion.

Fulcher holds that for a defendant to succeed, the government agent upon whom she relied must have had the actual authority to empower her to engage in the conduct in question. Contrary to the court's statement that this is the unanimous view, not all jurisdictions require proof that the agent had actual authority. *See* Michael L. Rich, *Brass Rings and Red-Headed Stepchildren: Protecting Active*

Criminal Informants, 61 AM. U. L. REV. 1433, 1502 n. 303 (2012) (collecting cases). Requiring proof of actual authority is, however, the majority approach. Why should the public authority defense turn on actual authority? From the perspective of blameworthiness, the rule is hard to justify. "No conceivable fairness rationale justifies this limitation on the public authority defense. From the individual informant's point of view, government assurances are no less an 'indefensible sort of entrapment' because the official who offered them lacked genuine authority to do so. Indeed, levels of official authority within the agency will often be entirely opaque to those on the outside." Zachary S. Price, *Reliance on Nonenforcement*, 58 WM. & MARY L. REV. 937, 981 (2017). Price argues that the actual authority requirement "reflect[s] structural concerns rooted in separation of powers," namely an interest in "declin[ing] to give every law enforcement official an effective dispensing power." *Ibid.*

3. Wiretaps

Wiretaps are another important tool for investigating drug crimes, though they are not as frequently employed as one might assume. According to the Administrative Office of the United States Courts, only 3,168 domestic wiretaps were authorized in 2016, 1,551 by federal judges and 1,617 by state judges. This figure does not include intercepts pursuant to the Foreign Intelligence Surveillance Act of 1978 (FISA) or recordings made with the consent of one of the principal parties to the conversation. Though wiretaps are not widespread, drug investigations are responsible for the great majority of them. In 2016, 82 percent of all wiretap applications cited illegal drugs as the most serious offense under investigation.

The high cost of wiretaps may partly explain why they are not used more often. The average cost of a wiretap in 2016 was $74,949. The most expensive single wiretap that year was for a 434-day wiretap in a drug case that cost just under $3 million and resulted in just 15 arrests and *zero* convictions. As a text written as a resource for law enforcement officers on drug investigations explains, because wiretaps require "a considerable amount of time and manpower, many departments often cannot justify [their] use." Michael D. Lyman, PRACTICAL DRUG ENFORCEMENT at 120 (3d ed. 2007). *See also*, Max Minzer, *Putting Probability Back Into Probable Cause*, 87 TEX. L. REV. 913, 926–29 (2009) (discussing a study concluding the high cost of wiretaps is a greater constraint on their use than the probable cause requirement).

In addition to the cost associated with employing and monitoring a wiretap, law enforcement officers must meet special statutory requirements before a wiretap is authorized. Though wiretaps are considered to be "searches" under the Fourth Amendment, the statutory requirements for wiretaps are stricter than the constitutional requirements. *See*, *United States v. Gaines*, 2011 WL 1662363 (8th Cir. 2011) (comparing Title III's particularity requirement with the Fourth Amendment's particularity requirement). The case that follows provides an overview of some of the legal issues that can arise in the context of a wiretap investigation.

United States v. Meléndez-Santiago

United States Court of Appeals for the First Circuit
644 F.3d 54 (2011)

Lynch, J.

After a twenty-eight-day trial in 2007 a jury found Elkin Meléndez-Santiago, one of twelve indicted co-conspirators, guilty of conspiracy to import five or more kilograms of cocaine and one or more kilograms of heroin, as well as actual importation of five or more kilograms of cocaine, as part of a massive cocaine and heroin importation organization. Only one other defendant went to trial and he was also convicted. The remainder pled guilty.

In the conspiracy, Meléndez provided cash to co-conspirators to cover expenses for some drug smuggling operations and purchased cocaine and heroin imported into Puerto Rico for further distribution. Millions of dollars worth of drugs were imported. During one importation attempt in 2004, federal officers who had been tipped off to the drugs' arrival seized the drugs after a shootout with some of Meléndez's co-conspirators. The district court found it was known or foreseeable that firearms were being carried in furtherance of the conspiracy, justifying a sentence enhancement.

Meléndez was a cocaine addict who used cocaine daily, but he had no prior criminal record. He was sentenced to 360 months' imprisonment, which was less than the life sentence advised by the U.S. Sentencing Guidelines.

His appeal argues . . . the district court committed reversible error in not suppressing evidence of conversations recorded in two Title III wiretaps because the affidavits in support of the wiretaps did not sufficiently explain why traditional investigative procedures were inadequate, necessitating wiretaps, see 18 U.S.C. § 2518(1)(c), (3)(c), and because the affidavits contained misleading information. He argues that the district court should have held a *Franks* hearing to permit him to establish that the affidavits included misleading information and that without such information, the affidavits would not have sufficed to establish probable cause for the wiretaps. See *Franks v. Delaware,* 438 U.S. 154, 155–56 (1978).

The initial determination as to compliance with the stringent standards for issuing a wiretap authorization is made by the judge to whom the application is made. At this later stage, appellate review of that authorization is not de novo, but deferential. We "decide if the facts set forth in the application were minimally adequate to support the determination that was made."

Here, two wiretap authorizations resulted from applications dated November 23 and December 9, 2004, both supported by sworn affidavits by FBI agent Jose Mena. Both applications targeted certain cell phone numbers and were approved by a district court judge. These cell phone numbers were used by the conspiracy leader, Luis Alfredo De La Rosa-Montero, also known as "Luis Viagra" or "El Compadre," to coordinate the drug conspiracy.

In order to be approved, the applications needed to show what is commonly referred to as the "necessity" of resort to wiretaps. To make this showing, wiretap applications must provide "a full and complete statement as to whether or not other investigative procedures have been tried and failed or why they reasonably appear to be unlikely to succeed if tried or to be too dangerous." 18 U.S.C. §2518(1)(c). In *United States v. Villarman-Oviedo,* we interpreted §2518(1)(c) "to mean that the statement should demonstrate that the government has made 'a reasonable, good faith effort to run the gamut of normal investigative procedures before resorting to means so intrusive as electronic interception of telephone calls.'" In such a statement, "[i]t is not necessary . . . to show that other methods have been entirely unsuccessful."

Our reading of the affidavits disproves Meléndez's contentions that they were insufficient to support issuance of the wiretap authorizations. Indeed, they were better than minimally adequate. The November 23 affidavit contained the available identifying information known about the conspirators, all Dominican or Puerto Rican nationals. The affidavit also described how three confidential sources and one confidential informant had at times aided the investigation, providing information about those who were working in the conspiracy and about particular prior shipments, information that had led to successful arrests and drug seizures. The affidavit described in twenty-five detailed pages the conversations and interactions the sources and informant had with De La Rosa, some of which were recorded by the sources and some of which were verified when transactions were interrupted and smugglers arrested by federal officials. The affidavit also described what information had been gleaned from existing pen register and trap and trace analysis of De La Rosa's phone numbers.

The November 23 affidavit also described the limited success of efforts to conduct physical surveillance of the conspiracy leader De La Rosa. Physical surveillance was especially difficult in St. Thomas, where De La Rosa lived, because the streets were narrow and foreigners easily spotted. De La Rosa and other conspirators stayed in areas frequented by other Dominican nationals who were part of the same criminal subculture. The conspirators were wary of surveillance and they, in fact, mounted vigilant counter-surveillance. The conspirators did not use their real names and distrusted others not like them. Federal agents either mounting surveillance or attempting to infiltrate the organization undercover who were not members of that subculture would be easily spotted, would not be trusted by other members of the conspiracy, and would consequently be at great risk. Importantly, at the time of the wiretap application, one of the confidential sources had been missing for five months and was presumed dead; another had been threatened with death and was no longer trusted by members of the organization.

The information from sources other than surveillance was also constrained. The affidavit explained why traditional investigative techniques that had not been used—a grand jury investigation, interviews with co-conspirators or their associates, or execution of search warrants—were, particularly given the limited information known about the co-conspirators' identities and roles, likely to tip off the co-conspirators as to the developing investigation without yielding much helpful information. Pen registers and trap and trace records were already being used and would continue to be used, but gleaned only limited information about the cell phones being used.

The December 9 application sought wiretap authorization for another, new cell phone number used by De La Rosa. The supporting affidavit was similar in its level of detail to the first, related affidavit.

The affidavits' exhaustive explanation of what facts were known, what details remained unknown, what investigative techniques had been used and what techniques were likely to be unhelpful in the specific context of this particular conspiracy clearly constituted "a full and complete statement as to whether or not other investigative procedures have been tried and failed or why they reasonably appear to be unlikely to succeed if tried or to be too dangerous." 18 U.S.C. § 2518(1)(c). The affidavits certainly supported the determination to authorize the wiretaps.

Meléndez argues that the affidavits failed to disclose that the agent who signed them was himself of Dominican origin, as was one of the confidential sources, and that they understated the scope of that source's knowledge about the internal workings of the criminal conspiracy. These arguments are in service of Meléndez's hypothesis that someone of Dominican origin could easily have been slipped into the organization as an undercover agent, and that alternatively, the confidential source must already have had sufficient knowledge about the conspiracy's organization, both facts obviating any need for wiretaps.

Meléndez takes it one step further and argues that because these facts were so obviously material, the affidavit misled the district court judges who authorized the wiretaps into authorizations they would not otherwise have granted. See *Franks*, 438 U.S. at 171–72 (holding that if "deliberate falsity or reckless disregard" for the truth in a warrant affidavit are specifically and reliably alleged, and if there is no longer sufficient material to support a finding of probable cause when the material in question "is set to one side," the court must grant the defendant a hearing to prove the allegations).

This house of cards is too flimsy to stand. To be of Dominican origin does not make one a natural undercover agent (or inconspicuous as part of a criminal subculture); nor does it mitigate the likelihood of an agent or confidential source being murdered by the conspiracy upon discovery.[1] Meléndez's speculation that the confidential source must already have known and shared with the investigators the details of the conspiracy's inner workings before the wiretap application is equally

1. Indeed, as the affidavit explained, the confidential source Meléndez refers to was in custody at the time of the application because members of the conspiracy already distrusted him and had threatened his life.

illogical and unsupported. No inference of falsity or reckless disregard of the truth can be drawn from the non-disclosure of these irrelevant bits of information. For that reason no hearing was required. Nor did the ample probable cause set forth in the affidavit for tapping the phones depend in any way on these alleged omissions, also obviating the need for a Franks hearing.

The judgment of conviction is affirmed.

B. Drug Investigations and the Fourth Amendment

The Fourth Amendment, covered in detail in Criminal Procedure courses, provides rules for when and how the police may gather evidence and detain suspects. Many (if not most) of the cases assigned in a Criminal Procedure course today involved drug investigations. This section does not attempt to duplicate the material covered in Criminal Procedure courses. Instead, it focuses on Fourth Amendment problems that are uniquely related to the enforcement and investigation of drug offenses.

Before looking at issues that arise in drug investigations, a review of Fourth Amendment basics is in order. The Fourth Amendment provides in full: "The right of the people to be secure in their persons, houses, papers, and effects, against unreasonable searches and seizures, shall not be violated, and no Warrants shall issue, but upon probable cause, supported by Oath or affirmation, and particularly describing the place to be searched, and the persons or things to be seized."

When applying the Fourth Amendment, courts first ask whether the police have performed a search or a seizure. After all, if the police conduct does not amount to a search or a seizure, then by definition it cannot be an "unreasonable" search or seizure. A search occurs when the police infringe on an expectation of privacy that society recognizes as reasonable or when the police make an unlicensed physical intrusion on a constitutionally protected area for purposes of obtaining information. A seizure has taken place when a reasonable person in the suspect's situation would not feel free to decline the officer's request or otherwise terminate the encounter.

To be constitutional, a search or seizure must be done pursuant to a warrant supported by probable cause or an exception to the warrant requirement. There is a long list of exceptions to the warrant requirement. Most relevant to the material to come, the police may conduct a stop (seizure) and frisk (search) based on reasonable suspicion, a lower standard than probable cause. If a police officer has probable cause to believe evidence of a crime is in a car, she can search it without a warrant under the automobile exception. Finally, the special needs exception allows the government to conduct certain searches, including some drug tests, if they are done in order to achieve a need that is separate from law enforcement.

1. Drug Dog Sniffs

In *Illinois v. Caballes*, the United States Supreme Court held that the use of a drug dog to sniff a vehicle does not amount to a "search" under the Fourth Amendment. As a result, the police do not need any suspicion in order to conduct a drug dog sniff of a vehicle. As discussed in the next section, the ability to use drug dogs to sniff stopped vehicles without suspicion has helped to fuel the phenomenon of pretextual car stops.

Illinois v. Caballes

Supreme Court of the United States
543 U.S. 405 (2005)

Justice Stevens delivered the opinion of the Court.

Illinois State Trooper Daniel Gillette stopped respondent for speeding on an interstate highway. When Gillette radioed the police dispatcher to report the stop, a second trooper, Craig Graham, a member of the Illinois State Police Drug Interdiction Team, overheard the transmission and immediately headed for the scene with his narcotics-detection dog. When they arrived, respondent's car was on the shoulder of the road and respondent was in Gillette's vehicle. While Gillette was in the process of writing a warning ticket, Graham walked his dog around respondent's car. The dog alerted at the trunk. Based on that alert, the officers searched the trunk, found marijuana, and arrested respondent. The entire incident lasted less than 10 minutes.

Respondent was convicted of a narcotics offense and sentenced to 12 years' imprisonment and a $256,136 fine. The trial judge denied his motion to suppress the seized evidence and to quash his arrest. He held that the officers had not unnecessarily prolonged the stop and that the dog alert was sufficiently reliable to provide probable cause to conduct the search. Although the Appellate Court affirmed, the Illinois Supreme Court reversed, concluding that because the canine sniff was performed without any "'specific and articulable facts'" to suggest drug activity, the use of the dog "unjustifiably enlarg[ed] the scope of a routine traffic stop into a drug investigation."

The question on which we granted certiorari is narrow: "Whether the Fourth Amendment requires reasonable, articulable suspicion to justify using a drug-detection dog to sniff a vehicle during a legitimate traffic stop." Thus, we proceed on the assumption that the officer conducting the dog sniff had no information about respondent except that he had been stopped for speeding.

Here, the initial seizure of respondent when he was stopped on the highway was based on probable cause and was concededly lawful. It is nevertheless clear that a seizure that is lawful at its inception can violate the Fourth Amendment if its manner of execution unreasonably infringes interests protected by the Constitution. A seizure that is justified solely by the interest in issuing a warning ticket to the driver can become unlawful if it is prolonged beyond the time reasonably required to complete that mission. In an earlier case involving a dog sniff that occurred during an unreasonably prolonged traffic stop, the Illinois Supreme Court held that use of the dog and the subsequent discovery of contraband were the product of an unconstitutional seizure. We may assume that a similar result would be warranted in this case if the dog sniff had been conducted while respondent was being unlawfully detained.

In the state-court proceedings, however, the judges carefully reviewed the details of Officer Gillette's conversations with respondent and the precise timing of his radio transmissions to the dispatcher to determine whether he had improperly extended the duration of the stop to enable the dog sniff to occur. We have not recounted those details because we accept the state court's conclusion that the duration of the stop in this case was entirely justified by the traffic offense and the ordinary inquiries incident to such a stop.

Despite this conclusion, the Illinois Supreme Court held that the initially lawful traffic stop became an unlawful seizure solely as a result of the canine sniff that occurred outside respondent's stopped car. That is, the court characterized the dog sniff as the cause rather than the consequence of a constitutional violation. In its view, the use of the dog converted the citizen-police encounter from a lawful traffic stop into a drug investigation, and because the shift in purpose was not supported by any reasonable suspicion that respondent possessed narcotics, it was unlawful. In our view, conducting a dog sniff would not change the character of a traffic stop that is lawful at its inception and otherwise executed in a reasonable manner, unless the dog sniff itself infringed respondent's constitutionally protected interest in privacy. Our cases hold that it did not.

Official conduct that does not "compromise any legitimate interest in privacy" is not a search subject to the Fourth Amendment. We have held that any interest in possessing contraband cannot be deemed "legitimate," and thus, governmental conduct that *only* reveals the possession of contraband "compromises no legitimate privacy interest." This is because the expectation "that certain facts will not come to the attention of the authorities" is not the same as an interest in "privacy that society is prepared to consider reasonable." In *United States v. Place*, 462 U.S. 696 (1983), we treated a canine sniff by a well-trained narcotics-detection dog as "*sui generis*" because it "discloses only the presence or absence of narcotics, a contraband item." Respondent likewise concedes that "drug sniffs are designed, and if properly conducted are generally likely, to reveal only the presence of contraband." Although respondent argues that the error rates, particularly the existence of false positives, call into question the premise that drug-detection dogs alert only to contraband, the record contains no evidence or findings that support his argument. Moreover, respondent does not suggest that an erroneous alert, in and of itself, reveals any legitimate private information, and, in this case, the trial judge found that the dog sniff was sufficiently reliable to establish probable cause to conduct a full-blown search of the trunk.

Accordingly, the use of a well-trained narcotics-detection dog—one that "does not expose noncontraband items that otherwise would remain hidden from public view"—during a lawful traffic stop, generally does not implicate legitimate privacy interests. In this case, the dog sniff was performed on the exterior of respondent's car while he was lawfully seized for a traffic violation. Any intrusion on respondent's privacy expectations does not rise to the level of a constitutionally cognizable infringement.

The judgment of the Illinois Supreme Court is vacated, and the case is remanded for further proceedings not inconsistent with this opinion.

It is so ordered.

Justice Souter, dissenting.

I would hold that using the dog for the purposes of determining the presence of marijuana in the car's trunk was a search unauthorized as an incident of the speeding stop and unjustified on any other ground. I would accordingly affirm the judgment of the Supreme Court of Illinois, and I respectfully dissent.

In *United States v. Place,* we categorized the sniff of the narcotics-seeking dog as "*sui generis*" under the Fourth Amendment and held it was not a search. The classification rests not only upon the limited nature of the intrusion, but on a further premise that experience has shown to be untenable, the assumption that trained sniffing dogs do not err. What we have learned about the fallibility of dogs in the years since *Place* was decided would itself be reason to call for reconsidering *Place*'s decision against treating the intentional use of a trained dog as a search. The portent of this very case, however, adds insistence to the call, for an uncritical adherence to *Place* would render the Fourth Amendment indifferent to suspicionless and indiscriminate sweeps of cars in parking garages and pedestrians on sidewalks; if a sniff is not preceded by a seizure subject to Fourth Amendment notice, it escapes Fourth Amendment review entirely unless it is treated as a search. We should not wait for these developments to occur before rethinking *Place*'s analysis, which invites such untoward consequences.

At the heart both of *Place* and the Court's opinion today is the proposition that sniffs by a trained dog are *sui generis* because a reaction by the dog in going alert is a response to nothing but the presence of contraband. Hence, the argument goes, because the sniff can only reveal the presence of items devoid of any legal use, the sniff "does not implicate legitimate privacy interests" and is not to be treated as a search.

The infallible dog, however, is a creature of legal fiction. Although the Supreme Court of Illinois did not get into the sniffing averages of drug dogs, their supposed infallibility is belied by judicial opinions describing well-trained animals sniffing and alerting with less than perfect accuracy, whether owing to errors by their handlers, the limitations of the dogs themselves, or even the pervasive contamination of currency by cocaine. See, *e.g., United States v. Scarborough,* 128 F.3d 1373, 1378, n. 3 (CA10 1997) (describing a dog that erroneously alerted 4 times out of 19 while working for the postal service and 8% of the time over its entire career); *United States v. $242,484.00*, 351 F.3d 499, 511 (CA11 2003) (noting that because as much as 80% of all currency in circulation contains drug residue, a dog alert "is of little value"). Indeed, a study cited by Illinois in this case for the proposition that dog sniffs are "generally reliable" shows that dogs in artificial testing situations return false positives anywhere from 12.55 to 60% of the time, depending on the length of the search. In practical terms, the evidence is clear that the dog that alerts hundreds of times will be wrong dozens of times.

Once the dog's fallibility is recognized, however, that ends the justification claimed in *Place* for treating the sniff as *sui generis* under the Fourth Amendment: the sniff alert does not necessarily signal hidden contraband, and opening the container or enclosed space whose emanations the dog has sensed will not necessarily reveal contraband or any other evidence of crime. This is not, of course, to deny that a dog's reaction may provide reasonable suspicion, or probable cause, to search the container or enclosure; the Fourth Amendment does not demand certainty of success to justify a search for evidence or contraband. The point is simply that the sniff and alert cannot claim the certainty that *Place* assumed, both in treating the deliberate use of sniffing dogs as *sui generis* and then taking that characterization as a reason to say they are not searches subject to Fourth Amendment scrutiny. And when that aura of uniqueness disappears, there is no basis in *Place*'s reasoning, and no good reason otherwise, to ignore the actual function that dog sniffs perform. They are conducted to obtain information about the contents of private spaces beyond anything that human senses could perceive, even when conventionally enhanced. The information is not provided by independent third parties beyond the reach of constitutional limitations, but gathered by the government's own officers in order to justify searches of the traditional sort, which may or may not reveal evidence of crime but will disclose anything meant to be kept private in the area searched. Thus in practice the government's use of a trained narcotics dog functions as a limited search to reveal undisclosed facts about private enclosures, to be used to justify a further and complete search of the enclosed area.

I would treat the dog sniff as the familiar search it is in fact, subject to scrutiny under the Fourth Amendment.

The Supreme Court's decision in *Caballes* does not mean that the use of drug-sniffing dogs can never be a search. In *Florida v. Jardines*, the Court held that "[t]he government's use of trained police dogs to investigate the home and its immediate surroundings is a 'search' within the meaning of the Fourth Amendment. 569 U.S. 1, 11–12 (2013). In contrast to a drug dog sniff of a vehicle on a public road, using a drug dog to sniff around a home requires the police to "physically enter[] and occupy[]" the curtilage of the home. *Id.* at 6. By intruding on the curtilage of the home to gather information, the *Jardines* Court found, the police had conducted a search within the meaning of the Fourth Amendment.

Jardines did not undermine the holding in *Caballes* in any way; it is still not a search for the police to conduct a drug dog sniff of a car on a public road. It is, however, a search for a police officer to *physically* inspect the interior of the car. To look inside a car in the absence of the owner's consent, the police need probable cause to believe contraband or evidence of a crime is inside. With probable cause, the police can search a car under the automobile exception to the warrant requirement.

Because of this, the question of when a drug dog's alert establishes probable cause is very important. If a drug dog's alert were not sufficient to give the police probable cause to search a car, then drug dog sniffs would not be a very helpful investigative tool. As the outcome in *Caballes* suggests, however, a drug dog's alert will almost always establish probable cause. In the next case, *Florida v. Harris*, the Supreme Court considered whether the government should be required to produce records of a dog's reliability and performance in the field to establish probable cause or if evidence of the dog's training is sufficient.

Florida v. Harris

Supreme Court of the United States
568 U.S. 237 (2013)

Justice Kagan delivered the opinion of the Court.

William Wheetley is a K-9 Officer in the Liberty County, Florida Sheriff's Office. On June 24, 2006, he was on a routine patrol with Aldo, a German shepherd trained to detect certain narcotics (methamphetamine, marijuana, cocaine, heroin, and ecstasy). Wheetley pulled over respondent Clayton Harris's truck because it had an expired license plate. On approaching the driver's-side door, Wheetley saw that Harris was "visibly nervous," unable to sit still, shaking, and breathing rapidly. Wheetley also noticed an open can of beer in the truck's cup holder. Wheetley asked Harris for consent to search the truck, but Harris refused. At that point, Wheetley retrieved Aldo from the patrol car and walked him around Harris's truck for a "free air sniff." Aldo alerted at the driver's-side door handle—signaling, through a distinctive set of behaviors, that he smelled drugs there.

Wheetley concluded, based principally on Aldo's alert, that he had probable cause to search the truck. His search did not turn up any of the drugs Aldo was trained to detect. But it did reveal 200 loose pseudoephedrine pills, 8,000 matches, a bottle of hydrochloric acid, two containers of antifreeze, and a coffee filter full of iodine crystals—all ingredients for making methamphetamine. Wheetley accordingly arrested Harris, who admitted after proper *Miranda* warnings that he routinely "cooked" methamphetamine at his house and could not go "more than a few days without using" it. The State charged Harris with possessing pseudoephedrine for use in manufacturing methamphetamine.

While out on bail, Harris had another run-in with Wheetley and Aldo. This time, Wheetley pulled Harris over for a broken brake light. Aldo again sniffed the truck's exterior, and again alerted at the driver's-side door handle. Wheetley once more searched the truck, but on this occasion discovered nothing of interest.

Harris moved to suppress the evidence found in his truck on the ground that Aldo's alert had not given Wheetley probable cause for a search. At the hearing on that motion, Wheetley testified about both his and Aldo's training in drug detection. In 2004, Wheetley (and a different dog) completed a 160-hour course in narcotics detection offered by the Dothan, Alabama Police Department, while Aldo (and a different handler) completed a similar, 120-hour course given by the Apopka, Florida Police Department. That same year, Aldo received a one-year certification from Drug Beat, a private company that specializes in testing and certifying K-9 dogs. Wheetley and Aldo teamed up in 2005 and went through another, 40-hour refresher course in Dothan together. They also did four hours of training exercises each week to maintain their skills. Wheetley would hide drugs in certain vehicles or buildings while leaving others "blank" to determine whether Aldo alerted at the right places. According to Wheetley, Aldo's performance in those exercises was "really good." The State introduced "Monthly Canine Detection Training Logs" consistent with that testimony: They showed that Aldo always found hidden drugs and that he performed "satisfactorily" (the higher of two possible assessments) on each day of training.

On cross-examination, Harris's attorney chose not to contest the quality of Aldo's or Wheetley's training. She focused instead on Aldo's certification and his performance in the field, particularly the two stops of Harris's truck. Wheetley conceded that the certification (which, he noted, Florida law did not require) had expired the year before he pulled Harris over. Wheetley also acknowledged that he did not keep complete records of Aldo's performance in traffic stops or other field work; instead, he maintained records only of alerts resulting in arrests. But Wheetley defended Aldo's two alerts to Harris's seemingly narcotics-free truck: According to Wheetley, Harris probably transferred the odor of methamphetamine to the door handle, and Aldo responded to that "residual odor."

The trial court concluded that Wheetley had probable cause to search Harris's truck and so denied the motion to suppress. Harris then entered a no-contest plea while reserving the right to appeal the trial court's ruling. An intermediate state court summarily affirmed.

The Florida Supreme Court reversed, holding that Wheetley lacked probable cause to search Harris's vehicle under the Fourth Amendment. "[W]hen a dog alerts," the court wrote, "the fact that the dog has been trained and certified is simply not enough to establish probable cause." To demonstrate a dog's reliability, the State needed to produce a wider array of evidence:

> "[T]he State must present ... the dog's training and certification records, an explanation of the meaning of the particular training and certification, field performance records (including any unverified alerts), and evidence concerning the experience and training of the officer handling the dog, as

> well as any other objective evidence known to the officer about the dog's reliability."

The court particularly stressed the need for "evidence of the dog's performance history," including records showing "how often the dog has alerted in the field without illegal contraband having been found." That data, the court stated, could help to expose such problems as a handler's tendency (conscious or not) to "cue [a] dog to alert" and "a dog's inability to distinguish between residual odors and actual drugs." Accordingly, an officer like Wheetley who did not keep full records of his dog's field performance could never have the requisite cause to think "that the dog is a reliable indicator of drugs."

We granted certiorari and now reverse.

A police officer has probable cause to conduct a search when "the facts available to [him] would 'warrant a [person] of reasonable caution in the belief'" that contraband or evidence of a crime is present. The test for probable cause is not reducible to "precise definition or quantification." "Finely tuned standards such as proof beyond a reasonable doubt or by a preponderance of the evidence . . . have no place in the [probable-cause] decision." All we have required is the kind of "fair probability" on which "reasonable and prudent [people,] not legal technicians, act."

In evaluating whether the State has met this practical and common-sensical standard, we have consistently looked to the totality of the circumstances.

The Florida Supreme Court flouted this established approach to determining probable cause. To assess the reliability of a drug-detection dog, the court created a strict evidentiary checklist, whose every item the State must tick off. Most prominently, an alert cannot establish probable cause under the Florida court's decision unless the State introduces comprehensive documentation of the dog's prior "hits" and "misses" in the field. (One wonders how the court would apply its test to a rookie dog.) No matter how much other proof the State offers of the dog's reliability, the absent field performance records will preclude a finding of probable cause. That is the antithesis of a totality-of-the-circumstances analysis.

Making matters worse, the decision below treats records of a dog's field performance as the gold standard in evidence, when in most cases they have relatively limited import. Errors may abound in such records. If a dog on patrol fails to alert to a car containing drugs, the mistake usually will go undetected because the officer will not initiate a search. Field data thus may not capture a dog's false negatives. Conversely (and more relevant here), if the dog alerts to a car in which the officer finds no narcotics, the dog may not have made a mistake at all. The dog may have detected substances that were too well hidden or present in quantities too small for the officer to locate. Or the dog may have smelled the residual odor of drugs previously in the vehicle or on the driver's person. Field data thus may markedly overstate a dog's real false positives. By contrast, those inaccuracies—in either direction—do not taint records of a dog's performance in standard training and certification settings. There, the designers of an assessment know where drugs are hidden and where they are not—and so where a dog should alert and where he should not. The better measure of a dog's reliability thus comes away from the field, in controlled testing environments.

For that reason, evidence of a dog's satisfactory performance in a certification or training program can itself provide sufficient reason to trust his alert. If a bona fide organization has certified a dog after testing his reliability in a controlled setting, a court can presume (subject to any conflicting evidence offered) that the dog's alert provides probable cause to search. The same is true, even in the absence of formal certification, if the dog has recently and successfully completed a training program that evaluated his proficiency in locating drugs. After all, law enforcement units have their own strong incentive to use effective training and certification programs, because only accurate drug-detection dogs enable officers to locate contraband without incurring unnecessary risks or wasting limited time and resources.

A defendant, however, must have an opportunity to challenge such evidence of a dog's reliability, whether by cross-examining the testifying officer or by introducing his own fact or expert witnesses. The defendant, for example, may contest the adequacy of a certification or training program, perhaps asserting that its standards are too lax or its methods faulty. So too, the defendant may examine how the dog (or handler) performed in the assessments made in those settings. Indeed, evidence of the dog's (or handler's) history in the field, although susceptible to the kind of misinterpretation we have discussed, may sometimes be relevant, as the Solicitor General acknowledged at oral argument. *See* Tr. of Oral Arg. 23–24 ("[T]he defendant can ask the handler, if the handler is on the stand, about field performance, and then the court can give that answer whatever weight is appropriate"). And even assuming a dog is generally reliable, circumstances surrounding a particular alert may undermine the case for probable cause—if, say, the officer cued the dog (consciously or not), or if the team was working under unfamiliar conditions.

In short, a probable-cause hearing focusing on a dog's alert should proceed much like any other. The court should allow the parties to make their best case, consistent with the usual rules of criminal procedure. And the court should then evaluate the proffered evidence to decide what all the circumstances demonstrate. If the State has produced proof from controlled settings that a dog performs reliably in detecting drugs, and the defendant has not contested that showing, then the court should find probable cause. If, in contrast, the defendant has challenged the State's case (by disputing the reliability of the dog overall or of a particular alert), then the court should weigh the competing evidence. In all events, the court should not prescribe, as the Florida Supreme Court did, an inflexible set of evidentiary requirements. The question—similar to every inquiry into probable cause—is whether all the facts surrounding a dog's alert, viewed through the lens of common sense, would make a reasonably prudent person think that a search would reveal contraband or evidence of a crime. A sniff is up to snuff when it meets that test.

And here, Aldo's did. The record in this case amply supported the trial court's determination that Aldo's alert gave Wheetley probable cause to search Harris's truck.

The State, as earlier described, introduced substantial evidence of Aldo's training and his proficiency in finding drugs. The State showed that two years before alerting to Harris's truck, Aldo had successfully completed a 120-hour program in narcotics detection, and separately obtained a certification from an independent company. And although the certification expired after a year, the Sheriff's Office required continuing training for Aldo and Wheetley. The two satisfied the requirements of another, 40-hour training program one year prior to the search at issue. And Wheetley worked with Aldo for four hours each week on exercises designed to keep their skills sharp. Wheetley testified, and written records confirmed, that in those settings Aldo always performed at the highest level.

Harris, as also noted above, declined to challenge in the trial court any aspect of Aldo's training. To be sure, Harris's briefs in *this* Court raise questions about that training's adequacy—for example, whether the programs simulated sufficiently diverse environments and whether they used enough blind testing (in which the handler does not know the location of drugs and so cannot cue the dog). Similarly, Harris here queries just how well Aldo performed in controlled testing. But Harris never voiced those doubts in the trial court, and cannot do so for the first time here. As the case came to the trial court, Aldo had successfully completed two recent drug-detection courses and maintained his proficiency through weekly training exercises. Viewed alone, that training record—with or without the prior certification—sufficed to establish Aldo's reliability.

And Harris's cross-examination of Wheetley, which focused on Aldo's field performance, failed to rebut the State's case. Harris principally contended in the trial court that because Wheetley did not find any of the substances Aldo was trained to detect, Aldo's two alerts must have been false. But we have already described the hazards of inferring too much from the failure of a dog's alert to lead to drugs; and here we doubt that Harris's logic does justice to Aldo's skills. Harris cooked and used methamphetamine on a regular basis; so as Wheetley later surmised, Aldo likely responded to odors that Harris had transferred to the driver's-side door handle of his truck. A well-trained drug-detection dog *should* alert to such odors; his response to them might appear a mistake, but in fact is not. For the reasons already stated, Wheetley had good cause to view Aldo as a reliable detector of drugs. And no special circumstance here gave Wheetley reason to discount Aldo's usual dependability or distrust his response to Harris's truck.

Because training records established Aldo's reliability in detecting drugs and Harris failed to undermine that showing, we agree with the trial court that Wheetley had probable cause to search Harris's truck. We accordingly reverse the judgment of the Florida Supreme Court.

It is so ordered.

Courts in states that have legalized marijuana have begun to wrestle with the question of how legalization impacts the constitutionality of drug dog sniffs. If not for federal law, the analysis would be fairly straightforward. Drug dogs are typically trained to detect a number of different illegal drugs, including marijuana. The rule that drug dog sniffs are not searches is premised on the fact that an alert reveals only the suspected presence of contraband. Where marijuana is legal, however, the alert of a dog that has been trained to detect marijuana reveals the suspected presence of a perfectly legal (under state law) substance. Similarly, the alert of a dog trained to detect marijuana would be very weak evidence of probable cause in a legalization state, again at least as far as state law is concerned. As a result, it would seem that a drug dog that had been trained to detect marijuana would need to be retrained or retired in a legalization state. Federal marijuana prohibition may complicate the issue, however. Should the fact that marijuana is considered contraband under federal law, even in legalization states, control for purposes of the Fourth Amendment analysis? Shortly before this book went to press, the Colorado Supreme Court held "that a sniff from a drug-detection dog that is trained to alert to marijuana constitutes a search under article 11, section 7 of the Colorado Constitution because that sniff can detect lawful activity, namely the legal possession of up to one ounce of marijuana by adults twenty-one and older." *People v. McKnight*, _ P.3d _(Colo., May 20, 2019).

2. Profiling and Pretextual Stops

Pretextual traffic stops are a widespread drug enforcement tactic. In a pretextual stop, the police will stop a driver for a minor traffic violation in order to question him. While issuing the traffic citation, the officer will ask the driver's permission to search the vehicle for drugs. In many cases, the driver will grant the police permission to search.

In cases where the driver refuses to allow a search of her vehicle, however, the police may employ a drug dog to sniff around the car while the citation is being issued. In *Canine Sniffs: The Search That Isn't*, criminal defense attorney Ken Lammers described the connection between drug dogs and pretextual traffic stops: "I practice criminal defense in a jurisdiction where the local drug interdiction unit uses drug-sniffing dogs extensively. Generally, one officer performs a blatant pretext stop, such as pulling someone over for having an air freshener hanging from the rear view mirror. Sometimes the police operate as a team and preposition the dog in anticipation of the stop. Sometimes the officer with the dog operates in a particular area and responds to nearby stops. In either case, the officers run the dog past both the stopped vehicle and its occupants." 1 N.Y.U. J.L. & Liberty 844 (2005).

Pretextual stops are also closely related to the phenomenon of racial profiling. By definition, a pretextual stop is one where the officer lacks reasonable suspicion or probable cause to suspect the driver is carrying contraband. Instead, the officer relies on a hunch or gut feeling to decide which cars to pull over for traffic violations as a pretext to search for drugs.

The next article describes the relationship between drug enforcement, pretextual stops, and racial profiling.

Marijuana Legalization and Pretextual Stops
Alex Kreit

50 UC Davis Law Review 741 (2016)

In a pretextual stop, the "police use traffic violation stops as a way to gain consent, plain view, or other justification for a search or seizure." In the context of most other crimes, this would be a strange investigative tactic. It is very unlikely that a police officer would pull someone over at random for speeding and ask for his consent to search in the hope of finding a murder weapon. Indeed, it is almost absurd to imagine a police officer doing this; why would she waste her time on this kind of fishing expedition? But, of course, this is an everyday feature of drug enforcement.

To understand why, consider the dynamics of policing drug possession. The police know that a not-insignificant percentage of citizens are walking the streets and driving the highways while in possession of drugs. In fact, drug possession is common enough that a completely random suspicionless search might well turn up drugs. In order to stop a person solely for the purpose of a drug investigation, however, an officer needs a "'particularized and objective basis' for suspecting" that the person has drugs—a "mere 'hunch' is insufficient . . . ." This makes policing drug possession and transportation quite challenging. Because drug possession is hidden and rarely reported to the police, it is very difficult for a police officer to develop reasonable suspicion or probable cause that a particular person is in possession of drugs in advance of stopping them.

Without an easy way to reliably distinguish the cars that contain drugs from the cars that do not, pretextual stops can seem effective relative to the other, quite limited, investigative options. If an officer spots a driver who she has a hunch might be carrying drugs, pretextual stops provide an avenue for investigation. Instead of having to try and develop reasonable suspicion that there are drugs in the car in advance of pulling it over, the officer can stop the car for a traffic violation with the ulterior motive of questioning the driver about drugs. As a result, relying on a gut feeling or a drug courier profile to check for drugs under the guise of a minor traffic violation—an incredibly inefficient method for investigating almost any other crime—became an encouraged drug war tactic in the 1980s and 1990s. The Drug Enforcement Administration ("DEA") went so far as to develop a training program that teaches state and local law enforcement how to use pretextual stops to interdict drugs. In the DEA's training program—Operation Pipeline—state and local "[o]fficers learn how to lengthen a routine traffic stop and leverage it into a search for drugs by extorting consent or manufacturing probable cause." Law enforcement enthusiasm for pretextual stops is such that the International Association of Chiefs of Police has created an annual award for it: the "Looking Beyond the License Plate award . . . [is] awarded to officers who have gone beyond the 'routine' traffic stop, resulting in the apprehension of dangerous criminals."

In addition to resulting in drug arrests, pretextual stops can also put money into police coffers through asset forfeiture. In 1984, the same year the DEA established

Operation Pipeline, Congress revised federal asset forfeiture laws to "allow[] the direct transfer of seized assets from drug dealers to the law enforcement agencies that seized the assets...." Asset forfeiture gives law enforcement a profit incentive to police drug crimes more heavily than they would otherwise. This profit incentive has also been a key contributor to the use of pretextual stops. A 2013 *New Yorker* investigation, for example, described how the small town of Tenaha, Texas (population 1,170) "amassed . . . $1.3 million in seized profits" within six months of implementing a highway drug interdiction program that "made heavy use of 'pretextual stops,' focusing on out-of-state . . . cars." The case of Tenaha is far from an outlier. A 2014 *Washington Post* investigation found that "[h]undreds of state and local departments and drug task forces appear to rely on seized cash" and that, since September 11, 2001, there have been "61,998 cash seizures made on highways and elsewhere . . . without search warrants or indictments" through the federal equitable sharing program alone. The *Post* report also described how, behind the rise in forfeitures, "is a little-known cottage industry of private-police training firms that teach the techniques of 'highway interdiction' to departments across the country."

Pretextual stops are also perfectly legal. In the 1996 case *Whren v. United States*, two plainclothes police officers on patrol in an unmarked car in Washington, D.C. became suspicious "when they passed a dark Pathfinder truck with temporary license plates and youthful occupants waiting at a stop sign, the driver looking down into the lap of the passenger at his right." Although the officers did not have reasonable suspicion that the "youthful occupants" were in possession of drugs, they decided to pull the Pathfinder over after it "turned suddenly to its right, without signaling, and sped off at an 'unreasonable' speed." During the stop, the officers spotted illegal drugs inside of the truck. The United States Supreme Court held that the officer's pretextual stop did not violate the Fourth Amendment. The Court reasoned that the police had sufficient cause to stop the truck for a traffic infraction. And while the stop may have been conducted with the ulterior motive of investigating for drugs, the Court held that an officer's "[s]ubjective intentions play no role in ordinary, probable-cause Fourth Amendment analysis."

If pretextual stops were nothing more than an effective law enforcement tool, there might be little reason to want their use curtailed. Though constitutional, critics argue that the practice of pretextual stops gives the police nearly limitless power to pull drivers over for investigative purposes. This is because, given the wide range of traffic regulations, "no driver can avoid violating some traffic law during a short drive, even with the most careful attention." The result is the potential for widespread infringement on civil liberties. Even more troubling is the relationship between pretextual stops and racial disparities.

Race has been closely linked to drug prohibition in the United States going back to the very first anti-opium laws, some of which were passed with the stated purpose of discriminating against Chinese immigrants. Though overt racism has mostly vanished from drug laws, a sharp racial disparity in drug enforcement persists. Blacks and whites use drugs at about the same rate. But blacks are significantly more likely to be arrested for drugs than whites, with blacks accounting for 12.6% of the population and 30.4% of drug arrestees. Drug enforcement disparities result from a number of systemic causes, "including demographics, the extent of community complaints, police allocation of resources, racial profiling, and the relative ease of making drug arrests." While the practice of pretextual stops is unrelated to most of these causes, it goes hand-in-hand with racial profiling.

When an officer has reasonable suspicion to stop a car, then the car stop is not pretextual. The purpose of requiring reasonable suspicion or probable cause for a seizure or a search is to prevent against arbitrary enforcement by ensuring intrusions on privacy are based on evidence. A pretextual stop, of course, is one where an officer who lacks reasonable suspicion of criminal activity uses a minor traffic violation as a pretext for conducting a stop and fishing for drugs or other contraband. By definition then, when making pretextual stops, officers rely on little more than intuition or a DEA-created profile to decide which cars to pull over and investigate. All too often, driver ethnicity consciously or unconsciously factors into an officer's hunch or a drug offender profile.

Beginning in the 1990s, a series of studies found that the police were more likely to pull over people of color than whites. On the New Jersey Turnpike, for example, data showed that 35% of drivers stopped for alleged traffic violations between 1988 and 1991 were black even though "only 15% of observed traffic violators were black . . . ." The disparities have persisted. In 2015, the *New York Times* looked at data from seven states with the most robust requirements for collecting and reporting data from traffic stops. The *Times* reported that in all seven states, "the data show police officers are more likely to pull over black drivers than white ones, given their share of the local driving-age population." The data also reveal that the disparities persist in the treatment of drivers who have been stopped. "In the four states that track the results of consent searches," the *Times* reported, "officers were more likely to conduct them when the driver was black . . . ." One especially striking study of traffic stops in Kansas City separated stops for minor violations done for purposes of investigation from stops for more significant traffic violations, where the purpose of the stop was to enforce the traffic laws. The results showed "that investigatory stops are the site of pervasive racially biased policing, whereas traffic-safety stops generally involve unbiased policing." Specifically, the study found blacks were twice as likely as whites to be subjected to a pretextual traffic stop done for purposes of investigation. In the case of traffic safety stops, by contrast, there was no racial disparity in who was stopped.

It is very difficult to combat the problem of racial disparities in pretextual stops in court. Under the Supreme Court's decision in *Whren*, of course, an officer's subjective intent in making a stop is irrelevant to the Fourth Amendment analysis. This includes cases in which race may have played a role in the officer's decision to stop a suspect. Although the Equal Protection Clause forbids purposeful racial profiling, it provides no protection against profiling animated by unconscious bias. And, even on the rare occasion where an officer has intentionally engaged in racial profiling and is willing to admit to it, the remedy for a violation in any individual case is "toothless." As a result, racial disparity in pretextual stops continues to be widespread, despite widespread concern about the problem.

The link between racial profiling and drug enforcement extends beyond pretextual stops. Samuel R. Gross and Katherine Y. Barnes explain the relationship this way: "Racial profiling depends on police discretion in choosing suspects. At one end of the continuum, racial profiling is impossible once the police are looking for a particular person—the victim's partner, the woman in the surveillance video, Osama bin Laden—although it may be a factor at an earlier stage, in determining who to look for. At the other extreme, racial profiling can flourish in proactive investigations in which the police scan large numbers of people in search of culprits in crimes that have not been reported or have not yet occurred." Samuel R. Gross and Katherine Y. Barnes, *Road Work: Racial Profiling and Drug Interdiction on the Highway*, 101 MICH. L. REV. 651, 654 (2002).

As noted in the excerpt above, the United States Supreme Court held that pretextual stops do not violate the Fourth Amendment in *Whren v. United States*, 517 U.S. 806 (1996). In *Whren*, the Court concluded that a police officer may constitutionally stop an individual for a traffic violation any time the officer has sufficient cause to believe a traffic violation has occurred. The officer's subjective intent is irrelevant to the Fourth Amendment analysis. With respect to racially motivated pretextual stops, the *Whren* Court explained: "We of course agree with petitioners that the Constitution prohibits selective enforcement of the law based on considerations such as race. But the constitutional basis for objecting to intentionally discriminatory application of laws is the Equal Protection Clause, not the Fourth Amendment. Subjective intentions play no role in ordinary, probable-cause Fourth Amendment analysis."

Two years before the Supreme Court's decision in *Whren*, the Sixth Circuit considered the constitutionality of pretextual stops under the Fourth Amendment in *United States v. Lamour*. The majority in *Lamour* adopted essentially the same rule as the Supreme Court ultimately would in *Whren*. Although *Lamour* pre-dates *Whren*, the case remains noteworthy because the officer who conducted the stop testified that race played a role in his decision. Specifically, the officer stated that one of the reasons he stopped the car was that "[t]here were three young black male occupants in an old vehicle." This testimony led to a vigorous dissent.

United States v. Lamour

United States Court of Appeals for the Sixth Circuit
16 F.3d 109 (1994)

Batchelder, J.

Marcus Harvey appeals from the judgment of conviction entered on his conditional plea of guilty following the district court's denial of his motion to suppress the evidence obtained from a warrantless search of the vehicle in which he was a passenger. For the reasons that follow, we affirm the conviction.

Briefly stated the facts are these. On May 22, 1990, on I-475 in Genesee County, Michigan, the defendant was a passenger in a 1978 Chevrolet automobile that had no front bumper or right front headlight and that was clocked by police officers exceeding the speed limit by several miles per hour. The officers stopped the vehicle for speeding and equipment violations and because, as one officer later testified at the suppression hearing, "the vehicle that I observed with the defective equipment was very similar in appearance and profile to several other vehicles that I have stopped which ultimately ended in arrests of drug traffickers." When the driver of the car was unable to produce a driver's license, he was asked to step out of the car. He admitted then that his license was suspended; he was placed under arrest for driving with a suspended license; and, while being searched incident to the arrest, he was found to have a rock of crack cocaine in his jacket pocket. The driver gave conflicting stories about who owned the car, but the vehicle registration that he produced showed defendant Marcus Harvey to be the owner. Neither Harvey nor the other passenger could produce a driver's license (Harvey's license had been suspended also and the other passenger had never obtained a license), or any other form of identification. Both passengers were asked to get out of the vehicle and were patted down for weapons by the officers; no weapons were found. Following the policy of their police department, the officers impounded the car because there was no licensed driver to drive it away, and conducted an inventory search of the car. Because none of the occupants had the key to the vehicle's trunk, the officers removed the back seat in order to inventory the trunk and found there a pair of men's sweat pants whose pockets contained 78 rocks of crack cocaine and six live .357 magnum revolver cartridges. Also in the trunk was a bulletproof vest. At this point the officers pried open the trunk of the car to more carefully search it and found a .357 magnum six-shot revolver.

Defendant Harvey was arrested for possession with intent to distribute cocaine and possession of a firearm during the commission of a felony. Defendant was subsequently indicted for possession with intent to distribute cocaine, conspiracy to distribute cocaine, and use of a firearm during a drug trafficking offense. The trial court denied defendant's motion to suppress the evidence seized during the search of the vehicle . . . and defendant entered this conditional plea.

Defendant's first assignment of error is foreclosed by this court's recent en banc decision in *United States v. Ferguson*, 8 F.3d 385 (6th Cir. 1993). Defendant does not dispute that the automobile in which he was riding was exceeding the speed limit at the time it was stopped, or that it was in violation of the applicable state laws because of its equipment deficiencies. Defendant concedes that had the officers stopped the car solely because of either or both of those violations, the stop would have been lawful. Rather, defendant argues that no reasonable police officer would have stopped the car for those violations absent some other motive, and that the actual reason for the stop in this instance was not the obvious violations of the law but the fact that the car and its occupants fit the officer's notion of a "drug profile." In *Ferguson*, we held that

> so long as the officer has probable cause to believe that a traffic violation has occurred or was occurring, the resulting stop is not unlawful and does not violate the Fourth Amendment. We focus not on whether a reasonable officer "would" have stopped the suspect (even though he had probable cause to believe that a traffic violation had occurred), or whether any officer "could" have stopped the suspect (because a traffic violation had in fact occurred), but on whether this particular officer in fact had probable cause to believe that a traffic offense had occurred, regardless of whether this was the only basis or merely one basis for the stop. The stop is reasonable if there was probable cause, and it is irrelevant what else the officer knew or suspected about the traffic violator at the time of the stop. It is also irrelevant whether the stop in question is sufficiently ordinary or routine according to the general practice of the police department or the particular officer making the stop.

There is no dispute about the fact that the traffic violations occurred, and the district court found that those violations would have been obvious to any officer observing the car. Because that finding is not clearly erroneous, we hold that, under *Ferguson*, the stop of the car was not pretextual and was lawful.

Nor did the district court err in determining that the search of the vehicle in which Harvey was a passenger was lawful. In fact, the district court found that the warrantless search of the automobile was permissible under either the "automobile exception" or as an inventory search. A review of the record of the suppression hearing persuades us that the district court's findings of fact cannot be said to be clearly erroneous, either as to the facts upon which it based its determination that the officers had probable cause to believe that the car contained drugs or other contraband, or as to the fact that the officers' impounding of the car and the subsequent inventory search were pursuant to departmental policy and not for the purposes of a "fishing expedition."

Having held that both the stop and the search of the vehicle were lawful, we hold that the district court did not err in refusing to suppress the evidence obtained in the search. The judgment of conviction is affirmed.[3]

---

3. We are constrained to respond briefly to the dissent. The dissent makes much—indeed, everything—of the fact that Officer Collardey testified that one of the reasons this vehicle caught his attention was that it fit his own empirically justified profile of drug couriers, which included a racial factor. And as the dissent's quotations from the record indicate, Collardey did indeed say that he took note of occupants' race. But the dissent entirely mischaracterizes this testimony when it says repeatedly that Collardey testified that he stopped the vehicle because the occupants were African-Americans; when it says that "Collardey testified [that] if the occupants had not been African-Americans, he would not have stopped the car"; and when it says that Collardey had a "primary race-based motivation" for the stop. There is no such testimony in the record; the dissent quotes the testimony that most supports its view of this case, and nowhere in that testimony

Keith, J., dissenting.

Because I strongly disagree with the majority's conclusion that the district court correctly denied Harvey's motion to suppress evidence, I respectfully dissent.

The Sixth Circuit recently discussed pretextual stops and held the correct inquiry is "whether this particular officer in fact had probable cause to believe that a traffic offense had occurred, regardless of whether this was the only basis or merely one basis for the stop." *United States v. Ferguson*, 8 F.3d 385 (6th Cir. 1993). I dissented in *Ferguson* because I believe this test is ripe for abuse. Today, although I am bound by the law of this circuit, I write separately to emphasize how the instant case illustrates the abuses of which I warned in *Ferguson* and to insist that egregious circumstances, such as in this case, warrant an exception to the *Ferguson* test.

In the instant case, Officer Collardey admits repeatedly he stopped the vehicle because the occupants were African-Americans. On redirect he testified:

> Q: Officer Collardey, you gave the Prosecutor two reasons for your effecting a traffic stop. One was the traffic infraction, speeding and equipment violation, and then you referred to something that I hadn't heard yet today, that was, fitting the general description of some sort of a profile?
>
> A: It did, yeah, it did fit.
>
> Q: Was it a certain way that the damage had been on this car that made it look like it fit a profile for you?
>
> A: No, I made that statement on the basis of my experience on that highway, and drug traffickers that I have arrested coming to the Flint area.

Officer Collardey continued:

> Q: What else was it that made you think this fits some sort of a profile?
>
> A: There were three young black male occupants in an old vehicle.
>
> Q: Three young black male occupants in a car?
>
> A: Yes, sir.
>
> Q: And that was the basis or part of the basis for your stopping that car?
>
> A: The age of the vehicle and the appearance of the occupants.

Under oath, Officer Collardey stated he stopped the vehicle because there were three African-American males in an old car. Recognizing Officer Collardey's use of the minor traffic violations as pretext for stopping the vehicle, the district judge improperly rehabilitated Officer Collardey's testimony:

---

is there any suggestion that Collardey's use of race was a "but for" cause of the stop. Nor is such an inference justified based on this record. It does not follow from the fact that Collardey testified that race was a factor in his "why I stopped the vehicle" calculus that the suspects' race was a "necessary" cause of the stop.

Q (district judge): What was it about the appearance of the occupants that got your attention?

A: It wasn't so much the appearance. *Almost every time that we have arrested drug traffickers from Detroit, they're usually young black males driving old cars.*

Q (district judge): Was that why you stopped the car, or did you stop the car for traffic violations?

A: I stopped them for traffic violations.

(emphasis added). Only after the court gave Officer Collardey an either/or question did he give the appropriate response.

My dissent in *United States v. Ferguson* emphasized that the test, as adopted by the majority, provides officers with unlimited discretion to determine whom they will stop for minor traffic violations. As a result, the court renders meaningless the Fourth Amendment's prohibition of unwarranted searches and seizures.

The Fourth Amendment imposes "a standard of 'reasonableness' upon the exercise of discretion by government officials." Under the *Ferguson* test, the court's failure to limit an officer's discretion to stop motorists once a traffic offense establishes probable cause negates any reasonableness inquiry. In essence, the absence of limitations allows pretext to serve as probable cause thus undermining the guarantees of the Fourth Amendment.

The instant case clearly pinpoints the abuses to which the *Ferguson* test is subject. By myopically focusing on whether probable cause exists to believe a motorist committed a traffic offense, the majority waived any meaningful review of the seizure and its legality, and allowed pretext (the traffic violations) to serve as probable cause. Here, Harvey and his companions committed minor traffic violations. They drove three miles over the speed limit in a car which was missing a bumper and a headlight. Indisputably, probable cause existed to believe a traffic offense occurred. The problem, however, is the officer said he stopped the vehicle because the occupants were African-Americans. Officer Collardey testified if the occupants had not been African-Americans, he would not have stopped the car. Officer Collardey's improper motivation for the stop inserted an unconstitutional illegality into the stop. Applying the *Ferguson* test, because a minor traffic violation was present, the majority concludes Collardey's primary race-based motivation, although illegal, is irrelevant.

Equal Protection principles absolutely and categorically prohibit state actors from using race to differentiate between motorists. Yet, the majority acquiesces to an officer's substitution of race for probable cause and essentially licenses the state to discriminate. Moreover, the majority states race-based motivation is irrelevant under these or any circumstances. Not only is the officer's race-based motivation relevant, it is patently unconstitutional.

The Fourteenth Amendment of the United States Constitution prohibits state actors from denying persons equal protection of the laws. In *Samaad v. City of Dallas*, the Fifth Circuit stated: "The heart of the *equal protection clause* is its prohibition of discriminatory treatment. If a governmental actor has imposed unequal burdens based upon race, it has violated the clause." Traditionally, courts review state action singling a person out solely on the basis of race with the strictest scrutiny, and generally condemn the action.

In my twenty-six years as a federal judge, although I have suspected discrimination by police officers, I have never heard an officer admit he stopped an individual based on the color of his skin. This case presents blatantly egregious circumstances and warrants an exception to the *Ferguson* test. Such an exception does not grant special treatment to African-Americans, but merely ensures equal treatment as guaranteed by the Equal Protection Clause. The majority's willful disregard of the flagrant discriminatory treatment in this case endorses a system where one set of traffic regulations exist for African-Americans, like myself, and a more lenient set exists for white Americans. For the same minor traffic infraction, a white motorist remains an unimpeded violator, whereas an African-American motorist automatically becomes a suspected felon and menace to society. Such disparate treatment alienates and ostracizes African-Americans, fortifying their badge of second-class citizenship.

As the old adage warns, the more things change, the more they remain the same. In Montgomery, Alabama, on January 26, 1956, police officers arrested and jailed Dr. Martin Luther King, Jr. for allegedly driving thirty miles per hour in a twenty-five mile per hour zone. *See* Randall Kennedy, *Martin Luther King's Constitution: A Legal History of the Montgomery Bus Boycott*, 98 Yale L.J. 999, 1028 (1989). Today, everyone readily acknowledges the police officers stopped, arrested, jailed and harassed Dr. King because he was an African-American and because he actively and vigorously sought equal protection and equal treatment for African-Americans. Today, almost thirty years later, the majority's actions in this case again allow police officers to stop individuals based on their race under the guise of an insignificant traffic violation. It is a sad commentary that this court not only approves disparate treatment based on race but legitimizes a "legal" basis for disparate treatment. Certainly this circuit cannot in good faith state that the decisions in *Ferguson* and in this case represent equal justice under law.

Unfortunately, the present case is not unique; rather, it eloquently illustrates the plight of many African-Americans. News reports detail unreasonable stops of African Americans by police motivated solely by irrational and illogical racial stereotypes. For example, a national newspaper reported "the same percentage of whites and blacks use drugs." Sam Meddis, *Suburbs 'Have Gotten Off Easy,' Whites' Drug Activity Often Better Hidden*, USA Today, (July 26, 1993), at 6A. Blacks, however, are four times as likely to be arrested for drugs in central cities, six times as likely in suburbs, and three times as likely in rural areas. *Id.* In Michigan, the ratios are much worse. For example:

Detroit	2:1
Warren	32:1
Royal Oak	27:1
Livonia	43:1
Dearborn Heights	40:1
Lincoln Park	46:1

Id. African-Americans are more likely to be arrested because drug courier profiles reflect the erroneous assumption that one's race has a direct correlation to drug activity. *See United States v. Taylor,* 956 F.2d 572, 580 (6th Cir. 1992) (*en banc*) (Keith dissenting) (citing Sheri Lynn Johnson, *Race and the Decision to Detain a Suspect*, 93 Yale L.J. 214, 234 (1983)); *see also* Morgan Cloud, *Search and Seizure by the Numbers: The Drug Courier Profile and Judicial Review of Investigative Formulas*, 65 B.U.L. Rev. 843 (1985) (discussing the historical use of drug profiles).

The deprivation of Defendant Harvey's constitutional rights in this case demonstrates the victimization of African-Americans by a flawed and stereotypical system. His case presents clear and articulated racial discrimination. National statistics illustrate how the insulation of the use of illegitimate, illegal and illogical stereotypes disproportionately impacts African-Americans. Concededly, disproportionate impact alone does not constitute a violation of the Equal Protection Clause; intentional discrimination, however, does. Here, Officer Collardey testified he stopped the vehicle because it contained three young African-Americans. The majority, however, blindly refuses to recognize this glaring constitutional violation and suppress the evidence that flowed from it.

This court's application of the *Ferguson* test to this case is repugnant to our Constitution and national conscience and does not reflect due regard for the integrity of our justice system. Courts exist to promote justice and judges have the duty to support and protect the Constitution as well as to observe its fundamental guarantees. Unfortunately, in this case, the Sixth Circuit abdicates that sacred duty.

3. Drug Testing

The United States Supreme Court has held that the government may not conduct suspicionless drug testing for law enforcement purposes. *See Ferguson v. City of Charleston*, 532 U.S. 67 (2001) (holding that suspicionless drug testing of pregnant women for law enforcement purposes violates the Fourth Amendment). Though drug testing is not commonly used to investigate drug crimes, it is nevertheless a part of daily life for many Americans. Employees—including government employees—are often asked to take a drug test in order to obtain or keep a job. *See, e.g.*, Mark A. Rothstein, *Workplace Drug Testing: A Case Study in the Misapplication of Technology*, 5 Harv. J. L. & Tech. 65 (1991) ("In less than a decade drug testing has become a way of life in public and private employment."). Many schools drug test their students as a condition of participating in extracurricular activities. Probationers, parolees, and drug court participants are also frequently drug tested. Indeed, based on the number of individuals who take (or have taken) a drug test, one could argue that no aspect of the drug war directly impacts more Americans than drug testing.

The Supreme Court has held that the suspicionless drug testing of public school students and public employees may be constitutional under certain circumstances. The Court's decisions in these cases have rested on the special needs exception to the warrant requirement, which can permit warrantless (and sometimes suspicionless) searches when "special needs, beyond the need for law enforcement, make the warrant and probable cause requirement impractical." *Griffin v. Wisconsin*, 483 U.S. 868, 873 (1987).

Public Employees: The United States Supreme Court first took up the constitutionality of public employee drug testing in a pair of cases decided on the same day in 1989, *Skinner v. Railway Labor Executives' Ass'n*, 489 U.S. 602 (1989) and *National Treasury Employees Union v. Von Raab*, 489 U.S. 656 (1989). In *Skinner*, the Court upheld the constitutionality of Federal Railway Administration regulations that required employees to submit to breath and urine testing after a railway accident. In addition, the regulations permitted—but did not require—railroads to test employees whenever a supervisor had reasonable suspicion that an employee was under the influence of drugs or alcohol. In *Von Raab*, the Court upheld a U.S. Customs Service policy requiring employees who applied for promotion to positions directly involving the interdiction of drugs or the carrying of firearms to submit to urine testing to detect drug use. In both *Skinner* and *Von Raab*, the Court upheld the drug testing programs primarily on the ground that they served important public safety interests beyond the need for law enforcement.

Based on the holdings in *Skinner* and *Von Raab*, courts focus on an employee's duties when assessing the constitutionality of public employee drug testing programs. For example, federal courts of appeals have upheld suspicionless drug testing "of categories of employees whose work involves heavy machinery or the operation of large vehicles, such as planes, trains, buses, or boats" along with "police officers, correctional officers who interact with parolees or inmates in a prison, and firefighters[.]" *American Federation of State, County and Mun. Employees Council 79 v. Scott*, 717 F.3d 851 (11th Cir. 2013). Outside of these types of job categories, however, public employee drug testing is on shaky grounds. In 2011, Florida enacted perhaps the most far-reaching government employment drug testing policy when Governor Rick Scott issued an Executive Order mandating suspicionless drug testing for nearly 85,000 employees. Specifically, the policy required "random testing of all employees at state agencies within [the Governor's] control, and pre-employment testing of all applicants to those agencies." *Id.* at 857. The Eleventh Circuit found the testing program unconstitutional as applied to most employees. It declined to enjoin the program in its entirety, however, remanding the case so that the State could be given the opportunity to "demonstrat[e] important special needs on a job category-by-category basis." *Id.* at 858.

Public School Students: The United States Supreme Court has heard two student drug testing cases. In *Vernonia School Dist. 47J v. Acton,* 515 U.S. 646 (1995), the Court upheld the suspicionless drug testing of school athletes. Seven years later, in *Board of Education v. Earls*, 536 U.S. 822 (2002), five Justices found constitutional a high school drug testing program that applied to all students engaged in extracurricular activities. The reasoning of the lead opinion in *Earls* gives the impression that the Court would be likely to find a high school testing program that applied to *all* students to be constitutional. In a concurring opinion, however, Justice Breyer indicated that his vote was contingent on leaving students the choice to opt out of drug testing programs by forgoing extracurricular activities. "[T]he testing program avoids subjecting the entire school to testing[,]" Breyer wrote in *Earls*. "And it preserves an option for a conscientious objector. He can refuse testing while paying a price (nonparticipation) that is serious, but less severe than expulsion from the school." Perhaps because of Breyer's opinion, it appears that few public high schools have adopted school-wide drug testing programs for all students.

Somewhere between one-quarter and one-fifth of public school students report that their school has a drug testing program for participants in athletics or extracurricular activities. Yet studies indicate student drug testing programs have a negligible impact on student drug use. An author of one study advised that their findings should "send[] a cautionary note to the estimated 20% or more of high schools that have joined the drug testing bandwagon. We find little evidence that this approach to minimizing teen drug use is having the deterrent effect its proponents claim." Shari Roan, *Student Drug Testing May Have Only Small Effect in Reducing Use*, L.A. Times, Aug. 17, 2011.

Recipients of Public Benefits: In recent years, an increasing number of states have considered proposals to drug test recipients of public benefits—specifically, welfare recipients. As of 2017, at least 15 states had passed laws to drug test welfare recipients. *See* Nat'l Conference of State Legislators, *Drug Testing for Welfare Recipients and Public Assistance*, http://www.ncsl.org/research/human-services/drug-testing-and-public-assistance.aspx. Some of these laws require reasonable suspicion to believe an individual has used an illegal drug in order to conduct a test. In 2011, Florida passed a much more sweeping drug testing law, which required every single welfare applicant in the state to undergo an annual suspicionless drug test. These laws have been quite controversial as a matter of public policy. Proponents of the laws argue that they might save the state money and that giving public benefits to individuals who have used an illegal drug is not a good use of funds. In response, critics note that these laws often cost much more to administer than they save in undistributed benefits—after all, it costs a good deal of money to properly conduct and process drug tests. The programs also risk imposing unseen costs in the form of increases in thefts by those who have lost benefits and harms to the children of those who have lost benefits. Finally, some question the motivation behind these laws, noting "the absence of any data to suggest that the incidence of drug abuse among the poor is appreciably greater than in the general population." Jordan C. Budd, *Pledge Your Body for Your Bread: Welfare, Drug Testing, and the Inferior Fourth Amendment*, 19 Wm. & Mary Bill of Rts. J. 751 (2011). Given this fact, critics argue that the drug testing of welfare recipients "evidently seeks to vindicate little more than the familiar impulse to stigmatize and stereotype the impoverished" *Ibid.*

Putting the policy wisdom of welfare drug testing programs aside, are they constitutional? The United States Supreme Court has not yet considered the question. But, in 2014, the Eleventh Circuit struck down Florida's drug testing statute on Fourth Amendment grounds.

Lebron v. Secretary of the Florida Department of Children and Families

United States Court of Appeals for the Eleventh Circuit
772 F.3d 1352 (2014)

Marcus, J.

A Florida statute mandates suspicionless drug testing of all applicants seeking Temporary Assistance for Needy Families ("TANF") benefits. Luis Lebron sued the Secretary of the Florida Department of Children and Families (the "State"), claiming that the statute violates the Fourth Amendment's prohibition against unreasonable searches and seizures, applied against the states through the Fourteenth Amendment. After we affirmed the entry of a preliminary injunction barring the application of the statute against Lebron, the State halted the drug-testing program. Since then, the district court granted final summary judgment to Lebron, declared § 414.0652 unconstitutional, and permanently enjoined its enforcement.

We affirm. On this record, the State has failed to meet its burden of establishing a substantial special need to drug test all TANF applicants without any suspicion. Even viewing the facts in the light most favorable to the nonmoving party, the State has not demonstrated a more prevalent, unique, or different drug problem among TANF applicants than in the general population. The ordinary government interests claimed in this case are nothing like the narrow category of special needs that justify blanket drug testing of railroad workers, certain federal Customs employees involved in drug interdiction or who carry firearms, or students who participate in extracurricular activities because those programs involve "surpassing safety interests," *Skinner v. Railway Labor Execs. Ass'n*, 489 U.S. 602 (1989), or "close supervision of school children," *Vernonia Sch. Dist. 47J v. Acton*, 515 U.S. 646, 655 (1995).

Moreover, . . . the State cannot circumvent constitutional concerns by requiring that applicants consent to a drug test to receive TANF payments. When a government benefit is conditioned on suspicionless drug testing, the voluntariness of the program is properly viewed as a factor baked into the special needs reasonableness analysis, not as an exception to it.

I.

A.

Congress created TANF in the Personal Responsibility and Work Opportunity Reconciliation Act of 1996, TANF provides federal block grants for state programs "that provide[ ] assistance to needy families with (or expecting) children and provide[ ] parents with job preparation, work, and support services to enable them to leave the program and become self-sufficient." Florida began disbursing TANF benefits, including Temporary Cash Assistance, to families in 1996 through its Department of Children and Families ("DCF" or the "Department"). To apply for TANF benefits in Florida, an individual must complete an application and must satisfy a number of eligibility requirements. Only expectant mothers and families with children qualify. In the application, an individual must disclose certain information, including medical history, immunization records, living arrangements, social security numbers, family income, employment history, and job-search activities. For families of two like Lebron and his son, the maximum Temporary Cash Assistance benefit currently is $241.00 per month. An individual generally may not receive TANF Temporary Cash Assistance for more than a lifetime cumulative total of 48 months.

Congress specified in the 1996 Act that states were not prohibited "from testing welfare recipients for use of controlled substances nor from sanctioning welfare recipients who test positive for use of controlled substances." In 2011, Florida enacted a statute requiring suspicionless drug screening for all TANF applicants as a condition of eligibility. Under that law, applicants must provide a DCF-approved laboratory with a urine sample to be tested for Amphetamines, Methamphetamines, Cannabinoids (THC), Cocaine, Phencyclidine (PCP), Opiates, Barbiturates, Benzodiazepines, Methadone, and Propoxyphene. The statute does not require testing for alcohol. DCF must "[a]dvise each individual to be tested, before the test is conducted, that he or she may, but is not required to, advise the agent administering the test of any prescription or over-the-counter medication he or she is taking." Applicants bear the cost of testing, which during the period of the statute's implementation generally ranged between $24 and $45. However, if an applicant tests negative for controlled substances, the Department increases the amount of TANF benefit to compensate for the testing expense. State law provides that "[a] sample shall be collected with due regard to the privacy of the individual providing the sample, and in a manner reasonably calculated to prevent substitution or contamination of the sample."[1] Notably, an applicant may arrange the timing of filing an application; after

1. State regulations further require "minimum precautions" to ensure the security of the urine specimen: "[t]he collection site person shall ask the individual to remove any unnecessary outer garments, such as a coat or jacket, and to empty all clothing pockets. . . . The individual may retain his or her wallet, provided that the collection site person shall check it for possible contaminants." "The individual may provide his or her urine specimen in a stall or otherwise partitioned enclosure that allows for individual privacy. The collection site person shall remain in the restroom or area,

the State determines that the applicant has satisfied all non-drug testing eligibility factors (e.g., income, assets, etc.), the applicant must pass a drug test within ten days.

Under § 414.0652, an individual who tests positive for controlled substances is ineligible for TANF benefits for one year, though those who fail drug tests may reapply for benefits after six months if they can document successful completion of a substance abuse treatment program and pass another drug test. A parent cannot receive benefits without passing a drug test, but the parent's failure of a test does not affect a child's eligibility to receive TANF benefits; instead, a protective payee would be designated to receive benefits for the child.

The ... drug-testing requirement went into effect on July 1, 2011, and was enforced until the district court entered a preliminary injunction on October 24, 2011. During that period, 4,046 TANF applicants submitted to drug testing. Only 108—2.67%—tested positive for drug use: 44 for cannabinoids (marijuana); 24 for benzodiazepines (e.g., Xanax); 10 for cocaine; 9 each for barbiturates and opiates; 10 for methadone; 3 for propoxyphene; 5 for amphetamines or methamphetamines; and 2 for PCP.[2] Throughout that period, 2,306 additional applicants did not complete applications and submit drug-test results to DCF, even though they were otherwise eligible for TANF Temporary Cash Assistance.

When he brought suit, Lebron had sole custody of his five-year-old son. A veteran of the United States Navy and a college student, Lebron was a thirty-five-year-old single-parent who lived with and cared for his disabled mother in Orlando, Florida. On July 16, 2011, Lebron applied to DCF for TANF benefits for himself and his son. Lebron initially signed a form agreeing to drug testing, but he later revoked his consent and refused to take the test. If Lebron had passed a drug test and submitted the results, the Department determined, he and his son would have been eligible for TANF benefits. Without the test, however, the Department deemed him ineligible to receive TANF assistance and denied his application on August 25, 2011.

B.

On behalf of himself and a class of similarly situated persons, Lebron commenced this lawsuit in the United States District Court for the Middle District of Florida on September 6, 2011, against the Secretary of DCF in his official capacity. Lebron sought a declaration that requiring suspicionless drug testing for TANF eligibility under § 414.0652 violated the Fourth Amendment right to be free from unreasonable searches. Lebron also asked for a permanent injunction barring the enforcement of § 414.0652. Lebron filed a motion for a preliminary injunction with his complaint.

---

but outside the stall or partitioned enclosure." In addition, if "a collection site person has reason to believe that a particular individual may alter or has altered or substituted a urine specimen," and a higher level supervisor agrees, a second specimen shall be collected "under the direct observation of an observer of the same gender as the donor."

2. Some applicants tested positive for more than one drug.

On October 24, 2011, the district court preliminarily enjoined the State from requiring that Lebron submit to a suspicionless drug test pursuant to § 414.0652 as a condition for receiving TANF benefits until the case was resolved. In response to the preliminary injunction, DCF suspended the § 414.0652 TANF drug-testing program statewide, approved all applications that had been pending based on drug testing, approved benefits for individuals who had tested positive, and reimbursed TANF applicants for drug tests to the extent they had not already received reimbursement. In total, the Department restored TANF Temporary Cash Assistance to approximately 1,727 families.

The Secretary appealed the preliminary injunction, and a panel of this Court affirmed.

After we issued our opinion in the preliminary injunction matter, and after the completion of discovery, the district court entered an order granting final summary judgment in favor of Lebron and denying the State's motion. The State argued in the district court that drug testing was constitutionally permissible because of three "special needs": "(1) ensuring TANF participants' job readiness; (2) ensuring the TANF program meets its child-welfare and family-stability goals; and (3) ensuring that public funds are used for their intended purposes and not to undermine public health." [T]he district court concluded, however, that the State failed to show that TANF recipients fell within the "closely guarded category" for whom the Supreme Court has allowed suspicionless drug testing, and also failed to demonstrate that the statute was necessary to protect children because the TANF testing has no impact on the familial and custodial relationships of applicants.

Significantly, the district court also found that the only competent record evidence addressing drug use among the Florida TANF population came from a 1998 study conducted by DCF that actually found a lower rate of drug usage among TANF applicants than among current estimates of the population of Florida as a whole. The district court concluded that "there simply is no competent evidence offered on this record of the sort of pervasive drug problem the State envisioned in the promulgation of this statute." Ultimately, because there was no set of circumstances under which § 414.0652 could be applied constitutionally, the court declared the statute facially unconstitutional and permanently enjoined the State from enforcing it. The State filed a timely notice of appeal of the district court's final order, which we have jurisdiction to review.

II.

We review the district court's grant of summary judgment in favor of Lebron *de novo,* viewing all facts in the light most favorable to the State.

III.

"The right of the people to be secure in their persons, houses, papers, and effects, against unreasonable searches and seizures, shall not be violated. . . ." U.S. Const. amend. IV. The drug testing by urinalysis required under § 414.0652 is undisputedly a Fourth Amendment search. The question is whether mandatory, suspicionless drug testing of all TANF applicants amounts to a *reasonable* search. While the Constitution generally prohibits government searches conducted without individualized suspicion, the Supreme Court has recognized exceptions in certain well-defined circumstances, including when the government has "special needs, beyond the normal need for law enforcement." The Secretary argues that the State has a "special need" for its drug-testing regime and, alternatively, that consent from TANF applicants renders the searches constitutionally valid. We are unpersuaded.

A.

The special needs doctrine recognizes that, "[i]n limited circumstances, where the privacy interests implicated by the search are minimal, and where an important governmental interest furthered by the intrusion would be placed in jeopardy by a requirement of individualized suspicion, a search may be reasonable despite the absence of such suspicion." In determining whether the State possesses a sufficiently substantial special need, "courts must undertake a context-specific inquiry, examining closely the competing private and public interests advanced by the parties." The Supreme Court has permitted suspicionless drug testing only "where the asserted special need addresses a substantial concern for public safety or where the state is fulfilling its well-recognized role as the guardian and tutor of public school children."

In *Skinner,* federal regulations required blood and urine testing of railroad employees involved in train accidents, and also allowed railroads to conduct breath and urine tests of employees who violated safety rules. The regulations were adopted in response to evidence of drug and alcohol abuse by some rail employees, the enormous safety hazards posed by such abuse, and the documented link between impaired employees and train accidents. The Supreme Court upheld the testing program as justified by "surpassing safety interests" because drug testing could deter rail workers who might "cause great human loss before any signs of impairment become noticeable to supervisors." Suspicionless testing was necessary, according to the Court, because blanket searches after (unpredictable) accidents prevented employees from avoiding detection by planning drug use around a testing schedule, and because waiting to establish suspicion about individuals after an accident "likely would result in the loss or deterioration of the evidence furnished by the tests."

For similar reasons, the Supreme Court upheld drug testing of United States Customs Service employees who were directly involved in drug interdiction or were required to carry firearms. *See Nat'l Treasury Emps. Union v. Von Raab,* 489 U.S. 656, (1989). Noting that the program was intended "to deter drug use among those eligible for promotion to sensitive positions within the Service and to prevent the promotion of drug users to those positions," the Court concluded that a substantial special need justified the search. Considering the hazardous and important work done by Customs employees, particularly their exposure to threats, bribes, and blackmail from drug traffickers, the Court held that "the Government has a compelling interest in ensuring that front-line interdiction personnel are physically fit, and have unimpeachable integrity and judgment." Similarly, employees "who may use deadly force plainly discharge duties fraught with such risks of injury to others that even a momentary lapse of attention can have disastrous consequences." "In light of the extraordinary safety and national security hazards that would attend the promotion of drug users to positions that require the carrying of firearms or the interdiction of controlled substances, the Service's policy of deterring drug users from seeking such promotions cannot be deemed unreasonable."

Outside the context of employees in especially hazardous occupations, the Supreme Court has recognized only one other circumstance giving rise to a substantial special need that justifies suspicionless drug testing: when testing "was undertaken in furtherance of the government's responsibilities, under a public school system, as guardian and tutor of children entrusted to its care." The *Vernonia* Court upheld a school board policy that required public school students to consent to suspicionless drug testing in order to participate in athletics. The Supreme Court highlighted the peculiar circumstances of public schools, where "[a] proper educational environment requires close supervision of schoolchildren, as well as the enforcement of rules against conduct that would be perfectly permissible if undertaken by an adult." As a result, "Fourth Amendment rights . . . are different in public schools than elsewhere; the 'reasonableness' inquiry cannot disregard the schools' custodial and tutelary responsibility for children." The Supreme Court found that the school board had an important interest in deterring drug use among student athletes because they are at an age "when the physical, psychological, and addictive effects of drugs are most severe," because "the effects of a drug-infested school are visited . . . upon the entire student body and faculty, as the educational process is disrupted," and because, with school athletics, "the risk of immediate physical harm to the drug user or those with whom he is playing his sport is particularly high."

After *Vernonia,* the Supreme Court also upheld a policy requiring drug tests for all public middle and high school students who participated in competitive extracurricular activities, including athletics but also the Academic Team, Future Farmers of America, band, choir, and cheerleading. The Supreme Court interpreted *Vernonia* as "depend[ing] primarily upon the school's custodial responsibility and authority" and explained that "[t]he health and safety risks identified in *Vernonia* apply with equal force" to the population of school children in *Earls,* particularly because the school district "presented specific evidence of drug use at [its] schools."

By contrast, in *Chandler* the Supreme Court refused to recognize a special need justifying Georgia's mandatory drug testing of candidates for designated state offices because the program did "not fit within the closely guarded category of constitutionally permissible suspicionless searches." Georgia claimed that suspicionless testing was justified by "the incompatibility of unlawful drug use with holding high state office," particularly because "the use of illegal drugs draws into question an official's judgment and integrity; jeopardizes the discharge of public functions, including antidrug law enforcement efforts; and undermines public confidence and trust in elected officials." The Supreme Court found no "indication of a concrete danger demanding departure from the Fourth Amendment's main rule." Unlike in *Skinner* and *Vernonia,* the Georgia "statute was not enacted . . . in response to any fear or suspicion of drug use by state officials." The Supreme Court saw no significance to the message the State sought to send by testing politicians: "The need revealed . . . is symbolic, not 'special,' as that term draws meaning from our case law."

These precedents establish and enforce the principle that "the proffered special need for drug testing must be substantial—important enough to override the individual's acknowledged privacy interest, sufficiently vital to suppress the Fourth Amendment's normal requirement of individualized suspicion." With that in mind, we turn to the application of the doctrine in this case. [W]e need not weigh competing individual and governmental interests unless the State satisfies its burden of establishing a special need for its suspicionless drug-testing program. The State argues that, by seeking TANF benefits, applicants voluntarily subject themselves to heightened regulation, and thus have limited legitimate expectations of privacy.

Of course, citizens do not abandon all hope of privacy by applying for government assistance. By virtue of poverty, TANF applicants are not stripped of their legitimate expectations of privacy—they are not employees in dangerous vocations or students subject to the *parens patriae* power of the state. And "the collection and testing of urine intrudes upon expectations of privacy that society has long recognized as reasonable." But even if TANF applicants had reduced expectations of privacy—and the record supports no such inference—the State first must demonstrate a substantial special need.

On this record the State has failed to meet its burden on the "core issue" of whether a special need justifies suspicionless searches of TANF applicants. The State argues that the following interests . . . qualify as special needs sufficient to permit mandatory drug testing of TANF applicants: "(1) ensuring TANF participants' job readiness; (2) ensuring the TANF program meets its child-welfare and family-stability goals; and (3) ensuring that public funds are used for their intended purposes and not to undermine public health." Encouraging employability, protecting children, and conserving public funds are general—and unquestionably legitimate—public concerns. But empirical evidence indicates these needs are not specific to or special for TANF applicants, nor is drug testing essential to ensuring the success of the TANF program as a whole. The government's stated needs are general concerns, proffered only at a high level of abstraction and without empirical evidence, and thus do not justify an exception to the Fourth Amendment. The State claims, nevertheless, an interest in preparing TANF applicants for the workplace. But government generally wants its citizens to be able to find and keep jobs—the State does not desire work-readiness only for the TANF population. Similarly, while it claims an interest in protecting children from drug use by TANF parents, the State has presented no evidence that children of TANF parents face a danger or harm from drug use that is different from the general threat to all children in all families. After all, the State acknowledges that drug use harms all individuals and families, but the State does not—and cannot—claim an entitlement to drug test all parents of all children.

Nor do we see a special need from the State's desire that government funds are spent wisely. An interest in fiscal responsibility inheres in all public programs, and the interest is real. "Every expenditure of state dollars, taxpayers hope, is for the purpose of achieving a desirable social goal. But that does not mean that a state is entitled to require warrantless and suspicionless drug testing of all recipients of state funds (e.g., college students receiving Bright Futures scholarships) to ensure that those funds are not being misused and that policy goals (e.g., the graduation of such students) are being achieved." "[T]he nature and immediacy of the governmental concern at issue here" is ordinary, not exceptional. The State has presented no evidence demonstrating that drug testing saves a significant portion of TANF funds that would otherwise be spent on drugs. Indeed, the State has made no attempt to quantify even in a general way the amount of TANF money that is otherwise wasted on the purchase or use of drugs. Nor could it do so on the record that was presented to the district court. A government concern that a wholly undefined, albeit a very small, share of a program's expenditures will be squandered cannot easily fit within the closely guarded category reserved for substantial special needs without exploding that carefully cultivated doctrine.

We do not foreclose (nor could we) the possibility that government could establish a special need if a voluntary benefits program as a whole would be rendered ineffective without suspicionless searches. [F]or example, if the government sponsored experimental pharmaceutical trials, it might have a unique concern in drug testing participants to ensure drug interactions did not compromise the results or endanger participants. Similarly, if a state provided a free drug treatment program, it might have a special need to test participants to monitor progress and tailor treatment. In this case, and on this record, however, suspicionless drug testing of all TANF applicants comes nowhere near meeting this standard—the State has not demonstrated that the TANF program as a whole has been compromised without suspicionless searches. Quite simply, we see no essential nexus between the legitimate state interest and the condition imposed. Put differently, the fit is not reasonably proportionated to the harms the State seeks to avoid.

The State argues, nevertheless, that its broadly applicable interests are special because drug use concerns are particularly strong for TANF applicants, but it has not presented a persuasive theoretical or empirical account of a unique problem among TANF applicants. First, no concrete danger exists as a theoretical matter: we have no reason to think impoverished individuals are necessarily and inherently prone to drug use, or, for that matter, are more prone to drug use than the general population. Nor does the State give a reason to think that, if TANF applicants use drugs, that use is somehow different from drug use by the general population. Without an obvious and palpable danger, the State makes an empirical claim that a drug-use problem exists among Florida TANF applicants. Notably, however, the district court found an absence of any showing of pervasive drug use among the Florida TANF population on the summary judgment record: "Even considering the State's evidence presented to date, the Court finds that there is no material dispute concerning whether drug use has been shown to be a 'demonstrated problem' among Florida TANF recipients."

Viewing all of the facts in the light most favorable to the State, we agree with the district court that the State has failed to establish a demonstrable or peculiar drug-use problem among TANF applicants. If anything, the evidence extant suggests quite the opposite: that rates of drug use in the TANF population are no greater than for those who receive other government benefits, or even for the general public.

Well before § 414.0652 was enacted, the State's own DCF, at the direction of the Florida legislature, conducted a study—dubbed the Demonstration Project—to test empirically whether TANF applicants were likely to abuse illegal drugs and whether that abuse affected employment opportunities. The study was conducted between January 1, 1999, through May 31, 2000, in select regions of the state by Dr. Robert E. Crew, a professor at Florida State University. Ultimately, . . . the study revealed that only 5.2% of those who completed their TANF applications tested positive for illegal use of a controlled substance (335 out of 6,462). Notably, the researchers also found no evidence that TANF recipients who tested positive for illicit substances were any less likely to find work than those who tested negative.

Data collected during the brief implementation of § 414.0652 suspicionless drug testing was altogether consistent with the Demonstration Project results. Preliminary numbers showed that only 2.67% of the TANF applicants who submitted to urinalyses under § 414.0652 tested positive for controlled substances—108 out of 4,046. The State argues that this number is artificially depressed because thousands of eligible TANF applicants failed to take the test and complete their application. As the district court pointed out, however, the State offers no way to tell how many incomplete applications came from drug users, and how many instead were cut short because applicants were deterred by other factors, including: the desire not to surrender Fourth Amendment rights; the inability to afford the test; or the difficulty finding a nearby testing location or securing transportation. And, as the Demonstration Project noted, historically a high number of applicants fail to complete their TANF applications, with or without a drug test requirement. The long and the short of it is that the district court fairly concluded on this record that the number of TANF applicants to test positive for illegal drugs during the brief operation of the program can only support the Demonstration Project findings of low rates of drug use. Whatever else can be said about these figures, they do not help the State meet its heavy burden of demonstrating a substantial special need.

In short, the State has not met its core burden of establishing a substantial special need justifying suspicionless drug testing.

B.

Alternatively, the State argues, even if its suspicionless drug-testing regime otherwise would run afoul of the Fourth Amendment, all constitutional concerns are cured by the consent of TANF applicants because "a search conducted pursuant to a valid consent is constitutionally permissible." *Schneckloth v. Bustamonte,* 412 U.S. 218, 222, (1973). After all, TANF is a voluntary program. Applicants must sign a form consenting to the drug test and must follow through with the screening themselves. Lebron responds that, when "the State attempts to justify a search on the basis of . . . consent, the Fourth and Fourteenth Amendments require that it demonstrate that the consent was in fact voluntarily given, and not the result of duress or coercion, express or implied."

[W]e need not ask separately whether consent to a suspicionless drug test was valid when conditioned on receipt of a government benefit because, in this case, the unconstitutional conditions inquiry is baked into the special needs analysis. [W]hen the government conducts suspicionless drug testing, consent exacted as a condition of receiving a benefit is a factor in the special needs analysis, not an alternative path around Fourth Amendment requirements.

Treating consent as a separate and dispositive inquiry would eviscerate the Supreme Court's carefully delineated special needs analysis in drug testing cases. After all, special needs balancing accounts for whether consent reduces an individual's legitimate expectation of privacy. Tellingly, the drug-testing programs in *Skinner, Von Raab, Vernonia, Chandler,* and *Earls* all required consent, but the Supreme Court each time applied the same special needs reasonableness analysis: "the Supreme Court has never held that such drug testing regimes were constitutionally reasonable because of consent." Allowing a government program that plainly fails the special needs balancing test to move forward solely on the basis of extracted consent would effect an end-run around the Supreme Court's well-established approach to suspicionless drug-testing cases. Consent to such a search is surely relevant, but it should be considered "through the prism of . . . special-needs balancing."

"Simply put, we have no reason to conclude that the constitutional validity of a mandated drug testing regime is satisfied by the fact that a state *requires* the affected population to 'consent' to the testing in order to gain access or retain a desired benefit."

In the final analysis, the warrantless, suspicionless urinalysis drug testing of every Florida TANF applicant as a mandatory requirement for receiving Temporary Cash Assistance offends the Fourth Amendment. We respect the State's overarching and laudable desire to promote work, protect families, and conserve resources. But, above all else, we must enforce the Constitution and the limits it places on government. If we are to give meaning to the Fourth Amendment's prohibition on blanket government searches, we must—and we do—hold that § 414.0652 crosses the constitutional line.

Drug testing policies only raise constitutional questions if they are part of a government program. A great deal of drug testing is conducted by private companies, however. Do the benefits of drug testing outweigh the costs in the workplace or in other environments? If not, or if the evidence is inconclusive, what might lead so many companies to drug test their employees? The next article describes some of the literature on the effectiveness of drug testing.

Testing Drugs versus Testing for Drug Use: Private Risk Management in the Shadow of Criminal Law
Robert J. MacCoun

56 DePaul Law Review 507 (2007)

Workplace drug testing is now fairly common, as exhibited in the 1994 and 1997 versions of the National Household Survey on Drug Abuse (NHSDA). These surveys show that 49% of workers in 1997, and 44% in 1994, reported that their workplaces conducted drug testing; testing was more common in large firms (74%) than in medium (58%) or small (28%) firms. According to the American Management Association, the proportion of its members using drug testing rose from 21% to 81% between 1987 and 1996. The NHSDA study found that pre-employment testing was more common (39%) than either testing for cause (30%) or random testing (25%). Similarly, a National Institute on Drug Abuse (NIDA) survey of workplace drug testing data in the early 1990s found that pre-employment testing was more common (44% of testing firms) than random testing (27% of testing firms).

In the NHSDA study, about 8% of full-time workers reported using illicit drugs during the month; a similar share reported heavy alcohol use. Full-time workers accounted for 70% of current illicit drug users aged 18 to 49. Because the household survey likely excluded a sizeable fraction of the addicted population, the true employment rate among current drug users is surely lower. Nevertheless, this suggests an upper-bound estimate that a third . . . of current adult drug users are subject to drug-testing surveillance.

In the 1998 Monitoring the Future survey of high school seniors, 14% of schools and 16% of students reported having some form of drug testing. Similar testing rates (16% of schools and 16% of students) were found in 2001. A somewhat lower rate was reported by the National Study of Delinquency Prevention in Schools (NSDPS), which relied on administrative rather than student respondents. It found that from 1997 to 1998, "approximately 9 percent of secondary schools conducted some sort of testing program, presumably focused on athletes." This estimate covers a time period just after the Supreme Court held in *Vernonia School District 47J v. Acton* that mandatory drug testing of student athletes is legal under the Fourth and Fourteenth Amendments. A later opinion by Justice Clarence Thomas in *Board of Education of Independent School District No. 92 of Pottawatomie County v. Earls* further established student drug testing by holding that it "is a reasonably effective means of addressing the School District's legitimate concerns in preventing, deterring, and detecting drug use" among schoolchildren.

Most of what we know about drug use among arrestees comes from urinalyses conducted for research purposes, rather than for criminal processing. Drug testing of arrestees is rare, except in Washington, D.C. and jurisdictions participating in the Treatment Alternatives for Special Clients (TASC) program or the recently cancelled Arrestee Drug Abuse Monitoring (ADAM) program. Most probationers and parolees are technically subject to testing, but it is very infrequent. Based on his recent study in Los Angeles, San Diego, and Santa Cruz Counties, Professor Mark Kleiman and his colleagues argue that testing of probationers is an inadequate means of surveillance and monitoring: "Once-a-week testing produces about a 35% chance of detecting any given incident of drug use; twice a week pushes that figure above 80%. By contrast, a probationer tested once a month—a far more typical pattern in the three departments studied—has less than one chance in ten of being detected for any given incident of use."

One might assume that the criminal justice system occupies the most intrusive and punitive end of the drug testing spectrum, but Eric Wish and Bernard Gropper of the National Institute of Justice note that in such settings "a single positive test result will seldom have the drastic consequences it can have in the employment setting." They argue that "the level of recent drug use in the offender population is so high that it would be counterproductive to attempt to revoke probation or parole or incarcerate all persons who tested positive." Instead, a positive test is usually "used to trigger more assessment, testing, or supervision and not to punish people or deprive them of their liberty."

Quest Diagnostics, "the leading provider of employer drug testing services in the United States," publishes a regular Drug Testing Index summarizing its results. Between January 2005 and June 2005, Quest conducted over 3.6 million drug tests; the positivity rate was 5% for the general U.S. workforce and 2% for federal workers in safety-sensitive positions. The results show a general decline in positivity rates in recent years, particularly for marijuana. An early 1990s NIDA survey of workplace drug testing found that almost 4% of samples were positive for an illicit substance: 2% for marijuana, 1% for cocaine, and less than 1% for opiates and benzodiazepines. Positive rates were highest in the construction sector at 6%, compared to only 3% for the retail sector and 2% for both the manufacturing and transportation sectors.

Not surprisingly, positive drug test rates are dramatically higher among criminal justice arrestees. The National Institute of Justice began collecting systematic drug testing data from arrestees with its Drug Use Forecasting (DUF) program in 1988. An improved methodology, the ADAM program, was implemented in 2000. The most recent data available are from 2000. In that year, more than half of thirty-five sites reported that 64% or more of their male arrestees tested positive for either cocaine, opiates, marijuana, methamphetamine, or PCP (the NIDA-5). The most common drugs present were marijuana (40%) and cocaine (30%).

Any consideration of drug test results should be qualified by the serious limitations of existing testing methods. Blood testing is the most accurate method for identifying drug influences at the moment of testing, but it is intrusive, expensive, and rare. Urine testing, which is also intrusive, is far more common. But it is a poor indicator of immediate drug status because drugs cannot be detected in urine until they have been metabolized, often many hours after consumption. Urine testing is particularly sensitive to cannabis use, and can detect use dating back several months for a heavy user, but it is far less likely to detect other "hard" drugs. Saliva and hair testing are less intrusive and are becoming more common. In fact, hair testing can detect use dating back two to three months, and can even date the use with some accuracy.

Use testing is vulnerable to false positives due to contaminants (for urine testing), as well as false negatives due to temporary abstention (for blood, urine, and saliva testing), "water loading" (for urine testing), and even a haircut (for hair testing). Detailed advice on defeating a drug test is available on various websites. For example, false positives for marijuana can be triggered by many different prescription and over-the-counter medications.

Another reason to be wary of the accuracy of use testing results is problems with sampling. "Random testing" may sound a lot like "random sampling," but there is selection into and out of the sample, because users and others who object to testing may avoid the testing organization altogether—whether it be the military, a workplace, or a school sports program.

From a deterrence perspective, use testing should be an effective way to reduce drug use. Use testing increases the certainty of sanctioning, and even when it does not lead to arrest, the consequences of a positive test are effectively punitive, because it damages one's reputation with family, friends, and colleagues. Nevertheless, support for a general deterrent effect of drug testing is mixed.

The available studies are correlational and hence subject to a variety of inferential problems. It is astonishing that such an intrusive intervention is being implemented so widely in the absence of a carefully controlled experiment group, with random assignment to testing condition either at the individual, site, or organizational level.

On the basis of the special workplace modules, the NHSDA 1994/1997 project noted the effect of information availability in the workplace: "There is evidence that workplace policies matter. Employees in three of the four occupations with the lowest rates of drug use (protective service, extraction and precision production, and administration support) were also among employees in the four occupations with the highest rates of drug information and policies in the workplace."

In 1981, the U.S. military implemented a tough "zero-tolerance" drug policy, which imposed mandatory drug testing and threatened job termination for violations. Two studies have examined the effects of the policy. Professor Jerald Bachman and his colleagues used the Monitoring the Future cohort data from young adults who graduated from high school between 1976 and 1995. They found declining rates of drug use among active duty military personnel and nonmilitary cohort members in the two years after graduation, but beginning in 1981, the rate of decline was steeper for the military group, at least for illicit drugs. This is a pattern "strongly suggestive of causal relationships." In a separate study, economists Stephen Mehay and Rosalie Pacula compared NHSDA and Department of Defense health survey data collected before and after the military adopted the zero-tolerance policy. They estimated a 16% drop in the prevalence of past-year drug use in the military, with a lower bound estimate of 4%.

Dr. W. Robert Lange and his colleagues examined the effects of a decision at Johns Hopkins hospital to shift from "for cause" employee testing in 1989 to universal pre-employment testing in 1991. In 1989, 10.8% of 593 specimens were positive—55% of them for marijuana—and there were seven "walkouts" who refused to be tested. In 1991, 5.8% of 365 specimens tested positive—28% for marijuana—with no walkouts. The authors interpreted these results as evidence of the deterrent effect of drug testing. But Professors M.R. Levine and W.P. Rennie offer a variety of alternative explanations, including the fact that in 1991 users had advance warning of the test and could abstain, water load, or ingest legal substances that would confound the test.

The most comprehensive study of the effects of school testing on student drug use comes from analyses of data from the Monitoring the Future survey. This analysis found no measurable association between either random or "for cause" drug testing and students' self-reported drug use. The study is cross-sectional, rather than prospective, and is somewhat limited by the relative rarity of exposure to testing.

At present, the evidence suggests that the military's testing program had a deterrent effect, but no such effect was found in workplaces or in schools. Still, the absence of evidence is not evidence of absence. There are very few rigorous studies; low statistical power, noisy measurement, and other factors may hide genuine effects. Alternatively, the military program may be more effective as a deterrent due to differences in its implementation, its target population, its consequences for users, or its institutional setting.

The National Research Council (NRC) took a comprehensive look at the evidence for a safety-promoting benefit of drug testing in the workplace. They concluded that the evidence linking alcohol and drug use to workplace accidents was largely inconclusive, partly because both workplace accidents and workplace intoxication were relatively rare events: "Despite the wide variety of research in the studies reviewed above, few definitive statements can be made about the impact of using alcohol and other drugs on job performance. The abundance of evidence presented here indicates that the relationship between use and job behaviors and outcomes is clearly negative. However, the magnitude of the relationships found is generally small, and causal spuriousness and direction are problems that have not been adequately addressed in the literature."

The intuition that drug testing might prevent accidents involves an implicit causal chain: drug use impairs psychomotor functioning, which in turn enhances accident risk. Drug testing is designed to detect drug use, the earliest link in the chain, and hopefully to deter or prevent it. But the model also explicitly demonstrates some of the drawbacks of relying on drug use to prevent accidents. This point is illustrated by the statistical logic of "path analysis," first articulated by mathematician Sewall Wright in 1934. In a causal chain (for example, A—>B—>C) where the effect of a variable at one end (A) on the other end (C) is "mediated" by a variable in the middle (B), the distal A—>C correlation equals the product of the two intermediate correlations, and will thus be smaller than either one. The percentage of variance in accident risk due to drug use will drop rapidly with less than perfect correlation in the two intermediate links in the chain.

From a prediction standpoint, one might argue that drug tests can serve as a double proxy for drug use and low self-control. But psychometrically, a better strategy would be to directly assess low self-control and psychomotor functioning. Psychologists and ergonomic specialists have developed a wide variety of valid psychomotor tests, and many are already in use in the military and other "mission-critical" organizations. The private sector has also begun to recognize the potential advantages of directly testing impaired psychomotor performance. There are a variety of psychometrically reliable and valid measures of impulsivity, sensation-seeking, and self-control. More controversially, there are paper-and-pencil "integrity tests" that allow corporations to assess drug and alcohol use, honesty, and other behavioral factors.

A preference for drug testing over psychomotor testing suggests that use testing is really about drug control rather than safety. This is also shown by the fact that drug testing is more common than alcohol testing, even though the link between alcohol and accidents is better established. Granted, it may be easier to consume alcohol without intoxication than cannabis or other drugs. And alcohol is far more prevalent, meaning far more positive test results—though from a safety perspective that is not much of an argument at all.

Use testing may also have some unintended consequences. Theoretically, it could encourage users to substitute less detectable intoxicants. In 1995, 20% of worksites tested for illicit drugs but not for alcohol. The most commonly tested substances are the NIDA-5: marijuana, cocaine, PCP, opiates, and amphetamines. Thus, users might shift from the NIDA-5 to other illicit drugs like MDMA (Ecstasy) and barbiturates, or from illicit drugs to alcohol. I am unaware of studies examining such substitution effects, but these effects have been linked to other policies. There is some evidence that users substitute marijuana for hard drugs when marijuana is decriminalized, and that users substitute marijuana for alcohol when the legal drinking age is raised or beer prices increase. Because marijuana has the longest window of detectability in urinalysis, one might see a shift toward less readily detectable substances like MDMA, amphetamines, and barbiturates.

A related concern is that use testing will drive users away from testing organizations—workplaces, schools, sports teams, and the military. This might make those particular organizations safer, but it displaces the harm to other settings where use might even escalate.

A similar argument is suggested by "labeling theory" in criminology. Labeling theory predicts that legal controls can actually enhance the likelihood of future offenses if the stigma associated with criminal sanctioning alienates the individual from conventional society. Alienation encourages contact with criminally involved referent groups, and weakens the reputational costs that may restrain deviance—thus creating a self-fulfilling prophecy.

Evidence supports this prediction, but the results are not conclusive. Neither Mehay and Pacula nor Bachman found any evidence linking past drug use to self-selection into the military. On the other hand, using the 1994 NHSDA survey, John Hoffmann and Cindy Larison of the National Opinion Research Center found that those using marijuana or cocaine at least weekly were more likely to work for companies that had no testing program. And the NHSDA 1994/1997 workplace analysis suggested that current users were more likely than nonusers to say they would avoid working for an employer who conducts pre-employment screening (22% versus 4%), random drug testing (29% versus 6%), or "for cause" testing (24% versus 10%).

In addition to testing for current drug use, some government agencies refuse to hire applicants based on their past drug use. The Federal Bureau of Investigation, for example, requires candidates for some positions to "swear that they have not used any illegal substances recently—three years for marijuana and 10 years for other drugs." Prior to 2007, the hiring restrictions were even more stringent, "barr[ing] FBI employment to anyone who had used marijuana more than 15 times in their lives or who had tried other illegal narcotics more than five times." Dan Eggen, *FBI Bows to Modern Realities, Eases Rules on Past Drug Use*, Wash. Post, Aug. 7, 2007. The Department of Justice won't hire an applicant who has used an illegal drug less than one year prior to their application for employment and has an "absolute post-bar [exam] prohibition on any drug use, including marijuana" for attorney applicants. "Any other drug use is reviewed on a case-by-case basis." Loyola University of Chicago School of Law, Government Security Clearance Information, http://www.luc.edu/law/career/govt_security.html. Needless to say, neither agency's policy bars past or present alcohol users from employment.

4. "No-Knock" Drug Raids and Police Militarization

In *Wilson v. Arkansas*, 514 U.S. 927 (1995) and *Richards v. Wisconsin*, 520 U.S. 385 (1997), the United States Supreme Court held that the police must typically knock and announce their presence before searching a residence pursuant to a warrant. In *Richards*, the Court described the circumstances in which the police may search a residence without knocking as follows: "In order to justify a 'no-knock' entry, the police must have a reasonable suspicion that knocking and announcing their presence, under the particular circumstances, would be dangerous or futile, or that it would inhibit the effective investigation of crime by, for example, allowing the destruction of evidence." 520 U.S. 385, 594 (1997). In the 2006 case *Hudson v. Michigan*, 547 U.S. 586 (2006), however, the Court held that the exclusionary rule does not forbid the use of evidence obtained after a violation of the knock and announce requirement. As a result of the holding in *Hudson*, the rule limiting no-knock searches that was announced in *Richards* is largely toothless and no-knock searches have become widespread. *Wilson, Richards,* and *Hudson* are addressed in detail in most Criminal Procedure courses. This section focuses on the link between no-knock searches and drug enforcement. The following excerpt from a 2006 report on paramilitary style raids in domestic law enforcement provides an overview of their history and relationship to drug enforcement.

Overkill: The Rise of Paramilitary Police Raids in America
Radley Balko

The Cato Institute 2006

"They [police officers] made a mistake. There's no one to blame for a mistake. The way these people were treated has to be judged in the context of a war." — *Hallandale, Florida, attorney Richard Kane, after police officers conducted a late night drug raid on the home of Edwin and Catherine Bernhardt. Police broke into the couple's home and threw Catherine Bernhardt to the floor at gunpoint. Edwin Bernhardt, who had come down from his bedroom in the nude after hearing the commotion, was also subdued and handcuffed at gunpoint. Police forced him to wear a pair of his wife's under-wear, then took him to the police station, where he spent several hours in jail. Police later discovered they had raided the wrong address.*

The typical SWAT team carries out its missions in battle fatigues: Lace-up, combat-style boots; black, camouflage, or olive-colored pants and shirts, sometimes with "ninja-style" or balaclava hoods; Kevlar helmets and vests; gas masks, knee pads, gloves, communication devices, and boot knives; and military-grade weapons, such as the Heckler and Koch MP5 submachine gun, the preferred model of the U.S. Navy Seals. Other standard SWAT-team weaponry includes battering rams, ballistic shields, "flashbang" grenades, smoke grenades, pepper spray, and tear gas. Many squads are now ferried to raid sites by military-issue armored personnel carriers. Some units have helicopters. Others boast grenade launchers, tanks (with and without gun turrets), rappelling equipment, and bayonets.

Paramilitary raids are generally carried out late at night, or just before dawn. Police are technically bound by law to "knock and announce" themselves, and give occupants time to answer the door before forcing entry. But . . . that requirement is today commonly either circumvented through court-sanctioned loopholes, ignored completely with little consequence, or only ceremoniously observed, with a knock and announcement unlikely to be noticed by anyone inside.

Police generally break open doors with a battering ram, or blow them off their hinges with explosives. Absent either, police have pried doors open with sledgehammers or screwdrivers, ripped them off by attaching them to the back ends of trucks, or entered by crashing through windows or balconies. After an entryway is cleared, police sometimes detonate a flashbang grenade or a similar device designed to disorient the occupants in the targeted house. They then enter the home under its cover. SWAT teams have entered homes through fire escapes, by rappelling down from police helicopters, and by crashing through second-story windows. Once police are inside, the occupants are quickly and forcefully incapacitated. They're instructed to remain in the prone position, generally at gunpoint, while police carry out the search warrant. Any perceived noncompliance is typically met with force, which can potentially be lethal, depending on the nature of the noncompliance.

Once rare, these procedures are now performed dozens of times per day in cities and towns all across the country.

Longtime Los Angeles police chief Daryl F. Gates is widely credited with inventing the SWAT team in early 1966, though there's some evidence that the idea was brought to Gates a year earlier, when he was inspector general, by Los Angeles Police Department officer John Nelson. The inspiration for the modern SWAT team was a specialized force in Delano, California, made up of crowd control officers, riot police, and snipers, assembled to counter the farm worker uprisings led by Cesar Chavez. In search of new methods to counter the snipers and guerrilla tactics used against L.A. police during the Watts riots, Gates and other L.A. police officials quickly embraced the idea of an elite, military-trained cadre of law enforcement officers who could react quickly, accurately, and with overwhelming force to particularly dangerous situations. Gates brought in a team of ex-Marines to train a small group of police officers Gates handpicked for the new endeavor. Gates called his unit the Special Weapons Attack Team, or SWAT. City officials liked the idea, including the acronym, but balked at the word "attack." They persuaded Gates to change the units name to Special Weapons and Tactics, though the new moniker was purely cosmetic—no change in training or mission accompanied the name change.

SWAT quickly gained favor with public officials, politicians, and the public. In August 1966, former Marine Charles Whitman barricaded himself at the top of a clock tower at the University of Texas and opened fire on the campus below. Whitman shot 46 people and killed 15. Police struggled for more than 90 minutes to remove Whitman from his tower perch. Public horror at Whitman's slaughter quickly turned into support for Gates's idea of training elite teams to complement city policing in dangerous situations like the Whitman massacre. SWAT teams subsequently began to pop up in larger urban areas across the country.

Three years later, the L.A. SWAT team engaged in a highly publicized shootout with the city's Black Panther militia. Publicity from the standoff won the L.A. SWAT team and the concept of SWAT teams in general widespread public acclaim.

Gates's experiment soon became a celebrated part of American pop culture. A SWAT-themed television show debuted in 1975, and the show's theme song hit the Billboard Top Forty. In 1995, Gates launched a SWAT video game franchise with Sierra Entertainment. The SWAT series spawned several award winning "first-person" style shooter games, the most recent version of which was released in early 2005. In January 2006, cable television channel A&E debuted a new reality television show called Dallas SWAT, which follows the lives of the members of a Dallas, Texas, SWAT team. Court TV now carries the show Texas SWAT, in which seasoned war journalist Jeff Chagrin tags along with several SWAT teams across the state.

But despite the American public's fascination with SWAT, until the 1980s, actual deployments of the paramilitary units were still largely confined to extraordinary, emergency situations such as hostage takings, barricades, hijackings, or prison escapes. Though the total number of SWAT teams gradually increased throughout the 1970s, they were mostly limited to larger, more urbanized areas, and the terms surrounding their deployment were still for the most part narrowly and appropriately defined. That changed in the 1980s.

The election of Ronald Reagan in 1980 brought new funding, equipment, and a more active drug-policing role for paramilitary police units across the country. Reagan's new offensive in the War on Drugs involved a more confrontational, militaristic approach to combating the drug supply, a policy enthusiastically embraced by Congress. During the next 10 years, with prodding from the White House, Congress paved the way to widespread military-style policing by carving yawning drug war exceptions to the Posse Comitatus Act, the Civil War-era law prohibiting the use of the military for civilian policing. These new exceptions allowed nearly unlimited sharing of drug interdiction intelligence, training, tactics, technology, and weaponry between the Pentagon and federal, state, and local police departments.

The first of these exemptions was the Military Cooperation with Law Enforcement Act, passed in 1981. This wide-reaching legislation encouraged the military to give local, state, and federal police access to military bases, research, and equipment for drug interdiction. It also authorized the military to train civilian police officers to use the newly available equipment, and not only encouraged the military to share drug-war-related information with civilian police but authorized the military to take an active role in preventing drugs from entering the country.

In a 1999 paper for the Cato Institute on the militarization of American policing, Diane Cecilia Weber outlined ensuing laws passed in the 1980s and 1990s that further eroded the clear demarcation between military and civilian drug enforcement set forth by Posse Comitatus. Among the laws cited by Weber are the following:

- In 1986, President Reagan issued a National Security Decision Directive, which declared drugs a threat to U.S. "national security." The directive allowed for yet more cooperation between local, state, and federal law enforcement and the military.
- In 1988, Congress ordered the National Guard to assist state drug enforcement efforts. Because of this order, National Guard troops today patrol for marijuana plants and assist in large-scale anti-drug operations in every state in the country.
- In 1989, President Bush created a series of regional task forces within the Department of Defense, charged with facilitating cooperation between the military and domestic police forces.

- In 1994, the Department of Defense issued a memorandum authorizing the transfer of equipment and technology to state and local police. The same year, Congress created a "reutilization program" to facilitate handing military gear over to civilian police agencies.

Despite the fact that these laws were a significant departure from longstanding domestic policy, most were passed without much media attention or public debate. What debate there was muted by assurances from politicians and drug war supporters that (a) the scourge of drugs was too threatening and too pervasive to be fought with traditional policing and (b) critics who feared for the civil liberties of American civilians under a more militarized system were alarmist and overstating their case. Rep. Charles Bennett (D-FL), for example, called the century-old Posse Comitatus Act—a law whose principles can be traced directly to concerns expressed by the Founding Fathers—a "sinful, evil law." In 1989, Drug Enforcement Agency administrator Francis Mullen forthrightly asserted that Congress should green-light the use of the U.S. military in law enforcement because "there is sufficient oversight on the part of Congress and others to deter infringement on individual liberties." Also in 1989, then-secretary of defense Dick Cheney declared, "The detection and countering of the production, trafficking and use of illegal drugs is a high priority national security mission of the Department of Defense."

After each of these policies was enacted, police departments across the country helped themselves to the newly available equipment, training, and funding. By the late 1990s, the various laws, orders, and directives softening Posse Comitatus had added a significant military component to state and local police forces. The National Defense Authorization Security Act of 1997, commonly called "1033" for the section of the U.S. Code assigned to it, created the Law Enforcement Support Program, an agency headquartered in Ft. Belvoir, Virginia. The new agency was charged with streamlining the transfer of military equipment to civilian police departments. It worked. Transfers of equipment took off at an even greater clip than before. The National Journal reports that between January 1997 and October 1999, the agency handled 3.4 million orders of Pentagon equipment from over 11,000 domestic police agencies in all 50 states. By December 2005, the number was up to 17,000. The purchase value of the equipment comes to more than $727 million. The National Journal reported that included in the bounty were 253 aircraft (including six- and seven-passenger airplanes, and UH-60 Blackhawk and UH-1 Huey helicopters), 7,856 M-16 rifles, 181 grenade launchers, 8,131 bulletproof helmets, and 1,161 pairs of night-vision goggles.

Civilian police departments suddenly found themselves flush with military arms. The Los Angeles Police Department was offered bayonets. The city of St. Petersburg, Florida, bought an armored personnel carrier from the Pentagon for just $1,000. The seven police officers of Jasper, Florida—which has all of 2,000 people and hasn't had a murder in 14 years—were each given a military-grade M-16 machine gun, leading one Florida paper to run the headline, "Three Stoplights, Seven M-16s."

The sheriff 's office in landlocked Boone County, Indiana, was given an amphibious armored personnel carrier.

In a 1997 60 Minutes segment on the trend toward militarization, the CBS news magazine profiled the Sheriff 's Department of Marion County, Florida, a rural, agricultural area known for its horse farms. Courtesy of the various Pentagon giveaway programs, the county sheriff proudly showed reporter Lesley Stahl the department's 23 military helicopters, two C-12 luxury executive aircraft (often called the "Rolls Royce with wings"), a motor home, several trucks and trailers, a tank, and a "bomb robot." This, in addition to an arsenal of military-grade assault weapons.

With all of this funding and free or discounted equipment and training from the federal government, police departments across the country needed something to do with it. So they formed SWAT teams—thousands of them. SWAT teams have since multiplied and spread across the country at a furious clip.

In a widely cited survey, criminologist Peter Kraska found that as of 1997, 90 percent of cities with populations of 50,000 or more had at least one paramilitary police unit, twice as many as in the mid-1980s. The increase has been even more pronounced in smaller towns: In a separate study, Kraska found that the number of SWAT teams serving towns with populations between 25,000 and 50,000 increased 157 percent between 1985 and 1996. They've popped up in college towns like South Bend, Indiana, and Champaign, Illinois, where they're increasingly used for routine marijuana policing. The University of Central Florida's campus police department actually has its own, separate SWAT team, independent of the city and county. As of 1996, 65 percent of towns within the 25,000–50,000-population range had a SWAT team, with another 8 percent planning to form one. Given that the trends giving rise to SWAT proliferation in the 1990s haven't gone away, it's safe to assume that all of these numbers have continued to rise and are significantly higher today. In fact, SWAT teams are increasingly popping up in even smaller towns.

In 2002, . . . the Miami Herald ran a prophetic report about the SWAT teams proliferating across small-town Florida, including in Broward County suburbs like Miramar (population 101,000), Pembroke Pines (150,000), and Davie (82,579). "Police say they want [SWAT teams] in case of a hostage situation or a Columbine-type incident," the paper reported, "But in practice, the teams are used mainly to serve search warrants on suspected drug dealers. Some of these searches yield as little as few grams of cocaine or marijuana."

A subsequent investigation by the St. Petersburg Times found that many Florida police departments even fudged crime statistics and exaggerated local drug crimes in an effort to get more military weaponry. The "panhandle town of Lynn Haven (pop. 12,451) reported a 900 percent rise in armed robberies," the paper wrote, "without telling regulators that the raw number of robberies rose from one to 10, then fell to one again just as quickly." The investigation also found that without the military's sophisticated anti-theft system tracking the weapons once they reached the police departments, many went missing or were stolen, meaning many officers could potentially later encounter the same weapons in the hands of criminals.

As the Miami Herald reported was happening in Florida, it's commonplace for police officials who want a SWAT team to attempt to assuage community concerns by arguing the units are necessary to thwart the possibility of terrorism, school shootings, or violent crime. Once in place, however, SWAT teams are inevitably used far more frequently, mostly in the service of drug warrants.

In 2001, Madison, Wisconsin's Capital Times reported that as of 2001, 65 of the state's 83 local SWAT teams had come into being since 1980, 28 since 1996, and 16 since 2000. Many of those newly established teams had popped up in absurdly small towns like Forest County (population 9,950), Mukwonago (7,519), and Rice Lake (8,320).

Like the Miami Herald . . . the Capital Times investigation found that though paramilitary units are often justified to town councils and skeptical citizens as essential to fight terrorism, deal with hostage situations, and diffuse similarly rare but volatile situations; once established, they're rarely deployed for those reasons. Instead, they're almost always sent to serve routine search warrants, make drug arrests, and conduct similar drug-related proactive policing.

One sheriff, for example, convinced his county to give him a SWAT team after one of his deputies was killed in a shootout. Now, he told the Capital Times, he uses the unit primarily for "drug searches and stuff." A police captain in Green Bay noted that armed barricades are happening "less and less," and so the SWAT team instead "assists the drug task force on a regular basis." The Jackson County, Wisconsin, SWAT captain likewise told the paper that the most common use of the teams is for "drug search warrants." Columbia County, Wisconsin, put its $1.75 million Pentagon bounty to use at "Weedstock" in nearby Sauk County, where cops in full SWAT attire stood guard to intimidate while, as the Times reports, "hundreds of young people gather[ed] peacefully to smoke marijuana and listen to music."

The Capital Times also found that in addition to free equipment, the federal government gave money to the states for drug control, primarily through the Byrne Justice Assistance Grant program, as well as various federal law enforcement block grants. The states then disbursed the money to local police departments on the basis of each department's number of drug arrests. The extra funding was only tied to anti-drug policing. In some cases, the funding could offset the entire cost of establishing and maintaining a SWAT team, with funds left over. The paper found that the size of the disbursements was directly tied to the number of city or county drug arrests, noting that each arrest in theory would net a given city or county about $153 in state and federal funding. Jackson County, Wisconsin, for example, quadrupled its drug arrests between 1999 and 2000. Correspondingly, the county's federal subsidy quadrupled, too.

Thanks to the federal subsidies for drug arrests, then, not only did the number of SWAT teams soar through the 1980s and 1990s, so too did the frequency with which they were deployed. In 1972, there were just a few hundred paramilitary drug raids per year in the United States. According to Kraska, by the early 1980s there were 3,000 annual SWAT deployments, by 1996 there were 30,000, and by 2001 there were 40,000. The average city police department deployed its paramilitary police unit about once a month in the early 1980s. By 1995, that number had risen to seven. To give one example, the city of Minneapolis, Minnesota, deployed its SWAT team on no-knock warrants 35 times in 1987. By 1996, the same unit had been deployed for drug raids more than 700 times that year alone.

In small-to medium-sized cities, Kraska estimates that 80 percent of SWAT callouts are now for warrant service. In large cities, it's about 75 percent. These numbers, too, have been on the rise since the early 1980s. Orange County, Florida, deployed its SWAT team 619 times during one five-year period in the 1990s. Ninety-four percent of those call-outs were to serve search warrants, not for hostage situations or police standoffs.

For several years, the heavily armed Fresno SWAT team mentioned earlier was used for routine, full-time patrolling in high-crime areas. The Violent Crime Suppression Unit, as it was called, was given carte blanche to enter residences and apprehend and search occupants in high-crime, mostly minority neighborhoods. The unit routinely stopped pedestrians without probable cause, searched them, interrogated them, and entered their personal information into a computer. "It's a war," one SWAT officer told a reporter from the Nation. Said another, "If you're 21, male, living in one of these neighborhoods, and you're not in our computer, then there's something definitely wrong." The VCSU was disbanded in 2001 after a series of lawsuits alleging police brutality and wrongful shootings, though officials claim the unit was dissolved because it had "fulfilled its goals."

The deployment of SWAT teams for routine police work, even independent of the drug war, has reaped unfortunate—though predictable—results, from general police overreaction to mass raids on entire neighborhoods, to the deaths of innocent people. In January 1999, for example, a SWAT team in Chester, Pennsylvania, outraged the local community when it raided Chester High School in full tactical gear to break up a half dozen students who had been loitering outside the school in the early afternoon. An incident like that is troubling enough. But the use of heavily armed police tactics in response to nonviolent offenses can have far more tragic consequences. In 1998, the Virginia Beach SWAT team shot and killed security guard Edward C. Reed in a 3 a.m. gambling raid on a private club. Police say they approached the tinted car where Reed was working security, knocked, and identified themselves, at which point Reed refused to drop his handgun. Reed's family insists that the police version of events is unlikely, given that Reed was a security guard and had no criminal record. More likely, they say, Reed mistakenly believed the raiding officers were there to do harm, particularly given that the club had been robbed not long before. According to police, Reed's last words were, "Why did you shoot me? I was reading a book." Club owner Darrin Hyman actually shot back at the SWAT team. Prosecutors would later decline to press felony charges against

Hyman, concluding he had good reason to believe he was under attack. Hyman was convicted of a misdemeanor gambling offense (playing a game of dice with friends) and of discharging a firearm.

The most obvious problem with the militarization of civilian policing is that the military and the police have two distinctly different tasks. The military's job is to seek out, overpower, and destroy an enemy. Though soldiers attempt to avoid them, collateral casualties are accepted as inevitable. Police, on the other hand, are charged with "keeping the peace," or "to protect and serve."

Given that civilian police now tote military equipment, get military training, and embrace military culture and values, it shouldn't be surprising when officers begin to act like soldiers, treat civilians like combatants, and tread on private property as if it were part of a battlefield. Of course, it's hard to overlook the fact that the soldiering-up of civilian police forces is taking place as part of the larger War on Drugs, which grows more saturated with war imagery, tactics, and phraseology every day.

War imagery and the endorsement of indiscriminate, military battle tactics for the War on Drugs has become common in political discourse. For example, the nation's first Drug Czar, William Bennett, recommended in 1989 that the United States abolish habeas corpus for drug offenders. "It's a funny war when the 'enemy' is entitled to due process of law and a fair trial," Bennett later told Fortune magazine. On the Larry King Show Bennett suggested that drug dealers be publicly beheaded.

Given such rhetoric, it isn't all that surprising when civilian agencies police drug crimes like soldiers instead of peacekeepers and treat civilians like combatants instead of citizens with rights.

The most obvious criticism of paramilitary drug raids is that, contrary to assertions from proponents that they minimize the risk of violence, they actually escalate provocation and bring unnecessary violence to what would otherwise be a routine, nonviolent police procedure. SWAT teams typically serve drug warrants just before dawn, or late at night. They enter residences unannounced, or just seconds after announcing. Targets, then, are suddenly awoken from sleep, and confronted with the prospect that their homes are being invaded. Police sometimes deploy diversionary devices such as flashbang grenades, designed to cause temporary blindness and deafness, intentionally compounding the confusion.

It isn't difficult to see why a gun owner's first instinct upon waking under such conditions would be to disregard whatever the intruders may be screaming at him, and reach for a weapon to defend himself. Even public officials have expressed that sentiment. In 1992, police in Venice, Illinois, mistakenly raided the wrong home on a paramilitary narcotics raid. Fortunately, no one was home. But the house turned out to be the home of Tyrone Echols, Venice's mayor. "To tell the truth, I don't remember what they said because I was furious," Echols told the St. Louis Post-Dispatch. "If I'd been here and heard that going on I probably would have taken my pistol and shot through the door. I'd probably be dead. And some of the officers would probably be dead, too."

Even former police officers have instinctively reached for their weapons when SWAT teams have mistakenly entered their homes on faulty, no-knock search warrants. So have many civilians—some guilty of drug crimes, some completely innocent—who were then shot and killed by police officers who understandably mistook an otherwise nonviolent suspect's attempt to defend himself as an act of aggression. Should a suspect or any occupant of the residence be asleep in a room far away from the point of entry, or perhaps on another floor, it's not difficult to see how he might be awoken by the commotion but not hear the announcement that the intruders are police (assuming such an announcement was made in the first place).

Another problem with military-style, late-night drug raids is that there's good reason for civilians to suspect late night intruders aren't police. Spurred on in part by the frequent nature and popularization of surprise drug raids, it is not uncommon for criminals to disguise themselves as raiding police to gain entry into homes and businesses.

One infamous example took place in 1994, when a group of men entered the home of Lisa Renee and abducted her as retribution for a drug deal, which they'd conducted with her brothers, gone wrong. In a chilling 911 call, as Renee pleads with the operator to send help, one of the men announces through the door that he's the "FBI." Renee says to the operator, "Oh, they're the FBI." One intruder then says, "Open the door and we'll talk." Renee says again, "They're the FBI. They say they're the FBI, ma'am," and opens the door. The call ends with screaming. The men kidnapped Renee, raped and beat her over the next several days, then buried her alive in a shallow grave. Given its sensational elements, the Renee case is perhaps the most famous case of armed intruders posing as police. But it's by no means the only example. New York City alone reports more than 1,000 cases each year of people pretending to be police officers, many of them in attempts to rob homes and businesses.

An overwhelming number of mistaken raids take place because police relied on information from confidential informants. Police routinely secure warrants for paramilitary drug raids on the basis of a tip from a single, confidential informant, many of whom are paid, or rewarded with leniency in their own criminal cases. Back in 1995, National Law Journal estimated that money paid to informants jumped from $25 million in 1985 to about $97 million in 1993. It's safe to assume that number is significantly higher now. Those figures also don't include money seized by police from drug suspects, a portion of which often gets filtered back to informants.

One of the more egregious examples of how the informant system can lead to tragedy is the case of Pedro Oregon Navarro. In the summer of 1998, two police officers in Houston pulled over a car with three men inside. One of them was subsequently arrested for public intoxication. Already on probation, the suspect came up with a bargain for the arresting officers. He'd give them a tip on a drug dealer if they'd let him off. They agreed. The man made up a story and gave police Navarro's address. At 1:40 a.m., six police from the city's anti-gang task force raided Navarro's house. The informant knocked on the door, and Navarro's brother-in-law answered. At that point, the officers stormed Navarro's bedroom, where the man awoke, startled and frightened, and reached for his gun. Police opened fire. They shot Navarro 12 times, killing him. Navarro never fired his gun.

There isn't much data available on just how often judges or prosecutors turn down search warrants because of the untrustworthiness of a confidential informant or on how often they turn down drug search warrants in general. But most criminal justice experts agree that it's rare.

A 2000 Denver Post investigation found that judges exercise almost no discretion at all when it comes to issuing no-knock warrants. The Post found that Denver judges had denied just five of 163 no-knock applications over a 12-month period (local defense attorneys were surprised to learn there were even five). "No-knock search warrants appear to be approved so routinely that some Denver judges have issued them even though police asked only for a regular warrant," the Post wrote. "In fact, more than one of every 10 no-knock warrants issued over the past seven months was transformed from a regular warrant with just a judge's signature." Among the paper's other findings: In 8 of 10 raids, police assertions in affidavits that weapons would be present turned out to be wrong.

Judge Robert Patterson, the presiding judge for Denver's criminal court system provided an astonishing defense. "We are not the fact gatherers," he said. "It's pretty formulaic how it's done. If you sign your name 100 times, you can look away and sign in the wrong place. We read a lot of documents. We may, just like anyone else, sign something and realize later that it's the wrong place or the wrong thing. Is it wrong not to be paying attention? No. It's just that we're doing things over and over again."

Perhaps what's most troubling about the use of no-knock and quick-knock raids is that for all the peril and confrontation associated with them, the little evidence available suggests they aren't even all that effective. The public scrutiny that followed [a] botched no-knock raid in Denver that killed immigrant Ismael Mena in 2000, for example, enabled Denver's Rocky Mountain News to get access to warrants and court records for all of the no-knock raids conducted in the city in 1999. The paper's findings were alarming: Of 146 no-knock raids conducted in the city that year, only 49 produced charges of any kind. And of those, just 2 resulted in prison time for the targets of the raids. In comparison, the paper noted that while 21 percent of the city's felony defendants on average are sent to prison, just 4 percent of its no-knock defendants were. One former prosecutor said of the results, "When you have that violent intrusion on people's homes with so little results, you have to ask why." The Rocky Mountain News continued: "Almost all of the 1999 no-knock cases were targeted at people suspected of being drug dealers.... Often the tips went unsubstantiated, and little in the way of narcotics was recovered. The problem doesn't stem only from the work of inexperienced street cops, which city officials have maintained. Even veteran narcotics detectives sometimes seek no-knock warrants based on the word of an informant and without conducting undercover buys to verify the tips."

A 1997 investigation by the Palm Beach Post found that in a sampling of 50 of the 309 arrests made by Palm Beach County's 12 SWAT teams, the longest jail sentence meted out from any of the raids was five years. The vast majority produced sentences of less than six months, parole, or no sentence at all. Of the defendants actually found guilty, most were sentenced to less than six months in jail, suggesting they were hardly the hardened, violent, dangerous criminals police and prosecutors say require the use of a heavily fortified paramilitary team.

After [a] New York City raid that [resulted in the death of the suspect], Police Chief Raymond Kelly estimated that at least 10 percent of the city's 450+ monthly no-knock drug raids were served on the wrong address, under bad information, or otherwise didn't produce enough evidence for an arrest. Kelly conceded, however, that NYPD didn't keep careful track of botched raids, leading one city council member to speculate the problem could be even worse.

Supporters of the increased use of paramilitary tactics often say that such aggressive tactics are necessary because drug dealers are increasingly arming themselves with heavier and more sophisticated weaponry. The only way to counter that trend, they say, is to keep police well ahead in the arms race, and to show overwhelming force when serving drug search and arrest warrants.

[However], there's simply not much evidence that criminals are arming themselves with heavy weaponry. In a paper by David Kopel and Eric Morgan published by the Independence Institute in 1991, about a decade into the militarization of civilian policing that began in 1980, the authors point to a number of statistics showing that high-powered weapons, which are often cumbersome and difficult to conceal, simply aren't favored by criminals, including drug peddlers. The authors surveyed dozens of cities and found that, in general, less than 1 percent of weapons seized by police fit the definition of an "assault weapon." Nationally, they found that fewer than 4 percent of homicides across the United States involved rifles of any kind. And fewer than one-eighth of 1 percent involved weapons of military caliber.

The massive increase in SWAT callouts over the last two decades ought to be of concern for reasons other than the fact that it presents more opportunities for a botched raid on an innocent person to end in gunfire. It represents the needless terrorizing of American citizens and an increased perception that the drug war is just that: a war. It suggests that in terms of civil liberties, American citizens are given little more consideration than the citizens of a country with which the United Sates is at war: No real rights or protections against unwarranted searches, and in some neighborhoods, the real possibility that lives and homes could become collateral damage. It's striking how many police and government officials have responded to paramilitary raids on the homes of innocents by dismissing them as regrettable, but inevitable and acceptable, consequences of the War on Drugs.

C. Other Constitutional Issues

1. Is There a "Drug Exception" to the Constitution?

Some commentators—and even some judges—have argued that courts have developed an implicit "drug exception" to the Constitution. *See, e.g.,* Steven Wisotsky, *Crackdown: The Emerging 'Drug Exception' to the Bill of Rights*, 38 HASTINGS L. J. 889 (1987). How, if at all, has the drug war impacted the scope of constitutional protections?

Drug Exceptionalism
Erik Luna

47 Villanova Law Review 753 (2002)

A particularly powerful illustration of both macro- and micro-level exceptionalism is provided by America's second war on drugs—the ongoing ban on the sale, possession and use of illegal narcotics. Like alcohol Prohibition, the modern drug war pits deeply held ideological values against one another: individualism, which would limit government interference with a person's choice to ingest a substance, versus moralism, which would demand state involvement to prevent self-destructive and anti-social behavior from unraveling the moral fabric of society. As was true at the height of the Temperance Movement, morality has won out over privacy and autonomy in society's current drug war. This is evidenced by, among other things, the very use of the term war—a state-sponsored metaphor intended to emphasize the seriousness of the underlying threat, as well as the righteous and unyielding efforts of government to enforce drug laws. "To endorse a war," Seymour Martin Lipset suggests in his book on exceptionalism, "Americans must define their role in a conflict as being on God's side against Satan—for morality, against evil." And in the war on drugs, God and the good society are with the prohibitionists.

Criminal procedure is independent of substantive criminal law, or so we are led to believe. On their face, the relevant constitutional provisions do not discriminate among the various categories of crime, as the texts specify general methods for administering justice rather than drawing lines between suspects entitled to procedural protections and those who receive process only as a matter of grace. Pickpockets and bank robbers alike are supposed to be informed of their *Miranda* warnings prior to custodial interrogation, while the ban on unreasonable searches and seizures is not subject to a "murder scene" exception. And for the most part, the courts have outwardly refused to incorporate a substantive variable into constitutional criminal procedure.

This substantive neutrality allegedly applies to narcotics offenses as well. "Those suspected of drug offenses," the Court has argued, "are no less entitled to [constitutional] protection than those suspected of non-drug offenses." Yet scholars and jurists have recognized that the Constitution seems to bend when the criminal procedure rights of drug offenders are at stake. They are accorded, for instance, lesser expectations of privacy in their homes, cars, personal effects and so on. What has emerged from the case law, as just mentioned, is drug exceptionalism in constitutional interpretation—although no majority opinion of any court in the land would dare admit as much.

As these scholars have noted, drug exceptionalism in judicial decisionmaking is wide-ranging and can be seen in a number of areas of constitutional jurisprudence, including the Court's interpretation of First Amendment religious freedom, the Sixth Amendment right to counsel, Eighth Amendment limitations on detention and punishment and the Fourteenth Amendment's guarantee of equal protection. Nonetheless, this [discussion] will focus on the "hors de combat of the government's so-called War on Drugs"—the Fourth Amendment.

Since its 1967 decision in *Katz v. United States*, the Supreme Court's search and seizure jurisprudence has been based on notions of privacy rather than property, holding that "the Fourth Amendment protects people, not places," and, in particular, expectations of privacy that society is prepared to consider reasonable. The *Katz* formula was clearly intended to provide individuals with a higher level of security against government surveillance, but in an ironic twist, the decision has frequently been used to constrict constitutional rights rather than expand them. As Fourth Amendment scholars have noted, "reasonableness" may well be the law's favorite weasel word, beyond hard definition, simple in application and sufficiently elastic to reach nearly any result. Nowhere does this seem more evident than in the Court's drug-related cases testing reasonable expectations of privacy.

Consider a series of decisions during the mid-to late-1980s on drug enforcement activities around private dwellings. Police can ignore "no trespassing" signs and jump over locked fences to sneak onto the property surrounding homes. They may snoop into the buildings adjacent to a residence, peering at whatever activity is occurring in private sheds or barns. Narcotics agents may parse through garbage bags to uncover what a citizen is doing in the privacy of his own home. And law enforcement may fly over houses in planes or helicopters, spying on an individual's otherwise private backyard activities. According to the Supreme Court, no reasonable expectation of privacy is implicated in any of these cases, meaning that such drug war-driven intrusions can be undertaken without judicial oversight and in the absence of a warrant or probable cause.

Each of these decisions appeared doctrinally and logically suspect. In the first case, *Oliver v. United States*, the Supreme Court decided that narcotics agents could ignore a "no trespassing" sign, enter onto a private farm and thereby violate state trespassing laws in search of marijuana—all without a warrant or probable cause. Dissenting Justice Thurgood Marshall and scholars such as Stephen Saltzburg dissected the majority's tortured reasoning on a number of fronts: The Court utilized a strict form of textualism that was impossible to square with nearly two decades of prior precedents and the majority's own holding; it misused the common law and stretched a sixty-year-old case to create a sweeping limitation on the Fourth Amendment, despite the fact that the hoary precedent likely did not survive Katz;

the Court's analysis of land use and "our societal understanding" of constitutional protection demonstrated only conclusory, result-oriented reasoning; and it left undefined legally dispositive terms for future police searches while simultaneously rejecting a case-by-case approach as too ambiguous for law enforcement.

The apparent distortion of Fourth Amendment doctrine is further demonstrated by a pair of Supreme Court decisions on the search and seizure rights of houseguests. In *Minnesota v. Olson*, the police entered the home where a suspected robber and murderer had been spending the night as a guest and arrested him without a warrant or any exigency. In *Minnesota v. Carter*, a police officer peered through a small gap in an apartment's drawn window blind and witnessed the resident bagging up cocaine with her house guests. Despite the fact that in both cases the defendants were neither the homeowners nor long-term occupants but instead were solely present with the permission of their respective hosts, only the robber-murderer maintained a legitimate expectation of privacy that had been violated by the state. According to the Carter Court, the drug dealers had no Fourth Amendment protection because they were engaged in a "purely commercial" transaction, were in the home for a relatively short period of time and had no previous association with the resident.

As with *Oliver* and its descendants, Carter presents a troubled opinion. The case largely ignores the special solicitude given to private dwellings, while, in turn, encouraging law enforcement to bust into homes on the chance that someone inside is not an overnight guest. The decision also seems doctrinally jarring when placed along side prior case law: Apparently, an individual has greater Fourth Amendment protection when executing a business deal by public phone (for example, placing an illegal bet in *Katz*) than when performing a commercial transaction in a residence (bagging up drugs in *Carter*).

2. Drug Policy and the First Amendment

The Second Casualty of War: Civil Liberties and the War on Drugs

Paul Finkelman

66 Southern California Law Review 1389 (1993)

There is an old saying that truth is the first casualty of war. In the United States it seems safe to add that the Bill of Rights is the second casualty of war. In most of our wars the Bill of Rights has suffered as individual liberties were subordinated to the needs of "national security." This seems to be true as well in the war on drugs.

Law enforcement activities, government policies, legislative innovations, and court decisions related to the drug war threaten to diminish the First, Fourth, Fifth, Sixth, Seventh, and Eighth Amendments of the Constitution. Depending on how one understands the meaning of the Second and Ninth amendments, they too are under assault. More importantly, the very philosophy behind the Bill of Rights is in danger.

At first glance it would seem that the First Amendment has been untouched by the war on drugs. Unlike in other wars, there seem to be no limitations on the free speech of those who oppose this war. Sessions at a national meeting of academics—and entire academic conferences—criticizing the war on drugs seem to attest that our free speech has not been harmed by this war. It is unlikely that comparable sessions and conferences decrying American involvement in World War I would have been possible after April, 1917. Similarly, only the bravest of academics dared speak out against McCarthyism at its peak.

Despite the ability of scholars, politicians, judges, lawyers, and scientists to speak out against current drug policy, the war on drugs has led to the suppression of ideas and speech. It has also led to a contraction of religious liberty.

In 1990 High Times, a monthly magazine with a circulation of about 250,000, was under investigation by federal prosecutors. High Times is one of the nation's few magazines devoted to the legalization of marijuana, and editors there believed the government was trying to silence their investigative reports on the value of marijuana and hemp. The executive director of the Reporters Committee for Freedom of the Press noted at the time that "this is the first instance . . . where the war on drugs has been directed at a publishing organization . . . where it has gone right into the newsroom."

In May 1990 High Times sought to quash grand jury subpoenas issued to its editors. The motion to quash noted that the manner in which the United States Attorney in New Orleans issued the subpoenas violated Justice Department regulations on investigation of the press. The motion argued that "by intimidating High Times advertisers and subscribers the government is attempting to exercise unlawful prior restraint and self-censorship by intimidation" and that "the forms of harassment currently being applied towards High Times magazine have a substantial effect on its ability to disseminate information to the public."

Canada, with its weak protection of a free press, already prohibits the sale of High Times. In the United States an outright ban of the magazine would probably not withstand a court challenge. But law enforcement officials at the state and federal level have found other, less reviewable, ways to suppress the magazine. A Montana police chief has tried to convince newsstands not to carry High Times. Such behavior by a high ranking public official is bound to have a chilling effect on the First Amendment. This sort of pressure borders on a new form of seditious libel. The Montana police chief argued, "The point of the magazine is, 'Hey, let's make pot legal.'" In other words, at least some police officials are interested in suppressing the magazine because it promotes ideas which undermine the war effort against drugs and challenge the scientific and cultural basis for the war itself.

Besides articles on drugs, the magazine contains discussions of politics, music, and culture. The government pressure on the magazine thus threatens a broad range of expression. While a Montana police chief honestly says he would ban High Times because it advocates legalizing marijuana, the federal government's crusade against the magazine is more shrewd, and is couched in terms that do not focus on the ideas for which the magazine stands. Federal officials claim that High Times is part of a national conspiracy to distribute drugs. The federal prosecutors claim that their subpoenas are "demands for purely commercial or financial information unrelated to the news-gathering function." The government is arguing that High Times has violated the law by running advertisements for a Dutch seed catalogue which sells marijuana seeds. The government does not allege that High Times has advertised to sell the seeds themselves, but only that the magazine has printed advertisements for catalogues from the Dutch company that sells the seeds. It is worth noting that in Holland it is not illegal to possess or sell marijuana seeds. Because the magazine's advertisers sell drug paraphernalia, equipment to grow indoor plants, and marijuana seeds, federal prosecutors claim that the magazine may be a "continuing criminal enterprise," a status which would subject it to the severe penalties of the federal RICO statute.

The DEA and state authorities have also raided numerous stores and mail-order houses which sell horticultural equipment because these businesses have advertised in High Times. The agents have confiscated business records in an attempt to discover who is growing marijuana in their homes. In one case, police officials from the North Carolina State Bureau of Investigation conducted a warrantless search on a man's home because he had ordered three light meters from a firm which advertised in High Times. The man grew orchids.

The raids on advertisers and consumers of perfectly legal products raise serious questions about the protection of a free press. Harassing a magazine's advertisers is an effective form of censorship. After raids on businesses that advertised in High Times in October 1989, the magazine initially lost two-thirds of its advertisers. Over a six month period following the raids the magazine's total advertising revenue dropped by a third. If this type of government behavior continues the magazine may be forced out of business.

Drying up a source of talent in journalism is a second way drug warriors can silence a magazine that they find annoying. As part of its investigation, federal prosecutors have also asked for the names, addresses, and phone numbers of every "current and past" employee of the magazine. Such an investigation is likely to intimidate any current or potential High Times employee.

In 2007, the Supreme Court appeared to establish a free speech exception for some drug-related speech in public schools. In *Morse v. Frederick*, Juneau, Alaska high school senior Joseph Frederick unfurled a 14-foot banner emblazoned with the inscrutable phrase "BONG HiTS 4 JESUS" at a school event connected with the 2002 Olympic Torch Relay. The school's principle, Deborah Morse, "told Frederick to take the banner down because she thought it encouraged illegal drug use" in violation of a Juneau School Board Policy prohibiting "any assembly or public expression that . . . advocates the use of substances that are illegal to minors[.]" Frederick refused and he was ultimately suspended from school for 10 days. Frederick sued the school board, alleging that his First Amendment rights had been violated. Five members of the Supreme Court disagreed, holding that "'[t]he special characteristics of the school environment' and the governmental interest in stopping student drug abuse . . . allows schools to restrict student expression that they reasonably regard as promoting illegal drug use." In a concurring opinion, Justices Alito and Kennedy cautioned that they joined the majority opinion "on the understanding that . . . it provides no support for any restriction of speech that can plausibly be interpreted as commenting on a political or social issue, including speech on issues such as 'the wisdom of the war on drugs or of legalizing marijuana for medicinal use." *Morse v. Frederick*, 551 U.S. 393 (2007).

Writing in dissent in *Morse*, Justice Stevens worried that the majority's holding will permit "the censorship of any student speech that mentions drugs, at least so long as someone could perceive that speech to contain a latent pro-drug message." He argued that "it would be profoundly unwise to create special rules for speech about drug and alcohol use," citing his personal recollection from the era of alcohol prohibition. "[T]he current dominant opinion supporting the war on drugs in general, and our antimarijuana laws in particular, is reminiscent of the opinion that supported the nationwide ban on alcohol consumption when I was a student. While alcoholic beverages are now regarded as ordinary articles of commerce, their use was then condemned with the same moral fervor that now supports the war on drugs. . . . But just as prohibition in the 1920s and early 1930s was secretly questioned by thousands of otherwise law-abiding patrons of bootleggers and speakeasies, today the actions of literally millions of otherwise law-abiding users of marijuana, and the majority of voters in each of the several States that tolerate medicinal uses of the product, lead me to wonder whether the fear of disapproval by those in the majority is silencing opponents of the war on drugs. Surely our national experience with alcohol should make us wary of dampening speech suggesting—however inarticulately—that it would be better to tax and regulate marijuana than to persevere in a futile effort to ban its use entirely." *Id.* (Stevens, J., dissenting). For more on *Morse v. Frederick*, see JAMES C. FOSTER, BONG HITS 4 JESUS: A PERFECT CONSTITUTIONAL STORM IN ALASKA'S CAPITAL (2010).

Allegations of government censorship of statements in favor of drug policy reform have also emerged in the law enforcement setting. In 2011, for example, former Border Patrol agent Bryan Gonzalez said he was fired after remarking to a fellow agent that "[i]f marijuana were legalized . . . the drug-related violence across the border in Mexico would cease" and discussing "an organization called Law Enforcement Against Prohibition that favors ending the war on drugs. . . . After an investigation, a termination letter arrived that said Mr. Gonzalez held 'personal views that were contrary to the core characteristics of Border Patrol Agents, which are patriotism, dedication and esprit de corps.'" Marc Lacey, *Police Officers Find That Dissent on Drug Laws May Come With a Price*, N.Y. TIMES, Dec. 3, 2011 at A11.

In addition to cases concerning speech rights, a number of individuals have attempted to bring First Amendment challenges to drug laws based on freedom of religion. Courts have rejected these challenges, finding drug laws may be constitutionally applied to religious users because the burden on religion is "merely the incidental effect of a generally applicable and otherwise valid" law and not the object of the law. *See Employment Division v. Smith*, 494 U.S. 872, 878 (1990). Though the First Amendment does not grant a religious exception to generally applicable drug laws, the Religious Freedom Restoration Act of 1993 (RFRA) provides statutory protection to religiously motivated activities beyond what is constitutionally required. In *Gonzales v. O Centro Espirita Beneficente Uniao Do Vegetal*, 546 U.S. 418 (2006), the United States Supreme Court applied RFRA in the context of the religious use of a hallucinogenic controlled substance.

Gonzales v. O Centro Espirita Beneficente Uniao Do Vegetal

Supreme Court of the United States
546 U.S. 418 (2006)

Chief Justice Roberts delivered the opinion of the Court.

In *Employment Div., Dept. of Human Resources of Ore. v. Smith,* 494 U.S. 872 (1990), this Court held that the Free Exercise Clause of the First Amendment does not prohibit governments from burdening religious practices through generally applicable laws. In *Smith*, we rejected a challenge to an Oregon statute that denied unemployment benefits to drug users, including Native Americans engaged in the sacramental use of peyote. In so doing, we rejected the interpretation of the Free Exercise Clause announced in *Sherbert v. Verner,* 374 U.S. 398 (1963), and, in accord with earlier cases held that the Constitution does not require judges to engage in a case-by-case assessment of the religious burdens imposed by facially constitutional laws.

Congress responded by enacting the Religious Freedom Restoration Act of 1993 (RFRA), which adopts a statutory rule comparable to the constitutional rule rejected in *Smith*. Under RFRA, the Federal Government may not, as a statutory matter, substantially burden a person's exercise of religion, "even if the burden results from a rule of general applicability." § 2000bb-1(a). The only exception recognized by the statute requires the Government to satisfy the compelling interest test—to "demonstrate that application of the burden to the person—(1) is in furtherance of a compelling governmental interest; and (2) is the least restrictive means of furthering that compelling governmental interest." A person whose religious practices are burdened in violation of RFRA "may assert that violation as a claim or defense in a judicial proceeding and obtain appropriate relief."

The Controlled Substances Act regulates the importation, manufacture, distribution, and use of psychotropic substances. The Act classifies substances into five schedules based on their potential for abuse, the extent to which they have an accepted medical use, and their safety. Substances listed in Schedule I of the Act are subject to the most comprehensive restrictions, including an outright ban on all importation and use, except pursuant to strictly regulated research projects. The Act authorizes the imposition of a criminal sentence for simple possession of Schedule I substances and mandates the imposition of a criminal sentence for possession "with intent to manufacture, distribute, or dispense" such substances.

O Centro Espirita Beneficente Uniao do Vegetal (UDV) is a Christian Spiritist sect based in Brazil, with an American branch of approximately 130 individuals. Central to the UDV's faith is receiving communion through *hoasca* (pronounced "wass-ca"), a sacramental tea made from two plants unique to the Amazon region. One of the plants, *psychotria viridis*, contains dimethyltryptamine (DMT), a hallucinogen whose effects are enhanced by alkaloids from the other plant, *banisteriopsis caapi*. DMT, as well as "any material, compound, mixture, or preparation, which contains any quantity of [DMT]," is listed in Schedule I of the Controlled Substances Act.

In 1999, United States Customs inspectors intercepted a shipment to the American UDV containing three drums of *hoasca*. A subsequent investigation revealed that the UDV had received 14 prior shipments of *hoasca*. The inspectors seized the intercepted shipment and threatened the UDV with prosecution.

The UDV filed suit against the Attorney General and other federal law enforcement officials, seeking declaratory and injunctive relief. The complaint alleged that applying the Controlled Substances Act to the UDV's sacramental use of *hoasca* violates RFRA.

The Government contends that the Act's description of Schedule I substances as having "a high potential for abuse," "no currently accepted medical use in treatment in the United States," and "a lack of accepted safety for use . . . under medical supervision," by itself precludes any consideration of individualized exceptions such as that sought by the UDV. The Government goes on to argue that the regulatory regime established by the Act—a "closed" system that prohibits all use of controlled substances except as authorized by the Act itself—"cannot function with its necessary rigor and comprehensiveness if subjected to judicial exemptions." According to the Government, there would be no way to cabin religious exceptions once recognized, and "the public will misread" such exceptions as signaling that the substance at issue is not harmful after all. Under the Government's view, there is no need to assess the particulars of the UDV's use or weigh the impact of an exemption for that specific use, because the Controlled Substances Act serves a compelling purpose and simply admits of no exceptions.

RFRA, and the strict scrutiny test it adopted, contemplate an inquiry more focused than the Government's categorical approach. RFRA requires the Government to demonstrate that the compelling interest test is satisfied through application of the challenged law "to the person"—the particular claimant whose sincere exercise of religion is being substantially burdened.

Under the more focused inquiry required by RFRA and the compelling interest test, the Government's mere invocation of the general characteristics of Schedule I substances, as set forth in the Controlled Substances Act, cannot carry the day. It is true, of course, that Schedule I substances such as DMT are exceptionally dangerous. Nevertheless, there is no indication that Congress, in classifying DMT, considered the harms posed by the particular use at issue here—the circumscribed, sacramental use of *hoasca* by the UDV. Congress' determination that DMT should be listed under *Schedule I* simply does not provide a categorical answer that relieves the Government of the obligation to shoulder its burden under RFRA.

This conclusion is reinforced by the Controlled Substances Act itself. The Act contains a provision authorizing the Attorney General to "waive the requirement for registration of certain manufacturers, distributors, or dispensers if he finds it consistent with the public health and safety." 21 U.S.C. § 822(d). The fact that the Act itself contemplates that exempting certain people from its requirements would be "consistent with the public health and safety" indicates that congressional findings with respect to Schedule I substances should not carry the determinative weight, for RFRA purposes, that the Government would ascribe to them.

And in fact an exception has been made to the Schedule I ban for religious use. For the past 35 years, there has been a regulatory exemption for use of peyote—a Schedule I substance—by the Native American Church. In 1994, Congress extended that exemption to all members of every recognized Indian Tribe. Everything the Government says about the DMT in *hoasca*—that, as a *Schedule I* substance, Congress has determined that it "has a high potential for abuse," "has no currently accepted medical use," and has "a lack of accepted safety for use . . . under medical supervision"—applies in equal measure to the mescaline in peyote, yet both the Executive and Congress itself have decreed an exception from the Controlled Substances Act for Native American religious use of peyote. If such use is permitted in the face of the congressional findings in § 812(b)(1) for hundreds of thousands of Native Americans practicing their faith, it is difficult to see how those same findings alone can preclude any consideration of a similar exception for the 130 or so American members of the UDV who want to practice theirs.

The Government argues that the existence of a *congressional* exemption for peyote does not indicate that the Controlled Substances Act is amenable to *judicially crafted* exceptions. RFRA, however, plainly contemplates that *courts* would recognize exceptions—that is how the law works. See 42 U.S.C. § 2000bb-1(c) ("A person whose religious exercise has been burdened in violation of this section may assert that violation as a claim or defense in a judicial proceeding and obtain appropriate relief against a government").

We do not doubt that there may be instances in which a need for uniformity precludes the recognition of exceptions to generally applicable laws under RFRA. But it would have been surprising to find that this was such a case, given the longstanding exemption from the Controlled Substances Act for religious use of peyote, and the fact that the very reason Congress enacted RFRA was to respond to a decision denying a claimed right to sacramental use of a controlled substance. And in fact the Government has not offered evidence demonstrating that granting the UDV an exemption would cause the kind of administrative harm recognized as a compelling interest in [other cases]. The Government failed to convince the District Court at the preliminary injunction hearing that health or diversion concerns provide a compelling interest in banning the UDV's sacramental use of *hoasca*. It cannot compensate for that failure now with the bold argument that there can be no RFRA exceptions at all to the Controlled Substances Act.

We have no cause to pretend that the task assigned by Congress to the courts under RFRA is an easy one. Indeed, the very sort of difficulties highlighted by the Government here were cited by this Court in deciding that the approach later mandated by Congress under RFRA was not required as a matter of constitutional law under the Free Exercise Clause. But Congress has determined that courts should strike sensible balances, pursuant to a compelling interest test that requires the Government to address the particular practice at issue. Applying that test, we conclude that the courts below did not err in determining that the Government failed to demonstrate, at the preliminary injunction stage, a compelling interest in barring the UDV's sacramental use of *hoasca*.

Chapter 6

The Controlled Substances Act

A. The Controlled Substances Act: Overview

The previous chapters have focused on the criminalization of controlled substances, examining the wisdom of prohibition, the elements of a variety of controlled substances offenses, sentencing of drug offenders and the investigation of drug crimes. The foundation for these criminal laws is a complex regulatory scheme that raises a range of legal and policy issues in its own right.

The federal Controlled Substances Act of 1970 (CSA), which is administered primarily by the Drug Enforcement Administration (DEA), aims to provide a comprehensive and uniform structure for classifying drugs of abuse and regulating their manufacture, distribution, and use in medical studies. Under the CSA, controlled substances are divided into five "schedules" based on their potential for abuse, medicinal value, and addictiveness.

Classification under the Controlled Substances Act, 21 U.S.C. § 812(b)

	Abuse Potential	Medical Use	Safety and Dependence
Schedule I	High potential for abuse	No currently accepted medical use	Lack of accepted safety for use under medical supervision
Schedule II	High potential for abuse	Has a currently accepted medical use	Abuse may lead to severe dependence
Schedule III	Potential for abuse less than Schedules I and II	Has a currently accepted medical use	Abuse may lead to moderate or low physical dependence or high psychological dependence
Schedule IV	Low potential for abuse relative to Schedule III	Has a currently accepted medical use	Abuse may lead to limited dependence relative to Schedule III
Schedule V	Low potential for abuse relative to Schedule IV	Has a currently accepted medical use	Abuse may lead to limited dependence relative to Schedule IV

Although the basic scheduling criteria are easily stated, several features of the CSA make the application of these criteria much more complicated than it might at first seem.

First, the term "United States" "is the only portion of the Schedule I criteria that Congress has expressly defined in the CSA[.]" *Grinspoon v. Drug Enforcement Admin.*, 828 F.2d 881 (1st Cir. 1987). The CSA is silent as to the meaning of potential for abuse, accepted medical use, and physical dependence The lack of congressional guidance in combination with the deferential administration process has given the DEA a great deal of control over the scheduling criteria.

Second, the CSA does not say how the criteria fit together. This omission is particularly problematic because the CSA's scheduling criteria "cannot logically be read as cumulative in all situations. For example, finding (B) for Schedule I requires that 'The drug or other substance has no currently accepted medical use in treatment in the United States.' Finding (B) for the other four schedules specifies that the drug has a currently accepted medical use. At the same time, finding (A) requires that the drug has a 'high potential for abuse' for placement in Schedule I, but a 'potential for abuse less than the drugs or other substances in schedules I and II' for placement in Schedule III. If the findings are really cumulative, where would one place a drug that has no accepted medical use but also has a potential for abuse less than the drugs in Schedules I and II? According to finding (A) for Schedule III it belongs in Schedule III, but finding (B) for that schedule precludes Schedule III; according to finding (B) for Schedule I it belongs in Schedule I, but finding (A) for that schedule appears to preclude Schedule I." *United States v. Maiden*, 355 F. Supp. 743, 748 n.4 (D. Conn. 1973). More than 40 years after the CSA's enactment, this basic problem has not yet been definitively tested in the courts.

Finally, although one provision of the CSA (21 U.S.C. § 812(b)) seems to suggest that the three scheduling criteria outlined in the chart above are a self-contained and exclusive list of the "findings required for each schedule," a different provision of the CSA itemizes eight additional factors that can also inform scheduling decisions. Specifically, 21 U.S.C. § 811(c) provides:

> In making any finding under [the CSA's three scheduling criteria], the Attorney General shall consider the following factors with respect to each drug or other substance proposed to be controlled or removed from the schedules:
>
> (1) Its actual or relative potential for abuse.
>
> (2) Scientific evidence of its pharmacological effect, if known.
>
> (3) The state of current scientific knowledge regarding the drug or other substance.
>
> (4) Its history and current pattern of abuse.
>
> (5) The scope, duration, and significance of abuse.
>
> (6) What, if any, risk there is to the public health.
>
> (7) Its psychic or physiological dependence liability.
>
> (8) Whether the substance is an immediate precursor of a substance already controlled under this title.

The CSA does not specify exactly how these eight factors relate to the three scheduling criteria. Some of section 811's factors—for example, the "actual or relative potential for abuse" factor—mirror the scheduling criteria. Others, like "[w]hether the substance is an immediate precursor of a substance already controlled under this title," are more difficult to fit into the framework of the three scheduling criteria.

Though the CSA's scheduling criteria have withstood vagueness challenges, at least one government official has acknowledged that the CSA provides administrators with little guidance and few meaningful constraints. Shortly after passage of the CSA, an employee of the Department of Health Education and Welfare (the predecessor agency to the Department of Health and Human Services) voiced concern about the classification scheme in an internal department memo: "These eight factors [found in §811(c)] unfortunately are for the most part vague and redundant. The list exhibits circular reasoning and lack of parallelism, particularly when viewed together with the definitions of the schedules. Most importantly, the list of factors and the definitions of the schedules leave undefined the concepts of drug abuse potential, of drug dependence, and of risk to public health. In short, the factors provide little practical guidance in deciding particular cases." *United States v. Pastor*, 419 F. Supp. 1318, 1339 n.6 (S.D. N.Y. 1975)(quoting memo by HEW employee Henry E. Simmons).

In sum, nearly five decades after its passage, much about the CSA remains surprisingly unclear. One certainty is that that the three scheduling criteria are what ultimately control the federal classification of controlled substances.

Before examining the scheduling criteria in depth, the article that follows, which was published shortly after passage of the CSA, provides a helpful history of the federal drug legislation that preceded the CSA.

The Evolution of Federal Drug Control Legislation
Thomas M. Quinn and Gerald T. McLaughlin

22 Catholic University Law Review 586 (1973)

The earliest mention of opium (or for that matter, any narcotic drug) in Federal legislation appears in the Tariff Act of 1832. The Act—exempting opium from all import duties—attempted neither to interdict the flow of drugs nor produce substantial revenue. Ten years later in 1842, however, the narcotic was placed on the tariff lists for the first time and a duty of seventy-five cents per pound was levied on all imported opium. In 1862, morphine was added to the tariff list and taxed at the rate of two dollars per pound. The tariff rates on medicinal or raw opium and morphine fluctuated throughout the nineteenth century. Raw opium even reappeared on the duty free list in 1890. This use of imported opium as a source of governmental revenue was consistent with the flourishing international opium traffic of the nineteenth century. British traffic in opium had led to the Opium Wars with China and generated a series of diplomatic concessions extorted from the Chinese, concessions which assured continuance of the lucrative opium trade. For example, in an

1858 treaty between China and the United States, China agreed to remove opium from its list of contraband items, permitting American merchants to sell the drug at various Chinese ports. With opium traffic so open and obvious, it was not surprising that the Unite States government should view opium as nothing more than another imported item to be taxed.

Smoking opium, however, was singled out for special treatment during this earliest period of federal concern. [S]moking opium was first associated with the Chinese immigrant but gradually, as the practice spread, it became a national concern. The response was an eighty per cent ad valorem tax on all imported smoking opium. In succeeding years, it continued to be taxed at ever increasing rates, reflecting the growing fear with which the practice was regarded.

A second and quite different theme in federal narcotic drug control appeared on the scene in 1906. It came in response to a growing national concern with the use of patent medicines. These commodities—heavily laced with opium, morphine and cocaine—were widely sold throughout the country and served as familiar preparations for such ailments as headaches, menstrual pains, cold symptoms, alcoholism, and general fatigue. What resulted from the heavy dependence on such patented medicines was a widespread pattern of national addiction. The federal response conceived of the patent medicine problem as one of consumer deception. Thus, to control the trade in these medicines, Congress enacted labeling regulations in 1906, the idea being that an informed consumer could protect himself if he chose to do so.

The Pure Food and Drug Act of 1906 prohibited the interstate shipment of misbranded or adulterated food and drugs. An article of food or drugs was considered to be misbranded if it contained any alcohol, morphine, cocaine, heroin, or any derivatives or preparations of these substances where such ingredients were not clearly marked on the label. Similarly, confectionaries were considered to be adulterated if they contained any narcotic drug as an ingredient. The Act also provided that food would be considered adulterated if it contained any added poisonous or deleterious ingredients which might be injurious to health. By requiring labeling of medicines which contained opium and cocaine, and by prohibiting outright the interstate shipment of food containing deleterious substances, the Act exposed to public view the dangerous and addictive capacities of non-prescription medicines and sodas being marketed in the country. It should be noted, however, that this legislation was entirely consistent with a legitimate domestic traffic in opium, morphine, heroin, and cocaine. Indeed, heroin was sold by one pharmaceutical company under the heroin trade name and widely touted; morphine could be purchased over the counter along with opium or cocaine. While the Pure Food and Drug Act alerted consumers to the presence of narcotic drugs in various products, the sales of these drugs continued to flourish. For example, a 1910 pharmaceutical journal reported that one drug store earned a profit of $60 a day from sales of cocaine alone.

In 1909 the federal government shifted from its earlier pattern of taxing opium to outright suppression of the traffic in the drug. In response to the Shanghai Opium Conference in 1909, the United States banned the importation of all smoking opium and restricted the importation of all other opium except for limited amounts authorized by the Secretary of the Treasury for medical purposes. This had the effect of closing the United States ports of entry to the legal flow of opium except in controlled quantities for regulated purposes. Since the Act also forbade any person from receiving or selling illegally imported opium knowing it to be illegally imported, the Act represented the first serious federal attempt to use the criminal law to curtail domestic trafficking in opium.

Five years later, the United States took a second major step in the border control of opium traffic when it set controls on the export of opium. With these controls, Congress effectively took the United States out of the international drug traffic by prohibiting the use of its ports for either the import or export of opium and other harmful drugs. Controls on export, like the earlier controls on import, came in response to international pressures. At the Hague International Opium Conference in 1912, the signatory powers, including the United States, had agreed to place various restrictions on prepared opium, cocaine, and morphine—one of these restrictions was to align export controls with the import controls of other nations. Consequently, Congress enacted the Narcotic Drug Export Act, absolutely prohibiting any smoking opium from being admitted into the United States for transshipment to another country and, more importantly, banning the export of cocaine and opium—other than smoking opium, the export of which was absolutely forbidden—to any country which did not regulate the importation of these drugs. On the very same day that it passed the Narcotic Drug Export Act, Congress also adopted a statute which levied a prohibitive tax of $300 per pound on all opium manufactured in the United States for smoking purposes. Thus, Congress had now forbidden the import or export of smoking opium, heavily taxed its domestic manufacture, and severely restricted the import of other forms of opium.

With the Harrison Act [of 1914] the federal government interjected itself decisively into the domestic traffic in narcotic drugs. This statute was by far the most significant of all the early federal drug control laws, setting the main lines for domestic narcotic control and regulation which persisted until 1970. The thrust of the Harrison Act was twofold. First the Act sought to expose to federal surveillance the legal traffic in narcotics from its point of entry or manufacture to its point of consumption. Second, the Act provided criminal penalties for any trafficking in narcotics outside the legally established patterns. The stage was thus set for the regulation of the legal narcotic flow and the suppression of the illegal flow.

To achieve such broad purposes, the actual legislative scheme of the Harrison Act might be considered cumbersome to say the least. Congress chose to assert jurisdiction through its revenue powers rather than through its power to regulate interstate commerce. This rather curious approach was justified, however, since in 1914 the interstate commerce clause was still read rather restrictively by the courts. In all probability, that clause would not have supported any congressional controls over local drug manufacturers or distributors. Of course, Congress' decision to use its revenue powers placed the domestic control of narcotics in the hands of the Internal Revenue Service, then deeply involved in the enforcement of the newly created federal income tax, and later the Prohibition laws. Contrary to certain state patterns of narcotic control, this placed enforcement of the Harrison Act in the hands of a special enforcement unit rather than in the hands of general law enforcement officers.

By its terms, the Harrison Act required registration with the local Internal Revenue Collector and payment of a special occupational tax by every person, with certain exceptions, who produced, imported, manufactured, compounded, dealt in, dispensed, sold, distributed, or gave away opium or coca leaves or any compound or preparation of these drugs. The Act also stipulated that any sale, exchange, or transfer of these drugs must be pursuant to the written order of the person to whom the drugs were to be transferred. Written orders could only be executed on forms specially provided by the Commissioner of Internal Revenue and the forms themselves could only be purchased by a registered person. Everyone in the drug distribution system was subject to stringent record-keeping. Finally, it was unlawful for any unregistered or unpaid person to possess or control any restricted drug; such possession or control was presumptive evidence of failure to register and pay the occupational tax.

The Harrison Act was amended in 1919[.] The 1919 amendments made it unlawful for any person to purchase, sell, dispense or distribute any of the aforementioned drugs or their compounds except in the original stamped packages or from the original stamped packages. The absence of appropriate tax-paid stamps became prima facie evidence of a violation of the Harrison Act.

From the viewpoint of federal law enforcement officer, there was one glaring gap in the coverage of the Harrison Act—the medical profession. Section 2 of the Act specifically exempted from its coverage the dispensing or distribution of drugs "to a patient by a physician . . . in the course of his professional practice only." With narcotics tightly regulated, the physician represented the sole legitimate source of supply open to the addict. For the unscrupulous doctor, this presented a lucrative opportunity to push drugs legitimately under the guise of practicing medicine.

Huge profits could be made. The "script doctor," as he came to be called, became a prime concern of the early Internal Revenue Service personnel charged with enforcement of the Harrison Act. For the responsible physician, the Harrison exemption was not a source of new income; if anything, it was a source of unexpected problems. As long as an addict was not confined to a hospital for treatment, a doctor could minister to him in one of two ways—either by personally administering the drug to the addict in his office or by prescribing the drug for the addict to administer to himself at home. If he treated the addict in his office, the physician could minimize possible drug diversion into the illicit market but at the expense of turning his office into a drug clinic with long lines of addicts awaiting treatment. If he prescribed drugs for self administration, the doctor created serious problems of illegal diversion. The dilemma was real and with no apparent solution. Because of the possibility of diversion, law enforcement officials soon began to move to curtail the medical profession's freedom to prescribe narcotics in the treatment of addicts. The unfortunate consequence of this policy was to drive from the field of drug treatment not only the unethical "script doctor" but the legitimate doctor as well.

At the outset, the Harrison Act was not interpreted as interfering with the physician's medical treatment of the addict, whether by prescription or otherwise. Thus, for example, providing an addict with morphine in the treatment of his addiction was considered valid medical treatment to the extent that it suppressed and alleviated withdrawal symptoms. In 1919, however, with the Supreme Court's decision in *Webb v. United States*, a series of cases maintained otherwise. Although Webb was a "script doctor," the Court was asked to decide whether a practicing physician's order for morphine was exempt as a physician's prescription within the meaning of section 2 where the order was not in the course of professional treatment in an attempt to cure the addict but solely to keep the addict comfortable by maintaining his customary use? The Court said no: "[T]o call such an order for the use of morphine a physician's prescription would be so plain a perversion of meaning that no discussion of the subject is required."

One year later, in *Jin Fuey Moy v. United States*, the Supreme Court was faced with another case involving a "script doctor." In elaborating on its holding in *Webb*, the Court stated that the Harrison Act's immunity for physicians dispensing or distributing drugs in the course of their professional practice did not "include a sale to a dealer or a distribution intended to cater to the appetite or satisfy the craving of one addicted to the use of the drug. A "prescription" issued for either of the latter purposes protects neither the physician who issues it, nor the dealer who knowingly accepts and fills it."

The most controversial decision in this area, however, was neither *Webb* nor *Jin Fuey Moy*, but *United States v. Behrman*, decided in 1922. Behrman, a physician like Webb and Jin Fuey Moy, dispensed drugs indiscriminately. At one time, for instance, he had given an addict prescriptions for 150 grains of heroin, 360 grains of morphine and 210 grains of cocaine. The Government, however, grounded its indictment on a holding that "prescribing drugs for an addict was a crime regardless of the physician's intent in the matter." Although the Supreme Court stressed the large amount of the drugs dispensed by Behrman, the decision could be read by nervous physicians as prohibiting all doctors from prescribing, in good faith, even small quantities of narcotics for self-administration in an attempt to treat an addict. After *Behrman*, it seemed that a physician could only prescribe narcotics for conditions such as ulcers or cancer, but not for relief of addiction itself.

The *Behrman* holding was soon tested in *Linder v. United States*. Dr. Linder had personally dispensed to one of his patients one tablet of morphine and three tablets of cocaine. Limiting the *Behrman* rationale, the Court stated: "[The Harrison Act] says nothing of 'addicts' and does not undertake to prescribe methods for their medical treatment. They are diseased and proper subjects for such treatment, and we cannot possibly conclude that a physician acted improperly or unwisely or for other than medical purposes solely because he has dispensed to one of them, in the ordinary course and in good faith, four small tablets of morphine or cocaine for relief of conditions incident to addiction."

The Court further asserted that *Behrman* could not be interpreted as precluding a physician, acting in good faith and according to fair medical standards, from ever giving an addict moderate amounts of drugs for self-administration in order to relieve the conditions incident to addiction.

Although the language in *Linder* could be read to repudiate *Behrman*, doctors were genuinely afraid to treat addicts. This fear increased as lower federal courts seemingly disregarded the clear intent of the *Linder* rationale. Now the addict could no longer turn to the medical profession for help: he was forced to turn to a new source of supply—the growing illicit drug market. As Rufus King remarks: "The addict-patient vanished; the addict-criminal emerged in his place."

In 1922, Congress passed the Narcotic Drug Import and Export Act which continued the existing ban on opium importation while adding cocaine to the list of drugs which were forbidden entry into the country. Limited amounts of crude opium and coca leaves, however, were permitted to be imported for medical and other legitimate needs. It is interesting to note that, for the first time, all restricted drugs were classified under the generic category of "narcotic drugs." A Federal Narcotics Control Board (composed of three Cabinet members) was created to administer various provisions of the Act. For instance, the Board was empowered to determine exactly what amounts of crude opium and coca leaves were needed to be imported for legitimate and medical purposes.

By the late twenties, the federal government was faced with a new problem—large numbers of addicts in its prison system. As the patterns of addiction grew and became associated with domestic crime, it was perhaps inevitable that the addict population in prisons would increase. Congress responded to the problem by enacting the Porter Act in 1929. The Act established two United States Narcotic Farms designed to provide care and treatment of convicted addicts. The first was opened in Lexington, Kentucky in 1935; the second at Fort Worth, Texas in 1938.

The growing narcotic problem also led to the emergence of a new federal agency within the Treasury Department. Enforcement of the Harrison Act of 1914 was entrusted to the narcotics division of the prohibition unit of the Internal Revenue Service. In 1927 this division was incorporated into the newly created Prohibition Bureau of the Treasury Department. In 1930 law enforcement in the federal narcotics field was further developed and consolidated into its own separate agency, the Federal Bureau of Narcotics. Of equal importance with the establishment of the agency was the appointment of Harry J. Anslinger as the new agency's first commissioner. Anslinger had risen through the diplomatic service and established himself later at the Department of the Treasury as Assistant Commissioner of Prohibition. With the establishment of the Bureau of Narcotics, Anslinger shifted his main concern from prohibition to narcotic law enforcement. Under his vigorous leadership the Bureau of Narcotics was shaped and developed into a powerful law enforcement agency.

While the Harrison Act was cast in terms of a regulatory statute designed to publicly expose the legitimate narcotic drug flow on the domestic scene, its collateral and less obvious goal was to interdict the domestic flow of illegal narcotics. This latter purpose obviously led to heavy criminal law enforcement work. To facilitate this effort the Commissioner of Narcotics was empowered by Congress in 1930 to pay informers for information concerning violations of the drug laws.

Although early federal legislation was mainly concerned with controlling opium and cocaine, a new "drug menace" had appeared by the 1930s—that "menace" was marihuana. In 1937, under the prodding of the newly created Federal Bureau of Narcotics, Congress passed the Marihuana Tax Act—which was similar, in many respects, to the Harrison Act. The Marihuana Tax Act required those in the chain of marihuana distribution to register and pay an occupational tax. A commodity tax of $1.00 per ounce was levied on transfers of marihuana to persons registered under the Act. Unlike the Harrison Act where transfers could only be made to registered persons, the Marihuana Tax Act allowed transfers to non-registered persons but provided ample deterrents to such transfers by a prohibitive tax of $100 an ounce. To effect a legal transfer both registered and non-registered persons were required to file special order forms. Increasing federal control over marihuana distribution even further, various reports and record-keeping requirements were mandated. In short, Congress placed virtually identical controls over marihuana as over the narcotic drugs.

The unintended effect of the Harrison Act and its subsequent enforcement was the closing of legitimate sources of supply to the addict, resulting in the rise to a flourishing black market in illegal drugs. With the repeal of Prohibition, organized crime in turn became more involved with the illegal distribution of drugs. The inevitable result was an expanding drug problem. The years between 1946 and 1960 were times of a rising drug trade in the United States and, equally important, times of growing fears regarding the drug problem.

In 1960 the federal government once again broke new ground in the field of narcotics control. For approximately forty years, the United States had closed its ports of entry to the import and export of narcotic drugs and then regulated and controlled the internal distribution processes with the Harrison Act. However, the Act exercised no direct control over the quantities of narcotic drugs legally manufactured within the country itself. The Narcotic Manufacturing Act of 1960 sought to remedy this. Under this Act the Secretary of the Treasury was empowered to license manufacturers of narcotic drugs and to set an individual quota for each drug classification. The Government could not be assured that only those quantities of narcotic drugs actually required for legitimate needs would be domestically manufactured.

This Act was significant in another respect. Before 1960, licensing was always viewed as a peculiarly local concern left to the several states. Now Congress asserted jurisdiction over licensing and, interestingly enough, based its power—at least in part—on the interstate commerce clause, an approach which had been rejected in

1914 when the Harrison Act was enacted. The cumbersome fiction of a tax statute to justify local control over drug distribution was no longer needed.

Dangerous drugs are not to be confused with narcotic drugs which have been previously discussed[.] Dangerous drugs include basically three categories of drug—depressants [including barbiturates and tranquillizers], stimulants, and hallucinogens.

When compared to narcotics, dangerous drugs became subject to federal regulation rather late in time. It was not until 1965—with the amendments to the Federal Food, Drug and Cosmetic Act—that Congress imposed controls on the distribution of these drugs comparable to those in the Harrison Act. Before this time, individuals who unlawfully dispensed dangerous drugs could only be prosecuted through certain misbranding provisions of the Food, Drug and Cosmetic Act.

The 1965 amendments cover[ed] all dangerous drugs—whether in interstate or intrastate commerce. Unlike the Harrison Act which was based on federal taxing powers, Congress justified intrastate regulation of dangerous drugs on interstate commerce theories.

The amendments categorize[d] dangerous drugs as either depressants or stimulants. Depressant drugs include[d] all drugs containing "any quantity of barbituric acid or any of the salts of barbituric acid" (a definition which does not encompass many common tranquilizers); stimulant drugs [were] those containing "any quantity of amphetamine, any of its optical isomers, or any salt of amphetamine." The definition of a depressant or stimulant drug, however, include[d] the following significant language: "any drug which contains any quantity which the Secretary, after investigation, has found to have, and by regulation designates as having, a potential for abuse because of its depressant or stimulant effect on the central nervous system or its hallucinogenic effect[.]"

This language [provided] the authority for controlling hallucinogens and non-barbituric tranquilizers under the amendments.

With certain exceptions the 1965 amendments forbade the manufacture of depressant or stimulant drugs. Permitted to manufacture, however, were manufacturers who were properly registered and who produced drugs for use in research, teaching, medicine or for chemical analysis. Sales were prohibited except by those legitimately in the chain of distribution and only in the ordinary and authorized course of their business. Finally, possession (a) other than for personal use of the possessor or a member of his household or (b) for administration to an animal owned by him or by a member of his household, was forbidden.

It is interesting that enforcement of the dangerous drug laws was first placed in the hands of the Food and Drug Administration in the Department of Health, Education, and Welfare—an agency responsible for the general health and not particularly involved with law enforcement. In 1968, however, jurisdiction over dangerous drugs was transferred from the FDA to the Justice Department.

These amendments were the final piece of legislation which preceded the Comprehensive Drug Abuse Prevention and Control Act of 1970, with Title II of that Act otherwise known as the Controlled Substances Act.

The Comprehensive Drug Abuse Prevention and Control Act of 1970 repealed almost all prior federal drug legislation and created a new and comprehensive scheme for federal drug control. For the first time, one statute governed both narcotics and dangerous drugs. Enforcement of all drug laws was placed in the hands of the Bureau of Narcotics and Dangerous Drugs (BNDD)—an agency created in the Justice Department in 1968 [and which was the predecessor agency of the Drug Enforcement Administration, established in 1973]. Although the 1970 Act totally revamped the existing pattern of drug control, a great deal was borrowed from prior legislation[.]

B. Classifying Substances under the Controlled Substances Act

Literally hundreds of substances are scheduled under the CSA. *See* 21 CFR § 1308 (providing the current list of controlled substances). The table below provides a short representative list, showing where some of the more well-known substances are classified.

Representative List of Drugs Classifications Under the CSA, 21 CFR § 1308

Schedule I	Schedule II	Schedule III	Schedule IV	Schedule V
Heroin, LSD, marijuana, MDMA	Cocaine, Codeine, Methadone, Methamphetamine, Oxycodone	Anabolic steroids, Tylenol with Codeine, Marinol (synthetic THC), Ketamine	Xanax, Valium, Rohypnol, Modafinil, Ambien	Robitussin A-C, Lyrica

Note: In some cases a brand or street name has been substituted for the chemical name of the substance as it identified under the CSA.

In the cases that follow, courts and administrative decision makers apply the CSA's scheduling criteria to classify substances. When reading these cases, consider whether you believe the Controlled Substances Act achieves its aim of facilitating consistent, predictable, and science-based classifications of substances of abuse. Is the term "accepted medical use," for example, sufficiently well defined? Are you able to discern from the cases how much weight each of the scheduling criteria is to be given in scheduling decisions? If a substance were found to have a negligible potential for abuse and no currently accepted medical use, in what schedule would it fall?

Before you continue, be sure to take a moment to refer to the table on the first page of this chapter, which outlines the factors for each of the five schedules so that you have the CSA's basic classification structure in mind while reading the material that follows.

Grinspoon v. Drug Enforcement Administration

United States Court of Appeals for the First Circuit
828 F.2d 881 (1987)

Coffin, J.

On November 13, 1986, the Administrator of the Drug Enforcement Administration ("DEA") issued a final rule placing the substance 3,4-methylenedioxymetham phetamine ("MDMA")* into Schedule I of the Controlled Substances Act ("CSA"). In reaching this decision, the Administrator found that MDMA met all three of the statutory requirements for classification as a Schedule I substance, namely, (A) The drug or other substance has a high potential for abuse. (B) The drug or other substance has no currently accepted medical use in treatment in the United States. (C) There is a lack of accepted safety for use of the drug or other substance under medical supervision. 21 U.S.C. § 812(b)(1).

Dr. Lester Grinspoon, a psychiatrist and faculty member of the Harvard Medical School, petitions this court to review the final rule. Dr. Grinspoon seeks to conduct research on the therapeutic use of MDMA and believes that the imposition of Schedule I controls will effectively foreclose such research. He cites four reasons for vacating the Administrator's scheduling determination. The first reason advanced is that the Administrator applied the wrong legal standards for "currently accepted medical use in treatment in the United States" and for "accepted safety for use ... under medical supervision" in 21 U.S.C. § 812(b)(1). The other three reasons contained in Dr. Grinspoon's petition challenge the scheduling determination as arbitrary and capricious because (a) the Administrator's determination that MDMA had a "high" potential for abuse was flawed by his failure to articulate a legal standard and his reliance on insufficient record evidence; (b) the Administrator failed to give adequate weight to the evidence showing that placing MDMA into Schedule I would create a barrier to medical research on the drug; and (c) the rule is based upon incomplete and arbitrary recommendations from the Secretary of Health and Human Services. Petitioner urges this court to remand the case to the DEA with instructions to place the substance MDMA into Schedule III.

Although we are satisfied that these final three claims do not require us to overturn the rule, we believe that Dr. Grinspoon's first claim has considerable merit and requires us to remand the scheduling determination for reconsideration by the Administrator.

---

* MDMA is also commonly referred to as "ecstasy" or "Molly." [*Footnote by casebook author.*]

In January of 1984, the DEA prepared a document entitled "Schedule I Control Recommendation Under the CSA for 3,4-Methylenedioxymethamphetamine (MDMA)." The control recommendation, which was based upon information compiled from various DEA data sources and scientific and medical literature, considered all three Schedule I criteria listed in section 812(b)(1) and concluded that (1) MDMA has a high potential for abuse; (2) MDMA has no known legitimate medical use for treatment in the United States; and (3) there is a lack of accepted safety for the use of MDMA under medical supervision. Based upon these findings, the DEA recommended that MDMA be placed into Schedule I of the CSA.

In March of 1984, pursuant to the procedures set out in the CSA, 28 U.S.C. 811(b),[2] the Administrator submitted the DEA's control recommendation to the Assistant Secretary for Health of the Department of Health and Human Services ("HHS") for scientific and medical evaluation and for an HHS recommendation as to whether MDMA should be controlled. The HHS evaluation was conducted by Dr. Charles Tocus, Chief of the Drug Abuse Staff of the Food and Drug Administration ("FDA"). Dr. Tocus stated in his affidavit that he searched the FDA files and found no reference to MDMA. Based upon this absence of information in the FDA files and a review of the information contained in the DEA control recommendation carried out by Dr. Tocus, HHS responded by making minor (typographical) corrections in the DEA's eight-factor analysis[3] and concurring in the recommendation that MDMA be placed into Schedule I.

Upon receiving the HHS evaluation and recommendation, the Administrator issued a Notice of Proposed Rulemaking with regard to placing MDMA into Schedule I of the CSA. Later, following the receipt of several comments and requests for a hearing, the Administrator referred the matter to an Administrative Law Judge ("ALJ") with instructions to "conduct a hearing for the purpose of receiving factual evidence and expert opinion regarding the proposed scheduling of MDMA." During the course of the hearing, the ALJ heard 33 witnesses and received 95 exhibits into evidence.[4] On May 22, 1986, the ALJ issued a comprehensive opinion finding

2. 21 U.S.C. § 811(b) provides that[:] "The Attorney General shall, before initiating proceedings under subsection (a) of this section to control a drug or other substance . . . , and after gathering the necessary data, request from the Secretary a scientific and medical evaluation, and his recommendations, as to whether such drug or other substance should be so controlled."

3. Section 811(c) requires the Administrator to consider the following eight factors for each drug proposed to be controlled under the CSA: "(1) [The drug's] actual or relative potential for abuse. (2) Scientific evidence of its pharmacological effect, if known. (3) The state of current scientific knowledge regarding the drug or other substance. (4) Its history and current pattern of abuse. (5) The scope, duration, and significance of abuse. (6) What, if any, risk there is to the public health. (7) Its psychic or physiological dependence liability. (8) Whether the substance is an immediate precursor of a substance already controlled under this subchapter." 21 U.S.C. § 811(c).

4. On July 1, 1985, while the hearing was proceeding, the Administrator placed MDMA into Schedule I of the Controlled Substances Act pursuant to the emergency scheduling provisions of the Act, 21 U.S.C. § 811(h)(1). The Administrator determined that this action was necessary to avoid an imminent hazard to the public safety.

that MDMA fit none of the three criteria prerequisite to placement in Schedule I. Relying on the hearing testimony of experts in the health care community, the ALJ concluded that MDMA had an accepted medical use for treatment in the United States, and an accepted safety for use under medical supervision. The ALJ also found that the record did not establish that MDMA had a "high" potential for abuse. The ALJ therefore recommended that MDMA be placed into Schedule III of the CSA.

The Administrator, however, declined to accept the reasoning and scheduling recommendation of the ALJ. In his October 13, 1986, decision, the Administrator held that the phrases "currently accepted medical use in treatment in the United States" and "accepted safety for use . . . under medical supervision" as used in the CSA both mean that the FDA has evaluated the substance for safety and approved it for interstate marketing in the United States pursuant to the Federal Food, Drug, and Cosmetic Act of 1938 ("FDCA"), 21 U.S.C. § 355. From these premises, the Administrator reasoned that because the FDA has not approved a new drug application ("NDA") or investigational new drug application ("IND") authorizing interstate marketing of MDMA under the FDCA, MDMA cannot be lawfully marketed and has neither a currently accepted medical use in treatment in the United States nor an accepted safety for use under medical supervision. Finally, the Administrator found that the DEA had sustained its burden of proving that MDMA has a high potential for abuse. The Administrator's final rule, effective November 13, 1986, placed MDMA into Schedule I. Dr. Grinspoon appeals from this final rule under the CSA.

We turn first to petitioner's claim that the Administrator erred in interpreting the phrases "accepted medical use in treatment in the United States" and "accepted safety for use . . . under medical supervision" in section 812(b)(1) to mean, in essence, "approved for interstate marketing by the FDA under the FDCA." Before embarking on an analysis of that issue, however, we begin by explaining the appropriate standard of review in a case, such as this, where a court must assess an agency's interpretation of a statute it administers.

The Administrator argues correctly that we must review his interpretation of the CSA in light of the guidelines set forth by the Supreme Court in *Chevron U.S.A., Inc. v. Natural Resources Defense Council, Inc.*, 467 U.S. 837 (1984). In *Chevron* the Court explained that a reviewing court must employ a two-step analysis that focuses initially on the intentions of Congress:

> First, always, is the question whether Congress had directly spoken to the precise question at issue. If *the intent of Congress is clear*, that is the end of the matter; for the court, as well as the agency, must give effect to the unambiguously expressed intent of Congress.

In the absence of congressional intent, however, the court must proceed to a second inquiry:

> If . . . the court determines Congress has not directly addressed the precise question at issue, the court does not simply impose its own construction on the statute, as would be necessary in the absence of an administrative

> interpretation. Rather, if the statute is silent or ambiguous with respect to the specific issue, the question for the court is whether the agency's answer is based on a *permissible construction of the statute.*

It is undisputed that Congress has not directly spoken to the question at issue here, namely, the proper means of interpreting the second and third criteria of section 812(b)(1). The absence of express intent, however, does not compel us to proceed to the deferential second step of the *Chevron* scheme. As the Supreme Court indicated in a footnote to its *Chevron* opinion, "if a court, employing traditional tools of statutory construction, ascertains that Congress had an intention on the precise question at issue, that intention is law and must be given effect."

The Administrator contends that congressional intent favoring his interpretation of the CSA can be gleaned from the language of the statute, its legislative history, and the language and history of subsequent legislative enactments designed to enhance the regulatory system established by the CSA in 1970. In the alternative, he argues that if the intent of Congress is ambiguous, then his construction of the statute is permissible in view of the statutory scheme. Our review of the sources identified by the litigants convinces us that Congress neither expressed nor implied an affirmative intent regarding how the second and third Schedule I criteria should be interpreted. Nevertheless, these same sources—the language and structure of the CSA and FDCA, the legislative history of the CSA, and the subsequent handiwork of Congress in the area of controlled substance regulation—lead us to conclude that the Administrator's construction is contrary to congressional intent.

The Administrator begins by arguing that the language of the CSA itself is evidence of congressional intent favoring his construction of the statute. His argument is based on the definitions of terms chosen by Congress in drafting the relevant provisions of the CSA. He first cites the definition of the term "United States" as used in "accepted medical use in treatment in the United States." This term is the only portion of the Schedule I criteria that Congress has expressly defined in the CSA, providing that "the term 'United States,' when used in a geographic sense, means *all places* . . . subject to the jurisdiction of the United States." Coupling this statutory definition of "United States" with the dictionary definition of "accepted"—which means "generally approved" or "generally agreed upon"—the Administrator argues that the phrase "*accepted* medical use in treatment in the *United States*," must contemplate an administrative determination that the substance has been "generally approved" for use in treatment in "all places" subject to United States jurisdiction. In other words, FDA interstate marketing approval is necessary to satisfy this criterion because, otherwise, the substance could not be deemed to be "generally approved" *everywhere* in the United States.[7]

7. The Administrator does not confine this argument to section 812(b)(1)(B), but also states that "*accepted* Safety for use . . . under medical supervision, 21 U.S.C. § 812(b)(1)(C), is equivalent to FDA approval because, otherwise, the safety of the substance could never be "generally agreed upon."

We find this argument to be strained and unpersuasive. The CSA's definition of "United States" plainly does not require the conclusion asserted by the Administrator simply because section 802(28) defines "United States" as "*all places* subject to the jurisdiction of the United States." Congress surely intended the reference to "all places" in section 802(28) to delineate the broad jurisdictional scope of the CSA and to clarify that the CSA regulates conduct occurring *any place*, as opposed to *every place*, within the United States. As petitioner aptly notes, a defendant charged with violating the CSA by selling controlled substances in only two states would not have a defense based on section 802(28) if he contended that his activity had not occurred in "all places" subject to United States jurisdiction.

Nor does the dictionary definition of "accepted" offered by the Administrator convince us that Congress intended FDA approval to be the equivalent of the second and third Schedule I criteria. Use of the term "accepted" in sections 812(b)(1)(B) and 812(b)(1)(C) may indicate that Congress intended the medical use or safety of the substance to be "generally agreed upon," but this alone does not inform us as to *who* must generally be in agreement. The Administrator reads "accepted" to mean that *the FDA* must have approved the drug for interstate marketing. Dr. Grinspoon, on the other hand, prefers to interpret "accepted" as meaning that the *medical community* generally agrees that the drug in question has a medical use and can be used safely under medical supervision. Our conclusion is that the term "accepted" does not cure the statute's ambiguity. We are simply unable to extrapolate from the drafters' choice of the word "accepted" and thereby ascertain a general congressional intention favoring the interpretation advanced by the Administrator.

In another argument focusing upon the language of the statute, the Administrator urges us to adopt his interpretation of the CSA because it is entirely consistent with the interpretation of the phrase "accepted medical use in treatment in the United States" employed in the Commissioners' Notes to the Uniform Controlled Substances Act ("Uniform CSA").[8] At first glance, this argument appears to have considerable merit. The Uniform CSA, like its federal counterpart, creates five schedules of controlled substances and, indeed, was modeled on the federal CSA.[9] But, while we agree that the Uniform CSA offers an interesting comparison, we fail to see how the interpretation of the Uniform CSA offered by the Commissioners has any bearing at all on the intent of Congress, which enacted the federal CSA *prior to* the creation of the Uniform CSA. We can only conclude, therefore, that this argument, despite its facial appeal, has no bearing on the claim that the language of the

8. "Experimental substances found to have a potential for abuse in early testing will also be included in Schedule I. When those substances are accepted by the Federal Food and Drug Administration as being safe and effective, they will then be considered to have an accepted medical use for treatment in the United States, and thus, will be eligible to be shifted to an appropriate schedule based upon the criteria set out in Sections 205, 207, 209, and 211." 9 U.L.A. at 221.

9. The Uniform CSA was approved for adoption by the states in 1970. To date, 48 states, the District of Columbia, Guam, and the Virgin Islands have adopted the Uniform CSA. 9 U.L.A. Supp. 123–24 (1986).

federal CSA evidences congressional intent to adopt the construction of the statute favored by the Administrator.

While the Administrator's arguments fail to persuade us that Congress affirmatively intended his construction of the CSA, we believe nevertheless that the language and structure of the two relevant statutes, the CSA and the FDCA, are helpful in determining whether the Administrator's interpretation squares with congressional intent. Although, as the District of Columbia Circuit has stated, "the interrelationship between the two Acts [CSA and FDCA] is far from clear," we are persuaded that this interrelationship precludes the Administrator's reliance on the absence of FDA approval as a substitute for the second and third Schedule I criteria under the CSA.

The CSA clearly provides that a substance may not be placed in Schedule I unless it lacks *both* a "currently accepted medical use in treatment in the United States" *and* "accepted safety for use . . . under medical supervision." The FDCA, on the other hand, provides that a substance may fail to obtain FDA interstate marketing approval (or exemption) for any of seven specific reasons. 21 U.S.C. § 355(d)(1)–(7). Although approval may be withheld because the substance lacks both "safety", and "efficacy" for a particular use, it is equally possible for a substance to be disapproved for interstate marketing because it lacks only *one* of these attributes, or because the application fails to contain relevant patent information, or even because the labeling proposed for the drug "is false or misleading in any particular." Thus, we find no necessary linkage between failure to obtain FDA interstate marketing approval and a determination that the substance in question is unsafe *and* has no medical use. Indeed, the FDCA does not even mention the term "medical use." In short, it is plainly possible that a substance may fail to obtain interstate marketing approval even if it has an accepted medical use.

Another possible reason for failure to obtain FDA new drug approval is that the manufacture, distribution, and use of a substance might not involve interstate marketing. Unlike the CSA scheduling restrictions, the FDCA interstate marketing provisions do not apply to drugs manufactured and marketed wholly intrastate. Thus, it is possible that a substance may have both an accepted medical use and safety for use under medical supervision, even though no one has deemed it necessary to seek approval for interstate marketing. Indeed, as Dr. Grinspoon argues, there is no economic or other incentive to seek interstate marketing approval for a drug like MDMA because it cannot be patented and exploited commercially. The prospect of commercial development, of course, is irrelevant to one who, like Grinspoon, seeks only to do research.

These considerations tend to indicate that the absence of FDA approval for interstate commerce does not foreclose the possibility that a substance might still possess an accepted medical use or even be considered safe for use under medical supervision. It appears, instead, that blind reliance on the lack of FDA interstate marketing approval could cause a substance to be placed in Schedule I, even though one or two of the three requirements prescribed by Congress for placement of a drug in Schedule I have not been proven. Based solely on the language of the CSA and the FDCA, therefore, we find it unlikely that substituting the lack of FDA interstate marketing approval for the statutory requirements that a substance lack both an "accepted medical use" and "accepted safety for use . . . under medical supervision" is consistent with the intent of Congress in enacting the CSA. We turn now to consider whether the legislative history of the CSA confirms or rebuts this tentative conclusion.

The Administrator purports to have identified portions of the CSA's legislative history that support his construction of the statutory language. [H]e cites a passage from the House Committee Report that states:

> Under Reorganization Plan No. 1 of 1968 a Bureau of Narcotics and Dangerous Drugs has been established in the Department of Justice to regulate all these drugs (including legitimate importation, exportation, manufacture, and distribution) to prevent diversion from legitimate channels. Safety and efficacy will continue to be regulated under the Federal Food, Drug, and Cosmetic Act by [HHS].

From this, the Administrator draws the proposition that "Congress clearly intended that the 'safety and efficacy' of narcotic and dangerous drugs (*e.g.*, whether such drugs are acceptable for medical use and safe for such use) be determined by [HHS] under the [FDCA]." The Administrator's conclusion is objectionable, however, because his parenthetical comment—equating a finding of "safety and efficacy" by the FDA with a finding of "accepted medical use" and "accepted safety for use . . . under medical supervision"—is totally unsupported by the quoted passage from the House Committee Report. Nowhere does Congress equate "safety and efficacy" under the FDCA with the second and third Schedule I criteria contained in section 812(b)(1). This, indeed, is the point at issue in this litigation, and we are loath to accept such a disingenuous argument.

The Administrator has cited subsequent legislative enactments as support for his position that Congress has approved his construction of the second and third criteria for Schedule I substances. Our review of these legislative enactments, however, leads us to find that the subsequent legislation tends to weaken, not strengthen, the position espoused by the Administrator in this litigation.

[I]n 1984, Congress amended the CSA to include an "emergency scheduling" provision. This provision allows the Attorney General to place certain substances into Schedule I on a temporary basis without regard to the regular scheduling criteria and procedures if such emergency scheduling is "necessary to avoid an imminent hazard to the public safety." This amendment to the CSA, however, expressly states that the Attorney General's authority to schedule substances in this expedited manner does not apply where an "exemption or approval is in effect for the substance under section 355 of this title,"[11] *i.e.*, where the FDA has permitted the substance to be marketed in interstate commerce. The fact that Congress expressly authorized

11. 21 U.S.C. § 355 is the section of the FDCA describing the standards and procedures for FDA interstate marketing approvals and exemptions.

the Attorney General to use expedited procedures and rely upon the absence of FDA interstate marketing approval, rather than the usual Schedule I criteria, only in temporary emergency situations suggests to us that these shorthand methods are not appropriate in routine (i.e., nonemergency) situations such as the one before us in the instant case. We do not interpret the explicit reference to FDA approval in the "emergency scheduling" provision to mean, as the Administrator would have us believe, that Congress sought to permit blind reliance on FDA standards as a legitimate shortcut in the general run of cases.

We believe there is yet one additional policy reason, no doubt related to some of the other factors already discussed, for rejecting the construction of the CSA advanced by the Administrator as contrary to congressional intent. Under the statutory scheme set up by Congress, the Attorney General may not schedule a substance under the CSA without first obtaining the recommendation of the FDA, through its parent agency, HHS, and providing an "opportunity for a hearing pursuant to the rulemaking procedures prescribed by [the Administrative Procedure Act]." It is plain, therefore, that while Congress intended the recommendation of HHS to have significant weight in the decisionmaking process, it also intended that there be an opportunity for a meaningful hearing *after* receipt of the HHS report. It would surely be anomalous if the FDA's recommendation, based solely on the absence of approval for interstate marketing, sufficed to determine the ultimate conclusion prior to the hearing.

If we were to accept the Administrator's construction of section 812(b)(1) in this case, the opportunity for a meaningful hearing would be lost, and satisfaction of the "accepted medical use" and "accepted safety" criteria would turn solely on the existence of FDA approval for interstate marketing. A hearing on issues of the sort required by the statute—Does the substance have an accepted medical use in treatment in the United States? Is the substance safe for use under medical supervision?—would be reduced to an empty formality and, for participants like Dr. Grinspoon, would amount to an exercise in futility. We hesitate to interpret the CSA in a manner that would cause its important provision requiring a[n] administrative hearing to be meaningless as to two of the three requirements for scheduling a substance in Schedule I. We believe instead that, for the hearing opportunity to be a significant one on these issues, the agency must remain flexible enough to weigh and consider claims raised at the administrative hearing to the effect that a substance has an accepted use and is accepted as safe even though it is not approved for distribution in interstate commerce.

For the reasons listed above, we conclude that the Administrator erroneously applied an interpretation of the "accepted medical use in treatment in the United States" and "accepted safety for use . . . under medical supervision" criteria of section 812(b)(1) that directly conflicts with congressional intent. We therefore vacate the Administrator's determination that MDMA should be placed in Schedule I of the CSA and remand the rule for further consideration by the DEA. On remand, the Administrator will not be permitted to treat the absence of FDA interstate marketing approval as conclusive evidence that MDMA has no currently accepted medical use and lacks accepted safety for use under medical supervision.

Petitioner Grinspoon has offered his own theory concerning the type of inquiry the Administrator must make under the statute. He urges us to adopt a standard for the second and third criteria that is based upon the opinion of members of the medical community. He contends that Congress drafted the CSA with this type of standard in mind. To support this contention, Grinspoon cites the testimony of two representatives of the Bureau of Narcotics and Dangerous Drugs ("BNDD"), DEA's predecessor agency, during legislative consideration of the Comprehensive Drug Abuse Prevention and Control Act of 1970. Michael R. Sonnenreich, Deputy Chief Counsel of the BNDD, testified that drugs in Schedule I would "have no medical use as determined by the medical community," and that "the medical community" would decide "whether or not the drug has [a] medical use. . . ." Likewise, John Ingersoll, Director of the BNDD, testified that substances placed in Schedule I would be those drugs that "the medical profession has already determined to have no legitimate medical use in the United States."

While we acknowledge that the statements by the BNDD witnesses before the House Subcommittee tend to support Dr. Grinspoon's position, we do not believe they are entitled to much weight as indicia of congressional intent in fashioning the "accepted medical use" and "accepted safety for use . . . under medical supervision" criteria. This is especially true where, as here, there is no indication whatsoever in either the legislative history or the history of any subsequent amendments that Congress concurred with the views expressed by the witnesses. In short, we do not find Grinspoon's evidence to be persuasive on the issue of affirmative congressional intent to have certain members of the medical community determine whether a substance has an "accepted medical use in treatment in the United States" or "accepted safety for use . . . under medical supervision."

The nature of our review further constrains us from requiring the Administrator to adopt Dr. Grinspoon's proposed construction of section 812(b)(1). Although we find that the Administrator's present interpretation of the second and third Schedule I criteria contravenes congressional intent, we are unable to ascertain with any certainty what Congress intended to be the proper interpretation of subsections (B) and (C). In other words, while we are satisfied that Congress intended to preclude reliance on the absence of FDA approval in assessing whether a substance has an "accepted medical use" and "accepted safety for use . . . under medical supervision," we have found nothing to indicate how Congress affirmatively intended these two ambiguous statutory phrases to be construed and applied. It appears to us that Congress has implicitly delegated to the Administrator the authority to interpret these portions of the CSA, and we must therefore refrain from imposing our own statutory interpretation upon the agency. Hence, to avoid unduly infringing upon the Administrator's legitimate discretion to develop a legally acceptable standard—i.e., one that does not conflict with the intentions of Congress, and makes sense in light of the statutory language, the legislative history, and the purposes of the entire legislative scheme—we remand the rule to the Administrator for reconsideration and for further proceedings not inconsistent with this opinion.

Although a remand is necessary due to our above holding, we nonetheless feel compelled to address the other issues raised in Dr. Grinspoon's petition because they are likely to arise again when the Administrator reconsiders the rule.

In addition to the "accepted medical use" and "accepted safety" criteria discussed above, the CSA also requires substances identified for placement in Schedule I to have a "high potential for abuse." Dr. Grinspoon contends that the Administrator's placement of MDMA in Schedule I is arbitrary and capricious because the Administrator failed to articulate a legal standard for assessing MDMA's potential for abuse and because the evidence in the record is insufficient to support a finding that MDMA has a "high" potential for abuse. While conceding that MDMA has some potential for abuse, and therefore should be scheduled under the CSA, Dr. Grinspoon insists that the Administrator has not proved, as he must for a Schedule I substance, that MDMA's potential for abuse is high.

The CSA provides no definition of the phrase "high potential for abuse," but both parties agree that the legislative history of the statute provides guidance in this regard. Specifically, the report of the House Committee on Interstate and Foreign Commerce accompanying the bill that eventually became the CSA sets forth four alternative legal standards for determining when a substance possesses a "potential for abuse." Borrowing from regulations promulgated under the FDCA, the House Committee Report provides that the Administrator may determine a substance has potential for abuse if:

> (1) There is evidence that individuals are taking the drug or drugs containing such a substance in amounts sufficient to create a hazard to their health or to the safety of other individuals or of the community; *or*
>
> (2) There is significant diversion of the drug or drugs containing such a substance from legitimate drug channels; *or*
>
> (3) Individuals are taking the drug or drugs containing such a substance on their own initiative rather than on the basis of medical advice from a practitioner licensed by law to administer such drugs in the course of his professional practice; *or*
>
> (4) The drug or drugs containing such a substance are new drugs so related in their action to a drug or drugs already listed as having a potential for abuse to make it likely that the drug will have the same potentiality for abuse as such drugs, thus making it reasonable to assume that there may be significant diversions from legitimate channels, significant use contrary to or without medical advice, or that it has a substantial capability of creating hazards to the health of the user or to the safety of the community.

The Committee Report goes on to state that "potential for abuse" exists only when there is "a substantial potential for the occurrence of significant diversions from legitimate channels, significant use by individuals contrary to professional advice, or substantial capability of creating hazards to the health of the user or the safety of the community."

The Administrator argues that he applied the standards expressly approved by Congress, but Dr. Grinspoon complains that the Administrator articulated no standard for showing that MDMA had a *relative* potential for abuse sufficient to warrant placement in Schedule I. As Grinspoon notes, the passage from the legislative history quoted above provides guidance only as to the minimum needed to show *any* potential for abuse, in other words, enough to justify a level of CSA control as low as placement in Schedule V. It offers no guidance for assessing whether a substance should be subject to Schedule I controls, the strictest imposed under the CSA, which require a "high" potential for abuse. For this, argues Grinspoon, the Administrator must prove that MDMA has a high potential for abuse *relative* to other scheduled substances and must base its proof on existing levels of actual abuse "on the streets."

While we acknowledge that the Administrator's final rule is silent with respect to the legal standard required for a finding of "high" potential for abuse, we do not find the Administrator's action to be arbitrary and capricious. The fourth standard contained in the segment of the Committee Report quoted above makes it quite clear that the Administrator can permissibly reach a conclusion regarding a substance's level of potential for abuse by comparing the substance to drugs already scheduled under the CSA. Here the Administrator has done just that, offering several findings concerning the evidence of close structural and pharmacological similarity between MDMA and other substances, such as MDA, which already have been found to have a high potential for abuse and have been placed in Schedule I or II. The Administrator also cited animal studies, human behavioral studies, and a survey of MDMA users which suggest that MDMA is related in its effects to Schedule I and II substances such as LSD, cocaine, mescaline, and MDA. We believe this approach to ascertaining MDMA's potential for abuse is entirely consistent with the statutory scheme developed by Congress and therefore hold that the Administrator's method is not arbitrary and capricious.[12] The question remains, of course, whether the evidence collected by the Administrator is sufficient to justify his conclusion that MDMA has a high potential for abuse. Since Dr. Grinspoon has also challenged this aspect of the scheduling determination as arbitrary and capricious, we turn next to a discussion of this issue.

---

12. While we appreciate Dr. Grinspoon's point that MDMA abuse is low relative to other drugs that seem to be more popular "on the street," we do not believe that this fact precludes the Administrator from finding that MDMA has a high *potential* for abuse. Grinspoon's argument overlooks the importance of the term "potential" in section 812(b)(1)(A) and runs contrary to the explicit intent of Congress that the Administrator "not be required to wait until a number of lives have been destroyed or substantial problems have already arisen before designating a drug as subject to the controls of the bill." So long as the Administrator can marshal substantial evidence to demonstrate that MDMA is sufficiently similar to scheduled drugs with a "high potential for abuse," we will sustain his determination regardless of existing levels of actual abuse.

In reviewing the Administrator's conclusion regarding MDMA's potential for abuse, we must determine whether it is based on "substantial evidence," a term the Supreme Court has defined as "'such relevant evidence as a reasonable mind might accept as adequate to support a conclusion.'"

The question before us, therefore, is whether there is substantial evidence in the administrative record to support the Administrator's determination that MDMA is "so related in [its] action to a drug or drugs already listed as having a [high] potential for abuse" that it is likely MDMA "will have the same potentiality for abuse as such drugs." In support of his conclusion, the Administrator made 46 numbered findings related to MDMA's similarity to other drugs with a high potential for abuse. These findings were based on scientific evidence concerning the chemical structural similarity between MDMA and other Schedule I and II drugs; the similar pharmacological effects of MDMA and these other drugs; animal drug discrimination studies; animal self-administration studies; and recent studies of the neurotoxic effects of MDMA and related drugs on rats.

Dr. Grinspoon, in an item-by-item analysis contained in the proposed findings of fact and conclusions of law he submitted to the DEA, calls into question many of the Administrator's findings concerning MDMA's similarity to other drugs with a high potential for abuse. For instance, Grinspoon agrees that MDMA is a member of a family of psychoactive drugs, but disputes the validity of the inference drawn from the similarity by the Administrator. According to Grinspoon, "chemical similarity is not necessarily a good guide to the actual effects of a compound in the human body." Grinspoon notes that of the 28 known phenethylamines, 17 were not scheduled under the CSA as late as December 1983. Even a subsequent review of these 17 substances by the World Health Organization's Expert Committee on Drug Dependence resulted in a recommendation that only nine of the substances be scheduled by member nations. Eight were thought harmless enough to remain unscheduled.

We have reviewed Dr. Grinspoon's item-by-item analysis closely, but find no basis sufficient to overturn the Administrator's decision. Grinspoon's reinterpretation of the scientific evidence before the agency surely demonstrates that the available evidence does not inexorably lead to a conclusion that MDMA is similar to drugs possessing a high potential for abuse. But, faced with such uncertainty, we must defer to the conclusion reached by the Administrator, even if we may have favored Dr. Grinspoon's approach had we studied the evidence in a *de novo* fashion. In reaching this conclusion, we follow the well-established maxim that "where the agency presents scientifically respectable evidence which the petitioner can continually dispute with rival, and we will assume, equally respectable evidence, the court must not second-guess the particular way the agency chooses to weigh the conflicting evidence or resolve the dispute." We find this maxim to have particular force in a case such as this because, as one court has explained, "appellate courts have neither the expertise nor the resources to evaluate complex scientific claims."

Dr. Grinspoon also takes issue with the Administrator's alleged failure to consider evidence tending to show that placement of MDMA in Schedule I would strongly discourage medical research on the drug. Grinspoon contends that failure to consider the impact of a scheduling decision on legitimate research amounts to arbitrary and capricious action on the part of the Administrator because he did not weigh all relevant factors in making his decision. To buttress his contention, Grinspoon recites a litany of legal, administrative, and practical obstacles that hinder researchers seeking to conduct experiments with Schedule I drugs. These obstacles include mandatory FDA approval of research involving Schedule I substances; mandatory special registration with the DEA; mandatory reporting and security procedures beyond those required for drugs placed in Schedules II through V; unavoidable bureaucratic delays; and other adverse impacts due to the grave concern caused by a substance's placement in Schedule I, such as difficulty in obtaining volunteers for clinical studies and, for academic researchers, difficulty in securing approval from institutional review boards.

Again, we do not doubt that Dr. Grinspoon has correctly identified several ways in which the placement of MDMA in Schedule I will impede his research and the efforts of other researchers interested in exploring the possibility of clinical uses for MDMA. We must conclude, nevertheless, that the existence of such hurdles does not render the Administrator's scheduling decision arbitrary and capricious.

Dr. Grinspoon has identified nothing in the CSA, its legislative history, or its implementing regulations that can be read to require the Administrator to consider the impact of a scheduling determination upon legitimate scientific research. From our review of the CSA, we can only conclude that Congress has already weighed the costs and benefits of legitimate research on dangerous drugs and has determined, in a categorical manner, that if the three Schedule I criteria are satisfied, then the substance should be subject to Schedule I controls even if this action will create administrative and other burdens for researchers. Here there is no dispute that the Administrator *considered* all of the section 812(b)(1) criteria in arriving at his final rule, so we are left with a situation in which there can be no complaint that the Administrator failed to consider any relevant factor.

Dr. Grinspoon's final dissatisfaction with the final rule is the Administrator's alleged reliance on the conclusions recommended by HHS on the criteria enumerated in section 812(b)(1). Grinspoon argues that the determination by the Secretary of HHS was arbitrary and capricious and not in accordance with law, and that all relevant scientific and medical evidence was not before the Secretary at the time of the determination. The record, in fact, reveals that HHS performed in a less than admirable fashion in making its recommendation to the Administrator. The record indicates that HHS failed to look beyond its own files upon receiving the Administrator's section 811(b) request for a scientific and medical evaluation; neglected to consult any organization of medical professionals or even the FDA's own panel of experts, the Drug Abuse Advisory Committee; and simply rubber-stamped the Administrator's conclusion by adopting the section 811(c) eight-factor analysis already performed by the DEA. There is also evidence that FDA analysts failed to forward a letter received from the National Institute of Drug Abuse, which stated that the evidence cited by the DEA did not support the existence of abuse potential in animals, to either the FDA Commissioner or the Assistant Secretary of HHS prior to the issuance of the HHS recommendation to the Administrator.

Despite these alleged procedural shortcomings, we fail to see how the procedure followed by HHS tainted the Administrator's determination. The CSA does not specify the steps to be taken by HHS; it simply requires the Administrator to request from the Secretary of HHS a scientific and medical evaluation. Moreover, the HHS recommendation to schedule a substance is not binding[18] and, indeed, serves to trigger an administrative hearing at which interested persons may introduce evidence to rebut the Secretary's scheduling recommendation. Ultimately, of course, responsibility rests with the Administrator, not HHS, to ensure that the final rule rests on permissible legal standards and substantial evidence. It is true that the Administrator twice mentioned the HHS recommendation in his final rule, once in relation to the "accepted medical use" criterion and once in relation to the "high potential for abuse" criterion. With regard to the first mention, however, we have already determined that this aspect of the case must be remanded and reconsidered because the Administrator interpreted the statutory language in a manner that is contrary to the intent of Congress. Because, on remand, the Administrator will not be able to rely on lack of FDA approval to demonstrate the absence of an accepted medical use, we need not discuss any possible reliance on the HHS recommendation regarding the absence of an accepted medical use. With regard to the second mention, we believe that the Administrator's conclusion that MDMA has a high potential for abuse is amply supported by a substantial amount of independent evidence. Because we believe that the Administrator's finding with regard to MDMA's potential for abuse is justified even in the absence of the HHS recommendation to place MDMA in Schedule I, we hold that any reliance on the HHS evaluation by the Administrator constitutes, at most, harmless error.

For the foregoing reasons, the rule is vacated and remanded to the Administrator for further proceedings consistent with this opinion.

On remand in *Grinspoon*, the Administrator concluded, once again, that MDMA should be placed in Schedule I. The Administrator declined to hold a new hearing and, instead, reached his determination by applying the following definition of "accepted medical use" to the existing evidentiary record: "The characteristics of a drug or other substance with an accepted medical use in treatment include scientifically determined and accepted knowledge of its chemistry; the toxicology and pharmacology of the substance in animals; establishment of its effectiveness

18. According to section 811(b), the HHS recommendation is binding as to "scientific and medical" matters, but not with respect to the appropriate schedule in which to place a particular substance. The exception to this rule is that, "if the Secretary recommends that a drug or other substance *not* be controlled, the Attorney General shall not control the drug or other substance." 21 U.S.C. § 812(b) (emphasis supplied).

in humans through scientifically designed clinical trials; general availability of the substance and information regarding its use; recognition of its clinical use in generally accepted pharmacopeia, medical references, journals or textbooks; specific indications for the treatment of recognized disorders; recognition of the use of the substance by organizations or associations of physicians; and recognition and use of the substance by a substantial segment of the medical practitioners in the United States." 53 Fed. Reg. 5156 (1988).

While *Grinspoon* introduces many of the key questions raised by the CSA's scheduling provisions, no scheduling issue has generated as much interest (or litigation) as marijuana's classification as a Schedule I substance. Over the years, a number of different groups have petitioned the DEA to reschedule marijuana, and these efforts remain ongoing. The most significant rescheduling petition was filed in 1972 by the National Organization for the Reform of Marijuana Laws (NORML). The matter worked its way through the administrative process and the courts for *22 years* before it was finally resolved in 1994. During that time, the United States Court of Appeals for the District of Columbia considered appeals related to NORML's petition on five separate occasions.

The final series of administrative and court decisions in response to NORML's 1972 petition provide a particularly illuminating look at the CSA's classification scheme. This is in part because the NORML litigation served as a vehicle for the DEA to settle on a definition for the second scheduling criterion—whether or not a substance has a currently accepted medical use in treatment in the United States. By the conclusion of the NORML litigation, the DEA had adopted a five-factor test for determining whether a substance has a currently accepted use in treatment in the United States:

1. The drug's chemistry must be known and reproducible;
2. There must be adequate safety studies;
3. There must be adequate and well-controlled studies proving efficacy;
4. The drug must be accepted by qualified experts; and
5. The scientific evidence must be widely available.

This is the definition that the DEA continues to apply today. The DEA's definition requires *all* five factors to be met for it to conclude that a substance has a currently accepted medical use under the CSA.

Presented below are three decisions from the NORML petition: a 1988 opinion by Administrative Law Judge Francis Young recommending marijuana be transferred to Schedule II; the Drug Enforcement Administrator's 1989 order rejecting Young's recommendation; and a 1991 District of Columbia Court of Appeals decision that addressed the Administrator's order. These decisions were key points on the path to the DEA's five-factor test for the currently accepted medical use criterion and they help to explain why—despite the widespread acceptance of medical marijuana among the states and many physicians—the DEA continues to conclude that marijuana has no "accepted" medical use.

As you read these decisions, pay particular attention to how each of them defines "currently accepted medical use." Which definition do you find the most compelling? Can you imagine other possible definitions of the term that you think would be better than any of the definitions offered in the opinions below?

In the Matter of Marijuana Rescheduling Petition

September 6, 1988

Opinion and Recommended Ruling, Findings of Fact, Conclusions of Law and Decision of Administrative Law Judge Francis L. Young.

This is a rulemaking pursuant to the Administrative Procedure Act to determine whether the marijuana plant (Cannabis sativa L) considered as a whole may lawfully be transferred from Schedule I to Schedule II of the schedules established by the Controlled Substances Act (the Act). None of the parties is seeking to "legalize" marijuana generally or for recreational purposes. Placement in Schedule II would mean, essentially, that physicians in the United States would not violate Federal law by prescribing marijuana for their patients for legitimate therapeutic purposes. It is contrary to Federal law for physicians to do this as long as marijuana remains in Schedule I. This proceeding had its origins on May 18, 1972 when the National Organization for the Reform of Marijuana Laws (NORML) and two other groups submitted a petition to the Bureau of Narcotics and Dangerous Drugs (BNDD), predecessor agency to the Drug Enforcement Administration (DEA or the Agency), asking that marijuana be removed from Schedule I and freed of all controls entirely, or be transferred from Schedule I to Schedule V where it would be subject to only minimal controls. The Act by its terms had placed marijuana in Schedule I thereby declaring, as a matter of law that it had no legitimate use in therapy in the United States and subjecting the substance to the strictest level of controls. The Act had been in effect for just over one year when NORML submitted its 1972 petition.

On September 1, 1972 the Director of BNDD announced his refusal to accept the petition for filing, stating that he was not authorized to institute proceedings for the action requested because of the provisions of the Single Convention on Narcotic Drugs, 1961. NORML appealed this action to the United States Court of Appeals for the District of Columbia Circuit. The court held that the Director had erred in rejecting the petition without "a reflective consideration and analysis," observing that the Director's refusal "was not the kind of agency action that promoted the kind of interchange and refinement of views that is the lifeblood of a sound administrative process." The court remanded the matter in January 1974 for further proceedings not inconsistent with its opinion, "to be denominated a consideration on the merits."

A three-day hearing was held at DEA by Administrative Law Judge Lewis Parker in January 1975. The judge found in NORML's favor on several issues but the Acting

Administrator of DEA entered a final order denying NORML's petition "in all respects." NORML again petitioned the court for review. Finding fault with DEA's final order the court again remanded for further proceedings not inconsistent with its opinion. The Court directed the then-Acting Administrator of DEA to refer NORML's petition to the Secretary of the Department of Health, Education and Welfare (HEW) for findings and, thereafter, to comply with the rulemaking procedures outlined in the Act at 21 U.S.C. § 811 (a) and (b).

On remand the Administrator of DEA referred NORML's petition to HEW for scientific and medical evaluation. On June 4, 1979 the Secretary of HEW advised the Administrator of the results of the HEW evaluation and recommended that marijuana remain in Schedule I. Without holding any further hearing the Administrator of DEA proceeded to issue a final order ten days later denying NORML's petition and declining to initiate proceedings to transfer marijuana from Schedule I. NORML went back to the Court of Appeals.

When the case was called for oral argument there was discussion of the then-present status of the matter. DEA had moved for a partial remand. The court found that "reconsideration of all the issues in this case would be appropriate" and again remanded it to DEA, observing: "We regrettably find it necessary to remind respondents [DEA and HEW] of an agency's obligation on remand not to 'do anything which is contrary to either the letter or spirit of the mandate construed in the light of the opinion of [the] court deciding the case.'" DEA was directed to refer all the substances at issue to the Department of Health and Human Services (HHS), successor agency to HEW, for scientific and medical findings and recommendations on scheduling. DEA did so and HHS has responded. In a letter dated April 1, 1986 the then-Acting Deputy Administrator of DEA requested this administrative law judge to commence hearing procedures as to the proposed rescheduling of marijuana and its components.

After the Judge conferred with counsel for NORML and DEA, a notice was published in the Federal Register on June 24, 1986 announcing that hearings would be held on NORML's petition for the rescheduling of marijuana and its components commencing on August 21, 1986 and giving any interested person who desired to participate the opportunity to do so.

Of the three original petitioning organizations in 1972 only NORML is a party to the present proceeding. In addition the following entities responded to the Federal Register notice and have become parties, participating to varying degrees: the Alliance for Cannabis Therapeutics (ACT), Cannabis Corporation of America (CCA) and Carl Eric Olsen, all seeking transfer of marijuana to Schedule II; the Agency, National Federation of Parents for Drug-Free Youth (NFP) and the International Association of Chiefs of Police (IACP), all contending that marijuana should remain in Schedule I.

Preliminary pre-hearing sessions were held on August 21 and December 5, 1986 and on February 20, 1987. During the preliminary stages, on January 20, 1987,

NORML filed an amended petition for rescheduling. This new petition abandoned NORML's previous requests for the complete descheduling of marijuana or rescheduling to Schedule V. It asks only that marijuana be placed in Schedule II.

All Parties present stipulated, for the purpose of this proceeding, that marijuana has a high potential for abuse and that abuse of the marijuana plant may lead to severe psychological or physical dependence.

During the Spring and Summer of 1987 the parties identified their witnesses and put the direct examination testimony of each witness in writing in affidavit form. Copies of these affidavits were exchanged. Similarly, the parties assembled their proposed exhibits and exchanged copies. Opportunity was provided for each party to submit objections to the direct examination testimony and exhibits proffered by the others. The objections submitted were considered by the administrative law judge and ruled on. The testimony and exhibits not excluded were admitted into the record. Thereafter hearing sessions were held at which witnesses were subjected to cross-examination. These sessions were held in New Orleans, Louisiana on November 18 and 19, 1987; in San Francisco, California on December 8 and 9, 1987; and in Washington, D.C. on January 5 through 8 and 26 through 29, and on February 2, 4 and 5, 1988. The parties have submitted proposed findings and conclusions and briefs. Oral arguments were heard by the judge on June 10, 1988 in Washington.

The Act provides (21 U.S.C. § 812(b)) that a drug or other substance may not be placed in any schedule unless certain specified findings are made with respect to it. The findings required for Schedule I and Schedule II are as follows:

> Schedule I. (A) The drug or other substance has a high potential for abuse. (B) The drug or other substance has no currently accepted medical use in treatment in the United States. (C) There is a lack of accepted safety for use of the drug or other substance under medical supervision.
>
> Schedule II. (A) The drug or other substance has a high potential for abuse. (B) The drug or other substance has a currently accepted medical use in treatment in the United States or a currently accepted medical use with severe restrictions. (C) Abuse of the drug or other substances [sic] may lead to severe psychological or physical dependence.

As noted above the parties have stipulated, for the purpose of this proceeding, that marijuana has a high potential for abuse and that abuse of it may lead to severe psychological or physical dependence. Thus the dispute between the two sides in this proceeding is narrowed to whether or not marijuana has a currently accepted medical use in treatment in the United States, and whether or not there is a lack of accepted safety for use of marijuana under medical supervision.

With respect to whether or not marijuana has a "currently accepted medical use in treatment in the United States" for chemotherapy patients, the record shows the following facts to be uncontroverted.

One of the most serious problems experienced by cancer patients undergoing chemotherapy for their cancer is severe nausea and vomiting caused by their reaction to the toxic (poisonous) chemicals administered to them in the course of this treatment. This nausea and vomiting at times becomes life threatening. The therapy itself creates a tremendous strain on the body. Some patients cannot tolerate the severe nausea and vomiting and discontinue treatment. Beginning in the 1970s there was considerable doctor-to-doctor communication in the United States concerning patients known by their doctors to be surreptitiously using marijuana with notable success to overcome or lessen their nausea and vomiting.

Many physicians, some engaged in medical practice and some teaching in medical schools, have accepted smoking marijuana as effective in controlling or reducing the severe nausea and vomiting (emesis) experienced by some cancer patients undergoing chemotherapy for cancer.

Such physicians include board-certified internists, oncologists and psychiatrists. (Oncology is the treatment of cancer through the use of highly toxic chemicals, or chemotherapy.) Doctors who have come to accept the usefulness of marijuana in controlling or reducing emesis resulting from chemotherapy have done so as the result of reading reports of studies and anecdotal reports in their professional literature, and as the result of observing patients and listening to reports directly from patients.

In many cases doctors have found that, in addition to suppressing nausea and vomiting, smoking marijuana is a highly successful appetite stimulant. The importance of appetite stimulation in cancer therapy cannot be overstated. Patients receiving chemotherapy often lose tremendous amounts of weight. They endanger their lives because they lose interest in food and in eating. The resulting sharp reduction in weight may well affect their prognosis. Marijuana smoking induces some patients to eat. The benefits are obvious, doctors have found. There is no significant loss of weight. Some patients will gain weight. This allows them to retain strength and makes them better able to fight the cancer. Psychologically, patients who can continue to eat even while receiving chemotherapy maintain a balanced outlook and are better able to cope with their disease and its treatment, doctors have found.

The vomiting induced by chemotherapeutic drugs may last up to four days following the chemotherapy treatment. The vomiting can be intense, protracted and, in some instances, is unendurable. The nausea which follows such vomiting is also deep and prolonged. Nausea may prevent a patient from taking regular food or even much water for periods of weeks at a time.

The State of New Mexico set up a program in 1978 to make marijuana available to cancer patients pursuant to an act of the State legislature. The legislature had accepted marijuana as having medical use in treatment. It overwhelmingly passed this legislation so as to make marijuana available for use in therapy, not just for research. Marijuana and synthetic THC were given to patients, administered under medical supervision, to control or reduce emesis. The marijuana was in the form of cigarettes obtained from the Federal government. The program operated from

1979 until 1986, when funding for it was terminated by the State. During those seven years about 250 cancer patients in New Mexico received either marijuana cigarettes or THC. Twenty or 25 physicians in New Mexico sought and obtained marijuana cigarettes or THC for their cancer patients during that period. All of the oncologists in New Mexico accepted marijuana as effective for some of their patients. At least ten hospitals [were] involved in this program in New Mexico, in which cancer patients smoked their marijuana cigarettes. The hospitals accepted this medicinal marijuana smoking by patients. Voluminous reports filed by the participating physicians make it clear that marijuana is a highly effective anti-emetic substance. It was found in the New Mexico program to be far superior to the best available conventional anti-emetic drug, compazine, and clearly superior to synthetic THC pills. More than 90% of the patients who received marijuana within the New Mexico program reported significant or total relief from nausea and vomiting. Before the program began cancer patients were surreptitiously smoking marijuana in New Mexico to lessen or control their emesis resulting from chemotherapy treatments. They reported to physicians that it was successful for this purpose. Physicians were aware that this was going on.

Certain law enforcement authorities have been outspoken in their acceptance of marijuana as an antiemetic agent. Robert T. Stephan, Attorney General of the State of Kansas, and himself a former cancer patient, said of chemotherapy in his affidavit in this record: "The treatment becomes a terror." His cancer is now in remission. He came to know a number of health care professionals whose medical judgment he respected. They had accepted marijuana as having medical use in treatment. He was elected Vice President of the National Association of Attorneys General (NAAG) in 1983. He was instrumental in the adoption by that body in June 1983 of a resolution acknowledging the efficacy of marijuana for cancer and glaucoma patients. The resolution expressed the support of NAAG for legislation then pending in the Congress to make marijuana available on prescription to cancer and glaucoma patients. The resolution was adopted by an overwhelming margin. NAAG's President, the Attorney General of Montana, issued a statement that marijuana does have accepted medical uses and is improperly classified at present. The Chairman of NAAG's Criminal Law and Law Enforcement Committee, the Attorney General of Pennsylvania, issued a statement emphasizing that the proposed rescheduling of marijuana would in no way affect or impede existing efforts by law enforcement authorities to crack down on illegal drug trafficking.

[The Administrative Law Judge then recounted a number of additional stories of patients and doctors who had concluded that marijuana had medicinal value.]

From the foregoing uncontroverted facts it is clear beyond any question that many people find marijuana to have, in the words of the Act, an "accepted medical use in treatment in the United States" in effecting relief for cancer patients. Oncologists, physicians treating cancer patients, accept this. Other medical practitioners and researchers accept this. Medical faculty professors accept it. Nurses performing hands-on patient care accept it. Patients accept it.

Of relevance, also, is the acceptance of marijuana by state attorneys-general, officials whose primary concern is law enforcement. A large number of them have no fear that placing marijuana in Schedule II, thus making it available for legitimate therapy, will in any way impede existing efforts of law enforcement authorities to crack down on illegal drug trafficking.

The Act does not specify by whom a drug or substance must be "accepted [for] medical use in treatment" in order to meet the Act's "accepted" requirement for placement in Schedule II. Department of Justice witnesses told the Congress during hearings in 1970 preceding passage of the Act that "the medical Profession" would make this determination, that the matter would be "determined by the medical community." The Deputy Chief Counsel of BNDD, whose office had written the bill with this language in it, told the House subcommittee that "this basic determination . . . is not made by any part of the federal government. It is made by the medical community as to whether or not the drug has medical use or doesn't".

No one would seriously contend that these Justice Department witnesses meant that the entire medical community would have to be in agreement on the usefulness of a drug or substance. Seldom, if ever, do all lawyers agree on a point of law. Seldom, if ever, do all doctors agree on a medical question. How many are required here? A majority of 51%? It would be unrealistic to attempt a plebiscite of all doctors in the country on such a question every time it arises, to obtain a majority vote.

In determining whether a medical procedure utilized by a doctor is actionable as malpractice the courts have adopted the rule what it is acceptable for a doctor to employ a method of treatment supported by a respectable minority of physicians.

As noted above, there is no question but that this record shows a great many physicians, and others, to have "accepted" marijuana as having a medical use in the treatment of cancer patients' emesis. True, all physicians have not "accepted" it. But to require universal, 100% acceptance would be unreasonable. Acceptance by "a respectable minority" of physicians is all that can reasonably be required. The record here establishes conclusively that at least "a respectable minority" of physicians has "accepted" marijuana as having a "medical use in treatment in the United States." That others may not makes no difference.

It is not for [the DEA] to tell doctors whether they should or should not accept a drug or substance for medical use. The statute directs the Administrator merely to ascertain whether, in fact, doctors have done so.

The overwhelming preponderance of the evidence in this record establishes that marijuana has a currently accepted medical use in treatment in the United States for nausea and vomiting resulting from chemotherapy treatments in some cancer patients. To conclude otherwise, on this record, would be unreasonable, arbitrary and capricious.

[The Administrative Law Judge then analyzed other claimed medical uses of marijuana and concluded that marijuana also had an accepted medical use in treatment in the United States for spasticity resulting from multiple sclerosis and for hyperparathyroidism. The Judge found, however, that marijuana did not have an accepted medical use in treatment in the United States for glaucoma because the record "fail[ed] to show that the preponderance of the evidence that a respectable minority of physicians accepts marijuana as being useful in the treatment of glaucoma in the United States."]

With respect to whether or not there is "a lack of accepted safety for use of [marijuana] under medical supervision", the record shows the following facts to be uncontroverted.

The most obvious concern when dealing with drug safety is the possibility of lethal effects. Can the drug cause death?

Nearly all medicines have toxic, potentially lethal effects. But marijuana is not such a substance. There is no record in the extensive medical literature describing a proven, documented cannabis-induced fatality.

This is a remarkable statement. First, the record on marijuana encompasses 5,000 years of human experience. Second, marijuana is now used daily by enormous numbers of people throughout the world. Estimates suggest that from twenty million to fifty million Americans routinely, albeit illegally, smoke marijuana without the benefit of direct medical supervision. Yet, despite this long history of use and the extraordinarily high numbers of social smokers, there are simply no credible medical reports to suggest that consuming marijuana has caused a single death.

By contrast aspirin, a commonly used, over-the-counter medicine, causes hundreds of deaths each year.

Drugs used in medicine are routinely given what is called an LD-50. The LD-50 rating indicates at what dosage fifty percent of test animals receiving a drug will die as a result of drug induced toxicity. A number of researchers have attempted to determine marijuana's LD-50 rating in test animals, without success. Simply stated, researchers have been unable to give animals enough marijuana to induce death.

At present it is estimated that marijuana's LD-50 is around 1:20,000 or 1:40,000. In layman terms this means that in order to induce death a marijuana smoker would have to consume 20,000 to 40,000 times as much marijuana as is contained in one marijuana cigarette. A smoker would theoretically have to consume nearly 1,500 pounds of marijuana within about fifteen minutes to induce a lethal response.

Another common medical way to determine drug safety is called the therapeutic ratio. This ratio defines the difference between a therapeutically effective dose and a dose which is capable of inducing adverse effects.

A commonly used over-the-counter product like aspirin has a therapeutic ratio of around 1:20. Two aspirins are the recommended dose for adult patients. Twenty times this dose, forty aspirins, may cause a lethal reaction in some patients, and will almost certainly cause gross injury to the digestive system, including extensive internal bleeding.

The therapeutic ratio for prescribed drugs is commonly around 1:10 or lower. Valium, a commonly used prescriptive drug, may cause very serious biological damage if patients use ten times the recommended (therapeutic) dose.

There are, of course, prescriptive drugs which have much lower therapeutic ratios. Many of the drugs used to treat patients with cancer, glaucoma and multiple sclerosis are highly toxic. The therapeutic ratio of some of the drugs used in antineoplastic therapies, for example, are regarded as extremely toxic poisons with therapeutic ratios that may fall below 1:1.5. These drugs also have very low LD-50 ratios and can result in toxic, even lethal reactions, while being properly employed.

By contrast, marijuana's therapeutic ratio, like its LD-50, is impossible to quantify because it is so high.

In strict medical terms marijuana is far safer than many foods we commonly consume. For example, eating ten raw potatoes can result in a toxic response. By comparison, it is physically impossible to eat enough marijuana to induce death.

Marijuana, in its natural form, is one of the safest therapeutically active substances known to man. By any measure of rational analysis marijuana can be safely used within a supervised routine of medical care.

[By contrast, for example,] Cisplatin, one of the most powerful chemo-therapeutic agents used on humans may cause deafness; may lead to life-threatening kidney difficulties and kidney failure; adversely affects the body's immune system, suppressing the patient's ability to fight a host of common infections.

[Many currently used cancer treatment] agents cause a number of disturbing adverse effects. Most of these drugs cause hair loss. Studies increasingly indicate all of these drugs may cause other forms of cancer. Death due to kidney, heart or respiratory failure is a very real possibility with all of these agents and the margin for error is minimal. Similarly, there is a danger of overdosing a patient weakened by his cancer. Put simply, there is very great risk associated with the medical use of these chemicals agents. Despite these high risks, all of these drugs are considered "safe" for use under medical supervision and are regularly administered to patients on doctor's orders in the United States today.

There have been occasional instances of panic reaction in patients who have smoked marijuana. Such persons have responded to simple person-to-person communication with a doctor and have sustained no long term mental or physical damage. If marijuana could be legally obtained, and administered in an open, medically-supervised session rather than surreptitiously, the few instances of such adverse reaction doubtless would be reduced in number and severity.

Other reported side effects of marijuana have been minimal. Sedation often results. Sometimes mild euphoria is experienced. Short periods of increased pulse rate and of dizziness are occasionally experienced. Marijuana should not be used by persons anxious or depressed or psychotic or with certain other health problems. Physicians could readily screen out such patients if marijuana were being employed as an agent under medical supervision.

All drugs have "side effects" and all drugs used in medicine for their therapeutic benefits have unwanted, unintended, sometimes adverse effects.

The [Controlled Substances] Act, at 21 U.S.C. § 812(b)(1)(C), requires that marijuana be retained in Schedule I if "[t]here is a lack of accepted safety for use of [it] under medical supervision." If there is no lack of such safety, if it is accepted that this substance can be used with safety under medical supervision, then it is unreasonable to keep it in Schedule I.

Again we must ask[:] "accepted" by whom?

The gist of the Agency's case against recognizing marijuana's acceptance as safe is to assert that more studies, more tests are needed. The Agency has presented highly qualified and respected experts, researchers and others, who hold that view. But, as demonstrated in the discussion above, it is unrealistic and unreasonable to require unanimity of opinion on the question confronting us. For the reasons there indicated, acceptance by a significant minority of doctors is all that can reasonably be required. This record makes it abundantly clear that such acceptance exists in the United States.

Based upon the facts established in this record and set out above one must reasonably conclude that there is accepted safety for use of marijuana under medical supervision. To conclude otherwise, on this record, would be unreasonable, arbitrary and capricious.

Based upon the foregoing facts and reasoning, the administrative law judge concludes that the provisions of the Act permit and require the transfer of marijuana from Schedule I to Schedule II. The Judge realizes that strong emotions are aroused on both sides of any discussion concerning the use of marijuana. Nonetheless it is essential for this Agency, and its Administrator, calmly and dispassionately to review the evidence of record, correctly apply the law, and act accordingly.

Marijuana can be harmful. Marijuana is abused. But the same is true of dozens of drugs or substances which are listed in Schedule II so that they can be employed in treatment by physicians in proper cases, despite their abuse potential.

Transferring marijuana from Schedule I to Schedule II will not, of course, make it immediately available in pharmacies throughout the country for legitimate use in treatment. Other government authorities, Federal and State, will doubtless have to act before that might occur. But this Agency is not charged with responsibility, or given authority, over the myriad other regulatory decisions that may be required before marijuana can actually be legally available. This Agency is charged merely with determining the placement of marijuana pursuant to the provisions of the Act. Under our system of laws the responsibilities of other regulatory bodies are the concerns of those bodies, not of this Agency.

There are those who, in all sincerity, argue that the transfer of Marijuana to Schedule II will "send a signal" that marijuana is "OK" generally for recreational use. This argument is specious. It presents no valid reason for refraining from taking an action required by law in light of the evidence. If marijuana should be placed in Schedule II, in obedience to the law, then that is where marijuana should be placed, regardless of misinterpretation of the placement by some. The reasons for the placement can, and should, be clearly explained at the time the action is taken. The fear of sending such a signal cannot be permitted to override the legitimate need, amply demonstrated in this record, of countless suffers for the relief marijuana can provide when prescribed by a physician in a legitimate case.

The evidence in this record clearly shows that marijuana has been accepted as capable of relieving the distress of great numbers of very ill people, and doing so with safety under medical supervision. It would be unreasonable, arbitrary and capricious for DEA to continue to stand between those sufferers and the benefits of this substance in light of the evidence in this record.

The administrative law judge recommends that the Administrator conclude that the marijuana plant considered as a whole has a currently accepted medical use in treatment in the United States, that there is no lack of accepted safety for use of it under medical supervision and that it may lawfully be transferred from Schedule I to Schedule II. The judge recommends that the Administrator transfer marijuana from Schedule I to Schedule II.

Marijuana Scheduling Petition; Denial of Petition

Drug Enforcement Administration
54 F.R. 53767

December 29, 1989

John C. Lawn, Administrator.

This is a final order of the Administrator of the Drug Enforcement Administration (DEA) denying the petition of the National Organization for Reform of Marijuana Laws (NORML) to reschedule the plant material marijuana from Schedule I to Schedule II of the Controlled Substances Act. This order follows a rulemaking on the record as prescribed by the Controlled Substances Act and the Administrative Procedures Act. There are seven parties in the rulemaking proceeding. Four parties, NORML, the Alliance for Cannabis Therapeutics (ACT), the Cannabis Corporation of America (CCA), and Carl Eric Olsen, comprised the pro-marijuana parties, those advocating the rescheduling of marijuana from Schedule I to Schedule II. The three remaining parties, who advocated that marijuana remain in Schedule I, were DEA, the National Federation of Parents for a Drug-Free Youth, and the International Association of Chiefs of Police (IACP).

The two issues involved in a determination of whether marijuana should be rescheduled from Schedule I to Schedule II are whether marijuana plant material has a currently accepted medical use in treatment in the United States, or a currently accepted medical use with severe restrictions; and whether there is a lack of accepted safety for use of marijuana plant material under medical supervision. After a thorough review of the record in this matter, the Administrator rejects the recommendation of the administrative law judge to reschedule marijuana into Schedule II and finds that the evidence in the record mandates a finding that the marijuana plant material remain in Schedule I of the Controlled Substances Act.

The pro-marijuana parties advocate the placement of marijuana plant material into Schedule II for medical use in the treatment of a wide variety of ailments, including nausea and vomiting associated with chemotherapy, glaucoma, spasticity in amputees and those with multiple sclerosis, epilepsy, poor appetite, addiction to drugs and alcohol, pain, and asthma. The evidence presented by the pro-marijuana parties includes outdated and limited scientific studies; chronicles of individuals, their families and friends who have used marijuana; opinions from over a dozen psychiatrists and physicians; court opinions involving medical necessity as a defense to criminal charges for illegal possession of marijuana; state statutes which made marijuana available for research; newspaper articles; and the opinions of laypersons, including lawyers and associations of lawyers. The Administrator does not find such evidence convincing in light of the lack of reliable, credible, and relevant scientific studies documenting marijuana's medical utility; the opinions of highly respected, credentialed experts that marijuana does not have an accepted medical use; and statements from the American Medical Association, the American Cancer Society, the American Academy of Ophthalmology, the National Multiple Sclerosis Society, and the Federal Food and Drug Administration that marijuana has not been demonstrated as suitable for use as a medicine.

The record contains many research studies which have been published in scientific journals and many unpublished studies conducted by individual states. In order to evaluate the validity of any research study many factors must be considered. Certain scientific practices have been generally accepted by the scientific community which are designed to increase the validity of experimental studies. Studies or research projects which do not follow these accepted scientific practices have very limited, if any, credibility. A review of such studies must first examine the degree to which researchers control, or hold constant, all the variables which could affect the results, except the variable being studied. For example, if you wish to evaluate the effectiveness of marijuana on a group of glaucoma patients, you must control any other medication which the patient is taking. Otherwise, it is impossible to conclude that the results are attributable to the marijuana.

The second factor, or aspect of the design of a research project which must be evaluated, is the placebo effect. This is the tendency of research subjects to act and respond in a manner they believe is expected of them. To eliminate this factor, research subjects are usually "blinded," or not informed, of what drug they are receiving. Results of non-blind studies are questionable since they could be attributable, in large part, to psychological reactions of subjects rather than any real effects from the experimental drug. The next factor which must be minimized or eliminated for a research study to be valid is the expectation of the researcher. This is especially true where the effect being measured is subjective and not objective. For example, if the researcher is evaluating if the patient is nauseated, that is very subjective. If the researcher knows which patients are receiving the experimental drug, his perception of the results could be significantly altered.

Other factors to be considered when evaluating the validity of research include the number of subjects in the study, how the subjects are selected for the study, the length of the study, or how many times the experimental drug is administered, and the measurement of results in quantifiable, objective terms. The fewer the subjects in a research study, the less valid the results. If the sample of subjects is not statistically significant, the chances of the same results being duplicated in other individuals is reduced. Subjects for a research study should be randomly selected and representative of the population that is targeted to use the drug. Testing of marijuana in cancer patients for relief of nausea and vomiting should not be limited to those who have previously used marijuana recreationally and request its use in the study. The length of a study is particularly significant when the drug is to be used to treat a chronic condition such as glaucoma or spasticity. Studies based upon acute or one-time administration of the drug must be viewed with caution when the goal is treatment of a chronic condition. The effectiveness of the drug for long-time administration and the existence of side effects resulting from chronic use will not be revealed in acute studies.

In addition to factors related to the design and execution of a research study, there are two other factors which must be reviewed in evaluation of a research study. Research results are always considered tentative or preliminary until they have been replicated or confirmed by another researcher. The research study must be reported in sufficient detail to permit others to repeat it. Finally, publication of a study in a scientific journal, especially a journal which subjects an article to review prior to publication, adds validity to a study. Journal publication subjects a study to review and scrutiny by the scientific community and opens the door to replication of the studies. Unpublished studies are inherently suspect.

While research studies with the limitations mentioned above may provide useful and preliminary data which will be valuable in designing further studies, research studies with substantial limitations are not sufficient to support a determination that a drug has an accepted medical use. Both the published and unpublished research studies submitted by the pro-marijuana parties in this proceeding to support marijuana's medical use suffer from many deficiencies. They are, in essence, preliminary studies. None of these studies has risen to the level of demonstrating that marijuana has an accepted medical use for treatment of any medical condition.

Five studies were presented by the pro-marijuana parties to support the medical use of marijuana [to treat nausea and vomiting associated with chemotherapy.] [One] study compared a combination of pure THC and marijuana to placebo cigarettes. This study by Chang, et al., *Delta-9-Tetrahydrocannabinol as an Antiemetic in Cancer Patients Receiving High-Dose Methotrexate,* 91 Annals of Internal Medicine, 819–824 (1979), was randomized, double-blind, and placebo controlled. The study concluded, "that a combination of oral and smoked THC is a highly effective antiemetic compared to placebo[.]" This study was limited to 15 subjects, some of whom received both marijuana and THC at the same time. The validity of the results of this study is severely limited by its small size and administration of the mixture of the two drugs, THC and marijuana. The study is not helpful in determining the therapeutic utility of marijuana alone in treating nausea and vomiting.

[Another] study conducted by Dr. Thomas J. Ungerleider, a psychiatrist, involved the administration of marijuana to 16 bone marrow transplant patients suffering from severe nausea and vomiting from radiation therapy. The results of this study are of little value due to the limited number of patients, the subjective nature of the data, and the fact that the results of the study were never published. The conclusion that there was less nausea and vomiting with use of marijuana was based upon the subjects' and researcher's subjective determination. There were no objective measurements, such as number of incidents or frequency of vomiting. During cross-examination, Dr. Ungerleider indicated that the results of the study were not published because there was not enough hard data.

[One of the claimed] stud[ies] presented by the pro-marijuana parties is actually a group of programs, collectively labeled "Controlled Substances Therapeutic Research Programs," conducted by six states in the 1970s and 1980s. These programs involved the use of both marijuana cigarettes and synthetic THC capsules. The programs were given Investigational New Drug (IND) approval by the Food and Drug Administration (FDA) and the marijuana and THC were supplied by the Federal Government. The protocols of these programs were very loosely constructed. There were no controls. That is, there were no individuals who did not take the experimental drugs to compare with those who did. The studies were not blind or double-blind. Every research subject knew what drug they were receiving and, in many cases, were permitted to request either marijuana or THC. The studies were not randomized. In most instances, the results were measured by the subject's subjective evaluation of the drug's effectiveness. This is even more of a problem where the drug in question is a psychotropic or mind-altering substance like marijuana, which by its very nature makes some individuals feel "high," and may distort their perception of physical symptoms. There were no objectively measured results. The results were not published in scientific journals and, in some cases, data were lost or not recorded. The number of individuals who actually smoked marijuana in these studies was relatively small. These state studies were born of compassion and frustration. They abandoned traditional scientific methods in favor of dispensing marijuana to as many individuals as possible on the chance that it might help them. Though well-intentioned, these studies have little scientific value.

The research studies presented by the pro-marijuana parties in this proceeding do not support a conclusion that marijuana has a therapeutic use for treatment of nausea and vomiting associated with chemotherapy.

The pro-marijuana parties presented many testimonials from cancer patients, their families, and friends about the use of marijuana to alleviate nausea and vomiting associated with chemotherapy. These stories of individuals who treat themselves with a mind-altering drug, such as marijuana, must be viewed with great skepticism. There is no scientific merit to any of these accounts. In many cases the individuals were taking a variety of other medications and were using anything which might help treat the cancer as well as the nausea. They were using marijuana purchased on the street, and were unaware of the strength of the drug. They were not using the drug under medical supervision. Many of these individuals had been recreational users of marijuana prior to becoming ill. These individuals' desire for the drug to relieve their symptoms, as well as a desire to rationalize their marijuana use, removes any scientific value from their accounts of marijuana use. There is no doubt that these individuals and their loved-ones believed that marijuana was beneficial. The accounts of these individuals' suffering and illnesses are very moving and tragic; they are not, however, reliable scientific evidence, nor do they provide a basis to conclude that marijuana has an accepted medical use as an antiemetic.

There were many physicians and other medical experts who testified in this proceeding. In reviewing the weight to be given to an expert's opinion, the facts relied upon to reach that opinion and the credentials and experience of the expert must be carefully examined. The experts presented by the pro-marijuana parties were unable to provide a strong scientific or factual basis to support their opinions. In addition, many of the experts presented by the pro-marijuana parties did not have any expertise in the area of research in the specific medical area being addressed. The pro-marijuana parties presented the testimony of five psychiatrists to support the use of marijuana as an antiemetic. None of these individuals is an oncologist, nor have they treated cancer patients. Three of the psychiatrists, Drs. Grinspoon, Ungerleider and Zinberg are current or former board members of NORML or ACT. All these physicians indicated that they relied on scientific studies which they had read, their experience with cancer patients, or stories from others, to reach their conclusions. When questioned on cross-examination as to which studies they relied upon, most were unable to list one study. A review of the available literature has already demonstrated the unreliability of the studies that exist. The testimonials upon which these psychiatrists relied are also scientifically suspect. The opinions of these psychiatrists are, therefore, of little value in determining whether marijuana is therapeutically useful as an antiemetic.

Two general practitioners, Drs. Weil and Kaufman, also provided testimony on behalf of the pro-marijuana parties. Neither are oncologists, nor do they treat cancer patients. Dr. Weil is a wellness counselor at a health spa, and Dr. Kaufman is an officer of a company that audits hospital quality control programs. Dr. Weil has written a number of books on drugs and admitted that he has personally used every mind-altering, illicit drug he has written about. Dr. Kaufman stopped practicing medicine in 1974, and was unable to provide any information on cross-examination regarding the basis for his opinion that marijuana has an accepted medical use. Neither Dr. Weil nor Dr. Kaufman has a credible basis for their opinions regarding marijuana, and, therefore, their testimony will be disregarded.

Four oncologists presented testimony on behalf of the pro-marijuana parties. They were Drs. Goldberg, Silverberg, Bickers, and Stephens. Dr. Goldberg is a board certified oncologist, but practices primarily internal medicine. She only administers chemotherapy to one or two patients a year. In her career, she has administered chemotherapy to no more than ten patients whom she believed to be using marijuana. On cross-examination, she could not recall any studies regarding marijuana. Dr. Goldberg was a member and financial contributor to NORML. Dr. Silverberg has practiced oncology for 20 years. He is a Professor of Clinical Oncology at the University of California at San Francisco, but is not a board certified oncologist. In his testimony, Dr. Silverberg indicated that there was voluminous medical research regarding marijuana's effectiveness in treating nausea and vomiting. On cross-examination, Dr. Silverberg could not identify any studies, and was forced to admit that he had been incorrect and that there were, in fact, very few studies conducted using marijuana as an antiemetic. Although Dr. Silverberg has advised patients to use marijuana to control nausea and vomiting associated with chemotherapy, he has never been involved in any research nor has he documented any of his observations. Dr. Bickers is an oncologist in New Orleans and is a Professor of Medicine at the Louisiana University School of Medicine. Although Dr. Bickers claims that young patients have better control over nausea and vomiting after using marijuana, he has never documented this claim. Dr. Bickers was unable to identify any scientific information which he relied upon in reaching his conclusion regarding marijuana. Dr. Stephens, an oncologist, Professor of Medicine and Director of Clinical Oncology at the University of Kansas, characterized marijuana as a "highly effective, and in some cases, critical drug in the reduction of chemotherapeutically-induced emesis." During cross-examination, Dr. Stephens stated that he was unaware of any scientific studies which had been done with marijuana, and that he had never done research or treated patients with marijuana. He indicated that he received his information about the patient's use of marijuana from the nursing staff or the patient's family. None of these oncologists based their opinions about marijuana on scientific studies or their own research. Most did not base their opinions on their direct observations, but on the opinions of others. In light of lack of scientific basis for these opinions, they will be given little regard.

The agency presented the testimony of nationally recognized experts in oncology. Dr. Ettinger, a Professor of Oncology at Johns Hopkins School of Medicine, is the author of over 100 published articles on cancer treatment. Dr. Ettinger testified: "There is no indication that marijuana is effective in treating nausea and vomiting resulting from radiation treatment or other causes. No legitimate studies have been conducted which make such conclusions."

Dr. Laszlo, currently Vice President of Research for the American Cancer Society, is an expert who has devoted the majority of his over 30 years in medicine to the treatment of cancer. During his career, he spent eleven years as the Director of Clinical Programs at the Duke University Comprehensive Cancer Center. Dr. Laszlo has authored numerous scientific articles about cancer research and treatment and has written a book titled, *Antiemetics and Cancer Chemotherapy.* In his testimony for this proceeding, Dr. Laszlo stated that he does not advocate the use of marijuana as an antiemetic, in part, because there has not been sufficient testing of marijuana to show that it is a safe and effective drug. He also indicated that because there are other available, highly effective antiemetics, a physician does not need to resort to a crude drug such as marijuana. Dr. Laszlo concluded that marijuana does not have a currently accepted medical use in the United States for treatment of nausea and vomiting resulting from cancer chemotherapy.

The American Cancer Society provided DEA with its policy statements regarding medical use of marijuana. The American Cancer Society has, and continues to, support research with substances which may provide relief to cancer patients, including marijuana. It states, however, that the results of clinical investigations are insufficient to warrant the decontrol of marijuana for medical use. The American Medical Association has expressed a similar opinion.

The Food and Drug Administration has provided DEA with a scientific and medical evaluation of marijuana, as well as testimony from one of its leading pharmacologists. Evaluating marijuana against its criteria for safety and effectiveness, FDA has concluded that there is inadequate scientific evidence to support a finding that marijuana is safe and effective for treating nausea and vomiting experienced by patients undergoing chemotherapy.

The numerous testimonials and opinions of lay persons which were presented in this proceeding by the pro-marijuana parties are not useful in determining whether marijuana has a medical use. While experiences of individuals with medical conditions who use marijuana may provide a basis for research, they cannot be substituted for reliable scientific evidence. For the many reasons stated in the previous discussion of scientific evidence, these statements can be given little weight. Similarly, endorsements by such organizations as the National Association of Attorneys General, that marijuana has a medical use as an antiemetic, are of little persuasive value when compared with statements from the American Cancer Society and the American Medical Association.

[The Administrator then discussed the evidence related to the use of marijuana as a medicine to treat glaucoma and spasticity.]

In order to be effective, a drug's therapeutic benefits must be balanced against, and outweigh, its negative or adverse effects. This has not been established with marijuana. As the previously discussed evidence has demonstrated, there is as yet no reliable scientific evidence to support marijuana's therapeutic benefit. It is, therefore, impossible to balance the benefit against the negative effects. The negative effects of marijuana use are well-documented in the record. Marijuana smoking, the route of administration advocated by many witnesses presented by the pro-marijuana parties, causes many well-known and scientifically documented side effects. These include decreased blood pressure, rapid heart rate, drowsiness, euphoria, disphoria and impairment of motor function, not to mention various negative effects on the respiratory and pulmonary systems. Therefore, the only conclusion is that marijuana is not safe for use under medical supervision, because its safety has not been established by reliable scientific evidence.

In summary, the Administrator finds that there is insufficient, and in many instances no, reliable, credible, scientific evidence, supported by properly conducted scientific research, to support a conclusion that marijuana has a medical use to treat any ailment or disease. In addition, there is a lack of scientific evidence to support a conclusion that marijuana is safe for use under medical supervision. This agency, and the Government as a whole, would be doing the public a disservice by concluding that this complex psychoactive drug with serious adverse effects has a medical use based upon anecdotal and unreliable evidence. The evidence presented by the pro-marijuana parties in this proceeding consisted of a few published scientific studies involving marijuana and THC, testimony of general practice physicians and psychiatrists, and testimony of individuals who have used marijuana for various medical conditions. The majority of these individuals did not use marijuana under medical supervision and used "street" marijuana. In contrast, recognized, credentialed specialists in the fields of oncology, glaucoma and multiple sclerosis, and organizations involved in medical research in these areas, have concluded that marijuana does not have an accepted medical use in treatment in the United States. The Administrator would be abdicating his responsibility to the public if he concluded that marijuana has a medical use and is safe for use under medical supervision.

The Administrator finds that the administrative law judge failed to act as an impartial judge in this matter. He appears to have ignored the scientific evidence, ignored the testimony of highly-credible and recognized medical experts and, instead, relied on the testimony of psychiatrists and individuals who used marijuana.

The Administrator rejects the administrative law judge's findings and conclusions. They were erroneous; they were not based upon credible evidence; nor were they based upon evidence in the record as a whole. Therefore, in this case, they carry no weight and do not represent the position of the agency or its Administrator. The inadequacy of Judge Young's analysis of the case is exemplified by his acceptance of, and reliance upon, irresponsible and irrational statements propounded by the pro-marijuana parties. Such statements include the following: "marijuana is far safer than many of the foods we commonly consume. For example, eating ten raw potatoes can result in a toxic response. By comparison, it is physically impossible to eat enough marijuana to induce death." That such a statement would come from the proponents of marijuana is understandable. To give it the weight of an administrative law judge's finding is appalling.

The Administrator has accepted the agency's findings of fact as his own. In order to conclude that these facts support a conclusion that marijuana remain in Schedule I, they must be applied to the criteria set forth in the Controlled Substances Act for substances in Schedule I.

The three criteria are found at 21 U.S.C. 812(b)(1) and are as follows:

(a) The drug or other substance has a high potential for abuse.

(b) The drug or other substance has no currently accepted medical use in treatment in the United States.

(c) There is lack of accepted safety for use of the drug or other substance under medical supervision.

For purposes of this proceeding, the parties stipulated that marijuana has a high potential for abuse. The criteria for substances listed in Schedule II also includes that the drug has a high potential for abuse.

The issue of what "currently accepted medical use in treatment in the United States," and "accepted safety for use . . . under medical supervision" mean, has been the subject of a previous scheduling proceeding involving the drug MDMA. In that proceeding, the Administrator did not adopt Judge Young's recommendation and defined both phrases to mean approved for marketing as safe and effective pursuant to the Food, Drug, and Cosmetic Act. The Administrator's decision was reviewed by the United States Court of Appeals for the First Circuit in *Grinspoon v. DEA*, 828 F.2d 881 (1987). The Court remanded the matter to the Administrator finding that his standard was too restrictive. The Court did not suggest a standard to be adopted and, instead, stated that "Congress has implicitly delegated to the Administrator the authority to interpret these portions of the CSA[.]" The Administrator then published a revised final rule in which he listed several characteristics of a drug or other substance which has an "accepted medical use in treatment in the United States." These characteristics are:

1. Scientifically determined and accepted knowledge of its chemistry;

2. The toxicology and pharmacology of the substance in animals;

3. Establishment of its effectiveness in humans through scientifically designed clinical trials;

4. General availability of the substance and information regarding the substance and its use;

5. Recognition of its clinical use in generally accepted pharmacopeia, medical references, journals or textbooks;

6. Specific indications for the treatment of recognized disorders;

7. Recognition of the use of the substance by organizations or associations of physicians; and

8. Recognition and use of the substance by a substantial segment of the medical practitioners in the United States.

These characteristics rely heavily on verifiable scientific data and acceptance by the medical community. These two areas go hand-in-hand, as aptly demonstrated by the record in this proceeding. Most physicians and organizations of physicians rely on scientific data in formulating their opinions regarding the safety and effectiveness of a drug and whether they will provide it for their patients. Many of the experts and organizations who concluded that marijuana did not have an "accepted medical use in treatment in the United States," stated that they reached this conclusion because of the lack of adequate scientific data to support the safety and efficacy of marijuana. The Administrator also notes that the Controlled Substances Act and its legislative history require him to consider scientific evidence in determining the schedule in which a drug should be placed. For example, the Controlled Substances Act at 21 U.S.C. 811(c) lists eight factors to be considered in evaluating the three scheduling criteria. Included among those factors are "scientific evidence of its pharmacological effect, if known" and "the state of current scientific knowledge regarding the drug or other substance." In addition, the Controlled Substances Act requires the Administrator to request a scientific and medical evaluation from the Secretary of Health and Human Services. The Administrator is then bound by the Secretary's recommendation as to scientific and medical matters. In this proceeding, the Assistant Secretary for Health has provided the Administrator with an extensive scientific and medical evaluation in which it was recommended that marijuana remain in Schedule I because there is insufficient scientific and medical evidence to conclude that marijuana is a safe and effective drug.

It is clear from the evidence presented in this proceeding that marijuana does not have the characteristics of a drug which has an "accepted medical use in treatment in the United States." Because of the complex composition of marijuana, containing over 400 separate constituents (many of which have not been tested) varying from plant to plant, the chemistry, toxicology and pharmacology of marijuana is not established. As discussed previously, the effectiveness of marijuana has not been documented in humans with scientifically-designed clinical trials. While many individuals have used marijuana and claim that it is effective in treating their ailments, these testimonials do not rise to the level of scientific evidence. Marijuana is available from the Federal Government to those researchers who obtain proper licensure. However, the evidence suggests that only small numbers of researchers and physicians have obtained marijuana for this purpose, and that some research programs sponsored by states had trouble getting physicians to participate. The vast majority of physicians do not accept marijuana as having a medical use. Marijuana is not recognized as medicine in generally accepted pharmacopeia, medical references, journals or textbooks. As evidenced by expert physician testimony and the statements of many professional medical and research organizations, marijuana is not accepted by organized medicine or a substantial segment of the physician population.

The administrative law judge's conclusion that a "respectable minority" of physicians is all that is necessary to establish accepted medical use in treatment in the United States is preposterous. By placing a substance in Schedule II, the Administrator, and through him, the Federal Government, establishes a national standard for drug use. Using the same criteria as medical malpractice cases to determine a national standard of medical acceptance is untenable. It must be recognized that in every profession, including the medical and scientific community, there are those that deviate from the accepted practices of the profession. These deviations may be the beginning of new revolutionary treatments or they may be rejected as quackery. The opinions of those few physicians and scientists are not sufficient to create a finding of national acceptance. The Administrator feels that, in light of the potential risks of declaring a drug has an accepted medical use in treatment in the United States, he must adhere to the strict standard that was established in the MDMA proceeding. It is clear that the evidence conclusively demonstrates that marijuana does not have an accepted medical use in treatment in the United States or an accepted medical use with severe restrictions.

The Administrator's standard for "accepted safety for use . . . under medical supervision" was also stated in the second MDMA final rule published on February 22, 1988. The tests for determining accepted safety of a drug were stated as follows: "The first requirement in determining safety of a substance is that the chemistry of the substance must be known and reproducible. The next step is to conduct animal toxicity studies to show that the substance will not produce irreversible harm to organs at proposed human doses. Limited clinical trials may then be initiated, but they must be carefully controlled so that adverse effects can be monitored and studies terminated if necessary . . . safety in humans is evaluated as a risk/benefit ratio for a specific use."

It is clear that marijuana cannot meet the criteria set forth above for safety under medical supervision. The chemistry of marijuana is not known and reproducible. The record supports a finding that marijuana plant material is variable from plant to plant. The quantities of the active constituents, the cannabinoids, vary considerably. In addition, the actions and potential risks of several of the cannabinoids have not been studied. Animal toxicity studies with marijuana show several potential risks or hazards of marijuana use, especially when the marijuana is smoked. These hazards have not been evaluated against the benefit or effectiveness of the drug. This is due, in great part, to the fact that marijuana's effectiveness in treating specific medical conditions has not been established by reliable scientific studies. Since a proper risk/benefit ratio cannot be made, the safety of marijuana for medical use cannot be demonstrated. Such lack of information is the basis for the majority of the medical and scientific community, and the Food and Drug Administration, concluding that marijuana does not have "accepted safety for use . . . under medical supervision." The Administrator, therefore, concludes that marijuana lacks "accepted safety for use . . . under medical supervision."

As a final note, the Administrator expresses his displeasure at the misleading accusations and conclusions leveled at the Government and communicated to the public by the pro-marijuana parties, specifically NORML and ACT. These two organizations have falsely raised the expectations of many seriously ill persons by claiming that marijuana has medical usefulness in treating emesis, glaucoma, spasticity and other illnesses. These statements have probably caused many people with serious diseases to experiment with marijuana to the detriment of their own health, without proper medical supervision, and without knowing about the serious side effects which smoking or ingesting marijuana may cause. These are not the Dark Ages. The Congress, as well as the medical community, has accepted that drugs should not be available to the public unless they are found by scientific studies to be effective and safe. To do otherwise is to jeopardize the American public, and take advantage of desperately ill people who will try anything to alleviate their suffering. The Administrator strongly urges the American public not to experiment with a potentially dangerous, mind-altering drug such as marijuana in an attempt to treat a serious illness or condition. Scientific and medical researchers are working tirelessly to develop treatments and drugs to treat these diseases and conditions. As expressed in the record, treatments for emesis (nausea and vomiting) associated with cancer chemotherapy have advanced significantly in the last ten years. Recent studies have shown an over 90 percent rate of effectiveness for the new antiemetic drugs and therapies. NORML and ACT have attempted to perpetrate a dangerous and cruel hoax on the American public by claiming marijuana has currently accepted medical uses. The Administrator again emphasizes that there is insufficient medical and scientific evidence to support a conclusion that marijuana has an accepted medical use for treatment of any condition, or that it is safe for use, even under medical supervision.

Based upon the evidence in the record and the conclusions discussed previously, the Administrator, under the authority vested in the Attorney General by section 201(a) of the Controlled Substances Act and delegated to the Administrator of the Drug Enforcement Administration by regulations of the Department of Justice, 28 CFR 0.100(b), hereby orders that marijuana remain a Schedule I controlled substance as listed in 21 CFR 1308.11(d)(14).

Alliance for Cannabis Therapeutics v. Drug Enforcement Administration

United States Court of Appeals for the District of Columbia
930 F.2d 936 (1991)

Silberman, J.

This is a petition for review of a final order of the Administrator of the Drug Enforcement Administration (DEA). The order maintains the classification of marijuana as a narcotic drug under Schedule I of the Controlled Substances Act. Petitioners, Alliance for Cannabis Therapeutics (ACT) and National Organization for the Reform of Marijuana Laws (NORML), who claim that marijuana should be reclassified in Schedule II, argue that the DEA Administrator's decision rests on an improper application of the statutory standards and an incorrect determination that petitioners failed to meet them. We think that the Administrator's interpretation of the statute was in the main acceptable, but he appears to have relied on several factors that are unreasonable because logically impossible to satisfy; therefore, we remand.

The Controlled Substances Act (CSA) is a comprehensive regulatory measure that divides the universe of hazardous drugs into five different categories of substances (so-called schedules), which determine the severity of restrictions on doctors' and patients' access to controlled drugs.[1] Drugs can be "re-scheduled" or "de-scheduled" only if the DEA makes certain statutorily-mandated findings. Schedule I drugs are subject to the most severe controls and give rise to the harshest penalties for violations of these controls; they are deemed to be the most dangerous substances, possessing no redeeming value as medicines.

[O]ne salient concept distinguishing the two schedules is whether a drug has "no currently accepted medical use in treatment in the United States." This case turns on the appropriate definition and application of that phrase.

The Administrator is guided by a set of statutory factors in making a classification decision as to which schedule is appropriate. And two of those factors bear on the Administrator's definition of generally accepted medical use—the "scientific evidence of [the drug's] pharmacological effect, if known" and "the state of current scientific knowledge regarding the drug or other substance."

Petitioners argued below that marijuana has medical uses for the treatment of cancer, glaucoma, and other diseases and therefore it cannot properly be maintained in Schedule I. The ALJ agreed with petitioners and found, based on testimony of a number of physicians and patients, that a "respectable minority" of American physicians accept those uses, which was sufficient, according to the ALJ, to say that marijuana had a currently accepted medical use. The Administrator rejected the ALJ's recommendation, however, determining that the phrase "currently accepted medical use" required a greater showing than that a minority—even a respectable minority—of physicians accept the usefulness of a given drug.

In a prior proceeding, the Administrator had employed an additional eight factor test to further elaborate the characteristics of a drug that he thought had a "currently accepted medical use": "(1) Scientifically determined and accepted knowledge of its chemistry; (2) The toxicology and pharmacology of the substance in animals; (3) Establishment of its effectiveness in humans through scientifically designed clinical trials; (4) General availability of the substance and information regarding the substance and its use; (5) Recognition of its clinical use in generally accepted pharmacopeia, medical references, journals or textbooks; (6) Specific indications for the treatment of recognized disorders; (7) Recognition of the use of the substance by organizations or associations of physicians; and (8) Recognition and use of the substance by a substantial segment of the medical practitioners in the United States."

---

1. When it enacted the CSA in 1970, Congress placed marijuana in Schedule I. From that time, petitioners have indefatigably sought to obtain a change in marijuana's classification. The long and checkered history of this proceeding and an explanation of the complex statutory scheme are detailed in *National Org. for the Reform of Marijuana Laws v. Ingersoll*, 497 F.2d 654 (D.C. Cir. 1974); *National Org. for the Reform of Marijuana Laws v. Drug Enforcement Admin.*, 559 F.2d 735 (D.C. Cir. 1977).

The Administrator, in his opinion in this proceeding, reaffirmed this eight factor test. Most important to the Administrator was his conclusion that "the chemistry, toxicology, and pharmacology of marijuana is not established" and its effectiveness has not been documented in humans with scientifically-designed clinical trials (such as double-blind studies where neither the patient nor the observer knows who received the placebo and who received the actual substance). Therefore, "the vast majority of physicians do not accept marijuana as having a medical use" and it is "not recognized as medicine in generally accepted pharmacopoeia, medical references, journals, or textbooks." The Administrator exercised with a vengeance his prerogative under *Universal Camera Corp. v. NLRB,* 340 U.S. 474 (1951), to reject the ALJ's recommended decision, labelling the ALJ's standard for "currently accepted medical use" as use by a "respectable minority" of physicians as "preposterous."

The petitioners renew their argument that the Administrator unreasonably rejected the evidence they presented (largely anecdotal) that a number of physicians believe marijuana is medically useful and, instead, improperly predicated his determination on the absence of demonstrated scientific evidence that the drug is medically useful and safe. The difficulty we find in petitioners' argument is that neither the statute nor its legislative history precisely defines the term "currently accepted medical use"; therefore, we are obliged to defer to the Administrator's interpretation of that phrase if reasonable. And since Congress required the Administrator, in making scheduling determinations with respect to any drug, to consider the "scientific evidence of [the drug's] pharmacological effect" and the "state of current scientific knowledge regarding the drug," we do not see how it can be thought an unreasonable application of the statutory phrase to emphasize the lack of exact scientific knowledge as to the chemical effects of the drug's elements. Perhaps if virtually all doctors in the United States were vociferous in their espousal of marijuana for medical treatment—notwithstanding scientific uncertainties—the Administrator's position would be more vulnerable. But that is not the case; the ALJ's finding (not contested by the petitioners) is only that a "respectable minority" take that position. The determination as to how much weight to place on scientific uncertainties as opposed to anecdotal evidence in applying the statutory phrase "currently accepted medical uses," then, is very much a policy judgment which we have no authority to challenge. We certainly have no grounds, on this record, to dispute the Administrator's premise that without much more complete scientific data American physicians will not "accept" marijuana.

Petitioners, however, mount something of a flanking attack on that premise. They assert that the Administrator's eight factor test, which emphasizes, in factors 1, 2 and 3, scientific knowledge of the chemistry of the drug and its effectiveness in humans established through scientifically-designed clinical trials, is improperly drawn from the Food, Drug and Cosmetic Act (administered by the Food and Drug Administration) and not the Controlled Substances Act which the Administrator is authorized to apply. The First Circuit in *Grinspoon v. Drug Enforcement Administration,* 828 F.2d 881, 891–92 (1st Cir. 1987), upon which petitioners rely, had held that earlier criteria the Administrator had employed to define "currently accepted medical use" were contrary to the statute because they were a carbon copy of those used by the FDA in licensing new drugs. The present criteria, it is argued, duplicate a number of those original criteria. But the criteria challenged in *Grinspoon* included several elements, such as the availability of patent information or FDA-required labelling, which were necessary only to market the drug in interstate commerce. These criteria are clearly relevant to the FDA's mission, but not to the DEA's. The First Circuit never suggested the DEA Administrator was foreclosed from incorporating and relying on those standards employed by the FDA that are relevant to the pharmaceutical qualities of the drug. The court merely held that while FDA approval is sufficient to establish the existence of an accepted medical use, the converse is not true—that absent FDA approval, commonly accepted medical use cannot be proven. Nor can we conceive of a reason the Administrator should be barred from employing notions developed by a sister agency insofar as those notions serve the missions of both agencies.

Which brings us to the most troubling part of the Administrator's decision—the part which we think obliges us to order a remand. Petitioners, almost in passing, point out that three of the factors in the Administrator's eight-factor test appear impossible to fulfill and thus must be regarded as arbitrary and capricious. Impossible requirements imposed by an agency are perforce unreasonable[.] These three factors are: "(4) General availability of the substance and information regarding the substance and its use; (5) Recognition of its clinical use in generally accepted pharmacopeia, medical references, journals or textbooks; (8) Recognition and use of the substance by a substantial segment of the medical practitioners in the United States."

Petitioners argue that one cannot logically show that a drug enjoys general "availability" or "use" by a substantial segment of medical practitioners if the drug remains in Schedule I. One of the very purposes in placing a drug in Schedule I is to raise significant barriers to prevent doctors from obtaining the drugs too easily. DEA regulations require doctors who wish to use such drugs to submit a scientific research protocol to the FDA for approval and permit use only in accordance with the protocol. And the FDA insists that a developed scientific study program be presented in order to gain approval of the protocol. The DEA regulations further impose mandatory registration with the DEA and mandatory record-keeping and safe-keeping requirements, presenting additional barriers to widespread use. We are therefore hard-pressed to understand how one could show that *any* Schedule I drug was in general use or generally available. We are also concerned that the fifth factor "recognition of [a drug's] clinical use in generally accepted pharmacopeia, medical references, journals, or textbooks" might be subject to the same objection. Petitioners assert that if a drug is not widely prescribed—regardless of its safety or use—it will not appear in a pharmaceutical listing of medically useful drugs. Since the government did not respond clearly to the argument, we are left in doubt as to the argument's validity. Under these circumstances, we think the appropriate course is to remand to the agency for an explanation as to how all three of these factors were utilized by the Administrator in reaching his decision.[4]

To be sure, the Administrator did not explicitly rely on factors (4) and (8) in the analytical portion of his opinion (he did say "marijuana is not recognized as a medicine in generally accepted pharmacopeia, medical references, and textbooks," indicating his reliance on factor (5)). But since he did reaffirm the eight criteria's applicability to this case, we simply cannot be certain what role, if any, factors (4) and (8) played in his decision. Under our governing cases, we must remand for the requisite explanation.

For the foregoing reasons, the case is remanded.

It is so ordered.

On remand, the Administrator discarded his eight-part test in favor of the five-part test described above in the introduction to this trio of decisions. As noted there, the five-factor test for determining whether a controlled substance has a currently accepted medical use requires that "(1) The drug's chemistry must be known and reproducible; (2) there must be adequate safety studies; (3) there must be adequate and well-controlled studies proving efficacy; (4) the drug must be accepted by qualified experts; and (5) the scientific evidence must be widely available." *Alliance for Cannabis Therapeutics v. Drug Enforcement Administration*, 15 F.3d 1131, 1135 (1994). The DEA continues to apply this test to determine whether or not a substance has an accepted medical use within the meaning of the CSA.

The DEA's most recent rejection of a petition to reschedule marijuana came in 2016. The agency's reasoning on the question of medical use in its 2016 denial was particularly noteworthy for its suggestion that the marijuana plant may never be able to meet the DEA's current five-factor definition for accepted medical use. This is because the first factor requires that a drug's chemistry be known and reproducible. The DEA left open the possibility that a specific marijuana plant strain may one day be able to meet this test, however. As explained in the DEA's denial of the rescheduling petition:

> [T]he chemistry of marijuana, as defined in the petition, is not reproducible in terms of creating a standardized dose. The petition defines marijuana as including all Cannabis cultivated strains. Different marijuana samples derived from various cultivated strains may have very different chemical constituents including delta9-THC and other cannabinoids. As a consequence, marijuana products from different strains will have different safety, biological, pharmacological, and toxicological profiles. Thus, when

---

4. Petitioners also quarrel with the Administrator's decision that marijuana lacks "accepted safety for use." Since the Administrator based this determination on his decision that no medical uses are possible (and thus any use lacks "accepted safety"), we do not see that "safety" issue as raising a separate analytical question.

> considering all Cannabis strains together, because of the varying chemical constituents, reproducing consistent standardized doses is not possible. Additionally, smoking marijuana currently has not been shown to allow delivery of consistent and reproducible doses. However, if a specific Cannabis strain is grown and processed under strictly controlled conditions, the plant chemistry may be kept consistent enough to produce reproducible and standardized doses.

Denial of Petition to Initiate Proceedings To Reschedule Marijuana, 81 Fed. Reg. 53688, 53700 (2016).

Although NORML's 1972 rescheduling petition ultimately led the DEA to adopt a definitive test for the CSA's accepted medical use factor, the CSA's other two criteria—potential for abuse and safety and dependence—remain comparatively imprecise.

The Safety and Dependence Finding: The safety and dependence finding is perhaps the most puzzling of the CSA's three scheduling criteria. This finding relates to safety or dependence, depending on the Schedule. Under Schedule I, the third criterion is that "[t]here is a lack of accepted safety for use of the drug or other substance under medical supervision." By contrast, the third criterion in Schedules II through V focuses on the likelihood that abuse of a drug may lead to dependence. Schedule II's third finding provides that "[a]buse of the drug or other substances may lead to severe psychological or physical dependence." Schedules III, IV, and V are pegged to a progressively lower dependence finding. 21 U.S.C. § 812(b).

Though the text of the CSA places all three findings on equal footing, as footnote four of the D.C. Circuit's *Alliance for Cannabis Therapeutics* decision excerpted immediately above suggests, the third criterion is often treated as an afterthought in scheduling decisions. Indeed, the DEA's current position with respect to Schedule I substances appears to be that the third scheduling finding is not, in fact, an independent requirement at all. As DEA Administrator Robert C. Bonner concluded in his 1992 decision denying NORML's petition to reschedule marijuana following the D.C. Circuit's remand:

> It must be emphasized that while the existence of adequate safety tests is a separate analytical question, the ultimate determination of whether a drug is safe for a specific use is not a distinct issue. Safety and effectiveness are inextricably linked in a risks-benefits calculation. A determination that a drug is ineffective is tantamount to a determination that it is unsafe.
>
> The scheduling criteria of the Controlled Substances Act appear to treat the lack of medical use and lack of safety as separate considerations. Prior rulings of this Agency purported to treat safety as a distinct factor. In retrospect, this is inconsistent with scientific reality. Safety cannot be treated as a separate analytical question.

57 Fed. Reg. 10499 (1992). The "prior rulings" referenced by Bonner in this quote included his predecessor John Lawn's 1988 decision excerpted above.

The Potential for Abuse Finding: By the time NORML's rescheduling petition was before Administrative Law Judge Francis Young in 1988, the group had dropped its request to move marijuana below Schedule II and stipulated that marijuana has a "high potential for abuse and that abuse of the marijuana plant may lead to severe psychological or physical dependence."

As discussed in *Grinspoon*, excerpted above, the DEA has traditionally relied on four factors outlined in the CSA's legislative history to guide its scheduling findings regarding potential for abuse. The House Committee on Interstate and Foreign Commerce report accompanying the bill that became the CSA provided "that the Administrator may determine a substance has a potential for abuse if:

> (1) There is evidence that individuals are taking the drug or drugs containing such a substance in amounts sufficient to create a hazard to their health or to the safety of other individuals or of the community; *or*
>
> (2) There is significant diversion of the drug or drugs containing such a substance from legitimate drug channels; *or*
>
> (3) Individuals are taking the drug or drugs containing such a substance on their own initiative rather than on the basis of medical advice from a practitioner licensed by law to administer such drugs in the course of his professional practice; *or*
>
> (4) The drug or drugs containing such a substance are new drugs so related in their action to a drug or drugs already listed as having a potential for abuse to make it likely that the drug will have the same potentiality for abuse as such drugs, thus making it reasonable to assume that there may be significant diversions from legitimate channels, significant use contrary to or without medical advice, or that it has a substantial capability of creating hazards to the health of the user or to the safety of the community."

Grinspoon v. Drug Enforcement Admin., 828 F.2d 881, 893 (1st Cir. 1987) (quoting H.R. Rep. No. 91–1444 (1970), reprinted in 1971 U.S.C.C.A.N. 4566, 4601).

These factors give the DEA a great deal of flexibility in determining the abuse potential for any given substance. There is perhaps no better example of this than the classification of synthetic THC in comparison to marijuana.

Dronabinol, a synthetic THC pill marketed under the trade name Marinol, is currently a Schedule III drug, meaning that the DEA has determined the substance has both a currently accepted medical use and a "potential for abuse less than the drugs or other substances in schedules I and II."

How can it be that marijuana is in Schedule I, meaning it has the highest potential for abuse in the DEA's eyes, while a version of synthetic THC is in Schedule III? The relatively small number of recreational users of Marinol has been the decisive consideration.

In rejecting marijuana rescheduling petitions, the DEA has consistently emphasized the large number of marijuana users in the United States. In the DEA's 2011 denial of a petition to reschedule marijuana, for example, the agency found: "The large number of individuals using marijuana on a regular basis, its widespread use, and the vast amount of marijuana that is available for illicit use are indicative of the high abuse potential for marijuana." *Denial of petition to initiate proceedings to reschedule marijuana*, 76 Fed. Reg. 40552 (2011)

By contrast, the DEA has concluded that because few people use Marinol recreationally, it has a lower abuse potential than marijuana. In 1995, the DEA placed Marinol in Schedule III (from 1986 to 1995, it had been in Schedule II). With respect to Marinol's abuse potential, the DEA acknowledged that "[t]here are few scientific studies that directly evaluate the pharmacologeutical and behavioral effects of the product Marinol to indicate that there are differences in its abuse liability compared to oral THC. Nevertheless, there is little evidence of actual abuse of Marinol, despite modest annual increases in the total number of prescriptions written. Although excessive use of Marinol may result in the development of psychological dependence, there has been no evidence of such use. The scientific data reviewed to date and the minimal evidence of actual abuse and trafficking support the transfer of dronabinol to Schedule III of the CSA." 63 Fed. Reg. 59751 (1998).

The Uniform Controlled Substances Act: The federal Controlled Substances Act only governs the classification and control of drugs under federal law. States are free to adopt their own regulatory schemes for controlled substances. By and large, however, the state regulatory structure governing controlled substances mirrors federal law. This is because of the Uniform Controlled Substances Act (UCSA), which was originally drafted in 1970 by the National Conference of Commissioners on Uniform State Laws.

The UCSA was designed to maintain consistency between state and federal law and the Commissioners have promulgated revisions to the UCSA in 1990 and 1994 to account for changes in federal law. As noted by the *Grinspoon* court in footnote 9, the vast majority of states have adopted a version of the UCSA. While the UCSA serves as the foundation for controlled substances laws across the country, each state has modified the UCSA in various ways. For example, while many states follow the UCSA in making distribution and possession with the intent to distribute a crime, others criminalize "sale" or possession for "sale." *See* Elaine M. Chiu, *The Challenge of Motive in the Criminal Law*, 8 Buff. Crim. L. R. 653, 699–700 (2005). The UCSA has intentionally left some issues to the discretion of the states. Perhaps most notably, the UCSA does not prescribe specific sentences for drug offenders. As a result, sentences between states for the same offense can vary widely.

With respect to the classification of controlled substances, the UCSA has been especially influential. The UCSA is built around the same five-schedule structure as the federal CSA, classifying substances on the basis of their potential for abuse (and addiction) and usefulness in medical treatment. But uniformity in the classification scheme does not always translate into uniformity regarding whether a specific substance has been scheduled (and, if so, which schedule it falls under) at any given time. This is because the scheduling process is not self-executing; scheduling a substance requires administrative action. *See, e.g., Ruiz-Vidal v. Gonzales*, 473 F.3d 1072, 1078 (9th Cir. 2007) ("We note that California law regulates the possession and sale of numerous substances that are not regulated by the CSA. For instance, the possession of apomorphine is specifically excluded from Schedule II of the CSA, but California's Schedule II specifically includes it.").

To account for this problem, the UCSA provides for a "short-form" scheduling process in addition to the standard scheduling procedure. The short form method allows states to incorporate DEA scheduling decisions into their own regulatory scheme in a streamlined fashion. A number of state courts have struck down this aspect of the UCSA, however, on the grounds that their legislatures cannot delegate "legislative power to a federal agency, nor to Congress." *Louisiana v. Rodriguez*, 379 So. 2d 1084, 1087 (1980). As a result, the process for scheduling or rescheduling a substance can vary from state to state. But the UCSA's substantive criteria for scheduling decisions and the five-schedule classification scheme has been adopted in almost every state.

C. Constitutional Challenges to Scheduling Under the Controlled Substances Act

The Drug Enforcement Administration enjoys a great deal of discretion over scheduling determinations. Over the years, some litigants have sought to challenge the CSA's classification system on constitutional grounds, particularly as it has been applied to marijuana. Courts have consistently rejected these efforts. In the next case, for example, the National Organization for the Reform of Marijuana Laws argued the CSA's classification of marijuana as a Schedule I substance was so irrational that it should be declared unconstitutional. The court applied the familiar rational basis test to reject NORML's constitutional challenge. As a matter of constitutional law, the decision is unexceptional. The case does, however, provide a useful vehicle for thinking more about how substances of abuse should be classified as a matter of policy.

The National Organization for the Reform of Marijuana Laws (NORML) v. Bell

United States District Court for the District of Columbia
488 F. Supp. 123 (1980)

Tamm, J.

In this action, the National Organization for The Reform of Marijuana Laws (NORML or plaintiff) challenges the provisions of the Controlled Substances Act, 21 U.S.C. §§ 801–904 (CSA or Act), that prohibit the private possession and use of marijuana.

NORML filed this action October 10, 1973, seeking a declaratory judgment that the CSA and District of Columbia Uniform Narcotic Drug Act are unconstitutional in prohibiting the private possession and use of marijuana and requesting a permanent injunction enjoining enforcement of those statutes. This court stayed the proceedings for a year while NORML tried to obtain administrative relief through a proceeding to reclassify marijuana.[3] After the stay was vacated, the parties battled over preliminary motions for two years. Finally, in June 1978, this court heard five days of evidentiary hearings. Both sides presented live and documentary evidence concerning the effects of marijuana. Shortly thereafter, the parties submitted proposed findings of fact on the effects of marijuana and legal arguments for the court's consideration.

Congress passed the Comprehensive Drug Abuse Prevention and Control Act of 1970 (DAPCA), 21 U.S.C. §§ 801–966 (1976), to fight this nation's growing drug problem. The act was designed to "deal in a comprehensive fashion with the growing menace of drug abuse in the United States (1) through providing authority for increased efforts in drug abuse prevention and rehabilitation of users, (2) through providing more effective means for law enforcement aspects of drug abuse prevention and control, and (3) by providing for an overall balanced scheme of criminal penalties for offenses involving drugs." H.R. Rep. No. 1444, 91st Cong., 2d Sess. 1 (hereinafter cited as 1970 House Report). It ended the patchwork federal effort against drug abuse and signaled a national commitment to deal with this problem by committing federal funds for rehabilitation programs.[4]

In addition to the rehabilitation programs, DAPCA also revised completely the federal drug laws dealing with drug control.[5] Title II, called the Controlled Substances Act (CSA), establishes five schedules for classifying controlled substances according to specified criteria. Two criteria—the potential for abuse and the medical applications of a drug—are the major bases for classification, along with certain

---

3. On May 18, 1972, NORML filed an application with the Attorney General to remove marijuana from control under the CSA or, in the alternative, to reclassify the drug in a different schedule. This endeavor continues today. The Drug Enforcement Administration (DEA) twice rejected these efforts at reclassification, citing American treaty obligations under the Single Convention on Narcotic Drugs. The United States Court of Appeals for the District of Columbia Circuit reversed these determinations. *NORML v. DEA*, 559 F.2d 735 (D.C. Cir. 1977); *NORML v. Ingersoll*, 497 F.2d 654 (D.C. Cir. 1974). In the DEA case, the court directed the DEA to "refer the NORML petition to the Secretary of HEW for medical and scientific findings and recommendations for rescheduling, consistent with the requirements of the Single Convention." On remand the DEA again declined to reclassify marijuana. The Administrator of the DEA followed the recommendation of the Secretary of HEW that marijuana remain in Schedule I. NORML is appealing this ruling to the District of Columbia Circuit. NORML v. DEA, No. 79-1660 (D.C.Cir., filed June 27, 1979).

4. Title I of DAPCA deals with the rehabilitation of drug abusers and authorizes federal funds for treatment centers and drug abuse programs. Title II establishes controls and registration requirements for drugs, while Title III regulates the import and export of controlled substances.

5. Previous federal laws dealing with drug abuse included the Harrison Act, ch. 1, 38 Stat. 785 (1914) (repealed 1970), and the Marihuana Tax Act, ch. 553, 50 Stat. 551 (1937) (repealed 1970). For a discussion of federal efforts against drug abuse before passage of DAPCA, see Bonnie and Whitebread, The Forbidden Fruit and the Tree of Knowledge: An Inquiry into the Legal History of American Marijuana Prohibition, 56 Va.L.Rev. 976 (1970).

social and medical information. Congress, on the basis of information gathered from extensive hearings, made the initial classifications. Recognizing that scientific information concerning controlled substances would change, Congress empowered the Attorney General to hear petitions for the reclassification or removal of drugs from the schedules.

Marijuana (cannabis sativa L.) is a psychoactive drug made of the leaves, flowers, and stems of the Indian Hemp plant. It derives its psychoactive properties from delta-9-tetrahydrocannabinol (THC), which exists in varying concentrations in the plant, depending on its origin, growing conditions, and cultivation. The concentration of THC within the sections of the plant also varies widely. The resin contains the greatest concentration of THC; smaller amounts are found, respectively, in the flowers, the leaves, and the stems. The most potent form of the drug, hashish, is prepared from the resins of the flowers and contains 5–12% THC. Marijuana generally found in the United States is weaker, with around 1% THC.

The drug produces a number of physiological and psychological effects. The short-term physiological effects have been well documented. They are reddening of the whites of the eye, dryness in the mouth, increased pulse rate, and impaired motor responses. The short-term psychological effects are equally well known:

> At low, usual "social" doses, the intoxicated individual may experience an increased sense of well-being; initial restlessness and hilarity followed by a dreamy, carefree state of relaxation; alteration of sensory perceptions including expansion of space and time; and a more vivid sense of touch, sight, smell, taste, and sound; a feeling of hunger, especially a craving for sweets; and subtle changes in thought formation and expression. To an unknowing observer, an individual in this state of consciousness would not appear noticeably different from his normal state.
>
> At higher, moderate doses, these same reactions are intensified. . . . The individual may experience rapidly changing emotions, changing sensory imagery, dulling of attention, more altered thought formation and expression such as fragmented thought, flight of ideas, impaired immediate memory, disturbed associations, altered sense of self-identity and, to some, a perceived feeling of enhanced insight.
>
> At very high doses, psychotomimetic phenomena may be experienced. These include distortions of body image, loss of personal identity, sensory and mental illusions, fantasies and hallucinations.

The intensity of these reactions depends on dosage, method of use, metabolism, attitude and setting, tolerance, duration of use, and pattern of use.

Experiences under marijuana intoxication are usually pleasurable, but negative reactions are not infrequent. These negative reactions include distortion of body image, depersonalization, acute panic anxiety reaction, nausea, and, more rarely, psychosis. These reactions may be caused or exaggerated by pre-existing psychological problems.

Studies have dispelled many of the myths about the drug: marijuana is not a narcotic, not addictive,[15] and generally not a stepping-stone to other, more serious drugs. Furthermore, it causes neither aggressive behavior nor insanity.

Despite these findings, questions about long-term use remain. Studies have indicated that marijuana may affect adversely the lungs and the endocrine, the immunity, and the cardiovascular systems. Some of these studies are disputed, but an examination of these adverse findings illustrates the important questions still remaining about marijuana use.

In addition to these problems, other tests have found negative aspects to marijuana use. Amotivational difficulties and changes in brain cells, chromosomes, and cell metabolism have been noted in various studies. These findings have not been corroborated, however, and other research has reached contradictory conclusions. As with the other areas, these questions demand further scientific study to determine conclusively the long-term effects of marijuana. Although we now know that marijuana is not the "killer" drug, as branded in the past, its long-term effects are still an open question and must be approached as unresolved. These lingering questions must be kept in mind in considering the legal issues.

NORML contends that the CSA violates the equal protection component of the due process clause. First, it argues that the classification of marijuana, a relatively harmless drug, as a controlled substance violates equal protection. Second, NORML believes that, even if marijuana may be controlled, its classification as a Schedule I drug is infirm: placement in Schedule I is both underinclusive in failing to include as a controlled substance drugs such as alcohol and nicotine, which satisfy Schedule I criteria, and overinclusive for establishing the same penalties for possession of marijuana as for all other controlled substances and for including marijuana in Schedule I with the more dangerous narcotics and opiates. For the reasons stated below, this court rejects these contentions.

Legislation that does not affect a "fundamental" right or a "suspect" class need only bear a rational relationship to a legitimate state interest. This standard of judicial review gives legislatures wide discretion and permits them to attack problems in any rational manner. The classification will be upheld unless "the varying treatment of different groups or persons is so unrelated to the achievement of any combination of legitimate purposes that (a court) can only conclude that the legislature's actions were irrational."

The inclusion of marijuana as a controlled substance under the CSA easily satisfies this deferential rationality standard. Congress gave the CSA provisions concerning marijuana considerable attention. It recognized that much of the information regarding marijuana was inaccurate and that bias and ignorance had perpetuated many myths about the consequences and dangers of marijuana use. Despite all the

15. Marijuana is not physically addictive, but some studies have found that long-term users develop a psychological addiction.

concern over the drug, few reliable scientific studies existed that could give accurate information to the legislators. Representative Cohelan acknowledged this lack of accurate information on marijuana during the House discussion of the bill: "Much remains to be done to find out the effects of marijuana. Assertions from both sides are not hard to find, but there is precious little hard clinical data on this subject." Unsure of marijuana's effects, Congress placed marijuana in Schedule I, with its program of strict controls, until it could obtain more scientific information on the drug's effects. In so doing, Congress followed the recommendation of the Department of Health, Education, and Welfare, which had suggested classification in Schedule I until further tests could be completed.[32]

Inclusion of marijuana as a controlled substance in 1970 certainly was rational. The information then available indicated that marijuana might well have substantial detrimental effects, and Congress thus reasonably could decide to include the drug as a controlled substance rather than leave it unregulated. NORML argues that, although classification of marijuana as a controlled substance in 1970 might have been rational, the scientific evidence available today establishes that "private possession and use of marijuana by adults (do) not pose any significant danger to the public health, safety or welfare." NORML therefore asserts the classification of marijuana as a controlled substance is no longer rational and invokes *United States v. Carolene Products Co.*, 304 U.S. 144, 153 (1938): "the constitutionality of a statute predicated upon a particular state of facts may be challenged by a showing to the court that those facts have ceased to exist."

The record, however, is not so clear as NORML contends. Experts still strongly disagree about the safety of marijuana, and its long-term effects remain an open question. Studies indicate that marijuana may impair the circulatory, the endocrine, and the immunity systems of the body, alter chromosomes, and change cell metabolism. Although many dispute these findings, this contradictory evidence demonstrates that important questions about marijuana use persist.

Given the continuing debate over marijuana, this court must defer to the legislature's judgments on disputed factual issues. The classification need not change continually as more information becomes available. Congressional action must be upheld as long as a rational basis still exists for the classification. The continuing questions about marijuana and its effects make the classification rational.

In a related equal protection challenge, NORML argues that classification of marijuana in Schedule I is irrational as being both underinclusive and overinclusive. The CSA does not regulate alcohol and tobacco, which are more harmful than marijuana, and it places marijuana in the same schedule with such dangerous

32. In an effort to secure more information about marijuana, Congress established the Commission on Marihuana and Drug Abuse to study marijuana use and its effects. The Commission, headed by Governor Raymond P. Shafer, issued its report, Marihuana: A Signal of Misunderstanding, in 1972. The Commission recommended that federal and state penalties for private possession of marijuana be eliminated and that governmental efforts should focus on discouraging marijuana use.

substances as heroin and other narcotics. Thus, even if the classification of marijuana as a controlled substance is rational, the plaintiff believes that the legislation nonetheless is unconstitutional because marijuana's treatment within the Act is irrational in relation to other controlled substances.

"Underinclusive classifications do not include all who are similarly situated with respect to a rule, and thereby burden less than would be logical to achieve the intended government end." L. Tribe, American Constitutional Law, § 16-4, at 997 (1978). To be successful in a challenge based on underinclusiveness, plaintiff must show that the governmental choice is "clearly wrong, a display of arbitrary power, not an exercise of judgment[.]" *Mathews v. de Castro,* 429 U.S. 181, 185 (1976). Few challengers can sustain such a heavy burden of proof. Courts have recognized the very real difficulties under which legislatures operate difficulties that arise due to the nature of the legislative process and the society that legislation attempts to reshape. As Professor Tribe has explained: "underinclusive" or "piecemeal legislation is a pragmatic means of effecting needed reforms, where a demand for completeness may lead to total paralysis. . . ."

Legislatures have wide discretion in attacking social ills. "A State may direct its law against what it deems the evil as it actually exists without covering the whole field of possible abuses, and it may do so none the less that the forbidden act does not differ in kind from those that are allowed." *Hughes v. Superior Court,* 339 U.S. 460, 468 (1950). Failure to address a certain problem in an otherwise comprehensive legislative scheme is not fatal to the legislative plan.

Given this policy of legislative freedom in confronting social problems, the exclusion of alcohol and tobacco from the CSA does not render the scheme unconstitutional. Different legislative schemes control the sale and distribution of alcohol and tobacco. The specific exemption of alcohol and tobacco from the provisions of the CSA, 21 U.S.C. § 802(6), reflects Congress's view that other regulatory schemes are more appropriate for alcohol and tobacco.[36] That alcohol and tobacco may have adverse effects on health does not mean the CSA is the only proper means of regulating these drugs, nor does it mean that marijuana should be treated identically. As a Presidential commission on drug abuse pointed out, "While alcoholism constitutes a major social problem, surely it is not valid to justify the adoption of a new abuse on the basis that it is no worse than a presently existing one. The result could only be added social damage from a new source." Congress, having the power to deal with drug abuse in any reasonable manner, decided to exclude alcohol and tobacco from the CSA. This court will not disturb that judgment.

---

36. In discussing the regulation of alcohol and tobacco, one district court observed: "The legislative judgment concerning alcohol and nicotine may well have taken into account the degree to which their dangers are known, the adverse consequences of prohibition, and the economic significance of their production. Whether such factors should lead to similar judgments concerning marijuana is within legislative discretion." *United States v. Maiden,* 355 F. Supp. 743, 747–48 (D .Conn.1973).

A law also may be challenged for including within a prohibited class an item that does not rationally belong with the other members of that class. NORML once again draws its support from the *Carolene Products* decision: "[T]he constitutionality of a statute, valid on its face, may be assailed by proof of facts tending to show that the statute as applied to a particular article is without support in reason because the article, although within the (particular) class, is so different from others of the class as to be without the reason for the prohibition." *United States v. Carolene Products Co.*, 304 U.S. at 153–54. The plaintiff here argues marijuana's classification in Schedule I is impermissible because the drug does not fit the statutory criteria for placement in that schedule.

NORML argues that marijuana does not belong in Schedule I, for it does not satisfy that schedule's statutory criteria high potential for abuse, no medically accepted use, and no safe use of the drug even under medical supervision. The Government disagrees and contends that all three criteria are met. It claims the drug has a "high potential for abuse," in that millions of Americans use marijuana on their own initiative rather than on the basis of medical advice. While tests have indicated that marijuana may have therapeutic uses in the treatment of glaucoma and cancer, the Food and Drug Administration does not currently accept it for any form of medical treatment. Finally, the Government claims that marijuana cannot be used safely due to the differing concentrations of THC in cannabis.

Even assuming, arguendo, that marijuana does not fall within a literal reading of Schedule I, the classification still is rational. Placing marijuana in Schedule I furthered the regulatory purposes of Congress. The statutory criteria of section 812(b)(1) are guides in determining the schedule to which a drug belongs, but they are not dispositive. Indeed, the classifications at times cannot be followed consistently, and some conflict exists as to the main factor in classifying a drug potential for abuse or possible medical use.[40] The district court in *United States v. Maiden*, 355 F. Supp. 743 (D.Conn.1973), discussed this problem in rejecting the identical claim raised here by NORML:

> [The statutory classifications] cannot logically be read as cumulative in all situations. For example finding (B) for Schedule I requires that "The drug or other substance has no currently accepted medical use in treatment in the United States." Finding (B) for the other four schedules specifies that

---

40. According to the House Report, "(a) key criterion for controlling a substance, and the one which will be used most often, is the substance's potential for abuse." Senator Hughes, on the other hand, believed the existence of an accepted medical use was the primary factor in a drug's classification. Discussing the penalties for possession of marijuana and heroin, he noted: "Classification in the bill depends primarily upon whether there is an accepted medical use for the drug. Because heroin and marijuana have no recognized medical use, they are classified in the same category.... If there is no valid use for a drug, there is a sound reason to impose the strictest recordkeeping controls. But criminal sanctions for illegal distribution and use should be based upon the danger to society and the individual, not upon whether there is any valid medical use."

Other members of Congress indicated the two criteria were equally important.

> the drug has a currently accepted medical use. At the same time, finding (A) requires that the drug has a "high potential for abuse" for placement in Schedule I, but a "potential for abuse less than the drugs or other substances in Schedules I and II" for placement in Schedule III. If the findings are really cumulative, where would one place a drug that has no accepted medical use but also has a potential for abuse less than the drugs in Schedules I and II? According to finding (A) for Schedule III it belongs in Schedule III, but finding (B) for that schedule precludes Schedule III; according to finding (B) for Schedule I it belongs in Schedule I, but finding (A) for that schedule appears to preclude Schedule I.

The legislative history also indicates the statutory criteria are not intended to be exclusive. The House report states that "[a]side from the criterion of actual or relative potential for abuse, subsection (c) of section 201 (21 U.S.C. § 811(c)) lists seven other criteria . . . which must be considered in determining whether a substance meets the specific requirements specified in section 202(b) (21 U.S.C. § 812(b)) for inclusion in particular schedules. . . ." 1970 House Report, *supra* at 35, reprinted in (1970) U.S. Code Cong. & Admin. News at 4602. The criteria listed in section 811(c)[41] include the state of current knowledge, the current pattern of abuse, the risk to public health, and the significance of abuse. These more subjective factors significantly broaden the scope of issues to be considered in classifying a drug. Given these other concerns, Congress might well want marijuana in Schedule I for regulatory purposes.

In addition, Congress itself made the initial classifications and established a procedure for reclassifying drugs and controlled substances: "Schedules I, II, III, IV, and V shall, unless and until amended pursuant to section 811 of this title, consist of the following drugs and other substances. . . ." 21 U.S.C. § 812(c). In making the initial determination, Congress placed marijuana in Schedule I. The clear meaning of section 812(c) is that Congress intended marijuana to remain in Schedule I until such time as it might be reclassified by the Attorney General on the basis of more complete scientific information about the drug. In such a reclassification hearing, the statutory criteria would be the guides to determining the most appropriate schedule for marijuana. By providing for periodic review and constant revision

---

41. This section states: "In making any finding under subsection (a) of this section or under subsection (b) of section 202 (21 U.S.C. § 812(b)), the Attorney General shall consider the following factors with respect to each drug or other substance proposed to be controlled or removed from the schedules:

(1) Its actual or relative potential for abuse.
(2) Scientific evidence of its pharmacological effect, if known.
(3) The state of current scientific knowledge regarding the drug or other substance.
(4) Its history and current pattern of abuse.
(5) The scope, duration, and significance of abuse.
(6) What, if any, risk there is to the public health.
(7) Its psychic or physiological dependence liability.
(8) Whether the substance is an immediate precursor of a substance already controlled under this title. 21 U.S.C. § 811(c)."

of drug classifications, Congress enacted a sensible mechanism for scrutinizing the classification of marijuana. As Judge Feinberg stated in *United States v. Kiffer*:

> [T]he very existence of the statutory scheme indicates that, in dealing with the "drug" problem, Congress intended flexibility and receptivity to the latest scientific information to be the hallmarks of its approach. This . . . is the very antithesis of the irrationality (plaintiff) attributes to Congress.

The legislative scheme under section 811 offers a flexible means of reclassifying controlled substances, and the Attorney General may reclassify marijuana pursuant to that scheme. The propriety of any administrative determination on the reclassification of marijuana is not before this court. The constitutional legitimacy of the classification of marijuana in Schedule I is challenged, however, and this court concludes that the classification is constitutionally permissible. Thus, plaintiff's equal protection challenge must be rejected.

In this case, NORML has asked this court to overturn the CSA prohibition on private possession of marijuana. In so doing, NORML misdirects its efforts. This challenge presents the difficult social questions that legislatures are especially adept at resolving, and we do not sit to second-guess their judgments. Under our system of checks and balances, it is the court's duty to examine legislation and to determine the legality or illegality of that legislation within the confines of the law. The legislative system may not always work efficiently, or fairly, but we have staked our fortunes on it, and our history would support the wisdom of our forefathers' judgment.

NORML's efforts have seared the conscience of many representatives. Eleven states have decriminalized possession of marijuana and efforts to decriminalize are continuing in many others. The legislative branch, and not the judicial, is the proper battleground for the fight to decriminalize the possession of marijuana. The people, and not the courts, must decide whether the battle will be won or lost.

The court in *NORML v. Bell* suggests that advocates for marijuana law reform should pursue their arguments through the legislative process or the Controlled Substances Act's administrative procedure for rescheduling controlled substances. But was it constitutional for Congress to delegate the power to criminalize substances under the CSA to the same administrative entity responsible for enforcing the CSA? In *Touby v. United States,* 500 U.S. 160 (1991), defendants who had been convicted of manufacturing "Euphoria" argued that the CSA's delegation of scheduling power to the Attorney General conflicted with Article I of the Constitution, which provides that "all legislative Powers herein granted shall be vested in a Congress of the United States." The Supreme Court rejected the challenge, concluding that the CSA "place[s] multiple specific restrictions on the Attorney General's discretion to define criminal conduct. These restrictions satisfy the constitutional requirements of the nondelegation doctrine." In *Touby,* the Court also upheld the Attorney General's subdelegation of scheduling authority to the Drug Enforcement Administration.

D. Research of Controlled Substances

In explaining his rejection of NORML's rescheduling petition in 1989, Drug Enforcement Administration head John Lawn emphasized the absence of "scientifically-designed clinical trials" documenting marijuana's value as a medicine. Lawn's order even seemed to imply that researchers were not conducting clinical trials because they thought the idea that marijuana could have medicinal uses was not plausible enough to be worth their attention: "Marijuana is available from the Federal Government to those researchers who obtain proper licensure," Lawn wrote. "However, the evidence suggests that only small numbers of researchers and physicians have obtained marijuana for this purpose, and that some research programs sponsored by states had trouble getting physicians to participate."

But if clinical trials of Schedule I controlled substances are rare, it may say more about the bureaucratic hurdles that await researchers who seek to study them than anything else. Even though accepted medical use is one of the three scheduling criteria under the Controlled Substances Act, the CSA does not require that any research into the potential medical value of a substance actually be performed before it is scheduled. And once a substance has been placed in Schedule I, it becomes significantly more difficult for researchers to study it.

Indeed, as discussed in *Grinspoon v. Drug Enforcement Administration*, Dr. Grinspoon objected to the placement of MDMA in Schedule I on precisely this basis, arguing that it "would strongly discourage medical research on the drug" and that the "failure to consider the impact of a scheduling decision on legitimate research" was "arbitrary and capricious on the part of the Administrator." The court in *Grinspoon* summarized some of the obstacles facing researchers who wish to study Schedule I substances, noting that they "include mandatory FDA approval of research involving Schedule I substances; mandatory special registration with the DEA; mandatory reporting and security procedures beyond those required for drugs placed in Schedules II through V; unavoidable bureaucratic delays; and other adverse impacts due to the grave concern caused by a substance's placement in Schedule I, such as difficulty in obtaining volunteers for clinical studies and, for academic researchers, difficulty in securing approval from institutional review boards." In addition to administrative hurdles, there is often little financial incentive for private companies to fund studies into the potential medicinal effects of Schedule I controlled substances. Many of the substances are not patent-protected. In addition, even if studies were to reveal that a Schedule I substance has medicinal value, the procedure for rescheduling it under the CSA is time-consuming and uncertain.

Though obtaining the necessary permission and funding to research Schedule I substances can be difficult, it is not impossible. Researchers have undertaken studies into potential medicinal uses of psychedelic substances, including MDMA and psilocybin (the psychoactive ingredient found in hallucinogenic mushrooms). *See* John Tierney, *Hallucinogens Have Doctors Tuning in Again*, N.Y. TIMES, Apr. 11, 2010. In 2010, researchers released a study on the use of MDMA to combat posttraumatic stress disorder (PTSD). The paper, which was published in the *Journal of Psychopharmacology*, "showed that ecstasy is not only safe when administered in controlled settings but also remarkably effective in treating PTSD in conjunction with psychotherapy." John Cloud, *Ecstasy Shows Promise in Relieving PTSD*, TIME, July 20, 2010. It took researchers more than a decade to get approval for the study, however, and "[b]ecause of budget and time restraints, only 20 participants could be recruited." *Id.* In 2017, the FDA granted Breakthrough Therapy Designation to MDMA for the treastment of PTSD, which will help to speed up Phase 3 trials of the drug.

The article below describes some of the requirements researchers must meet in order to conduct studies using Schedule I substances. As you read it, consider what purposes these restrictions serve. Are they in place to prevent Schedule I substances used in research from being diverted to the black market? Were they designed with the health and safety of the participants who would be using Schedule I substances during clinical trials in mind? Do the restrictions have any drawbacks? If so, do you think the current approach strikes the proper balance between the risks and benefits of studying Schedule I drugs?

Medical Marijuana: The Conflict between Scientific Evidence and Political Ideology
Peter J. Cohen

2009 Utah Law Review 35

[T]he first objective study of the safety and efficacy of smoked marijuana was published less than two years ago. Why did it take so long for this study to appear in the peer-reviewed scientific literature? Why did the pharmaceutical industry fail to show any interest in this promising compound?

In 1992, Dr. Donald Abrams, a clinical pharmacologist, Professor of Medicine at the University of California San Francisco, and Chair of the Bay Area's Community Consortium on HIV research, proposed a study "designed to provide objective data about whether or not smoked marijuana could ease subjective symptoms of AIDS wasting and produce objective gains in body weight." The University of California planned to fund the study, the FDA approved the I[nvestigational] N[ew] D[rug application], and the ethics of the study protocol were approved by the University Hospital's Institutional Review Board. However, Dr. Abrams was denied permission to import marijuana from the Netherlands as he had originally planned or to use illegal marijuana that had been seized by the DEA.

Since the National Institute on Drug Abuse (NIDA) grows marijuana and is the only domestic source for scientific investigators, Dr. Abrams requested their assistance, a request that would have involved only a minimal expense to NIDA. However, it was then the policy of the NIH to restrict its provision of marijuana only to investigators who had received a peer-reviewed NIH grant to conduct a study. Because Abrams's funding had originated at his university, and not the National Institutes of Health (NIH) of which NIDA is a part, he was refused access to NIH's marijuana.

In May of 1996, hoping that the NIH had changed its policies, Dr. Abrams resubmitted his study proposal to the NIH. At that time, the study had again been approved and funded at the university level; thus, NIH approval was required not for funding, but to allow him to obtain federally grown marijuana. In October 1996, four years after he had first initiated requests to obtain marijuana legally, he was again informed that the NIH would not supply it.

In 1998, after six years of frustrating attempts to obtain marijuana either in the United States or abroad, the NIH finally approved Dr. Abrams's request and he was able to obtain marijuana legally. Abrams then initiated the first federally funded effort to study the effects of marijuana on patients with AIDS, an investigation that was eventually published in the peer-reviewed scientific literature.

This was not the only instance in which the federal government appeared to place significant roadblocks in the way of university-sponsored research directed toward obtaining information about the possible medical uses of marijuana. Because of difficulties in obtaining marijuana from NIDA's "marijuana farm," Lyle E. Craker, PhD, a professor in the Department of Plant and Soil Sciences at the University of Massachusetts Amherst, petitioned the Drug Enforcement Agency (DEA) in 2003 for permission to cultivate marijuana to use in university-approved clinical studies that would evaluate marijuana's ability to provide pain relief and control nausea in patients with cancer, as well as to alleviate some of the symptoms of multiple sclerosis in other patients. His petition was denied by the DEA in spite of DEA Administrative Law Judge Mary Ellen Bittner's nonbinding opinion that it would be in the public interest to grant it. She stated in that opinion that the federal government's system for evaluating requests for marijuana for clinical study had hindered investigation of the drug's safety and effectiveness. As of mid-2008, the case is still pending. Four years after the petition was filed, DEA spokesman Steve Robertson told the American Medical News that the agency was reviewing the decision but he declined to comment other than to declare that "the government maintains that no sound scientific studies exist to support marijuana's medical value."

The federal government's stance regarding scientific investigation of medical marijuana has, however, been far from monolithic. While those individuals within the NIH who acted on Dr. Abrams's request appeared to reject even minimal support of scientific study of the medical use of marijuana, other NIH personnel appeared to take an opposite stance. After considerable "wide-ranging public discussion on the potential medical use of marijuana, particularly smoked marijuana," the National Institutes of Health convened a conference "to review the scientific data concerning the potential therapeutic uses for marijuana and the need for and feasibility of additional research" in February 1997.

At this forum, a group of experts in anesthesiology, internal medicine, neurology, oncology, ophthalmology, pharmacology and psychiatry maintained that there was a need for accurate and nonbiased scientific investigation of medical marijuana. The participants suggested that although [DELTA] 9-tetrahydrocannabinol, the major psychoactive component of marijuana, is currently available as a separate and approved medication, this should not obviate the need to study the efficacy of smoked marijuana itself. They noted the plant may also contain other compounds with important therapeutic properties. Moreover, "the bioavailability and pharmacokinetics of THC from smoked marijuana are substantially different than those of the oral dosage form."

The expert group proposed that the possibly beneficial (or even superior) role of smoked marijuana cannot be delineated without proper investigation. They maintained that studies of marijuana should not be precluded because effective approved therapy was currently available for the diseases in which it might also be efficacious.

This was not the only expert discussion suggesting that the use of medical marijuana should not be dismissed out of hand. A meeting sponsored by the National Academies of Sciences-Institute of Medicine to discuss the medical use of marijuana (Workshop on Prospects for Cannabinoid Drug Development, National Academies of Sciences-Institute of Medicine) was held in February 1998; the proceedings were published in 1999. Discussion at this meeting centered on both the adverse effects and potential benefits of smoked marijuana. Participants indicated that smoked marijuana could be a valuable agent in the treatment of chemotherapy-induced nausea and vomiting, HIV-related gastrointestinal disorders, AIDS wasting, severe pain, and some forms of spasticity. Some participants stressed—as had those at the NIH conference held the preceding year—that since the whole marijuana plant contains many possibly active cannabinoids besides THC, its possible efficacy may not be replicated by medications containing only THC.

Nonetheless, the suggestion by an impartial conference of experts that marijuana might have some medical utility that should be discussed and that its properties should be subjected to scientific investigation evoked a forceful but inaccurate response from the federal government[, which released the following statement shortly after the Institute of Medicine report]: "A past evaluation by several Department of Health and Human Services (HHS) agencies, including the Food and Drug Administration (FDA), Substance Abuse and Mental Health Services Administration (SAMHSA) and National Institute for Drug Abuse (NIDA), concluded that no sound scientific studies supported medical use of marijuana for treatment in the United States, and no animal or human data supported the safety or efficacy of marijuana for general medical use."

This "authoritative" statement did not go unnoticed by the media. A reporter for the New York Times observed that: "The Food and Drug Administration said Thursday that 'no sound scientific studies' supported the medical use of marijuana, contradicting a 1999 review by a panel of highly regarded scientists. [It] directly contradicts a 1999 review by the Institute of Medicine [IOM], a part of the National Academy of Sciences, the nation's most prestigious scientific advisory agency. That review found marijuana to be 'moderately well suited for particular conditions, such as chemotherapy-induced nausea and vomiting and AIDS wasting.'"

Dr. John Benson, cochairman of the IOM committee and professor of internal medicine at the University of Nebraska Medical Center, whose report had suggested that smoked marijuana could have therapeutic value, strongly disputed the FDA's stance. "The federal government loves to ignore our report," said Dr. Benson, "They would rather it never happened." Dr. Jerry Avorn, a medical professor at Harvard Medical School, declared, "Unfortunately, this is yet another example of the F.D.A. making pronouncements that seem to be driven more by ideology than by science."

E. The Classification of Hemp Under the Controlled Substances Act

Until late 2018, the CSA's classification of marijuana as a Schedule I substance also encompassed industrial hemp. This feature of the CSA was particularly controversial. Industrial hemp has a variety of uses, including in paper, textiles, clothing, and health food. The CSA did not bar companies from importing hemp and hemp products into the United States. It did, however, prohibit the manufacture of industrial hemp in the United States.

Congress began to chip away at the prohibition against growing hemp in 2014, by creating a carve-out for state pilot programs. In 2018, Congress went further by removing hemp from the definition of marijuana under the CSA. The opinion that follows discusses some of the key developments in the status of hemp under federal law since 2014.

United States v. Mallory

United States District Court for the Southern District of West Virginia
372 F. Supp. 3d 377 (2019)

Chambers, J.

Pending before the Court are Motions to Dismiss by Defendants Matthew Mallory (Mr. Mallory) and Commonwealth Alternative Medicinal Options, LLC (collectively the "CAMO Defendants") and Gary Kale and the Grassy Run Farms, LLC, (collectively the "Grassy Run Defendants"). For the following reasons, the Court GRANTS the motions to dismiss.

The United States brought this action on September 11, 2018, seeking an Ex Parte Temporary Restraining Order (TRO) and Preliminary Injunction, with the ultimate goal of securing a Permanent Injunction and other relief. With respect to the TRO, the Court GRANTED the motion and scheduled a preliminary injunction hearing for September 17, 2018. In the meantime, the TRO prevented the CAMO Defendants and the Grassy Run Defendants from, *inter alia*, harvesting and transporting certain cannabis plants across state lines.

The cannabis at issue in this case was grown under an "industrial hemp" pilot program in West Virginia. At the time, "industrial hemp" was defined as "the plant

Cannabis sativa L. and any part of such plant, whether growing or not, with a delta-9 tetrahydrocannabinol concentration [(THC)] of not more than 0.3 percent on a dry weight basis." 7 U.S.C. § 5940.[1] Mr. Mallory, using the business name CAMO HEMP WV LLC, applied for and received a Research and Marketing Cultivation of Industrial Hemp License from the West Virginia Department of Agriculture (WVDA) to grow the plants. The seeds used by Defendants were purchased from a supplier in Kentucky[2] and shipped directly to Grassy Run Farms in West Virginia. The seeds were then planted and grown on property located in Mason County, West Virginia. The United States claims the property is owned by Grassy Run Farms, LLC, and Gary Kale is an employee of that company.

In its Verified Complaint, the United States alleges Defendants conspired together to violate the law with respect to the project, and they failed to follow the project description submitted by the CAMO Defendants to the WVDA. Specifically, the United States argues that Defendants violated the Controlled Substances Act (CSA) when they obtained the cannabis seeds from Kentucky. Additionally, the United States asserts Defendants will continue to violate the CSA if, as intended, they transport harvested portions of those plants to Pennsylvania.

Upon hearing the parties' arguments, the Court converted the TRO into a preliminary injunction. The Court allowed Defendants to harvest, dry, and process the cannabis, but the Court prohibited Defendants from transporting or selling it after it was processed.[3] The harvesting, drying, and milling process took several weeks to complete. In the interim period, the parties filed and briefed the current motions.

The CAMO Defendants then moved to lift the stay because they had a time-sensitive contractual obligation to deliver cannabidiol (CBD) isolate, a hemp extract, by the end of January 2019. The CAMO Defendants represented to the Court that they had to take the plant material to a facility in Pennsylvania to be processed in order to fulfill the contract. Given that the passage of time had changed the circumstances of the CAMO Defendants because of the looming contractual deadlines, and the fact the Court had become increasingly doubtful as to the merits of the United States' case, the Court lifted the stay and exercised its inherent authority to

1. Hemp is now defined in 7 U.S.C. § 1639*o* as "the plant Cannabis sativa L. and any part of that plant, including the seeds thereof and all derivatives, extracts, cannabinoids, isomers, acids, salts, and salts of isomers, whether growing or not, with a delta-9 tetrahydrocannabinol concentration of not more than 0.3 percent on a dry weight basis." 7 U.S.C. § 1639*o* (effective Dec. 20, 2018).

2. The seeds were shipped from Hickman Seed & Grain, LLC in Kentucky. *Delivery Receipt*, ECF No. 3-5. It appears that Hickman Seed & Grain is a duly licensed participant of Kentucky's pilot program. *See* Kentucky Department of Agriculture Industrial Hemp Research Pilot Program, "2018 License Holder List," http://www.kyagr.com/marketing/documents/HEMP_OV_License-Holder-List_2018.pdf (last visited on March 1, 2019).

3. On October 22, 2018, the Court entered an Order prohibiting Defendants from transporting the hemp outside of West Virginia.

dissolve the preliminary injunction.[5] The Court permitted Defendants to immediately transport the product to Pennsylvania to be processed into CBD isolate. Now, upon consideration of the merits of Defendants' motions to dismiss, the Court rules in their favor.

Pursuant to the dismissal standard, courts must look for "plausibility" in the complaint. In other words, the United States in this case must set forth the "grounds" for an "entitle[ment] to relief" that is more than mere "labels and conclusions, and a formulaic recitation of the elements of a cause of action will not do." If the allegations in the complaint, assuming their truth, do "not raise a claim of entitlement to relief, this basic deficiency should . . . be exposed at the point of minimum expenditure of time and money by the parties and the court."

The fundamental question this Court must resolve is a legal one, that is whether Defendants violated any federal laws in procuring, cultivating, processing, or selling the cannabis at issue. Under the CSA, controlled substances are divided into five schedules. Schedule I substances, which includes marijuana, are the most tightly controlled. The CSA expressly prohibits the manufacture, distribution, or disbursement of a Schedule I controlled substance without a Drug Enforcement Administration (DEA) registration. Notably, at the time this action was brought, the CSA defined "marihuana" as including "all parts of the plant Cannabis sativa L., whether growing or not; the seeds thereof; the resin extracted from any part of such plant; and every compound, manufacture, salt, derivative, mixture, or preparation of such plant, its seeds or resin." CBD is a derivative product of the Cannabis sativa L. plant.

In 2014, Congress passed the Agriculture Act of 2014 (the "2014 Farm Bill"). As part of the Act, Congress carved out a special exception to the CSA under certain circumstances, for the domestic growth, cultivating, and marketing of industrial hemp. This exception, set forth in 7 U.S.C. § 5940(a) provided:

> (a) In general
>
> Notwithstanding the Controlled Substances Act . . . or any other Federal law, an institution of higher education . . . or a State department of agriculture may grow or cultivate industrial hemp if—
>
> > (1) the industrial hemp is grown or cultivated for purposes of research conducted under an agricultural pilot program or other agricultural or academic research; and
> >
> > (2) the growing or cultivating of industrial hemp is allowed under the laws of the State in which such institution of higher education or State department of agriculture is located and such research occurs.

---

5. After the Court entered its Memorandum Opinion and Order, the United States immediately moved to stay and argued for the first time that the plants may have a THC level that exceeds the limit to qualify it as hemp. The Court entered a temporary stay and an expedited briefing schedule. In Response, the CAMO Defendants provided documentation showing the THC level was well below the legal limit. Based upon this testing and the fact the United States' argument was pure speculation and conjecture, the Court denied the United States' motion.

Thereafter, an "agricultural pilot program" is defined as:

> a pilot program to study the growth, cultivation, or marketing of industrial hemp—
>
> (A) in States that permit the growth or cultivation of industrial hemp under the laws of the State; and
>
> (B) in a manner that—
>
> (i) ensures that only institutions of higher education and State departments of agriculture are used to grow or cultivate industrial hemp;
>
> (ii) requires that sites used for growing or cultivating industrial hemp in a State be certified by, and registered with, the State department of agriculture; and
>
> (iii) authorizes State departments of agriculture to promulgate regulations to carry out the pilot program in the States in accordance with the purposes of this section.

Pursuant to the 2014 Farm Bill, industrial hemp includes "any part" of the plant Cannabis sativa L., "whether growing or not," so long as it has a delta-9 tetrahydrocannabinol concentration (THC) of 0.3 percent or less based on dry weight. THC is the psychoactive component of Cannabis sativa L. THC at 0.3 percent or less is insufficient to have a narcotic effect. Thus, rather than defining industrial hemp on the part of the plant used, the 2014 Farm Bill defined industrial hemp on the level of THC it contains. However, as the CSA continued to define marijuana broadly as the entire Cannabis sativa L. plant, including its seeds and extracts, conflicts arose between agencies charged with enforcing the CSA and those who sought to promote and explore the hemp industry under the 2014 Farm Bill.

In reaction to this tension, in December 2015, Congress adopted language in the Consolidated Appropriations Act of 2016 (the "2016 Spending Bill") to address the issue. This Spending Bill provided, in part:

> None of the funds made available by this Act or any other Act may be used—
>
> (1) in contravention of section 7606 of the Agricultural Act of 2014 (7 U.S.C. 5940); or
>
> (2) *to prohibit the transportation, processing, sale, or use of industrial hemp that is grown or cultivated in accordance with subsection section 7606 of the Agricultural Act of 2014, within or outside the State in which the industrial hemp is grown or cultivated.*

Consolidated Appropriations Act of 2016, Pub. L. No. 114-113, § 763, 129 Stat. 2242, 2285 (2015) (italics added).

In the 2018 Spending Bill, which was passed on March 23, 2018 and was effective through the 2018 fiscal year, the phrase "or seeds of such plant" was added to subsection (2) to provide: "None of the funds . . . may be used . . . to prohibit the transportation, processing, sale, or use of industrial hemp, or seeds of such plant. . . ."

Thus, by the time the seeds were purchased in this case, these Spending Bills made it clear that agencies, such as the United States Attorney's Office and the Drug Enforcement Agency (DEA),* cannot use federal funds to prohibit the interstate or intrastate "transportation, processing, sale, or use of industrial hemp, or seeds of such plant, that is grown or cultivated in accordance" with the 2014 Farm Bill.

After the passage of the 2016 Spending Bill, however, the United States Department of Agriculture, the DEA, and the Food and Drug Administration (FDA) issued a Statement of Principles on Industrial Hemp (SOP) on August 12, 2016. Although they recognized in the SOP that States could adopt industrial hemp agricultural pilot projects, they took the position that "[i]ndustrial hemp plants and seeds may not be transported across State lines." *Statement of Principles on Industrial Hemp*, 81 FR 53395-01, 2016 WL 4240092 (Aug. 12, 2016). In addition, the SOP provided that, while authorized entities could "grow or cultivate" industrial hemp under the 2014 Farm Bill, it "did not eliminate the requirement under the Controlled Substances Import and Export Act that the importation of viable cannabis seeds must be carried out by persons registered with the DEA to do so." Although the SOP acknowledged that it "does not establish any binding legal requirements," on December 14, 2016, the DEA established a new drug code for marijuana extract, codified at 21 C.F.R. § 1308.11(d)(58). This Rule created a new DEA Controlled Substance Code Number under Schedule I for "marihuana extract," which is defined as an "extract containing one or more cannabinoids that has been derived from any plant of the genus Cannabis, other than the separated resin (whether crude or purified) obtained from the plant."

In the meantime, and despite the DEA's position, individual States seized upon the opportunity under the 2014 Farm Bill to grow, cultivate, and market industrial hemp. Capitalizing on this burgeoning market, both West Virginia and Kentucky established industrial hemp agricultural pilot programs under the auspices of their respective Departments of Agriculture. West Virginia's Industrial Hemp Development Act provides that the Commissioner of Agriculture is responsible to regulate industrial hemp and "license qualified persons . . . to lawfully grow or cultivate industrial hemp in this state[.]" An individual licensed in West Virginia "may plant, grow, harvest, possess, process, sell or buy industrial hemp." Additionally, if an individual is licensed by the Commissioner, that individual "is presumed to be growing industrial hemp for commercial purposes." Similarly, Kentucky's Department of Agriculture has the authority to regulate hemp pilot programs and "[l]icense persons who wish to participate in an industrial hemp research pilot program by cultivating, handling, processing, or marketing industrial hemp[.]" Under Kentucky's program, "it is lawful for a licensee, or his or her agent, to cultivate, handle, or process industrial hemp or industrial hemp products in the Commonwealth."

---

* The court's opinion mistakenly referred to the DEA as the "Drug Enforcement Agency." Its true name is the Drug Enforcement Administration. [*Footnote by casebook author.*]

In this case, however, the United States contends that Defendants violated the CSA because they obtained the seeds without a DEA registration number and, thus, were not authorized under the CSA's definition of "marihuana" to manufacture, distribute, or dispense it, or possess it with the intent to manufacture, distribute or dispense it. Additionally, the United States argues that those licensed under a State program cannot exceed the scope of the State's DEA registration. *See* 21 U.S.C. § 822(b) (providing that those with a DEA registration only may act "to the extent authorized by their registration"). In this case, the WVDA's registration number is limited to the international importation of Schedule I Cannabis sativa L. seeds. Instead of receiving the seeds directly from the supplier in Kentucky, the United States contends Defendants only could get the seeds legally from the WVDA pursuant to its DEA registration number. As the seeds here were sent across State lines directly from the seed supplier in Kentucky to Defendants in West Virginia, the United States asserts the seeds were illegally obtained.

However, upon review, the Court disagrees with the United States' position. The relevant section of 2014 Farm Bill begins with the phrase "[n]otwithstanding the Controlled Substances Act . . . or any other Federal law," industrial hemp can be grown and cultivated in a State under certain conditions. 7 U.S.C. § 5940. Although at the time the 2014 Farm Bill was passed Congress did not amend the definition of "marihuana" under the CSA, its use of the term "notwithstanding" indicates Congress intended to override any conflicting provisions in the CSA.

The 2014 Farm Bill expressly permits growing, cultivating, and marketing industrial hemp under State pilot programs. When tensions arose between enforcement of the broad language in the CSA and the narrow exception for industrial hemp carved out from the 2014 Farm Bill, Congress reacted by inserting language in the 2016 Spending Bill to bar enforcement agencies from using appropriations "to prohibit the transportation, processing, sale, or use of industrial hemp that is grown or cultivated in accordance with [the 2014 Farm Bill], within or outside the State in which the industrial hemp is grown or cultivated." Consolidated Appropriations Act of 2016, Pub. L. No. 114-113, § 763, 129 Stat. 2242, 2285 (2015). This language was repeated in both the 2017 and 2018 Spending Bills, with the addition of the phrase "or seeds of such plant" in the 2018 version.

Obviously, this language was included in the Spending Bills to clear up any doubt that Congress did not want these enforcement agencies from interfering with industrial hemp under the 2014 Farm Bill. Notably, the Spending Bills provided that such agencies were not to prevent the transportation or sale of industrial hemp within or outside a State. This language certainly suggests that Congress contemplated there would be both intrastate and interstate transportation and sale of industrial hemp and its seeds, and it undermines the United States' argument the seeds only could be purchased from international sources. Furthermore, this conclusion drawn from the pronouncements in the Spending Bills is consistent with the legislative history and the recently passed 2018 Farm Bill.

Prior to the 2014 Farm Bill, industrial hemp could not be grown in the United States. As a result, the seeds and oil had to be imported. When introducing an amendment to H.R. 1947, the Federal Agriculture Reform and Risk Management Act of 2013, to allow colleges and universities to grow and cultivate hemp, Representative Earl Blumenauer (D-OR-3), expressed his frustration with that system by stating:

> "[b]ecause of outdated federal drug laws, our farmers can't grow industrial hemp and take advantage of a more than $300 million dollar market. We rely solely on imports to sustain consumer demand. It makes no sense, ... Our fear of industrial hemp is misplaced—it is not a drug. By allowing colleges and universities to cultivate hemp for research, Congress sends a signal that we are ready to examine hemp in a different and more appropriate context."

On December 20, 2018, the President also signed the 2018 Farm Bill that makes this conclusion unmistakably clear. The 2018 Farm Bill expressly allows hemp, its seeds, and hemp-derived products to be transported across State lines. *See* § 10114 of the 2018 Farm Bill (providing "[n]othing in this title or an amendment made by this title prohibits the interstate commerce of hemp (as defined in section 297A of the Agricultural Marketing Act of 1946 (as added by section 10113)) or hemp products"). Additionally, to further clarify the law, Congress finally statutorily removed hemp from the definition of "marihuana" under the CSA and amended 21 U.S.C. § 812(c)(17) to exclude tetrahydrocannabinols in hemp from Schedule I. *See* § 12619 of the 2018 Farm Bill, Conforming Changes to Controlled Substances Act (providing "[t]he term 'marihuana' does not include—(i) hemp, as defined in section 297A of the Agricultural Marketing Act of 1946" and excepting "tetrahydrocannabinols in hemp (as defined under section 297A of the Agricultural Marketing Act of 1946)" from § 812(c)(17)).[10] Congress also ensured that States with approved plans exercise primary control over hemp production. *See* 7 U.S.C. § 1639p(a)(1) ("A State . . . desiring to have primary regulatory authority over the production of hemp in the State . . . shall submit to the Secretary [of Agriculture], through the State department of agriculture . . . a plan under which the State . . . monitors and regulates that production. . . ."). Despite being enacted after the issues in this case arose, the

---

10. "Marijuana" under the CSA is now defined in full as:

> (16)(A) Subject to subparagraph (B), the term "marihuana" means all parts of the plant Cannabis sativa L., whether growing or not; the seeds thereof; the resin extracted from any part of such plant; and every compound, manufacture, salt, derivative, mixture, or preparation of such plant, its seeds or resin.
>
> (B) *The term "marihuana" does not include—*
>
> (i) *hemp, as defined in section 1639o of Title 7; or*
>
> (ii) the mature stalks of such plant, fiber produced from such stalks, oil or cake made from the seeds of such plant, any other compound, manufacture, salt, derivative, mixture, or preparation of such mature stalks (except the resin extracted therefrom), fiber, oil, or cake, or the sterilized seed of such plant which is incapable of germination.

21 U.S.C. § 802(16) (2018) (emphasis added).

2018 Farm Bill provides further evidence that Congress did not intend for industrial hemp to be classified as a Schedule I drug.

In light of the language of the 2014 Farm Bill, the Spending Bills, and the legislative history, the Court finds that Congress intended to carve out an exception to the CSA for industrial hemp. Under the 2014 Farm Bill, there is no requirement that hemp seeds be imported from international sources, and it was contemplated that, if in compliance, industrial hemp and industrial hemp seeds could be shipped domestically. As an exception to the CSA, it also was not necessary for qualifying individuals operating under a State's pilot program to be registered with the DEA. Indeed, the 2018 Spending Bill, which was passed before the seeds were shipped in this case, made it clear that Congress did not want enforcement agencies interfering with the growth, cultivating, and marketing of industrial hemp and industrial hemp seeds. Quite simply, industrial hemp is not a controlled substance under the CSA.[12]

The United States . . . argues, however, that Mr. Mallory stated in the Hemp Research Project Description submitted to the WVDA that he would be ordering the seeds through the WVDA. In addition, Mr. Mallory wrote on the application that signs would be erected on the farm to inform the public that the plants contained no THC. Neither of these things were done. The United States also submitted a handout Mr. Mallory distributed before the seeds were obtained which acknowledges the SOP provides that hemp and hemp seeds cannot be transported across state lines and that the seeds must be imported by those registered with the DEA. Thus, the United States asserts it is undeniable that the CAMO Defendants understood the requirement and violated West Virginia's pilot program by not complying with this requirement and for not fulfilling their other obligations.

However, Congress vested authority over such pilot programs with the States and their respective departments of agriculture. *See* 7 U.S.C. § 5940(b)(1)(B)(iii) (2014) (authorizing "State departments of agriculture to promulgate regulations to carry out the pilot program"). Although the United States believes Defendants did not adhere to West Virginia's requirements, it is the obligation of the WVDA, not the United States, to enforce those requirements. Therefore, the Court declines to accept the United States' argument that it should be able to bring an enforcement

12. The United States requests that this Court wait to rule on this issue until after the Fourth Circuit issues an Opinion in *Palomo Farms, LLC v. DEA*, No. 4:17-cv-169-BO, 2018 WL 2768676 (E.D. N.C. Sept. 6, 2018). In *Palomo Farms*, the DEA had issued an importer registration number to the plaintiff, and the plaintiff ordered seeds from an international source. 2018 WL 2768676, at *1. When the seeds arrived at the airport, they were seized by U.S. Customs and Border Protection, and the DEA stated the plaintiff's importer registration number was issued by mistake. *Id.* at *1-2. The plaintiff then filed an action. In considering the arguments by the parties, the district court determined it was without subject matter jurisdiction to resolve the plaintiff's challenge to the DEA's "decision as any such challenge must be brought in the appropriate court of appeals." *Id.* at *3 (citing 21 U.S.C. § 877). These facts are clearly distinguishable from the facts at issue in this case. Therefore, the Fourth Circuit's decision in *Palomo* may not have any impact on this case, and the Court declines to put this case on hold until it is decided.

action against an applicant for what it believes are violations of the WVDA's pilot program.

In fact, as background and not as an underpinning of this Court's legal conclusion, the Court notes that the WVDA rejected the United States' position that the WVDA should take an action against the CAMO Defendants for their alleged violations of the pilot program. On the same day this action was filed, the WVDA sent a letter to the United States Attorney's Office responding to a letter sent by the United States Attorney's Office the previous week. [In the letter], the WVDA rejected the United States' request it summarily revoke Mr. Mallory's permit. The WVDA specifically stated that "the alleged inaccuracies on Mr. Mallory's application do not rise to the level of materiality that would normally trigger our revocation procedures." Moreover, the WVDA's practice is to allow permit holders to correct any inaccuracies, which is what occurred. Thus, although the United States believed there were material violations of West Virginia's pilot program, the WVDA, which is the department authorized under federal and state law to administer program, did not.

Accordingly, for the foregoing reasons, the Court GRANTS the Motions to Dismiss by Matthew Mallory and CAMO Hemp WV LLC and Gary Kale and Grass Run Farm, LLC.

F. Listed Chemicals

In addition to criminalizing the manufacture of controlled substances, the Controlled Substances Act also regulates and criminalizes some of the chemicals that are used in the production of controlled substances. These substances, sometimes referred to as drug precursors, are classified as "listed chemicals" under the controlled substances act.

> The CSA was amended in 1988 to include the regulation of listed chemicals. Listed chemicals are those chemicals that can be either directly used to illicitly manufacture controlled substances (List I chemicals), such as pseudoephedrine, or chemicals that are important to the manufacture of controlled substances (List II chemicals), such as phosphorous. As problems with the misuse and diversion of these chemicals have increased, the CSA has been further amended to place more controls and restrictions on the import, manufacture and distribution of controlled substances. Currently, the regulation of listed chemicals is approaching a level similar to that of controlled substances; that is, there are certain registration, recordkeeping, security and reporting requirements for importing, manufacturing or distributing these substances.

John A. Gilbert, Jr., *DEA Regulation of Controlled Substances and Listed Chemicals*, 65 Food & Drug L. J. 623, 628–29 (2010).

Criminal prosecutions for trafficking in listed chemicals can sometimes raise difficult legal and policy questions. This is because listed chemicals are perfectly legal to distribute in certain circumstances. Distributing a listed chemical is a crime, however, if the distributor knows or has "reasonable cause to believe" that it will be used to manufacture a controlled substance. Arguably, this statutory scheme has the potential to result in criminal liability for legitimate business owners who are simply careless.

United States v. Kim

United States Court of Appeals for the Ninth Circuit
449 F.3d 933 (2006)

Berzon, J.

Pseudoephedrine, a "listed chemical" under a federal drug statute, 21 U.S.C. § 802(33) & (34)(K), is an ingredient in many over-the-counter cold medications. It can also be used to manufacture methamphetamine, a controlled substance under 21 U.S.C. § 812. Both the United States and California have statutes prohibiting over-the-counter sales of drugs containing pseudoephedrine in certain instances.

This case concerns the conviction of the proprietor of a small pharmacy for selling cold remedies containing pseudoephedrine. Jae Gab Kim was convicted of violating 21 U.S.C. § 841(c)(2), which prohibits the distribution of listed chemicals, including pseudoephedrine, "knowing, or having reasonable cause to believe, that [the pseudoephedrine] will be used to manufacture a controlled substance." He argues that, because drugs containing pseudoephedrine can be legally sold over the counter and there is no bright line in the law demarcating a legal sale from an illegal sale, the law allowing conviction upon "reasonable cause to believe" is unconstitutionally vague. We have previously held that § 841(c)(2) contains a mens rea requirement. With that mens rea standard, the statute is not unconstitutionally vague. We therefore affirm Kim's conviction.

Kim owned and operated the San Jacinto Pharmacy. After receiving information about the law regarding the sale of pseudoephedrine from an industry newsletter, Kim instructed his clerk, Virginia Garcia, not to sell more than 150 sixty-milligram pills per person, per day. Kim believed that sales under this quantity were legal.

Kim purchased drugs containing pseudoephedrine from Bergen Brunswig. In May 2000, the Drug Enforcement Administration (DEA) received a report from Bergen Brunswig that Kim's purchases of drugs containing pseudoephedrine had sharply increased.[1]

The DEA began an investigation of Kim, sending undercover agents to purchase cold remedies containing pseudoephedrine from his pharmacy. Two transactions

1. Evidence at trial showed that Kim's purchases increased from a total of 347.28 grams in December 1999 to 1712.16 grams in April 2000. The quantity continued to increase, reaching a high of 4396.32 grams in July 2000. Kim's purchases of the larger-count bottles (stock bottles) also increased drastically over the same time period.

are relevant to this appeal:[2] On January 4, 2001, three undercover agents entered Kim's pharmacy. Kim was standing in an elevated section at the rear of the pharmacy, filling prescriptions. Kim nodded and smiled at the three agents. The agents attempted to purchase all the packages of cold medication on display. After Garcia started to tell the agents that one person could not buy all the medication, Kim interjected to ask what was going on and who was buying what. Kim instructed them to return some of the medication so that his stock would not be depleted. The three agents returned some of the boxes and divided the remainder for purchase. Ultimately, the agents were each allowed to purchase two boxes of 96-count thirty-milligram tablets and one box of 24-count thirty-milligram tablets, for a total of around 6 grams of pseudoephedrine. Additionally, in Kim's presence and conspicuously, the men inquired about and purchased hydrogen peroxide, iodine, and rubbing alcohol, all of which are used to manufacture methamphetamine. One of the men mumbled, in connection with the purchase of alcohol, that he needed alcohol to "break it down." One of the agents provided all the money for the purchases, although the purchases were rung up separately. There were confusing statements as to whether the person who supplied the money was holding the others' money for them or, instead, paying for all the purchases himself.

As Garcia was completing the transaction, one of the agents asked, "Can we get some more of this tomorrow?" Garcia answered, "Well hopefully." Kim, however, answered, "We're not selling every day." He added that the purchase "lasts for you, normally."

The next day, January 5, 2001, the same three undercover officers returned to the pharmacy. Kim again nodded to them as they entered. Although the officers assumed that he recognized them, there is no direct evidence that he did. One officer attempted to purchase multiple bottles of pseudoephedrine. Again, Garcia would not allow this sale to proceed. She did, however, allow each man to purchase one 100-count sixty-milligram bottle. As on the previous day, one officer held all the money initially and handed it to the other two so they could pay for their pseudoephedrine. Afterwards, the officers also each purchased two 24-count boxes of thirty-milligram pseudoephedrine, for a total of about 7.5 grams each. Kim was not involved in this transaction, but he was in the store at the time.

Kim was indicted for violating 21 U.S.C. § 841(c)(2), for distributing a listed chemical when the merchant "knows or has reasonable cause to believe" that the chemical will be used to manufacture illicit drugs. At trial, at the close of the government's case-in-chief, the district court granted Kim's motion for judgment of acquittal on three counts. The jury found Kim not guilty of another count. The district court later granted a post-verdict judgment of acquittal as to yet another count.

---

2. There were seven total purchases by undercover agents, each one eventually resulting in a count in Kim's indictment. As noted below, Kim was ultimately convicted of only two counts in the indictment.

In the end, Kim was convicted only on counts six and seven, covering the incidents described above.

Both after the government's case-in-chief and after the jury returned its verdict, Kim challenged the vagueness of the statute under which he was indicted. The district court denied both motions. Kim was sentenced to five months incarceration, three years supervised release—during which he was to spend five months in home detention—and a $15,000 fine. We were informed at oral argument that he lost his pharmacist's license as a result of the convictions.

The federal statute under which Kim was convicted provides that "[a]ny person who knowingly or intentionally . . . possesses or distributes a listed chemical knowing, or having reasonable cause to believe, that the listed chemical will be used to manufacture a controlled substance except as authorized by this subchapter" shall be fined or imprisoned, or both. 21 U.S.C. § 841(c)(2). The federal law also contains a requirement that sales of certain packages of pseudoephedrine be recorded.[5] The recording statute contains a confusing maze of rules, exceptions to the rules, and exceptions to the exceptions. First, "[e]ach regulated person who engages in a regulated transaction involving a listed chemical . . . shall keep a record of the transaction for two years after the date of the transaction." 21 U.S.C. § 830(a)(1). Not all sales of listed chemicals, however, are considered "regulated transactions." "[A]ny sale of ordinary over-the-counter pseudoephedrine . . . by retail distributors shall not be a regulated transaction." § 802(39)(A)(iv)(I)(aa). Over-the-counter sales of pseudoephedrine that are not "ordinary," however, may be regulated transactions, because they are not necessarily included in the exemption from regulated transactions.[6] With respect to pseudoephedrine in particular, "The term 'ordinary over-the-counter pseudoephedrine . . . product' means any product containing pseudoephedrine . . . sold in package sizes of not more than 3.0 grams of pseudoephedrine base . . . that is packaged in blister packs, each blister containing not

---

5. Certain of those sales that must be recorded must also be *reported* to the government. "Each regulated person shall report to the Attorney General . . . any regulated transaction involving an extraordinary quantity of a listed chemical, an uncommon method of payment or delivery, or any other circumstance that the regulated person believes may indicate that the listed chemical will be used in violation of this subchapter." 21 U.S.C. § 830(b)(1)(A). The statute contains no definition of "extraordinary quantity."

6. The definition of "regulated transaction" generally allows the "Attorney General [to] establish[ ] a threshold amount for a specific listed chemical." § 802(39)(A). Section 802(39)(A)(iv)(II) provided at the time of Kim's offense "the threshold for any sale of products containing pseudoephedrine . . . products by retail distributors or by distributors required to submit reports by section 830(b)(3) of this title shall be 24 grams of pseudoephedrine . . . in a single transaction."

At the time of the relevant transactions in this case, the Attorney General had not established single transaction thresholds for retail sales of pseudoephedrine, but he has done so since then. *Compare* 21 C.F.R. 1310.04(f) (2000) with 21 C.F.R. 1310.04(f) (2006). The details of the quantity or quality of pseudoephedrine that must be recorded and reported are not dispositive in this case and the statute has been amended recently, *see* infra note 8, so we do not address the recording and reporting requirements further.

more than two dosage units, or where the use of blister packs is technically infeasible, that is packaged in unit dose packets or pouches." § 802(45)(B)(i).[7] Additionally, sales of twenty-four grams or more of pseudoephedrine were automatically subject to the recording requirements of § 830. § 802(39)(A)(iv)(II). The upshot is that over-the-counter sales of pseudoephedrine had to be recorded if the items purchased totaled twenty-four grams or more and (1) were not in blister packs or (2) were in packages of more than three grams per package.[8]

California makes it a felony for people to sell certain substances "with knowledge or the intent that the recipient will use the substance to unlawfully manufacture a controlled substance." Cal. Health & Safety Code § 11104(a). The prohibited substances, which include pseudoephedrine, are listed in California Health and Safety Code section 11100(a), which also requires merchants to report sales of regulated substances. The California reporting statute, section 11100, incorporates federal law by exempting from its reporting requirements those transactions involving chemicals "lawfully sold, transferred, or furnished over the counter without a prescription pursuant to the federal Food, Drug, and Cosmetic Act (21 U.S.C. Sec. 301 et seq.) or regulations adopted thereunder." The California statute, however, specifically *does not exempt* from its reporting requirement sales "where the individual transaction involves more than three packages or nine grams of" pseudoephedrine. Thus, a pharmacist who sells more than nine grams of pseudoephedrine must report the sale to the California government, whereas a pharmacist who sells less must only report the sale to California if the drugs were sold in violation of the federal law—a category which would include, as we have noted, sales made "knowing or having reasonable cause to believe" that the purchase of drugs would be used to manufacture methamphetamine.

The upshot is that neither state nor federal law specifies any "safe harbor" amount of pseudoephedrine that may be sold over the counter. Instead, the seller's actual or imputed knowledge that the chemical will be used to manufacture methamphetamine is determinative of criminal liability, regardless of the amount sold.

Kim sold quantities below the per se reporting limits of the California statute, never selling to the undercover DEA agents more than three packages or nine grams of pseudoephedrine during a single transaction. Kim argues that because the California provision makes a sale of nine grams "otherwise authorized," he did not have

7. In the case of liquids, however, if they are "sold in package sizes of not more than 3.0 grams of pseudoephedrine base," they qualify as "ordinary over-the-counter" sales. § 802(45)(B)(ii).

8. The federal law has very recently been amended. On March 9, 2006, President Bush signed into law an amendment to the USA PATRIOT Improvement and Reauthorization Act of 2005, which contained a section entitled the Combat Methamphetamine Epidemic Act of 2005. The Combat Methamphetamine Epidemic Act strengthened the recording requirements of the federal statute and further restricted sales of pseudoephedrine. It contains no amendment, however, to § 841(c)(2), the criminal liability section.

adequate notice that a sale of less than nine grams could subject him to federal prosecution.[10] We reject Kim's claim.

First, Kim points to no support for his assumption that the federal statute exempts from criminal liability transactions permitted under state law. There is no provision in the federal law providing a safe harbor for transactions "otherwise authorized"; the term is entirely of Kim's own construction. Furthermore, unless a federal law states otherwise, state law cannot empower a citizen to act contrary to a federal prohibition.

Second, Kim appears to have confused the reporting requirements under California law with the criminal liability standards. The California provision does not "authorize[ ]" single transactions of less than nine grams. As noted above, the California law requires merchants to report to the California Department of Justice transactions involving sales of certain chemicals. A merchant need not report a *lawful* (under federal law) sale of less than nine grams; he or she *must* report a sale of more than nine grams, whether or not lawful under federal law. The more-than-nine-grams standard is thus significant for the purposes of California law only because it delineates those sales that must automatically be reported from those that *may* not need to be reported.

The California *felony* provision covering sales of pseudoephedrine, in contrast, contains *no* dosage safe harbor. Section 11104(a), the criminal liability provision, makes it a felony conviction to sell certain chemicals "with knowledge or the intent" that those chemicals will be used to manufacture illicit drugs. A sale of *any* quantity can violate California law if it is entered into with the requisite mental state; the quantity is irrelevant except as circumstantial evidence of intent. Although Kim allowed the undercover agents to purchase only quantities of pseudoephedrine below the per se *reporting* requirement of the California statute, he was not necessarily acting within the bounds of state law by consummating the sale for those quantities.

Kim argues that there is inadequate notice "of where (and how) the line is drawn to indicate when an [over-the-counter] sale that is otherwise authorized becomes one that is unlawful." As noted above, however, Kim's sales were *not* authorized by the California statute, although they were not explicitly prohibited either; the mens rea requirement was determinative.

Third, Kim's arguments based solely on federal law fare no better. He contends that because pseudoephedrine is legally sold over-the-counter for personal use, he

---

10. Kim does not challenge the sufficiency of the evidence on his conviction. In particular, he does not argue that because he did not directly participate in the January 5 transaction, he could not be guilty of distributing pseudoephedrine with any knowledge or reasonable cause to believe that this particular sale would result in the production of methamphetamine. We therefore do not decide whether a supervising pharmacist or proprietor who does not participate directly in a specific transaction can be criminally liable under § 841(c)(2).

must have protection against criminal liability under federal law for those personal use sales that are below the level at which they must be recorded. Pointing to provisions of federal law that mention "legitimate medical use" and "personal use," § 802(46)(A) & (B), Kim contends that "other than limiting the dosage level, there is nothing in the law to provide a retail distributor with assurance or guidance as to what is required for his over-the-counter sales to be deemed sales for legitimate medical use."

Kim is correct that, under federal law, a retail distributor is one who engages in sales for personal use, which are "below-threshold" sales for legitimate medical purposes. 21 U.S.C. § 802(46). He forgets, however, that retail distributors are *only* exempted from the definition of "regulated transaction" (which triggers the *recording* requirements of § 830) when they sell "not more than 3.0 grams of pseudoephedrine base . . . that is packaged in blister packs, each blister containing not more than two dosage units, or where the use of blister packs is technically infeasible, that is packaged in unit dose packets or pouches." § 802(45)(B)(i).

Kim is therefore correct that a bright-line rule exists establishing a threshold for sales of pseudoephedrine. This bright-line rule, however, applies only to the recording requirements and *not* to the criminal liability provision. The criminal liability provision contains no cross-reference to the recording requirements, nor does it include the terms "legitimate medical use" or "personal use." Whether the over-the-counter sale was for a legitimate medical purpose within the meaning of the recording requirement is therefore technically irrelevant to the criminal liability provision at issue here. In practical terms, however, when a pharmacist knows or has reasonable cause to believe that a below-threshold quantity of pseudoephedrine will be used for the production of methamphetamine, that is not a legitimate medical use.

In any event, whether or not Kim had to report the sales he entered into with the undercover DEA agents to the U.S. Attorney General, he could still be subject to criminal prosecution if those sales violated § 841(c)(2). Kim's criminal liability instead turns on whether he "kn[e]w or ha[d] reasonable cause to believe" that his conduct would lead to manufacture of illicit drugs. § 841(c)(2). As is true with other criminal statutes, conduct is prohibited not solely because of its objective contours, but because of the defendant's state of mind regarding such an effect. There is no quantity threshold exempting a merchant from criminal liability under § 841(c)(2).

Kim argues that, construed as containing no quantity threshold, the statute is unconstitutionally vague because it does not provide a reasonably intelligent person with sufficient notice concerning whether he is violating it. Essentially, he argues that absent designation of a "safe harbor" amount that he may sell to each individual each day, he cannot be expected to conform his behavior to legal requirements and thus avoid criminal liability. There is, however, no constitutional principle—and Kim points to none—requiring the federal government to spell out a specific amount of pseudoephedrine that pharmacists may sell in each transaction without incurring criminal liability. Nor do more general vagueness principles support his contention.

Vague laws that do not infringe upon First Amendment rights have two principle evils: (1) they do not give a "person of ordinary intelligence a reasonable opportunity to know what is prohibited, so that he may act accordingly"; and (2) they encourage arbitrary and discriminatory enforcement by not providing explicit standards for policemen, judges, and juries. Thus, if a statute is not sufficiently clear to provide guidance to citizens concerning how they can avoid violating it and to provide authorities with principles governing enforcement, a defendant cannot be punished for violating that statute.[16]

We have previously held that § 841(c)(2) contains a mens rea requirement. *United States v. Johal*, 428 F.3d 823, 827 (9th Cir. 2005). The statute "requires that a defendant subjectively know facts that either cause him or would cause a reasonable person to believe that the ingredients are being used to produce illegal drugs." Whether a defendant is guilty of having "reasonable cause to believe" that the pseudoephedrine will be used to produce illicit drugs "turns on *the facts actually known by the defendant* in a particular case." Also, the requirement includes the specification that the defendant had reasonable cause to believe that the chemical he sold "*will be used* to manufacture a controlled substance," § 841(c)(2) (emphasis added); mere probability of use is insufficient.[17] For all these reasons, the statutory "reasonable cause to believe" mens rea standard "limits the likelihood that a defendant will be prosecuted for mere inadvertent conduct and is consistent with the longstanding principle presuming a mens rea requirement for criminal activity." *Johal*, 428 F.3d at 827.

The holding in *Johal* forecasts our decision here, because "a scienter requirement may mitigate a law's vagueness, especially with respect to the adequacy of notice to the complainant that his conduct is proscribed." Significantly, here, a person of ordinary intelligence can base his behavior on his factual knowledge of the situation at hand and thereby avoid violating the law.

Kim argues that larger chain stores escape liability because of their larger size and mechanized checkouts, demonstrating that the statute is subject to arbitrary enforcement and therefore vague. We do not have any evidence on the record

16. As we noted earlier, we are assuming sufficient evidence because sufficiency was not challenged.

17. *Johal* rejected the defendant's contention that the "statute requires the actual production of methamphetamine." *Johal*, 428 F.3d at 828. It is therefore of no consequence that Kim sold the pseudoephedrine to undercover federal agents who presumably did not actually manufacture illicit drugs with their purchases. The key question is whether *Kim* had "reasonable cause to believe the chemical will be used to make drugs." The inquiry therefore centers on defendant's understanding, or imputed understanding, of the situation at the time of the sale.

supporting Kim's differential enforcement accusation. Even assuming that it is accurate, however, lack of prosecution of some cases that could be covered by a statute "is not sufficient reason to hold the language too ambiguous to define a criminal offense." *United States v. Petrillo,* 332 U.S. 1, 7 (1947).

Furthermore, any discrepancy in enforcement could well be the result of a structural difference between the chain stores and small pharmacies, rather than of arbitrary enforcement. It is not that the statute has no guidelines, such that the authorities can arbitrarily prosecute one class of merchants instead of another, but rather that the statute allows for a situation in which a store's structure can, intentionally or not, cause its employees and managers to avoid criminal liability. The disincentive to prosecute may be a matter of proof—that it is difficult for the government to prove the existence of an actor in the chain stores who knows or has reasonable cause to believe that a sale of pseudoephedrine will lead to the manufacture of methamphetamine, because checkout stands are covered by many different people at different times or not covered at all. Alternatively, the reason for any discrepancy in prosecution may be a matter of there not *being* an actor in the store who has such mens rea, because the larger stores have ways of monitoring their sales to assure that suspicious sales do not occur. Or it may be that the smaller, nonchain stores are targeted by the methamphetamine manufacturers themselves and so are more likely to come on the DEA's radar screen through pseudoephedrine manufacturers' reports or personal observation. As these examples show, given the reach of prosecutorial discretion, there are many explanations for differential prosecution—not all of them indicative of the most efficient policy—other than the vagueness of the statute involved.

Kim has misinterpreted, whether deliberately or not, his obligations under the federal and state laws restricting the sale of pseudoephedrine. We clarify here that the recording and reporting statutes establish no safe harbor from prosecution under § 841(c)(2). Instead, retailers must refrain from selling *any* amount of pseudoephedrine knowing or having reasonable cause to believe that the buyer intends to use the chemical to manufacture methamphetamine. Here, the jury determined that Kim knew or had reasonable cause to believe that the sales to the undercover DEA agents would lead to the manufacture of methamphetamine. Kim apparently thought he could rely on some magic formula, rather than his own informed observation of his customers, to decide which sales were legal and which were not. Congress has chosen not to provide such a formula. Balancing its desire to continue to allow sales of cold medicines without a prescription against the apparent propensity of methamphetamine manufacturers to accumulate chemicals for their manufacturing processes through purchases from ordinary retail stores, Congress has placed responsibility to monitor pseudoephedrine sales on those who are profiting from them.

There may be circumstances more marginal than this one in which that approach could yield an unfair result. Careful attention to the sufficiency of the evidence in cases under § 841(c)(2) is therefore of critical importance, so as not to dissuade legitimate retailers from selling these useful home remedies at all, for fear of prosecution.[18] That Kim was acquitted by the judge and the jury on most of the counts against him indicates that such care was taken in this case.

In sum, we conclude that because it has a sufficiently clear mens rea provision, § 841(c)(2) is not unconstitutionally vague. Kim's conviction was therefore valid.

AFFIRMED.

18. Although he did not raise a sufficiency argument, Kim's case is somewhat close compared to others that have been reported. There was, however sufficient evidence supporting the jury's conclusion, at least to the January 4 offense: Before the sting operation, Kim was warned by investigators from the California Pharmacy Board about the dangers of pseudoephedrine and his potential liability. There was a large spike in his sales, especially of the larger stock bottles. On January 4, Kim directly encountered three men who were acting suspiciously while purchasing substantial quantities of pseudoephedrine—specifically, stating a desire to "break it down"; purchasing alcohol, hydrogen peroxide, *and* iodine; attempting to purchase the entire supply of pseudoephedrine packages; and paying through a single person, suggesting one transaction rather than three—and yet he allowed the sale to proceed.

Chapter 7

The Regulation of Controlled Substances with Accepted Medical Uses

When it comes to Schedule I drugs like marijuana and heroin, the Controlled Substances Act (CSA) has a single objective: prohibition. But most substances that are regulated under the CSA have more legal medical users than illegal users. For substances in Schedules II through V of the CSA, the goal of prohibiting recreational use must be balanced against the need to ensure lawful medical users can obtain the substances prescribed to them. This chapter focuses on the CSA's treatment of controlled substances that are also legally recognized as medicines under federal law.

A. The Relationship Between the Controlled Substances Act and the Food, Drug, and Cosmetic Act

An examination of the Food and Drug Administration (FDA) and the Food, Drug, and Cosmetic Act (FDCA) is the domain of a course on Food and Drug Law. But a basic understanding of how the FDA and FDCA relate to the Drug Enforcement Administration (DEA) and the CSA helps to illuminate some of the issues that can arise in the regulation of substances that have both medicinal and recreational uses.

Prescription drugs that the DEA believes have a negligible potential for abuse, like penicillin, are not regulated under the CSA at all. Schedule I substances that have no currently accepted medical use are not regulated under the FDCA. But many substances are regulated both as controlled substances by the DEA and as medicines by the FDA. The "aims and regulatory mechanisms" of the FDA and the DEA "differ sharply." Kimani Paul-Emile, *Making Sense of Drug Regulation: A Theory of Law for Drug Control Policy*, 19 Cornell J. L. & Pub. Pol'y 691 (2010). The FDA is principally concerned with ensuring drug safety and efficacy while the DEA's mission is to try to eliminate illicit traffic in controlled substances, primarily through criminal investigations and prosecutions. As we have seen already, however, there is sometimes regulatory overlap between the FDA and DEA and the federal laws they administer—the FDCA and the CSA respectively. Recall, for example, that in

Grinspoon v. Drug Enforcement Administration, the DEA unsuccessfully argued that a drug could not have an "accepted medical use" under the Controlled Substances Act unless "the FDA ha[d] evaluated the substance for safety and approved it for interstate marketing in the United States pursuant to the Federal Food, Drug, and Cosmetic Act."

The next case examines the relationship between the FDCA and the CSA. In it, the court holds that the FDA overstepped its authority when it enacted regulations to guard against the diversion of methadone on the grounds that "[t]he problem of unlawful diversion is one presently consigned by Congress to the Drug Enforcement Administration."

American Pharmaceutical Association v. Weinberger

United States District Court for the District of Columbia
377 F. Supp. 824 (1974)

Pratt, J.

This is an action for judicial review of a regulation of the Food and Drug Administration (FDA) which restricts the distribution of methadone to certain specified outlets as set forth in the regulation. In effect, it prohibits virtually all licensed pharmacies from dispensing this drug when lawfully prescribed by a physician, despite the fact that methadone was invented and was first used as a safe, useful and effective agent in the treatment of severe pain and for antitussive purposes. Decision is not made easier by the fact that in recent years methadone has become a widely known maintenance agent in the treatment of heroin addicts and there is evidence of serious abuses in the distribution of this drug. In their efforts to control improper distribution of methadone, there are strong public policy arguments on the side of defendants. At the same time, the popularity of methadone for use as a pain killer has declined because of the introduction of effective new drugs, and as recently as 1972 the plaintiff Association formally recommended that FDA withdraw its approval of methadone for its indications as an analgesic and antitussive and expressed its philosophic non-disagreement with a course of regulation which would restrict the distribution and use of methadone to approved methadone treatment programs.

The challenged regulation, while ruling out most so-called community pharmacies in the dispensing of methadone for any purpose, still permits approved hospital pharmacies to dispense methadone for analgesic and antitussive purposes. Stripped of the rhetoric which abounds in the papers before us, this appears to be the basis of plaintiffs' complaint. Whether the FDA has the authority to enact the challenged regulation depends on the interplay and connection between two complementary but distinct statutes, the Food, Drug and Cosmetic Act of 1938 and the Comprehensive Drug Abuse Prevention & Control Act of 1970 and the respective roles assigned by Congress to the agencies which administer these Acts. With this brief background, we proceed to the issues presented.

This cause came on for hearing on defendants' motion to dismiss, or in the alternative, for summary judgment and plaintiffs' cross-motion for summary judgment on May 8, 1974. Plaintiffs challenge the validity of certain provisions of the Food and Drug Administration's methadone regulations, 21 C.F.R. § 130.44 ("Conditions for use of methadone") and § 130.48 ("Drugs that are subjects of approved new-drug applications and that require special studies, records and reports.") Specifically, plaintiffs object to those parts of the regulations which purport to restrict the distribution of methadone to direct shipments from the manufacturer to (a) approved maintenance treatment programs, (b) approved hospital pharmacies, and (c) in cases where hospital pharmacies are unavailable in a particular area, to selected community pharmacies.

Plaintiffs include the American Pharmaceutical Association (APhA), a professional association of pharmacists with a membership in excess of 50,000, three individual professional pharmacists and an individual physician. They argue that the restrictions imposed on the channels of distribution exceed the limits of FDA's authority. Plaintiffs seek declaratory relief holding said restrictions invalid and enjoining defendants from enforcing them.

Defendants are the Secretary of Health, Education and Welfare, the Commissioner of Food and Drugs, the Attorney General and the Acting Administrator of the Drug Enforcement Administration. They counter plaintiffs' contentions by citing FDA's authority under the Federal Food, Drug and Cosmetic Act (the Act) to control access to the public market of all new drugs and to promulgate regulations for the efficient enforcement of the Act and their authority under the Comprehensive Drug Abuse Prevention & Control Act of 1970 "[to] determine the appropriate methods of professional practice in the medical treatment of . . . narcotic addicts. . . ."

The drug methadone, a synthetic substitute for morphine, is a "new" drug within the meaning of section 201(p) of the Federal, Food, Drug and Cosmetic Act and, as a new drug, requires FDA's approval of a NDA, filed with the Commissioner of Food and Drugs pursuant to section 505(b) of the Act. The drug was first approved by FDA in the 1950s as safe for use as an analgesic and antitussive agent as well as for short-term detoxification of persons addicted to heroin. Subsequently, investigation of methadone for use in long-term maintenance of narcotic addicts (methadone maintenance) was approved by FDA pursuant to its authority under 21 U.S.C. § 355(i), the investigational new-drug (IND) exemption. Section 355(i) of the Act empowers FDA to exempt from NDA approval requirements those new drugs "intended solely for investigational use by experts qualified by scientific training and experience to investigate the safety and effectiveness of drugs." Final guidelines for long-term maintenance programs were promulgated by FDA in 1971. A year later FDA determined that "retention of the drug [methadone] solely on an investigational status appears to be no longer warranted" and published a notice of proposed rulemaking which resulted, with certain modifications, in the regulations now in question.

The final regulation gave notice that pursuant to FDA's authority under 21 U.S.C. § 355(c), the Commissioner was withdrawing approval of all outstanding NDA's because of "a lack of substantial evidence that methadone is safe and effective for detoxification, analgesia, or antitussive use *under the conditions of use that presently exist*."[5] Having withdrawn all approved NDA's, the Commission's new regulatory scheme is presently the exclusive means of distribution for the drug methadone. The Commissioner has thereby created an admittedly unique classification for methadone since on the one hand he has determined that methadone should not be limited solely to investigational status while at the same time concluding that the drug is inappropriate for regular NDA approval. As statutory support for this novel solution to the methadone dilemma, defendants rely on an expansive interpretation of the Commissioner's NDA authority under § 355 of the Act.

Under the Federal Food, Drug and Cosmetic Act, the FDA (through the Secretary of HEW) has the responsibility of passing on the merits of NDA's. The grounds upon which an NDA can be denied approval are explicitly stated in subsection (d) of § 355 and the NDA shall be approved "if [FDA] . . . finds that none of the grounds for denying approval . . . applies." The NDA must be supported by "substantial evidence" defined to mean "evidence consisting of adequate and well-controlled investigations, including clinical investigations, by experts qualified by scientific training and experience to evaluate the effectiveness of the drug involved, on the basis of which it could be fairly and responsibly concluded by such experts that the drug will have the effect it purports or is represented to have under the conditions of use prescribed, recommended, or suggested in the labeling or proposed labeling thereof."

One of the six enumerated grounds for refusing approval of a new drug application (NDA) specifically deals with the "methods" or "controls" used in connection with the proffered drug. Subsection (d)(3) of § 355 reads as follows: "(d) If the Secretary finds . . . (3) the methods used in, and the facilities and controls used for, the *manufacture, processing*, and *packing* of such drug are inadequate to preserve its identity, strength, quality, and purity; . . . he shall issue an order refusing to approve the application." (emphasis added.)

This is the only provision of § 355 which speaks of the Secretary's authority with respect to "controls." The Congress apparently intended that the Secretary, or his delegate, FDA, be responsible for the adequacy of premarketing methods and controls inasmuch as the provision delineates the scope of the provision to the manufacturing, processing and packaging stage of a drug's genesis.

The defendants point out, however, that § 355(d) also gives the Secretary the authority to refuse to approve an NDA where the reports of the investigations submitted do not include adequate tests showing whether the new drug is "safe for use under the conditions prescribed, recommended, or suggested in the proposed labeling thereof." Defendants argue that the term "safe" should be interpreted with

5. Although the Commissioner notes a lack of evidence with respect to methadone's effectiveness for the enumerated uses, defendants have relied exclusively on the drug's alleged safety hazard in attempting to justify the challenged restrictions on distributions.

reference not only to the inherent qualities of the drug under consideration but also in the sense of the drug's being secure from possible misuse. Such a broad interpretation would, according to defendants' theory, serve as the statutory foundation for FDA's exercise of authority in restricting methadone's channels of distribution because FDA's principal rationale for restricting distribution was "to help reduce the likelihood of diversion."

As a general proposition of statutory construction, a general term should not be construed in isolation but should be interpreted according to the context of the statute within which it is found. As noted above, the term "safe" is used in conjunction with the phrase "for use under the conditions prescribed, recommended, or suggested in the proposed labeling thereof." When taken in this context, a determination of whether a drug is "safe" is premised on the drug's use in the "prescribed, recommended, or suggested" manner. Thus the context of the statute indicates that the term "safe" was intended to include only the inherent safety of the drug when used in the manner intended. Moreover, as also noted above, the subject of "controls" is specifically covered in provision (3) of the same subsection (d) wherein the term "safe" appears. Provision (3) extends the Secretary's authority to pass on the adequacy of methods, facilities and *controls* only with respect to *manufacturing, processing* and *packaging.* Under the doctrine of "expressio unius est exclusio alterius" any stage of the drug's genesis not specifically mentioned in provision (3) was presumably intended to be excluded from the Secretary's authority. Thus by examining the term "safe" in the context of those provisions of the Act in which it appears as well as in relationship to the provision of the Act which specifically deals with controls, the Court concludes that the term "safe" was intended to refer to a determination of the inherent safety or lack thereof of the drug under consideration when used for its intended purpose.

Finally, the legislative history of the Act fully supports this conclusion. In enacting the Comprehensive Drug Abuse Prevention and Control Act of 1970, Congress was presented with a conscious decision as to how the lines of authority should be drawn with respect to the regulation of dangerous drugs. Congress decided to continue all control authority over the distribution of dangerous drugs in the Justice Department despite a recommendation of the Prettyman Commission that this function be transferred to HEW. The House Committee on Interstate and Foreign Commerce in their report on the Comprehensive Drug Abuse Prevention and Control Act of 1970 indicated that Title II of that Act, known as the Controlled Substances Act, was designed to "provide authority for the Department of Justice to keep track of all drugs subject to abuse manufactured or distributed in the United States in order to prevent diversion of these drugs from legitimate channels of commerce." Although it is nowhere specifically stated that Congress contemplated that the Justice Department would have exclusive authority to prevent diversion, this result would appear logically to follow from a comparison of the functions delegated to the Secretary of HEW with those assigned to the Attorney General.

In addition to being a "new" drug and thus within the jurisdiction of the FDA, methadone is a controlled substance within Schedule II of the Controlled Substances Act. Under this Act the Attorney General is made responsible for the registration of any person who manufactures, distributes or dispenses any controlled substance. An applicant may be refused registration if the Attorney General makes a determination that registering the applicant would be inconsistent with the public interest. Congress has also provided the specific means for revoking or suspending the authority of a registrant to distribute controlled substances. In addition, Congress has specified the precise procedure to be followed by the Attorney General in attempting to revoke or suspend a registration.

The Court concludes that Congress intended to create two complementary institutional checks on the production and marketing of new drugs. At the production or pre-marketing stage, the FDA is given the primary responsibility in determining which new drugs should be permitted to enter the flow of commerce. The Commissioner must approve or deny every NDA, or he may determine that a particular new drug qualifies for IND status in order to permit additional experimentation. When an IND exemption is approved, the Commissioner may, of course, severely restrict the distribution of the exempted drug to bona fide researchers and clinicians. But once a drug is cleared for marketing by way of a NDA-approval, for whatever uses the Commissioner deems appropriate, the question of permissible distribution of the drug, when that drug is a controlled substance, is one clearly within the jurisdiction of the Justice Department. The diversion of the particular drug to a use not approved by the Commissioner would be grounds for revocation of the offending distributor's registration. FDA attempts to accomplish peremptorily by way of its challenged regulation, that which could only be accomplished, according to the scheme of the Controlled Substances Act, by way of show-cause proceedings initiated by the Attorney General, i.e., revoking the authority of otherwise duly-registered distributors with respect to the drug methadone. To allow the challenged portions of the methadone regulations to stand, therefore, would be to abrogate the collective judgment of Congress with regard to the appropriate means of controlling unlawful drug diversion.

This is particularly true of the regulations' denial of authority to the plaintiffs at bar. Although the Attorney General generally has discretion to register applicants wishing to distribute or dispense controlled substances [under the Controlled Substances Act] in the case of "practitioners" the Attorney General *must* register them "if they are authorized to dispense under the law of the State in which they regularly conduct business." Congress has thereby specifically sanctioned the registration of all State-licensed practitioners with the clear intent of permitting them to dispense controlled substances on an equal basis with all other approved distributors. In the face of such clear-cut Congressional intent, it would be anomalous to suggest that an agency, by the mere issuance of a regulation, could modify these mandated channels of distribution. Accordingly, the Court concludes that FDA has overstepped the bounds of its authority in purporting to limit the distribution of methadone in the manner contemplated by its regulations.

It is undoubtedly true that methadone poses unique problems of medical judgment, law enforcement and public policy but this fact alone cannot justify a federal agency of specifically delimited jurisdiction from implementing equally unique control solutions not authorized by Congress. The problem of unlawful diversion is one presently consigned by Congress to the Drug Enforcement Administration (DEA, formerly the Bureau of Narcotics and Dangerous Drugs) of the Department of Justice. FDA, on the other hand, has the responsibility of making the initial decision, based on all available medical and scientific data, as to whether a particular new drug is safe and effective for its intended use. While the functions of FDA and DEA are not entirely exclusive of one another,[16] a certain division of authority and responsibility was clearly intended by Congress and must be recognized by this Court in order to preserve the integrity of the legislative scheme. Under these circumstances, the relative merits of FDA's plan to control the distribution of methadone, a controlled substance, must first be passed upon by Congress.

Wherefore, for all the foregoing reasons, . . . plaintiffs' motion for summary judgment . . . is, granted[.]

The D.C. Circuit Court affirmed *American Pharmaceutical Association v. Weinberger* in a *per curiam* opinion "on the basis of the opinion of the District Court." *American Pharmaceutical Association v. Matthews*, 530 F. 2d 1054 (1976). The decision included a brief concurring opinion by Judge McGowan describing the distinction between the FDA's power to authorize the distribution of a drug on a prescription-only basis and its effort to place restrictions on the distribution of methadone out of concern that the drug would be misused:

> The pivotal provision of the Federal Food, Drug and Cosmetic Act [in this case] is 21 U.S.C. § 355(d), which prohibits the approval of a new drug application unless there are adequate data to establish that the "drug is safe for use under the conditions prescribed, recommended, or suggested in the proposed labeling thereof. . . ." The FDA contends that where there exists a documented pattern of drug misuse contrary to the intended uses specified in the labelling, the drug is unsafe for approval unless controls over distribution are imposed. As a corollary, it asserts that for a drug such as methadone, for which there is substantial evidence of misuse, the FDA

16. For example, the Attorney General, in exercising his authority under 21 U.S.C. § 811(a) to add or remove drugs from the schedules of controlled substances established by the Controlled Substances Act, must first call upon FDA for its recommendation. The recommendations of FDA, insofar as they concern "scientific and medical matters" relating to the "appropriate schedule, if any, under which such drug or substance should be listed" are binding on the Attorney General. 21 U.S.C. § 811(b).

must have the power to restrict distribution to avoid the dilemma of either disapproving a drug with important therapeutic benefits or of placing on the market a drug likely to be misused. The FDA claims that section 355(d) authorized restricting distribution to a prescription-only basis before the FDA was explicitly granted that authority in 1951, and that the regulations at issue differ only in degree from a prescription-only restriction.

Although these arguments have some weight, I do not find them ultimately convincing. The word "safe" in section 355(d) is, to my mind, best interpreted as requiring the labelling to include the evidence from drug testing, and the inferences therefrom, indicating the therapeutic benefits, possible dangers, and uncertainties involved in use of a drug, as an aid to a conscientious physician in determining appropriate medical treatment. That view seems to me to accord with both the most reasonable interpretation of the statutory language and the common understanding of the FDA's mission. Thus, methadone is safe for its intended use notwithstanding the possibility that it will be employed in unintended fashions.

The controls on distribution here are different in kind from prescription-only restrictions. The latter restrictions prevent self-diagnosis by the layman. If such restrictions had not been permitted before 1951, drug labelling would have had to include both specific medical evidence about a drug and all the general medical knowledge that a physician must possess in order to decide, after reading a labelling, whether to administer a drug. Although one might contend in theory that any drug is safe for its intended use if the labelling contains enough information, it is evident that a layman cannot be expected to digest a mass of complicated medical information and bring to bear upon it the medical judgment of a practicing physician. Thus, restrictions to a prescription-only basis are necessary to ensure that persons intending to use drugs in accordance with the implications of medical evidence gathered by the FDA and contained in a drug labelling can do so. The restrictions on methadone involved here are quite different. Without them an informed and sound medical judgment about medical safety and effectiveness can still be made. They are designed instead to control drug misuse by persons who have no intent to try to use drugs for medical purposes.

There would be almost no limit to the FDA's authority were its view adopted. If, for example, it had concluded before 1970 that without restrictions on methadone of the sort now contained in the Controlled Substances Act, the possibility of drug misuse remained high, there would be no barrier under its argument to its having established a regulatory scheme of the complexity of that ultimately adopted in that Act. Thus, under the authority of section 355(d) (and the general power to promulgate implementing regulations in section 371(a)), the FDA might have established a comprehensive registration scheme, complete with detailed record-keeping, security, and inspection requirements. I do not believe that the current grant of statutory authority contemplates such activity by the FDA, but accepting the FDA's view would require upholding far-ranging regulation of that sort.

B. The Controlled Substances Act and Prescription Drugs

As discussed in Chapter 2, the opioid crisis is arguably the most damaging drug epidemic in at least 100 years, with 47,600 overdose deaths involving an opiod in 2017. The problem is not limited to pharmaceutical painkillers. A study released in 2017 found that just over one-third of opioid users initiated use with heroin and not a prescription medicine. TJ Cicero et al., *Increased Use of Heroin as an Initiating Opioid of Abuse*, 74 ADDICTIVE BEHAVIORS 63 (2017). Nevertheless, prescription medicines remain at the center of the epidemic. While prescription opioids have understandably attracted a great deal of attention and concern, there are a number of other pharmaceuticals with significant numbers of non-medical users—from sleep medications like Ambien to stimulants like Adderall.

The non-medical use of prescription medications presents particularly difficult legal and policy challenges. In addition to the policy issues explored at the beginning of this casebook—such as whether it is legitimate for the government to criminalize the distribution or use of a substance for recreational purposes—the regulation of prescription drugs raises the question of how to balance a patient's interest in having convenient and affordable access to her medication with the government's desire to stop recreational use. This is because every administrative and criminal control aimed at preventing the diversion of prescription drugs to recreational users will inevitably add an additional cost or hurdle that may be borne by patients. Unlike FDA regulations which, as discussed in *American Pharmaceutical Association v. Weinberger*, are promulgated with the aim of furthering the interest of patients (e.g., by ensuring that a drug is properly labeled and its side effects identified and disclosed), the Controlled Substances Act's provisions related to pharmaceuticals exist in order to try to prevent non-medical use and abuse. When reading the materials that follow, consider whether you think the law has struck the proper balance between these interests.

1. Regulation and Prosecution of Physicians

Should a physician who prescribes a controlled substance outside the bounds of legitimate medical practice be subject to the "same penalties as street pushers with no claim to legitimacy"? *United States v. Moore*, 423 U.S. 122, 139 (1975). Or should lesser (or no) criminal penalties apply in light of the availability of a civil sanction that might be adequate to deter misconduct by doctors—namely, the loss of their license to prescribe controlled substances or even to practice medicine?

In *Moore*, presented below, the Supreme Court considered this issue. Three different sections of the Controlled Substances Act's criminal provisions were at issue in *Moore*.

First was 21 U.S.C. § 841(a), which applies to "street pushers" and is the provision that Dr. Moore was convicted of having violated. It provides that "[e]xcept as authorized by this subchapter, it shall be unlawful for any person knowingly or intentionally . . . to manufacture, distribute, or dispense, or possess with intent to manufacture, distribute, or dispense, a controlled substance." Before the Supreme Court, Moore argued that he could not have been guilty of violating 21 U.S.C. § 841(a) because "registered physicians may be prosecuted only under [21 U.S.C.] §§ 842 and 843." *Moore, supra*, 423 U.S. at 128. Sections 842 and 843 apply to people who are registered to handle controlled substances under the CSA. Each makes it a federal crime for CSA registrants, including physicians, to violate various regulatory provisions of the CSA. Section 842 makes it unlawful for any CSA registrant or prospective registrant "to distribute or dispense a controlled substance in violation of" the part of the CSA that outlines requirements for prescribing controlled substances. 21 U.S.C. § 842(a)(1). Section 843 makes it a crime for "a registrant to distribute a controlled substance classified in schedule I or II, in the course of his legitimate business, except pursuant to an order or an order form as required by section 828 of this title." 21 U.S.C. § 843(a)(1). Notably, sections 842 and 843 both provide for much lighter maximum penalties than section 841.

Moore argued that the statutory scheme suggested that Congress intended for CSA registrants like him to be subject to the more lenient penalties of sections 842 and 843 and to be excluded from the harsher penalties of section 841. The Supreme Court rejected Moore's position and held that the doctors can be subject to the same criminal penalties for controlled substances violations as anyone else.

United States v. Moore

Supreme Court of the United States
423 U.S. 122 (1975)

Mr. Justice Powell delivered the opinion of the Court.

Dr. Moore was charged, in a 639-count indictment, with the knowing and unlawful distribution and dispensation of methadone (Dolophine), a Schedule II controlled substance, in violation of 21 U.S.C. § 841(a)(1). That subsection provides:

> "Except as authorized by this subchapter, it shall be unlawful for any person knowingly or intentionally—
>
> "(1) to manufacture, distribute, or dispense, or possess with intent to manufacture, distribute, or dispense, a controlled substance. . . ."

The indictment covered a 5 1/2-month period from late August 1971 to early February 1972. It was reduced before trial to 40 counts, and the jury convicted respondent on 22 counts. He was sentenced to concurrent terms of five to 15 years' imprisonment on 14 counts, and to concurrent terms of 10 to 30 years on the remaining eight counts. The second set of sentences was to be consecutive with the first. Fines totaling $150,000 were also imposed.[2]

Methadone is an addictive drug used in the treatment of heroin addicts. If taken without controls it can, like heroin, create euphoric "highs," but if properly administered it eliminates the addict's craving for heroin without providing a "high." The two principal methods of treating heroin addicts with methadone are "detoxification" and "maintenance." Under a maintenance program, the addict is given a fixed dose once a day for an indefinite period to keep him from using heroin. In detoxification the addict is given a large dose of methadone during the first few days of treatment to keep him free of withdrawal symptoms. Then the dose is gradually reduced until total abstinence is reached.

Maintenance is the more controversial method of treatment. During the period covered by the indictment, registration under § 822, in itself, did not entitle a physician to conduct a maintenance program. In addition to a § 822 registration, the physician who wished to conduct such a program was required to obtain authorization from the Food and Drug Administration for investigation of a new drug. Dr. Moore's authorization by the FDA was revoked in the summer of 1971, and he does not claim that he was conducting an authorized maintenance program. Instead, his defense at trial was that he had devised a new method of detoxification based on the work of a British practitioner. He testified that he prescribed large quantities of methadone to achieve a "blockade" condition, in which the addict was so saturated with methadone that heroin would have no effect, and to instill a strong psychological desire for detoxification. The Government's position is that the evidence established that Dr. Moore's conduct was inconsistent with all accepted methods of treating addicts, that in fact he operated as a "pusher."

Respondent concedes in his brief that he did not observe generally accepted medical practices. He conducted a large-scale operation. Between September 1971 and mid-February 1972 three District of Columbia pharmacies filled 11,169 prescriptions written by Dr. Moore. These covered some 800,000 methadone tablets. On 54 days during that period respondent wrote over 100 prescriptions a day. In billing his patients he used a "sliding-fee scale" pegged solely to the quantity prescribed, rather than to the medical services performed. The fees ranged from $15 for a 50-pill prescription to $50 for 150 pills. In five and one-half months Dr. Moore's receipts totaled at least $260,000.

When a patient entered the office he was given only the most perfunctory examination. Typically this included a request to see the patient's needle marks (which in more than one instance were simulated) and an unsupervised urinalysis (the results

2. In addition, Dr. Moore's license to practice medicine was revoked pursuant to D.C. Code Ann. § 2-131 (1973), which authorizes revocation upon the conviction of "any felony." An appeal from the conviction acts "as a supersedeas to the judgment . . . revoking his license. . . ."

of which were regularly ignored). A prescription was then written for the amount requested by the patient. On return visits—for which appointments were never scheduled—no physical examination was performed and the patient again received a prescription for whatever quantity he requested. Accurate records were not kept, and in some cases the quantity prescribed was not recorded. There was no supervision of the administration of the drug. Dr. Moore's instructions consisted entirely of a label on the drugs reading: "Take as directed for detoxification." Some patients used the tablets to get "high"; others sold them or gave them to friends or relatives. Several patients testified that their use of methadone increased dramatically while they were under respondent's care.

The Court of Appeals, with one judge dissenting, assumed that respondent acted wrongfully but held that he could not be prosecuted under § 841. The court found that Congress intended to subject registered physicians to prosecution only under §§ 842 and 843, which prescribe less severe penalties than § 841.[6] The court reasoned:

> ". . . Congress intended to deal with registrants primarily through a system of administrative controls, relying on modest penalty provisions to enforce those controls, and reserving the severe penalties provided for in § 841 for those seeking to avoid regulation entirely by not registering."

It said, further, that §§ 842 and 843 were enacted to enforce that scheme, while § 841 was reserved for prosecution of those outside the "legitimate distribution chain." Persons registered under the Act were "authorized by [the] subchapter" within the meaning of § 841 and thus were thought to be immunized against prosecution under that section.

Respondent advances two basic arguments, contending that each requires affirmance of the Court of Appeals: (i) as that court held, registered physicians may be prosecuted only under §§ 842 and 843; and (ii) in any event, respondent cannot be prosecuted under § 841 because his conduct was "authorized by [the] subchapter" in question. We now consider each of these arguments.

Section 841(a)(1) makes distribution and dispensing of drugs unlawful "[e]xcept as authorized by this subchapter. . . ." Relying on this language, the Court of Appeals held that a physician registered under the Act is *per se* exempted from prosecution under § 841 because of his status as a registrant. We take a different view, and hold that only the lawful acts of registrants are exempted. By its terms § 841 reaches "any person." It does not exempt (as it could have) "all registrants" or "all persons registered under this Act."

---

6. Violations of § 841, under which respondent was convicted, carry sentences of up to 15 years, fines as high as $25,000, or both. Knowing violators of § 842 are subject at most to imprisonment for one year, a fine of $25,000, or both. There also may be a civil penalty of $25,000 for violation of § 842. The penalties for violation of § 843 are imprisonment for not more than four years, a fine of not more than $30,000, or both. All three sections impose higher penalties for violations after the first conviction.

The Court of Appeals relied also on § 822 (b), which provides: "Persons registered . . . under this subchapter to distribute, or dispense controlled substances are authorized to possess, . . . distribute, or dispense such substances . . . to the extent authorized by their registration and in conformity with the other provisions of this subchapter." This is a qualified authorization of certain activities, not a blanket authorization of all acts by certain persons. We think the statutory language cannot fairly be read to support the view that all activities of registered physicians are exempted from the reach of § 841 simply because of their status.

If § 822 (b) were construed to authorize all such activities, thereby exempting them from other constraints, it would constitute a sharp departure from prior laws. But there is no indication that Congress had any such intent. Physicians who stepped outside the bounds of professional practice could be prosecuted under the Harrison Act (Narcotics) of 1914, the predecessor of the CSA. In *Jin Fuey Moy v. United States,* 254 U.S. 189 (1920), the Court affirmed the conviction of a physician on facts remarkably similar to those before us (*e.g.,* no adequate physical examination, the dispensing of large quantities of drugs without specific directions for use, and fees graduated according to the amount of drugs prescribed). A similar conviction was upheld in *United States v. Behrman,* 258 U.S. 280 (1922), where the defendant-doctor had prescribed heroin, morphine, and cocaine to a person whom he knew to be an addict.

In enacting the CSA Congress attempted to devise a more flexible penalty structure than that used in the Harrison Act. Penalties were geared to the nature of the violation, including the character of the drug involved. But the Act was intended to "strengthen," rather than to weaken, "existing law enforcement authority in the field of drug abuse."

Section 822 (b) was added to the original bill at a late date to "make it clear that persons registered under this title are authorized to deal in or handle controlled substances." It is unlikely that Congress would seek, in this oblique way, to carve out a major new exemption, not found in the Harrison Act, for physicians and other registrants. Rather, § 822 (b) was added merely to ensure that persons engaged in lawful activities could not be prosecuted.

Respondent nonetheless contends that §§ 841 and 822 (b) must be interpreted in light of a congressional intent to set up two separate and distinct penalty systems: Persons not registered under the Act are to be punished under § 841, while those who are registered are to be subject only to the sanctions of §§ 842 and 843. The latter two sections, the argument goes, establish modest penalties which are the sole sanctions in a system of strict administrative regulation of registrants.

The operative language of those sections provides no real support for the proposition that Congress intended to establish two mutually exclusive systems. It is true that the term "registrants" is used in §§ 842 and 843, and not in § 841. But this is of limited significance. All three sections provide that "[i]t shall be unlawful for any person . . . [to commit the proscribed acts]." Two of the eight subsections of § 842 (a), one of the five subsections of § 843 (a), and § 842 (b) further qualify "any person" with "who is a registrant." The other subsections of §§ 842 and 843 are not so limited. In context, "registrant" is merely a limiting term, indicating that the only "persons" who are subject to these subsections are "registrants."[10] There is no indication that "persons" means "nonregistrants" when introducing the other subsections.

There are other indications that § 841, and §§ 842 and 843, do not constitute two discrete systems. Section 843 (b), for example, makes it unlawful for any person to use a communication facility in committing a felony under any provision of the subchapter. But violations of both § 841 and § 843 lead to felony convictions; criminal violations of § 842 are misdemeanors. And counsel for respondent agreed at oral argument that registrants can be prosecuted under § 841 (a)(2), which prohibits the creation, distribution, dispensing, or possession with intent to distribute or dispense of a "counterfeit substance."

The legislative history indicates that Congress was concerned with the nature of the drug transaction, rather than with the status of the defendant. The penalties now embodied in §§ 841–843 originated in §§ 501–503 of the Controlled Dangerous Substances Act of 1969. The Report of the Senate Judiciary Committee on that bill described § 501 (the counterpart of § 841) as applying to "traffickers." Section 502 provided "[a]dditional penalties . . . for those involved in the legitimate drug trade," and "[f]urther penalties . . . for registrants" were specified in § 503. The House Committee Report on the bill that was to become the CSA explains: "The bill provides for control . . . of problems related to drug abuse through registration of manufacturers, wholesalers, retailers, and all others in the legitimate distribution chain, and makes transactions outside the legitimate distribution chain illegal." Although this language is ambiguous, the most sensible interpretation is that the penalty to be imposed for a violation was intended to turn on whether the "transaction" falls within or without legitimate channels. All persons who engage in legitimate transactions must be registered and are subject to penalties under §§ 842 and 843 for "[m]ore or less technical violations." But "severe criminal penalties" were imposed on those, like respondent, who sold drugs, not for legitimate purposes, but "primarily for the profits to be derived therefrom."

Congress was particularly concerned with the diversion of drugs from legitimate channels to illegitimate channels. It was aware that registrants, who have the greatest access to controlled substances and therefore the greatest opportunity for diversion, were responsible for a large part of the illegal drug traffic.

Recognizing this concern the Court of Appeals suggested that Dr. Moore could be prosecuted under § 842 (a)(1) for having violated the provisions of § 829 with

---

10. This represents a commonsense recognition by Congress that only a registrant could, for example, distribute drugs "not authorized by his registration," § 842 (a)(2), or manufacture substances "not expressly authorized by his registration" or "in excess of [his] quota." §§ 842 (b)(1), (2). Nor would there be any reason to apply to nonregistrants the penalties for distributing drugs without complying with the labeling and order-form requirements of the Act, §§ 842 (a)(3), 843 (a)(1), for nonregistrants are barred from making any distributions whatsoever.

respect to the issuing of prescriptions.[12] Whether Dr. Moore could have been so prosecuted is not before the Court.[13] We note, however, that the penalties for such a violation could hardly have been deemed by Congress to be an appropriate sanction for drug trafficking by a registered physician. Indeed, the penalty for conviction under § 842 would be significantly lighter than, for example, that applicable to a registrant convicted under § 843 for using a suspended registration number. Moreover, a physician who wished to traffic in drugs without threat of criminal prosecution could, if violation of § 829 were the sole basis for prosecution, simply dispense drugs directly without the formality of issuing a prescription. Direct dispensing is exempt from § 829 and thus is not reached by any subsection of § 842 or § 843 so long as the technical requirements are complied with.

But we think it immaterial whether Dr. Moore also could have been prosecuted for his violation of statutory provisions relating to dispensing procedures. There is nothing in the statutory scheme or the legislative history that justifies a conclusion that a registrant who may be prosecuted for the relatively minor offense of violating § 829 is thereby exempted from prosecution under § 841 for the significantly greater offense of acting as a drug "pusher."

Respondent argues that even if Congress did not intend to exempt registrants from all prosecutions under § 841, he cannot be prosecuted under that section because the specific conduct for which he was prosecuted was "authorized by [the] subchapter" and thus falls within the express exemption of the section.

---

12. Section 829 provides, in part: "Except when dispensed directly by a practitioner, other than a pharmacist, to an ultimate user, no controlled substance in schedule II, which is a prescription drug as determined under the Federal Food, Drug, and Cosmetic Act, may be dispensed without the written prescription of a practitioner, except that in emergency situations, as prescribed by the Secretary by regulation after consultation with the Attorney General, such drug may be dispensed upon oral prescription in accordance with section 353 (b) of this title. Prescriptions shall be retained in conformity with the requirements of section 827 of this title. No prescription for a controlled substance in schedule II may be refilled."

The Attorney General's regulations enacted pursuant to § 829 required "A prescription for a controlled substance to be effective must be issued for a legitimate medical purpose by an individual practitioner acting in the usual course of his professional practice. The responsibility for the proper prescribing and dispensing of controlled substances is upon the prescribing practitioner, but a corresponding responsibility rests with the pharmacist who fills the prescription. An order purporting to be a prescription issued not in the usual course of professional treatment or in legitimate and authorized research is not a prescription within the meaning and intent of section 309 of the Act (21 U.S.C. 829) and the person knowingly filling such a purported prescription, as well as the person issuing it, shall be subject to the penalties provided for violations of the provisions of law relating to controlled substances." 21 CFR § 306.04 (a) (1973) (redesignated as 21 CFR § 1306.04 (a) (1975)).

13. On its face § 829 addresses only the form that a prescription must take. A written prescription is required for Schedule II substances. § 829 (a). Either a written or an oral prescription is adequate for drugs in Schedules III and IV. § 829 (b). The only limitation on the distribution or dispensing of Schedule V drugs is that it be "for a medical purpose." The medical purpose requirement explicit in subsection (c) could be implicit in subsections (a) and (b). Regulation § 306.04 makes it explicit. But § 829 by its terms does not limit the authority of a practitioner.

The trial judge assumed that a physician's activities are authorized only if they are within the usual course of professional practice. He instructed the jury that it had to find

> "beyond a reasonable doubt that a physician, who knowingly or intentionally, did dispense or distribute [methadone] by prescription, did so other than in good faith for detoxification in the usual course of a professional practice and in accordance with a standard of medical practice generally recognized and accepted in the United States."

The Court of Appeals did not address this argument because it concluded that registrants could not be prosecuted under § 841 under any circumstances. But it suggested that if a registrant could be reached under § 841 he could not be prosecuted merely because his activities fall outside the "usual course of practice."

Under the Harrison Act physicians who departed from the usual course of medical practice were subject to the same penalties as street pushers with no claim to legitimacy. Section 2 of that Act required all persons who sold or prescribed certain drugs to register and to deliver drugs only to persons with federal order forms. The latter requirement did not apply to "the dispensing or distribution of any of the aforesaid drugs to a patient by a physician . . . registered under this Act in the course of his professional practice only." As noted above, Congress intended the CSA to strengthen rather than to weaken the prior drug laws. There is no indication that Congress intended to eliminate the existing limitation on the exemption given to doctors.[16] The difficulty arises because the CSA, unlike the Harrison Act, does not spell out this limitation in unambiguous terms.

Instead of expressly removing from the protection of the Act those physicians who operate beyond the bounds of professional practice, the CSA uses the concept of "registration." Section 822 (b) defines the scope of authorization under the Act in circular terms: "Persons registered . . . under this subchapter . . . are authorized [to dispense controlled substances] . . . to the extent authorized by their registration and in conformity with the other provisions of this subchapter." But the scheme of the statute, viewed against the background of the legislative history, reveals an intent to limit a registered physician's dispensing authority to the course of his "professional practice."

---

16. The Narcotic Addict Treatment Act of 1974 (NATA) modified the registration and revocation procedures provided in the CSA in order to facilitate "more expeditious" criminal prosecutions by making revocation easier.

There was no indication that Congress thought that trafficking doctors could escape felony prosecution altogether under pre-NATA law. Rather, it sought to "cure the present difficulty in such prosecutions because of the intricate and nearly impossible burden of establishing what is beyond 'the course of professional practice' for criminal law purposes when such a practitioner speciously claims that the practices in question were ethical and humanitarian in nature." Dr. Moore's conviction was cited to illustrate that successful criminal actions could be brought only "in the most aggravated of circumstances . . . after prolonged effort to make undercover penetrations."

Registration of physicians and other practitioners is mandatory if the applicant is authorized to dispense drugs or conduct research under the law of the State in which he practices. In the case of a physician this scheme contemplates that he is authorized by the State to practice medicine and to dispense drugs in connection with his professional practice. The federal registration, which follows automatically, extends no farther. It authorizes transactions within "the legitimate distribution chain" and makes all others illegal. Implicit in the registration of a physician is the understanding that he is authorized only to act "as a physician."

This is made explicit in § 802 (20), which provides that "practitioner" means one who is "registered . . . by the United States or the jurisdiction in which he practices or does research, to distribute, dispense, conduct research with respect to, administer, or use in teaching or chemical analysis, a controlled substance in the course of professional practice or research." This section defines the term "practitioner" for purposes of the Act. It also describes the type of registration contemplated by the Act. That registration is limited to the dispensing and use of drugs "in the course of professional practice or research."

The evidence presented at trial was sufficient for the jury to find that respondent's conduct exceeded the bounds of "professional practice."[20] As detailed above, he gave inadequate physical examinations or none at all. He ignored the results of the tests he did make. He did not give methadone at the clinic and took no precautions against its misuse and diversion. He did not regulate the dosage at all, prescribing as much and as frequently as the patient demanded. He did not charge for medical services rendered, but graduated his fee according to the number of tablets desired. In practical effect, he acted as a large-scale "pusher"—not as a physician.

Respondent further contended at trial that he was experimenting with a new "blockade" theory of detoxification. The jury did not believe him. Congress understandably was concerned that the drug laws not impede legitimate research and that physicians be allowed reasonable discretion in treating patients and testing new theories. But respondent's interpretation of the Act would go far beyond authorizing legitimate research and experimentation by physicians.

In enacting the Comprehensive Drug Abuse Prevention and Control Act of 1970, Title II of which is the CSA, Congress faced the problem directly. Because of the potential for abuse it decided that some limits on free experimentation with drugs were necessary. But it was also aware of the concern expressed by the Prettyman Commission:*

> "[A] controversy has existed for fifty years over the extent to which narcotic drugs may be administered to an addict solely because he is an addict.

20. The jury was instructed that Dr. Moore could not be convicted if he merely made "an honest effort" to prescribe for detoxification in compliance with an accepted standard of medical practice.

* The Prettyman Commission, was established by President John F. Kennedy to review and make recommendations regarding federal drug policy. [*Footnote by casebook author.*]

> "The practicing physician has . . . been confused as to when he may prescribe narcotic drugs for an addict. Out of a fear of prosecution many physicians refuse to use narcotics in the treatment of addicts except occasionally in a withdrawal regimen lasting no longer than a few weeks. In most instances they shun addicts as patients."

Congress' solution to this problem is found in §4 of Title I of the 1970 Act. That section requires the Secretary of Health, Education, and Welfare, after consultation with the Attorney General and national addict treatment organizations, to "determine the appropriate methods of professional practice in the medical treatment of . . . narcotic addiction. . . ." It was designed "to clarify for the medical profession . . . the extent to which they may safely go in treating narcotic addicts as patients." Congress pointed out that "criminal prosecutions" in the past had turned on the opinions of federal prosecutors. Under the new Act, "[t]hose physicians who comply with the recommendations made by the Secretary will no longer jeopardize their professional careers. . . ." The negative implication is that physicians who go beyond approved practice remain subject to serious criminal penalties.

In the case of methadone treatment the limits of approved practice are particularly clear. As Dr. Moore admitted at trial, he was authorized only to dispense methadone for detoxification purposes. His authorization by the FDA to engage in a methadone maintenance program had been revoked. Nor was respondent unfamiliar with the procedures for conducting a legitimate detoxification program. Charges arising out of his 1969 treatment program, which involved a combination of "long term" and "short term" detoxification, were dropped after he testified before a grand jury and agreed to abide by certain medical procedures in future methadone programs. These included obtaining a medical history of each patient, conducting a reasonably thorough physical examination, abiding by the results of urine tests, recording times and amounts of dosages, and either administering the methadone in his office or prescribing no more than a daily dosage. At trial respondent admitted that he had failed to follow these procedures.

The judgment of the Court of Appeals is reversed.

So ordered.

The majority of states follow *Moore* and hold that physicians can be prosecuted under the same criminal provisions that apply to non-physicians engaged in the distribution of controlled substances. In some states, however, doctors accused of prescribing controlled substances for illegitimate purposes can only be prosecuted under statutes that pertain specifically to registered practitioners, which generally carry significantly lower penalties. *See* State v. Young, 185 W. Va. 327, 338–40 (1991) (collecting cases). *Moore* distinguishes between physicians who dispense controlled substances for legitimate medical purposes and those who operate as "pushers." Not surprisingly, this issue can present difficult line-drawing problems.

United States v. Hurwitz

United States Court of Appeals for the Fourth Circuit
459 F.3d 463 (2006)

Traxler, J.

A jury convicted Dr. William E. Hurwitz of multiple counts of drug trafficking for prescribing narcotic pain medicine in violation of 21 U.S.C.A. §§ 841(a)(1) and 846.

Hurwitz is a medical doctor who operated a practice in McLean, Virginia, dedicated to the treatment of patients suffering from pain. Hurwitz's approach to pain management involved the use of opioids, including methadone, oxycodone (typically Oxycontin, a brand-name version of a time-release form of oxycodone), and hydromorphone (usually the brand-name Dilaudid). Many of Hurwitz's patients were on a protocol that used very high doses of opioids to control their pain.

Hurwitz came to the attention of federal authorities in 2002, after several of his patients were arrested for attempting to sell illicit and prescription drugs. The patients identified Hurwitz as the source of their prescription drugs, and they began cooperating with the investigators. The information these patients provided eventually led to Hurwitz's indictment on numerous drug-related charges—one count of conspiracy to engage in drug trafficking; one count of engaging in a continuing criminal enterprise; two counts of healthcare fraud; and 58 counts of drug trafficking, including two counts each of drug-trafficking resulting in serious bodily injury and drug-trafficking resulting in death.

The government's evidence at trial painted a picture of a doctor who operated well outside the boundaries of usual medical practice. The government contended that Hurwitz was little more than a common drug dealer who operated out of a medical office rather than on a street corner. The government's expert witnesses testified that a doctor who knowingly prescribed opioids to an addict or to a patient the doctor knew was selling the drugs on the street was acting outside the bounds of legitimate medical practice, and the government presented compelling evidence suggesting that Hurwitz did just that—continued to prescribe large quantities of opioids to patients that he knew were selling the drugs or abusing them (for example, by injecting drugs that were directed to be taken orally).

Several of the patients who were cooperating with the authorities tape-recorded their appointments with Hurwitz. In one recording, Hurwitz indicated that it was "not inconceivable" to him that some patients were "selling part of their medicines so they could buy the rest." In another recording Hurwitz stated, "so I have kind of a huge conspiracy of silence because I, in fact, even, even knowing what I'll call the suspicious nature of you guys, assumed that you weren't stupid enough to—to not protect my practice and preserve your own . . . access to medications." Hurwitz told another patient to get an x-ray or an MRI "for the files to cover our butts."

The government presented evidence of what seemed to be extraordinarily high doses of opioids prescribed by Hurwitz. An expert witness for the government testified that high-dose opioid therapy typically involved doses of the equivalent of approximately 195 milligrams of morphine a day, although there had been a study involving doses of 350 milligrams a day and another involving doses of up to two grams a day.

The doses prescribed by Hurwitz, however, vastly exceeded those quantities. Hurwitz often wrote prescriptions calling for a patient to take thirty 80-milligram Oxycontins per day. For Hurwitz's patients in the high-dose program, a prescribed opioid dosage of 100 pills per day was not uncommon. Hurwitz testified that between 1998 and 2002, the median daily dosage for his patients was approximately 2000 milligrams (2 grams) of morphine or its equivalent. (Because Oxycontin is stronger than morphine, Hurwitz testified that 2000 milligrams of morphine would translate to about 1000 milligrams of Oxycontin.) Between July 1999 and October 2002, Hurwitz prescribed to one patient a total of more than 500,000 pills, which amounted to more than 400 pills per day. Towards the end of the time that Hurwitz treated the patient, the prescribed dosage included 1,600 5-milligram Roxicodones (a non-timed release version of Oxycontin) per day.[1] Still another patient was prescribed 10,000 Roxicodones as a one-month supply. Patients with limited visible sources of income spent tens of thousands of dollars a month on narcotics prescribed by Hurwitz.

The government also presented evidence showing that Hurwitz had previously been disciplined for improper prescribing practices. In 1992, the District of Columbia Board of Medicine had reprimanded Hurwitz and placed him on probation for prescribing drugs when not authorized to do so and for failing to conform to the prevailing standards of acceptable medical practice. In 1996, the Virginia Board of Medicine revoked his license upon finding that he had prescribed excessive amounts of controlled substances. The Virginia Board also required Hurwitz to attend classes on proper prescription practices and how to detect when patients were trying to use him as a source for prescription drugs rather than a doctor to treat pain.

Not surprisingly, the defense painted an entirely different picture. Hurwitz and his witnesses contended that the high-dose protocol was a proper medical procedure for treating patients with intractable pain. They testified that the body quickly develops resistance to the dangerous side-effects of opioids (such as respiratory depression), which then permits an escalation of the dosage until pain relief is obtained. One expert testified that once a patient becomes tolerant of the side-effects, there is effectively "no ceiling" on the quantity of opioids that can be prescribed if necessary to control pain. That expert also testified that many patients over time will require an increase in their opioid dosage in order to maintain control of their pain.

1. At trial, Hurwitz contended that the 1,600 pills per day dosage was the product of a clerical error.

Hurwitz's experts also testified that there is no medical reason to stop treating a patient for pain simply because that patient may be abusing illicit drugs and that, in some cases, stopping such treatment may even be more problematic.

Hurwitz testified about his practices and the patients he treated. He discussed how patients were generally asked to fill out questionnaires and submit medical records before receiving treatment and how he often included patients' family members during visits as a part of his approach to treating pain. Hurwitz participated in an e-mail discussion group with other professionals about how to approach various situations in pain treatment, and he would confer with other physicians concerning the treatment of certain patients. Hurwitz also discussed how he based his pain-management approach on what he learned at pain management conferences and what he understood other doctors would do.

Some of Hurwitz's patients testified on his behalf, explaining that Hurwitz was the only physician who had managed to relieve their debilitating pain. Molly Shaw, for example, discussed her futile attempts to treat what the Mayo Clinic had diagnosed as neuropathic pain, a pain so severe that it forced her to retire at age 47 and remain almost completely bedridden. She testified that Hurwitz's treatments allowed her to regain her life and live in considerably less pain. The patients' testimony, as well as the testimony of Hurwitz's staff, portrayed Hurwitz as a caring physician whose sole focus was providing pain relief for his patients.

Hurwitz was convicted of one count of drug trafficking conspiracy, one count of drug trafficking resulting in death, two counts of drug trafficking resulting in serious bodily injury, and forty-six counts of drug trafficking. The jury acquitted Hurwitz of six counts of drug trafficking, as well as one count of engaging in a continuing criminal enterprise and two counts of healthcare fraud. The jury failed to reach a decision on the remaining drug trafficking counts. The district court sentenced Hurwitz to 25 years in prison. This appeal followed.

Section 841 provides that, "[e]xcept as authorized by this subchapter, it shall be unlawful for any person knowingly or intentionally . . . to . . . distribute, or dispense, or possess with intent to . . . distribute, or dispense, a controlled substance." Doctors who are "registered" by the Attorney General are authorized to write prescriptions for or to otherwise dispense controlled substances, so long as they comply with the requirements of their registration.

As authorized by the Controlled Substances Act, the Attorney General has promulgated regulations addressing the conditions under which registrants are authorized to dispense controlled substances. The regulations provide that a prescription for a controlled substance is effective only if it is "issued for a legitimate medical purpose by an individual practitioner acting in the usual course of his professional practice." 21 C.F.R. § 1306.04(a) (2006). The regulation further provides that:

> An order purporting to be a prescription issued not in the usual course of professional treatment or in legitimate and authorized research is not a prescription within the meaning and intent of section 309 of the Act (21 U.S.C.

> 829) and the person knowingly . . . issuing [such a purported prescription] shall be subject to the penalties provided for violations of the provisions of law relating to controlled substances.

Synthesizing the requirements of the relevant statutes and regulations, we have held that to convict a doctor for violating § 841, the government must prove: (1) "that the defendant distributed or dispensed a controlled substance"; (2) that the defendant "acted knowingly and intentionally"; and (3) "that the defendant's actions were not for legitimate medical purposes in the usual course of his professional medical practice or were beyond the bounds of medical practice." *United States v. Tran Trong Cuong,* 18 F.3d 1132, 1141 (4th Cir. 1994).[7]

Hurwitz contends that the district court erred by rejecting his request for a "good faith" instruction. Hurwitz argues that his good faith in issuing the challenged prescriptions was relevant to his intent when treating his patients and thus relevant to the jury's determination of whether he acted outside the bounds of accepted medical practice or without a legitimate medical purpose.

The district court agreed with the government's position that Hurwitz's good faith was legally irrelevant to the drug-trafficking charges, and the court declined to include Hurwitz's requested instruction. However, as to the two healthcare fraud charges, the district court agreed to give a good-faith instruction. As to those counts, the district court instructed the jury that it could not convict Dr. Hurwitz if he "acted in good faith in dispensing any of the prescriptions alleged to constitute the crime of healthcare fraud." The court defined "good faith" to mean "good intentions in the honest exercise of best professional judgment as to a patient's needs. It means the doctor acted according to what he believed to be proper medical practice." The district court instructed the jury that "good faith applies only" to the healthcare fraud counts. Thus, the district court not only declined to give a good-faith instruction with regard to the drug counts, but also informed the jury that it *could not* consider good faith when deciding whether to convict Hurwitz of drug trafficking under § 841.[8]

As an initial premise, we agree with Hurwitz that a doctor's good faith generally is relevant to a jury's determination of whether the doctor acted outside the bounds of medical practice or with a legitimate medical purpose when prescribing narcotics.

In *United States v. Moore,* 423 U.S. 122 (1975), the seminal case addressing the prosecution of physicians under § 841, the Supreme Court concluded that "registered

7. Other circuits have concluded that whether the defendant's actions were for legitimate medical purposes or were beyond the bounds of medical practice is not an essential element of a § 841 charge against a doctor. *See, e.g., United States v. Steele,* 147 F.3d 1316, 1318 (11th Cir. 1998) (en banc); *United States v. Polan,* 970 F.2d 1280, 1282 (3d Cir. 1992); *United States v. Seelig,* 622 F.2d 207, 211–12 (6th Cir. 1980).

8. The jury acquitted Hurwitz of the healthcare fraud charges.

physicians can be prosecuted under § 841 when their activities fall outside the usual course of professional practice." In the course of concluding that the evidence was sufficient to support the jury's conclusion that the defendant acted beyond the bounds of professional practice, the Court noted two good-faith instructions that had been given to the jury. The district court had instructed the jury that the defendant could be convicted if the jury found that he knowingly distributed controlled substances "other than in good faith for detoxification in the usual course of a professional practice and in accordance with a standard of medical practice generally recognized and accepted in the United States," and that the defendant "could not be convicted if he merely made 'an honest effort' to prescribe . . . in compliance with an accepted standard of medical practice."

Building on the Supreme Court's approach in *Moore*, lower courts have concluded that when resolving the ultimate question in a § 841 prosecution against a doctor—whether the doctor acted without a legitimate medical purpose or beyond the bounds of accepted medical practice—some latitude must be given to doctors trying to determine the current boundaries of acceptable medical practice. Thus, courts have consistently concluded that it is proper to instruct juries that a doctor should not be held criminally liable if the doctor acted in good faith when treating his patients. Accordingly, the district court erred by concluding that good faith is not relevant when a registered physician is charged with violating § 841.

The question we must next consider is Hurwitz's argument that the district court erred by refusing his proffered good-faith charge. While the government objected below to any suggestion that a good-faith instruction was appropriate, the government on appeal does not contend that a good-faith instruction is never warranted in a case where a registered physician is prosecuted under § 841. Instead, the government argues that Hurwitz is not entitled to reversal on this point because the good-faith instruction Hurwitz offered below was an incorrect statement of the law. We agree with the government that the good-faith instruction offered by Hurwitz was not an accurate statement of the law.

The good-faith instruction offered by Hurwitz at trial stated that: "If a doctor dispenses a drug in good faith to medically treat a patient, then the doctor has dispensed the drug for a legitimate medical purpose and in the course of medical practice. That is, he has dispensed the drug lawfully. 'Good faith' in this context means good intentions in the honest exercise of best professional judgment as to a patient's needs. It means the doctor acted according to what *he believed to be proper medical practice*." This proposed instruction clearly sets forth a subjective standard, permitting Hurwitz to decide for himself what constitutes proper medical treatment. As the government contends, however, allowing criminal liability to turn on whether the defendant-doctor complied with his own idiosyncratic view of proper medical practices is inconsistent with the Supreme Court's decision in *Moore*.

In *Moore*, the Supreme Court discussed the circumstances under which doctors could be prosecuted under § 841 using language that strongly suggests the inquiry is an objective one. For example, the Court held that "registered physicians can be prosecuted under § 841 when their activities fall outside the *usual course of professional practice*." The Court also noted that, when passing the Controlled Substances Act, Congress intended to "confine authorized medical practice within *accepted limits*," and that "physicians who go beyond *approved practice* remain subject to serious criminal penalties." And as discussed above, the Supreme Court when concluding that the evidence was sufficient to support the defendant's conviction noted two good-faith instructions that had been given to the jury. Those instructions clearly set forth an objective standard.

Hurwitz, however, contends that his proffered good-faith instruction was proper because it was derived from our opinion in *United States v. Tran Trong Cuong*, 18 F.3d 1132 (4th Cir. 1994). In that case, the defendant argued that the district "court and the prosecution used a medical malpractice standard rather than a criminal standard to judge his actions." In the course of addressing the defendant's arguments, we reviewed the jury instructions given by the district court and concluded that the instructions correctly set forth a criminal standard of liability.

The jury instructions in *Tran Trong Cuong* included the following language: "[If a] doctor dispenses a drug in good faith in medically treating a patient, then the doctor has dispensed the drug for a legitimate medical purpose in the usual course of medical practice. That is, he has dispensed the drug lawfully. Good faith in this context means good intentions in the honest exercise of best professional judgment as to a patient's need. It means the doctor acted in accordance with what he believed to be proper medical practice." This charge is essentially identical to the good-faith instruction proffered by Hurwitz. Since we described the instructions in *Tran Trong Cuong* as correctly establishing a criminal standard of liability, Hurwitz argues that we approved of the good-faith portion of those instructions. We disagree.

No issue was raised by the defendant in *Tran Trong Cuong* that required us to consider the precise contours of a good-faith instruction. Instead, the only challenge to the jury instructions was the defendant's claim that the instructions set forth a civil rather than criminal liability standard. Because in *Tran Trong Cuong* we were not called on to consider the defendant's good faith . . . it simply cannot be said that in *Tran Trong Cuong* we *approved* the good-faith instruction sought by Hurwitz.

In this case, however, we are squarely presented with the question of whether, in a § 841 prosecution against a doctor, the inquiry into the doctor's good faith in treating his patients is a subjective or objective one. We believe that the inquiry must be an objective one, a conclusion that has been reached by every court to specifically consider the question. As the Second Circuit explained,

> "[P]rofessional practice" [as used in 21 C.F.R. § 1306.04(a)] refers to generally accepted medical practice; a practitioner is not free deliberately to disregard prevailing standards of treatment. . . .
>
> . . . .

> To permit a practitioner to substitute his or her views of what is good medical practice for standards generally recognized and accepted in the United States would be to weaken the enforcement of our drug laws in a critical area.

Vamos, 797 F.2d at 1151, 1153; *see also* 3 Leonard B. Sand et al., *Modern Federal Jury Instructions*, Instruction 56-19, comment (2003) ("Every court to examine the issue has held that the objective standard that the doctor acted in accordance with what he *reasonably* believed to be proper medical practice should apply.").

Because the instruction proffered by Hurwitz set forth a subjective standard for measuring his good faith, the instruction was not a correct statement of the law. Accordingly, although we conclude that good faith generally is relevant in a § 841 case against a registered physician, we nonetheless conclude that the district court did not err by refusing the particular charge sought by Hurwitz.

Though the district court did not err by refusing Hurwitz's good-faith charge, there remains a separate issue regarding the court's good-faith instructions. As mentioned above, the district court gave a good-faith instruction with regard to the healthcare fraud charges and then specifically instructed the jury that good faith was relevant *only* to the fraud charges. As we have explained, however, a doctor's good faith in treating his patients is relevant to the jury's determination of whether the doctor acted beyond the bounds of legitimate medical practice.

The government contends that because Hurwitz's proposed instruction was not a correct statement of the law, any errors in the district court's good-faith instructions cannot justify a new trial. We disagree. The government's argument confuses two separate issues—whether the district court erred by refusing to use the good-faith charge proposed by Hurwitz, and whether the district court erred by affirmatively informing the jury that good faith was relevant only to the fraud charges. Hurwitz timely objected to that instruction, thus preserving that error of commission as a separate issue for review on appeal. The district court's incorrect instruction on good faith is not insulated from review on appeal simply because Hurwitz's proposed good-faith instruction was incorrect.

The government also contends that any error with regard to the good-faith instruction is harmless, because a good-faith instruction was not warranted in this case.

The government first suggests that any error is harmless because Hurwitz's attorney admitted during closing argument that Hurwitz's actions were beyond the bounds of accepted medical practice. The government argues that this admission is binding on Hurwitz and amounts to a concession that the jury could not reasonably have concluded that Hurwitz acted in good faith. We disagree.

Although counsel stated that Hurwitz "did practice outside the bounds of medicine," the statement referred to Hurwitz's dealings with various state medical boards. Given counsel's statement that the medical boards "were back in the Stone Age," the statement could be understood as meaning only that Hurwitz in the past acted outside the bounds of what *those boards* believed to be proper medical practice. That Hurwitz practiced outside the bounds of an out-of-step medical board's view of proper medical practices does not necessarily mean that his actions were beyond the bounds of *generally accepted* medical practices. The attorney's statement therefore cannot be viewed as a clear and unambiguous admission that Hurwitz knowingly acted outside the bounds of accepted medical practice.

A more difficult question, however, is presented by the government's contention that the evidence presented at trial so overwhelmingly demonstrated that Hurwitz was acting well beyond the bounds of accepted medical practice that the jury could not reasonably have found that he acted in good faith. *See Mathews v. United States*, 485 U.S. 58, 63 (1988) ("As a general proposition a defendant is entitled to an instruction as to any recognized defense for which there exists evidence sufficient for a reasonable jury to find in his favor."). Under the government's view, then, any error in the instructions was necessarily harmless, because Hurwitz was not entitled to a good-faith instruction under the evidence presented at trial.

While the government's evidence was powerful and strongly indicative of a doctor acting outside the bounds of accepted medical practice, we cannot say that no reasonable juror could have concluded that Hurwitz's conduct fell within an objectively-defined good-faith standard. Hurwitz presented expert testimony showing that it was proper to use opioids when treating addicts who suffered from pain. Hurwitz's experts testified that his high-dose opioid therapy was a medically appropriate way to treat intractable pain and that the quantities of opioids he prescribed were appropriate. Even as to the patients whose dosages appeared extraordinarily high, such as the patient who was prescribed over 500,000 pills during the course of his treatment, the record contains expert testimony showing that Hurwitz's treatment and the quantities of opioids prescribed was medically proper. In addition, the testimony of Hurwitz and his staff indicated that he ran a legitimate medical practice, requiring patients to submit medical records and questionnaires before visits, conferring with other physicians outside of his practice about proper procedures, and relying on information from professional conferences when determining proper treatment practices. Thus, the record reveals a sufficient evidentiary basis for a good-faith instruction.

Good faith was at the heart of Hurwitz's defense. Hurwitz did not dispute the bulk of the government's factual evidence—that is, he did not argue that he did not prescribe the narcotics that were the basis for the charges against him. Instead, Hurwitz argued that the manner in which he used narcotics to treat chronic and debilitating pain was a medically proper approach to a difficult medical issue. By concluding that good faith was not applicable to the § 841 charges and affirmatively instructing the jury that good faith was not relevant to those charges, the district court effectively deprived the jury of the opportunity to consider Hurwitz's defense.

Thus, while we recognize that the government's evidence was strong, we simply cannot conclude that the district court's error in removing good faith from the jury's consideration was harmless.

Accordingly, we conclude that Hurwitz was prejudiced by the district court's error in instructing the jury that Hurwitz's good faith was relevant only to the fraud charges.

To summarize, we conclude that good faith is relevant to § 841 charges against a registered physician and that the district court erred by incorrectly instructing the jury that Hurwitz's good faith was relevant only to the healthcare fraud charges. This error in the court's instructions to the jury cannot be considered harmless, and a new trial is therefore required. On remand, the district court shall include a good-faith instruction (if requested by Hurwitz and if supported by the evidence presented at re-trial), but that instruction must reflect an objective rather than subjective standard for measuring Hurwitz's good faith.

Accordingly, for the foregoing reasons, we vacate Hurwitz's convictions under 21 U.S.C.A. §§ 841 and 846, and we remand for a new trial in accordance with this opinion.

Hurwitz was retried in 2007. The jury found him guilty on 16 counts, acquitted on 17 counts, and deadlocked on 12 counts. The court imposed a sentence of four years and eight months. Hurwitz's case was the subject of a feature-length documentary released in 2016 titled *Dr. Feelgood: Dealer or Healer?*

The judge who sentenced Hurwitz indicated that she had "some sympathy" for him. But "she felt that the sentence was warranted because Hurwitz was 'willfully blind' to the actions of his patients who were diverting their drugs." Diane E. Hoffmann, *Treating Pain v. Reducing Drug Diversion and Abuse: Recalibrating the Balance in Our Drug Control Laws and Policies*, 18 St. Louis U. J. Health L. & Pol'y 231, 250 (2008). Application of the willful blindness doctrine in this setting is controversial because, some argue, it can put doctors in a difficult position:

> At issue in many of the cases brought against physicians prescribing opioids is what constitutes "legitimate medical practice," which is not defined in the law or regulations. While this definitional issue is often at the heart of the relevant court cases, the more significant question may be whether the current standard for violation of the law, i.e., failure to prescribe within "the usual course of . . . professional practice" and "for a legitimate medical purpose," is appropriate. Arguably, the standard draws the line too far on the side of prosecutions and does not adequately take into account the range of patients seen by physicians treating pain.
>
> At this point in time, "[t]here is no objective test for pain." Neither is there an easy test to determine whether the patient is telling the truth. The

> determination of whether or not a patient is lying is a judgment call a physician must make by observing the patient's behavior.
>
> In response to prosecutor claims that doctors should know when individuals are feigning pain solely to obtain prescriptions for opioids, Drs. Jung and Reidenberg did a study to determine how readily physicians can tell when patients lie. They found that physicians correctly identified patients who were lying (pretending to be patients when they were not) only 10% of the time. The authors attributed this result to an observation that doctors operate with a "truth bias," i.e., they "assume that patients come to see them because they have a problem for which they want treatment." Given this bias, second guessing a physician's judgment in these matters, after the fact, seems patently unfair.
>
> Additionally, physicians may see patients who are diverting or abusing narcotics but who are also legitimately in pain. Arguably, prosecuting a physician who prescribes opioids to such patients is unfair if he or she is attempting to relieve the patient's pain, even if the physician knows, based on past behavior, that the patient may abuse or divert the drugs. Despite the possibility for abuse or diversion, "in the absence of some kickback or tangible benefit . . . , or incontrovertible evidence that the doctor has simply exercised no medical judgment at all, it is difficult to justify criminal prosecution of a doctor for his prescribing or dispensing" of opioids for patients complaining of chronic pain.

Id. at 284–86. *See also* Deborah Hellman, *Prosecuting Doctors for Trusting Patients*, 16 Geo. Mason L. Rev. 701 (2009) (arguing that applying the willful blindness doctrine to physician prosecutions under the CSA is inappropriate because doctors have a professional duty to trust their patients).

Cases like *Hurwitz* have the potential to carry unintended consequences. Penalties for misprescribing are meant to reduce substance abuse. But if physicians become worried that an honest mistake could result in a criminal prosecution, they might decide not to prescribe a particular substance at all. This risk is especially high if physicians fear that they might be penalized for being tricked by a patient, since "[a]ny physician who prescribes opioids is vulnerable to being duped by a deceptive patient; there is no degree of conscientiousness that can prevent it." Kelly K. Dineed and James M. DuBois, *Between a Rock and a Hard Place: Can Physicians Prescribe Opioids to Treat Pain Adequately While Avoiding Legal Sanction?*, 42 Am. J.L. & Med. 7, 17 (2016). To what extent do you think that prosecutors should consider the risk of overdeterrence when deciding whether to pursue charges in a case like *Hurwitz*?

Though the DEA's administrative power over doctors does not generate as many headlines as criminal charges based on misprescribing, it is likely of greater practical relevance for the average physician. The following excerpt briefly describes the DEA's physician registration system.

Did You Forget to Say You're Sorry? Litigating a Show Cause Hearing for a Physician's DEA Registration

Douglas J. Behr

9 Quinnipiac Health Law Journal 99 (2005)

A physician must be registered with the DEA in order to purchase, prescribe, administer, or dispense controlled substances. As of November 27, 2005, more than a million practitioners held such registrations.

The registration process requires only the completion of an application listing the doctor's name, address, identification of the schedules for which the doctor seeks to be registered, and payment of the required fee. A separate registration is required for each "principal place of professional practice." Pursuant to statute, the DEA "shall register an applicant" unless it "determines that the issuance of such registration is inconsistent with the public interest." An application for registration can be denied only if the DEA finds, after providing notice and, if requested, a hearing, that the registration is not in the public interest. This process applies, even if the prospective registrant has previously lost a registration.

Registration, once obtained, can be lost only by being voluntarily surrendered to the DEA or by revocation through notice and, if requested, a hearing. In order to revoke an existing registration, the DEA must determine that continued registration is no longer in the public interest.

Under 21 U.S.C. 824, a registration application may be denied or revoked upon a finding that the registrant: "(1) has materially falsified any application . . . ; (2) has been convicted of a felony under federal or state law relating to controlled substances or a list I chemical; (3) has had his State license or registration suspended, revoked, or denied and is no longer authorized to handle controlled substances in the State in which he maintains a DEA registration (4) has committed acts that would render his registration inconsistent with the public interest as determined pursuant to 21 U.S.C. 823(f); or (5) has been excluded from participation in a program pursuant to 42 U.S.C. 1320a-7(a) of Title 42."

Violation of any one of the statutory factors justifies revocation/denial of registration.

The fourth statutory factor, acts inconsistent with the public interest, was added to the statute in 1984. The "public interest" factor invests the Administrator with discretion to consider any relevant information. Oftentimes, the "public interest" basis is cited in conjunction with another statutory factor or as encompassing it. However, the Administrator has found violations of the "public interest" factor based primarily on conduct that does not fit within any of the other statutory factors. The Administrator examines the factors set out in 21 U.S.C. 823(f) in determining the "public interest" and has found that a registration was not in the public interest in cases where the physician had been prescribing controlled substances without a legitimate medical need, or engaged in other abusive practices, including illegally obtaining drugs for his own use even though no criminal charges had been brought. On one occasion, the public interest factor was the basis for the revocation of the registration of a physician who prescribed large quantities of narcotics to three individuals who were either drug addicts or were diverting the drugs, where the doctor's medical license had been placed on probation, and the doctor had been ordered not to prescribe Schedule II controlled substances even though no criminal charges had been filed. Additionally, this public interest factor was cited when a physician had issued prescriptions for controlled substances that he did not have the authority to write as well as when a physician was arrested and charged with possession with intent to distribute street cocaine but no conviction had yet occurred.

According to the DEA, the public interest, consistent with section 823(f), is evaluated using the following criteria, "1. The recommendation of the appropriate State licensing board or professional disciplinary authority; 2. The applicant's experience in dispensing, or conducting research with respect to controlled substances; 3. The applicant's conviction record under Federal or State laws relating to manufacture, distribution, or dispensing of controlled substances 4. Compliance with applicable State, Federal, or local laws relating to controlled substances; and, 5. Such other factors which may threaten the public health and safety." These factors are considered in the disjunctive. "The Deputy Administrator may properly rely on any one or any combination of these factors, and may give each factor the weight he deems appropriate. . . ." While any of the specifically defined criteria can support a revocation or denial of an application, no one criteria requires revocation or denial.

In determining whether to grant or continue a registration, the DEA generally evaluates each of the five "public interest" factors set out above. In determining whether registration is in the public interest, the Administrator looks at the totality of the circumstances. The governing statute is discretionary. The Administrator gives each factor the weight she deems appropriate in the exercise of her discretion. While the factors to be considered are varied . . . a review of the decisions leaves the clear impression that whether the applicant has recognized the error of his ways and dealt with the motivations and causes that brought about those errors is of particular importance. The Respondent must demonstrate that he can "be entrusted with the authority to prescribe and dispense controlled substances . . ." that a DEA registration represents. "Poor medical judgment, and the dispensing of controlled substances that resulted from such judgment, is sufficient to establish that Respondent cannot be trusted to responsibly handle such substances. . . ." The failure to "admit to the full extent of his involvement in documented misconduct involving controlled substances [has led] the Deputy Administrator [to doubt] such a Respondent's commitment to compliance with the Controlled Substances Act. . . ." Thus, "[t]he revocation of a DEA Certificate of Registration is not a penalty or a punitive measure. It is a remedial measure, based upon the public interest and the necessity to protect the public from those individuals who have misused controlled substances or their DEA Certificate of Registration, and who have not presented sufficient mitigating evidence to assure the Administrator that they can be trusted with the responsibility carried by such a registration."

While the prosecution and registration of doctors may deter them from prescribing controlled substances for non-medical purposes, these measures do not address the phenomenon of "doctor shopping" whereby an individual may seek to obtain prescriptions from multiple doctors. To try to combat doctor shopping, states have adopted prescription drug monitoring programs (PDMPs).

> PDMPs digitally store controlled substance dispensing information in a centralized, statewide database and make that information accessible to "authorized users," including prescribers, pharmacists, and sometimes law enforcement officials and state medical boards. When they query the system about a patient, authorized users typically see the dose, supply, and prescriber of scheduled drugs that the patient has recently filled. Authorized users can only access the data with log-in credentials provided upon registering with the PDMP.
>
> PDMPs seek to satisfy many goals, most prominently to support providers in facilitating the legitimate medical use of controlled substances, while avoiding prescription drug misuse. Armed with PDMP-supplied information about a patient, prescribers and pharmacists can communicate with the patient about his or her prescription histories, address potentially dangerous co-prescribing of substances, refrain from supplying opioids to a doctor shopper or diverter, comfortably provide prescription drugs to an individual who doesn't raise concerns about misuse, and direct individuals into substance abuse treatment therapy when clinically indicated. When enough providers share dispensing information and access patient profiles via PDMPs, opioid misusers and diverters have a harder time "gaming" the system by seeking drugs from multiple providers or pharmacies. As well, PDMPs are intended to help regulators investigate clinicians with inappropriate prescribing and dispensing patterns as well as patients with drug fill behaviors indicative of misuse or diversion. In sum, PDMPs aim to improve individual as well as population health, by improving prescribing and dispensing decisions made for each patient, and by limiting the negative externalities generated by the over-supply of opioids.
>
> State legislatures create PDMPs by statute and outline program details by regulation, often leaving many of the operational particulars to the executive agency in which the program is housed. Advances in information technology facilitated state implementation of electronic PDMPs in the 1990s-20000s. These programs succeeded earlier, less-widespread paper prescription monitoring systems (also known as carbon copy or triplicate paper programs), the first of which was created in California in 1939. Since the first electronic PDMP was established in Oklahoma in 1990, these

> programs have rapidly proliferated. In 2001, sixteen states had authorized the creation of a program by statute; and by June 2012, forty-nine states and one territory had passed such laws (with forty-one states having an operational program). Today, every state except Missouri has an operational PDMP.
>
> PDMPs vary widely along a number of dimensions, including: who can query the data (and for what purposes); whether unsolicited reports are sent to users; whether prescribers and/or dispensers can delegate access to an authorized agent; whether notification of a patient is required when his/her data is accessed; the extent to which data is shared with other states; how frequently the data is updated; and whether training is required for users. PDMPs increasingly monitor (or track) drugs that are included in Schedules II through V of the DEA's controlled substances schedules.

Rebecca L. Haffajee, *Preventing Opioid Misuse with Prescription Drug Monitoring Programs: A Framework for Evaluating the Success of State Public Health Laws*, 67 Hastings L.J. 1621, 1634–36 (2016). Despite the widespread adoption of PMDPs, their effect on public health outcomes is not entirely clear. A 2018 review of the literature on whether PMDPs decrease overdoses found that the evidence was mixed. One reason for this may be that when a patient who is dependent on prescription opioids loses access to them as a result of prescription drug monitoring, the patient will not necessarily simply stop using opioids. Some patients who lose access to prescription opioids may turn to heroin as a substitute. David S. Fink et al., *Association between Prescription Drug Monitoring Programs and Nonfatal and Fatal Drug Overdoses: A Systematic Review*, Annals of Internal Medicine (2018).

2. Controlled Substances and Medication-Assisted Treatment

Restrictions on the distribution of controlled substances in Schedules II through V are designed to limit the market for these substances to medical uses and to prevent diversion to recreational users. As the previous section suggests, what constitutes a legitimate medical use is not always clear. This has been especially true with respect to the use of controlled substances for medication-assisted treatment. In medication-assisted treatment, a patient suffering from a substance use disorder is given medication that prevents withdrawal symptoms in combination with counseling. In essence, the strategy is to use medicine to maintain the patient and keep her from relapsing into illegal drug use while she receives addiction counseling.

Before passage of the Harrison Narcotics Act in 1914, "physicians prescribed opioid medications for the care of addicted patients without legal restrictions." Ellen M. Weber, *Failure of Physicians to Prescribe Pharmacotherapies for Addiction: Regulatory Restrictions and Physician Resistance*, 13 J. Health Care L. & Pol'y 49, 56 (2010). After the Harrison Act took effect, there was a question as to whether prescribing narcotics for addiction maintenance—in other words, to keep addicted patients from suffering withdrawal symptoms—was a legitimate medical use under the law.

Starting in the late 1910s, a series of cases on this issue made its way to the United States Supreme Court. In these cases, the Court interpreted the Harrison Act to "bar[] physicians from prescribing heroin and cocaine to patients with addictions, putting an end to medication maintenance of addiction." *Id.* at 58. *See also,* ALFRED R. LINDESMITH, THE ADDICT AND THE LAW 3–17 (1967) (discussing these early cases).

Maintenance treatment remains subject to a number of restrictions and obstacles in the United States. Perhaps most notably, because Schedule I substances cannot be prescribed to end-users for any purpose other than research, the Controlled Substances Act prevents cities and states from establishing heroin-assisted treatment programs of the kind discussed in Chapter 2. By contrast, medication-assisted treatment using substances in Schedule II or below is permitted. But, as outlined in the article that follows, medication-assisted treatment is subject to a number of additional restrictions beyond those that apply to typical medicines and controlled substances.

The Law and Policy of Opioids for Pain Management, Addiction Treatment, and Overdose Reversal

Corey S. Davis and Derek H. Carr

14 Indiana Health Law Review 1 (2017)

[O]pioid use is associated with severe adverse effects, including, in some cases, addiction and death. Somewhat counterintuitively, opioids can also be used to treat opioid misuse and addiction. Indeed, medication-assisted treatment ("MAT"), which combines counseling with medication therapy, is widely recognized as the most effective treatment for [opioid use disorder] OUD.

The federal Food and Drug Administration ("FDA") has approved three medications for the treatment of OUD: methadone, buprenorphine, and naltrexone. However, effective MAT for OUD generally involves methadone or buprenorphine. Methadone, approved by the FDA in 1972 for treating opioid addiction, is a long-acting full mu opioid agonist with a half-life between twenty-four to thirty-six hours, thereby allowing for once-a-day treatment. The drug has a relatively safe profile when used for treating opioid addiction. Buprenorphine received FDA approval for use in treating opioid addiction in 2002. The drug can remain effective for up to seventy-two hours with proper dosing, and because it is only a partial mu opioid agonist, increased dosages generally only produce a longer duration of action rather than greater agonist effects. This "ceiling effect" renders buprenorphine generally safer than methadone. Between 2009 and 2013, the number of opiate-dependent individuals receiving methadone and buprenorphine increased by 17% and 100%, respectively.

Numerous studies have demonstrated MAT's efficacy. For example, one study found that individuals receiving MAT are 50% less likely to relapse than those receiving non-medication-assisted therapy. Others note the significantly lower mortality rates associated with the availability and use of MAT. In a meta-analysis of studies on MAT in prison settings, researchers found increased participation in treatment post-release, as well as substantially reduced heroin use and syringe sharing. More generally, MAT is "associated with decreased injecti[on] drug use, decreased criminal activity, increased retention in treatment for chemical dependence, increased adherence to HIV medication, improved family relations, and successful return to employment."

Despite its proven efficacy, MAT has been implemented in less than 50% of private sector addiction treatment programs and only 34.4% of opiate-dependent individuals in such programs receive MAT. Numerous factors contribute to this low utilization of MAT, including misconceptions, stigma, and the lack of available prescribers. The legal regime controlling access to methadone and buprenorphine for opioid addiction treatment presents another significant barrier to increasing the use of MAT.

At the turn of the twentieth century, medical professionals commonly provided opioids and other drugs without legal restrictions, including for the treatment of addiction. Between 1912 and 1920, federal, state, and local agencies promoted maintenance clinics for drug-dependent individuals. However, in 1914, Congress passed the Harrison Narcotics Tax Act, which imposed licensing, tax, prescription, and record requirements on physicians providing opiate and cocoa products, as well as restricted physicians from dispensing and distributing such products except "in the course of his professional practice." Importantly federal officials interpreted the law as prohibiting physicians from prescribing opiate and cocoa products to drug-dependent individuals. As a result, enforcement of the Harrison Narcotics Act effectively ended addiction maintenance treatment for nearly a half-century.

In 1965, two doctors, Vincent Dole and Marie Nyswander, published a landmark study in the *Journal of the American Medical Association* highlighting the effectiveness of methadone to treat heroin addiction. This and similar research lead to the rapid increase in using methadone to treat opioid addiction under Investigational New Drug ("IND") applications issued by the FDA, and the number of methadone maintenance patients rose from less than 400 in 1968 to 73,000 in 1973.

At the same time, the legal landscape for opioid addiction treatment was also evolving. In 1970, responding to concerns over methadone diversion and addiction, the FDA proposed a new rule establishing protocols for methadone treatment under INDs; the rule was finalized in April 1971. In October 1970, Congress passed the Comprehensive Drug Abuse Prevention and Control Act ("CDAPCA") addressing "research, treatment, and prevention of drug abuse and drug dependence, and with drug abuse law enforcement authority." In April 1972, the FDA proposed new regulations on methadone treatment. These regulations, finalized in December 1972, established the modern regulatory framework for methadone treatment. The regulations limited methadone dispensing to federally licensed programs and approved hospital pharmacies, restricted patient eligibility for participation, required physician justification for high dosages, and specified criteria for granting and rescinding take-home doses.

Congress complemented these new FDA regulations with the passing of the Narcotic Addict Treatment Act of 1974 ("NATA"). NATA, which amended the CSA, required medical professionals treating opioid addiction with opioids to obtain a separate DEA registration, established the National Institute on Drug Abuse, and retained the Secretary of Health, Education, and Welfare's role in setting medical practice standards for addiction treatment. The law represented Congress' formal recognition of the practice of using opioids to treat opioid addiction and was the first time that federal statutes defined "detoxification" and "maintenance" treatment. Minor revisions to the methadone treatment regulations in 1980 and 1989 represented the only changes to this federal legal landscape between 1974 and 2000.

At the federal level, the legal requirements for prescribing and dispensing methadone depend on its intended purpose. When used to treat pain, methadone is subject to the same requirements and restrictions applicable to all other Schedule II controlled substances, such as OxyContin. However, federal regulations specify more rigorous requirements and limitations for methadone detoxification and maintenance therapy ("methadone therapy") for treating opioid addiction. These include requirements on who can provide and receive methadone therapy, as well as where and how methadone therapy can be provided. States and local governments may also impose additional requirements on methadone therapy.

Subject to limited exception, federal law limits methadone therapy to accredited and certified opioid treatment programs ("OTP"). As a condition to this certification, OTPs must provide the methadone therapy in accordance with federal treatment standards, although the programs may apply for exemptions from these requirements. Moreover, practitioners providing methadone therapy must obtain a separate annual registration from the DEA.

Federal law also requires individuals seeking methadone therapy to meet specified criteria based on their age and the type of treatment sought. For maintenance treatment, an individual must meet the DSM-IV criteria for addiction to an opioid drug and must have become "addicted at least 1 year before admission for treatment." The one-year requirement may be waived for individuals recently released from incarceration, pregnant women, and previously treated patients. Persons under age eighteen must also "have two documented unsuccessful attempts at short-term detoxification or drug-free treatment within a 12-month period." Although detoxification treatment is available for any person meeting the diagnostic criteria established by the OTP, individuals are limited to two detoxification treatment episodes per year.

In addition to these provider and patient qualifications, federal regulations also specify the services OTPs must provide and how OTPs may dispense the methadone. At the most general level, OTPs must provide "adequate medical, counseling, vocational, educational, other assessment and treatment services." This includes an initial full medical examination, as well as initial and periodic assessment services to create and revise treatment plans. Counseling must cover not only substance abuse but also prevention of exposure to and transmission of HIV, community resources, vocational rehabilitation, education, and employment services.

The provision of the methadone itself is also strictly regulated. OTPs may only provide methadone in oral form. The initial dose must not exceed 30 milligrams, and the entire dose provided on the first day of treatment must not exceed 40 milligrams. By default, patients must take the methadone under supervision; however, patients in comprehensive maintenance treatment may receive unsupervised "take-home" dosages under limited circumstances, such as when the clinic is closed. If an OTP medical director determines based on specified factors that "a patient is responsible in handling opioid drugs for unsupervised use," an individual may receive a specified number of take-home doses based on how long the individual has been in treatment.

In 2002, the FDA approved buprenorphine for treating opioid dependence, and the DEA rescheduled the drug from a Schedule V to a Schedule III controlled substance. Two years earlier, in October 2000, Congress passed the Drug Addiction Treatment Act of 2000 ("DATA 2000"). The law amended the CSA to allow practitioners meeting certain qualifying criteria to prescribe and dispense Schedule III, IV, and V controlled substances approved by the FDA for addiction treatment outside OTPs and without receiving a separate DEA registration. These two events created the current regulatory scheme for buprenorphine-based MAT.

DATA 2000 requires physicians to obtain a waiver by submitting a notification to the Secretary of Health and Human Services of the physician's intent to prescribe and dispense buprenorphine (or other Schedule III-V controlled substances) for the treatment of opioid dependence. This waiver must contain a certification that the physician is qualified to prescribe the medications for treating opioid dependence, "has the capacity to refer [ ] [their] patients ... for appropriate counseling and other appropriate ancillary services," and will comply with limitations on the total number of patients the physician may treat at any one time. Physicians are considered qualified to dispense buprenorphine to treat opioid dependence if they are licensed under state law and meets at least one specified educational or experience requirements. A physician may treat only up to thirty patients at any one time during the first year the physician treats opiate-dependent patients under a DATA 2000 waiver. In subsequent years and upon notifying the Secretary of Health and Human Services, a physician may treat up to 100 patients at any one time.

On July 8, 2016, SAMHSA, a division of the Department of Health and Human Services, finalized revisions to the OTP regulations relating to buprenorphine-based MAT. Effective August 8, 2016, these new regulations increase the patient limit to 275 for qualified practitioners providing buprenorphine-based MAT. To qualify for these increased patient limits, the practitioner must both (1) possess a DATA 2000 waiver allowing them to treat up to 100 patients for at least one year and (2) possess a subspecialty board certification in addiction medicine or addiction psychiatry or practice in a "qualified practice setting." These qualified practice settings must ensure patients can access emergency care when the practice is closed, provide access to case management services, use health information technology systems such as electronic health records, utilize their state prescription drug monitoring program ("PDMP"), and accept third-party payment.

Similarly, the Comprehensive Addiction and Recovery Act of 2016 ("CARA"), signed into law on July 22, 2016, makes additional changes to federal law aimed at increasing access to MAT. Most prominently, CARA amends the CSA to allow certain nurse practitioners and physician assistants to provide MAT with Schedule II, IV, or V controlled substances, including buprenorphine. To qualify, the nurse practitioner or physician assistant must be "licensed under State law to prescribe schedule II, IV, or V medications for the treatment of pain" and have sufficient training. CARA also includes more specific content requirements for physician education when used by the physician to qualify for a DATA 2000 waiver.

Historically, many insurance plans, particularly those available to lower income people, provided poor or no coverage for OUD treatment. Moreover, health insurance providers legally could, and generally did, impose more stringent requirements and limitations on coverage for mental health services, including treatment for OUD, than for other medical services. These requirements and limitations made it extraordinarily difficult and costly for individuals with OUD-even those with health insurance-to obtain needed care. Beginning in 1996, Congress took several steps to increase access to mental health care, but the impact on access to substance use disorder ("SUD") treatment, and more specifically MAT, remains unclear.

In 1996, Congress enacted the Mental Health Parity Act ("MPHA"), prohibiting large group insurers from imposing more restrictive annual and lifetime financial limitations on mental health services than those applicable to other medical care. However, the law did not address SUD, did not require insurers to offer mental health coverage at all, and explicitly permitted cost sharing and utilization limitations. In 2008, the Paul Wellstone and Pete Domenici Mental Health Parity and Addiction Equity Act of 2008 ("MHPAEA") strengthened the MPHA by adding SUD benefits and prohibiting insurers from imposing more restrictive financial and treatment limitations on mental health and SUD benefits. Moreover, regulations promulgated under the MHPAEA required that health plans, that offered benefits for a specific substance use condition, in any one of six classifications (inpatient, in-network; inpatient, out-of-network; outpatient, in-network; outpatient, out-of-network; emergency care; and prescription drugs), also provide benefits for that condition in every other classification in which medical or surgical benefits were offered. However, the law's exemption for small employers left a large segment of the population without its protections.

The Patient Protection and Affordable Care Act ("ACA"), signed into law on March 23, 2010, requires all individual and small group health insurance policies to provide coverage for SUD as an essential health benefit ("EHB")-the first such requirement in federal law. It also extended the MHPAEA's requirements to all insurance plans offered through an ACA Marketplace, all benchmark and benchmark-equivalent Medicaid plans, and Medicaid plans operated by managed care organizations. Moreover, the ACA prohibits insurers from refusing to cover people currently experiencing SUD or with a history of SUD, as well as prohibits insurers from charging individuals with SUD higher premiums or cost sharing based on their condition.

Although these changes are welcome and will likely continue to increase access to SUD treatment, including MAT for OUD, they are not a panacea. One study examining the MHPAEA found that the law did not increase the number of individuals receiving SUD treatment and found "no significant change in identification, treatment initiation or treatment engagement." Another recent study revealed that approximately half of individuals with unmet mental health treatment needs, including substance use disorder, reported cost and insurance coverage as a barrier to access. Noncompliance with federal requirements likely contributes to these results. A June 2016 report from the National Center on Addiction and Substance Abuse revealed that the vast majority of ACA benchmark plans do not satisfy the ACA and MHPAEA's requirements. More aggressive enforcement may be necessary to ensure the ACA fulfills its promise of expanding access to SUD.

Some object to medication-assisted treatment on the grounds that it is inconsistent with the abstinence-only model of drug treatment. This outlook may partly account for the extensive federal regulation of methadone and buprenorphine. It has also resulted in resistance to medication-assisted treatment in some quarters, including drug courts:

> A recent national survey of adult drug courts found that, while 98% of courts reported that at least some participants were addicted to opioids upon entering the drug court program, two-thirds of these courts did not provide medication-assisted treatment to individuals who were using illegal opioids at the time they began drug court. This study concluded that while drug courts were "originally conceived as a more treatment-based and less punitive approach to substance abuse than incarceration," the procedures and policies in place in many of these courts did not reflect current understandings of evidence-based pharmacological treatment for drug abuse. In response to open-ended questions in the survey, some respondents reported concern about participants substituting "one high for another" and a resulting "new addiction." Other cited barriers included court policies against medication assisted treatment and treatment provider policies against medication assisted treatment. So while "copious medical and scientific research has established that for many opioid-addicted people, the need for prolonged, sometimes lifetime medication assisted treatment is necessary to prevent relapse to illicit opioid use," many drug courts continue to limit the availability of these pharmacological treatments to participants.

> According to the Multi-Site Adult Drug Court Evaluation, only 23% of drug courts provide pharmacological interventions to participants. And while the National Association of Drug Court Professionals recently released a resolution noting that "[d]rug court professionals have an affirmative obligation to learn about current research findings related to the safety and efficacy of [medication assisted treatment] for addiction," and should "not impose blanket prohibitions against the use of [medication assisted treatment] for their participants," it is still the case that 12-step groups like AA and NA are the most commonly accessed treatment for individuals in the country with a substance use disorder.

Sara Gordon, *The Use and Abuse of Mutual-Support Programs in Drug Courts*, 2017 U. Ill. L. Rev. 1503, 1540.

Although some continue to believe that medication-assisted therapy is inconsistent with abstinence-only treatment, the goal of abstinence has remained part of the FDA's calculus when considering whether to approve maintenance drugs. In 2018 the FDA pulled back slightly from this position by announcing that it "plans to begin permitting pharmaceutical companies to sell medications that help temper cravings, even if they don't fully stop addiction." Sheila Kaplan, *F.D.A. to Expand Medication-Assisted Therapy for Opioid Addicts*, N.Y. Times (Feb. 25, 2018). Specifically, "the agency said it would soon publish two guidances, recommendations for drugmakers, on the issue." *Id.* One will encourage "the development of new, longer-acting formulations of existing drugs for opioid treatment" while the second will make new drugs "eligible for [FDA] approval that don't end addiction but help with aspects of it, such as cravings, or overdoses." *Id.*

For more on the history of medication-assisted treatment in the United States, see Center for Substance Abuse Treatment, *Medication-Assisted Treatment for Opioid Addiction in Opioid Treatment Programs* 11–23 (2005).

3. Regulation and Prosecution of Pharmacies

The DEA's regulatory authority extends to all CSA registrants, not just doctors. Although pharmacists do not write prescriptions, they have a legal duty to independently assess them. This is because "DEA regulations have long explained that the responsibility required of a pharmacy registrant in ensuring that controlled substance prescriptions are legitimately issued is not identical to the responsibility of prescribers, but is instead a 'corresponding responsibility.'" John J. Mulrooney II and Katherine E. Legel, *Current Navigation Points in Drug Diversion Law: Hidden Rocks in Shallow, Murky, Drug-Infested Waters*, 101 Marq. L. Rev. 333, 369 (2017). Under these regulations, "a pharmacy can violate its corresponding responsibility by ignoring red flags raised by prescriptions and the circumstances in which they are presented." *Id.* at 370. The next case examines the corresponding responsibility of pharmacists under the CSA.

Jones Total Health Care Pharmacy, LLC v. Drug Enforcement Administration

United States Court of Appeals for the Eleventh Circuit
881 F.3d 823 (2018)

Per curiam:

Before this Court is a petition for review of a final order of the United States Drug Enforcement Administration ("DEA") revoking Jones Total Health Care Pharmacy, LLC's ("Jones Pharmacy") certificate of registration under the Controlled Substances Act ("CSA") to dispense controlled substances. The DEA Acting Administrator revoked Jones Pharmacy's registration after determining that it unlawfully dispensed controlled substances and that Cherese Jones, the pharmacy's owner and operator, failed to accept full responsibility for the misconduct. Jones Pharmacy . . . ("Petitioners") then filed this petition for review, arguing that the DEA's decision is arbitrary and capricious. We disagree, so we deny the petition for review.

Jones Pharmacy is a community pharmacy started by Jones in Fort Lauderdale. Jones graduated from Texas A & M University with a Doctor of Pharmacy degree in 2000 and worked in clinical and retail pharmacy positions before opening Jones Pharmacy in February 2010.

Jones Pharmacy was registered with the DEA to dispense substances controlled by the CSA.

The CSA creates "a closed regulatory system making it unlawful to manufacture, distribute, dispense, or possess any controlled substance except in a manner authorized by the CSA." Pharmacies that dispense prescription medications that are controlled substances are required to obtain proper registration from the Attorney General. Under the CSA, the responsibility for the proper prescribing and dispensing of controlled substances, which must be for "a legitimate medical purpose," is on the prescribing practitioner, "but a corresponding responsibility rests with the pharmacist who fills the prescription." 21 C.F.R. § 1306.04(a). Thus, pharmacists have a "corresponding responsibility" to refuse to fill prescriptions that are not issued for a legitimate medical purpose. *See id.*

The Attorney General has the authority to deny, revoke, or suspend registrations. The Attorney General has delegated this authority to the DEA. When an existing registration is proposed for revocation, the DEA must serve an "order to show cause" on the registrant and give the registrant an opportunity for a hearing before an Administrative Law Judge ("ALJ") in order to contest the proposed action.

On October 6, 2014, the DEA issued an order to show cause proposing to revoke Jones Pharmacy's existing registration. In the order, the DEA alleged that, from February 2010 to July 2012, Jones Pharmacy "repeatedly failed to ensure that it filled only prescriptions issued for legitimate medical purposes within the usual course of professional practice." Jones Pharmacy, according to the order, repeatedly ignored "obvious and unresolvable red flags of diversion." The order also alleged record-keeping violations.

Petitioners requested a hearing, which was held before an ALJ in March 2015. At the hearing, the ALJ heard testimony from several persons, including Domingo Gonzales (a DEA diversion investigator), Mary Crane (a Pharmacy Inspector for the Florida Department of Health), Dr. Tracy Gordon (the government's expert), Donna Horn (Jones Pharmacy's expert), and Jones.

After the hearing, the ALJ issued her findings of fact, conclusions of law, and recommendations that the DEA Acting Administrator revoke Jones Pharmacy's registration. The ALJ credited the testimony of Gordon, who reviewed over one-hundred prescriptions filled by Jones Pharmacy between February 2010 and July 2012 and found that they had one or more "red flags"—indicia that the prescriptions were not issued for a legitimate medical purpose—and should not have been filled. According to Gordon, these red flags included the following: (1) individuals traveling long distances to fill prescriptions; (2) prescriptions for drug "cocktails," known for their abuse potential, such as oxycodone and Xanax; (3) individuals who arrived together with identical or nearly identical prescriptions; (4) purported pain patients with prescriptions for immediate-release rather than long-acting narcotics; (5) cash purchases; and (6) doctors prescribing outside the scope of their usual practice. The ALJ credited Gordon's testimony that many of these red flags could not have been resolved by the pharmacists. Accordingly, the ALJ determined that Jones Pharmacy violated its "corresponding responsibility" by filling controlled-substances prescriptions with unresolved red flags.

Crediting Gonzales's testimony and other evidence submitted by the government, the ALJ also found additional indicators that Jones Pharmacy dispensed controlled substances unlawfully. The ALJ cited statistics showing that, from February 2010 to July 2012, Jones Pharmacy's business was based primarily on sales of controlled substances. In addition, of the more than 3,000 controlled-substance prescriptions filled, 99% were for immediate-release drugs, 89% were for "cocktail" drugs, and 93% were paid for in cash. The ALJ noted that these statistics were "unusually high compared to national averages." For instance, according to a report from the IMS Institute of Healthcare Informatics, the national average for cash sales between 2007 and 2011 was 6%. The ALJ also found that Jones Pharmacy's high markup on the price per pill—including 415 instances where the markup on the price per pill was over 1,000%—combined with the high rate of cash-based customers indicated diversion because "it elucidates a customer base willing to pay exorbitant prices for a drug the customer could otherwise purchase at a nearby pharmacy for much less."

The ALJ rejected Petitioners' contentions that Jones was unaware of the concept of "red flags" and that she did not know or have reason to know that the prescriptions filled by Jones Pharmacy were not written for a legitimate medical purpose. The ALJ was unpersuaded by testimony offered by Jones Pharmacy's expert Horn, who stated that pharmacists were generally unaware of the concept of red flags during the relevant time period. Instead, the ALJ credited the contrary testimony of the government's expert, Gordon, and concluded that "the concept of red flags has long been recognized as a reflection of the norms of the pharmacy profession," so Jones Pharmacy's purported ignorance was not a credible defense.

Having found that the government met its burden of establishing a *prima facie* case that revocation of Jones Pharmacy's registration was in the public interest, the ALJ then addressed whether Jones Pharmacy put forward sufficient evidence to show that it could be trusted with a registration going forward. The ALJ explained that a registrant must establish two things to rebut the government's *prima facie* face: (1) full acceptance of responsibility and (2) remedial measures so that such violations will not happen in the future. Based on Jones's testimony at the hearing, the ALJ determined that she had not fully accepted responsibility for Jones Pharmacy's unlawful dispensing of controlled substances. Citing agency precedent holding that acceptance of responsibility is an independent and essential requirement for rebutting the government's *prima facie* case, the ALJ declined to address Jones Pharmacy's remedial efforts.

Petitioners filed exceptions in May 2015, which the Acting Administrator overruled in a 54-page final order issued on October 31, 2016. Addressing and rejecting many of the arguments we are faced with here, and which we address in more detail below, the Acting Administrator adopted the ALJ's recommendations. This petition for review followed. *See* 21 U.S.C. § 877.

We may set aside the Acting Administrator's final decision if it is "arbitrary, capricious, an abuse of discretion, or otherwise not in accordance with the law." "The arbitrary and capricious standard is exceedingly deferential." We may not substitute our judgment for that of the agency so long as its conclusions are rational and based on the evidence before it. Nevertheless, we may set aside a decision as "arbitrary and capricious when, among other flaws, the agency has relied on factors which Congress has not intended it to consider, entirely failed to consider an important aspect of the problem, [or] offered an explanation for its decision that runs counter to the evidence before the agency."

The Acting Administrator's factual findings are conclusive if supported by substantial evidence. Substantial evidence is less than a preponderance of the evidence, but rather such relevant evidence as a reasonable person would accept as adequate to support a conclusion. An administrative agency's finding is supported by substantial evidence even if "two inconsistent conclusions [could be drawn] from the evidence."

The DEA may revoke registration to dispense controlled substances upon a finding that the registrant "has committed such acts as would render his registration . . . inconsistent with the public interest."

Section 823 lists five factors that "shall be considered" in determining the public interest. These factors include "[t]he applicant's experience in dispensing, or conducting research with respect to controlled substances," as well as "[c]ompliance with applicable State, Federal, or local laws relating to controlled substances."[1] The Acting "Administrator must consider each factor, though he need not make explicit findings as to each one and can give each factor the weight [he] determines is appropriate."

The government bears the initial burden of proving that registration is inconsistent with the public interest. If the government proves its *prima facie* case, the burden of proof shifts to the registrant to show why it can be trusted with a registration.

Here, Petitioners do not dispute that the government met its initial burden of proving that Jones Pharmacy's registration was inconsistent with the public interest. The record supports the agency's determination that Jones Pharmacy unlawfully filled numerous controlled substance prescriptions that were not issued for a legitimate medical purpose. As discussed above, the evidence showed that Jones Pharmacy from February 2010 through July 2012 filled over one-hundred prescriptions that had at least one red flag that Jones Pharmacy did not attempt to resolve and that could not have been resolved. The government also put forward other substantial evidence indicating that the controlled substances dispensed by Jones Pharmacy were being diverted for improper use. Accordingly, the agency reasonably determined that revocation of Jones Pharmacy's registration was in the public interest because of Jones Pharmacy's failure to comply with federal laws relating to controlled substances.

Petitioners instead challenge as arbitrary and capricious the DEA's determination that Jones Pharmacy did not prove that it could be trusted with a registration notwithstanding the prior misconduct. In particular, Petitioners argue that the agency's finding that Jones, the owner and operator of Jones Pharmacy, did not credibly accept full responsibility is fatally flawed for a number of reasons. The agency, according to Petitioners, misconstrued Jones's testimony, relied too heavily on the severity of the misconduct, and unreasonably refused to consider the remedial measures Jones Pharmacy put in place after the time period at issue. Petitioners also contend that the agency's choice of the most severe sanction—revocation—was inconsistent with prior agency decisions that either suspended or continued registrations despite more egregious misconduct.

---

1. In full, the statute directs that the following five factors shall be considered in determining the public interest:

> (1) The recommendation of the appropriate State licensing board or professional disciplinary authority.
>
> (2) The applicant's experience in dispensing, or conducting research with respect to controlled substances.
>
> (3) The applicant's conviction record under Federal or State laws relating to the manufacture, distribution, or dispensing of controlled substances.
>
> (4) Compliance with applicable State, Federal, or local laws relating to controlled substances.
>
> (5) Such other conduct which may threaten the public health and safety.

21 U.S.C. § 823(f).

We address Petitioners' arguments in three parts. First, we conclude that substantial evidence supports the agency's determination that Jones did not credibly accept full responsibility. Second, we hold that the agency's refusal to consider Jones Pharmacy's remedial measures does not render its decision arbitrary or capricious in the circumstances of this case. Finally, we find that the chosen sanction was not arbitrary or capricious.

A. Acceptance of Responsibility

At the outset, we agree with the other circuits that have addressed this issue that the DEA may properly consider a registrant's acceptance of responsibility in determining if registration should be revoked. *See MacKay v. Drug Enf't Admin.*, 664 F.3d 808, 820 (10th Cir. 2011) ("The DEA may properly consider whether a physician admits fault in determining if the physician's registration should be revoked."). If a pharmacy has failed to comply with its responsibilities in the past, it makes sense for the agency to consider whether the pharmacy will change its behavior in the future.

Turning to the facts at hand, substantial evidence supports the DEA's determination that Jones did not fully accept responsibility for Jones Pharmacy's unlawful dispensing practices. The ALJ, who heard Jones testify in person and was therefore in the best position to assess Jones's credibility, extensively reviewed Jones's testimony and found her admission of fault to be equivocal at best. In relevant part, the ALJ summarized Jones's testimony as follows:

> Ms. Jones claimed that she was following her corresponding responsibility [to fill only legitimate prescriptions] as she understood it from 2010–2012 when over a hundred prescriptions that were presented with multiple unresolved red flags were dispensed at Jones Pharmacy. Ms. Jones purported to accept responsibility for Jones Pharmacy's dispensing practices by repeatedly asserting that she did what she knew at the time, but now she knows she could have done more.

The ALJ found, however, that Jones made other statements that demonstrated she "does not fully understand her corresponding responsibility even yet today." For example, Jones indicated on cross-examination that she did not understand that the law required her to make sure that prescriptions were issued for legitimate medical purposes before filling them. And, significantly, she did not admit that Jones Pharmacy's past dispensing practices failed to comply with its legal obligations. Thus, the ALJ concluded that Jones did not accept responsibility and that her claimed ignorance about her legal responsibilities, particularly her continued lack of understanding of those responsibilities, was no excuse. The Acting Administrator agreed with the ALJ's findings after conducting his own review of Jones's testimony.

Petitioners maintain that the agency's assessment of whether Jones accepted responsibility is fatally flawed for a number of reasons. They insist that Jones accepted responsibility by acknowledging and correcting her mistakes, and that the ALJ's interpretation of her testimony was strained and unreasonable. The ALJ, according to Petitioners, failed to properly consider Jones's explanation that her misunderstanding of her responsibilities was based in part on what she learned while working at other pharmacies earlier in her career. Petitioners also contend that the ALJ, by drawing a negative inference from Jones's attempt to explain why she failed to comply with her corresponding responsibility in the past, imposed a test for acceptance of responsibility "that can only be met by the most blatant offenders" who knowingly violate their responsibilities.

Petitioners' arguments are unpersuasive. To begin with, both the ALJ and the Acting Administrator considered Jones's explanation of her conduct and reasonably concluded that her purported confusion or ignorance was not a valid excuse. Jones believed that it was the prescribing physician's responsibility to issue medically legitimate prescriptions. That may be true, but as a pharmacist registered with the DEA, Jones had a "corresponding responsibility" not to fill prescriptions that were not issued for a medically legitimate purpose. The "corresponding responsibility" rule is not new, *see United States v. Hayes*, 595 F.2d 258, 261 & n.6 (5th Cir. 1979) (holding that pharmacists have an obligation "not to fill an order that purports to be a prescription but is not a prescription within the meaning of the statute"), nor is it unreasonable for the DEA to expect a pharmacist entrusted with dispensing highly regulated, addictive, and potentially destructive substances to fully understand her obligations under the law, regardless of prior work experience.

As the Acting Administrator stated, . . . "notwithstanding the obvious and compelling evidence that the prescriptions lacked a legitimate medical purpose, [Jones] continued to deny that the prescriptions were unlawfully dispensed." To be sure, Jones indicated in her testimony that she was naïve, made mistakes, and could and should have done "more digging" to verify prescriptions. But Petitioners have not identified any clear admission by Jones—regardless of whether she acted knowingly or not—that she understood Jones Pharmacy violated its obligations under the CSA. Instead, Jones reiterated her belief that Jones Pharmacy was fulfilling its responsibilities as she understood them at the time.

Jones's refusal to admit that Jones Pharmacy's dispensing practices violated its obligations under federal law reflects that she did not "recognize[] the extent of [the] misconduct." It also supports the factual finding, critical to both the ALJ's and the Acting Administrator's decisions, that Jones did not fully understand her legal obligations as a pharmacist.

[W]e reject Petitioners' argument that the ALJ impermissibly required Jones to admit to knowing misconduct in order to accept responsibility. For starters, the record supports an inference of knowing misconduct, even though Jones maintained that the misconduct was not intentional. More significantly, however, Jones could have maintained that the misconduct was not intentional while, at the same time, recognizing at the hearing that it nonetheless violated the pharmacy's obligations under the CSA. We do not know whether the agency would have credited that testimony, of course, but it was reasonable for the agency to conclude that her failure to clearly acknowledge even unintentional misconduct demonstrated a lack of understanding of her legal obligations.

Because the record supports the Acting Administrator's findings that Jones did not acknowledge the prior misconduct and still did not understand the scope of her responsibilities under the CSA, we conclude that the determination that Jones did not fully accept responsibility for Jones Pharmacy's misconduct was rational and supported by substantial evidence.

B. Remedial Measures

We acknowledge that Jones Pharmacy appears to have implemented policies to address the misconduct at issue here. According to Petitioners, these remedial efforts are evidence that they can be trusted with registrations going forward, so it was unreasonable for the DEA to ignore that evidence even if Jones did not unequivocally admit fault.

Of course, corrective measures undertaken by a pharmacy are certainly relevant to whether it can be trusted with a registration to dispense controlled substances. At the same time, though, the DEA must have confidence that, if the registration is continued, the pharmacy will faithfully comply with its obligations under the CSA. If a pharmacy shows that it does not understand the extent of the past misconduct or its current responsibilities under the law, the DEA rationally could doubt that the pharmacy would faithfully comply in the future with its obligations under the CSA.

Here, the DEA's refusal to consider Jones Pharmacy's remedial measures does not render the decision to revoke its registration arbitrary and capricious. The Acting Administrator explained that, based on the scope and duration of misconduct, Jones's failure to acknowledge that misconduct, and her testimony that she still does not understand the scope of a pharmacist's obligations under the CSA, he had no confidence that . . . Jones . . . would faithfully comply with the CSA. We conclude that the Acting Administrator's determination was rational and supported by substantial evidence in the record. Accordingly, the Acting Administrator's decision to revoke Jones Pharmacy's registration as inconsistent with the public interest was not arbitrary, capricious, or an abuse of discretion.

C. Choice of Sanction

Petitioners contend that the Acting Administrator unreasonably recommended the severe sanction of revocation when the DEA has imposed lesser sanctions under equal or more egregious circumstances. We disagree.

Under the APA, the agency's "choice of sanction is entitled to substantial deference." It is not to be overturned unless it is "unwarranted in law or without justification in fact." Where, as here, Congress intended to grant the agency significant discretion, "mere unevenness in the application of the sanction does not render its application in a particular case 'unwarranted in law.'" The agency's sanction may be set aside, however, if it represents a "flagrant departure" from agency policy and practice.

Here, Petitioners have not shown that the agency's choice of sanction was unwarranted in law or without justification in fact. The DEA decisions Petitioners rely on are distinguishable because, in each of the decisions, the agency found that the registrant had rebutted the government's case by, among other things, admitting fault or expressing remorse. The general pattern of the cited decisions is that a physician engaged in misconduct attributable in part to alcoholism or drug abuse, sought treatment, did not engage in other misconduct since obtaining treatment, and expressed remorse or otherwise accepted responsibility for the misconduct.

Petitioners focus on the past misconduct in these cases, but they do not cite any decision in which the DEA has continued a registration despite finding that the registrant did not fully accept responsibility. Because substantial evidence supports the DEA's finding that Jones did not accept responsibility for the misconduct in this case, Petitioners have not shown that the agency's choice of sanction represented a flagrant departure from prior practice. Therefore, the agency's decision to revoke Jones Pharmacy's registration was not arbitrary or capricious.

For the reasons stated, the DEA Acting Administrator's decision to revoke Jones Pharmacy's registration to dispense controlled substance was not "arbitrary, capricious, an abuse of discretion, or otherwise not in accordance with the law." The factual findings underlying that decision were supported by substantial evidence, and Petitioners have demonstrated no fatal flaw in the proceedings or reasoning leading to the revocation decision. Accordingly, we deny Petitioners' petition for review.

4. Regulation and Prosecution of Manufacturers

Manufacturers of controlled substances with medical uses are also subject to a wide range of regulations under the CSA. In contrast to physicians and pharmacies, however, manufacturers of controlled substances who are accused of wrongdoing in connection with overprescribing, such as Purdue Pharma, are more often prosecuted under the Food, Drug, and Cosmetic Act's misbranding provisions than the Controlled Substances Act. Purdue's involvement in the opioid epidemic was discussed in an article presented in Chapter 2, *The Opioid Epidemic: Fixing a Broken Pharmaceutical Market.* The excerpt that follows describes the FDA's case against Purdue in more detail. As you read it, consider how the prosecution of Purdue compares to prosecutions of physicians like Dr. Hurwitz.

"There's Danger Here, Cherie!": Liability for the Promotion and Marketing of Drugs and Medical Devices for Off-Label Uses
Richard C. Ausness

73 Brooklyn Law Review 1253 (2008)

Physicians often prescribe prescription drugs and other medications for uses that are not approved by the Food and Drug Administration ("FDA"), and such "off label" prescription is widely accepted within the medical community as a legitimate form of treatment. However, the federal government discourages off-label prescription and use in various ways. For example, the FDA restricts the dissemination of information by drug companies about potential off-label therapies.

An off-label use is one that is not provided for on the product's FDA-approved labeling. A doctor makes an off-label prescription when he or she prescribes a drug or medical device to treat a medical condition other than the one the drug or device was approved to treat. Off-label prescription also involves using a different method of applying the treatment as well as prescribing a drug or device to patient groups other than those for whom the FDA approved it. In addition, off-label use includes prescriptions for drug dosages that are different from the recommended dosage or for periods that exceed the recommended use in the labeling.

Off-label uses are not necessarily unusual or experimental. In fact, they are widely accepted within the medical community and may sometimes be the most effective treatment for certain types of medical conditions. It is estimated that between twenty and sixty percent of all prescriptions are for off-label uses. For example, a large percentage of prescriptions for pediatric use are off-label because many drugs are not tested or approved for use by children. Off-label uses are also common in cancer therapy and are often considered to be among the most effective treatments.

Courts have repeatedly held that certain off-label uses are legitimate forms of therapy. The FDA has also tacitly recognized that off-label uses are legitimate. Nevertheless, the FDA severely restricts the ability of drug manufacturers to promote off-label uses for their products. Thus, drug companies are forced to circumvent, or even violate, the law if they wish to inform physicians about beneficial off-label therapies (and make money from the increased sales of their products). The drug companies that cross the line and get caught face substantial civil and criminal liability.

The recent experience of Purdue Pharma, manufacturer of the prescription pain medication OxyContin, illustrates the perils of misbranding and other violations of the FDCA. The company was accused of encouraging physicians to prescribe OxyContin for use every eight hours instead of the twelve-hour dosage approved by the FDA. It eventually agreed to pay $19.5 million to twenty-six states and the District of Columbia to settle a civil suit based on its alleged promotion of off-label use of the painkiller. This led Connecticut Attorney General Richard Blumenthal to declare, "We are raising the bar on off-label marketing—and other promotion tactics—that lead to abuse and diversion of prescription drugs." However, Purdue Pharma suffered an even more serious blow when the U.S. Department of Justice brought criminal charges against the company and three of its top executives. Federal prosecutors contended that Purdue Pharma had engaged in a fraudulent and deceptive marketing campaign that falsely claimed that OxyContin, because of its timed-release formula, was more resistant to abuse and less likely to cause addiction than competing products such as Percocet. The federal government also charged some company sales representatives with giving doctors misleading scientific data to support their fraudulent claims.

Pursuant to an agreement, Purdue Pharma and the three corporate officers pleaded guilty to these criminal charges. As part of the plea bargain deal, Purdue Pharma acknowledged that it had made false statements, and it agreed to pay $470 million in fines and payments to various state and federal agencies as well as $130 million to settle civil lawsuits brought against the company by former patients who claimed to have become addicted to OxyContin. According to federal prosecutors, the $600 million in fines and civil penalties that Purdue Pharma agreed to pay amounted to ninety percent of the profits that it initially made from OxyContin sales. Furthermore, as part of the plea bargain deal, the court sentenced the company to five years' probation.

Three company executives also pleaded guilty to misdemeanor charges of misbranding OxyContin, a violation of the FDCA that does not require proof that the defendants intended to defraud doctors or consumers or that they knew about the wrongdoing of others. These officials agreed to pay a total of $34.5 million in fines. At a "lengthy and highly emotional hearing" in federal district court, parents of those who had died from overdoses of OxyContin condemned the company officials and urged the court to reject the plea agreements and sentence the officials to jail terms. However, the court accepted the plea agreements and only sentenced the three officials to three years' probation and 400 hours each of community service in drug treatment programs. Nevertheless, the judge expressed disappointment that he was unable to send the defendants to prison because federal prosecutors had not produced evidence that the company officials were aware of the wrongdoing at Purdue Pharma.

United States v. The Purdue Frederick Company, Inc.

United States District Court for the Western District of Virginia
495 F.Supp.2d 569 (2007)

Jones, J.

The issue before the court is whether or not to accept the plea agreements in this case.

The Purdue Frederick Company, Inc. ("Purdue") has pleaded guilty to misbranding OxyContin, a prescription opioid pain medication, with the intent to defraud or mislead, a felony under the federal Food, Drug, and Cosmetic Act. The individual defendants, Michael Friedman, Howard R. Udell, and Paul D. Goldenheim, have pleaded guilty to the misdemeanor charge of misbranding, solely as responsible corporate officers.[2] The individual defendants are not charged with personal knowledge of the misbranding or with any personal intent to defraud.

---

2. Friedman is the former president and CEO of Purdue, Udell is the executive vice president and chief legal officer, and Goldenheim is the former chief scientific officer.

The Information in this case charges, among other things, that

> [b]eginning on or about December 12, 1995, and continuing until on or about June 30, 2001, certain PURDUE supervisors and employees, with the intent to defraud or mislead, marketed and promoted OxyContin as less addictive, less subject to abuse and diversion, and less likely to cause tolerance and withdrawal than other pain medications as follows:
>
> a. Trained PURDUE sales representatives and told some health care providers that it was more difficult to extract the oxycodone from an OxyContin tablet for the purpose of intravenous abuse, although PURDUE's own study showed that a drug abuser could extract approximately 68% of the oxycodone from a single 10mg OxyContin tablet by crushing the tablet, stirring it in water, and drawing the solution through cotton into a syringe;
>
> b. Told PURDUE sales representatives they could tell health care providers that OxyContin potentially creates less chance for addiction than immediate-release opioids;
>
> c. Sponsored training that taught PURDUE sales supervisors that OxyContin had fewer "peak and trough" blood level effects than immediate-release opioids resulting in less euphoria and less potential for abuse than short-acting opioids;
>
> d. Told certain health care providers that patients could stop therapy abruptly without experiencing withdrawal symptoms and that patients who took OxyContin would not develop tolerance to the drug; and
>
> e. Told certain health care providers that OxyContin did not cause a "buzz" or euphoria, caused less euphoria, had less addiction potential, had less abuse potential, was less likely to be diverted than immediate-release opioids, and could be used to "weed out" addicts and drug seekers.

(Information ¶ 19.) Purdue has agreed that these facts are true, and the individual defendants, while they do not agree that they had knowledge of these things, have agreed that the court may accept these facts in support of their guilty pleas.

The plea agreements have been submitted pursuant to Federal Rule of Criminal Procedure 11(c)(1)(C), which allows the parties to agree to a specific sentence to be imposed. The court is not bound by the plea agreements, and may reject them. If a plea agreement is rejected, that defendant must be given an opportunity to withdraw the guilty plea. The government has agreed in this case that if the court rejects any of the plea agreements, the government will dismiss the Information filed in the case, without prejudice to the government's right to later indict the defendants or any other entity or individual on any charge. Accordingly, if the court rejects any of the plea agreements, the present case may end, and it will be up to the government to decide whether to re-prosecute the defendants, or any of them.

In addition to a lengthy hearing on the present issue, the parties were required to submit extensive written material, including financial information, for the court's consideration.

The Supreme Court has held that defendants have "no absolute right to have a guilty plea accepted." The Court stated, "A court may reject a plea in exercise of sound judicial discretion." But as the Sixth Circuit stated, "By leaving the decision whether to accept or reject a plea to the exercise of sound judicial discretion, the Supreme Court did not intend to allow district courts to reject pleas on an arbitrary basis."

While the court's decision must not be arbitrary, "Rule 11 does not limit the reasons for which the district court may reject a proposed plea agreement." Rule 11 explicitly states that a court cannot accept a plea if it is not supported by the factual record or if the court believes that that the plea is not voluntary. But Rule 11 also allows a district judge to reject a plea agreement if it is too lenient or too harsh.

Under the law, Purdue is subject to a penalty of five years probation and a fine of up to $500,000. In its plea agreement, Purdue has agreed to substantial additional monetary sanctions totaling $600 million, reported to be one of the largest in the history of the pharmaceutical industry. The amount includes the following:

1. $100,615,797.25 payable to federal government health care agencies under a Civil Settlement Agreement;

2. $59,384,202.75 in escrow for those states that elect to settle their claims against Purdue. These civil settlements to the federal and state government total $160 million, of which the federal government is receiving sixty percent;

3. $3,471,220.68 to Medicaid programs for improperly calculated rebates;

4. $500,000 fine to the United States;

5. $20 million in trust to the Commonwealth of Virginia for operating the Virginia Prescription Monitoring Program;

6. $5.3 million to the Virginia Medicaid Fraud Control Unit's Program Income Fund;

7. $276.1 million forfeiture to the United States;

8. $130 million to settle private civil claims related to OxyContin; and

9. $4,628,779.32 to be expended by Purdue for monitoring costs in connection with a Corporate Integrity Agreement with the U.S. Department of Health and Human Services.

The individual defendants are subject to a punishment of twelve months imprisonment and a fine of up to $100,000. In their plea agreements, they have agreed to pay a total of $34.5 million to the Virginia Medicaid Fraud Unit's Program Income

Fund.[3] In return, the government has agreed to sentences for them without any imprisonment.

There have been several reasons suggested why the court should reject the plea agreements.

Lack of Restitution.

The plea agreements preclude restitution other than as set forth in the agreements and a number of alleged victims object to this provision, contending that the amounts allocated to private parties are insufficient, compared to the recovery by governmental victims. BlueCross BlueShield of Tennessee has filed a Request for Notice, an Opportunity to be Heard at Sentencing, and an Order of Restitution. Other third-party health care payors have joined in this motion. In addition, an individual who considers herself a victim because of her addiction to OxyContin has objected to the plea agreements and has filed a formal Motion to Assert Victim's Rights, in which she complains about restitution, as well as other matters.

These parties have received notice of this present proceedings and the court has allow them an opportunity to speak.

The government and the defendants, in agreeing to preclude other restitution, rely on the Victim and Witness Protection Act of 1982 ("VWPA"), which states in relevant part as follows:

> To the extent that the court determines that the complication and prolongation of the sentencing process resulting from the fashioning of an order of restitution under this section outweighs the need to provide restitution to any victims, the court may decline to make such an order.

In order to award an alleged victim restitution under either the VWPA . . . , the court would have to determine whether that person was "directly and proximately" harmed by the misbranding offense that was the subject of the plea agreements. The Fourth Circuit has held that to be considered "directly and proximately harmed" under either the VWPA or the MVRA, a person must show that the harm resulted from "conduct underlying an element of the offense of conviction."

Purdue argues that third-party payors cannot show that they were directly and proximately harmed by Purdue's misbranding, unless they can prove the following:

> 1. That a Purdue sales representative misstated to a specific prescribing physician that OxyContin was less addictive, less subject to abuse and diversion, or less likely to cause tolerance or withdrawal than other pain medications;
>
> 2. That specific prescribing physician relied upon that misstatement by that Purdue sales representative and, in reliance on that misstatement, prescribed OxyContin rather than an alternative pain medication (e.g. Percocet) for one of the private third-party payor's insured individuals;

3. Defendant Friedman has agreed to pay $19 million, whereas defendants Udell and Goldenheim have agreed to pay $8 million and $7.5 million, respectively.

3. That the physician prescribed OxyContin for the insured because of the misstatement and not because of the other attributes of OxyContin (e.g., twelve-hour dosing or the absence of acetaminophen, which risks liver toxicity);

4. That the private third-party payor paid for that prescription of OxyContin; and

5. That the private third-party payor paid more for the OxyContin prescription than the particular alternative pain medication that the prescribing physician would have prescribed if he or she had not relied on the misstatement and prescribed OxyContin.

Purdue further argues that the chain of causation between the harm alleged and the misbranding offense could have been broken by any intervening act on behalf of the insured patient or the prescribing health care professional. For example, if patients obtained OxyContin improperly by deceiving their physicians or by altering an otherwise proper prescription, the third-party payors would not be entitled to restitution for those prescriptions since the misbranding did not directly and proximately caused any financial loss to the third-party payor. Or if a physician negligently prescribed OxyContin, the third-party payor that paid for that prescription is also not entitled to restitution because the misbranding once again did not directly and proximately cause the third-party payor's financial loss.

Even if third-party payors can show that they were directly harmed by Purdue's misbranding, Purdue claims that each payor would have to present to this court the facts of every instance of overpayment in order for the Court to determine the proper amount of restitution for each third-party payor.

As to any individuals injured by the use of OxyContin, the difficulties of establishing causation are demonstrated by the numerous civil suits that have been filed by such persons against Purdue, including two before this court, *McCauley v. Purdue Pharma, L.P.*, 331 F.Supp.2d 449 (W.D.Va.2004), and *Ewing v. Purdue Pharma, L.P.*, No. 2:02CV00150, 2004 WL 1856002 (W.D.Va. Aug. 19, 2004). Courts have consistently found that despite extensive discovery, plaintiffs were unable to show that Purdue's misbranding proximately caused their injuries. *See, e.g., Bodie v. Purdue Pharma Co.*, No. 05-13834, 2007 WL 1577964, at *3 (11th Cir. June 1, 2007) (affirming the district court's conclusion that the plaintiff's claims failed because he could not show that he was proximately harmed by Purdue's allegedly inadequate warnings); *Koenig v. Purdue Pharma Co.*, 435 F.Supp.2d 551, 556 (N.D.Tex.2006) ("Because plaintiffs have failed to show that an adequate warning would have changed [the physician]'s decision to prescribe OxyContin, and because [the physician] testified that he would not have changed his decision, the Court finds that Plaintiffs have failed to raise a genuine fact issue.").

It is argued that restitution might be handled in this case as with a civil class action claim, but class certification has been generally denied in OxyContin claims because of the variety of causation issues.

It is true that the governmental health care providers have been allotted a portion of Purdue's payment in settlement of their civil claims for the misbranding of OxyContin ($160 million) that is greater than the portion to be used by Purdue to settle private claims ($130 million). However, Purdue's liability for private claims is not capped by the plea agreements. Purdue agrees to pay at least $130 million to settle private claims, but no maximum limit is imposed. I do not find that the plea agreements are inherently unfair in this regard.

Accordingly, in spite of the arguments by putative victims, I agree that the restitution process would unduly complicate and prolong the sentencing process. In order to prove causation, litigation over many months, if not years, would be required before final judgment in this case could be entered. Such delay would be contrary to the basic principles of our criminal justice system.

I would have preferred that the plea agreements had allocated some amount of the money for the education of those at risk from the improper use of prescription drugs, and the treatment of those who have succumbed to such use. Prescription drug abuse is rampant in all areas of our country, particularly among young people, causing untold misery and harm. The White House drug policy office estimates that such abuse rose seventeen percent from 2001 to 2005. That office reports that currently there are more new abusers of prescription drugs than new users of any illicit drugs.

On the other hand, I am forbidden by law to participate in plea discussions, Fed.R.Crim.P. 11(c)(1), and I will not reject these agreements simply because they do not contain provisions that I would have preferred. The government has represented that it did not demand inclusion of a treatment provision in the plea agreements because national drug policy has been placed by Congress in the Substance Abuse and Mental Health Service Administration, an agency of the U.S. Department of Health and Human Services. The government prosecutors were reluctant to direct treatment funds in a manner beyond their expertise and possibly contrary to national policy. I will not second-guess their decision in this regard.

Political Interference.

It has been suggested that Purdue may have received a favorable deal from the government solely because of politics.

I completely reject this claim. I have had long experience with the United States Attorney for this district, and I am convinced that neither he nor the career prosecutors who handled this case would have permitted any political interference. In fact, I am sure that they would have refused to accept a plea agreement that they did not sincerely feel was in the best interests of justice.

Lack of Incarceration.

The plea agreements provide for no incarceration for the individual defendants. The government points out that a sentence of incarceration under the federal sentencing guidelines would be unusual based on the facts of the case. The government is also convinced that the nature of the convictions of the individual defendants—based on strict liability for misbranding—will send a strong deterrent message to the pharmaceutical industry. The defendants point to their lack of prior criminal record, their strong commitment to civic and charitable endeavors, as well as their other positive personal attributes. On the other hand, the potential damage by the misbranding disclosed in this case was substantial and I do not minimize the danger to the public from this crime. The defendants voluntarily accepted responsibility over this business enterprise, for which they were generously rewarded. However, while the question is a close one, I find that in the absence of government proof of knowledge by the individual defendants of the wrongdoing, prison sentences are not appropriate.

Summary.

In summary, I find that the plea agreements are supported by the facts and the law and impose adequate punishment on the defendants and I accept them. Moreover, for the reasons stated, I will deny the third party motions.

In 2018, the *New York Times* reported that federal prosecutors had recommended that the three Purdue Pharma executives "be indicted on felony charges, including conspiracy to defraud the United States, that could have sent the men to prison if convicted." Barry Meier, *Origins of an Epidemic: Purdue Pharma Knew its Opioids Were Widely Abused*, N.Y. Times (May 29, 2018). The recommendation was based on a four-year investigation that reportedly showed that "[c]ompany officials had received reports that the pills were being crushed and snorted; stolen from pharmacies; and that some doctors were being charged with selling prescriptions . . . [b]ut the drug maker continued 'in the face of this knowledge' to market OxyContin as less prone to abuse and addiction than other prescription opioids." *Id.* The recommendation to bring felony charges against the executives was rejected by "top Justice Department officials in the George W. Bush administration," which led to the 2007 plea agreement. *Id.*

As the court alluded to in accepting Purdue's guilty plea, the company has faced a number of civil suits in connection with OxyContin, including class actions, cases brought by individual litigants, and parens patriae cases brought by state attorneys general. Purdue has won most of these cases, although the parens patriae cases "have been more successful than other forms of civil litigation for various reasons. In the first place, state officials can muster more effective legal resources than individual litigants. Secondly, governmental litigants are not subject to the conduct-based defenses that have been invoked to defeat individual plaintiffs in product misuse cases." Richard C. Ausness, *The Role of Litigation in the Fight against Prescription Drug Abuse*, 116 W. Va. L. Rev. 1117, 1121 (2014).

Chapter 8

State Marijuana Reforms and the Federal Response

As discussed in Chapter 6, federal law classifies marijuana as a Schedule I substance. But if you were to spend a few days in Denver, Seattle, Las Vegas, or a number of other cities, it would be easy to forget that federal law still criminalizes the distribution, manufacture, and possession of marijuana. Since 2012, ten states—Alaska, California, Colorado, Illinois, Maine, Massachusetts, Michigan, Nevada, Oregon, and Washington—have legalized marijuana. Vermont and Washington, D.C., have both legalized the possession and cultivation of small amounts of marijuana, although commercial manufacture and sale remain prohibited. State medical marijuana laws are even more prevalent. Because there is so much variation in state medical marijuana laws, there is some disagreement about how robust a state law should have to be to count as a medical marijuana legalization law. At the time of this writing, however, the National Conference on State Legislatures classified 34 states as having a "comprehensive public medical marijuana and cannabis program" and an additional 12 states as having narrower laws permitting the use of low-THC marijuana for medical purposes. This chapter examines state marijuana reforms and the federal response, with a focus on laws legalizing marijuana for recreational use.

A. State Marijuana Legalization

California was the first state to legalize medical marijuana in 1996, but it missed the chance to be the first to fully legalize when state voters narrowly rejected a legalization ballot measure in 2010. After campaigns informed by the California experience, Colorado and Washington voters passed the first state marijuana legalization laws via ballot measure in 2012. It was not until the beginning of 2014, however, that marijuana retail stores opened their doors in Colorado (in Washington, the first stores opened in the middle of 2014).

Because marijuana legalization laws are comparatively new, it is hard to draw any firm conclusions about their impact on the economy, the criminal justice system, and public health. The available evidence suggests that, so far, marijuana legalization has generated substantial tax revenue and savings in the criminal justice system, all without resulting in significant increases in use of the drug. But the impact of marijuana legalization after five years may not necessarily tell us much about what the impact may be after 10 or 15 years. If the price of retail marijuana drops substantially, as has recently happened in a few jurisdictions, spikes in use and decreases in tax revenue could follow. Bearing in mind that today's data can only tell us so much about whether or not to view legalization as a success, the following article provides an overview of the experience of state marijuana legalization laws after the first few states implemented their legalization regimes. The article, excerpted from a report on criminal justice reform by the Academy of Justice, provides an overview of what we know about the impact of marijuana legalization laws so far.

Marijuana Legalization
Alex Kreit

1 Reforming Criminal Justice 115 (Erik Luna ed., 2017)

Not long ago, marijuana legalization was considered to be far outside the political mainstream. The idea that it could actually become law seemed so remote that when President Barack Obama was asked for his thoughts on marijuana legalization in a 2009 online town-hall event, he treated the question as a joke. "I don't know what this says about the online audience," he chuckled, before tersely answering that, no, he did not think legalizing marijuana would be "a good strategy to grow our economy." President Obama's drug czar was similarly dismissive when asked about the topic in 2009, saying that "[l]egalization was not in the President's vocabulary." On the same night Obama was elected to a second term, however, Colorado and Washington became the first states to pass marijuana-legalization ballot measures. All of a sudden, marijuana legalization was no longer a laughing matter.

The story of state marijuana legalization dates back to 1996, when California passed the first statewide medical-marijuana legalization law. The federal government did all that it could to try to stop the law in its tracks, raiding medical-marijuana dispensaries and prosecuting some of the operators. Despite its best efforts, however, the federal government was not able to stop the trend. Throughout the 2000s, more and more states passed medical-marijuana laws, and marijuana stores started opening faster than the federal government could shut them down. The problem came down to resources. The federal government has the legal authority to prosecute any marijuana offense, from a marijuana kingpin to a user in possession of a single joint. But it only has the manpower to go after a small fraction of marijuana offenders—almost all marijuana enforcement is carried out by state and local police. As a result, the federal government did not succeed in shutting down state medical-marijuana laws. Instead, federal enforcement served mostly to make it more difficult for states to implement effective regulations.

By the time Colorado and Washington passed the first laws legalizing marijuana for all adult use in 2012, it was clear to most observers that the federal government was fighting a losing battle. Perhaps in recognition of this dynamic, the DOJ announced a cease-fire in its war on state-legal marijuana in late 2013, in the form of a memorandum advising federal law-enforcement officials not to use scarce resources to go after people in compliance with state marijuana laws.

Since Colorado and Washington voters legalized marijuana, six more states have followed suit. In 2014, Oregon and Alaska passed marijuana-legalization ballot measures. And, in 2016, California, Maine, Massachusetts, and Nevada joined the club. Since 2012, voters in only two states have rejected marijuana-legalization proposals. In 2015, Ohioans decisively rejected a controversial ballot measure that would have legalized marijuana by giving the initiative's backers a monopoly on marijuana production. In 2016, an Arizona legalization ballot measure was narrowly defeated, with 51.32% against and 48.68% in favor.

Manufacture and distribution. Perhaps the most important element of any state legalization law concerns marijuana manufacture and distribution. To date, state legalization laws have adopted an alcohol-style commercial model, but with much stricter oversight of the supply chain. States have gone to great length to track marijuana in order to avoid diversion to the black market in prohibition states and to minors in their own states. Diversion is an especially important concern, in part because under the Department of Justice's 2013 non-enforcement guidelines, "[p]reventing the diversion of marijuana from states where it is legal under state law in some form to other states" is one of the things that states must do to avoid federal interference.

To guard against diversion of marijuana, the four states that have already implemented marijuana legalization—Alaska, Colorado, Oregon, and Washington—all require "seed-to-sale" tracking of the product. (The legalization laws in California, Maine, Massachusetts, and Nevada, which were passed by voters in 2016, have not yet been implemented with respect to marijuana manufacture and retail sale.) These tracking systems "offer[] the state the ability to track product in ways that far surpass product tracking in most other commodity markets in the U.S."

Other considerations for regulating manufacturers and producers include whether to permit licensees to manufacture and distribute unlimited amounts of marijuana, which may contribute to driving the price down. Or, whether to place limits on the amount of marijuana a licensee can produce. California's marijuana-legalization law, for example, establishes 19 different license types, including 13 different cultivation license types and a "microbusiness" license. Each cultivation license type is based on the size of the grow operation and its location (indoors, outdoors, etc.). Notably, the law places a moratorium on the three "large" cultivation license types—which would allow a licensee to grow up to one acre of marijuana outdoors or 22,000 square feet indoors. The state may not issue these licenses until after January 1, 2023.

Of course, it is also possible to legalize marijuana without allowing commercial manufacture and distribution. Leaving all or part of the supply chain in the hands of the state is an attractive option for legalization supporters who are concerned that commercialization could result in increased use. Uruguay is in the process of implementing a marijuana-legalization law under which production is controlled by state-commissioned companies. This model is not entirely unfamiliar to the United States: In a number of states, liquor is sold at state-run stores. Unfortunately, state-run marijuana stores are unlikely to be a legally viable option so long as federal prohibition remains on the books. This is because, unlike a state marijuana law that merely permits private actors to grow and sell marijuana, a system in which the state itself is violating federal marijuana law would almost surely be struck down under the Constitution's Supremacy Clause.

Possession limits. Marijuana legalization proponents often use the tagline of taxing and regulating marijuana "like alcohol." Unlike alcohol, however, marijuana-legalization laws strictly limit the amount a person can purchase and possess. As with seed-to-sale tracking, this feature is designed to help prevent against diversion. If consumers were allowed to buy unlimited amounts of marijuana, smuggling legally produced marijuana into other states for sale would be easy and cost-effective. These limits might also have public health benefits by preventing stores from offering bulk discounts to consumers and keeping prices high.

With the exception of Maine, legalization states limit the amount of marijuana a person can buy to one ounce. In Maine, the limit is substantially higher, at 2.5 ounces. At least as long as most states retain prohibition, legalization laws should probably include a limit on the amount of marijuana a person can purchase and possess. Although one ounce is a nice, round number, states could probably adopt a lower limit. Studies suggest daily marijuana users consume between 1.3 and 1.9 grams of marijuana per day, so half an ounce would last a very heavy user a little more than a week. A half-ounce limit would further reduce the risk of diversion and help to keep prices relatively high (a goal of many public health advocates). On the other hand, a lower limit on personal possession could expose more users to arrest for having more marijuana than the law allows.

Cultivation for personal use. Cultivation for personal use, or "homegrows," warrants special attention from policymakers. Most state legalization laws allow individuals to grow small amounts of marijuana for personal use. In Colorado, for example, adults can legally grow up to six marijuana plants for personal use. Although there is a requirement that the marijuana be secured "in an enclosed, locked space," homegrows are essentially unregulated. No license is needed to legally grow six marijuana plants or fewer for personal use in Colorado. Similarly, under Oregon's legalization law, adults may grow up to four plants per residence. By contrast, Washington did not legalize home cultivation—there, the only way to legally grow marijuana for recreational use is if you have a commercial license to do so.

If marijuana were legal nationwide, letting people grow small amounts of marijuana in their homes probably would not present many challenges. Growing marijuana "is much more difficult than most people understand," not to mention resource intensive: "[t]he investment—in hydroponics, proper lighting, and humidity controls—can be substantial." It would seem, then, that home marijuana cultivation would be left mostly to hobbyists, much like home brewing by beer enthusiasts.

There is little evidence that small marijuana homegrows that comply with state laws have become a problem in the states that permit them. There is, however, reason to "worry that homegrowers may grow *more* marijuana than they are allowed and present an opportunity to divert product to illegal markets" in other states. Anecdotal evidence suggests that this may be happening in Colorado, where law enforcement officials report that illegal growers are attempting to use Colorado's homegrow law as a cover. The illegal growers take advantage of the fact that it is hard for police to distinguish the legal and illegal homegrows without gaining access to a home. But, without some evidence that a homegrower is operating outside the law, the police will not be able to get a search warrant.

The data so far. A few organizations have released reports assessing state marijuana-legalization laws. Because marijuana-legalization laws are so new—in Colorado and Washington, the provisions permitting marijuana businesses did not take effect until 2014—the findings are necessarily preliminary. Based on the early results, however, marijuana-legalization laws appear to be succeeding at reducing law enforcement expenditures and generating tax revenue, without significantly impacting rates of marijuana use.

The Cato Institute has released the most comprehensive analysis of state marijuana-legalization laws to date, with its September 2016 report *Dose of Reality: The Effect of State Marijuana Legalizations.*[64] The report examines the legalization laws in Colorado, Washington, Oregon, and Alaska, and it considers data on marijuana use, marijuana pricing, health indicators, crime rates, and road safety. Overall, the report concludes "that state marijuana legalizations have had a minimal effect on marijuana use and related outcomes." Specifically, the data shows that "state-level marijuana legalizations to date have been associated with, at most, modest changes in marijuana use and related outcomes." Meanwhile, tax revenue following marijuana legalization has generally met or exceeded expectations. In Colorado, the state "collects well over $10 million per month from recreational marijuana alone" and in Washington "recreational marijuana generated approximately $70 million in tax revenue in the first year of sales—double the original forecast."

A 2016 report by the Drug Policy Alliance (DPA) reaches a similar conclusion.[68] The DPA report looked at data on youth marijuana use, marijuana arrests, road safety, and tax revenue. It found that while "[i]t is too early to draw any line-in-the-sand conclusion about the effects of marijuana legalization," the preliminary data "suggest that the effects of legalization have been either positive or negligible." Thus far, legalization appears to have had "little to no impact on the overall rate

64. Angela Dills et al., Dose of Reality: The Effect of State Marijuana Legalizations (Cato Inst. Pol'y Analysis No. 799, 2016), https://object.cato.org/sites/cato.org/files/pubs/pdf/pa799.pdf.

68. Drug Policy Alliance, So Far, So Good: What We Know About Marijuana Legalization in Colorado, Washington, Alaska, Oregon, and Washington, D.C. (2016), https://www.drugpolicy.org/sites/default/files/Marijuana_Legalization_Status_Report_101316.pdf.

of youth marijuana use." The data also indicates that "[l]egalization has not led to more dangerous road conditions," with "the post-legalization fatality rate" remaining consistent with pre-legalization levels in Colorado and Washington and early data from Oregon and Alaska showing the same. DPA found that states are realizing substantial cost savings and tax revenue. Arrests for marijuana have (not surprisingly) "plummeted since voters legalized the adult use of marijuana, saving those jurisdictions millions of dollars and preventing the criminalization of thousands of people." Tax revenue exceeded expectations in both Colorado and Washington in 2015, and early data from Oregon show the state collecting about $4 million a month in marijuana taxes. (Alaska did not issue its first retail marijuana license until September 8, 2016.)

This is not to say that marijuana-legalization laws are costless or that they do not carry public health risks. Hospital admissions and poison-control calls related to marijuana have jumped in legalization states. In both Colorado and Washington, poison-center calls involving marijuana roughly doubled following legalization, although in absolute terms the numbers are still quite low. In Washington, calls increased from 156 in 2012 to 280 in 2016. In Colorado, there were 110 calls in 2012 and 224 in 2016. This is a small fraction of marijuana users and much lower than poison-center calls for many common household goods (for example, 2014 saw just under 200,000 poison-control calls nationwide for cosmetics and personal-care products). Nevertheless, policymakers should certainly pay close attention to this trend, particularly as it concerns the regulation of edible marijuana products.

In addition, it appears adult marijuana use has increased slightly following state marijuana legalization. Legalization opponents, such as Smart Approaches to Marijuana (SAM), argue that this is cause for alarm.[80] But the data so far show at most a small increase in use, and nothing close to "the sometimes dire predictions made by legalization opponents." Past-month use in Colorado rose from 14.93% of the population in 2013–2014 to 16.57% in 2014–2015. Past-month use in Washington actually *decreased* slightly during that same period, from 12.79% to 11.22%, although use rates in Washington had been rising in the years leading up to 2014–2015. Still, basic economic theory would suggest that as marijuana becomes less expensive and easier for adults to purchase, adult use will increase, at least somewhat.

Of course, policymakers should be mindful that early data may not necessarily reflect the impact of marijuana legalization over the long term. As the RAND Corporation's Beau Kilmer recently wrote in the *New England Journal of Medicine*, "we should be skeptical of people who claim to know what the net effect of cannabis legalization on public health will be." Marijuana prices in legalization states are still higher than they are likely to be as the industry matures. Already, prices have begun to drop in Colorado and Washington. With this in mind, future rates of marijuana use may depend a great deal on details like the extent to which legalization states

80. *See* Smart Approaches to Marijuana, Lessons Learned After 4 Years of Marijuana Legalization (2016), https://learnaboutsam.org/wp-content/uploads/2016/11/SAM-report-on-CO-and-WA-issued-31-Oct-2016.pdf.

deploy taxes and other regulatory measures to prevent prices from dropping too far. It is also worth noting that the data we have on use is limited—rates of past-year or past-month use do not account for other important measures like the amount of marijuana people are consuming or its potency.

Still, while no one can predict the future, the experience of marijuana-legalization states so far is, on the whole, encouraging. States that have legalized marijuana have raised tax revenue in excess of pre-legalization estimates while redirecting law-enforcement and judicial resources that were previously spent on enforcing marijuana prohibition. Youth marijuana use does not appear to have increased as a result of legalization, adult marijuana use has risen at most modestly, and the overall impact of legalization on public health and safety has been small.

Marijuana prohibition has been a costly failure, requiring states to invest a significant amount of money on enforcement while losing out on potential tax revenue, all with little to show for it. Marijuana legalization may not be as perfect as some advocates make it out to be. But if implemented well, it is far better than the status quo.

B. Comparing Regulatory Models

Marijuana legalization can encompass a range of policy options. Tobacco and caffeine are both legal, for example, but one is much more tightly regulated than the other. To date, state marijuana legalization laws have followed an alcohol-style model. As you read the material that follows, consider whether you think this is the best approach or whether a different model would be preferable.

1. Overview

The following analysis, excerpted from a report prepared by the RAND Corporation for the Vermont legislature, provides an overview of some of the different possible legal regimes for regulating marijuana.

Considering Marijuana Legalization: Insights for Vermont and Other Jurisdictions

Jonathan P. Caulkins, Beau Kilmer, Mark A. R. Kleinman, Robert J. MacCoun, Gregory Midgette, Pat Oglesby, Rosalie Liccardo Pacula and Peter H. Reuter

RAND Corporation (2015)

One of the key elements of a plan for implementing legalization is determining how marijuana will be supplied. Specifically, what kinds of organizations will be allowed to produce and distribute marijuana? Historically, the answer under prohibition has been "none." In November 2012, Colorado and Washington State made a dramatic break with past practice by voting to allow a for-profit commercial marijuana industry that is licensed and regulated somewhat like the alcohol industry.

But there is a lot of policy space between traditional prohibition and such commercial legalization. Voters in Colorado and Washington skipped over many intermediate options, such as barring for-profit corporations but allowing co-ops or nonprofits whose boards include public-health and child-welfare advocates.

Each of these supply strategies is really a broad category of options encompassing considerable scope for fine-tuning. And a bad implementation of a good strategy might underperform relative to a wise implementation of an inferior one. Therefore, picking a strategy is more the beginning of a discussion and design process than an answer to the question of what should be done. However, some consequences inevitably flow from selecting who is allowed to produce and supply marijuana that no amount of fine-tuning can overcome.

The Commonly Discussed Options

Implement an Alcohol-Style Commercial Model (Regulate Like Alcohol)

When people use the term *legalize* without further elaboration, they might often have in mind what might be called the standard commercial model, leaving production, distribution, and sale to the competitive private market, subject both to the standard laws and regulations that apply to all economic activity and to some additional rules specific to that product. For marijuana, these additional rules mostly pertain to the following:

- who can use (e.g., anyone over 21)
- quality control (e.g., testing requirements)
- packaging (e.g., requiring certain labeling)
- industry structure (e.g., requiring or banning vertical integration between producers, distributors, and retailers)
- product selection (e.g., whether to allow the sale of concentrates and edibles, whether to restrict potency)
- retail operations (e.g., rules that keep a minimum distance between stores and sensitive locations, such as schools; require vendor training; ban special sales and volume discounts; limit amount either per transaction or per user per day or month).

To reduce the risk of exports to other states, Washington State has also sought to limit the amount produced to that needed to serve its own domestic market.

[T]his approach is [often] referred to as "regulate like alcohol."

Washington State and Colorado (and soon Oregon and Alaska) limit marijuana sales to dedicated stores, as opposed to allowing other retail stores to stock marijuana products alongside other items. That helps keep minors away from retail selling and renders impractical some cross-price subsidization tactics. (If convenience stores could sell marijuana, one might expect them to use marijuana as a loss leader, selling below cost in order to increase customer volumes and recoup forgone marijuana revenue through greater sales of other items.) It also keeps marijuana sales separate from alcohol and tobacco sales.

The guiding spirit of this approach is to let the market evolve to maximize the efficiency of production, the appeal of products to consumers, and the size, scale, and scope of the market—subject only to remaining within the regulatory parameters. This spirit is reflected in which types of agencies are charged with implementing the rules: a revenue-raising agency in Colorado and the Liquor Control Board in Washington, rather than a public-health agency. A public-health agency might instead view the problem as one of killing off the black market while suffering the smallest possible increase in use. However, creating a public-health agency with the requisite capacity to issue licenses, monitor production, issue and enforce regulations, and collect taxes would constitute a challenge, while those activities are among the core competencies of revenue departments and liquor boards.

No one knows how a dynamic competitive market in marijuana would evolve, but we think that some plausible conjectures include the following:

- Production costs of usable marijuana will be much lower at production scales above 10,000 to 100,000 sq. ft. than they have been in traditional (indoor) operations that were smaller than a few thousand square feet, so average firm size will grow.
- Production will shift from indoors to greenhouses (greenhouses are cheaper, artificial lighting is expensive, and densely packed plants are more prone to pests and disease) and possibly to outdoor production (cheaper still but subject to some caveats explored below).
- The marijuana industry will want to shift consumption patterns away from traditional loose marijuana (for pipes and roll-your-own joints) that could require labor-intensive hand trimming via some combination of the following:
    - mechanization of trimming (viewed skeptically by many in the industry)
    - production and sale of extract-based products
    - sale of rolled joints (akin to conventional manufactured versus roll-your-own tobacco cigarettes).
- Declining costs of production per unit of intoxicant will shift profit opportunities toward
    - firms that promote brand identification via mass marketing
    - boutique brands for affluent consumers
    - on-premise consumption (compare cost of a muffin at a café with that of one from a grocery store)
    - high-touch retailers
    - bundling (marijuana in candy bars might yield higher margins than just marijuana)

- cross-subsidization (e.g., promoting ski vacations with complimentary marijuana).

The great unknown is the direction of product innovation:

- toward (or away from?) very-high-potency products
- toward (but how far toward?) concentrates and edibles
- the biggest wild card of all: the potential development of new products based on systematic extraction and blending of the hundreds of possibly psychoactive chemicals in the cannabis plant, of which today only two (THC and CBD) have reasonably well-characterized activity.

The contrast between extracts and conventional usable marijuana is important, so it bears elaboration—albeit with a reemphasis on the caveat that these projections are all speculative. *These considerations are also not necessarily germane only to a commercial market model.* A government monopoly could promote the production and sale of extracts despite the associated public-health concerns, just as government monopolies promote lotteries despite various concerns they raise.

Usable marijuana generally refers to the flowering tops of cannabis plants and sometimes the leaves, suitably prepared. The flowering tops have the highest concentrations of THC but constitute only a modest proportion of the plant's weight. So a considerable proportion of the THC produced by the plant resides in leaves and trim, material that, in the past, has often been discarded because machines that can efficiently extract that THC were too expensive and bulky to maintain while evading police detection. After legalization, one would expect this THC to be extracted for sale as cooking oils, edibles, wax for dabbing, and oils to be used in vaporizers (which release THC by heating but not combusting, akin to e-cigarettes versus conventional cigarettes). So whereas with traditional patterns of production the market equilibrium had the bulk of marijuana being consumed in raw form, after legalization, extracted THC might be produced in volumes that will induce industry to promote a shift toward greater consumption of extract-based products.

If demand for extract-based products takes off (e.g., because e-cigarettes displace combustion as the principal route of inhalation) and marijuana is legalized nationally, not just at the state level, there could be a further radical shift away from labor-intensive cultivation for flowering tops and toward outdoor mechanized farming. Production costs per acre are very low when cannabis plants are grown for seed or fiber and harvested with tractors and combines. By design, cannabis varieties grown for hemp have near-zero THC content, but THC-bearing strains can be farmed in the same way. They likely would not approach the THC content achieved with intensive indoor cultivation, but industrial farming would more than make up for lower potency through much lower costs per pound of material harvested. If the extraction process can be scaled up to deal with larger volumes of lower-THC material, this might radically reduce the cost structure for producing extract and, hence, extract-based products, such as hash oils. This might also push the efficient operating scale for marijuana firms up again, beyond the 10,000- to 100,000-square-foot range, to farm-sized operations. At that point, the production sector might be commoditized; all of the THC consumed in the entire country could be grown on a dozen or so modest farms of 1,000 acres, a common size in the Midwest.

If the industry goes down this path, then market power and profits could shift to firms with the marketing expertise to develop and promote brands that consumers recognize and for which they are willing to pay more. That is, the industry could shift from being product- or production process-dominated to one in which producers achieve dominance through marketing. Arguably, that is the situation today with cigarettes and mass-market (as opposed to craft) beer.

It is hard to predict whether consumers will accept an overall shift from combustion to vaporization. On the one hand, it is already taking place to some extent in states with wide-open medical dispensaries, such as California, and in Colorado and Washington. Also, by (largely) eliminating the odor, vaporizing makes it much easier to use marijuana discreetly, without being detected by disapproving friends, parents, teachers, or co-workers, and . . . vaporization avoids the carcinogens and irritants in conventional marijuana smoke. Nevertheless, the tradition of smoking marijuana—and hence of inhaling combustion by-products—is very well-entrenched.

Another possible product shift that might prompt a transition from greenhouse-based production to outdoor industrial farming would be a shift from roll-your-own to rolled joints if—and this remains unclear—lower-THC material could be fortified with additional THC from extracts. Large-scale farming might not match either the potency or the aesthetic (e.g., appearance, smell) of the artisanally grown usable marijuana that dominates the high-end market today. But if THC levels could be pumped up by supplementing the basic organic material with additional THC, large-scale manufacturing might offer rolled marijuana cigarettes at far lower prices than is possible with current production methods. That would mirror the way in which the introduction of manufactured, rolled cigarettes in the 1880s revolutionized patterns of tobacco consumption in the United States and eventually the world.

It is entirely unclear how long it will take the industry to evolve. Where growing is legal or quasi-legal, some of the more-successful firms have been teaming a skilled grower with someone with a good head for business . . . in order to expand production volume and leverage the (high-salaried) marijuana expert with larger numbers of lower-skilled workers. As those operations grow a bit more, one might expect them to begin to hire other specialists, such as industrial engineers and professional agronomists, and perhaps professionals with expertise in marketing and brand management.

The specific trajectory just outlined is far from certain. Nevertheless, one would expect there to be, in some form, considerable product innovation, declining production costs, increasing firm sizes, and greater marketing. A regulated-like-alcohol industry can present consumers with a tantalizing array of high-quality products at prices well below what they are today; that is a service at which free markets excel.

One should also expect the industry to maintain a lobbying presence in state capitols; indeed, a trade group, the National Cannabis Industry Association, already does so in some states. But whether a mature marijuana industry looks more like that for tobacco or beer, with a few giant corporations dominating, or whether it looks more like the wine industry, is hard to predict.

The prediction challenge is amplified because much depends on policy. Legalizing only usable marijuana and not extract-based products would slow the evolution of the industry. Banning or taxing outdoor and greenhouse-based production would help keep production costs high. Instituting minimum pricing would thwart sharp price declines, as would production quotas set below the amount demanded at market prices, with or without a quota auction to capture the increase in price as revenue for the state.

The Middle-Ground Options

Allow Adults to Grown Their Own

In 1975, Alaska's Supreme Court ruled that the privacy rights granted by its state constitution cover possession of marijuana in the home, a right later quantified as possession of up to 4 oz. or 25 plants. (The right was challenged by a 1990 voter proposition that passed but reaffirmed in a 2003 court case.) Likewise, Washington, D.C., voted [in] fall [2014] to pass ballot Initiative 71, which allows people to grow up to six plants (three mature) in their principal residences, with up to two people per residence exercising this right (i.e., up to 12 plants per residence).

So there is considerable experience with allowing users to grow their own marijuana, and overall the effects of doing so seem not to be very dramatic. [In a 2013 study, Robert] MacCoun reviewed the scarce and conflicting evidence concerning Alaska's home-growing policy changes and concluded that there was no compelling evidence that they affected use appreciably.

[The National Survey on Drug Use and Health] asks respondents how they obtained the marijuana they used most recently, with one of the four response options being "grew it yourself." The number of respondents checking this option hovered somewhat above 200,000 from 2002 through 2007 but has since risen sharply to nearly 500,000 in 2012. One grower could supply several friends, and own-growers tend to be heavier-than-average users, but those are still modest numbers compared with 25 million past-month users. Although home growing could help siphon some demand away from the black market, it might not ever win a large market share. Black-market marijuana could be just too cheap and available for the opportunity to grow one's own to appeal to many customers.

Grow-your-own plus sharing (also known as grow and give) offers little opportunity for the government to generate revenue and provides less scope for enforcing product quality and labeling standards; however, regulations are indeed a possibility.

There is also some risk of enabling illegal commercial production, particularly if the limits on home production are set too high. Enterprising entrepreneurs could distribute production across friends' houses, with each house staying below the threshold limit, and aggregate the production into (illegal) wholesale quantities only when it was time to harvest the marijuana and ship it to market.

This distributed production strategy, akin to the putting-out system of early textile manufacturing, is viable because it is possible to grow very large plants with yields of approximately 1 lb. per plant. That is not the usual practice when the constrained factor is area (as when trying to avoid police detection), but, if the limit is set only in terms of number of plants, growers can achieve very high yields per plant. Legislators seeking to allow limited home-grow without creating such a loophole might opt to restrict not only the number of plants but also their area and perhaps the wattage of lights used to grow them.

Of course, from the perspective of someone who favors outright legalization, this loophole could be seen as a feature rather than a bug, and one could make that loophole larger by setting generous limits on the number of plants or, as in the Washington, D.C., Initiative 71, allowing multiple adults within a single residence to each have a set of plants.

Whether to allow home growing remains a question even if a state permits large-scale commercial growing. Colorado allows unlicensed home growing; Washington State does not allow home growing for recreational marijuana. The preferred option might depend on a state's aspiration for taxation. High tax rates provide an incentive to grow one's own, thereby placing some limits on potential tax revenue.

As a final note, there is a matter of principle; allowing own-growing provides a mechanism through which someone who cared enough about avoiding illegal activity could do so and still enjoy using marijuana. That principle could be important to some people, even if, in practice, allowing home growing would not change the behavior of most market participants, either users or producers.

Allow Distribution Only Within Small Co-Ops or Buyers' Clubs (The Co-Op or Buyers' Club Model)

One limitation of grow-your-own is that it suffers from the "zucchini problem" of feast-or-famine production. If you are going to grow any at all, it is hard not to grow too much for one person. An experienced grower can produce 300 to 400 g from one large plant, which is a year's supply for even many daily users. Also, there are many varieties of cannabis plants, varying in potency, ratio of THC to CBD, and other ways, which exacerbates the problem. Growing one of each type of plant risks an even greater surfeit.

Some Spanish jurisdictions have addressed this issue by allowing so-called cannabis clubs, which amount to grow-your-own plus sharing with others within the club (or grow-your-own plus selling at cost, depending on the club).

The Spanish model is not perfect. It falls into a legal gray area, and some strictly illegal producers feign being cannabis clubs in order to provide cover for their black-market activities. Uruguay is currently in the process of implementing and regulating collectives, and time will tell whether they can prevent diversion.

Nevertheless, unlike a strict version of own-growing, the cannabis-club model appears to have the potential to undercut a meaningful segment of the illegal market while nonetheless confining the industry to traditional craft or artisanal production methods that avert the sort of price collapse that could accompany legalization of large-scale commercial production. Likewise, if clubs confine distribution to members, the clubs have little incentive to advertise their product to the public generally.

Permit Locally Controlled Retail Sales (Dutch Coffee-Shop Model)

A common misconception is that the Netherlands has legalized marijuana production and sale. That is incorrect. Laws against production and wholesale distribution remain on the books and are enforced with considerable energy. Rather, starting in the 1970s, the Netherlands established de facto (though not de jure) legalization of possession, use, and retail sale via an explicit and formal policy of nonenforcement against sale of small amounts. (The quantity threshold was originally set at 30 g—roughly 1 oz.—but, in response to problems with drug tourism, was subsequently dropped to 5 g.)

The result was the famous Dutch coffee-shop system in which adults can buy (and use) cannabis with no risk of arrest, but proprietors may not sell alcohol or hard drugs or sell to minors.

Eliminating arrests for possession and retail sale is no mere half-measure. The great majority of marijuana arrests in the United States are for possession, many of which are for possession of small amounts. So for a typical state, legalizing retail sale, possession, and use might eliminate a large proportion of the criminal sanctioning.

The Dutch choice of nonenforcement against retail selling is restricted to shops that meet certain well-established criteria, such as the limit on amounts sold and a prohibition on most forms of traditional advertising. This provides levers for controlling the nature and behavior of the industry, but the Dutch system is nonetheless probably not best thought of as a national regulatory model. The Dutch national government does not, for example, collect special taxes on cannabis sales or mandate testing or labeling standards. Rather, regulatory control over coffee shops is mostly devolved to local governments.

The Dutch system is widely praised in the academic literature and by marijuana advocates. In particular, it is credited with substantially achieving its original policy objective, which was to separate the soft-drug (cannabis) and hard-drug (e.g., heroin) markets by allowing people to obtain cannabis without coming into contact with people selling hard drugs.

The policy also continues to enjoy support from the Dutch public, although there is some lingering dissatisfaction, in no small part because of the inherent tension that what the shops legally sell to retail customers out the front door is illegal when it enters through the back door in wholesale amounts.

Also, over the years, the Netherlands has grappled with drug tourism, meaning people coming to the Netherlands from other countries to purchase marijuana and other drugs. Marijuana tourism is not all bad; it would generate revenues for hoteliers and restaurateurs just as fall leaves and ski slopes do. But with tourism comes traffic, congestion, and—for marijuana tourism—some risk of drivers who are impaired on their return journey. That could lead—as it has in a few Dutch towns—to problems with disorder.

Have the Government Operate the Supply Chain (Government Monopoly)

Throughout history, governments have maintained monopoly control over the supply of certain intoxicants, including British control of the opium trade between India and China (through the East India Company), national monopolies on tobacco production in various European countries in the post-World War II era, and various levels of the alcohol supply chain at various times in the United States and elsewhere.

Indeed, after repeal of federal alcohol prohibition in 1933, some states chose to move beyond mere licensing and regulation to directly own and operate parts of the supply chain in order to limit the influence of for-profit businesses. It was a partial—not a pure—government monopoly because none of the states produced its own alcohol, but, in many places, the state was the only wholesale distributor or the retail shops were state-run. Deregulation of these markets occurred over time, really accelerating after 1980. As of January 2013, only 17 states retained state-run wholesale liquor-distribution systems.

Given the wealth of research suggesting that alcohol monopolies are better for public health than less regulated options, we focus special attention on this particular supply alternative. However, we want to stress at the outset that direct state participation in the supply chain could cause the state to violate federal law. Such a violation would seem to exist unless and until the CSA is amended or an equivalent suitable workaround is implemented.

Direct government control of the supply chain would offer at least four categories of potentially beneficial effects.

Potential Benefit 1: Control of Diversion

If the state itself operates the production and distribution chain, limiting diversion could become somewhat easier. It could transform diversion from a regulatory violation by an independent private company to theft or unlawful sale by a supervised government employee. Also, unless the regulatory system is extremely efficient, distributing licenses for legal production to private entities might help provide cover for illegal production, in somewhat the way owning a cash-based business can provide cover for a money-laundering operation. Minimizing diversion from private production is possible, but it could require more effort, partially offsetting legalization's anticipated benefit of eliminating the government's costs of enforcing a prohibition.

Potential Benefit 2: Reversibility

If monopoly proves the best method of legalization, it will be easy to retain monopoly if Vermont adopts that method from the beginning. If Colorado- and Washington-style commercial legalization proves to be a better choice for Vermont, it will be relatively easy to switch from monopoly to private commerce. But, if Vermont adopts commercial legalization from the beginning and later realizes that it prefers another supply architecture, change might be more difficult. Commercial interests, at that point vested, would presumably oppose any proposal to take away their profits. Because it is more readily reversible in light of information yet to be obtained, monopoly is a more adaptable method of legalizing than private commerce.

Potential Benefit 3: Avoiding Advertising and Product Innovation

Private companies in the United States can advertise; their First Amendment protections of commercial free speech are very strong. Most of the limits on alcohol and tobacco advertising have come from voluntary agreements and court settlements, not legislation. However, if a government monopoly controlled supply, firms would have no incentive to spend their money promoting consumption of the government's product, even if they technically retained that right. So placing the entire distribution system in the government's hands sidesteps concerns about commercial advertising.

Government monopoly of just the retail stores would achieve a bit of this benefit; the government could directly control signage and point-of-sale displays, as opposed to merely issuing constitutionally questionable regulations of those practices. However, if the government stores sold name-brand merchandise produced by private companies, then those companies would continue to have an interest in promoting their brands.

The government could also outsource production but sell only a generic commodity with no branding or other labeling that identified the producer. In theory, that might limit producers' incentive to advertise as much as government operation of production would.

Limiting advertising is a mixed blessing. Advertising that promotes underage use (e.g., the infamous Joe Camel campaign) is highly undesirable in the eyes of most public-health advocates. But advertising can also provide consumers with information that makes the markets operate more efficiently by reducing search time, facilitating comparison-shopping, and generally balancing the information asymmetry between suppliers and consumers. Losing those functions represents a real loss to society, although the loss could be partially offset by peer-to-peer sharing of user-generated information, which has long been prominent for marijuana, perhaps because of the scarcity of traditional advertising.

Potential Benefit 4: Preventing a Price Collapse

We expect that in the medium to long run, a free-market industry would innovate in ways that drive down production costs, and competitive pressures would force companies to pass along those savings to consumers in the form of lower prices. For most consumer goods, lower prices are a cause for celebration, but, if consumers are vulnerable to overindulging, low prices might be problematic. For example, some view innovation that has led to very low prices for soda pop, junk food, and candy to be a curse, not a blessing, for the American public.

The typical response of economists is that low production costs remain a blessing even if one prefers moderately high prices because one can always use taxes to prop prices up to whatever level is deemed socially optimal. Indeed, public-health advocates frequently suggest higher taxes for tobacco and alcohol; environmentalists do the same for gasoline.

Propping up prices with high taxes always works in the classroom, and usually works in the real world, but there are two caveats. The first is that, if the industry gets too powerful, it could lobby successfully for lower taxes. Arguably, that applies to alcohol, federal taxes for which have not been adjusted for inflation since 1991 and so have fallen enormously in real terms. The second catch is that, if taxes are too high, they invite evasion.

A government monopoly will not solve this problem completely. If the prices are too high either in government stores or in private stores subject to large taxes, then that might induce black-market production. However, a government monopoly might be able to sustain a higher retail price because it would be easier to detect and suppress illegal activity if legitimate production were a government monopoly. Then any production outside of the identified government facilities would necessarily be illegal, whereas, if tax-evading activity could hide amid legal private production, it might be hard for enforcement agents to ascertain quickly whether a particular production site or a particular shipment in transit is legal or illegal.

Potential Cost and Its Possible Irrelevance

One of the usual arguments against government monopolies is that they are inefficient and unimaginative. Oddly, inefficiency might not be a serious problem with regard to marijuana production. Freed from the obligation to produce discreetly, marijuana-production costs might be quite low in the long run. So if the government wastefully produces at double the cost of an efficient free-market enterprise, that deadweight loss to society might not be all that large in absolute terms.

Waste and inefficiency are never good, but it is important to keep a sense of perspective. Economizing on production cost is not necessarily the most important consideration when selecting an architecture governing who gets to supply marijuana. If there are other compelling reasons for preferring a government monopoly, the problem of inefficient production costs might not be severe enough to warrant abandoning that approach.

Have a Public Authority Operate the Supply Chain (Near Monopoly)

Another option would obtain many, but not all, of the advantages of monopoly without having the state itself directly violate federal laws against possession or sale of marijuana. Legislation, rather than limiting commerce to licensed sellers, could create a single, special-purpose entity, call it a public authority, that would be the sole supplier and distributor of marijuana.

Under a public-authority model, the state would not itself possess or distribute marijuana. Rather, the public authority, like for-profit businesses in Colorado and Washington, would be the one violating any federal law. The state would appoint members of the public authority and set policy (for instance, to control diversion, control interactions with consumers, restrict sale to particular types of products, avoid advertising and product innovation, and prevent a price collapse). The hope is that those actions, in substance, might prove no more offensive to federal interests than a state's actions in a for-profit commercial model of hiring regulators and tax collectors, issuing licenses, writing regulatory and tax law, and collecting taxes.

There is a tension in the decision about how much independence to grant the authority. The more the state puts the authority at arm's length, the better the case for the authority being equivalent to a private business, so its position vis-à-vis the [federal Controlled Substances Act] would rise and fall with the Colorado and Washington models. For example, the state could *authorize* the authority to do various things but not require it and, hence, would not require the authority to violate federal law. Indeed because, like a public monopoly, a public authority could pursue policies that serve the public, not just a profit interest, a rational and selective federal government might well let the public authority proceed, even if more-provocative for-profit commercial sales in other states came under federal attack.

On the other hand, if the authority is entirely separate from the state in form and substance, the state loses control, and the authority could disregard the state's preferences.

Permit Only Nonprofit Organizations to Sell

[Another option is] granting licenses only to organizations that are chartered to operate in the public interest (e.g., nonprofits). By design, nonprofits operate to serve the public interest, not to maximize shareholders' profit (although boards of nonprofits might nevertheless seek profits, whether to advance the mission of the group or to extend their personal influence).

One could go a step further and place specific requirements on the types of nonprofit organizations that are eligible. For example, one could require licensees to be nonprofits whose boards include members who are chosen by child-welfare and public-health groups, whose charters include language about operating only to meet existing demand rather than promoting greater use, or that pledge to donate any excess operating revenue to drug treatment and use-prevention organizations.

Of course, limiting participation in the marijuana market to nonprofits does not guarantee that the industry will not attempt to exert political influence or try to increase revenues. Although nonprofits should, in theory, not be inherently interested in expanding sales or streamlining production, nonprofit hospitals and universities compete aggressively. Board members might have a tendency to see growth as a sign of success. Term limits for board members of the nonprofit could be considered, along with other mechanisms to deter empire building.

Restricting the industry to nonprofits would also likely slow its growth—for better and for worse. Raising capital has been challenging for nonprofit medical-marijuana producers because they cannot sell equity shares in future profit streams the way for-profit companies can. Their capital comes primarily from loans. Furthermore, under federal prohibition, banks might be reluctant to make commercial loans, so the loans might come from private individuals.

Permit Only For-Benefit Companies to Sell (Sustainable Businesses)

Another supply option serves as a hybrid between the nonprofit and commercial options: Permit only for-benefit companies to sell. This structure would limit participation in the marijuana industry to companies that are concerned with improving environmental and social conditions in addition to making a profit. Although most companies have a fiduciary responsibility only to maximize profits for shareholders, for-benefit companies incorporate social goals into their governing documents.

This could be a particularly attractive option for Vermont, which is one of 27 states that allows new companies to incorporate as benefit corporations or amend their articles of incorporation to become benefit corporations. In Vermont, these companies must create "a material positive impact on society and the environment, as measured by a third-party standard, through activities that promote some combination of specific public benefits," such as improving the environment or human health.

In addition, a benefit corporation's board of directors must have at least one member designated as the benefit officer. Among other responsibilities, the benefit officer is charged with preparing the annual benefit report, which includes his or her statement about whether the "benefit corporation acted in accordance with its general public benefit purpose and any specific public benefit purpose in all material respects during the period covered by the report." The company must make this report available to the public.

Have Very Few Closely Monitored For-Profit Licensees (Structured Oligopoly)

If a commercial free market would not serve the social interest and the other middle-ground options are not politically viable, it is natural to ask whether there is some way to get for-profit businesses to behave in the public interest. The answer is "Perhaps."

The challenge is to figure out how to insulate the regulatory agencies from industry influence, empower regulators with big sticks, structure incentives so that companies prefer complying with regulations voluntarily to breaking the rules and taking the chance of getting hit by that stick, and get regulators to see their task as promoting public health rather than simply keeping the industry lawful.

One key might be restricting licensing to the appropriate number of firms that are of appropriate size. Colorado makes no effort to limit the number of licenses.

Applicants have to meet certain criteria, but the state awards licenses to all who meet the criteria, depending on market competition to balance supply and demand. Economists would predict that, in such circumstances, competition would drive the value of a license down to zero. If obtaining a license were a ticket to easy profits, then more firms would join the market until those potential rents were bid away.

States might prefer instead to offer only a limited number of licenses, creating artificial scarcity that makes the licenses valuable—valuable enough that firms will have a strong incentive to cooperate with regulators rather than risk revocation. Requiring the payment of license fees on an annual basis, rather than issuing permanent licenses, could also help nudge prices in a useful direction.

Limiting the number of licensees also makes monitoring their behavior easier. A rogue company could more easily break the rules if it were one of 1,000 licensees than if it were one of just ten.

So a structured-oligopoly strategy might involve licensing a limited number of firms, monitoring them closely, and not being shy about rescinding a firm's license if it behaves in ways contrary to the public interest.

2. The Netherlands

The most well-known and well-established alternative to marijuana prohibition is the Dutch coffee shop policy. Although the policy is often described as legalization in popular media, as mentioned in the RAND Corporation's report above, the Netherlands has not technically legalized marijuana sales. Instead, their system rests on "a formal written policy of non-enforcement for" possession and sale of certain quantities of marijuana. Robert J. MacCoun, *What Can We Learn from the Dutch Cannabis Coffeeshop System?*, 106 Addiction 1899 (2011). For users and retail marijuana outlets—known as coffee shops—the non-enforcement policy operates as a form of de facto legalization. But the Dutch non-enforcement policy does not extend to marijuana growers and wholesale distributors. This has resulted in what is sometimes called the back door problem—the "front door" (retail sales) are permitted and regulated but the "back door" (manufacture and wholesale distribution) remains in the hands of the black market.

The next article, written by a researcher at the Research and Documentation Centre of the Ministry of Justice and Security in the Netherlands, discusses the motivations for the Dutch coffee shop policy, its distinctive characteristics, and its impact on marijuana use and public health.

The Dutch Coffee Shop System, Tensions and Benefits
Marianne M. J. van Ooyen-Houben

25 Michigan State International Law Review 623 (2017)

Coffee shops are a typical Dutch phenomenon. They are commercial enterprises where the sale of small amounts of cannabis to adult users is tolerated, which means that the police and the Public Prosecutor won't arrest or prosecute the coffee shop owner for selling cannabis, although this is a criminal act according to the Dutch Opium Act. The user won't be arrested for buying and possessing cannabis either. The first coffee shop started in 1968 in the city of Utrecht. There was no official tolerance policy back then, that's why the coffee shops' door was closed and customers had to knock on the door in order to enter the shop. A 'house dealer' sold the cannabis and you could consume a coffee or a tea. In the 1970s coffee shops in Amsterdam started their business: Mellow Yellow in 1972, the Bulldog in 1975. After a change in the Opium Act in 1976, coffee shops developed into open enterprises. They became one of the most salient features of the Dutch drug policy. Their number grew explosively in the 1980s and 1990s. In 1995, the number of coffee shops was estimated at 1100–1200. Since then, the policy towards them became more restrictive and the number slowly and gradually decreased to 582 in March 2015. The coffee shops of 2016 look like normal cafés where adults can walk in and buy and use cannabis.

If we want to understand the reason for the existence of coffee shops, we have to go back in history and look at the attitude towards drugs and drug use in the Netherlands back in the 1970s and 1980s. An important year for the Dutch drug policy was 1976. [That year, t]he [Dutch] Opium Act was revised [and p]ossession of cannabis for personal use was reduced from a crime to a minor infraction of the law. But the most important change was that a distinction was made between two types of drugs: drugs with an unacceptable risk for the health ('hard drugs' like heroin, LSD, amphetamine or cocaine) and, on the other hand, drugs with less risks ('soft drugs,' cannabis being the most important one). By making a distinction between cannabis and other, more harmful drugs, a differentiated judicial reaction could be given to crimes with regard to hard drugs or cannabis. Offenses were punished more severely when hard drugs were involved.

The change was considered necessary because of radical changes in the drug situation in the Netherlands in the 1960s. The use of drugs, . . . and especially the use of cannabis, LSD and amphetamine, increased substantially. In the 1970s, the use of heroin (and the international organized trafficking of heroin) started demanding a lot of attention because of the severe problems with addiction and crime related to it. The initial reaction to all this new drug use was repression, but a big difference was noticed between the cannabis users on the one hand, who were well-integrated members of society and functioned in a socially normal way, and heroin users on the other hand, who were often addicted and marginalized (the 'junkies'). This soon led to an informal tolerance policy towards cannabis users: they were left as they were by police and Public Prosecutor. During the 1970s, the Public Prosecutor was dropping the majority of cannabis charges.

This differentiated, more lenient attitude towards cannabis and cannabis users was consolidated in the Opium Act of 1976. The aim of the policy with regard to cannabis users since then has been to prevent them from becoming marginalized, stigmatized, and criminalized and to reduce the risk that they start using more harmful 'hard drugs' like heroin or amphetamine.

This opened the way for a tolerant attitude of police and Public Prosecutor towards house dealers of cannabis at music events and in public premises, and later in coffee shops. By tolerating sales outlets where cannabis users can buy their cannabis quietly and safely, users will be kept away from the hands of criminal street drug dealers who also sell hard drugs.

This is the key function of coffee shops in the Dutch cannabis policy: contributing to a separation of the hard drugs consumer market in the streets and the cannabis consumer market. Coffee shops are, thus, a consequence of the Dutch cannabis policy, which aims at normalization of users, is primarily focused on the health of users, and which wants to keep cannabis users away from hard drugs. This is embedded in a health-oriented drug policy in which the ministry of Health, Welfare and Sports plays the coordinating role.

The settlement of coffee shops was a bottom-up development. Individuals took the initiative to start a commercial cannabis outlet. The official policy followed and shaped the conditions.

On the national level, the policy with regards to enforcement is that coffee shops are 'tolerated.' This means that there is no enforcement of the law, despite the fact that this is legally and practically possible. Strictly speaking, coffee shops commit a crime against the Opium Act when they sell cannabis, because the sale of cannabis as well as the possession of (large amounts of) cannabis is forbidden. But this criminal act is not investigated by the police, nor prosecuted by the Public Prosecutor. Coffee shops can do their business without being arrested. Not that the police turns a blind eye to the coffee shops, no, it is the formal and explicit policy.

The judicial basis for the tolerance is the principle of discretionary powers of the Public Prosecutor, the "expediency principle." This principle, laid down in the Code of Criminal Procedure, gives the Public Prosecutor the power to refrain from prosecution of offences if this serves a general public interest. This principle is systematically applied in the Dutch coffee shop policy. This is explicitly stated in the Directive for Opium Act crimes for the Public Prosecutor:

> The basis for the policy of tolerance lies in the balancing of interests which the importance of enforcement must give way to a more identifiable public interest. In the context of the drug policy is this higher interest found in public health (separation of markets) and the public order.

For this higher public interest, coffee shops are left un-arrested and un-prosecuted.

The tolerance is, however, bound to strict rules. In the course of time, when more and more coffee shops opened their doors, rules for tolerance developed in practice, initially in the city of Amsterdam. In 1991, the National Office of the Public Prosecutor decided that these rules would be applicable to coffee shops nationwide. The national rules, or "criteria for tolerance" are described explicitly in the Directive Opium Act for the Public Prosecutor. [Under the rules, c]offee shops [are] only tolerated when they do not advertise (apart from a minor reference on the shop); when they have no hard drugs in the shop and do not sell hard drugs; when they do not cause public nuisance in their direct vicinity; when they do not sell to or give access to youngsters [defined as people under the age of 18]; and when they do not sell large quantities of cannabis to a customer per transaction, which means quantities larger than [5 grams]. [In addition,] coffee shops are not allowed to have more than 500 grams of cannabis in stock and they may not serve alcohol. [S]ince 2013, [the criteria for tolerance have also stated that] coffee shops are not allowed to give access to non-residents of the Netherlands. [In practice, however, the rule simply] gives municipalities the option to ban nonresidents from the coffee shops. [Thus far, most municipalities that permit coffee shops have decided not to enforce the residence criterion and continue to allow tourists to buy marijuana from coffee shops.]

The coffee shop policy . . . is implemented and gets its concrete shape on the local level. Local authorities take some basic decisions about coffee shops and they play, in fact, a key role. First of all, the mayor, together with the Public Prosecutor and the Chief of the police in the city, decide whether they will allow the establishment of (one or more) coffee shops in their municipality. Every coffee shop needs a license from the mayor. The majority of municipalities in the Netherlands, especially the smaller ones, have such a local "zero policy" of *not* allowing any coffee shop within their municipality, 69.7% in 2014. The others do allow coffee shops and give out licenses for a certain number of them. The local authorities also decide how many coffee shops they will allow. Most municipalities limit the number of coffee shops to a certain maximum. No more licenses will be given out by the mayor when this maximum is reached.

When the local authorities decide to allow coffee shops, the mayor can apply additional local rules for the coffee shops. A wide spread local rule is that no coffee shop is allowed within a certain distance (mostly 250 meters) from a secondary school. The cities of Amsterdam and Rotterdam, for instance, apply such a "distance criterion." Rotterdam introduced this criterion in 2009, and, as a consequence, 16 coffee shops had to close.

The mayor plays an important role in enforcement. He can apply administrative sanctions, like a temporary or definitive closure of a coffee shop when it does not comply with the rules. This authority of the mayor is laid down in the Opium Act. Additionally, the Public Prosecutor can prosecute a coffee shop when it does not comply with the rules, but administrative sanctions have priority. Police and municipal authorities in co-operation mostly carry out controls of compliance in the coffee shops. They take place unannounced periodically, or in reaction to complaints or speculations about noncompliance. The frequency of controls is determined on the local level.

The criteria and the sanctions must be described in a local 'enforcement plan' so that everybody is informed about the local policy and knows what to expect. This is important with regard to the necessary transparency and predictability of authorities; coffee shops must know how to behave and they must be able to trust the authorities. The judge will weigh this when a case of noncompliance comes to court.

Only coffee shops that fit in the local policy and that adhere to the national and local criteria will be tolerated by the police, Public Prosecutor, and mayor. The tolerance, thus, is bound to strict conditions. This is an active and systematic way of tolerance: authorities and Public Prosecutor decide officially and explicitly to *not* enforce the law under certain conditions.

Ever since its existence, the coffee shop system has been struggling with tensions and frictions on [the] national and international level.

The coffee shop system can be defined as a "regulatory system for adults." The system, however, regulates only the sale of cannabis to consumers. The authorities never regulated the supply of cannabis to the coffee shops. This leads to a central paradox in the coffee shop system: coffee shops can sell cannabis at their "front door," but they are not allowed to buy cannabis at their "back door." Although policy makers in the 1970s preferred a legalization of cannabis, they realized that this was not feasible within the United Nations [Drug] Treaties. [At the time, t]hey expected that the international treaties would be adapted on the mid-range term in order to give national states the freedom to follow their own regimes with regard to cannabis and cannabis cultivation. However, this never happened. [Today, i]n the view of the International Narcotics Control Board, the committee that is responsible for the control and supervision of the implementation of the UN Narcotic Drugs Conventions . . . the Dutch policy of tolerance with regard to coffee shops contravenes the Conventions.

The most vulnerable spot, the Achilles heel, [of the tolerance policy] is the purchase of cannabis [by the coffee shop]. The Netherland's coffee shop policy [is] somehow stuck in the middle of a regulated system. The retail sale is regulated with an increasing number of rules on national and local level, but the supply [has] stayed completely illegal.

[S]upply [of cannabis] is a criminal act, which implies that coffee shops have to deal with criminals for their supply. How far coffee shop owners or their personnel are involved in supply or in (organized) criminal networks that cultivate cannabis is not clear. Research into . . . coffee shops in the center of Amsterdam indicated that some of them were indeed involved, but others were not.

[Because, t]he regulation of the sale of cannabis does not cover the so-called "back door" of the coffee shops, . . . [w]e know little about what happens there. The police turn a blind eye to the "back door," as long as the supply is low profile and not too visible. Whereas a coffee shop is not allowed to have more than 500 grams in stock at any given moment, this small-scale supply takes place discretely several times a day when more is needed. A coffee shop does not pay value added tax (VAT) over its cannabis sales because these activities are illegal and no VAT can be applied on such activities. A coffee shop does pay income tax and has to keep an administration about sourcing and sales, but whereas the 'back door' is a 'black box' nobody can check what was bought and what prices were paid for the cannabis. This means that the suppliers at the "back door" are uncontrollable for authorities or taxes and that the insight in benefits is only fragmentary, even for the tax authorities. In cases of cannabis cultivation or violation of the stock-rule by coffee shops, the police do not do any deep investigation into the interweaving.

Despite the lack of exact figures about the profits of coffee shops, it is clear that a lot of money is involved in cannabis cultivation, as well as in the retail sale of cannabis. The turnover of coffee shops was estimated (in 2006) at a total of 211 to 283 million euros. In 2013, the total turnover over of the then 606 coffee shops was estimated to be between € 875 million and € 1.25 billion (with a 95% confidence interval).

[Though there are] differences in amounts estimated, it is clear that a reasonable amount of money must be involved in the supply of cannabis at the "back door" of the coffee shops. At the same time, the cannabis cultivation in the Netherlands became professionalized and criminal networks became involved, which implies that coffee shops (to an unknown extent) have to deal with those networks. Because investment via banks is difficult for coffee shops, there is a risk that they become involved in money laundering or get dependent from criminal investments. The municipalities therefore use a license system for coffee shops, for which they can screen, on the basis of a law, the potential criminal engagement of coffee shop entrepreneurs before a license is given. It can be assumed that, by implementing this law on screening on criminal involvement, investments in coffee shops becomes less attractive for criminal networks.

The halfway regulation [has] caused numerous political debates in the Netherlands, a debate which has continued over the years. While some parties in the Parliament want to include cannabis cultivation in the coffee shop system in order to be able to control the cannabis and to exclude criminals and criminal networks from the coffee shop cannabis chain, other parties are vigorously opposed. There is also a dividing line between a majority of municipalities and the national authorities, represented by the minister of Security and Justice.

Time and again the cabinet and the minister of Security and Justice [have] state[d] that international obligations forb[ids] any kind of regulation of cannabis cultivation and that they will not take any step in the direction of regulation or legalization.

Municipalities did not give up, though. The mayors prefer a clear system, which makes a distinction between illegal cultivation—that has to be combatted—and cultivation as part of the tolerance system—which can be tolerated. A bill from the liberal party Democrats 66 to regulate the supply to the coffee shops by a system in which not only coffee shops, but also the cultivation and the sales for the coffee shops are tolerated was accepted in the Lower House of the Dutch parliament in February 2017. The bill is now on the agenda of the Senate.

The frictions and tensions inherent to the coffee shop system are undeniable. But what about the benefits of the system? Does it reach its goals? Why has the system survived?

If the idea behind the coffee shop system is right, then the coffee shop system should contribute to a separation of the cannabis retail market and the hard drug retail markets in the Netherlands. We should also observe that cannabis users in the Netherlands move less often to hard drugs use than in a system without coffee shops. A third hypothesis is that cannabis users in the Netherlands are well integrated in society and do not get in contact with the criminal justice system.

These hypotheses are supported by evidence. Coffee shops are not only the most important retail channel for cannabis in the Netherlands, but also contribute to a separation of markets: they keep cannabis users for a large part away from illegal dealers and thus reduce the risk that they get in contact with hard drugs. Cannabis users are, in general, well integrated in society. In this respect, the system was good for the consumers.

International comparisons support the evidence that coffee shops indeed contribute to the separation of cannabis and hard drug consumer markets. The retail markets of cannabis and those of hard drugs like heroin, crack, cocaine or amphetamine are more separated in the Netherlands than in other European countries or the US. The correlation between the use of cannabis and the use of cocaine and amphetamines is weaker in the Netherlands and the step from cannabis use towards use of hard drugs is less probable here. Cannabis users in the Netherlands use relatively few hard drugs like cocaine, amphetamine, heroin, and crack, and there are few hard drug addicts among the cannabis users compared to other countries. The use of ecstasy, though, is higher and cannabis users with a regular or frequent pattern of use have more experience with hard drugs than in the general population. The use of hard drugs is relatively low in the Netherlands, with ecstasy as an exception.

[T]he evidence shows that the majority of the customers of coffee shops are students or people who have a job. A recent thesis shows that young adult frequent cannabis users are generally rather "normal" people, generally living a conventional life, including social and romantic activities, jobs, education, sports, and incidental minor delinquency (not related to cannabis). Cannabis users in the Netherlands are (in principle) not prosecuted for possession of cannabis for personal use (no more than five grams), which is what they can buy in a coffee shop. They will not be sentenced or imprisoned or end up with a criminal record, like in other countries. The fact that the majority of the coffee shop customers in the Netherlands are students or employed could be interpreted as an indication that they are not marginalized and, in general, function normally in society.

The coffee shop system thus contributes to a separation of markets and counteracts the stepping-stone idea that cannabis use will lead to hard drug use. Cannabis users and coffee shop customers are, usually, not marginalized.

Did the coffee shops contribute to an increase in use or addiction? Were there other adverse effects? The evidence teaches us that the potential dangers of the system with regard to cannabis use are reasonably limited.

Coffee shops do not necessarily lead to 'uncontrolled,' rampant use and they do not appear to encourage escalation into heavier use or lengthier use careers. In fact, the prevalence of use among youngsters of 12–16 years in regular secondary schools has been decreasing since 2003.

There is only a modest correlation between the number of coffee shops and the prevalence of use. If there are no coffee shops, users will find a way to cannabis via other channels. That's why prevalence of cannabis use is even higher in France, Spain or the US than in the Netherlands, although the other countries have no coffee shops. Other factors than the presence of coffee shops are more important for the prevalence of use in a country, like perceived harmfulness, availability and price, severity of sanctions, or characteristics of the youth culture.

From the evidence described above it can be concluded that the coffee shop system functions well for the mainstream cannabis users. They benefit from the non-marginalization and non-criminalization without getting into trouble with their use.

It is difficult to say which direction the system will take in the future. Shall the coffee shop system survive? How will the Senate vote about the bill to regulate the supply of cannabis to coffee shops? The ideology of the ruling parties after the elections in the Netherlands of 2017, in combination with international developments (in Uruguay, the US, Spain, harmonization on European level), might facilitate a change in one direction or the other. Change in the case of coffee shops and their supply seems to depend not so much on scientific evidence, but rather on the political will of national policy makers.

In a 2011 review of the evidence on the Dutch coffee shop policy, Robert MacCoun found that "Dutch citizens use cannabis at more modest rates than some of their neighbors, and they do not appear to be particularly likely to escalate their use relative to their counterparts in Europe and the United States." Robert J. MacCoun, *What Can We Learn from the Dutch Cannabis Coffeeshop System?*, 106 ADDICTION 1899 (2011). Perhaps even more notably, marijuana prices in the Netherlands are still relatively high. Indeed, "[t]he 'typical' retail price reported by government officials circa 2007 was about $7 per gram of cannabis herb in the Netherlands, slightly higher than in Spain ($4), lower than in the United States ($10), and considerably lower than in Norway ($27)." *Id.* Some researchers have speculated that the relatively high price of marijuana in the Netherlands, along with the relatively low use rates, may be at least partly due to the continued prohibition of manufacture and wholesale distribution. After all, "[i]f high-level Dutch traffickers face an enforcement risk, they presumably pass this along in higher prices down the supply chain." *Id.*

The Dutch back door problem may soon be a thing of the past. As of this writing in May 2019, a modified version of the proposal to regulate marijuana supply discussed in the article above is continuing to move forward. Specifically, the Dutch have been moving forward with "a pilot program to explore the effects of legalizing, standardizing and taxing" marijuana production. Christopher F. Schuetze, *Solving the Dutch Pot Paradox: Legal to Buy, but Not to Grow*, N.Y. Times, March 25, 2018. Under the plan, "a minimum of six and no more than 10 Dutch municipalities" could participate and allow marijuana growers to apply for a permit and "coffee shops to switch from illegal suppliers to legal providers." Alfredo Pascual, *Netherlands Prepares Legal Recreational Cannabis Cultivation Experiment*, Marijuana Business Daily (May 9, 2019). The pilot project would run for four years, with an assessment planned at the end of that period.

3. Uruguay

Uruguay's Cannabis Law: Pioneering a New Paradigm
John Hudak, Geoff Ramsey, and John Walsh

The Brookings Institution (2018)

Uruguay is the first country to legalize and regulate its domestic non-medical cannabis market. In light of this pioneering role, the choices and experiences of Uruguayan authorities hold important lessons for other jurisdictions that may consider whether and how to regulate cannabis. Uruguay's breakthroughs and challenges related to banking, international treaties, access to the product, enforcement, medical cannabis, tourism, and research and evaluation in particular hold immense value to policymakers and analysts elsewhere. To this end, this report examines the conditions that led Uruguay's government to pass its cannabis law in 2013, studies its progress so far, and identifies areas that policymakers should consider addressing in order to maximize the law's potential benefits.

In important ways, Uruguay's cannabis law is in line with its historical approach to drug policy. Even during the 1973–85 dictatorship, the country was out of step with the highly punitive "drug war" approaches being implemented in many other countries. Though the dictatorship maintained strict sentences for drug trafficking, it decriminalized possession of "a minimum quantity [of illicit substances], intended solely for personal use," in 1974. Over the years, the fact that Uruguayans could possess cannabis under the law, but could not legally acquire it, was consistently highlighted by civil society groups pressing for legal forms of access to the drug.

Eventually, legislators addressed this issue. In early 2012, the governing Broad Front (FA) majority in Uruguay looked set to pass a bill that would legalize the home cultivation of up to eight plants and the possession of up to 25 grams of cannabis. In the face of this momentum, then-President José Mujica saw an opportunity. In June 2012, his administration released a 15-point document titled the "Strategy for Life and Coexistence," which proposed to "legalize and control cannabis sales." Unlike the home-grow bill in the legislature, however, President Mujica proposed the creation of a state monopoly over cannabis production and distribution.

Mujica's proposal and the bill already under debate were merged into a bill that allowed for home cultivation as well as commercial sales, in addition to "cannabis clubs" that allowed users to grow in state-authorized collectives. This bill was passed in the legislature's lower house in July 2013, cleared the Senate in December, and was signed into law on December 20, 2013.

Uruguayan officials have publicly provided a wide range of justifications for the law since its passage. At various times authorities have said the law could reduce crime, or lower the demand for more harmful drugs such as a crack cocaine-like substance known locally as "pasta base." However, the text of the law expresses its goals through three main objectives:

1. Reducing drug trafficking-related violence by taking cannabis off the black market.
2. Promoting public health through education and prevention campaigns.
3. Eliminating the existing legal paradox that allowed for possession but effectively blocked users from accessing cannabis.

When Mujica proposed that Uruguay legalize and regulate cannabis, he proclaimed that "someone has to be first." In opting to regulate cannabis from cultivation through sale, Uruguay was the first country to leave behind the global ban on non-medical cannabis that began with the United Nations' 1961 Single Convention on Narcotic Drugs. The UN drug control treaty regime, to which nearly every country on the planet is a signatory, expressly limits cannabis use to medical and scientific purposes.

In taking such an audacious step, Uruguay's authorities knew that they would need to contend with criticisms from other countries and from the monitors of the UN drug treaties, in particular the International Narcotics Control Board (INCB, the Board). Mindful of the international dimensions of their decision to move forward with cannabis regulation, Uruguayan lawmakers designed a tightly controlled regulatory system and fashioned arguments that justified their reform as upholding Uruguay's fundamental obligation to protect the human rights of its citizens. Thus, Uruguay's reform was at once bold and cautious; concerned that their policy would come under intense scrutiny from their neighbors and from the broader international community, Uruguayan authorities deliberately opted for a strict approach to regulation, such as a user registry and monthly sales limits.

As passed, Uruguay's cannabis law forbids cannabis use in indoor public spaces where it is forbidden to smoke tobacco and prohibits advertising or any form of promotion. The law also created a new regulatory body charged with overseeing implementation, the Institute for the Regulation and Control of Cannabis (IRCCA). Under the law there are three methods of access to cannabis, with specific parameters set forth in subsequent regulations:

1. **Homegrow:** Adults can grow up to six female flowering cannabis plants per household for their own consumption, so long as they have first registered their plants with authorities. The total annual production of the drug must not exceed 480 grams, but cultivation of more than six plants is allowed so long as they are either male or not flowering. At time of writing, 8,266 Uruguayans had registered as homegrowers.

2. **Cannabis clubs:** Adults can join cooperatives to grow cannabis collectively. These "cannabis clubs" must first be registered with the IRCCA and other authorities, and must have between 15 and 45 members. The clubs may plant up to 99 plants in the same space, but cannot dispense more than 480 grams of the drug to each of their members per year. Any surplus yield must be turned over to authorities. So far, authorities have registered 83 such clubs across the country.
3. **Commercial purchase:** Individuals can purchase up to 40 grams per month (10 grams per week, according to subsequent regulations) at sales points. The law specifies that pharmacies will act as points of sale, though the government has expressed interest in creating new, specifically-designated outlets for this purpose. Under the law, pharmacies are not required to sell cannabis; they can opt into the system if they desire. Under the law a handful of commercial growers can be licensed by the state to produce cannabis for commercial sales. Currently, two companies have been licensed to produce commercial cannabis, and 22,077 Uruguayans have registered as purchasers.

Since its passage, the executive branch has issued a series of presidential decrees further fleshing out the law. The most significant of these was issued in May 2014, when the Mujica government issued the main set of regulations on implementation. In addition to limiting purchase to 10 grams per week, the regulations specified that only Uruguayan citizens and permanent residents over the age of 18 are legally able to acquire cannabis, effectively banning marijuana tourism. The regulations also state that the above three methods of access would be mutually exclusive, meaning that individuals must choose to grow their own cannabis, access it via a club, or purchase it in pharmacies, but cannot legally do more than one of these at the same time. Authorities have described this element of the law as intended to discourage problematic use. In addition, the regulations stipulate that drivers will be considered intoxicated if any THC is detected in their system, and instruct the IRCCA to regulate the potency of THC in commercially-sold cannabis. Authorities have so far said that no product will be sold with THC levels higher than 15 percent.

Following the May 2014 regulations, authorities proceeded to implement the law at a slow but deliberate pace. The IRCCA began registering interested home-growers in August 2014, and started club registration in October 2014. In February 2015, Mujica's last month in office, the outgoing government issued additional regulations that permit the IRCCA to authorize the scientific community to obtain the substance for research purposes and lay out a framework specifically allowing physicians to dispense medical cannabis.

Unlike the cannabis legalization measures that have been approved by voters in various U.S. states—beginning in Colorado and Washington in 2012—Uruguay's cannabis law was ushered to passage by the national government despite evident skepticism and disapproval of the effort among Uruguayans. Since Mujica first proposed the reform, public opinion surveys have consistently shown most Uruguayans to be doubtful about the government's initiative. The issue, however, has never been especially salient with respect to national political dynamics. The ruling Broad Front coalition, sensing enough backing among its own supporters, used its majority control of both chambers of the legislature to secure the law's passage in December 2013. In taking this step, Broad Front lawmakers were hopeful that, over time, most Uruguayans would come to approve of regulating cannabis, or at least accept it.

The first major political test came with the October and November 2014 elections, when the Broad Front retained control of both legislative chambers and once again won the presidency. The law to regulate cannabis may not have actually boosted the ruling coalition's fortunes, but nor did it obviously harm them. Since then, the law's implementation has unfolded slowly

After a months-long bidding process, in October 2015, the government selected two companies out of more than twenty applicants to grow cannabis for sale in pharmacies. The two, Simbiosis and ICC, are both of mixed Uruguayan and foreign ownership. The latter has links to Uruguayan agroindustry magnate Juan Sartori, president and founder of the largest agriculture firm in Uruguay, the Union Agriculture Group. The companies carry out cultivation through a perpetual harvest system in green- houses located on a 24-acre plot of land adjacent to a maximum security prison in San Jose Department, just northwest of Montevideo, the capital. Although Simbiosis and ICC began operating in 2016, there was an extended delay before the first sales began, as the IRCCA finalized the details of distribution and sales with pharmacy owners. During this time, authorities established a secure database system that allowed potential buyers to scan their fingerprint at pharmacies, which would be checked with the IRCCA's registry of individuals signed up to purchase.

On July 19, 2017, Uruguay launched the last remaining stage of the cannabis law, with sales finally beginning in 16 pharmacies across the country. The onset of sales saw a surge in interest, with the number of Uruguayans on the IRCCA's purchaser registry increasing from roughly 4,900 to over 13,000 in the first month. Initially, only two varieties of cannabis (referred to on their packaging Alpha I, an indica, and Beta I, a sativa) were made available, sold in five-gram containers at the price of 187.04 Uruguayan pesos each. In January 2018, this price was increased to 200 Uruguayan pesos (or roughly seven U.S. dollars) but at about US$1.40 per gram, the figure remains very competitive with the black market.

There was initial concern regarding the potency of cannabis in Uruguay, as both of the initially available varieties had THC levels at two percent, with CBD at six-to-seven percent. However, this did not dissuade purchasers, and anecdotal reports have suggested that Alpha I and Beta I do indeed have a psychoactive effect. Additionally, in late 2017, the IRCCA made two new varieties available—Alpha II and Beta II—both of which are indica/sativa hybrids and have THC levels of nine percent and CBD levels of roughly three percent.

Uruguay has forged ahead with cannabis regulation despite repeated criticisms from the International Narcotics Control Board (INCB).

In opting for regulation notwithstanding such criticisms, Uruguay has argued that its policy is fully in line with the original objectives that the UN drug control treaties emphasized but have subsequently failed to achieve: namely, the protection of the health and welfare of humankind. While there can be little doubt that, as the INCB has pointed out, Uruguay is contravening its obligations under the 1961 Single Convention to limit cannabis exclusively to medical and scientific purposes, Uruguay has sought to side step the question of drug treaty non-compliance by placing its new law in the context of the country's adherence to its more foundational obligations under international law.

Uruguayan authorities have specifically argued that the creation of a regulated market for adult use of cannabis is driven by health and security imperatives and is therefore an issue of human rights. As such, officials point to wider UN human rights obligations that need to be respected, specifically appealing to the precedence of human rights principles over drug control obligations within the UN system as a whole. In the event of a conflict between human rights obligations and drug control requirements, they argue, Uruguay is bound to give priority to its human rights obligations.

Uruguay's ability to move forward with a policy clearly beyond the bounds of the UN drug treaties owes to a combination of factors. First, Uruguayan authorities foresaw the international criticism their move would likely trigger, and fashioned an argument based on human rights obligations that was consistent with the country's international reputation, and that was coherent with the country's rationale for revising its cannabis law in the first place.

Second, as a practical matter, the UN drug control treaty bodies, including the INCB, do not have the kind of enforcement authority or practical political power that would be necessary to prevent Uruguay from moving ahead with implementation of its new law. Countries such as the United States have historically wielded their political influence and power to encourage full implementation of the drug treaties. However, with Uruguay's law entering its fifth year since passage, there has not been a concerted U.S. government effort to punish Uruguay bilaterally or in an international arena, suggesting that Uruguay's reforms will not be stymied because of international pressures.

In this regard, Uruguay has taken advantage of felicitous timing, with its law's passage having come in the midst of a major shift toward cannabis regulation within the United States. In the wake of the Colorado and Washington ballot initiatives, the U.S. federal government was suddenly in an awkward spot. The United States was the key architect and for decades the chief enforcer of the UN drug treaties, including vigorous enforcement of the global prohibition on non-medical uses of cannabis. To oppose Uruguay's new law or even pressure Uruguay to revise or annul it—as it is easy to imagine previous administrations attempting to do so—would open the United States to charges of hypocrisy.

For the foreseeable future, the United States is unlikely to be in a position to oppose efforts to legalize and regulate cannabis, such as that now underway in Uruguay.

Banking

Because Uruguay was the first nation to legalize the cultivation, processing, distribution, and sale of cannabis, it was anticipated it would avoid some of the challenges faced by other nations with less comprehensive reforms. The Dutch model that tolerates cannabis use at the point of sale still relies on an illegal supply model complicated by the risks of drug importation. The U.S. situation of legalization among some states created interstate commerce, tax, banking, and other challenges.

By legalizing the entire production and distribution process nationwide, Uruguay's reforms were designed in ways that learned from other nation's experiences. In many ways, the Dutch and American systems' shortcomings were avoided. Uruguay's model provides a clear framework for a legal nationwide market, but leaves important flexibility to the executive branch on key matters such as pricing, distribution, enforcement, and accessibility. However, shortly after commercial sales began through the nation's pharmacies, one of the biggest challenges to the reform model appeared: banking.

Because cannabis was legalized nationwide, Uruguayan banks continued their existing relationships with pharmacies—as the nation's pharmacies already used financial institutions as part of their pre-cannabis business operations. Soon after, two of the largest U.S. financial institutions, Bank of America and CitiBank, notified the Uruguayan banks with whom they have relationships that they needed to discontinue serving pharmacies that sell cannabis. These large American banks, which have shied away from serving even U.S. domestic markets with recreational or medical cannabis, cited the USA PATRIOT Act as a basis for their claim and demand to shutter the accounts. Under Section 320 of the law, banks cannot serve accounts that commit an offense that "involves the manufacture, importation, sale, or distribution of a controlled substance (as that term is defined for purposes of the Controlled Substances Act) . . ." and that includes cannabis.

While some argued that the operations within Uruguay and serviced by Uruguayan banks should be outside the reach of that law, they are not. Section 319 of the USA PATRIOT Act extends the reach of the law to foreign (non-U.S.) banks with "an interbank account in the United States with a covered financial institution." Given that Uruguayan banks, even government-operated ones such as the Central Bank of Uruguay and the Bank of the Republic (BROU) fall under that definition, the U.S. banks' threats were real. This situation left Uruguayan banks with a choice: shut down cannabis-selling pharmacies or risk the withdrawal of major American financial institutions from the country. The latter came with significant economic risk. The former would affect only a handful of pharmacies. For Uruguayan banks, the choice was an obvious one, and pharmacies were notified that their accounts would be closed.

Cannabis-dispensing pharmacies faced a choice, as well. They could switch their entire operations (cannabis and non-cannabis) to a cash-only system, or they could stop selling cannabis, continue as a standard pharmacy, and maintain their access to banking—a choice that Uruguayan banks made clear in their communications with pharmacies. Pharmacies chose different options.

In the authors' discussions with pharmacy owner Alicia Chavert Riverós—who operates Farmacia La Cabina in Las Flores, Maldonado Department—Chavert Riverós noted that while she does not use cannabis herself, she agrees with the aims of the law and wants to afford the community's users with legal access to cannabis. She explained that while the switch to cash-only makes it difficult to pay bills (relying on cash transfers through Abitab), she has seen an increase in revenue for other products in her pharmacy since cannabis sales began. If her pharmacy discontinued sales due to the banking obstacles, people in the area would have to travel to either Atlantida (25 miles away) or Minas (38 miles away) to find the next nearest pharmacy that sells cannabis.

In response to financial institutions' decisions not to bank the cannabis industry in Uruguay, alternative ideas have arisen. The first was to create a central, cannabis-only account through the Central Bank of Uruguay. However, given the Central Bank's dealings with international financial institutions, legitimate worries arose that those same American banks would shutter their relations.

In the immediate term, the IRCCA is reacting to the situation—and in particular to the hesitancy of pharmacies to participate as suppliers in light of the banking difficulties—by preparing to set up new points of sales that operate on a cash-only basis. According to authorities, these new establishments will be privately owned, and unlike pharmacies would exclusively sell cannabis (though they may also sell paraphernalia like rolling papers and grinders, and perhaps other items that would allow them to be economically viable).

Supply issues

In any new, legal cannabis market, managing supply poses a serious challenge. Often, cultivators (growers) are unaware of what market demand will be, and in order to avoid product losses, they underestimate consumer demand, leading to huge product shortages and high prices. Over time, as cultivators better understand demand, they supply a level of product that better meets it.

Supply challenges in Uruguay arose because of a combination of typical economic forces and ones particular to the Uruguayan model. Uruguay faced the traditional information challenges regarding how much cannabis would be consumed, even as the law requires people to register to purchase at pharmacies and the law limits the monthly quantity that can be purchased. Growth in the number of registrants can happen quickly, while changes to cultivation (and consequently, output) take months to adjust.

At the same time, in an effort to limit the size of the market, prevent diversion, ensure security, and signal to the world a model of strict regulation, Uruguay authorized only two cultivators—the firms Simbiosis and ICC—to produce cannabis. In addition, it was required that all cannabis produced be tested and approved by IRCCA before it could be supplied to pharmacies. IRCCA (so far) only authorizes cannabis with between two and nine percent THC and also tests for genetic specificity, mold, bacteria, pesticides, metals, etc. Initially, one of the approved cultivators (Simbiosis) was delayed in getting up and running, and once they were, their product did not meet the standards required by the government. The initial Simbiosis crop was turned away from market. So, for several months, only ICC was supplying the entire commercial market with two strains: "Alpha I" and "Beta I."

This limited production meant that pharmacies were undersupplied—not given the maximum product allowed monthly—and that pharmacies sold product so quickly that there would be days of shortages before the next cannabis shipment. This was complicated by some basic aspects of the Uruguayan model. In the month following the opening of sales, more than 13,000 Uruguayans were registered to purchase from pharmacies, each buyer being able to purchase up to 40 grams per month. However, there were initially only 16 pharmacies registered to dispense cannabis, and a pharmacy could only receive two kilograms of cannabis monthly in deliveries every 14 days. That created not just a shortage from the lopsided purchaser to dispensary ratio, but also in terms of the purchaser maximum to pharmacy monthly supply ratio.

Supply challenges compounded because of the failure of one firm to bring approved product to market and the decisions of some pharmacies to end commercial sales (due to the banking challenges mentioned above). At the time of publication there are only 12 pharmacies to serve more than 22,000 buyers, with five of those pharmacies being located in Montevideo. And while the concentration of so many pharmacies in Montevideo closely reflects the population distribution of Uruguay, 11 of Uruguay's 19 departments do not have a single cannabis-dispensing pharmacy. This has led to periods of deep shortages nationwide, with the most notable occurring in October 2017 and February 2018.

To the government's credit, it has maintained its commitment to a heavily regulated market. It has allowed neither the supply shortages nor the banking challenges to push them to weaken regulation. Instead, the government has sought alternative solutions including a government-regulated dispensary model, rather than an exclusive pharmacy model for sales. In the interim, the government could entertain (temporarily or permanently) increasing the monthly maximum that pharmacies (and eventually dispensaries) are allowed to receive.

Enforcement

In implementing Uruguay's law, authorities have placed a clear emphasis on law enforcement aimed at non-compliant clubs and homegrows, hoping to prevent them from fueling a black market. One clear priority for the government in this effort is the tourist market, particularly during peak summer months of November through February. Because sales to tourists are prohibited, some Uruguayan homegrowers and clubs have attempted to get around the ban by offering "cannabis tours," which are framed more as social and educational experiences, in which participants are free to sample cannabis while on a paid tour. Others simply sell directly to tourists behind closed doors, a gray market quietly operating via word of mouth. The IRCCA is aware of this dynamic and has relied on a combination of stern warnings and police action to dissuade such activity. In February 2017, for instance, police seized some 800 plants associated with a cannabis club that was offering cannabis samples to tourists through a hostel in Maldonado Department. The club also had its license revoked by the IRCCA.

In carrying out enforcement, however, IRCCA authorities are aware that they face a dilemma. While they are eager to curtail the black market, they also know that the law is still young. If regulatory authorities were to launch an aggressive strategy of raids against any registered actor suspected of fueling the black market, they are concerned that this would risk discouraging individuals from registering with the IRCCA at all. For this reason the IRCCA has largely followed a more quiet enforcement strategy, prioritizing verbal warnings for those running afoul of the law and only pursuing police action in severe, emblematic cases such as the hostel in Maldonado.

However, the IRCCA's careful enforcement strategy is occasionally complicated by the National Police. In the period following the law's passage, Uruguay saw some disconnect between the letter of the law and how police enforced it. Reports surfaced of IRCCA-registered growers being arrested and falsely accused of violating the law.

The IRCCA is aware of the need for better education of police, and has taken steps to provide it. In August 2015, the Ministry of Interior (which controls the National Police) issued a new set of guidelines meant to train growers and police alike about the proper procedures in cannabis-related police encounters. Among other items, the protocol establishes that the sole existence of cannabis plants is not, by itself, sufficient cause for criminal suspicion. Instead, the Interior Ministry asserts that police should only respond to allegations that refer to "the existence in some way of trafficking, sales, commerce, supply or other illicit behavior in order to constitute a crime."

Tourism

Uruguay's regulations allow only Uruguayan citizens and permanent residents to access cannabis legally. Non-citizen tourists are therefore not eligible to legally purchase cannabis. During debate over the bill, lawmakers were concerned about attracting "marijuana tourism," which they perceived as a potential threat to both Uruguay's international reputation and its existing tourism trade. Due to the lack of public support for the law, authorities also expressed concerns that an influx of tourists seeking cannabis could widen opposition to the law.

Nevertheless, since the law's passage there has been an increasing number of tourists who, if not primarily coming in the hope of accessing cannabis, have sought to acquire it once in Uruguay. There are no official estimates, but reports of tourists paying for "marijuana tours" and inquiring about purchasing cannabis in pharmacies have been widespread in local media. During an October 2017 research trip, this report's authors witnessed this dynamic firsthand, observing illicit sales at a Montevideo paraphernalia shop that itself catered to tourists.

Ultimately, this dynamic suggests a tourism market exists, despite the preferences of Uruguayan authorities. And as the Uruguayan tourism industry continues to grow (official data shows that the flow of tourists is on track to increase by 20 percent in the November 2017–February 2018 tourist season) the cannabis tourism market is likely to increase.

Confronted with this dynamic, so far the IRCCA has responded with enforcement, making an example of those who are most flagrantly catering to tourists. But this response is unlikely to eliminate the market, in the same way that prohibition of cannabis has been ineffective at stemming its use. For this reason, Uruguayan authorities will likely see an increasing rationale to create a legal tourist market in the coming years. Some figures have already publicly mused about such a fix. In January 2018, lawmaker Sebastian Sabini—one of the two original sponsors of the law in Uruguay's legislature—told La Republica newspaper: "Many come to Uruguay to get to know the legal [cannabis] system. However, they end up buying in illicit drug markets because pharmacies still can't sell to tourists. In the medium term we are evaluating the possibility of changing this situation."

* * *

Uruguay makes no claims of being a blueprint for others to follow, but its legal regulation of cannabis is a pioneering effort from which other governments will surely learn. Although Uruguay has done well in rolling out the implementation of non-medical cannabis, the country has encountered some significant challenges. That is not necessarily a flaw in the system, but a reality of cutting-edge public policy. As the world's first country to legalize cannabis fully, it was bound to encounter problems. And, as the country continues to implement this program, more problems will arise. Good public policy making requires governments to anticipate problems before they happen and respond effectively when they do.

C. The Conflict Between State Legalization and Federal Prohibition

As discussed in Chapter 6, marijuana is classified as a Schedule I substance under the federal Controlled Substances Act. Marijuana's status under federal law has posed an array of challenges for the implementation of state legalization laws. This section reviews some of the more pressing legal and policy issues presented by the conflict between state legalization and federal prohibition.

1. Federal Prosecution of State-Legal Marijuana Operations

a. Federal Enforcement Policies

Anyone who grows, sells, or even buys marijuana is guilty of a federal crime, even if it is legal under state law. Although some litigants continue to try to mount constitutional challenges to the federal prohibition on marijuana, current Supreme Court precedent leaves little doubt about the federal government's power to prosecute marijuana crimes.

In *Gonzales v. Raich,* 545 U.S. 1 (2005), a case that is read in most Constitutional Law courses, the Supreme Court considered the scope of Congress's power to regulate state-legal marijuana activity under the Commerce Clause. In 2002, DEA agents raided the home of Dianne Monson, a California medical marijuana patient, and seized six marijuana plants. Although the government did not bring charges against her, Monson, along with fellow patient Angel Raich and her two caregivers, filed suit to enjoin the DEA from enforcing the Controlled Substances Act against them for cultivating medical marijuana.

The *Raich* plaintiffs relied on two Supreme Court decisions, *United States v. Lopez*, 514 U.S. 549 (1995), and *United States v. Morrison*, 529 U.S. 598 (2000), which had restricted the federal government's authority under the Commerce Clause. In essence, *Lopez* and *Morrison* had held that the commerce power did not extend to purely local "noncommercial" activity, placing such activity beyond the reach of federal law. Thus, for example, the Court in *Lopez* struck down a provision of the Gun Free School Zones Act of 1990 that made possession of a gun in a school zone a federal crime on the grounds that it was not commercial activity. Raich and Monson argued that, like possession of a gun in a school zone, the cultivation and possession of marijuana for personal medical use was the sort of noncommercial activity that fell outside the federal government's authority under the Commerce Clause.

In a 6-3 decision, the Supreme Court held the federal government could reach Monson and Raich's activities under the commerce power. The Court reasoned that regulation of the possession and noncommercial cultivation of marijuana was a necessary part of Congress's efforts to criminalize the interstate market for the drug under the Controlled Substances Act. This distinguished *Raich* from *Lopez* and *Morrison*, according to the majority, because regulation of the noncommercial possession and cultivation of marijuana was an "essential part of a larger regulation of economic activity, in which the regulatory scheme could be undercut unless the intrastate activity were regulated."

Raich made clear that the federal government can prosecute individuals whose conduct is in compliance with state marijuana laws, including even individual patients for possessing personal use amounts of marijuana. In her dissent in *Raich*, Justice O'Connor lamented that the Court's decision had "sanction[ed] an application of the federal Controlled Substances Act that extinguishes" California's medical marijuana laws.

Yet, in the years following *Raich*, states continued to enact medical marijuana laws at a similar rate as they had before the decision. The 2000s also saw the proliferation of medical marijuana dispensaries in a number of medical marijuana states. By the time President George W. Bush left office in 2009, it was estimated that more than 700 medical marijuana dispensaries were operating in California alone. During this period, a small number of unlucky state-legal marijuana growers and sellers were sentenced to lengthy federal prison terms—some are still incarcerated today. But many more marijuana businesses operated out in the open, without any federal interference whatsoever. Despite the federal government's legal authority to prosecute marijuana users and providers, it was unable to stop the implementation of state marijuana laws.

Resource constraints account for the disconnect between the federal government's legal authority and practical ability to shut down state marijuana laws. As Robert Mikos explained in his article *On the Limits of Supremacy: Medical Marijuana and the Overlooked Power to Legalize Federal Crime*, 62 Vand. L. Rev. 1421 (2009):

> If the government wants to promote a certain type of behavior, it must reward that behavior (with a subsidy). Conversely, if the government wants to curtail the behavior, it must punish the behavior (with fines or jail time). Viewed from this perspective, the federal ban on medical marijuana does not actually deter possession or cultivation/distribution of the drug. Though the CSA certainly threatens harsh sanctions, the federal government does not have the resources to impose them frequently enough to make a meaningful impact on proscribed behavior.
>
> To begin, the federal law enforcement apparatus is small. The federal government employs 105,000 law enforcement agents, only about 4,400 of whom work for the DEA, the lead federal agency on drug crimes. The remainder work for dozens of departments—FBI, ICE, ATF, and so on—and spend only a fraction of their time handling drug crimes. All told, federal agents made 154,000 arrests in 2007—30,000 for all drug offenses, including 7,276 for marijuana. These figures amount to only 1 percent of all criminal arrests, 1.6 percent of all drug arrests, and less than 1 percent of all marijuana arrests made in the United States that year. Compared to the number of federal law enforcement agents, the number of potential targets in the war on marijuana is enormous.

Perhaps in recognition of this dynamic, after Colorado and Washington became the first states to legalize marijuana in 2012, the Department of Justice issued a non-enforcement policy that advised federal prosecutors not to expend resources going after people who are operating in compliance with state law. This non-enforcement policy, which followed two earlier Obama-era marijuana enforcement policies, was in effect from the time it was issued in 2013 until January of 2018, when it was rescinded by former Attorney General Jeff Sessions.

Although the non-enforcement policy has been rescinded, it is still helpful for understanding the current state of affairs as it relates to federal interference with state marijuana laws.

Memorandum For All United States Attorneys: Guidance Regarding Marijuana Enforcement
James M. Cole, Deputy Attorney General

August 29, 2013

In October 2009 and June 2011, the Department issued guidance to federal prosecutors concerning marijuana enforcement under the Controlled Substances Act (CSA). This memorandum updates that guidance in light of state ballot initiatives that legalize under state law the possession of small amounts of marijuana and provide for the regulation of marijuana production, processing, and sale. The guidance set forth herein applies to all federal enforcement activity, including civil enforcement and criminal investigations and prosecutions, concerning marijuana in all states.

As the Department noted in its previous guidance, Congress has determined that marijuana is a dangerous drug and that the illegal distribution and sale of marijuana is a serious crime that provides a significant source of revenue to large-scale criminal enterprises, gangs, and cartels. The Department of Justice is committed to enforcement of the CSA consistent with those determinations. The Department is also committed to using its limited investigative and prosecutorial resources to address the most significant threats in the most effective, consistent, and rational way. In furtherance of those objectives, as several states enacted laws relating to the use of marijuana for medical purposes, the Department in recent years has focused its efforts on certain enforcement priorities that are particularly important to the federal government:

- Preventing the distribution of marijuana to minors;
- Preventing revenue from the sale of marijuana from going to criminal enterprises, gangs, and cartels;
- Preventing the diversion of marijuana from states where it is legal under state law in some form to other states;
- Preventing state-authorized marijuana activity from being used as a cover or pretext for the trafficking of other illegal drugs or other illegal activity;
- Preventing violence and the use of firearms in the cultivation and distribution of marijuana;
- Preventing drugged driving and the exacerbation of other adverse public health consequences associated with marijuana use;
- Preventing the growing of marijuana on public lands and the attendant public safety and environmental dangers posed by marijuana production on public lands; and
- Preventing marijuana possession or use on federal property.

These priorities will continue to guide the Department's enforcement of the CSA against marijuana-related conduct. Thus, this memorandum serves as guidance to Department attorneys and law enforcement to focus their enforcement resources and efforts, including prosecution, on persons or organizations whose conduct interferes with any one or more of these priorities, regardless of state law.

Outside of these enforcement priorities, the federal government has traditionally relied on states and local law enforcement agencies to address marijuana activity through enforcement of their own narcotics laws. For example, the Department of Justice has not historically devoted resources to prosecuting individuals whose conduct is limited to possession of small amounts of marijuana for personal use on private property. Instead, the Department has left such lower-level or localized activity to state and local authorities and has stepped in to enforce the CSA only when the use, possession, cultivation, or distribution of marijuana has threatened to cause one of the harms identified above.

The enactment of state laws that endeavor to authorize marijuana production, distribution, and possession by establishing a regulatory scheme for these purposes affects this traditional joint federal-state approach to narcotics enforcement. The Department's guidance in this memorandum rests on its expectation that states and local governments that have enacted laws authorizing marijuana-related conduct will implement strong and effective regulatory and enforcement systems that will address the threat those state laws could pose to public safety, public health, and other law enforcement interests. A system adequate to that task must not only contain robust controls and procedures on paper; it must also be effective in practice. Jurisdictions that have implemented systems that provide for regulation of marijuana activity

In jurisdictions that have enacted laws legalizing marijuana in some form and that have also implemented strong and effective regulatory and enforcement systems to control the cultivation, distribution, sale, and possession of marijuana, conduct in compliance with those laws and regulations is less likely to threaten the federal priorities set forth above. Indeed, a robust system may affirmatively address those priorities by, for example, implementing effective measures to prevent diversion of marijuana outside of the regulated system and to other states, prohibiting access to marijuana by minors, and replacing an illicit marijuana trade that funds criminal enterprises with a regulated market in which revenues are tracked and accounted for. In those circumstances, consistent with the traditional allocation of federal-state efforts in this area, enforcement of state law by state and local law enforcement and regulatory bodies should remain the primary means of addressing marijuana-related activity. If state enforcement efforts are not sufficiently robust to protect against the harms set forth above, the federal government may seek to challenge the regulatory structure itself in addition to continuing to bring individual enforcement actions, including criminal prosecutions, focused on those harms.

The Department's previous memoranda specifically addressed the exercise of prosecutorial discretion in states with laws authorizing marijuana cultivation and distribution for medical use. In those contexts, the Department advised that it likely was not an efficient use of federal resources to focus enforcement efforts on seriously ill individuals, or on their individual caregivers. In doing so, the previous guidance drew a distinction between the seriously ill and their caregivers, on the one hand, and large-scale, for-profit commercial enterprises, on the other, and advised that the latter continued to be appropriate targets for federal enforcement and prosecution. In drawing this distinction, the Department relied on the common-sense judgment that the size of a marijuana operation was a reasonable proxy for assessing whether marijuana trafficking implicates the federal enforcement priorities set forth above.

As explained above, however, both the existence of a strong and effective state regulatory system, and an operation's compliance with such a system, may allay the threat that an operation's size poses to federal enforcement interests. Accordingly, in exercising prosecutorial discretion, prosecutors should not consider the size or commercial nature of a marijuana operation alone as a proxy for assessing whether marijuana trafficking implicates the Department's enforcement priorities listed above. Rather, prosecutors should continue to review marijuana cases on a case-by-case basis and weigh all available information and evidence, including, but not limited to, whether the operation is demonstrably in compliance with a strong and effective state regulatory system. A marijuana operation's large scale or for-profit nature may be a relevant consideration for assessing the extent to which it undermines a particular federal enforcement priority. The primary question in all cases—and in all jurisdictions—should be whether the conduct at issue implicates one or more of the enforcement priorities listed above.

As with the Department's previous statements on this subject, this memorandum is intended solely as a guide to the exercise of investigative and prosecutorial discretion. This memorandum does not alter in any way the Department's authority to enforce federal law, including federal laws relating to marijuana, regardless of state law. Neither the guidance herein nor any state or local law provides a legal defense to a violation of federal law, including any civil or criminal violation of the CSA. Even in jurisdictions with strong and effective regulatory systems, evidence that particular conduct threatens federal priorities will subject that person or entity to federal enforcement action, based on the circumstances. This memorandum is not intended to, does not, and may not be relied upon to create any rights, substantive or procedural, enforceable at law by any party in any matter civil or criminal. It applies prospectively to the exercise of prosecutorial discretion in future cases and does not provide defendants or subjects of enforcement action with a basis for reconsideration of any pending civil action or criminal prosecution. Finally, nothing herein precludes investigation or prosecution, even in the absence of any one of the factors listed above, in particular circumstances Where investigation and prosecution otherwise serves an important federal interest.

As a candidate, President Trump said that he thought the federal government should not interfere with state marijuana laws. But his choice for Attorney General,

Jeff Sessions, was known for his strident opposition to marijuana. As a Senator in 2016, Sessions remarked at a committee hearing on drug enforcement that marijuana "is dangerous, you cannot play with it, it is not funny, it's not something to laugh about" and called on the federal government "to send that message with clarity that good people don't smoke marijuana." With respect to legalization specifically, Sessions continued, "we need grown-ups in charge in Washington to say marijuana is not the kind of thing that ought to be legalized, it ought not to be minimized, that it's in fact a very real danger."

The appointment of Sessions to be Attorney General raised the possibility of a return to federal interference with state marijuana laws. In January 2018, Sessions rescinded the Department of Justice's 2013 non-enforcement policy in the memo that follows.

Memorandum For All United States Attorneys: Marijuana Enforcement
Jefferson B. Sessions, III, Attorney General

January 4, 2018

In the Controlled Substances Act, Congress has generally prohibited the cultivation, distribution, and possession of marijuana. 21 U.S.C. § 801 *et seq.* It has established significant penalties for these crimes. These activities also may serve as the basis for the prosecution of other crimes, such as those prohibited by the money laundering statutes, the unlicensed money transmitter statute, and the Bank Secrecy Act. These statutes reflect Congress's determination that marijuana is a dangerous drug and that marijuana activity is a serious crime.

In deciding which marijuana activities to prosecute under these laws with the Department's finite resources, prosecutors should follow the well-established principles that govern all federal prosecutions. Attorney General Benjamin Civiletti originally set forth these principles in 1980, and they have been refined over time, as reflected in chapter 9-27.000 of the U.S. Attorneys' Manual. These principles require federal prosecutors deciding which cases to prosecute to weigh all relevant considerations, including federal law enforcement priorities set by the Attorney General, the seriousness of the crime, the deterrent effect of criminal prosecution, and the cumulative impact of particular crimes on the community.

Given the Department's well-established general principles, previous nationwide guidance specific to marijuana enforcement is unnecessary and is rescinded, effective immediately.[1] This memorandum is intended solely as a guide to the exercise of

1. Previous guidance includes: David W. Ogden, Deputy Att'y Gen., Memorandum for Selected United States Attorneys: Investigations and Prosecutions in States Authorizing the Medical Use of Marijuana (Oct. 19. 2009); James M. Cole, Deputy Att'y Gen., Memorandum for United States Attorneys: Guidance Regarding the Ogden Memo in Jurisdictions Seeking to Authorize Marijuana for Medical Use (June 29, 2011); James M. Cole, Deputy Att'y Gen., Memorandum for All United

investigative and prosecutorial discretion in accordance with all applicable laws, regulations, and appropriations. It is not intended to, does not, and may not be relied upon to create any rights, substantive or procedural, enforceable at law by any party in any matter civil or criminal.

Sessions's withdrawal of the non-enforcement policy generated a lot of news coverage and, for those in the marijuana industry, a good deal of apprehension. But a federal crackdown on state-legal marijuana operators did not materialize. Why do you think federal prosecutions did not resume?

In late 2018, Sessions resigned as Attorney General. His replacement, William Barr, told Congress during his confirmation hearings that he would not "go after companies that have relied on the Cole memoranda," referring to the Obama-era non-enforcement policy.

b. Appropriations Limits on Enforcement

There have been a number of different proposals to try to resolve the conflict between state and federal marijuana laws.

To date, however, the only federal marijuana reform proposal to pass Congress has been a restriction on Department of Justice spending. In spring 2014, the House of Representatives narrowly passed a budget appropriations amendment that prevents the Department of Justice from spending any money to block states from implementing their medical marijuana laws. (The amendment only applies to medical marijuana laws. It does not apply to state laws that have legalized all adult use.) The Senate never voted on the provision directly and, for much of 2014, it seemed unlikely ever to become law. Ultimately, however, it made its way into the final budget for 2015. The budget rider blocks the Department of Justice (DOJ) from using funds "to prevent . . . States from implementing their own State laws that authorize the use, distribution, possession, or cultivation of medical marijuana." Consolidated and Further Continuing Appropriations Act, 2015, Pub. L. No. 113-235, § 538, 128 Stat. 2130 (2014). Ever since, the federal budget has continued to include a similar appropriations rider and at the time this book went to press, the provision was still in place.

Politically, passage of this budget rider was a significant development—the first congressional vote in favor of accommodating state-level marijuana reforms. But to what extent does it actually restrict the federal government from prosecuting people who are in compliance with state medical marijuana laws? The Ninth Circuit considered the question in the case that follows.

States Attorneys: Guidance Regarding Marijuana Enforcement (Aug. 29, 20 I3); James M. Cole. Deputy Att'y Gen., Memorandum for All United States Attorneys: Guidance Regarding Marijuana Related Financial Crimes (Feb. 14, 2014); and Monty Wilkinson, Director of the Executive Office for U.S. Att'ys, Policy Statement Regarding Marijuana Issues in Indian Country (Oct. 28, 2014).

United States v. McIntosh

United States Court of Appeals for the Ninth Circuit
833 F.3d 1163 (2016)

O'Scannlain, J.

We are asked to decide whether criminal defendants may avoid prosecution for various federal marijuana offenses on the basis of a congressional appropriations rider that prohibits the United States Department of Justice from spending funds to prevent states' implementation of their own medical marijuana laws.

I. A

These ten cases are consolidated interlocutory appeals and petitions for writs of mandamus arising out of orders entered by three district courts in two states within our circuit. All Appellants have been indicted for various infractions of the Controlled Substances Act (CSA). They have moved to dismiss their indictments or to enjoin their prosecutions on the grounds that the Department of Justice (DOJ) is prohibited from spending funds to prosecute them.

In *McIntosh*, five codefendants allegedly ran four marijuana stores in the Los Angeles area known as Hollywood Compassionate Care (HCC) and Happy Days, and nine indoor marijuana grow sites in the San Francisco and Los Angeles areas. These codefendants were indicted for conspiracy to manufacture, to possess with intent to distribute, and to distribute more than 1000 marijuana plants in violation of 21 U.S.C. §§ 846, 841(a)(1), 841(b)(l)(A). The government sought forfeiture derived from such violations under 21 U.S.C. § 853.

In *Lovan*, the U.S. Drug Enforcement Agency* and Fresno County Sheriff's Office executed a federal search warrant on 60 acres of land located on North Zedicker Road in Sanger, California. Officials allegedly located more than 30,000 marijuana plants on this property. Four codefendants were indicted for manufacturing 1000 or more marijuana plants and for conspiracy to manufacture 1000 or more marijuana plants in violation of 21 U.S.C. §§ 841(a)(1), 846.

In *Kynaston*, five codefendants face charges that arose out of the execution of a Washington State search warrant related to an investigation into violations of Washington's Controlled Substances Act. Allegedly, a total of 562 "growing marijuana plants," along with another 677 pots, some of which appeared to have the root structures of suspected harvested marijuana plants, were found. The codefendants were indicted for conspiring to manufacture 1000 or more marijuana plants, manufacturing 1000 or more marijuana plants, possessing with intent to distribute 100 or more marijuana plants, possessing a firearm in furtherance of a Title 21 offense, maintaining a drug-involved premise, and being felons in possession of a firearm in violation of 18 U.S.C. §§ 922(g)(1), 924(c)(1)(A)(i) and 21 U.S.C. §§ 841, 856(a)(1).

* The court's opinion mistakenly refers to the DEA as the "Drug Enforcement Agency." Its true name is the Drug Enforcement Administration. [*Footnote by casebook author.*]

B

In December 2014, Congress enacted the following rider in an omnibus appropriations bill funding the government through September 30, 2015:

> None of the funds made available in this Act to the Department of Justice may be used, with respect to the States of Alabama, Alaska, Arizona, California, Colorado, Connecticut, Delaware, District of Columbia, Florida, Hawaii, Illinois, Iowa, Kentucky, Maine, Maryland, Massachusetts, Michigan, Minnesota, Mississippi, Missouri, Montana, Nevada, New Hampshire, New Jersey, New Mexico, Oregon, Rhode Island, South Carolina, Tennessee, Utah, Vermont, Washington, and Wisconsin, to prevent such States from implementing their own State laws that authorize the use, distribution, possession, or cultivation of medical marijuana.

Consolidated and Further Continuing Appropriations Act, 2015, Pub. L. No. 113-235, § 538, 128 Stat. 2130, 2217 (2014). Various short-term measures extended the appropriations and the rider through December 22, 2015. On December 18, 2015, Congress enacted a new appropriations act, which appropriates funds through the fiscal year ending September 30, 2016, and includes essentially the same rider in § 542. Consolidated Appropriations Act, 2016, Pub. L. No. 114-113, § 542, 129 Stat. 2242, 2332–33 (2015) (adding Guam and Puerto Rico and changing "prevent such States from implementing their own State laws" to "prevent any of them from implementing their own laws").

Appellants in *McIntosh*, *Lovan*, and *Kynaston* filed motions to dismiss or to enjoin on the basis of the rider. The motions were denied from the bench in hearings in *McIntosh* and *Lovan*, while the court in *Kynaston* filed a short written order denying the motion after a hearing. In *McIntosh* and *Kynaston*, the court concluded that defendants had failed to carry their burden to demonstrate their compliance with state medical marijuana laws. In *Lovan*, the court concluded that the determination of compliance with state law would depend on facts found by the jury in a federal prosecution, and thus it would revisit the defendants' motion after the trial.

Appellants in all three cases filed interlocutory appeals, and Appellants in *McIntosh* and *Lovan* ask us to consider issuing writs of mandamus if we do not assume jurisdiction over the appeals.

II

We note the unusual circumstances presented by these cases. In almost all federal criminal prosecutions, injunctive relief and interlocutory appeals will not be appropriate. Federal courts traditionally have refused, except in rare instances, to enjoin federal criminal prosecutions. Thus, in almost all circumstances, federal criminal defendants cannot obtain injunctions of their ongoing prosecutions, and orders by district courts relating solely to requests to stay ongoing federal prosecutions will not constitute appealable orders under § 1292(a)(1).

Here, however, Congress has enacted an appropriations rider that specifically restricts DOJ from spending money to pursue certain activities. It is "emphatically . . .

the exclusive province of the Congress not only to formulate legislative policies and mandate programs and projects, but also to establish their relative priority for the Nation. Once Congress, exercising its delegated powers, has decided the order of priorities in a given area, it is for . . . the courts to enforce them when enforcement is sought." *Tenn. Valley Auth. v. Hill*, 437 U.S. 153, 194 (1978). Even if Appellants cannot obtain injunctions of their prosecutions themselves, they can seek—and have sought—to enjoin DOJ from spending funds from the relevant appropriations acts on such prosecutions.[2] When Congress has enacted a restriction like § 542 that expressly prohibits DOJ from spending funds on certain actions, federal criminal defendants may seek to enjoin the expenditure of those funds, and we may exercise jurisdiction over a district court's direct denial of a request for such injunctive relief.

Here, Appellants complain that DOJ is spending funds that have not been appropriated by Congress in violation of the Appropriations Clause of the Constitution. See U.S. Const. art. I, § 9, cl. 7 ("No Money shall be drawn from the Treasury, but in Consequence of Appropriations made by Law . . . ."). This "straightforward and explicit command . . . means simply that no money can be paid out of the Treasury unless it has been appropriated by an act of Congress." *Office of Pers. Mgmt. v. Richmond*, 496 U.S. 414, 424 (1990) (citation omitted). "Money may be paid out only through an appropriation made by law; in other words, the payment of money from the Treasury must be authorized by a statute." *Id.*

The Appropriations Clause plays a critical role in the Constitution's separation of powers among the three branches of government and the checks and balances between them. "Any exercise of a power granted by the Constitution to one of the other branches of Government is limited by a valid reservation of congressional control over funds in the Treasury." Without it, Justice Story explained, "the executive would possess an unbounded power over the public purse of the nation; and might apply all its moneyed resources at his pleasure." *Id.* at 427, 110 S.Ct. 2465 (quoting 2 Joseph Story, Commentaries on the Constitution of the United States § 1348 (3d ed. 1858)).

Thus, if DOJ were spending money in violation of § 542, it would be drawing funds from the Treasury without authorization by statute and thus violating the Appropriations Clause. That Clause constitutes a separation-of-powers limitation that Appellants can invoke to challenge their prosecutions.

---

2. We need not decide in the first instance exactly how the district courts should resolve claims that DOJ is spending money to prosecute a defendant in violation of an appropriations rider. We therefore take no view on the precise relief required and leave that issue to the district courts in the first instance. We note that district courts in criminal cases have ancillary jurisdiction, which "is the power of a court to adjudicate and determine matters incidental to the exercise of its primary jurisdiction over a cause under review." *United States v. Sumner*, 226 F.3d 1005, 1013–15 (9th Cir. 2000); *see Kokkonen v. Guardian Life Ins. Co. of Am.*, 511 U.S. 375, 378–80, 114 S.Ct. 1673, 128 L. Ed.2d 391 (1994); *Garcia v. Teitler*, 443 F.3d 202, 206–10 (2d Cir. 2006).

III

The parties dispute whether the government's spending money on their prosecutions violates § 542.

We focus, as we must, on the statutory text. Section 542 provides that "[n]one of the funds made available in this Act to the Department of Justice may be used, with respect to [Medical Marijuana States[3]] to prevent any of them from implementing their own laws that authorize the use, distribution, possession, or cultivation of medical marijuana." Consolidated Appropriations Act, 2016, Pub. L. No. 114-113, § 542, 129 Stat. 2242, 2332–33 (2015). Unfortunately, the rider is not a model of clarity.

[I]n order to decide whether the prosecutions of Appellants violate § 542, we must determine the plain meaning of "prevent any of [the Medical Marijuana States] from implementing their own laws that authorize the use, distribution, possession, or cultivation of medical marijuana." The pronoun "them" refers back to the Medical Marijuana States, and "their own laws" refers to the state laws of the Medical Marijuana States. And "implement" means:

> To "carry out, accomplish; esp.: to give practical effect to and ensure of actual fulfillment by concrete measure." Implement, Merriam-Webster's Collegiate Dictionary (11th ed. 2003);
>
> "To put into practical effect; carry out." Implement, American Heritage Dictionary of the English Language (5th ed. 2011); and
>
> "To complete, perform, carry into effect (a contract, agreement, etc.); to fulfil (an engagement or promise)." Implement, Oxford English Dictionary, www.oed.com.

In sum, § 542 prohibits DOJ from spending money on actions that prevent the Medical Marijuana States' giving practical effect to their state laws that authorize the use, distribution, possession, or cultivation of medical marijuana.

DOJ argues that it does not prevent the Medical Marijuana States from giving practical effect to their medical marijuana laws by prosecuting private individuals, rather than taking legal action against the state. We are not persuaded.

Importantly, the "[s]tatutory language cannot be construed in a vacuum. It is [another] fundamental canon of statutory construction that the words of a statute

---

3. To avoid repeating the names of all 43 jurisdictions listed, we refer to Alabama, Alaska, Arizona, California, Colorado, Connecticut, Delaware, Florida, Georgia, Hawaii, Illinois, Iowa, Kentucky, Louisiana, Maine, Maryland, Massachusetts, Michigan, Minnesota, Mississippi, Missouri, Montana, Nevada, New Hampshire, New Jersey, New Mexico, New York, North Carolina, Oklahoma, Oregon, Rhode Island, South Carolina, Tennessee, Texas, Utah, Vermont, Virginia, Washington, Wisconsin, Wyoming, the District of Columbia, Guam, and Puerto Rico as the "Medical Marijuana States" and their laws authorizing "the use, distribution, possession, or cultivation of medical marijuana" as the "State Medical Marijuana Laws." While recognizing that the list includes three non-states, we will refer to the listed jurisdictions as states and their laws as state laws without further qualification.

must be read in their context and with a view to their place in the overall statutory scheme." Here, we must read § 542 with a view to its place in the overall statutory scheme for marijuana regulation, namely the CSA and the State Medical Marijuana Laws. The CSA prohibits the use, distribution, possession, or cultivation of any marijuana. See 21 U.S.C. §§ 841(a), 844(a).[4] The State Medical Marijuana Laws are those state laws that authorize the use, distribution, possession, or cultivation of medical marijuana. Thus, the CSA prohibits what the State Medical Marijuana Laws permit.

In light of the ordinary meaning of the terms of § 542 and the relationship between the relevant federal and state laws, we consider whether a superior authority, which prohibits certain conduct, can prevent a subordinate authority from implementing a rule that officially permits such conduct by punishing individuals who are engaged in the conduct officially permitted by the lower authority. We conclude that it can.

DOJ, without taking any legal action against the Medical Marijuana States, prevents them from implementing their laws that authorize the use, distribution, possession, or cultivation of medical marijuana by prosecuting individuals for use, distribution, possession, or cultivation of medical marijuana that is authorized by such laws. By officially permitting certain conduct, state law provides for non-prosecution of individuals who engage in such conduct. If the federal government prosecutes such individuals, it has prevented the state from giving practical effect to its law providing for non-prosecution of individuals who engage in the permitted conduct.

We therefore conclude that, at a minimum, § 542 prohibits DOJ from spending funds from relevant appropriations acts for the prosecution of individuals who engaged in conduct permitted by the State Medical Marijuana Laws and who fully complied with such laws.

Appellants in *McIntosh* and *Kynaston* argue for a more expansive interpretation of § 542. They contend that the rider prohibits DOJ from bringing federal marijuana charges against anyone licensed or authorized under a state medical marijuana law for activity occurring within that state, including licensees who had failed to comply fully with state law.

For instance, Appellants in *Kynaston* argue that "implementation of laws necessarily involves all aspects of putting the law into practical effect, including interpretation of the law, means of application and enforcement, and procedures and processes for determining the outcome of individual cases." Under this view, if the federal government prosecutes individuals who are not strictly compliant with state law, it

4. This requires a slight caveat. Under the CSA, "the manufacture, distribution, or possession of marijuana [is] a criminal offense, with the sole exception being use of the drug as part of a Food and Drug Administration preapproved research study." *Gonzales v. Raich*, 545 U.S. 1, 14, 125 S.Ct. 2195, 162 L.Ed.2d 1 (2005); *see* 21 U.S.C. §§ 812(c), 823(f), 841(a)(1), 844(a). Thus, except as part of "a strictly controlled research project," federal law "designates marijuana as contraband for *any* purpose." *Raich*, 545 U.S. at 24, 27, 125 S.Ct. 2195.

will prevent the states from implementing the entirety of their laws that authorize medical marijuana by preventing them from giving practical effect to the penalties and enforcement mechanisms for engaging in unauthorized conduct. Thus, argue the *Kynaston* Appellants, the Department of Justice must refrain from prosecuting "unless a person's activities are so clearly outside the scope of a state's medical marijuana laws that reasonable debate is not possible."

To determine whether such construction is correct, we must decide whether the phrase "laws that authorize" includes not only the rules authorizing certain conduct but also the rules delineating penalties and enforcement mechanisms for engaging in unauthorized conduct. In answering that question, we consider the ordinary meaning of "laws that authorize the use, distribution, possession, or cultivation of medical marijuana." "Law" has many different meanings, including the following definitions that appear most relevant to § 542:

> "The aggregate of legislation, judicial precedents, and accepted legal principles; the body of authoritative grounds of judicial and administrative action; esp., the body of rules, standards, and principles that the courts of a particular jurisdiction apply in deciding controversies brought before them."
>
> "The set of rules or principles dealing with a specific area of a legal system <copyright law>."

Law, Black's Law Dictionary (10th ed. 2014); and:

> "1. a. The body of rules, whether proceeding from formal enactment or from custom, which a particular state or community recognizes as binding on its members or subjects. (In this sense usually the law.)."
>
> "One of the individual rules which constitute the 'law' (sense 1) of a state or polity. . . . The plural has often a collective sense . . . approaching sense 1."

The relative pronoun "that" restricts "laws" to those laws authorizing the use, distribution, possession, or cultivation of medical marijuana. In sum, the ordinary meaning of § 542 prohibits the Department of Justice from preventing the implementation of the Medical Marijuana States' laws or sets of rules and only those rules that authorize medical marijuana use.

We also consider the context of § 542. The rider prohibits DOJ from preventing forty states, the District of Columbia, and two territories from implementing their medical marijuana laws. Not only are such laws varied in composition but they also are changing as new statutes are enacted, new regulations are promulgated, and new administrative and judicial decisions interpret such statutes and regulations. Thus, § 542 applies to a wide variety of laws that are in flux.

Given this context and the restriction of the relevant laws to those that authorize conduct, we conclude that § 542 prohibits the federal government only from preventing the implementation of those specific rules of state law that authorize the use, distribution, possession, or cultivation of medical marijuana. DOJ does not prevent the implementation of rules authorizing conduct when it prosecutes individuals who engage in conduct unauthorized under state medical marijuana laws. Individuals who do not strictly comply with all state-law conditions regarding the use, distribution, possession, and cultivation of medical marijuana have engaged in conduct that is unauthorized, and prosecuting such individuals does not violate § 542. Congress could easily have drafted § 542 to prohibit interference with laws that address medical marijuana or those that regulate medical marijuana, but it did not. Instead, it chose to proscribe preventing states from implementing laws that authorize the use, distribution, possession, and cultivation of medical marijuana.

The parties cite various pieces of legislative history to support their arguments regarding the meaning of § 542.

We cannot consider such sources. It is a fundamental principle of appropriations law that we may only consider the text of an appropriations rider, not expressions of intent in legislative history. "An agency's discretion to spend appropriated funds is cabined only by the 'text of the appropriation,' not by Congress' expectations of how the funds will be spent, as might be reflected by legislative history."

We recognize that some members of Congress may have desired a more expansive construction of the rider, while others may have preferred a more limited interpretation. However, we must consider only the text of the rider. If Congress intends to prohibit a wider or narrower range of DOJ actions, it certainly may express such intention, hopefully with greater clarity, in the text of any future rider.

We therefore must remand to the district courts. If DOJ wishes to continue these prosecutions, Appellants are entitled to evidentiary hearings to determine whether their conduct was completely authorized by state law, by which we mean that they strictly complied with all relevant conditions imposed by state law on the use, distribution, possession, and cultivation of medical marijuana. We leave to the district courts to determine, in the first instance and in each case, the precise remedy that would be appropriate.

We note the temporal nature of the problem with these prosecutions. The government had authority to initiate criminal proceedings, and it merely lost funds to continue them. DOJ is currently prohibited from spending funds from specific appropriations acts for prosecutions of those who complied with state law. But Congress could appropriate funds for such prosecutions tomorrow. Conversely, this temporary lack of funds could become a more permanent lack of funds if Congress continues to include the same rider in future appropriations bills. In determining the appropriate remedy for any violation of § 542, the district courts should consider the temporal nature of the lack of funds along with Appellants' rights to a speedy trial under the Sixth Amendment and the Speedy Trial Act, 18 U.S.C. § 3161.[5]

---

5. The prior observation should also serve as a warning. To be clear, § 542 does not provide immunity from prosecution for federal marijuana offenses. The CSA prohibits the manufacture, distribution, and possession of marijuana. Anyone in any state who possesses, distributes, or manufactures marijuana for medical or recreational purposes (or attempts or conspires to do so) is

For the foregoing reasons, we vacate the orders of the district courts and remand with instructions to conduct an evidentiary hearing to determine whether Appellants have complied with state law.

In *McIntosh*, the Ninth Circuit held that the appropriations rider restricts the Department of Justice from spending money to prosecute people who are operating in strict compliance with state medical marijuana laws. The decision left a number of other important questions unresolved, however. Would a single non-state-compliant sale open a medical marijuana business to a conspiracy prosecution for *all* of its activity? How would a minor regulatory violation—not having proper signage, for example—impact the strict compliance standard? Who has the burden regarding proof of compliance with state law?

In a subsequent case, *United States v. Kleinman*, 880 F.3d 1020 (9th Cir. 2017), the Ninth Circuit indicated that a single violation of state law could potentially expose a medical marijuana business to serious federal criminal liability, notwithstanding the appropriations rider. The court in *Kleinman* held that the appropriations rider "focuses on the conduct forming the basis of a particular charge, which requires a count-by-count analysis to determine which charges, if any, are restricted" by the rider. *Id.* at 1028.

Kleinman's count-by-count holding means that the government "cannot use a prosecutable charge (for conduct that violates state medical marijuana law) to bootstrap other charges that rely solely upon conduct that would fully comply with state law." *Ibid.* At first blush, this holding might seem to provide a great deal of protection to state medical marijuana operators. But when applied to the crime of conspiracy, *Kleimann*'s count-by-count approach could potentially expose marijuana operators to sweeping charges based on a single violation of state law. In *Kleinman* itself, the Ninth Circuit held that the rider did not apply to a conspiracy conviction that involved two out-of-state sales, rejecting the defendant's argument that those sales "should not taint his entire marijuana operation." *Id.* at 1029. By that logic, *Kleinman*'s holding might also give the Department of Justice the power to prosecute a medical marijuana business operator for conspiracy following a minor

---

committing a federal crime. The federal government can prosecute such offenses for up to five years after they occur. *See* 18 U.S.C. § 3282. Congress currently restricts the government from spending certain funds to prosecute certain individuals. But Congress could restore funding tomorrow, a year from now, or four years from now, and the government could then prosecute individuals who committed offenses while the government lacked funding. Moreover, a new president will be elected soon, and a new administration could shift enforcement priorities to place greater emphasis on prosecuting marijuana offenses.

Nor does any state law "legalize" possession, distribution, or manufacture of marijuana. Under the Supremacy Clause of the Constitution, state laws cannot permit what federal law prohibits. U.S. Const. art VI, cl. 2. Thus, while the CSA remains in effect, states cannot actually authorize the manufacture, distribution, or possession of marijuana. Such activity remains prohibited by federal law.

state law regulatory violation. Under federal weight-based sentencing laws, such a prosecution could easily result in a lengthy mandatory minimum sentence based on the amount of marijuana the business had sold throughout its existence (i.e., the amount of marijuana sold during the existence of the conspiracy).

Of course, the limits of *Kleinman* will only be tested if the Department of Justice decides to bring federal charges against medical marijuana operators based on relatively minor state-law violations. For a discussion of the various legal issues raised by the appropriations rider, see Florence Shu-Acquaye, *Rohrbacher-Blumenauer Amendment, Case Law and the Department of Justice: Who Prevails in the Medical Marijuana Legalization Debate?*, 54 Gonz. L. Rev. 127 (2018).

c. Preemption

The federal government's legal authority to prosecute people who grow, sell, or possess marijuana is clear—subject, of course, to the appropriations rider that is currently in effect. Less clear is whether, and to what extent, the state marijuana legalization laws themselves could be found preempted by federal law.

As the Ninth Circuit mentioned in footnote 5 of *McIntosh*, "[u]nder the Supremacy Clause of the Constitution, state laws cannot permit what federal law prohibits." Specifically, Article Six, Clause 2 of the U.S. Constitution (known as the Supremacy Clause) provides that federal statutes are "the supreme law of the land." At first glance, the Supremacy Clause might seem to present a straightforward and cost-effective method for the federal government to block state marijuana legalization laws. Marijuana legalization laws certainly make it more difficult to enforce the federal Controlled Substances Act, after all. So, don't they stand "as an obstacle to the accomplishment of Congress's full objectives under the" Controlled Substances Act? *Crosby v. Nat'l Foreign Trade Council*, 530 U.S. 363, 373 (2000).

To date, preemption challenges to state marijuana legalization laws have been mostly unsuccessful. In a few cases, courts have struck down specific provisions of state legalization laws. A Colorado statute requiring the police to return marijuana to an individual later acquitted of a state drug charge was found preempted by federal law, for example. *People v. Crouse*, 350 P.3d 849 (Colo. 2017). But no court has struck down the core provisions of a state medical or recreational legalization law on a preemption theory. One reason for this is that, although the federal government can prosecute marijuana cases under the Controlled Substances Act, it cannot conscript state and local actors into doing so. The anti-commandeering principle forbids the federal government from forcing states to criminalize conduct, which arguably means that state marijuana legalization laws cannot be preempted. See *Printz v. United States*, 521 U.S. 898, 935 (1997).

In May 2018, the United States Supreme Court issued an anti-commandeering decision that appears to significantly strengthen the legal standing of state marijuana legalization laws in relation to the Supremacy Clause. The case, *Murphy v. National Collegiate Athletic Association (NCAA)*, 138 S. Ct. 1461 (2018), held that

New Jersey can legalize sports gambling at its casinos, despite a federal law that purported to make it unlawful for a state to "authorize" sports betting. The Supreme Court concluded that the federal law unconstitutionally commandeered state authority and that New Jersey's law was not preempted by federal law. Although the federal gambling statute at issue in *Murphy* operated much differently from the Controlled Substances Act, the logic of the Court's decision appears to "provide states the clear precedent they need to debunk lingering claims that their marijuana reforms are preempted because they 'authorize' drug activities that federal law forbids." Rob Mikos, *The Implications of* Murphy v. NCAA *for State Marijuana Reforms*, Marijuana Law, Policy, and Authority Blog, May 17, 2018.

2. Access to Banking Services

Even if the Department of Justice continues to refrain from prosecuting state-legal marijuana operators, the federal prohibition of marijuana has resulted in a number of other legal and practical problems for marijuana businesses. These problems include the inability to secure federal trademark rights, the potential inability to receive bankruptcy relief, and a tax penalty that applies to businesses that traffic in Schedule I drugs (known as the Section 280E tax penalty).

Of all the challenges posed by federal prohibition, access to banking services warrants special attention. Marijuana's status under federal law has made it difficult, if not impossible, for marijuana businesses to access banking services. This is because federal money laundering statutes and related regulations consider marijuana to be no different from any other illegal drug, regardless of the legal status of marijuana businesses under state law. As a result, many marijuana businesses are forced to operate on a cash basis—a fact that can make them an enticing target for robberies. This is a concern for marijuana businesses and law enforcement agencies alike. As former Attorney General Eric Holder explained, "Huge amounts of cash, substantial amounts of cash just kind of lying around with no place for it to be appropriately deposited, is something that would worry me, just from a law enforcement perspective." Jack Healy and Matt Apuzzo, *Legal Marijuana Businesses Should Have Access to Banks, Holder Says*, N.Y. Times, Jan. 24, 2014 at A20.

In *Banks, Marijuana, and Federalism*, Julie Anderson Hill described some of the key banking rules that stand in the way of banking access for marijuana businesses.

Banks, Marijuana, and Federalism
Julie Anderson Hill

65 Case Western Reserve Law Review 597 (2015)

Lack of banking services stands as a formidable barrier to growth of the state-legal marijuana industry. Without access to banking services, marijuana businesses must conduct transactions in cash and spend an inordinate amount of time and resources on cash management. From vaults, to cameras, to security personnel, to finding suppliers that accept cash payment, managing cash can quickly become a logistical and security nightmare. In Colorado, the controller of one recreational marijuana retailer described cash management as "a full-time job." Stories abound concerning marijuana retailers attempting to surreptitiously drive large quantities of concealed cash across town just to pay tax bills.

At the same time, lack of banking services equates to a lack of capital for the marijuana industry. Banks are the traditional backbone of small business financing, but banks will not lend to marijuana-related businesses. The state-legal marijuana industry must instead "rely on short-term loans from individuals, usually with higher interest rates." Even if a marijuana-related business finds financing, there is still the problem of not having a bank account. As a marijuana retailer hoping to finance the one-million-dollar purchase of a new building explains, "What do you say? . . . I want it in cash, guys?"

At its root, the issue of marijuana banking—like the issue of state legalization of marijuana more broadly—is a federalism issue.

The United States has a dual banking system: banks can choose a federal charter issued by the Office of the Comptroller of the Currency or a state charter from a state banking regulator. Likewise, credit unions can generally choose a federal charter from the National Credit Union Administration (NCUA) or a state charter from a state credit union regulator. Indeed, the federalism represented by the dual banking system has been described as "competitive" because regulators compete to charter institutions. In general, national financial institutions must follow a set of federal laws while state institutions must follow state law. If the dual banking system were truly dichotomous (federal law only regulated national institutions and state law only regulated state institutions), the answer for marijuana banking would be clear: state-chartered institutions in states where marijuana is legal would be free to provide banking services to marijuana-related entities.

But state and federal financial institution regulators do not "operate in distinct spheres." The federal government has some regulatory control over state institutions, and state government has some control over federal institutions.

Federal law . . . expects financial institutions to do more than merely avoid assisting those who manufacture, distribute, or dispense marijuana. Financial institutions must discover illegal activity, report it to federal officials, and prevent wrongdoers from accessing the banking system.

The Money Laundering Control Act makes individuals and entities subject to criminal liability for money laundering. There are several ways to commit the offense of money laundering, but two are especially relevant to financial institutions considering marijuana banking. First, a financial institution commits money laundering by conducting a financial transaction involving the proceeds of a known "specified unlawful activity" while "knowing that the transaction is designed in whole or in part to conceal or disguise the nature, the location, the source, the ownership or the control of the proceeds of specified unlawful activity or to avoid a transaction reporting requirement under State or Federal law." Second, a financial institution commits money laundering if it "knowingly engages or attempts to engage in a monetary transaction in criminally derived property of a value greater than $10,000." Lest there be any doubt, the "manufacture, importation, sale, or distribution of a controlled substance," including marijuana, is a "specified unlawful activity" under the money laundering statute. Both types of money laundering can result in substantial fines and imprisonment.

Press reports suggest that because financial institutions are well aware of the anti-money laundering laws, some marijuana businesses attempt to gain access to banking services by disguising the nature of their business. As one owner of medical marijuana dispensaries in Washington explains, "Your savvy business owners know how to open a holding company, get a banking account through that holding company, and put their assets underneath that holding company . . . . The only way to really get banking is to not give the bank the entire story."

Of course, these surreptitious businesses may be subject to money laundering charges themselves. Moreover, it is far from clear that such measures result in long-term access to the banking system; banking law does not allow financial institutions to simply take customer assertions at face value.

Under the Bank Secrecy Act and the USA PATRIOT Act, financial institutions must maintain robust programs designed to prevent money laundering. Every financial institution must implement a customer identification program to make reasonable efforts to "verify the identity of any person seeking to open an account." Even when the "person" opening an account is a business, a financial institution must verify the identity of the prospective accountholder.

Verifying the identity of the customer is only the beginning. Federal regulators expect institutions to undertake sufficient due diligence on each customer to adequately assess the risk associated with that customer. For "higher-risk" accounts (like accounts belonging to "cash-intensive businesses"), financial institutions must know the purpose of each account, the source of funds in the account, and the customer's primary trade area.

Armed with information about the normal business of each customer, financial institutions are then tasked with identifying suspicious transactions. The Bank Secrecy Act requires that financial institutions report illegal and suspicious activities to the federal Financial Crimes Enforcement Network (FinCEN).

FinCEN has authority to seek substantial civil money penalties from financial institutions and individuals who violate the Bank Secrecy Act. Such fines often reach well into the millions of dollars. Federal officials also have an even bigger hammer: criminal prosecution.

> For example, a person, including a bank employee, willfully violating the BSA or its implementing regulations is subject to a criminal fine of up to $250,000 or five years in prison, or both. A person who commits such a

> violation while violating another U.S. law, or engaging in a pattern of criminal activity, is subject to a fine of up to $500,000 or ten years in prison, or both.

Institutions face criminal money penalties of "not less than 2 times the amount of the transaction, but not more than $1,000,000."

In sum, a financial institution that knowingly processes transactions for marijuana-related businesses commits the crime of money laundering. Even if financial institutions believe that prosecutorial discretion will spare them criminal penalties, the Bank Secrecy Act requires costly due diligence and reporting for all marijuana-related transactions. Ignoring Bank Secrecy Act obligations is a recipe for incurring civil and criminal penalties.

The federal government also wields significant control over payment systems. The Federal Reserve provides four important payment services: (1) a centralized check collection system, (2) the Automated Clearinghouse (ACH) network for processing batched electronic small-dollar payments, (3) the Fedwire system for larger electronic payments, and (4) coin and currency services.

Financial institutions use each of these systems to provide customers payment services. The Monetary Control Act of 1980 requires that the Federal Reserve offer payment system services to all "depository institutions," regardless of whether the institution is a member of the Federal Reserve System. Thus, the Federal Reserve currently provides services to banks and credit unions alike. By establishing regulations and policies governing access to its payment systems, the Federal Reserve has the ability to impact practices at all financial institutions using these systems.

Accessing the Federal Reserve's payment systems is not administratively difficult. It requires only a resolution from the financial institution's board of directions and the completion of forms designating individuals authorized to initiate transactions and identifying the types of services wanted. Under normal circumstances, once a financial institution receives a charter, the Federal Reserve grants the institution a "master account" and access to payment services. This process makes sense because the prospective financial institution has already been vetted by the chartering authority, and usually by the deposit or share insurer as well.

Of course, nothing prevents the Federal Reserve from adjusting the terms and conditions for use of the Federal Reserve's payment systems. It is possible that future terms and conditions could cut off access to financial institutions that provide services to the marijuana industry.

In 2014, the federal government issued advisory guidelines that were designed to try to address the problem of banking services for marijuana businesses. Unlike the Department of Justice's non-enforcement policy, which was rescinded by former Attorney General Jeff Sessions in 2018, the banking guidelines are still in place. As you read through the memo that follows, put yourself in the place of an attorney for a bank in a state with a marijuana business. Would you advise the bank to take on a marijuana business as a customer in light of this guidance?

Guidance: BSA Expectations Regarding Marijuana-Related Businesses

Department of the Treasury, Financial Crimes Enforcement Network
February 14, 2014

The Financial Crimes Enforcement Network ("FinCEN") is issuing guidance to clarify Bank Secrecy Act ("BSA") expectations for financial institutions seeking to provide services to marijuana-related businesses. FinCEN is issuing this guidance in light of recent state initiatives to legalize certain marijuana-related activity and related guidance by the U.S. Department of Justice ("DOJ") concerning marijuana-related enforcement priorities. This FinCEN guidance clarifies how financial institutions can provide services to marijuana-related businesses consistent with their BSA obligations, and aligns the information provided by financial institutions in BSA reports with federal and state law enforcement priorities. This FinCEN guidance should enhance the availability of financial services for, and the financial transparency of, marijuana-related businesses.

The Controlled Substances Act ("CSA") makes it illegal under federal law to manufacture, distribute, or dispense marijuana. Many states impose and enforce similar prohibitions. Notwithstanding the federal ban, as of the date of this guidance, 20 states and the District of Columbia have legalized certain marijuana-related activity. In light of these developments, U.S. Department of Justice Deputy Attorney General James M. Cole issued a memorandum (the "Cole Memo") to all United States Attorneys providing updated guidance to federal prosecutors concerning marijuana enforcement under the CSA. The Cole Memo guidance applies to all of DOJ's federal enforcement activity, including civil enforcement and criminal investigations and prosecutions, concerning marijuana in all states.

[T]he Cole Memo provides guidance to DOJ attorneys and law enforcement to focus their enforcement resources on persons or organizations whose conduct interferes with any one or more of the following important priorities (the "Cole Memo priorities").

This FinCEN guidance clarifies how financial institutions can provide services to marijuana-related businesses consistent with their BSA obligations. In general, the decision to open, close, or refuse any particular account or relationship should be made by each financial institution based on a number of factors specific to that institution. These factors may include its particular business objectives, an evaluation of the risks associated with offering a particular product or service, and its capacity to manage those risks effectively. Thorough customer due diligence is a critical aspect of making this assessment.

In assessing the risk of providing services to a marijuana-related business, a financial institution should conduct customer due diligence that includes: (i) verifying with the appropriate state authorities whether the business is duly licensed and registered; (ii) reviewing the license application (and related documentation) submitted by the business for obtaining a state license to operate its marijuana-related business; (iii) requesting from state licensing and enforcement authorities available information about the business and related parties; (iv) developing an understanding of the normal and expected activity for the business, including the types of products to be sold and the type of customers to be served (e.g., medical versus recreational customers); (v) ongoing monitoring of publicly available sources for adverse information about the business and related parties; (vi) ongoing monitoring for suspicious activity, including for any of the red flags described in this guidance; and (vii) refreshing information obtained as part of customer due diligence on a periodic basis and commensurate with the risk. With respect to information regarding state licensure obtained in connection with such customer due diligence, a financial institution may reasonably rely on the accuracy of information provided by state licensing authorities, where states make such information available.

As part of its customer due diligence, a financial institution should consider whether a marijuana-related business implicates one of the Cole Memo priorities or violates state law. This is a particularly important factor for a financial institution to consider when assessing the risk of providing financial services to a marijuana-related business. Considering this factor also enables the financial institution to provide information in BSA reports pertinent to law enforcement's priorities. A financial institution that decides to provide financial services to a marijuana-related business would be required to file suspicious activity reports ("SARs") as described below.

The obligation to file a SAR is unaffected by any state law that legalizes marijuana-related activity. A financial institution is required to file a SAR if, consistent with FinCEN regulations, the financial institution knows, suspects, or has reason to suspect that a transaction conducted or attempted by, at, or through the financial institution: (i) involves funds derived from illegal activity or is an attempt to disguise funds derived from illegal activity; (ii) is designed to evade regulations promulgated under the BSA, or (iii) lacks a business or apparent lawful purpose.[5] Because federal law prohibits the distribution and sale of marijuana, financial transactions involving a marijuana-related business would generally involve funds derived from illegal activity. Therefore, a financial institution is required to file a SAR on activity involving a marijuana-related business (including those duly licensed under state law), in accordance with this guidance and FinCEN's suspicious activity reporting requirements and related thresholds.

5. *See, e.g.*, 31 CFR § 1020.320. Financial institutions shall file with FinCEN, to the extent and in the manner required, a report of any suspicious transaction relevant to a possible violation of law or regulation. A financial institution may also file with FinCEN a SAR with respect to any suspicious transaction that it believes is relevant to the possible violation of any law or regulation but whose reporting is not required by FinCEN regulations.

One of the BSA's purposes is to require financial institutions to file reports that are highly useful in criminal investigations and proceedings. The guidance below furthers this objective by assisting financial institutions in determining how to file a SAR that facilitates law enforcement's access to information pertinent to a priority.

"Marijuana Limited" SAR Filings

A financial institution providing financial services to a marijuana-related business that it reasonably believes, based on its customer due diligence, does not implicate one of the Cole Memo priorities or violate state law should file a "Marijuana Limited" SAR. The content of this SAR should be limited to the following information: (i) identifying information of the subject and related parties; (ii) addresses of the subject and related parties; (iii) the fact that the filing institution is filing the SAR solely because the subject is engaged in a marijuana-related business; and (iv) the fact that no additional suspicious activity has been identified. Financial institutions should use the term "MARIJUANA LIMITED" in the narrative section.

A financial institution should follow FinCEN's existing guidance on the timing of filing continuing activity reports for the same activity initially reported on a "Marijuana Limited" SAR. The continuing activity report may contain the same limited content as the initial SAR, plus details about the amount of deposits, withdrawals, and transfers in the account since the last SAR. However, if, in the course of conducting customer due diligence (including ongoing monitoring for red flags), the financial institution detects changes in activity that potentially implicate one of the Cole Memo priorities or violate state law, the financial institution should file a "Marijuana Priority" SAR.

"Marijuana Priority" SAR Filings

A financial institution filing a SAR on a marijuana-related business that it reasonably believes, based on its customer due diligence, implicates one of the Cole Memo priorities or violates state law should file a "Marijuana Priority" SAR. The content of this SAR should include comprehensive detail in accordance with existing regulations and guidance. Details particularly relevant to law enforcement in this context include: (i) identifying information of the subject and related parties; (ii) addresses of the subject and related parties; (iii) details regarding the enforcement priorities the financial institution believes have been implicated; and (iv) dates, amounts, and other relevant details of financial transactions involved in the suspicious activity. Financial institutions should use the term "MARIJUANA PRIORITY" in the narrative section to help law enforcement distinguish these SARs.[7]

---

7. FinCEN recognizes that a financial institution filing a SAR on a marijuana-related business may not always be well-positioned to determine whether the business implicates one of the Cole Memo priorities or violates state law, and thus which terms would be most appropriate to include (i.e., "Marijuana Limited" or "Marijuana Priority"). For example, a financial institution could be providing services to another domestic financial institution that, in turn, provides financial services to a marijuana-related business. Similarly, a financial institution could be providing services to a non-financial customer that provides goods or services to a marijuana-related business

"Marijuana Termination" SAR Filings

If a financial institution deems it necessary to terminate a relationship with a marijuana-related business in order to maintain an effective anti-money laundering compliance program, it should file a SAR and note in the narrative the basis for the termination. Financial institutions should use the term "MARIJUANA TERMINATION" in the narrative section. To the extent the financial institution becomes aware that the marijuana-related business seeks to move to a second financial institution, FinCEN urges the first institution to use Section 314(b) voluntary information sharing (if it qualifies) to alert the second financial institution of potential illegal activity.

Red Flags to Distinguish Priority SARs

The following red flags indicate that a marijuana-related business may be engaged in activity that implicates one of the Cole Memo priorities or violates state law. These red flags indicate only possible signs of such activity, and also do not constitute an exhaustive list. It is thus important to view any red flag(s) in the context of other indicators and facts, such as the financial institution's knowledge about the underlying parties obtained through its customer due diligence. Further, the presence of any of these red flags in a given transaction or business arrangement may indicate a need for additional due diligence, which could include seeking information from other involved financial institutions under Section 314(b). These red flags are based primarily upon schemes and typologies described in SARs or identified by our law enforcement and regulatory partners, and may be updated in future guidance.

- A customer appears to be using a state-licensed marijuana-related business as a front or pretext to launder money derived from other criminal activity (i.e., not related to marijuana) or derived from marijuana-related activity not permitted under state law. Relevant indicia could include:
  - The business receives substantially more revenue than may reasonably be expected given the relevant limitations imposed by the state in which it operates.
  - The business receives substantially more revenue than its local competitors or than might be expected given the population demographics.
  - The business is depositing more cash than is commensurate with the amount of marijuana-related revenue it is reporting for federal and state tax purposes.
  - The business is unable to demonstrate that its revenue is derived exclusively from the sale of marijuana in compliance with state law, as opposed to

(e.g., a commercial landlord that leases property to a marijuana-related business). In such circumstances where services are being provided indirectly, the financial institution may file SARs based on existing regulations and guidance without distinguishing between "Marijuana Limited" and "Marijuana Priority." Whether the financial institution decides to provide indirect services to a marijuana-related business is a risk-based decision that depends on a number of factors specific to that institution and the relevant circumstances. In making this decision, the institution should consider the Cole Memo priorities, to the extent applicable.

revenue derived from (i) the sale of other illicit drugs, (ii) the sale of marijuana not in compliance with state law, or (iii) other illegal activity.

- The business makes cash deposits or withdrawals over a short period of time that are excessive relative to local competitors or the expected activity of the business.
- Deposits apparently structured to avoid Currency Transaction Report ("CTR") requirements.
- Rapid movement of funds, such as cash deposits followed by immediate cash withdrawals.
- Deposits by third parties with no apparent connection to the accountholder.
- Excessive commingling of funds with the personal account of the business's owner(s) or manager(s), or with accounts of seemingly unrelated businesses.
- Individuals conducting transactions for the business appear to be acting on behalf of other, undisclosed parties of interest.
- Financial statements provided by the business to the financial institution are inconsistent with actual account activity.
- A surge in activity by third parties offering goods or services to marijuana-related businesses, such as equipment suppliers or shipping servicers.

- The business is unable to produce satisfactory documentation or evidence to demonstrate that it is duly licensed and operating consistently with state law.
- The business is unable to demonstrate the legitimate source of significant outside investments.
- A customer seeks to conceal or disguise involvement in marijuana-related business activity. For example, the customer may be using a business with a non-descript name (e.g., a "consulting," "holding," or "management" company) that purports to engage in commercial activity unrelated to marijuana, but is depositing cash that smells like marijuana.
- Review of publicly available sources and databases about the business, its owner(s), manager(s), or other related parties, reveal negative information, such as a criminal record, involvement in the illegal purchase or sale of drugs, violence, or other potential connections to illicit activity.
- The business, its owner(s), manager(s), or other related parties are, or have been, subject to an enforcement action by the state or local authorities responsible for administering or enforcing marijuana-related laws or regulations.
- A marijuana-related business engages in international or interstate activity, including by receiving cash deposits from locations outside the state in which the business operates, making or receiving frequent or large interstate transfers, or otherwise transacting with persons or entities located in different states or countries.

- The owner(s) or manager(s) of a marijuana-related business reside outside the state in which the business is located.
- A marijuana-related business is located on federal property or the marijuana sold by the business was grown on federal property.
- A marijuana-related business's proximity to a school is not compliant with state law.
- A marijuana-related business purporting to be a "non-profit" is engaged in commercial activity inconsistent with that classification, or is making excessive payments to its manager(s) or employee(s).

FinCEN's enforcement priorities in connection with this guidance will focus on matters of systemic or significant failures, and not isolated lapses in technical compliance. Financial institutions with questions about this guidance are encouraged to contact FinCEN's Resource Center at (800) 767-2825, where industry questions can be addressed and monitored for the purpose of providing any necessary additional guidance.

It appears that most bankers have remained wary of doing business with marijuana companies following the Department of Justice and Financial Crimes Enforcement Network memos. The CEO of the Colorado Bankers Association, Don Childears, said of the guidance: "At best, this amounts to 'serve these customers at your own risk' and it emphasizes all of the risks." Matt Ferner, *Obama's Marijuana Banking Rules Don't Change Anything, Bankers Say,* HuffingtonPost.com, February 21, 2014.

In a section of *Marijuana, Banks, and Federalism* that was not included in the excerpt above, Julie Anderson Hill explained why the FinCEN and Department of Justice guidance did not solve the marijuana banking problem:

> It is not hard to see why financial institutions are still skittish. Marijuana is still illegal under federal law. The FinCEN and Department of Justice guidance does not change that. Any bank or credit union providing services could face criminal prosecution at any time. Even if financial institutions were willing to rely on public statements about enforcement priorities, the Department of Justice's assurance to banks is quite weak. Actual enforcement practices could change anytime—with or without warning.
>
> Furthermore, the federal guidance seems to set the bar for financial institution compliance quite high. When comparing compliance costs with the profits available from the growing but still small marijuana industry, banking the industry may not make economic sense. The paperwork associated with anti-money laundering reporting may be enough to dissuade some institutions from banking some marijuana businesses. And then there is the problem of confirming that none of the institution's customers deal with marijuana in a way that implicates the Department of Justice's enforcement priorities. Among other things, a financial institution needs

> to ensure that its customers do not sell marijuana to minors and do not sell marijuana to customers that may transport it across state lines. Such due diligence efforts will be costly. Due to these concerns, some financial institutions that will accept accounts from marijuana growers will not accept accounts from marijuana dispensaries. Most financial institutions, however, seem to avoid marijuana businesses altogether.

Although most banks continue to stay away from marijuana businesses, a few "local banks and credit unions have been quietly taking on marijuana businesses as customers. A 2015 report from American Banker showed 266 of the nation's nearly 6,200 financial institutions had accounts with marijuana-related businesses." Brooke Edwards Staggs, *California Seeks Role in Linking Pot Industry to Banking Services*, ORANGE COUNTY REGISTER (Jan. 4, 2017). Still, reports suggest that many, perhaps most, marijuana businesses have not been able to get banking services. A survey conducted in late 2015 by *Marijuana Business Daily*, for example, found that about 60% of the 400 marijuana companies polled did not have bank accounts. Becky Olson, *Chart of the Week: 60% of Cannabis Companies Don't Have Bank Accounts*, MARIJUANA BUSINESS DAILY (Dec. 14, 2015).

3. Options for Resolving the Conflict between Federal and State Marijuana Laws

A number of different bills have been introduced in Congress over the years to try to resolve the conflict between federal prohibition and state legalization. Until recently, none of these proposals seemed to have a realistic chance of passing, or even of receiving a vote on the floor of the House or the Senate.

In June 2018, however, two prominent Senators—Elizabeth Warren (D-MA) and Cory Gardner (R-CO)—introduced a bipartisan bill that would change federal marijuana law to accommodate state reforms. Not long after the legislation was introduced, President Donald Trump said that he would "probably end up supporting" the bill, known as the Strengthening the Tenth Amendment Through Entrusting States (STATES) Act. With bipartisan support in the Senate and the possible backing of the President, some observers think there is an outside possibility that the proposal could become law. Below is an official summary of the bill, followed by the bill itself.

Do you think this is an effective way to resolve the conflict between state and federal marijuana laws? Are there other options that you think might work better?

The STATES Act

Senator Elizabeth Warren and Senator Cory Gardner (2018)

Background:

- Today, 46 states have laws permitting or decriminalizing marijuana or marijuana-based products. Washington D.C., Puerto Rico, Guam, and a number of tribes have similar laws.

- As states began developing their own approaches to marijuana enforcement the Department of Justice issued guidance to support these state actions and focus law enforcement resources.
- However, this guidance was withdrawn in 2018, causing legal uncertainty that severely limits these state laboratories of democracy, creates public health and safety issues, and undermines the state regulatory regimes.
- As more states, territories, and tribes thoughtfully consider updates to marijuana regulations, often through voter-initiated referendums, it is critical that Congress take immediate steps to safeguard their right to do so.

Purpose:

- The Strengthening the Tenth Amendment Through Entrusting States (STATES) Act ensures that each State has the right to determine for itself the best approach to marijuana within its borders. The bill also extends these protections to Washington D.C, U.S. territories, and federally recognized tribes, and contains common-sense guardrails to ensure that states, territories, and tribes regulating marijuana do so in a manner that is safe and respectful of the impacts on their neighbors.

What The Bill Does:

- Amends the Controlled Substances Act (21 U.S.C. § 801 *et seq.*) (CSA) so that—as long as states and tribes comply with a few basic protections—its provisions no longer apply to any person acting in compliance with State or tribal laws relating to the manufacture, production, possession, distribution, dispensation, administration, or delivery of marijuana.
- Amends the definition of "marihuana" under the CSA (21 U.S.C. § 802(16)) to exclude industrial hemp, as defined in section 7606(b) of the Agricultural Act of 2014 (7 U.S.C. § 5940(b)).
- The bill does not alter CSA Section 417 (prohibition on endangering human life while manufacturing a controlled substance) and maintains the prohibition on employing persons under age 18 in marijuana operations, two federal requirements with which states, territories, and tribes must continue to comply.
- The bill prohibits the distribution of marijuana at transportation safety facilities such as rest areas and truck stops (Section 409).
- The bill does not allow for the distribution or sale of marijuana to persons under the age of 21 (Section 418) other than for medical purposes.
- To address financial issues caused by federal prohibition, the bill clearly states that compliant transactions are not trafficking and do not result in proceeds of an unlawful transaction.

Strengthening the Tenth Amendment Through Entrusting States Act

S.3032

115th Congress (2017–2018)

SECTION 1. SHORT TITLE.

This Act may be cited as the "Strengthening the Tenth Amendment Through Entrusting States Act" or the "STATES Act".

SEC. 2. RULE REGARDING APPLICATION TO MARIHUANA.

(a) In General.—Part G of the Controlled Substances Act (21 U.S.C. 801 et seq.) is amended by adding at the end the following:

"RULE REGARDING APPLICATION TO MARIHUANA

"Sec. 710. (a) Notwithstanding any other provision of law, the provisions of this title as applied to marihuana, other than the provisions described in subsection (c) and other than as provided in subsection (d), shall not apply to any person acting in compliance with State law relating to the manufacture, production, possession, distribution, dispensation, administration, or delivery of marihuana.

"(b) Notwithstanding any other provision of law, the provisions of this title related to marihuana, other than the provisions described in subsection (c) and other than as provided in subsection (d), shall not apply to any person acting in compliance with the law of a Federally recognized Indian tribe within its jurisdiction in Indian Country, as defined in section 1151 of title 18, United States Code, related to the manufacture, production, possession, distribution, dispensation, administration, or delivery of marihuana so long as such jurisdiction is located within a state that permits, respectively, manufacture, production, possession, distribution, dispensation, administration, or delivery of marihuana.

"(c) The provisions described in this subsection are—

"(1) section 401(a)(1),[*] with respect to a violation of section 409[**] or 418;[***]

"(2) section 409;

"(3) section 417;[****] and

"(4) section 418.

---

* Codified at 21 U.S.C. § 841(a)(1), this section makes it unlawful "to manufacture, distribute, or dispense, or possess with intent to manufacture, distribute, or dispense, a controlled substance." [*Footnote by casebook author.*]

** Codified at 21 U.S.C. § 849, this section makes it unlawful to distribute or possess with intent to distribute "a controlled substance in or on, or within 1,000 feet of, a truck stop or a safety rest area." [*Footnote by casebook author.*]

*** Codified at 21 U.S.C. § 859, this section makes it unlawful to distribute "a controlled substance to a person under twenty-one years of age." [*Footnote by casebook author.*]

**** Codified at 21 U.S.C. § 858, this section makes it unlawful to "create[] a substantial risk of harm to human life" while manufacturing a controlled substance. [*Footnote by casebook author.*]

"(d) Subsection (a) shall not apply to any person who—

"(1) violates the Controlled Substances Act with respect to any other controlled substance;

"(2) notwithstanding compliance with State or tribal law, knowingly or intentionally manufactures, produces, possesses, distributes, dispenses, administers, or delivers any other marihuana in violation of the laws of the State or tribe in which such manufacture, production, possession, distribution, dispensation, administration, or delivery occurs; or

"(3) employs or hires any person under 18 years of age to manufacture, produce, distribute, dispense, administer, or deliver marihuana.".

(b) Definition Of Marihuana.—Section 102(16) of the Controlled Substances Act (21 U.S.C. 802(16)) is amended—

(1) by striking "or the sterilized" and inserting "the sterilized"; and

(2) by striking the period at the end and inserting ", or industrial hemp (as defined in section 7606(b) of the Agricultural Act of 2014 (7 U.S.C. 5940(b)))."

. . .

SEC. 4. DISTRIBUTION TO PERSONS UNDER AGE 21.

Section 418 of the Controlled Substances Act (21 U.S.C. 859) is amended—

. . .

(3) by adding at the end the following:

"(c) Subsections (a) and (b) shall not apply to any person at least 18 years of age who distributes medicinal marihuana to a person under 21 years of age in compliance with section 710.".

SEC. 5. RULE OF CONSTRUCTION.

(a) In General.—Conduct in compliance with this Act and the amendments made by this Act—

(1) shall not be unlawful;

(2) shall not constitute trafficking in a controlled substance under section 401 of the Controlled Substances Act (21 U.S.C. 841) or any other provision of law; and

(3) shall not constitute the basis for forfeiture of property under section 511 of the Controlled Substances Act (21 U.S.C. 881) or section 981 of title 18, United States Code.

(b) Proceeds.—The proceeds from any transaction in compliance with this Act and the amendments made by this Act shall not be deemed to be the proceeds of an unlawful transaction under section 1956 or 1957 of title 18, United States Code, or any other provision of law.

The STATES Act appears to have the best chance of passing Congress (although the odds of this happening in the current Congress are still quite low). A more far-reaching proposal from Senator Cory Booker may have longer odds of becoming law, but is no less noteworthy. Senator Booker introduced his Marijuana Justice Act proposal in 2017. The bill is reproduced below. Do you think the Marijuana Justice Act is preferable to the STATES Act? Or would you favor another approach to resolving the conflict between federal and state marijuana laws?

Marijuana Justice Act of 2017

S.1689

115th Congress (2017–2018)

A Bill

To amend the Controlled Substances Act to provide for a new rule regarding the application of the Act to marihuana, and for other purposes.

Be it enacted by the Senate and House of Representatives of the United States of America in Congress assembled,

SECTION 1. SHORT TITLE.

This Act may be cited as the "Marijuana Justice Act of 2017".

SEC. 2. DE-SCHEDULING MARIHUANA.

(a) Marihuana Removed From Schedule Of Controlled Substances.—Subsection (c) of schedule I of section 202(c) of the Controlled Substances Act (21 U.S.C. 812) is amended—

(1) by striking "marihuana"; and

(2) by striking "tetrahydrocannabinols".

(b) Removal Of Prohibition On Import And Export.—Section 1010(b) of the Controlled Substances Import and Export Act (21 U.S.C. 960) is amended—

(1) in paragraph (1)—

(A) in subparagraph (F), by inserting "or" after the semicolon;

(B) by striking subparagraph (G); and

(C) by redesignating subparagraph (H) as subparagraph (G);

(2) in paragraph (2)—

(A) in subparagraph (F), by inserting "or" after the semicolon;

(B) by striking subparagraph (G); and

(C) by redesignating subparagraph (H) as subparagraph (G);

(3) in paragraph (3), by striking "paragraphs (1), (2), and (4)" and inserting "paragraphs (1) and (2)";

(4) by striking paragraph (4); and

(5) by redesignating paragraphs (5), (6), and (7) as paragraphs (4), (5), and (6), respectively.

(c) Conforming Amendments To Controlled Substances Act.—The Controlled Substances Act (21 U.S.C. 801 et seq.) is amended—

(1) in section 102(44) (21 U.S.C. 802(44)), by striking "marihuana,";

(2) in section 401(b) (21 U.S.C. 841(b))—

(A) in paragraph (1)—

(i) in subparagraph (A)—

(I) in clause (vi), by inserting "or" after the semicolon;

(II) by striking (vii); and

(III) by redesignating clause (viii) as clause (vii);

(ii) in subparagraph (B)—

(I) by striking clause (vii); and

(II) by redesignating clause (viii) as clause (vii);

(iii) in subparagraph (C), in the first sentence, by striking "subparagraphs (A), (B), and (D)" and inserting "subparagraphs (A) and (B)";

(iv) by striking subparagraph (D);

(v) by redesignating subparagraph (E) as subparagraph (D); and

(vi) in subparagraph (D)(i), as so redesignated, by striking "subparagraphs (C) and (D)" and inserting "subparagraph (C)";

(B) by striking paragraph (4); and

(C) by redesignating paragraphs (5), (6), and (7) as paragraphs (4), (5), and (6), respectively;

(3) in section 402(c)(2)(B) (21 U.S.C. 842(c)(2)(B)), by striking ", marihuana,";

(4) in section 403(d)(1) (21 U.S.C. 843(d)(1)), by striking ", marihuana,";

(5) in section 418(a) (21 U.S.C. 859(a)), by striking the last sentence;

(6) in section 419(a) (21 U.S.C. 860(a)), by striking the last sentence;

(7) in section 422(d) (21 U.S.C. 863(d))—

(A) in the matter preceding paragraph (1), by striking "marijuana,"; and

(B) in paragraph (5), by striking ", such as a marihuana cigarette,"; and

(8) in section 516(d) (21 U.S.C. 886(d)), by striking "section 401(b)(6)" each place the term appears and inserting "section 401(b)(5)".

(d) Other Conforming Amendments.—

(1) NATIONAL FOREST SYSTEM DRUG CONTROL ACT OF 1986.—The National Forest System Drug Control Act of 1986 (16 U.S.C. 559b et seq.) is amended—

(A) in section 15002(a) (16 U.S.C. 559b(a)) by striking "marijuana and other";

(B) in section 15003(2) (16 U.S.C. 559c(2)) by striking "marijuana and other"; and

(C) in section 15004(2) (16 U.S.C. 559d(2)) by striking "marijuana and other".

(2) INTERCEPTION OF COMMUNICATIONS.—Section 2516 of title 18, United States Code, is amended—

(A) in subsection (1)(e), by striking "marihuana,"; and

(B) in subsection (2) by striking "marihuana,".

SEC. 3. INELIGIBILITY FOR CERTAIN FUNDS.

(a) Definitions.—In this section—

(1) the term "covered State" means a State that has not enacted a statute legalizing marijuana in the State;

(2) the term "disproportionate arrest rate" means—

(A) the percentage of minority individuals arrested for a marijuana related offense in a State is higher than the percentage of the non-minority individual population of the State, as determined by the most recent census data; or

(B) the percentage of low-income individuals arrested for a marijuana offense in a State is higher than the percentage of the population of the State that are not low-income individuals, as determined by the most recent census data;

(3) the term "disproportionate incarceration rate" means the percentage of minority individuals incarcerated for a marijuana related offense in a State is higher than the percentage of the non-minority individual population of the State, as determined by the most recent census data;

(4) the term "low-income individual" means an individual whose taxable income (as defined in section 63 of the Internal Revenue Code of 1986) is equal to or below the maximum dollar amount for the 15 percent rate bracket applicable to the individual under section 1 of the Internal Revenue Code of 1986;

(5) the term "marijuana" has the meaning given the term "marihuana" in section 102 of the Controlled Substances Act (21 U.S.C. 802); and

(6) the term "minority individual" means an individual who is a member of a racial or ethnic minority group.

(b) Ineligibility For Certain Funds.—

(1) IN GENERAL.—For any fiscal year beginning after the date of enactment of this Act in which the Attorney General, acting through the

Director of the Bureau of Justice Assistance, determines that a covered State has a disproportionate arrest rate or a disproportionate incarceration rate for marijuana offenses, the covered State—

(A) shall not be eligible to receive any Federal funds for the construction or staffing of a prison or jail; and

(B) shall be subject to not more than a 10-percent reduction of the funds that would otherwise be allocated for that fiscal year to the covered State under subpart 1 of part E of title I of the Omnibus Crime Control and Safe Streets Act of 1968 (42 U.S.C. 3750 et seq.), whether characterized as the Edward Byrne Memorial State and Local Law Enforcement Assistance Programs, the Local Government Law Enforcement Block Grants Program, the Edward Byrne Memorial Justice Assistance Grant Program, or otherwise.

(2) FUNDS FOR CERTAIN PROGRAMMING.—For purposes of paragraph (1)(A), Federal funds for the construction or staffing of a prison or jail shall not include Federal funds used by a prison or jail to carry out recidivism reduction programming or drug addiction treatment.

(3) REALLOCATION.—Any amounts not awarded to a covered State because of a determination under paragraph (1) shall be deposited in the Community Reinvestment Fund established under section 4.

(c) Expungement Of Marijuana Offense Convictions.—Each Federal court shall issue an order expunging each conviction for a marijuana use or possession offense entered by the court before the date of enactment of this Act.

(d) Sentencing Review.—

(1) IN GENERAL.—For any individual who was sentenced to a term of imprisonment for a Federal criminal offense involving marijuana before the date of enactment of this Act and is still serving such term of imprisonment, the court that imposed the sentence, shall, on motion of the individual, the Director of the Bureau of Prisons, the attorney for the Government, or the court, conduct a sentencing hearing.

(2) POTENTIAL REDUCED RESENTENCING.—After a sentencing hearing under paragraph (1), a court may impose a sentence on the individual as if this Act, and the amendments made by this Act, were in effect at the time the offense was committed.

(e) Right Of Action.—

(1) IN GENERAL.—An individual who is aggrieved by a disproportionate arrest rate or a disproportionate incarceration rate of a State may bring a civil action in an appropriate district court of the United States.

(2) RELIEF.—In a civil action brought under this subsection in which the plaintiff prevails, the court shall—

(A) grant all necessary equitable and legal relief, including declaratory relief; and

(B) issue an order requiring the Attorney General, acting through the Director of the Bureau of Justice Assistance, to—

(i) declare the State to be ineligible to receive any Federal funds for the construction or staffing of a prison or jail in accordance with subsection (b)(1)(A); and

(ii) reduce grant funding of the State in accordance with subsection (b)(1)(B).

SEC. 4. COMMUNITY REINVESTMENT FUND.

(a) Establishment.—There is established in the Treasury of the United States a fund, to be known as the "Community Reinvestment Fund" (referred to in this section as the "Fund").

(b) Deposits.—The Fund shall consist of—

(1) any amounts not awarded to a covered State because of a determination under section 3(b)(1); and

(2) any amounts otherwise appropriated to the Fund.

(c) Use Of Fund Amounts.—Amounts in the Fund shall be available to the Secretary of Housing and Urban Development to establish a grant program to reinvest in communities most affected by the war on drugs, which shall include providing grants to impacted communities for programs such as—

(1) job training;

(2) reentry services;

(3) expenses related to the expungement of convictions;

(4) public libraries;

(5) community centers;

(6) programs and opportunities dedicated to youth;

(7) the special purpose fund discussed below; and

(8) health education programs.

(d) Availability Of Fund Amounts.—Amounts in the Fund shall be available without fiscal year limitation.

(e) Authorization Of Appropriations.—There are authorized to be appropriated to the Fund $500,000,000 for each of fiscal years 2018 through 2040.

Chapter 9

International Drug Control

Most criminal law and public health issues are primarily matters of domestic concern. To be sure, countries can learn from one another by sharing knowledge about questions like how to combat drunk driving or how to improve access to health care. But the criminal laws governing driving under the influence in one country are not likely to impact the citizens of other countries.

This is not the case when it comes to drug control. As with any consumer good, the production and sale of a controlled substance in one country has the potential to impact the price, availability, and usage of the drug in other countries. For this reason, a group of treaties and international agencies aim to control the international market for controlled substances.

This chapter examines the international drug control regime. It begins with an overview of the international market for illegal drugs in Section A. Section B moves from the drug market to drug laws with an examination of drug control treaties and implementing organizations. Finally, Section C focuses on the role of the United States in international drug control, covering issues including the extraterritorial application of United States drug laws, United States-led crop eradication campaigns, and methods the United States employs to encourage cooperation by so-called drug producer countries in its drug war strategy.

A. The International Market for Controlled Substances

Disciplining Globalization: International Law, Illegal Trade, and the Case of Narcotics
Chantal Thomas

24 Michigan Journal of International Law 549 (2003)

While the omni-term "globalization" can mean many (probably too many) different things, from a purely material standpoint the term refers to the dramatic increase in contemporary times of international production and consumption.

After World War II, world trade in goods "grew at a rate twice as fast as the overall world economy." For the United States, "trade volume multiplied nearly twentyfold" during the same time frame. In the globalized economy, intricate chains of manufacture, assembly, distribution, and retail link together an ever greater number of countries. Lan Cao's description of modern automobile production is classic: "A Chevy may be built in Mexico from imported parts and then re-imported into the United States; a Ford built in German plants by Turkish workers and sold in Hong Kong and Nigeria; a Toyota Camry designed by an American designer at Toyota's Newport Beach California Calty Design Research Center, assembled at the Georgetown, Kentucky plant from American-made parts (except that the engine and drive trains are still Japanese) and then test driven at Toyota's Arizona proving ground."

Car production seems a typical facet of the global production. Illegal drug production, however, exceeds car production as a proportion of the global economy. The United Nations Office for Drug Control and Crime Prevention (UNODCCP) reports that the last two decades have witnessed "the global spread of drug trafficking," rendering it "now truly a global phenomenon." The complexity of narcotics trade rivals that of multinational corporations. The United States Bureau for International Narcotics and Law has observed that "the relatively simple charts of drug flows" of previous eras "now resemble schematic drawings of intricate . . . networks tying nearly every country in the world to the . . . drug production and trafficking countries."

In addition to sharing the same characteristics, the globalization of licit goods and illicit narcotics share many of the same causes. Advances in communications technology constitute one such cause; for example, the telecommunications network that facilitates international capital investment also facilitates money laundering for the illicit narcotics trade. In addition, modern transportation (such as air, rail, road, and even national mail and commercial courier services) facilitates the production and distribution of narcotics. Further, because narcotics are so frequently smuggled in otherwise legal distribution chains, often it is not only the same types of technology, but the same actual shipment, that drives trade in both licit goods and illicit narcotics.

There is one final connection between the globalization of licit and illicit trade, found in international trade law itself. The primary multilateral trade agreements name the expansion of world trade as their central objective. Most believe that these agreements have largely achieved their objective: John Jackson, for example, has asserted that "to a great extent, contemporary international economic interdependence can be attributed to the success" of the multilateral trade regime in expanding global trade. The expansion in communications, transportation, and trade volume also facilitates trafficking, so that the institutionalized expansion of legal trade has generated "spillover effects" expanding illegal trade.

In the twentieth century, the licit international trade regime progressed from a relatively antagonistic approach to imports to an ever more liberal one. In the period after World War I and before World War II, the governments of Europe and the United States engaged in unabashed protectionism. The United States, for example, adopted tariff levels under its Smoot-Hawley Tariff Act of 1930 that resulted in the highest average tariff imposed on dutiable goods in U.S. history. Following World War II, most economists and statesmen concluded that the ills of the interwar period—both the economic decline and the political hostilities—had been exacerbated by the protectionist policies of the world's major powers. Consequently, the leading governments after World War II sought to construct a trade regime that would prevent a return to such widespread protectionism. The resulting General Agreement on Tariffs and Trade (hereinafter GATT) established basic principles of non-discrimination and a mechanism through which governments could negotiate the gradual reduction of trade barriers.

At the same time that the international regime for governing trade in licit goods was slowly shifting from a protectionist to a liberal approach, the international narcotics regime was effecting a shift in the opposite direction.

For most of the nineteenth century, the British championed the expansion of international trade in narcotics. Indeed, through its production stronghold in India, the narcotics trade provided a significant source of revenue for the British Empire. So dear was the opium market that Britain went to war with China over the latter's refusal to admit British imports of opium. Of course, the preference for liberalization was not total—the British trade in opium traveled through monopolies—but the British unquestionably favored the minimization of import restrictions on narcotics at this time. At the turn of the twentieth century, both opium and cocaine were widely used by consumers in the developed world in a variety of over-the-counter food and medicine products.

Between the conclusion of the Opium War and the first modern multilateral agreement regulating trade in narcotics—the Hague Convention of 1912—the prevalent attitude in the West toward narcotics shifted considerably. The Hague Convention of 1912 obliged signatories to "confine to medical and legitimate purposes the manufacture, sale and use of" opium, heroin, morphine, and cocaine. The next several agreements built on this model of medical control. The Geneva Convention of 1925 required Member States to furnish statistics supporting their estimates of "medical and legitimate" narcotics imports and exports. The Geneva Convention of 1931 required Member States to extend their export control schemes to all States, not just other members. Finally, the 1948 Paris Protocol required Member States to report information about any "medical and scientific" drugs not listed in the 1931 Convention that could have harmful effects or could be subject to abuse. The Protocol also provided for the application of the 1931 Convention's controls to any drug deemed harmful by the World Health Organization.

Thus, the agreements in the first half of the twentieth century gradually strengthened the medical controls narcotics trade. In doing so, the agreements evinced an "administrative" approach—neither liberal, nor prohibitive—that sought to circumscribe, but not to prevent, narcotics production and trade. These early agreements sought neither to expand nor to eliminate narcotics production and trade, but rather to control it in accordance with "medical and scientific" concerns.

The second half of the twentieth century saw the U.N. narcotics regime shift from an administrative model toward an increasingly prohibitionist one. The 1961 United Nations Single Convention on Narcotic Drugs marked the beginning of this shift. On the one hand, the 1961 Convention retained the administrative focus, though it tightened controls on members' ability to produce and trade narcotics for medical purposes. On the other, it sowed the seeds of a punitive approach by requiring Member States to establish as criminal offenses the production or trade of narcotics. The 1961 Convention also required States to establish conspiracy as a crime.

The 1961 Convention's intermingling of the medical-administrative and punitive approaches is perhaps best found in an important exception to the criminalization provisions: where unauthorized narcotics production or trade occurred at the hands of "abusers of drugs," a signatory could adopt measures of "treatment, education, after-care, rehabilitation and social reintegration" as an alternative response.

The medical, rehabilitative tone of the 1961 Convention shifted to a more punitive register in the 1988 Convention on Narcotic Drugs and Psychotropic Substances. The 1961 Convention's "drug abuser" exception narrowed in 1988 to production only "for personal consumption," or otherwise to "cases of a minor nature." Moreover, the 1988 Convention multiplied the number of offenses deemed criminal: Now not only were production, trade and conspiracy criminal, but knowing acquisition, possession, use, conversion or transfer of property derived the reform. By expanding the scope of the criminal and reducing the reach of the rehabilitative, the 1988 Convention shifted away from the administrative and toward the prohibitive mode.

The latest U.N. agreement, the Convention on Transnational Organized Crime of 2000, expands the range of criminal offenses even further. In addition to the offenses identified by the 1961 and 1988 Conventions, the 2000 Convention adds anti-racketeering type provisions, criminalizing "participation in an organized criminal group" and "laundering of the proceeds of crime." The 2000 Convention also makes criminal both the promise, offer, or gift of reward to, and the solicitation or acceptance of reward by, a public official to facilitate criminal activity.

Comparing the development of the international trade regime to the international narcotics regime reveals opposing trends. The regime governing general trade in goods has shifted from a protectionist regulatory model, to an administrative model, and finally toward a liberalized model. The regime governing trade in narcotics, however, has moved from a liberalized model to an administrative model, to an expansively prohibitionist model.

The GATT/WTO system operates on the foundational belief that liberalization of international trade in goods will maximize world welfare. The international narcotics regime operates on the belief that prohibition of trade in narcotic drugs will do the same. Why should liberalization of one set of goods be desirable, but liberalization in another set of goods be undesirable?

Like any species of market control, the criminalization of the international narcotics trade betrays the ambivalent impulses of "liberal governance." On the one hand, the market provides a grand theater for individual choice that is the *sine qua non* of prevailing liberal theory. On the other hand, governments maintain an infinite array of controls on the choices available to individuals in the market.

The tension between principles of liberalism and practices of market control emerges in both the trade regimes for legal goods and for illegal narcotics. In the GATT/WTO system, the principles of free trade are offset by exceptions allowing for trade restrictions. In the international narcotics regime, the backdrop of a liberalized international economic order contrasts with the foreground of narcotics prohibitionism.

Such puzzles should not be dismissed as unrelated idiosyncrasies of modern international governance. These conflicting regimes do relate to each other in an underlying framework, in which the discrepancy between liberalization and prohibition is mediated through the concept of normalcy in international trade: liberalization for "normal" international trade; restriction and prohibition for "abnormal" international trade. The normalcy concept organizes the apparent contradiction along parallel sides of a dichotomy.

World Drug Report, 2017

United Nations Office on Drugs and Crime (2017)

Harm caused by drug use remains considerable

An estimated quarter of a billion people, or around 5 per cent of the global adult population, used drugs at least once in 2015. Even more worrisome is the fact that about 29.5 million of those drug users, or 0.6 per cent of the global adult population, suffer from drug use disorders. This means that their drug use is harmful to the point that they may experience drug dependence and require treatment.

The magnitude of the harm caused by drug use is underlined by the estimated 28 million years of "healthy" life (disability-adjusted life years (DALYs)) lost worldwide in 2015 as a result of premature death and disability caused by drug use.

Of those years lost, 17 million were attributable solely to drug use disorders across all drug types. DALYs attributable to morbidity and mortality resulting from all causes of drug use have increased overall in the past decade.

Yet, with fewer than one in six persons with drug use disorders provided with treatment each year, the availability of and access to science-based services for the treatment of drug use disorders and related conditions remain limited.

Opioids, including heroin, remain the most harmful drug type in health terms. The use of opioids is associated with the risk of fatal and non-fatal overdoses; the risk of acquiring infectious diseases (such as HIV or hepatitis C) through unsafe injecting practices; and the risk of other medical and psychiatric co-morbidities.

The large number of premature deaths related to drugs are mostly avoidable. A significant proportion of those deaths is attributable to opioids. In addition, opioid use disorders account for the heaviest burden of disease attributable to drug use disorders: in 2015, almost 12 million DALYs, or 70 per cent of the global burden of disease attributable to drug use disorders, were attributable to opioids.

A problem in many countries, the harm caused by opioids is particularly evident in the United States of America. The misuse of pharmaceutical opioids, coupled with an increase in heroin and fentanyl use, has resulted in a combined and interrelated epidemic in the United States, as well as in an increase in morbidity and mortality related to opioids.

The United States accounts for approximately one quarter of the estimated number of drug-related deaths worldwide, including overdose deaths, which continue to rise. Mostly driven by opioids, overdose deaths in the United States more than tripled during the period 1999–2015, from 16,849 to 52,404 annually, and increased by 11.4 per cent in the past year alone, to reach the highest level ever recorded.

The emergence of derivatives of prescription medicines, classified as new psychoactive substances (NPS), particularly fentanyl analogues, has been associated with rising numbers of overdoses, including fatal overdoses, among opioid users. In recent years, several emergent synthetic opioids have been associated with increasing numbers of serious adverse events and deaths. The pills and powders containing synthetic opioids sold on the illicit market pose a threat to public health, a problem that is compounded by the variation in both the quantity and potency of their active components.

Disorders related to the use of amphetamines account for a considerable share of the global burden of disease attributable to drug use disorders, second only to those related to the use of opioids. Available data show that, among amphetamines, methamphetamine represents the greatest global health threat. Methamphetamine use is spreading and an increasing number of methamphetamine users are seeking treatment. In addition to the established and expanding market for methamphetamine in East and South-East Asia and Oceania, there are growing concerns about methamphetamine use in North America, South-West Asia and parts of Europe.

Although the number of cocaine users is decreasing or stabilizing in parts of Europe, wastewater analysis suggests that cocaine consumption in that region may be increasing. Following several years of decline, there are also indications of an increase in cocaine use in North America. Moreover, drug overdose cases involving cocaine increased markedly in the United States between 2012 and 2015. Much of that increase is linked, however, to the use of cocaine in combination with opioids.

The drug market is thriving

Overall, drug trafficking seems to have increased slightly in 2015 and some drug markets, particularly the cocaine and synthetic drugs markets, appear to be thriving.

Data on drug production, trafficking and use point to an overall expansion of the market for cocaine worldwide. Following a long-term decline, coca bush cultivation increased by 30 per cent during the period 2013–2015, mainly as a result of increased cultivation in Colombia. Total global manufacture of pure cocaine hydrochloride reached 1,125 tons in 2015, representing an overall increase of 25 per cent over 2013.

Cocaine use appears to be increasing in the two largest markets, North America and Europe. The prevalence of use of cocaine among the general population and testing in the workforce suggest an increase in cocaine use in the United States. In Europe, early signs of increases in cocaine consumption, based on wastewater analysis in selected cities, have been reported, with an increase of 30 per cent or more during the period 2011–2016.

The quantities of cocaine seized are also on the increase. Worldwide, they increased by 30 per cent to reach 864 tons (of varying purities) in 2015, the highest level ever reported. In North America, they increased by 40 per cent to reach 141 tons; in Europe, they increased by 35 per cent to reach 84 tons.

In 2016, global opium production increased by one third compared with the previous year. Although there was also an increase in the size of the area under opium poppy cultivation, the major increase in opium production was primarily the result of an improvement in opium poppy yields in Afghanistan compared with the previous year. At 6,380 tons, however, total global opium production was still some 20 per cent lower than at its peak in 2014, and was close to the average reported in the past five years.

Seizures of both opium and heroin have remained quite stable at the global level in recent years, suggesting a smooth supply of heroin, irrespective of annual changes in opium production. The quantity of heroin seized in North America increased sharply in 2015. This went in parallel with reports of increasing heroin use and heroin-related deaths in that subregion.

Flux in drug flows

Drug flows are in a constant state of flux. With the changes brought by globalization and the spread of new communication technologies, drug flows are characterized more than ever by rapid changes in trafficking routes, modi operandi and concealment methods.

With about 40 per cent of global heroin and morphine seizures in 2015 being made in countries on the so-called "Balkan route", the route appears to remain the world's principal opiate trafficking route. While overall quantities seized on the Balkan route declined in 2015, an alternative branch of the route, through the Caucasus countries, appears to have been gaining in importance in recent years.

That route circumvents Turkey, where the recent increase in flows of refugees heading towards countries in the European Union may have pushed traffickers to seek other options.

Data show that quantities of heroin and morphine seized declined in Bulgaria, Greece and Turkey during the period 2014–2015 compared with the period

Main Opiate Trafficking Flows, 2011–2015

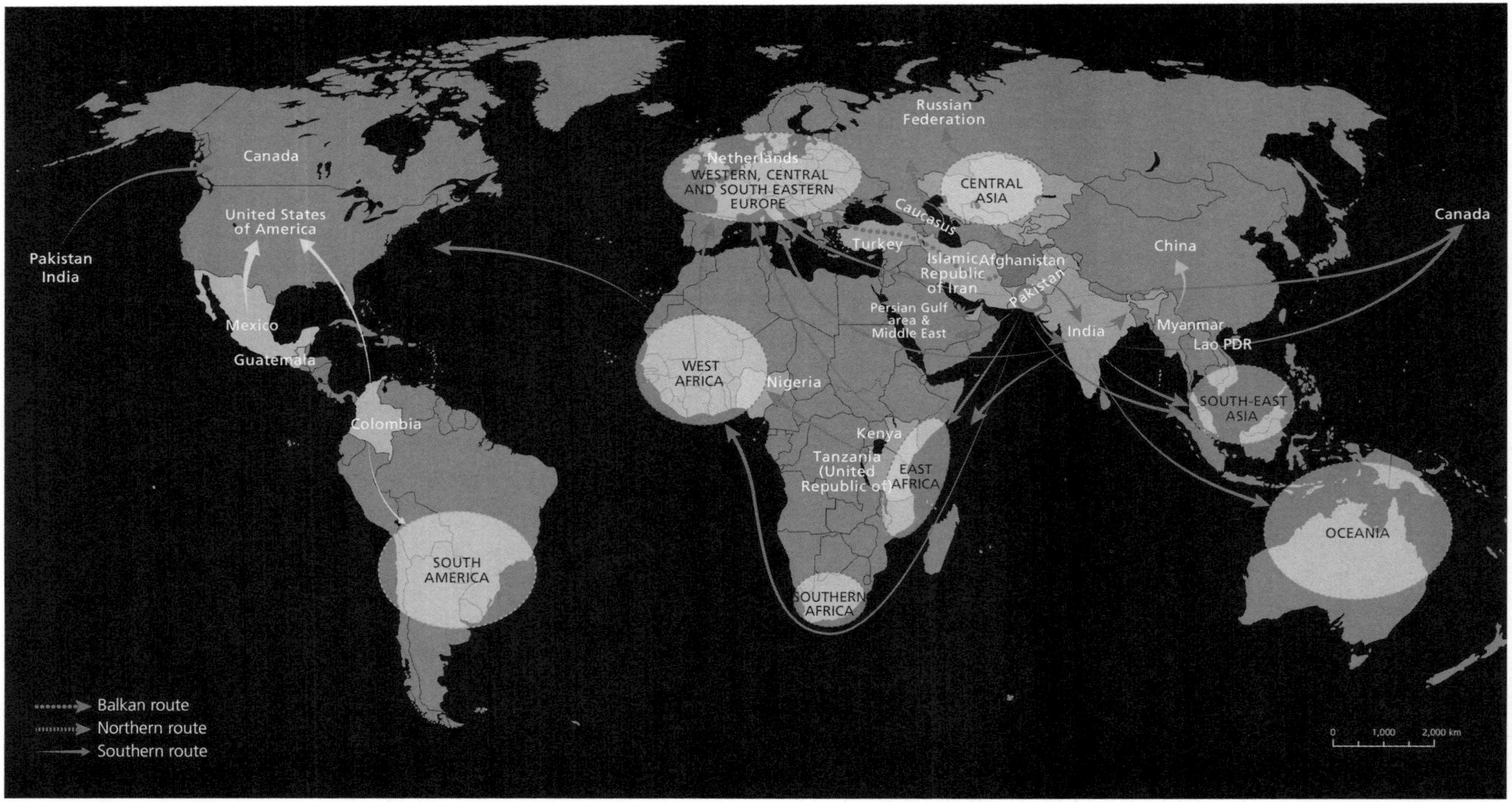

Sources: UNODC elaboration, based on responses to annual report questionnaire and individual drug seizure database.

2012–2013. By contrast, the amounts intercepted on the trafficking route through Armenia, Azerbaijan and Georgia, and via the Black Sea to Ukraine and Romania, increased sharply between those two periods.

A major geographical shift appears to have occurred in the methamphetamine market in the last five years. In 2015, the quantity of methamphetamine intercepted in East and South-East Asia surpassed the quantity intercepted in North America for the first time, making East and South-East Asia the leading subregions for methamphetamine seizures worldwide. While this may be a reflection of an increase in the effectiveness of law enforcement in East and South-East Asia, methamphetamine trafficking routes appear to be increasingly connecting previously unconnected markets in various subregions. Of particular note is the large increase in methamphetamine seizures in China.

In contrast to methamphetamine, amphetamine has been confined to fewer subregions, such as the Near and Middle East and Western and Central Europe. The quantities of amphetamine seized in 2015 point to a possible recent expansion of the amphetamine market in South-Eastern Europe, but this may be simply related to the large amphetamine market in the neighbouring Near and Middle East. Quantities of amphetamine seized also sharply increased in Central America and South-West Asia.

Although still comparatively small overall, there are indications that cocaine markets in several countries in Asia continue to rise. Possible proof of this was a very large seizure (900 kg) of cocaine in Sri Lanka in 2016 and another of 500 kg in Djibouti in 2017, which was probably en route to Asia. That was the single largest cocaine seizure in East Africa since 2004.

Overall, in 2015, the quantities of cocaine intercepted in Asia increased by more than 40 per cent compared with the previous year, with increases reported across all subregions. The largest proportions of the total quantity of cocaine seized in Asia over the period 2010–2015 were seized in East and South-East Asia (56 per cent) and in the Near and Middle East (40 per cent).

Changing business models for drug trafficking and organized crime

Organized crime groups have widened their port- folio of illicit activities. New crime areas such as cybercrime and environmental crime have emerged. Fewer groups are exclusively dedicated to drug trafficking, while more are also operating in other illicit sectors.

Almost two thirds of drug trafficking groups operating in countries in the European Union are involved in more than one crime area, according to research by the European Police Office (Europol), and that figure has been rising for years. Drug trafficking groups in Europe are frequently also involved in the counterfeiting of goods, trafficking in human beings, smuggling of migrants and trafficking in weapons.

In 2014, transnational organized crime groups across the globe were estimated to have generated between approximately one fifth and one third of their revenues from drug sales.

Europol identified some 5,000 international organized crime groups operating in countries in the European Union in 2017, and estimated that more than one third were involved in drug trafficking. This makes drug trafficking more widespread across organized crime than organized property crime, smuggling of migrants, trafficking in human beings, excise fraud or any other illicit activity.

Groups with a strong hierarchical structure, such as those in Mexico and Japan, and to some extent in the Russian Federation, continue to be involved in the drug trade. Hierarchical, top-down organizations are still the most widespread type of organized crime group in Europe, according to Europol.

However, there is evidence that looser, horizontal networks are becoming increasingly significant. In 2017, Europol estimated that such networks accounted for 30–40 per cent of organized crime groups operating in countries in the European Union.

The mobile communications revolution has offered new opportunities to traffickers. They no longer need personal contact with clients; instead, low-level "runners" can collect cash and dealers can let the customer know where to collect their drugs using messages sent over encrypted networks.

The darknet allows users to buy drugs with a cryptocurrency, such as bitcoin, and have their purchases delivered to them in a concealed manner. Typical buyers are recreational users of cannabis, "ecstasy", cocaine, hallucinogens and NPS. They are less likely to order heroin or methamphetamine. Although the darknet accounts for only a small percentage of drug sales, the market has been growing rapidly in recent years.

Corruption facilitates illicit drug markets, which fuel corruption

At each stage of the drug supply chain, there are opportunities for corruption. At the production level, farmers may bribe eradication teams, producers may bribe judges and police officers, and manufacturers may exploit workers in chemical companies in order to get hold of precursor chemicals. Further down the chain, traffickers bribe customs officials and take advantage of weaknesses in transport firms. At the consumer level, users can get drugs through corrupt doctors and pharmacists.

Corruption entrenches poverty by discouraging foreign investment, according to World Bank research. In a narco-economy, this is doubly true. Foreign firms, seeing the corrupted justice system and pervasive money-laundering that characterize narco-economies, are unlikely to make or increase investments.

Corruption also increases the level of income inequality, according to International Monetary Fund research. Higher levels of income inequality are known to encourage drug trafficking and corruption. In fact, the drug industry may perpetuate and exacerbate income inequality, which may in turn cause the expansion of drug production and trafficking.

A Report on Global Illicit Drugs Markets 1998–2007: Assessing the Operation of the Global Drug Market, Report 1
Peter H. Reuter

RAND Corporation, Prepared for the European Commission (2009)

Illicit drugs, predominantly cocaine and heroin, now generate a substantial international and domestic trade. For these two drugs, production is concentrated in poor nations and the bulk of revenues, though not of consumption, is generated by users in wealthy countries. Earnings have an odd shape; most of the money goes to a very large number of low level retailers in wealthy countries while the fortunes are made by a small number of entrepreneurs, many of whom come from the producing countries. Actual producers and refiners receive one or two percent of the total; almost all the rest is payment for distribution labour. The industry is in general competitive, though some sectors in some countries have small numbers of competing organisations.

It is not difficult to explain why cocaine heroin production occurs primarily in poor countries and only a little harder to understand why the accounting profits are downstream. Almost everything else about the trade presents a challenge, both descriptively and analytically. Why is the production of cocaine and heroin concentrated in such a small number of poor countries? How are the different sectors organized, in terms of enterprise size and internal structure? What is the relationship of drug trafficking and distribution to other transnational and organized criminal activities?

Cannabis and [Amphetamine Type Stimulants (ATS)] provide a contrast in several dimensions. For cannabis a high percentage is produced in rich consuming countries and a larger share goes to the growers. ATS is produced in both rich and poor countries and traded in both directions.

Table 1. Prices of Cocaine and Heroin through the Distribution System ca. 2000 (per pure kilogram equivalent)

Stage	Cocaine	Heroin
Farm gate	$650 (Leaf in Colombia)	$550 (Opium in Afghanistan)
Export	$1,000 (Colombia)	$2,000–$4,000 (Afghanistan)
Import	$15–20,000 (Miami)	$35,000
Wholesale (Kilo)	$33,000 (Chicago)	$50,000 (London)
Wholesale (Ounce)	$52,000 (Chicago)	$65,000
Retail (100 mg. pure)	$120,000 (Chicago)	$135,000 (London)

Source: Drug Enforcement Administration; EMCDDA; UNODC; Matrix, 2007.

A small number of nations account for the vast bulk of production of coca and opium. According to official estimates (e.g. U.S. Department of State, 2008; UNODC, 2008), Myanmar and Afghanistan have accounted for over 80 percent of global production of opium since the mid-1980s. Since the turn of the century, Afghanistan has increasingly dominated, so that in 2007 it was estimated to account for 93% of the total (8,200 tons out of 8,870 tons). A total of six countries account for 98% of world production.

Bolivia, Colombia and Peru account for all of coca production. The distribution of production among them has changed over time. In the 1980s, when the illegal market in the U.S. first emerged, it was produced primarily in Peru, Bolivia was second and Colombia a distant third. Since the mid-1990s this has changed markedly, with Colombia responsible for about two thirds of total production. Though other nations in the Andes, particularly Ecuador, are always rumoured to be about to enter the coca growing sector, none has so far done so.

There is no technical reason for not producing cocaine or heroin in the United States or Western Europe. Hydroponic techniques could be used for both coca and opium poppies. However the enforcement risks faced by producers in the U.S. or Western Europe are substantial and the risk compensation costs sufficiently high, that even with transportation costs and associated interdiction risks, local production of coca and opium poppies have never developed; indeed, these drugs are not even refined in the Western world.

Francisco Thoumi contrasts the distribution of coca and opium production across nations with that for legitimate agricultural products. Coffee can be grown in many countries; in fact, a large number of those countries do have coffee producing and exporting industries. Many countries are capable of producing opium or coca; very few of them do. For example, opium has at various times been grown in China, Lebanon, Macedonia and Turkey. However none of these are currently active producers for the illicit market.

It is useful to contrast this configuration with that for cannabis. One hundred and thirty four countries report to UNODC that cannabis is produced in their territory. U.S. production accounts for a substantial (though unknown) share of U.S. consumption, apparently much of it grown indoors. The Netherlands estimates domestic production that approximately 18,000 "cannabis farms" produced between 130 and 300 tons of cannabis in the early part of this decade, far more than might be consumed by Dutch users and the coffee shop visitors (less than 80 tons). Some of this is exported to other Western European nations.

Mexico and Morocco are the only nations identified as major exporters, Mexico exclusively to the United States and Morocco to Europe. There are no estimates of what share of consumption in these markets are accounted for by imports from these producers. However it is unlikely that the total international trade component of the cannabis trade is large.

Cannabis' exceptional status in terms of disbursed production probably rests on four factors: the bulkiness per unit value,[2] which raises smuggling costs substantially; the high yields per square meter, which allow a grower to produce substantial revenues from a small area; and the existence of a boutique market of user/growers interested in developing better breeds of the plant; and the ease of entry, since the seeds are widely available and there are probably few economies of scale beyond quite a small number of plants.

ATS production is scattered around the world but not in many countries and not always in developing countries. It is useful to consider the three component drugs (amphetamine, ecstasy and methamphetamine) separately.

Amphetamine is primarily consumed in Europe and that is the locus of production as well. Manufacturing requires neither highly specialized skills nor sophisticated facilities. The United Kingdom was for some years the principal production centre but other Western and Eastern European nations (notably Belgium, the Netherlands and Poland) have become more prominent in recent years.

Methamphetamine is produced mostly in East Asia and North America. In Asia the UNODC (2008) reports substantial methamphetamine production in China, Indonesia, Myanmar and the Philippines; these countries service both large domestic markets and markets in other Asian countries such as Japan and Korea. However methamphetamine is also produced in Australia, where a substantial domestic market has developed. Mexico produces for the U.S. market; however tough enforcement at the border and perhaps effective precursor controls in Mexico itself have led to the development of a U.S. based production capacity.

For ecstasy on the other hand, rich nations (such as the Netherlands and the U.K.) are major exporters to many countries, including developing countries such as Brazil. The production process requires considerable sophistication both of technicians and equipment; this may explain the location of the producers in the developed world.

Risks and the costs of bearing them provide a plausible, though still untested, explanation for all these observations. Coca and opium are grown in countries characterized by labour and land that have low prices relative to those in Europe and North America. The comparative advantage of these countries is reinforced by the reluctance or inability of governments in Bolivia, Colombia and Peru (for coca) and Afghanistan and Myanmar (for opium/heroin) to act aggressively against growers or early stage refiners. Low opportunity cost for factors of production plus low enforcement risks produce very modest prices for the refined product and also ensure that production does not move upstream geographically.

2. A kilogram of cocaine might have a border price of 10,000 Euros entering Europe; a kilogram of cannabis would be only a few hundred Euros.

It is also useful to consider why neighbouring countries, involved in transhipment, have not been major producers. Consider for example Thailand. In the early 1970s it was a major producer of opium. It also has had a substantial addict population (predominantly heroin using). It continues to suffer from high levels of corruption, both in the powerful military and in the civilian government. It would seem to be a strong candidate for a large opium production sector.

Yet Thailand now produces little and serves primarily as a consuming and transhipment country for Myanmar. The explanation can probably be found in economic factors. Over the past thirty years Thailand has had high rates of growth, raising the opportunity cost of land and labour relative to impoverished Myanmar. Thus, Thai farmers have not been able to compete in the opium growing sector, particularly since the illegality of the product has inhibited the development of more technologically advanced growing methods. Targeted alternative development programs, sponsored by the Thai king, may also have contributed to the decline of production in Thailand. The Thai government, despite the corruption of its border drug controls, has also been more willing to act aggressively against growers.

Until the mid-1990s Colombia was the other anomaly, a nation that would have been expected to dominate coca growing, given that coca grew readily there and domestic production would reduce the risk of interdiction. Though the principal source of refined exports to the United States, and an important source for Western Europe, it was a distant third in coca production until the mid-1990s. The subsequent and rather sudden expansion of coca growing in Colombia, which has accompanied a decline in Peruvian and, to a lesser extent, Bolivian production may be the result of specific political factors and developments in the other two producers. The upturn in political violence in Colombia has led to a large internal migration from more settled agricultural regions, where the paramilitary are most active, to unsettled areas in which there are few economic opportunities other than coca growing and in which the guerrillas can provide effective protection. The decline in Peruvian production may also be the consequence of an extended blight, the first to hit the coca crop in recent decades, and a period of intense enforcement against air traffic of coca base between Peru and Colombia. In Bolivia a broad program of developmental support in the principal producing area (the Chapare) and perhaps actions of the governments prior to the 2006 election of Evo Morales as president led to sharp decline in production. If peace and stability ever return to rural Colombia, the coca trade may shift back to the poorer Bolivia; the recent loss of leadership and membership in the FARC, along with the demilitarisation of the paramilitary, may allow a test of that proposition.

Both in the Andes and in Afghanistan the growers are small producers and there is no suggestion that they have any collective power in bargaining. Mansfield, in a series of studies over the last decade has shown that opium is just another crop that farmers choose to grow with the amount grown depending on access to water, availability of infrastructure, prices of other agricultural commodities, availability of family labour etc. At that level, it is a typical agricultural product, produced by many independent decision makers. Even at the level of traders, the market appears to be competitive. Only at the highest level of the domestic Afghanistan trade is there any indication of possible market power. While there are no similarly detailed studies of the coca producing and cocaine refining sectors in Colombia, there is little indication of any control.

There is an emerging literature on cannabis production in wealthy countries. For example, Bouchard provides a fine-grained description of marijuana growing in Quebec, an important supplier to the U.S. market according to his careful estimates. Again what emerges is an industry of many small producers with minimal co-ordination, often employing teenagers as workers. Less is available on production in poor countries that serve as suppliers to the West. In Morocco, cannabis growing is a major agricultural activity in some regions, again involving small farmers who sell to numerous middle-men. There are no published studies of cannabis production in Mexico.

The modest share of retail price associated with international cocaine and heroin smuggling is easily explained. First, consider cocaine, which travels in large bundles at that stage; seizures suggest that shipments of 250–500 kilograms are quite common. Though large sums may be paid to pilots for flying small planes carrying cocaine or to Honduran colonels in return for ignoring their landing, these costs are defrayed over a large quantity. A pilot who demands $500,000 for flying a plane with 250 kilograms is generating costs of only $2,000 per kilogram, about 2 percent of the retail price in the United States. Even if the plane has to be abandoned after one flight, that adds only another $2,000 to the kilogram price. For Europe, where courier smuggling may be more important, since it is remote from production areas for both cocaine and heroin, payments to the couriers again amount to only a few thousand Euros per kilo. For shipments in container cargo, seizure constitutes little more than random tax collection; replacement cost of the seized drugs is substantially less than the landed price, so high seizure rates have modest effect even on wholesale prices.

A large share of cocaine in the 1980s was smuggled to the United States in dedicated vessels, either small boats or planes. Intense interdiction has changed both routes and patterns. Small (and sometimes not so small) planes are still used to carry a substantial fraction of cocaine to Mexico, from where it enters the U.S. in regular cargo, either by truck or cargo vessel. Patterns of seizure also suggest that in recent years even shipments direct from Colombia have tended to travel in commercial traffic, both air and sea. The drug is found concealed in an enormous variety of cargoes; frozen fruit pulp containers, wooden furniture and suspended in other liquids. European smuggling patterns are influenced by the simple distance from Colombia to Western Europe; dedicated small planes and boats are less feasible. An increasing share is now coming through West African transit countries, such as Ghana and Guinea-Bissau.

Heroin smuggling appears to be less efficient, at least as measured in dollars per kilogram. Heroin that exits Myanmar at $1,000 per kilogram (in bundles of ten kilograms or more) sells on arrival in the United States for $50,000 per kilogram. There have been a few multi-hundred kilogram shipments of heroin but they are very rare compared to those for cocaine. The drug often travels in small bundles carried internally by individual couriers. "Body-packing" where the couriers are low wage earners, produces per kilogram smuggling costs of less than $10,000. A body-packer can apparently carry about 3/4 of a kilogram. A payment of $5,000 for incurring a 1 in 10 risk in prison (perhaps acceptable for couriers whose legitimate wages are only about $2,000 per annum), along with $3,000 in travel expenses, produces a kilogram cost of just over $11,000 compared to a retail price of $1 million. The remainder of the smugglers' margin is for assuming other kinds of risk. Body packing is also a common mode of smuggling from Central Asia, particularly Tajikistan, into Russia. The payments to couriers there are much lower, perhaps as little as $200, reflecting both the greater poverty of that region compared to Mexico (a Middle Income country now by World Bank standards) and the lower risk of apprehension.

Nigeria is an interesting anomaly, a nation that seems to have little potential role in the international drug trade. It is isolated from any of the principal producer or consumer countries and lacks a significant base of traditional domestic production or consumption. Nonetheless, Nigerian traffickers have come to play a significant role in the shipping of heroin between Southeast Asia and the U.S. and also to Europe. They have even been identified as important figures in the early stages of heroin trafficking in Central Asia. More recently Nigerian traffickers have even entered the cocaine business, though the production centres are still more remote from their home country.

The explanation is probably to be found in a complex of factors. Nigerians are highly entrepreneurial, have been misruled by corrupt governments over a long time, have large overseas populations, weak civil society, very low domestic wages and moderately good commercial links to the rest of the world. Thus it is relatively easy to buy protection for transactions in Nigerian airports (corruption and a weak governmental tradition), to establish connections in both the source and consumption nations (large overseas populations) and to use existing commercial transportation; smuggling labour is cheap (low domestic wages) and the entrepreneurial tradition produces many competent and enthusiastic smuggling organizers. Nigeria is not unique in most of these dimensions (except for size and connections with the rest of the world) and there is perhaps an accidental quality to its initiation into the trade, but these other factors plausibly play a major role. The country of Nigeria may have been supplanted by other West African states as a transit location in recent years, as indicated by the origin of seizures at London's Heathrow Airport, but it is less clear that Nigerians have been supplanted as smugglers.

Immigrants have advantages in exporting, with better knowledge of potential sellers and corruption opportunities. Few potential US importers speak any of the languages of the Golden Triangle (Myanmar, Laos and Thailand); English has more currency in Pakistan but not much in Afghanistan. Corrupt officials may be much more at ease in dealing with traffickers whose families they can hold in mutual hostage. Moreover, non-native traffickers are likely to be conspicuous in the growing regions. Nor are the exporters merely agents for wealthy country nations, in sharp contrast to the international trade in refined agricultural products. Khun Sa, an exotic figure associated with irredentist ethnic groups on the periphery of Myanmar was the dominant figure in opium exports from the Golden Triangle for many years. The Colombian cocaine trade has spawned some spectacular figures, such as Pablo Escobar and Carlos Lehder, all of them of Colombian descent. If there are major US or European exporters in the source countries, they have managed to escape detection.

The smuggling sector is where great fortunes appear to be made. Most prominent have been the Colombian entrepreneurs such as Carlos Lehder and Pablo Escobar whose extravagant lifestyles provided an important part of the imagery of the failure of the state to prevent their accumulation of power and wealth. Though there are no documented estimates of their actual earnings, there is no doubt that they accumulated many hundreds of millions of Euros during their careers. Khun Sa, the dominant figure in Myanmar's heroin industry (both production and exporting) also became extraordinarily wealthy and was able to negotiate with the national government an exit from the trade that may well have involved payment of large sums. The principal figures in the Mexican drug trade, which is mostly smuggling to the U.S., are also reputed to have very large fortunes.

Though for a long time it was assumed that illegal drug markets were typically monopolized in fact monopoly control is rare. Prior to 1980, it was widely believed that the Mafia had dominated the major illegal markets such as those for bookmaking and loan sharking, and even for heroin importation into New York City until the late 1960s. Despite finding that some dealers within the U.S. have enormous incomes and traffic in large quantities, no researcher has found evidence, except on the most local basis (e.g., a few blocks), that a dealer organisation has the ability to exclude others or to set prices, the hallmarks of market power.

Even at the trafficker level, market power seems elusive. Notwithstanding references to the Medellin and Cali "cartels", these groups seem to have been only loose syndicates of independent entrepreneurs, who sometimes collabourated but also had to compete with other, smaller, Colombian smuggling enterprises. The small share of the retail price accounted for by all activities up to import is strong, but not conclusive, evidence of competition at this level. The continuing decline of prices over an almost twenty year period at all levels of the market suggests that, if market power ever existed, it has now been dissipated.

Some characteristics of smuggling organisations seem quite general. For example, smuggling is rarely integrated with downstream distribution activities. Organisations which import 250 kilogram shipments of cocaine do not distribute beyond the initial transaction, selling in loads of 10 kilograms or more. The explanation for this probably lies in risk management; lower level transactions are more visible and the purchasers less reliable. Integration thus increases risk of arrest. Only very small scale importers are likely to operate close to the retail level.

Markets for smuggling services contain many forms and sizes of organisation. A credible case can be made that the 1990s US cocaine market has been dominated by a few large organisations. For other eras, countries and drugs, smaller and more ephemeral organisations may account for a significant share of the total.

If drugs travel in legitimate commerce and traffic, then transportation companies, as well as financial institutions, may be active accomplices. For example, American Airlines has paid substantial fines in the past for inadequate monitoring; its planes were importing clandestine cocaine shipments. Revelations at the Miami International Airport in the late 1990s showed that employees of the airline have continued to find opportunities for large scale smuggling; these ones involved baggage handlers at the U.S. landing point.

Corruption in the consuming countries seems to be less central to the business, an assertion that arouses considerable scepticism in producer countries. Corruption, like scientific hypotheses, presents a problem of epistemological asymmetry. Scientific hypotheses can only be disproved, not proven; corruption can be found but its existence never disproved. Nonetheless, U.S. prosecutors pursue corrupt agents with considerable zeal when they find them; at the same time the overlapping authority of enforcement agencies creates a situation in which any corrupt agent, no matter how well protected in her own department, has to be concerned with possible investigation by another agency. The market for corruption will shrink in such an environment. In many Western European countries with large drug markets, such as the United Kingdom and Switzerland, there simply is a dearth of credible corruption allegations beyond the occasional individual police officer who takes drugs or money.

The final sale of drugs to users is the sector accounting for most of the enforcement effort, participants and revenues. It is the easiest and best studied sector of the market, resulting in studies in many Western countries.

The large fraction of sellers operating at the retail level is simply a consequence of the incentives for concealment, which lead to a very tiered distribution system. High level dealers will seek to sell to small numbers of customers in order to reduce the number of potential informants against them. It is plausible, though empirically untested, that the number of customers a dealer is willing to transact with will rise as the drug moves down the distribution system; since the higher level dealers earn more and face higher penalties if caught, they are likely to be more cautious than those further down the distribution system. If each high level dealer will transaction with, say, only five customers (themselves dealers) and there are just three distribution levels in the market, retailers will account for almost five sixths of sellers. Thus is it hardly surprising that most of those who are incarcerated for drug selling operate at the bottom of the system.

The low level of earnings of participants in the retail markets is shown in a number of studies. Levitt and Venkatesh used the financial records of a cocaine dealing organisation in Chicago to show that most participants earned less than the minimum wage; they worked in the organisation in the hope of rising to the top, where earnings were very large indeed. Reuter, MacCoun and Murphy, collecting data ten years earlier when the crack and cocaine markets in Washington, D.C. were near their peak, found that street level dealers earned more than the minimum wage but still quite modest sums, in part because they were able to work profitably only for a few hours each week.

The high share of the retail price accounted for by low level distributors is easily explained in the standard risk compensation model used by economists. Assume that a higher level trafficker sells 1 kilogram of cocaine and has a 1 percent probability of being imprisoned for one year as a result of the transaction; the rich trafficker values a year in prison at 100,000 Euros. Assume a retailer sells 1 gram of cocaine and has only a 1 in 1,000 chance of the same imprisonment; he values a year in prison at 25,000 Euros. The trafficker will charge 1 Euro per gram to cover the risk, while the retailer, even though he has a lower chance of being jailed and values that less highly, needs 25 Euros to cover the risk associated with one gram. The figures are intended to be illustrative only.

Drug markets lend themselves to mythologising, because they are difficult to study and because the effects of the drugs themselves create a good deal of glamour to what is in fact a banal and grubby business. The common view that drug markets are lucrative, violent and monopolistic is, for most drugs, places and time exactly wrong. Mostly participants earn low incomes from engaging in routine activities in the context of small organisations with no capacity to control their customers. There are important exceptions at the higher levels of the markets, particularly for cocaine and heroin, in which a few individuals earn large incomes and control great violence. These constitute a specific social problem which needs to be dealt with but nothing is gained by generalising the exceptional few to the mass market in which millions of participants are engaged on a daily basis.

Peter Reuter suggests that "[c]orruption in [drug] consuming countries"—like the United States—"seems to be less central to the [drug] business" than in drug-producing countries. The recent experiences of Mexico and the United States are consistent with this view. Though drug consumption is much higher in the United States than in Mexico, to say that drug prohibition-related violence and corruption is worse in Mexico than in the United States would be an understatement. Mexican drug cartels have become so powerful that in 2009 former U.S. drug czar Barry McCaffrey said he believed the country was at risk of becoming a failed "narco-state." David Luhnow and José de Cordoba, *The Perilous State of Mexico*, WALL ST. J., Feb. 21, 2009. Former Mexican President Vicente Fox, who once "declared the 'mother of all battles' against drug cartels while in office, has reversed course and now favors legalization, saying that because of the drug war Mexico is 'losing in many things: tourism is stagnant, trade on the border, nightclubs, hotels are all stuck. We don't deserve to pay this price.'" Ioan Grillo and San Francisco del Rincon, *Mexico's Ex-President Vicente Fox: Legalize Drugs*, TIME, Jan. 19, 2011.

The idea that drug consumption in the United States is fueling drug cartel violence across the border has become a common refrain; but shouldn't logic dictate that the country with the greater amount of use and accompanying retail sales also have more violence and corruption? What might explain this imbalance? Was there a similar imbalance in the costs and benefits of prohibition among countries during alcohol prohibition? If not, what accounts for the difference?

Note: *Globalization of the U.S. Black Market: Prohibition, the War on Drugs, and the Case of Mexico* Seth Harp

85 New York University Law Review 1661 (2010)

On Valentine's Day, 1929, seven members and hangers-on of the Bugs Moran gang arrived at a garage in the Lincoln Park neighborhood of Chicago, supposedly to receive a shipment of hijacked whiskey at a discount. It was a set-up. Members of the rival Capone gang, some dressed as police officers, led the seven underground, lined them up against a brick wall, and machine-gunned them to death. The uniformed killers led the plain-clothed killers outside at gunpoint to mislead bystanders into believing the shooting was under official control.

The hit had targeted Bugs Moran, Al Capone's chief rival for control of the illegal alcohol market, but Moran was either late or saw the "police" car in time and eluded assassination. However, Moran's evasion was not the primary failure of the attempted hit. The murders were at that time the most heinous offenses associated with the high-profile world of larger-than-life bootleggers and the crime syndicates they controlled, and the media backlash was severe. The murders were, in Capone's words, "lousy public relations." "MURDER COPS HUNTED IN MASSACRE" shouted the headline of *the Daily Mirror*, which devoted its entire front page to the story, including a large, gruesome photo of the crime scene and mug shots of each victim. "The viciousness of the killing and the powerlessness of police were both part of the abiding image of Prohibition." Public opinion had reached an inflection point, and it was not long before Prohibition was abandoned.

On September 2, 2009, hitmen working for the Sinaloa Cartel, a powerful Mexican drug-trafficking organization, broke into an addiction rehabilitation center in a northern sector of Juarez, Mexico, within view of the U.S. border, pushed eighteen people up against a wall, and machine-gunned them to death. The mass-murder was not directed at a rival cartel, but at a few recovering addicts regarded by the Sinaloa Cartel as potential informants.

Juarez and El Paso, Texas, are essentially one city split by the Rio Grande, an international border; the metropolis is home to more than two million people, making it the world's most populous binational area. Despite the depravity of the killings and the fact that Juarez is geographically contiguous with the United States, CNN declined to cover the event in lieu of such topics as President Obama's speech to schoolchildren, a football coach charged with homicide, Michael Jackson's funeral, the weather phenomenon El Nino, environmental terrorism, the sale of human body parts, Twitter, and the kidnapping of Jaycee Dugard.

The editorial decision was partly understandable, as the killings were nothing new: From January 2008 to the date of the killings described above, more than 1800 people had been murdered in Juarez, the most violent place in the world. It is in no sense metaphorical to describe the city as a war zone, as rival cartels have for years been engaged in open battle with one another, the federal army, the local police (ambiguously allied), and American agents, in a multifaceted, overlapping, and perpetually mutating conflict.

It is more likely that the lack of attention to the bloodshed in Juarez was due to the understandable human tendency to care less about what happens to people in other countries. But the war in Mexico does not properly belong to Mexico. It is caused by exactly the same phenomenon that caused the Saint Valentine's Day Massacre: competition between outlaw organizations that supply the American black market for recreational drugs.

The United States consumes more drugs and alcohol than any other country in the world. The U.S. legal strategy for reducing recreational drug consumption has long emphasized outright criminalization of possession and police interdiction of supply. "Prohibition," the ban on the drug alcohol from 1919 to 1933, is a dramatic example of such a policy. The "War on Drugs," the current campaign against a number of drugs, but especially cocaine, heroin, marijuana, and methamphetamine, is another. The similarities between the two are many, and the subject of much literature. Most notably, both failed or are failing to eliminate consumption of the targeted drug(s) while generating secondary costs that outweigh the problems caused by the drugs themselves, and both failed or are failing for the same reason: the futility of trying to eliminate, by fiat, flourishing markets for highly demanded goods.

This much has been well argued by many authors, but this Note explores the most salient difference between the two regimes, namely that Prohibition was met with a decisive backlash and repeal, while the War on Drugs manages to retain popular support, even though it has created violence on a scale beyond anything seen during Prohibition. This Note argues that the divergence in public choice is substantially explained by drug production taking place outside the United States, a fact that lowers the visibility of corruption and murder to those who support the War on Drugs. Simply because drugs are produced abroad, much of the human misery immanent in black markets of every kind has been offloaded onto people in third world countries. By contrast, black market alcohol was mostly produced in the United States, where Prohibition's bad effects were concentrated. The visibility of local costs led to relatively quick repeal of the 18th Amendment.

Reducing consumption of drugs and alcohol is a social goal with widespread support. How effective are prohibitions at achieving this goal? In general, they probably reduce consumption by a small to moderate margin. This is the primary benefit of a drug prohibition regime.

There is now tentative consensus among historians that Prohibition probably decreased alcohol consumption by a small to moderate margin that diminished over time.

[I]t is reasonable to conclude that the War on Drugs has decreased consumption by an unknown but almost certainly small margin. So the principal benefit of prohibitions, whether of alcohol or other drugs, is a slight or moderate reduction in consumption.

If it were as simple as that, if banning drugs were like banning, say, lead paint—that is, if taxpayers paid no more than the dollar price of administering the newly prohibited substance's removal from the market and the disutility, if any, of its absence—drug prohibitions might be reasonable or even good laws. But that is not how it works in practice.

When the sale of a popular recreational drug is banned, wealth and power flowing from productive capital are amplified and transferred from the arena of competition between legitimate firms to the monopoly control of entrepreneurs whose competitive advantage is a willingness to break the law. The government then invests in thwarting the criminals, who counterinvest in resistance and subterfuge. Meanwhile, large numbers of transactions take place without recourse to private property rights or the civil courts, leaving violence as the only mechanism for adjudicating contractual disputes and enforcing industry norms. Violence is used to take over and hold supply routes and distribution territory, with each gangster knowing that to succeed he must be more brutal than the gangster whom he has just supplanted. Over time, violence and expenditures ratchet upward, making it increasingly more expensive to bring the good to market, exacerbating the cycle. Meanwhile, consumers whose demand for drugs is inelastic (in some cases due to addiction) resort to theft to pay for artificially priced drugs they can no longer afford. The only constant in this uncontrollable spiral is a steady supply. The only change to consumers is increased price and reduced quality. Instead of champagne or powder cocaine, they get moonshine or crack, the latter substances being cheaper to produce clandestinely, more compact for transportation, and providing greater per-unit intoxication to consumers wishing to minimize their transactions with criminal suppliers.

[Alcohol p]rohibition is generally regarded to have been a disastrous experience because it was much more costly than expected. The murder rate rose sharply following the passage of the Eighteenth Amendment, remained high for fourteen years, and then, after repeal and passage of the Twenty-First Amendment, declined for eleven straight years. Once regulated alcohol was removed from the market, death and severe illnesses from adulterated homemade liquor became epidemic. Meanwhile, judicial criminal dockets were overwhelmed, and, given the difficulty of securing convictions against participants in voluntary transactions, prosecutors resorted to disproportionate punishments against bootleggers, up to life in prison in some cases. In fact, the origins of the American mass prison system trace to the Prohibition era, when the number of federal prisons had to be doubled. Yet illegal alcohol production and consumption was a "respectable crime." Like the presence of women in saloons, it became socially acceptable, for the first time, to be seen intoxicated in public. Most infamously, corruption among law enforcement became rampant, due in part to the large number of officials at every level of the executive branch, including the White House, who themselves were "ready to drink anything that burns, at the same time giving thanks to God." These unintended effects bent public opinion against Prohibition and produced a reexamination of policy at a national level.

Like Prohibition, the War on Drugs is expensive, even when the measurement is confined to U.S. borders. "The War on Drugs [costs the government] more . . . than the Commerce, Interior, and State Departments put together." To American taxpayers, the cost of the War on Drugs, including the opportunity cost of drug peace, is estimated to be more than eighty billion dollars annually. How does enforcing bans on a few rudimentary chemicals come to be so expensive?

First, the War on Drugs causes violence. Violent conflict arises from competition between gangs that buy drugs wholesale and distribute them to consumers.

In addition to causing violence, the War on Drugs increases property crime. It is estimated that users seeking to finance purchases of drugs, some of which are 50 to 100 times more expensive than the predicted free market equilibrium price, commit around forty percent of all property crime in the United States.

In addition to causing violence and property crime, the War on Drugs increases official corruption. Bribery and graft are the result of a surfeit of drug profits, the lack of real moral revulsion directed against the use of drugs (compared to crimes that immediately cause tangible harm to others), and police fatigue with the Sisyphean struggle. Over the last half century the War on Drugs has led to serious and widespread corruption, especially in the police departments of high-crime cities and in the federal agencies tasked with controlling the southern border.

Because the U.S. War on Drugs pits large costs against moderate benefits, the criminalization of drugs has long been a controversial legal policy, but not as controversial as it should be: Despite the similarities between Prohibition and the War on Drugs, pressure to end the latter is clearly lower than pressure to end the former was at the height of Prohibition. This must be in substantial part because most of the violence caused by the War on Drugs is realized outside the United States.

As discussed, the War on Drugs causes violence in the United States. Yet that violence, mostly inner-city shootings, is trivial compared to the mayhem caused in illegal-drug-producing countries, like Mexico, the primary supplier of U.S. demand. Were these effects manifested in the United States, even if confined to marginalized and impoverished communities, the War on Drugs would probably go the same way as Prohibition—written off as a social experiment that proved too costly.

Mexico is currently embroiled in a major national conflict with a 2009 body count that surpassed the body count in Iraq and Afghanistan combined. Steadily enriched by the constant flow of money from American drug sales, the cartels have infiltrated every layer of society in Mexico.

Al Capone's thugs were farmboys and immigrants with sawed-off shotguns and tommyguns. Retail gangs in American cities wield pistols, knives, and fists. The armed wings of Mexico's cartels, by contrast, are manned by disciplined soldiers well equipped with increasingly sophisticated arsenals now reported to go beyond mere assault rifles, machine guns, and grenades, to include such military materiel as anti-aircraft guns and semisubmersible submarines. Cartel operatives coordinate their operations from sophisticated command centers using cell phones, two-way radios, scanner devices, Voice Over Internet Protocol, broadband satellite instant messaging, and encrypted text messages. Street battles between them and the federal army are sustained infantry engagements that can last hours and leave dozens dead.

Los Zetas, a private army that rose to prominence as the enforcement branch of the Gulf Cartel, originated out of the Grupo Aeromovil de Fuerzas Especiales, the special forces branch of the Mexican army. Its defection to entrepreneurial endeavors was a stark testament to the ability of the drug trade to compete with the Mexican state.

As of 2010, large swaths of the country are under cartel control. As much as thirty percent of Mexico's arable land is under drug crop cultivation. Every political party takes drug money, the Federal Investigative Agency has been corrupted, and one-fifth of the Attorney General's office is under investigation. Vigilantism is rampant. The Central Intelligence Agency (CIA) and Department of Defense are preparing for the possibility of the failure of the Mexican state. The cartels are believed to be actively trying to kill the head of state, and some business leaders have even called for the U.N. to occupy the country.

In short, Mexico is a country pushed to the brink of a particularly awful kind of failure, the cause of which is its status as the leading producer and transporter of drugs bound for the U.S. black market.

Imagine instead, however implausibly, that the United States produced all of the drugs it consumes. To be sure, eradication efforts would be more efficient, because the United States is wealthier and more developed. But the resulting scarcity would drive the price of drugs higher, making them an even more lucrative product. The higher price commanded by drugs would induce more determined, better-financed criminals to enter the illegal market. This would increase production, again spurring an increase in corresponding antinarcotics efforts, making drugs even more costly. Those increased costs would in turn be passed on to drug consumers, again raising the price of drugs, again exacerbating the cycle, until an equilibrium were reached at which the price of drugs would be much higher than at the outset but the total quantity supplied would have changed little or not at all. All the while counternarcotics efforts would be increasing, and domestic criminal syndicates would be gaining money, power, and reputational capital. Eventually, with the two upward trajectories pitted against one another, the conflict would approach an outright war.

In response to such a pointless conflagration, the country would likely seek an alternative means to regulate drugs other than a criminal ban. That is precisely what happened at the end of Prohibition. Nowadays, by contrast, the violence inherent in the War on Drugs is out of sight and out of mind of the average voter.

But how did the violence come to be outsourced in the first place?

In the absence of some barrier, production of a commodity will take place where it is cheapest. During Prohibition, it was cheapest to produce alcohol in the United States because significant productive capital already existed, and alcohol was easy to make at home and expensive to warehouse and transport. Although a significant amount of marijuana is produced in the United States, most illegal drugs are produced abroad.

It is cheapest to produce drugs for the American market abroad for a number of reasons.

To begin with, when marijuana, cocaine, and heroin were made illegal there was little demand for any of them, so there was not much productive capital to eliminate. Unlike the Eighteenth Amendment and the Volstead Act, the bans on these drugs were not in response to a perceived problem of widespread use among the general population; rather, they were directed most particularly at blacks and immigrants.

But the illegality of these drugs did not stop them from becoming popular among the middle classes. Indeed, to 1960s counterculturists, that very illegality was part of the attraction, illustrating another counterproductive tendency of prohibition. By the 1970s, demand for opium, cannabis, and cocaine was substantial.

When alcohol was banned, the de facto tax of illegality was insufficient to drive production abroad wherever sunken investment outweighed the cost of subterfuge. But entrants to the rapidly expanding drug market in the second half of the twentieth century faced a different cost structure. For them, investment in productive capacity anywhere in the United States necessarily entailed a high risk of detection, seizure, fines, and imprisonment. At the outset, then, not only did suppliers face the usual pressure to locate production where conventional inputs—e.g., land and labor—were cheapest, they also had an incentive to invest in countries that had not banned the substance to be produced, or where law enforcement was lax or the central state weak.

Some of the plants from which drugs are made are highly particular to certain regions. Varietals of the coca plant containing the cocaine alkaloid are essentially confined to Bolivia, Colombia, and Peru. Cocaine, once in demand, was bound to be produced there—and other drugs as well—due to economies of scope.

Sometimes a climate amenable to indigenous narcotic botanicals combines with a forbidding terrain and social factors of the kind already discussed (a weak state, lax enforcement, cheap labor) to give a country a near monopoly over a specific drug crop. The Andean-Amazonian region, for example, has a near monopoly on coca, not only because of its traditional use there and the coca plant's poor survival elsewhere, but also because of the protection provided by high mountain ranges, dense jungles, and low population density. In the United States, California and federal police fight a losing battle to eradicate cannabis plots in a handful of national forests. Consider, then, the impossibility for Latin American security forces, who have their own policing priorities, of eradicating millions of acres of plants hidden high in the Andes or deep in the Amazon rain forest amongst recalcitrant campesinos to whom the opportunity cost of growing such crops approaches zero, the alternative being sustenance farming. To take another example, poppy grows well throughout much of Europe, South America, and Asia, yet Afghanistan produces approximately 94 percent of the global heroin supply. Afghanistan's arid climate and long history of poppy cultivation explain less of its dominance than the country's lawlessness, tribal balkanization, lack of available economic alternatives for laborers, and a rugged terrain that is arguably impossible to police.

The comparative advantage enjoyed by overseas drug producers outlined above is lessened, however, by the necessity of international transportation. Drugs produced in Latin America, or elsewhere, have to be shipped to the United States in order to be sold. But because of the rapid growth of international transportation and communications networks in the twentieth and twenty-first centuries, globalization, and the implementation of international free trade accords like the WTO, GATT, and NAFTA, these exportation costs are declining rapidly.

International liberalization—opening markets and freeing the movement of goods and services—is at odds with efforts to control the international drug trade. First, expansion of neoliberal free trade policies tends to reduce the price of precursor commodities, such as land, labor, and chemicals, used to make saleable narcotics and makes legally controlled chemical precursors more difficult to restrict. A global reduction in the price commanded by more mundane agricultural commodities also makes drug crops more attractive to peasant farmers. Second, international economic liberalization lowers the price of transportation, improves international infrastructure, and enhances distribution networks, all of which make transportation of drugs across long distances more affordable. Third, by increasing the overall volume in world trade, globalization gives smugglers more hiding places for drugs. Fourth, streamlined customs procedures lower the probability of seizures. Finally, financial deregulation, the proliferation of offshore banking, and increasingly rapid capital flows across borders make money laundering easier.

For all these reasons, globalized criminal networks concentrate drug production in about a dozen countries—including Mexico, Colombia, Bolivia, Peru, Afghanistan, Pakistan, Kazakhstan, Myanmar, Thailand, Morocco, Jamaica, and Laos—countries that are generally large, fertile, mountainous or jungly, and underdeveloped, with a weak or war-hobbled central state. These countries supply the developed world with drugs. Currently, Mexico has a lock on the U.S. drug market, but, in the past, Colombia has held that position (making use of maritime rather than overland importation channels), and in the future it could be any one of them. As global trade grows more laissez-faire, competition increases: In an industry that operates outside law, this translates directly to more violence.

Three decades of campaigning by the United States and the security forces of client regimes have done little to dislodge this arrangement, and there is little reason to expect change soon.

The externalization of War on Drugs costs described above would be a boon to the United States if the country received the benefits of a moderate reduction in drug consumption without paying the concomitant price in blood, unless it were conceded that the value of a human life does not depend on nationality. Even though governments clearly owe the greatest duty of consideration to their own citizens, it is unreasonable, not to mention uncompassionate, in a globally interconnected and interdependent world to knowingly sacrifice tens of thousands of foreign lives for a marginal reduction in the amount of recreational drugs consumed by Americans. Taking into account the suffering borne by noncitizens, it is necessary to search for some other method of regulating drugs: a regulatory framework the costs of which are as moderate as its benefits.

Seth Harp argues that "Mexico is a country pushed to the brink of a particularly awful kind of failure, the cause of which is its status as the leading producer and transporter of drugs bound for the U.S. black market." The following excerpt examines the state of drug war-related violence in Mexico in more detail.

Drug Violence in Mexico: Data and Analysis through 2017
Laura Calderón, Octavio Rodríguez, and David A. Shirk

University of San Diego Justice in Mexico Project (2018)

Mexico has experienced dramatic surges in crime and violence over the last decade, most visibly exemplified by an increased number of homicides. The number of intentional homicides documented by Mexico's National Institute of Statistics and Geography (INEGI) had declined significantly under both presidents Ernesto Zedillo (1994–2000) and Vicente Fox (2000–2006), but rose dramatically after 2007, the first year in office for President Felipe Calderón (2006–2012). Throughout the Calderón administration, INEGI reported 121,669 homicides, an average of over 20,000 people per year, more than 55 people per day, or just over two people every hour.

While homicides declined from 2011 through 2014, the number began to rebound during the last half of the administration of President Enrique Peña Nieto (2012–2018), with levels exceeding those of the Calderón administration. Figures for 2017 appear to have matched or surpassed the record levels set in 2011, a year in which the country saw more than 27,000 homicides. Over the course of Peña Nieto's five years in office, there have been 64 homicides per day, or more than 2.6 murders every hour. All told, since the start of the twenty-first century, more than a quarter of a million people have been murdered in Mexico.

A large portion of Mexico's surge in homicides over the last decade has been attributed to organized crime groups engaged in drug trafficking and other illicit activities. This study is the latest in a series of annual reports produced by Justice in Mexico since 2010 in an attempt to examine trends in violence and organized crime in Mexico using the latest available data. Over the years, these reports have attempted to reconcile often imperfect, confusing, and even conflicting information from both official and non-governmental sources regarding trends in violence and organized crime, and particularly "drug-related" violence.

As the ninth annual report on *Drug Violence in Mexico,* this study compiles the latest available data and analysis of crime and violence trends in Mexico. According to this and past reports, a major portion—between a third and half—of Mexico's homicides have been attributable to drug trafficking organizations (DTOs) and other organized crime groups (OCGs). According to Mexican newspapers *Reforma* and *Milenio*, respectively, the tally amounts to between 82,000 and 100,000 killings attributable to "drugs" and organized criminal violence since 2007.[1] All told, roughly a third to half of Mexico's murders bore characteristics that are frequently associated with organized crime groups, including execution-style killings, the presence of multiple victims and assailants, the use of high-powered weaponry, messages left by the perpetrators, and other telltale signs. This report presents a comprehensive assessment of the publicly available data to help understand Mexico's recent violence, and specifically the role of organized crime in relation to this problem.

In the analysis of crime and violence, alarm or frustration about a given situation sometimes makes it easy to slip into impassioned claims and hyperbole. In 2008, in the face of Mexico's rapidly mounting security crisis, a worst-case scenario analysis by the U.S. Joint Forces Command contemplated Mexico as one of two countries—along with Pakistan—that could suffer a sudden collapse into a "failed state." A decade later, in 2017, a widely-publicized report from the International Institute for Strategic Studies suggested that Mexico was the second most violent country in the world (after Syria), and asserted that all 23,000 homicides in 2016 were attributable to organized crime. This claim was seized on by U.S. President Donald Trump as a means to proliferate fear and animosity toward Mexico.

Yet, while Mexico is often characterized as having extreme levels of violence, homicide rates per 100,000 inhabitants are actually far worse elsewhere in the Western Hemisphere. With nearly two times Mexico's population, Brazil continues to lead the hemisphere in the total number of homicides, as it has for at least the last decade according to the latest available cross-national data from the United Nations Office of Drugs and Crime (UNODC). Also, in per capita terms, Mexico's national homicide rate is close to "average" for the region and, due to the magnifying effect

1. More Mexicans have been killed by organized crime-style homicides than the number of U.S. soldiers reported killed in "battle deaths" and "other deaths (in theater)" in the U.S. War for Independence (4,000), the Mexican-American War (13,000), the Spanish American War (2,000), World War I (53,000), the Korean Conflict (36,000), the Vietnam War (58,000), or the current conflicts in Afghanistan (2,000), and Iraq (4,000). All figures indicated here are rounded down to the nearest thousand.

of population-based homicide rate calculations, ranks well below those of smaller countries, like Belize, Colombia, Guatemala, Honduras, Jamaica, and Venezuela. Meanwhile, by the various measures used to compile the so-called Fragile States Index (formerly known as the Failed State Index), the health of the Mexican state ranks about average for Latin American countries. In short, considering the size of its population and capacity for basic governance, Mexico is far from becoming the world's most violent country and does not appear to be on the verge of collapse.

Still, while Mexico's levels of violence may be "average," the fact that its population exceeds 110 million means that the overall toll of violence is much greater in Mexico than in smaller countries with higher homicide rates. Indeed, the number of homicides in Mexico from 2000 through 2015 (256,347) amounted to more than the combined total for several countries with much higher homicide rates, including Belize (1,523), Dominican Republic (28,208), El Salvador (54,548), Guatemala (70,012), Honduras (75,679), and Jamaica (20,508). During that same period, the total number of homicides in Mexico was also slightly higher than the total for the United States (254,983), which has nearly three times Mexico's population. Based on available data since 2000, roughly 1 in 8 murders in the Western Hemisphere occurred in Mexico.

Mexico also stands out because the problem of violence is relatively new. For many Latin American countries, political violence was a recurring problem during much of the 20th century, due to military interventions, civil wars, and insurgencies that led to mass killing, disappearances, and human rights violations. In contrast, from the 1930s onward, Mexico experienced a relatively high degree of political stability and low levels of internal conflict for the remainder of the 20th century. In terms of interpersonal violence, historical data show that homicide in Mexico generally declined from the 1930s into the mid-2000s. Thus, the rise in violence in Mexico over the past decade presents a disconcerting and urgent problem that merits serious consideration from scholars and policy makers.

[A] review of available data shows that a many homicides in recent years bore characteristics typically associated with organized crime-style violence: group executions, torture, beheadings, dismemberment, assault weapons, "narco" messages, mass graves, and other methods used by organized crime groups.

In total, for 2017, *Lantia* reported 18,898 organized-crime-style homicides, *Milenio* reported 12,532, and *Reforma* reported 9,883, showing across-the-board increases in such tallies.

Given the substantial variation across different sources, there appear to be important differences in methodology and/or data compilation for tallies of organized-crime-style homicides. Still, regardless which datasets are being compared, there is a very strong statistical relationship between the variables being measured. That is, the various sources of data on both homicides and organized-crime-style homicides are highly correlated, moving in the same direction with a high degree of statistical correlation.

Of course, there is the possibility of false positives or negatives (Type I and Type II errors) in the data. Thus, in estimating the share of organized-crime-style homicides, it is arguably best to consider the range. With this in mind, available sources indicate that as few as a 34% and as many as 57% of all homicides in Mexico from 2006–2017 bore characteristics of organized-crime-style violence. Moreover, limiting the comparison to the years from 2008–2017 raises the proportion of homicides attributable to organized crime by about 2% on average across all sources. For 2017, the most conservative estimate suggests that roughly a third of all homicides in Mexico were attributable to organized crime.

Among the major centers of violence, Tijuana stands out. While Tijuana was ranked as Mexico's second most violent municipality (after Acapulco) from 2013 to 2016, it moved into first place in 2017 largely because of an 85% increase in homicide cases over the course of that year. Whereas Tijuana saw 871 homicide cases in 2016, the number rose to 1,618 cases in 2017. Tijuana has not ranked as the most violent municipality since 2007, when violence was considerably lower throughout the country. Since many had lauded the city for regaining control of its security situation after a wave of violence in the municipality between 2008–2010, the resurgence of violence in Tijuana has accordingly become a matter of significant alarm and frustration for local authorities.

In a policy brief published by Justice in Mexico earlier this year, Arredondo, et. al. (2018) point out that one out of twenty murders in Mexico took place in Tijuana, and only 10% of these were cleared by law enforcement investigations. The authors point out that the increase in homicides in Tijuana reflects the influence of a new violent organized crime group in Tijuana: the Jalisco New Generation Cartel (Cartel de Jalisco Nueva Generación, CJNG). Since the fall of Sinaloa Cartel leader Joaquín "El Chapo" Guzmán, the CJNG has battled elements of the Sinaloa Cartel for control over drug trafficking routes in Tijuana and other parts of the country, according to a separate Justice in Mexico policy brief published in March 2018.

Assassination of current, former, elected, or substitute candidates to the mayoral position in Mexico is a serious concern. The murder of elected authorities threatens the democratic process and undermines the rule of law. According to newspaper *El País,* nine mayors were assassinated in Mexico in 2017, making it the most violent year for sitting mayors in the last two decades, reaching a total of over 50 victims, with 23 murdered during the current administration.

Justice in Mexico's *Memoria* dataset includes 152 mayors, candidates and former mayors killed from 2005 through 2017. While the peak of violence in Mexico occurred during 2011, the year with the most killings of mayors, as documented in *Memoria*, was actually 2010, with 20 cases reported. With the increase of the total number of homicides in Mexico since 2015 until 2017, there have been a total of 41 current, former, and aspiring mayors killed, with 14 victims in 2015, six in 2016, and 21 in 2017.

Of the 21 murdered the past year, Justice in Mexico found eleven mayors (11) and ten former mayors (10). According to Justice in Mexico's data, the party affiliation of the victims in 2017 was diverse.

Justice in Mexico acknowledges that, while the *Memoria* database includes information on mayors, former mayors, and mayoral candidates, it currently does not account for all relevant cases of local political assassinations. For example, in 2017, Jorge Hernández Jiménez, a PRI municipality council (*regidor*) of Quecholac, Puebla was murdered. Likewise, Saúl Galindo, a PRD Local Deputy (*diputado local*) and aspiring candidate seeking his party's nomination for mayor in Tomatlán, Jalisco was also killed in 2017.

As reported in previous years, dozens of reporters and media workers have been killed or disappeared in Mexico, making it one of the world's most dangerous places for journalists. The various organizations tallying homicides involving reporters in Mexico use different criteria for tallying and classifying this violence, since motives are often difficult to confirm. For example, one of the most respected sources, the Committee to Protect Journalists (CPJ), focuses primarily on cases where a murder was confirmed to have been committed in relation to the journalist's profession. From 1992 through 2017, CPJ reported that there were 40 such confirmed cases, 52 unconfirmed cases, and four media-support workers killed in Mexico. Nearly 78% of those confirmed cases involved reporters working the crime beat, approximately 38% involved reporters working on issues related to corruption, and almost one-third involved reporters working on political issues. CPJ considers Mexico the third deadliest country worldwide, placing in 2017 only behind Iraq (at least 8 journalists killed) and Syria (7).

CPJ's criteria for identifying the murders of reporters and media workers are fairly conservative, since they focus only on cases where there is a confirmed motive associated with the journalist's profession. The organization known as Article 19, meanwhile, documented 11 murders of media workers in 2017, almost double CPJ's count. Taking into account all attacks on media and journalists, including homicides and non-lethal attacks, Article 19 reports that 2017 was the most violent year on record in Mexico, which has been experiencing an increasing trend since 2015, where there were 397 attacks against journalists registered. In 2017, Article 19 recorded 507 attacks, an increase of 19% from 2016's 426 attacks. To put this increase into perspective, according to Article 19's *Violencia Contra la Prensa en México* report, during the first half of 2017 a journalist was attacked every 15.7 hours, totaling 1.5 aggressions every day.

[I]n 2017 the number of homicides in Mexico increased for the third time in three years, continuing a troubling upward trend at a 20% rate of increase. Among the factors noted in our previous reports, Mexico's recent economic difficulties (e.g., stagnant economic growth, a devalued peso, a serious fiscal crisis due to falling oil prices) are often cited as major contributors to the recent increases in violence. Yet socio-economic conditions alone are insufficient to understand the surge in violence, since the dynamics of conflict or equilibrium among organized crime groups—particularly those involved in international drug trafficking—tend to have perceptible effects on patterns of violence at both at the national and local level.

What is clear is that government intervention to disrupt (or sometimes facilitate) organized criminal activities has an important effect, and one that is not always positive or predictable. Despite assurances from government officials that Mexico's drop in violence from 2012 through mid-2014 was attributable to effective law enforcement at the national and local level, other factors—including the dominance of Mexico's Sinaloa cartel—seem to have played an important role. As made evident by the rise in violence following the recapture and extradition of Joaquín "El Chapo" Guzmán, Mexican law enforcement has a long way to go before it can provide a lasting protective effect against organized crime and violence. In Guzmán's place, a new violent criminal organization known as the Jalisco New Generation Cartel has emerged, and its efforts to establish itself as Mexico's dominant criminal organization has contributed to the dramatic increase in violence throughout the country.

A major portion of the increase in violence in Mexico over the last few years is attributable to competition between organized crime groups, particularly those battling for control of the drug trade. For this reason, the Mexican government has focused heavily on counter-drug efforts targeting major drug trafficking organizations, including efforts to eradicate production, interdict illicit goods in transit, and disrupt organized crime leadership structures. In a major milestone for counter-drug efforts, the Mexican government extradited famed drug trafficker Joaquín "El Chapo" Guzmán to the United States in January 2017 to stand trial for various drug-related crimes in New York. A March 2018 Justice in Mexico policy brief entitled "The New Generation: Mexico's Emerging Organized Crime Threat" identifies Guzmán's downfall as a major contributor to the dramatic increase in violence over the past three years. In [that] report, La Rosa and Shirk argue that Guzmán's removal as the purported head of the Sinaloa Cartel, gave rise to conflicts involving splinter groups and rival organizations competing to take over the drug's lord lucrative drug trafficking routes. A relatively new organized crime syndicate, the Jalisco New Generation Cartel (Cartel Jalisco Nueva Generación, CJNG), has been behind much of this violence. An offshoot of the Sinaloa Cartel, the CJNG is based in Guadalajara, Jalisco, and has a growing presence throughout the country.

The CJNG's emerged from the drug trafficking syndicate founded by the Valencia in Michoacán in the 1970s, which relocated to the state of Jalisco in the late 1990s and became known as the Milenio Cartel. In the early 2000s, the Milenio Cartel operated under the umbrella of the Sinaloa Cartel, reporting to regional organized crime boss, Ignacio "Nacho" Coronel. Coronel helped connect Milenio's leaders to Taiwanese immigrant Ye Gon, who provided the chemical precursors that helped their organization become one of the world's leading sources of methamphetamine. In this sense, the CJNG demonstrates the manner in which Mexican drug trafficking organizations have diversified their operations into new product areas, including heroin, methamphetamines, and other synthetic drugs in the face of more intensive counter-drug efforts and the partial legalization of marijuana [in the United States].

After Coronel was killed in 2010, the Milenio Cartel suffered internal schisms that ultimately led to the eventual emergence of the CJNG. The organization was initially led by Erick Valencia Salazar, a descendant of the founders of the Milenio Cartel. However, after Valencia Salazar's arrest in 2012, a U.S. deportee and long-time cartel operative named Ruben Oseguera Cervantes rose to become the leader of the CJNG. Oseguera has proved to be an effective and assertive leader of the CJNG. Following Valencia Salazar's arrest in 2012, Oseguera responded by deploying blockades and a series of explosions throughout the state of Jalisco. Under his leadership, the CJNG also directly challenged Mexican law enforcement and military forces, killing dozens of police and shooting down a Cougar EC 725 helicopter from the Mexican Air Force.

In this sense, the rise of the CJNG also illustrates how organized crime groups fragment and adapt following the disruption of leadership structures. Indeed, while numerous factors have contributed to the rise and resurgence of violence in Mexico, the reliance of U.S. and Mexican law enforcement on leadership disruption, or "kingpin" removal, stands out as a particularly counter-productive strategy. The CJNG is just the latest of a series of Mexican organized crime groups to emerge from the power vacuums that result when major drug traffickers like Joaquín "El Chapo" Guzmán are arrested. This process of leadership removal and regeneration is so well understood by researchers that it is frequently described as the "hydra-effect." Like the mythological beast of ancient times, cutting off the head of a drug cartel almost always results in the emergence of a new one that is just as dangerous, if not more so.

That said, Justice in Mexico has long pointed out that in addition to the hydra effect, the kingpin strategy has another unintended consequence, organized crime group splintering. When an organized crime group loses top leaders, lower level cells and individual operatives are more likely to splinter away to form their own criminal enterprises. In this sense, the Mexican government's efforts are akin to those of the fabled sorcerer's apprentice, a Germanic fairy tale that was made famous by the Disney film Fantasia. When magical spells go awry, the apprentice tries to break an enchanted broom into smaller and smaller pieces, causing his problems to multiply. Unlike the Fantasia example, however, no magical wizard will be able to come to Mexico's rescue, perhaps not even the Mexican military.

Drug prohibition-related violence has led a number of prominent international political figures to call for a dramatic reassessment of international drug control strategy over the past decade. As noted above, former Mexican President Vicente Fox raised the prospect of ending drug prohibition in late 2010. But the trend began before then. In 2009, the Latin American Commission on Drugs and Democracy issued a striking report criticizing the United States-led drug war. The Commission was comprised of a blue-ribbon panel of experts from throughout Latin America and headed by three former Latin American Presidents: Fernando Henrique Cardoso of Brazil, César Gaviria of Colombia, and Ernesto Zedillo of Mexico. The Commission concluded that the war on drugs is a "failed war" that has led to an increase in organized crime and drug-related violence without reducing drug use or availability. The group called for a paradigm shift in drug policy toward an approach that focuses on demand reduction and "[c]hanges the status of addicts from drug buyers in the illegal market to that of patients cared for in the public health system." THE LATIN AM. COMM'N ON DRUGS AND DEMOCRACY, DRUGS AND DEMOCRACY: TOWARD A PARADIGM SHIFT 1 (2009).

In 2011, the Global Commission on Drug Policy released a report that was perhaps even more critical of the war on drugs. The Global Commission on Drug Policy, which included the three former Presidents who had convened the Latin American Commission on Drugs and Democracy among its 19 members, was formed to build on the Latin American Commission's work. In addition, at the time of the 2011 report's release, the Global Commission's membership also included former Secretary General of the United Nations, Kofi Annan, and former U.S. Secretary of State under President Ronald Reagan, George P. Shultz.

War on Drugs

Report of The Global Commission on Drug Policy (2011)

The global war on drugs has failed. When the United Nations Single Convention on Narcotic Drugs came into being 50 years ago, and when President Nixon launched the US government's war on drugs 40 years ago, policymakers believed that harsh law enforcement action against those involved in drug production, distribution and use would lead to an ever-diminishing market in controlled drugs such as heroin, cocaine and cannabis, and the eventual achievement of a 'drug free world'. In practice, the global scale of illegal drug markets—largely controlled by organized crime—has grown dramatically over this period. While accurate estimates of global consumption across the entire 50-year period are not available, an analysis of the last 10 years alone shows a large and growing market.

In spite of the increasing evidence that current policies are not achieving their objectives, most policymaking bodies at the national and international level have tended to avoid open scrutiny or debate on alternatives.

This lack of leadership on drug policy has prompted the establishment of our Commission, and leads us to our view that the time is now right for a serious, comprehensive and wide-ranging review of strategies to respond to the drug phenomenon. The starting point for this review is the recognition of the global drug problem as a set of interlinked health and social challenges to be managed, rather than a war to be won.

Commission members have agreed on four core principles that should guide national and international drug policies and strategies, and have made eleven recommendations for action.

PRINCIPLES

> 1. Drug policies must be based on solid empirical and scientific evidence. The primary measure of success should be the reduction of harm to the health, security and welfare of individuals and society.

In the 50 years since the United Nations initiated a truly global drug prohibition system, we have learned much about the nature and patterns of drug production, distribution, use and dependence, and the effectiveness of our attempts to reduce these problems. It might have been understandable that the architects of the system would place faith in the concept of eradicating drug production and use (in the light of the limited evidence available at the time). There is no excuse, however, for ignoring the evidence and experience accumulated since then. Drug policies and strategies at all levels too often continue to be driven by ideological perspectives, or political convenience, and pay too little attention to the complexities of the drug market, drug use and drug addiction.

Effective policymaking requires a clear articulation of the policy's objectives. The 1961 UN Single Convention on Narcotic Drugs made it clear that the ultimate objective of the system was the improvement of the 'health and welfare of mankind'.

This reminds us that drug policies were initially developed and implemented in the hope of achieving outcomes in terms of a reduction in harms to individuals and society—less crime, better health, and more economic and social development. However, we have primarily been measuring our success in the war on drugs by entirely different measures—those that report on processes, such as the number of arrests, the amounts seized, or the harshness of punishments. These indicators may tell us how tough we are being, but they do not tell us how successful we are in improving the 'health and welfare of mankind'.

> 2. Drug policies must be based on human rights and public health principles. We should end the stigmatization and marginalization of people who use certain drugs and those involved in the lower levels of cultivation, production and distribution, and treat people dependent on drugs as patients, not criminals.

Certain fundamental principles underpin all aspects of national and international policy. These are enshrined in the Universal Declaration of Human Rights and many international treaties that have followed. Of particular relevance to drug policy are the rights to life, to health, to due process and a fair trial, to be free from torture or cruel, inhuman or degrading treatment, from slavery, and from discrimination. These rights are inalienable, and commitment to them takes precedence over other international agreements, including the drug control conventions. As the UN High Commissioner for Human Rights, Navanethem Pillay, has stated, "Individuals who use drugs do not forfeit their human rights. Too often, drug users suffer discrimination, are forced to accept treatment, marginalized and often harmed by approaches which over-emphasize criminalization and punishment while under-emphasizing harm reduction and respect for human rights."

A number of well-established and proven public health measures (generally referred to as *harm reduction*, an approach that includes syringe access and treatment using the proven medications methadone or buprenorphine) can minimize the risk of drug overdose deaths and the transmission of HIV and other blood-borne infections. However, governments often do not fully implement these interventions, concerned that by improving the health of people who use drugs, they are undermining a 'tough on drugs' message. This is illogical—sacrificing the health and welfare of one group of citizens when effective health protection measures are available is unacceptable, and increases the risks faced by the wider community.

An indiscriminate approach to 'drug trafficking' is similarly problematic. Many people taking part in the drug market are themselves the victims of violence and intimidation, or are dependent on drugs. An example of this phenomenon are the drug 'mules' who take the most visible and risky roles in the supply and delivery chain. Unlike those in charge of drug trafficking organizations, these individuals do not usually have an extensive and violent criminal history, and some engage in the drug trade primarily to get money for their own drug dependence. We should not treat all those arrested for trafficking as equally culpable—many are coerced into their actions, or are driven to desperate measures through their own addiction or economic situation. It is not appropriate to punish such individuals in the same way as the members of violent organized crime groups who control the market.

Finally, many countries still react to people dependent on drugs with punishment and stigmatization. In reality, drug dependence is a complex health condition that has a mixture of causes—social, psychological and physical (including, for example, harsh living conditions, or a history of personal trauma or emotional problems). Trying to manage this complex condition through punishment is ineffective—much greater success can be achieved by providing a range of evidence-based drug treatment services. Countries that have treated citizens dependent on drugs as patients in need of treatment, instead of criminals deserving of punishment, have demonstrated extremely positive results in crime reduction, health improvement, and overcoming dependence.

> 3. The development and implementation of drug policies should be a global shared responsibility, but also needs to take into consideration diverse political, social and cultural realities. Policies should respect the rights and needs of people affected by production, trafficking and consumption, as explicitly acknowledged in the 1988 Convention on Drug Trafficking.

The UN drug control system is built on the idea that all governments should work together to tackle drug markets and related problems. This is a reasonable starting point, and there is certainly a responsibility to be shared between producing, transit and consuming countries (although the distinction is increasingly blurred, as many countries now experience elements of all three).

However, the idea of shared responsibility has too often become a straitjacket that inhibits policy development and experimentation. The UN (through the International Narcotics Control Board), and in particular the US (notably through its 'certification' process), have worked strenuously over the last 50 years to ensure that all countries adopt the same rigid approach to drug policy—the same laws, and the same tough approach to their enforcement. As national governments have become more aware of the complexities of the problems, and options for policy responses in their own territories, many have opted to use the flexibilities within the Conventions to try new strategies and programs, such as decriminalization initiatives or harm reduction programs. When these involve a more tolerant approach to drug use, governments have faced international diplomatic pressure to 'protect the integrity of the Conventions', even when the policy is legal, successful and supported in the country.

A current example of this process (what may be described as 'drug control imperialism'), can be observed with the proposal by the Bolivian government to remove the practice of coca leaf chewing from the sections of the 1961 Convention that prohibit all non-medical uses. Despite the fact that successive studies have shown that the indigenous practice of coca leaf chewing is associated with none of the harms of international cocaine markets, and that a clear majority of the Bolivian population (and neighboring countries) support this change, many of the rich 'cocaine consumer' countries (led by the US) have formally objected to the amendment.

The idea that the international drug control system is immutable, and that any amendment—however reasonable or slight—is a threat to the integrity of the entire system, is short-sighted. As with all multilateral agreements, the drug conventions need to be subject to constant review and modernization in light of changing and variable circumstances. Specifically, national governments must be enabled to exercise the freedom to experiment with responses more suited to their circumstances. This analysis and exchange of experiences is a crucial element of the process of learning about the relative effectiveness of different approaches, but the belief that we all need to have exactly the same laws, restrictions and programs has been an unhelpful restriction.

> 4. Drug policies must be pursued in a comprehensive manner, involving families, schools, public health specialists, development practitioners and civil society leaders, in partnership with law enforcement agencies and other relevant governmental bodies.

With their strong focus on law enforcement and punishment, it is not surprising that the leading institutions in the implementation of the drug control system have been the police, border control and military authorities directed by Ministries of Justice, Security or Interior. At the multilateral level, regional or United Nations structures are also dominated by these interests.

Although governments have increasingly recognized that law enforcement strategies for drug control need to be integrated into a broader approach with social and public health programs, the structures for policymaking, budget allocation, and implementation have not modernized at the same pace.

These institutional dynamics obstruct objective and evidence-based policymaking. This is more than a theoretical problem—repeated studies have demonstrated that governments achieve much greater financial and social benefit for their communities by investing in health and social programs, rather than investing in supply reduction and law enforcement activities. However, in most countries, the vast majority of available resources are spent on the enforcement of drug laws and the punishment of people who use drugs.

The lack of coherence is even more marked at the United Nations. The development of the global drug control regime involved the creation of three bodies to oversee the implementation of the conventions—the UN Office on Drugs and Crime (UNODC), the International Narcotics Control Board (INCB), and the Commission on Narcotic Drugs (CND). This structure is premised on the notion that international drug control is primarily a fight against crime and criminals. Unsurprisingly, there is a built-in vested interest in maintaining the law enforcement focus and the senior decisionmakers in these bodies have traditionally been most familiar with this framework.

Now that the nature of the drug policy challenge has changed, the institutions must follow. Global drug policy should be created from the shared strategies of all interested multilateral agencies—UNODC of course, but also UNAIDS, WHO, UNDP, UNICEF, UN Women, the World Bank, and the Office of the High Commissioner on Human Rights. The marginalization of the World Health Organization is particularly worrisome given the fact that it has been given a specific mandate under the drug control treaties.

While national governments have considerable discretion to move away from repressive policies, the UN drug control system continues to act largely as a straitjacket, limiting the proper review and modernization of policy. For most of the last century, it has been the US government that has led calls for the development and maintenance of repressive drug policies. We therefore welcome the change of tone emerging from the current administration—with President Obama himself acknowledging the futility of a 'war on drugs' and the validity of a debate on alternatives. It will be necessary, though, for the US to follow up this new rhetoric with real reform, by reducing its reliance on incarceration and punishment of drug users, and by using its considerable diplomatic influence to foster reform in other countries.

The Global Commission on Drug Policy has remained actively involved in the discussion of international drug control. The Commission issued major reports in 2014, 2016, and 2017, all building on the themes and policy recommendations of its 2011 report. Although the Global Commission on Drug Policy's 2011 report spoke positively of "the change of tone emerging from" President Barack Obama's administration, the White House Office of National Drug Control Policy (ONDCP) did not respond favorably to the Commission's report. An ONDCP spokesperson criticized the report, saying that "[m]aking more drugs available—as this report suggests—will make it harder to keep our communities healthy and safe." Ken Ellingwood and Brian Bennett, *High-profile Panel Urges Non-criminal Approach to World Drug Policy*, L.A. TIMES, June 1, 2011. Former U.S. President Jimmy Carter was much more receptive to the report and wrote an editorial in support of the Commission's recommendations in the *New York Times*. Carter praised the report for "describ[ing] the total failure of the present global antidrug effort, and in particular America's 'war on drugs'" and argued that "to make drug policies more humane and more effective, the American government should support and enact the reforms laid out by the Global Commission on Drug Policy." Jimmy Carter, *Call Off the Global Drug War*, N.Y. TIMES, June 17, 2011 at A35.

The phrase "global war on drugs" has taken on a new dimension over the last two decades as drug trafficking organizations and terrorist groups have become increasingly intertwined. *See, e.g.*, VANDA FELBAB-BROWN, SHOOTING UP: COUNTERINSURGENCY AND THE WAR ON DRUGS (2009). The Global Commission on Drug Policy pointed to this development to critique the drug war, arguing "it is the illicit nature of the market that creates much of the market-related violence . . . and, in some cases, fund[s] insurgency and terrorism." However, others believe that the link between terrorism and the illegal drug market means we should prosecute the drug war even more vigorously. Which conclusion do you think is correct? Consider the following remarks by former U.S. Secretary of Homeland Security, Michael Chertoff, from a speech he gave at a law review symposium.

The Nexus between Drug Trafficking, Terrorism and Organized Crime
Michael Chertoff

13 Chapman Law Review 681 (2010)

We have a tendency to say everything is war, the war on poverty, the war on drugs, the war on this—but some of these areas really do have a war. There's repeated violence and destruction, and when we look at the intersection between terrorism and international drug trafficking, I think we really do have a war. So, what I thought I'd do is give you a little bit of a sense of change from the beginning of this decade through the next decade. I'll tell you right up front, I'm not recommending legalizing drugs. I think that would be a major mistake.

I first looked at the nexus between drug trafficking and terrorism when I was head of the Criminal Division at the Department of Justice. Some of you may remember that the FARC, the Revolutionary Army in Colombia, which was a left wing political organization, was very strong in the 1990s and the early part of this decade. It has lost a considerable amount of ground since then, partly because of our work with President Uribe of Colombia and his people in really reforming the military and pushing back against the FARC. But certainly they remain a potent force, and they were very potent in the late 1990s and the early 2000s.

We brought a series of indictments against the FARC for various terrorism-related violations which included, among other things, kidnapping people—including Americans—and holding them for ransom. But one of the things that emerged as we investigated was that the FARC had begun to migrate toward becoming a classic drug organization. What happened first was they began to encounter drug traffickers in the areas of Columbia that they controlled, and then they began to charge them a tax or a protection fee. This is similar to what organized crime often does in the United States. They don't directly engage in the sale of drugs, but they essentially reap the benefits by extorting money from the drug dealers, or taxing them and protecting them against being ripped off.

So the FARC began to move into the protection racket, but pretty soon that migrated into something a little bit more enabling. They'd be involved in managing staging areas, helping load airplanes, and ultimately they became full-fledged partners in drug trafficking. And, in fact, we had indictments issued against the FARC that included both terrorism and drug trafficking charges. In many ways, that was the first concrete example of the intersection between a global criminal organization involved in the drug trade—one that has access to the modern tools of money, movement, communications, and travel—with terrorist organizations who benefit from the money and the enabling capabilities of the drug organizations, and who can provide violence and the support of violence, which of course is important for the drug organizations.

We've now seen this problem migrate from Colombia around the world. It's no secret in Afghanistan, for example, where the cultivation of poppies creates a major source for heroin. It's no secret that the Taliban has protected and, in fact, is cooperating with drug dealers, because they receive money from the drug dealing and the drug trafficking. That money enables them to buy arms and, not coincidentally, the drug activity winds up also hurting the West and the enemies of the Taliban, so they get a double bang for their buck. They have the ability both, in some general sense, to strike at their enemies and, in a more specific, narrow sense, to get the kinds of financing that they need in order to acquire the weapons and trading capabilities which allow them to be such lethal adversaries.

What we've now seen, however, is that this is moving into South America, as well in places apart from Colombia. For example, recent information tells us that there has been an increase in the movement of cocaine from South America into Europe. That's partly a reflection of some of the progress we've made in making it more difficult to bring drugs into the United States. Partly, it's a rise in demand in Europe, but what's interesting, for the purpose of my talk, is how it's getting there. And the way a lot of it is getting there is via North Africa. The cocaine moves out of South America, often through Venezuela, where, of course, Hugo Chavez is really a dedicated enemy of the United States and the West and, therefore, very happy to be in a neighborhood of drug trafficking. It then moves from Venezuela into North Africa, where it is staged and ultimately sent into Europe to be sold.

What we have learned is that in North Africa, groups affiliated with terrorism, including Al-Qaeda in the Maghreb (which is a North African group that is sympathetic and, in fact, formally linked with the core Al-Qaeda in Pakistan and Afghanistan), have become involved in protecting the loads when they arrive and while they're being held in staging to be ultimately shipped into Europe. And the reason for that, again, is perfectly obvious, because it's a source of money which enables them to recruit and buy arms and further their own political goals. So, once again, we begin to see the capabilities of drug organizations, and the money they generate, to create an attractive partner for terrorist organizations. Terrorist organizations also have the ability to provide the violence and the security that is very important to the drug traffickers.

What I predict is going to happen is, at some point, some trafficker is going to look in the mirror and say: "You know, I'm not a drug trafficker. I'm a political insurgent." We're very close to having that cross-over of political ideology, no matter how far-fetched it is, beginning to engraft itself into the violence and the mayhem that is part of the drug trade. That, of course, is going to bring two dangerous adversaries together in a way which is only going to multiply the problems for those of us around the world who are trying to protect society.

Where this might touch this country most seriously is in Northern Mexico. I know people in California know this, but it's not that well-known in other parts of the country—there's currently nothing less than a war going on in Northern Mexico for the control and governance of the country. It is underway because the President of Mexico has done a courageous thing—he has recognized that tolerating the rule of drug organizations in various cities in Northern Mexico is not an acceptable alternative for a modern democracy. You cannot surrender parts of your country to organized crime or narcotics trafficking gangs. And so he made it his top priority when he came into office several years ago to take these groups on.

Not surprisingly, when you strike at organized criminal groups, they strike back. And the tactics that they've adopted in many of the cartels in Northern Mexico are directly derived from what they have seen on television or over the Internet in Iraq and Afghanistan. We have beheadings. We have kidnappings. We have bombings. We have torture. All the things that Al-Qaeda and the Taliban have done are now being used by these organized crime cartels.

The reason is quite explicit. It is to terrorize the population of Mexico so that either this President at some point will be forced to pull back, or when the next election comes, it is more likely to go to somebody who is either tacitly or overtly willing to make peace with the cartels. That would be a disaster for the United States. It would be the equivalent of putting Waziristan on our southern border. It's one of the reasons that, when I was Secretary, we put into effect a process of contingency planning against the remote—but nevertheless certainly not unthinkable—possibility that we might have an increase in cross-border violence coming from Mexico into the United States.

The short answer here, of course, is to support President Calderon in his effort. It's one of the reasons that President Bush pushed very hard for an initiative to send not only money but weapons, training, and modern technology to Mexico to help the Mexicans ramp up their own ability to fight the drug gangs. This policy is continuing into the current administration, which is also firmly committed to supporting Mexico in this endeavor. But, again, I want to put before you the notion that if one of these drug leaders one day decides that rather than thinking of himself as a thug, he'd rather think of himself as a political leader, we will have completed that merger between terrorism and organized criminality, which I think we've seen in its incipient phases in various places of the world.

B. International Drug Treaties and Control Organizations

1. Overview

Three treaties form the foundation of the international drug control regime: the 1961 Single Convention on Narcotic Drugs, the 1971 Convention on Psychotropic Substances, and the 1988 United Nations Convention Against Illicit Traffic in Narcotic Drugs and Psychotropic Substances. The excerpt that follows discusses these three treaties and the international bodies that oversee them. It also provides a brief history of international drug control agreements.

The International Control of Illegal Drugs and the U.N. Treaty Regime: Preventing or Causing Human Rights Violations?
Daniel Heilmann

19 Cardozo Journal of International and Comparative Law 237 (2011)

International drug control, administered under the auspices of the United Nations, rests on three pillars: The [1961] Single Convention on Narcotic Drugs as amended by the Protocol (1972) (Single Convention), the Convention on Psychotropic Substances (1971 Convention), and the United Nations Convention Against Illicit Traffic in Narcotic Drugs and Psychotropic Substances (1988 Convention).

The status of the international drug control regime in international law is noteworthy because the system is almost universally recognized. Almost every State in the world is a party to at least one of the conventions, including: 184 State parties to the Single Convention, 183 State parties to the 1971 Convention, and 184 State parties to the 1988 Convention.... Alcohol, despite its psychoactive effect, is not included in the conventions and therefore falls outside the scope of international drug control.

By defining control measures to be maintained within each State party's jurisdiction and by prescribing rules to be obeyed by the parties in their relations with each other, the system provides a legal framework for drug control. The rules focus on commodity control on one hand (regulation of licit production, supply and consumption of drugs) and sanctions on the other (suppression of illicit production, supply and possession mainly through criminal law). Thus, the control system has been developed on the premise that a reduction in the illicit drug markets will be achieved predominantly through prohibition-oriented measures.

Concerted drug control efforts have evolved over a period of more than 100 years. At the end of the nineteenth century, the increased consumption of psychoactive substances such as morphine, heroin and cocaine, and the globally unregulated market for these substances led to serious concerns in the United States. However, for the other colonial powers, such as the United Kingdom or the Netherlands, narcotic drugs, especially opium, were a commodity of enormous economic significance. For example, the export of Indian opium to China created significant revenues and ultimately led to the two Opium Wars between Britain and China (1839–42 and 1857–60) in which Britain defended the interests of British merchants in the region.

Opium consumption was at a record level when the United States convened an international opium conference in Shanghai in 1909. Due to its relative lack of overseas possessions and slight trading presence in Asia, the United States had no genuine interest in maintaining the global opium market. Therefore, the US approach emphasized that the prohibition of opium was a moral question. However, other countries were not ready to concede a total ban on the opium trade. They preferred controlled trade over a complete prohibition. Due to these discrepancies in strategic interest, no final agreement (besides a set of non-binding resolutions) was reached at the Shanghai conference. But, in retrospect, the conference proved to be crucial because it paved the way for a follow-up conference in The Hague in 1911. These follow-up negotiations resulted in the 1912 International Opium Convention. In addition to opium and morphine, cocaine and heroin were also included as controlled substances. The main principles stipulated in the convention are still valid today. For example, the axiom that the manufacture, trade and use of narcotic drugs should be limited to medical and scientific purposes governs the control system to this day. Under the 1912 Opium Convention, national governments were required to enact laws to control the production and distribution of narcotic drugs.

Nevertheless, due to the aforementioned differences in strategic interests between the participating governments, the 1912 Opium Convention was only ratified by China, Norway, the Netherlands, the United States and Honduras before the outbreak of World War I. This changed when the Convention was imposed on the losing parties of the war by linking the ratification of the Opium Convention to the Versailles Peace Treaty of 1919. Thus, by the mid-1920s close to sixty States were party to the 1912 Opium Convention. Furthermore, in the aftermath of World War I the League of Nations assumed responsibility for overseeing the Opium Convention, and specialized bodies, in particular the Advisory Committee on the Traffic in

Opium and Other Dangerous Drugs, were created under its auspices. This proved to be a strong foundation for the successful establishment of a comprehensive international drug control system.

A further cornerstone of the international drug control system was established a few years later by the 1925 Geneva Opium Convention and the Agreement Concerning the Manufacture of, Trade in, and Use of Prepared Opium. Now States were required to annually submit statistics on the production of opium and coca leaves to the newly established Permanent Central Opium Board (PCOB). The obligatory control system included mandatory import certification and export authorization by government. Unfortunately, the system failed to prevent legally manufactured drugs from seeping into the illegal market. One more major drug control treaty was adopted in the period between the First World War and the Second World War: the Convention for the Suppression of the Illicit Traffic in Dangerous Drugs. It emphasized the importance of agreement by States on the implementation of provisions into their domestic laws on severe punishment, for, *inter alia*, the production, trafficking, and sale of illicit substances. Articles 7 to 10 were novel in that they dealt in great detail with extradition for drug related crimes. Overall, the inter-war drug control system achieved considerable success in limiting and screening the production and trade of narcotic drugs.

After World War II, the administration of the drug control regime was transferred from the defunct League of Nations to the United Nations by the Protocol amending the Agreements, Conventions and Protocols on Narcotic Drugs (Protocol of Lake Success). The Commission on Narcotic Drugs (CND), which replaced the Opium Advisory Committee, was established by the Economic and Social Council (ECOSOC) at its first session. From then on it has been the main body advising ECOSOC on all drug-related matters.

In 1948, the Paris Protocol supplemented the 1931 Convention and provided for bringing under international control the drugs outside the scope of the 1931 Convention. This measure was much needed because of the rise of "designer drugs" (in particular opiate derivatives with harmful effects, such as methadone or pethidine), which had been developed to evade international restrictions. A new opium protocol was signed in New York in 1953 (1953 Opium Protocol). The intention behind the protocol was to eliminate the overproduction of opium by authorizing only seven states to produce opium for export (Bulgaria, India, Iran, Greece, the Soviet Union, Turkey and Yugoslavia).

Despite the passage of the 1953 Opium Protocol and its predecessors—due to the increasing complexity of the drug control system—the international community felt an increasing need to consolidate the numerous conventions introduced since the initial Opium Convention of 1912 into one treaty. The resultant efforts led to the drug control regime in force today.

The main underlying objectives of the [1961] Single Convention, besides the codification of the existing laws into one multilateral treaty, were the streamlining of the control mechanisms and the extension of existing controls. The Single Convention was intended to be the final and definitive document that supersedes all previous treaties, i.e. terminates and replaces them. Covered by the Single Convention are . . . the definitions of controlled substances; the framework for the operations of the drug control bodies; reporting obligations of Member States regarding manufacture, trade and consumption of controlled substances; and penal provisions and actions to be taken against illicit trafficking. The scope of the Single Convention includes the classic plant-based drugs, such as opium, heroin, cocaine, and cannabis. It consists of fifty-one articles and four schedules: over one-hundred illicit substances are listed in the four schedules, with drugs grouped according to their perceived dependence-creating properties.

The Preamble stipulates that "addiction to narcotic drugs constitutes a serious evil for the individual and is fraught with social and economic danger to mankind." Article 4(c), the central operational provision of the Convention, manifests a prohibitionist approach by stipulating that "the parties shall take such legislative and administrative measures . . . to limit exclusively to medical and scientific purposes the production, manufacture, export, import distribution of, trade in, use and possession of drugs." However, it must be noted that medical purposes include veterinary and dental purposes and that the meaning of the term "medical purpose" may change and is not exclusive to the use permitted under the system of "western medicine."

Article 2 of the Single Convention addresses control measures for the respective substances; the action of two agencies, the WHO and the CND, is required to put a narcotic drug under control. First, the WHO must determine whether a substance has dangerous properties and should therefore be listed on one of the schedules. Then the CND can either act in accordance with the recommendation of the WHO, or take no action at all.

Countries allowing for the cultivation of coca bushes and opium poppies were required to establish national monopolies and subsequently centralize and phase out their cultivation and production. The ultimate goal of these efforts is a universal international prohibition of the non-medical use of these substances. In regard to manufacturing, trade and distribution, and international trade of controlled narcotic drugs, a strict licensing system and extensive control measures are prescribed to the parties. Under Article 39, parties are allowed to adopt laws with stricter measures of control than those provided by the Single Convention if they deem them desirable or necessary.

The Single Convention of 1961 was amended by a Protocol in 1972 (1972 Protocol). The objective of the adoption of the 1972 Protocol was to further strengthen the international drug control system. This objective was furthered by introducing provisions on technical and financial assistance and the establishment of regional centers for scientific research and education to combat illegal use and traffic in drugs. Article 22(2) of the 1972 Protocol provided for the seizure and destruction of illegally cultivated opium poppies and cannabis. In addition, the 1972 Protocol modified the penal provisions of the Single Convention by providing extradition provisions similar to those in the 1936 Convention for the Suppression of the Illicit Traffic in Dangerous Drugs.

In the late 1960s, the technical advances in the manufacture of synthetic drugs led to an unregulated global market for psychotropic substances, (such as amphetamines, barbiturates and hallucinogens). After careful analysis, the CND concluded that the existing drug control system was limited to narcotic drugs and that the Single Convention was not applicable to psychotropic substances. Nonetheless, the international community felt that a control mechanism over those substances was urgently needed, and the CND was called upon to draft a convention, which would bring those substances under control.

The result of the CND's efforts was the 1971 Convention, which consists of thirty-three articles and four schedules. It can fairly be described as being based on the Single Convention, and its general purpose to limit the manufacture, trade, and use of psychotropic substances to medical and scientific purposes is similar to Article 4 of the Single Convention in respect to narcotic drugs. Any substance included in the schedules must be licensed by the government for manufacture, trade, and distribution. However, compared with the strict controls imposed on plant-based drugs under the Single Convention, the 1971 Convention imposes a somewhat weaker control mechanism. Similar to the control mechanism of the Single Convention, the WHO recommends whether a drug should be controlled. But, the CND is not bound by the recommendation of the WHO. It may, (provided that the WHO has made and communicated its findings on control measures), place the substance concerned under a control regime, change the control regime, or free a substance from a control regime—contrary to the recommendations of the WHO. This obviously gives the CND much wider discretion under the 1971 Convention than under the Single Convention.

Detailed provisions deal with licences, prescriptions, and warnings on packages and advertisements. Concerning prescriptions, the main difference between the Single Convention and the 1971 Convention is that under the 1971 Convention a medical prescription is, in general, required for individual use of all psychotropic substances or preparations, whereas under the Single Convention a medical prescription is only required for certain drugs in its Schedule I. According to Article 10 of the 1971 Convention, directions for use, including cautions and warnings, need to be given only if they are necessary for the safety of the patients using them. What is necessary for the safety of the user is left to the judgment of the party concerned. Advertisements to the general public for psychotropic substances are prohibited under the 1971 Convention; this includes newspapers, television and radio, but not announcements in technical journals, e.g. published specifically for medical practitioners.

Article 20 of the 1971 Convention also addresses measures to be taken against the abuse of psychotropic substances, including treatment, education, rehabilitation and social reintegration. Article 20 acknowledges that a system of penal sanctions and administrative control alone is not sufficient to keep drugs from the users and should therefore not form the sole subject of international cooperation against drug abuse. However, the penal provisions are similar to those in the Single Convention, (but without the extradition provisions which were added to the Single Convention by the 1972 Protocol).

Although the international drug control system satisfactory regulated the lawful production of narcotic drugs and psychotropic substances, the situation regarding illicit production did not noticeably improve. By the mid-1980s it was apparent that global drug abuse had reached unprecedented dimensions. Of special concern was the growing illegal opium production in Asia and the illegal cocaine production in the Andean countries. Against this background, the CND was requested by the General Assembly to prepare a draft convention against illicit traffic in narcotic drugs. Three years of deliberations by expert and review groups resulted in the 1988 United Nations Convention Against Illicit Traffic in Narcotic Drugs and Psychotropic Substances.

The main accomplishment of the 1988 Convention is that it extends controls to the entire market chain, including precursors at the beginning of the chain, to anti-money laundering measures at the end of the chain. The Convention consists of thirty-four articles (together with an annex containing two lists of substances frequently used in the illicit manufacture of narcotic drugs and psychotropic substances) and aims at strengthening compliance with the established drug control system. Member States are required to cooperate and to coordinate their efforts to prevent global drug trafficking. However, some States were worried that the Convention could be misused for other political objectives, i.e. be used to undermine their sovereign rights. Article 2(2) therefore clarifies that "the parties shall carry out their obligations under this Convention in a manner consistent with the principles of sovereign equality and territorial integrity of States and that of non-intervention in the domestic affairs of other States."

While under the Single Convention, Member States are obliged to make trafficking in drugs "punishable offenses," Article 3 of the 1988 Convention goes a step further and obliges Parties to make them "criminal offenses." According to Article 3(2) this includes the possession, purchase, or cultivation of drugs for personal consumption. Nevertheless, States are allowed to provide for alternatives to punishment (e.g. treatment, education, or rehabilitation) in cases of a minor nature and personal consumption. Furthermore, States are called upon to introduce domestic legislation to prevent drug related money laundering. Although money laundering was in principle already a punishable offense under the Single Convention, the provisions of the 1988 Convention are much more precise. Article 3(1)(b) establishes drug related money laundering as a criminal offense, and, in targeting criminal proceeds, the 1988 Convention asks State Parties to confiscate proceeds from drug related offenses and to empower courts to seize bank and financial records.

As previously mentioned, the establishment of a control system for precursor chemicals was a novelty to the drug control regime. According to Article 12, the manufacture, transport or distribution of precursor chemicals should be deemed criminal offenses. This is reflected in the extension of criminal offenses for which extradition can be sought: they include the offenses of drug related money laundering and the manufacture, transport, and distribution of equipment and precursor chemicals.

Some confusion was created by Article 14(2), which stipulates that measures adopted to prevent illicit cultivation of narcotic plants "shall respect fundamental human rights and take due account of traditional licit uses, where there is a historic evidence of such use." Some States tried to interpret this as an acknowledgement that traditional licit uses still existed and had to be taken into account. However, the Single Convention had already outlawed the traditional habits of [coca] chewing and opium smoking. The maximum transitional period granted by the Single Convention ended for opium in 1979 and for cannabis and the [coca]-leaf in 1989. Thus, it is clear that the drug conventions, including the 1988 Convention, do not provide for the production of these controlled drugs for licit traditional use. Such a conclusion is underpinned by Article 14(1) of the 1988 Convention, which points out that "any measures taken pursuant to this Convention by Parties shall not be less stringent than the provisions applicable to the eradication of illicit cultivation of plants containing narcotic and psychotropic substances . . . under the provisions of the 1961 Convention."

Although during the 1990s law enforcement measures based on the international drug control system had been successfully employed in the dismantling of some of the most notorious drug cartels (e.g. the Cali and Medellin cartels), global drug abuse did not, as had been hoped for, decrease. A remarkable initiative to refocus international attention on the global drug problem was therefore taken by the UN General Assembly in 1998 when a Special Session (UNGASS) was convened. UNGASS focused on a number of measures to enhance international cooperation, and the UN General Assembly adopted a Declaration on the Guiding Principles of Drug Demand Reduction, a Political Declaration, and various action plans to this end.

The Political Declaration is notable for various reasons, but particularly so for linking, for the first time, the illicit production and trafficking of drugs with terrorism and arms trafficking. States were called upon to consider the documents agreed on at UNGASS when formulating national drug strategies. Moreover, they were encouraged to report biennially to the CND on their efforts to meet the goals of the action plans. However, in contrast to the three drug conventions, the Political Declaration does not set up a system for monitoring compliance with the Declaration and the accompanying action plans. Article 20 of the Political Declaration solely declares that the CND will analyze the reports that it obtains from member States and use them for the enhancement of cooperation, but there is no formal sanction system foreseen in the Political Declaration. It thus remains a soft instrument.

The year 2008 was envisaged as a target date by which measurable results of the implementation of the action plans were to be achieved, and indeed, considerable success was achieved in reducing the cultivation of coca in South America and opium in some regions of Southeast Asia. But these achievements were overshadowed by the rapid expansion of opium production in Afghanistan. Overall the problem of global drug abuse did not improve significantly during the UNGASS period. Based on the review, the CND at its fifty-second session in 2009 considered further action and adopted a new political declaration and action plan. The new action plan addresses novel trends in drug trafficking, such as the use of information technology, and calls for better regulation of online pharmacies and enhanced intelligence exchange and judicial cooperation.

In order to complete the overview of the functioning of the admittedly complex control regime, some remarks are warranted on the agencies coordinating and developing international drug policies. Compliance with the drug control system outlined in the preceding chapter is managed (rather than enforced) by the United Nations. Three bodies carry out the UN's main activities in this area: the Commission on Narcotic Drugs (CND), the International Narcotics Control Board (INCB), and the UN Office on Drugs and Crime (UNODC). Other UN related agencies are also involved, on the periphery, in administering the global drug control effort, most notably the World Health Organization (WHO) and the United Nations Educational, Scientific, and Cultural Organization (UNESCO).

The CND is a functional commission of ECOSOC and the central policy-making body concerning all drug related matters in the UN. It was created by ECOSOC at its first session in 1946 and although initially composed of fifteen States, membership increased over time to fifty-three States.

Summed up, the main task of the CND is to analyze the global situation on drug control and, when necessary, advise ECOSOC on changes to enhance the drug control system. In this context, the CND acts as guardian of the three international drug conventions. For example, according to Article 8 of the Single Convention, the CND is authorized to consider all matters pertaining to the aims of the Single Convention. Similar blanket clauses can be found in Article 17 of the Convention on Psychotropic Substances and Article 21 of the Convention Against the Illicit Traffic in Narcotic Drugs and Psychotropic Substances.

Furthermore, special functions are assigned to the CND under the drug control conventions. Most important in the catalogue of competencies is the CND's supervision of the classification of controlled substances. The CND's authority to decide—on the basis of recommendations by the WHO—whether a drug is listed on, deleted from, or transferred to the schedules, is powerful. Similarly, the CND decides pursuant to the 1988 Convention on the recommendation of the INCB, on placing precursor chemicals on the Convention's list of controlled substances. Whereas general decisions of the CND—as those of any other functional commission of the UN system—remain subject to approval by the ECOSOC or the General Assembly, this is not the case when the CND decides on amending the schedules annexed to the conventions. Although a decision on amending the schedules is not subject to an initial review by ECOSOC or the General Assembly, the CND's powers are restricted by the right of any party to file an appeal against such a decision.

ECOSOC may then confirm, alter or reverse the decision of the CND. Recently the position of the CND has been strengthened by the mandate to receive reports on States' efforts to meet the goals agreed upon at the UNGASS.

The INCB differs from the CND and UNODC in that it is an independent treaty body rather than a UN agency. Notably, it is not purely an inter-governmental body, as the members are elected by ECOSOC from candidates proposed by governments and the WHO. However, the elected members do not represent governments, but act in their personal capacity as experts on drug related matters.

The INCB was established in 1968 as the monitoring body for the implementation of the Single Convention. Today it monitors the implementation of all three drug conventions and is concerned with the monitoring and screening of the production, trade, and use of licit and illicit drugs. To this end it works closely with national governments to ensure that adequate supplies of drugs are available for medical and scientific uses, and that weaknesses in national approaches to combating the production, trafficking, and use of illicit drugs are identified. The INCB collects and administers the statistical data for drug production, trade, and consumption; a measure aimed at helping governments to establish a balance between (licit) supply and demand. The main task in this regard is the administration of the estimates and statistical returns systems. States have an obligation to report their statistical data at certain deadlines, and, if they fail to submit estimates, the INCB might establish the estimates for them. If the INCB has objective reason to believe that the aims of the Convention are being seriously endangered by a party (e.g. if a State is under the risk of becoming a centre of the illicit cultivation or production of narcotic drugs), the INCB may request the State to explain the condition, and it may propose the opening of consultations or the initiation of a study. The mandate of the INCB includes entering into a continuing dialogue with governments relating to their obligations under the drug control conventions, and ultimately, if all measures of cooperation with the respective government fail, the INCB may recommend that other States stop the import and export of drugs to and from a country that fails to explain properly its activities. However, the authority is much weaker than that of the INCB's predecessor, the Permanent Central Board, which actually could impose sanctions on States. Although the INCB does not have the power to administer sanctions, it may well censure States which it judges not to be in compliance; such censure may have a positive effect in and of itself on compliance with the control regime.

The set-up of the UN programs and initiatives on drug control has changed frequently in recent decades. In 1991, the secretariat of the INCB (but not the Board itself), the functions of the Division of Narcotic Drugs (DND), and the UN Fund for Drug Abuse Control (UNFDAC) were integrated into the UN Drug Control Programme (UNDCP). A further streamlining took place in 1997, when UNDCP was merged with the Centre for International Crime Prevention to form the UN Office for Drug Control and Crime Prevention (UNODCCP). This agency finally became the UN Office on Drugs and Crime (UNODC) in 2002. With a staff of about five hundred worldwide, UNODC is a rather small office, but carries out important activities.

Besides providing secretarial services for the other drug control bodies, UNODC is also responsible for the coordination of the UN anti-drug programs. Its mission involves close cooperation and assistance to national governments on the domestic and regional level. A variety of programs, mainly in developing and transitional countries, are executed under the supervision of UNODC. One of the most prominent initiatives is the Global Programme on Monitoring Illicit Crops, which covers the cultivation of illegal crops in the most troubled countries, such as Myanmar, Laos, Afghanistan in Asia, and Bolivia, Colombia, and Peru in South America. In pursuing its mandate UNODC follows a twofold approach: on the one side research and awareness-raising by publishing material on global trends in drug cultivation and trafficking (e.g., the annual World Drug Report, which is the most cited document on the state of the global drug problem), and on the other side programs on drug abuse prevention and drug dependence treatment/rehabilitation.

The UN-guided international drug control effort must be put into perspective by acknowledging that it does not operate in a vacuum. In fact, it is interdependent with unilateral efforts at the domestic level and with numerous bilateral initiatives (for example between the United States and various Latin American countries). Additionally, regional and sub-regional cooperation on drug control takes place on all continents. To a considerable extent these multilateral efforts are also supervised by the United Nations through the CND. Five subsidiary bodies have been established, in which the Heads of National Drug Law Enforcement Agencies (HONLEA) coordinate and strengthen their efforts in drug law enforcement activities. The HONLEA bodies meet annually to identify policy and enforcement issues and to establish respective working groups.

But, regional organizations and action plans have also been launched outside of the UN system. Although these initiatives oftentimes cooperate with UNODC on some level, they are not directly affiliated with the United Nations. For example, the European Council, in December 2004, endorsed a European Union Drugs Strategy. This was followed by two successive Drugs Action Plans, which aimed at strengthening cross-border cooperation with third countries and international organizations. In Asia, members of The Association of Southeast Asian Nations (ASEAN) and China endorsed an action plan called Drug Free ASEAN 2015, under which the respective States plan to improve their bilateral and regional cooperation. In South America, the Inter-American Drug Abuse Control Commission (CICAD) was established in 1986 under the framework of the Organization of American States (OAS). Furthermore, a Permanent Commission for the Eradication of the Illicit Production, Trafficking, Consumption and Use of Illicit Narcotic Drugs and Psychotropic Substances was established for Central America in 1993. Also the African Union has recently taken action by adopting in 2008 the Plan of Action on Drug Control and Crime Prevention. An important inter-regional drug control initiative worth mentioning is the Paris Pact Initiative. It is a partnership of more than fifty countries and international organizations aimed at combating the trafficking and consumption of Afghan opiates and focuses on enhanced border control and law enforcement on the drug trafficking routes from Central Asia to Europe. In addition to the aforementioned high-level institutions and programs, various other regional and bilateral initiatives have been created, e.g., in the field of intelligence sharing, joint investigations, and the establishment of permanent task forces.

2. Marijuana Legalization and the Drug Treaties

As discussed in Chapter 8, at the time of this writing in 2019, ten U.S. states have legalized the manufacture and retail sale of marijuana for adult use. In mid-2017, Uruguay fully implemented a tightly controlled version of marijuana legalization. In October 2018, Canada became the second country in the world to legalize marijuana nationwide. These laws and others have begun to test the power of the international drug control regime.

The leaders of the United Nations Office on Drugs and Crime (UNODC) and the International Narcotics Control Board (INCB) have both taken the position that the drug treaties forbid member countries, or states within member countries, from legalizing marijuana. Shortly after Colorado and Washington voted to legalize marijuana, the INCB's then-president Raymond Yans "warned bluntly that permitting recreational use of marijuana 'would be a violation of international law, namely the United Nations Single Convention on Narcotic Drugs of 1961, to which the United States is party.' He also asserted that the 'United States has a treaty obligation to ensure the implementation of the treaties on the entirety of its territory.' No one was surprised, then, when the Board's annual report covering developments in 2013 (released in March 2014) also disapproved of the legalization-and-regulation move as 'not in conformity' with the drug treaties, and recommended that the United States fully implement its treaty obligations 'on its entire territory.'" Wells Bennett and John Walsh, Ctr. for Effective Pub. Mgmt. at Brookings, Marijuana Legalization Is an Opportunity to Modernize International Drug Treaties 9–10 (2014). More recently, in response to Canada's marijuana legalization proposal, the INCB issued a brief stating that "the legalisation and regulation of cannabis for non-medical and non-scientific purposes, including by the Government of Canada, would constitute a breach of the country's international obligations under the 1961 Single Convention on Narcotic Drugs." International Narcotics Control Board, Brief on the Conformity of Bill C-45 3 (2018).

So far, the INCB's opposition has not stopped U.S. states or countries like Canada and Uruguay from moving forward with marijuana legalization. How can a country that is a party to the Single Convention legalize marijuana given its treaty obligations?

The answer may lie, in part, on the process for ensuring compliance with the drug control treaties. The INCB is tasked with overseeing domestic application of the three drug conventions, but "while often vocal in its criticism of national policy, the

INCB . . . has no formal power to enforce implementation of the Convention provisions. Nor has the Board the formal power to punish parties for non-compliance." David R. Bewley-Taylor, *Challenging the UN Drug Control Conventions: Problems and Possibilities*, 14 Int'l J. Drug Pol'y 171 (2003). This does not mean the treaties are entirely toothless. The INCB has mechanisms for applying "informal pressure in its attempts to encourage what it perceives to be treaty compliance" including recommending to other convention parties "that they 'stop the import of drugs, the export of drugs, or both, from or to the country or territory concerned' for a designated period or until [the INCB] is satisfied with the situation within the country or territory." David R. Bewley-Taylor and Mike Trace, *The International Narcotics Control Board: Watchdog or Guardian of the UN Drug Control Conventions?*, The Beckley Foundation Drug Policy Programme (2006). Moreover, even in the absence of external pressure, nations commit to interpret and implement treaties to which they are a party in good faith. If a country is set on passing a law that the INCB believes violates the drug treaties, however, there are relatively few options to try to compel compliance.

The paper below examines the tension between marijuana legalization laws and the drug treaties in more detail, along with options for addressing the conflict.

Cannabis Regulation and the UN Drug Treaties: Strategies for Reform

David Bewley-Taylor, Martin Jelsma, Steve Rolles, and John Walsh

The Global Drug Policy Observatory (2016)

Cannabis prohibition has not proven to be an effective strategy for reducing the extent of the illicit market or cannabis health harms. The legal regulation of cannabis markets has therefore become an increasingly attractive policy option for countries to consider, creating obvious tensions within the prohibitionist United Nations drug control treaty framework. Cannabis is one of the psychoactive substances included within the UN drug control regime, based on three treaties: the 1961 Single Convention on Narcotic Drugs, the 1971 Convention on Psychotropic Substances, and the 1988 Convention against Illicit Traffic in Narcotic Drugs and Psychotropic Substances. Current tensions arise from the decision to place cannabis under strict controls as part of the bedrock of the contemporary regime, the 1961 Single Convention. This states that, as with a range of other listed substances, "the production, manufacture, export, import, distribution of, trade in, use and possession" of cannabis should be limited "exclusively to medical and scientific purposes."

Cannabis, the world's most widely used illicit drug, is categorized within the Single Convention alongside cocaine and heroin.[2] This decision, taken more than

2. Cannabis has a double or composite classification within the Single Convention. Cannabis, cannabis resin, and extracts and tincture of cannabis are in Schedule I among substances whose

50 years ago, had very little to do with consideration of the available scientific evidence concerning relative health risks. Today the drug conventions are, on the surface, among the most widely adhered to of all UN instruments. This veneer of virtually universal support, however, masks a number of important considerations.

First, nations signed on to the Single Convention in an era dramatically different from the one we live in today. The treaty was being drafted and negotiated during the 1940s and 1950s, consolidating the structures and philosophy of a series of multilateral drug control treaties dating back to 1912. This was a period when drug issues were of only marginal concern for many states, permitting a few nations to dominate proceedings and steer the development of the international control system in their preferred prohibition-oriented direction.

Authoritative studies suggesting that there was no need to impose international prohibition-oriented controls on cannabis were largely ignored. Remarkably, the World Health Organization's (WHO) Expert Committee on Drug Dependence (ECDD), the body charged by the 1961 and 1971 Conventions with the scientific and medical review of scheduling proposals, has never engaged in a formal review of cannabis' place within the Convention. As the Committee itself noted in 2014, "Cannabis and cannabis resin has not been scientifically reviewed by the Expert Committee since the review by the Health Committee of the League of Nations in 1935."

Second, dissatisfaction with the implications of cannabis' status within the treaty system is not a new phenomenon. Numerous national and sub-national jurisdictions have questioned and increasingly moved away from the punitive prohibitions on cannabis encouraged by the Conventions. This has manifested in successive waves of what might be regarded as "soft defection," whereby authorities tried to remain within the flexibility afforded by the treaty framework, but deviate from the prohibitive norm at the heart of the regime.

As early as the 1970s, . . . Dutch authorities re-evaluated cannabis policies, leading to the development of the current cannabis "coffee shop" system. The International Narcotics Control Board (INCB, the "independent, quasi-judicial expert body" overseeing implementation of the treaties) has long criticized the Dutch model as falling outside the bounds of the Conventions (although without providing the detailed legal reasoning behind that criticism).

A second wave of reforms—which has been referred to as a "quiet revolution" of decriminalization—has occurred more recently in several Latin American and European countries and within Australian states and territories. In Spain,

---

properties might give rise to dependence and that present a serious risk of abuse and so are subject to all control measures envisaged by the Convention. Cannabis and cannabis resin are also listed in Schedule IV, along with some other substances listed in Schedule I, and are deemed especially dangerous by virtue of what are regarded to be their harmful characteristics, risk of abuse, and extremely limited therapeutic value.

an increasingly popular local approach by cannabis users to bypass the problems of the illicit market has been the establishment of Cannabis Social Clubs. These are intended to provide a de facto source of legal supply operating informally on a small-scale, non- profit basis within a decriminalized model.

Meanwhile at the multilateral level, recent sessions of the Commission on Narcotic Drugs (CND)—the UN's central policymaking body on drug issues—have seen some Member States, including Argentina, the Czech Republic, Ecuador, and Mexico, call openly for a re-evaluation of some aspects of the current treaty framework.

The tensions around cannabis within the treaty framework have come most dramatically to the fore in the Americas, with recent passage of laws that explicitly legalize and regulate cannabis for non-medical, non-scientific uses, a policy that is expressly forbidden by the UN drug treaties. Successful ballot initiatives in 2012 in the U.S. states of Colorado and Washington to establish legally taxed and regulated cannabis markets have been followed by initiatives in Alaska and Oregon.

At the national level, in December 2013, Uruguay became the first country in the world to legally regulate the cannabis market, with the passage of Law 19.172 granting the government control over the import, export, cultivation, production, and sale of cannabis through the newly established Institute for the Regulation and Control of Cannabis (*Instituto de Regulación y Control del Cannabis,* IRCCA). Even more recently, Canada's new government was elected in 2015 pledging to legalize and regulate cannabis for non-medical, non-scientific use. And, with varying levels of political support, legislative proposals for cannabis regulation are also under consideration in Guatemala, Italy, Mexico, and Morocco.

Clearly, tensions in the treaty regime around cannabis are long-standing and growing. The international community, including the UN drug control bureaucracy, has been well aware of these tensions for some time. Indeed, in a much-remarked 2008 report, "Making Drug Control Fit for Purpose," the Executive Director of the UN Office on Drugs and Crime (UNODC) wrote that "Cannabis is the most vulnerable point in the whole multilateral edifice. In the Single Convention, it is supposed to be controlled with the same degree of severity as cocaine and the opiates. In practice, this is seldom the case, and many countries vacillate in the degree of control they exercise over cannabis."

Since then, "soft defections" with regard to cannabis policy have given way to direct breaches of the Conventions' ban on cannabis for non-medical or non-scientific purposes. As more jurisdictions appear likely to enact reforms to legalize and regulate adult use of cannabis, these treaty tensions have become the "elephant in the room" in key high-level forums, including the 2016 United Nations General Assembly Special Session (UNGASS) on drugs—obviously present, but studiously ignored. Different countries and international agencies have different reasons for seeking to avoid directly engaging the question of what to do about these tensions. But the kinds of treaty breaches that may have seemed merely hypothetical only a few years ago are already a reality today, and will not simply disappear. Governments and the UN system should give serious consideration to options for managing these policy shifts in ways that can help to modernize the drug treaty regime itself, and to thereby reinforce the UN pillars of human rights, development, peace and security, and the rule of law.

A difficult dilemma has thus entered the international drug policy arena. There is no doubt that recent policy developments with regard to cannabis regulation have moved beyond the legal latitude of the treaties. Initiating a formal procedure to review or amend the current treaty framework, however, would not only immediately trigger an avalanche of political frictions with some of the most powerful countries in the world, but could even lead to unintended negative outcomes. Indeed, even as many governments continue to tout the supposed global consensus on drug policy, officials are quite aware of the significant and growing policy differences among drug treaty Member States; to the extent that a truly global consensus ever existed, it is now fractured, and there is no new consensus to take its place.

Under such conditions, it is not difficult to understand why many countries would prefer to avoid or delay confronting the treaty questions raised by cannabis regulation. Indeed, such concerns go far in explaining the attraction of the legally fallacious—but politically potent—stance that the drug treaties as they stand are flexible enough to accommodate the regulation of adult-use cannabis. Different countries have different reasons for finding appeal in the notion of treaty flexibility. During the March 2016 negotiations in Vienna of the UNGASS Outcome Document, different strands of support for the idea of flexibility converged around language declaring that new challenges "should be addressed in conformity with the three international drug control conventions, which allow for *sufficient flexibility* for States parties to design and implement national drug policies according to their priorities and needs . . ." (Emphasis added). The same language was able to serve different, even contradictory, purposes.

The wording of "sufficient flexibility" originates from the European Union (EU) common position on the UNGASS, where it was accompanied by the EU's commitment to "maintain a strong and unequivocal commitment to the UN conventions." For the EU then, flexibility applies to policies such as harm reduction, decriminalization of possession and cultivation of cannabis for personal use, and alternatives to incarceration, but certainly not to cannabis regulation, which the EU considers as falling outside the scope of policy options allowed under the treaties.

However, for governments for whom it would be politically convenient to maintain that cannabis regulation fits within the boundaries of the Conventions—especially the United States—"sufficient flexibility" could be read as covering cannabis regulation.

Lest there be doubt about the INCB's views, INCB President Werner Sipp directly addressed the issue of flexibility in his keynote speech at the March 2016 session of the CND, as the UNGASS document was under negotiation. Some proponents of new laws that permit the non-medical use of cannabis, he said, "pretend that the flexibility of the conventions allows such regulations. In fact, the debate on flexibility is at the core of the general debate on future drug policy because it regards the possibilities and the limitations of the Conventions. Undoubtedly, there exists flexibility in the Conventions—but not in each and every respect." For example, Sipp explained, there is "no obligation stemming from the conventions to incarcerate drug users having committed minor offences," and they "provide for flexibility in the determination of appropriate sanctions." However, there is "*no flexibility* in the conventions for allowing and regulating any kind of non-medical use" (Emphasis in the original).

The UNGASS document negotiators—in settling on language with such different and even contradictory meanings to different sets of countries—did achieve what most countries wanted: a way to avoid opening a debate on the adequacy of the treaties themselves.

The fact remains, however, that the accelerating process of national reforms has already moved cannabis policies beyond the boundaries of what the Conventions can legally accommodate. To move the debate forward, this paper aims to illuminate the available options for countries to ensure that their new domestic cannabis laws and policies are aligned with their international obligations, thereby modernizing the global drug control system in ways consistent with international law and the overarching purposes of the UN system.

Treaty Amendment

Any State party can notify the UN Secretary General of a proposed amendment, including the reasoning behind the move. The Secretary General then communicates the proposed amendment and the reasons for it to the State parties and to the Economic and Social Council (ECOSOC), which can decide to: (1) Convene a Conference of all the Parties (COP) of the treaty to consider the amendment; (2) Ask the Parties if they accept the amendment; or (3) Take no action and wait to see whether any State party submits any objection.

In the event of no Party rejecting the amendment within 18 months (24 months for the 1988 Convention), the amendment is automatically accepted.

In the event State parties register objections to a proposed amendment, ECOSOC can decide to: (1) Still approve the amendment (in which case it would not be applicable to the objecting states); (2) Reject it (if multiple objections are raised that argue convincingly that such an amendment would compromise the object and purpose of the treaty); or (3) Convene a COP to consider the amendment.

In theory, all three UN drug control conventions could be amended using these procedures. While many consider this to be a politically unlikely scenario for the foreseeable future, it is important to recall that the 1961 Single Convention was amended with the 1972 Protocol, after a COP was convened and agreed to substantial treaty changes. At that stage, the U.S. government argued that it was "time for the international community to build on the foundation of the Single Convention, since a decade has given a better perspective of its strengths and weaknesses." The latitude under the 1961 Single Convention with regard to alternatives to incarceration—which has been the focus of many recent debates—only exists due to a treaty amendment agreed in the 1972 Protocol.

For historical perspective, it is also useful to recall that many decisions in the process of negotiating the drug treaties were taken by majority vote. The false perception that the UN drug control system has always relied on full consensus is a more recent construct, intended to reinforce an image of universal agreement even as tensions were becoming ever more visible. Moreover, in the event that treaty amendments are approved, States can opt not to become part of the amended agreement. As the 1969 Vienna Convention on the Law of Treaties (VCLT) makes clear: "The amending agreement does not bind any State already a party to the treaty which does not become a party to the amending agreement." As such, States that do not wish to be bound by the treaty as amended may retain the older obligations.

Most modern treaties, including the 2000 Transnational Organized Crime Convention (UNTOC), the 2003 Convention against Corruption (UNCAC), and the 2003 WHO Framework Convention on Tobacco Control (FCTC) have an inbuilt COP mechanism that requires them to undergo periodic reviews and enables them to evolve and modernize if necessary. The international drug control treaty regime, however, with its roots predating the UN, lacks such a periodic review mechanism—which helps to explain its outdated nature and resistance to reform. The challenge of modernizing the drug control regime via a COP mechanism is further complicated by the fact that that the regime consists of three separate treaties, all of which would require amendment. A more rational course of systemic evolution could be to try and resolve the inconsistencies between the 1961 and 1971 Conventions by merging them, together with the precursor controls under the 1988 Convention, into a new Single Convention.

Discussions on more substantive reforms of this nature have yet to occur formally, although they have been suggested in the Organization of American States' 2013 report *Scenarios for the Drug Problem in the Americas.*

Rescheduling

The 1961 Single Convention allows for the WHO or any State party to initiate, at any time, the modification process that could reschedule a specified drug or delete it from the Conventions. The WHO is the only body mandated to make scheduling recommendations, which must subsequently be agreed by the Commission on Narcotic Drugs (CND). Modifying schedules does not require consensus; these are the only decisions the CND takes by vote. New substances are routinely scheduled in this way, and the treaty system is thus constantly being modified.

In the case of cannabis, scheduled under the Single Convention, a rescheduling decision would be taken by a simple majority of its "members present and voting."

For cannabis, . . . this process is further complicated by the fact that it (along with coca and opium) is also mentioned explicitly in specific articles within the 1961 and 1988 Conventions. Re-scheduling or de-scheduling cannabis may therefore not be sufficient to allow for fully regulated markets along the lines of the changes now being enacted in various jurisdictions today. Most likely, some form of amendment, modification, or reservation to those treaties would also be required.

"Inter Se" Treaty Modification

The 1969 Vienna Convention on the Law of Treaties (VCLT) also allows for the option to modify treaties between certain parties only, offering in this context an intriguing and under-explored legal option. According to Article 41 of the VCLT, "Two or more of the parties to a multilateral treaty may conclude an agreement to modify the treaty as between themselves alone," as long as it "does not affect the enjoyment by the other parties of their rights under the treaty or the performance of their obligations" and it is not "incompatible with the effective execution of the object and purpose of the treaty as a whole."

In principle, both conditions could be met. It would require that the agreement include a clear commitment to the original treaty obligations vis- à-vis countries not party to the *inter se* modification agreement, especially concerning prevention of trade or leakage to prohibited jurisdictions. All the provisions in the treaties—including those pertaining to cannabis—would remain in force vis- à-vis the treaty's State parties that are not part of the *inter se* agreement. Over time, such an *inter se* agreement might evolve into an alternative treaty framework to which more and more countries could adhere, while avoiding the cumbersome (if not impossible) process of unanimous approval of amendments to the current regime.

In theory, modification *inter se* could be used by a group of like-minded countries that wish to resolve the treaty non-compliance issues resulting from national decisions to legally regulate the cannabis market, as Uruguay has already done, and Canada appears poised to do. Such countries could sign an agreement with effect only among themselves, modifying or annulling the cannabis control provisions of the UN conventions. This could also be an interesting option to explore in order to provide a legal basis justifying international trade between national jurisdictions that allow or tolerate the existence of a licit market of a substance under domestic legal provisions, but for which international trade is not permitted under the current UN treaty obligations.

The drafters of the 1969 VCLT considered the option of *inter se* modification as a core principle for international law, and the issue was discussed at length at the International Law Commission in 1964: "The importance of the subject needed no emphasis; it involved reconciling the need to safeguard the stability of treaties with the requirements of peaceful change."

A leading authority on international treaty law, Jan Klabbers, describes the *inter se* option as "perhaps the most elegant way out," but also notes that though *inter se* modification is based on an ancient principle of international law, "practical examples are hard to come by." Indeed, it seems this is essentially uncharted legal territory, but a good case could be made that the increasing tensions between cannabis policy trends and the frozen drug treaty system provides a clear example of circumstances for which this exceptional option was designed and deemed to be of crucial importance.

Withdrawing from the Treaties

In light of the outdated nature of the drug control treaties and the seemingly insurmountable procedural and political obstacles to modernizing them, the question is often raised why countries should not simply withdraw from the UN drug control treaty regime. The option exists for any signatory Member States to withdraw from the treaties via the process of denunciation; treaty exit would technically "solve" the problems of breach or non-compliance from a legal perspective.

However, a key reason reform-minded states may wish to remain party to the UN drug control treaties is that they also regulate the global trade in drugs for licit medical purposes, including substances on the WHO list of essential medicines. Inadequate access to controlled medicines is already a severe problem in most developing countries, and withdrawing from the INCB-administered global system of estimates and requirements operating under the UN drug control conventions could risk making it even worse.

For countries receiving development aid or benefitting from preferential trade agreements, denunciation would also risk triggering economic sanctions. Being State party to all three of the drug control conventions is a condition in a number of preferential trade agreements or for accession to the European Union. The U.S. government—though now more likely to be lenient towards cannabis reforms elsewhere due to the changes underway within U.S. borders—still maintains the disciplinary certification mechanism,* and withdrawal from the drug control treaties altogether would almost certainly lead to decertification and sanctions. Denunciation can therefore have serious political and economic implications, especially for less powerful and poor countries. Even for countries that are less economically vulnerable, simply withdrawing from the drug treaties could carry the risk of reputational costs.

Denunciation Followed by Re- Accession with a Reservation

At the moment of signing, acceding, or ratifying a treaty, states have the option to make reservations regarding specific provisions, as many countries in fact did in the case of all three drug control treaties. Reservations or other formal unilateral "interpretive declarations" are meant to exclude or modify the legal effect of certain provisions of a treaty for the reserving state.

Under the procedure of treaty denunciation followed by re-accession with a reservation, a country can withdraw itself from the treaty entirely, with the intention of rejoining with specific reservations. In the case of the 1961 Convention, if one

---

* The United States drug certification process is discussed in Section C.5 of this Chapter. [*Footnote by casebook author.*]

third or more State parties object, the country would be blocked from re-acceding. Denunciation and re-accession with a reservation is recognized as a legitimate procedure, although its practice has been limited to exceptional cases.

In the case of the drug treaties, there is a recent precedent: in 2011, Bolivia notified the Secretary General that it had decided to exit the Single Convention, taking effect in January 2012, intending to re-accede with reservations regarding coca. The INCB condemned the move, and 15 countries—including every member of the G8—submitted formal objections. But the number of objections fell far short of the 62 (one third of all State parties to the Convention) that were needed to block Bolivia from re-acceding. In early 2013, Bolivia's re-adherence to the treaty was formally accepted, with reservations upholding the right to allow in its territory traditional coca leaf chewing, the use of the coca leaf in its natural state, and the cultivation, trade, and possession of the coca leaf to the extent necessary for these licit purposes. (Bolivia had initially tried to amend the treaties, but was blocked by a small number of objections.) The procedure thus successfully resolved the legal tensions, at least for Bolivia, between the 1961 Single Convention's obligation to abolish its indigenous coca culture, versus Bolivia's legal obligations under the 2007 UN Declaration on the Rights of Indigenous Peoples and its national Constitution to protect it.

A reservation by which a state would exempt itself from implementing the Convention's obligations for cannabis could therefore be attempted following the same treaty procedure, but there are differences to be taken into account. The main legal issue relates to article 19 of the VCLT, which requires that a reservation must not be "incompatible with the object and purpose of the treaty." Those overall aims of the Single Convention are expressed in the preamble's opening paragraph regarding concern about "the health and welfare of mankind" and the treaty's general obligation to limit controlled drugs "exclusively to medical and scientific purposes."

Implementing Cannabis Regulation in Situations of Treaty Non-Compliance

The treaty reform options described above—with their varying procedural and political considerations—all assume a decision on the part of at least one State to proactively alter its relationship to the current treaties with respect to cannabis. States might opt to sidestep the treaty questions that arise in the context of their cannabis reforms, or assert that the changes underway within their countries are allowable under the treaties as they stand, therefore denying that treaty reform options of any sort ought or need to be considered. Another option—acknowledging the fact of temporary non-compliance and working toward an eventual realignment of domestic law and treaty obligations—would open the door to deliberately pursuing some set of treaty reform options.

Side-Stepping or Denying Issues of Non-Compliance

The two States that have thus far proceeded with development and implementation of formal non-medical cannabis markets are the United States and Uruguay. Their situations are very different and they have provided contrasting commentaries on the implications of their moves, while both arguing that policy shifts within their borders do not put them in breach of the UN drug control conventions.

Uruguay has argued its policy is fully in line with the original objectives that the drug control treaties emphasized, but have subsequently failed to achieve—namely, the protection of the health and welfare of humankind. Uruguayan authorities have specifically argued that the creation of a regulated market for adult use of cannabis is driven by health and security imperatives and is therefore an issue of human rights. As such, officials point to wider UN human rights obligations that need to be respected, specifically appealing to the precedence of human rights principles over drug control obligations. As the first country courageous enough to take the step of regulating cannabis for all uses, it is enormously significant that Uruguay has explained its reform with reference to its overarching human rights obligations under international law. Moreover, while reluctant to acknowledge its cannabis regulation model represents non-compliance with the drug treaties, Uruguay has noted that it creates legal tensions within the treaty system that may require revision and modernization. At the 2013 CND session, for example, Diego Cánepa, head of the Uruguayan delegation, declared: "Today more than ever we need the leadership and courage to discuss if a revision and modernization is required of the international instruments adopted over the last fifty years."

U.S. officials, for their part, have argued that since the cultivation, trade, and possession of cannabis taking place in multiple U.S. states remain criminal offenses under U.S. federal law, the federal government as State party to the Conventions is not in breach. This is despite the federal government's decision to accommodate the state-level developments, provided they proceed within certain parameters. A recent U.S. discourse, promoted by Ambassador William Brownfield (Assistant Secretary for International Narcotics and Law Enforcement Affairs), maintains that the extant treaty framework possesses sufficient flexibility to allow for regulated cannabis markets. This argument is strained by any reasonable understanding of the treaties and their overtly prohibitionist object and purpose—and appears to reflect political expediency rather than convincing legal reasoning. [Indeed,] the INCB has made clear statements that both Uruguayan and U.S. cannabis regulation models are not in compliance with the treaties, and Brownfield has himself acknowledged the INCB's authority in determining whether or not State parties are in compliance.

Proceeding in "Principled Non-Compliance"

Rather than attempting to argue why legally regulating cannabis would not constitute a compliance problem with the 1961 and 1988 Conventions, States that wish to proceed with legal regulation could instead openly acknowledge that doing so would result in non-compliance. Crucially, this option requires that the State sets out its reasons for national policy reform, how this affects compliance, and in particular why this is necessary for the realization of other international legal and policy commitments. Moreover this situation of non-compliance should be seen and presented as temporary, with the aim of ensuring the realignment of the country's new domestic laws and practice with its treaty obligations as part-and-parcel of the reform initiative. The State should, in parallel, request multilateral discussions to resolve the situation, for example through supporting an expert advisory group on the reform of the conventions, and supporting a later Conference of the Parties (COP). Pending those developments, the State would carry on in conformity with its remaining commitments under the treaties, report as usual to the INCB, and report to the CND on the outcomes of its policies.

Clearly, open non-compliance with international legal obligations is not desirable, but all of the reform options set out in this paper are driven by necessity. The problem here is not that countries are opting for regulatory approaches. Rather, outmoded and unworkable treaty provisions are the problem that gives rise to the need for a temporary and transitional period of principled non-compliance. In this context the recognition of the fact that a State can no longer fully comply with the Conventions' obligations regarding cannabis need not be seen as disrespect for the rule of law. To the contrary, it confirms that treaty commitments matter. Indeed, treaty non-compliance as domestic laws and practice change is a fairly common feature of regime evolution and modernization. Waving away worries about non-compliance by resorting to dubious legal justifications is much more an expression of disrespect for international law.

3. Drug Control and the International Criminal Court

Though the international drug control regime is built on domestic enforcement of treaty-based laws, some commentators have proposed granting an international court the power to hear serious drug trafficking cases directly. *See, e.g.*, Faiza Patel, *Crime without Frontiers: A Proposal for an International Narcotics Court*, 22 N.Y.U. J. INT'L L. & POL., 709 (1990). By and large, supporters of this approach argue that the International Criminal Court (ICC) should be given jurisdiction over drug cases. Others argue that the ICC's jurisdiction should be reserved for more serious offenses.

The ICC is a "treaty-based international criminal court established to help end impunity for perpetrators of genocide, crimes against humanity, and war crimes." Yvonne M. Dutton, *Explaining State Commitment to the International Criminal Court: Strong Enforcement Mechanisms as a Credible Threat*, 10 WASH. U. GLOBAL STUDIES L. REV. 477 (2011).

> Although the United Nations first began considering the prospect of an international criminal court after World War II, it was not until 1990, following a request submitted by Trinidad and Tobago, that work again commenced in earnest towards drafting a statute for the creation of such a court.
>
> The statute creating the court—the Rome Statute—was finally adopted [in 1998] at the conclusion of the Rome Conference. Attending the conference were 160 states, 33 international governmental coalitions, and a coalition of more than 200 non-governmental organizations (NGOs). Of the states in attendance, 120 voted in favor of adopting the statute, 7 voted

> against, and 21 abstained. In July 2002 after the required 60 states had ratified the statute, the ICC came into existence.
>
> As of August 2010, some 139 countries had signed the Rome Statute, and 113 had actually become States Parties to it. Of the States Parties, 20 are from Western Europe, 17 are from Eastern Europe, 31 are from Africa, 14 are from Asia, and 25 are from Latin America and the Caribbean. The United States, Israel, China, Russia, Indonesia, and India are notable powerful states that have declined to ratify the treaty. Also not parties to the treaty are a number of Islamic and African states, including: Bahrain, Iran, Iraq, Kuwait, Pakistan, Qatar, Syria, Turkey, United Arab Emirates, Yemen, Algeria, Angola, Cameroon, Cape Verde, Cote d'Ivoire, Egypt, Morocco, Sudan, and Zimbabwe. In June 2010, Bangladesh became the first country from southern Asia to join the court.
>
> [T]he ICC's jurisdiction is not circumscribed to dealing with particular atrocities in particular states. Nor can states decide whether or not to accede to the court's jurisdiction on a case-by-case basis. Rather, by committing to the treaty creating the ICC, states agree that investigations may be commenced against the state's own nationals for the covered crimes of genocide, crimes against humanity, or war crimes, as long as those crimes were committed after the court came into existence or after the state ratified the treaty, whichever is later. Furthermore, the ICC treaty is not only backward-looking; by joining the court, states agree that the court can prosecute any future atrocities in the event the state itself does not prosecute those atrocities domestically. Moreover, the treaty does not recognize any immunity that states may otherwise grant to heads of state who engage in criminal activities.
>
> The treaty creating the ICC also has stronger enforcement mechanisms than those traditionally associated with international human rights treaties. According to the terms and provisions of the Rome Statute, an independent ICC prosecutor may initiate investigations against nationals of States Parties for the covered crimes on his own with the approval of the court, or based on referrals from a State Party or the United Nations Security Council. The prosecutor and the court operate without direct Security Council oversight, with the Council having no veto power over what situations are investigated or prosecuted. Not only have States Parties to the ICC delegated authority to independent decision makers, but they have also given those decision makers power to enforce those decisions. Most importantly, the ICC is empowered to issue arrest warrants to bring those who have committed mass atrocities to stand trial for their crimes in The Hague.

Id.

The excerpt that follows discusses efforts to expand the ICC's jurisdiction to include drug trafficking offenses.

Just Say No: The Case against Expanding the International Criminal Court's Jurisdiction to Include Drug Trafficking
Heather L. Kiefer

31 Loyola of Los Angeles International and Comparative Law Review 157 (2008)

Currently, those who are responsible for drug trafficking and related offenses cannot be prosecuted in the International Criminal Court (ICC). The ICC is not a court of general jurisdiction; it has jurisdiction only over the offenses enumerated in the Rome Statute. Because drug trafficking is not among the offenses included in the Statute, it falls outside the Court's subject matter jurisdiction. But the contents of the Rome Statute are not set in stone. The Statute, including its jurisdictional provisions, may be amended at any time "[a]fter the expiry of seven years from the [Statute's] entry into force. . . ." That date—July 2, 2008—has now arrived. Any state party to the Statute may now propose an amendment. If the Assembly chooses to consider the proposal, it can either "deal with the proposal directly or convene a Review Conference if the issue involved so warrants."

Although there are numerous multilateral treaties addressing the issue of drug trafficking, it is debatable whether the global issue of drug trafficking is sufficiently addressed through the current regime or if it should also be incorporated into another multilateral treaty that contains a stronger enforcement mechanism, namely the ICC.

Currently, the jurisdiction of the International Criminal Court encompasses genocide, crimes against humanity, war crimes, and crimes of aggression. Given the present contents of the Rome Statute, the origins and motivation of the effort to establish the International Criminal Court are somewhat surprising. While international tribunals of various sorts existed prior to the creation of the ICC, the ICC itself was initially conceived as a means to combat a crime not previously within the jurisdiction of any international tribunal: drug trafficking. Led by Arthur Robinson, the Prime Minister of Trinidad and Tobago, [in 1989] seventeen Caribbean and Latin American states proposed the idea of an international court with subject matter jurisdiction covering drug trafficking offenses—a proposal the UN General Assembly quickly embraced.

In 1994, the International Law Commission (ILC) prepared a Draft Statute for an International Court. The Draft Statute created a court with broader jurisdiction than the original proponents of the ICC had envisioned, but the Court's function as an international tribunal to try drug trafficking offenses was nevertheless preserved.

Following the release of the Draft Statute, the General Assembly created the Preparatory Committee on the Establishment of an International Criminal Court. The Committee's main function was to consider and resolve the more controversial points of the Draft Statute. During the Committee's proceedings, two schools of thought emerged regarding the question of whether to include drug trafficking crimes within the subject matter jurisdiction of the ICC. On one hand, some delegations argued: "[D]rug trafficking should not be included because these crimes were not of the same nature as those listed in other paragraphs of Article 20 and were of such a quantity as to flood the court; the court would not have the necessary resources to conduct lengthy and complex investigations required to prosecute the crimes; the investigation of the crimes often involved highly sensitive information and confidential strategies; and the crimes could be more effectively investigated and prosecuted by national authorities under existing international cooperation arrangements."

On the other hand, another group of delegations to the Preparatory Committee "expressed the view that particularly serious drug trafficking offenses which involved an international dimension should be included" because the current regime of controlling and punishing trafficking had serious shortcomings.

The literature predating the convening of the Committee also helps to illuminate the reasons for supporting the creation of an international court with subject matter jurisdiction over drug trafficking offenses. To proponents of the inclusion of such offenses within the jurisdiction of an international court, drug trafficking was viewed as international in character, having very serious and harmful effects, and requiring international cooperation. These characteristics supported the notion that drug trafficking was an international crime even in the absence of positive law . . . establishing its criminality. Given the magnitude of the trafficking problem, its perceived status as an international crime, and great discrepancies in the willingness and ability of states to prosecute traffickers, proponents urged the creation of an international court to handle the prosecution of drug crimes. Proponents believed that such a court was not only eminently desirable, but also feasible.

By 1998, states came to a consensus regarding the subject matter jurisdiction of the ICC. The consensus was on the side of a narrower, more limited jurisdiction that did not include drug trafficking offenses. Despite that consensus, however, the second version of the Draft Statute, finalized in 1998, still included drug trafficking among the offenses within the Court's jurisdiction. Although the second Draft Statute was transmitted to the Rome Conference, the final product of the Rome Conference, the Rome Statute of the International Criminal Court, contained no mention of drug trafficking—neither explicitly nor by incorporation—because there were problems with defining the scope of the offense with an acceptable degree of precision. There is some measure of irony in this result: the impetus for the movement to create the ICC was the desire to create an international court to try drug traffickers, and yet, the result of that movement, the Rome Statute, deprived the Court of jurisdiction over drug trafficking offenses.

This irony was not lost on those who had started the movement. Trinidad and Tobago, widely cited as the state behind the movement to create the ICC, abstained from voting to adopt the Rome Statute. It abstained for two reasons. First, as discussed above, the Rome Statute did not expressly provide for jurisdiction over drug trafficking—the very reason Trinidad and Tobago had pushed for an international criminal court. Second, some delegations, including Trinidad and Tobago, wanted the Rome Statute to provide for capital punishment, and the final version of the treaty did not allow for that penalty. Despite the abstention, however, Trinidad and Tobago became the second state to ratify the Statute.

One of the most persuasive arguments for not allowing the ICC to have jurisdiction over drug trafficking cases is the lack of ICC resources.

Cannabis alone is cultivated in 172 countries and territories. In order to collect the evidence needed for prosecution, the ICC would have to undertake the expensive and time-consuming task of sending investigators around the globe. Mahnoush Arsanjani, the Director of the Codification Division of the UN's Office of Legal Affairs, points out that the evidence-gathering obstacles shaped the development of the Rome Statute's jurisdictional provisions: "The opposition [to including drug trafficking] was based on the fact that the nature of investigating the crimes of drug trafficking and terrorism, which requires long-term planning, infiltration into the organizations involved . . . makes them better suited for national prosecution."

There are good reasons to think these perceptions were, and are correct. In 2005, the ICC budget totaled approximately € 69,564,000 or $86,634,310 at then-prevailing exchange rates. In contrast, the United States appropriated $2.141 billion dollars to its Drug Enforcement [Administration] in 2005 alone. Some might argue that this demonstrates that states need to dedicate more resources to the ICC as well as other international institutions. But the gap between the investigative expenditures of international institutions and states is so large that it is hard to imagine that the latter would be willing, or could even afford, to dedicate similar resources to the ICC. Moreover, if states completely ceded their investigative role to the ICC, it would render the principle of complementarity irrelevant.

The problem of drug trafficking is dealt with in part through the comprehensive treaty regime currently in place. Under the Rome Statute, however, the existence of a wide-scale problem is not sufficient to vest in the ICC jurisdiction over the offense. Specific provisions must instead provide for the Court's jurisdiction over particular categories of offenses.

Debates over the Statute itself and the Draft Code show that there is no real consensus over whether drug trafficking offenses rise to the same level of severity as the other offenses currently included in Article 5. With no consensus on the subject, the inclusion of the offense would ignore the significant differences in cultural attitudes toward drug use and trafficking, as well as the appropriate punishment for such offenses. Moreover, the investigation of drug trafficking is complex and expensive. These problems, taken together, could create insurmountable obstacles for a court trying to establish its institutional competence and legitimacy.

In 2010, a Review Conference was convened to consider proposed amendments to the Rome Statute. At that conference, Trinidad and Tobago put forward a proposal to add drug trafficking to the list of crimes over which the ICC has jurisdiction, but the proposal was not adopted. In the aftermath of the 2010 Review Conference, efforts to add drug trafficking offenses to the ICC's jurisdiction have waned.

Though the ICC does not have jurisdiction over drug crimes, in February 2018 it opened a preliminary investigation into allegations of human rights abuses committed as part of Philippine President Rodrigo Duterte's war on drugs. Duterte won "a landslide victory in 2016 on a pledge to kill tens of thousands of criminals and eradicate drugs from Philippine society." Michael Plachta, *The Philippines' Withdrawal from the ICC Rome Statute: Background and Context*, 34 No. 3 Int'l Enforcement L. Rep. 118 (2018). As of 2017, Duterte's drug war has resulted in the killings of more than 12,000 people according to Human Rights Watch. "The bloodshed during [Duterte's] war on drugs has caused international alarm and fierce criticism from several U.N. rapporteurs and human rights officials. But Duterte refused to change his approach, or accept that police may have executed suspected drug dealers, as activists allege." *Id.* One month after the ICC announced its investigation, Duterte formally served notice to the United Nations that the Philippines would be withdrawing from the ICC. Under the Rome statute, the withdrawal took effect one year after the United Nations' receipt of the notice on March 17, 2019.

Duterte's withdrawal does not offer legal protection from acts committed while the Philippines was a party to Rome Statute. This is because, "[a]ccording to Article 127 of the Rome Statute, a state party's withdrawal should not affect its cooperation with the Court on criminal investigations and proceedings initiated prior to the effectivity of the state's withdrawal. The withdrawal should also not 'prejudice in any way the continued consideration of any matter which was already under consideration by the Court prior to the date on which the withdrawal became effective.'" *Id.*

This is not the first time activists have called on the ICC to investigate allegations of human rights abuses done in the pursuit of drug enforcement. In 2011, Mexican human rights lawyer Netzai Sandoval filed a complaint before the ICC asking it to investigate whether war crimes and crimes against humanity have been committed in connection with Mexico's war against drugs. The complaint, signed by 23,000 Mexican citizens, alleged that "President Felipe Calderón, other top officials and the country's most-wanted drug trafficker" have "allow[ed] subordinates to kill, torture and kidnap victims." Sara Webb and Manuel Rueda, *Activists Seek International Probe of Mexican Drug War*, Chicago Trib., Nov. 27, 2011. Several similar complaints have been filed since and in 2016 the Open Society Justice Initiative issued a detailed report concluding that there is "a reasonable basis to believe that both state and non-state actors have committed crimes against humanity in Mexico." Open Society Foundations, Undeniable Atrocities: Confronting Crimes Against Humanity in Mexico 12 (2016). Thus far, however, the ICC has not opened an investigation into Mexico's drug war. For more analysis of these issues, see Rodolfo D. Saenz, *Confronting Mexico's Enforced Disappearance Monsters: How the ICC Can Contribute to the Process of Realizing Criminal Justice Reform in Mexico*, 50 Vand. J. Transnat'l L. 45, 47 (2017); Taylor Baronich, *Bleeding Mexico*, 17 Or. Rev. Int'l L. 111, 112 (2015).

C. U.S. Influence on International Drug Control

The United States has been a driving force behind drug prohibition efforts internationally, pursuing drug enforcement with war-like intensity both at home and abroad. As William B. McAllister observes in his authoritative history of international drug control, "in the late twentieth-century the United States promoted adoption of American-style drug control laws in other countries as vigorously as any commercial export, often threatening the domestic stability of other states in the process." WILLIAM B. MCALLISTER, DRUG DIPLOMACY IN THE TWENTIETH CENTURY 254 (2000). This section considers the role of the United States and its "war on drugs" strategy in international drug control.

1. Extraterritorial Application of U.S. Drug Laws

As discussed above, although there is a significant amount of international cooperation among nations in drug control, there is no international body that has jurisdiction over drug investigations or prosecutions. As a result, drug law enforcement remains a fundamentally national task. Inevitably, however, some domestic drug prosecutions will involve international conduct. Imagine, for example, a drug business operator living in Mexico whose organization sends marijuana into the United States. Should the U.S. be allowed to prosecute the drug operator, even if he has never stepped foot on U.S. soil?

There are five accepted principles of jurisdiction under international law that guide the reach of domestic criminal statutes: (1) the territorial principle; (2) the nationality principle; (3) the protective principle; (4) the passive personality principle; and (5) the universality principle. *See generally*, RESTATEMENT (THIRD) OF FOREIGN RELATIONS LAW OF THE UNITED STATES§§ 401–404. The territorial principle grants nations jurisdiction over crimes committed within their own territory. This principle includes typical domestic crimes as well as crimes that produce an effect within the country exercising jurisdiction, even though the conduct occurred in a different country. This is referred to as "objective territorial jurisdiction." The nationality principle allows states to exercise jurisdiction over their own nationals. The protective principle "recognizes the right of a state to punish . . . offenses directed against the security of the state or other offenses threatening the integrity of governmental functions[.]" *Id.* at § 402 cmt. f. Under the passive personality principle, nations may exercise jurisdictions over crimes committed against their nationals. Finally, the universality principle gives states the "jurisdiction to define and prescribe punishment for certain offenses recognized by the community of nations as of universal concern, such as piracy, slave trade, attacks on or hijacking of aircraft, genocide, war crimes, and perhaps certain acts of terrorism, even where none of the [other] bases of jurisdiction . . . is present." *Id.* at § 404.

Though the basic principles of the extraterritorial application of domestic law are easily stated, determining whether a specific statute should be applied extraterritorially in a particular case can be a much more difficult task. As one scholar has observed, "[t]he increasing phenomenon of U.S. extraterritoriality, or extension of federal law to activity outside U.S. borders, embroils a complex tangle of multifaceted and often overlapping legal doctrines." Anthony J. Colangelo, *A Unified Approach to Extraterritoriality*, 97 VA. L. REV. 1019, 1020–21 (2011).

Over the past few decades, the U.S. has increasingly sought to prosecute international drug crimes in its courts. Some of the resulting cases have presented courts with particularly controversial and challenging questions about the extraterritorial reach of U.S. drug laws.

a. Prosecution of Foreign Drug Producers and Distributors

United States v. Noriega

United States District Court for the Southern District of Florida
746 F. Supp. 1506 (1990)

Hoeveler, J.

The case at bar presents the Court with a drama of international proportions, considering the status of the principal defendant and the difficult circumstances under which he was brought before this Court. The pertinent facts are as follows:

On February 14, 1988, a federal grand jury sitting in Miami, Florida returned a twelve-count indictment charging General Manuel Antonio Noriega with participating in an international conspiracy to import cocaine and materials used in producing cocaine into and out of the United States. Noriega is alleged to have exploited his official position as head of the intelligence branch of the Panamanian National Guard, and then as Commander-in-Chief of the Panamanian Defense Forces, to receive payoffs in return for assisting and protecting international drug traffickers, including various members of the Medellin Cartel, in conducting narcotics and money laundering operations in Panama.

Specifically, the indictment charges that General Noriega protected cocaine shipments from Columbia through Panama to the United States; arranged for the transshipment and sale to the Medellin Cartel of ether and acetone, including such chemicals previously seized by the Panamanian Defense Forces; provided refuge and a base for continued operations for the members of the Medellin Cartel after the Columbian government's crackdown on drug traffickers following the murder of the Columbian Minister of Justice, Rodrigo Lara-Bonilla; agreed to protect a cocaine laboratory in Darien Province, Panama; and assured the safe passage of millions of dollars of narcotic proceeds from the United States into Panamanian banks. Noriega also allegedly traveled to Havana, Cuba and met with Cuban president Fidel Castro, who, according to the indictment, mediated a dispute between Noriega and the Cartel caused by the Panamanian troops' seizure of a drug laboratory that Noriega was paid to protect. All of these activities were allegedly undertaken for General Noriega's own personal profit. Defendant [Lt. Col. Luis] Del Cid, in addition to being an officer in the Panamanian Defense Forces, was General Noriega's personal secretary. He is charged with acting as liaison, courier, and emissary for Noriega in his transactions with Cartel members and other drug traffickers.

Because of the activities alleged, Defendants are charged with engaging in a pattern of racketeering activity, in violation of the RICO statutes, 18 U.S.C. §§ 1962(c) and 1962(d); conspiracy to distribute and import cocaine into the United States, in violation of 21 U.S.C. § 963; and distributing and aiding and abetting the distribution of cocaine, intending that it be imported into the United States, in violation of 21 U.S.C. § 959 and 18 U.S.C. § 2. Defendant Noriega is further charged with aiding and abetting the manufacture of cocaine destined for the United States, in violation of 21 U.S.C. § 959 and 18 U.S.C. § 2; conspiring to manufacture cocaine intending that it be imported into the United States, in violation of 21 U.S.C. § 963; and causing interstate travel and use of facilities in interstate commerce to promote an unlawful activity, in violation of 18 U.S.C. § 1952(a)(3) and 18 U.S.C. § 2.

Subsequent to the indictment, the Court granted General Noriega's motion to allow special appearance of counsel, despite the fact that Noriega was a fugitive and not before the Court at that time. Noriega's counsel then moved to dismiss the indictment on the ground that United States laws could not be applied to a foreign leader whose alleged illegal activities all occurred outside the territorial bounds of the United States. Counsel further argued that Noriega was immune from prosecution as a head of state and diplomat, and that his alleged narcotics offenses constituted acts of state not properly reviewable by this Court.

Upon hearing arguments of counsel, and after due consideration of the memoranda filed, the Court denied Defendant's motion, for reasons fully set forth below. At that time, the Court noted that this case was fraught with political overtones, but that it was nonetheless unlikely that General Noriega would ever be brought to the United States to answer the charges against him. The former observation proved to be considerably more correct than the latter, in light of subsequent events.

In the interval between the time the indictment was issued and Defendants were arrested, relations between the United States and General Noriega deteriorated considerably. Shortly after charges against Noriega were brought, the General delivered a widely publicized speech in which he brought a machete crashing down on a podium while denouncing the United States. On December 15, 1989, Noriega declared that a "state of war" existed between Panama and the United States. Tensions between the two countries further increased the next day, when U.S. military forces in Panama were put on alert after Panamanian troops shot and killed an American soldier, wounded another, and beat a Navy couple. Three days later, on December 20, 1989, President Bush ordered U.S. troops into combat in Panama City on a mission whose stated goals were to safeguard American lives, restore democracy, preserve the Panama Canal treaties, and seize General Noriega to face federal drug charges in the United States. Before U.S. troops were engaged, American officials arranged a ceremony in which Guillermo Endara was sworn in as president and recognized by the United States as the legitimate head of the government of

Panama. Endara was reported to have won the Panamanian presidential election held several months earlier, the results of which were nullified and disregarded by General Noriega.

Not long after the invasion commenced, Defendant Del Cid, the commander of about two thousand Panamanian troops located in the Chiriqui Province, surrendered to American forces. He was then transferred into the custody of agents from the United States Drug Enforcement Agency,* who thereupon arrested Del Cid for the offenses for which he is under indictment in this Court. The apprehension of General Noriega was not quite so easy. He successfully eluded American forces for several days, prompting the United States government to offer a one million dollar bounty for his capture. Eventually, the General took sanctuary in the Papal Nunciature in Panama City, where he apparently hoped to be granted political asylum. Noriega's presence in the Papal Nunciature touched off a diplomatic impasse and a round of intense negotiations involving several countries. Vatican officials initially refused to turn Noriega over to the United States. While he was still ensconced in the nunciature, American troops stationed outside pelted the building with loud rock-and-roll music blasted through loudspeakers. The music was played continuously for three days until church authorities protested the action as offensive. After an eleven-day standoff, Noriega finally surrendered to American forces, apparently under pressure from the papal nuncio and influenced by a threatening crowd of about 15,000 angry Panamanian citizens who had gathered outside the residence. On January 3, 1990, two weeks after the invasion began, Noriega walked out of the Papal Nunciature and surrendered himself to U.S. military officials waiting outside. He was flown by helicopter to Howard Air Force Base, where he was ushered into a plane bound for Florida and formally arrested by agents of the Drug Enforcement Agency. During the course of this litigation, which has included several hearings, no evidence was presented nor suggestion made that Noriega was in any way physically mistreated.

As is evident from the unusual factual background underlying this case, the Court is presented with several issues of first impression. This is the first time that a leader or de facto leader of a sovereign nation has been forcibly brought to the United States to face criminal charges. The fact that General Noriega's apprehension occurred in the course of a military action only further underscores the complexity of the issues involved. In addition to Defendant Noriega's motion to dismiss based on lack of jurisdiction over the offense and sovereign immunity, Defendants Noriega and Del Cid argue that they are prisoners of war pursuant to the Geneva Convention. This status, Defendants maintain, deprives the Court of jurisdiction to proceed with the case. Additionally, Noriega contends that the military action which brought about his arrest is "shocking to the conscience", and that due process considerations require the Court to divest itself of jurisdiction over his person.

---

* The court's opinion mistakenly referred to the DEA as the "Drug Enforcement Agency." Its true name is the Drug Enforcement Administration. [*Footnote by casebook author.*]

Noriega also asserts that the invasion occurred in violation of international law. Finally, Noriega argues that, even in the absence of constitutional or treaty violations, the Court should dismiss the indictment pursuant to its supervisory powers so as to prevent the judicial system from being party to and tainted by the government's alleged misconduct in arresting Noriega. The Court examines each of these issues, in turn, below.

The first issue confronting the Court is whether the United States may exercise jurisdiction over Noriega's alleged criminal activities. Noriega maintains that "the extraterritorial application of the criminal law is unreasonable under the unique facts of this case, and cannot be relied upon to secure jurisdiction over a leader of a sovereign nation who has personally performed no illegal acts within the borders of the United States." Although the defendant attempts to weave his asserted status as a foreign leader into his challenge to the extraterritorial application of this country's criminal laws, the question of whether the United States may proscribe conduct which occurs beyond its borders is separate from the question of whether Noriega is immune from prosecution as a head of state. The Court therefore reserves analysis of Noriega's claim to head of state immunity and confines its discussion here to the ability of the United States to reach and prosecute acts committed by aliens outside its territorial borders. While the indictment cites specific instances of conduct occurring within the United States, including the shipment of cocaine from Panama to Miami and several flights to and from Miami by Noriega's alleged co-conspirators, the activity ascribed to Noriega occurred solely in Panama with the exception of the one trip to Cuba. Noriega is charged with providing safe haven to international narcotic traffickers by allowing Panama to be used as a location for the manufacture and shipment of cocaine destined for this country's shores.

Where a court is faced with the issue of extraterritorial jurisdiction, the analysis to be applied is 1) whether the United States has the power to reach the conduct in question under traditional principles of international law; and 2) whether the statutes under which the defendant is charged are intended to have extraterritorial effect. As Noriega concedes, the United States has long possessed the ability to attach criminal consequences to acts occurring outside this country which produce effects within the United States. For example, the United States would unquestionably have authority to prosecute a person standing in Canada who fires a bullet across the border which strikes a second person standing in the United States. *See* Restatement (Third) [of the Foreign Relations Laws of the United States] § 402, Comment d. "All the nations of the world recognize 'the principle that a man who outside of a country willfully puts in motion a force to take effect in it is answerable at the place where the evil is done. . . .'" The objective territorial theory of jurisdiction, which focuses on the effects or intended effects of conduct, can be traced to Justice Holmes' statement that "acts done outside a jurisdiction, but intended to produce or producing effects within it, justify a State in punishing the cause of the harm as if he had been present at the effect, if the State should succeed in getting him within its power." *Strassheim v. Daily*, 221 U.S. at 285. Even if the extraterritorial conduct produces no effect within the United States, a defendant may still be reached if he was part of a conspiracy in which some co-conspirator's activities took place within United States territory. The former Fifth Circuit, whose decisions establish precedent for this Court, has on numerous occasions upheld jurisdiction over foreigners who conspired to import narcotics into the United States but never entered this country nor personally performed any acts within its territorial limits, as long as there was proof of an overt act committed within the United States by a co-conspirator.

More recently, international law principles have expanded to permit jurisdiction upon a mere showing of *intent* to produce effects in this country, without requiring proof of an overt act or effect within the United States. According to the Restatement (Third):

> Cases involving intended but unrealized effect are rare, but international law does not preclude jurisdiction in such instances, subject to the principle of reasonableness. When the intent to commit the proscribed act is clear and demonstrated by some activity, and the effect to be produced by the activity is substantial and foreseeable, the fact that a plan or conspiracy was thwarted does not deprive the target state of jurisdiction to make its law applicable.

In the drug smuggling context, the 'intent doctrine' has resulted in jurisdiction over persons who attempted to import narcotics into the United States but never actually succeeded in entering the United States or delivering drugs within its borders. The fact that no act was committed and no repercussions were felt within the United States did not preclude jurisdiction over conduct that was clearly directed at the United States. *United States v. Wright-Barker, supra* ("The purpose of these [narcotics laws] is to halt smugglers *before* they introduce their dangerous wares into and distribute them in this country.") (emphasis in original).

These principles unequivocally support jurisdiction in this case. The indictment charges Noriega with conspiracy to import cocaine into the United States and alleges several overt acts performed within the United States in furtherance of the conspiracy. Specifically, the indictment alleges that co-conspirators of Noriega purchased a Lear jet in Miami, which was then used to transport drug proceeds from Miami to Panama. Moreover, Noriega's activities in Panama, if true, undoubtedly produced effects within this country as deleterious as the hypothetical bullet fired across the border. The indictment alleges that, as a result of Noriega's facilitation of narcotics activity in Panama, 2,141 pounds of cocaine were illegally brought into Miami from Panama. While the ability of the United States to reach and proscribe extraterritorial conduct having effects in this country does not depend on the amount of narcotics imported into the United States or the magnitude of the consequences, the importation of over 2,000 pounds of cocaine clearly has a harmful impact and merits jurisdiction. Finally, even if no overt acts or effects occurred within the territorial borders, the object of the alleged conspiracy was to import cocaine into the United States and therefore an intent to produce effects is present.

The defendant's argument that the exercise of jurisdiction over his alleged activities in Panama is unreasonable is simply unsupportable in light of established principles of international law and the overwhelming case law in this Circuit upholding jurisdiction under similar circumstances. Other than asserting his status as a foreign leader, which presents a different question from the one posed here, Noriega does not distinguish this case from those cited above. He cites the principle of reasonableness recently articulated in the Restatement (Third) § 403, but fails to say how extending jurisdiction over his conduct would be unreasonable. In fact, the defendant's invocation of a reasonableness requirement supports rather than undermines the application of jurisdiction in the present case. Thus, for example, Noriega quotes the following language from the Restatement:

> In applying the principle of reasonableness, the exercise of criminal (as distinguished from civil) jurisdiction in relation to acts committed in another state may be perceived as particularly intrusive. . . . It is generally accepted by enforcement agencies of the United States government that criminal jurisdiction over activity with substantial foreign elements should be exercised more sparingly than civil jurisdiction over the same activity, and only upon strong justification.

However, the same section of the Restatement establishes that narcotics offenses provide the strong justification meriting criminal jurisdiction: "Prosecution for activities committed in a foreign state have generally been limited to serious and universally condemned offenses, such as treason or traffic in narcotics, and to offenses by and against military forces. In such cases the state in whose territory the act occurs is not likely to object to regulation by the state concerned." The Restatement therefore explicitly recognizes the reasonableness of extending jurisdiction to narcotics activity such as that alleged here. *See also United States v. Wright-Barker,* 784 F.2d at 168 (construing § 403 to permit jurisdiction over extraterritorial narcotics trafficking). Even if another state were likely to object to jurisdiction here, the United States has a strong interest in halting the flow of illicit drugs across its borders. In assessing the reasonableness of extraterritorial jurisdiction, one of the factors to be considered is the character of the activity to be regulated, including the importance of regulation to the regulating state and the degree to which the desire to regulate is generally accepted. Restatement (Third) § 403(1)(c). The consensus of the American public on the need to stem the flow of drugs into this country is well publicized and need not be elaborated upon in detail. Further, the Court notes that the United States has an affirmative duty to enact and enforce legislation to curb illicit drug trafficking under the Single Convention on Narcotics Drugs. Given the serious nature of the drug epidemic in this country, certainly the efforts of the United States to combat the problem by prosecuting conduct directed against itself cannot be subject to the protests of a foreign government profiting at its expense. In any case, the Court is not made aware of any instance in which the Republic of Panama objected to the regulation of drug trafficking by the United States. In sum, because Noriega's conduct in Panama is alleged to have resulted in a direct effect within the United States, the Court concludes that extraterritorial jurisdiction is appropriate as a matter of international law.

This conclusion does not end the Court's analysis, however, since a further requirement is that the criminal statutes under which the defendant is charged be intended to apply to conduct outside the United States. Noriega is charged with violations of 21 U.S.C. § 959 (distributing a controlled substance with the knowledge that it would be unlawfully imported into the United States); 21 U.S.C. § 952 (importing a controlled substance into the United States from a place outside thereof); 21 U.S.C. § 963 (conspiring to commit the above offenses); and 18 U.S.C. § 2 (aiding and abetting the violation of § 959). The indictment also alleges that Noriega participated in a pattern of racketeering activity consisting of the above crimes, in violation of the Racketeer Influenced and Corrupt Organizations Act (RICO), §§ 1962(c) and 1962(d), and caused the travel and use of facilities in interstate and foreign commerce in furtherance of a narcotics conspiracy, in violation of 18 U.S.C. § 1952 (a)(3).

Section 959, prohibiting the distribution of narcotics intending that they be imported into the United States, is clearly meant to apply extraterritorially. The statute expressly states that it is "intended to reach acts of manufacture or distribution committed outside the territorial jurisdiction of the United States." 21 U.S.C. § 959(c). The remaining statutes, by contrast, do not on their face indicate an express intention that they be given extraterritorial effect. Where a statute is silent as to its extraterritorial reach, a presumption against such application normally applies. However, "such statutes may be given extraterritorial effect if the nature of the law permits it and Congress intends it. Absent an express intention on the face of the statutes to do so, the exercise of that power may be inferred from the nature of the offenses and Congress' other legislative efforts to eliminate the type of crime involved."

With respect to 21 U.S.C. § 952, it is apparent from the very nature of the offense that the statute was intended to reach extraterritorial acts. Section 952 makes it unlawful to import narcotics "into the United States from *any place outside* thereof . . ." (emphasis added). Because importation by definition involves acts originating outside of the territorial limits of the United States, the Court can only infer that § 952 applies to conduct which begins abroad; any interpretation to the contrary would render the statute virtually meaningless. With jurisdiction over the substantive violations of §§ 959 and 952 established, jurisdiction over the conspiracy and aiding and abetting counts likewise follows. Since a conspiracy to commit an offense is closely related to the offense itself, courts have regularly inferred the extraterritorial reach of the § 963 conspiracy statute on the basis of a finding that the substantive statutes apply abroad. The same must be said for an aiding and abetting charge; if anything, the act of aiding and abetting is even more intimately connected to the underlying crime. In short, the Court perceives no sound jurisdictional reason for distinguishing the conspiracy and aiding and abetting charges from the substantive offense for purposes of extraterritorial application. Section 963 and 18 U.S.C. § 2 must therefore be given extraterritorial effect as well.

Whether the RICO and Travel Act statutes reach conduct abroad is a more difficult question. None of the cases cited by the parties address this point and the Court is unaware of any case reaching the issue. The question of these statutes' extraterritorial effect is therefore a matter of apparent first impression.

Section 1962(c) makes it unlawful for "*any* person associated with *any* enterprise engaged in, or the activities of which affect, interstate or foreign commerce, to conduct or participate. in the conduct of such enterprise's affairs through a pattern of racketeering activity. . . ." 18 U.S.C. § 1962(c) (emphasis added). Section 1962(d) similarly makes it illegal for "*any* person to conspire to violate" Section 1962(c). These prohibitions are on their face all-inclusive and do not suggest parochial application. Indeed, if any statute reaches far and wide, it is RICO.

When Congress passed RICO, it was primarily concerned with eradicating the destructive influence of organized crime on our society[.] Though its emphasis is on economic effects, RICO itself is not so limited; its history demonstrates concern with our domestic security and welfare as well as our gross national product.

Given the Act's broad construction and equally broad goal of eliminating the harmful consequences of organized crime, it is apparent that Congress was concerned with the effects and not the locus of racketeering activities. The Act thus permits no inference that it was intended to apply only to conduct within the United States. Such a narrow construction would frustrate RICO's purpose by allowing persons engaged in racketeering activities directed at the United States to escape RICO's bite simply by moving their operations abroad. Yet in the context of narcotics activities, perhaps the greatest threat to this country's welfare comes from enterprises outside the United States such as the Columbian cocaine cartels. Keeping in mind Congress' specific instruction that RICO be applied liberally to effect its remedial purpose, the Court cannot suppose that RICO does not reach such harmful conduct simply because it is extraterritorial in nature. As long as the racketeering activities produce effects or are intended to produce effects in this country, RICO applies.

Noriega is also charged with violating the Travel Act, 18 U.S.C. § 1952(a)(3), by causing foreign travel and the use of facilities in foreign and interstate commerce to promote an unlawful activity. The indictment alleges that, on two separate occasions, co-conspirators of Noriega used an airplane to transport drug proceeds from Miami to Panama.

Like RICO, the Travel Act was originally designed to combat organized crime. Specifically, "the purpose of the Travel Act was to aid local law enforcement officials. In many instances, the 'top men' of a given criminal enterprise resided in one State but conducted their illegal activities in another; by creating a federal interest in limiting the interstate movement necessary to such operations, criminal conduct beyond the reach of local officials could be controlled." *United States v. Nardello,* 393 U.S. 286, 290 (1969). The Act was thus an attempt to reach criminal activities uniquely broad and transitory in scope, i.e., those whose influence extend beyond state and national borders and therefore require federal assistance. While courts have sometimes, as above, referred to persons "residing in one state," the Act itself indicates no such territorial limitation; the reference is therefore more properly understood as calling attention to the interstate character of the activity rather than the defendant's location. Stated more broadly, the Act "constitutes an effort to deny individuals who act for criminal purposes access to the channels of commerce."

In this case, the defendant allegedly participated in a criminal syndicate which utilized the channels of commerce to carry out illegal drug activities in the United States. His location may have differed from the typical defendant charged under the Travel Act but the nature and effect of the alleged activity is the same, and implicates the same congressional desire to reach conduct which transcends state lines both physically and symbolically.

Jurisdiction over Defendant's extraterritorial conduct is therefore appropriate both as a matter of international law and statutory construction.

[The Court went on to reject Noriega's additional arguments that (1) he was immune from prosecution based on head of state immunity, the act of state doctrine, and diplomatic immunity; (2) the Court did not have jurisdiction to proceed with the case because Noriega was a prisoner of war within the meaning of the Geneva Convention; and (3) the Court should divest itself of jurisdiction because he was illegally arrested.]

In view of the above findings and observations, it is the Order of this Court that the several motions presented by Defendants relating to this Court's jurisdiction as well as that suggesting dismissal under supervisory authority be and each is DENIED.

Manuel Noriega was tried and convicted in 1992. Though Noriega completed his sentence in 2007, he was not released from custody. Instead, Noriega was extradited to France where he received a seven-year prison sentence for money laundering offenses. Not long after his conviction in France, Noriega was extradited to Panama to serve a 20-year sentence for the disappearances of political opponents. Noriega died in 2017. Interestingly, before Noriega became a target of the United States, he spent decades as a paid informant for the United States. According to one former DEA officer, the United States suspected Noriega of involvement in drug trafficking "[a]s early as 1972" but "the State Department told the [DEA] in no uncertain terms that Noriega and his boss, Panamanian strongman Omar Torrijos, were too important to be touched [because t]hey provided critical intelligence on Soviet influence on Latin American countries." ROBERT M. STUTMAN AND RICHARD ESPOSITO, DEAD ON DELIVERY: INSIDE THE DRUG WARS, STRAIGHT FROM THE STREET 98–99 1992. For more on Noriega's prosecution, see Geoffrey S. Corn and Sharon C. Finegan, *America's Longest Held Prisoner of War: Lessons Learned from the Capture, Prosecution, and Extradition of General Manuel Noriega*, 71 LA. L. REV. 1111 (2011).

In *Noriega*, the Court found that the objective territorial principle of international law gave U.S. courts jurisdiction over cases "upon a mere showing of *intent* to produce effects in" the United States. But is an intent to produce effects in the United States necessary for the extraterritorial application of federal drug laws? Or can federal courts exercise jurisdiction over drug cases with a weaker connection to the United States?

United States v. Manuel

United States District Court for the Southern District of New York 371 F. Supp. 2d 404 (2005)

Lynch, J.

Defendant Virgilio Martinus Manuel was charged, along with six other defendants, in two different conspiracy counts. Count One charged defendants with conspiring to import over 300,000 ecstasy pills into the United States, in violation of 21 U.S.C. §§ 963, 812, 952(a)(2) and 960(b)(3). Count Two charged them with conspiring to distribute or possess with intent to distribute ecstasy, in violation of 21 U.S.C. §§ 846, 841(a)(1), and 841(b)(1)(C). Manuel was tried before a jury from March 23 through March 30, 2005. At the close of the Government's case, the Court dismissed Count One, holding that the evidence was insufficient to prove beyond a reasonable doubt that Manuel knew that the drugs were destined for the United States. However, the Court ruled at that time that this insufficiency did not require acquittal on Count Two. The jury subsequently found Manuel guilty on that count. Manuel now renews his motion for acquittal on that charge, arguing that the evidence was insufficient to permit his conviction and that the court lacks subject matter jurisdiction over the offense. The motion will be denied.

Manuel does not contest that the Government's evidence was sufficient to establish the following facts. Beginning in the spring of 2001, a skillful German undercover police officer insinuated himself into a group of conspirators in the Netherlands, who hoped to export large quantities of ecstasy (a controlled substance whose distribution is illegal in the Netherlands, Germany, and the United States) from Europe to the United States. The undercover officer persuaded the chief conspirators, Beatriz Henao, Armando Enano, Valderama Ruiz, and Victor deBoer, that, for a fee, he could safely transport large quantities of pills to the United States.

The conspirators decided to try an initial test run of 47,000 pills in June 2001. DeBoer delivered the pills to the undercover officer in Germany, for transportation to America. From the criminals' perspective, the test went off almost without a hitch: The pills were delivered undetected (so far as they knew) to their courier in New York, Ricardo Quintero. Through a clever ruse, by making it appear that the drugs were discovered by accident after a successful delivery to the courier, the investigators were able to arrest Quintero and seize the drugs without bringing the undercover officer under suspicion. Writing that seizure off to bad luck and the incompetence of their New York courier, the leaders of the enterprise decided to go ahead with a larger shipment in August 2001.

Because deBoer was in Colombia at that time, the conspirators arranged to use a different courier to deliver the second shipment, of 301,000 pills, to the undercover officer at a highway rest stop in Germany. The conspirators advised the undercover officer that the courier would be driving a white car and wearing a white hat. That courier was Manuel, who arrived at the designated location in a white car wearing a white cap, made contact with the undercover, and delivered the drugs. On September 29, 2001, the undercover delivered the pills, as instructed by the conspiracy's leaders, to Carlos Ruiz in New York. Ruiz was arrested and the drugs seized.

So far as the evidence at trial revealed, Manuel's sole role in the conspiracy was to deliver the pills from Holland to Germany on August 7, 2001. For purposes of this motion, he does not dispute that a reasonable jury could infer that he knew that he was delivering illegal drugs, since (among other reasons) professional drug dealers would hardly entrust an unwitting dupe to carry drugs worth over $1,000,000 wholesale in Europe (and $6,000,000 to $9,000,000 retail at their eventual destination in the streets and clubs of New York) across an international border. There was no evidence whatsoever, on the other hand, suggesting that Manuel knew the eventual destination of the pills.[2]

The point of departure for analysis of Manuel's claims is *United States v. Londono-Villa,* 930 F.2d 994 (2d Cir. 1991). In Londono-Villa, as in this case, an undercover narcotics officer negotiated with foreign drug dealers (in that case, cocaine smugglers in Panama, rather than ecstasy sellers in the Netherlands) regarding drugs to be shipped to the United States. The negotiations having been successfully concluded, the undercover agent was advised that his pilot could pick up the drugs at a hidden airfield in Colombia and bring them back to Panama for eventual transshipment to the United States. Londono, an experienced pilot who had frequently used that airfield, was recruited by the conspirators to guide the undercover agent's plane to the secret landing strip; Londono would then remain in Colombia while the plane returned to Panama with the drugs. Londono unquestionably knew of the illegal purpose of the flight; indeed, he inspected the cocaine at the landing field,

2. The Government halfheartedly argues in a footnote that the jury could have found, by the same process of inference, that Manuel must have had a high enough rank in the conspiracy to be privy to the details of the conspiracy. This claim is without merit. It is reasonable to assume that a courier entrusted the task of transporting valuable illegal commodities across an international border would be aware of the nature of his cargo; the conspirators would be foolish to run the risk that an unwitting courier would steal or neglect the cargo, attract police attention by violating traffic laws, or fail to take action to evade customs patrols. There is no reason to assume, however, that a mere courier, albeit one with criminal intent, would be advised of the business plans of the leaders. On the contrary, it would presumably be advisable to keep subordinates in the dark. Moreover, as evidence in the record indicates that the Netherlands is the leading source country for ecstasy, and that there is a thriving market for ecstasy in Germany, there is no reason why a courier would assume that the drugs were destined for further transshipment.

and was sufficiently intimate with the drug sellers that when the shipment turned out to be short, the parties relied on him to verify the amount of cocaine actually delivered to the plane. The cocaine was eventually transported to the United States.

Nevertheless, the Second Circuit held that the evidence was insufficient to convict Londono of conspiracy to import the drugs into the United States. The Court held that in order to be guilty of this offense, an individual must by definition have knowledge that the illegal drugs are intended to enter the United States. This holding is rooted in the language of the statute. The very definition of the offense that is the object of the conspiracy requires that the defendant "knowingly or intentionally import[]" a controlled substance in violation of § 952. 21 U.S.C. § 960(a)(1). Section 952 is even more explicit, making it illegal "to import [a controlled substance] into the United States from any place outside thereof." 21 U.S.C. § 952. In order to conspire to "import [cocaine] into the United States," in violation of 21 U.S.C. § 963, one would necessarily have to agree not merely to possess the drug or to distribute it to others, but specifically to bring the drugs into the United States. Absent knowledge that the United States was the destination for the drug, one could not so agree.

This precedent compelled the dismissal of Count One of the present indictment. Manuel, like Londono, was directly involved in smuggling illegal drugs across an international border. There was no evidence, however that Manuel, a mere courier so far as the evidence shows, was aware of the larger goal of the conspiracy. As in Londono-Villa, Manuel "was not involved in any of the lengthy negotiations for the sale of the [ecstasy]; he was not present at most of the meetings but rather came into the picture only at the end, in order to serve as a [courier] who was to pick up the [ecstasy] in [the Netherlands] and take it [to Germany]. There was no evidence that [Manuel] had been told that the United States was to be the ultimate destination of the cocaine, and no evidence that the United States was ever mentioned in his presence."

Count Two, however, charges a different offense. The definition of the crime that is the object of the conspiracy charged in Count Two does not refer to importation, nor does it refer to the United States. Instead, the statute in question merely makes it a crime to "distribute, . . . or possess with intent to . . . distribute . . . a controlled substance." 21 U.S.C. § 841(a)(1). It is not questioned, for purposes of this motion, that Manuel conspired with others to do exactly that: by agreeing to undertake, by prearrangement with others, the delivery of over 300,000 ecstasy pills to the undercover in Germany, he joined a conspiracy whose object was the retail distribution of that controlled substance.

It is beyond dispute, as Manuel points out, that this offense requires a jurisdictional nexus to the United States. Congress did not intend to prohibit every act of distributing drugs anywhere in the world, but only distribution within the United States. See *United States v. Hayes*, 653 F.2d 8, 15–16 (1st Cir. 1981) (declining to "impute to Congress an intent to punish all whom its courts can catch, for conduct which has no consequences in the United States" by applying § 841(a)(1) to possession of a controlled substance outside the United States with intent to distribute, unless the "intent to distribute" is an intent to distribute within the United States) (quoting *United States v. Aluminum Co. of America,* 148 F.2d 416, 443 (2d Cir. 1945) (Hand, J.)). But the distribution of ecstasy that was the object of this conspiracy was indeed to occur in the United States. That was the very purpose of the conspiracy, which enlisted the undercover officer precisely for his supposed prowess in smuggling goods into the United States. Nor was this intention purely hypothetical: the conspirators arranged for colleagues in the Southern District of New York to receive the drugs, and both shipments were accepted by those co-conspirators here in New York. The quantity of drugs in both shipments makes plain that the importation was for the purpose of further distribution here.

These facts doom Manuel's argument that "the court lacks subject matter jurisdiction over the defendant for the offenses charged." In the first place, the argument misstates the question. A court has subject matter jurisdiction over a case, not over a person, and the Court plainly has jurisdiction over the case, because the indictment charged a violation of federal law. What Manuel means to argue is either that Congress lacked legislative jurisdiction to prohibit his actions, or that he is not guilty of the offense charged because Congress did not intend the law to have extraterritorial application to his acts.

But however defined, Manuel's argument fails on the merits. Any challenge to the legislative jurisdiction of Congress must fail, since there is no constitutional bar to the extraterritorial application of penal laws. Whether a statute has such extraterritorial application is solely a question of legislative intent. *United States v. Bowman,* 260 U.S. 94, 97–98 (1922).[4] The Supreme Court has specifically upheld the exercise of jurisdiction over conspirators who have never entered the United States, where the conspiracy "was directed to violation of the United States law within the United States." *Ford v. United States,* 273 U.S. 593, 620 (1927). Where, as here, the object of a conspiracy is the violation of American law, and co-conspirators committed extensive overt acts within American territory, there can be no serious question of the jurisdiction of the United States to punish all members of the conspiracy.

The sole remaining question is whether Congress intended to do so in enacting the statutes at issue in this case. Although there is a presumption that Congress does not intend a statute to apply to conduct outside the United States, that presumption can be overcome if Congress clearly expresses its intent. It is well-established that Congress intended to give extraterritorial reach to the statutes at issue here. Thus, the Second Circuit has held that jurisdiction to prosecute violations of § 841(a)(1) exists both where defendants possess drugs outside the United States with intent to

4. While international law standards of national jurisdiction are not binding on the Congress, it should be noted that extraterritorial application of United States law to Manuel is entirely in keeping with international law, since international law permits a country to exercise jurisdiction over acts committed outside it that have harmful effects within it. See Restatement (Third) of the Foreign Relations Law of the United States §§ 402–403.

distribute them in the United States, or possess drugs inside the United States with intent to distribute them elsewhere. *United States v. Muench,* 694 F.2d 28, 32–33 (2d Cir. 1982).

There is no question that *both* bases of jurisdiction applied here. The heads of the conspiracy possessed ecstasy in the Netherlands with intent to distribute it in the United States, and the conspirators in New York actually possessed the drug here with the intent to distribute it. Thus, the crime that was the object of the conspiracy Manuel joined was a violation of United States law.

Where a crime is within the jurisdiction of the United States, it is not necessary that the offender be aware of the facts that establish jurisdiction. Thus, for example, a defendant need not know that the person he is assaulting is a federal officer in order to be guilty of violating 18 U.S.C. § 111, *United States v. Feola,* 420 U.S. 671, 684 (1975); a defendant need not know that securities were transported across a state line to be guilty of interstate transportation of stolen securities under 18 U.S.C. § 2314, *United States v. Eisenberg,* 596 F.2d 522, 526 (2d Cir. 1979); and a defendant need not know he was stealing from an interstate shipment to be guilty of violating 18 U.S.C. § 659, *United States v. Green,* 523 F.2d 229, 233–34 (2d Cir. 1975). If the defendant knowingly commits the acts that cause the harm that the legislature intended to prevent (here, the distribution of narcotics), and jurisdiction exists (because, objectively speaking, the crime satisfies the condition that creates jurisdiction), the statute has been violated. Had the defendants in *Muench* inadvertently wandered into United States territory from Canada, rather than being carried (unwillingly, but knowingly) into the United States by a diverted flight, it could have made no difference: in either case, they committed the crime of possessing narcotics with intent to distribute, and their actions in doing so came within the legislative jurisdiction of the United States in a manner that Congress intended to reach.

Nor does the fact that the crime charged is a conspiracy, and thus requires an intentional agreement to violate the statute, alter the result. Conviction for conspiracy requires no greater *mens rea* than that required to violate the underlying statute. Indeed, ordinary doctrines of conspiracy law confirm the conclusion that Manuel is guilty of the conspiracy charged in Count Two. It is axiomatic that a conspirator does not need to know all of the details of a conspiracy in order to be guilty of joining the agreement and it is equally axiomatic that a conspirator is responsible for the overt acts of co-conspirators, including those necessary to establish venue. Here, it is unquestioned for purposes of this motion that Manuel and his co-conspirators were in "agreement on the essential nature of the plan, and on the kind of criminal conduct . . . in fact contemplated." His co-conspirators committed acts on American soil, and other acts abroad with the specific intention of having effects in the United States. Under basic conspiracy law, he is guilty of joining their conspiracy, and is brought under American jurisdiction by their acts.

There is nothing unfair about this conclusion. Like the defendants in *Feola,* Manuel clearly "knew from the very outset that his planned course of conduct [was] wrongful. The situation is not one where legitimate conduct becomes unlawful solely because of the identity of the [country] affected.... The concept of criminal intent does not extend so far as to require that the actor understand not only the nature of his act but also its consequence for the choice of a judicial forum." Unlike *Londono-Villa,* and Count One of this indictment, in which the object of the conspiracy by its nature required an intention to cross the American border, and in which the defendant did not share in the plan to send drugs into the United States that was the very essence of the conspiracy charged, the effect on the United States in Count Two is a mere jurisdictional element, which does not require knowledge or intent on the part of Manuel.

It was established beyond a reasonable doubt at trial that the conspiracy here was to possess a controlled substance with intent to distribute; that Manuel joined the conspiracy, with full knowledge that its goal was to possess and distribute ecstasy; and that that conspiracy came under the jurisdiction of the United States because co-conspirators both possessed the drugs in the United States and intended to distribute them here. Nothing more is required to convict Manuel of the charge in Count Two.

For these reasons, defendant's motion for acquittal under Federal Rule of Criminal Procedure 29(c) is denied.

In a footnote in *Manuel*, Judge Lynch suggests that a drug courier is likely to "be aware of the nature of his cargo" because "the conspirators would be foolish to run the risk that an unwitting courier would steal or neglect the cargo, attract police attention by violating traffic laws, or fail to take action to evade customs patrols." Is this really the case? In 2012, the federal government revealed that Mexican drug trafficking groups have been using "unwitting courier[s]"—so called "blind mules"—near the San Diego border. The traffickers place classified advertisements for seemingly legitimate jobs that require travel into the United States, such as work as a housecleaner or furniture mover. The driver is not told that the company vehicle is loaded with drugs, however. *See* Elliot Spagat, *Drug Smugglers Placing Job Ads In Mexican Newspapers*, Associated Press, April 11, 2012. Why might a drug trafficker use a "blind mule" in light of the considerations outlined by Judge Lynch?

In *Manuel*, Judge Lynch also noted that the intent to distribute ecstasy was not "purely hypothetical: the conspirators arranged for colleagues in the Southern District of New York to receive the drugs, and both shipments were accepted by those co-conspirators in New York." Could a defendant like Manuel be prosecuted in the United States even if the intent to send drugs into the country was "purely hypothetical"?

The Drug Enforcement Administration has put this question to the test by manufacturing jurisdiction in a number of international drug investigations. Though the details vary, in the typical case an undercover DEA agent or informant will pose as a drug trafficker in order to infiltrate an overseas drug operation. If it turns out that the drug traffickers are shipping drugs outside of the United States, "[i]n order to establish U.S. jurisdiction, [the undercover agent or informant will] tell suspects that some of the drugs will be sold in the United States[.]" Chris Hawley, *Swede Charged in NYC With Guns-for-Coke Scheme*, Associated Press, May 10, 2011. None of the actual traffickers plan to bring drugs into the United States. The only link to the United States is the undercover agent's stated intention. Is this manufactured connection to the United States sufficient to ground jurisdiction?

In one case, four defendants—a Nigerian, a Russian, and two Ghanaians—faced charges based on drug shipments between South America and West Africa. A DEA informant participating in the scheme "stated clearly to the defendants he planned to import cocaine from them to the United States." Colin Moynihan, *Jury Convicts 2 and Acquits 2 in Scheme to Funnel Cocaine into U.S.*, N.Y. Times, April 28, 2011 at A25. Of course, the informant never actually intended to send drugs to the United States; the story was devised as a tool to give U.S. courts jurisdiction over the case. At least one of the defendants moved to dismiss the indictment, arguing that the U.S. had improperly "manufactured jurisdiction." The Judge denied the motion, however, finding that the indictment alleged the defendant had taken "affirmative, voluntary actions implicating federal jurisdiction" because he "understood that from Liberia, portions of this cocaine would subsequently be imported into the United States" by the informant. *United States v. Umeh*, 762 F. Supp. 2d 658, 665 (2011). At trial, three of the defendants conceded that they were involved in international drug trafficking but argued that they had no knowledge of the informant's statements that he planned to send some of the drugs into the U.S. The jury convicted two of the four defendants and acquitted the other two.

Cases like *Umeh* and *Manuel* demonstrate the broad extraterritorial reach of federal law when drugs are destined for the United States. Is the same true if drug traffickers are involved in shipping drugs between two foreign countries, but hold meetings to plan their conspiracy on U.S. soil? In the next case, *Lopez-Vanegas*, the Eleventh Circuit considered this question.

United States v. Lopez-Vanegas

United States Court of Appeals for the Eleventh Circuit
493 F.3d 1305 (2007)

Walter, J.

Doris Mangeri Salazar ("Salazar") and Ivan Lopez-Vanegas ("Lopez") appeal their convictions on one count each of conspiracy to possess with the intent to distribute five kilograms or more of a mixture and substance containing cocaine, in violation of 21 U.S.C. §§ 841(a)(1) and (b)(1)(A)(ii), and 21 U.S.C. § 846. The Government alleged that Salazar and Lopez brokered a deal between a Colombian drug trafficking organization headed by Juan Gabriel Usuga ("Usuga") and a Saudi Arabian Prince, Nayef Al-Shaalan (the "Prince"), to transport cocaine on the Prince's airplane from Caracas, Venezuela to Paris, France, for distribution in Europe.

On appeal, Lopez and Salazar assert, inter alia, that the conduct of which they were accused, and for which they have been convicted, does not violate 21 U.S.C.

§§ 841 and 846. Finding that Salazar and Lopez have committed no crime against the United States, the judgments of conviction and sentences issued by the district court are VACATED.

By 1998, Usuga, Carlos Ramon ("Ramon"), Oscar Campuzano ("Campuzano") and Bernard Sanchez ("Sanchez") (collectively, the "Usuga Group") had become partners in a large-scale Colombian cocaine trafficking organization out of Medellin, Colombia. Usuga was the leader; Campuzano was in charge of collecting money; Sanchez was responsible for transporting, packaging, warehousing and labeling the cocaine in South America; Ramon handled transportation abroad, including the receipt and delivery of cocaine at its destination. Clemente, a Spaniard, was also closely affiliated with the group, though not a member, and specialized in laundering the Usuga Group's drug money.

Evidence at trial showed that the Usuga Group exported at least 50 tons of cocaine during the 1990s throughout Europe and North America. The Group also provided transportation services to other traffickers. The Usuga Group's trademark transportation method was to hide cocaine within isotanks containing petro chemicals.

By January 2000, all four members of the Usuga Group had been indicted in Miami and elsewhere in connection with, among other investigations, Operation Millennium, which targeted high-level narcotics traffickers for extradition. All four members of the Usuga Group surrendered, entered into plea agreements and cooperated with the Government. In particular, Usuga and Campuzano pleaded guilty only to money laundering in connection with Operation Millennium, and each received a reduced sentence of 34 months. Their sentences were later reduced to 22 and 23 months, respectively. Both Usuga and Campuzano had served their time before testifying at trial.

Sanchez pleaded guilty to drug trafficking and received a reduced sentence of 156 months[.] Ramon pleaded guilty to drug trafficking and received a reduced sentence of six years, with the hope of an additional sentence reduction.

Usuga testified at trial that the plans behind the Paris Load began in 1998, when Lopez approached Usuga in Medellin and told him about a "friend of a woman friend of mine" with whom they could engage in financial transactions or deals in Europe. Usuga later learned that Salazar was Lopez's "woman friend," and that the Prince was Salazar's friend. Over the course of a year, the Usuga Group, Clemente, Lopez, the Prince and Salazar had meetings across the globe[5] where, according to the Government, the group conspired to purchase cocaine in Colombia, to be shipped from Venezuela to Paris, France, for distribution in Europe. For purposes of this appeal, the Court will assume that all facts alleged by the Government are uncontested. With that in mind, the following meetings took place in Miami, Florida:

5. Meetings were held in Marbella, Spain, Geneva, Switzerland, Saudi Arabia, Aruba, Colombia and Miami. The Court will focus on the Miami meetings as they are the only events related to the charged conspiracy that took place in the United States.

a. Miami, Florida ("Porto Fino")—Mid-September 1998. In mid-September, 1998, Usuga, Ramon and Campuzano met at the "Porto Fino," Ramon's South-Beach condominium. Neither Lopez nor Salazar was present. At this meeting, the group discussed "the way we were going to set up this organization." "Various tasks" were assigned after Usuga told his cohorts that "he had been able to confirm that in fact . . . [the Prince] had a bank in Geneva and that [the Prince] was who he said he was." Usuga told the group that he would soon be traveling to Saudi Arabia for further discussions. Campuzano confirmed Usuga's account of this Miami meeting.

At this meeting, it was agreed that "there would be two groups . . . [the Prince's] group would consist of [the Prince] and [Salazar] . . . [Salazar would] receive a commission from [the Prince]." Lopez would receive his commission from the Usuga Group for each kilogram transported. Usuga would handle direct communications with the Prince; Ramon would be responsible for the movement of the cocaine; and Campuzano "would be responsible for setting up the straw corporations abroad."

Usuga presented two proposals: one possibility involved the shipment of ten or twenty tons of cocaine using isotanks from Venezuela to Saudi Arabia for re-export to New York;[6] the second proposal was to transport cocaine in the Prince's airplane from Venezuela to Saudi Arabia.

b. Miami, Florida (Dinner at The Forge Restaurant)—November/December 1998. In November or December of 1998, Ramon, Salazar, Clemente, Lopez, Usuga and Pepe Gugliatto met for dinner at The Forge. There, Lopez and Salazar introduced Gugliatto to Usuga. Salazar assured Usuga that Gugliatto was a close friend akin to a relative "with whom [Usuga] could comfortably talk." According to Ramon, Gugliatto was Lopez's personal friend and came with good references from Lopez and

---

6. There is no dispute that Usuga, not the Prince, wanted to send the shipment to New York. Further, the Government has not asserted that shipment to New York was anything more than a one-sided fleeting thought.

In its appellate brief, the Government relies solely upon the "domestic conspiratorial conduct" of Lopez and Salazar to support its argument that the district court had jurisdiction, or as is discussed below, that a crime was actually committed under 21 U.S.C. §§ 841(a)(1) and 846. Further, the Government's subsequent arguments presume that there was no agreement to distribute illegal narcotics in the United States, e.g., "[t]he law does not impose upon §§ 846 and 841(a)(1) any requirement that the object of such a conspiracy must be to possess or distribute cocaine in the United States"; "[b]ecause a defendant may be convicted of a substantive offense under § 841(a)(1) without intending to distribute narcotics in the United States, it follows that defendants like Salazar and Lopez may be guilty of conspiracy to possess with intent to distribute cocaine, in violation of § 846, as long as they or others have engaged in conspiratorial activities to violate that statute in the United States." Brief for the United States, pp. 29–30. Further, as noted above, in response to Salazar's motion for judgment of acquittal, the Government argued that "the drug conspiracy touches here" because the conspirators held meetings in Miami.

In other words, the Government does not rely upon Usuga's statement that he initially wanted to ship cocaine to New York rather than Paris. Thus, this Court finds that the Government has abandoned any such argument. See *Sepulveda v. United States Attorney General,* 401 F.3d 1226, 1228 n. 2 (11th Cir. 2002) (concluding that the petitioners abandoned an issue by failing to raise it in their initial appellate brief).

Salazar. Two matters were discussed at this Miami meeting: the Brazil shoe deal,[7] and Gugliatto's potential for "partnership" with the Prince. Salazar sat with the group at the Forge; "she gave her opinions" though Ramon could not recall her exact words.

Ramon testified that another meeting occurred at the Biltmore Hotel in Miami, involving Usuga, Ramon, Clemente, Salazar and Gugliatto. At that meeting, "some comments were made" about the potential Prince deal, but nothing specific. Usuga, however, testified that they did not discuss the deal at this meeting.

c. Miami, Florida (Don Shula Hotel)—March 5, 1999. On March 5, 1999, Usuga met Salazar, Lopez and Gugliatto at the Don Shula Hotel in Miami. The brief discussion at this meeting centered on the upcoming arrival of the Prince in Caracas, Venezuela for which "everything was ready." Lopez stated that he would notify Usuga of the Prince's arrival date, a few days prior to that date. Usuga replied "that we would be waiting for that."

d. Miami, Florida (Tides Hotel)—July 1999. After the Paris Load was successfully purchased in Colombia, transported to Caracas, Venezuela, and shipped to Paris, France on May 16, 1999, most of the load was distributed, but 804 kilograms of cocaine were seized by French law enforcement on June 3, 1999. In July 1999, Usuga, Campuzano, Clemente and Salazar met at the Tides Hotel in Miami Beach to discuss the amount of money owed to the Prince, who had already been paid $5,000,000 from Lopez's sale of 250 kilograms of cocaine. According to Usuga and Campuzano, Salazar demanded payment of her commission "for the Paris operation" and an additional $10,000,000 owed the Prince, but Usuga refused. Salazar insisted "that the money was owed to the Prince and it had to be paid." Salazar further insisted that Usuga was "responsible for the incident" and, thus, was responsible for her commission.

e. Recorded Conversations With Lopez. After Usuga was arrested and was cooperating with the Government, he recorded a number of conversations with Lopez between April 2000 and March 2001. After Campuzano surrendered and agreed to cooperate with the Government, Lopez called and Campuzano also recorded their conversation. Lopez's conversations with Campuzano and Usuga centered on the debts owed to the Prince, and those owed by and to Lopez as a result of the Paris Load.

Whether a criminal statute reaches a defendant's conduct is reviewed de novo.

Appellants assert that the agreement to ship cocaine from Colombia to Venezuela to Saudi Arabia to France for distribution throughout Europe does not violate

---

7. Gugliatto proposed sending cocaine from Brazil to the Port of Miami; the cocaine would be hidden in a commercial cargo container of shoes where Gugliatto could access them "before Customs could touch them." Lopez contributed $350,000 to be part of the Brazil shoe deal, which would have involved "a ton of units," but that deal never materialized. The Government conceded, and the district court acknowledged and *instructed the jury*, that the Brazil shoe deal was a separate *uncharged* conspiracy that was offered simply to explain the relationship among the participants.

21 U.S.C. § 846 because the object of the conspiracy—the possession and distribution of cocaine on foreign soil—is not a violation of 21 U.S.C. § 841(a)(1). Thus, the district court should have granted defendants' motion for acquittal at the close of the Government's case. The Government asserts that the defendants' conduct was encompassed by the prohibitions of 21 U.S.C. § 846 and § 841(a)(1), forbidding conspiracy to possess with intent to distribute cocaine. The issue of whether discussions occurring in the United States related to possession of controlled substances outside of the United States with intent to distribute those substances outside of the United States is a crime in the United States is *res nova* in the Eleventh Circuit. We squarely address that issue now.

Title 21 U.S.C. § 841(a)(1), in conjunction with § 846, makes it unlawful for any person to conspire to possess with the intent to distribute a controlled substance, such as cocaine. Neither statute expressly requires that possession, distribution nor an act in furtherance of the conspiracy occur in the United States. A silent statute is presumed to apply only domestically. *Small v. United States,* 544 U.S. 385, 388 (2005). Such statutes may be given extraterritorial application if the nature of the law permits it *and* Congress intends it. "Absent an express intention on the face of the statutes to do so, the exercise of that power may be inferred from the nature of the offenses and Congress' other legislative efforts to eliminate the type of crime involved." The United States Supreme Court explained the issues involved with a statute silent as to its extraterritorial application:

> The necessary locus, when not specially defined, depends upon the purpose of Congress as evinced by the description and nature of the crime and upon the territorial limitations upon the power and jurisdiction of a government to punish crime under the law of nations. Crimes against private individuals or their property, like assaults, murder, burglary, larceny, robbery, arson, embezzlement, and frauds of all kinds, which affect the peace and good order of the community must, of course, be committed within the territorial jurisdiction of the government where it may properly exercise it. If punishment of them is to be extended to include those committed out side {*sic*} of the strict territorial jurisdiction, it is natural for Congress to say so in the statute, and failure to do so will negative the purpose of Congress in this regard.
>
> But the same rule of interpretation should not be applied to criminal statutes which are, as a class, not logically dependent on their locality for the government's jurisdiction, but are enacted because of the right of the government to defend itself against obstruction, or fraud wherever perpetrated, especially if committed by its own citizens, officers, or agents. Some such offenses can only be committed within the territorial jurisdiction of the government because of the local acts required to constitute them. Others are such that to limit their locus to the strictly territorial jurisdiction would be greatly to curtail the scope and usefulness of the statute and leave open a large immunity for frauds as easily committed by citizens on the high seas

> and in foreign countries as at home. In such cases, Congress has not thought it necessary to make specific provision in the law that the locus shall include the high seas and foreign countries, but allows it to be inferred from the nature of the offense. *United States v. Bowman,* 260 U.S. 94, 97–98 (1922).

Our case law, and that of our sister circuits, has applied § 841(a)(1) and § 846 extraterritorially in certain circumstances, even though Congress has not specifically expressed its intent on the matter. See *United States v. Baker,* 609 F.2d 134, 139 (5th Cir. 1980). However, in each of those cases some other nexus to the United States allowed for extraterritorial application of § 841(a)(1): defendants either possessed or conspired to possess controlled substances within the United States, or intended to distribute controlled substances within the United States. Our predecessor Court made clear in *Baker* that § 841(a)(1) does not apply to possession outside United States territory unless the possessor intends to distribute the contraband within the United States. *[S]ee Muench,* 694 F.2d at 33 (discussing Baker and Hayes). Furthermore, there can be no violation of § 846 if the object of the conspiracy is not a violation of the substantive offense. 21 U.S.C. § 846 ("Any person who . . . conspires to commit any offense defined in this subchapter. . . ."). Accordingly, where, as here, the object of the conspiracy was to possess controlled substances outside the United States with the intent to distribute outside the United States, there is no violation of § 841(a)(1) or § 846.

Further, Congress has shown it is capable of addressing acts involving controlled substances occurring outside of the United States, and has shown it thinks it necessary to make specific provisions in the law that allow the locus to include acts of manufacture or distribution of controlled substances on foreign soil when there is an intent to unlawfully import such substances or chemicals into the United States. In 21 U.S.C. § 959, Congress specifically stated that the statute "is intended to reach acts of manufacture or distribution committed outside the territorial jurisdiction of the United States." Under 21 U.S.C. §§ 841 and 846, Congress has not stated its intent to reach discussions held in the United States in furtherance of a conspiracy to *possess* controlled substances *outside* the territorial jurisdiction of the United States, with intent to *distribute* those controlled substances *outside* of the territorial jurisdiction of the United States.

Because the Court holds that 21 U.S.C. §§ 841 and 846 do not apply extraterritorially, the conduct of Lopez and Salazar does not violate those statutes. The judgments of conviction and sentences issued by the district court are VACATED.

Lopez-Vanegas highlights the distinction between the two key questions involved in the extraterritorial application of the law. In *Lopez-Vanegas,* there is no doubt that application of U.S. drug laws would have been consistent with accepted international principles of jurisdiction. For example, the territorial principle would have permitted jurisdiction because meetings at which the conspiracy was planned occurred in the United States. *Cf, e.g., Kauthar SDN BHD v. Sternberg,* 149 F.3d 659 (7th Cir. 1998) (upholding the extraterritorial application of U.S. securities laws where "the conduct occurring in the United States directly cause[d] the plaintiff's alleged loss in that the conduct form[ed] a substantial part of the alleged fraud and [was] material to its success"). But, the fact that international law would allow for jurisdiction says nothing about whether the statute at issue does, in fact, apply extraterritorially. As *Lopez-Vanegas* indicates, to determine extraterritorial reach of a particular law, courts are guided by congressional intent.

Are you persuaded by the *Lopez-Vanegas* court's conclusion with respect to congressional intent? Is there a reason that Congress would intend for 21 U.S.C. § 841 and 21 U.S.C. § 846 to apply to a defendant like Virgilio Martinus Manuel (who delivered drugs from Holland to Germany without knowing that the recipient planned to send the cargo to the United States) but not Lopez-Vanegas and Salazar (who planned their drug conspiracy on U.S. soil)?

b. Prosecution of Drug Possession on the High Seas

Lopez-Vanegas held that the drug distribution and conspiracy statutes—21 U.S.C. § 841 and 21 U.S.C. § 846—did not apply where the defendants, while in the United States, facilitated a drug deal to transport cocaine from Venezuela to France for distribution in Europe. Can the United States exercise jurisdiction over drug traffickers even when there is no evidence the defendants intended to bring drugs into the United States? Two federal laws—the Drug Trafficking Vessel Interdiction Act (DTVIA) and the Maritime Drug Law Enforcement Act (MDLEA)—target ships transporting drugs on the high seas seemingly without regard to where they set sail or where they are headed. In some cases, these ships have no direct connection to the United States, but courts have upheld extraterritorial application of the laws nonetheless, citing the protective principle of jurisdiction and (less frequently) the universal principle of jurisdiction. Is the application of U.S. law to drug shipments with no direct connection to the United States consistent with principles of international law, due process, and Congress's enumerated powers? The next three cases examine these questions.

United States v. Saac

United States Court of Appeals for the Eleventh Circuit
632 F.3d 1203 (2011)

Martin, J.

This case consolidates criminal appeals by four co-defendants challenging the constitutionality of the Drug Trafficking Vessel Interdiction Act of 2008 ("DTVIA"), 18 U.S.C. § 2285.

On January 6, 2009, a United States helicopter crew observed defendants on board a self-propelled, semi-submersible vessel that was dead in the international waters of the eastern Pacific Ocean. Defendants' semi-submersible vessel lacked a flag, registration number, homeport, or navigational lights. The next day, as the United States Coast Guard approached defendants' vessel, a helicopter crew saw the four defendants, three of whom were wearing life vests, emerge from the vessel's hatch and jump into the water. The vessel sank within minutes. The Coast Guard recovered all four defendants the same day. Mr. Rodriguez Renegifo identified himself as the master of the vessel but claimed no nationality for it. Defendants asserted that they were Colombian citizens.

The government filed a two-count indictment in federal district court. The first count charged defendants with knowingly conspiring to operate a semi-submersible vessel without nationality and with the intent to evade detection in violation of 18 U.S.C. §§ 2285(a) and (b). The second charged defendants with knowingly and intentionally, while aiding and abetting each other, operating and embarking in a semi-submersible vessel without nationality, with the intent to evade detection in violation of 18 U.S.C. § 2285(a) and (b).

The DTVIA provides that: "[w]hoever knowingly operates, or attempts or conspires to operate, by any means, or embarks in any submersible vessel or semi-submersible vessel that is without nationality and that is navigating or has navigated into, through, or from waters beyond the outer limit of the territorial sea of a single country or a lateral limit of that country's territorial sea with an adjacent country, with the intent to evade detection, shall be fined under this title, imprisoned not more than 15 years, or both."

A submersible vessel is one that "is capable of operating completely below the surface of the water, including both manned and unmanned watercraft." A semi-submersible vessel is "any watercraft constructed or adapted to be capable of operating with most of its hull and bulk under the surface of the water, including both manned and unmanned watercraft."

Defendants pleaded not-guilty at arraignment. Mr. Rodriguez Renegifo filed a motion to dismiss the indictment, arguing that 18 U.S.C. § 2285 is unconstitutional. The other defendants each filed a "motion to adopt co-defendant Rodriguez Renegifo's motion to dismiss indictment," and the district court considered Mr. Rodriguez Renegifo's motion as to all defendants. The district court denied the motion to dismiss the indictment, concluding that § 2285 is not unconstitutionally vague, does not violate the Due Process Clause, and does not exceed Congress's power under Article I, Section 8, Clause 10 of the Constitution.

After the district court denied the motion to dismiss, defendants entered unconditional guilty pleas, without plea agreements, as to both counts of the indictment. At the change of plea hearing, defendants informed the district court that, based on binding precedent, they understood that their guilty pleas would not preclude them from contesting the constitutionality of the DTVIA on appeal. The district court agreed with defendants' reading of the relevant precedent. The government made no argument to the contrary.

The court sentenced each defendant to 108 months imprisonment and 3 years of supervised release for each count, all to run concurrently. The court assessed each defendant $100 per count. Defendants each filed separate, timely notices of appeal.

Defendants challenge the constitutionality of the DTVIA. [They argue] that in enacting the DTVIA Congress exceeded its power under the High Seas Clause of the Constitution, Article I, § 8, cl. 10. The High Seas Clause enables Congress "[t]o define and punish Piracies and Felonies committed on the high Seas, and Offences against the Law of Nations." U.S. Const., art. I, § 8, cl. 10. While there is a dearth of authority interpreting the scope of Congress's power under the High Seas Clause, early Supreme Court opinions intimate that statutes passed under the High Seas Clause may properly criminalize conduct that lacks a connection to the United States. For instance, in *United States v. Palmer,* 16 U.S. (3 Wheat.) 610, 630 (1818), the Court explained that "[t]he constitution having conferred on congress the power of defining and punishing piracy, there can be no doubt of the right of the legislature to enact laws punishing pirates, although they may be foreigners, and may have committed no particular offence against the United States."

Defendants argue that for Congress to criminalize conduct by statute under the High Seas Clause, the conduct must have a nexus with the United States. We first observe that the text of the clause makes no mention of such a jurisdictional nexus requirement. The clause gives Congress the power "[t]o define and punish Piracies and Felonies committed on the high Seas, and Offences against the Law of Nations." The clause's text does not limit that power to only those piracies and felonies committed in waters within the territorial jurisdiction of the United States. Neither does the clause expressly limit Congress's power to only those offenses committed on or by United States citizens.

Defendants rely on *United States v. Furlong,* 18 U.S. (5 Wheat.) 184, 185 (1820), as support for the proposition that the High Seas Clause allows Congress to reach only conduct with a connection to the United States. But in Furlong the Supreme Court examined the scope of a statute Congress passed pursuant to the High Seas Clause, rather than the scope of Congress's power under the High Seas Clause itself. The Court held that because the particular statute at issue included the phrase "out of the jurisdiction of any particular *State*" its scope was limited to murders committed "out of any *one of the United States.*" *Id.* at 200 (emphasis added). The Court reasoned that "[b]y examining the context, it will be seen that *particular State* is uniformly used in contradistinction to *United States* [within the statute]." Thus, the Court's analysis is a textual one, confined to an interpretation of the language and structure of the statute before it. *Furlong,* a statutory interpretation case, therefore, does not resolve the parties' debate over the scope of Congress's constitutional authority.

When analyzing a constitutional challenge to the Maritime Drug Law Enforcement Act ("MDLEA"), 46 U.S.C. app. § 1901 et seq., we rejected the same argument that defendants make here—that Congress exceeded its constitutional authority under the High Seas Clause in passing a statute that punishes conduct without a nexus to the United States. See *United States v. Estupinan,* 453 F.3d 1336, 1338 (11th Cir. 2006). In doing so, we explained that "this circuit and other circuits have not embellished the MDLEA with the requirement of a nexus between a defendant's criminal conduct and the United States." *Id.* (quotation marks omitted). In the MDLEA cases, the appellants argued that offenses other than piracies may not be punished under Congress's High Seas Clause power when there is no nexus to the United States. In each case, the court concluded, however, that Congress's High Seas Clause power includes the authority to punish offenses other than piracies outside the territorial limits of the United States. This Court, and our sister circuits, have refused to read a jurisdictional nexus requirement into the clause.

In examining the constitutionality of the MDLEA, we concluded that the statute's extraterritorial reach was justified under the universal principle of international law. *Estupinan,* 453 F.3d at 1339. According to this principle, a nation may pass laws to define and punish certain crimes considered to be of "universal concern." We adopted the reasoning of the Third Circuit, which opined that "[i]nasmuch as the trafficking of narcotics is condemned universally by law-abiding nations, we see no reason to conclude that it is 'fundamentally unfair' for Congress to provide for the punishment of persons apprehended with narcotics on the high seas." *Estupinan,* 453 F.3d at 1339 (citing *Martinez-Hidalgo,* 993 F.2d at 1056). Thus, we reasoned that because the MDLEA criminalizes conduct that is condemned universally, the statute's extraterritorial reach was permissible.

We now conclude that the DTVIA is also justified under the universal principle and thus a constitutional exercise of Congress's power under the High Seas Clause. In passing the DTVIA, Congress reported that it: "finds and declares that operating or embarking in a submersible vessel or semi-submersible vessel without nationality and on an international voyage is a serious international problem, facilitates transnational crime, including drug trafficking, and terrorism, and presents a specific threat to the safety of maritime navigation and the security of the United States."[3] Congress's findings show that the DTVIA targets criminal conduct that facilitates drug trafficking, which is "condemned universally by law-abiding nations." *Estupinan,* 453 F.3d at 1339 (citing *Martinez-Hidalgo,* 993 F.2d at 1056).

Given Congress's findings, the "protective principle" of international law provides an equally compelling reason to uphold the DTVIA. Under that principle, a nation may "assert jurisdiction over a person whose conduct outside the nation's territory threatens the nation's security or could potentially interfere with the operation of its governmental functions." *United States v. Gonzalez,* 776 F.2d 931, 938 (11th Cir. 1985). "The protective principle does not require that there be proof of an actual or intended effect inside the United States." *Id. at 939.* Those who engage

3. Vessels without nationality include: "(A) a vessel aboard which the master or individual in charge makes a claim of registry that is denied by the nation whose registry is claimed; (B) a vessel aboard which the master or individual in charge fails, on request of an officer of the United States authorized to enforce applicable provisions of United States law, to make a claim of nationality or registry for that vessel; and (C) a vessel aboard which the master or individual in charge makes a claim of registry and for which the claimed nation of registry does not affirmatively and unequivocally assert that the vessel is of its nationality."

in conduct the DTVIA targets threaten our nation's security by evading detection while using submersible vessels to smuggle illegal drugs or other contraband, such as illegal weapons, from one country to another, and often into the United States.

The United States Coast Guard reported to Congress that semi-submersible vessels present "one of the emerging and most significant threats we face in maritime law enforcement today." These vessels pose a formidable security threat because they are difficult to detect and easy to scuttle or sink. These vessels therefore facilitate the destruction of evidence and hinder prosecution of smuggling offenses.

Based on the foregoing, we conclude that Congress acted properly within its constitutional authority under the High Seas Clause in passing the DTVIA. The fact that defendants are challenging the constitutionality of a statute other than the MDLEA does not alter our conclusion about the scope of Congress's power under the High Seas Clause. We declined to embellish one statute passed under the High Seas Clause with a nexus requirement. We now decline defendants' invitation to rewrite the Constitution to create one.

Notice what the Drug Trafficking Vessel Interdiction Act of 2008 criminalizes: "operat[ing] . . . or embark[ing] in any submersible vessel or semi-submersible vessel that is without nationality and that is navigating or has navigated into, through, or from waters beyond the outer limit of the territorial sea of a single country . . . with the intent to evade detection." 18 U.S.C. § 2285. In *United States v. Ibarguen-Mosquera*, the defendants argued that the law was unconstitutional "because it effectively redefines the offense of drug trafficking, eliminating the requirement of drug possession." In rejecting the challenge, the court explained that despite the law's title, "Congress determined to criminalize *not only* the underlying conduct . . . but also traveling on the vessel itself. . . . Even if Appellants proved that they were not trafficking drugs, they would still be guilty of violating the DTVIA if the government proved, beyond a reasonable doubt, all of the elements of the crime." The court continued that "[t]here is no defense if a defendant is found not to be trafficking in narcotics." 634 F.3d 1370 (11th Cir. 2011).

The Maritime Drug Law Enforcement Act, passed in 1986, is the basis for more prosecutions than the DTVIA. Although the MDLEA requires proof of the defendant's involvement in drug activity, its reach is still quite broad, as the next two decisions demonstrate. The MDLEA makes it a crime to, "[w]hile on board a covered vessel, . . . knowingly or intentionally manufacture or distribute, or possess with intent to manufacture or distribute, a controlled substance." 46 U.S.C. § 70503(a)(1). The law defines a covered vessel as "a vessel of the United States or a vessel subject to the jurisdiction of the United States; or any other vessel if the individual is a citizen of the United States or a resident of the United States." *Id.* at (c)(1)–(2). Federal prosecutors have taken the position that a vessel subject to the jurisdiction of the United States includes "any foreign vessels on the high seas, or even in foreign territorial waters, so long as the relevant foreign nation consents."

Eugene Kontorovich, *Beyond the Article I Horizon: Congress's Enumerated Powers and Universal Jurisdiction Over Drug Crimes*, 93 Minn. L. Rev. 1191, 1200 (2009).

In the next case, *United States v. Bellaizac-Hurtado*, the Eleventh Circuit overturned convictions under the MDLEA on the grounds that they exceeded Congress' enumerated powers under the Constitution. The *Bellaizac-Hurtado* defendants succeeded in their claims because they were arrested not on the high seas but in Panamanian waters. As a result, the prosecutions could not be justified under Congress' authority to define and punish felonies committed on the high seas. Keep this fact in mind as you read the opinion, particularly the portion distinguishing the decision in *Saac*.

United States v. Bellaizac-Hurtado

United States Court of Appeals for the Eleventh Circuit
700 F. 3d 1245 (2012)

Pryor, J.

This appeal presents a novel issue about the scope of congressional power to proscribe conduct abroad: whether the Maritime Drug Law Enforcement Act, 46 U.S.C. §§70503(a), 70506, exceeds the power of Congress to "define and punish . . . Offences against the Law of Nations," U.S. Const. Art. I, §8, cl. 10, as applied to the drug-trafficking activities of Yimmi Bellaizac-Hurtado, Pedro Felipe Angulo-Rodallega, Albeiro Gonzalez-Valois, and Luis Carlos Riascos-Hurtado in the territorial waters of Panama. Because we conclude that drug trafficking is not an "Offence[ ] against the Law of Nations" and that Congress cannot constitutionally proscribe the defendants' conduct under the Offences Clause, we vacate their convictions.

During a routine patrol of Panamanian waters in 2010, the United States Coast Guard observed a wooden fishing vessel operating without lights and without a flag. The Coast Guard informed the Panamanian National Aero-Naval Service of the vessel. The Panamanian Navy pursued the vessel until its occupants abandoned the vessel and fled into a jungle. When members of the Panamanian Navy searched the vessel the next morning, they discovered approximately 760 kilograms of cocaine. The Panamanian National Frontier Service searched on land for the occupants of the abandoned vessel and arrested Bellaizac-Hurtado, Angulo-Rodallega, Gonzalez-Valois, and Riascos-Hurtado in various locations on the beach and in the jungle. After an exchange of diplomatic notes, the Foreign Ministry of the Republic of Panama consented to the prosecution of the four suspects in the United States.

A federal grand jury indicted Bellaizac-Hurtado, Angulo-Rodallega, Gonzalez-Valois, and Riascos-Hurtado for conspiracy to possess with intent to distribute five kilograms or more of cocaine, and for actual possession with intent to distribute five kilograms or more of cocaine, on board a vessel subject to the jurisdiction of the United States. The defendants moved to dismiss the indictment "based upon the lack of jurisdiction and the unconstitutionality of the Maritime Drug Law Enforcement Act as applied to [their] conduct." A magistrate judge recommended that the motion be denied. The magistrate judge reasoned that the district court had jurisdiction because the defendants were operating a stateless vessel and that the Act was constitutional as applied because Congress and several courts had determined that drug trafficking was "universally condemned" by various nations with "reasonably developed" legal systems. The district court adopted the magistrate judge's report. The district court also explained that section 70505 of the Act "limits the actors that have standing to challenge the validity of an MDLEA prosecution on international law grounds."

The defendants conditionally pleaded guilty to the conspiracy charge. The defendants appealed their convictions on the ground that the Act, as applied, exceeded the power of Congress under Article I, Section 8, Clause 10. We consolidated their appeals.

The United States argues that the Maritime Drug Law Enforcement Act, as applied to the defendants, is a constitutional exercise of the power granted to Congress "[t]o define and punish Piracies and Felonies committed on the high Seas, and Offences against the Law of Nations." U.S. Const., Art. I, § 8, cl. 10. The Supreme Court has interpreted that Clause to contain three distinct grants of power: the power to define and punish piracies, the power to define and punish felonies committed on the high seas, and the power to define and punish offenses against the law of nations. The first two grants of power are not implicated here: piracy is, by definition, robbery on the high seas and the Felonies Clause is textually limited to conduct on the high seas, *see* U.S. Const., Art. I, § 8, cl. 10. The United States relies instead on the third grant—the Offences Clause—as the source of congressional power to proscribe the defendants' drug trafficking in the territorial waters of Panama. The question whether Congress has the power under the Offences Clause to proscribe drug trafficking in the territorial waters of another nation is an issue of first impression in our Court.

We divide our discussion in two parts. First, we explain why the power of Congress to define and punish conduct under the Offences Clause is limited by customary international law. Second, we explain why drug trafficking is not a violation of customary international law and, as a result, falls outside of the power of Congress under the Offences Clause.

The power granted to Congress in the Offences Clause is limited by customary international law for two reasons. First, the related Supreme Court precedent and the text, history, and structure of the Constitution confirm that the power to "define" is limited by the law of nations. Second, the phrase "Offences against the Law of Nations" is understood today to mean violations of customary international law.

The power to "define" offenses against the law of nations does not grant Congress the authority to punish conduct that is not a violation of the law of nations. The Supreme Court has explained that the power to "define" in Article I, Section 8, Clause 10, is limited by the three specific subjects of the Clause. For example, the Supreme Court has explained that Congress may not define murder as "piracy" to punish it under the Piracies Clause:

> Nor is it any objection to this opinion, that the law declares murder to be *piracy.* These are things so essentially different in their nature, that not even the omnipotence of legislative power can confound or identify them. Had Congress, in this instance, declared piracy to be murder, the absurdity would have been felt and acknowledged; yet, with a view to the exercise of jurisdiction, it would have been more defensible than the reverse, for, in one case it would restrict the acknowledged scope of its legitimate powers, in the other extend it. If by calling murder *piracy,* it might assert a jurisdiction over that offence committed by a foreigner in a foreign vessel, what offence might not be brought within their power by the same device? The most offensive interference with the governments of other nations might be defended on the precedent. Upon the whole, I am satisfied that Congress neither intended to punish murder in cases with which they had no right to interfere, nor leave unpunished the crime of piracy in any cases in which they might punish it . . . .

Furlong, 18 U.S. (5 Wheat.) at 198. And, on the issue whether Congress must declare the conduct to be an offense against the law of nations to exercise its power under the Offences Clause, the Supreme Court has explained that "[w]hether the offense as defined is an offense against the law of nations depends on the thing done, not on any declaration to that effect by Congress." *United States v. v. Arjona*, 120 U.S. 479, 488 (1887).

This precedent is consistent with the original understanding of the word "define." During the Founding period, the word "define" meant "[t]o give the definition; to explain a thing by its qualities" and "[t]o circumscribe; to mark limits." Samuel Johnson, *A Dictionary of the English Language*, at DEF, DEF (10th ed. 1792). These definitions reveal that the word "define" would not have been understood to grant Congress the power to create or declare offenses against the law of nations, but instead to codify and explain offenses that had already been understood as offenses against the law of nations.

The records of the debates at the Constitutional Convention confirm that the Framers also understood the word "define" to be limited by international law. In an early draft of the clause, Congress would have been given the power "[t]o declare the law and punishment of piracies and felonies." 2 *Records of the Federal Convention of 1787*, at 315 (Max Farrand, ed. 1966). After Gouverneur Morris successfully moved to strike out "declare the law" and insert "punish," James Madison and Edmund Randolph moved to insert the power to "define." Morris suggested that they should use the word "designate" as opposed to "define" because he felt that "define" was limited to the preexisting meaning of felonies. But the delegates rejected this suggestion and adopted Madison and Randolph's proposal to insert the more limited word "define." About one month later, the delegates considered a new draft of the clause, which granted Congress the power "[t]o define & punish piracies and felonies on the high seas, and 'punish' offences against the law of nations." Morris moved to strike out "punish" before the offenses provision, so that the offenses could also be definable. Wilson objected on the ground that "[t]o pretend to *define* the law of nations which depended on the authority of all the Civilized Nations of the World, would have a look of arrogance" and "would make us ridiculous." Morris responded by noting that "[t]he word *define* is proper when applied to *offences* in this case; the law of nations being often too vague and deficient to be a rule." Although this last sentence might suggest that Morris believed that the word "define" would enable Congress to create offenses not already recognized as contrary to the law of nations, his statement a month earlier that the word "define" would limit the "law of nations" to its preexisting meaning proves otherwise. *See* J. Andrew Kent, *Congress's Under–Appreciated Power to Define and Punish Offenses Against the Law of Nations*, 85 Tex. L.Rev. 843, 899 (2007) (explaining that "Morris's desire for prior notice and clear definition sound[ed] in the due process and legality principle concerns that we still have today about vague criminal statutes"). The insertion of the power to "define" enabled Congress to provide notice to the people through codification; it did not enable Congress to create offenses that were not recognized by the law of nations.

The structure of the Constitution also confirms the limited power of Congress under the Offences Clause. If Congress could define any conduct as "piracy" or a "felony" or an "offence against the law of nations," its power would be limitless and contrary to our constitutional structure. "The Constitution creates a Federal Government of enumerated powers. As James Madison wrote: 'The powers delegated by the proposed Constitution to the federal government are few and defined. Those which are to remain in the State governments are numerous and indefinite.'" *United States v. Lopez*, 514 U.S. 549, 552 (1995) (citation omitted) (quoting The Federalist No. 45, pp. 292–93 (C. Rossiter ed. 1961)). For these reasons, we look to international law to ascertain the scope of power granted to Congress under the Offences Clause.

We and our sister circuits agree that the eighteenth-century phrase, the "law of nations," in contemporary terms, means customary international law. And although the Supreme Court has never held that the "law of nations" is synonymous with "customary international law," its decision in *Sosa v. Alvarez-Machain*, 542 U.S. 692 (2004), confirms that it is. *See id.* at 735 (evaluating whether the "prohibition of arbitrary arrest has attained the status of binding customary international law" to determine whether Alvarez could bring a claim under the Alien Tort Statute). These decisions interpreted the Alien Tort Statute, instead of the Offences Clause, but the Alien Tort Statute was enacted by the First Congress and uses the same term of art—"the law of nations"—that is used in the Offences Clause. Given the proximity in time between the writing of these provisions and the substantial overlap between the delegates of the Constitutional Convention and the members of the First Congress, one would expect that the Framers understood the term "the law of nations" in the Offences Clause and the Alien Tort Statute to mean the same thing. The more difficult question involves how to determine whether a crime violates customary international law.

Our Court has referred to customary international law several times, but we have never defined it. Five of our sister circuits have adopted the definition in the Restatement (Third) of Foreign Relations, which provides that customary international law is the "general and consistent practice of states followed by them from a sense of legal obligation," Restatement (Third) of Foreign Relations § 102(2) (1987).

We agree with our sister circuits that customary international law is determined by examining state practice and *opinio juris*:

> Customary international law . . . consists of two components. First, there must be a general and consistent practice of states. This does not mean that the practice must be universally followed; rather it should reflect wide acceptance among the states particularly involved in the relevant activity. Second, there must be a sense of legal obligation, or *opinio juris sive necessitatis*. In other words, a practice that is generally followed but which states feel legally free to disregard does not contribute to customary law; rather, there must be a sense of legal obligation. States must follow the practice because they believe it is required by international law, not merely because that they think it is a good idea, or politically useful, or otherwise desirable.

Buell, 274 F.3d at 372 (internal quotation marks and citations omitted). As evidence of customary international law, we consider "the works of jurists and commentators who by years of labor, research, and experience have made themselves peculiarly well acquainted with the subjects of which they treat."

Private criminal activity will rarely be considered a violation of customary international law because private conduct is unlikely to be a matter of mutual legal concern:

> Matters of "mutual" concern between States are those involving States' actions performed . . . towards or with regard to the other—matters that, as Judge Friendly aptly noted, concern the dealings of States "inter se." Matters of "several" concern among States are matters in which States are separately and independently interested. Even if certain conduct is universally proscribed by States in their domestic law, that fact is not necessarily significant or relevant for purposes of customary international law . . . . Therefore, for example, murder of one private party by another, universally proscribed by the domestic law of all countries (subject to varying definitions), is not actionable . . . as a violation of customary international law because the nations of the world have not demonstrated that this wrong is of mutual, and not merely several, concern.

Flores, 414 F.3d at 249 (internal quotation marks and citations omitted).

The text of the Offences Clause does not resolve the question whether it limits the power of Congress to define and punish only those violations of customary international law that were established at the Founding or whether the power granted under the Clause expands and contracts with changes in customary international law. The Supreme Court has not resolved the issue in either of the two cases in which it upheld federal statutes as a constitutional exercise of the power granted under the Offences Clause. *See Ex Parte Quirin*, 317 U.S. 1, 27–28 (1942); *Arjona*, 120 U.S. at 488. In both cases, the Court explained that the conduct at issue had been condemned as a violation of the law of nations since the time of the Founding. Scholars have long debated whether the Offences Clause is affected by the later development of customary international law.

We need not decide whether the power granted to Congress under the Offences Clause changes with the evolution of customary international law because, under either approach, the result is the same. Drug trafficking was not a violation of customary international law at the time of the Founding, and drug trafficking is not a violation of customary international law today.

When the Constitution was ratified, the range of conduct that could be viewed as a violation of customary international law was even more limited than it is today. In his *Commentaries on the Laws of England*, William Blackstone explained that, because offenses against the law of nations are "principally incident to whole states or nations," they "can rarely be the object of the criminal law of any particular state." 4 William Blackstone, *Commentaries* at *68. As a result, "[t]he principal offences against the law of nations [that could be committed by private individuals and punished criminally] . . . [we]re of three kinds: 1. Violation of safe conducts; 2. Infringement of the rights of ambassadors; and, 3. Piracy." *Id.*

Drug trafficking was not a matter of international concern in 1789, let alone a violation of customary international law. Vattel's *Law of Nations* contains no references to narcotics, opium, or drug trafficking. And the international community did not even begin its efforts to limit the drug trade until the turn of the twentieth century. As the United Nations Office on Drugs and Crime has observed, "[p]rior to the 1909 Shanghai Opium Commission, national governments and state-sponsored monopolies played an active role in peddling opium across borders. The profits to be made were enormous, generating as much as half of the national revenues of some island states serving as redistribution centres." United Nations Office on Drugs and Crime, *A Century of International Drug Control* 7 (2008). Because violations of customary international law during the Founding Period were so limited, and narcotics then were not even a subject of international concern, we cannot conclude that drug trafficking was an offense against the law of nations when the Constitution was ratified.

Drug trafficking is also not a violation of contemporary customary international law.

The United States argues that the widespread ratification of the 1988 United Nations Convention Against Illicit Traffic in Narcotic Drugs and Psychotropic Substances establishes that drug trafficking violates a norm of customary international law, but we disagree. Treaties may constitute evidence of customary international law, but "will only constitute *sufficient proof* of a norm of customary international law if an overwhelming majority of States have ratified the treaty, *and* those States uniformly and consistently act in accordance with its principles." *Flores*, 414 F.3d at 256. "Of course, States need not be universally successful in implementing the principle in order for a rule of international law to arise .... But the principle must be more than merely professed or aspirational." *Id.* at 248. And as the International Court of Justice has explained, a customary international law norm will not form if specially affected States have not consented to its development through state practice consistent with the proposed norm. *North Sea Continental Shelf Cases* (Fed. Republic of Ger. v. Den.; Fed. Republic of Ger. v. Neth.), 1969 I.C.J. 3, 43 (Feb. 20).

The 1988 Convention was ratified by an overwhelming majority of States and currently has 188 States Parties but the drug trade continues to flourish in many specially affected States despite their ratification of the Convention. In 2011, the President of the United States designated 21 of these States Parties as "major drug transit or major illicit drug producing countries." Memorandum from Barack Obama, President of the United States, to Hillary Rodham Clinton, Secretary of State (Sept. 15, 2011). And the President described Bolivia, Burma, and Venezuela "as countries that have failed demonstrably during the previous 12 months to make substantial efforts to adhere to their obligations under international counternarcotics agreements." The International Narcotic Control Board—the independent, quasi-judicial body established by the United Nations to monitor compliance with international drug treaties—has reported that drug-related corruption "has increasingly weakened the criminal justice systems in Central America and the Caribbean." International Narcotics Control Board, *Report of the International Narcotics Control Board for 2011,* at 52, E/INCB/2011/1 (Feb. 28, 2012). The 2011 Report of the Board found that "[c]orruption and limited law enforcement capacity in Central America and the Caribbean have facilitated the use of smuggling channels and drug trafficking activities." The Board also has expressed concern about corruption and lack of progress in reducing illicit opium poppy cultivation in Afghanistan.

The practice of these specially affected States evidences that drug trafficking is not yet considered a violation of customary international law. Governments corrupted by the interests of drug traffickers are not simply unable to prosecute drug traffickers, but are often unwilling to do so because their economies are dependent upon the drug trade. The persistent failure of these specially affected States to comply with their treaty obligations suggests that they view the curtailment of drug trafficking as an aspirational goal, not a matter of mutual legal obligation under customary international law.

The international community has also distinguished drug trafficking from established violations of customary international law in its efforts to combat drug trafficking. Comparing the 1988 Drug Convention with the Genocide Convention is instructive. Article 2 of the 1988 Drug Convention described drug trafficking as conduct "having an international dimension." But Article 1 of the Genocide Convention defined genocide as a "crime under international law." And, unlike genocide, the international community has addressed drug trafficking at the domestic, instead of international, level. The 1988 Drug Convention, for example, relied on domestic enforcement mechanisms to combat drug trafficking and prohibited States Parties from interfering in the domestic enforcement efforts of other States Parties. By contrast, the Genocide Convention provided for trial by international tribunals, in addition to domestic tribunals, and permitted States Parties to appeal to the United Nations to take further action to prevent and suppress genocide.

The drafters of the Rome Statute, which established the International Criminal Court, considered and rejected a proposal to make drug trafficking a crime within the jurisdiction of the court. The negotiators of the Rome Statute repeatedly referred to drug crimes as "treaty crimes" only, in contrast to genocide, war crimes, and crimes against humanity, which are violations of customary international law. And several delegates expressed the opinion that drug crimes "had no place in a statute dealing with international crimes" and should be addressed at the national level.

Scholars who have considered the status of drug trafficking in international law agree too that it is not a violation of customary international law. Antonio Cassesse, a noted international criminal law scholar, has explained, for example, that drug trafficking is not an international crime because it is not a crime under customary international law and is not a matter of mutual concern:

> [T]he notion of international crimes does not include illicit traffic in narcotic drugs and psychotrophic substances.... For one thing, this broad range of crimes is only provided for in international *treaties* or *resolutions* of international organizations, not in customary law. For another, normally it is private individuals or criminal organizations which perpetrate these offences; States fight against them, often by joint official action. In other words, as a rule these offences are committed *against* States. Usually they do not involve States as such or, if they involve State agents, these agents typically act for private gain, perpetrating what national legislation normally regards as ordinary crimes.

Antonio Cassesse, *International Criminal Law* 24 (2003). Another scholar has explained that "there is a vast difference between conduct that all nations criminalize and international crimes. Uniform condemnation and criminalization does not make something an international crime. Murder and rape, and indeed, most malum in se offenses, are also universally condemned, and all fall outside of international law." Eugene Kontorovich, *Beyond the Article I Horizon: Congress's Enumerated Powers and Universal Jurisdiction Over Drug Crimes*, 93 Minn. L.Rev. 1191, 1226 (2009).

The United States argues that this appeal is controlled by our decision in *United States v. Saac*, 632 F.3d 1203 (11th Cir.2011), but we disagree. In *Saac*, we considered a constitutional challenge to the Drug Trafficking Vessel Interdiction Act, which provides for the punishment of any person who "knowingly operates ... or embarks in any submersible vessel or semi-submersible vessel that is without nationality" on the high seas "with the intent to evade detection." 18 U.S.C. § 2285(a). In *Saac*, we held that Congress had the authority, under the High Seas Clause, to prohibit this conduct. We did not hold that drug trafficking was an "Offence against the Law of Nations." Instead, we held that Congress had the authority under the High Seas Clause to punish the operation of these stateless vessels. *Saac* is inapposite.

Moreover, none of our earlier precedents about the extraterritorial application of our drug trafficking laws have answered the constitutional question presented in this appeal. Indeed, all of the appeals in which we have considered the constitutionality of those laws involved conduct on the high seas. Congress possesses additional constitutional authority to restrict conduct on the high seas, including the Piracies Clause, U.S. Const., Art. I, § 8, cl. 10; the Felonies Clause, *id.*; and the admiralty power, *United States v. Flores*, 289 U.S. 137, 148–49, 53 S.Ct. 580, 582, 77 L.Ed. 1086 (1933). And we have always upheld extraterritorial convictions under our drug trafficking laws as an exercise of power under the Felonies Clause. But we have never held that Congress has the power, under the Offences Clause, to apply our drug trafficking laws to conduct in the territorial waters of another State.

Judge Barkett argues in her special concurrence that we should decide this appeal on the ground that drug trafficking is not an offense of universal jurisdiction and, as a result, Congress may not punish the defendants' conduct under the Offences Clause, but that reasoning raises issues that we need not decide. We need not decide whether the Offences Clause, which makes no mention of the requirements of prescriptive jurisdiction under international law in its grant of power to "define and punish . . . Offences against the Law of Nations," U.S. Const. Art. I, § 8, cl. 10, nevertheless incorporates those jurisdictional principles. We need not decide whether the Constitution imposes any limit on the power of Congress to violate international law. And we need not decide whether international law would permit the exercise of prescriptive jurisdiction by the United States over a stateless vessel in territorial waters when, as here, the sovereign of those waters has consented to that jurisdiction.

Because drug trafficking is not a violation of customary international law, we hold that Congress exceeded its power, under the Offences Clause, when it proscribed the defendants' conduct in the territorial waters of Panama. And the United States has not offered us any alternative ground upon which the Act could be sustained as constitutional. As applied to these defendants, the Act is unconstitutional, and we must vacate their convictions.

Barkett, J., specially concurring.

I concur in the majority's conclusion that drug trafficking does not constitute an "Offence[ ] against the Law of Nations" and agree with much of the majority's opinion. However, my conclusion is based on my view that when conduct has no connection to the United States, such as the conduct at issue here, it can only be punished as an "Offence[ ] against the Law of Nations" if it is subject to universal jurisdiction.

I agree with the majority that the "Offences against the Law of Nations" Clause must be interpreted in accordance with principles of customary international law. That is to say, customary international law necessarily informs what conduct may be punished as an "Offence[ ] against the Law of Nations."[1] However, I believe that customary international law contains both a substantive and a jurisdictional component. Thus, when analyzing Congress's authority to proscribe conduct under the Offences Clause in light of customary international law, a court determines both whether the conduct at issue violates a "'norm[ ] of international law'" that is "'well-established' and 'universally recognized'" and whether customary international law provides some basis for the exercise of jurisdiction over that conduct. Only conduct that violates a norm of customary international law *and* is subject to United States jurisdiction under customary international law principles may be prosecuted in United States courts as an "Offence[ ] against the Law of Nations."

Customary international law recognizes five theories of jurisdiction: territorial, protective, national, passive personality, and universality. The first four theories permit nations to exercise jurisdiction over offenses that implicate domestic interests—that is, offenses that occur within a nation's territory and those that occur outside the territory but have effects within it. In contrast, the universality theory authorizes any nation to exercise jurisdiction over certain offenses, even when no domestic interests are directly implicated. Here, because the drug trafficking occurred outside of United States territory and had no direct impact on the interests of the United States, the only potential basis for jurisdiction is the universality principle.

Although the class of offenses that triggers universal jurisdiction has expanded over the last century, the scope of universal jurisdiction remains exceedingly narrow[.]

The government argues that drug trafficking is an "Offence[ ] against the Law of Nations" that is subject to universal jurisdiction because Congress, when enacting the MDLEA, stated that drug trafficking is "universally condemned" and is a "threat to the security and societal well-being of the United States [.]" 46 U.S.C. § 70501. However, it is not Congress's declaration that establishes conduct as subject to universal jurisdiction under customary international law. Rather, the scope of universal jurisdiction is "ascertained by consulting the works of jurists, writing professedly on public law; or by the general usage and practice of nations; or by judicial decisions recognising and enforcing that law." *United States v. Smith*, 18 U.S. (5 Wheat.) 153, 160–61 (1820).

Furthermore, universal condemnation is by itself insufficient to place an offense within the scope of universal jurisdiction. As noted by the Supreme Court in *United*

1. The majority questions whether the constitution imposes any limit on the power of Congress to violate international law. However, Congress may only violate international law to the extent that it is acting within the authority granted to it by the Constitution. In other words, while Congress may violate international law when invoking its authority under other constitutional clauses, it cannot do so when acting under the Offences Clause, which is *defined* by customary international law. Congress cannot violate international law when the constitution says that it is bound by international law.

States v. Furlong, murder may be universally condemned, but it is not subject to universal jurisdiction. For universal jurisdiction to apply to an offense, the international community must reach both a "substantive agreement" that the offense is "universally condemned" and a "procedural agreement that universal jurisdiction exists to prosecute [that offense]." *Sosa v. Alvarez-Machain*, 542 U.S. 692, 762 (2004) (Breyer, J., concurring). Thus, "because universal jurisdiction over a crime is established by international consensus, a state can only invoke universal jurisdiction for those acts that fall within the specific 'subset of [universally condemned] behavior' that the international community has agreed warrants the assertion of universal jurisdiction."[4]

Drug trafficking does not fall within that subset. No source of customary international law has designated drug trafficking as being subject to universal jurisdiction. The academic community is in accord that drug trafficking is not considered a universal jurisdiction offense. Although "[i]nternational criminal law evidences the existence of twenty-seven crime categories[,]"[5] only the so-called *jus cogens* crimes of "piracy, slavery and slave-related practices, war crimes, crimes against humanity, genocide, apartheid, and torture" have thus far been identified as supporting universal jurisdiction.

Nor are there any judicial decisions recognizing Congress's authority to punish drug trafficking that has no connection to the United States as an "Offence[ ] against the Law of Nations." Indeed, several courts of appeals have held that drug trafficking

---

4. I agree with the majority that drug trafficking probably does not violate a norm of customary international law as of yet. However, I do not believe that this is because the drug trade continues to exist or because some signatories to an international drug treaty have not complied with their obligations under the treaty. There are undisputed violations of customary international law, such as torture, that also continue to exist and with regard to which countries may not comply with their treaty-based obligations.

However, as explained above, even if drug trafficking were to be considered a violation of a norm of customary international law, I do not believe that the United States would have the authority to prosecute drug trafficking that has no connection to the United States as an "Offence[ ] against the Law of Nations" because drug trafficking is not subject to universal jurisdiction and no other jurisdictional basis exists.

5. These international crimes are:

> aggression, genocide, crimes against humanity, war crimes, crimes against the UN and associated personnel, unlawful possession and/or use of weapons, theft of nuclear materials, mercenarism, apartheid, slavery and slave-related practices, torture, unlawful human experimentation, piracy, aircraft hijacking, unlawful acts against civil maritime navigation, unlawful acts against internationally protected persons, taking of civilian hostages, unlawful use of the mail, nuclear terrorism, financing of international terrorism, unlawful traffic in drugs and dangerous substances, destruction and/or theft of national treasures and cultural heritage, unlawful acts against the environment, international traffic in obscene materials, falsification and counterfeiting of currency, unlawful interference with submarine cables, and bribery of foreign public officials.

M. Cherif Bassiouni, *Universal Jurisdiction for International Crimes: Historical Perspectives and Contemporary Practice*, 42 Va. J. Int'l L. 81, 107 (2001).

is not a universal jurisdiction offense, albeit discussing drug trafficking as an offense occurring on the "high Seas" rather than as an "Offence[ ] against the Law of Nations." *See, e.g., United States v. Perlaza*, 439 F.3d 1149, 1161–63 (9th Cir.2006) (rejecting the government's argument that it had jurisdiction over drug trafficking conducted on a go-fast vessel under the principle of universal jurisdiction); *United States v. Wright-Barker*, 784 F.2d 161, 168 n.5 (3d Cir.1986) ("[I]nternational agreements have yet to recognize drug smuggling . . . as a heinous crime subject to universal jurisdiction."). Nor have we been able to find any case decided by any international court defining drug trafficking as an offense subject to universal jurisdiction.

Because the drug trafficking at issue here is not subject to universal jurisdiction and no other internationally recognized jurisdictional basis applies, Congress does not have the authority to proscribe these defendants' conduct under Article I, Section 8, Clause 10 of the Constitution. The government's argument that this authority can be supplied by another nation's consent to United States jurisdiction is without merit. As Judge Torruella illustrates in *United States v. Cardales-Luna*, accepting this argument leads to absurd results:

> Perhaps an even more relevant example would be if Congress passed legislation attempting to apply the criminal laws of the United States, with the Bolivian government's consent, to the conduct of Colombian nationals in Bolivia traveling over its mountain roads carrying a load of coca leaves destined for Peru. The power of Congress to legislate in such a case cannot be countenanced even with the consent of Bolivia, whose consent is ultimately irrelevant, for Bolivia cannot grant Congress powers beyond those allotted to it by the Constitution.

632 F.3d 731, 741 (1st Cir.2011) (Torruella, J., dissenting).

United States v. Ballestas

United States Court of Appeals for the District of Columbia
795 F.3d 138 (2015)

Srinivasan, Circuit Judge:

Javier Eduardo Juan Ballestas, a Colombian citizen, was indicted under the Maritime Drug Law Enforcement Act (MDLEA) and extradited to the United States for prosecution. Ballestas pleaded guilty to a charge of conspiracy to distribute drugs "on board . . . a vessel subject to the jurisdiction of the United States," in violation of the MDLEA. 46 U.S.C. §§ 70503(a), 70506(b). He reserved the right to bring an appeal on certain issues, including whether the MDLEA's conspiracy provision reaches extraterritorially to encompass his charged conduct in Colombia, and whether the application of the MDLEA against him violates the Due Process Clause of the Fifth Amendment because of the absence of an adequate nexus between his conduct and the United States. Because we are unpersuaded by Ballestas's arguments on those and other issues, we affirm.

I.

A long-term investigation conducted by United States and Colombian officials uncovered an international drug-trafficking operation based in Colombia. The organization used stateless vessels to transport large quantities of cocaine from Colombia through international waters, ultimately destined for the United States. Email and phone surveillance revealed that Ballestas supported the organization's drug smuggling activities. He provided maps and law enforcement reports purporting to reveal the location of United States, Colombian, and other nations' air and maritime forces in the vicinity of the Caribbean Sea at specific times. Vessels engaged in trafficking runs used those reports to evade detection and capture.

Between May 2008 and September 2010, law enforcement agents seized or attempted to seize eight of the organization's cocaine shipments. Intercepted communications linked Ballestas to at least four of the seized shipments, which together accounted for thousands of kilograms of seized cocaine.

The government sought indictment of Ballestas and six co-conspirators for violating the MDLEA, 46 U.S.C. §§ 70501 *et seq.* The MDLEA provides that an "individual may not knowingly or intentionally manufacture or distribute, or possess with intent to manufacture or distribute, a controlled substance on board . . . a vessel subject to the jurisdiction of the United States," *id.* § 70503(a), or attempt or conspire to do the same, *id.* § 70506(b). The statute defines a "vessel subject to the jurisdiction of the United States" to include "vessel[s] without nationality."

In February, 2011, a federal grand jury returned an indictment charging Ballestas with conspiring to distribute drugs "on board . . . a vessel subject to the jurisdiction of the United States" in violation of the MDLEA. Ballestas was arrested in Colombia and extradited to the United States to stand trial.

In September, 2012, Ballestas filed a motion to dismiss the indictment. He contended that the MDLEA's conspiracy provision did not extend extraterritorially to reach individuals (like Ballestas) who never came "on board" the relevant vessels. Ballestas also argued that applying the MDLEA against him violated the Due Process Clause because of the absence of a nexus between his conduct and the United States.

In response to Ballestas's motion, the government proffered facts supporting the conspiracy charge. Two boats in particular, the government submitted, supported Ballestas's prosecution under the MDLEA for conspiring to distribute drugs on board a vessel without nationality. First, a boat intercepted in international waters near Panama on March 3, 2010, displayed no visible flag and held no valid registration. Second, another boat, seized in Panamanian waters on March 11, 2010, similarly had no flag or registration. Officials observed the vessel in international waters, pursued the vessel into Panamanian waters, and then seized it. According to the government's proffer, Ballestas provided assistance with the cocaine shipments aboard both of those vessels.

In February 2013, the district court denied Ballestas's motion to dismiss the indictment. The court concluded that the conspiracy provision of the MDLEA applied extraterritorially to Ballestas's actions in Colombia. Physical presence "on board" a vessel, the district court held, is not an essential element of a conspiracy offense under the MDLEA. The court further held that the vessels apprehended on March 3rd and 11th qualified as stateless vessels "subject to the jurisdiction of the United States." In addition, the court rejected Ballestas's due process challenge, finding that there is no requirement to show a nexus to the United States when the alleged crimes involve stateless vessels.

Ballestas sought reconsideration of the district court's denial of his motion to dismiss. He argued that certain intervening decisions undermined the court's extraterritoriality and due process holdings. The district court denied the motion for reconsideration, and, shortly thereafter, Ballestas pleaded guilty.

Ballestas's plea agreement reserved his right to appeal "the specific and limited issue" of the denial of his motion to dismiss and motion for reconsideration. The agreement also preserved his right to appeal his sentence on the grounds that it "exceeds the maximum permitted by statute or results from an upward departure from the guideline range established by the Court at sentencing." In connection with his plea agreement, Ballestas and the government entered a joint statement of stipulated facts. Those facts established Ballestas's awareness of and involvement with the vessel interdicted on March 3rd and also established that the vessel was "without nationality" and therefore subject to the jurisdiction of the United States. The district court accepted Ballestas's plea after conducting a colloquy in accordance with Federal Rule of Criminal Procedure 11.

In November 2013, the district court calculated Ballestas's sentencing guidelines range to be seventy to eighty-seven months based on the quantity of drugs stipulated to have been recovered from the March 3rd vessel. The court sentenced Ballestas to a below-guidelines sentence of sixty-four months of imprisonment followed by three years of supervised release. Ballestas now appeals, challenging the denial of his motion to dismiss, the denial of his motion for reconsideration, and his sentence.

II.

Ballestas first contends that the MDLEA's conspiracy provision does not apply extraterritorially to reach his conduct in Colombia. We disagree.

The MDLEA's conspiracy provision, 46 U.S.C. § 70506(b), provides that a "person attempting or conspiring to violate section 70503 of this title is subject to the same penalties as provided for violating section 70503." The underlying substantive offense set forth in § 70503 prohibits "knowingly or intentionally manufactur[ing] or distribut[ing], or possess[ing] with intent to distribute, a controlled substance on board," *inter alia,* "a vessel subject to the jurisdiction of the United States," which includes "a vessel without nationality."

In arguing that the MDLEA's conspiracy provision fails to reach extraterritorially, Ballestas relies on two canons of statutory interpretation. First, he invokes the presumption against extraterritoriality, which dictates that, "[w]hen a statute gives no clear indication of an extraterritorial application, it has none." Second, he relies on the so-called *Charming Betsy* canon, which takes its name from a decision in which the Supreme Court explained that "an act of Congress ought never to be construed to violate the law of nations if any other possible construction remains." *Murray v. Schooner Charming Betsy,* 6 U.S. (2 Cranch) 64, 118, 2 L.Ed. 208 (1804).

Each of those "principle[s]," however, "represents a canon of construction, or a presumption about a statute's meaning, rather than a limit upon Congress's power to legislate." Thus, notwithstanding the presumption against extraterritoriality, a statute will be construed to apply extraterritorially if Congress gives a "clear indication" of that intention. With regard to the *Charming Betsy* canon, similarly, if "a statute makes plain Congress's intent," a court "must enforce the intent of Congress irrespective of whether the statute conforms to customary international law." After all, "Congress is not bound by international law," so "it may legislate with respect to conduct outside the United States, in excess of the limits posed by international law."

Here, the extraterritorial reach of the MDLEA's substantive prohibitions is clear. Section 70503(b), entitled "extension beyond territorial jurisdiction," provides that § 70503(a), which sets forth the substantive prohibitions, "applies even though the act is committed outside the territorial jurisdiction of the United States." 46 U.S.C. § 70503(b). That straightforward expression of extraterritorial application settles the extraterritorial reach of § 70503(a).

Ballestas, however, attempts to draw a line between the extraterritorial reach of the MDLEA's substantive offense in § 70503(a) and the reach of the MDLEA's conspiracy offense in § 70506(b). He relies on the understanding that, "[w]hen a statute provides for some extraterritorial application, the presumption against extraterritoriality operates to limit that provision to its terms." *Kiobel v. Royal Dutch Petroleum Co.,* 133 S.Ct. 1659, 1667 (2013). In Ballestas's view, the MDLEA's extraterritorial application therefore should be confined to the substantive prohibitions set forth in § 70503(a), and should not extend to conspiracy (or attempt) to commit those substantive crimes under § 70506. We are unpersuaded.

Under the presumption against extraterritoriality, the extraterritorial reach of a particular provision will not necessarily be imputed to an entire statute. But in the particular context of "an ancillary offense like aiding and abetting or conspiracy," we have held that, "[g]enerally, the extraterritorial reach of [the] ancillary offense ... is coterminous with that of the underlying criminal statute." As a result, "when the underlying criminal statute's extraterritorial reach is unquestionable, the presumption [against extraterritoriality] is rebutted with equal force" for ancillary offenses in the same statute. Here, because the substantive offense established in § 70503(a) applies extraterritorially, we conclude that conspiracy to commit that substantive offense under § 70506 also has extraterritorial reach. And with the extraterritorial reach of the conspiracy provision clearly established, we have no occasion to apply the *Charming Betsy* canon.

Our conclusion that the MDLEA's conspiracy provision applies extraterritorially is consistent with Congress's purpose in enacting it. As the Senate Report for the MDLEA explains, Congress sought to address concerns about difficulties encountered in prosecuting persons involved with shipments of drugs to the United States on vessels, both with respect to the crew on board and others associated with the enterprise. Before the MDLEA's enactment, when the Coast Guard seized illegal drug shipments, the government could not "prosecute the crew *or others involved in the smuggling operation* " in the absence of often elusive evidence that the drugs were destined for the United States. S.Rep. No. 96855, at 2 (1980) (emphasis added). In light of the obstacles to successful prosecution in the United States, the Coast Guard's drug interdiction efforts had "little deterrent effect on the crews *or the trafficking organizations.*" *Id.* (emphasis added).

Recognizing that "trafficking in controlled substances aboard vessels is a serious international problem, is universally condemned, and presents a specific threat to the security and societal well-being of the United States," 46 U.S.C. § 70501, Congress enacted the MDLEA to enhance the government's ability to prosecute members of drug trafficking organizations. Giving the MDLEA's conspiracy provision the construction suggested by Ballestas would effectively inoculate many members of such organizations—including organizations targeting the United States—against prosecution. Drug kingpins and other conspirators who facilitate and assist in carrying out trafficking schemes would fall beyond the reach of the statute, compromising the overriding intent of Congress in enacting it. Those considerations reinforce our conclusion that the MDLEA's conspiracy provision reaches Ballestas's extraterritorial conduct in this case.

III.

Ballestas next challenges Congress's authority to criminalize his actions under the Define and Punish Clause, U.S. Const. art. I, § 8, cl. 10. That clause grants Congress the authority "[t]o define and punish Piracies and Felonies committed on the high Seas, and Offenses against the Law of Nations." The clause encompasses three distinct powers: (i) to define and punish piracy; (ii) to define and punish felonies committed on the high seas; and (iii) to define and punish offenses against the Law of Nations. *See United States v. Smith,* 18 U.S. (5 Wheat.) 153, 158–59 (1820). In defending Congress's constitutional authority to apply the MDLEA in the circumstances of this case, the government relies solely on Congress's power under the Felonies Clause, *i.e.,* its power to define and punish felonies committed on the high seas. We agree that the Felonies Clause grants Congress authority to criminalize Ballestas's conduct.

Ballestas's argument relies in substantial part on the Eleventh Circuit's decision in *United States v. Bellaizac-Hurtado,* 700 F.3d 1245 (11th Cir.2012). In that case, Panamanian officials apprehended the defendants on board a stateless vessel in Panamanian waters. Panama consented to the prosecution of the defendants in the

United States, but the Eleventh Circuit found that the application of the MDLEA to the defendants' conduct lay beyond Congress's constitutional authority. Critically, however, the government in *Bellaizac-Hurtado* relied solely on the Law of Nations Clause to support the constitutionality of the MDLEA's application. Responding to the government's argument, the Eleventh Circuit held that "drug trafficking is not a violation of customary international law and, as a result, falls outside the power of Congress under the [Law of Nations] Clause." *Bellaizac-Hurtado* did not address whether any alternative source of congressional authority—such as the Felonies Clause—could serve to criminalize the defendants' conduct. In fact, the court observed that "all of the [other] appeals in which we have considered the constitutionality of [drug trafficking] laws involved conduct on the high seas," and those convictions were upheld "as an exercise of [Congress's] power under the Felonies Clause." Because the government in this case defends Congress's authority under the Felonies Clause, not the Law of Nations Clause, *Bellaizac-Hurtado* is of little assistance to Ballestas.

In assessing whether the Felonies Clause grants Congress the power to criminalize Ballestas's behavior, we again rely on the established principles of conspiracy law set forth above. "[T]he overt act of one partner in a crime is attributable to all," as long as the act "was done in furtherance of the conspiracy, and was reasonably foreseeable as a 'necessary or natural consequence of the unlawful agreement[.]'" Here, the stipulated facts establish that Ballestas's co-conspirators committed felonious acts on the high seas, and also that those acts are directly attributable to him. Ballestas acknowledged that one of the drug trafficking organization's vessels was apprehended on March 3, 2010, carrying approximately 1500 kilograms of cocaine. He further acknowledged that the vessel had "traveled through the high seas." As an admitted co-conspirator of the crew members, the acts of the crew—committed on the high seas—are attributable to Ballestas. The Felonies Clause therefore provides Congress with authority to "punish" Ballestas for his role in that conspiracy.

IV.

We next consider Ballestas's argument that the application of the MDLEA in his case violated the Due Process Clause because the government failed to demonstrate a nexus between his actions abroad and the United States. Our circuit has yet to decide "whether the Constitution limits the extraterritorial exercise of federal criminal jurisdiction." Several other courts of appeals, though, have found that the Due Process Clause imposes limits on the extraterritorial application of federal criminal laws. *See, e.g., United States v. Brehm,* 691 F.3d 547, 552–54 (4th Cir.2012); *United States v. Ibarguen-Mosquera,* 634 F.3d 1370, 1378–79 (11th Cir.2011). Those courts generally require a showing of "sufficient nexus between the defendant and the United States, so that . . . application [of the law] would not be arbitrary or fundamentally unfair."

[W]e need not definitively resolve whether the Due Process Clause constrains the extraterritorial application of federal criminal laws. Even assuming the existence of a due process limitation, the extraterritorial application of the MDLEA in this case would not run afoul of it. [N]exus with the United States merely serves as a "proxy for due process" requirements. "The 'ultimate question'" under the Due Process Clause is not nexus, but is "whether 'application of the statute to the defendant [would] be arbitrary or fundamentally unfair.'" There is no arbitrariness or fundamental unfairness in the circumstances of this case.

Again, Ballestas's factual stipulations establish that he was part of an international drug smuggling organization that used stateless vessels to transport drugs across the high seas, bound ultimately for the United States. The conduct to which Ballestas pleaded guilty involved obtaining and selling reports and maps "indicat[ing] where *U.S.*, Colombian and other countries' . . . maritime assets were operating in the Caribbean Sea on a particular day." He stipulated to his knowledge that his coconspirators used the maps to "plan the best route to be taken by the cocaine-laden vessels so as to avoid detection by maritime and law enforcement authorities," including, specifically, United States authorities. Those admissions establish that application of a United States drug trafficking law (the MDLEA) to Ballestas was neither arbitrary nor fundamentally unfair.

* * * * * *

For the foregoing reasons, we reject Ballestas's challenges and affirm the judgment of the district court.

So ordered.

The D.C. Circuit rejected Ballestas' Due Process Clause challenge, finding that even if there is a due process limit on the extraterritorial application of federal criminal laws, applying the MDLEA to Ballestas would not be arbitrary or fundamentally unfair. This was so, because "[t]he conduct to which Ballestas pleaded guilty involved obtaining and selling reports and maps 'indicat[ing] where U.S., Colombian and other countries' . . . maritime assets were operating in the Caribbean Sea on a particular day.'" This analysis seems to imply that it would not be unfair to apply the MDLEA to Ballestas because he knew that the drugs were bound for the United States.

But does the fact that Ballestas knew drugs were headed for the United States necessarily mean that criminally prosecuting him in the United States is fundamentally fair? Michael Farbiarz argues that due process should take into account the potential for "inaccuracies when a litigant is forced to defend in a distant forum." Michael Farbiarz, *Accuracy and Adjudication: The Promise of Extraterritorial Due Process*, 116 COLUM. L. REV. 625, 670 (2016). When a crime has taken place outside of the United States, "important evidence will virtually always be outside of the United States." *Id.* at 673. This can make it much more difficult for defendants to present a defense. In an extraterritorial prosecution, for example, "eyewitnesses will likely also be outside the United States. And if those witnesses do not want to take the trip to an American court, there is no ready way to force them." *Id.* at 672. The government often has much greater access to evidence in these cases, both because of resources and because of Mutual Legal Assistance Treaties (MLATs). MLATs "generally empower[] the United States to ask other countries to gather documents within their own borders, or to compel a witness to attend a deposition." *Id.* 680. If defendants are unable to gather evidence and call key witnesses, the potential for an innocent person to be found guilty increases. To address this procedural mismatch, Farbiarz proposes that courts recognize robust due process limits on personal jurisdiction over criminal defendants, similar to the longstanding "due process limits on personal jurisdiction" in civil cases. *Id.* at 633.

2. Extradition of Drug Offenders

The extraterritorial application of U.S. drug laws typically begins with an extradition request. Extradition cases can present challenging and esoteric legal problems. *See, e.g.,* Ann Powers, *Justice Denied? The Adjudication of Extradition Applications*, 37 TEX. INT'L L. J. 277 (2002) (noting that "[e]ven counsel who deal regularly with immigration and deportation matters rarely deal with extradition, and they may be unaware of its unusual elements"); David Aronofsky and Jie Qin, *U.S. International Narcotics Extradition Cases: Legal Trends and Developments with Implications for U.S.-China Drug Enforcement Activities*, 19 MICH. ST. J. INT'L L. 279 (2011) (surveying some of the difficult legal issues that have been raised in drug extradition cases). The excerpt that follows provides an overview of the role of extradition in U.S. prosecutions of international drug cases.

Traffic Circles: The Legal Logic of Drug Extraditions
Edward M. Morgan

31 University of Pennsylvania Journal of International Law 373 (2009)

[E]xtradition, as opposed to domestic prosecution, has become the law enforcement vehicle of choice for governments willing to engage with the United States in the anti-drug campaign.

Despite the plethora of U.N.-sponsored, multilateral conventions relating to narcotics trafficking, drugs have not been the focus of much adjudication by international judicial organs. The negotiations culminating in the Statute of the International Criminal Court raised the possibility of categorizing drug trafficking as an international offense; however, the sessions concluded only with a resolution that the state parties consider including it at a future review conference. Although drug policy plays a central role in international legal discourse and the United Nations monitors narcotics treaty implementation by its member states, actual enforcement and prosecution has been left to the unilateral and coordinated actions of domestic legal systems.

The vision of nationals as a cog in the societal wheel and that of the citizen as a self-standing force in opposition to state action have met directly, and clashed, in the law of extradition. As a starting point, international theorists have long perceived the community of nations to operate under a natural duty to extradite offenders from neighboring states. This duty is most frequently translated into an interstate obligation to ensure that no one jurisdiction stands as a safe haven or refuge for serious offenders fleeing another jurisdiction. Some early theorists limited the sphere of operation of extradition only to those international relations backed by an enforceable treaty. However, Grotius' maxim: "extradite or prosecute," has long placed the international exchange of fugitives between nations at the epicenter of the contest between the national as owing duties and allegiance to the state community of which he is a member, and the citizen as holding rights to be asserted against any combination of sovereign states.

The compromise followed by most civil law jurisdictions, and a number of common law countries, has been to extradite only third-party nationals, protecting citizens of the requested state from being the subject of an international exchange. In contrast, the United States has, since its first extradition agreements with England, France, and Switzerland, been prepared to extradite its own citizens on the same basis as nationals of the treaty partners or of third countries. While it is possible for a treaty to preclude the extradition of nationals, U.S. policy has generally been antagonistic to the idea. In fact, in 1913, the Supreme Court ruled that reciprocity is not a necessary ingredient to extradition treaty enforcement, and American fugitives can be sent by the United States to countries which refuse to send their own nationals in return.

While the blanket exemption of nationals from the extradition process has been condemned as a matter of international law theory, several prominent civil law countries in Western Europe continue to refuse extradition of their own citizens. Among Latin American countries, the practice has also tended to exempt nationals, despite substantial American pressure to change policies to accommodate the war on drugs. Thus, for example, Colombia agreed in 1982 in a revised extradition treaty to send fugitive citizens to the United States, but the treaty was declared unenforceable by the Colombia Supreme Court in 1986 in a decision widely perceived to be a capitulation to the power of narcotics cartels. Extraditions were reinstated for Colombians, without judicial review, by executive order of the President in 1989, but were . . . eliminated [again] in 1991 when extradition of citizens was rendered unconstitutional by means of a specific constitutional amendment.

The extradition treaty between the United States and Mexico has likewise proved to be a highly contentious instrument in terms of the two-way flow of nationals. In the first place, although the treaty was negotiated in terms meant to grant each of the signing governments the discretionary power to extradite its own nationals, the governing clause is stated in the negative: "neither contracting parties shall be bound to deliver up its own nationals. . . ." For its part, the United States government has been willing to extradite U.S. citizens even in the face of a credible claim that the evidence supporting the Mexican allegations were obtained through torture. Moreover, the Courts of Appeals have specifically rejected the argument that the United States should put a moratorium on extraditions of U.S. citizens to

Mexico until such time as Mexico determines that it will extradite its nationals for trial in the United States.

By contrast, the Mexican legal system has traditionally barred extradition of citizens, although it has reserved for the executive branch the discretion to determine case by case whether exceptional circumstances warranting extradition of a Mexican citizen exist. This has typically been justified on the ground that the Mexican courts have inherent jurisdiction over and are competent to try all crimes, wherever committed, that are perpetrated by Mexican nationals. Despite assurances to the contrary, through most of the twentieth century Mexican officials so rarely acted on extradition warrants aimed at their citizens that the U.S. Drug Enforcement [Administration] developed a practice of bypassing the extradition process altogether by kidnapping fugitives and smuggling them into U.S. territory for trial. In recent years, in response to increased pressure to follow U.S. law enforcement policies, Mexico has been more willing to deem drug traffickers as falling under the "exceptional circumstances" category denying selected Mexican nationals from the exemption otherwise applicable to all Mexican nationals. That said, the Mexican policy has been enforced inconsistently, with protection from extradition frequently applied even to fugitives accused of crimes of extreme violence.

The controversy over extraditing nationals strikes the dual chords of which the international and constitutional norms surrounding nationality and citizenship are composed. On one hand, the image of citizens as non-extraditable parts of the nation stands opposite that of citizens as rights holder as against her nation, although both lead to the same result. By contrast, the image of fugitives as extraditable individuals imbued with personal stature and responsibility stands opposite that of accused persons wedded to the society and locale in which their crime was committed, although again both lead to the same result. Whether the state in question chooses to extradite its nationals or to keep them at home, the dual strands of nationality law are inevitably in play. Persons are both part of society and apart from it, and their citizenship can potentially stand for both positions.

Among U.S. policymakers and critics, it has often been debated whether the anti-narcotics campaign of the past several decades is a product of law enforcement necessity or cynical politics; likewise, it has been debated whether the global drug prohibition has been a winning or a losing endeavor. Additionally, in U.S. legal commentary, it has frequently been debated whether the Constitution supports the fight against drug use and trafficking or is contrary to the "war" effort. Whatever side one prefers in these debates, it is clear from the U.S. interventions in the Colombian and Mexican drug wars that international politics cannot be factored out of the debates over extraditing nationals.

Running parallel with the explicit linkage of drug law enforcement to foreign policy goals, are the judicial politics that underscore recent judgments. The dual nature of nationality, as an identity marker that affiliates persons with sovereign states and as a rights emblem that sets persons apart from state power, has given rise to a set of cases that reflect a confusion of ideological motifs. The nationality cases in extradition law bring to the surface the fact that courts appear unable to determine whether due process is owed by states to persons or to each other. This dilemma, in turn, has led adjudicators to confuse the civil libertarianism of criminal law with state self-interest, and the authoritarianism of law enforcement with international cooperation.

Three contemporary extradition cases, each sending a suspected drug fugitive to the United States, will illustrate the phenomenon.

In December of 2000, a federal grand jury in Florida indicted Samuel "Ninety" Knowles—a colorful Bahamian national who, as reported by the local press, "got his nickname by blowing $90,000 in one day"—on several counts of conspiracy to possess, distribute, and import cocaine and marijuana into the United States. The indictment formed the basis of an extradition request from the U.S. government to the Republic of Bahamas, which was in turn challenged in *habeas corpus* proceedings on the grounds that the statutory conditions for extradition had not been met. During the course of lengthy appeal and review proceedings, and well before the signing of an extradition order by the Bahamian Foreign Minister, the President of the United States exercised his statutory authority to designate Knowles as a foreign drug "kingpin," thereby seizing his U.S. assets and barring him from using the U.S. financial system prior to any judicial finding of guilt.

In one of his two trips to the Privy Council, Knowles challenged the extradition to the United States on the grounds that the "kingpin" designation was widely published, notorious, and tantamount to a public declaration of his guilt. As the defense put it, once in the United States, "the jurors at his trial might well know or learn of his designation . . . [and] his trial would not be fair if a juror were prejudiced by such knowledge." Moreover, the U.S. statute triggered a citizenship issue, the other half of Knowles' challenge being that the prejudice against his fair trial "derived from his nationality, since the [Foreign Narcotics Kingpin Designation] Act did not apply to U.S. citizens." Thus, although the terms of the U.S.-Bahamas Extradition Treaty specify that "extradition shall not be refused on the grounds that the fugitive is a citizen or national of the Requested State", the citizenship question played a central role in the fairness/discrimination argument both in court and in the public discourse that accompanied the Bahamian proceedings.

The "kingpin" issue barely got off the ground when "Ninety" was sent fifty miles across the Gulf Stream to face the federal charges in Miami. Indeed, the Bahamas Court of Appeal ruled after his departure that the government had acted prematurely in sending him to stand trial. The identical question of prejudice to foreign extraditees, however, had in the meantime been considered by the Privy Council in yet another drug extradition from yet another Caribbean jurisdiction, the islands of St. Kitts and Nevis. Two cocaine co-conspirators, Noel Heath and Glenroy Mathews, had been designated as foreign drug "kingpins" on June 1, 2000, and, according to the Privy Council, had been announced as such on a U.S. government website despite provisions in the legislation for non-disclosure of the designee's name if such disclosure could jeopardize the integrity of the ongoing criminal trial.

In a relatively brief judgment, Lord Brown of Eaton-under-Heywood gave the kingpin argument relatively short shrift. Analogizing the problem to one of ordinary domestic publicity, the law lords were willing to leave it to the ultimate trial judge to determine an appropriate remedy. Turning to the particular problem of foreign proceedings, and the fact that the domestic extradition court cannot predict the remedies that a foreign trial court will invoke, the court fell back on a presumption of judicial innocence. Lord Brown cited the 1987 judgment of the Supreme Court of Canada in *Argentina v. Mellino* in order to invoke what he found to be the commonplace principle that "our courts must assume that [the defendant] will be given a fair trial in the foreign country."

In September of 2004, a grand jury in southern Florida indicted Ze'ev Rosenstein—a stocky, domineering figure in the Tel Aviv underworld referred to as "The Fat Man" by undercover U.S. investigators in taped telephone conversations—on charges of heading an international conspiracy to traffic in the drug methylenedioxymethamphetamine ("MDMA," more generally known as "ecstasy"). The indictment formed the basis of an extradition request from the government of the United States to the State of Israel. That request, in turn, prompted a challenge by the defense in the Jerusalem District Court on the grounds that extradition would violate Israeli constitutional safeguards.

In his appeal to Israel's Supreme Court, Rosenstein presented a long list of legal arguments, the crux of which contended that since he is "an Israeli citizen and resident, and the alleged offense was committed entirely in Israel, extradition to another country deviates from the balance required by Basic Law: Human Dignity and Freedom, and by fundamental principles of penal law." Although by the time of his arrest Israel had revised its law to permit the extradition of Israeli citizens under certain circumstances, the defense argued that for a person whose center of life is in the territory of the State, "the prosecution's policy on drug offenses has long been to conduct trials in Israel, even if the act was committed outside of Israel." Under the circumstances, the due process demanded by the alleged ecstasy financier was presented as a counterweight to the lead prosecutor's assertion that extradition "is good for the country and good for the cooperation between countries against international crime."

In rejecting the defendant's challenges and arriving at its conclusion that Rosenstein can be sent to the United States, the court relied heavily on American investigatory evidence. [T]his appears to be part of an ongoing law enforcement strategy by Israeli authorities to contract large drug prosecutions out to the United States[.]

[I]n *Lake v. Canada* (Minister of Justice)[,] Talib Steven Lake was caught selling roughly 100 grams of crack cocaine in a series of transactions in Windsor, Ontario, and across the bridge in Detroit, Michigan, with an undercover officer of the Ontario Provincial Police. He was tried and convicted for the Canadian transactions. After serving a relatively light sentence of three years in prison, he was processed for extradition to the United States where an indictment had been issued in the U.S. District Court for the Eastern District of Michigan relating to the Detroit transaction. Upon losing his committal battle in the Ontario courts, Lake requested that the Minister of Justice exercise his discretion not to order him extradited, but the Minister decided against him and ordered him sent back to Michigan in February 2005.

The Minister incorrectly determined that Canada had no jurisdiction to try Lake on the Michigan charge, and thus, the extradition did not infringe his mobility rights under the Charter. The Minister also considered the prospect of Lake facing a mandatory minimum sentence of ten years under U.S. law—a far more severe punishment than would be meted out by the Canadian judicial system. However, the Minister rejected Lake's potential punishment under U.S. law as grounds for exercising his discretion in the fugitive's favor because the minimum incarceration term was not seen to shock the conscience of Canadians. Lake sought judicial review of the Minister's discretionary decision, and on appeal the Supreme Court of Canada determined that, whatever its failings, the ministerial decision deserved a level of deference with which the court should not interfere. Although he argued heatedly that "the Minister is required to respect a fugitive's constitutional rights in deciding whether to exercise his or her discretion . . . ," the court effectively threw cold water on Lake.

The case law reveals that when the United States calls for drug extraditions, the fugitives tend to come; or, more accurately, tend to be sent.

Drugs have reintroduced the national to the sovereign nation, removing the protections afforded by a sovereign law. The American insistence on policing the worlds of narcotics trade, and the changes wrought by that insistence on the character of global society, has had this transformative effect on extradition policy around the world. Although the "war on drugs" has been a failure if measured by the goal of eradication it has set for itself, it has had remarkable impact on judicial opinions among neighbors and allies of the United States.

3. Extraterritorial Drug Investigation and Enforcement by U.S. Officials

Though the United States increasingly has been successful at convincing other countries to extradite their nationals, some countries remain hesitant to send their citizens abroad for prosecution. If a country does not wish to extradite one of its citizens, can the U.S. send its own agents into that country to arrest him or pay a third party to kidnap him and bring him into the U.S.? The question implicates a distinct aspect of extraterritorial jurisdiction: the jurisdiction to enforce. *See* Restatement (Third) of the Law of Foreign Relations of the United States § 401 (1986) (explaining the distinction between the jurisdiction to prescribe, the jurisdiction to adjudicate, and the jurisdiction to enforce).

United States v. Alvarez-Machain

Supreme Court of the United States
504 U.S. 655 (1992)

Chief Justice Rehnquist delivered the opinion of the Court.

The issue in this case is whether a criminal defendant, abducted to the United States from a nation with which it has an extradition treaty, thereby acquires a defense to the jurisdiction of this country's courts. We hold that he does not, and that he may be tried in federal district court for violations of the criminal law of the United States.

Respondent, Humberto Alvarez-Machain, is a citizen and resident of Mexico. He was indicted for participating in the kidnap and murder of United States Drug Enforcement Administration (DEA) special agent Enrique Camarena-Salazar and a Mexican pilot working with Camarena, Alfredo Zavala-Avelar. The DEA believes that respondent, a medical doctor, participated in the murder by prolonging Agent Camarena's life so that others could further torture and interrogate him. On April 2, 1990, respondent was forcibly kidnaped from his medical office in Guadalajara, Mexico, to be flown by private plane to El Paso, Texas, where he was arrested by DEA officials. The District Court concluded that DEA agents were responsible for respondent's abduction, although they were not personally involved in it.[2]

Respondent moved to dismiss the indictment, claiming that his abduction constituted outrageous governmental conduct, and that the District Court lacked jurisdiction to try him because he was abducted in violation of the extradition treaty between the United States and Mexico. The District Court rejected the outrageous governmental conduct claim, but held that it lacked jurisdiction to try respondent because his abduction violated the Extradition Treaty. The District Court discharged respondent and ordered that he be repatriated to Mexico

[T]he Court of Appeals affirmed the District Court's finding that the United States had authorized the abduction of respondent, and that letters from the Mexican Government to the United States Government served as an official protest of the Treaty violation. Therefore, the Court of Appeals ordered that the indictment against respondent be dismissed and that respondent be repatriated to Mexico. We granted certiorari and now reverse.

Although we have never before addressed the precise issue raised in the present case, we have previously considered proceedings in claimed violation of an extradition treaty and proceedings against a defendant brought before a court by means of a forcible abduction. We addressed the former issue in *United States v. Rauscher,* 119 U.S. 407 (1886); more precisely, the issue whether the Webster-Ashburton Treaty

---

2. Apparently, DEA officials had attempted to gain respondent's presence in the United States through informal negotiations with Mexican officials, but were unsuccessful. DEA officials then, through a contact in Mexico, offered to pay a reward and expenses in return for the delivery of respondent to the United States.

of 1842, 8 Stat. 576, which governed extraditions between England and the United States, prohibited the prosecution of defendant Rauscher for a crime other than the crime for which he had been extradited. Whether this prohibition, known as the doctrine of specialty, was an intended part of the treaty had been disputed between the two nations for some time. Justice Miller delivered the opinion of the Court, which carefully examined the terms and history of the treaty; the practice of nations in regards to extradition treaties; the case law from the States; and the writings of commentators, and reached the following conclusion: "[A] person who has been brought within the jurisdiction of the court *by virtue of proceedings under an extradition treaty*, can only be tried for one of the offences described in that treaty, and for the offence with which he is charged in the proceedings for his extradition, until a reasonable time and opportunity have been given him, after his release or trial upon such charge, to return to the country from whose asylum he had been forcibly taken under those proceedings." *Id.*, at 430 (emphasis added). Unlike the case before us today, the defendant in *Rauscher* had been brought to the United States by way of an extradition treaty; there was no issue of a forcible abduction.

In *Ker v. Illinois,* 119 U.S. 436 (1886), also written by Justice Miller and decided the same day as *Rauscher*, we addressed the issue of a defendant brought before the court by way of a forcible abduction. Frederick Ker had been tried and convicted in an Illinois court for larceny; his presence before the court was procured by means of forcible abduction from Peru. A messenger was sent to Lima with the proper warrant to demand Ker by virtue of the extradition treaty between Peru and the United States. The messenger, however, disdained reliance on the treaty processes, and instead forcibly kidnaped Ker and brought him to the United States. We distinguished Ker's case from *Rauscher*, on the basis that Ker was not brought into the United States by virtue of the extradition treaty between the United States and Peru, and rejected Ker's argument that he had a right under the extradition treaty to be returned to this country only in accordance with its terms. We rejected Ker's due process argument more broadly, holding in line with "the highest authorities" that "such forcible abduction is no sufficient reason why the party should not answer when brought within the jurisdiction of the court which has the right to try him for such an offence, and presents no valid objection to his trial in such court."

In *Frisbie v. Collins,* 342 U.S. 519 (1952), we applied the rule in *Ker* to a case in which the defendant had been kidnaped in Chicago by Michigan officers and brought to trial in Michigan. We upheld the conviction over objections based on the Due Process Clause and the federal Kidnaping Act and stated: "This Court has never departed from the rule announced in [*Ker*] that the power of a court to try a person for crime is not impaired by the fact that he had been brought within the court's jurisdiction by reason of a 'forcible abduction.'"

The only differences between *Ker* and the present case are that *Ker* was decided on the premise that there was no governmental involvement in the abduction and Peru, from which Ker was abducted, did not object to his prosecution. Respondent finds these differences to be dispositive, as did the Court of Appeals[.] The

Government, on the other hand, argues that *Rauscher* stands as an "exception" to the rule in *Ker* only when an extradition treaty is invoked, and the terms of the treaty provide that its breach will limit the jurisdiction of a court. Therefore, our first inquiry must be whether the abduction of respondent from Mexico violated the Extradition Treaty between the United States and Mexico. If we conclude that the Treaty does not prohibit respondent's abduction, the rule in *Ker* applies, and the court need not inquire as to how respondent came before it.

In construing a treaty, as in construing a statute, we first look to its terms to determine its meaning. The Treaty says nothing about the obligations of the United States and Mexico to refrain from forcible abductions of people from the territory of the other nation, or the consequences under the Treaty if such an abduction occurs. Respondent submits that Article 22(1) of the Treaty, which states that it "shall apply to offenses specified in Article 2 [including murder] committed before and after this Treaty enters into force" evidences an intent to make application of the Treaty mandatory for those offenses. However, the more natural conclusion is that Article 22 was included to ensure that the Treaty was applied to extraditions requested after the Treaty went into force, regardless of when the crime of extradition occurred.

More critical to respondent's argument is Article 9 of the Treaty, which provides:

> "1. Neither Contracting Party shall be bound to deliver up its own nationals, but the executive authority of the requested Party shall, if not prevented by the laws of that Party, have the power to deliver them up if, in its discretion, it be deemed proper to do so.
>
> "2. If extradition is not granted pursuant to paragraph 1 of this Article, the requested Party shall submit the case to its competent authorities for the purpose of prosecution, provided that Party has jurisdiction over the offense."

According to respondent, Article 9 embodies the terms of the bargain which the United States struck: If the United States wishes to prosecute a Mexican national, it may request that individual's extradition. Upon a request from the United States, Mexico may either extradite the individual or submit the case to the proper authorities for prosecution in Mexico. In this way, respondent reasons, each nation preserved its right to choose whether its nationals would be tried in its own courts or by the courts of the other nation. This preservation of rights would be frustrated if either nation were free to abduct nationals of the other nation for the purposes of prosecution. More broadly, respondent reasons, as did the Court of Appeals, that all the processes and restrictions on the obligation to extradite established by the Treaty would make no sense if either nation were free to resort to forcible kidnaping to gain the presence of an individual for prosecution in a manner not contemplated by the Treaty.

We do not read the Treaty in such a fashion. Article 9 does not purport to specify the only way in which one country may gain custody of a national of the other country for the purposes of prosecution. In the absence of an extradition treaty, nations are under no obligation to surrender those in their country to foreign authorities for prosecution. Extradition treaties exist so as to impose mutual obligations to surrender individuals in certain defined sets of circumstances, following established procedures. The Treaty thus provides a mechanism which would not otherwise exist, requiring, under certain circumstances, the United States and Mexico to extradite individuals to the other country, and establishing the procedures to be followed when the Treaty is invoked.

The history of negotiation and practice under the Treaty also fails to show that abductions outside of the Treaty constitute a violation of the Treaty. As the Solicitor General notes, the Mexican Government was made aware, as early as 1906, of the *Ker* doctrine, and the United States' position that it applied to forcible abductions made outside of the terms of the United States-Mexico Extradition Treaty.[11] Nonetheless, the current version of the Treaty, signed in 1978, does not attempt to establish a rule that would in any way curtail the effect of *Ker*. Moreover, although language which would grant individuals exactly the right sought by respondent had been considered and drafted as early as 1935 by a prominent group of legal scholars sponsored by the faculty of Harvard Law School, no such clause appears in the current Treaty.

Thus, the language of the Treaty, in the context of its history, does not support the proposition that the Treaty prohibits abductions outside of its terms. The remaining question, therefore, is whether the Treaty should be interpreted so as to include an implied term prohibiting prosecution where the defendant's presence is obtained by means other than those established by the Treaty.

Respondent contends that the Treaty must be interpreted against the backdrop of customary international law, and that international abductions are "so clearly prohibited in international law" that there was no reason to include such a clause in the Treaty itself. The international censure of international abductions is further evidenced, according to respondent, by the United Nations Charter and the Charter of the Organization of American States. Respondent does not argue that these sources of international law provide an independent basis for the right respondent asserts not to be tried in the United States, but rather that they should inform the interpretation of the Treaty terms.

[T]he difficulty with the support respondent garners from international law is that none of it relates to the practice of nations in relation to extradition treaties.

11. In correspondence between the United States and Mexico growing out of the 1905 Martinez incident, in which a Mexican national was abducted from Mexico and brought to the United States for trial, the Mexican Charge wrote to the Secretary of State protesting that as Martinez' arrest was made outside of the procedures established in the extradition treaty, "the action pending against the man can not rest [on] any legal foundation." Letter of Balbino Davalos to Secretary of State, *reprinted in* Papers Relating to the Foreign Relations of the United States, H. R. Doc. No. 1, 59th Cong., 2d Sess., pt. 2, p. 1121 (1906). The Secretary of State responded that the exact issue raised by the Martinez incident had been decided by *Ker*, and that the remedy open to the Mexican Government, namely, a request to the United States for extradition of Martinez' abductor, had been granted by the United States.

In *Rauscher*, we implied a term in the Webster-Ashburton Treaty because of the practice of nations with regard to extradition treaties. In the instant case, respondent would imply terms in the Extradition Treaty from the practice of nations with regards to international law more generally. Respondent would have us find that the Treaty acts as a prohibition against a violation of the general principle of international law that one government may not "exercise its police power in the territory of another state." There are many actions which could be taken by a nation that would violate this principle, including waging war, but it cannot seriously be contended that an invasion of the United States by Mexico would violate the terms of the Extradition Treaty between the two nations.

In sum, to infer from this Treaty and its terms that it prohibits all means of gaining the presence of an individual outside of its terms goes beyond established precedent and practice. In *Rauscher*, the implication of a doctrine of specialty into the terms of the Webster-Ashburton Treaty, which, by its terms, required the presentation of evidence establishing probable cause of the crime of extradition before extradition was required, was a small step to take. By contrast, to imply from the terms of this Treaty that it prohibits obtaining the presence of an individual by means outside of the procedures the Treaty establishes requires a much larger inferential leap, with only the most general of international law principles to support it. The general principles cited by respondent simply fail to persuade us that we should imply in the United States-Mexico Extradition Treaty a term prohibiting international abductions.

Respondent and his *amici* may be correct that respondent's abduction was "shocking" and that it may be in violation of general international law principles. Mexico has protested the abduction of respondent through diplomatic notes and the decision of whether respondent should be returned to Mexico, as a matter outside of the Treaty, is a matter for the Executive Branch.[16] We conclude, however, that respondent's abduction was not in violation of the Extradition Treaty between the

16. The Mexican Government has also requested from the United States the extradition of two individuals it suspects of having abducted respondent in Mexico, on charges of kidnaping.

The advantage of the diplomatic approach to the resolution of difficulties between two sovereign nations, as opposed to unilateral action by the courts of one nation, is illustrated by the history of the negotiations leading to the treaty discussed in *Cook v. United States*. The United States was interested in being able to search British vessels that hovered beyond the 3-mile limit and served as supply ships for motor launches, which took intoxicating liquor from them into ports for further distribution in violation of prohibition laws. The United States initially proposed that both nations agree to searches of the other's vessels beyond the 3-mile limit; Great Britain rejected such an approach, since it had no prohibition laws and therefore no problem with United States vessels hovering just beyond its territorial waters. The parties appeared to be at loggerheads; then this Court decided *Cunard S. S. Co. v. Mellon*, 262 U.S. 100 (1923), holding that our prohibition laws applied to foreign merchant vessels as well as domestic within the territorial waters of the United States, and that therefore the carrying of intoxicating liquors by foreign passenger ships violated those laws. A treaty was then successfully negotiated, giving the United States the right to seizure beyond the 3-mile limit (which it desired), and giving British passenger ships the right to bring liquor into United States waters so long as the liquor supply was sealed while in those waters (which Great Britain desired).

United States and Mexico, and therefore the rule of *Ker* v. *Illinois* is fully applicable to this case. The fact of respondent's forcible abduction does not therefore prohibit his trial in a court in the United States for violations of the criminal laws of the United States.

The judgment of the Court of Appeals is therefore reversed, and the case is remanded for further proceedings consistent with this opinion.

Justice Stevens, with whom Justice Blackmun and Justice O'Connor join, dissenting.

The Court correctly observes that this case raises a question of first impression. The case is unique for several reasons. It does not involve an ordinary abduction by a private kidnaper, or bounty hunter, as in *Ker v. Illinois,* 119 U.S. 436 (1886); nor does it involve the apprehension of an American fugitive who committed a crime in one State and sought asylum in another, as in *Frisbie v. Collins,* 342 U.S. 519 (1952). Rather, it involves this country's abduction of another country's citizen; it also involves a violation of the territorial integrity of that other country, with which this country has signed an extradition treaty.

A Mexican citizen was kidnaped in Mexico and charged with a crime committed in Mexico; his offense allegedly violated both Mexican and American law. Mexico has formally demanded on at least two separate occasions[1] that he be returned to Mexico and has represented that he will be prosecuted and, if convicted, punished for his offense.[2] It is clear that Mexico's demand must be honored if this official abduction violated the 1978 Extradition Treaty between the United States and Mexico. In my opinion, a fair reading of the treaty in light of our decision in *United States v. Rauscher,* 119 U.S. 407 (1886), and applicable principles of international law, leads inexorably to the conclusion that the District Court and the Court of Appeals for the Ninth Circuit correctly construed that instrument.

The extradition treaty with Mexico is a comprehensive document containing 23 articles and an appendix listing the extraditable offenses covered by the agreement. The parties announced their purpose in the preamble: The two governments desire "to cooperate more closely in the fight against crime and, to this end, to mutually render better assistance in matters of extradition." From the preamble, through the

---

1. The abduction of respondent occurred on April 2, 1990. Mexico responded quickly and unequivocally. On April 18, 1990, Mexico requested an official report on the role of the United States in the abduction, and on May 16, 1990, and July 19, 1990, it sent diplomatic notes of protest from the Embassy of Mexico to the United States Department of State. In the May 16th note, Mexico said that it believed that the abduction was "carried out with the knowledge of persons working for the U.S. government, in violation of the procedure established in the extradition treaty in force between the two countries" and in the July 19th note, it requested the provisional arrest and extradition of the law enforcement agents allegedly involved in the abduction.

2. Mexico has already tried a number of members involved in the conspiracy that resulted in the murder of the Drug Enforcement Administration agent. For example, Rafael -Caro-Quintero, a co-conspirator of Alvarez-Machain in this case, has already been imprisoned in Mexico on a 40-year sentence.

description of the parties' obligations with respect to offenses committed within as well as beyond the territory of a requesting party, the delineation of the procedures and evidentiary requirements for extradition, the special provisions for political offenses and capital punishment, and other details, the Treaty appears to have been designed to cover the entire subject of extradition. Thus, Article 22, entitled "Scope of Application," states that the "Treaty shall apply to offenses specified in Article 2 committed before and after this Treaty enters into force," and Article 2 directs that "extradition shall take place, subject to this Treaty, for willful acts which fall within any of [the extraditable offenses listed in] the clauses of the Appendix." Moreover, as noted by the Court, Article 9 expressly provides that neither contracting party is bound to deliver up its own nationals, although it may do so in its discretion, but if it does not do so, it "shall submit the case to its competent authorities for purposes of prosecution."

The Government's claim that the Treaty is not exclusive, but permits forcible governmental kidnaping, would transform these, and other, provisions into little more than verbiage. For example, provisions requiring "sufficient" evidence to grant extradition, withholding extradition for political or military offenses, withholding extradition when the person sought has already been tried, withholding extradition when the statute of limitations for the crime has lapsed, and granting the requested country discretion to refuse to extradite an individual who would face the death penalty in the requesting country, would serve little purpose if the requesting country could simply kidnap the person. As the Court of Appeals for the Ninth Circuit recognized in a related case, "each of these provisions would be utterly frustrated if a kidnapping were held to be a permissible course of governmental conduct." In addition, all of these provisions "only make sense if they are understood as *requiring* each treaty signatory to comply with those procedures whenever it wishes to obtain jurisdiction over an individual who is located in another treaty nation."

It is true, as the Court notes, that there is no express promise by either party to refrain from forcible abductions in the territory of the other nation. Relying on that omission, the Court, in effect, concludes that the Treaty merely creates an optional method of obtaining jurisdiction over alleged offenders, and that the parties silently reserved the right to resort to self-help whenever they deem force more expeditious than legal process.[11] If the United States, for example, thought it more expedient to torture or simply to execute a person rather than to attempt extradition, these options would be equally available because they, too, were not explicitly prohibited by the Treaty.[12] That, however, is a highly improbable interpretation of a consensual

11. To make the point more starkly, the Court has, in effect, written into Article 9 a new provision, which says: "Notwithstanding paragraphs 1 and 2 of this Article, either Contracting Party can, without the consent of the other, abduct nationals from the territory of one Party to be tried in the territory of the other."

12. It is ironic that the United States has attempted to justify its unilateral action based on the kidnaping, torture, and murder of a federal agent by authorizing the kidnaping of respondent, for which the American law enforcement agents who participated have now been charged by Mexico.

agreement, which on its face appears to have been intended to set forth comprehensive and exclusive rules concerning the subject of extradition. In my opinion, "the manifest scope and object of the treaty itself" plainly imply a mutual undertaking to respect the territorial integrity of the other contracting party.

In *Rauscher*, the Court construed an extradition treaty that was far less comprehensive than the 1978 Treaty with Mexico. The 1842 treaty with Great Britain determined the boundary between the United States and Canada, provided for the suppression of the African slave trade, and also contained one paragraph authorizing the extradition of fugitives "in certain cases." In Article X, each nation agreed to "deliver up to justice all persons" properly charged with any one of seven specific crimes, including murder. After Rauscher had been extradited for murder, he was charged with the lesser offense of inflicting cruel and unusual punishment on a member of the crew of a vessel on the high seas. Although the treaty did not purport to place any limit on the jurisdiction of the demanding state after acquiring custody of the fugitive, this Court held that he could not be tried for any offense other than murder. Thus, the treaty constituted the exclusive means by which the United States could obtain jurisdiction over a defendant within the territorial jurisdiction of Great Britain.

The Court noted that the treaty included several specific provisions, such as the crimes for which one could be extradited, the process by which the extradition was to be carried out, and even the evidence that was to be produced, and concluded that "the fair purpose of the treaty is, that the person shall be delivered up to be tried for that offence and for no other." The Court reasoned that it did not make sense for the treaty to provide such specifics only to have the person "pas[s] into the hands of the country which charges him with the offence, free from all the positive requirements and just implications of the treaty under which the transfer of his person takes place." To interpret the treaty in a contrary way would mean that a country could request extradition of a person for one of the seven crimes covered by the treaty, and then try the person for another crime, such as a political crime, which was clearly not covered by the treaty; this result, the Court concluded, was clearly contrary to the intent of the parties and the purpose of the treaty.

Thus, the Extradition Treaty, as understood in the context of cases that have addressed similar issues, suffices to protect the defendant from prosecution despite the absence of any express language in the Treaty itself purporting to limit this Nation's power to prosecute a defendant over whom it had lawfully acquired jurisdiction.

Although the Court's conclusion in *Rauscher* was supported by a number of judicial precedents, the holdings in these cases were not nearly as uniform[19] as the

---

This goes to my earlier point that extradition treaties promote harmonious relations by providing for the orderly surrender of a person by one state to another, and without such treaties, resort to force often followed.

19. In fact, both parties noted in their respective briefs several authorities that had held that a person could be tried for an offense other than the one for which he had been extradited.

consensus of international opinion that condemns one nation's violation of the territorial integrity of a friendly neighbor. It is shocking that a party to an extradition treaty might believe that it has secretly reserved the right to make seizures of citizens in the other party's territory.[21] Justice Story found it shocking enough that the United States would attempt to justify an American seizure of a foreign vessel in a Spanish port: "But, even supposing, for a moment, that our laws had required an entry of The Apollon, in her transit, does it follow that the power to arrest her was meant to be given, after she had passed into the exclusive territory of a foreign nation? We think not. *It would be monstrous* to suppose that our revenue officers were authorized to enter into foreign ports and territories, for the purpose of seizing vessels which had offended against our laws. It cannot be presumed that congress would voluntarily justify such a clear violation of the laws of nations." *The Apollon*, 22 U.S. 362 (1824) (emphasis added).

The law of nations, as understood by Justice Story in 1824, has not changed. Thus, a leading treatise explains: "A State must not perform acts of sovereignty in the territory of another State.... It is ... a breach of International Law for a State to send its agents to the territory of another State to apprehend persons accused of having committed a crime. Apart from other satisfaction, the first duty of the offending State is to hand over the person in question to the State in whose territory he was apprehended." 1 Oppenheim's International Law 295, and n. 1 (H. Lauterpacht 8th ed. 1955).[23]

In the *Rauscher* case, the legal background that supported the decision to imply a covenant not to prosecute for an offense different from that for which extradition had been granted was far less clear than the rule against invading the territorial integrity of a treaty partner that supports Mexico's position in this case. If *Rauscher* was correctly decided—and I am convinced that it was—its rationale clearly dictates a comparable result in this case.

A critical flaw pervades the Court's entire opinion. It fails to differentiate between the conduct of private citizens, which does not violate any treaty obligation, and conduct expressly authorized by the Executive Branch of the Government, which unquestionably constitutes a flagrant violation of international law, and in my opinion, also constitutes a breach of our treaty obligations. Thus, at the outset of its opinion, the Court states the issue as "whether a criminal defendant, abducted to the United States from a nation with which it has an extradition treaty, thereby

---

21. When Abraham Sofaer, Legal Adviser of the State Department, was questioned at a congressional hearing, he resisted the notion that such seizures were acceptable: "'Can you imagine us going into Paris and seizing some person we regard as a terrorist ... ? How would we feel if some foreign nation—let us take the United Kingdom—came over here and seized some terrorist suspect in New York City, or Boston, or Philadelphia, ... because we refused through the normal channels of international, legal communications, to extradite that individual?'"

23. *See* Restatement § 432, Comment c ("If the unauthorized action includes abduction of a person, the state from which the person was abducted may demand return of the person, and international law requires that he be returned").

acquires a defense to the jurisdiction of this country's courts." That, of course, is the question decided in *Ker v. Illinois,* 119 U.S. 436 (1886); it is not, however, the question presented for decision today.

The importance of the distinction between a court's exercise of jurisdiction over either a person or property that has been wrongfully seized by a private citizen, or even by a state law enforcement agent, on the one hand, and the attempted exercise of jurisdiction predicated on a seizure by federal officers acting beyond the authority conferred by treaty, on the other hand, is explained by Justice Brandeis in his opinion for the Court in *Cook v. United States,* 288 U.S. 102 (1933). That case involved a construction of a Prohibition Era treaty with Great Britain that authorized American agents to board certain British vessels to ascertain whether they were engaged in importing alcoholic beverages. A British vessel was boarded 11 1/2 miles off the coast of Massachusetts, found to be carrying unmanifested alcoholic beverages, and taken into port. The Collector of Customs assessed a penalty which he attempted to collect by means of libels against both the cargo and the seized vessel.

The Court held that the seizure was not authorized by the treaty because it occurred more than 10 miles off shore. The Government argued that the illegality of the seizure was immaterial because, as in *Ker,* the court's jurisdiction was supported by possession even if the seizure was wrongful. Justice Brandeis acknowledged that the argument would succeed if the seizure had been made by a private party without authority to act for the Government, but that a different rule prevails when the Government itself lacks the power to seize.

The same reasoning was employed by Justice Miller to explain why the holding in *Rauscher* did not apply to the *Ker* case. The arresting officer in *Ker* did not pretend to be acting in any official capacity when he kidnaped Ker. As Justice Miller noted, "the facts show that it was a clear case of kidnapping within the dominions of Peru, without any pretence of authority under the treaty *or from the government of the United States.*" *Ker v. Illinois,* 119 U.S. at 443 (emphasis added). The exact opposite is true in this case, as it was in *Cook.*

As the Court observes at the outset of its opinion, there is reason to believe that respondent participated in an especially brutal murder of an American law enforcement agent. That fact, if true, may explain the Executive's intense interest in punishing respondent in our courts. Such an explanation, however, provides no justification for disregarding the Rule of Law that this Court has a duty to uphold.[33]

---

33. As Justice Brandeis so wisely urged: "In a government of laws, existence of the government will be imperilled if it fails to observe the law scrupulously. Our Government is the potent, the omnipresent teacher. For good or for ill, it teaches the whole people by its example. Crime is contagious. If the Government becomes a law-breaker, it breeds contempt for law; it invites every man to become a law unto himself; it invites anarchy. To declare that in the administration of the criminal law the end justifies the means—to declare that the Government may commit crimes in order to secure the conviction of a private criminal—would bring terrible retribution. Against that

That the Executive may wish to reinterpret[34] the Treaty to allow for an action that the Treaty in no way authorizes should not influence this Court's interpretation. Indeed, the desire for revenge exerts "a kind of hydraulic pressure . . . before which even well settled principles of law will bend" but it is precisely at such moments that we should remember and be guided by our duty "to render judgment evenly and dispassionately according to law, as each is given understanding to ascertain and apply it." The way that we perform that duty in a case of this kind sets an example that other tribunals in other countries are sure to emulate.

The significance of this Court's precedents is illustrated by a recent decision of the Court of Appeal of the Republic of South Africa. Based largely on its understanding of the import of this Court's cases—including our decision in *Ker*—that court held that the prosecution of a defendant kidnaped by agents of South Africa in another country must be dismissed. *S* v. *Ebrahim*, S. Afr. L. Rep. (Apr.–June 1991). The Court of Appeal of South Africa—indeed, I suspect most courts throughout the civilized world—will be deeply disturbed by the "monstrous" decision the Court announces today. For every nation that has an interest in preserving the Rule of Law is affected, directly or indirectly, by a decision of this character.[37] As Thomas Paine warned, an "avidity to punish is always dangerous to liberty" because it leads a nation "to stretch, to misinterpret, and to misapply even the best of laws." To counter that tendency, he reminds us: "He that would make his own liberty secure must guard even his enemy from oppression; for if he violates this duty he establishes a precedent that will reach to himself."

I respectfully dissent.

Following the Supreme Court's decision, Humberto Alvarez-Machain was tried and acquitted. In 1993, he returned to Mexico and filed a civil action in the United States under the Federal Tort Claims Act, 28 U.S.C. §§ 1346(b)(1), and the Alien Tort Statute, 28 U.S.C. § 1350. Alvarez-Machain sued the United States for false arrest and sued the individuals (including four DEA agents) who were involved in his abduction for "a violation of the law of nations." The civil suit also made its way to the United States Supreme Court, where the Justices unanimously held against

---

pernicious doctrine this Court should resolutely set its face." *Olmstead v. United States,* 277 U.S. 438, 485, (1928) (dissenting opinion).

34. Certainly, the Executive's view has changed over time. At one point, the Office of Legal Counsel advised the administration that such seizures were contrary to international law because they compromised the territorial integrity of the other nation and were only to be undertaken with the consent of that nation. 4B Op. Off. Legal Counsel 549, 556 (1980). More recently, that opinion was revised, and the new opinion concluded that the President did have the authority to override customary international law. Hearing before the Subcommittee on Civil and Constitutional Rights of the House Committee on the Judiciary, 101st Cong., 1st Sess., 4–5 (1989) (statement of William P. Barr, Assistant Attorney General, Office of Legal Counsel, U.S. Department of Justice).

37. As Judge Mansfield presciently observed in a case not unlike the one before us today: "Society is the ultimate loser when, in order to convict the guilty, it uses methods that lead to decreased respect for the law." *United States v. Toscanino,* 500 F.2d 267, 274 (CA2 1974).

Alvarez-Machain, albeit with some disagreement as to the legal rationale. *Sosa v. Alvarez-Machain*, 542 U.S. 692 (2004).

Not surprisingly, the U.S. practice of kidnapping Mexican citizens for drug prosecutions only contributed to Mexico's reluctance to extradite its nationals to the United States. *See, e.g.*, María Celia Toro, *The Internationalization of Police: The DEA in Mexico*, 86 J. AM. HIST. 623, 636 (1999) ("The kidnapping of Alvarez Machaín, for instance, had an immediate effect on Mexico's laws regarding DEA agents in its territory."). In recent years, however, "Mexico's long-standing reluctance to extradite has vanished." Devin C. McNulty, *The Changing Face of Extraditions Between Mexico and the United States*, 31 CHAMPION 32 (2007) (describing how a number of developments, including the U.S. drug enforcement certification program, has led Mexico to begin extraditing its nationals to the U.S. for prosecution).

The DEA's involvement in kidnappings is a particularly striking example of the scope of the agency's drug enforcement efforts outside of the U.S. Since its creation in 1973, the DEA has been "transformed into a global intelligence organization with a reach that extends far beyond narcotics, and an eavesdropping operation so expansive it has to fend off foreign politicians who want to use it against their political enemies[.]" Ginger Thompson and Scott Shane, *Cables Portray Expanded Reach of Drug Agency*, N.Y. TIMES, Dec. 26, 2010 at A1. Today, the DEA has 87 offices in 63 countries and "has steadily built its international turf, an expansion primarily driven by the multinational nature of the drug trade, but also by forces within the agency seeking a larger mandate." *Ibid. See also, e.g.*, PETER ANDREAS AND ETHAN NADELMANN, POLICING THE GLOBE: CRIMINALIZATION AND CRIME CONTROL IN INTERNATIONAL RELATIONS 129 (2006) (noting that in 1967 the U.S. drug enforcement budget was approximately $3 million and only 12 U.S. drug agents were stationed outside of the U.S.).

Do constitutional constraints on police investigations within the U.S. apply to investigations by U.S. drug enforcement agents abroad?

United States v. Verdugo-Urquidez

Supreme Court of the United States
494 U.S. 259 (1990)

Chief Justice Rehnquist delivered the opinion of the Court.

The question presented by this case is whether the Fourth Amendment applies to the search and seizure by United States agents of property that is owned by a nonresident alien and located in a foreign country. We hold that it does not.

Respondent Rene Martin Verdugo-Urquidez is a citizen and resident of Mexico. He is believed by the United States Drug Enforcement Agency (DEA)* to be one of

* The court's opinion mistakenly refers to the DEA as the "Drug Enforcement Agency." Its true name is the Drug Enforcement Administration. [*Footnote by casebook author.*]

the leaders of a large and violent organization in Mexico that smuggles narcotics into the United States. Based on a complaint charging respondent with various narcotics-related offenses, the Government obtained a warrant for his arrest on August 3, 1985. In January 1986, Mexican police officers, after discussions with United States marshals, apprehended Verdugo-Urquidez in Mexico and transported him to the United States Border Patrol station in Calexico, California. There, United States marshals arrested respondent and eventually moved him to a correctional center in San Diego, California, where he remains incarcerated pending trial.

Following respondent's arrest, Terry Bowen, a DEA agent assigned to the Calexico DEA office, decided to arrange for searches of Verdugo-Urquidez's Mexican residences located in Mexicali and San Felipe. Bowen believed that the searches would reveal evidence related to respondent's alleged narcotics trafficking activities and his involvement in the kidnaping and torture-murder of DEA Special Agent Enrique Camarena Salazar (for which respondent subsequently has been convicted in a separate prosecution). Bowen telephoned Walter White, the Assistant Special Agent in charge of the DEA office in Mexico City, and asked him to seek authorization for the search from the Director General of the Mexican Federal Judicial Police (MFJP). After several attempts to reach high ranking Mexican officials, White eventually contacted the Director General, who authorized the searches and promised the cooperation of Mexican authorities. Thereafter, DEA agents working in concert with officers of the MFJP searched respondent's properties in Mexicali and San Felipe and seized certain documents. In particular, the search of the Mexicali residence uncovered a tally sheet, which the Government believes reflects the quantities of marijuana smuggled by Verdugo-Urquidez into the United States.

The District Court granted respondent's motion to suppress evidence seized during the searches, concluding that the Fourth Amendment applied to the searches and that the DEA agents had failed to justify searching respondent's premises without a warrant. A divided panel of the Court of Appeals for the Ninth Circuit affirmed. It cited this Court's decision in *Reid v. Covert*, 354 U.S. 1 (1957), which held that American citizens tried by United States military authorities in a foreign country were entitled to the protections of the Fifth and Sixth Amendments, and concluded that "The Constitution imposes substantive constraints on the federal government, even when it operates abroad." Relying on our decision in *INS v. Lopez-Mendoza*, 468 U.S. 1032 (1984), where a majority of Justices assumed that illegal aliens in the United States have Fourth Amendment rights, the Ninth Circuit majority found it "difficult to conclude that Verdugo-Urquidez lacks these same protections." It also observed that persons in respondent's position enjoy certain trial-related rights, and reasoned that "it would be odd indeed to acknowledge that Verdugo-Urquidez is entitled to due process under the fifth amendment, and to a fair trial under the sixth amendment, . . . and deny him the protection from unreasonable searches and seizures afforded under the fourth amendment." Having concluded that the Fourth Amendment applied to the searches of respondent's properties, the court went on to decide that the searches violated the Constitution because the DEA agents failed to procure a search warrant. Although recognizing that "an American search warrant would be of no legal validity in Mexico," the majority deemed it sufficient that a warrant would have "substantial constitutional value in this country," because it would reflect a magistrate's determination that there existed probable cause to search and would define the scope of the search.

The dissenting judge argued that this Court's statement in *United States v. Curtiss-Wright Export Corp.*, 299 U.S. 304, 318 (1936), that "neither the Constitution nor the laws passed in pursuance of it have any force in foreign territory unless in respect of our own citizens," foreclosed any claim by respondent to Fourth Amendment rights. More broadly, he viewed the Constitution as a "compact" among the people of the United States, and the protections of the Fourth Amendment were expressly limited to "the people." We granted certiorari.

Before analyzing the scope of the Fourth Amendment, we think it significant to note that it operates in a different manner than the Fifth Amendment, which is not at issue in this case. The privilege against self-incrimination guaranteed by the Fifth Amendment is a fundamental trial right of criminal defendants. Although conduct by law enforcement officials prior to trial may ultimately impair that right, a constitutional violation occurs only at trial. The Fourth Amendment functions differently. It prohibits "unreasonable searches and seizures" whether or not the evidence is sought to be used in a criminal trial, and a violation of the Amendment is "fully accomplished" at the time of an unreasonable governmental intrusion. For purposes of this case, therefore, if there were a constitutional violation, it occurred solely in Mexico. Whether evidence obtained from respondent's Mexican residences should be excluded at trial in the United States is a remedial question separate from the existence *vel non* of the constitutional violation.

The Fourth Amendment provides: "The right of the people to be secure in their persons, houses, papers, and effects, against unreasonable searches and seizures, shall not be violated, and no Warrants shall issue, but upon probable cause, supported by Oath or affirmation, and particularly describing the place to be searched, and the persons or things to be seized."

That text, by contrast with the Fifth and Sixth Amendments, extends its reach only to "the people." Contrary to the suggestion of *amici curiae* that the Framers used this phrase "simply to avoid [an] awkward rhetorical redundancy," "the people" seems to have been a term of art employed in select parts of the Constitution. The Preamble declares that the Constitution is ordained and established by "the People of the United States." The Second Amendment protects "the right of the people to keep and bear Arms," and the Ninth and Tenth Amendments provide that certain rights and powers are retained by and reserved to "the people." While this textual exegesis is by no means conclusive, it suggests that "the people" protected by the Fourth Amendment, and by the First and Second Amendments, and to whom rights and powers are reserved in the Ninth and Tenth Amendments, refers to a class of persons who are part of a national community or who have otherwise developed sufficient connection with this country to be considered part of that community.

See *United States ex rel. Turner v. Williams*, 194 U.S. 279, 292 (1904) (Excludable alien is not entitled to First Amendment rights, because "he does not become one of the people to whom these things are secured by our Constitution by an attempt to enter forbidden by law"). The language of these Amendments contrasts with the words "person" and "accused" used in the Fifth and Sixth Amendments regulating procedure in criminal cases.

What we know of the history of the drafting of the Fourth Amendment also suggests that its purpose was to restrict searches and seizures which might be conducted by the United States in domestic matters. The Framers originally decided not to include a provision like the Fourth Amendment, because they believed the National Government lacked power to conduct searches and seizures. Many disputed the original view that the Federal Government possessed only narrow delegated powers over domestic affairs, however, and ultimately felt an Amendment prohibiting unreasonable searches and seizures was necessary. Madison, for example, argued that "there is a clause granting to Congress the power to make all laws which shall be necessary and proper for carrying into execution all of the powers vested in the Government of the United States," and that general warrants might be considered "necessary" for the purpose of collecting revenue. The driving force behind the adoption of the Amendment, as suggested by Madison's advocacy, was widespread hostility among the former colonists to the issuance of writs of assistance empowering revenue officers to search suspected places for smuggled goods, and general search warrants permitting the search of private houses, often to uncover papers that might be used to convict persons of libel. The available historical data show, therefore, that the purpose of the Fourth Amendment was to protect the people of the United States against arbitrary action by their own Government; it was never suggested that the provision was intended to restrain the actions of the Federal Government against aliens outside of the United States territory.

There is likewise no indication that the Fourth Amendment was understood by contemporaries of the Framers to apply to activities of the United States directed against aliens in foreign territory or in international waters. Only seven years after the ratification of the Amendment, French interference with American commercial vessels engaged in neutral trade triggered what came to be known as the "undeclared war" with France. In an Act to "protect the Commerce of the United States" in 1798, Congress authorized President Adams to "instruct the commanders of the public armed vessels which are, or which shall be employed in the service of the United States, to subdue, seize and take any armed French vessel, which shall be found within the jurisdictional limits of the United States, or elsewhere, on the high seas." This public naval force consisted of only 45 vessels, so Congress also gave the President power to grant to the owners of private armed ships and vessels of the United States "special commissions," which would allow them "the same license and authority for the subduing, seizing and capturing any armed French vessel, and for the recapture of the vessels, goods and effects of the people of the United States, as the public armed vessels of the United States may by law have." Under the latter provision, 365 private armed vessels were commissioned before March 1, 1799; together, these enactments resulted in scores of seizures of foreign vessels under congressional authority. Some commanders were held liable by this Court for unlawful seizures because their actions were beyond the scope of the congressional grant of authority, but it was never suggested that the Fourth Amendment restrained the authority of congress or of United States agents to conduct operations such as this.

The global view taken by the Court of Appeals of the application of the Constitution is also contrary to this Court's decisions in the *Insular Cases,* which held that not every constitutional provision applies to governmental activity even where the United States has sovereign power. See, *e.g., Balzac v. Porto Rico,* 258 U.S. 298 (1922) (Sixth Amendment right to jury trial inapplicable in Puerto Rico); *Dorr v. United States,* 195 U.S. 138 (1904) (jury trial provision inapplicable in Philippines). In *Dorr,* we declared the general rule that in an unincorporated territory—one not clearly destined for statehood—Congress was not required to adopt "a system of laws which shall include the right of trial by jury, and that *the Constitution does not, without legislation and of its own force, carry such right to territory so situated.*" 195 U.S., at 149 (emphasis added). Only "fundamental" constitutional rights are guaranteed to inhabitants of those territories. If that is true with respect to territories ultimately governed by Congress, respondent's claim that the protections of the Fourth Amendment extend to aliens in foreign nations is even weaker. And certainly, it is not open to us in light of the *Insular Cases* to endorse the view that every constitutional provision applies wherever the United States Government exercises its power.

To support his all-encompassing view of the Fourth Amendment, respondent points to language from the plurality opinion in *Reid v. Covert,* 354 U.S. 1 (1957). *Reid* involved an attempt by Congress to subject the wives of American servicemen to trial by military tribunals without the protection of the Fifth and Sixth Amendments. The Court held that it was unconstitutional to apply the Uniform Code of Military Justice to the trials of the American women for capital crimes. Four Justices "rejected the idea that when the United States acts *against citizens* abroad it can do so free of the Bill of Rights." *Id., at 5* (emphasis added).

Respondent urges that we interpret this discussion to mean that federal officials are constrained by the Fourth Amendment wherever and against whomever they act. But the holding of *Reid* stands for no such sweeping proposition: it decided that United States citizens stationed abroad could invoke the protection of the Fifth and Sixth Amendments. The concurring opinions by Justices Frankfurter and Harlan in *Reid* resolved the case on much narrower grounds than the plurality and declined even to hold that United States citizens were entitled to the full range of constitutional protections in all overseas criminal prosecutions. Since respondent is not a United States citizen, he can derive no comfort from the *Reid* holding.

Verdugo-Urquidez also relies on a series of cases in which we have held that aliens enjoy certain constitutional rights. See, *e.g., Plyler v. Doe,* 457 U.S. 202, 211–212 (1982) (illegal aliens protected by Equal Protection Clause); *Kwong Hai Chew v. Colding, 344 U.S. 590, 596 (1953)* (resident alien is a "person" within the meaning of the Fifth Amendment). These cases, however, establish only that aliens receive constitutional protections when they have come within the territory of the United States and developed substantial connections with the country. See, *e.g., Plyler, supra,* at 212 (The provisions of the Fourteenth Amendment "'are universal in their application, *to all persons within the territorial jurisdiction* . . .'"). Respondent is an alien who has had no previous significant voluntary connection with the United States, so these cases avail him not.

Justice Stevens' concurrence in the judgment takes the view that even though the search took place in Mexico, it is nonetheless governed by the requirements of the Fourth Amendment because respondent was "lawfully present in the United States . . . even though he was brought and held here against his will." But this sort of presence—lawful but involuntary—is not of the sort to indicate any substantial connection with our country. The extent to which respondent might claim the protection of the Fourth Amendment if the duration of his stay in the United States were to be prolonged—by a prison sentence, for example—we need not decide. When the search of his house in Mexico took place, he had been present in the United States for only a matter of days. We do not think the applicability of the Fourth Amendment to the search of premises in Mexico should turn on the fortuitous circumstance of whether the custodian of its nonresident alien owner had or had not transported him to the United States at the time the search was made.

The Court of Appeals found some support for its holding in our decision in *INS v. Lopez-Mendoza,* 468 U.S. 1032 (1984), where a majority of Justices assumed that the Fourth Amendment applied to illegal aliens in the United States. We cannot fault the Court of Appeals for placing some reliance on the case, but our decision did not expressly address the proposition gleaned by the court below. The question presented for decision in *Lopez-Mendoza* was limited to whether the Fourth Amendment's exclusionary rule should be extended to civil deportation proceedings; it did not encompass whether the protections of the Fourth Amendment extend to illegal aliens in this country. The Court often grants certiorari to decide particular legal issues while assuming without deciding the validity of antecedent propositions and such assumptions—even on jurisdictional issues—are not binding in future cases that directly raise the questions. Our statements in *Lopez-Mendoza* are therefore not dispositive of how the Court would rule on a Fourth Amendment claim by illegal aliens in the United States if such a claim were squarely before us. Even assuming such aliens would be entitled to Fourth Amendment protections, their situation is different from respondent's. The illegal aliens in *Lopez-Mendoza* were in the United States voluntarily and presumably had accepted some societal obligations; but respondent had no voluntary connection with this country that might place him among "the people" of the United States.

Not only are history and case law against respondent, but as pointed out in *Johnson v. Eisentrager,* 393 U.S. 763 (1950), the result of accepting his claim would have significant and deleterious consequences for the United States in conducting activities beyond its boundaries. The rule adopted by the Court of Appeals would apply not only to law enforcement operations abroad, but also to other foreign policy operations which might result in "searches or seizures." The United States frequently employs armed forces outside this country—over 200 times in our history—for the protection of American citizens or national security. Application of the Fourth Amendment to those circumstances could significantly disrupt the ability of the political branches to respond to foreign situations involving our national interest. Were respondent to prevail, aliens with no attachment to this country might well bring actions for damages to remedy claimed violations of the Fourth Amendment in foreign countries or in international waters.

We think that the text of the Fourth Amendment, its history, and our cases discussing the application of the Constitution to aliens and extraterritorially require rejection of respondent's claim. At the time of the search, he was a citizen and resident of Mexico with no voluntary attachment to the United States, and the place searched was located in Mexico. Under these circumstances, the Fourth Amendment has no application.

For better or for worse, we live in a world of nation-states in which our Government must be able to "function effectively in the company of sovereign nations." Some who violate our laws may live outside our borders under a regime quite different from that which obtains in this country. Situations threatening to important American interests may arise halfway around the globe, situations which in the view of the political branches of our Government require an American response with armed force. If there are to be restrictions on searches and seizures which occur incident to such American action, they must be imposed by the political branches through diplomatic understanding, treaty, or legislation.

The judgment of the Court of Appeals is accordingly

Reversed.

Justice Kennedy, concurring.

I agree that no violation of the Fourth Amendment has occurred and that we must reverse the judgment of the Court of Appeals. Although some explanation of my views is appropriate given the difficulties of this case, I do not believe they depart in fundamental respects from the opinion of the Court, which I join.

I cannot place any weight on the reference to "the people" in the Fourth Amendment as a source of restricting its protections. With respect, I submit these words do not detract from its force or its reach. Given the history of our Nation's concern over warrantless and unreasonable searches, explicit recognition of "the right of the people" to Fourth Amendment protection may be interpreted to underscore the importance of the right, rather than to restrict the category of persons who may assert it. The restrictions that the United States must observe with reference to aliens beyond its territory or jurisdiction depend, as a consequence, on general principles of interpretation, not on an inquiry as to who formed the Constitution or a construction that some rights are mentioned as being those of "the people."

I take it to be correct, as the plurality opinion in *Reid* v. *Covert* sets forth, that the Government may act only as the Constitution authorizes, whether the actions in question are foreign or domestic. But this principle is only a first step in resolving this case. The question before us then becomes what constitutional standards apply when the Government acts, in reference to an alien, within its sphere of foreign operations. [W]e must interpret constitutional protections in light of the undoubted power of the United States to take actions to assert its legitimate power and authority abroad.

The conditions and considerations of this case would make adherence to the Fourth Amendment's warrant requirement impracticable and anomalous. Just as the Constitution in the *Insular Cases* did not require Congress to implement all constitutional guarantees in its territories because of their "wholly dissimilar traditions and institutions," the Constitution does not require United States agents to obtain a warrant when searching the foreign home of a nonresident alien. If the search had occurred in a residence within the United States, I have little doubt that the full protections of the Fourth Amendment would apply. But that is not this case. The absence of local judges or magistrates available to issue warrants, the differing and perhaps unascertainable conceptions of reasonableness and privacy that prevail abroad, and the need to cooperate with foreign officials all indicate that the Fourth Amendment's warrant requirement should not apply in Mexico as it does in this country. For this reason, in addition to the other persuasive justifications stated by the Court, I agree that no violation of the Fourth Amendment has occurred in the case before us. The rights of a citizen, as to whom the United States has continuing obligations, are not presented by this case.

I do not mean to imply, and the Court has not decided, that persons in the position of the respondent have no constitutional protection. The United States is prosecuting a foreign national in a court established under Article III, and all of the trial proceedings are governed by the Constitution. All would agree, for instance, that the dictates of the Due Process Clause of the Fifth Amendment protect the defendant. Indeed, as Justice Harlan put it, "the question of which specific safeguards . . . are appropriately to be applied in a particular context . . . can be reduced to the issue of what process is 'due' a defendant in the particular circumstances of a particular case." Nothing approaching a violation of due process has occurred in this case.

Justice Stevens, concurring in the judgment.

In my opinion aliens who are lawfully present in the United States are among those "people" who are entitled to the protection of the Bill of Rights, including the Fourth Amendment. Respondent is surely such a person even though he was brought and held here against his will. I therefore cannot join the Court's sweeping opinion. I do agree, however, with the Government's submission that the search conducted by the United States agents with the approval and cooperation of the Mexican authorities was not "unreasonable" as that term is used in the first Clause of the Amendment. I do not believe the Warrant Clause has any application to searches of noncitizens' homes in foreign jurisdictions because American magistrates have no power to authorize such searches. I therefore concur in the Court's judgment.

Justice Brennan, with whom Justice Marshall joins, dissenting.

Today the Court holds that although foreign nationals must abide by our laws even when in their own countries, our Government need not abide by the Fourth Amendment when it investigates them for violations of our laws. I respectfully dissent.

Particularly in the past decade, our Government has sought, successfully, to hold foreign nationals criminally liable under federal laws for conduct committed entirely beyond the territorial limits of the United States that nevertheless has effects in this country. Foreign nationals must now take care not to violate our drug laws,[1] our antitrust laws, our securities laws, and a host of other federal criminal statutes. The enormous expansion of federal criminal jurisdiction outside our Nation's boundaries has led one commentator to suggest that our country's three largest exports are now "rock music, blue jeans, and United States law." Grundman, *The New Imperialism: The Extraterritorial Application of United States Law,* 14 Int'l Law. 257, 257 (1980).

The Constitution is the source of Congress' authority to criminalize conduct, whether here or abroad, and of the Executive's authority to investigate and prosecute such conduct. But the same Constitution also prescribes limits on our Government's authority to investigate, prosecute, and punish criminal conduct, whether foreign or domestic. As a plurality of the Court noted in *Reid v. Covert,* 354 U.S. 1, 5–6 (1957): "The United States is entirely a creature of the Constitution. Its power and authority have no other source. It can only act in accordance with all the limitations imposed by the Constitution."

The Court today creates an antilogy: the Constitution authorizes our Government to enforce our criminal laws abroad, but when Government agents exercise this authority, the Fourth Amendment does not travel with them. This cannot be. At the very least, the Fourth Amendment is an unavoidable correlative of the Government's power to enforce the criminal law.

The Fourth Amendment guarantees the right of "the people" to be free from unreasonable searches and seizures and provides that a warrant shall issue only upon presentation of an oath or affirmation demonstrating probable cause and particularly describing the place to be searched and the persons or things to be seized. According to the majority, the term "the people" refers to "a class of persons who are

---

1. Federal drug enforcement statutes written broadly enough to permit extraterritorial application include laws proscribing the manufacture, distribution, or possession with intent to manufacture or distribute of controlled substances on board vessels, see 46 U.S.C. App. § 1903(h) (1982 ed., Supp. V) ("This section is intended to reach acts . . . committed outside the territorial jurisdiction of the United States"), the possession, manufacture, or distribution of a controlled substance for purposes of unlawful importation, see 21 U.S.C. § 959(c) (same), and conspiracy to violate federal narcotics laws, see *Chua Han Mow v. United States,* 730 F.2d 1308, 1311–1312 (CA9 1984) (applying 21 U.S.C. §§ 846 and 963 to conduct by a Malaysian citizen in Malaysia).

part of a national community or who have otherwise developed sufficient connection with this country to be considered part of that community." The Court admits that "the people" extends beyond the citizenry, but leaves the precise contours of its "sufficient connection" test unclear. At one point the majority hints that aliens are protected by the Fourth Amendment only when they come within the United States and develop "substantial connections" with our country. At other junctures, the Court suggests that an alien's presence in the United States must be voluntary and that the alien must have "accepted some societal obligations." At yet other points, the majority implies that respondent would be protected by the Fourth Amendment if the place searched were in the United States.

What the majority ignores, however, is the most obvious connection between Verdugo-Urquidez and the United States: he was investigated and is being prosecuted for violations of United States law and may well spend the rest of his life in a United States prison. The "sufficient connection" is supplied not by Verdugo-Urquidez, but by the Government. Respondent is entitled to the protections of the Fourth Amendment because our Government, by investigating him and attempting to hold him accountable under United States criminal laws, has treated him as a member of our community for purposes of enforcing our laws. He has become, quite literally, one of the governed. Fundamental fairness and the ideals underlying our Bill of Rights compel the conclusion that when we impose "societal obligations," such as the obligation to comply with our criminal laws, on foreign nationals, we in turn are obliged to respect certain correlative rights, among them the Fourth Amendment.

By concluding that respondent is not one of "the people" protected by the Fourth Amendment, the majority disregards basic notions of mutuality. If we expect aliens to obey our laws, aliens should be able to expect that we will obey our Constitution when we investigate, prosecute, and punish them. We have recognized this fundamental principle of mutuality since the time of the Framers. James Madison, universally recognized as the primary architect of the Bill of Rights, emphasized the importance of mutuality when he spoke out against the Alien and Sedition Acts less than a decade after the adoption of the Fourth Amendment: "It does not follow, because aliens are not parties to the Constitution, as citizens are parties to it, that, whilst they actually conform to it, they have no right to its protection. Aliens are not more parties to the laws than they are parties to the Constitution; yet it will not be disputed that, as they owe, on one hand, a temporary obedience, they are entitled, in return, to their protection and advantage." Madison's Report on the Virginia Resolutions (1800), reprinted in 4 Elliot's Debates 556 (2d ed. 1836).

Mutuality is essential to ensure the fundamental fairness that underlies our Bill of Rights. Foreign nationals investigated and prosecuted for alleged violations of United States criminal laws are just as vulnerable to oppressive Government behavior as are United States citizens investigated and prosecuted for the same alleged violations. Indeed, in a case such as this where the Government claims the existence of an international criminal conspiracy, citizens and foreign nationals may be codefendants, charged under the same statutes for the same conduct and facing the same penalties if convicted. They may have been investigated by the same agents pursuant to the same enforcement authority. When our Government holds these codefendants to the same standards of conduct, the Fourth Amendment, which protects the citizen from unreasonable searches and seizures, should protect the foreign national as well.

Mutuality also serves to inculcate the values of law and order. By respecting the rights of foreign nationals, we encourage other nations to respect the rights of our citizens. Moreover, as our Nation becomes increasingly concerned about the domestic effects of international crime, we cannot forget that the behavior of our law enforcement agents abroad sends a powerful message about the rule of law to individuals everywhere.

If we seek respect for law and order, we must observe these principles ourselves. Lawlessness breeds lawlessness.

Finally, when United States agents conduct unreasonable searches, whether at home or abroad, they disregard our Nation's values. For over 200 years, our country has considered itself the world's foremost protector of liberties. The privacy and sanctity of the home have been primary tenets of our moral, philosophical, and judicial beliefs. Our national interest is defined by those values and by the need to preserve our own just institutions. We take pride in our commitment to a Government that cannot, on mere whim, break down doors and invade the most personal of places. We exhort other nations to follow our example. How can we explain to others—and to ourselves—that these long cherished ideals are suddenly of no consequence when the door being broken belongs to a foreigner?

In its effort to establish that respondent does not have sufficient connection to the United States to be considered one of "the people" protected by the Fourth Amendment, the Court relies on the text of the Amendment, historical evidence, and cases refusing to apply certain constitutional provisions outside the United States. None of these, however, justifies the majority's cramped interpretation of the Fourth Amendment's applicability.

The majority looks to various constitutional provisions and suggests that "'the people' seems to have been a term of art." But the majority admits that its "textual exegesis is by no means conclusive." The majority suggests a restrictive interpretation of those with "sufficient connection" to this country to be considered among "the people," but the term "the people" is better understood as a rhetorical counterpoint to "the Government," such that rights that were reserved to the "the people" were to protect all those subject to "the Government." "The people" are "the governed."

In drafting both the Constitution and the Bill of Rights, the Framers strove to create a form of Government decidedly different from their British heritage. Whereas the British Parliament was unconstrained, the Framers intended to create a Government of limited powers. The colonists considered the British government dangerously omnipotent. After all, the British declaration of rights in 1688 had been enacted not by the people, but by Parliament. Americans vehemently attacked the notion that rights were matters of "'favor and grace,'" given to the people from the Government.

Thus, the Framers of the Bill of Rights did not purport to "create" rights. Rather, they designed the Bill of Rights to prohibit our Government from infringing rights and liberties presumed to be pre-existing. See, e.g., U.S. Const., Amdt. 9 ("The enumeration in the Constitution of certain rights, shall not be construed to deny or disparage others retained by the people"). The Fourth Amendment, for example, does not create a new right of security against unreasonable searches and seizures. It states that "[t]he right of the people to be secure in their persons, houses, papers, and effects, against unreasonable searches and seizures, shall not be violated. . . ." The focus of the Fourth Amendment is on what the Government can and cannot do, and how it may act, not on against whom these actions may be taken. Bestowing rights and delineating protected groups would have been inconsistent with the drafters' fundamental conception of a Bill of Rights as a limitation on the Government's conduct with respect to all whom it seeks to govern. It is thus extremely unlikely that the Framers intended the narrow construction of the term "the people" presented today by the majority.

The Court also relies on a series of cases dealing with the application of criminal procedural protections outside of the United States to conclude that "not every constitutional provision applies to governmental activity even where the United States has sovereign power." None of these cases, however, purports to read the phrase "the people" as limiting the protections of the Fourth Amendment to those with "sufficient connection" to the United States, and thus none gives content to the majority's analysis. The cases shed no light on the question whether respondent—a citizen of a nonenemy nation being tried in a United States federal court—is one of "the people" protected by the Fourth Amendment.

The majority's rejection of respondent's claim to Fourth Amendment protection is apparently motivated by its fear that application of the Amendment to law enforcement searches against foreign nationals overseas "could significantly disrupt the ability of the political branches to respond to foreign situations involving our national interest." The majority's doomsday scenario—that American Armed Forces conducting a mission to protect our national security with no law enforcement objective "would have to articulate specific facts giving them probable cause to undertake a search or seizure"—is fanciful. Verdugo-Urquidez is protected by the Fourth Amendment because our Government, by investigating and prosecuting him, has made him one of "the governed." Accepting respondent as one of "the governed," however, hardly requires the Court to accept enemy aliens in wartime as among "the governed" entitled to invoke the protection of the Fourth Amendment.

Moreover, with respect to non-law-enforcement activities not directed against enemy aliens in wartime but nevertheless implicating national security, doctrinal exceptions to the general requirements of a warrant and probable cause likely would be applicable more frequently abroad, thus lessening the purported tension between the Fourth Amendment's strictures and the Executive's foreign affairs power. Many situations involving sensitive operations abroad likely would involve exigent circumstances such that the warrant requirement would be excused. Therefore, the Government's conduct would be assessed only under the reasonableness standard, the application of which depends on context.

In addition, where the precise contours of a "reasonable" search and seizure are unclear, the Executive Branch will not be "plunge[d] . . . into a sea of uncertainty" that will impair materially its ability to conduct foreign affairs. Doctrines such as official immunity have long protected Government agents from any undue chill on the exercise of lawful discretion. Similarly, the Court has recognized that there may be certain situations in which the offensive use of constitutional rights should be limited. In most cases implicating foreign policy concerns in which the reasonableness of an over-seas search or seizure in unclear, application of the Fourth Amendment will not interfere with the Executive's traditional prerogative in foreign affairs because a court will have occasion to decide the constitutionality of such a search only if the Executive decides to bring a criminal prosecution and introduce evidence seized abroad. When the Executive decides to conduct a search as part of an ongoing criminal investigation, fails to get a warrant, and then seeks to introduce the fruits of that search at trial, however, the courts must enforce the Constitution.

Because the Fourth Amendment governs the search of respondent's Mexican residences, the District Court suppressed the evidence found in that search because the officers conducting the search did not obtain a warrant. I cannot agree with Justice Blackmun and Justice Stevens that the Warrant Clause has no application to searches of noncitizens' homes in foreign jurisdictions because American magistrates lack the power to authorize such searches. The Warrant Clause would serve the same primary functions abroad as it does domestically, and I see no reason to distinguish between foreign and domestic searches.

The primary purpose of the warrant requirement is its assurance of neutrality. As Justice Jackson stated for the Court in *Johnson v. United States*, 333 U.S. 10, 13–14 (1948): "The point of the Fourth Amendment, which often is not grasped by zealous officers, is not that it denies law enforcement the support of the usual inferences which reasonable men draw from evidence. Its protection consists in requiring that those inferences be drawn by a neutral and detached magistrate instead of being judged by the officer engaged in the often competitive enterprise of ferreting out crime. When the right of privacy must reasonably yield to the right of search is, as a rule, to be decided by a judicial officer, not by a policeman or government enforcement agent." A warrant also defines the scope of a search and limits the discretion of the inspecting officers. These purposes would be served no less in the foreign than in the domestic context.

The Warrant Clause cannot be ignored simply because Congress has not given any United States magistrate authority to issue search warrants for foreign searches.

Congress cannot define the contours of the Constitution. If the Warrant Clause applies, Congress cannot excise the Clause from the Constitution by failing to provide a means for United States agents to obtain a warrant.

Nor is the Warrant Clause inapplicable merely because a warrant from a United States magistrate could not "authorize" a search in a foreign country. Although this may be true as a matter of international law, it is irrelevant to our interpretation of the Fourth Amendment. As a matter of United States constitutional law, a warrant serves the same primary function overseas as it does domestically; it assures that a neutral magistrate has authorized the search and limited its scope. The need to protect those suspected of criminal activity from the unbridled discretion of investigating officers is no less important abroad than at home.

When our Government conducts a law enforcement search against a foreign national outside of the United States and its territories, it must comply with the Fourth Amendment. Absent exigent circumstance or consent, it must obtain a search warrant from a United States court. When we tell the world that we expect all people, wherever they may be, to abide by our laws, we cannot in the same breath tell the world that our law enforcement officers need not do the same. Because we cannot expect others to respect our laws until we respect our Constitution, I respectfully dissent.

Justice Blackmun, dissenting.

I cannot accept the Court of Appeals' conclusion, echoed in some portions of Justice Brennan's dissent, that the Fourth Amendment governs every action by an American official that can be characterized as a search or seizure. American agents acting abroad generally do not purport to exercise sovereign authority over the foreign nationals with whom they come in contact.

I am inclined to agree with Justice Brennan, however, that when a foreign national is held accountable for purported violations of United States criminal laws, he has effectively been treated as one of "the governed" and therefore us entitled to Fourth Amendment protections. Although the Government's exercise of power abroad does not ordinarily implicate the Fourth Amendment, the enforcement of domestic criminal law seems to me to be the paradigmatic exercise of sovereignty over those who are compelled to obey. In any event, as Justice Stevens notes, respondent was lawfully (though involuntarily) within this country at the time the search occurred. Under these circumstances I believe that respondent is entitled to invoke protections of the Fourth Amendment. I agree with the Government, however, that an American magistrate's lack of power to authorize a search abroad renders the Warrant Clause inapplicable to the search of a noncitizen's residence outside this country.

The Fourth Amendment nevertheless requires that the search be "reasonable." And when the purpose of a search is the procurement of evidence for a criminal prosecution, we have consistently held that the search, to be reasonable, must be based upon probable cause. Neither the District Court not the Court of Appeals addressed the issue of probable cause, and I do not believe that a reliable determination could be made on the basis of the record before us. I therefore would vacate the judgment of the Court of Appeals and remand the case for further proceedings.

The increased presence of U.S. drug enforcement abroad extends beyond the DEA. Throughout the 1980s, the Reagan and Bush Administrations worked to integrate the nation's military into the "war on drugs." *See, e.g.*, Mark Bowden, Killing Pablo: The Hunt for the World's Greatest Outlaw 140 (2001) (reporting that in 1989, then-Defense Secretary Dick Cheney "sent a memo to all top military commanders directing them to define counterdrug efforts as 'a high priority mission' and requesting them to submit plans for increased military involvement" in drug enforcement); Sean J. Kealy, *Reexamining the Posse Comitatus Act: Toward a Right to Civil Law Enforcement,* 21 Yale L. & Pol'y Rev. 383 (2003). Today, both the U.S. military and private military contractors are involved in international drug enforcement work. The Defense Department's Counter Narco-Terrorism Program Office issues billions of dollars to private contractors for tasks ranging from training Naval Commandos in Azerbaijan to "building 'anti-terrorism/force protection enhancements' for the Pakistani border force in the tribal areas abutting Afghanistan." Spencer Ackerman, *Pentagon's War on Drugs Goes Mercenary,* Wired, Nov. 22, 2011.

4. Crop Eradication Initiatives

U.S. efforts to try to reduce the supply of drugs extend beyond interdiction. One particularly controversial supply reduction measure has been the fumigation of coca and opium crops. Critics of crop eradication policies argue that they cause environmental damage and displace farmers in developing countries without resulting in an overall decrease in drug production. A 2008 report by the Brookings Institute's Partnership for the America's Commission found that "[e]radication efforts have not delivered sustained reductions in drug production. Total coca leaf and cocaine production in the Andean region is currently at historic highs, with Colombia still the dominant producer." According to the report, eradication programs are not successful because they simply cause drug production to shift elsewhere. "Though policymakers can point to pockets of success at specific times in particular countries, counternarcotics policies have simply displaced cultivation and trafficking from one country or region to another, without reducing the overall supply of drugs." The report concludes that "[t]he only long-run solution to the problem of illegal narcotics is to reduce the demand for drugs in the major consuming countries, including the United States." *Rethinking U.S.-Latin American Relations: A Hemispheric Partnership for a Turbulent World, Report of the Partnership for the Americas Commission*, The Brookings Institution, 25–26 (2008).

Note: *A New Approach to Extraterritorial Application of Environmental Statutes? Uncovering the Effects of Plan Colombia*
Joanne Sum-Ping

31 Colombia Journal of Environmental Law 139 (2006)

The drug trade creates problems extending much further than the drugs themselves. In Colombia, both paramilitaries and insurgents admit to funding their operations through "taxes" levied on farmers of illicit crops and have been accused of direct involvement in drug production and trafficking. Referred to as the "Hobbesian Trinity," narco-traffickers, paramilitaries, and insurgents wage violent battles. This violence, which the Colombian government has been unable to control, has created a brutal society rife with kidnappings, tortures, murders, and other human rights abuses. These brutal conditions threaten democracy in Colombia and surrounding countries.

Despite the destructive nature of the drug trade, poor farmers in southern Colombia turn to drug crops because it is their best option to make a living—a farmer with a 3-acre cocaine field earns almost ten times the minimum wage of 1200 dollars a year. Further, while narco-traffickers pick up drug crops directly from farmers' fields, the roads, markets, and other infrastructural elements necessary to support legitimate crops do not exist in Colombia. As one opium farmer in southern Colombia explains, "Opium is bad for people, but what am I going to do? If there was something else to grow, I wouldn't touch it."

To address these problems, the U.S. Congress approved 1.289 billion dollars in aid to Colombia in 2000, a package that came to be known as Plan Colombia, with funding approved every year since. A major component of Plan Colombia is the aerial fumigation of coca (cocaine) and poppy (heroin) crops. Illegal crops are sprayed with a mixture of water, herbicide (glyphosate), and surfactants (polyoxyethylene alkylamine, cosmoflux 411f, and an unknown surfactant). Spray aircraft, escort helicopters, pilots, fuel, herbicide, and technical and scientific advice are provided by the U. S. Department of State.

This aerial fumigation is extremely unpopular among the Colombian people and some branches of the Colombian government. Governors of four Colombian provinces have spoken out against the herbicide sprayings for causing "economic destruction, environmental degradation and illness, including birth defects."

It is unclear whether the aerial fumigation is successful in decreasing the amount of drug crops grown in Colombia. Some reports indicate that after their fields are fumigated, drug farmers simply move their fields elsewhere in Colombia or to neighboring Peru and Bolivia. Known as the "balloon effect," this phenomenon results in the destruction of virgin rainforest to create new coca fields and irreversibly damages delicate ecosystems. Another source claims that land devoted to coca production has decreased by 38% in Colombia and by 22% in South America. A State Department official, while claiming that overall production of illicit crops in Colombia has decreased, conceded that production in some areas of Bolivia and Peru increased.

The glyphosate spraying has triggered many complaints of negative health effects including headaches, dizziness, fever, skin rashes, red eyes, and vomiting. In 2003, the Department of State logged thousands of health complaints related to the spraying, but dismissed all as caused by other factors.

The spraying also damages ecosystems. U.N. experts described an area in which a coca field was aerially eradicated as a "desolate scene" with "indiscriminate destruction of the jungle, legal crops, medicinal plants, and fish-ponds. There is clear evidence that wildlife has fled, rivers are contaminated and production in the region has fallen."

Furthermore, the herbicide spraying has profound economic and social effects. Many farmers have no other way to support themselves and "tens of thousands have fled the [coca growing] region, a vast exodus of poor, uneducated people looking for money to feed themselves in an economy in which unemployment hovers at 15%." These farmers converge in Colombia's cities or flee to neighboring countries, alarming those countries' governments. While some funding for alternative crop programs exists, alternative crop programs are not comprehensive and are only meant to last a few years. Without the infrastructure to assure long-term success, it is unlikely that these farmers will have any choice but to resume growing drug crops.

Several commentators have vehemently criticized Plan Colombia for its failure to provide viable economic alternatives to farmers. Noam Chomsky writes that "the 'drug war' is crafted to target poor peasants abroad and poor people at home; by the use of force, not constructive measures to alleviate the problems that allegedly motivate it, at a fraction of the cost." Another commentator argues, "emphasis on aerial eradication undermines the economic stability of the country, exacerbates international displacement, and creates resentment of the citizens toward the state, undermining citizen confidence." Finally, "the rural population of Colombia . . . is unlikely to be weaned off of drug traffickers or guerrillas without fundamental political reform and economic development. It will take the equivalent of a Marshall Plan to turn the tide."

Concerned about the potential environmental and social effects of aerial fumigation, Congress attached an environmental reporting requirement to the Foreign Operations Appropriations Act of 2002. This provision placed conditions on the funds to be used for herbicides and aerial fumigation of coca plants in Colombia. The Department of State was required to certify that "(1) aerial coca fumigation is being carried out in accordance with regulatory controls required by the Environmental Protection Agency as labeled for use in the United States, and after consultation with the Colombian Government to ensure that the fumigation is in accordance with Colombian laws; (2) the chemicals used in the aerial fumigation of coca, in the manner in which they are being applied, do not pose unreasonable risks or adverse effects to humans or the environment; and (3) procedures are available to evaluate claims of local citizens that their health was harmed or their licit agricultural crops were damaged by such aerial coca fumigation, and to provide fair compensation for meritorious claims; and such funds may not be made available for such purposes after six months from the date of enactment of this Act unless alternative development programs have been developed, in consultation with communities and local authorities in the departments in which such aerial coca fumigation is planned . . ." The certification requirement was renewed in 2003, 2004, and 2005.

In its 2002 Certification report, the State Department claimed that the glyphosate spraying in Colombia was being conducted in accordance with Congressional requirements. The report mentions that EPA expressed concern about the herbicide's potential for acute eye toxicity, and recommended use of a lower toxicity glyphosate formulation until further testing could be done. The Department promised to switch to a lower toxicity formula as soon as one became available.

In the 2003 report, the Department again claimed to have met Congress's requirements and noted that it had switched to lower toxicity glyphosate formula. In this report, the EPA expressed concern that the spray would drift and that nearby, non-targeted vegetation would be killed by the herbicide spraying. The Department reported that it was developing mechanisms and pilot training programs to minimize spray drift.

In the 2004 report, the Department noted that it had expanded monitoring of human and environmental issues related to Plan Colombia. According to this report, effects from spray drift are "temporary in nature and small in extent" and "to date, no relation of reported human health problems to spraying has been substantiated by the rigorous evaluations of toxicologists hired by the Embassy's Narcotics Affairs Section (NAS)." The 2005 report made similar claims.

These certification reports have been heavily criticized as misleading and incomplete. For example, the Institute for Science and Interdisciplinary Studies notes that the State Department report assumes that glyphosate is being used in accordance with the manufacturer's instructions, which is not the case in Colombia. The State Department also focuses its report on the effects of the herbicide itself, and does not take into account potential toxic effects of the added surfactant. The Inter-American Association for Environmental Defense raised similar concerns, adding that the State Department did not study health effects suffered by those directly sprayed with the herbicide mixture. The Senate Appropriations Committee also expressed dissatisfaction with the report, delaying the release of funding until after State Department staff appeared before the Senate to answer questions.

However, even if it were established that the Department of State did not fulfill the environmental conditions attached to Plan Colombia funding, reports to Congress are arguably not subject to judicial review.

While Colombia's crop eradication program is perhaps the most well-known, the United States has supported fumigation efforts in other nations as well. *See, e.g.*, Luz Estella Nagle, *Global Terrorism in Our Own Backyard: Colombia's Legal War Against Illegal Armed Groups*, 15 TRANSNAT'L L. & CONTEMP. PROBS. 5, 60–62 (2005) (describing crop eradication efforts in other South American countries and reporting that in 2001, 10,000 Ecuadorians filed a complaint against Virginia-based DynCorp. based on its involvement in that country's aerial spraying program); Alyssa Greenspan, Note: *Are We Fighting the Right War?*, 16 CARDOZO J. INT'L & COMP. L. 493, 518–23 (2008) (describing U.S.-led opium eradication efforts in Afghanistan).

5. The U.S. Drug Certification Process

As discussed above, a number of international leaders—particularly within Latin America—have begun to call for an end to the global drug war. This development is consistent with Seth Harp's argument in *Globalization of the U.S. Black Market: Prohibition, the War on Drugs, and the Case of Mexico* that the costs and benefits of drug prohibition are unevenly distributed, with consumer countries like the United States receiving the benefits of any decrease in use and producer countries bearing the costs of violence and corruption. But if drug prohibition visits its costs primarily on producer countries, why haven't any legalized the manufacture of drugs within their borders? The answer may lie, at least partially, in United States policies designed to encourage producer countries to adopt and actively enforce drug prohibition laws. *See generally* Allegra M. McLeod, *Exporting U.S. Criminal Justice*, 29 YALE L. & POL'Y REV. 83 (2010) (examining methods used by the U.S. to advance its transnational criminal enforcement priorities abroad). In particular, the U.S. has developed a certification process that ties trade status and aid packages to participation in the drug war.

Fighting Bad Guys with International Trade Law
Raj Bhala

31 University of California Davis Law Review 1 (1997)

Congress and the President have used international trade law not only to deal with the threat to Americans from terrorists, but also to combat the scourge of drugs in American society. As former Secretary of State James Baker suggested, both are national security threats: "there is no foreign policy issue short of war or peace which has a more direct bearing on the well-being of the American people" than the international trade of illicit drugs. Secretary Baker's statement is not hyperbole. The United Nations estimates that the international trade in illicit drugs is worth $400 billion—approximately 8% of world trade—more than the trading in iron, steel, or motor vehicles. There are very few commodities that the United States is more heavily dependent upon foreign countries than drugs. Approximately 95% of the illegal narcotics consumed in the United States is imported.

Among the particularly severe drug threats to the United States are cocaine and heroin.

Both drugs originate almost entirely from overseas: Bolivia, Colombia, and Peru account for essentially all of the world's coca cultivation, and the "Golden Triangle" countries of Myanmar (Burma), Laos, and Thailand account for 75% of the world's opium production. Most of the balance of the world's opium production occurs in the "Golden Crescent" countries of Iran, Afghanistan, and Pakistan. During the early 1990s, the share of the illicit drug industry in the gross domestic product was 6% in Peru, more than 7% in Colombia, and more than 9% in Bolivia. The most important Burmese and Afghan exports are also drugs.

In an effort to combat the scourge of drugs, Congress amended the Trade Act of 1974 with title IX of the Drug Enforcement, Education, and Control Act in 1986, also known as the 1986 Narcotics Act. The 1986 Narcotics Act is a "carrot and stick" approach to dealing with the problem of illegal drug smuggling into the United States and the threat of foreign[-]sourced drug production. The 1986 Narcotics Act empowers the President to take unilateral trade actions against a country producing or transporting drugs if that country does not cooperate fully with the U.S. government in keeping drugs out of the United States. These "stick" actions are to be taken as of March 1 of each year. The "carrot" is the possibility of obtaining presidential certification that would exempt a country from trade sanctions.

The carrot and stick approach of the 1986 Narcotics Act reflects an important development in U.S. strategy in the war on drugs. Until Congress passed this Act, the United States concentrated much of its effort on interdiction—intercepting drug shipments during transit from the source countries of the drugs to the U.S. border. Interdiction is a game of cat and mouse that raises the cost of doing business for drug producers and traffickers each time a seizure occurs. However, interdiction cannot stem the wave of drug smuggling. As the State Department declared in 1995, "We are not satisfied with simply raising the cost of doing business for the traffickers." The 1986 Narcotics Act reflects what might be called a "source country" strategy. The major source countries of drugs are identified; the weak link in the chain from drug production overseas to drug sales in the United States is attacked, namely the drug crops lying dormant in the field. This strategy is attractive because the bulk of world production of cocaine and heroin is concentrated in a relatively small number of countries.

The 1986 Narcotics Act identifies two target classes of possible unilateral trade sanctions: "major drug producing countries," and "major drug-transit countries." A major drug producing country is defined by the annual output of opium, cocaine base, or marijuana produced in that country. Specifically, it is a country that illegally produces at least five metric tons of opium or opium derivative, 500 metric tons of coca, or 500 metric tons of marijuana during one fiscal year. A major drug-transit country is a conduit for narcotics or a money laundering center. It is a country "that is a significant direct source of illicit narcotic or psychotropic drugs or other controlled substances significantly affecting" the United States. In addition, the country's government must either know or be in complicity with drug transporting and money-laundering of significant sums of drug-related profits. To establish a suspect country as a major drug producing country, it is unnecessary to demonstrate that a country's government is involved in producing or trafficking drugs.

The 1986 Narcotics Act establishes the stick—five sanctions the President must impose on a major drug producing or drug[-]transit country. Although the sanctions are mandatory in most cases, the President has some discretion whether to impose any or all of the sanctions. First, the President may revoke any preferential treatment afforded to the country's products under the Generalized System of Preferences ("GSP"), Caribbean Basin Initiative ("CBI"), or other preferential scheme. Second, the President may impose an additional duty of up to 50% ad valorem on any or all of the country's products, and he may impose a duty of up to 50% on duty-free products. Third, the President may suspend air carrier transportation between the United States and the country, and may terminate any air service agreement with the country. Fourth, the President may withdraw U.S. personnel and resources that are participating in a service arrangement for customs pre-clearance. Finally, a country whose government is involved in illegal drug trade or that fails to cooperate with U.S. narcotics enforcement activities cannot receive a quota allocation for sugar imports into the United States. In the abstract, these sanctions may not appear particularly severe. In some cases, however, the first and second sanctions may inflict harm on another country and thereby cause it to alter its behavior with respect to drug production or transit.

The 1986 Narcotics Act contains an important exception to these sanctions. The United States will not impose sanctions on a major drug producing or drug-transit country if the President determines and certifies to Congress that, during the previous year, the country "has cooperated fully" with the United States, or "has taken adequate steps on its own," to change its behavior. The four certification criteria are the carrot in the 1986 Narcotics Act because they attempt to compel a major drug producing or drug-transit country to alter its behavior and thereby avoid the stick of trade sanctions. Because there is no definition of "cooperation fully" or "adequate steps," the President has considerable discretion in using the carrot.

First, a major drug producing or drug-transit country must reach a bilateral or multilateral narcotics agreement with the United States and cooperate fully with the U.S. government in satisfying the agreement's goals. The statute contemplates an agreement with specific objectives: to reduce drug production, consumption, and trafficking within the country, and address illicit crop eradication and crop substitution. Under the agreement's terms, a nation must also increase drug interdiction and enforcement, drug education and treatment programs, cooperate with U.S. drug enforcement officials, and participate in extradition, mutual legal assistance, sharing of evidence, and other treaties aimed at drug enforcement. The country must also identify and eliminate illicit drug laboratories, as well as the trafficking of essential precursor chemicals used to produce illegal drugs. If a country has already been designated as a major drug producing or drug-transit country during the previous year, the President similarly cannot certify a country as cooperating fully with the United States unless that country enacts a bilateral or multilateral narcotics agreement. This requirement induces countries to enter into such an agreement.

Second, a country must cooperate fully with the United States to prevent illegal drug sales and transports to U.S. government personnel and their dependents. Unfortunately, the statute does not specify how a country is to prevent drugs from being sold to U.S. government personnel, particularly where a U.S. government official is determined to buy drugs. Certainly, a country cannot be expected to police the behavior of U.S. officials within a U.S. embassy, which is U.S. property, and where U.S. officials may enjoy diplomatic immunity.

Third, before the President certifies a major drug producing or drug-transit country, that country must also cooperate fully with the United States to prevent and punish the laundering of drug-related profits in that country. This requirement may prove especially difficult for smaller countries with limited law enforcement resources and little experience in prosecuting sophisticated white-collar crimes. Money laundering cases typically involve extensive and painstaking investigation. For example, it may be necessary to trace wire transfers of funds among banks around the world, which may require obtaining exemptions from applicable bank secrecy laws. These tasks are likely to require the assistance of bank regulators in relevant countries. Further, money laundering is a criminal offense requiring proof that the funds in question were generated by drug sales and that they were laundered.

The final requirement for certification takes aim at official corruption that often is connected with drug production and trade. A major drug producing or transit country must cooperate fully with the United States to prevent and punish bribery and other public corruption that facilitates the production, processing, and shipment of illegal drugs, or that discourages the investigation and prosecution of these acts. This requirement may prove difficult in a country whose government is riddled with corruption. "Clean" government officials may lack the political clout to punish bribery and other corrupt acts by "dirty" officials. Indeed, they may fear for their own lives. Even in a less extreme situation, rooting out corruption may be difficult.

The statute imposes one further requirement to obtain presidential certification, pertaining to a major drug producing or drug-transit country that produces licit opium. The opium producing country must take steps to prevent significant diversion of its licit cultivation and production into the illicit market, maintain production and stockpiles at levels no higher than those consistent with licit market demand, and prevent illicit cultivation and production. This requirement acknowledges the legitimate reasons for producing opium and induces countries to act against the illicit market.

Consider the 1997 certification of Mexico granted by President Clinton under the Foreign Assistance Act of 1961 ("1961 Assistance Act"), as amended. The President certified Mexico as a full partner in the U.S. war on drugs despite the arrest of Mexico's top anti-narcotics law enforcement official on charges of collaboration with drug traffickers. The House of Representatives voted 251 to 175 against the President's certification, and the Senate voted ninety-four to five in favor of a non-binding resolution criticizing the certification. This congressional action was not surprising in the wake of the arrest. While the arrest signified that Mexico was making some progress, many members of Congress questioned the integrity of Mexico's entire law enforcement apparatus. Moreover, by 1996, more than half of all cocaine entering the United States came through Mexico. Mexico had become a major money laundering center even though it had introduced legislation to criminalize money laundering and fight organized crime.

However, the President's certification was foreseeable. The Clinton administration had invested considerable time and money in forging closer ties with Mexico and helping it develop economically through two controversial events: Mexico's inclusion in the North American Free Trade Agreement ("NAFTA") and the multi-billion dollar rescue package arranged for Mexico after its peso crisis. Politically, President Clinton was not in a position to reverse course and impose trade sanctions on Mexico. At the same time, the Republican Congress assuredly did not fail to point out Mexico's shortcomings in the war on drugs. The end result reflected this political stand-off.

The 1961 Assistance Act and 1986 Narcotics Act work in tandem, in a manner analogous to a cross-default clause in an international loan agreement. For example, suppose a country fails to obtain certification and does not qualify for the "vital national interests waiver," discussed below, under the 1961 Assistance Act. Because the certification and waiver criteria are similar to the criteria in the 1986 Narcotics Act, the country should not be certified under the 1986 Narcotics Act. The result would be a loss of foreign assistance and the imposition of trade sanctions under the 1961 Assistance Act.

The 1986 Narcotics Act provides guidance to the President in administering the above four certification criteria to determine whether the government of a major drug producing or transit country is cooperating fully with the United States, or making adequate efforts on its own in the war on drugs. The 1986 Narcotics Act lists eleven issues the President must consider when evaluating a government for potential certification. First, has the government of that country acted to effect "the maximum reductions in illicit drug production" that the U.S. government has determined to be achievable? Second, has the foreign government adopted judicial and law enforcement measures to eliminate illicit drug production and trafficking, as evidenced by seizures of drugs and illicit laboratories and prosecutions of violators? Third, has the foreign government adopted judicial and law enforcement measures to eliminate money laundering, as evidenced by the enactment of anti-money laundering laws and cooperation with U.S. anti-money laundering efforts? Fourth, has the foreign government adopted judicial and law enforcement measures to eliminate bribery and other forms of public corruption that facilitate drug production and trafficking and discourage investigation and prosecution? Fifth, has the foreign government, as a matter of policy, encouraged or facilitated the production or distribution of illegal drugs? Sixth, does any senior official of the foreign government engage in, encourage, or facilitate the production or distribution of illegal drugs? Seventh, has the foreign government aggressively investigated cases in which a U.S. drug enforcement official has been the victim of acts or threats of violence, inflicted by or in complicity with a law enforcement officer, and has the government "energetically sought to bring the perpetrators . . . to justice?" Eighth, has the foreign government failed to provide reasonable cooperation to U.S. drug enforcement officials, including the refusal to allow these officials to pursue aerial smugglers a reasonable distance into the airspace of the foreign country? Ninth, has the foreign government revised its conspiracy and asset seizure laws to combat drug traffickers more effectively? Tenth, has the foreign government expeditiously processed U.S. extradition requests relating to drug traffickers? Finally, has the foreign government protected or granted safe haven to known drug traffickers?

While the President must consider these eleven questions in applying the certification criteria, the precise statutory language used to frame several of these questions leaves considerable room for the President to maneuver. For example, the second, third, and fourth questions contain the phrase "to the maximum extent possible." Thus, using the fourth question as an example, the President must decide whether a foreign government has taken measures against money laundering to the maximum extent possible. Similar flexible wording is contained in other questions. For instance, the sixth question uses the term "senior official" but does not define this term; the seventh question asks the President to determine whether a foreign government has investigated cases aggressively and brought perpetrators to justice energetically; the eighth question inquires about reasonable cooperation and a reasonable invasion of airspace; and the ninth question addresses expeditious processing of extradition requests. In sum, while the statute provides the President with a checklist of issues to consider in applying the certification criteria, this subjective checklist invites the President to exercise discretion.

Even if a country is a major drug producing or transit country and even if it fails to meet the four certification criteria, the country may still avoid the stick of sanctions under the 1986 Narcotics Act. This possibility depends upon whether, from the U.S. perspective, sanctions would be counterproductive. The President may determine and certify to Congress that the "vital national interests" of the United States require that it not apply sanctions.

Countries are likely to obtain a vital national interests waiver in five scenarios. For example, in 1987 and 1988, President Reagan found that Laos had failed to cooperate fully with the United States on narcotics control and to take adequate steps on its own. Nonetheless, he gave Laos a vital national interests certification in both years to promote continuing investigations of Americans missing in action and prisoners of the Vietnam War. Plainly, the United States has a unique issue to address with Laos that qualifies as a vital national interest. Second, suppose the non-certified country is a principal U.S. supplier of a precious commodity, and there is no other readily available substitute source. Examples include oil from

Saudi Arabia, or certain minerals like uranium from countries such as Russia. The non-certified country's supplier status may effectively immunize it from sanctions. Third, suppose the non-certified country could inflict significant economic damage to U.S. businesses through a denial of market access or government procurement contracts. China would be an obvious example of a country that may be too big to penalize. A fourth category of non-certified country is one that might be too dangerous to penalize. Such a country may be able to inflict significant damage to American military and civilian personnel working abroad. Egypt and Turkey might be examples. Finally, consider a country in which the United States has too much invested to sanction. Surely Mexico, a partner in NAFTA, is a case in point.

Our trading partners may consider the 1986 Narcotics Act to be an imperialistic statute.

[T]he 1986 Narcotics Act focuses and visits blame entirely on drug-supplying countries. It pays no attention to the tremendous demand for drugs by Americans. Consider the statement of former Singapore Prime Minister Lee Kuan Yew: "Let me give you an example that encapsulates the whole difference between America and Singapore. America has a vicious drug problem. How does it solve it? It goes around the world helping other anti-narcotic agencies to try and stop the suppliers. It pays for helicopters, defoliating agents and so on. And when provoked, it captures the President of Panama and brings him to trial in Florida. Singapore does not have that option. We can't go to Burma and capture the warlords there. What we can do is pass a law which says that any customs officer or policeman who sees anybody in Singapore behaving suspiciously, leading him to suspect the person is under the influence of drugs, can require the man to have his urine tested. If the sample is found to contain drugs, the man immediately goes for treatment.... In America if you did that it would be an invasion of the individual's rights and you would be sued."

[Moreover,] even the State Department admits that some governments of drug-supplying countries lack the ability, assuming they have the will, to reduce or eliminate drug production in their territory. Consider the context in which the governments of Laos, Afghanistan, and Burma, all major heroin-producing countries, must lead an anti-heroin campaign. Laos has "a difficult geography, an impecunious central government that has delegated fiscal responsibility to regional entities and thus lost some measure of control, and a dependency on international institutions for external financing." In Afghanistan, years of warfare diverted government attention from the problem of poppy cultivation; without a vigorous central government, Afghanistan fell under the thumb of regional commanders who are akin to feudal warlords. Moreover, Afghanistan is plagued by a "devastated economy and a large refugee population." In Burma, the ruling State Law and Order Restoration Commission is hardly a sympathetic government. Insurgent armies in Burma control the poppy fields in areas largely out of the central government's reach. The Rangoon government allows poppy cultivation in return for peaceful coexistence with these armies.

Imagine the reaction in the United States if our trading partners enacted a converse piece of legislation. This hypothetical bill would mandate the identification and publication of major drug-consuming countries; the United States surely would be blacklisted. Such legislation would require the United States to cooperate fully with its trading partners to reduce drug demand or take steps on its own according to criteria set by our trading partners. These criteria would include creating drug rehabilitation programs, prosecution initiatives, and the commitment of specific budgetary allocations to support these efforts. Failure to satisfy these criteria could lead to denial of access to our trading partners' markets in key sectors like agriculture, services, and aviation. This hypothetical legislation, if enacted by a trading partner, would undoubtedly provoke outrage in the United States; however, the 1986 Narcotics Act is precisely this sort of legislation visited upon our partners.

In 2011, Bolivian President Evo Morales called for the development of a certification process for drug-consuming countries like the United States. "The origins of drug trafficking are in the demand, not the supply," said Morales. "So I'd like for some international organism to certify or decertify the United States for their responsibility on the issue of drug trafficking." CNN Wire Staff, *Morales Wants Drug Certification for U.S.*, CNN.com, Sept. 21, 2011. Thus far, Morales's proposal has not come to fruition. Meanwhile, even though the federal government has permitted U.S. states to implement marijuana legalization laws without interference, the 1986 Narcotics Act's drug certification policy remains in place.

Index

Substances

Countries and Regions

People and Organizations

U.S. and International Agencies

Commissions

Constitutional Provisions

Legislation

International Meetings and Agreements

Legal and Policy Issues